LABOR RELATIONS LAW

MICHIE CONTEMPORARY
LEGAL EDUCATION SERIES

Labor Relations Law

CASES AND MATERIALS

Tenth Edition

THEODORE J. St. ANTOINE
James E. & Sarah A. Degan Professor of Law
University of Michigan

CHARLES B. CRAVER
Leroy S. Merrifield Research Professor of Law
The George Washington University

MARION G. CRAIN
Paul Eaton Professor of Law
University of North Carolina

LEXIS® LAW PUBLISHING
CHARLOTTESVILLE, VIRGINIA

LEXIS® LAW PUBLISHING
P.O. Box 7587, Charlottesville, VA 22906-7587

Law School Publications
Phone: 800/446-3410, ext. 5578 or 804/961-5578
E-mail: llplawschool@lexis-nexis.com

Customer Service
Phone: 800/533-1646
E-mail: customer.support@bender.com

Library of Congrass Catalog Card No. 99-60689
ISBN 0-327-00929-2

1311712

Preface to the Tenth Edition

The last couple of decades have seen an explosive growth in the law governing the workplace. Even the name of the subject has often changed from Labor Relations Law to Labor and Employment Law to reflect the new emphasis on the direct governmental regulation of employer-employee relations, as distinct from traditional union-management relations. The question fairly arises whether the "basic" Labor Law course should attempt to cover the recent legal developments concerning job safety, employee benefit plans, wrongful discharge, civil rights, and the like, in addition to the traditional National Labor Relations Act materials. Most law schools have resolved this dilemma by creating separate courses covering Employment Discrimination Law and Individual Employment Rights. We agree with this trend, because we believe that there is a grave risk of superficiality and lack of focus if someone tries to include all of these areas in a single three- or four-hour offering. We also think that those two almost unique American institutions—the representative labor union and the collective bargaining process as they have evolved in this country—deserve study in a setting in which they occupy center stage.

Like its predecessors, therefore, the tenth edition of this casebook is designed for an intensive examination of the union-management relationship throughout its major phases. Kind words from many readers, both faculty members and students, indicate that the structure of recent editions has been conducive to that purpose. We generally follow the chronology of organizing, bargaining, contract enforcement, and internal union affairs.

As in the past, we have tried to respond generously to the most significant current developments in the field, while simultaneously providing a set of materials that will be truly manageable in the usual three- or four-hour courses. For this revision, we shall continue our practice of publishing an annual softbound supplement so that the book will be up-to-date at the beginning of each school year.

We dedicate this tenth edition to Leroy S. Merrifield, the Lobingier Professor Emeritus of Jurisprudence and Comparative Law at George Washington University, who was our collaborator on earlier editions. For forty years, Professor Merrifield was an outstanding teacher, a highly respected legal scholar, and a wonderful collaborator who set a standard of excellence we hope to approach in this edition.

We must finally express our appreciation to Jeffrey Pearlman, whose capable and conscientious research assistance contributed substantially to this revision.

Ann Arbor, Michigan   *Theodore J. St. Antoine*
Washington, D.C.   *Charles B. Craver*
Chapel Hill, North Carolina   *Marion G. Crain*

Summary Table of Contents

PART FIVE: INTERNAL UNION AFFAIRS

Table of Contents

PART FOUR: COLLECTIVE BARGAINING

PART FIVE: INTERNAL UNION AFFAIRS

PART ONE

HISTORICAL BACKGROUND AND INTRODUCTION

FOREWORD

Labor relations law is dynamic, philosophically divisive, and highly sensitive both to last November's elections and to this morning's headlines. For adequate understanding, the student and the lawyer must examine much more than the law itself. The perspective of history, as well as some knowledge of the economic, social, and political aspects of unionism, all are essential aids in evaluating the efforts of courts and legislatures to create suitable legal standards.

Most of the information presented below concerning American labor organizations is to be found in the literature produced by the labor historians and economists, and there is no pretense of originality in any of it. The objective has been to reduce a mass of material to fairly comfortable dimensions and to make it easily available for immediate consultation as the student begins to work in this field. Principal sources used in preparing this summary are as follows: I. Bernstein, A History of the American Worker—The Lean Years: 1920-1933 (1960); I. Bernstein, The Turbulent Years: 1933-1941 (1969); I. Bernstein, A Caring Society: The New Deal, the Workers, and the Great Depression (1985); A. Blum, A History of the American Labor Movement (1972); D. Bok & J. Dunlop, Labor and the American Community (1970); D. Brody, Workers in Industrial America (1980); S. Cohen, Labor in the United States (5th ed. 1979); J. Commons & Associates, History of Labor in the United States (1918); F. Dulles & M. Dubofsky, Labor in America (4th ed. 1984); A. Faulkner & M. Starr, Labor in America (rev. ed. 1957); Forbath, *The Shaping of the American Labor Movement,* 102 Harv. L. Rev. 1109 (1989); A. Goldberg, AFL-CIO: Labor United (1956); S. Gompers, Seventy Years of Life and Labor (1925) (P. Taft & J. Sessions abr. ed. 1957); G. Hildebrand, American Unionism: An Historical and Analytical Survey (1979); R. Morris, Government and Labor in Early America (1946); H. Pelling, American Labor (1960); S. Perlman, A History of Trade Unionism in the United States (1935); S. Perlman & P. Taft, History of Labor in the United States, 1896-1932 (1935); J. Rayback, A History of American Labor (1966); P. Taft, Organized Labor in American History (1964); P. Taft, The AF of L from the Death of Gompers to the Merger (1959); P. Taft, The AF of L in the Time of Gompers (1957); C. Tomlins, The State and the Unions: Labor Relations, Law and the Organized Labor Movement in America, 1880-1960 (1985); L. Ulman, The Rise of the National Trade Union (1955); U.S. Department of Labor, Brief History of the

American Labor Movement (1964); U.S. Department of Labor, Bicentennial History of the American Worker (R. Morris, ed. 1976).

SECTION I. Historical Background

A. THE PRE-CIVIL WAR PERIOD

1. EARLY DEVELOPMENT OF LABOR UNIONS

In the early years of this country's history there were comparatively few free workers. The great majority of laborers were either African slaves or indentured servants who, to secure passage to America, had bound themselves in servitude for a term of years. As trade and commerce increased, however, there was an increased demand for free workers. The skilled craftsmen, as they began to open small shops and use helpers, soon found it to their advantage to employ free workers whom they could dismiss when business was poor and for whose maintenance they had no responsibility. Other factors such as the seasonal nature of many trades and the danger of loss of a large investment in runaway slaves made free labor desirable. As the terms of the bondsmen expired, and as craftsmen immigrated from Europe in large numbers, lured by the comparatively high prices paid for skilled labor and the glowing accounts of a laborer's life in America, the group of free wage earners steadily increased.

In these times the master worked side by side with his journeymen and apprentices, and there was as yet no well-defined distinction between the interests of master and workmen. Journeymen looked forward to the time when they would become master craftsmen. The market was local and the master bargained directly with his customers for the price of his product. Because of the scarcity of skilled labor and because the master could set his prices noncompetitively, wage rates were generally high, as compared, for example, with wages paid in England. This, however, did not necessarily mean that the Colonial worker's lot as a whole was an enviable one; in some colonies there was maximum wage legislation; workers had to compete with slave labor and, during the winter months, with farmers who sought temporary employment in town. When work was slack, the jails were filled with workers who could not meet their debts, and poverty was widespread. The worker had not yet conceived the idea that he could improve his lot through self-organization.

There were, it is true, labor organizations of a sort existing in America as early as the seventeenth century, but they were not trade unions in the modern sense—that is, permanent organizations of workers created to achieve, by concerted action, improvements in wages, hours, and other terms and conditions of employment. Rather, they were primarily guilds of artisans who marketed their own products. They sought to maintain working standards by regulation of apprenticeship requirements and exertion of control over wage rates and prices. The few so-called "strikes" which occurred in the Colonial period were not strikes by workers against their masters for increased wages, but for the most part were protests by master craftsmen against local government regulations relaxing apprenticeship requirements or setting ceilings on prices.

The Philadelphia printers who "turned out" in 1786 for a minimum wage of $6.00 per week are credited with having called the first genuine labor strike. However, it was not until 1792 that any continuous organization of wage earners appeared. In that year the Philadelphia shoemakers formed an organization, which existed for about a year. In 1794 the shoemakers created the Federal Society of Journeymen Cordwainers, which survived until 1806. Other localized craft unions quickly sprang up throughout the country. Besides providing the customary services of fraternal societies, their usual aims were to achieve shorter hours, higher wages, the enforcement of apprenticeship regulations, and the closed shop.

2. THE "CRIMINAL CONSPIRACY" DOCTRINE

Judicial reaction to these early attempts of labor to organize in order to improve working conditions was highly unfavorable. Applying the doctrine as established in England in the early eighteenth century, the courts in this country began to condemn the concerted activities of workers' associations as "criminal conspiracies." The following case, digested from the full report which appears in the monumental documentary history compiled by John R. Commons and associates, is a classic in the history of labor law. It is fully analyzed in its social setting in Nelles, *The First American Labor Case,* 41 Yale L.J. 165 (1931).

PHILADELPHIA CORDWAINERS' CASE
[COMMONWEALTH v. PULLIS]

Philadelphia Mayor's Court (1806)
3 Doc. Hist. of Am. Ind. Soc. 59 (2d ed. Commons 1910)

Indictment for common law conspiracy, tried before a jury consisting of two inn-keepers, a tavern-keeper, three grocers, a merchant, a hatter, a tobacconist, a watchmaker, a tailor, a bottler.

The indictment charged in substance: (1) That defendants conspired and agreed that none of them would work at the shoemaking craft except at certain specified prices higher than prices which had theretofore customarily been paid; (2) that defendants conspired and agreed that they would endeavor to prevent "by threats, menaces, and other unlawful means" other craftsmen from working except at said specified rates; and (3) that defendants, having formed themselves into an association, conspired and agreed that none of them would work for any master who should employ a cordwainer who had broken any rule or bylaw of the association, and that defendants, in accordance with such agreement refused to work at the usual rates and prices.

Counsel for the prosecution were Jared Ingersol and Joseph Hopkinson. Counsel for the defendants were Caesar A. Rodney and Walter Franklin.

During his address to the jury, Mr. Joseph Hopkinson, for the prosecution, stated, among other things, the following:

If the court and jury shall decide, that journeymen may associate together, and determine that none shall work under certain prices; then, when orders arrive for considerable quantities of any article, the association may determine to raise the wages, and reduce the contracts to diminish their profit; to sustain a loss, or to abandon the execution of the orders, as was done in Bedford's case, who told you he could have afforded to execute the orders he obtained at the southward, had wages remained the same as when he left Philadelphia. When they found he had a contract, they took advantage of his necessity. What was done by the journeymen shoemakers, may be done by those of every other trade, or manufacturer in the city.... A few more things of this sort, and you will break up the manufactories; the masters will be afraid to make a contract, therefore he must relinquish the export trade, and depend altogether upon the profits of the work of Philadelphia, and confine his supplies altogether to the city. The last turn-out had liked to have produced that effect: Mr. Ryan told you he had intended to confine himself to bespoke work.

It must be plain to you, that the master employers have no particular interest in the thing ... if they pay higher wages, you must pay higher for the articles. They, in truth, are protecting the community. Nor is it merely the advance of wages that encreases the price to the consumer, the master must have some compensation for the advance of his cash, and the credit he frequently gives. They have no interest to serve in the prosecution; they have no vindictive passions to gratify ... they merely stand as the guardians of the community from imposition and rapacity. [pp. 137-8.]

If this conspiracy was to be confined to the persons themselves, it would not be an offense against the law, but they go further. There are two counts in the indictment; you are to consider each, and give your verdict on each. The first is for contriving, and intending, unjustly and oppressively, to encrease and augment the wages usually allowed them. The other for endeavouring to prevent, by threats, menaces, and other unlawful means, other journeymen from working at the usual prices, and that they compelled others to join them.

If these persons claim the right to put the price on their own work, if they say their labour is their own, and they are the judges of its value, why not admit the same right to others? If it is the right of Dubois, and the other defendants, is it not equally the right of Harrison and Cummings? We stand up for the right of the journeymen, as well as of the masters. The last turn-out was carried by a small majority ... 60 against 50, or thereabout: shall 60 unreasonable men, perhaps single men, having no one to provide for but themselves, distress and bring to destruction, 50 married men with their families? Let the 60 put what price they please on their own work; but the others are free agents also: leave them free, or talk no more of equal rights, of independence, or of liberty.

It may be answered, that when men enter into a society they are bound to conform to its rules; they may say, the majority ought to govern the minority ... granted ... but they ought to leave a man free to join, or not to join the society. If I go into a country I am bound to submit to its laws, but surely I may judge, whether or not I will go there. The society has no right to force you into its body, and then say you shall obey its rules under severe penalties. By their constitution you find, and from their own lips I must take the words, that though a man wants no more wages than he gets, he must join in a turn-out. The man who seeks an asylum in this country, from the arbitrary laws of other nations, is coerced into this society, though he does not work in the article intended to be raised; he must leave his seat and join the turn-out. [pp. 138-9.]

Recorder Levy, in his charge to the jury, made the following statements, among others:

It is proper to consider, is such a combination consistent with the principles of our law, and injurious to the public welfare? The usual means by which the prices of work are regulated, are the demand for the article and the excellence of its fabric. Where the work is well done, and the demand is considerable, the prices will necessarily be high. Where the work is ill done, and the demand is inconsiderable, they will unquestionably be low. If there are many to consume, and few to work, the price of the article will be high; but if there are few to consume, and many to work, the article must be low. Much will depend, too, upon these circumstances, whether the materials are plenty or scarce; the price of the commodity, will in consequence be higher or lower. These are the means by which prices are regulated in the natural course of things. To make an artificial regulation, is not to regard the excellence of the work or quality of the material, but to fix a positive and arbitrary price, governed by no standard, controlled by no impartial person, but dependent on the will of the few who are interested; this is the unnatural way of raising the price of goods or work. This is independent of the number who are to do the work. It is an unnatural, artificial means of raising the price of work beyond its standard, and taking an undue advantage of the public. Is the rule of law bottomed upon such principles, as to permit or protect such conduct? Consider it on the footing of the general commerce of the city. Is there any man who can calculate (if this is tolerated) at what price he may safely contract to deliver articles, for which he may receive orders, if he is to be regulated by the journeymen in an arbitrary jump from one price to another? It renders it impossible for a man, making a contract for a large quantity of such goods, to know whether he shall lose or gain by it. If he makes a large contract for goods today, for delivery at three, six or nine months hence, can he calculate what the prices will be then, if the journeymen in the intermediate time, are permitted to meet and raise their prices, according to their caprice or pleasure? Can he fix the price of his commodity for a future day? It is impossible that any man can carry on commerce in this way. There cannot be a large contract entered into, but what the contractor will make at his peril. He may be ruined by the difference of prices made by the journeymen in the intermediate time. What then is the operation of this kind of conduct upon the commerce of the city? It exposes it to inconveniences, if not to ruin; therefore, it is against the public welfare....

What is the case now before us? ... A combination of workmen to raise their wages may be considered in a two fold point of view; one is to benefit themselves ... the other is to injure those who do not join their society. The rule of law condemns both. If the rule be clear, we are bound to conform to it even though we do not comprehend the principle upon which it is founded. We are not to reject it because we do not see the reason of it. It is enough, that is the will of the majority. It is law because it is their will—if it is law, there may be good reasons for it though we cannot find them out. But the rule in this case is pregnant with sound sense and all the authorities are clear upon the subject. Hawkins, the greatest authority on the criminal law, has laid it down, that a combination to maintaining one another, carrying a particular object, whether true or false, is criminal ... the authority cited from 8 Mod. Rep. does not rest merely upon the reputation of that book. He gives you other authorities to which he refers. It is adopted by Blackstone, and laid down as the law by Lord Mansfield 1793, that an act innocent in an individual, is rendered criminal by a confederacy to effect it....

One man determines not to work under a certain price and it may be individually the opinion of all; in such a case it would be lawful in each to refuse to do so, for if each stands, alone, either may extract from his determination when he pleases. In the turn-out of last fall, if each member of the body had stood alone, fettered by no promises to the rest, many of them might have changed their opinion as to the price of wages and gone to work; but it has been given to you in evidence, that they were bound down by their agreement, and pledged by mutual engagements, to persist in it, however contrary to their own judgment. The continuance in improper conduct may therefore well be attributed to the combination. The good sense of those individuals was prevented by this agreement, from having its free exercise....

The defendants were found guilty and were fined eight dollars each plus costs.

———

It wasn't until the decision in *Commonwealth v. Hunt,* 45 Mass. (4 Met.) 111, 38 Am. Dec. 346 (1842), that the first break in the doctrine of criminal conspiracy occurred, enabling labor to shift its emphasis from political action towards "business unionism" (which seeks improvement through collective bargaining).

In that case certain workmen had been found guilty of criminal conspiracy. On appeal, however, exceptions to the indictment were sustained and the conviction was reversed. The opinion of Chief Justice Shaw is confusing as to its rationale, and therefore difficult to dissect, but in some respects it seemed to be in disagreement with the prevailing views concerning the legality of trade union activities. For example, allegations in the indictment that defendants had agreed not to work for any employer who should employ a nonunion workman were held to be insufficient, at least on the assumption that defendants were not under contractual obligations to the employer. The court also ruled that a conspiracy to impoverish another workman, who was alleged to have lost his employment because he was not a union member, was not in itself unlawful; that illegality would depend upon the means used. "If it is to be carried into effect by fair or honorable and lawful means, it is, to say the least, innocent; if by falsehood or force, it may be stamped with the character of conspiracy." For a detailed examination of the case, *see* Nelles, *Commonwealth v. Hunt,* 32 Colum. L. Rev. 1128 (1932).

B. THE POST-CIVIL WAR ERA

1. THE GROWTH OF NATIONAL UNIONS AND LABOR UNREST

Several present-day unions—the typographers, hatters, machinists, and molders—had their origins in the 1850s, but they suffered setbacks in the depression of 1857. During the years of the Civil War there was a heavy demand for labor due to the shortage of manpower. Prices were high, wages lagged behind, and hours were long. As the size of the business unit increased, the impersonalized employer-employee relationship introduced by the factory system became more evident. With improved transportation conditions workers tended to move about more freely in search of suitable employment so that standardized working conditions became increasingly important. Workers came to realize the need for broader organization of their unions. Local units were federated into local trades' associations and many crafts were organized nationally. There were thirty-two national and international (so-called because of affiliates in Canada) unions in 1866. Among the more important of these were organizations of locomotive engineers, bricklayers and masons, carpenters and joiners, cigar makers and shoemakers. The shoemakers, one of the first of the groups to feel the effects of the factory system, organized in 1867 under the designation of the Order of Knights of St. Crispin. The purpose of the union was to protect its members against unemployment occasioned by the introduction of machinery and the attendant use of unskilled labor. By 1868 the Order had chartered 600 chapters, numbered 50,000 members, and was the largest craft union then in existence.

In 1866 the National Labor Union was formed under the leadership of William H. Silvis, a leader in the iron molders' union. This was a loosely built federation of national trades unions, city trades assemblies, local trade unions, and reform organizations of various kinds. Among the contributions of this union to the development of the trade union movement in the United States was its leadership in the movement for an eight-hour day, its insistence upon organization of women and Negro workers, and its emphasis upon equal pay for equal work for these two categories of workers most frequently and flagrantly discriminated against. Various reasons have been advanced to explain the ultimate failure of the Union: internal dissension which divided the organization when it became involved in politics; the failure of its commercial enterprises, causing many to lose confidence in its leaders; the fact that many of its members, who were primarily interested in local and craft matters, thought its aims too broad; and the loss of the outstanding leadership of Silvis by reason of his death in 1869. By 1872 it had virtually disappeared.

The panic of 1873 began a six-year period of hard times for the worker and with the depression came a severe weakening of labor organization, which frustrated plans for further federation. Only a few of the national craft unions survived and these were depleted in membership and financial strength. It was a period of turbulence in management-union relationships. The railroad strikes in the summer of 1877 on the three main trunk lines running west, which were precipitated by reductions in wages, were particularly violent. Federal troops and state militia were called out to "restore order."

One of the two important survivors among the labor unions of the depression years of 1873-1879 was the Noble Order of the Knights of Labor, which was organized in 1869 by the tailors of Philadelphia. The sponsors of this union conceived that the weaknesses which the trade unions had shown in the depression period were in part attributable to lack of unity, and that strength would come from a consolidation in one organization of all labor groups, including the unskilled as well as the skilled. They therefore welcomed into their ranks all who worked, even some employers and members of the professions.

The "Knights" was thus an attempt at amalgamation of local unions into a nationwide organization. The union was highly organized, each local union being subordinate to a district organization which, in turn, was directly responsible to a central supreme council. Since the local assemblies were mixed in craft and industrial character, the sympathetic strike became a powerful weapon in their hands with the bargaining power of the skilled workers reinforcing that of the unskilled. On the other hand, opposing points of view of the constituent groups became the basis for serious internal dissension later on. The general aims of the organization were to oppose the accumulation of wealth in the hands of a few and in other ways to secure for workers a fuller enjoyment of the wealth they created. These aims were to be achieved by legislation and education rather than by strikes and other forms of economic action.

This idealistic program for a co-operative society found its most ardent supporter in Terence V. Powderly who became president (Master Workman) of the Knights in 1878. But despite the philosophy which was written into the Preamble of the Order and was referred to as the "First Principles"—that improvement of the worker's condition should be sought through political action and not by means of the militant methods of industrial warfare—a more pragmatic element in the union ultimately got control and turned to typical economic action in an effort to achieve immediate results. Threats of strikes became common and the fear of a general strike made even such a powerful capitalist as Jay Gould seek terms with the union. In 1885 strikes had been called on Gould-controlled railroads because of a reduction in wages. These strikes were successful, largely because engineers, firemen, brakemen, and conductors all along the lines joined with the strikers. Shortly thereafter another strike was called because of a reduction in labor force on one of the roads. Even though the operating employees did not support the strikers this time, Gould, fearing a general strike, held a conference with members of the executive board of the Order and the receivers of his railroads at which time he threw his influence in favor of the union. This was the first time a great capitalist had discussed the workers' problems with a labor organization. The Order received a great deal of publicity for this achievement and the masses of the laboring population rushed to join up. S. Perlman, History of Trade Unionism in the United States 87 (1937). But Powderly did not on this occasion even ask for union recognition, bargaining machinery, or other conventional union objectives, so that victory was not enduring. *See* H. Harris, American Labor, A History 78-79 (1939). In 1886 the Order reached its peak membership of 700,000.

The year 1886 has sometimes been called the period of "the great upheaval." It was a period of nationwide strikes, sympathetic strikes which were set in motion on the least provocation, violence and turbulence including the famous "Haymarket" riots in Chicago, the widespread use of the boycott, and the rise of a strong feeling of labor class consciousness, particularly among the unskilled. A meeting of strikers was held in Haymarket Square, Chicago, in May, 1886, to protest against the killing of four strikers the day before by police who had attacked strikers at the McCormick reaper works. As police advanced to disperse the meeting, a bomb was thrown into their midst, killing many. Although this action was blamed on anarchists, Chicago citizens were thrown into panic and the incident turned many former sympathizers against the strikers. H. Harris, American Labor, A History 85-89 (1939). It has been asserted that the conviction of the "Haymarket Martyrs" followed one of the most unfair trials in history. *See generally* H. David, History of the Haymarket Affair (1936). During the latter half of 1886, however, the strikes ended, for the most part disastrously for labor.

From 1886 on, the Knights of Labor declined in popularity and membership. One of the reasons for this was the presence of conflicting interests within the Order. Other causes of the disintegration of the organization were the weak, utopian, vacillating leadership of Powderly, the persistent efforts of the newspapers to link the Knights with the famous Haymarket incident, and the efficient spy and blacklist system of the Pinkerton agency, much used by employers. Whatever the reasons, the Knights were practically defunct by the early nineties.

The ideology of the Knights of Labor was in direct contrast with that of the trade unions, one of which, the Cigar Makers' International Union, was the other important survivor of the labor movement of the sixties. Both Adolph Strasser, president of this union in 1877, and Samuel Gompers, then president of its New York local, had been influenced by men trained in the Marxist school, some of whom, formerly workers in the revolutionary labor movements of Europe, were leaders in the cigar makers' unions in New York. Both Strasser and Gompers eventually turned away from the philosophies of the more radical element in the union in support of a program which they believed would bring more immediate benefits to the worker. "The philosophy which these new leaders developed might be termed a philosophy of pure wage consciousness. It signified a labor movement reduced to an opportunistic basis, accepting the existence of capitalism and having for its object the enlarging of the bargaining power of the wage earner in the sale of his labor." S. Perlman, A History of Trade Unionism in the United States 78 (1937).

Gompers and other leaders also stood for craft union autonomy and accused the Knights of Labor of trying to make the craft unions subservient to the interest of the less skilled workers. This bitter rivalry eventually led to the reorganization of the Federation of Organized Trades and Labor Unions, which had been impotent since its birth in 1881. The reorganization occurred in 1886, at which time the name of the organization was changed to "The American Federation of Labor." The AFL placed its emphasis upon business unionism rather than upon reform through legislation, relegating to subordinate state federations its legislative interests. Said Samuel Gompers in his autobiography: "The secret of this continuous progress [of the AFL] has been understanding of the nature and possibilities of economic power and concentration on mobilization of that power. The Federation has maintained that economic organization is adequate to deal with all of the problems of wage earners. Its political action is simply to utilize the functions of the trade union in another field." 2 S. Gompers, Seventy Years of Life and Labor 268 (1925).

While an officer of the Cigar Makers' Union, Gompers had recognized the need for union organization on a business-like basis. He saw that there should be sustained office work and paid union administrators. He believed that financial strength was the foundation of stable unionism and that dues should be paid regularly. In searching for something to make it worthwhile for the worker to maintain continuous membership in the union, he adopted the plan of unemployment benefits and sickness and death provisions from the program of the British trades unions. Another policy adopted from the British was equalization of funds. Under this plan, the central office retained for operating expenses a certain sum from the dues and fees collected, and each local union kept for itself a certain sum proportionate to its membership. Any excess over and above these deductions was used to build up the treasury of any locals whose funds had been depleted by strike or other unusual expenditures.

Originally, the AFL was a federation of national and international craft unions and such locals as were not organized in nationals or internationals. The national and international organizations retained their autonomy. They chartered their locals, determined membership requirements, disciplined their members, conducted strikes, negotiated with employers, and otherwise acted as independent unions with respect to their particular craft problems. The function of the federation was to act in those matters which were of general interest to all. It arbitrated jurisdictional matters, maintained the craft autonomy of its affiliates, and gave financial aid and moral encouragement during strikes.

After 1893, business was depressed, but the AFL and other trade unions were able to maintain their organizations and ride out hard times despite membership losses. Later in the decade business conditions improved but the federation had many obstacles to overcome, the most important of which was the problem of coping with the expansion of corporate power. Giant corporations such as the Carnegie Steel Company and the Pullman Company succeeded in smashing important strikes in 1892 and 1894. When negotiations failed to end in an agreement, a strike was called on June 29, 1892, by the Amalgamated Iron and Steelworkers against the Carnegie Steel Company in protest against a wage reduction. Pinkerton detective agents had been hired by the company to serve as guards. When they arrived by boat at Homestead, Pennsylvania, a battle with the strikers ensued. At least half a dozen men were killed and many were seriously wounded. The Pinkerton men were defeated and left, but the state militia was called and remained in Homestead for several months, with the result that the strike was eventually broken and the union dismembered. *See* S. Perlman, A History of Trade Unionism in the United States 134 (1937).

The American Railway Union, formed in 1893 by Eugene V. Debs, supported a strike of its members at the paternalistic company town of Pullman, Illinois, by refusing to handle trains containing Pullman cars. This sympathetic boycott by railroad employees was accompanied by considerable violence, despite Debs' warnings against it. Upon petition of the United States Attorney General, a federal court issued a sweeping injunction against interfering with the railroads or inducing railroad employees to refrain from doing their work. Debs was found guilty of contempt and sentenced to six months in jail. *In re Debs,* 158 U.S. 564 (1895). The report of the United States Strike Commission which investigated the Pullman strike is important as an early expression of public concern with a national labor policy recognizing collective bargaining. By 1898 the AFL had proved its stability, and had even managed to keep out of the violent political campaign of 1896 when, despite the seductive allure of Bryan and "free silver," Gompers' nonpartisan "reward your friends and punish your enemies" policy was approved and supported. By 1904 there were no less than ninety stable national and international unions, most of which, excepting the railroad and postal unions, were affiliated with the AFL.

Employers at this time began to adopt numerous new anti-union tactics. During the depression of 1907 they disregarded collective agreements made when business had been good and labor had been in demand. "Scientific management" and "efficiency" (speed-up) systems were introduced in plants which forced the workers to work harder and faster for the same wages. Vigilante groups and citizens' committees were fostered by employers to resist union activities. Employer associations took a hand. The National Founders' Association and the National Metal Trades Association, for example, each maintained a "labor bureau," which kept a card index of every man in the employ of its members, and facilitated the use of the "black list" against unionists. These associations also furnished workers when needed, so that resort to the unions for employees was unnecessary, and they furnished strikebreakers upon request. There was also the National Association of Manufacturers, whose chief effort lay in the legislative field where it attempted, through lobbying, to nullify labor's political influence.

2. JUDICIAL REACTION AND THE LABOR INJUNCTION

Opposition to the trade union movement came not only from employers. The courts began to issue injunctions against strikes and picketing. This form of remedy, with its obvious advantages of speed and flexibility, especially when issued ex parte, quickly became standard in this country almost to the exclusion of criminal prosecutions, except insofar as such prosecutions were based on statutes such as the antitrust laws or miscellaneous local statutes and ordinances. In consequence, the development of the common law concerning trade unionism has been substantially the work of the equity judges proceeding, by easy transition, from the inheritance of the early common law of criminal conspiracy to the creation of a body of tort law dealing with the propriety of labor union objectives and means.

The majority opinion in the following landmark case exemplifies the prevailing judicial approach around the turn of the century, and the dissent of Judge Oliver Wendell Holmes, Jr., is a forerunner of later developments in labor law.

VEGELAHN v. GUNTNER

Supreme Judicial Court of Massachusetts
167 Mass. 92, 44 N.E. 1077 (1896)

… The following decree was entered at a preliminary hearing upon the bill: "This cause came on to be heard upon the plaintiff's motion for a temporary injunction; and after due hearing, at which the several defendants were represented by counsel, it is ordered, adjudged, and decreed that an injunction issue *pendente lite,* to remain in force until the further order of this court, or of some justice thereof, restraining the respondents and each and every one of them, their agents and servants, from interfering with the plaintiff's business by patrolling the sidewalk or street in front or in the vicinity of the premises occupied by him, for the purpose of preventing any person or persons, who now are or may hereafter be in his employment, or desirous of entering the same, from entering it, or continuing in it; or by obstructing or interfering with such persons, or any others, in entering

the exist of the injunctn was to prevent ? union ? "from intimidating ? others ? workers

or leaving the plaintiff's said premises; or by intimidating, by threats or otherwise, any person or persons who now are or may hereafter be in the employment
of the plaintiff, or desirous of entering the same, from entering it, or continuing
in it; or by any scheme or conspiracy among themselves or with others, organized
for the purpose of annoying, hindering, interfering with, or preventing any person
or persons who now are, or may hereafter be, in the employment of the plaintiff,
or desirous of entering the same, from entering it, or from continuing therein."

Hearing upon the bill and the answers before Holmes, J., who reported the case
for the consideration of the full court, as follows:

> The facts admitted or proved are that, following upon a strike of the
> plaintiff's workmen, the defendants have conspired to prevent the plaintiff
> from getting workmen, and thereby to prevent him from carrying on his
> business unless and until he will adopt a schedule of prices which has been
> exhibited to him, and for the purpose of compelling him to accede to that
> schedule, but for no other purpose. If he adopts that schedule, he will not be
> interfered with further. The means adopted for preventing the plaintiff from
> getting workmen are (1) in the first place, persuasion and social pressure.
> And these means are sufficient to affect the plaintiff disadvantageously, al-
> though it does not appear, if that be material, that they are sufficient to crush
> him. I ruled that the employment of these means for the said purpose was
> lawful, and for that reason refused an injunction against the employment of
> them. If the ruling was wrong, I find that an injunction ought to be granted.

> (2) I find also, that, as a further means for accomplishing the desired end,
> threats of personal injury or unlawful harm were conveyed to persons seek-
> ing employment or employed, although no actual violence was used beyond
> a technical battery, and although the threats were a good deal disguised, and
> express words were avoided. It appeared to me that there was danger of
> similar acts in the future. I ruled that conduct of this kind should be en-
> joined.

> The defendants established a patrol of two men in front of the plaintiff's
> factory, as one of the instrumentalities of their plan. The patrol was changed
> every hour, and continued from half-past six in the morning until half-past
> five in the afternoon, on one of the busy streets of Boston. The number of
> men was greater at times, and at times showed some little inclination to stop
> the plaintiff's door, which was not serious, but seemed to me proper to be
> enjoined. The patrol proper at times went further than simple advice, not
> obtruded beyond the point where the other person was willing to listen, and
> conduct of that sort is covered by (2) above, but its main purpose was in aid
> of the plan held lawful in (1) above. I was satisfied that there was probabil-
> ity of the patrol being continued if not enjoined. I ruled that the patrol, so far
> as it confined itself to persuasion and giving notice of the strike, was not
> unlawful, and limited the injunction accordingly.

Holmes - Such injs can no longer be granted

There was some evidence of persuasion to break existing contracts. I ruled that this was unlawful, and should be enjoined.

I made the final decree appended hereto. If, on the foregoing facts, it ought to be reversed, or modified, such decree is to be entered as the full court may think proper; otherwise, the decree is to stand.

The final decree was as follows: "This cause came on to be heard, and was argued by counsel; and thereupon, on consideration thereof, it is ordered, adjudged, and decreed that the defendants, and each and every [one] of them, their agents and servants, be restrained and enjoined from interfering with the plaintiff's business by obstructing or physically interfering with any persons in entering or leaving the plaintiff's premises numbered 141, 143, 145, 147 North Street in said Boston, or by intimidating, by threats, express or implied, of violence or physical harm to body or property, any person or persons who now are or hereafter may be in the employment of the plaintiff, or desirous of entering the same, from entering or continuing in it, or by in any way hindering, interfering with, or preventing any person or persons who now are in the employment of the plaintiff from continuing therein, so long as they may be bound so to do by lawful contract...."

ALLEN, J. The principal question in this case is whether the defendants should be enjoined against maintaining the patrol. The report shows that, following upon a strike of the plaintiff's workmen, the defendants conspired to prevent him from getting workmen, and thereby to prevent him from carrying on his business, unless and until he should adopt a certain schedule of prices. The means adopted were persuasion and social pressure, threats of personal injury, or unlawful harm, conveyed to persons employed or seeking employment, and a patrol of two men in front of the plaintiff's factory, maintained from half-past six in the morning till half-past five in the afternoon, on one of the busiest streets in Boston. The number of men was greater at times, and at times showed some little disposition to stop [at] the plaintiff's door. The patrol proper at times went further than simple advice, not obtruded beyond the point where the other person was willing to listen; and it was found that the patrol would probably be continued, if not enjoined. There was also some evidence of persuasion to break existing contracts.

The patrol was maintained as one of the means of carrying out the defendants' plan, and it was used in combination with social pressure, threats of personal injury or unlawful harm, and persuasion to break existing contracts. It was thus one means of intimidation indirectly to the plaintiff, and directly to persons actually employed, or seeking to be employed, by the plaintiff, and of rendering such employment unpleasant or intolerable to such persons. Such an act is an unlawful interference with the rights both of employer and of employed. An employer has a right to engage all persons who are willing to work for him, at such prices as may be mutually agreed upon; and persons employed or seeking employment have a corresponding right to enter into, or remain in, the employment of any person or corporation willing to employ them. These rights are secured by the

[handwritten marginalia: Distinctly at law; picketing]

constitution itself [citing cases]. No one can lawfully interfere by force or intimidation to prevent employers or persons employed or wishing to be employed from the exercise of these rights. In Massachusetts, as in some other states, it is even made a criminal offense for one by intimidation or force to prevent or seek to prevent a person from entering into or continuing in the employment of a person or corporation. Pub. Sts. c. 74, Section 2. Intimidation is not limited to threats of violence or of physical injury to person or property. It has a broader signification, and there also may be a moral intimidation which is illegal. Patrolling or picketing, under the circumstances stated in the report, has elements of intimidation like those which were found to exist in *Sherry v. Perkins,* 147 Mass. 212. It was declared to be unlawful in *Regina v. Druitt,* 10 Cox C.C. 592; *Regina v. Hibbert,* 13 Cox C.C. 82, and *Regina v. Bauld,* 13 Cox C.C. 282. It was assumed to be unlawful in *Trollope v. London Bldg. Trades Fed'n,* 11 T.L.R. 228, though in that case the pickets were withdrawn before the bringing of the bill. The patrol was an unlawful interference both with the plaintiff and with the workmen, within the principle of many cases, and, when instituted for the purpose of interfering with his business, it became a private nuisance....

The defendants contend that these acts were justifiable, because they were only seeking to secure better wages for themselves by compelling the plaintiff to accept their schedule of wages. This motive or purpose does not justify maintaining a patrol in front of the plaintiff's premises, as a means of carrying out their conspiracy. A combination among persons merely to regulate their own conduct is within allowable competition, and is lawful, although others may be indirectly affected thereby. But a combination to do injurious acts expressly directed to another, by way of intimidation or constraint, either of himself or of persons employed or seeking to be employed by him, is outside of allowable competition, and is unlawful....

Nor does the fact that the defendants' acts might subject them to an indictment prevent a court of equity from issuing an injunction. It is true that ordinarily a court of equity will decline to issue an injunction to restrain the commission of a crime; but a continuing injury to property or business may be enjoined, although it may also be punishable as a nuisance or other crime....

A question is also presented whether the court should enjoin such interference with persons in the employment of the plaintiff who are not bound by contract to remain with him, or with persons who are not under any existing contract, but who are seeking or intending to enter into his employment. A conspiracy to interfere with the plaintiff's business by means of threats and intimidation, and by maintaining a patrol in front of his premises in order to prevent persons who are in his employment from continuing therein, is unlawful, even though such persons are not bound by contract to enter into or to continue in his employment; and the injunction should not be so limited as to relate only to persons who are bound by existing contracts. *Walker v. Cronin,* 107 Mass. 555, 565; *Carew v. Rutherford,* 106 Mass. 1; *Sherry v. Perkins,* 147 Mass. 212; *Temperton v. Russell* [1893] 1 Q.B. 715, 728, 731; *Flood v. Jackson,* 11 T.L.R. 276.

In the opinion of a majority of the court the injunction should be in the form originally issued.

So ordered....

HOLMES, J. In a case like the present, it seems to me that, whatever the true result may be, it will be of advantage to sound thinking to have the less popular view of the law stated, and therefore, although when I have been unable to bring my brethren to share my convictions my almost invariable practice is to defer to them in silence, I depart from that practice in this case, notwithstanding my unwillingness to do so in support of an already rendered judgment of my own.

In the first place, a word or two should be said as to the meaning of the report. I assume that my brethren construe it as I meant it to be construed, and that, if they were not prepared to do so, they would give an opportunity to the defendants to have it amended in accordance with what I state my meanings to be. There was no proof of any threat or danger of a patrol exceeding two men, and as of course an injunction is not granted except with reference to what there is reason to expect in its absence, the question on that point is whether a patrol of two men should be enjoined. Again, the defendants are enjoined by the final decree from intimidating by threats, express or implied, of physical harm to body or property, any person who may be desirous of entering into the employment of the plaintiff so far as to prevent him from entering the same. In order to test the correctness of the refusal to go further, it must be assumed that the defendants obey the express prohibition of the decree. If they do not, they fall within the injunction as it now stands, and are liable to summary punishment. The important difference between the preliminary and the final injunction is that the former goes further, and forbids the defendants to interfere with the plaintiff's business "by any scheme ... organized for the purpose of ... preventing any person or persons who now are or may hereafter be ... desirous of entering the [plaintiff's employment] from entering it." I quote only a part, and the part which seems to me most objectionable. This includes refusal of social intercourse, and even organized persuasion or argument, although free from any threat of violence, either express or implied. And this is with reference to persons who have a legal right to contract or not to contract with the plaintiff, as they may see fit. Interference with existing contracts is forbidden by the final decree. I wish to insist a little that the only point of difference which involves a difference of principle between the final decree and the preliminary injunction which it is proposed to restore, is what I have mentioned, in order that it may be seen exactly what we are to discuss. It appears to me that the judgment of the majority turns, in part, on the assumption that the patrol necessarily carries with it a threat of bodily harm. That assumption I think unwarranted, for the reasons which I have given. Furthermore, it cannot be said, I think, that two men walking together up and down a sidewalk and speaking to those who enter a certain shop do necessarily and always thereby convey a threat of force. I do not think it possible to discriminate, and to say that two workmen, or even two representatives of an organization of workmen, do,—

especially when they are, and are known to be, under the injunction of this court not to do so. *See* Stimson, "Handbook to Labor Law," Section 60, esp. pp. 290, 298, 299, 300; *Regina v. Shepherd,* 11 Cox C.C. 325. I may add, that I think the more intelligent working men believe as fully as I do that they no more can be permitted to usurp the State's prerogative of force than can their opponents in their controversies. But if I am wrong, then the decree as it stands reaches the patrol, since it applies to all threats of force. With this I pass to the real difference between the interlocutory and the final decree.

I agree, whatever may be the law in the case of a single defendant, *Rice v. Albee,* 164 Mass. 88, that when plaintiff proves that several persons have combined and conspired to injure his business, and have done acts producing that effect, he shows temporal damage and a cause of action, unless the facts disclose, or the defendants prove, some ground of excuse or justification. And I take it to be settled, and rightly settled, that doing that damage by combined persuasion is actionable, as well as doing it by falsehood or by force. *Walker v. Cronin,* 107 Mass. 555; *Morasse v. Brochu,* 151 Mass. 567; *Tasker v. Stanley,* 153 Mass. 148.

Nevertheless, in numberless instances, the law warrants the intentional infliction of temporal damage because it regards it as justified. It is on the question of what shall amount to a justification, and more especially on the nature of the consideration which really determine or ought to determine the answer to that question, that judicial reasoning seems to me often to be inadequate. The true grounds of decision are considerations of policy and of social advantage, and it is vain to suppose that solutions can be attained merely by logic and the general propositions of law which nobody disputes. Propositions as to public policy rarely are unanimously accepted, and still more rarely, if ever, are capable of unanswerable proof. They require a special training to enable any one even to form an intelligent opinion about them. In the early stages of law, at least, they generally are acted on rather as inarticulate instincts than as definite ideas for which a rational defense is ready.

To illustrate what I have said in the last paragraph, it has been the law for centuries that a man may set up a business in a country town too small to support more than one, although he expects and intends thereby to ruin someone already there, and succeeds in his intent. In such a case, he is not held to act "unlawfully and without justifiable cause," as was alleged in *Walker v. Cronin* and *Rice v. Albee.* The reason, of course, is that the doctrine generally has been accepted that free competition is worth more to society than it costs, and that on this ground the infliction of the damage is privileged. *Commonwealth v. Hunt,* 4 Met. 111, 134. Yet even this proposition nowadays is disputed by a considerable body of persons, including many whose intelligence is not to be denied, little as we may agree with them.

I have chosen this illustration partly with reference to what I have to say next. It shows without the need of further authority that the policy of allowing free competition justifies the intentional inflicting of temporal damage, including the damage of interference with a man's business, by some means, when the damage is done, not for its own sake, but as an instrumentality in reaching the end of victory in the battle of trade. In such a case it cannot matter whether the plaintiff is the only rival of the defendant, and so is aimed at specifically, or is one of a class all of whom are hit. The only debatable ground is the nature of the means by which such damage may be inflicted. We all agree that it cannot be done by force or threats of force. We all agree, I presume, that it may be done by persuasion to leave a rival's shop and come to the defendant's. It may be done by the refusal or withdrawal of various pecuniary advantages which, apart from this consequence, are within the defendant's lawful control. It may be done by the withdrawal, or threat to withdraw, such advantages from third persons who have a right to deal or not to deal with the plaintiff, as a means of inducing them not to deal with him either as customers or servants [citing cases].

I pause here to remark that the word "threats" often is used as if, when it appeared that threats had been made, it appeared that unlawful conduct had begun. But it depends on what you threaten. As a general rule, even if subject to some exceptions, what you may do in a certain event you may threaten to do, that is, give warning of your intention to do in that event, and thus allow the other person the chance of avoiding the consequences. So as to "compulsion," it depends on how you "compel." *Commonwealth v. Hunt,* 4 Met. 111, 133. So as to "annoyance" or "intimidation." *Connor v. Kent, Curran v. Treleaven,* 17 Cox C.C. 354, 367, 368, 370. In *Sherry v. Perkins,* 147 Mass. 212, it was found as a fact that the display of banners which was enjoined was part of a scheme to prevent workmen from entering or remaining in the plaintiff's employment, "by threats and intimidation." The context showed that the words as there used meant threats of personal violence, and intimidation by causing fear of it.

I have seen the suggestion made that the conflict between employers and employed is not competition. But I venture to assume that none of my brethren would rely on that suggestion. If the policy on which our law is founded is too narrowly expressed in the term free competition, we may substitute free struggle for life. Certainly the policy is not limited to struggles between persons of the same class competing for the same end. It applies to all conflicts of temporal interests.

So far, I suppose, we are agreed. But there is a notion which latterly has been insisted on a good deal, that a combination of persons to do what any one of them lawfully might do by himself will make the otherwise lawful conduct unlawful. It would be rash to say that some as yet unformulated truth may not be hidden under this proposition. But in the general form in which it has been presented and accepted by many courts, I think it plainly untrue, both on authority and on principle. *Commonwealth v. Hunt,* 4 Met. 111; *Randall v. Hazleton,* 12 Allen 412, 414. There was combination of the most flagrant and dominant kind in *Bowen v. Matheson* and in the *Mogul Steamship Company's* case, and combination was essential to the success achieved. But it is not necessary to cite cases; it is plain from the slightest consideration of practical affairs, or the most superficial reading of industrial history, that free competition means combination, and that the organization of the world, now going on so fast, means an ever increasing might and scope of combination. It seems to me futile to set our faces against this tendency. Whether beneficial on the whole, as I think it, or detrimental, it is inevitable, unless the fundamental axioms of society, and even the fundamental conditions of life, are to be changed.

One of the eternal conflicts out of which life is made up is that between the effort of every man to get the most he can for his services, and that of society, disguised under the name of capital, to get his services for the least possible return. Combination on the one side is patent and powerful. Combination on the other is the necessary and desirable counterpart, if the battle is to be carried on in a fair and equal way. I am unable to reconcile *Temperton v. Russell* [1893] 1 Q.B. 715, and the cases which follow it, with the *Mogul Steamship Company* case. But *Temperton v. Russell* is not a binding authority here, and therefore I do not think it necessary to discuss it.

If it be true that workingmen may combine with a view, among other things, to getting as much as they can for their labor, just as capital may combine with a view to getting the greatest possible return, it must be true that when combined they have the same liberty that combined capital has to support their interests by argument, persuasion, and the bestowal or refusal of those advantages which they otherwise lawfully control. I can remember when many people thought that, apart from violence or breach of contract, strikes were wicked, as organized refusals to work. I suppose that intelligent economists and legislators have given up that notion today. I feel pretty confident that they equally will abandon the idea that an organized refusal by workmen of social intercourse with a man who shall enter their antagonist's employ is wrong, if it is dissociated from any threat of violence, and is made for the sole object of prevailing, if possible, in a contest with their employer about the rate of wages. The fact, that the immediate object of the act by which the benefit to themselves is to be gained is to injure their antagonist, does not necessarily make it unlawful, any more than when a great house lowers the price of certain goods for the purpose, and with the effect, of driving a smaller antagonist from the business. Indeed, the question seems to me to have been decided as long ago as 1842 by the good sense of Chief Justice Shaw, in *Commonwealth v. Hunt*, 4 Met. 111. I repeat at the end, as I said at the beginning, that this is the point of difference in principle, and the only one, between the interlocutory and the final decree. See *Regina v. Shepherd*, 11 Cox C.C. 325; *Connor v. Kent, Gibson v. Lawson, Curran v. Treleaven*, 17 Cox C.C. 354.

The general question of the propriety of dealing with this kind of case by injunction I say nothing about, because I understand that the defendants have no objection to the final decree if it goes no further and that both parties wish a decision upon the matters which I have discussed.

———

It would require no particular omniscience to speculate that American courts would be conservative in their approach to the problems thrown up by unionism, even after the atrophy of the doctrine of criminal conspiracy. A judiciary nurtured in the culture of contract and property, and recruited largely from the middle and upper classes of society, would very naturally have moved slowly in the adaptation of its legal system to accommodate and privilege the injuries to recognized interests which collective action in its typical forms necessarily inflicts. It was to be anticipated that organized labor would face an uphill struggle in gaining legal acceptance of its normal modes of conduct in the absence of legislative approbation, and so it has been.

There were, it is true, occasional judicial pronouncements exhibiting tolerance and understanding of the labor movement. Examples are the opinion (in dissent) of Judge Holmes in 1900 in *Plant v. Woods,* 176 Mass. 492, 57 N.E. 1011 (1900), decided by the Massachusetts Supreme Judicial Court, and the earlier opinion of Judge Macomber of the New York Supreme Court in *Johnston Harvester Co. v. Meinhardt,* 60 How. Pr. 168 (N.Y. 1880). And it is also true that there was a gradual amelioration of the harsh standards of the common law as unions slowly gained ground in numbers and acceptability, a movement in which the New York Court of Appeals played a leading role. But the progress of organized labor at the hands of the courts was slow and halting; employers had easy access to the courts, especially in equity; by and large the judges were quite ready to supply the policy standards by which to condemn many forms of collective action, and they were able to find in the common law an extraordinarily rich supply of doctrine with which to rationalize the results reached.

A sampling of the common-law torts cases dealing with collective action would disclose that the following are some of the principles of law that have been used:

(1) Although economic injuries inflicted for the purpose of promoting some legitimate interest are privileged, they are actionable if inflicted without justification, maliciously, in bad faith, or where the primary object is to harm others and not to benefit the actors. Thus, in *National Fireproofing Co. v. Mason Bldrs.' Ass'n,* 169 F. 259, 265 (2d Cir. 1909), the court held that "laborers and builders may combine for mutual advantage, and, so long as the motive is not malicious, the object not unlawful, nor oppressive and the means neither deceitful nor fraudulent, the result is not a conspiracy, although it may necessarily work injury to other persons."

(2) Combinations in restraint of trade are illegal. The use of this theory is illustrated in *Berry v. Donovan,* 188 Mass. 353, 74 N.E. 603 (1905), where it was held that a contract whereby an employer agrees to hire only members of the Boot and Shoe Workers' Union was not within the ambit of fair competition.

(3) Acts which are privileged if done by individuals may be actionable if done in combination. This view is reflected by Justice Harlan's majority opinion in *Arthur v. Oakes,* 63 F. 310, 322 (7th Cir. 1894), where he stated:

> An intent upon the part of a single person to injure the rights of others or of the public is not in itself a wrong of which the law will take cognizance, unless some injurious act be done in execution of the unlawful intent. But a combination of two or more persons with such an intent, and under circumstances that give them, when so combined, a power to do an injury they would not possess as individuals acting singly, has always been recognized as in itself wrongful and illegal.

(4) An action will lie for a nonprivileged interference in business and contractual relations. *Hitchman Coal & Coke Co. v. Mitchell,* 245 U.S. 229 (1917), is the leading case in this country on the application of this doctrine to union-management relations. In it the "inducement of breach of contract" principle of law was used to found union liability for interfering with a "yellow-dog" contractual arrangement under which the company had exacted of each employee a warranty that he would not, while employed, become a member of a union.

(5) Concerted action subjects the actors to liability for injuries inflicted if either the object sought or the means used is improper. This theory was adopted by the Restatement of Torts in § 775 where it was stated:

> Workers are privileged intentionally to cause harm to another by concerted action if the object and the means of their concerted action are proper; they are subject to liability to the other for harm so caused if either the object or the means of their concerted action is improper.

Probably the most frequently cited doctrine, and certainly the most potent, is the so-called "ends-means" or civil conspiracy test. This has all the flexibility of the older law of criminal conspiracy. It has permitted the judges, in the light of the mores of the times, to pass judgment on the entire gamut of union objectives and methods of collective action. In passing on the propriety of union "methods" the test has been the more effective because the common inquiry has been whether the action taken was "coercive," and this in turn has been a standard so broad and indefinite as to have enabled some courts to condemn even picketing of the most peaceful kind.

Writers have sometimes referred to the various traditional legal standards of union liability as if they were well defined and clearly differentiated. The fact, however, is that they have frequently been confusingly scrambled in judicial opinions. The doctrine of civil conspiracy, for example, has often been used in conjunction with inducement of breach of contractual relations and with restraint of trade, the illegality of the conspiracy being made to rest on the commission of acts which would presumably be independently tortious under some one of the other cited theories. On occasion, when a given objective has been present which the court has felt obliged to uphold under the ends-means test (as, for example, inducing workers to join the union, or pressing for higher wages for a class of workers), illegality has been predicated on a finding that such objective was only "secondary" or that the union was motivated by malice rather than self-interest.

We would discover quickly enough, upon examining the cases, that the plethora of legal principle has not made decisions either easy or automatic, and that, however the rule for the particular case has been phrased, the primary problem has really been to what extent, in the light of the various competing interests involved, the action of the unionists carried a privilege to inflict economic or other injury upon others. Unfortunately the courts have not always recognized this. Many opinions are doctrinaire in the extreme, and hence are useless except in cataloging legal formulae. A famous observation of Justice Holmes is peculiarly apt in the field of labor law:

> But whether, and how far, a privilege shall be allowed is a question of policy. Questions of policy are legislative questions, and judges shy of reasoning from such grounds. Therefore, decisions for or against the privilege, which really can stand only upon such grounds, often are presented as hollow deductions from empty general propositions like sic utere tuo ut alienum non laedas, which teaches nothing but a benevolent yearning, or else are put as if they themselves embodied a postulate of the law and admitted of no further deduction, as when it is said that, although there is temporal damage, there is no wrong; whereas, the very thing to be found out is whether there is a wrong or not, and if not, why not....
>
> Perhaps one of the reasons why judges do not like to discuss questions of policy, or put a decision in terms upon their views as law-makers, is that the moment you leave the path of merely logical deduction you lose the illusion of certainty which makes legal reasoning seem like mathematics. Views of policy are taught by experience of the interests of life. Those interests are fields of battle. Whatever decisions are made must be against the wishes and opinion of one party, and the distinctions on which they go will be distinctions of degree.

Holmes, *Privilege, Malice, and Intent,* 8 Harv. L. Rev. 1, 3, 7 (1894). *See generally* Hovenkamp, *Labor Conspiracies in American Law, 1880-1930,* 66 Tex. L. Rev. 919 (1988).

3. EARLY LEGISLATIVE REACTION

During the period after the Civil War, there were sporadic state and federal legislative efforts to correct some of the inequities in the law with respect to trade unionism. These included attempts to outlaw the use of "yellow-dog" contracts, to limit the use of labor injunctions, to abolish the crime of conspiracy as applied to labor combinations, to exempt labor organizations from the antitrust laws, to protect union labels, to outlaw employer "blacklisting" of employees for union activity, and to provide for the mediation and arbitration of labor disputes.

Sooner or later it was inevitable not only that worker organizations should be tolerated under the law, but that they should be regarded as necessary and desirable institutions in promoting an effective democracy and as having commensurate legal privileges and responsibilities. So it was natural, if not inevitable, that ultimately the legislative "bit" treatment should give way to something more positive and comprehensive, and that responsibility for social policies with respect to unionism should gradually be withdrawn from the courts and assumed by the legislative branch of government.

a. Railway Labor Legislation

In view of the rail strikes of 1886, 1892, and 1894, and the close relation between railroad transportation and the public welfare, it was to be expected that the first legislative efforts directed toward establishing a federal labor policy should be in the railroad field.

The first major pieces of legislation to be passed were the Arbitration Act of 1888 and the Erdman Act of 1898, 25 Stat. 501 (1888); 30 Stat. 424 (1898). They provided for voluntary arbitration, and the latter inaugurated the policy of government mediation and conciliation. Also included was a provision outlawing "yellow-dog" contracts, which was later nullified by the Supreme Court in *Adair v. United States,* 208 U.S. 161 (1908).

The Erdman Act was followed by the Newlands Act of 1913, 38 Stat. 103 (1913), which established a permanent Board of Mediation and Conciliation, and the Adamson Act of 1916, 39 Stat. 721 (1916), upheld in *Wilson v. New,* 243 U.S. 332 (1917), which established the eight-hour-day principle.

During the wartime period of federal operation of the railroads, from 1917 to 1920, the government under the urgent necessity of maintaining efficient transportation service first formulated the policy of protecting the workers' right to unionize, a policy somewhat foreshadowed by the earlier attempt to outlaw the "yellow-dog" contract. General Order No. 8 of the Director General of the railroads provided for the right of self-organization of workers without discrimination. A bipartisan Board of Railroad Wages and Working Conditions was established with advisory duties with respect to wages and other working conditions. The Director General entered into several nationwide agreements with labor organizations, in which wage awards made by the board were incorporated. Disputes arising out of these agreements were required to be referred, after local adjustment machinery failed, to boards of adjustment set up by agreement of the regional directors and the labor organizations to function with respect to the various crafts. This system marked a distinct advance toward a solution of the problem of interpretation of collective agreements, which had proved to be a source of friction under the earlier legislation.

The next phase in the development of railroad labor legislation occurred in connection with the return of the roads to their owners in 1920. Out of a welter of conflicting ideas, Title III of the Transportation Act of 1920, 41 Stat. 456 (1920), (the Esch-Cummins law) emerged. In substance, this statute provided with respect to labor relations (1) that all disputes should be considered first in conference between representatives of the carriers and of the employees, and (2) that failing of disposition in such conferences, they should be referred to a bipartisan board of adjustment, if one had been created and if the dispute concerned "grievances, rules or working conditions," otherwise to the Railroad Labor Board, created by the act, for "hearing and decision." The principle of mediation which had been the main forte of the earlier statutes was completely abandoned. A basic premise of the legislation was that an agency on which the carriers, labor, and the public were equally represented could settle basic nongrievance disputes simply by decision, as if they were justiciable matters. Its decisions were not legally enforceable, the thought being that public opinion would provide sufficient sanction. The act contained no provisions concerning the right of workers to self- organization, although the Railroad Labor Board did in one of its decisions espouse the right to self-organization without interference and the principle of "majority rule" in labor representation. From the point of view of labor this had the anomalous, and perhaps intended, result of encouraging the formation of company unions. An important innovation was the provision in the act placing upon the parties a duty to bargain, but no penalties or other means of enforcement were provided. The weaknesses of the statute made new legislation imperative.

The Railway Labor Act of 1926, 44 Stat. 577 (1926), 45 U.S.C. §§ 151-63 (*see* The Railway Labor Act at Fifty: Collective Bargaining in the Railroad and Airline Industries (C. Rehmus, ed. 1976)), represented an attempt to incorporate into law the best features of all preceding legislation, and was supported both by the railroads and by the railroad unions. The policy of mediation was again brought to the fore, with the creation of a nonpartisan Board of Mediation whose primary duty was to mediate, and, failing in that, to urge arbitration. Arbitration procedures were specified and awards were made enforceable. Bipartite boards of adjustment could be set up to consider secondary disputes involving questions of interpretation of collective agreements, as under the act of 1920. An additional feature was that, if mediation failed and if the parties to a dispute were unwilling to arbitrate, an emergency board of investigation could be named by the President upon the recommendation of the Board of Mediation, whereupon no strike nor change in the terms or conditions of employment could be undertaken until thirty days after the emergency board's report to the President, such report to be made within thirty days after the board's appointment. Finally, the statute reincorporated, in substance, a provision of the act of 1920 placing a duty upon carriers and employees to make reasonable efforts to make and maintain agreements, and also included a declaration of the right of employers and employees to designate representatives without interference, influence, or coercion. No penalties or other means of enforcement of any of the obligations imposed by the act were provided, however. Reliance was to be placed upon collective bargaining through real representatives, and upon the processes of mediation and voluntary arbitration and the avoidance of hasty action in an effort to effectuate the peaceful settlement of disputes.

The Railway Labor Act of 1926 remains the basic labor legislation for the railroads, but it has been amended on several occasions. In 1934, the act was modified in the following main respects: (1) by creating the National Railroad Adjustment Board, which was to function in four divisions, to decide grievances arising under collective agreements; (2) by creating the National Mediation Board, in lieu of the Board of Mediation, which was to mediate disputes other than those arising out of existing agreements and was also to decide representation disputes; and (3) by clarifying the right to organize and to bargain collectively, the principle of "majority rule" with respect to representation being expressly adopted. Penalties were added for violation of certain of the obligations declared.

In 1936, most of the provisions of the act were extended to cover interstate air carriers. In 1951, the act was further amended to authorize the union shop and the check-off, under certain conditions. And in 1966, the act was amended to provide for special boards of adjustment to decide grievances. *Compare* Stone, *Labor Relations on the Airlines: The Railway Labor Act in the Era of Deregulation*, 42 Stan. L. Rev. 1485 (1990), *with* Northrup, *The Railway Labor Act—Time for Repeal?* 13 Harv. J.L. & Pub. Pol. 441 (1990). The Railway Labor Act, as amended, is found in the companion volume, *Selected Federal Statutes and Sample Bargaining Agreement (1999 Edition)* (hereinafter *Selected Federal Statutes*).

b. The Clayton Act .

In the noncarrier field the initial effort of the national government toward the creation of a statutory labor relations policy consisted of an attempt to free unions of some of the curse of the labor injunction and of the application of the antitrust laws, which had been a prolific source of federal court jurisdiction to deal with union activities. The Clayton Act, enacted in 1914, declared "that the labor of a human being is not a commodity or article of commerce," that the antitrust laws were not to be construed to forbid the existence and operation of labor organizations, that courts of the United States were not to grant injunctions restraining certain specified types of conduct in cases involving labor disputes, and that such nonenjoinable conduct was not to be held to violate any law of the United States, including, of course, the Sherman Act, 38 Stat. 730 (1914), §§ 6, 20, 15 U.S.C. § 17, 29 U.S.C. § 52.

The high hopes of organized labor generated by this legislation were not realized because of a combination of legislative obscurantism and a reactionary judicial approach, which largely nullified the statute and left both the Sherman Act and the federal court injunction substantially intact as important legal tools for shaping labor law as administered in the federal courts. Not until some twenty years later were the alleged evils of the labor injunction again the subject of congressional attention.

4. LABOR UNIONS FROM 1900 TO 1932

After 1898 the membership of the AFL increased considerably and by 1913 it was almost 2,000,000. There was extensive organization in previously unorganized trades, as well as expansion into the South and West, with continued concentration on the skilled and semiskilled groups. For a time some competition came from the Industrial Workers of the World, or "Wobblies," a movement of militant syndicalists that aimed at bringing all workers, without regard to craft or skill, into "One Big Union," Although the IWW was never a serious rival of the AFL, its espousal of the cause of the unskilled brought these workers' problems to the attention of the federation's leaders, who were finally forced to alter the organizational structure of the AFL so as to give the unskilled at least limited recognition.

In 1912 Congress created the United States Commission on Industrial Relations to conduct public hearings on labor problems, which had been accentuated in the public mind because of increased industrial unrest throughout the country and numerous acts of violence in connection with strikes. These hearings popularized the labor cause, and with the passage in 1914 of the Clayton Act, organized labor began to exert a more important influence in the government.

The period of World War I resembled that of the Civil War in that the usual peacetime considerations were forced to yield to the exigencies of war. A code of rules was drawn up by the Taft-Walsh War Labor Conference Board, created by president Wilson, for the guidance of management and labor during wartime. This code recognized the basic eight-hour day and the right to a living wage. The status quo with respect to the union or closed shop was to be maintained for the duration and although no penalties were provided if strikes and lockouts were employed, the principle was recognized that such tactics should be suspended for the duration. The National Council of Defense appointed by President Wilson included Samuel Gompers, president of the AFL, as one of the seven members comprising the advisory commission which was in charge of government labor policies. It insisted that standards previously won by organized labor be maintained. Such government recognition was a stimulus to union membership, which increased phenomenally. In 1920, the AFL had a total membership of over 4,000,000.

At the end of the war, however, organized labor began to realize it had been living in a false paradise of government concessions. Many employers withdrew union recognition and countered union efforts with personnel management plans, profit-sharing arrangements, and company unions. Union demands and strikes were played up in the press as "un-American" and "Bolshevistic." The big coal and steel strikes of 1919 reflected the results of this reaction. The steel strike, in which 300,000 workers participated, was lost because the craft unions failed to co-operate fully with each other and because "an almost hysterical public opinion" turned against the strikers in favor of the corporations. The use of a federal court injunction in the coal strike convinced the unions that they were again face-to-face with unsympathetic courts.

In 1921, after production had caught up with the demand for goods which had not been available during the war, a two-year recession set in. During this interval total union membership declined to approximately 3,600,000. The next eight years saw little union progress. Various factors contributed toward worker apathy about unionism. Real wages were high. Management was finding it necessary to combat high labor turnover. The wider use by employers of welfare and pension plans, group life insurance and medical services, and personnel department grievance procedures helped to reduce labor discontent. Company unions flourished. By 1929 total union membership had declined to less than 3,500,000, and during the ensuing depression of the early "thirties," it was reduced another 500,000.

5. THE NORRIS-LA GUARDIA ACT

Judicial intervention in labor disputes came under increasing criticism, not only from the labor movement but also from those who were concerned for the prestige of the courts. Federal Judge Amidon, in *Great N. Ry. v. Brosseau,* 286 F. 414 (D.N.D. 1923), commented at length on a number of the abusive aspects of the labor injunction, and Professor Felix Frankfurter of the Harvard Law School wrote a book in 1930 with Nathan Greene, entitled The Labor Injunction, which was very influential in calling for reform. Criticisms which were aired at this time were:

(1) temporary restraining orders against union conduct in strikes and picketing were usually issued ex parte;

(2) they were frequently based upon affidavits submitted on behalf of the employers by guards or private detectives—"an untrustworthy guide for judicial action";

(3) the complaints and accompanying affidavits were in stereotyped form, raising "more than a suspicion that conformity to legal formula rather than accuracy of narrative guides oaths";

(4) the temporary restraining order or temporary injunction, while in theory providing merely interlocutory relief, was actually in many instances the means of breaking the union's strike;

(5) the injunction was often phrased in complex terminology, so that the ordinary workman would not be able to know clearly what he had been enjoined from doing;

(6) the armed guards supplied by private detective agencies, who had given the affidavits, were often sworn in as deputy marshals to enforce the decree; and

(7) if violence or breaches of the peace occurred, the unionists did not have the safeguards of ordinary criminal prosecutions before a jury, but were subject to contempt of court proceedings before the judge who had issued the injunction.

All of this led to a widespread feeling that the labor injunction was impairing public confidence in the judicial system. In addition, the point was made that the weight of the law was being thrown into labor disputes on one side, and that the

injunctions were not making any contribution to the solution of the industrial relations problems which has caused the disputes.

The continued application of the antitrust laws to labor unions during the
1920s in such cases as *Duplex Printing Press Co. v. Deering,* 254 U.S. 443
(1921), and *Bedford Cut Stone Co. v. Journeymen Stone Cutter's Ass'n,* 274 U.S.
37 (1927), where injunctions were issued against secondary boycotts, contributed
greatly to the increasing agitation for a stronger federal anti-injunction law.

In 1932, Congress passed the Norris-La Guardia Act, 47 Stat. 70 (1932), 29
U.S.C. §§ 101-15, which made sweeping reforms in federal court labor injunction procedure, forbade injunctions altogether that would prohibit what might be
described as peaceful collective action, and repudiated the "yellow-dog" contract
as the basis for legal or equitable relief in the federal courts. Perhaps most important as a portent of legislative policy was the preamble of the act, which recognized the impotence of the individual unorganized employee in establishing
the terms and conditions of employment in industry, and declared that he should
have "full freedom of association, self-organization, and designation of representatives of his own choosing, to negotiate the terms and conditions of his employment" and that he should be "free from the interference, restraint, or coercion
of employers of labor, or their agents, in the designation of such representatives
or in self-organization or in other concerted activities for the purpose of collective bargaining or other mutual aid or protection." Section 2 of the act, 29 U.S.C.
§ 102. This statute remains in force today, and constitutes an important part of
present day labor law, which must later be examined in some detail, particularly
in its interrelation with other federal statutes. But, for now, the student should
read the act itself, as it appears in *Selected Federal Statutes.*

One knowledgeable observer assessed Norris-La Guardia this way:

> The Norris-La Guardia Act had practical economic origins. It was enacted
> at the bottom of the Great Depression. Employees were weak, ill-paid, and
> working under deplorable conditions. Its sponsors believed that the workers'
> bargaining power could be enhanced and their earnings and working condi-
> tions improved by concerted action. Labor injunctions were obstacles; there-
> fore they deprived the courts of power to issue injunctions.

> Perhaps these economic forces were alone sufficient to carry the day, but
> the Norris-La Guardia Act also rested upon closely reasoned theory. The
> central proposition was that law served no useful purpose in labor disputes,
> save possibly to protect tangible property and preserve public order. Its
> philosophical underpinning was the belief that the government should not
> resolve labor disputes or substitute its wage or price determinations for pri-
> vate contracts in a free market. Union organization, strikes, boycotts, and
> picketing were held to be part of the competitive struggle for life, which so-
> ciety tolerates because the freedom is worth more than it costs.... The Nor-

ris-La Guardia Act introduced the only period of unqualified laissez faire in labor relations.

A. Cox, Law and the National Labor Policy 5, 8 (1960).

C. THE PERIOD SINCE 1933

1. THE INITIAL NEW DEAL LABOR POLICIES

The Roosevelt administration attempted to make effective a national labor policy favorable to trade unionism. An effort in this direction was made in the ill-starred National Industrial Recovery Act, 48 Stat. 198 (1933), § 7a of which provided as follows:

> Every code of fair competition, agreement, and license approved, prescribed, or issued under this title shall contain the following conditions: (1) That employees shall have the right to organize and bargain collectively through representatives of their own choosing, and shall be free from the interference, restraint, or coercion of employers of labor, or their agents, in the designation of such representatives or in self-organization or in other concerted activities for the purpose of collective bargaining; (2) that no employee and no one seeking employment shall be required as a condition of employment to join any company union or to refrain from joining, organizing, or assisting a labor organization of his own choosing; and (3) that employers shall comply with the maximum hours of labor, minimum rates of pay, and other conditions of employment, approved or prescribed by the President.

Even prior to the adoption of codes of fair competition under the act, the principles stated in § 7a had been incorporated into the "President's Re-Employment Agreement." Then, in order to compose differences that might arise under such agreement, the President, on August 5, 1933, created the National Labor Board, with Senator Robert F. Wagner as chairman, which subsequently assumed jurisdiction also of labor disputes arising under the codes of fair competition. When the board's authority was questioned, the President issued executive orders on February 1 and 23, 1934, purporting to give the board the right to conduct employee representation elections and to report its findings and recommendations concerning violations of § 7a to the Attorney General for possible prosecution, or to the Compliance Division of the National Recovery Administration for appropriate action.

After a period of considerable activity, the National Labor Board was superseded, on July 9, 1934, by the (first) National Labor Relations Board, which was established pursuant to a joint resolution of Congress approved June 19, 1934, 48 Stat. 1183 (1934). This resolution authorized the designation by the President of one or more boards to investigate the facts in labor controversies arising under § 7a with power to conduct elections among employees to determine their collective bargaining representatives, any orders issued in connection therewith to be reviewable by the circuit courts of appeal. The Board adopted procedures of "investigation" similar to the method of complaint, hearing, and decision later prescribed under the National Labor Relations Act. As in the case of the National Labor Board, however, its authority was definitely limited, since its orders could merely take the form of advisory recommendations to the Attorney General and to the Compliance Division of NRA.

The Board functioned until the decision of the Supreme Court in the *Schechter* case invalidated the NIRA on May 27, 1935. *Schechter Poultry Corp. v. United States,* 295 U.S. 495 (1935). It had an active life while it lasted, however. Possibly its most important contribution consisted of a total of 202 formal decisions in which an attempt was made to build up a body of labor law involving the principles of § 7a, which were later of material assistance in interpreting and applying similar principles set out in the National Labor Relations Act.

2. THE NATIONAL LABOR RELATIONS ACT (WAGNER ACT), 1935

Senator Wagner was determined that the labor relations policies, at least, of the NIRA should not be sacrificed but, indeed, should be reinforced, if possible. In little more than two months following the demise of the NIRA, the original National Labor Relations Act was enacted on July 5, 1935. This statute declared it to be "the policy of the United States" to encourage the practice of collective bargaining and full freedom of worker self-organization, as a means of facilitating the free flow of interstate commerce. Employees covered by the act were given the "right" to organize and to bargain collectively and this right was made effective by proscribing as "unfair labor practices" five kinds of employer conduct vis-à-vis unionism. The principle of "majority rule" among employees in selecting union representatives was adopted, and a three-member National Labor Relations Board was created with authority to settle representation questions and to prosecute violations of the unfair labor practice provisions of the act, 49 Stat. 449 (1935), 29 U.S.C. §§ 151-68. This Board, in accordance with the then prevailing vogue as to administrative agencies, combined the functions of prosecutor and judge, although its orders had no binding force until "enforced" by a circuit court of appeals upon petition. All employers whose labor practices might "affect" interstate commerce were subject to the act, with the exception of those covered by the Railway Labor Act, and the United States and states or political subdivisions thereof. *See* Casebeer, *Drafting Wagner's Act: Leon Keyserling and the Precommittee Drafts of the Labor Disputes Act and the National Labor Relations Act*, 11 Indus. Rel. L.J. 73 (1989).

This, then, was the statute which placed the full power and influence of the national government behind trade unionism. A detailed study of the principles embodied in this legislation will constitute an important part of this course; hence, their exposition will not be undertaken as a part of this introductory survey. It is noteworthy at this point, however, that the statute was partisan legislation in that restraints were placed upon employers but not upon unions. Moreover, it had a relatively narrow compass, as compared, for example, with the Railway Labor Act. The right of self-organization was secured and collective bargaining was made compulsory, but there was no attempt to deal with the problems of disputes persisting despite good faith bargaining or arising out of collective agreements, although it should be mentioned that facilities for voluntary mediation and arbitration of such disputes continued to be made available through the Conciliation Service of the Department of Labor.

The constitutionality of the Wagner Act was in doubt until the following landmark case in 1937, together with its associated cases. *NLRB v. Freuhauf Trailer Co.,* 301 U.S. 49 (1937); *NLRB v. Friedman-Harry Marks Clothing Co.,* 301 U.S. 58 (1937); *NLRB v. Associated Press,* 301 U.S. 103 (1937); *NLRB v. Washington, V. & M. Coach Co.,* 301 U.S. 142 (1937). For a discussion of this litigation in its historical context, *see* Cortner, The Wagner Act Cases (1964).

NLRB v. JONES & LAUGHLIN STEEL CORP.

Supreme Court of the United States
301 U.S. 1, 57 S. Ct. 615, 81 L. Ed. 893 (1937)

[The corporation was engaged in the manufacture of steel in Pennsylvania, importing iron ore from Michigan and Minnesota and shipping steel products to many states. The NLRB found that the corporation had committed an unfair labor practice by discharging ten men because of their union activities. The court of appeals declined to enforce the Board's order to cease and desist. The Supreme Court granted certiorari.]

MR. CHIEF JUSTICE HUGHES delivered the opinion of the Court (four justices dissenting):....

The scheme of the National Labor Relations Act—which is too long to be quoted in full—may be briefly stated. The first section sets forth findings with respect to the injury to commerce resulting from the denial by employers of the right to organize and from the refusal of employers to accept the procedure of collective bargaining. There follows a declaration that it is the policy of the United States to eliminate these causes of obstruction to the free flow of commerce. The act then defines the terms it uses, including the terms "commerce" and "affecting commerce." § 2. It creates the National Labor Relations Board and prescribes its organization. §§ 3-6. It sets forth the right of employees to self-organization and to bargain collectively through representatives of their own choosing. § 7. It defines "unfair labor practices." § 8. It lays down rules as to the representation of employees for the purpose of collective bargaining. § 9. The Board is empowered to prevent the described unfair labor practices affecting commerce and the act prescribes the procedure to that end. The Board is authorized to petition designated courts to secure the enforcement of its orders.... Any person aggrieved by a final order of the Board may obtain a review in the designated courts with the same procedure as in the case of an application by the Board for the enforcement of its order....

The Scope of the Act.—The act is challenged in its entirety as an attempt to regulate all industry, thus invading the reserved powers of the States over their local concerns. It is asserted that the references in the Act to interstate and foreign commerce are colorable at best; that the Act is not a true regulation of such commerce or of matters which directly affect it but on the contrary has the fundamental object of placing under the compulsory supervision of the federal government all industrial labor relations within the nation.

... We think it clear that the National Labor Relations Act may be construed so as to operate within the sphere of constitutional authority.... The grant of authority to the Board does not purport to extend to the relationship between all industrial employees and employers. Its terms do not impose collective bargaining upon all industry regardless of effects upon interstate or foreign commerce. It purports to reach only what may be deemed to burden or obstruct that commerce and, thus qualified, it must be construed as contemplating the exercise of control within constitutional bounds. It is a familiar principle that acts which directly burden or obstruct interstate or foreign commerce, or its free flow, are within the reach of the congressional power. Acts having that effect are not rendered immune because they grow out of labor disputes. *See Texas & N.O.R. Co. v. Railway Clerks,* 281 U.S. 548, 570 (1930); *A.L.A. Schechter Corp. v. United States,* 295 U.S. 495 (1935); *Virginian Railway Co. v. System Federation, No. 40, R.E.D.,* 300 U.S. 515 (1937). It is the effect upon commerce, not the source of the injury, which is the criterion. Second Employers' Liability Cases, 223 U.S. 1 (1912). Whether or not particular action does affect commerce in such a close and intimate fashion as to be subject to federal control, and hence to lie within the authority conferred upon the Board, is left by the statute to be determined as individual cases arise. We are thus to inquire whether in the instant case the constitutional boundary has been passed....

[I]n its present application, the statute goes no further than to safeguard the right of employees to self-organization and to select representatives of their own choosing for collective bargaining or other mutual protection without restraint or coercion by their employer.

That is a fundamental right. Employees have as clear a right to organize and select their representatives for lawful purposes as the respondent has to organize its business and select its own officers and agents. Discrimination and coercion to prevent free exercise of the right of employees to self-organization and representation is a proper subject for condemnation by competent legislative authority. Long ago we stated the reason for labor organizations. We said that they were organized out of the necessities of the situation; that a single employee was helpless in dealing with an employer; that he was dependent ordinarily on his daily wage for the maintenance of himself and family; that if the employer refused to pay him the wages that he thought fair, he was nevertheless unable to leave the employ and resist arbitrary and unfair treatment; that union was essential to give laborers opportunity to deal on an equality with their employer. *American Steel Foundries v. Tri-City Central Trades Council,* 257 U.S. 184, 209 (1921). We reiterated these views when we had under consideration the Railway Labor Act of 1926. Fully recognizing the legality of collective action on the part of employees in order to safeguard their proper interests, we said that Congress was not required to ignore this right but could safeguard it. Congress could seek to make appropriate collective action of employees an instrument of peace rather than of strife. We said that such collective action would be a mockery if representation were made futile by interference with freedom of choice. Hence the prohibition by Congress of interference with the selection of representatives for the purpose of negotiation and conference between employers and employees, "instead of being an invasion of the constitutional rights of either, was based on the recognition of the rights of both." *Texas & N.O.R. Co. v. Railway Clerks, supra.* We have reasserted the same principle in sustaining the application of the Railway Labor Act as amended in 1934. *Virginian Railway Co. v. System Federation, No. 40, R.E.D., supra....*

Experience has abundantly demonstrated that the recognition of the right of employees to self-organization and to have representatives of their own choosing for the purpose of collective bargaining is often an essential condition of industrial peace. Refusal to confer and negotiate has been one of the most prolific causes of strife. This is such an outstanding fact in the history of labor disturbances that it is a proper subject of judicial notice and requires no citation of instances. The opinion in the case of *Virginian Railway Co. v. System Federation, No. 40, R.E.D., supra,* points out that, in the case of carriers, experience has shown that before the amendment, of 1934, of the Railway Labor Act "when there was no dispute as to the organizations authorized to represent the employees and when there was a willingness of the employer to meet such representative for a discussion of their grievance, amicable adjustment of differences had generally followed and strikes had been avoided." That, on the other hand, "a prolific source of dispute had been the maintenance by the railroad of company unions and the denial by railway management of the authority of representatives chosen by their employees." The opinion in that case also points to the large measure of success of the labor policy embodied in the Railway Labor Act. But with respect to the appropriateness of the recognition of self-organization and representation in the promotion of peace, the question is not essentially different in the case of employees in industries of such a character that interstate commerce is put in jeopardy from the case of employees of transportation companies. And of what avail is it to protect the facility of transportation, if interstate commerce is throttled with respect to the commodities to be transported!

These questions have frequently engaged the attention of Congress and have been the subject of many inquiries. The steel industry is one of the great basic industries of the United States, with ramifying activities affecting interstate commerce at every point. The Government aptly refers to the steel strike of 1919-1920 with its far-reaching consequences. The fact that there appears to have been no major disturbance in that industry in the more recent period did not dispose of the possibilities of future and like dangers to interstate commerce which Congress was entitled to foresee and to exercise its protective power to forestall. It is not necessary again to detail the facts as to respondent's enterprise. Instead of being beyond the pale, we think that it presents in a most striking way the close and intimate relation which a manufacturing industry may have to interstate commerce and we have no doubt that Congress had constitutional authority to safeguard the right of respondent's employees to self-organization and freedom in the choice of representatives for collective bargaining....

Questions Under the Due Process Clause and Other Constitutional Restrictions.—Respondent asserts its right to conduct its business in an orderly manner without being subjected to arbitrary restraints. What we have said points to the fallacy in the argument. Employees have their correlative right to organize for the purpose of securing the redress of grievances and to promote agreements with employers relating to rates of pay and conditions of work. *Texas & N.O.R. Co. v. Railway Clerks, supra; Virginian Railway Co. v. System Federation, No. 40, R.E.D.* Restraint for the purpose of preventing an unjust interference with that right cannot be considered arbitrary or capricious....

3. UNION GROWTH UNDER THE WAGNER ACT: THE CIO AND INDUSTRIAL UNIONS

Both the NIRA and the NLRA, with their guarantees of the right to self-organization without employer interference, gave a tremendous impetus to the organization of the millions of unskilled and semiskilled workers in the mass production industries. As a result there came to a head within the AFL the issue of industrial unionism, which had been all but forgotten since the demise of the Knights of Labor in the nineties. The AFL Convention of 1934 recognized that these potential new recruits to the ranks of organized labor would not fit very well into the traditional pattern of craft unionism, but took an equivocal stand as to just what was to be done.

In the 1934 convention a resolution to organize new industrial type unions within the AFL was decisively defeated. The leading craft unionists took the position that the problem could be handled by using local federal unions within plants already partially organized by craft unions and by enlarging the jurisdiction of the established craft unions. Chartering industrial type unions would have precluded the expansion of the craft unions into certain industries, and the Carpenters, Teamsters, Machinists, Plumbers, and other unions could not face this result with equanimity, nor could they, in fact, easily have resolved the competitive problems which would have attended an attempt to enlarge their respective jurisdictions so as to bring in groups of hitherto unorganized employees. On the other hand, the industrial union partisans maintained that to split up workers within an industry among the various craft unions would weaken the bargaining position of such workers by preventing timely and concerted action.

Personal animosity and rivalry for power and control, unfortunately, also loomed large in AFL conclaves. Certain of the federation's affiliates, such as the United Mine Workers, the Ladies Garment Workers and the Amalgamated Clothing Workers, had become very strong and had successfully used the industrial type of organization. Few of the affiliated craft unions had done so well in rate or extent of growth and the successful pro-industrialist union leaders were impatient with the craft unionists who were dominant in high federation councils. The convention of 1935 was a scene of bitterness and some violence. "Big Bill" Hutcheson, head of the Carpenters union, objected to UMW President John L. Lewis' vociferations in favor of industrial unionism, and harsh words between them ended in fisticuffs. Finally, the industrial union protagonists decided to undertake organizing campaigns in mass production industries on their own, and in November 1935 the presidents of eight AFL unions created the Committee for Industrial Organization, the purpose of which was stated to be "encouragement and promotion of organization of unorganized workers in mass production and other industries on an industrial basis." John L. Lewis was chosen chairman.

In June 1936, a drive was undertaken by this group through the "Steelworkers Organizing Committee" to organize the iron and steel industry. It met with great success the following year when the United States Steel Corporation capitulated and entered into an agreement with the committee. Many other steel companies followed suit. There were also important membership gains in other fields, especially in the automobile, electrical manufacturing, and textile industries.

The Committee for Industrial Organization had stated its purpose was purely "educational" and "advisory" to convince the rank and file of the federation of the need of organizing the millions of workers in the mass production industries. However, the Executive Committee of the AFL considered the committee a "dual" organization and ordered its dissolution. When the ultimatum was disregarded, the member unions of the committee were suspended from the federation. Thereafter many attempts were made to reunite the two groups in the interest of labor harmony, but no agreement could be reached on the question of jurisdiction. At meetings of the AFL Executive Council in January and April 1938, it was decided to revoke the charters of the offending unions, which action was endorsed at the convention that fall.

In November 1938, the various groups then forming the Committee for Industrial Organization broke away completely from the AFL and changed the name of the organization to the "Congress of Industrial Organizations" (CIO). Its avowed purpose was to promote union organization, to extend the benefits of collective bargaining, and to obtain legislation safeguarding the economic security and social welfare of the workers of America. John L. Lewis was the organization's first president. When he resigned in 1940, Philip Murray, president of the CIO's United Steelworkers and a vice-president of the CIO, became president. For years he had handled difficult organizational assignments, and he was welcomed to the presidency of the CIO as a brilliant organizer and a skillful negotiator.

Both the CIO and the AFL had undertaken very active organizational campaigns which were accompanied by an unprecedented number of strikes, and union membership rose to over 7,000,000 in 1937. The business recession in 1937 and the public reaction against the aggressive organizing tactics of the unions, especially the "sit-down" strikes, led to a temporary decrease in membership, but with returning prosperity the uptrend was resumed. Both federations became active in organizing industries which previously had been substantially neglected. This was true particularly in such war production industries as shipbuilding, aircraft production, and aluminum.

The period following the passage of the NLRA was not, therefore, one of tranquility in labor relations. Coupled with the AFL-CIO rift was the fact that countless employers, who had neither the desire nor the experience which makes for successful collective bargaining, were forced to deal with unions. And the fact that many of them had to negotiate with young, militant, and inexperienced unions did not improve the opportunity for good relations. The result was a sharp increase, over the previous decade, in the number of strikes and in the number of production man-days lost as a result of labor disputes. *See* 62 Monthly Lab. Rev. 720 (1946). The short range consequence of the enactment of the statute was certainly not to mitigate, but rather to increase, those "substantial obstructions to the free flow of commerce" to which the preamble of the act referred. Indeed, any other result could hardly have been anticipated. Amicable labor relations through unionism could only be viewed as a long range objective to be achieved after the organizational stage was completed and both employers and unions had learned the art of collective bargaining.

4. LABOR STANDARDS AND SOCIAL SECURITY LEGISLATION

The Norris-La Guardia Act, the Railway Labor Act, and the National Labor Relations Act were directed toward the problems of trade unionism as such. In addition to these and to certain other federal statutes dealing with specific union-management relations problems there is an important body of federal legislation which represents the quite different policy of direct intervention in the determination of terms and conditions of employment. Section 1231 of the United States Code, Title 18 (Crimes and Criminal Procedure) prohibits the interstate transportation of strike-breakers; § 1951 makes it a felony to obstruct interstate commerce by robbery or extortion; the "Lea Act" of 1946 makes it unlawful, by use of threats, force, or other means to compel a broadcasting company to hire more employees than it needs. 60 Stat. 89 (1946), 47 U.S.C. § 506.

Of the statutes in this area, one of the most important is the Fair Labor Standards Act of 1938, 52 Stat. 1060 (1938), 29 U.S.C. §§ 201-19. Enacted as a humanitarian and "spread the work" depression measure, this Act prescribes minimum wage rates, discourages "overtime" employment by requiring premium rates for overtime work, and prohibits the use of child labor—all with respect to employees engaged in interstate commerce or in the production of goods for such commerce. In *National League of Cities v. Usery,* 426 U.S. 833 (1976), the Supreme Court held (5-4) that the 1974 amendments that extended the Act's minimum wage and maximum hour provisions to nearly all state and local government employees interfered with governmental functions traditionally performed by states and their local governments in their capacities as sovereign governments and were accordingly not within the authority granted to Congress by the commerce clause. In *Garcia v. San Antonio Metro. Transit Auth.,* 469 U.S. 528 (1985), however, a closely divided Supreme Court decided that the *National League of Cities'* "traditional governmental functions" test was not only unworkable, but inconsistent with established principles of federalism. The majority thus overruled *National League of Cities* and sustained the authority of the federal government to apply the FLSA to state and municipal personnel. It concluded that the sovereign rights of states would be adequately and appropriately protected through the political process.

The Public Contracts (Walsh-Healey) Act of 1936 requires contractors with the government to meet specified wage, hour, and child-labor standards, 49 Stat. 2036 (1936), 41 U.S.C. §§ 35-45; the Davis-Bacon Act of 1931 sets minimum wage standards on public projects, 46 Stat. 1494 (1931), 40 U.S.C. § 276a; the Selective Training and Service Act of 1940 and the Universal Military Training and Service Act give reemployment right to veterans, 54 Stat. 885 (1940), as amended, 50 U.S.C. App. §§ 301-18; 62 Stat. 604 (1948), as amended, 50 U.S.C. App. §§ 451-71.

The federal government has also made a major effort toward the equitable adjustment of the problems of superannuation and unemployment in industry. Again, the railroad industry was the subject of initial consideration, when the Railroad Retirement Act of 1934, 48 Stat. 1283 (1938), declared unconstitutional in *Railroad Ret. Bd. v. Alton R.R.,* 295 U.S. 330 (1935), was enacted, to be followed by the acts of 1935, 49 Stat. 967 (1935), and 1937, 50 Stat. 307 (1937), 45 U.S.C. §§ 228a-s. Of most importance, however, is the "social security" legislation, which began with the Social Security Act of 1935, 49 Stat. 620 (1935), 42 U.S.C. §§ 1301-1307. This statute and its amendments are the foundation for a comprehensive system of old-age and survivors' insurance benefits, and unemployment compensation, carried financially by means of payroll taxes on employers and employees.

5. THE WORLD WAR II PERIOD

During World War II unions cooperated with management in converting to war production, and offered their services in supplying skilled workers as instructors in training centers. In numerous plants labor-management committees were established under the auspices of the War Production Board for the purpose of meeting such problems as the maximum use of equipment and manpower, the spreading of war orders, and the production of strategic war materials. A "no-strike" pledge had been given at a conference of representatives of industry and labor which had been called by the President in December 1941 to consider the problems of labor relations and the war effort. The group agreed that, following the precedent of World War I, a federal agency should be established "for the peaceful adjustment" of labor disputes. Accordingly, by Executive Order, the President on January 12, 1942, created a "National War Labor Board" of twelve members, tripartite in composition, with authority to "finally determine" labor disputes certified to it by the Secretary of Labor or brought before it on its own motion.

The board had to function for a time without benefit of statutory sanction or guidance, and even after the enactment of the Stabilization Act of 1942 and the War Labor Disputes Act of 1943 the board continued, as a practical matter, to have the basic policy responsibility for wage stabilization and the settlement of labor disputes. Its policy with respect to wage issues was to establish a stabilization front, without, however, attempting a wage freeze. Its cost of living "Little Steel" formula, and companion doctrines relating to "inequalities" and "substandard" wages, were directed to this end, as was its resort to "industry or area practice" in passing on nonwage issues. Among its more famous policies was the "maintenance of membership" compromise solution of the union security issue.

During the first part of the war the "no-strike" pledge was substantially observed. However, after the early flush of patriotism had subsided, irritation at the settlement delays produced by the elaborate procedures of the War Labor Board and its tremendous case load resulted in a fairly large number of work stoppages, most of them "wildcat." There were also stoppages in protest against the "hold the line" policies of the administration. On the whole, however, giving due consideration to the unprecedented power of organized labor, and to the fact that many of the unions were young and undisciplined, the record of union devotion to war production must be regarded as good. The board's decisions with relatively few exceptions were respected. While they were without legal force, they were effectively supported by the possibility, and in some cases the actuality, of plant seizure by presidential directive.

6. THE LABOR MANAGEMENT RELATIONS ACT (TAFT-HARTLEY ACT), 1947

After VJ Day (August 14, 1945), labor-management relations took a turn for the worse. The no-strike, no-lockout pledges were considered as no longer operative. Restraint born of patriotic and emotional impulses, so effective during the war years, lost its force as workers and management faced reconversion problems.

In November 1945 President Truman called a Labor Management Conference on Industrial Relations. It proved fruitless in so far as the reaching of agreement on specific issues is concerned; but, in contrast to the situation after World War I, the principle of collective bargaining was firmly established. Perhaps the most significant outcome of the conference was the recommendation by both labor and management that disputes involving the application of collective agreements should be settled under a grievance procedure with arbitration as a final step and without resorting to work stoppages. This recognition was followed during the post-war period by a phenomenal growth in voluntary arbitration of grievances.

The process of reconversion during late 1945 and 1946 from a wartime to a peacetime economy was accompanied by a wave of strikes in many vital industries, including steel, coal, oil, automobiles, meat packing, and electrical products. In contrast to the post-World War I situation, the unions, particularly in the mass production industries, demonstrated their cohesiveness and strength of organization. The strikes involved a loss of 116,000,000 worker-days—an all-time record.

A reaction to this showing of union power became evident in 1947 when the Eightieth Congress enacted the Labor Management Relations Act (Taft-Hartley Act), 61 Stat. 136 (1947), 29 U.S.C. §§ 141-97, over President Truman's veto.

Title I of this statute amended the original National Labor Relations Act in numerous ways, the significance of which will become apparent as each of the topics of labor relations law are taken up in succeeding chapters. Before launching into this detailed study, however, the student should take time now to read through the amended National Labor Relations Act (Title I of LMRA, 1947), especially §§ 7, 8, 9, and 10, which are the heart of the act. Title I of LMRA is set out in *Selected Federal Statutes* in a manner which highlights the changes which were made in 1947.

In § 7, a basic change in emphasis can be seen in the addition of the right to refrain from organization and concerted activities. This was implemented in § 8(b)(1) by the prohibition of union restraint and coercion against employees exercising such rights.

In § 8(a), the various employer unfair labor practices were retained, but § 8(c) made it clear that employers may express their opinions about unionism unless they threaten reprisal or wrongfully promise benefits. Under § 8(a)(3), the closed shop was no longer authorized and the union shop was subjected to limitations.

Most important, the Taft-Hartley Act noted in § 1 that certain union practices obstruct commerce, and § 8(b) outlawed a number of them, including secondary boycotts (§ 8(b)(4)(A) and (B)) and jurisdictional strikes (§ 8(b)(4)(D)).

The changes in § 9 placed various restrictions on the NLRB in conducting representation proceedings, and those in § 10 tightened up procedures in unfair labor practice cases.

The NLRB was increased from three to five members, and the final authority to investigate charges, issue complaints, and present them before the Board was placed in the hands of the General Counsel, in order to avoid casting the Board in the role of both prosecutor and judge.

In addition to these and many other amendments to the Wagner Act, the Taft-Hartley Act contained much entirely new material. In Title II, the Federal Mediation and Conciliation Service was set up as an independent agency, and an elaborate procedure was outlined for the handling of national emergency disputes. Various important matters were dealt with in Title III of the LMRA, including a provision for suits in federal courts to enforce collective agreements (§ 301), restrictions on payments to employee representatives and on health and welfare funds (§ 302), damage suits in federal courts for secondary boycotts (§ 303), restrictions on political contributions (§ 304), and the outlawing of strikes by government employees (§ 305).

7. LABOR UNIONS FROM 1947 TO 1959: THE AFL-CIO MERGER

This statute became a political issue of the first magnitude in connection with the national elections of 1948, in which President Truman defeated Governor Dewey. The repeal of the act was promptly attempted by administration forces, but a coalition of Republicans and conservative Democrats successfully resisted this effort.

In spite of their inability to obtain the repeal of the Taft-Hartley Act, and their signal lack of success in organizing the unorganized, labor unions have remained strong and have won substantial wage increases and fringe benefits through collective bargaining during the post-World War II period.

Union membership had continued to grow steadily during World War II, passing the 15,000,000 mark by 1947. After 1947, however, the rate of growth in union membership leveled off, about 2,000,000 members being added during the following decade. During that period, the ratio of union members to the total labor force remained fairly constant at about twenty-five percent. U.S. Bureau of Labor Statistics, Dep't of Labor, Directory of National and International Unions in the United States (Bull. No. 1222, 1957). It should be noted that the "labor force" includes many "unorganizables."

In 1949 and 1950, as the "cold war" tightened and the conflict with the Communists in Korea drew near, a major effort was made to remove Communists from positions of power in the labor unions. The CIO Convention in November 1949 voted to expel the United Electrical, Radio and Machine Workers (UE), and within a year ten other unions were expelled from the CIO on charges of pursuing Communist policies. New unions, such as the International Union of Electrical Workers (IUE), were chartered by the CIO to take the place of the expelled unions.

The Korean crisis from mid-1950 to the end of 1952 presented the labor unions with the problems attendant upon a wage and price stabilization program. The AFL and the CIO cooperated in setting up a United Labor Policy Committee to advise the administration on labor policies. Early in 1951, the labor representatives on the Wage Stabilization Board and other defense agencies withdrew in protest against unduly rigid wage controls and the alleged failure of the administration to give weight to labor's views. The issues were eventually settled and labor representatives returned to a reorganized Wage Stabilization Board and a new Advisory Board on Mobilization. The United Labor Policy Committee was dissolved in August 1951.

In November 1952 Philip Murray, President of the CIO since 1940, and William Green, President of the AFL for nearly thirty years, both died. They were succeeded, respectively, by Walter Reuther and George Meany, both men of vigor and wide outlook and interests. As the original issues in the split in the labor movement had faded into history and the areas of economic and political cooperation between the two federations had grown, the time seemed auspicious for the long-thought-of merger.

In June 1953 a no-raiding agreement was negotiated, which was gradually ratified by a large majority of the constituent unions in the AFL and the CIO. Its purpose was to minimize the fruitless and costly efforts to claim jurisdiction over workers already organized by another union. A forerunner of the actual merger of the AFL and CIO, it went into effect in June 1954 for the sixty-five AFL and twenty-nine CIO affiliates which had ratified it.

In February 1955 a joint committee announced that full agreement had been reached for the merger of the two organizations. In December 1955 the merger became an accomplished fact. The new AFL-CIO, with about 15,000,000 members, was headed by George Meany, and Walter Reuther became head of the Industrial Union Department.

Beginning in 1957, the Senate Select Committee on Improper Activities in the Labor or Management Field (McClellan Committee) held a series of hearings lasting over two years, in the course of which instances were brought into public view of misuse of union funds; lack of democratic procedures in internal union affairs; improper imposition of trusteeships over locals by parent unions; collusive dealings between management and union officials, resulting in "sweetheart" contracts and payoffs to union officials; improper use of "middlemen" to discourage genuine union organization; infiltration of certain unions by gangsters and racketeers; laxity in local law enforcement dealing with violence and racketeering; misuse of picketing and secondary boycotting as an instrument of power, sometimes for extortion; and the existence of a "no-man's land," under which employers and employees were without either a federal or a state forum to hear and determine their complaints.

The McClellan Committee, in its first interim report in 1958 urged legislation to deal with a number of these abuses, and the Kennedy-Ives bill, S. 3974, 85th Cong., 2d Sess., designed to accomplish such objectives, passed the Senate but died in the House of Representatives. Congress did pass legislation requiring disclosure of the operations of welfare and pension plans, the Welfare and Pension Plans Disclosure Act.

8. THE LABOR-MANAGEMENT REPORTING AND DISCLOSURE ACT (LANDRUM-GRIFFIN ACT), 1959

In the first session of the Eighty-sixth Congress, Senator Kennedy introduced a revised version (S. 505) of the 1958 bill. The Senate Labor Committee, after extensive hearings, reported out a "clean bill," S. 1555, incorporating a number of changes. In April 1959 the Senate debated the bill at length, finally passing it with a number of amendments, including a modified version of a "bill of rights" for union members which had been introduced by Senator McClellan. The House Labor Committee held its own lengthy hearings and finally reported out a bill (the Elliott bill, H.R. 8342), which was somewhat less restrictive of labor unions than the Senate bill. In August 1959 the House debated this bill, along with the Shelley bill (H.R. 8490), which was favored by most unions, and the Landrum-Griffin bill (H.R. 8400), which was the "toughest" or most restrictive of union power of the three bills. Following an intensive effort on all sides to mobilize public opinion, including a radio-television appeal for "an effective labor reform bill" by President Eisenhower, the Landrum-Griffin bill was passed by the House of Representatives.

Senate-House conferees labored for twelve days, finally emerging with a compromise measure, basically following the House Landrum-Griffin bill, but with a number of important amendments. In early September, the resulting Labor-Management Reporting and Disclosure Act of 1959, 73 Stat. 519 (1959), 24 U.S.C. §§ 401-531, was accepted by both Houses; it was signed into law by the President September 14, 1959.

The full text is found in *Selected Federal Statutes*, and the various provisions are taken up in the appropriate chapters of this volume. Briefly, the 1959 labor reform legislation implements the recommendations of the McClellan Committee by establishing a "bill of rights" for union members; requiring periodic financial and other reports from unions and their officers and employees, employers and labor relations consultants; regulating trusteeships over local unions; regulating union election procedures; regulating misappropriation of union funds and loans from union treasuries; and prohibiting Communists and persons convicted of certain crimes within the preceding five years from holding union office.

In addition, a number of important amendments were made to the Labor Management Relations Act of 1947 (Taft-Hartley Act): in order to fill the "no-man's land," states were permitted to handle cases declined by the NLRB, but the Board was prohibited from further restricting its jurisdiction; economic strikers, though permanently replaced, were given limited voting rights in NLRB elections; the secondary boycott prohibitions of the Taft-Hartley Act were tightened up so as to prevent direct pressure upon secondary employers; hot cargo clauses were outlawed, with certain exceptions for the garment and construction industries; and organizational and recognition picketing was placed under explicit restrictions.

9. LABOR DEVELOPMENTS SINCE 1959

A wide range of social legislation was enacted by the Congress in the sixties as part of President Johnson's "Great Society" program, including increases in the minimum wage and greatly expanded coverage of the Fair Labor Standards Act, improvement of Social Security benefits and the introduction of Medicare for the aged. As part of a broad-scale attack on poverty, Congress enacted legislation dealing with area redevelopment, manpower development and training, and economic opportunity for disadvantaged portions of the population.

a. Equal Employment Opportunity Laws

Most directly related to labor relations law is Title VII of the Civil Rights Act of 1964, 78 Stat. 241, 253-66 as amended by Pub. L. No. 92-261 (1972), 86 Stat. 103, and Pub. L. No. 102-166, 105 Stat. 1071 (1991), 42 U.S.C. §§ 2000e— 2000e-15, declaring that it is an unfair employment practice for any employer, employment agency, or labor organization to discriminate against any individual because of race, color, religion, gender, or national origin, and creating the Equal Employment Opportunity Commission (EEOC) to investigate and conciliate charges of discrimination filed by the public. From 1965 until 1972, the EEOC received many charges and was able to conciliate many of them, but its effectiveness was limited by the lack of full enforcement powers. In the Equal Employment Opportunity Act of 1972, Congress gave the EEOC power to institute suits in the federal courts and substantially expanded the Commission's jurisdiction. Congress continues, however, to withhold from the agency the authority to issue its own enforcement orders. Nevertheless, Title VII already has had an enormous impact on hiring, promotions, wage rate differentials, job application forms, want ads, employment testing and record keeping. This is due in part to the attorney's fees provisions in the Act which have made it possible for those who allege discrimination, who are often poor, to obtain representation by the private bar on an individual or class-wide basis. The text of Title VII, as amended by the Equal Employment Opportunity Act of 1972 and the Civil Rights Act of 1991. Discrimination on the basis of gender in the payment of wages is also prohibited by the Equal Pay Act of 1963, 77 Stat. 56, 29 U.S.C. § 206(d).

In 1965, President Johnson issued Executive Order 11246, 30 Fed. Reg. 12319 (1965), amended by E.O. 11375, 32 Fed. Reg. 14303 (1967), requiring nondiscrimination in federal employment and in employment by government contractors. The Office of Federal Contract Compliance Programs has formulated affirmative action plans to increase minority employment on federally financed projects. Federal contractors are required to establish goals and timetables designed to increase the employment rates for trades in which minority groups and women are not adequately represented. See 41 C.F.R. Part 60 (1973).

Noting that it is not only minority and women employees who find themselves disadvantaged in the face of rising productivity and affluence, Congress in 1967 passed the Age Discrimination in Employment Act, 81 Stat. 602 (1967), 29 U.S.C. §§ 621-634. The Act, which was substantially amended in 1978 by Pub. L. 95-256 and in 1986 by Pub. L. 99-592, now prohibits age discrimination against employees forty and older. The Act gives the EEOC authority to investigate, conciliate, and prosecute age discrimination complaints against employers, unions, and employment agencies under the procedures of the Fair Labor Standards Act.

The Americans with Disabilities Act of 1990 (ADA), 104 Stat. 327, 42 U.S.C. § 12101 et seq., provides expansive protection for individuals with mental and physical disabilities. Title I of that enactment prohibits employment discrimination against a "qualified individual with a disability" because of that person's disability, and it requires employers to make reasonable accommodations for disabled persons, when those accommodations can be accomplished without undue hardship. The ADA is enforced through the procedures set forth in Title VII.

b. Job Safety Laws

A 1968 coal mine explosion in Farmington, W. Va., killed seventy-eight men and thrust the issue of job safety to the head of labor's list of legislative concerns. A total of three job safety acts soon emerged from Congress. The Construction Safety Act of 1969, 83 Stat. 96 (1969), 40 U.S.C. § 333, sets safety standards that the construction industry must meet on all federal and federally financed projects. The Act is enforced by way of a three-year blacklisting of any contractor found guilty of noncompliance. The Coal Mine Health and Safety Act of 1969, 83 Stat. 742 (1969), 30 U.S.C. §§ 801-960, codifies strict standards designed to prevent coal mine disasters, provides for compensation for victims of coal miners' "black lung" disease, and authorizes a study of ways of improving coal mine health and safety. The Act establishes fines of up to $10,000 for mine operators found not in compliance.

The third and most comprehensive statute is the Occupational Safety and Health Act of 1970, 84 Stat. 1590, 29 U.S.C. §§ 651-678. This important statute, passed as a compromise measure, gives the Secretary of Labor broad authority to promulgate safety and health standards for the millions of workers in businesses affecting interstate commerce. The discretion of the Secretary is generally limited by the various procedural safeguards expected in the administrative rule-making process, including notice and public hearings. The enforcement power is lodged in an independent three-member Commission appointed by the President. In contrast to the wide discretion granted to the Secretary to set standards, the Act provides a highly structured set of rules governing penalties. In the event of imminent danger to workers, the Secretary of Labor can petition a district court for an injunction to stop employee exposure to the danger.

In *Marshall v. Barlow's, Inc.,* 436 U.S. 307 (1978), the Supreme Court declared § 8(a) of the Occupational Safety and Health Act of 1970 violative of the Fourth Amendment insofar as it authorizes warrantless inspections of employment facilities within the Act's jurisdiction. The majority stated, however, that a showing that a particular business had been chosen for an OSHA search on the basis of a general enforcement plan derived from neutral sources would justify the issuance of a warrant even in the absence of "probable cause" that violations existed. Justices Stevens, Blackmun, and Rehnquist dissented, insisting that the ultimate question was whether the category of warrantless searches authorized by the statute was "unreasonable" within the meaning of the first clause of the fourth amendment.

The Supreme Court held, in *Donovan v. Dewey,* 452 U.S. 594 (1981), that warrantless inspections under the Federal Mine Safety and Health Act of 1977, 30 U.S.C. § 801 et seq. (which replaced the Coal Mine Health and Safety Act of 1969), do not violate the fourth amendment, but instead are reasonable within the meaning of that amendment. *Marshall v. Barlow's, Inc.,* was distinguished.

c. Public Employee Unionism

One area of increasing labor interest is the development of collective bargaining for federal, state, and local government employees. Public employee unions more than doubled their membership during the 1960s and currently represent about 37 percent of all government personnel. Organizational activity among federal employees was spurred by President Kennedy's issuance of Executive Order 10988, 27 Fed. Reg. 551 (1962), in 1962, which established an executive policy favorable to the organization of federal workers and the recognition of those organizations for collective negotiations. By 1969 President Nixon had fleshed out the Kennedy policy with an elaborate statement of recognition and grievance procedures in Executive Order 11491. 34 Fed. Reg. 17605 (1969), amended by E.O. 11616, 36 Fed. Reg. 17319 (1971). Statutory status was given to the federal program in 1978 with the enactment of Title VII of the Civil Service Reform Act of 1978, 92 Stat. 1111, 5 U.S.C. §§ 7101-7135. A number of states enacted legislation to deal with the problem of labor relations for government employees at the state and local level, and a coalition of public employee unions pledged in 1973 to seek federal legislation to govern public employee-management relations at all levels of government. Strikes by local government employees, particularly teachers, presented an increasingly difficult problem, and legislators and administrators turned their attention to devising procedures for resolving collective bargaining impasses. *See generally* H. Edwards, R. Clark & C. Craver, Labor Relations Law in the Public Sector (4th ed. 1991).

d. Organized Labor in the 1970s and 1980s

Union membership in the United States exceeded 19 million in 1970, much of the growth in recent years coming in the public sector. However, the workforce expanded faster than unionization; the proportion of the nonagricultural workforce comprised of union members declined from a high of 35.0 percent in 1953 to 27.3 percent in 1970, 23.0 percent in 1980, and 16.1 percent in 1990. Unions that had won 70-86 percent of NLRB representation elections during the 1940s and 60-75 percent of elections during the 1950s prevailed in less than half of Labor Board elections conducted during the late 1980s. Much of this decline has resulted from the shift in employment from industrial production, the traditional center of union strength, to white-collar and service work, the substitution of new technology for manufacturing workers, and the migration of millions of jobs from unionized north eastern and north central states to less unionized southern and south western states and to low-wage foreign countries. *See generally* C. Craver, Can Unions Survive? (1993); M. Goldfield, The Decline of Organized Labor in the United States (1987); D. Montgomery, The Fall of the House of Labor (1987).

A number of problems confronted labor unions during the 1970s, evidenced by a large number of rank-and-file rejections of negotiated settlements, apparent feelings by skilled workers that their interests were not being adequately represented, and coolness on the part of members living in middle-class suburbs to the traditional social legislation goals of the AFL-CIO. Unions faced increasing pressure from minorities and women for a greater recognition of their distinct interests.

The early 1980s saw "concession bargaining," in which a number of labor unions, under pressure from foreign competition, high unemployment, and an expanding unorganized sector, were forced to agree to reduced compensation in an effort to preserve some measure of job security. *See* Craver, *The Impact of Financial Crises Upon Collective Bargaining Relationships,* 56 Geo. Wash. L. Rev. 465 (1988).

e. Organized Labor in the Twenty-First Century

By 1999, union membership had declined to 16,211,000 members, comprising 13.9 percent of the nonagricultural workforce. While union members currently comprise 37.5 percent of government workers, private sector union membership constitutes a mere 9.6 percent of workforce participants. If the downward trend of the past two decades continues, labor organizations will only represent 5 percent of private sector workers by the early part of the new millennium.

If the labor movement is to remain an established and powerful force in American society, unions will have to adapt to the challenge of changed conditions. The traditional goal of achieving bigger bargaining "gains" may have to be supplemented with new goals concerned with greater job security and improved quality of life, both on the job and in the communities surrounding the work place.

Two contrasting trends seem apparent: (1) a hardening of the adversarial position by some employers, including a willingness to operate during strikes and to employ consultants in an effort to preserve or obtain "union-free" environments, and (2) a movement in the direction of greater cooperation between some managements and some unions in the effort to improve productivity. There has been some reflection in the United States, although still very limited, of a world-wide trend toward greater worker participation in managerial decisions. *See* Merrifield, *Worker Participation in Decisions within Undertakings,* 5 Comp. Lab. L. 1 (1982); Weiler, *Promises to Keep: Securing Workers' Rights to Self-Organization under the NLRA,* 96 Harv. L. Rev. 1769 (1983) ("Contemporary American labor law more and more resembles an elegant tombstone for a dying institution"). For a long-range view of the changing industrial, economic, and managerial environment and the changes which labor organizations must make to adapt to it. *See generally* C. Craver, Can Unions Survive? (1993); W. Gould, Agenda For Reform (1993); B. Bluestone & I. Bluestone, Negotiating the Future (1992); P. Weiler, Governing the Workplace (1990); C. Heckscher, The New Unionism (1988); T. Kochan, H. Katz & R. McKersie, The Transformation of American Industrial Relations (1986); Craver, *Why Labor Unions Must [and Can] Survive*, 1 U. Pa. J. Lab. & Empl. L. 15 (1998); Crain, *Building Solidarity Through Expansion of NLRA Coverage: A Blueprint for Worker Empowerment*, 74 Minn. L. Rev. 953 (1990); Crain, *Feminism, Labor, and Power*, 65 S. Cal. L. Rev. 1819 (1992); Crain, *Feminizing Unions: Challenging the Gendered Structure of Wage Labor*, 89 Mich. L. Rev. 1155 (1991); Stone, *The Legacy of Industrial Pluralism: The Tension Between Individual Employment Rights and the New Deal Collective Bargaining System*, 59 U. Chi. L. Rev. 575 (1992); Forbath, *The Shaping of the American Labor Movement*, 102 Harv. L. Rev. 1109 (1989); Atleson, *Reflections on Labor, Power, and Society,* 44 Md. L. Rev. 841 (1985); Symposium, *The Conceptual Foundations of Labor Law,* 51 U. Chi. L. Rev. 945 ff. (1984); Weiler, *Striking a New Balance: Freedom of Contract and the Prospects for Union Representation,* 98 Harv. L. Rev. 351 (1984); Craver, *The Vitality of the American Labor Movement in the Twenty-First Century,* 1983 U. Ill. L. Rev. 634 (1983). *See also* St. Antoine, *National Labor Policy: Reflections and Distortions of Social Justice,* 29 Catholic U.L. Rev. 535 (1980); St. Antoine, *Federal Regulation of the Workplace in the Next Half Century,* 61 Chi.-Kent L. Rev. 631 (1985); Craver, *The Declining Status of the National Labor Relations Act,* N.Y.U. Forty-first Annual Conf. on Labor 3-1 (1988); Symposium, *The National Labor Relations Act After Fifty Years,* 38 Stan. L. Rev. 935 ff. (1986).

SECTION II. Introductory Materials

A. COVERAGE OF THE NATIONAL LABOR RELATIONS ACT

1. SCOPE OF THE CONCEPT "AFFECTING COMMERCE"

In the *Jones & Laughlin* case the Supreme Court approved the interpretation by the NLRB (*see* First Annual Report 195 (1936)) that Congress had given the Board jurisdiction coextensive with congressional power to legislate under the commerce clause of the Constitution. As stated in § 10(a) of the National Labor Relations Act, the NLRB is empowered "to prevent any person from engaging in any unfair labor practice (listed in § 8) affecting commerce."

A long series of later cases have made it clear that federal power (and hence the jurisdiction of the NLRB) over industries in which a labor dispute would "affect commerce" is very broad. As we shall see later, the NLRB has, in its discretion, chosen not to exercise its jurisdiction to the full in some cases; but the power remains in the Board to exercise its jurisdiction to the fullest extent to which the courts have expanded the concept, "affecting commerce."

In general, the NLRA applies to:

(a) employers producing goods which are destined directly or indirectly to go out into interstate commerce;

(b) employers receiving goods from out-of-state, directly or indirectly, so that a labor dispute would tend to slow down the flow of goods in interstate commerce;

(c) employers engaged in commerce—communications, transportation, etc.—or performing services for such industries, so that a labor dispute would interfere with the movement of commerce.

The company need not do a majority of its business across state lines, and the company may do a very small percentage of the total business in its industry. It is immaterial whether the same goods or services could be obtained from another company in the event of a labor dispute. *NLRB v. Bradford Dyeing Ass'n,* 310 U.S. 318 (1940).

As the Supreme Court said in *NLRB v. Fainblatt,* 306 U.S. 601, 605-07 (1939):

> The power of Congress to regulate interstate commerce is plenary and extends to all such commerce be it great or small.... The amount of commerce regulated is of special significance only to the extent that Congress may be taken to have excluded commerce of small volume from the operation of its regulatory measure by express provision or fair implication.... Examining the Act in the light of its purpose and of the circumstances in which it must be applied we can perceive no basis for inferring any intention of Congress to make the operation of the Act depend upon any particular volume of commerce affected more than that to which courts would apply the maxim *de minimis.*

In *Polish Nat'l Alliance v. NLRB,* 322 U.S. 643, 648 (1944), the Court recognized that NLRA jurisdiction "is not to be determined by confining judgment to the effect of the activities immediately before the Board. Appropriate for judgment is the fact that the immediate situation is representative of many others throughout the country, the total incidence of which if left unchecked may well become far-reaching in its harm to commerce."

The Supreme Court has shown no tendency since the NLRA was amended by the Taft-Hartley Act to narrow its concept of the range of businesses in which a labor dispute would be regarded as "affecting commerce." *See NLRB v. Reliance Fuel Oil Corp.,* 371 U.S. 224 (1963); *Amalgamated Meat Cutters v. Fairlawn Meats, Inc.,* 353 U.S. 20 (1957); *Howell Chevrolet Co. v. NLRB,* 346 U.S. 482 (1953); *NLRB v. Denver Bldg. & Constr. Trades Council,* 341 U.S. 675 (1951).

2. NLRB EXERCISE OF ITS JURISDICTION

NLRB, A GUIDE TO BASIC LAW AND PROCEDURES UNDER THE NATIONAL LABOR RELATIONS ACT 41-43 (1987)

Although the National Labor Relations Board could exercise its powers to enforce the Act in all cases involving enterprises whose operations affect commerce, the Board does not act in all such cases. In its discretion it limits the exercise of its power to cases involving enterprises whose effect on commerce is substantial. The Board's requirements for exercising its power or jurisdiction are called "jurisdictional standards." These standards are based on the yearly amount of business done by the enterprise, or on the yearly amount of its sales or of its purchases. They are stated in terms of total dollar volume of business and are different for different kinds of enterprises. The Board's standards in effect since July 1, 1976, are as follows:

1. *Nonretail business:* Direct sales of goods to consumers in other States, or indirect sales through others (called outflow), of at least $50,000 a year; or direct purchases of goods from suppliers in other States, or indirect purchases through others (called inflow), of at least $50,000 a year.

2. *Office buildings:* Total annual revenue of $100,000 of which $25,000 or more is derived from organizations which meet any of the standards except the indirect outflow and indirect inflow standards established for nonretail enterprises.

3. *Retail enterprises:* At least $500,000 total annual volume of business.

4. *Public utilities:* At least $250,000 total annual volume of business, or $50,000 direct or indirect outflow or inflow.

5. *Newspapers:* At least $200,000 total annual volume of business.

6. *Radio, telegraph, television, and telephone enterprises:* At least $100,000 total annual volume of business.

7. *Hotels, motels, and residential apartment houses:* At least $500,000 total annual volume of business.

8. *Privately operated health care institutions:* At least $250,000 total annual volume of business for hospitals; at least $100,000 for nursing homes, visiting nurses associations, and related facilities; at least $250,000 for all other types of private health care institutions defined in the 1974 amendments to the Act. The statutory definition includes: "any hospital, convalescent hospital, health maintenance organization, health clinic, nursing home, extended care facility, or other institution devoted to the care of the sick, infirm, or aged person." Public hospitals are excluded from NLRB jurisdiction by Section 2(2) of the Act.

9. *Transportation enterprises, links and channels of interstate commerce:* At least $50,000 total annual income from furnishing interstate passenger and freight transportation services; also performing services valued at $50,000 or more for businesses which meet any of the jurisdictional standards ex-

cept the indirect outflow and indirect inflow standards established for non-retail enterprises.

10. *Transit systems:* At least $250,000 total annual volume of business.

11. *Taxicab companies:* At least $500,000 total annual volume of business.

12. *Associations:* These are regarded as a single employer in that the annual business of all association members is totaled to determine whether any of the standards apply.

13. *Enterprises in the Territories and the District of Columbia:* The jurisdictional standards apply in the Territories; all businesses in the District of Columbia come under NLRB jurisdiction.

14. *National defense:* Jurisdiction is asserted over all enterprises affecting commerce when their operations have a substantial impact on national defense, whether or not the enterprises satisfy any other standard.

15. *Private universities and colleges:* At least $1 million gross annual revenue from all sources (excluding contributions not available for operating expenses because of limitations imposed by the grantor).

16. *Symphony orchestras:* At least $1 million gross annual revenue from all sources (excluding contributions not available for operating expenses because of limitations imposed by the grantor).

17. *Law firms and legal assistance programs:* At least $250,000 gross annual revenues.

18. *Employers that provide social services:* At least $250,000 gross annual revenues.

19. *Lawful gambling casinos:* At least $500,000 gross annual revenues.

Through enactment of the Postal Reorganization Act of 1970, NLRA coverage was extended to U.S. Postal Service personnel, but Post Office employees are expressly denied the right to strike.

Enterprises that satisfy the Board's monetary standards are ordinarily engaged in activities that "affect" commerce. The NLRB must find, however, based on evidence, that each enterprise does in fact "affect" commerce. When an employer whose operations "affect" commerce refuses to supply the Board with information concerning total annual business, etc., the Board generally dispenses with the monetary requirement and asserts jurisdiction.

Finally, Section 14(c)(1) authorizes the Board, in its discretion, to decline to exercise jurisdiction over any class or category of employers where a labor dispute involving those firms is not sufficiently substantial to warrant the exercise of jurisdiction, but it cannot refuse to exercise jurisdiction over any labor dispute over which it would have asserted jurisdiction under the standards it had in effect on August 1, 1959. In accordance with this provision, the Board has declined to exercise jurisdiction over racetracks, owners, breeders, and trainers of racehorses, and real estate brokers. State substantive law governs disputes pertaining to industries over which the NLRB refuses to assert jurisdiction. *See Eatz v. IBEW Local 3*, 973 F.2d 64 (2d Cir. 1992).

NOTE

The NLRB asserts jurisdiction over the following types of employers, if they satisfy the appropriate monetary standard: charitable institutions, *St. Aloysius Home,* 224 N.L.R.B. 1344 (1976); agencies or instrumentalities of a foreign state engaged in commercial activity within the United States, *Bank of India,* 229 N.L.R.B. 838 (1977).

3. EXCLUSIONS FROM COVERAGE

a. Independent Contractors

The Wagner Act did not contain any specific exclusion of independent contractors, and the Supreme Court in *NLRB v. Hearst Publications, Inc.,* 322 U.S. 111, 126-28 (1944), sustained the NLRB in its finding that the newsmen selling papers at fixed spots on the streets were employees entitled to the protection of the act. The Court reasoned:

> The mischief at which the Act is aimed and the remedies it offers are not confined exclusively to "employees" within the traditional legal distinctions separating them from "independent contractors." ...
>
> Unless the common-law tests are to be imported and made exclusively controlling, without regard to the statute's purposes, it cannot be irrelevant that the particular workers in these cases are subject, as a matter of economic fact, to the evils the statute was designed to eradicate and that the remedies it affords are appropriate for preventing them or curing their harmful effects in the special situation. Interruption of commerce through strikes and unrest may stem as well from labor disputes between some who, for other purposes, are technically "independent contractors" and their employers as from disputes between persons who, for those purposes, are "employees" and their employers. *Cf. Milk Drivers' Union v. Lake Valley Farm Products,* 311 U.S. 91. Inequality of bargaining power in controversies over wages, hours and working conditions may as well characterize the status of the one group as of the other. The former, when acting alone, may be as "helpless in dealing with an employer," as "dependent ... on his daily wage" and as "unable to leave the employ and to resist arbitrary and unfair treatment" as the latter. For each, "union ... [may be] essential to give ... opportunity to deal on equality with their employer." And for each, collective bargaining may be appropriate and effective for the "friendly adjustment of industrial disputes arising out of differences as to wages, hours, or other working conditions." 49 Stat. 449. In short, when the particular situation of employment combines these characteristics, so that the economic facts of the relation make it more nearly one of employment than of independent business enterprise with respect to the ends sought to be accomplished by the legislation, those characteristics may outweigh technical legal classifi-

cation for purposes unrelated to the statute's objectives and bring the relation within its protections.

The Court took the position, moreover, that the task of making "a completely definitive limitation around the term 'employee'" had been assigned primarily to the NLRB to perform, since the everyday experience of the Board equips it with knowledge as to the circumstances and backgrounds of employment relationships in various industries, and of the abilities and needs of the workers for self-organization and collective bargaining. "Resolving that question, like determining whether unfair labor practices have been committed, 'belongs to the usual administrative routine' of the Board," and under the act, according to Justice Rutledge, the reviewing function of the Court was limited.

The Eightieth Congress reacted strongly in 1947, as the following committee report indicates.

HOUSE COMMITTEE ON EDUCATION AND LABOR, H.R. Rep. No. 245 on H.R. 3020, 80th Cong., 1st Sess. 18 (1947)

An "employee," according to all standard dictionaries, according to the law as the courts have stated it, and according to the understanding of almost everyone, with the exception of members of the National Labor Relations Board, means someone who works for another for hire. But in the case of *NLRB v. Hearst Publications, Inc.,* 322 U.S. 111 (1944), the Board expanded the definition of the term "employee" beyond anything that it ever had included before, and the Supreme Court, relying upon the theoretic "expertness" of the Board, upheld the Board. In this case the Board held independent merchants who bought newspapers from the publisher and hired people to sell them to be "employees." The people the merchants hired to sell the papers were "employees" of the merchants, but holding the merchants to be "employees" of the publisher of the papers was most far reaching. It must be presumed that when Congress passed the Labor Act, it intended words it used to have the meanings that they had when Congress passed the Act, not new meanings that, nine years later, the Labor Board might think up. In the law there always has been a difference, and a big difference, between "employees" and "independent contractors." "Employees" work for wages or salaries under direct supervision. "Independent contractors" undertake to do a job for a price, decide how the work will be done, usually hire others to do the work, and depend for their income not upon wages, but upon the difference between what they pay for goods, materials, and labor and what they receive for the end result, that is, upon profits. It is inconceivable that Congress, when it passed the Act, authorized the Board to give to every word in the Act whatever meaning it wished. On the contrary, Congress intended then, and it intends now, the Board to give to words not farfetched meanings but ordinary meanings. To correct what the Board has done, and what the Supreme Court, putting misplaced reliance upon the Board's expertness, has approved, the bill excludes "independent contractors" from the definition of "employee."

The NLRB subsequently explained its understanding of the distinction as follows:

> The Board has consistently held that the act requires that the question whether an individual is an independent contractor be determined by applying the "right-of-control" test. Under this test an independent contractor relationship will be found where the record shows that the person for whom services are performed reserves control only as to the result sought. On the other hand, where the record shows that control is retained over the manner and means by which the result is to be accomplished, an employer-employee relationship will be found.

NLRB, Twenty-Third Annual Report 40 (1958). For cases illustrating the ordinary tests of the law of agency as required by the Taft-Hartley Act, *see Teamsters Local 221 v. NLRB*, 899 F.2d 1238 (D.C. Cir. 1990); *Cardinal McCloskey Children's Servs.*, 298 N.L.R.B. 434 (1990); *Brown v. NLRB*, 462 F.2d 699 (9th Cir. 1972); *Herald Co. v. NLRB*, 444 F.2d 430 (2d Cir. 1971); *NLRB v. United Ins. Co.*, 390 U.S. 254 (1968); *National Van Lines v. NLRB*, 273 F.2d 402 (7th Cir. 1960); *Seven-Up Bottling Co. v. NLRB*, 506 F.2d 596 (1st Cir. 1974). *Compare Dial-A-Mattress*, 326 N.L.R.B. No. 75, 159 L.R.R.M. 1166 (1998) (owner-operators who use their own equipment and hire own helpers to deliver mattresses are independent contractors) *with Roadway Package Sys.*, 326 N.L.R.B. No. 72, 159 L.R.R.M. 1153 (1998) (pickup and delivery drivers are covered "employees" because of degree of control exercised by employer over their activities). *See generally* Perritt, *Should Some Independent Contractors Be Redefined as "Employees" Under Labor Law?* 33 Vill. L. Rev. 989 (1988); Comment, *Employees and Independent Contractors under the NLRA*, 2 Indus. Rel. L.J. 278 (1977).

The taxicab industry has proved to be a particularly difficult area in which to distinguish between employees and independent contractors. For a summary, *see Yellow Taxi of Minneapolis v. NLRB*, 721 F.2d 366 (D.C. Cir. 1983) ("In the past 10 years, the Board has been overruled in 10 independent contractor cases. Five of these involved lessee cab drivers.").

b. Supervisory and Managerial Employees

The status of supervisory employees presented one of the most troublesome problems to confront the NLRB under the original NLRA. The question was to what extent, if at all, supervisory groups were to be accorded the rights of "employees" under the statute. It was early and consistently held by the Board with judicial support that supervisory employees were protected against acts of discrimination under § 8(3) of the act.

The next question was whether, as employees protected in some respects under the act, supervisors also had bargaining rights, and, if so, in what form of bargaining unit. After considerable difference of opinion among members of the NLRB, the Board certified the Foreman's Association of America as representative of a bargaining unit of foremen, and the Supreme Court enforced an order to bargain in *Packard Motor Car Co. v. NLRB,* 330 U.S. 485 (1947). In *Jones & Laughlin Steel Corp.,* 66 N.L.R.B. 386 (1946), the Board held that District 50 of the United Mine Workers could represent mine foremen even though the UMW also represented the rank and file miners.

The Board's policy of according to supervisory personnel the full status of employees under the original act was the subject of bitter attack by employers, with the result that in the Taft-Hartley Act of 1947 Congress expressly excluded from the definition of "employee" "any individual employed as a supervisor" (§ 2(3)), and adopted an apparently broad definition of "supervisors" (§ 2(11)). At the same time it was provided in § 14(a) that "Nothing herein shall prohibit any individual employed as a supervisor from becoming or remaining a member of a labor organization, but no employer subject to this act shall be compelled to deem individuals defined herein as supervisors as employees for the purpose of any law, either national or local, relating to collective bargaining." While the act thus established a new national policy with respect to the status of such employees, the debate on the merits will doubtless continue, especially since supervisors remain free of any legislative prohibition against unionization.

The NLRB has commented:

> The supervisory status of an employee under the act depends on whether he possesses authority to act in the interest of his employer in the matters and the manner specified in Section 2(11) which defines the term "supervisors." Generally, it is the existence rather than the exercise of authority within the meaning of Section 2(11) that determines an employee's supervisory status.
>
> In determining the existence of supervisory authority in contested cases, the Board has continued to take into consideration such record facts as the ratio of supervisory to supervised employees in the particular department or plant.... Manner and rate of pay is also considered relevant in ascertaining the status of employees.
>
> Employees who possess some supervisory authority may be included in a bargaining unit if the exercise of their supervisory functions is only sporadic or occasional. On the other hand, employees who substitute regularly and periodically for their superior during his absence are generally excluded from bargaining units.

NLRB Twenty-Third Annual Report 40-41 (1958).

Overruling a long line of precedent, the Labor Board held that "system supervisors" who responsibly "direct" employees are supervisors within the meaning of the NLRA even though they do not hire, fire, transfer, lay off, recall, or promote, etc. It is enough to establish "any one of the statutory criteria listed, regardless of the frequency of its use." *Big Rivers Elec. Corp.*, 266 N.L.R.B. 618 (1983). *But cf. Anamag*, 284 N.L.R.B. 621 (1987) (leaders of cooperative work teams not supervisors when decisions regarding individual group members made by entire team). In *Schnuck Markets v. NLRB*, 961 F.2d 700 (8th Cir. 1992), the court reversed the Board and held that a night manager who spent 30-40 percent of his time on manual work was a "supervisor," since he was the highest ranking person on duty at night and had complete authority to manage the store.

Because of the unique relationships among practical nurses, nurse's aides, and patients, the Labor Board and the courts have had a difficult time determining when practical nurses who can direct the work of nurse's aides constitute excluded "supervisors." In *NLRB v. Health Care & Retirement Corp.*, 511 U.S. 571 (1994), the Supreme Court tried to clarify this area. The Board had held that "a nurse's direction of less-skilled employees, in the exercise of professional judgment incidental to the treatment of patients, is not authority exercised 'in the interest of the employer'" thus rendering those nurses "employees" under the Act. The Court rejected this approach, and held that nurses who exercise independent judgment of more than a routine nature when they direct the work of less-skilled employees are acting "in the interest of the employer" under § 2(11) and are supervisory personnel. Nonetheless, in *Providence Hosp.*, 320 N.L.R.B. 717 (1996), *enforced*, 121 F.3d 548 (9th Cir. 1997), the Board held that charge nurses who served as lead employees in a hospital department were not supervisors, because it found end-of-shift reporting to be clerical in nature and the monitoring of lower level personnel skills to be routine. *Compare Beverly Enterprises v. NLRB*, 129 F.3d 1269 (D.C. Cir. 1997) (sustaining Board finding licensed practical nurses not supervisors when direction of other employees merely routine) *with Caremore Inc. v. NLRB*, 129 F.3d 365 (6th Cir. 1997) (rejecting Board finding that licensed practical nurses not supervisors). *See also Beverly Enterprises, Virginia, Inc. v. NLRB*, ___ F.3d ___ (*en banc*) (4th Cir. 1999) (7-5 decision finding licensed practical nurses functioning as "charge nurses" to be "supervisors").

Although supervisors are no longer directly protected by the NLRA, they may gain the benefit of Labor Board remedial orders if employer action against them has adversely affected *employee* rights. *See, e.g., NLRB v. Advertisers Mfg. Co.*, 823 F.2d 1086 (7th Cir. 1987) (supervisor reinstated when discharged because of her son's union activity); *Howard Johnson Co. v. NLRB*, 702 F.2d 1 (1st Cir. 1983) (supervisor reinstated when fired for refusing to spy on employees). *Compare United Exposition Serv. v. NLRB*, 945 F.2d 1057 (8th Cir. 1991) (denial of supervisory position because of employee's prior strike activities unlawful since it was related to his conduct as an employee) *with Parker-Robb Chevrolet, Inc.*, 262 N.L.R.B. 402 (1982) (supervisor not protected merely because allied with rank-and-file employees).

Managerial employees (those who are in a position to formulate and effectuate management policies) are excluded from the coverage of the Act, even though they are not supervisors or persons involved with labor relations policies. *NLRB v. Textron, Inc.,* 416 U.S. 267 (1974). *See NLRB v. Yeshiva Univ.,* 444 U.S. 672 (1980), where the U.S. Supreme Court held that the faculty of a "mature" private university are more than simply professional employees. The Court held that they are "managerial employees" and thus excluded from the coverage of the Act because of their significant role in formulating and implementing university policy. The Ninth Circuit, in *Stevens Ins. v. NLRB,* 620 F.2d 720 (1980), declined to apply *Yeshiva* concepts where the institution involved was not found to be a "mature" university. The employer's claim was unpersuasive where faculty members had no input on policy matters, no duties of a supervisory nature, and fit easily within the normal definition of "employees" under the Act. *Accord Bradford College,* 261 N.L.R.B. 565 (1982) (faculty, departmental chairmen, and librarians not "managerial" employees). *See generally* Rabban, *Distinguishing Excluded Managers From Covered Professionals Under the NLRA,* 89 Colum. L. Rev. 1775 (1989); Rabban, *Can American Labor Law Accommodate Collective Bargaining by Professional Employees?* 99 Yale L.J. 689 (1990); Crain, *Building Solidarity Through Expansion of NLRA Coverage: A Blueprint for Worker Empowerment,* 74 Minn. L. Rev. 953 (1990).

Confidential employees (those who assist and act in a confidential capacity to persons who formulate and effectuate management labor relations policies) are also excluded from NLRA coverage. Nonetheless, in *NLRB v. Hendricks County Rural Elec. Membership Corp.,* 454 U.S. 170 (1981), the Supreme Court sustained the Labor Board holding that the personal secretary to the chief executive officer of a rural cooperative was covered by the NLRA, because she did not act in a confidential capacity with respect to labor relations matters, even though she had access to other confidential business information. *See also E & L Transport Co. v. NLRB*, 85 F.3d 1258 (7th Cir. 1996) (employer did not violate NLRA by refusing to consider union-affiliated applicants for confidential positions having "labor nexus," even though employer's only basis for fearing potential disloyalty or disclosure of confidential information was applicants' union affiliation).

See Weinstock, *§ 8(a)(1) Protection for Managerial, Confidential, and Supervisory Personnel,* 33 Lab. L.J. 509 (1982).

c. Other Exclusions

Other categories of persons who are excluded from the coverage of the Taft-Hartley Act by virtue of the definition of "employee" in § 2(3) include agricultural laborers and domestic servants. In *Holly Farms Corp. v. NLRB,* 517 U.S. 392 (1996), a closely divided Supreme Court held that the Labor Board could reasonably determine that "live-haul" crews, consisting of chicken catchers, forklift operators, and truck drivers employed by integrated poultry producers, who collect chickens raised by independent contract growers and transport them to a processing plant are "employees" rather than exempt agricultural workers. *See also Olaa Sugar Co.,* 118 N.L.R.B. 1442 (1957) ("employees who perform any regular amounts of non-agricultural work are covered by the Act with respect to the portion of the work that is non-agricultural" despite their performance of other agricultural work).

Other workers are excluded from NLRA coverage by virtue of the exclusion of their employers under § 2(2). These include employees of federal, state, and local governments and employers subject to the Railway Labor Act. In *Concordia Elec. Coop.*, 315 N.L.R.B. 752 (1994), the Board indicated that it will only refuse to assert jurisdiction over electrical cooperatives that are subject to popular political control. Since the Concordia cooperative included corporations and associations not eligible to vote in state elections, the NLRB found that it did not constitute an exempt political subdivision.

When it determines whether to assert jurisdiction over an employer with close ties to an exempt governmental entity, the Board only considers whether the enterprise fits the definition of "employer" and meets the applicable monetary jurisdictional standards. *Management Training Corp.*, 317 N.L.R.B. 1355 (1995). *Compare NLRB v. Potential Sch. for Exceptional Children*, 883 F.2d 560 (7th Cir. 1989) (sustaining jurisdiction over facility receiving public funding to provide special education for handicapped children) *with NLRB v. Princeton Mem. Hosp.*, 939 F.2d 174 (4th Cir. 1991) (private nursing home exempt when hospital board members are directly accountable to public officials).

The Taft-Hartley exemption for nonprofit hospitals was removed in 1974. In *Cedars-Sinai Med. Center*, 223 N.L.R.B. 251 (1976), the NLRB held that interns and residents are primarily students and not employees, because they participate in intern and resident programs not for the purpose of making a living, but to satisfy the requirements for entry into the medical profession. *See also St. Clare's Hosp.*, 229 N.L.R.B. 1000 (1977) (refusing to allow union representation for students performing services at their educational institutions directly related to their educational programs).

The Board and courts have recognized that undocumented aliens are entitled to employee status under § 2(3) of the Act, and share a sufficient "community of interest" to be included in bargaining units and to vote in NLRB elections. *See Garment Workers, Local 512 v. NLRB*, 795 F.2d 705 (9th Cir. 1986); *Duke City Lumber Co.*, 251 N.L.R.B. 53 (1980); *NLRB v. Apollo Tire Co.*, 604 F.2d 1180 (9th Cir. 1980).

The Supreme Court held (5-4) that the NLRB's assertion of jurisdiction over secondary schools operated by the Roman Catholic Church was not authorized by the NLRA, thus avoiding a first amendment question concerning the separation of church and state. *NLRB v. Catholic Bishop of Chicago*, 440 U.S. 490 (1979). The Labor Board has extended the Supreme Court's *Catholic Bishop* decision in two respects. First, concerns about risks to freedom of religion under the first amendment through the exercise of Board jurisdiction are not limited to parochial elementary and secondary schools, but apply to church-operated colleges and universities as well. *Trustee of St. Joseph's College*, 282 N.L.R.B. 65 (1986). Second, even when a school is not church-operated, the Board considers itself precluded from asserting jurisdiction when the purpose and function of the educational institution are, in substantial part, the propagation of a religious faith. *Jewish Day Sch. of Greater Washington, Inc.,* 283 N.L.R.B. 757 (1987). *Compare NLRB v. Hanna Boys Ctr.,* 940 F.2d 1295 (9th Cir. 1991), *cert. denied,* 504 U.S. 985 (1992) (sustaining exercise of jurisdiction over *non-teaching* parochial school employees who are not significantly involved with institution's religious mission).

The Senate's rejection of an amendment that would have excluded church-run hospitals from coverage and the addition of § 19 to the Act has convinced the Board that Congress intended to extend NLRA coverage to religious health care institutions. The Board thus determined that its assertion of jurisdiction over a hospital owned by a Roman Catholic religious order would not violate the first amendment, since there would be no "excessive entanglement" with the Catholic religion. *St. Elizabeth Community Hosp.,* 259 N.L.R.B. 1135 (1982).

4. STATE LABOR RELATIONS ACTS

A number of states have labor relations statutes with procedures for settling representation and unfair labor practice issues. Several of these states have "little Wagner Acts," listing unfair practices of employers only. The rest designate unlawful practices by both employers and unions.

Many states also have laws limiting the labor injunction, regulating picketing and boycotts, outlawing the union shop (so-called "right-to-work" laws), regulating internal union affairs and welfare and pension funds, and providing procedures for the settlement of labor disputes involving public utilities. These state laws are clearly applicable to disputes and parties that do not "affect" interstate commerce (*see* § 14(c)(2)). Where the industry is one in which a labor dispute would "affect" interstate commerce, however, and Congress has legislated on the matter, the states may be ousted from jurisdiction. The extent to which this "federal preemption" has occurred is one of the most controversial and complex issues in the labor law field. It will be considered after we have become more familiar with the federal labor relations law.

B. ORGANIZATION AND PROCEDURE OF THE NATIONAL LABOR RELATIONS BOARD

The functions of the NLRB in implementing the general policy of the NLRA are mainly two-fold: (1) the prevention of unfair labor practices, known as complaint or "C" proceedings; and (2) the settling of representation questions including the conduct of elections, known as representation or "R" proceedings. The Board's procedure in representation cases will be discussed later.

The Board, located in Washington, D.C., consists of five members, appointed by the President for staggered five-year terms. When it decides cases, it may sit in panels of three. Each Board member has a sizable staff of legal assistants.

The Administrative Law Judges, also located in Washington, with local offices in San Francisco, New York, and Atlanta, travel throughout the country to hold hearings. Although selected by the Board, they are independent and may not be removed except for cause after a hearing by the Civil Service Commission. The Administrative Law Judges were called Trial Examiners until 1972.

The General Counsel, appointed by the President for a four-year term, has final authority, under § 3(d) of the NLRA, over the investigation and prosecution of unfair labor practice charges. The forty-odd regional and sub-regional offices of the NLRB are under the supervision of the General Counsel. Each regional office is under the direction of a Regional Director, assisted by a Regional Attorney. Field examiners investigate charges and conduct elections, and field attorneys prosecute complaints before the Administrative Law Judges.

Our attention will be focused on the difficult, controversial cases which go to the Board and the courts. Consequently, it is well to take note of the fact that the vast bulk of the cases are disposed of at the regional office level and that most of them are disposed of without any formal proceedings. For example, in the fiscal year 1997, out of a total of 33,439 unfair labor practice cases closed, 30.5 percent were withdrawn before complaints were issued, 29.4 percent were administratively dismissed prior to the issuance of complaints, and 35.9 percent were settled or adjusted before issuance of administrative law judge decisions. Only 1.8 percent of the cases closed were decided by the Board in contested cases, and fewer than 1 percent reached the court of appeals via petitions for enforcement or review. NLRB, Sixty-Second Annual Report 5-7 (1998). *See generally Silverberg, Informal Procedures of the National Labor Relations Board,* 6 Syracuse L. Rev. 72 (1954); Weyand & Zarky, *Informal Procedure Before the National Labor Relations Board,* Prac. Law. 31 (Jan. 1955).

An unfair labor practice case begins when some person writes or visits an NLRB Regional Office and makes a charge against an employer or a union. The Board has no power to commence proceedings on its own. Indeed, the charging party may elect, when both the employer and the union are involved in an alleged unfair practice, to bring a charge against either or both.

The act contains a six-month statute of limitations, requiring the filing of a charge within six months of the date on which the alleged unfair practice occurred. When an individual is terminated, the § 10(b) statutory period begins to run on the date the employee is notified of the impending discharge, and not on the date the termination is effectuated. *See United States Postal Serv.,* 271 N.L.R.B. 397 (1984). *Compare Leach Corp. v. NLRB,* 54 F.3d 802 (D.C. Cir. 1995) (when employer gave union advance notice of intent to withdraw recognition and repudiate existing agreement once it transferred operations to a nonunion facility, statutory period did not begin to run at time of notice but only when the relocation was "substantially completed").

Under § 10(*l*) and (m) of the NLRA, as amended by the Labor-Management Reporting and Disclosure Act of 1959, priority handling must be given to cases involving secondary boycotts, hot cargo contracts, organizational or recognition picketing, and discrimination against individual employees.

After the case is assigned to a Board agent in the Regional Office, the charging party is usually asked to submit whatever evidence it has to support the charge, including the names and addresses of witnesses. The charged party is then asked to submit its version of the facts and circumstances surrounding the alleged unfair labor practices. The Board agent makes an investigation, interviews witnesses, and prepares a report with recommendations. The Regional Director decides whether to issue a complaint.

Short of issuance of a complaint, a charge may be disposed of in three ways: (1) withdrawal (sometimes pursuant to a non-Board settlement between the charging party and the charged party); (2) dismissal; or (3) settlement or adjustment. An adjustment means that the Regional Office has reached a settlement of the case, accomplishing the purposes of the act. It may be either informal, in which the charged party agrees to remedy its unfair practices, or formal, in which a consent decree is issued by the NLRB and a U.S. court of appeals. A decision by the General Counsel to accept an informal settlement after issuance of a complaint but before commencement of a hearing, over the objection of the charging party, is not subject to NLRB review and does not constitute a final Board order that is subject to judicial review. *NLRB v. Food & Commercial Workers Local 23,* 484 U.S. 112 (1987); *Sheet Metal Workers Local 28,* 306 N.L.R.B. 981 (1992). In *Pottsville Bleaching,* 301 N.L.R.B. 1095 (1991), the Board indicated that it will no longer permit the inclusion of non-admission clauses in NLRB notices that must be posted as part of informal or formal Board settlement agreements.

If the Regional Director decides to dismiss the charge, an appeal may be taken to the General Counsel (not the Board) in Washington. The General Counsel's decision whether to issue a complaint is final, and is not subject to judicial review. *Beverly Health Servs. v. Feinstein,* 103 F.3d 151 (D.C. Cir. 1996), *cert. denied,* 118 S. Ct. 65 (1997); *Lincourt v. NLRB,* 170 F.2d 306 (1st Cir. 1948). The nonreviewability of the General Counsel's discretionary decisions also applies to withdrawal of a previously issued complaint. *Machinists v. Lubbers,* 681 F.2d 598 (9th Cir. 1982).

When the General Counsel decides not to issue a complaint, the Freedom of Information Act requires the disclosure of the office's explanatory advice and appeals memorandum as a "final opinion" made in the adjudication of the case. Advice and appeals memoranda explaining decisions by the General Counsel to issue complaints are not "final opinions," however, falling instead within the Act's exemption for "intra-agency memoranda," and thus they need not be disclosed. *NLRB v. Sears, Roebuck & Co.,* 421 U.S. 132 (1975).

In *Kent Corp. v. NLRB,* 530 F.2d 612 (5th Cir. 1976), the Regional Director decided to issue a complaint on some charges and to dismiss other charges. The company sought to obtain under the FOIA certain "final investigative reports" prepared by regional office attorneys which were used by these staff members and the Regional Director in discussion on which charges, if any, a complaint would issue. The court held that these pre-decisional materials were not "final opinions" within the meaning of the *Sears* case, *supra,* and were exempt from disclosure under FOIA as intra-agency memoranda and attorney's work-products.

After the formal complaint has been issued, the Board has the power, under § 10(j) of the act, to seek a temporary injunction or restraining order against the unfair labor practice in a U.S. district court, but this is seldom done. Section 10(*l*) *requires* that an injunction be sought where there is reasonable cause to believe that a charge of certain union unfair labor practices is true.

The respondent is given time to file an answer to the complaint, and then the case proceeds to a hearing before an Administrative Law Judge. The case is presented by an attorney from the Regional Office, representing the General Counsel. The respondent may cross-examine witnesses, and may obtain, for this purpose, a copy of any written pretrial statement of the witness. *Ra-Rich Mfg. Corp.,* 121 N.L.R.B. 700 (1958). The charging party is permitted to participate in the hearing.

Exemption 7(A) of the Freedom of Information Act, covering investigatory records whose disclosure would "interfere with enforcement proceedings," does not require a case-by-case showing of particularized risk to each individual proceeding but may be invoked in specific types of enforcement proceedings. Thus, the statements of both employee and nonemployee witnesses are exempt from disclosure prior to an unfair labor practice hearing under the NLRA, since the risks posed by a prehearing release of statements, such as witness intimidation or coercion, would "interfere with enforcement proceedings." *NLRB v. Robbins Tire & Rubber Co.,* 437 U.S. 214 (1978).

The Administrative Law Judge (ALJ) is fully responsible for the conduct of hearings, ruling upon applications for subpoenas and depositions and other motions. He or she may call witnesses and cross-examine witnesses of the parties. Under § 10(b), the ALJ is required to conduct the proceedings in accordance with the rules of evidence applicable in the U.S. district courts, so far as practicable.

Parties may make an oral argument at the conclusion of the testimony and may file a brief with the ALJ. The ALJ then returns to his or her office with a transcript of the record and prepares the decision, which includes findings of fact, conclusions of law, and recommended order.

After receiving a copy of the ALJ's decision, parties are given an opportunity to file exceptions with the Board within twenty days. An alleged discriminatee who chose not to participate as a party in an unfair labor practice hearing does not have the right to file exceptions to the ALJ's order recommending dismissal of the complaint. *Giacalone v. NLRB,* 682 F.2d 427 (3d Cir. 1982). If no exceptions are filed, the Board adopts the decision of the ALJ as its own. If exceptions are filed, parties may file briefs in support of their exceptions, and the Board will consider the case on the record. Application may be made for oral argument before the NLRB in Washington, but it is seldom granted except where the Board wishes to examine or reexamine a basic policy question.

Although subject to change, the decisional process when the case goes to the Board is approximately as follows. The Executive Secretary assigns the case to one of the five Board members, and the record is read and analyzed by one of his or her legal assistants. This assistant meets with his or her supervisor and the chief counsel of the Board member, and if the case is a simple one, an affirmance of the ALJ's decision is prepared for the approval of the three Board members on the panel.

If more difficult questions are involved, the matter goes to a "sub-panel," consisting of the chief counsels of the Board members on the panel, who meet with the legal assistant and his or her supervisor and analyze the case. A draft of decision and order then goes to the three Board members for approval of changes. When necessary, the Board members hold a conference on it.

If the case involves novel issues or important questions of policy, it is sent to an "agenda" of the full Board. The legal assistant assigned to the case prepares a full memorandum for the consideration of the Board, and he or she attends the session. After discussion, a tentative decision is reached, and the legal assistant prepares a draft of the Board's decision. This is circulated to the members for approval or modification, and it may be discussed further at a later agenda. Finally, the decision is approved and issued by the Board.

Where the Board finds, upon a "preponderance of the testimony" (§ 10(c)), that an unfair labor practice had been committed, it makes findings of fact and issues a cease and desist order which may be accompanied by an order for affirmative action, such as reinstatement. According to the Sixth Circuit, the Board cannot refuse to rule on a complaint charging an unfair labor practice properly brought before it; the NLRA vests discretion solely in the General Counsel to determine whether complaints are sufficiently meritorious to bring to the Board. Moreover, if the Board finds a violation, it must issue a remedial order, even though it believes an order would serve no useful purpose. *UAW v. NLRB (Omni Spectra, Inc.)*, 427 F.2d 1330 (6th Cir. 1970).

If the party against whom the order is issued does not comply, the Board can seek an enforcement order from a U.S. court of appeals. An aggrieved party need not wait for Board enforcement; it may ask the appropriate court of appeals to review the Board's order. In either case, the test for judicial review of factual questions is whether the Board's findings are supported by "substantial evidence on the record considered as a whole" (§ 10(e)).

If the party against whom the court's enforcement order is issued does not comply, it runs the risk of being held in contempt of court.

The final possibility for review is to the U.S. Supreme Court upon petition for writ of certiorari, but the Supreme Court has warned: "Whether on the record as a whole there is substantial evidence to support agency findings is a question which Congress has placed in the Courts of Appeals. This Court will intervene only in what ought to be the rare instance when the standard appears to have been misapprehended or grossly misapplied." *Universal Camera Corp. v. NLRB,* 340 U.S. 474, 491 (1951).

For more detailed information as to NLRB procedure, *see* Statements of Procedures and Rules and Regulations of the National Labor Relations Board, 29 C.F.R. §§ 101-02; K. McGuiness, J. Norris & M. Shershin, How to Take a Case Before the National Labor Relations Board (6th ed. 1992); T. Kammholz & S. Strauss, Practice and Procedure Before the National Labor Relations Board (3d ed. 1980); L. Modjeska, NLRB Practice (1983); NLRB, Case-Handling Manual (1989).

C. THE PERCEIVED NEED FOR REFORM OF THE NATIONAL LABOR RELATIONS ACT

THE FAILURE OF LABOR LAW—A BETRAYAL OF AMERICAN WORKERS, Report of Subcommittee on Labor-Management Relations, House Committee on Education and Labor, 98th Cong., 2d Sess. (Oct. 1984)

Collective bargaining is the free market alternative to government imposition of adequate working conditions. It is based on the principle that an employer dealing directly with an organized workforce is the best way to assure not only fair and decent working conditions, but stability as well....

The Increase in Employer Resistance to Collective Bargaining

One of the most pronounced changes in labor-management relations in recent history has been management's increased resistance to unionization. Today, when employees undertake an effort to join a union and seek collective bargaining they run into intense opposition. Management has always resisted unions. Over the past twenty years, however, there is substantial evidence that the degree and sophistication of management's resistance has risen sharply. While there are differing views as to the cause, there is agreement that organizing campaigns have become far more hotly contested. Some have suggested that the resistance to unionization is more intense in this country than in virtually any other of the western democracies where collective bargaining rights exist....

The single most startling statistic presented at the hearings is that at least one in twenty workers who vote for a union today are illegally fired for their union support. This shocking number in all likelihood understates the reality because it is only based on a comparison of the number of workers voting for a union in NLRB elections with the number of unlawful discharges found by the Board. It does not include unlawfully fired workers who never pursue their legal remedies with the NLRB. One must also assume that, given the apparent adverse consequences, many pro-union employees hide their support from the employer. The fact that, in just the cases we know about, one in twenty pro-union voters are illegally fired, gives some idea of what is faced by workers today who are outspoken in their support of unions. It is also irrefutable evidence of the law's failure to deter violators.

Another indication of increased employer resistance is the sharp rise in the total number of unfair labor practices committed by employers. The following chart was compiled by Professor Weiler.

Unfair Labor Practices by Employers, 1950-80

Year	Certification Elections	Charges against employers	§ 8(a)(3) charges	Fraction found meritorious (percent)	Backpay awards (average amount)	Reinstates
1950	5,619	4,472	3,213	NA	2,259 ($477)	2,111
1955	4,215	4,362	3,089	NA	1,836 ($428)	1,275
1957	4,729	3,655	2,789	NA	1,457 ($354)	922
1960	6,380	7,723	6,044	[1]29.1	3,110 ($335)	1,885
1965	7,576	10,931	7,367	[1]35.5	4,644 ($599)	5,875
1970	7,773	13,601	9,290	[1]34.2	6,828 ($403)	3,779
1975	8,061	20,311	13,426	[2]32.3 [1]30.2	7,405 ($1,524)	3,816
1980	7,296	31,281	18,315	[2]39.0 [1]35.7	15,642 ($2,054)	10,033

[1]Overall.
[2]Employer.

....

Management's determination to resist unions created a demand for specialists to direct and orchestrate their campaign to defeat unionization drives. To meet the demand, the anti-union consultant industry sprang into existence. Consultants have played a significant role in translating management's resistance into a sophisticated and, when needed, protracted anti-union strategy. Consultants proudly point to their "success rates" in defeating employee efforts to unionize....

The Assault on the NLRA

....

Increased employer resistance has resulted in a broad assault on the basic provisions of the NLRA. We have seen how resistance has led to a dramatic rise in violations of the Act. While increased violations are visible evidence of the Act's failure, its vulnerabilities have proven more far-reaching. The assault has exposed several fundamental weaknesses in the Act, with two standing out in particular: protracted delay in the implementation of the law and ineffectual remedies. As resistance has increased, so has the exploitation of these weaknesses.

... [T]he average amount of time from the filing of an unfair labor practice charge to a court enforced remedy is currently nearly three years. This means that an employer can rely on the fact that the imposition of a sanction to remedy an unfair labor practice can easily be stalled for three years or more.

Delay has its most debilitating effect during a union organizing drive, when the Act's central purpose of protecting workers against retaliation for union activities is essential. It is during this period, when all employees are deciding whether they wish to be represented by a union, that it is most important for employees to be free of the fear that their views or activities might result in discriminatory treatment. While the law prohibits threats or coercion designed to influence this choice, when such unlawful acts occur during an organizing campaign, their chilling effect on employee free choice is not affected by a remedy applied several years after the election. The purpose of the remedy, to eliminate the intimidating effect of the illegal conduct, is meaningless if the intimidation has long had its desired impact....

Increased resistance has ... led employers to exploit the weakness of the Act's meager remedies, which, when combined with enforcement delays, has resulted in the law's failure to deter unlawful conduct. The remedies established by the NLRA are compensatory rather than punitive. For example, the remedy for the most extreme form of illegal conduct, the firing of a worker for supporting a union, is reinstatement with payment of lost wages. In addition, the employer is required to post a notice on a public bulletin board proclaiming that such unlawful conduct will not occur in the future. The employer is not subject to additional punishment.

Not only does this remedy fail to deter violations, it also fails to compensate the victim of the illegal conduct. It is the wronged worker who has to bear the financial burden of unemployment—frequently for years—before a remedy is forthcoming. The offer of reinstatement years after an unlawful firing does not begin to compensate the victim for the financial and emotional distress suffered. Studies have shown that fewer than a third of the employees who are offered reinstatement actually accept. Even the back-pay award is offset by interim earnings that an employee is obligated to pursue.

While the remedy is perhaps some consolation to the victimized employee, it is virtually useless in protecting the right of workers to unionize. Typically, the illegal discharge occurs at the height of an organizing campaign and is directed at the most active leaders of the unionization effort. The chilling effect that such a discharge has on the entire workforce is enormous. Reinstatement several years after an unlawful firing in most instances only further impresses on the workforce that favoring a union is a risky proposition. The remedy is focused on protecting an individual rather than guaranteeing workers an uncoerced opportunity to organize unions. The fact that at least one out of every twenty union supporters is illegally fired suggests that the practice of firing the leading union supporters to set an example is widespread....

The inadequacy of the Act's remedies has not been lost on employers determined to resist unionization. It has led employers to make the hard calculation that it often pays, in the crudest economic sense, to violate the law. The employer perceives the value of defeating a union to outweigh the cost of reinstating a worker with backpay several years later. The sanctions against the illegal firing of union supporters simply do not discourage employers from making such calculations....

The law's weaknesses are not confined to the period during which workers are seeking to organize. The law has also failed in the context of an already organized workforce where a collective bargaining relationship exists. In this situation, should problems arise requiring resort to the Board for resolution, the time delays, shortcomings of the available remedies, and adroit maneuvering at the peripheries of the law have the same effect in undermining the intent of the Act.

For example, a remedy directed at unlawful bargaining during the renegotiation of a contract, implemented years after the fact, cannot possibly remedy the effect of the illegal conduct, especially if the negotiation has effectively concluded. The typical remedy for bargaining in bad faith is an order to bargain fairly. Even the timely implementation of such a remedy is of negligible effect if an offending party is determined to ignore it.

The shortcomings of the law's bargaining remedies are particularly acute during the negotiation of a first contract. Another startling statistic presented at the hearings was that only slightly more than 60 percent of the time does a majority vote for a union ultimately result in a collective bargaining agreement. As 10% of these newly certified unions are in companies that already have a union somewhere in their organization, it is more accurate to say that only half the time will a new union achieve a first contract. Again the law fails to constrain an employer who continues to resist collective bargaining after the certification of a union....

Backlogs necessarily cause delays in the functioning of the agency. The time it takes from the filing of an unfair labor practice charge to the implementation of a remedy has steadily increased. The delays have long since reached the point that the effectiveness of the Act has been seriously undermined. Unfortunately, rather than addressing the problems the current Board has allowed the delays and inefficiencies to increase. The following chart reflects the total amount of time required for an NLRB decision, broken down into the time required at each procedural step from the filing of a charge to a decision by the Board. The figures show that in spite of productivity increases at the early stages of case handling, delays have continued to grow at the Board level of consideration.

NLRB Case
Processing Time
[in median days]

	Fiscal Year—			
	1980	1981	1982	1983
1. Filing of charge to issuance of complaint	46	44	45	45
2. Complaint to close of hearing	155	173	250	152
3. Close of hearing to ALJ decision	158	139	129	116

4. ALJ's decision to issuance of Board's decision............................	133	120	170	194
5. Filing of charge to issuance of Board decision	484	490	633	[1]627

[1]Based on preliminary Board estimate.

The above chart reflects the time required for a decision from the NLRB. Because Board orders are not self-enforcing, it is possible that court enforcement of a Board order is necessary. A party who loses before the Board can, in effect, appeal the decision to the federal courts. To arrive at an accurate estimate of the time required from the filing of an unfair labor practice charge to the implementation of a remedy, court processing time must be added to Board consideration. It now takes nearly a year and a half (501 days was the 1981 average) after the Board issues its decision before the decision is enforced by a federal court. This means a person filing an unfair labor practice charge with the NLRB can expect to wait nearly three years before a remedy is implemented by the courts. An employer who seeks delay can readily tie up the process for three years—three years during which a person illegally fired for advocating a union must wait....

NOTE

More recent assessments indicate that one in every twenty to thirty-five union supporters are unlawfully terminated during union organizing campaigns. *See* LaLonde & Meltzer, *Hard Times for Unions: Another Look at the Significance of Employer Illegalities,* 58 U. Chi. L. Rev. 953 (1991); Weiler, *Hard Times for Unions: Challenging Times for Scholars,* 58 U. Chi. L. Rev. 1015 (1991).

Regarding the extent and impact of NLRB delays, *see* "Delay, Slowness in Decision-Making, and the Case Backlog at the National Labor Relations Board," House Committee on Governmental Operations, H.R. Rep. 98-1141, 98th Cong., 2d Sess. (1984). What substantive or procedural changes would you formulate to make the NLRA more effective? *See generally* Becker, *Democracy in the Workplace: Union Representation Elections and Federal Labor Law,* 77 Minn. L. Rev. 495 (1993); Craver, *The National Labor Relations Act Must Be Revised to Preserve Industrial Democracy,* 34 Ariz. L. Rev. 397 (1992); Troy, *Will a More Interventionist NLRA Revive Organized Labor?* 13 Harv. J.L. & Pub. Pol. 583 (1990). In its Report and Recommendations of the Commission on the Future of Worker-Management Relations, January 9, 1995 (Special Supp. to BNA Daily Lab. Rep. No. 6 (Jan. 10, 1995), the so-called Dunlop Commission recommended expedited representation elections, greater union access to employer premises, the possibility of first-contract interest arbitration when parties are unable to achieve mutual accords, and more expansive use of worker participation committees designed to enhance product/service quality and productivity.

NLRB RULE-MAKING AUTHORITY

The NLRB generally adjudicates on a case-by-case basis, only occasionally exercising its rule-making authority—usually in setting guidelines for representation elections. In *NLRB v. Wyman-Gordon Co.,* 394 U.S. 759 (1969), the Supreme Court declared that the Board had promulgated a rule in violation of the rule-making requirements of the Administrative Procedure Act, 5 U.S.C. § 1, when it decided a case by announcing a rule for prospective application only. Since the rule was not applied to the parties immediately involved, the Board's decision was held not to be an "adjudication," which would have made it exempt from the procedural requirements of the APA. Relying on *Wyman-Gordon,* a court of appeals held that the Board must proceed by rulemaking, not adjudication, when it proposes to "reverse a long-standing and oft-repeated policy" in representation cases. *Textron, Inc. v. NLRB,* 475 F.2d 485 (2d Cir. 1973). The Supreme Court, however, held that the Board has the discretion to proceed either by adjudication or by rulemaking in effecting a change in policy, so long as the Board's holding does not amount to an abuse of discretion. Adjudication was found to be especially appropriate where the multiplicity and variety of possible applications made it "doubtful whether any generalized standard could be framed which would have more than marginal utility." *NLRB v. Textron, Inc.,* 416 U.S. 267 (1974).

What are the advantages and disadvantages of having the Board rely more on rule-making than on case-by-case adjudication? *See* Bernstein, *The NLRB's Adjudication—Rule Making Dilemma under the Administrative Procedure Act,* 79 Yale L.J. 571 (1970); Peck, *The Atrophied Rule Making Powers of the National Labor Relations Board,* 70 Yale L.J. 729 (1961); Peck, *A Critique of the National Labor Relations Board Performance in Policy Formation: Adjudication and Rule Making,* 117 U. Pa. L. Rev. 254 (1968); Shapiro, *The Choice of Rule Making or Adjudication in the Development of Administrative Policy,* 78 Harv. L. Rev. 921 (1965).

PART TWO

ORGANIZATION AND REPRESENTATION OF EMPLOYEES

SEMINAR ON FREE SPEECH AND PREELECTION CONDUCT, in SOUTHWESTERN LEGAL FOUNDATION, LABOR LAW DEVELOPMENTS, Proceedings of the Eleventh Annual Institute on Labor Law 239-46 (1965)*

A MANAGEMENT LAWYER: [T]he limitation of free speech in this area of the National Labor Relations Act primarily restricts the employer. Especially is this true of the inexperienced employer who finds out, frequently too late, that speech which comes instinctively is not permitted and, therefore, not free as far as he understands that term. His frustration is aggravated when he discovers the election process bears little resemblance to the democratic process which he understands as a fundamental part of American society.

Thus, the inexperienced employer is astounded to find that his employees are rugged and intelligent enough in a bitter presidential campaign to cast a ballot freely, based on their own judgment—or utter lack of it—for the man who in the next four years will have a life and death atomic choice over their destinies. Yet, the same employees' judgment must be protected by an untrammelled free choice, akin to "laboratory conditions," in the election determining whether or not he wants a union to represent him in dealing with his employer.

Also—and I cannot emphasize this point too much as we get into the area of the so-called great debate—the employer quickly discovers the basic fundamental that probably is the main issue in most elections: "Promise of future benefits" cannot be discussed by him but can be discussed by the union. Picture what would happen if, in the presidential campaign, they could take away all promises of future benefits....

A UNION LAWYER: [E]mployee fear ... takes this whole question completely outside the area with which we are used to dealing in political elections.... Think of a man whose whole livelihood is dependent upon a particular job. That is the loss he faces. This factor may vary. I can imagine that in the city of Pittsburgh an employer could make a certain kind of speech, using the language a lawyer has taken out of a book as being approved in past NLRB elections. He might not cause the least bit of fear in the employees listening to that speech.... But there are other places in our country where the identical speech would have a totally different impact. Out on the Great Plains, for example, you can get into a little

---

*Reprinted by permission from Labor Law Developments, copyright © 1965 by the Bureau of National Affairs, Inc., Washington, D.C. 20037.

town where one proprietary employer holds sway as economic emperor. In that little town the banker, the newspaper, the sheriff, and the entire community dance to the tune that employer calls. There, fear can be pervasive....

A much different problem is presented when you are trying to give everyone "equal time" and are trying to provide, as the union people urge, for a fair balance in the right to communicate with the employees.... We are not now talking about employee fear; we are talking about a chance to get your point of view across. Here the political analogy holds very well. As far as the unions are concerned, it is almost as if the Republican or the Democratic Party owned the television networks and prevented the opposition from appearing on them to address the voters....

BERNARD KARSH, DIARY OF A STRIKE 47, 117, 119-20 (1958)*

A UNION ORGANIZER: I organized a union and I ran a strike. When you have a job to do, you do it. If anyone tells you that there's a fixed way of running a strike, that you can plan it, they're insane. You build it from day to day, just like you build a union from day to day. There's nothing you can plan ahead. Sure, you can plan pickets, you can plan picket signs and songs, you can plan a kitchen and benefits. But your behavior, it varies from moment to moment according to the needs of the situation, and the important thing is to be there and be ready to do it, whatever it is, and go ahead and do it.

AN EMPLOYER: The management of this Company does not want a union, because we feel that our employees will not benefit by belonging to the union.... With the cooperation of our employees and without the interference of any outsiders, we have made the _____ Company a good place in which to work. Our wages, hours and working conditions compare favorably with those of other plants in this area and with the plants of others with whom we are in competition. You have received the benefits of this high standard without having to pay initiation fees, union dues and various special union assessments....

What the intervention of these strangers would mean in our relationship, no one can foretell. All of us know that unions engage in business interruptions and strikes and that frequently these cause substantial financial loss to the employees and their families....

AN EMPLOYEE: I was for it, but at the same time I didn't feel good about it. I had worked there so long, and I felt it wasn't right to strike. The Company had been very nice to me, and sometimes when I didn't feel well, they would let me come to work any time I felt like it and I appreciated that. But I felt we had to strike. We just weren't treated right in a lot of ways. I voted for the strike in the end.

---

*Copyright © 1958. Reprinted by permission of the University of Illinois Press.

SECTION I. The Right of Self-Organization; Protection Against Employer Unfair Labor Practices

Labor relations law deals with legal rights and duties. At the same time the student should not overlook the fact that we are dealing with a phase of human relations in which the parties—management and organized labor—through force of circumstances have established relationship which implies responsibilities greatly transcending those minimum standards which the law imposes. The labor union that establishes itself firmly in a plant acquires a status which, even without jural recognition, necessitates important changes in management's conception of its function. Even accepting the narrowest definition of this function, it must be obvious that the presence of a union possessing the power both to interfere with and to promote the processes of production, calls for the adoption of management policies that will enlist the union's interest in continuous and efficient plant operation. The keynote of a desirable relationship between the parties will be their mutual acceptance of the fact that each has a status in the enterprise. When they have accepted this elemental fact, the rudimentary legal obligations that the law may impose upon them will be of minor significance. Just as in the case of the citizen in the community, or the spouse in the family, so here the necessity of continuing relations calls for a code of conduct much above and beyond the call of legal duty.

This conception of management-union relations presupposes the existence of an established union and management acceptance of the "right" of employee self-organization. As shown in Part I, however, and as might be expected in a land in which much emphasis has been placed upon individual initiative and self-determinism, unionism has had to struggle hard against management resistance to gain a place for itself.

In this section, we will survey the statutory provisions that have given unions and workers legal protection against employer antiunion tactics. For supplementary reading, *see* The Developing Labor Law (3d ed. 1992), edited by Patrick Hardin on behalf of the ABA Section of Labor Relations Law; R. Gorman & M. Finkin, Basic Text on Labor Law (2d ed. forthcoming); F. Bartosic & R. Hartley, Labor Relations Law in the Private Sector (2d ed. 1986); D. Leslie, Labor Law in a Nutshell (3d ed. 1992); W. Gould, A Primer on American Labor Law (1982); C. Gregory & H. Katz, Labor and the Law (3d ed. 1979); J. Getman & B. Pogrebin, Labor Relations (1988).

A. EMPLOYER INTERFERENCE, RESTRAINT, OR COERCION

Section 8(a)(1) of the National Labor Relations Act is a broad, general provision. It may be violated by conduct which is contrary to any of the four following

You don't need to show actual coercion - just a tendency of the conduct to do so

subsections (*i.e.,* a "derivative" § 8(a)(1) violation). For example, a discharge on account of union activity would violate both §§ 8(a)(1) and 8(a)(3).

We shall deal first, however, with employer conduct which violates § 8(a)(1) independently of any other specific unfair labor practice. Such conduct ranges all the way from the crude and obvious to the ingenious and subtle.

It is not necessary, for proof of a violation, to show by direct evidence that any particular persons were in fact successfully restrained or coerced; it is enough if it is shown that the employer's conduct has a natural tendency to do so. *Time-O-Matic, Inc. v. NLRB,* 264 F.2d 96 (7th Cir. 1959); *NLRB v. Ford,* 170 F.2d 735 (6th Cir. 1948).

The Railway Labor Act, in § 2 (Third and Fourth), also makes it unlawful for a carrier to interfere with, influence, or coerce employees in organizing. Since the RLA does not provide an administrative procedure for the prevention of such practices, enforcement must be had through either criminal proceedings or petition for injunctive relief in the courts. *Virginian Ry. v. System Fed'n 40, Railway Emps.,* 300 U.S. 515 (1937); *Texas N.O.R.R. v. Brotherhood of Ry. & S.S. Clerks,* 281 U.S. 548 (1930). There has been very little litigation under these provisions of the RLA, probably because unionism had reached a fairly mature state in the railroad industry by the time these provisions were written into the law.

1. LIMITING ORGANIZATIONAL ACTIVITIES ON EMPLOYER'S PREMISES

LECHMERE, INC. v. NLRB

Supreme Court of the United States
502 U.S. 527, 112 S. Ct. 841, 117 L. Ed. 2d 79 (1992)

JUSTICE THOMAS delivered the opinion of the Court.

This case requires us to clarify the relationship between the rights of employees under § 7 of the National Labor Relations Act ... and the property rights of their employers.

I

This case stems from the efforts of Local 919 of the United Food and Commercial Workers Union, AFL-CIO, to organize employees at a retail store in Newington, Connecticut, owned and operated by petitioner Lechmere, Inc. The store is located in the Lechmere Shopping Plaza, which occupies a roughly rectangular tract measuring approximately 880 feet from north to south and 740 feet from east to west. Lechmere's store is situated at the Plaza's south end, with the main parking lot to its north. A strip of 13 smaller "satellite stores" not owned by Lechmere runs along the west side of the Plaza, facing the parking lot. To the Plaza's east (where the main entrance is located) runs the Berlin Turnpike, a four-lane divided highway. The parking lot, however, does not abut the Turnpike;

they are separated by a 46-foot-wide grassy strip, broken only by the Plaza's entrance. The parking lot is owned jointly by Lechmere and the developer of the satellite stores. The grassy strip is public property (except for a four-foot-wide band adjoining the parking lot, which belongs to Lechmere).

The union began its campaign to organize the store's 200 employees, none of whom was represented by a union, in June 1987. After a full-page advertisement in a local newspaper drew little response, nonemployee union organizers entered Lechmere's parking lot and began placing handbills on the windshields of cars parked in a corner of the lot used mostly by employees. Lechmere's manager immediately confronted the organizers, informed them that Lechmere prohibited solicitation or handbill distribution of any kind on its property,[1] and asked them to leave. They did so, and Lechmere personnel removed the handbills. The union organizers renewed this handbilling effort in the parking lot on several subsequent occasions; each time they were asked to leave and the handbills were removed. The organizers then relocated to the public grassy strip, from where they attempted to pass out handbills to cars entering the lot during hours (before opening and after closing) when the drivers were assumed to be primarily store employees. For one month, the union organizers returned daily to the grassy strip to picket Lechmere; after that, they picketed intermittently for another six months. They also recorded the license plate numbers of cars parked in the employee parking area; with the cooperation of the Connecticut Department of Motor Vehicles, they thus secured the names and addresses of some 41 nonsupervisory employees (roughly 20% of the store's total). The union sent four mailings to these employees; it also made some attempts to contact them by phone or home visits. These mailings and visits resulted in one signed union authorization card.

Alleging that Lechmere had violated the National Labor Relations Act by barring the nonemployee organizers from its property, the union filed an unfair labor practice charge with respondent National Labor Relations Board (Board). Applying the criteria set forth by the Board in *Fairmont Hotel Co.,* 282 N.L.R.B. 139 (1986), an administrative law judge (ALJ) ruled in the union's favor.... He recommended that Lechmere be ordered, among other things, to cease and desist from barring the union organizers from the parking lot and to post in conspicuous places in the store signs proclaiming in part:

---

[1]Lechmere had established this policy several years prior to the union's organizing efforts. The store's official policy statement provided, in relevant part: "Non-associates [*i.e.,* nonemployees] are prohibited from soliciting and distributing literature at all times anywhere on Company property, including parking lots. Non-associates have no right of access to the non-working areas and only to the public and selling areas of the store in connection with its public use." Brief for Petitioner 7. On each door to the store Lechmere had posted a 6 in. by 8 in. sign reading: "TO THE PUBLIC. No Soliciting, Canvassing, Distribution of Literature or Trespassing by Non-Employees in or on Premises." Lechmere consistently enforced this policy inside the store as well as on the parking lot (against, among others, the Salvation Army and the Girl Scouts).

WE WILL NOT prohibit representatives of Local 919, United Food and Commercial Workers, AFL-CIO ("the Union") or any other labor organization, from distributing union literature to our employees in the parking lot adjacent to our store in Newington, Connecticut, nor will we attempt to cause them to be removed from our parking lot for attempting to do so....

The Board affirmed the ALJ's judgment and adopted the recommended order, applying the analysis set forth in its opinion in *Jean Country,* 291 N.L.R.B. 11 (1988), which had by then replaced the short-lived *Fairmont Hotel* approach.... A divided panel of the United States Court of Appeals for the First Circuit denied Lechmere's petition for review and enforced the Board's order. 914 F.2d 313 (1990). This Court granted certiorari....

II

A

.... By its plain terms ... the NLRA confers rights only on *employees,* not on unions or their nonemployee organizers. In *NLRB v. Babcock & Wilcox Co.,* 351 U.S. 105 (1956), however, we recognized that insofar as the employees' "right of self-organization depends in some measure on [their] ability ... to learn the advantages of self-organization from others," *id.,* at 113, § 7 of the NLRA may, in certain limited circumstances, restrict an employer's right to exclude nonemployee union organizers from his property. It is the nature of those circumstances that we explore today.

Babcock arose out of union attempts to organize employees at a factory located on an isolated 100-acre tract. The company had a policy against solicitation and distribution of literature on its property, which it enforced against all groups. About 40% of the company's employees lived in a town of some 21,000 persons near the factory; the remainder were scattered over a 30-mile radius. Almost all employees drove to work in private cars and parked in a company lot that adjoined the fenced-in plant area. The parking lot could be reached only by a 100-yard-long driveway connecting it to a public highway. This driveway was mostly on company-owned land, except where it crossed a 31-foot-wide public right-of-way adjoining the highway. Union organizers attempted to distribute literature from this right-of-way. The union also secured the names and addresses of some 100 employees (20% of the total), and sent them three mailings. Still other employees were contacted by telephone or home visit.

The union successfully challenged the company's refusal to allow nonemployee organizers onto its property before the Board. While acknowledging that there were alternative, nontrespassory means whereby the union could communicate with employees, the Board held that contact at the workplace was preferable. *The Babcock & Wilcox Co.,* 109 N.L.R.B. 485, 493-494 (1954).... Concluding that traffic on the highway made it unsafe for the union organizers to distribute leaflets from the right-of-way, and that contacts through the mails, on the streets, at employees' homes, and over the telephone would be ineffective, the Board ordered the company to allow the organizers to distribute literature on its parking lot and exterior walkways.

The Court of Appeals for the Fifth Circuit refused to enforce the Board's order, *NLRB v. Babcock & Wilcox Co.*, 222 F.2d 316 (1955), and this Court affirmed.... [W]e explained that the Board had erred by failing to make the critical distinction between the organizing activities of employees (to whom § 7 guarantees the right of self-organization) and nonemployees (to whom § 7 applies only derivatively). Thus, while "[n]o restriction may be placed on the employees' right to discuss self-organization *among themselves,* unless the employer can demonstrate that a restriction is necessary to maintain production or discipline," 351 U.S., at 13 (emphasis added) (citing *Republic Aviation Corp. v. NLRB,* 324 U.S. 793, 803 (1945)), "no such obligation is owed nonemployee organizers," 351 U.S., at 113. As a rule, then, an employer cannot be compelled to allow distribution of union literature by nonemployee organizers on his property. As with many other rules, however, we recognized an exception. Where "the location of a plant and the living quarters of the employees place the employees beyond the reach of reasonable union efforts to communicate with them," *ibid.,* employers' property rights may be "required to yield to the extent needed to permit communication of information on the right to organize," *id.,* at 112.

Although we have not had occasion to apply *Babcock*'s analysis in the ensuing decades, we have described it in cases arising in related contexts. Two such cases, *Central Hardware Co. v. NLRB,* 407 U.S. 539 (1972), and *Hudgens v. NLRB,* 424 U.S. 507 (1976), involved activity by union supporters on employer-owned property. The principal issue in both cases was whether, based upon *Food Employees v. Logan Valley Plaza, Inc.,* 391 U.S. 308 (1968), the First Amendment protected such activities. In both cases we rejected the First Amendment claims, and in *Hudgens* we made it clear that *Logan Valley* was overruled. Having decided the cases on constitutional grounds, we remanded them to the Board for consideration of the union supporters' § 7 claims under *Babcock.* In both cases, we quoted approvingly *Babcock*'s admonition that accommodation between employees' § 7 rights and employers' property rights "must be obtained with as little destruction of the one as is consistent with the maintenance of the other," 351 U.S., at 112. There is no hint in *Hudgens* and *Central Hardware,* however, that our invocation of *Babcock*'s language of "accommodation" was intended to repudiate or modify *Babcock*'s holding that an employer need not accommodate nonemployee organizers unless the employees are otherwise inaccessible. Indeed, in *Central Hardware* we expressly noted that nonemployee organizers cannot claim even a limited right of access to a nonconsenting employer's property until "[a]fter the requisite need for access to the employer's property has been shown." 407 U.S., at 545.

If there was any question whether *Central Hardware* and *Hudgens* changed § 7 law, it should have been laid to rest by *Sears, Roebuck & Co. v. San Diego County District Council of Carpenters,* 436 U.S. 180 (1978). As in *Central Hardware* and *Hudgens,* the substantive § 7 issue in *Sears* was a subsidiary one; the case's primary focus was on the circumstances under which the NLRA pre-empts state law. Among other things, we held in *Sears* that arguable § 7 claims do not pre-empt state trespass law, in large part because the trespasses of nonemployee union organizers are "far more likely to be unprotected than protected," 436 U.S., at 205; permitting state courts to evaluate such claims, therefore, does not "create an unacceptable risk of interference with conduct which the Board, and a court reviewing the Board's decision, would find protected," *ibid*....

We further noted that, in practice, nonemployee organizational trespassing had generally been prohibited except where "unique obstacles" prevented non-trespassory methods of communication with the employees. *Id.,* at 205-206, n. 41.

B

Jean Country, as noted above, represents the Board's latest attempt to implement the rights guaranteed by § 7. It sets forth a three-factor balancing test:

> [I]n all access cases our essential concern will be [1] the degree of impairment of the § 7 right if access should be denied, as it balances against [2] the degree of impairment of the private property right if access should be granted. We view the consideration of [3] the availability of reasonably effective alternative means as especially significant in this balancing process. [291 N.L.R.B., at 14.]

The Board conceded that this analysis was unlikely to foster certainty and predictability in this corner of the law, but declared that "as with other legal questions involving multiple factors, the 'nature of the problem, as revealed by unfolding variant situations, inevitably involves an evolutionary process for its rational response, not a quick, definitive formula as a comprehensive answer.'" *Ibid.* (quoting *Electrical Workers v. NLRB,* 366 U.S. 667, 674 (1961))....

Like other administrative agencies, the NLRB is entitled to judicial deference when it interprets an ambiguous provision of a statute that it administers....

Before we reach any issue of deference to the Board, however, we must first determine whether *Jean Country*—at least as applied to nonemployee organizational trespassing—is consistent with our past interpretation of § 7. "Once we have determined a statute's clear meaning, we adhere to that determination under the doctrine of *stare decisis,* and we judge an agency's later interpretation of the statute against our prior determination of the statute's meaning." *Maislin Industries, U.S., Inc. v. Primary Steel, Inc.,* 497 U.S. 116, 131.

In *Babcock,* as explained above, we held that the Act drew a distinction "of substance," 351 U.S., at 113, between the union activities of employees and nonemployees. In cases involving *employee* activities, we noted with approval, the Board "balanced the conflicting interests of employees to receive information on self-organization on the company's property from fellow employees during nonworking time, with the employer's right to control the use of his property." *Id.,* at 109-110. In cases involving *nonemployee* activities (like those at issue in *Babcock* itself), however, the Board was not permitted to engage in that same balancing (and we reversed the Board for having done so). By reversing the Board's interpretation of the statute for failing to distinguish between the organizing activities of employees and nonemployees, we were saying ... that § 7 speaks to the issue of nonemployee access to an employer's property. *Babcock*'s teaching is straightforward: § 7 simply does not protect nonemployee union organizers *except* in the rare case where "the inaccessibility of employees makes ineffective the reasonable attempts by nonemployees to communicate with them through the usual channels," 351 U.S., at 112. Our reference to "reasonable" attempts was nothing more than a common-sense recognition that unions need not engage in extraordinary feats to communicate with inaccessible employees—*not* an endorsement of the view (which we expressly rejected) that the Act protects "reasonable" trespasses. Where reasonable alternative means of access exist, § 7's guarantees do not authorize trespasses by nonemployee organizers, even (as we noted in *Babcock, id.,* at 112) "under ... reasonable regulations" established by the Board.

Jean Country, which applies broadly to "all access cases," 291 N.L.R.B., at 14, misapprehends this critical point. Its principal inspiration derives not from *Babcock,* but from the following sentence in *Hudgens:* "[T]he locus of th[e] accommodation [between § 7 rights and private property rights] may fall at differing points along the spectrum depending on the nature and strength of the respective § 7 rights and private property rights asserted in any given context." 424 U.S., at 522. From this sentence the Board concluded that it was appropriate to approach every case by balancing § 7 rights against property rights, with alternative means of access thrown in as nothing more than an "especially significant" consideration. As explained above, however, *Hudgens* did not purport to modify *Babcock,* much less to alter it fundamentally in the way *Jean Country* suggests. To say that our cases require accommodation between employees' and employers' rights is a true but incomplete statement, for the cases also go far in establishing the locus of that accommodation where nonemployee organizing is at issue. So long as nonemployee union organizers have reasonable access to employees outside an employer's property, the requisite accommodation has taken place. It is only where such access is infeasible that it becomes necessary and proper to take the accommodation inquiry to a second level, balancing the employees' and employers' rights as described in the *Hudgens* dictum. See *Sears,* 436 U.S., at 205; *Central Hardware,* 407 U.S., at 545. At least as applied to nonemployees, *Jean*

Country impermissibly conflates these two stages of the inquiry—thereby significantly eroding *Babcock*'s general rule that "an employer may validly post his property against nonemployee distribution of union literature," 351 U.S., at 112. We reaffirm that general rule today, and reject the Board's attempt to recast it as a multifactor balancing test.

C

The threshold inquiry in this case, then, is whether the facts here justify application of *Babcock*'s inaccessibility exception. The ALJ below observed that "the facts herein convince me that reasonable alternative means [of communicating with Lechmere's employees] were available to the Union."... Reviewing the ALJ's decision under *Jean Country,* however, the Board reached a different conclusion on this point, asserting that "there was no reasonable, effective alternative means available for the Union to communicate its message to [Lechmere's] employees."...

We cannot accept the Board's conclusion.... As we have explained, the exception to *Babcock*'s rule is a narrow one. It does not apply wherever nontrespassory access to employees may be cumbersome or less-than-ideally effective, but only where "the *location of a plant and the living quarters of the employees* place the employees *beyond the reach* of reasonable union efforts to communicate with them," 351 U.S., at 113 (emphasis added). Classic examples include logging camps, see *NLRB v. Lake Superior Lumber Corp.,* 167 F.2d 147 (CA6 1948); mining camps, see *Alaska Barite Co.,* 197 N.L.R.B. 1023 (1972), *enforced mem.,* 83 LRRM 2992 (CA9), *cert. denied,* 414 U.S. 1025 (1973); and mountain resort hotels, see *NLRB v. S & H Grossinger's Inc.,* 372 F.2d 26 (CA2 1967). *Babcock*'s exception was crafted precisely to protect the § 7 rights of those employees who, by virtue of their employment, are isolated from the ordinary flow of information that characterizes our society. The union's burden of establishing such isolation is, as we have explained, "a heavy one," *Sears, supra,* 436 U.S., at 205, and one not satisfied by mere conjecture or the expression of doubts concerning the effectiveness of nontrespassory means of communication.

The Board's conclusion in this case that the union had no reasonable means short of trespass to make Lechmere's employees aware of its organizational efforts is based on a misunderstanding of the limited scope of this exception. Because the employees do not reside on Lechmere's property, they are presumptively not "beyond the reach," *Babcock, supra,* 351 U.S., at 113, of the union's message. Although the employees live in a large metropolitan area (Greater Hartford), that fact does not in itself render them "inaccessible" in the sense contemplated by *Babcock*. See *Monogram Models, Inc.,* 192 N.L.R.B. 705, 706 (1971). Their accessibility is suggested by the union's success in contacting a substantial percentage of them directly, via mailings, phone calls, and home visits. Such direct contact, of course, is not a necessary element of "reasonably effective" communication; signs or advertising also may suffice. In this case, the union tried advertising in local newspapers; the Board said that this was not reasonably effective because it was expensive and might not reach the employees.... Whatever the merits of that conclusion, other alternative means of communication were readily available. Thus, signs (displayed, for example, from the public grassy strip adjoining Lechmere's parking lot) would have informed the employees about the union's organizational efforts. (Indeed, union organizers picketed the shopping center's main entrance for months as employees came and went every day.) *Access* to employees, not *success* in winning them over, is the critical issue—although success, or lack thereof, may be relevant in determining whether reasonable access exists. Because the union in this case failed to establish the existence of any "unique obstacles," *Sears,* 436 U.S., at 205-206, n. 41, that frustrated access to Lechmere's employees, the Board erred in concluding that Lechmere committed an unfair labor practice by barring the nonemployee organizers from its property.

....

The judgment of the First Circuit is therefore reversed, and enforcement of the Board's order denied.

It is so ordered.

JUSTICE WHITE, with whom JUSTICE BLACKMUN joins, dissenting....

In the case before us, the Court holds that *Babcock* itself stated the correct accommodation between property and organizational rights; it interprets that case as construing §§ 7 and 8(a)(1) of the National Labor Relations Act to contain a general rule forbidding third-party access, subject only to a limited exception where the union demonstrates that the location of the employer's place of business and the living quarters of the employees place the employees beyond the reach of reasonable efforts to communicate with them. The Court refuses to enforce the Board's order in this case, which rested on its prior decision in *Jean Country,* 291 N.L.R.B. 11 (1988), because, in the Court's view, *Jean Country* revealed that the Board misunderstood the basic holding in *Babcock,* as well as the narrowness of the exception to the general rule announced in that case.

For several reasons, the Court errs in this case. First, that *Babcock* stated that inaccessibility would be a reason to grant access does not indicate that there would be no other circumstance that would warrant entry to the employer's parking lot and would satisfy the Court's admonition that accommodation must be made with as little destruction of property rights as is consistent with the right of employees to learn the advantages of self-organization from others. Of course the union must show that its "reasonable efforts," without access, will not permit proper communication with employees. But I cannot believe that the Court in *Babcock* intended to confine the reach of such general considerations to the single circumstance that the Court now seizes upon. If the Court in *Babcock* indicated that nonemployee access to a logging camp would be required, it did not

dissent that believes that the Court is misconstruing Babcock only in access in all circumstances

say that only in such situations could nonemployee access be permitted. Nor did *Babcock* require the Board to ignore the substantial difference between the entirely private parking lot of a secluded manufacturing plant and a shopping center lot which is open to the public without substantial limitation. Nor indeed did *Babcock* indicate that the Board could not consider the fact that employees' residences are scattered throughout a major metropolitan area; *Babcock* itself relied on the fact that the employees in that case lived in a compact area which made them easily accessible.

Moreover, the Court in *Babcock* recognized that actual communication with nonemployee organizers, not mere notice that an organizing campaign exists, is necessary to vindicate § 7 rights.... If employees are entitled to learn from others the advantages of self-organization, ... it is singularly unpersuasive to suggest that the union has sufficient access for this purpose by being able to hold up signs from a public grassy strip adjacent to the highway leading to the parking lot.

Second, the Court's reading of *Babcock* is not the reading of that case reflected in later opinions of the Court. We have consistently declined to define the principle of *Babcock* as a general rule subject to narrow exceptions, and have instead repeatedly reaffirmed that the standard is a neutral and flexible rule of accommodation. In *Central Hardware Co. v. NLRB,* 407 U.S. 539, 544 (1972), we explicitly stated that the "guiding principle" for adjusting conflicts between § 7 rights and property rights enunciated in *Babcock* is that contained in its neutral "accommodation" language. *Hudgens v. NLRB,* 424 U.S. 507 (1976), gave this Court the occasion to provide direct guidance to the NLRB on this issue. In that case, we emphasized *Babcock*'s necessity-to-accommodate admonition, pointed out the differences between *Babcock* and *Hudgens*, and left the balance to be struck by the Board.... *Hudgens* did not purport to modify *Babcock* and surely indicates that *Babcock* announced a more flexible rule than the narrow, iron-clad rule that the Court now extracts from that case. If *Babcock* means what the Court says it means, there is no doubt tension between that case and *Hudgens*. If that is so, *Hudgens* as the later pronouncement on the question, issued as a directive to the Board, should be controlling.

The majority today asserts that "[i]t is *only* where [reasonable alternative] access is infeasible that it becomes necessary and proper to take the accommodation inquiry to a second level, balancing the employees' and employers' rights."... Our cases, however, are more consistent with the *Jean Country* view that reasonable alternatives are an important factor in finding the least destructive accommodation between § 7 and property rights. The majority's assertion to this effect notwithstanding, our cases do not require a prior showing regarding reasonable alternatives as a precondition to any inquiry balancing the two rights. The majority can hardly fault the Board for a decision which "conflates ... two stages of the inquiry," ... when no two-stage inquiry has been set forth by this Court.

Third, and more fundamentally, *Babcock* is at odds with modern concepts of deference to an administrative agency charged with administering a statute. See *Chevron U.S.A. Inc. v. Natural Resources Defense Council, Inc.,* 467 U.S. 837 (1984). When reviewing an agency's construction of a statute, we ask first whether Congress has spoken to the precise question at issue.... If it has not, we do not simply impose our own construction on the statute; rather, we determine if the agency's view is based on a permissible construction of the statute.... *Babcock* did not ask if Congress had specifically spoken to the issue of access by third parties and did not purport to explain how the NLRA specifically dealt with what the access rule should be where third parties are concerned. If it had made such an inquiry, the only basis for finding statutory language that settled the issue would have been the language of § 7, which speaks only of the rights of employees; *i.e.,* the Court might have found that § 7 extends no access rights at all to union representatives. But *Babcock* itself recognized that employees have a right to learn from others about self-organization ... and itself recognized that in some circumstances, §§ 7 and 8 required the employer to grant the union access to parking lots. So have later Courts and so does the Court today.

That being the case, the *Babcock* Court should have recognized that the Board's construction of the statute was a permissible one and deferred to its judgment. Instead, the Court simply announced that as far as access is concerned, third parties must be treated less favorably than employees. Furthermore, after issuing a construction of the statute different from that of the Board, rather than remanding to the Board to determine how third parties should be dealt with, the *Babcock* Court essentially took over the agency's job, not only by detailing how union organizer access should be determined but also by announcing that the records before it did not contain facts that would satisfy the newly coined access rule.

Had a case like *Babcock* been first presented for decision under the law governing in 1991, I am quite sure that we would have deferred to the Board, or at least attempted to find sounder ground for not doing so. Furthermore, had the Board ruled that third parties must be treated differently than employees and held them to the standard that the Court now says *Babcock* mandated, it is clear enough that we also would have accepted that construction of the statute. But it is also clear, at least to me, that if the Board later reworked that rule in the manner of *Jean Country,* we would also accept the Board's change of mind....

As it is, the Court's decision fails to recognize that *Babcock* is at odds with the current law of deference to administrative agencies and compounds that error by adopting the substantive approach *Babcock* applied lock, stock, and barrel. And unnecessarily so, for, as indicated above, *Babcock* certainly does not require the reading the Court gives it today, and in any event later cases have put a gloss on *Babcock* that the Court should recognize.

Finally, the majority commits a concluding error in its application of the outdated standard of *Babcock* to review the Board's conclusion that there were no reasonable alternative means available to the union. Unless the Court today proposes to turn back time in the law of judicial deference to administrative agencies, the proper standard for judicial review of the Board's rulings is no longer for "'erroneous legal foundations,'" *ante* at —, but for rationality and consistency with the statute.... The Board's conclusion as to reasonable alternatives in this case was supported by evidence in the record. Even if the majority cannot defer to that application, because of the depth of its objections to the rule applied by the NLRB, it should remand to the Board for a decision under the rule it arrives at today, rather than sitting in the place Congress has assigned to the Board.

The more basic legal error of the majority today, like that of the Court of Appeals in *Chevron,* is to adopt a static judicial construction of the statute when Congress has not commanded that construction.... By leaving open the question of how § 7 and private property rights were to be accommodated under the NLRA, Congress delegated authority over that issue to the Board, and a court should not substitute its own judgment for a reasonable construction by the Board....

Under the law that governs today, it is *Babcock* that rests on questionable legal foundations. The Board's decision in *Jean Country,* by contrast, is both rational and consistent with the governing statute. The Court should therefore defer to the Board, rather than resurrecting and extending the reach of a decision which embodies principles which the law has long since passed by....

[The dissenting opinion of JUSTICE STEVENS is omitted.]

NOTES

1. *Babcock & Wilcox* and *Lechmere* indicate the law with respect to the validity of employer rules against solicitation and distribution of union literature by nonemployee organizers. *See, e.g., S. & H. Grossinger's,* 156 N.L.R.B. 233 (1965), *enforced as modified,* 372 F.2d 26 (2d Cir. 1967) (denial of union access to company premises violates § 8(a)(1) if it virtually insulates employees from the efforts of union organizers to reach them). *Compare NLRB v. New Pines, Inc.,* 468 F.2d 427 (2d Cir. 1972) (resort hotel in Catskill Mountains did not violate § 8(a)(1) by refusing hotel access by nonemployee organizers, where the union had not first sought to communicate with the employees through usual channels). *See Four B Corp. v. NLRB,* ___ F.3d ___ (10th Cir. 1999) (employer violated § 8(a)(1) by prohibiting nonemployee union solicitation in parking lots when it permitted nonemployee solicitation in parking lots for nonunion purposes).

In cases applying *Lechmere,* courts have frequently denied union agents access to areas open to public use. *See, e.g., UFCW Local 880 v. NLRB,* 74 F.3d 292 (D.C. Cir.), *cert. denied,* 519 U.S. 809 (1996) (sustaining ban on consumer picketing of Sears, Roebuck stores at different shopping malls); *Sparks Nugget, Inc. v. NLRB,* 968 F.2d 991 (9th Cir. 1992) (hotel/casino may prohibit handbilling and picketing by nonemployee union agents where tour buses arrive); *Oakwood Hosp. v. NLRB,* 983 F.2d 698 (6th Cir. 1993) (hospital may ban union organizer seeking to solicit employees in cafeteria).

Lechmere has been applied to prevent area standards *handbilling* by nonemployees where there was no showing of a lack of other means of communication. *See Galleria Joint Venture,* 317 N.L.R.B. 1147 (1995) (enclosed shopping mall); *Carpenters Dist. Council of Philadelphia v. NLRB,* 68 F.3d 71 (3d Cir. 1995) (condominium builder's property).

In *Monogram Models, Inc.,* 192 N.L.R.B. 705 (1971), the Board declined to adopt a "big city rule" and a different "small town rule" when applying *Babcock & Wilcox.* A plant's location in a metropolitan area is not enough in itself to open an employer's premises to nonemployee union organizers. The test is "not one of relative convenience, but rather whether the location of a plant and the living quarters of the employees place the employees beyond the reach of reasonable union efforts to communicate" by such conventional methods as mail, telephone, and home visits.

2. In *Brigadier Indus.,* 271 N.L.R.B. 656 (1984), *review denied,* 776 F.2d 365 (D.C. Cir. 1985), the Board indicated that an employer that does not act with antiunion animus may adopt an otherwise valid no-solicitation rule even after the commencement of a union organizing campaign:

> When faced with a union organizing campaign an employer may not for *union* reasons promulgate a no-solicitation and/or no-distribution rule or place other restrictions on employees. Nonetheless, during the union campaign, an employer maintains a legitimate interest in preserving production and discipline. When an employer adopts a rule during a union campaign, it does not automatically follow that the rule is invalid. If the employer has acted for legitimate business interests—rather than for union reasons—its promulgation of a rule cannot be deemed unlawful.

3. The law as to nondiscriminatory employer rules against solicitation and distribution of literature on company property by *employees* may be summarized as follows:

a. *Solicitation:*

(1) During working time—no violation of § 8(a)(1), *Peyton Packing Co.,* 49 N.L.R.B. 828, 843 (1943);

(2) During nonworking time—a violation, *Republic Aviation Corp. v. NLRB,* 324 U.S. 793 (1945), unless employer can show some special circumstances that make rules necessary to maintain production or discipline.

b. *Distribution of literature:*

(1) During working time—no violation of § 8(a)(1).

(2) During nonworking time—An employer may usually ban distribution in working areas of the plant even during nonworking time, because of its legiti-

mate interest in keeping the plant free of litter. It may not ban employee distribution in nonworking areas without a showing of special considerations. *Stoddard-Quirk Mfg. Co.,* 138 N.L.R.B. 615 (1962). *See also Eastex, Inc. v. NLRB,* 437 U.S. 556 (1978) (employer may not ban distribution of union literature opposing right-to-work law and supporting higher minimum wage law). An employer may prevent the distribution of literature that occurs in a manner that actually causes litter, even in nonworking areas. *Erie Marine, Inc.,* 192 N.L.R.B. 793 (1971), *enforced,* 465 F.2d 104 (3d Cir. 1972); *Genesee Merchants Bank & Trust Co.,* 206 N.L.R.B. 274 (1973).

Retail stores may generally ban solicitation and distribution in the *selling areas* even during employees' nonworking time, in order to avoid customer confusion. *Marshall Field & Co. v. NLRB,* 200 F.2d 375 (7th Cir. 1952); *May Dep't Stores Co.,* 59 N.L.R.B. 976 (1944), *enforced,* 154 F.2d 533 (8th Cir), *cert. denied,* 329 U.S. 725 (1946).

Health care facilities are generally permitted to prohibit employee solicitation and distribution at all times in *immediate patient care areas,* including locations in which patients receive treatment. Proscriptions which preclude such activities in nonpatient care areas during nonworking time contravene § 8(a)(1). *See NLRB v. Baptist Hosp.,* 442 U.S. 773 (1979), wherein the Court sustained the legality of a no-solicitation rule to the extent it applied to hospital corridors and sitting rooms on floors containing patient rooms, but struck down the rule to the extent it covered cafeterias, gift shops, and first floor corridors, since the employer failed to demonstrate that solicitation in such areas would have a significant effect on patient care. *See also Beth Israel Hosp. v. NLRB,* 437 U.S. 483 (1978).

The Board distinguishes between rules banning solicitation and distribution during "working time" (presumptively valid) and those phrased in terms of "working hours" (presumptively invalid), since the latter phrase is susceptible to an interpretation covering all paid time, including meal periods and breaktime. *See Our Way, Inc.,* 268 N.L.R.B. 394 (1983).

In *Southern Servs. v. NLRB,* 954 F.2d 700 (11th Cir. 1992), the court upheld the Labor Board's conclusion that employees of a janitorial subcontractor were entitled to distribute union literature among co-workers during nonworking time on the nonworking premises of a secondary business where the employees worked exclusively. *Republic Aviation* rather than *Babcock & Wilcox* was considered controlling on the rights of the subcontractor employees. *See also MBI Acquisition Corp.,* 324 N.L.R.B. No. 188, 156 L.R.R.M. 1257 (1997) (sustaining the right of electrical subcontractor employees to engage in area standards handbilling during their nonworking time in nonworking areas of a department store where their employer was working).

Absent "special circumstances based on legitimate production or safety reasons," an employer may generally not prohibit the wearing of union buttons or insignia by employees. *See Malta Constr. Co.,* 276 N.L.R.B. 1494 (1985), *en-*

forced, 806 F.2d 1009 (11th Cir. 1986). *See also St. Luke's Hosp.,* 314 N.L.R.B. 434 (1994) (allowing wearing of union buttons and stickers by hospital employees). In *Burger King Corp. v. NLRB,* 725 F.2d 1053 (6th Cir. 1984), however, the court held that a fast-food chain could lawfully ban the wearing of union buttons on employer-supplied uniforms by employees who had regular contact with the public. The rule was enforced in a nondiscriminatory manner, and the court found that the employer had the right "to project a clean, professional image to the public." *Accord, United Parcel Serv. v. NLRB,* 41 F.3d 1068 (6th Cir. 1994).

In *NLRB v. Magnavox Co.,* 415 U.S. 322 (1974), the Supreme Court held that representative unions may not agree to collective contract provisions waiving the solicitation or distribution rights of employees who support or oppose incumbent labor organizations, because such individual rights are not subject to union waiver.

c. *Off-duty Employees:*

A rule denying off-duty employees access to the employer's premises is valid only if it (1) limits access solely with respect to the interior of the plant and other working areas, (2) is clearly disseminated to all employees, and (3) applies to off-duty employees seeking access to the plant for any purpose and not just to those employees engaging in union activity. Unless justified by business reasons, a rule which denies off-duty employees entry to parking lots, gates, and other outside non-working areas is invalid. *Tri-County Med. Ctr.,* 222 N.L.R.B. 1089 (1976). *Accord, NLRB v. Ohio Masonic Home,* 892 F.2d 449 (6th Cir. 1989); *NLRB v. Pizza Crust Co. of Penn.,* 862 F.2d 49 (3d Cir. 1988).

d. *Discrimination:*

When employer rules discriminate against union solicitation and distribution— or against one union compared to another union—unfair labor practices are usually found. *See Restaurant Corp. of Am. v. NLRB,* 827 F.2d 799 (D.C. Cir. 1987). *See also NLRB v. Stowe Spinning Co.,* 336 U.S. 226 (1949) (employer violated § 8(a)(1) when it refused to rent company-owned meeting hall to union, since it was the only available hall in the company town and the company let other groups use it). *Compare Lucile Salter Packard Hosp. v. NLRB,* 97 F.3d 583 (D.C. Cir. 1996) (discriminatory to bar union solicitation while permitting many non-employee groups, mostly commercial and not charitable, to solicit) *with Cleveland Real Estate Partners v. NLRB,* 95 F.3d 457 (6th Cir. 1996) (no impermissible discrimination against union solicitation, despite Girl Scouts selling cookies, school kids selling candy, and other fraternal groups soliciting).

4. *See generally* Estlund, *Labor, Property, and Sovereignty After Lechmere,* 46 Stan. L. Rev. 305 (1994); Fanning, *Union Solicitation and Distribution of Literature on the Job—Balancing the Rights of Employers and Employees,* 9 Ga. L. Rev. 367 (1975); Gould, *The Question of Union Activity on Company Property,* 18 Vand. L. Rev. 73 (1964); Hanley, *Union Organization on Company Prop-*

erty—A Discussion of Property Rights, 47 Geo. L.J. 266 (1958); Vanderheyden, *Employee Solicitation and Distribution—A Second Look,* 14 Lab. L.J. 781 (1963); Note, *Property Rights and Job Security: Workplace Solicitation By Non-employee Union Organizers,* 94 Yale L.J. 374 (1984).

NLRB v. UNITED STEELWORKERS
[NUTONE, INC.]

Supreme Court of the United States
357 U.S. 357, 78 S. Ct. 1268, 2 L. Ed. 2d 1383 (1958)

[The Supreme Court's discussion of a companion case involving Avondale Mills has not been included in this excerpt from the Court's opinion.]

MR. JUSTICE FRANKFURTER delivered the opinion of the Court.

In April of 1953 the respondent Steelworkers instituted a campaign to organize the employees of respondent NuTone, Inc., a manufacturer of electrical devices.... In June the company began to distribute, through its supervisory personnel, literature that, although not coercive, was clearly anti-union in tenor. In August, while continuing to distribute such material, the company announced its intention of enforcing its rule against employees posting signs or distributing literature on company property or soliciting or campaigning on company time. The rule, according to these posted announcements, applied to "all employees—whether they are for or against the union."...

In a proceeding before the Board commenced at the instance of the Steelworkers, the company was charged with a number of violations of the Act ... including the discriminatory application of the no-solicitation rule.... The Board dismissed the allegation that the company had discriminatorily enforced its no-solicitation rule. 112 N.L.R.B. 1153. The Steelworkers sought review of this dismissal in the United States Court of Appeals for the District of Columbia Circuit.... The Court of Appeals concluded that it was an unfair labor practice for the company to prohibit the distribution of organizational literature on company property during working hours while the company was itself distributing antiunion literature....

Employer rules prohibiting organizational solicitation are not in and of themselves violative of the Act, for they may duly serve production, order and discipline. *See Republic Aviation Corp. v. NLRB,* 324 U.S. 793 (1945); *NLRB v. Babcock & Wilcox Co.,* 351 U.S. 105 (1956). In neither of the cases before us did the party attacking the enforcement of the no-solicitation rule contest its validity. Nor is the claim made that an employer may not, under proper circumstances, engage in noncoercive antiunion solicitation; indeed, his right to do so is protected by the so-called "employer free speech" provision of § 8(c) of the Act. Contrariwise, as both cases before us show, coercive antiunion solicitation and other similar conduct run afoul of the Act and constitute unfair labor practices irrespective of the bearing of such practices on enforcement of a no-solicitation rule. The very narrow and almost abstract question here derives from the claim that, when the employer himself engages in antiunion solicitation that if engaged in by employees would constitute a violation of the rule—particularly when his solicitation is coercive or accompanied by other unfair labor practices—his enforcement of an otherwise valid no-solicitation rule against the employees is itself an unfair labor practice. We are asked to rule that the coincidence of these circumstances necessarily violates the Act, regardless of the way in which the particular controversy arose or whether the employer's conduct to any considerable degree created an imbalance in the opportunities for organizational communication. For us to lay down such a rule of law would show indifference to the responsibilities imposed by the Act primarily on the Board to appraise carefully the interests of both sides of any labor-management controversy in the diverse circumstances of particular cases and in light of the Board's special understanding of these industrial situations....

No attempt was made in either of these cases to make a showing that the no-solicitation rules truly diminished the ability of the labor organizations involved to carry their message to the employees. Just as that is a vital consideration in determining the validity of a no-solicitation rule, *see Republic Aviation Corp. v. NLRB, supra* at 797-798; *NLRB v. Babcock & Wilcox Co., supra* at 112, it is highly relevant in determining whether a valid rule has been fairly applied. Of course the rules had the effect of closing off one channel of communication; but the Taft-Hartley Act does not command that labor organizations as a matter of abstract law, under all circumstances, be protected in the use of every possible means of reaching the minds of individual workers, nor that they are entitled to use a medium of communication simply because the employer is using it. *Cf. Bonwit Teller, Inc. v. NLRB,* 197 F.2d 640, 646 (2d Cir. 1952); *NLRB v. F. W. Woolworth Co.,* 214 F.2d 78, 84 (6th Cir. 1954) (concurring opinion). No such mechanical answers will avail for the solution of this non-mechanical, complex problem in labor-management relations. If, by virtue of the location of the plant and of the facilities and resources available to the union, the opportunities for effectively reaching the employees with a pro-union message, in spite of a no-solicitation rule, is at least as great as the employer's ability to promote the legally authorized expression of his antiunion message, there is no basis for invalidating these "otherwise valid" rules. The Board, in determining whether or not the enforcement of such a rule in the circumstances of an individual case is an unfair labor practice, may find relevant alternative channels available for communications on the right to organize. When this important issue is not even raised before the Board and no evidence bearing on it adduced, the concrete basis for appraising the significance of the employer's conduct is wanting.

We do not at all imply that the enforcement of a valid no-solicitation rule by an employer who is at the same time engaging in antiunion solicitation may not constitute an unfair labor practice. All we hold is that there must be some basis, in the actualities of industrial relations, for such a finding....

Employer or allowed to engage in no-coercal anti union speech

CHIEF JUSTICE WARREN ... concurring in part.

... In *United Steelworkers,* I concur in the result. The National Labor Relations Board declined to hold that the enforcement of an employer's no-distribution rule against a union was an unfair labor practice even though it was coupled with an antiunion campaign. The Court of Appeals reversed the Board on this point, modifying the Board's order accordingly. This Court sustains the Board. It is conceded that the enforcement of this no-distribution rule against the union is not by itself an unfair labor practice. The Board determined that the employer's expressions of his antiunion views were noncoercive in nature.... Being noncoercive in nature, the employer's expressions were protected by § 8(c) of the National Labor Relations Act and so cannot be used to show that the contemporaneous enforcement of the no-distribution rule was an unfair labor practice.

JUSTICES BLACK and DOUGLAS dissented for the reasons set forth in the opinion of the Court of Appeals.

NOTES

1. In what kinds of cases does the reasoning in *Babcock & Wilcox, Lechmere,* and *NuTone* require the NLRB to find that "reasonable efforts by the union through other available channels of communication will not enable it to reach the employees with its message" or that the employer's conduct has "created an imbalance in opportunities for organizational communication" or "truly diminished the ability of the labor organizations involved to carry their message to the employees"?

2. In *NLRB v. United Aircraft Corp.,* 324 F.2d 128 (2d Cir. 1963), *cert. denied,* 376 U.S. 951 (1964), the employer argued that the NLRB could not properly find a no-distribution rule as to nonworking areas to be an unfair labor practice where alternative means of communication with employees were readily available. The court said that the suggested requirement "would simply be an incitement to litigation and casuistry" and that "no such showing was required where employees alone were involved." The court commented: "It is inevitable that the thrust of an organizational drive would be blunted by rules which cut into a worker's use of his own time and made his association and expression subject to management limitations. Clearly the existence of available alternatives would not mitigate this deleterious effect or insure the employee the organization freedom which the Act seeks to give him." *Contra NLRB v. Rockwell Mfg. Co.,* 271 F.2d 109 (3d Cir. 1959).

2. ANTIUNION SPEECHES AND PUBLICATIONS

In a broad sense, any expression of antiunion opinion by the employer has a tendency to "interfere with, restrain or coerce" employees in the exercise of their right of self-organization. The attitude of the NLRB in the early days of the

Wagner Act was that the employer should remain neutral so that the employees could exercise a free choice as to organization. The Board said in its First Annual Report, at 73 (1936):

> [A]part from discrimination against union members ... the most common form of interference with self-organization engaged in by employers is to spread propaganda against unions and thus not only poison the minds of workers against them but also indicate to them that the employers are antagonistic to unions and are prepared to make this antagonism effective.

The ideas expressed in J. Rosenfarb, The National Labor Policy and How It Works 79 (1940), had a wide acceptance:

> An employer's "opinion" about unionism expressed to his employees is not the same as his opinion on what doctor to use or about the international situation.... When an employer addresses his antagonism toward unionism, however devoid his words may be of direct threats, there is always implicit the threat of economic compulsion if his wishes are not heeded.... Freedom of speech is possible only among those who approximate each other in equality of position.

See also International Ass'n of Machinists v. NLRB, 311 U.S. 72, 78 (1940):

> Slight suggestions as to the employer's choice between unions may have telling effect among men who know the consequences of incurring that employer's strong displeasure.

However, against these considerations must be weighed the public policy—indeed the constitutional right—of freedom of speech. In *NLRB v. Virginia Elec. & Power Co.,* 314 U.S. 469 (1941), the Supreme Court established the proposition that an employer's statements of opinion about unions should not be regarded as, or be evidence of, unfair labor practices unless, viewed against the "totality of conduct" of the employer, they appeared to be coercive. The Court said:

> The employer in this case is as free now as ever to take any side it may choose on this controversial issue. But, certainly, conduct, though evidenced in part by speech, may amount, in connection with other circumstances, to coercion, within the meaning of the Act.

The NLRB did not appear to construe the Supreme Court's *Virginia Electric* decision as requiring a marked departure from the Board's previous position with respect to employer publications. In *American Tube Bending Co.,* 44 N.L.R.B. 121 (1942), the publications consisted of letters sent to each employee and a speech made by the president to employees who were assembled for the purpose in the plant during working hours. There was no attempt to vilify the union, but the company did make clear that it thought the best interests of the employees would be served by voting against the union in the impending election. The "no-union" choice received 280 out of 413 votes counted. On petition of the losing AFL union, the Board held that the company had interfered with rights guaranteed to employees by § 7 of the Act, even though the case involved no other alleged unfair labor practices.

> Because of the relationship existing between the author of the utterances and the employees, as well as the circumstances under which the communications were delivered, they attained a force stronger than their intrinsic connotation, and beyond that of persuasion. They achieved a coercive effect that could not possibly be dissipated by the deft suggestion of Jones [the Company President] that the election would be "conducted in a fair and impartial manner ... give you absolute freedom to express your choice without any coercion."

Enforcement of the Board's order was refused on the authority of the *Virginia Electric* case. *NLRB v. American Tube Bending Co.,* 134 F.2d 993 (2d Cir. 1943), *cert. denied,* 320 U.S. 768 (1943).

In 1947, House and Senate bills containing provisions designed to preserve the free speech rights of employers and labor organizations were introduced. They culminated in the addition of § 8(c) to the NLRA.

The Senate Bill (S. 1126) contained the following provision:

> The Board shall not base any finding of unfair labor practice upon any statement of views or arguments, either written or oral, if such statement contains under all the circumstances no threat, express or implied, of reprisal or force, or offer, express or implied, of benefit.

The Senate Committee on Labor and Public Welfare explained the intent of this provision:

> Section 8(c): Another amendment to this section would insure both to employers and labor organizations full freedom to express their views to employees on labor matters, refrain from threats of violence, intimation of economic reprisal, or offers of benefit [*sic*]. The Supreme Court in Thomas v. Collins (323 U.S. 516) held, contrary to some earlier decisions of the Labor Board, that the Constitution guarantees freedom of speech on either side in labor controversies and approved the doctrine of the *American Tube Bending* case.
>
> The Board has placed a limited construction upon these decisions by holding such speeches by employers to be coercive if the employer was found guilty of some other unfair labor practice even though severable or unrelated (Monumental Life Insurance, 69 N.L.R.B. 247) or if the speech was made in the plant on working time (Clark Brothers, 70 N.L.R.B. 60). The committee believes these decisions to be too restrictive and, in this section, provides that if, under all the circumstances, there is neither an ex-

pressed or implied threat of reprisal, force, or offer of benefit, the Board shall not predicate any finding of unfair labor practice upon the statement. The Board, of course, will not be precluded from considering such statements as evidence. [S. Rep. No. 105, 80th Cong., 1st Sess. 23 (1947)]

Section 8(d) of the House Bill (H.R. 3020) contained the following provision:

The following shall not constitute or be evidence of unfair labor practice under any of the provisions of the Act:

(1) Expressing any views, argument, or opinion, or the dissemination thereof, whether in written, printed, graphic, or visual form, if it does not by its own terms threaten force or economic reprisal....

With reference to this provision, the House Committee on Education and Labor said:

Section 8(d)(1).—This guarantees free speech to employers, to employees, and to unions. Although the Labor Board says it does not limit free speech, its decisions show that it uses against people what the Constitution says they can say freely. Thus, if an employer criticizes a union, and later a foreman discharges a union official for gross misconduct, the Board may say that the official's misconduct warranted his being discharged, but "infer," from what the employer said, perhaps long before, that the discharge was for union activity, and reinstate the official with back pay. It has similarly abused the right of free speech in abolishing and penalizing unions of which it disapproved but which workers wished as their bargaining agents. The bill corrects this, providing that nothing that anyone says shall constitute or be evidence of an unfair labor practice unless it, by its own express terms, threatens force or economic reprisal. This means that a statement may not be used against the person making it unless it, standing alone, is unfair within the express terms of Sections 7 and 8 of the amended act. [H.R. Rep. No. 245, 80th Cong., 1st Sess. 33 (1947)]

The House Managers explained the import of the language finally included in § 8(c):

Section 8(d)(5). Both the House bill and the Senate amendment contained provisions designed to protect the right of both employers and labor organizations to free speech. The conference agreement adopts the provisions of the House bill in this respect with one change derived from the Senate amendment. It is provided that expressing any views, argument, or opinion or the dissemination thereof, whether in written, printed, graphic, or visual form, is not to constitute or be evidence of an unfair labor practice if such expression contains no threat of force or reprisal or promise of benefit. The practice which the Board has had in the past of using speeches and publications of employers concerning labor organizations and collective bargaining arrangements as evidence, no matter how irrelevant or immaterial, that some later act of the employer had an illegal purpose gave rise to the necessity for this change in the law. The purpose is to protect the right of free speech when what the employer says or writes is not of a threatening nature or does not promise a prohibited favorable discrimination. [H.R. Rep. No. 510, 80th Cong., 1st Sess. 45 (1947)]

NOTES

1. In the light of this legislative history, did Congress intend the coercive nature of an employer's communication to its employees to be judged "on the face" of the communication or as viewed in the "totality of conduct of the employer"? In *NLRB v. Kropp Forge Co.,* 178 F.2d 822 (7th Cir. 1949), *cert. denied,* 340 U.S. 810 (1950), the Seventh Circuit addressed this issue:

It ... seems clear to us that in considering whether such statements or expressions are protected by Section 8(c) of the Act, they cannot be considered as isolated words cut off from the relevant circumstances and background in which they are spoken. A statement considered only as to the words it contains might seem a perfectly innocent statement, including neither a threat nor a promise. But, when the same statement is made by an employer to his employees, and we consider the relation of the parties, the surrounding circumstances, related statements and events and the background of the employer's actions, we may find that the statement is part of a general pattern which discloses action by the employer so coercive as to entirely destroy his employees' freedom of choice and action. To permit statements or expressions to be so used on the theory that they are protected either by the First Amendment or by Section 8(c) of the Act, would be in violation of Section 7 and contrary to the expressed purpose of the Act. Therefore, in determining whether such statements and expressions constitute, or are evidence of unfair labor practice, they must be considered in connection with the positions of the parties, with the background and circumstances under which they are made, and with the general conduct of the parties. If, when so considered, such statements form a part of a general pattern or course of conduct which constitutes coercion and deprives the employees of their free choice guaranteed by Section 7, such statements must still be considered as a basis for a finding of unfair labor practice. To hold otherwise, would nullify the guaranty of employees' freedom of action and choice which Section 7 of the Act expressly provides. Congress, in enacting Section 8(c), could not have intended that result.

Accord, Irving Air Chute Co. v. NLRB, 350 F.2d 176 (2d Cir. 1965).

2. In *J.P. Stevens & Co. v. NLRB,* 380 F.2d 292 (2d Cir.), *cert. denied,* 389 U.S. 1005 (1967), the court considered an employer statement that "if this Union were to get in here, it would not work to your benefit but, in the long run, would itself operate to your serious harm." The court found that this statement was made in context of "massive" unfair labor practices.

> Apparently the Board has frequently characterized a substantially similar notice as an instrument of coercion. *E.g., Greensboro Hosiery Mills, Inc.,* 162 N.L.R.B. 1275 (1967); *White Oak Acres, Inc.,* 134 N.L.R.B. 1145, 1149-50 (1961). However, the Fourth and Sixth Circuits have disagreed with the Board, *see Wellington Mill Div., West Point Mfg. Co. v. NLRB,* 330 F.2d 579, 583 (4th Cir.), *cert. denied,* 379 U.S. 882 (1964); *Surprenant Mfg. Co. v. NLRB,* 341 F.2d 756, 758-60 (6th Cir. 1965). So has the Court of Appeals for the District of Columbia, with the important qualification that the notice may take a different coloration by virtue of the accompanying circumstances, *Amalgamated Clothing Workers v. NLRB,* 365 F.2d 898, 909-10 (D.C. Cir. 1966) (2-1 decision) .... There can hardly be disagreement with the view of the District of Columbia Court of Appeals that the words of a notice should not be so regarded [*in vacuo*], but may take on a darker hue when viewed in the perspective of the particular setting.

The court concluded that the setting in the *J.P. Stevens* case was of a sufficiently dark hue to warrant finding the "serious harm" statement as coercive under § 8(a)(1).

3. In *Daniel Constr. Co. v. NLRB,* 341 F.2d 805, 811 (4th Cir.), *cert. denied,* 382 U.S. 831 (1965), the court said: "Even if we assume that each of the key statements in the Daniel speeches considered separately would be lawful ... it still does not follow that we must accept the position pressed upon us by the company [that the whole cannot be greater than the sum of its parts]. Daniel may have accurately stated an accepted rule of mathematics, but words and speech are not governed entirely by mechanical mathematical concepts. Words and phrases, each lawful when considered alone, can be united in such a fashion as to yield an improper end product."

4. *Crown Stationers,* 272 N.L.R.B. 164 (1984), involved an employer that left a letter threatening to discharge a primary union organizer in a folder. The letter was discovered by a co-worker during the course of her duties, read by her, and disseminated to other employees. A violation was found, even though the employer did not intend to disclose the letter to any of the employees.

NLRB v. GISSEL PACKING CO.

Supreme Court of the United States
395 U.S. 575, 89 S. Ct. 1918, 23 L. Ed. 2d 547 (1969)

[The main part of the opinion in this case, dealing with the validity of bargaining orders based on authorization cards, is set out, *infra.* However, one of the four employers whose cases were consolidated before the Supreme Court—the

Sinclair Company—raised the issue of "employer free speech," and the portion of the Court's opinion which passed upon that point is reproduced below.]

MR. CHIEF JUSTICE WARREN delivered the opinion of the Court.

... The petitioner, a producer of mill rolls, wire, and related products at two plants in Holyoke, Massachusetts, was shut down for some three months in 1952 as the result of a strike over contract negotiations with the American Wire Weavers Protective Association (AWWPA), the representative of petitioner's journeymen and apprentice wire weavers from 1933 to 1952. The Company subsequently reopened without a union contract, and its employees remained unrepresented through 1964, when the Company was acquired by an Ohio corporation, with the Company's former president continuing as head of the Holyoke, Massachusetts, division. In July 1965, the International Brotherhood of Teamsters, Local Union No. 404, began an organizing campaign among petitioner's Holyoke employees and by the end of the summer had obtained authorization cards from 11 of the Company's 14 journeymen wire weavers choosing the Union as their bargaining agent. On September 20, the Union notified petitioner that it represented a majority of its wire weavers, requested that the Company bargain with it, and offered to submit the signed cards to a neutral third party for authentication. After petitioner's president declined the Union's request a week later, claiming, *inter alia,* that he had a good faith doubt of majority status because of the cards' inherent unreliability, the Union petitioned, on November 8, for an election that was ultimately set for December 8.

When petitioner's president first learned of the Union's drive in July, he talked with all of his employees in an effort to dissuade them from joining a union. He particularly emphasized the results of the long 1952 strike, which he claimed "almost put our company out of business," and expressed worry that the employees were forgetting the "lessons of the past." He emphasized secondly that the Company was still on "thin ice" financially, that the Union's "only weapon is to strike," and that a strike "could lead to closing the plant," since the parent company had ample manufacturing facilities elsewhere. He noted thirdly that because of their age and the limited usefulness of their skills outside their craft, the employees might not be able to find re-employment if they lost their jobs as a result of a strike. Finally, he warned those who did not believe that the plant could go out of business to "look around Holyoke and see a lot of them out of business." The president sent letters to the same effect to the employees in early November, emphasizing that the parent company had no reason to stay in Massachusetts if profits went down.

During the two or three weeks immediately prior to the election on December 9, the president sent the employees a pamphlet captioned "Do you want another 13-week strike?" stating, *inter alia,* that "We have no doubt that the Teamsters Union can again close the Wire Weaving Department and the entire plant by a strike. We have no hopes that the Teamsters Union bosses will not call a strike...."

The Teamsters Union is a strike happy outfit." Similar communications followed in late November, including one stressing the Teamsters' "hoodlum control." Two days before the election, the Company sent out another pamphlet that was entitled "Let's Look at the Record," and that purported to be an obituary of companies in the Holyoke-Springfield, Massachusetts, area that had allegedly gone out of business because of union demands, eliminating some 3,500 jobs; the first page carried a large cartoon showing the preparation of a grave for the Sinclair Company and other headstones containing the names of other plants allegedly victimized by the unions. Finally, on the day before the election, the president made another personal appeal to his employees to reject the Union. He repeated that the Company's financial condition was precarious; that a possible strike would jeopardize the continued operation of the plant; and that age and lack of education would make re-employment difficult. The Union lost the election 7-6, and then filed both objections to the election and unfair labor practice charges which were consolidated for hearing before the trial examiner.

The Board agreed with the trial examiner that the president's communications with the employees, when considered as a whole, "reasonably tended to convey to the employees the belief or impression that selection of the Union in the forthcoming election could lead [the Company] to close its plant, or to the transfer of the weaving production, with the resultant loss of jobs to the wire weavers." Thus, the Board found that under the "totality of the circumstances" petitioner's activities constituted a violation of § 8(a)(1) of the Act.

On appeal, the Court of Appeals for the First Circuit sustained the Board's findings and conclusions and enforced its order in full. 397 F.2d 157....

We consider finally petitioner Sinclair's First Amendment challenge to the holding of the Board and the Court of Appeals for the First Circuit. At the outset we note that the question raised here most often arises in the context of a nascent union organizational drive, where employers must be careful in waging their antiunion campaign. As to conduct generally, the above noted gradations of unfair labor practices, with their varying consequences, create certain hazards for employers when they seek to estimate or resist unionization efforts. But so long as the differences involve conduct easily avoided, such as discharge, surveillance, and coercive interrogation, we do not think that employers can complain that the distinctions are unreasonably difficult to follow. Where an employer's antiunion efforts consist of speech alone, however, the difficulties raised are not so easily resolved. The Board has eliminated some of the problem areas by no longer requiring an employer to show affirmative reasons for insisting on an election and by permitting him to make reasonable inquiries. We do not decide, of course, whether these allowances are mandatory. But we do note that an employer's free speech right to communicate his views to his employees is firmly established and cannot be infringed by a union or the Board. Thus, § 8(c) ... merely implements the First Amendment....

Any assessment of the precise scope of employer expression, of course, must be made in the context of its labor relations setting. Thus, an employer's rights cannot outweigh the equal rights of the employees to associate freely, as those rights are embodied in § 7 and protected by § 8(a)(1) and the proviso to § 8(c). And any balancing of those rights must take into account the economic dependence of the employees on their employers, and the necessary tendency of the former, because of that relationship, to pick up intended implications of the latter that might be more readily dismissed by a more disinterested ear. Stating these obvious principles is but another way of recognizing that what is basically at stake is the establishment of a nonpermanent, limited relationship between the employer, his economically dependent employee and his union agent, not the election of legislators or the enactment of legislation whereby that relationship is ultimately defined and where the independent voter may be freer to listen more objectively and employers as a class freer to talk. *Compare New York Times Co. v. Sullivan,* 376 U.S. 254 (1964).

Within this framework, we must reject the Company's challenge to the decision below and the findings of the Board on which it was based. The standards used below for evaluating the impact of an employer's statements are not seriously questioned by petitioner and we see no need to tamper with them here. Thus, an employer is free to communicate to his employees any of his general views about unionism or any of his specific views about a particular union, so long as the communications do not contain a "threat of reprisal or force or promise of benefit." He may even make a prediction as to the precise effects he believes unionization will have on his company. In such a case, however, the prediction must be carefully phrased on the basis of objective fact to convey an employer's belief as to demonstrably probable consequences beyond his control or to convey a management decision already arrived at to close the plant in case of unionization. *See Textile Workers v. Darlington Mfg. Co.,* 380 U.S. 263, 274, n.20 (1965). If there is any implication that an employer may or may not take action solely on his own initiative for reasons unrelated to economic necessities and known only to him, the statement is no longer a reasonable prediction based on available facts but a threat of retaliation based on misrepresentation and coercion, and as such without the protection of the First Amendment. We therefore agree with the court below that "conveyance of the employer's belief, even though sincere, that unionization will or may result in the closing of the plant is not a statement of fact unless, which is most improbable, the eventuality of closing is capable of proof." 397 F.2d, at 160. As stated elsewhere, an employer is free only to tell "what he reasonably believes will be the likely economic consequences of unionization that are outside his control," and not "threats of economic reprisal to be taken solely on his own volition." *NLRB v. River Togs, Inc.,* 382 F.2d 198, 202 (2d Cir. 1967)....

Equally valid was the finding by the court and the Board that petitioner's statements and communications were not cast as a prediction of "demonstrable economic consequences," 397 F.2d, at 160, but rather as a threat of retaliatory action. The Board found that petitioner's speeches, pamphlets, leaflets, and letters conveyed the following message: that the company was in a precarious financial condition; that the "strike-happy" union would in all likelihood have to obtain its potentially unreasonable demands by striking, the probable result of which would be a plant shut-down, as the past history of labor relations in the area indicated; and that the employees in such a case would have great difficulty finding employment elsewhere. In carrying out its duty to focus on the question "what did the speaker intend and the listener understand," Cox, Law and the National Labor Policy 44 (1960), the Board could reasonably conclude that the intended and understood import of that message was not to predict that unionization would inevitably cause the plant to close but to threaten to throw employees out of work regardless of the economic realities. In this connection, we need go no further than to point out (1) that petitioner had no support for his basic assumption that the union, which had not yet even presented any demands, would have to strike to be heard, and that he admitted at the hearing that he had no basis for attributing other plant closings in the area to unionism; and (2) that the Board has often found that employees, who are particularly sensitive to rumors of plant closings, take such hints as coercive threats rather than honest forecasts.

Petitioner argues that the line between so-called permitted predictions and proscribed threats is too vague to stand up under traditional First Amendment analysis and that the Board's discretion to curtail free speech rights is correspondingly too uncontrolled. It is true that a reviewing court must recognize the Board's competence in the first instance to judge the impact of utterances made in the context of the employer-employee relationship, *see NLRB v. Virginia Elec. & Power Co.,* 314 U.S. 469, 479 (1941). But an employer, who has control over that relationship and therefore knows it best, cannot be heard to complain that he is without an adequate guide for his behavior. He can easily make his views known without engaging in "'brinkmanship'" when it becomes all too easy to "overstep and tumble into the brink," *Wausau Steel Corp. v. NLRB,* 377 F.2d 369, 372 (7th Cir. 1967). At the least he can avoid coercive speech simply by avoiding conscious overstatements he has reason to believe will mislead his employees.

For the foregoing reasons, we affirm the judgment of the Court of Appeals for the First Circuit.

NOTES

1. The line between a permissible prediction or statement of legal position and an illegal threat has been a difficult one for the Board and the courts to draw.

Compare Crown Cork & Seal Co. v. NLRB, 36 F.3d 1130 (D.C. Cir. 1994) (company remarks about possible plant closure if workers voted for union permissible when based on reasonable fear that increased labor costs would render facility uncompetitive) *and NLRB v. Champion Labs.*, 99 F.3d 223 (7th Cir. 1996) (no threat to close plant in supervisor's casual remark to handbillers, "I hope you guys are ready to pack up and move to Mexico") *with Farris Fashions v. NLRB*, 32 F.3d 373 (8th Cir. 1994) (employer statements concerning possible plant closure if union prevailed § 8(a)(1) violation) *and Reeves Bros.*, 320 N.L.R.B. 1082 (1996) (company president who received letters from customers expressing concern about unionization "went over the brink" when he told employees that customers *would* remove their business if the union won).

Compare Eldorado Tool Div. of Quamco, 325 N.L.R.B. No. 16, 156 L.R.R.M. 1241 (1997) (creating "UAW WALL OF SHAME" tombstone depicting plant closures § 8(a)(1) violation as threat to close if union won) *with Be-Lo Stores v. NLRB*, 126 F.3d 268 (4th Cir. 1997) (no violation when employer handed out mock "pink slips" prior to Board election indicating that layoffs might be in employees' future if union won, since valid prediction about possible impact of unionization).

2. In *NLRB v. Herman Wilson Lumber Co.,* 355 F.2d 426 (8th Cir. 1966), the employer's speeches included the following remarks: "I will fight the Union in every legal way possible.... If the Union calls an economic strike, you place your job on the line. You can be permanently replaced. You can lose your job.... In dealing with the Union I'll deal hard with it—I'll deal cold with it—I'll deal at arm's length with it." The NLRB held that these statements violated § 8(a)(1), but the court of appeals denied enforcement.

The NLRB found no unfair labor practice when an employer referred to the lower wages being paid at unionized plants and suggested that the organization of its employees might result in similarly lower wages (*International Paper Co.,* 273 N.L.R.B. 615 (1984)) or when an employer told workers that wages and benefits are typically "frozen" during bargaining with a union, which could go on for more than a year (*Montrose-Haeuser Co.,* 306 N.L.R.B. 377 (1992)). On the other hand, unlawful threats were found when an employer made a slide presentation showing rental trucks replacing employee-driven trucks after the union won an election at another company (*Coronet Foods*, 305 N.L.R.B. 79 (1991), *enforced*, 981 F.2d 1284 (D.C. Cir. 1993)).

3. The Labor Board remains divided over the allowable forcefulness of an employer's language in urging employees not to sign union authorization cards. In *Airporter Inn Hotel,* 215 N.L.R.B. 824 (1974), the Board held (3-2) that a letter could lawfully conclude: "[A]void a lot of unnecessary turmoil.... [A] union ... can't and won't do anything for you except jeopardize your jobs." A divided Board ruled in *Munroe Co., 217* N.L.R.B. 1011 (1975), that an employer did not violate the NLRA when its president and two employer representatives told assembled employees that signing union cards could be "fatal." May an employer urge employees to withdraw authorization cards already signed? *See NLRB v. Monroe Tube Co.,* 545 F.2d 1320 (2d Cir. 1976).

4. The NLRB has indicated that § 8(c) is limited to unfair labor practice cases and has no application in representation cases. "Conduct that creates an atmosphere which renders improbable a free choice will sometimes warrant invalidating an election even though the conduct may not constitute an unfair labor practice." *General Shoe Corp.,* 77 N.L.R.B. 124 (1948), *enforced,* 192 F.2d 504 (6th Cir. 1951), *cert. denied,* 343 U.S. 904 (1952). Thus, employer statements that may not constitute a "threat of reprisal" under § 8(c), may so cloud the atmosphere as to warrant the setting aside of an election.

MAY DEPARTMENT STORES CO.

National Labor Relations Board
136 N.L.R.B. 797 (1962)

CHAIRMAN MCCULLOCH and MEMBERS BROWN and FANNING:
... The Respondent owns and operates two department stores in the Greater Cleveland, Ohio, area. During the years 1959 and 1960, the Joint Petitioners campaigned to organize the Respondent. During this time the Respondent had in effect and enforced a broad no-solicitation rule which prohibited, *inter alia,* union solicitation in the selling areas of the store during the employees' working and nonworking time. The Respondent's enforcement of this rule, as such, is not alleged by the General Counsel as a violation or as interference with the election. Just prior to the election held on April 28, 1960, at a time when it was enforcing its no-solicitation rule, the Respondent made noncoercive antiunion speeches to massed assemblies of employees on company property and thereafter denied the Union's request for equal opportunity and time to address the same employees. It is the theory of the General Counsel that the refusal to grant the Union's request to reply, on these uncontested facts, constitutes a violation of § 8(a)(1) of the Act and also warrants setting aside the election. We agree with position taken by the General Counsel.[4]

In the *Bonwit Teller* case, the employer had in effect a no-solicitation rule which forbade solicitation during working and nonworking time on the selling floors of the department store. The employer made preelection antiunion speeches to the employees in the selling areas but refused the Union's request for an opportunity to reply on equal terms. The Board found that such refusal interfered with the employees' organizational rights guaranteed by § 7, in violation of

---

[4] The no-solicitation rule in the instant case is of the broad but privileged type. Generally, in manufacturing industries, for example, a no-solicitation rule which interferes with the right of employees to solicit on nonworking time violates § 8(a)(1) of the Act. *See, Republic Aviation Corp. v. NLRB,* 324 U.S. 793 (1945). However, department stores have long been exempted from the application of the rule because the nature of the business is such that solicitation, even on nonworking time, in selling areas, would unduly interfere with the retail store operations. *See, e.g., Marshall Field & Co.,* 98 N.L.R.B. 88 and *Great A & P Co.,* 123 N.L.R.B. 747. *See also, Walton Mfg. Co.,* 126 N.L.R.B. 697.

§ 8(a)(1), and ordered the employer to cease and desist from such refusals. The Court of Appeals for the Second Circuit upheld the Board's finding of the violation.[6] In substance the Second Circuit reasoned as follows:

> The Board, however, has allowed retail department stores the privilege of prohibiting all solicitation within selling areas of the store during both working and nonworking hours [citations and footnote omitted]. Bonwit Teller chose to avail itself of that privilege and, having done so, was in our opinion required to abstain from campaigning against the Union on the same premises to which the Union was denied access; if it should be otherwise, the practical advantage to the employer who was opposed to unionization would constitute a serious interference with the rights of his employees to organize.[7]

In our opinion, the Board and court holding in the *Bonwit Teller* case, which we consider to be legally sound, squarely controls the issue in the present case.

Each of the contending parties herein relies upon *Livingston Shirt Corporation*[8] as supporting its respective position. The *Bonwit Teller* case itself, as noted, dealt with department store situations. Thereafter, for a time, the Board also applied the doctrine of *Bonwit Teller* to establishments other than retail department stores.[9]

However, in the *Livingston Shirt* case, the Board modified its approach to the problem in the following terms:

> Accordingly, we are convinced that absent special circumstances as hereinafter indicated, there is nothing improper in an employer refusing to grant to the union a right equal to his own in his plant. We rule therefore that, *in the absence of either an unlawful broad no-solicitation rule (prohibiting union access to company premises on other than working time) or a privileged no-solicitation rule (broad, but not unlawful because of the character of the business)* [citing *Marshall Field & Co.*, 98 N.L.R.B. 887] an employer does not commit an unfair labor practice if he makes a preelection speech on company time and premises to his employees and denies the union's request for an opportunity to reply....

> Our holding here finds support in the recent decision of Second Circuit Court of Appeals in *American Tube Bending* case [citation omitted] in

---

[6] *Bonwit Teller, Inc. v. NLRB*, 197 F.2d 640 (2d Cir. 1952), *cert. denied*, 345 U.S. 905 (1953).

[7] *Id.* at 645. *See also, NLRB v. American Tube Bending Co.*, 205 F.2d 45 (2d Cir. enfg. 102 N.L.R.B. 735, 1953), wherein the Second Circuit made it clear that its decision in *Bonwit Teller* gave the union a right of reply precisely *because* the broad rule was permitted.

[8] 107 N.L.R.B. 400 (1953).

[9] *E.g., Metropolitan Auto Parts*, 102 N.L.R.B. 1634 (unfair labor practices found); *Gruen Watch Co.*, 103 N.L.R.B. 3 (objections to election sustained).

which it explicated its views of permissible employer conduct within the scope of the *Bonwit Teller* doctrine [citation omitted].

We find no basis for the Respondent's contention that in *Livingston Shirt* the Board overruled the *Bonwit Teller* doctrine as it applies to department stores with broad but privileged no-solicitation rules.[11] It is clear that this latter situation was expressly excluded from the statement of allowable employer conduct and was particularly identified with the citation of the *Marshall Field* case and the explicit reliance upon the court opinions in *Bonwit Teller* and *American Tube Bending,supra.*[12]

However, the Respondent, in the alternative, maintains that certain decisions of the Supreme Court control and resolve the instant case. The Respondent contends in record argument and brief that the *NuTone*[13] and *Babcock & Wilcox*[14] cases stand for the proposition that retail store employers may: (1) enforce a broad but privileged rule; (2) make antiunion speeches to massed assemblies of employees; and (3) at the same time deny to organizing unions a similar right of reply.

We do not agree. Indeed, we believe that those decisions delineating the extent to which an employer can restrict the organizational activities of employees and nonemployees on its premises, require the result we have reached herein. The no-solicitation rule enforced by Respondent is one which seriously impaired the right of employees to discuss union organization on company premises during nonworking as well as working time and thus created an imbalance in the opportunities for organizational communication. Respondent's rule is broader than the valid rule involved in the *NuTone* case, which restricted employees' discussion of such matters only during their working time, but left them free to discuss and evaluate such matters during their nonworking time. Thus Respondent's rule, albeit privileged,[15] involved a significantly greater restriction on employees' self-organization rights than did the rule involved in *NuTone*.

---

[11] It is not necessary to, and we do not, pass upon the *Livingston Shirt* case insofar as it affects nondepartment store situations.

[12] In both cases, the Second Circuit indicated that enforcement of the Board's order would be confined to the specific situations, i.e., the employer's application of a "broad but privileged" no-solicitation rule while "availing itself of the privilege by campaigning against the union on the same premises, to which the union was denied access."

[13] *NLRB v. United Steelworkers (NuTone, Inc.),* 357 U.S. 357 (1958).

[14] *NLRB v. Babcock & Wilcox,* 351 U.S. 105 (1956).

[15] This rule, if promulgated by a nonretail store employer, would be presumptively invalid because it applies to nonworking time. The employer would have the burden of showing that factors relating to production, discipline and order at its particular plant made such additional restriction of employees' organizational activities necessary, thus overcoming the presumption of invalidity. *See Walton Mfg. Co.,* 126 N.L.R.B. 747. In effect the Board's rule for department stores eliminates this latter requirement and permits such employers to promulgate such a rule without a specific showing of such factors. Of course, Respondent's rule also precluded nonemployee organizers from coming

In *NuTone,* the Supreme Court discussed the right of an employer to enforce against its employees a no-solicitation rule relating only to working time, while itself engaging in an antiunion campaign during such time. It noted that the question at issue in such cases was whether such "conduct to any considerable degree created an imbalance in the opportunities for organizational communication." While holding that no such imbalance was shown therein, the Court indicated that the result might have been different had "the employees, or the union on their behalf, requested the employer, himself, engaging in antiunion solicitation, to make an exception to the rule for pro-union solicitation." Further, it indicated that even absent such a request, the employer's conduct might properly have been deemed unlawful, had it "truly diminished the ability of the labor organizations involved to carry their messages to the employees. *Just as that is a vital consideration in determining the validity of a no-solicitation rule, see Republic Aviation Corp. v. NLRB, supra* [324 U.S.] at 797-798; *NLRB v. Babcock & Wilcox Co., supra* [351 U.S.] at 112, *it is highly relevant in determining whether a valid rule has been fairly applied.*" (Emphasis supplied.)

Applying these principles, we find that a glaring "imbalance in opportunities for organizational communication" was created by Respondent's enforcement of the broad rule against union discussion during nonworking time as well as during working time, while it was engaged in utilizing such time to bring its antiunion message to the employees. By such conduct, Respondent seized for itself the most advantageous circumstances in which to present to employees its side of the organizational question. It spoke to them in massed assemblies during working time, thus gaining the not inconsiderable benefit flowing from the utilization of the employment relationship for such purposes, and insuring that its message would reach all of its employees in the most carefully thought out and coherent form of maximum effectiveness. At the same time, it relegated the union and its employee supporters to relatively catch-as-catch-can methods of rebuttal, such as home visits, advertised meetings on the employees' own time, telephone calls, letters, and the various mass media of communication. While it is true that the Supreme Court in *Babcock & Wilcox* held that an employer may normally put a union to the task of organizing employees through such channels, it indicated that such right was not absolute, but was limited to those circumstances, where the effectiveness of such channels of communication was not diminished by employer conduct, or by other circumstances.

The normal effectiveness of such channels stems not alone from the ability of a union to make contact with employees, away from their place of work, but also from the availability of normal opportunities to employees who have been contacted to discuss the matter with their fellow employees at their place of work. The place of work is the one place where all employees involved are sure to be

---

on its premises for purposes of distributing literature and soliciting employees. On this point we perceive no difference in the latitude allowed retail store employers and other employers.

together. Thus it is the one place where they can all discuss with each other the advantages and disadvantages of organization, and lend each other support and encouragement. Such full discussion lies at the very heart of the organizational rights guaranteed by the Act, and is not to be restricted, except as the exigencies of production, discipline and order demand.[16] It is only where opportunities for such discussion are available, limited, of course, by the need to maintain production, order and discipline, that the election procedures established in the Act can be expected to produce the peaceful resolution of representation questions on the basis of a free and informed choice. Where such discussion is not allowed, the normal channels of communication become clogged and lose their effectiveness. In such circumstances, the balance in "opportunities for organizational communication" is destroyed by an employer's utilization of working time and place for its antiunion campaign. Accordingly, while Respondent was under no obligation to forego utilizing such time and place for its antiunion campaign, we find that it was under an obligation to accede to the Union's request to address the employees under similar circumstances. Only by such action could it maintain the balance which the Supreme Court deemed so important a factor in this area. Respondent's failure to accede to the Union's request seriously impaired the employee's ability to learn of the advantages of union organization from others, and to discuss such advantages among themselves. It thereby interfered with their rights of self-organization as guaranteed in § 7 of the Act.

Accordingly, we find that Respondent's conduct as discussed above, violated § 8(a)(1) of the Act, and interfered with the conduct of the election of April 28, 1961. We shall therefore set aside that election and direct a new election....

MEMBER LEEDOM dissenting.

Under the principles established in the *NuTone* case,[31] which I deem dispositive of the issues in this case,[32] the enforcement of a valid no-solicitation rule by an employer who is at the same time engaging in antiunion solicitation may not constitute an unfair labor practice in the absence of substantial evidence that, when all alternative reasonably available channels of communication are considered, the ability of the Union to carry its message to the employees has been truly diminished.[33] Unlike the majority, I do not think such a true diminution can be established merely by showing that as a general proposition department store

---

[16] *NLRB v. Babcock & Wilcox Co., supra.*

[31] *NLRB v. United Steelworkers (NuTone, Inc.),* 357 U.S. 357 (1958); *see also NLRB v. Babcock & Wilcox Co.,* 351 U.S. 105 (1956).

[32] Although *NuTone* involved the rights of employees, its principles, insofar as they preclude a finding of violation, apply *a fortiori* to nonemployees; *see NLRB v. Babcock & Wilcox Co., supra.*

[33] To this extent I agree with Member Rodgers that a finding of violation cannot be predicated on *Bonwit Teller, Inc.,* 96 N.L.R.B. 608. In view of the *NuTone* and *Babcock* decisions, the question of the extent to which *Livingston Shirt Corp.,* 107 N.L.R.B. 400, overruled *Bonwit Teller* is largely academic and I see no need to join in the debate on that issue at this late date.

employees can be more easily reached through the avenues of communication open to their employer than through the avenues open to a union. As I find in this record no evidence of true diminution, I would find that the complaint should be dismissed and the objections to the election should be overruled.[34]

[MEMBER RODGERS dissented in an opinion which is omitted.]

NOTES

1. The Court of Appeals for the Sixth Circuit refused to enforce the Board's *May Department Stores* order, based on reasoning similar to that set forth in Member Leedom's dissent. *May Dep't Stores Co. v. NLRB,* 316 F.2d 797 (6th Cir. 1963). *Compare Montgomery Ward & Co. v. NLRB,* 339 F.2d 889 (6th Cir. 1965), wherein the court upheld the Board's § 8(a)(1) finding where the employer denied the union a chance to reply to its "captive audience" speech, banned all union solicitation on company property, and threatened employees with discharge if they solicited union memberships on their own time away from company property. The Sixth Circuit agreed that this situation created "an imbalance in organizational communication."

2. *See generally* Barbash, *Employer "Free Speech" and Employee Rights,* 14 Lab. L.J. 313 (1963); Becker, *Democracy in the Workplace: Union Representation Elections and Federal Labor Law,* 77 Minn. L. Rev. 495 (1993); Bloom, *Freedom of Communication Under the Labor Relations Act,* in N.Y.U. Eighth Annual Conference on Labor 219 (1955); Bok, *The Regulation of Campaign Tactics in Representation Elections Under the National Labor Relations Act,* 78 Harv. L. Rev. 38 (1964); Christensen, *Free Speech, Propaganda and the NLRA,* 38 N.Y.U. L. Rev. 243 (1963); Drotning, *Employer Free Speech: Two Basic Questions Considered by the NLRB and Courts,* 16 Lab. L.J. 131 (1965); Koretz, *Employer Free Speech Under the Taft-Hartley Act,* 6 Syracuse L. Rev. 82 (1954); Pokempner, *Employer Free Speech Under the National Labor Relations Act,* 25 Md. L. Rev. 111 (1965); Wollett & Rowen, *Employer Speech and Related Issues,* 16 Ohio St. L.J. 380 (1955).

3. INTERROGATION

BLUE FLASH EXPRESS, INC.

National Labor Relations Board
109 N.L.R.B. 591 (1954)

[Respondent, an interstate motor carrier, received a letter on May 19, 1953, from the union stating that it represented a majority of respondent's employees, that it was prepared to submit proof thereof, and that it desired to enter into col-

---

[34] As I find no violation on the facts in the case, I have not considered the impact, if any, which § 8(c) of the Act would have in other factual contexts.

lective bargaining negotiations. Before replying, respondent's general manager, Golden, interviewed each employee individually in his office, stating that he had received a letter from the union and that it was immaterial to him whether or not employees were union members, but that he desired to know whether they had joined so that he might know how to answer the letter. Each employee denied to Golden that he had signed any union card, although a majority of them had done so, designating the union as their representative, on or about May 17, 1953. Golden testified that this was the entire conversation. Several employees testified that Golden also stated on this occasion that the company was too small to operate with a union and that it would be impelled to sell out or reduce operations should the business be unionized. The Trial Examiner found that, since the witnesses appeared to be equally credible, the General Counsel had failed to establish the alleged threats of shutdown by a preponderance of the evidence and that the facts as to the interviews were as testified to by Golden.]

... [W]e are ... of the opinion that Golden's interrogation of the employees was not violative of the Act. At the time of the interrogation, the Respondent had just received a communication from the Union claiming majority status and the right to represent the Respondent's employees in collective bargaining. Golden so informed the employees. He further gave them assurances that the Respondent would not resort to economic reprisals and advised them that he wished to know whether they had signed union authorization cards in order to enable him to reply to the Union's request for collective bargaining. As found above, there is no credible evidence that the Respondent at any time made any threats or promises violative of the Act, resorted to any reprisals, or exhibited any antiunion animus. Although the employees who had signed union authorization cards gave false answers to Golden's inquiries, the Respondent did nothing to afford them a reasonable basis for believing that the Respondent might resort to reprisals because of their union membership or activity. The facts here are similar to those presented in *Atlas Life Ins. Co. v. NLRB*, 195 F.2d 136 (10th Cir. 1952), where the Employer tried to find out whether a union represented a majority of the employees so that he would know whether he was obligated to bargain with the union. In that case, the Court of Appeals for the Tenth Circuit held that such interrogation was proper. When such interrogation is conducted under proper safeguards, as was the situation in the instant case, the fact that the interrogation is systematic does not, in itself, impart a coercive character to the interrogation. The purpose of such interrogation could not be achieved without systematic inquiry.

Contrary to the assertion of our dissenting colleagues, we are not holding in this decision that interrogation must be accompanied by other unfair labor practices before it can violate the Act. We are merely holding that interrogation of employees by an employer as to such matters as their union membership or union activities, which, when viewed in the context in which the interrogation occurred, falls short of interference or coercion, is not unlawful.

If there is no interference or coercion then the interrogation is permissible

Test

Our dissenting colleagues rely upon the rationale of *Standard-Coosa-Thatcher,* 85 N.L.R.B. 1358, in which the Board held that interrogation *per se* is unlawful. They appear to overlook cases, for the most part of recent date, in which the courts of at least six circuits have explicitly or by necessary implication condemned the rationale of *Standard-Coosa-Thatcher.* We hereby repudiate the notion that interrogation *per se* is unlawful and overrule *Standard-Coosa-Thatcher* and the line of cases following it to the extent that they are inconsistent with our decision today.

In our view, the test is whether, under all the circumstances, the interrogation reasonably tends to restrain or interfere with the employees in the exercise of rights guaranteed by the Act. The fact that the employees gave false answers when questioned, although relevant, is not controlling. The Respondent communicated its purpose in questioning the employees—a purpose which was legitimate in nature—to the employees and assured them that no reprisal would take place. Moreover, the questioning occurred in a background free of employer hostility to union organization. These circumstances convince us that the Respondent's interrogation did not reasonably lead the employees to believe that economic reprisal might be visited upon them by Respondent.

The instant case is thus distinguishable from such cases as *Syracuse Color Press,* 103 N.L.R.B. 377, *enforced* by the Court of Appeals for the Second Circuit, 209 F.2d 596 (2d Cir. 1954), where the employer called the employees to the superintendent's office a week before a scheduled Board election, advocated adherence to 1 of 2 rival unions, and questioned them concerning their union membership and activities, as well as the membership and activities of other employees, without giving any legitimate explanation for the interrogation or any assurance against reprisal. In such cases, unlike the situation in the instant case, the surrounding circumstances together with the nature of the interrogation itself imparted a coercive character to the interrogation.

What to consider

This decision does not by any means grant employers a license to engage in interrogation of their employees as to union affiliation or activity. We agree with and adopt the test laid down by the Court of Appeals for the Second Circuit in the *Syracuse Color Press* case which we construe to be that the answer to whether particular interrogation interferes with, restrains, and coerces employees must be found in the record as a whole. And, as the court states "The time, the place, the personnel involved, the information sought and the employer's conceded preference [as in that case] must be considered...." Members of the majority have participated in a number of recent decisions in which we have joined in holding that certain acts of interrogation were violative of the Act, and we reaffirm that position here. Therefore, any employer who engages in interrogation does so with notice that he risks a finding of unfair labor practices if the circumstances are such that his interrogation restrains or interferes with employees in the exercise of their rights under the Act.

The rule which we adopt will require the Trial Examiners and the Board to carefully weigh and evaluate the evidence in such case, but that is what we believe the statute requires us to do. The only alternatives, both of which we reject, are either to find all interrogation *per se* unlawful, or to find that interrogation under all circumstances is permissible under the statute.

Our dissenting colleagues express disagreement with our decision, but do not make it clear precisely what rule they would follow. There is the strong implication that the dissenting members would hold interrogation to be coercive *per se,* which, of course, means wholly without regard to the circumstances in which it occurs. This would mean that a casual, friendly, isolated instance of interrogation by a minor supervisor would subject the employer to a finding that he had committed an unfair labor practice and result in the issuance of a cease and desist order, which, if enforced by the court, would subject the employer to punishment for contempt of court if the same or another minor supervisor repeated the question to the same or another employee. If this is not the position of our colleagues, and they agree that the Board is required to determine the significance of particular acts of interrogation in the light of the entire record in the case, the difference between their view and ours merely reflects disagreement as to the conclusion to be drawn from the particular facts of the case.

Hence, we conclude that the Respondent's interrogation of the employees under the circumstances of this case did not carry an implied threat of reprisal or in any other way interfere with, restrain, or coerce the employees in the exercise of the rights guaranteed in § 7 of the Act. Accordingly, we find that such conduct is not violative of § 8(a)(1) of the Act....

MEMBERS MURDOCK and PETERSON, dissenting:

The exact meaning and extent of the majority decision is not certain. Apparently, however, the majority has decided that interrogation unaccompanied by other unfair labor practices is not conduct which violates the Act. We cannot agree.

From the very beginning of the administration of this Act the Board has, with court approval, found that interrogation by an employer prevents employees from exercising freely their right to engage in concerted activities. After a substantial period of administrative experience and after amendment of the Act, the Board reaffirmed its position that when an employer questions his employees concerning any aspect of concerted activity he violates § 8(a)(1) of the Act. We believe that the carefully considered position on interrogation taken by the Board in previous cases is well founded, and we are aware of no recent development which warrants a departure from such precedent.

The rationale for finding interrogation violative of the Act is simple.... Employees can exercise fully their right to engage in or refrain from self-organizational and other concerted activities only if they are free from employer prying and investigation. When an employer inquires into organizational activity whether by espionage, surveillance, polling, or direct questioning, he invades the privacy in which employees are entitled to exercise the rights given them by the Act. When he questions an employee about union organization or any concerted activities he forces the employee to take a stand on such issues whether or not the employee desires to take a position or has had full opportunity to consider the various arguments offered on the subject. And the employer compels the employee to take this stand alone, without the anonymity and support of group action. Moreover, employer interrogation tends to implant in the mind of the employee the apprehension that the employer is seeking information in order to affect his job security and the fear that economic reprisal will follow the questioning. The fear induced by an employer's questions is illustrated by the fact that employees, as in this case, often give untruthful or evasive answers to such questions. The many cases in the Board's experience in which interrogation was the prelude to discrimination demonstrate the reasonableness of such fear. Interrogation thus serves as an implied threat or a warning to employees of the adverse consequences of organization and dissuades them from participating in concerted activity. It thereby undermines the bargaining agent chosen by the employees, thwarts self-organization, and frustrates employee attempts to bargain collectively. Such conduct tends to interfere with, restrain, or coerce employees in the exercise of the rights guaranteed by § 7 as prohibited by § 8(a)(1). Board condemnation of interrogation, which we believe is required by the Act, protects the right of employees to privacy in their organizational activities, removes the restraint and coercion resulting from the threat implicit in interrogation, and deters the commission of further unfair labor practices.

For these reasons the Board in its expert judgment and in the light of its administrative experience is warranted in concluding, as it has in the past, that interrogation generally inhibits employee self-organization and is violative of § 8(a)(1) whether or not other unfair labor practices are committed. This does not mean that all interrogation is automatically unlawful or requires remedial action by the Board. There are, of course, instances of interrogation which can be properly regarded as isolated, casual, and too inconsequential in their impact to constitute a violation of the Act or to warrant a Board remedy. In such situations we have participated in dismissing the allegations of illegal interrogation.

The test for determining the legality of interrogation—as the members of the majority profess to recognize—is whether the interrogation, reasonably interpreted, tends to impair the free exercise by employees of their rights under the Act. In applying this test in interrogation cases, the Board must, of course, carefully weigh and evaluate the evidence as it must in all cases. And it must do so in the light of its administrative experience and specialized knowledge. Viewing the interrogation in this case with these considerations in mind, we fail to see how the Respondent's questioning of its employees can be considered lawful. Certainly § 8(c) of the Act when it recognizes that an employer's expression of opinion is not an unfair labor practice does not privilege an employer to ferret out the views of his employees and to pry into their organizational activities. We see no circumstances in this case which would make unreasonable the fear which questions such as those of the Respondent usually tend to engender. Here a high managerial representative, the general manager, was the interrogator; all employees in the bargaining unit were subjected to the questioning; each employee was interviewed separately; the place of the interviews was the general manager's office. While the general manager did state to the employees that it was immaterial to him whether they were union members and explained that he was seeking information for the purpose of answering the Union's letter, his assurances were ineffective when the entire situation belied them. As the majority states, the interrogation was not accompanied by express threats or promises and was not followed by reprisals. The interrogation alone, however, we conclude, tended to create fear in the employees and to thwart organization. The facts demonstrate clearly the soundness of our conclusion: The employees obviously did not accept the assertions of the general manager and felt it necessary to misrepresent their union position. Each of the employees questioned denied that he had signed a union card although each had in fact signed a card only about 5 days before. The employees' denial of union adherence through fear furnished the Respondent grounds for refusing to bargain; the Union which had in fact represented all employees in the bargaining unit was deprived of the recognition to which it was entitled by reason of its actual majority status and was incapacitated as bargaining agent; and the employees were deprived of the opportunity for collective bargaining. The majority apparently believes, however, that the employees here, in concealing their union adherence in the face of the general manager's assurances and explanation, behaved in an unreasonable manner. But these employees acted in a manner typical of employees subjected to interrogation....

In addition to arriving at the unsound conclusion that the Respondent's interrogation did not reasonably tend to interfere with, restrain, or coerce its employees, the members of the majority encourage employers to engage in interrogation as a means of determining whether a labor organization represents a majority of their employees. They emphasize that the Respondent here questioned its employees to enable it to reply to the Union's request for recognition and that this purpose was legitimate in nature. An employer's purpose for inquiring into the union activities of his employees, we must point out, is not a significant or mitigating consideration in determining the legality of such conduct under § 8(a)(1). This section is concerned with the *effect* of the employer's conduct upon his employees' exercise of their statutory rights regardless of what motivates the conduct. The Act protects employees from an innocent or ignorant invasion of their rights as well as from an intended invasion. And the remedy for the invasion does not penalize the employer but merely restores freedom of activity to employees by requiring the employer to refrain from the conduct which impairs that freedom and to notify the employees that he will do so. Yet the majority sanctions interrogation, with its attendant discouraging effects upon collective bargaining, when engaged in for the purpose of resolving the question of a labor organization's majority status. We cannot understand this position nor can we see how our colleagues can approve such a method of determining a question concerning representation, a statutory function of the Board. This method places in the hands of an interested party, with obvious capacity to resort to economic reprisal against the voters, complete control over the timing, means of inquiry, the phrasing of the question, and compilation of results of the polling of employees, and it offers none of the traditional safeguards of voting such as a secret ballot and conduct of the poll by an impartial agency. The fallibility of such a method for testing a majority claim and the inaccuracy of the results it obtains is demonstrated in this case where all employees in the bargaining unit when subjected to individual interrogation by the Respondent denied the union adherence which they had earlier adopted.

Several approved methods of determining whether a labor organization represents a majority of his employees are available to an employer. He may ask the labor organization to offer proof of its majority; he may request the organization to file a petition for a Board determination by election; or he may file a similar petition himself. He may agree with the labor organization to submit authorization cards to an impartial third party for a check; and we note that in making its bargaining request the Union here stated its willingness to agree to such a check. Finally, if an employer has a *genuine* doubt as to the labor organization's majority status, he may simply refuse to recognize the organization, and his good-faith doubt is a defense to a charge of a violation of the duty to bargain. With all these avenues open to an employer, plainly there is no need for him to utilize interrogation, with its coercive effect, in order to reply to a union's request for recognition, and the Board should not approve such conduct....

NOTES

1. In response to a directive from the D.C. Circuit in *Operating Eng'rs Local 49 v. NLRB [Struksnes Constr. Co.]*, 353 F.2d 852 (D.C. Cir. 1965), the Board revised the *Blue Flash* tests and announced standards to be used to determine whether an employer "poll" is lawful:

> Absent unusual circumstances, the polling of employees by an employer will be violative of § 8(a)(1) of the Act unless the following safeguards are observed: (1) the purpose of the poll is to determine the truth of a union's claim of majority, (2) this purpose is communicated to the employees, (3) assurances against reprisal are given, (4) *the employees are polled by secret ballot* [emphasis added], and (5) the employer has not engaged in unfair labor practices or otherwise created a coercive atmosphere.
>
> The purpose of the polling in these circumstances is clearly relevant to an issue raised by a union's claim for recognition and is therefore lawful. The requirement that the lawful purpose be communicated to the employees,

along with assurances against reprisal, is designed to allay any fear of discrimination which might otherwise arise from the polling, and any tendency to interfere with employees' § 7 rights. Secrecy of the ballot will give further assurance that reprisals cannot be taken against employees because the views of each individual will not be known. And the absence of employer unfair labor practices or other conduct creating coercive atmosphere will serve as a further warranty to the employees that the poll does not have some unlawful object, contrary to the lawful purpose stated by the employer. In accord with presumptive rules applied by the Board with court approval in other situations, this rule is designed to effectuate the purposes of the Act by maintaining a reasonable balance between the protection of employee rights and legitimate interests of employers.

On the other hand, a poll taken while a petition for a Board election is pending does not, in our view, serve any legitimate interest of the employer that would not be better served by the forthcoming Board election. In accord with long-established Board policy, therefore, such polls will continue to be found violative of § 8(a)(1) of the Act.

Struksnes Constr. Co., 165 N.L.R.B. 1062 (1967).

2. The *Struksnes* standards have generally been followed by the Board, (*Northeastern Dye Works,* 203 N.L.R.B. 1222 (1973)), and by courts of appeals (*NLRB v. Super Toys, Inc.,* 458 F.2d 180 (9th Cir. 1972)). Nonetheless, in *Bushnell's Kitchens,* 222 N.L.R.B. 110 (1976), where the employer's polling was done at a meeting of the employees upon the suggestion of the union business agent, no violation was found. The Board said that the *Struksnes* requirements are "not a straight-jacket to be applied in any and all circumstances." *See also NLRB v. Lorben Corp.,* 345 F.2d 346 (2d Cir. 1965) (coercion may not be inferred simply from the employer's failure (1) to explain the purpose of a poll and (2) to assure employees against reprisal).

3. When an employer decides to conduct a *Struksnes* poll to determine whether an incumbent representative continues to enjoy majority support, the company must be able to demonstrate that objective considerations provide it with a "reasonable doubt" concerning the union's current majority status—the same burden applicable to cases in which the employer simply withdraws recognition. *Allentown Mack Sales & Service v. NLRB,* 118 S. Ct. 818 (1998).

4. *Bourne v. NLRB,* 332 F.2d 47, 48 (2d Cir. 1964), articulated the standards to be used to determine the legality of non-polling questioning of employees. "Under our decisions, interrogation, not itself threatening, is not held to be an unfair labor practice unless it meets certain fairly severe standards.... These include: (1) The background, *i.e.,* is there a history of employer hostility and discrimination? (2) The nature of the information sought, *e.g.,* did the interrogator appear to be seeking information on which to base taking action against individual employees? (3) The identity of the questioner, *i.e.,* how high was he in the company hierarchy? (4) Place and method of interrogation, *e.g.*, was employee called from work to the boss's office? Was there an atmosphere of 'unnatural formality'? (5) Truthfulness of the reply." In *Rossmore House,* 269 N.L.R.B. 1176, *affirmed,* 760 F.2d 1006 (9th Cir. 1985), the NLRB overruled recent decisions indicating that employer interrogation of employees regarding protected activities would generally violate § 8(a)(1) and adopted the *Bourne* totality-of-the-circumstances approach. The Board concluded that the non-coercive questioning of an open and active union supporter by both the manager and one of the owners did not violate the Act.

Although a supervisor may ask "casual" questions regarding the union sympathies of an employee who is not an open union adherent, so long as under the "totality of the circumstances" no coercion is found (*Sunnyvale Med. Clinic,* 277 N.L.R.B. 1217 (1985)), it is impermissible to ask such employees questions of a "probing, inquisitive and focused nature" (*Raytheon Co.,* 279 N.L.R.B. 245 (1986)).

5. Although the NLRB generally finds employer requests to employees for copies of written statements they have made to NLRB agents investigating alleged unfair labor practices to constitute per se § 8(a)(1) violations because of the inherently coercive effect of those requests, some courts have refused to apply a per se rule. *See, e.g., NLRB v. Martin A. Gleason, Inc.,* 534 F.2d 466 (2d Cir. 1976) (no violation when employer asked employees "if they would mind" supplying copies of their statements and indicated it was not requiring them to do so, and the employees willingly complied).

4. ECONOMIC COERCION AND INDUCEMENT

NLRB v. EXCHANGE PARTS CO.

Supreme Court of the United States
375 U.S. 405, 84 S. Ct. 457, 11 L. Ed. 2d 435 (1964)

[Respondent was engaged in the business of rebuilding automobiles and its employees were not represented by a union prior to 1959. On November 9, 1959, the Boilermakers Union announced that it was conducting an organizational campaign and on November 16 it petitioned the Board for a representation election which was ordered for March 18, 1960.]

MR. JUSTICE HARLAN delivered the opinion of the Court.

This case presents a question concerning the limitations which § 8(a)(1) of the National Labor Relations Act, 49 Stat. 452 (1935), as amended, 29 U.S.C. § 158(a)(1), places on the right of an employer to confer economic benefits on his employees shortly before a representation election. The precise issue is whether that section prohibits the conferral of such benefits, without more, where the employer's purpose is to affect the outcome of the election....

Ca employes bribe employees not to join?

At two meetings on November 4 and 5, 1959, C. V. McDonald, the Vice-President and General Manager of Exchange Parts, announced to the employees that their "floating holiday" in 1959 would fall on December 26 and that there would be an additional "floating holiday" in 1960. On February 25, six days after the Board issued its election order, Exchange Parts held a dinner for employees at which Vice-President McDonald told the employees that they could decide whether the extra day of vacation in 1960 would be a "floating holiday" or would be taken on their birthdays. The employees voted for the latter. McDonald also referred to the forthcoming representation election as one in which, in the words of the trial examiner, the employees would "determine whether ... [they] wished to hand over their right to speak and act for themselves." He stated that the union had distorted some of the facts and pointed out the benefits obtained by the employees without a union. He urged all the employees to vote in the election.

On March 4 Exchange Parts sent its employees a letter which spoke of "the *Empty Promises* of the Union" and "the *fact* that *it is the Company that puts things in your envelope....*" After mentioning a number of benefits, the letter said: "The Union can't put any of those things in your envelope—*only the Company can do that.*" [The italics appear in the original letter.] Further on, the letter stated: "... [I]t didn't take a Union to get any of those things and ... it won't take a Union to get additional improvements in the future." Accompanying the letter was a detailed statement of the benefits granted by the company since 1949 and an estimate of the monetary value of such benefits to the employees. Included in the statement of benefits granted by the company for 1960 were the birthday holiday, a new system for computing overtime during holiday weeks which had the effect of increasing wages for those weeks, and a new vacation schedule which enabled employees to extend their vacations by sandwiching them between two weekends. Although Exchange Parts asserts that the policy behind the latter two benefits was established earlier, it is clear that the letter of March 4 was the first general announcement of the changes to the employees. In the ensuing election the union lost.

The Board, affirming the findings of the trial examiner, found that the announcement of the birthday holiday and the grant and announcement of overtime and vacation benefits were arranged by Exchange Parts with the intention of inducing the employees to vote against the union. It found that this conduct violated § 8(a)(1) of the National Labor Relations Act and issued an appropriate order. On the Board's petition for enforcement of the order, the Court of Appeals rejected the finding that the announcement of the birthday holiday was timed to influence the outcome of the election. It accepted the Board's findings with respect to the overtime and vacation benefits, and the propriety of those findings is not in controversy here. However, noting that "the benefits were put into effect unconditionally on a permanent basis, and no one has suggested that there was any implication the benefits would be withdrawn if the workers voted for the union," 304 F.2d 368, 375, the court denied enforcement of the Board's order. It believed that it was not an unfair labor practice under § 8(a)(1) for an employer to grant benefits to its employees in these circumstances.

... We think the Court of Appeals was mistaken in concluding that the conferral of employee benefits while a representation election is pending, for the purpose of inducing employees to vote against the union, does not "interfere with" the protected right to organize.

... The danger inherent in well-timed increases in benefits is the suggestion of a fist inside the velvet glove. Employees are not likely to miss the inference that the source of benefits now conferred is also the source from which future benefits must flow and which may dry up if it is not obliged. The danger may be diminished if, as in this case, the benefits are conferred permanently and unconditionally. But the absence of conditions or threats pertaining to the particular benefits conferred would be of controlling significance only if it could be presumed that no question of additional benefits or renegotiation of existing benefits would arise in the future; and, of course, no such presumption is tenable.

... Other unlawful conduct may often be an indication of the motive behind a grant of benefits while an election is pending, and to that extent it is relevant to the legality of the grant; but when as here the motive is otherwise established, an employer is not free to violate § 8(a)(1) by conferring benefits simply because it refrains from other, more obvious violations. We cannot agree with the Court of Appeals that enforcement of the Board's order will have the "ironic" result of "discouraging benefits for labor." 304 F.2d, at 376. The beneficence of an employer is likely to be ephemeral if prompted by a threat of unionization which is subsequently removed. Insulating the right of collective organization from calculated good will of this sort deprives employees of little that has lasting value.

Reversed.

NOTES

1. The pertinent part of the Board's order in the *Exchange Parts* case reads: "Cease and desist from interfering with, restraining, or coercing its employees in the exercise of rights guaranteed in § 7 of the Act by granting them economic benefits or by changing the terms and conditions of their employment; provided, however, that *nothing in this recommended order shall be construed as requiring the Respondent to vary or abandon any economic benefit or any term or condition of employment which it has heretofore established.*" 131 N.L.R.B. at 807 (1961) (emphasis added). Such a roll-back would probably contravene the anti-retaliation proscription in § 8(a)(4).

2. Is it a forbidden "promise of benefit" for an employer to inform employees during an election campaign of its policy of providing benefits equal to or better than those provided in the industry generally or in a separate union-represented unit? *Compare John W. Galbreath & Co., 266 N.L.R.B. 96 (1983) with Pacific Tel. Co., 256 N.L.R.B. 449 (1981). See also B & D Plastics, 302 N.L.R.B. 245*

(1991) (employer interfered with election when it gave employees paid day off to attend company cookout held two days before election at which it conveyed anti-union sentiments); *Trencor, Inc. v. NLRB,* 110 F.3d 268 (5th Cir. 1997) (promise by union to host the "biggest party in the history of Texas" if it won may have tainted election victory).

3. Employer statements containing threats of reprisals or promises of benefits constitute unlawful interference, restraint, and coercion. If the employer actually effectuates such reprisals or benefits for the purpose of defeating unionization, this constitutes a separate unfair labor practice. "The Act does not preclude an employer from introducing benefits during an organizational period. But when an employer uses proposed benefits as an inducement not to join the union, his activity bears no shield of privilege." *Joy Silk Mills, Inc. v. NLRB,* 185 F.2d 732, 739 (D.C. Cir. 1950), *cert. denied,* 341 U.S. 914 (1951).

In *Idaho Falls Hosps. v. NLRB,* 731 F.2d 1384 (9th Cir. 1984), the court found that the Labor Board had erred in finding that a hospital violated § 8(a)(1) when, in a noncoercive discussion with employees over issues that had precipitated union organizing activity, a supervisor told employees that she had an "open door policy" and suggested that if workers had any problems they should consult with their head nurse. The court noted that the solicitation of grievances is unlawful only when accompanied by an implied or express promise they will be remedied and under circumstances giving rise to the inference that such redress will only be provided if the union is rejected. A mere expression of the willingness to listen to employee grievances is insufficient to establish an unfair labor practice.

4. The implementation of a health insurance plan during a union organizational effort was not a violation of § 8(a)(1), when preparations for the plan had begun nine months before the organizing campaign. *Pedro's, Inc. v. NLRB,* 652 F.2d 1005 (D.C. Cir. 1981). What if an employer customarily increases compensation levels at the same time each year, and a union organizing campaign is going on at that time? One court noted that such an employer confronts a "damned if you do, damned if you don't" situation in either granting or withholding a predetermined benefit prior to an election, since an employer that *withholds* a customary wage increase before an election may well be found in violation of § 8(a)(1). *J.J. Newberry Co. v. NLRB,* 645 F.2d 148, 151 (2d Cir. 1981). *See also Kauai Coconut Beach Resort,* 317 N.L.R.B. 996 (1995) (employer did not interfere with representation election when it announced it would not disclose amount of semiannual pay increase until after election, since it wished to avoid appearance of improper influence over election).

5. A unanimous Supreme Court ruled that the first amendment petition clause precluded a Board order seeking to halt an employer's state court defamation action against employees, even if the suit was in retaliation for their filing of unfair labor practice charges, so long as the lawsuit did not lack a reasonable basis in fact or law. The Court stated, however, that if the employer lost in the state proceeding, the Board could consider the matter further. If it determined the lawsuit was brought with retaliatory intent, the Board could find a violation of § 8(a)(1) and (4) of the NLRA. *Bill Johnson's Restaurants, Inc. v. NLRB*, 461 U.S. 731 (1983). *Compare H.W. Barss Co.*, 296 N.L.R.B. 1286 (1989) (employer's "baseless" retaliatory defamation action violated § 8(a)(1)); *IUOE Local 520 (Alberici Constr. Co.)*, 309 N.L.R.B. 1199 (1992) (union violated § 8(b)(1)(A) by filing meritless defamation action against member who filed charges with NLRB). *See generally* Wilson, *Retaliatory Lawsuits, the NLRA, and the First Amendment: A Proposed Accommodation of Competing Interests*, 38 Vand. L. Rev. 1235 (1985).

5. VIOLENCE, INTIMIDATION, ESPIONAGE, AND SURVEILLANCE

Violence and Intimidation. Violence and threats of violence to deter union organization are clearly unlawful. Examples were fairly common during the early days of the Wagner Act: an overseer offered to buy an employee a gallon of whiskey if he would "stamp hell out of" a union organizer (*Mansfield Mills, Inc.*, 3 N.L.R.B. 901 (1937)); a supervisor supplemented her attempt to dissuade employees from accepting union pamphlets by suggesting, with reference to the union organizer, "What do you say, girls, we give her a beating?" (*Tiny Town Togs, Inc.*, 7 N.L.R.B. 54 (1938)); a reign of terror was conducted by an employer association, of which the company was a member, with union organizers ordered out of the county at gun point by private police hired by the association (*Clover Fork Coal Co.*, 4 N.L.R.B. 202 (1937), *enforced*, 97 F.2d 331 (6th Cir. 1938)).

The Byrnes Act, 18 U.S.C. § 1231, makes unlawful and criminal the interstate transportation of persons employed for the purpose of obstructing, by force or threats, "(1) peaceful picketing by employees during any labor controversy affecting wages, hours or conditions of labor; or (2) the exercise by employees of any of the rights of self-organization, or collective bargaining."

A number of states have statutes specifically dealing with the use of professional strikebreakers. See the state law volumes of the loose-leaf labor services.

Espionage and Surveillance. In the period before the Wagner Act, the use of labor spies, often hired from detective agencies, to infiltrate unions and report on the "ringleaders" who were then discharged and blacklisted, received considerable publicity, and such practices were obviously included in the abuses aimed at in § 8(1). *See, e.g., Baldwin Locomotive Works*, 20 N.L.R.B. 1100 (1940), *enforced as modified*, 128 F.2d 39 (3d Cir. 1942).

It is not necessary to prove that employees knew they were being spied upon, since even surreptitious spying on protected activities is unlawful. *NLRB v. Grower-Shipper Vegetable Ass'n*, 122 F.2d 368 (9th Cir. 1941). *See also National Steel & Shipbuilding v. NLRB*, 156 F.3d 1268 (D.C. Cir. 1998) (videotaping of union rallies held outside main shipyard entrance to enhance worker bargaining position violates § 8(a)(1)). Furthermore, if employers merely give employees *the impression* they have been subject to improper surveillance, a violation will usually be found. *Idaho Egg Producers,* 111 N.L.R.B. 93 (1955), *enforced,* 229 F.2d 821 (9th Cir. 1956); *Filler Prod., Inc. v. NLRB,* 376 F.2d 369 (4th Cir. 1967). *Compare U.S. Steel Corp. v. NLRB,* 682 F.2d 98 (3d Cir. 1982) (refusing to find all employer surveillance of protected employee conduct unlawful, preferring a totality-of-the-circumstances approach). *See also National Tel. Directory Corp.,* 319 N.L.R.B. 420 (1995) (employer may not try to obtain names of union supporters by cross-examining union witness at Board hearing).

6. EMPLOYER RESPONSIBILITY FOR ANTIUNION CONDUCT OF SUBORDINATES AND OTHERS

The Wagner Act contained no test or standard of employer responsibility except that the term "employer" was defined in § 2(2) to include "any person acting in the interest of an employer, directly or indirectly."

Section 2(2), as amended, substituted the language of agency for "interest" in defining "employer." According to the House Committee, it was intended by the change in § 2(2) to make "employers responsible for what people say and do only when it is within the *actual* or *apparent* scope of their authority" and thus to make the "ordinary rules of the law of agency equally applicable to employers and to unions." H.R. Rep. No. 245, 80th Cong., 1st Sess. 11 (1947). The dissenters on the committee objected to this change. "It would make necessary proof that an employer had specifically authorized his foremen or superintendents to engage in unfair labor practices; matters which are easily concealed. In modern industrial enterprises foremen and superintendents *are* management to the workers under them and employers should be held responsible for their actions." H.R. Rep. No. 245, 80th Cong., 1st Sess. 68 (1947). Later the conference report recommended both the change proposed in the House bill *and* a new provision, § 2(13), providing: "In determining whether any person is acting as an 'agent' of another person so as to make such other person responsible for his acts, the question of whether the specific acts performed were actually authorized or subsequently ratified shall not be controlling." According to the report, this means that "both employers and labor organizations will be responsible for the acts of their agents in accordance with the ordinary common law rules of agency (and only ordinary evidence will be required to establish the agent's authority)." H.R. Conf. Rep. No. 510, 80th Cong., 1st Sess. 36 (1947).

(a) *Supervisors*—An employer is generally held responsible for the statements and acts of supervisors, since it can usually be said that they have apparent authority to speak for the employer. Even when the employer has instructed its supervisors not to interfere with the employees' organizational activities, it may still be responsible if it has not communicated these instructions to the rank-and-file employees. *Otis L. Broyhill Furn. Co.,* 94 N.L.R.B. 1452 (1951).

Isolated or sporadic instances of coercive statements by a supervisor do not give rise to employer responsibility, when the circumstances indicate no employer authorization. *Pittsburgh S.S. Co. v. NLRB,* 180 F.2d 731 (6th Cir. 1950), *aff'd,* 340 U.S. 498 (1951).

(b) *Nonsupervisory employees*—An employer is held responsible for the acts of its nonsupervisory employees when the employees act as agents of the employer. This may be shown when the employees are acting within the general scope of their employment, regardless of whether the specific acts have been authorized or even forbidden. *National Paper Co.,* 102 N.L.R.B. 1569 (1953), *enforcement denied,* 216 F.2d 859 (5th Cir. 1954) (armed guard made threatening and abusive phone calls to the union secretary, in a context of other coercive conduct by the employer).

When nonsupervisory employees are clothed with apparent authority to speak for the employer, the employer is held responsible for their acts. *NLRB v. Mississippi Prod., Inc.,* 213 F.2d 670 (5th Cir. 1954). The necessary agency relationship may also be found on the basis of implied authority or implicit ratification, when the employer condones or affirms violence by rank-and-file employees. *See, e.g., J.D. Jewell, Inc.,* 99 N.L.R.B. 61 (1952).

(c) *Nonemployees*—Whether an employer will be held responsible for threatening speeches and publications of local business people and town officials depends on evidence of an agency relationship, such as employer instigation, participation, express, implied, or apparent authority, or express or implied ratification. *Southland Mfg. Co.,* 94 N.L.R.B. 813 (1951) (a supervisor urged employees to attend a meeting addressed by the mayor and a bank official, was present at the meeting and failed to disavow threats). But when the employer refrains from "aiding, abetting, assisting, or co-operating" with the local citizens, coercive statements and conduct by them are not an unfair labor practices. *Clarke Mills,* 109 N.L.R.B. 666 (1954).

Note that the NLRB may set an election aside, without proof of agency, when community citizens have so inflamed the atmosphere with threats and appeals to passion and prejudice that employee free choice is prevented. *Universal Mfg. Co.,* 156 N.L.R.B. 1459 (1966).

B. EMPLOYER DOMINATION OR SUPPORT

During the 1920s and the early 1930s, "company unions" or "employee representation plans" flourished. *See* H. Pelling, American Labor 146, 160 (1960). With the Railway Labor Act as a precedent, prohibiting in § 2, Fourth, a carrier from interfering with the organization of its employees or using its funds in maintaining or assisting any labor organization, the "Wagner Act" Congress in 1935 attacked the company union problem by making it an unfair labor practice for an employer to dominate or interfere with the formation or administration of any labor organization or to contribute financial or other support to it. The prohibition is now embodied in § 8(a)(2) of the NLRA.

During the early days of the NLRB, there was substantial litigation against company unions. *See, e.g., NLRB v. Pennsylvania Greyhound Lines,* 303 U.S. 261 (1938), wherein the Supreme Court sustained the Board's unfair labor practice findings, based on evidence that company representatives were active in promoting the plan, in urging employees to join, in the preparation of the details of organization, including the bylaws, in presiding over organization meetings, and in selecting the employee representatives of the organization.

The problem with respect to "successor" unions. Employer-dominated unions have customarily been ordered "disestablished" as employee representatives, which means that they have lost, at least for a time, their capacity to represent employees for statutory purposes. Sometimes another unaffiliated or company union has been organized to replace the disestablished union, and the question has arisen whether the legal disability of the latter attached to the successor. The Board has taken the position that an organization is tainted with the illegality of its predecessor unless the employer, prior to the formation of the successor organization, has established a clear line of fracture between the two organizations, by publicly and unequivocally disestablishing the old organization and by assuring the employees of their freedom from further employer interference with their choice of bargaining representatives. NLRB, Sixteenth Annual Report 102 (1951).

Remedies for (a) domination or (b) illegal assistance or support not amounting to domination. During the Wagner Act period, the NLRB tended to order unaffiliated dominated unions disestablished, but, in the case of affiliated dominated unions, to merely order the employer to withdraw recognition until the affiliated union's majority status could be established by a secret Board election. The "Taft-Hartley" Congress amended § 10(c) of the Act to put an end to this disparate treatment. Although the NLRB believed that affiliated unions could probably eradicate the effects of illegal employer support, Congress thought this distinction was unfair to independent unions, which might also free themselves from employer control.

After examining this legislative history, the Board concluded in *Carpenter Steel Co.,* 76 N.L.R.B. 670 (1948), that it may no longer concern itself with the affiliation of a union, or lack thereof, in framing a remedy for violations of § 8(a)(2). Dominated unions will still be disestablished, with cease and desist orders being used for unlawfully supported unions. Domination is found only when the employer has interfered with the formation of the organization and has assisted and supported its administration to such an extent that it must be regarded as its own creation and subject to his control. Cases often refuse to find domination, but find the lesser offense of assistance and support. *NLRB v. Wemyss,* 212 F.2d 465 (9th Cir. 1954).

Employee participation programs. During World War II, in order to increase efficiency and productivity, the War Labor Board encouraged the formation of employee committees, which also handled grievances in plants without unions. The employer paid the expenses of these committees. After the War Labor Board authorization ceased, some of these committees continued. The Supreme Court held in *NLRB v. Cabot Carbon Co.,* 360 U.S. 203 (1959), that such committees were "labor organizations," within the meaning of § 8(a)(2), that the employer must disestablish, if they "deal with him concerning grievances." *See* § 2(5). Presentation to management of employee "views" and information, without specific recommendations as to what action is needed to accommodate those views, constitutes dealing with management under § 2(5)—if the purpose of the management-employee discussion is the correction of grievances. *NLRB v. Thompson Ramo Wooldridge, Inc.,* 305 F.2d 807 (7th Cir. 1962).

Electromation, Inc., 309 N.L.R.B. 990 (1992), *affirmed,* 35 F.3d 1148 (7th Cir. 1994), concerned a firm that established, in response to worker complaints, Action Committees comprised of employees and management representatives. The committees discussed various issues, including absenteeism, attendance bonuses, pay progression, and a no-smoking policy. Committee members could propose new policies regarding these matters, but management representatives retained final authority with respect to any recommendations. The NLRB found these committees to be "labor organizations" under § 2(5), since they acted in a representative capacity and "dealt with the employer" regarding basic terms of employment. Electromation defined the committee goals, determined how many employees would serve on each, and appointed the management participants. The Board decided that this significant involvement constituted unlawful domination. The Seventh Circuit affirmed the Board's decision. *Electromation, Inc. v. NLRB,* 35 F.3d 1148, 1170-71 (7th Cir. 1994):

> [T]he principal distinction between an independent labor organization and an employer-dominated organization lies in the unfettered power of the independent organization to determine its own actions.... The Electromation action committees, which were wholly created by the employer, whose continued existence depended upon the employer, and whose functions were essentially determined by the employer, lacked the independence of action and free choice guaranteed by Section 7. This is not to suggest that ... management representatives were anti-union or had devious intentions in proposing the creation of the committees. But, even assuming they acted from good intentions, their procedure in establishing the committees, their control of the subject matters to be considered or excluded, their membership and participation on the committees, and their financial support of the committees all combined to make the committees labor organizations dominated by the employer in violation of the Act.

E.I. Du Pont de Nemours & Co., 311 N.L.R.B. 893 (1993), involved a unionized company that created six employee-management safety committees and one joint fitness committee to discuss safety and fitness issues and to submit recommendations to management officials regarding those topics. The Board decided that these committees constituted "labor organizations," because they "dealt with" Du Pont regarding important working conditions. Since Du Pont determined the number of employee participants, decided which employee volunteers would be selected if an excessive number sought the available positions, and reserved the right to abolish any committee at will, unlawful employer domination was found. On the other hand, the Board found no § 8(a)(2) violation with respect to safety conferences conducted by company officials with employees. These "brainstorming" sessions simply enhanced employee-management communication and elicited worker input. The employee participants were not "dealing with" management with regard to discussed safety matters, and company officials openly acknowledged the role of union representative concerning these topics.

NLRB v. Peninsula Gen. Hosp., 36 F.3d 1262 (4th Cir. 1994), concerned the propriety of a nurses' committee that had been formed in 1968 as a forum for nurses to discuss practice issues. In 1989, the Vice President of Nursing, a member of the nurses' committee, encouraged the committee to communicate "major concerns" regarding weekend differential pay and the clinical ladder directly to management officials. When the committee communicated to management a list of concerns regarding wages, benefits, and working conditions, the Vice President indicated that the hospital had taken steps to deal with some. Although the Labor Board found this committee to constitute a management-dominated "labor organization," the Fourth Circuit rejected this conclusion. The court noted that while the § 2(5) "dealing with" language encompasses more than collective bargaining, it does not cover all employee committee communications to management concerning working conditions. The "dealing with" requirement is only satisfied when there is a pattern or practice over time of committee proposals and management responses. Isolated instances of committee proposals and management responses are insufficient to satisfy the "dealing with" prerequisite. When committees exist primarily to provide management with information with respect to employee concerns, they do not ipso facto contravene § 8(a)(2).

Keeler Brass Automotive Group, 317 N.L.R.B. 1110 (1995), considered the legality of a grievance committee comprised of elected employees that reviewed proposed management discipline and suggested appropriate changes. The Board found that this committee "dealt with" the employer with respect to employee grievances, and was thus a "labor organization." Since the employer established the term limits and the eligibility rules, conducted the elections, dictated the number of employees who could serve, and controlled the meeting days, unlawful employer domination was found.

NOTES

1. The Labor Board continues to struggle with *Electromation* issues. *Compare Stoody Co.*, 320 N.L.R.B. 18 (1995) ("handbook committee" designed to gather information about inconsistencies between existing handbook and current practices not "labor organization," even though at its single one-hour meeting employees raised concerns about vacation notification) *and Vons Grocery Co.*, 320 N.L.R.B. 53 (1995) (employer-employee "quality circle" established to discuss specific operational problems not "labor organization," since it did not follow "pattern or practice" of making proposals to management even though it did develop dress code and accident-point proposals) *with Webcor Packaging Inc.*, 319 N.L.R.B. 1203 (1995), *enforced*, 118 F.3d 1115 (6th Cir. 1997), *cert. denied*, 118 S. Ct. 1035 (1998) ("plant council" consisting of three managers and five employees elected by workers was an employer-dominated "labor organization," because it had the "pattern or practice" of proposing changes in working conditions to management, and the employer could set the council's agenda or disband it).

2. In 1996, Congress narrowly passed S. 295, the proposed TEAM (Teamwork for Employees and Managers) Act, to amend § 8(a)(2) to permit employers to establish employee committees to address subjects of mutual interest, but President Clinton vetoed it. 152 Lab. Rel. Rep. 429 (Aug. 5, 1996). The bill was strongly supported by the business community and vigorously opposed by organized labor which claimed it would generate company-dominated and sham unions.

3. The adoption of innovative worker participation programs involving shop level committees and/or board of director representation may raise substantial questions under § 8(a)(2), if such joint employee-management entities are found to constitute "labor organizations" under the *Cabot Carbon* rationale. When should such worker participation plans be found to contravene § 8(a)(2)? *Compare Hertzka & Knowles v. NLRB*, 503 F.2d 625 (9th Cir. 1974), *cert. denied*, 423 U.S. 875 (1975) *with Lawson Co. v. NLRB*, 753 F.2d 471 (6th Cir. 1985). *See also Modern Plastics Corp. v. NLRB*, 379 F.2d 201 (6th Cir. 1967). *See generally* Barenberg, *The Political Economy of the Wagner Act: Power, Symbol, and Workplace Cooperation*, 106 Harv. L. Rev. 1379 (1993); Barenberg, *Democracy and Domination in the Law of Workplace Cooperation: From Bureaucratic to Flexible Production*, 94 Colum. L. Rev. 753 (1994); Craver, *Mandatory Worker Participation is Required in a Declining Union Environment to Provide Employees with Meaningful Industrial Democracy*, 66 Geo. Wash. L. Rev. 135 (1997); J. Rogers & W. Streeck, Works Councils: Consultation, Representation, and Cooperation in Industrial Relations (1995); Gely, *Whose Team are You On? My Team or My TEAM? The NLRA's Section 8(a)(2) and the TEAM Act*, 49 Rutgers L. Rev. 323 (1997); O'Connor, *The Human Capital Era: Reconceptualizing Corporate Law to Facilitate Labor-Management Cooperation*, 78 Cornell L. Rev. 899

(1993); B. Bluestone & I. Bluestone, Negotiating the Future (1992); Kohler, *Models of Worker Participation: The Uncertain Significance of Section 8(a)(2),* 27 B.C.L. Rev. 499 (1986); Moberly, *New Directions in Worker Participation and Collective Bargaining,* 87 W. Va. L. Rev. 765 (1985); Schlossberg & Fetter, *U.S. Labor Law and the Future of Labor-Management Cooperation,* 3 Lab. Law. 11 (1987); Ryan, *The Encouragement of Labor-Management Cooperation: Improving American Productivity Through Revision of the National Labor Relations Act,* 40 U.C.L.A. L. Rev. 571 (1992); Note, *Collective Bargaining as an Industrial System: An Argument Against Judicial Revision of Section 8(a)(2) of the National Labor Relations Act,* 96 Harv. L. Rev. 1662 (1983); Note, *Participatory Management Under Sections 2(5) and 8(a)(2) of the National Labor Relations Act,* 83 Mich. L. Rev. 1736 (1985); Note, *Rethinking the Adversarial Model in Labor Relations: An Argument for Repeal of Section 8(a)(2),* 96 Yale L.J. 2021 (1987); Note, *New Standards for Domination and Support Under Section 8(a)(2),* 82 Yale L.J. 510 (1973).

INTERNATIONAL LADIES GARMENT WORKERS' UNION v. NLRB [BERNHARD-ALTMANN TEXAS CORP.]

Supreme Court of the United States
366 U.S. 731, 81 S. Ct. 1603, 6 L. Ed. 2d 762 (1961)

MR. JUSTICE CLARK delivered the opinion of the Court.

We are asked to decide in this case whether it was an unfair labor practice for both an employer and a union to enter into an agreement under which the employer recognized the union as exclusive bargaining representative of certain of his employees, although in fact only a minority of those employees had authorized the union to represent their interests. The Board found that by extending such recognition, even though done in the good-faith belief that the union had the consent of a majority of employees in the appropriate bargaining unit, the employer interfered with the organizational rights of his employees in violation of § 8(a)(1) of the National Labor Relations Act and that such recognition also constituted unlawful support to a labor organization in violation of § 8(a)(2). In addition, the Board found that the union violated § 8(b)(1)(A) by its acceptance of exclusive bargaining authority at a time when in fact it did not have the support of a majority of the employees, and this in spite of its bona fide belief that it did. Accordingly, the Board ordered the unfair labor practices discontinued and directed the holding of a representation election. The Court of Appeals, by a divided vote, granted enforcement, 108 U.S. App. D.C. 68, 280 F.2d 616. We granted certiorari. 364 U.S. 811. We agree with the Board and the Court of Appeals that such extension and acceptance of recognition constitute unfair labor practices, and that the remedy provided was appropriate.

In October 1956 the petitioner union initiated an organizational campaign at Bernhard-Altmann Texas Corporation's knitwear manufacturing plant in San

Antonio, Texas. No other labor organization was similarly engaged at that time. During the course of that campaign, on July 29, 1957, certain of the company's Topping Department employees went on strike in protest against a wage reduction. That dispute was in no way related to the union campaign, however, and the organizational efforts were continued during the strike. Some of the striking employees had signed authorization cards solicited by the union during its drive, and, while the strike was in progress, the union entered upon a course of negotiations with the employer. As a result of those negotiations, held in New York City where the home offices of both were located, on August 30, 1957, the employer and union signed a "memorandum of understanding." In that memorandum the company recognized the union as exclusive bargaining representative of "all production and shipping employees." The union representative asserted that the union's comparison of the employee authorization cards in its possession with the number of eligible employees representatives of the company furnished it indicated that the union had in fact secured such cards from a majority of employees in the unit. Neither employer nor union made any effort at that time to check the cards in the union's possession against the employee roll, or otherwise, to ascertain with any degree of certainty that the union's assertion, later found by the Board to be erroneous, was founded on fact rather than upon good-faith assumption. The agreement, containing no union security provisions, called for the ending of the strike and for certain improved wages and conditions of employment. It also provided that a "formal agreement containing these terms" would "be promptly drafted ... and signed by both parties within the next two weeks."

Thereafter, on October 10, 1957, a formal collective bargaining agreement, embodying the terms of the August 30 memorandum, was signed by the parties. The bargaining unit description set out in the formal contract, although more specific, conformed to that contained in the prior memorandum. It is not disputed that as of execution of the formal contract the union in fact represented a clear majority of employees in the appropriate unit. In upholding the complaints filed against the employer and union by the General Counsel, the Board decided that the employer's good-faith belief that the union in fact represented a majority of employees in the unit on the critical date of the memorandum of understanding was not a defense, "particularly where, as here, the Company made no effort to check the authorization cards against its payroll records." 122 N.L.R.B. 1289, 1292. Noting that the union was "actively seeking recognition at the time such recognition was granted," and that "the Union was [not] the passive recipient of an unsolicited gift bestowed by the Company," the Board found that the union's execution of the August 30 agreement was a "direct deprivation" of the nonconsenting majority employees' organizational and bargaining rights. At pp. 1292, 1293, note 9. Accordingly, the Board ordered the employer to withhold all recognition from the union and to cease giving effect to agreements entered into with the union; the union was ordered to cease acting as bargaining representative of any of the employees until such time as a Board-conducted election demonstrated its majority status, and to refrain from seeking to enforce the agreements previously entered....

At the outset, we reject as without relevance to our decision the fact that, as of the execution date of the formal agreement on October 10, petitioner represented a majority of the employees. As the Court of Appeals indicated, the recognition of the minority union on August 30, 1957, was "a *fait accompli* depriving the majority of the employees of their guaranteed right to choose their own representative." 280 F.2d, at 621. It is, therefore, of no consequence that petitioner may have acquired by October 10 the necessary majority if, during the interim, it was acting unlawfully. Indeed, such acquisition of majority status itself might indicate that the recognition secured by the August 30 agreement afforded petitioner a deceptive cloak of authority with which to persuasively elicit additional employee support.

Nor does this case directly involve a strike. The strike which occurred was in protest against a wage reduction and had nothing to do with petitioner's quest for recognition. Likewise, no question of picketing is presented. Lastly, the violation which the Board found was the grant by the employer of exclusive representation status to a minority union, as distinguished from an employer's bargaining with a minority union for its members only. Therefore, the exclusive representation provision is the vice in the agreement, and discussion of "collective bargaining," as distinguished from "exclusive recognition," is pointless. Moreover, the insistence that we hold the agreement valid and enforceable as to those employees who consented to it must be rejected. On the facts shown, the agreement must fail in its entirety. It was obtained under the erroneous claim of majority representation. Perhaps the employer would not have entered into it if he had known the facts. Quite apart from other conceivable situations, the unlawful genesis of this agreement precludes its partial validity.

In their selection of a bargaining representative, § 9(a) of the Wagner Act guarantees employees freedom of choice and majority rule. *J. I. Case Co. v. NLRB,* 321 U.S. 332, 339 (1944). In short, as we said in *Brooks v. NLRB,* 348 U.S. 96, 103 (1954), the Act placed "a nonconsenting minority under the bargaining responsibility of an agency selected by a majority of the workers." Here, however, the reverse has been shown to be the case. Bernhard-Altmann granted exclusive bargaining status to an agency selected by a minority of its employees, thereby impressing that agent upon the nonconsenting majority. There could be no clearer abridgement of § 7 of the Act, assuring employees the right "to bargain collectively through representatives of their own choosing" or "to refrain from" such activity. It follows, without need of further demonstration, that the employer activity found present here violated § 8(a)(1) of the Act which prohibits employer interference with, and restraint of, employee exercise of § 7 rights. Section 8(a)(2) of the Act makes it an unfair labor practice for an employer to "contribute ... support" to a labor organization. The law has long been settled that a grant of exclusive recognition to a minority union constitutes unlawful support in violation of that section, because the union so favored is given "a marked advantage over any other in securing the adherence of employees," *NLRB v. Pennsylvania Greyhound Lines,* 303 U.S. 261, 267 (1938). In the Taft-Hartley Law, Congress added § 8(b)(1)(A) to the Wagner Act, prohibiting, as the Court of Appeals held, "unions from invading the rights of employees under § 7 in a fashion comparable to the activities of employers prohibited under § 8(a)(1)." 280 F.2d at 620. It was the intent of Congress to impose upon unions the same restrictions which the Wagner Act imposed on employers with respect to violations of employee rights.

The petitioner, while taking no issue with the fact of its minority status on the critical date, maintains that both Bernhard-Altmann's and its own good-faith beliefs in petitioner's majority status are a complete defense. To countenance such an excuse would place in permissibly careless employer and union hands the power to completely frustrate employee realization of the premise of the Act—that its prohibitions will go far to assure freedom of choice and majority rule in employee selection of representatives. We find nothing in the statutory language prescribing *scienter* as an element of the unfair labor practices here involved. The act made unlawful by § 8(a)(2) is employer support of a minority union. Here that support is an accomplished fact. More need not be shown, for, even if mistakenly, the employees' rights have been invaded. It follows that prohibited conduct cannot be excused by a showing of good faith.

This conclusion, while giving the employee only the protection assured him by the Act, places no particular hardship on the employer or the union. It merely requires that recognition be withheld until the Board-conducted election results in majority selection of a representative. The Board's order here, as we might infer from the employer's failure to resist its enforcement, would apparently result in similarly slight hardship upon it. We do not share petitioner's apprehension that holding such conduct unlawful will somehow induce a breakdown, or seriously impede the progress of collective bargaining. If an employer takes reasonable steps to verify union claims, themselves advanced only after careful estimate—precisely what Bernhard-Altmann and petitioner failed to do here—he can readily ascertain their validity and obviate a Board election. We fail to see any onerous burden involved in requiring responsible negotiators to be careful, by cross-checking, for example, well-analyzed employer records with union listings or authorization cards. Individual and collective employee rights may not be trampled upon merely because it is inconvenient to avoid doing so. Moreover, no penalty is attached to the violation. Assuming that an employer in good faith accepts or rejects a union claim of majority status, the validity of his decision may be tested in an unfair labor practice proceeding. If he is found to have erred in extending or withholding recognition, he is subject only to a remedial order requiring him to conform his conduct to the norms set out in the Act, as was the case here. No further penalty results. We believe the Board's remedial order is the proper one in such cases. *NLRB v. District 50, U.M.W.,* 355 U.S. 453 (1958).

Affirmed.

[MR. JUSTICE DOUGLAS and MR. JUSTICE BLACK dissented in part.]

NOTES

1. Suppose the employer negotiates with a minority union an agreement purporting to bind all employees that is conditioned upon the union's attainment of majority status before the contract becomes effective. Such an agreement was found unlawful in *Majestic Weaving Co.,* 147 N.L.R.B. 859 (1964). Although the Second Circuit denied enforcement on a procedural ground, Judge Friendly noted "that 'the premature grant of exclusive bargaining status to a union,' even if conditioned on attainment of a majority before execution of a contract, is similar to formal recognition 'with respect to the deleterious effect upon employee rights.' 29 NLRB Ann. Rep. 69 (1964)." *NLRB v. Majestic Weaving Co.,* 355 F.2d 854, 859-61 (2d Cir. 1966).

2. When an employer and a labor organization agree to accrete to an existing bargaining unit a group of employees who have historically remained unorganized, they will be found in violation of § 8(a)(2) in the absence of evidence demonstrating that a majority of the nonunion personnel currently desire representation. *Teamsters Nat'l UPS Negotiating Comm. v. NLRB,* 17 F.3d 1518 (D.C. Cir. 1994), *cert. denied,* 513 U.S. 1076 (1995).

3. *Local 1814, ILA v. NLRB,* 735 F.2d 1384 (D.C. Cir.), *cert. denied,* 469 U.S. 1072 (1984), involved a situation in which union officials had agreed to steer business to an employer in return for union recognition and an illegal kickback. While the union claimed it was "the chosen representative of an uncoerced majority of [the company's] employees at all relevant times," the court sustained the authority of the Labor Board to remedy the employer's "extensive unlawful assistance" and the union's impermissible acceptance of that aid through an order directing the withdrawal of union recognition until it had obtained NLRB certification, the nullification of the existing bargaining agreement, and the reimbursement of all dues paid by employees who had joined the union during the term of that agreement pursuant to its union security clause. *See also Cascade Gen. v. NLRB,* 997 F.2d 571 (9th Cir. 1993) (dues reimbursement order appropriate to remedy premature recognition of labor organization).

4. In the construction industry, an employer does not violate § 8(a)(2) by making a "pre-hire" agreement with an unassisted union. Under § 8(f), such agreements are not illegal simply because "the majority status of such labor organization has not been established under the provisions of § 9 of this Act prior to the making of such agreement." If the employer hires on a job-by-job basis, its duty to honor the contract is contingent on the union's attaining majority support at the various construction sites. There is a rebuttable presumption of majority support when a union security agreement results in majority union membership on a project to which a § 8(f) pre-hire agreement applies. *See NLRB v. Pacific Erectors, Inc.,* 718 F.2d 1459 (9th Cir. 1983).

C. EMPLOYER DISCRIMINATION

1. GENERAL CONSIDERATIONS; PROBLEMS OF PROOF

STATUTORY REFERENCES

RLA § 2, Third, Fourth, Fifth and Eleventh;
NLRA §§ 8(a)(3), 8(b)(2) and 10(c)

These provisions of the federal acts and their state counterparts are, of course, directed against the most potent antiunion weapon possessed by the employer at common law, namely, its absolute legal control of the job in its plant. It was free to hire, fire, transfer, promote, demote, prefer, layoff, or otherwise deal with employees, subject only to the general pressures of the labor market. The labor relations acts have taken away some of this freedom by forbidding discriminatory treatment for the purpose of encouraging or discouraging union membership. The RLA does not expressly proscribe such discrimination, but the practice is easily encompassed by the broad language of § 2, Fourth and contractual discrimination of the "yellow-dog" variety is outlawed by § 2, Fifth.

It should be apparent at once that the possible kinds of prohibited discrimination are legion. Perhaps the most troublesome aspect of these cases lies in the fact that overt acts of the kind which are part of every day business management are laid open to interpretation as to motive and effect. It is not an exaggeration to say that *whenever* the employer makes a decision affecting adversely the employment situation of an employee who happens to belong to or to be interested in a union, and some other employee who happens not to belong to or to be interested in a union is not similarly treated, a charge of discrimination *may be made* with the possibility that it will be sustained. And it is important again to remember that the fact question is one which will be decided not by the courts (except under the RLA) but by an administrative tribunal.

Put yourself in the position of the Administrative Law Judge as you read the following problem cases and think about what factors seem most significant in deciding the employer's real reason for the discharges. In 1997, there were 13,127 discrimination charges filed—56 percent of the total filings against employers. NLRB, Sixty-Second Annual Report 6 (1998).

PROBLEMS

1. Mr. White was a trucker for ABC Corp. (engaged in interstate commerce) and had 30 years unblemished service with the company. Late last year, however, his performance at his position became somewhat erratic. He began arriving at work a little late, and leaving work a little early. He also began to pick up hitch-hikers along his truck route, thereby violating a seldom enforced regulation of the company. His supervisor, Mr. Rodriguez, expressed displeasure with Mr. White's tardiness on several occasions, but dismissal was never recommended because of Mr. White's excellent record and because the infractions appeared to be minor and easily remedied by docking Mr. White's pay.

Last week, Mr. White began to wear a rather inconspicuous union button to work and pasted a union decal onto the cab window of the truck he regularly drove, again contrary to a seldom enforced regulation against decals on trucks. Mr. Rodriguez noticed the button and decal and called Mr. White into his office for a talk. There, Mr. Rodriguez asked Mr. White to remove the decal from his truck, but Mr. White refused, countering with the argument that all the drivers had decals on their truck windows. Mr. Rodriguez insisted on the point, and also criticized Mr. White's tardiness, concluding with a threat of firing if the situation did not improve. Mr. White replied that he could not be fired because he was working with a union and was thereby protected against any discharge.

The next day, Mr. White was told by Mr. Rodriguez that he was immediately discharged and that his pay would be forwarded to him at the end of the pay period. The reasons for the discharge were given as repeated infractions of the company regulations, chronic tardiness, and insubordination.

2. Ms. Larson was a probationary employee for the XYZ Corp., a large manufacturing company engaged in interstate commerce, and as such had the lowest seniority in her 42-worker plant section. Last month, Ms. Larson began to actively advocate unionization of the plant among the other employees during lunch breaks. Mr. Miller, the supervisor, was told of Ms. Larson's organizational activities by a Mr. Sydney, an employee who had been specially recruited by Mr. Miller to keep management informed of such activities. Mr. Miller consequently called Ms. Larson into his office to review the latter's probationary period report, which was, by all accounts, unsatisfactory. Mr. Miller also lectured Ms. Larson on the evils of unionization, but asked Ms. Larson no questions about her own union activities.

Two weeks ago, without any prior warnings, Ms. Larson was told by Mr. Miller that she need not report in the next morning because the XYZ Corp. was being forced to cut back on employees due to an economic slowdown and Ms. Larson, having the least seniority, would be the first employee laid off. Ms. Larson complained that her probationary period was not yet over, and then accused Mr. Miller of antiunion bias in the discharge, to which Mr. Miller replied only that "I have my orders."

The XYZ Corp. retained all other employees, including several other union advocates. Proof was later offered which tended to show that last month was a very poor month for the XYZ Corp., but that business in the months both before and after was above the normal. A new employee was hired yesterday to perform substantially the same job as Ms. Larson had performed.

NOTES

1. *Burden of Proof.* Since the General Counsel is the moving party, he or she has the burden of proving a violation of the act. *Miller Elec. Mfg. Co. v. NLRB,* 265 F.2d 225 (7th Cir. 1959).

2. *Preponderance of the Testimony Taken.* Before the Board may find a violation of the act, it must find, under § 10(c), that a preponderance of the testimony taken shows that the employer committed an unfair labor practice.

Suppose the employer testifies that its real reason for discharging an employee was an infraction of company rules. What proof would be required to demonstrate that its real reason was to discourage union activity? In *Union-Tribune Pub. Co. v. NLRB,* 1 F.3d 486 (7th Cir. 1993), the court indicated that the mere finding that the reasons offered by a company to justify its discharge of a union official were pretextual does not ipso facto establish a § 8(a)(3) violation. Some additional evidence of antiunion animus must usually be provided. *See also NLRB v. Fluor Daniel, Inc.,* 102 F.3d 818 (6th Cir. 1996) (despite employer's antiunion animus in refusing to hire applicant, no § 8(a)(3) violation unless there was actually job vacancy for which applicant was qualified). *See generally* White, *Modern Discrimination Theory and the National Labor Relations Act,* 39 Wm. & Mary L. Rev. 99 (1997).

Suppose the employer denies that it knew that the discharged employee had been engaging in union activities. What kind of proof is needed to overcome this statement? *See* NLRB, Sixteenth Annual Report 163 (1952); *Long Island Airport Limousine Serv. Corp.,* 191 N.L.R.B. 94 (1971), *enforced,* 468 F.2d 292 (2d Cir. 1972).

3. Various employment decisions may contravene § 8(a)(3) when motivated by antiunion considerations. *See, e.g., NLRB v. CWI of Maryland,* 127 F.3d 319 (4th Cir. 1997) (employer that relocated reporting site of union supporter to new location 100 miles away constructively discharged that individual); *Matson Terminals v. NLRB,* 114 F.3d 300 (D.C. Cir. 1997) (*promotion* of bargaining unit members into supervisory positions violated Act when purpose was to deny them organizing rights).

4. *Effect of "For Cause" Provision of the Taft-Hartley Act, § 10(c).* NLRB General Counsel Robert N. Denham explained the impact of the "for cause" provision in a November 3, 1947, address before the St. Louis Bar Ass'n (21 L.R.R.M. 55):

> As I see it, "good cause," as the basis of a discharge, must be just as good under the provisions of this Act as it ever has been.... If a man is entitled to be discharged and the offenses he has committed are not offenses that customarily have been condoned in other employees, that constitutes good

cause. On the other hand, where the offenses are relatively minor and are of a character that have been more or less common within the plant and have been passed over without disciplinary action, but the employee involved is one who has been an active union leader in an atmosphere of some degree of antagonism on the part of the employer, everyone is entitled to look at such a discharge with much questioning. We still are not only entitled, but are obligated to, weigh the bona fides of the so-called "good cause" and to reject the "good cause" theory if it has all the earmarks of nothing but a subterfuge.

Thus the question still remains: What was the employer's real reason for discharge? Regarding a classic case of "condonation," *see Edward G. Budd Mfg. Co. v. NLRB,* 138 F.2d 86 (3d Cir.), *cert. denied,* 321 U.S. 778 (1943)

5. *Employer Antiunion Statements as Evidence.* In the light of § 8(c), may an antiunion statement of an employer be used as evidence that its reason for discharging an employee was to discourage union activity? In this connection, note the following exchange in Congress in the debate on the act (93 Cong. Rec. 6604 (1947)):

> *Senator Pepper.* ... If an employer were to say on Monday, 'I hate labor unions, and I think they are a menace to this country,' and if he fired a man on Thursday and the question was whether that man was fired for cause or fired because he was agitating for a union in the plant, would the statement made on Monday ... be admissible in evidence as bearing on the question of the reason for the discharge?
>
> *Senator Taft.* It would depend upon the facts. Under the facts generally stated by the Senator, I think that statement would not be evidence of any threat. There would have to be some other circumstances to tie in with the act of the employer. If the act of discharging is illegal and an unfair labor practice, consideration of such a statement would be proper. But it would not be proper to consider as evidence in such a case a speech which in itself contained no threat express or implied.

See also Pittsburgh S.S. Co. v. NLRB, 180 F.2d 731, 735 (6th Cir. 1950), *aff'd,* 340 U.S. 498 (1951); *and Indiana Metal Prod. Corp. v. NLRB,* 202 F.2d 613 (7th Cir. 1953), in which it was held that unless employer antiunion statements contained threats of reprisal or promises of benefit, they were not admissible as evidence of wrongful motivation regarding a discharge. *See generally* White, *The Statutory and Constitutional Limits of Using Protected Speech as Evidence of Unlawful Motive Under the National Labor Relations Act,* 53 Ohio St. L.J. 1 (1992).

6. *Scope of Judicial Review.* Prior to the Taft-Hartley Act, the findings of fact of the Board (on such issues as the employer's real reason for a discharge) were conclusive if supported "by evidence," and this was construed by the courts to mean "substantial evidence." The Taft-Hartley Act substituted the language "substantial evidence on the record considered as a whole."

The authoritative case in which the Supreme Court dealt with the scope of judicial review under the National Labor Relations Act was *Universal Camera Corp. v. NLRB,* 340 U.S. 474 (1951). On the point of immediate interest here Justice Frankfurter said:

> To be sure, the requirement for canvassing "the whole record" in order to ascertain substantiality does not furnish a calculus of value by which a reviewing court can assess the evidence. Nor was it intended to negative the function of the Labor Board as one of those agencies presumably equipped or informed by experience to deal with a specialized field of knowledge, whose findings within that field carry the authority of an expertness which courts do not possess and therefore must respect. Nor does it mean that even as to matters not requiring expertise a court may displace the Board's choice between two fairly conflicting views, even though the court would justifiably have made a different choice had the matter been before it *de novo.* Congress has merely made it clear that a reviewing court is not barred from setting aside a Board decision when it cannot conscientiously find that the evidence supporting that decision is substantial, when viewed in the light of evidence that the record in its entirety furnishes, including the body of evidence opposed to the Board's view.

Justice Frankfurter also addressed the situation in which the NLRB disagrees with the factual findings of the Administrative Law Judge (Trial Examiner):

> The "substantial evidence" standard is not modified in any way when the Board and its examiner disagree. We intend only to recognize that evidence supporting a conclusion may be less substantial when an impartial, experienced examiner who has observed the witnesses and lived with the case has drawn conclusions different from the Board's than when he has reached the same conclusion.

When reviewing discrimination cases, courts of appeals ordinarily give great weight to the Administrative Law Judge's findings on credibility. *MPC Restaurant Corp. v. NLRB,* 481 F.2d 75 (2d Cir. 1973); *NLRB v. A. & S. Elec. Die Corp.,* 423 F.2d 218 (2d Cir.), *cert. denied,* 400 U.S. 833 (1970). *See also NLRB v. Walton Mfg. Co.,* 369 U.S. 404 (1962), wherein the Supreme Court refused to apply a special, more onerous rule for review of cases in which the remedy would be reinstatement and back pay, since these remedies may impoverish an employer. "There is no place in the statutory scheme for one test of the substantiality of evidence in reinstatement cases and another test in other cases."

See generally Jaffe, *Judicial Review: "Substantial Evidence on the Whole Record,"* 64 Harv. L. Rev. 1233 (1951). *See also* Gibson, *The Trial Examiner's In-*

termediate Report and Its Role in Unfair Labor Practice Cases, 19 Geo. Wash. L. Rev. 2 (1950).

7. *Intervention by Successful Party in Enforcement and Review Proceedings.* In *UAW Local 283 v. Scofield,* 382 U.S. 205 (1965), the Court held that parties who are successful in unfair labor practice proceedings before the Board—a charged party when the complaint is dismissed and a charging party when the complaint is sustained in its entirety—have a right to intervene in court of appeals proceedings to review or enforce the Board's order. Note that giving the successful party before the NLRB the right to intervene in the court of appeal carries with it the right to petition the Supreme Court for a writ of certiorari, which the NLRB and the Solicitor General might not choose to do.

8. *"Mixed Motive" Cases. NLRB v. Transportation Mgt. Corp.,* 462 U.S. 963 (1983), involved a bus driver, Santillo, who was fired by his employer, Transportation Management Corp., shortly after he distributed union authorization cards. He was told that he was discharged for leaving his keys in the bus and for taking unauthorized breaks. Santillo filed a charge with the NLRB alleging that he was discharged because of his union activities. The NLRB applied the test used in "dual motive" cases that was formulated in *Wright Line,* 251 N.L.R.B. 1083 (1980). Under *Wright Line,* once the General Counsel proves by a preponderance of the evidence that the employer's action was based in whole or in part on antiunion animus, the employer will be found in violation—unless it can prove as an affirmative defense that the adverse action would have been taken even if the employee had not been involved in protected activities. The NLRB found that Transportation Management Corp. had failed to establish that Santillo's discharge would have taken place in the absence of the driver's protected activities.

The question before the Supreme Court was whether the burden placed on the employer under the *Wright Line* test is consistent with §§ 8(a)(1) and 8(a)(3), as well as with § 10(c) of the NLRA, which provides that the Board must prove an unlawful labor practice by a "preponderance of the evidence." The Court held the *Wright Line* allocation was proper under the Act. The Court reasoned that the Board has consistently held that a violation of the Act consists of an adverse action based in whole or in part on antiunion animus. This requires that the employee's protected conduct must have been a substantial or motivating factor in the adverse decision. The General Counsel is required by § 10(c) to prove this by a preponderance of the evidence. The Court stated that the Board's construction of the NLRA permits an employer to avoid being held in violation of the statute by showing that it would have taken the same action regardless of the employee's protected conduct. This does not change or add to the elements the General Counsel must prove, but merely extends to the employer what the Board considers to be an affirmative defense. While the Board's construction is not mandated by the Act, the Court concluded, it is permissible and entitled to deference.

9. In *NLRB v. Town & Country Elec.*, 516 U.S. 85 (1995), the Supreme Court unanimously held that full-time, paid union organizers constitute "employees" under the NLRA and that an employer violates § 8(a)(3) if it refuses to hire such individuals or terminates them once it learns of their union relationship. The Court cited § 226 of the *Restatement (Second) of Agency* to the effect that a "person may be the servant of two masters ... at one time as to one act, if the service to one does not involve abandonment of the service to the other." The Court countered the employer's argument that the union was trying to "salt" nonunion companies with paid union organizers who might harm the firms by observing that "nothing in this record suggests that such acts of disloyalty were present, in kind or degree, to the point where the company might lose control over the worker's normal workplace tasks."

The Labor Board has not been receptive to employer strategies for combating union "salting" campaigns. *See, e.g., Tualatin Elec.*, 319 N.L.R.B. 1237 (1995) (employer unlawfully prohibited employees from receiving compensation from any source other than the employer itself). *Compare Architectural Glass & Metal Co. v. NLRB*, 107 F.3d 426 (6th Cir. 1997) (employer did not have to hire full-time, paid union organizer when it had a nondiscriminatory general rule against dual full-time employment). In *H.B. Zachry Co.*, 319 N.L.R.B. 967 (1995), the Board held that an employer with a policy of disqualifying job applications that contained "nonresponsive information" unlawfully refused to consider applicants who wrote on their applications that they were "volunteer union organizers." Since the Eleventh Circuit found that the H.B. Zachry Company had applied its policy in a nondiscriminatory manner, it denied enforcement of the Board's decision. *Boilermakers v. NLRB*, 127 F.3d 1300 (11th Cir. 1997).

2. DISCRIMINATION TO ENCOURAGE UNION MEMBERSHIP

a. Hiring Halls and Other Practices

INTERNATIONAL BROTHERHOOD OF TEAMSTERS, LOCAL 357 v. NLRB

Supreme Court of the United States
365 U.S. 667, 81 S. Ct. 835, 6 L. Ed. 2d 11 (1961)

MR. JUSTICE DOUGLAS delivered the opinion of the Court.

Petitioner union (along with the International Brotherhood of Teamsters and a number of other affiliated local unions) executed a three-year collective bargaining agreement with California Trucking Associations which represented a group of motor truck operators in California. The provisions of the contract relating to hiring of casual or temporary employees were as follows:

> Casual employees shall, wherever the Union maintains a dispatching service, be employed only on a seniority basis in the Industry whenever such senior employees are available. An available list with seniority status

will be kept by the Unions, and employees requested will be dispatched
upon call to any employer who is a party to this Agreement. Seniority rating
of such employees shall begin with a minimum of three months service in
the Industry, *irrespective of whether such employee is or is not a member of*
the Union.

Discharge of any employee by any employer shall be grounds for removal
of any employee from seniority status. No casual employee shall be employed by any employer who is a party to this Agreement in violation of
seniority status if such employees are available and if the dispatching service for such employees is available. The employer shall first call the Union
or the dispatching hall designated by the Union for such help. In the event
the employer is notified that such help is not available, or in the event the
employees called for do not appear for work at the time designated by the
employer, the employer may hire from any other available source. (Emphasis added.)

Accordingly the union maintained a hiring hall for casual employees. One
Slater was a member of the union and had customarily used the hiring hall. But in
August 1955 he obtained casual employment with an employer who was a party
to the hiring-hall agreement without being dispatched by the union. He worked
until sometime in November of that year, when he was discharged by the employer on complaint of the union that he had not been referred through the hiring-
hall arrangement.

Slater made charges against the union and the employer. Though, as plain from
the terms of the contract, there was an express provision that employees would
not be discriminated against because they were or were not union members, the
Board found that the hiring-hall provision was unlawful *per se* and that the discharge of Slater on the union's request constituted a violation by the employer of
§ 8(a)(1) and § 8(a)(3) and a violation by the union of § 8(b)(2) and § 8(b)(1)(A)
of the National Labor Relations Act, as amended by the Taft-Hartley Act, 61
Stat. 140-141, as amended, 29 U.S.C. § 158. The Board ordered, *inter alia,* that
the company and the union cease giving any effect to the hiring-hall agreement;
that they jointly and severally reimburse Slater for any loss sustained by him as a
result of his discharge; and that they jointly and severally reimburse all casual
employees for fees and dues paid by them to the union beginning six months
prior to the date of the filing of the charge. 121 N.L.R.B. 1629.

The union petitioned the Court of Appeals for review of the Board's action,
and the Board made a cross-application for enforcement. That court set aside the
portion of the order requiring a general reimbursement of dues and fees. By a
divided vote it upheld the Board in ruling that the hiring-hall agreement was illegal *per se.* 107 App. D.C. 188, 275 F.2d 646 (1960). Those rulings are here on
certiorari, 363 U.S. 837, one on the petition of the union, the other on petition of
the Board.

Our decision in *Carpenters Locals 60 v. NLRB,* decided this day, *supra* at 651, is dispositive of the petition of the Board that asks us to direct enforcement of the order of reimbursement. The judgment of the Court of Appeals on that phase of the matter is affirmed.

The other aspect of the case goes back to the Board's ruling in *Mountain Pacific Chapter,* 119 N.L.R.B. 883. That decision, rendered in 1958, departed from earlier rulings and held, Abe Murdock dissenting, that the hiring-hall agreement, despite the inclusion of a nondiscrimination clause, was illegal, *per se:*

> Here the very grant of work at all depends solely upon union sponsorship, and it is reasonable to infer that the arrangement displays and enhances the Union's power and control over the employment status. Here all that appears is unilateral union determination and subservient employer action with no above-board explanation as to the reason for it, and it is reasonable to infer that the Union will be guided in its concession by an eye towards winning compliance with a membership obligation or union fealty in some other respect. The Employers here have surrendered all hiring authority to the Union and have given advance notice via the established hiring hall to the world at large that the Union is arbitrary master and is contractually guaranteed to remain so. From the final authority over hiring vested in the Respondent Union by the three AGC chapters, the inference of the encouragement of union membership is inescapable. [*Id.* 896].

The Board went on to say that a hiring-hall arrangement to be lawful must contain protective provisions. Its views were stated as follows:

> We believe, however, that the inherent and unlawful encouragement of union membership that stems from unfettered union control over the hiring process would be negated, and we would find an agreement to be nondiscriminatory on its face, only if the agreement explicitly provided that:
> (1) Selection of applicants for referral to jobs shall be on a nondiscriminatory basis and shall not be based on, or in any way affected by, union membership, bylaws, rules, regulations, constitutional provisions, or any other aspect or obligation of union membership, policies, or requirements.
> (2) The employer retains the right to reject any job applicant referred by the union.
> (3) The parties to the agreement post in places where notices to employees and applicants for employment are customarily posted, all provisions relating to the functioning of the hiring arrangement, including the safeguards that we deem essential to the legality of an exclusive hiring agreement. [*Id.* 897].

The Board recognizes that the hiring hall came into being "to eliminate wasteful, time-consuming, and repetitive scouting for jobs by individual workmen and haphazard uneconomical searches by employers." *Id.* 896, note 8. The hiring hall at times has been a useful adjunct to the closed shop. But Congress may have thought that it need not serve that cause, that in fact it has served well both labor and management—particularly in the maritime field and in the building and construction industry. In the latter the contractor who frequently is a stranger to the area where the work is done requires a "central source" for his employment needs; and a man looking for a job finds in the hiring hall "at least a minimum guarantee of continued employment."

Congress has not outlawed the hiring hall, though it has outlawed the closed shop except within the limits prescribed in the *provisos* to § 8(a)(3). Senator Taft made clear his views that hiring halls are useful, that they are not illegal *per se*, that unions should be able to operate them so long as they are not used to create a closed shop:

> In order to make clear the real intention of Congress, it should be clearly stated that the hiring hall is not necessarily illegal. The employer should be able to make a contract with the union as an employment agency. The union frequently is the best employment agency. The employer should be able to give notice of vacancies, and in the normal course of events to accept men sent to him by the hiring hall. He should not be able to bind himself, however, to reject nonunion men if they apply to him; nor should he be able to contract to accept men on a rotary-hiring basis....
>
> ... The National Labor Relations Board and the courts did not find hiring halls as such illegal, but merely certain practices under them. The Board and the court found that the manner in which the hiring halls operated created in effect a closed shop in violation of the law. Neither the law nor these decisions forbid hiring halls, even hiring halls operated by the unions as long as they are not so operated as to create a closed shop with all of the abuses possible under such arrangement, including discrimination against employees, prospective employees, members of union minority groups, and operation of a closed union. [S. Rep. No. 1827, 81st Cong., 2d Sess., pp. 13, 14].

There being no express ban of hiring halls in any provisions of the Act, those who add one, whether it be the Board or the courts, engage in a legislative act. The Act deals with discrimination either by the employers or unions that encourages or discourages union membership. As respects § 8(a)(3) we said in *Radio Officers' Union v. NLRB,* 347 U.S. 17, 42, 43 (1954):

> The language of § 8(a)(3) is not ambiguous. The unfair labor practice is for an employer to encourage or discourage membership by means of discrimination. Thus this section does not outlaw all encouragement or discouragement of membership in labor organizations; only such as is accomplished by discrimination is prohibited. Nor does this section outlaw dis-

crimination in employment as such; only such discrimination as encourages or discourages membership in a labor organization is proscribed.

It is the "true purpose" or "real motive" in hiring or firing that constitutes the test. *Id.* 347 U.S. 43. Some conduct may by its very nature contain the implications of the required intent; the natural foreseeable consequences of certain action may warrant the inference. *Id.* 347 U.S. 45. And see *Republic Aviation Corp. v. NLRB,* 324 U.S. 793 (1945). The existence of discrimination may at times be inferred by the Board, for "it is permissible to draw on experience in factual inquiries." *Radio Officers' Union v. NLRB, supra,* 49.

But surely discrimination cannot be inferred from the face of the instrument when the instrument specifically provides that there will be no discrimination against "casual employees" because of the presence or absence of union membership. The only complaint in the case was by Slater, a union member, who sought to circumvent the hiring-hall agreement. When an employer and the union enforce the agreement against union members, we cannot say without more that either indulges in the kind of discrimination to which the Act is addressed.

It may be that the very existence of the hiring hall encourages union membership. We may assume that it does. The very existence of the union has the same influence. When a union engages in collective bargaining and obtains increased wages and improved working conditions, its prestige doubtless rises and, one may assume, more workers are drawn to it. When a union negotiates collective bargaining agreements that include arbitration clauses and supervises the functioning of those provisions so as to get equitable adjustments of grievances, union membership may also be encouraged. The truth is that the union is a service agency that probably encourages membership whenever it does its job well. But as we said in *Radio Officers' Union v. NLRB, supra,* the only encouragement or discouragement of union membership banned by the Act is that which is "accomplished by discrimination." P. 43.

Nothing is inferable from the present hiring-hall provision except that employer and union alike sought to route "casual employees" through the union hiring hall and required a union member who circumvented it to adhere to it.

It may be that hiring halls need more regulation than the Act presently affords. As we have seen, the Act aims at every practice, act, source or institution which in fact is used to encourage and discourage union membership by discrimination in regard to hire or tenure, term or condition of employment. Perhaps the conditions which the Board attaches to hiring-hall arrangements will in time appeal to the Congress. Yet where Congress has adopted a selective system for dealing with evils, the Board is confined to that system. *NLRB v. Drivers Local Union,* 362 U.S. 274, 284-290 (1960). Where, as here, Congress has aimed its sanctions only at specific discriminatory practices, the Board cannot go farther and establish a broader, more pervasive regulatory scheme.

The present agreement for a union hiring hall has a protective clause in it, as we have said; and there is no evidence that it was in fact used unlawfully. We cannot assume that a union conducts its operations in violation of law or that the parties to this contract did not intend to adhere to its express language. Yet we would have to make those assumptions to agree with the Board that it is reasonable to infer the union will act discriminatorily.

Moreover, the hiring hall, under the law as it stands, is a matter of negotiation between the parties. The Board has no power to compel directly or indirectly that the hiring hall be included or excluded in collective agreements. *Cf. NLRB v. American Nat. Ins. Co.,* 343 U.S. 395, 404 (1952). Its power, so far as here relevant, is restricted to the elimination of discrimination. Since the present agreement contains such a prohibition, the Board is confined to determining whether discrimination has in fact been practiced. If hiring halls are to be subjected to regulation that is less selective and more pervasive, Congress not the Board is the agency to do it.

Affirmed in part and reversed in part.

MR. JUSTICE FRANKFURTER took no part in the consideration or decision of this case.

[The concurring opinion of MR. JUSTICE HARLAN, joined in by MR. JUSTICE STEWART, and the dissenting opinion of MR. JUSTICE CLARK, joined in by MR. JUSTICE WHITTAKER, are omitted.]

NOTES

1. In the leading *Radio Officers'* case, cited in the principal case, the Supreme Court held the following to constitute unlawful encouragement of union membership by discrimination: (a) reducing a truck driver's seniority standing because he did not keep up his union dues; (b) causing a ship's radio officer to be refused employment because he did not obtain union clearance, where there was no valid hiring-hall agreement; (c) granting a retroactive wage increase to union members and refusing such benefits to other employees because they were not union members.

In *Radio Officers'*, the Court discussed several evidentiary considerations:

Necessity for Proving Employer's Motive

The language of § 8(a)(3) is not ambiguous. The unfair labor practice is for an employer to encourage or discourage membership by means of discrimination. Thus this section does not outlaw all encouragement or discouragement of membership in labor organizations; only such as is accomplished by discrimination is prohibited. Nor does this section outlaw discrimination in employment as such; only such discrimination as encourages or discourages membership in a labor organization is proscribed.

The relevance of the motivation of the employer in such discrimination has been consistently recognized under both § 8(a)(3) and its predecessor....

That Congress intended the employer's purpose in discriminating to be controlling is clear. The Senate Report on the Wagner Act said: "Of course nothing in the bill prevents an employer from discharging a man for incompetence; from advancing him for special aptitude; or from demoting him for failure to perform...."

Proof of Motive

But it is also clear that specific evidence of intent to encourage or discourage is not an indispensable element of proof of violation of § 8(a)(3).... [A]n employer's protestation that he did not intend to encourage or discourage must be unavailing where a natural consequence of his action was such encouragement or discouragement. Concluding that encouragement or discouragement will result, it is presumed that he intended such consequence. In such circumstances intent to encourage is sufficiently established....

Power of Board to Draw Inferences

There is nothing in the language of the amendment itself that suggests denial to the Board of power to draw reasonable inferences. It is inconceivable that the authors of the reports intended such a result for a fact-finding body must have some power to decide which inferences to draw and which to reject. We therefore conclude that insofar as the power to draw reasonable inferences is concerned, Taft-Hartley did not alter prior law....

2. When the charge is brought against the employer for discriminating against an employee at the union's request, the test is not whether the employer subjectively wanted to encourage union membership (or the adherence to union rules or policies), but whether it should reasonably have known that its actions would tend to have that consequence. *See Printz Leather Co.,* 94 N.L.R.B. 1312 (1951) (employer complied with union demand to discharge employee who refused to cooperate in the concerted effort of his fellow employees to limit production).

3. Under a valid facially hiring-hall agreement, what kind of evidence would be required to prove that it actually functioned to encourage union membership by discrimination? *See Plumbers Local 198 v. NLRB,* 747 F.2d 326 (5th Cir. 1984) (union gave lower referral priority to members of other locals); *NLRB v. Southern Stevedoring & Contr'g Co.,* 332 F.2d 1017 (5th Cir. 1964) (union hiring hall gave direct preference to ILA members over IBL members); *NLRB v. Houston Maritime Ass'n,* 337 F.2d 333 (5th Cir. 1964) (union hiring hall selected members first and referred nonmembers only if members were not available).

4. Unions may charge nonmembers reasonable "service fees" when they use hiring halls, but organizations charging excessive fees will violate § 8(b)(1)(A). *See Pittsburgh Press Co. v. NLRB*, 977 F.2d 652 (D.C. Cir. 1992).

A union operating a *nonexclusive* hiring hall may lawfully refuse to refer nonmembers to jobs. *See Carpenters Local 537 (Dupont & Co.)*, 303 N.L.R.B. 419 (1991).

5. In *Hays v. NECA*, 781 F.2d 1321 (9th Cir. 1986), the court found that a labor organization did not act unlawfully when it adopted a rule that restricted preferential-work referral status to those individuals who resided within forty miles of the hiring hall. Such action disenfranchised few persons, and it constituted a legitimate exercise of union discretion.

————

Carpenters Local 60 v. NLRB, 365 U.S. 651, 81 S. Ct. 875, 6 L. Ed. 2d 1 (1961). A company and a union maintained an illegal closed-shop hiring system. Two job applicants were denied employment by the company because they could not obtain referrals from the union. The Labor Board included among other relief its so-called *"Brown-Olds"* remedy (*see* 115 N.L.R.B. 594 (1956)), requiring the reimbursement to *all* employees of all dues and fees collected by the union under the illegal contract during the six-months' period prior to the filing of the charges. The Supreme Court rejected the Board's refund order. "[T]he power of the Board 'to command affirmative action is remedial, not punitive....' Where no membership in the union was shown to be influenced or compelled by reason of any unfair practice, no 'consequences of violation' are removed by the order compelling the union to return all dues and fees collected from the members...."

NOTES

1. Contractual provisions granting shop stewards superseniority for purpose of *layoff* and *recall* are presumptively valid to ensure that there will be someone at the workplace to handle grievances and administer the bargaining agreement. Provisions granting such superseniority to stewards for other purposes, such as choice of lucrative delivery routes, are generally improper. *See NLRB v. Teamsters, Local 338 [Dairylea Coop.]*, 531 F.2d 1162 (2d Cir. 1976); *Mechanics Educ. Soc'y*, 287 N.L.R.B. 935 (1987). *But cf. NLRB v. Auto Warehousers, Inc.*, 571 F.2d 860 (5th Cir. 1978), wherein the court held that a contract clause permitting union stewards to exercise superseniority for purposes beyond layoff and recall is not *per se* invalid. In *Gulton Electro-Voice, Inc.*, 266 N.L.R.B. 406 (1983), *enforced*, 727 F.2d 1184 (D.C. Cir. 1984), the Board held that the grant of superseniority for layoff and recall purposes to union officials who do not handle grievances or exercise other on-the-job contract administrative responsibilities will be considered unlawful union-related discrimination. *See generally*

Note, *New Limits on Superseniority: Ignoring the Importance of Efficient Union Operations,* 86 Colum. L. Rev. 631 (1986).

2. A union operating a hiring hall may lawfully refer an employee it wants as steward at a job site ahead of another person who is higher on the out-of-work referral list. *See Plumbers & Pipefitters Local 520 (Aycock, Inc.),* 282 N.L.R.B. 1228 (1987).

3. A bargaining agreement may lawfully provide that employees serving as union officials may be granted two-year leaves without loss of seniority, even though employees taking other leaves are limited to six-month leaves. *See WPIX, Inc. v. NLRB,* 870 F.2d 858 (2d Cir. 1989).

b. Union Security Under Federal Legislation

STATUTORY REFERENCES

RLA § 2, Fourth, Fifth, and Eleventh
NLRA §§ 8(a)(3), 8(b)(2), 8(b)(5), 8(f), 9(e)

Unions ordinarily seek to make membership one hundred percent in occupational groups which they represent. To accomplish this, they may employ persuasion or economic pressure. They may also try to obtain so-called "union security" agreements from employers. The most common types of union security agreements are the following:

Closed Shop

From the union point of view, the most effective form of union security provision is the "closed shop." A standard version would read:

> The employer hereby agrees to employ only members in good standing of the Union.

Prior to the 1947 Taft-Hartley amendments that prohibited closed shop agreements, such provisions were quite common, especially in such industries as construction, printing, hosiery, clothing, baking, brewing, and trucking, where a majority of the workers covered by collective agreements were under closed shop contracts.

Union Shop

The "union shop" contract does not require the employer to hire only union members, but does require nonunion employees to become members of the union within a prescribed period after their initial employment. A typical clause would provide:

> Each employee covered by this agreement shall, as a condition of continued employment, become and remain a member of the Union on and after

the thirtieth day following the beginning of his or her employment or following the effective date of this agreement, whichever is the later.

Next to the closed shop, an agreement of this kind is the most favored by unions as a security device. Even though the Taft-Hartley amendments technically proscribed union shop provisions, many collective contracts continue to contain language that appears to require new employees to become actual union members within the first thirty days of their employment.

Agency Shop

In deference to the religious scruples or ethical principles of some employees, or in response to certain state statutes, or the express language of the Taft-Hartley amendments, some labor contracts expressly provide for a so-called "agency shop" instead of the usual union shop. Under an agency shop provision, employees do not have to become formal union members, but any employees electing not to join must pay to the union amounts equal to the customary initiation fee and the periodic dues required of regular members.

Maintenance of Membership

"Maintenance of membership" gained wide use as a form of union security during World War II, largely because it was employed by the National War Labor Board as a formula for compromising the demands of unions for the closed shop and the demands of employers for the maintenance of the status quo in their plants during the war. A typical maintenance of membership clause, as directed by the WLB, follows:

> All members who, 15 days after the date of the Directive Order of the National War Labor Board in this case, are members of the Union in good standing in accordance with the constitution and bylaws of the Union, and those employees who may thereafter become members, shall, as a condition of employment, remain members of the Union in good standing during the life of the agreement.

Checkoff

Another contractual arrangement is regarded as a form of union security, although it does not itself condition employment on union membership. This is the "checkoff," under which the employer agrees to deduct union dues from employee wages and to transmit them to the union. This is a great aid in keeping members in financial good standing. Sometimes unions have been satisfied with the checkoff as the sole security provision. More often, however, the checkoff has been used together with some type of provision conditioning employment on union membership. (Section 302(c)(4) of the LMRA requires written authorizations from employees before an employer can check off their dues.)

———————

Any agreement that conditions the right of employees to work on membership in a labor organization is a patent interference with their freedom of self-organization and an act of discrimination. In enacting the labor relations act limitations on employer discrimination, Congress and the state legislatures have perforce had to decide whether, (1) to equate such interferences with the "yellow-dog" contract and outlaw them altogether; (2) to exempt them altogether and leave them within the area of collective bargaining; or (3) to regulate their use by imposing conditions and limitations. A fourth alternative was to force employers and employees to accept union security, upon demand of qualified unions, but this was clearly not a practical possibility.

Legislative treatment of the problem has reflected its extremely troublesome nature. In the 1934 amendments to the Railway Labor Act, Congress prohibited all forms of union security arrangements, including the checkoff, a somewhat anomalous result since the RLA of 1926 was supposed to represent the views of both carriers and unions. In the original NLRA, and in the "little Wagner acts" which quickly followed, collective agreements conditioning employment on union membership were expressly exempted from the prohibition on employer discrimination when such agreements were made with unions having statutory bargaining rights. However, as the pendulum of public opinion, which had swung far toward unionism, began to return, some of the states either banned the closed shop and other forms of union security agreements or imposed various limitations.

In the 1947 Taft-Hartley amendments, Congress finally adopted a policy granting limited approval to union security arrangements. Under the amended proviso to § 8(a)(3), the closed shop was expressly outlawed. It appeared to many that union shop agreements continued to be permitted as a form of employer discrimination if the statutory conditions were satisfied. Nonetheless, as the following decision indicates, only agency shop obligations actually survived the Taft-Hartley amendments. In 1951, the RLA was amended to permit union shop and checkoff agreements subject to conditions approximating those contained in the LMRA amendments. And in 1952, the so-called "Taft-Humphrey" Act liberalized the restrictions of the LMRA by deleting the requirement of an affirmative vote of the employees before a union could negotiate a union security contract.

NLRB v. GENERAL MOTORS CORP.

Supreme Court of the United States
373 U.S. 734, 83 S. Ct. 1453, 10 L. Ed. 2d 670 (1963)

MR. JUSTICE WHITE delivered the opinion of the Court.

The issue here is whether an employer commits an unfair labor practice, National Labor Relations Act § 8(a)(5), when it refuses to bargain with a certified union over the union's proposal for the adoption of the "agency shop." More narrowly, since the employer is not obliged to bargain over a proposal that he commit an unfair labor practice, the question is whether the agency shop is an unfair labor practice under § 8(a)(3) of the Act or else is exempted from the prohibitions of that section by the proviso thereto. We have concluded that this type of arrangement does not constitute an unfair labor practice and that it is not prohibited by § 8.

Respondent's employees are represented by the United Automobile, Aerospace and Agricultural Implement Workers of America, UAW, in a single, multiplant, company-wide unit. The 1958 agreement between union and company provides for maintenance of membership and the union shop. These provisions were not operative, however, in such states as Indiana where state law prohibited making union membership a condition of employment.

In June 1959, the Indiana intermediate appellate court held that an agency shop arrangement would not violate the state right-to-work law. *Meade Elec. Co. v. Hagberg,* 129 Ind. App. 631, 159 N.E.2d 408 (1959). As defined in that opinion, the term "agency shop" applies to an arrangement under which all employees are required as a condition of employment to pay dues to the union and pay the union's initiation fee, but they need not actually become union members. The union thereafter sent respondent a letter proposing the negotiation of a contractual provision covering Indiana plants "generally similar to that set forth" in the *Meade* case. Continued employment in the Indiana plants would be conditioned upon the payment of sums equal to the initiation fee and regular monthly dues paid by the union members. The intent of the proposal, the NLRB concluded, was not to require membership but to make membership available at the employees' option and on nondiscriminatory terms. Employees choosing not to join would make the required payments and, in accordance with union custom, would share in union expenditures for strike benefits, educational and retired member benefits, and union publications and promotional activities, but they would not be entitled to attend union meetings, vote upon ratification of agreements negotiated by the union, or have a voice in the internal affairs of the union. The respondent made no counterproposal, but replied to the union's letter that the proposed agreement would violate the National Labor Relations Act and that respondent must therefore "respectfully decline to comply with your request for a meeting" to bargain over the proposal.

The union thereupon filed a complaint with the NLRB against respondent for its alleged refusal to bargain in good faith. In the Board's view of the record, "the union was not seeking to bargain over a clause requiring nonmember employees to pay sums equal to dues and fees as a condition of employment while at the same time maintaining a closed-union policy with respect to applicants for membership," since the proposal contemplated an arrangement in which "all employees are *given the option* of becoming, or refraining from becoming, members of the union." Proceeding on this basis and putting aside the consequences of a closed-union policy upon the legality of the agency shop, the Board assessed the union's proposal as comporting fully with the congressional declaration of policy in favor of union-security contracts and therefore a mandatory subject as to which the Act obliged respondent to bargain in good faith. At the same time, it stated that it had "no doubt that an agency-shop agreement is a permissible form of union-security within the meaning of §§ 7 and 8(a)(3) of the Act." Accordingly, the Board ruled that respondents had committed an unfair labor practice by refusing to bargain in good faith with the certified bargaining representative of its employees, and it ordered respondent to bargain with the union over the proposed arrangement; no back-pay award is involved in this case. 133 N.L.R.B. 451.

Respondent petitioned for review in the Court of Appeals, and the Board cross-petitioned for enforcement. The Court of Appeals set the order aside on the grounds that the Act tolerates only "an agreement requiring membership in a labor organization as a condition of employment" when such agreements do not violate state right-to-work laws, and that the Act does not authorize agreements requiring payment of membership dues to a union, in lieu of membership, as a condition of employment. It held that the proposed agency shop agreement would violate §§ 7, 8(a)(1), and 8(a)(3) of the Act and that the employer was therefore not obliged to bargain over it. 303 F.2d 428 (6th Cir. 1962). We granted certiorari ... and now reverse the decision of the Court of Appeals.

Section 8(3) under the Wagner Act was the predecessor to § 8(a)(3) of the present law. Like § 8(a)(3), § 8(3) forbade employers to discriminate against employees to compel them to join a union. Because it was feared that § 8(3) and § 7, if nothing were added to qualify them, might be held to outlaw union-security arrangements such as the closed shop, see 79 Cong. Rec. 7570 (statement of Senator Wagner), 7674 (statement of Senator Walsh); H.R. Rep. No. 972, at 17; H.R. Rep. No. 1147, at 19, the proviso to § 8(3) was added expressly declaring:

> "*Provided,* That nothing in this Act ... or in any other statute of the United States, shall preclude an employer from making an agreement with a labor organization ... to require as a condition of employment membership therein, if such labor organization is the representative of the employees as provided in section 9(a)...."

The prevailing administrative and judicial view under the Wagner Act was or came to be that the proviso to § 8(3) covered both the closed and union shop, as well as less onerous union security arrangements, if they were otherwise legal. The NLRB construed the proviso as shielding from an unfair labor practice charge less severe forms of union-security arrangements than the closed or the union shop, including an arrangement in *Public Service Co. of Colorado,* 89 N.L.R.B. 418, requiring nonunion members to pay to the union $2 a month "for the support of the bargaining unit." And in *Algoma Plywood & Veneer Co. v.*

Wisconsin Employment Relations Board, 336 U.S. 301, 307 (1949), which involved a maintenance of membership agreement, the Court, in commenting on petitioner's contention that the proviso of § 8(3) affirmatively protected arrangements within its scope, *cf. Garner v. Teamsters Union,* 346 U.S. 485 (1953), said of its purpose: "The short answer is that § 8(3) merely disclaims a national policy hostile to the closed shop *or other forms of union-security agreement.*" (Emphasis added.)

When Congress enacted the Taft-Hartley Act, it added ... to the language of the original proviso to § 8(3).... These additions were intended to accomplish twin purposes. On the one hand, the most serious abuses of compulsory unionism were eliminated by abolishing the closed shop. On the other hand, Congress recognized that in the absence of a union-security provision "many employees sharing the benefits of what unions are able to accomplish, like collective bargaining, will refuse to pay their share of the cost." S. Rep. No. 105, 80th Cong., 1st Sess., at 6, 1 Leg. Hist. L.M.R.A. 412. Consequently, under the new law "employers would still be permitted to enter into agreements requiring all employees in a given bargaining unit to become members thirty days after being hired" but "expulsion from a union cannot be a ground of compulsory discharge if the worker is not delinquent in paying his initiation fees or dues." S. Rep. No. 105, at 7, 1 Leg. Hist. L.M.R.A. 413. The amendments were intended only to "remedy the most serious abuses of compulsory union membership and yet give employers and unions who feel that such agreements promoted stability by eliminating 'free riders' the right to continue such arrangements." *Ibid.* As far as the federal law was concerned, all employees could be required to pay their way. The bill "abolishes the closed shop but permits voluntary agreements for requiring such forms of compulsory membership as the union shop or maintenance of membership...." S. Rep. No. 105, at 3, 1 Leg. Hist. L.M.R.A. 409.

We find nothing in the legislative history of the Act indicating that Congress intended the amended proviso to § 8(a)(3) to validate only the union shop and simultaneously to abolish, in addition to the closed shop, all other union-security arrangements permissible under state law. There is much to be said for the Board's view that, if Congress desired in the Wagner Act to permit a closed or union shop and in the Taft-Hartley Act the union shop, then it also intended to preserve the status of less vigorous, less compulsory contracts, which demanded less adherence to the union.

Respondent, however, relies upon the express words of the proviso which allow employment to be conditioned upon "membership": since the union's proposal here does not require actual membership but demands only initiation fees and monthly dues it is not saved by the proviso. This position, of course, would reject administrative decisions concerning the scope of § 8(3) of the Wagner Act, *e.g., Public Service Co. of Colorado, supra,* reaffirmed by the Board under the Taft-Hartley amendments, *American Seating Co.,* 98 N.L.R.B. 800. Moreover, the 1947 amendments not only abolished the closed shop but also made significant alterations in the meaning of "membership" for the purposes of union security contracts. Under the second proviso to § 8(a)(3), the burdens of membership upon which employment may be conditioned are expressly limited to the payment of initiation fees and monthly dues. It is permissible to condition employment upon membership, but membership, insofar as it has significance to employment rights, may in turn be conditioned only upon payment of fees and dues. "Membership" as a condition of employment is whittled down to its financial core. This Court has said as much before in *Radio Officers' Union v. NLRB,* 347 U.S. 17, 41 (1954):

> ... This legislative history clearly indicates that Congress intended to prevent utilization of union security agreements for any purpose other than to compel payment of union dues and fees. Thus, Congress recognized the validity of unions' concern about 'free riders,' i.e., employees who receive the benefits of union representation but are unwilling to contribute their fair share of financial support to such union, and gave the unions the power to contract to meet that problem while withholding from unions the power to cause the discharge of employees for any other reason....

We are therefore confident that the proposal made by the union here conditioned employment upon the practical equivalent of union "membership," as Congress used that term in the proviso to § 8(a)(3). The proposal for requiring the payment of dues and fees imposes no burdens not imposed by a permissible union shop contract and compels the performance of only those duties of membership which are enforceable by discharge under a union shop arrangement. If an employee in a union shop unit refuses to respect any union-imposed obligations other than the duty to pay dues and fees, and membership in the union is therefore denied or terminated, the condition of "membership" for § 8(a)(3) purposes is nevertheless satisfied and the employee may not be discharged for nonmembership even though he is not a formal member. Of course, if the union chooses to extend membership even though the employee will meet only the minimum financial burden, and refuses to support or "join" the union in any other affirmative way, the employee may have to become a "member" under a union shop contract, in the sense that the union may be able to place him on its rolls. The agency shop arrangement proposed here removes that choice from the union and places the option of membership in the employee while still requiring the same monetary support as does the union shop. Such a difference between the union and agency shop may be of great importance in some contexts, but for present purposes it is more formal than real. To the extent that it has any significance at all, it serves rather than violates, the desire of Congress to reduce the evils of compulsory unionism while allowing financial support for the bargaining agent.[12]

---

[12] Also wide of the mark is respondent's further suggestion that Congress contemplated the obligation to pay fees and dues to be imposed only in connection with actual membership in the un-

In short, the employer categorically refused to bargain with the union over a proposal for an agreement within the proviso to § 8(a)(3) and as such, lawful, for the purposes of this case. By the same token, § 7, and derivatively § 8(a)(1), cannot be deemed to forbid the employer to enter such agreements, since it too is expressly limited by the § 8(a)(3) proviso. We hold that the employer was not excused from his duty to bargain over the proposal on the theory that his acceding to it would necessarily involve him in an unfair labor practice. Whether a different result obtains in States which have declared such arrangements unlawful is an issue still to be resolved in *Retail Clerks Union v. Schermerhorn,* 373 U.S. 746 (1963), and one which is of no relevance here because Indiana law does not forbid the present contract proposal. In the context of this case, then, the employer cannot justify his refusal to bargain. He violated § 8(a)(5), and the Board properly ordered him to return to the bargaining table.

Reversed and remanded.

MR. JUSTICE GOLDBERG took no part in the consideration or decision of this case.

———

Marquez v. Screen Actors Guild, Inc., 119 S. Ct. 292 (1998). The Screen Actors Guild (SAG) negotiated a bargaining agreement with Lakeside Productions, a movie producer. The contract contained a union security clause requiring each employee with thirty days of employment in the motion picture industry to become "a member of the Union in good standing." Since Marquez had previously been employed in the industry for over thirty days, SAG insisted that she become a member as a condition of employment on a one-day job with Lakeside. When she failed to join, Lakeside hired another performer. Marquez filed suit alleging that SAG had breached its duty of fair representation by negotiating and enforcing a union security clause that required "membership" in SAG without expressly indicating that under *General Motors* employees need only become "financial core" members, by failing to explicitly apprise employees of their right to object to dues expenditures for reasons unrelated to collective bargaining, contract administration, and grievance handling under *Communications Workers v. Beck,* 487 U.S. 735 (1988), *infra,* and by requiring individuals with thirty days

———

ion, so as to insure the enjoyment of all union benefits and rights by those from whom money is extracted. Congress, it is said, had no desire to open the door to compulsory contracts which extract money but exclude the contributing employees from union membership. But, as analyzed by the Board and as the case comes to us, there is no closed-union aspect to the present proposal by the union. Membership remains optional with the employee and the significance of desired, but unavailable, union membership, or the benefits of membership, in terms of permissible § 8(a)(3) security contracts, we leave for another case....

of employment in the motion picture industry to become SAG members as soon as they accept employment with any production company.

The Supreme Court unanimously held that the mere negotiation of a union security clause tracking the language of the proviso to § 8(a)(3) requiring "membership" in the union does not itself constitute a breach of the duty of fair representation. A plaintiff must provide additional information from which a court could find that the union in negotiating this language acted arbitrarily, discriminatorily, or in bad faith. To prevail on such a claim, a plaintiff would have to establish that the union had used the language in question in a bad faith effort to mislead employees. Marquez did not claim that SAG had used dues money to support inappropriate expenditures under *Beck*, thus no fair representation claim could be maintained with respect to this issue. The Court declined to decide whether the failure of a representative labor organization to notify bargaining unit members in a non-bargaining agreement publication of their right to become "financial core" members and their right to challenge improper expenditures under *Beck* might constitute a fair representation breach, because the lower appellate court had properly decided to remand this question to the district court for further proceedings.

The Supreme Court finally held that the challenge to the thirty-day-in-the-industry provision did not raise an independent fair representation question but merely raised unfair labor practice issues under §§ 8(a)(3) and 8(b)(2) that are within the primary jurisdiction of the NLRB. As a result, neither a federal court nor a state court had jurisdiction to determine this question.

NOTES

1. *Duty to Inform Employees of Union Security Rights/Obligations.* Does a union retain a significant practical advantage in being able to include union shop, rather than agency shop, language in a collective agreement? The Labor Board thinks so, and in *California Saw & Knife Works*, 320 N.L.R.B. 224 (1995), *enforced*, 133 F.3d 1012 (7th Cir. 1998), it held that: (1) fair representation principles apply to the writing of union-security agreements under the NLRA; and (2) a union must inform all bargaining unit employees, including both union members and nonmembers, of their rights under *General Motors* to become and remain "financial core members" and under *Communications Workers v. Beck*, 487 U.S. 735 (1988), to pay only for the support of union activities germane to collective bargaining. Should these obligations be imposed under the union security proviso to § 8(a)(3) to extend similar duties to both labor organizations *and* employers that enter into collective agreements containing union security clauses? Could the Labor Board adopt a rule requiring employers to post notices generally describing the rights and obligations of employees under the NLRA, including those arising under § 7 and under the union security proviso to § 8(a)(3)?

In *Nielsen v. Machinists Lodge 2569*, 94 F.3d 1107 (7th Cir. 1996), *cert. denied*, 520 U.S. 1165 (1997), the court held that a union security clause was not facially invalid because it failed to inform members of their *Beck* rights. Enforcement did not violate the union's duty of fair representation, since the union newspaper had provided a well marked notice about *Beck* rights.

2. *Discharge for Reasons Other than Nonpayment of Dues.* Is there any practical difference between the "union shop" and the "agency shop"? In *Union Starch & Ref. Co.*, 87 N.L.R.B. 779 (1949), *enforced*, 186 F.2d 1008 (7th Cir.), *cert. denied*, 342 U.S. 815 (1951), the Labor Board held employees could not lawfully be discharged so long as they tendered their initiation fees and dues, even though they refused to comply with a union rule requiring all applicants to attend a union meeting and to take a membership oath. Similarly, workers meet the "membership" requirement as long as they continue to pay union dues, despite their formal resignation from the union ("financial core members"). *Marlin Rockwell Corp.*, 114 N.L.R.B. 553 (1955).

A union or agency shop provision may not be used to enforce membership obligations not relating to dues payments. Thus, for example, a discharge for failure to pay a union fine is an unfair labor practice. *Electric Auto-Lite Co.*, 92 N.L.R.B. 1073 (1950), *enforced per curiam*, 196 F.2d 500 (6th Cir.), *cert. denied*, 344 U.S. 823 (1952). In *Transportation Workers Local 525 (Johnson Controls World Servs.)*, 326 N.L.R.B. No. 3, 159 L.R.R.M. 1 (1998), the Board held that a union that had lawfully and permanently expelled a member for circulating a petition seeking to replace the incumbent union with a rival could not invoke the union security clause against him if he stopped paying his dues. Carefully distinguished was *Boilermakers (Kaiser Cement Corp.)*, 312 N.L.R.B. 218 (1993), *affirmed*, 56 F.3d 1438 (D.C. Cir. 1995), *cert. denied*, 516 U.S. 1171 (1996), in which the Board had held that a labor organization that merely suspended members from union activities could continue to enforce union security clause obligations against those individuals. The Board's *Transportation Workers Local 525* holding relied on the portion of the § 8(a)(3) union security proviso indicating that "no employer shall justify any discrimination against an employee for non-membership in a labor organization ... if he has reasonable grounds for believing that membership was denied or terminated for reasons other than the failure of the employee to tender the periodic dues."

Although unions may refund a portion of monthly dues to members who attend union meetings, requiring those who do not attend to pay the full amount (*Pulp & Paper Workers Local 171 (Boise Cascade Corp.)*, 165 N.L.R.B. 971 (1967)), they may not impose higher dues as a penalty on those who do not attend meetings (*Electric Auto-Lite Co.*, 92 N.L.R.B. 1073 (1950), *enforced*, 196 F.2d 500 (6th Cir.), *cert. denied*, 344 U.S. 823 (1952)).

3. *Belated Tender of Dues.* Employees expelled from a union for dues delinquency may lawfully be discharged even though they make a belated tender of all back dues after their discharge has been requested but before it actually occurs. *General Motors Corp., Packard Elec. Div.*, 134 N.L.R.B. 1107 (1961).

4. *Duration of Obligation.* A union and an employer may lawfully agree that employees on layoff must continue to pay dues to the union or lose their accrued vacation benefits and their seniority for purposes of recall. *See Machinists Lodge 1561 (Bendix Corp.)*, 205 N.L.R.B. 770 (1973). *Cf. Machinists Dist. 9 (Borg-Warner Corp.)*, 237 N.L.R.B. 1278 (1978) (requiring "full and timely notification" to an employee on sick leave).

5. *Oral Arrangements.* An oral union security agreement is enforceable. Both union and employer have a stringent burden of proof, however, in establishing the existence and precise terms of the agreement, and in establishing that affected employees have been fully and unmistakably notified about it. *Pacific Iron & Metal Co.*, 175 N.L.R.B. 604 (1969).

6. *Dues Checkoff Authorizations.* An employee who resigns from a union may still be subject to a dues checkoff, unless there is a timely revocation of the checkoff authorization. *UAW Local 1752 (Schweizer Aircraft Corp.)*, 320 N.L.R.B. 528 (1995), *affirmed*, 105 F.3d 787 (2d Cir. 1996); *Williams v. NLRB*, 105 F.3d 787 (2d Cir. 1996). In *United Food & Commercial Workers v. NLRB*, 975 F.2d 40 (2d Cir. 1992), the court held that in the absence of express language forbidding the partial revocation of dues checkoff agreements, employees could partially revoke their checkoff authorizations to prevent the deduction of money to support union organizing campaigns.

7. *Excessive Initiation Fees.* In the first court case to arise under § 8(b)(5), which makes it unlawful to "require of employees covered by an agreement authorized under subsection (a)(3) the payment, as a condition precedent to becoming a member of such organization, of a fee in an amount which the Board finds excessive or discriminatory under all the circumstances," the Third Circuit in *Television & Radio Broadcasting Studio Employees, Local 804*, 315 F.2d 398 (3d Cir. 1963), upheld the Board's finding that a union's increase of its initiation fee from $50 to $500 was excessive, discriminatory, and violative of the Act. *See also Longshoremen Local 1419 (New Orleans S.S. Ass'n)*, 186 N.L.R.B. 646 (1970) (increase from $500 to $1000).

The Board has held that a union can lawfully charge members who have become delinquent in their dues payments a "reinstatement fee" in excess of the initiation fee charged to new members. *See Food Mach. & Chem. Corp.*, 99 N.L.R.B. 1430 (1952).

8. *Religious Accommodation.* Section 19 of the NLRA was amended in 1980 to extend special protection to persons with religious scruples against "joining or financially supporting labor organizations." Such individuals may be required to contribute amounts equal to the initiation fees and periodic dues to non-labor, non-religious charitable organizations, and they may be charged the reasonable cost of grievance processing if they invoke contractual grievance procedures. The Sixth Circuit has found that § 19 unconstitutionally discriminates among religions, since it only protects members of "bona fide" religious organizations that have "traditional tenets" precluding financial support of unions. *Wilson v. NLRB*, 920 F.2d 1282 (6th Cir. 1990), *cert. denied*, 505 U.S. 1218 (1992).

9. *See generally* Haggard, *Union Checkoff Arrangements Under the National Labor Relations Act*, 39 DePaul L. Rev. 567 (1990); Haggard, *A Clarification of the Types of Union Security Agreements Affirmatively Permitted by Federal Statutes,* 5 Rutgers-Camden L. Rev. 418 (1974); Mayer, *Union Security and the Taft-Hartley Act,* 1961 Duke L.J. 505; Rosenthal, *The National Labor Relations Act and Compulsory Unionism,* 1954 Wis. L. Rev. 53.

ELLIS v. BROTHERHOOD OF RAILWAY, AIRLINE & STEAMSHIP CLERKS

Supreme Court of the United States
466 U.S. 435, 104 S. Ct. 1883, 80 L. Ed. 2d 428 (1984)

JUSTICE WHITE delivered the opinion of the Court.

In 1951, Congress amended the Railway Labor Act (the Act or RLA) to permit what it had previously prohibited—the union shop. Section 2, Eleventh of the Act permits a union and an employer to require all employees in the relevant bargaining unit to join the union as a condition of continued employment. 45 U.S.C. § 152, Eleventh. In *Machinists v. Street,* 367 U.S. 740 (1960), the Court held that the Act does not authorize a union to spend an objecting employee's money to support political causes. The use of employee funds for such ends is unrelated to Congress' desire to eliminate "free riders" and the resentment they provoked. *Id.,* at 768-769. The Court did not express a view as to "expenditures for activities in the area between the costs which led directly to the complaint as to 'free riders,' and the expenditures to support union political activities." *Id.,* at 769-770 and n. 18. Petitioners challenge just such expenditures.

I

In 1971, respondent Brotherhood of Railway, Airline and Steamship Clerks (the union or BRAC) and Western Airlines implemented a previously negotiated agreement requiring that all Western's clerical employees join the union within 60 days of commencing employment. As the agreement has been interpreted, employees need not become formal members of the union, but must pay agency fees equal to members' dues. Petitioners are present or former clerical employees of Western who objected to the use of their compelled dues for specified union activities. They do not contest the legality of the union shop as such, nor could they. *See Railway Employees' Department v. Hanson,* 351 U.S. 225 (1956). They do contend, however, that they can be compelled to contribute no more than their pro rata share of the expenses of negotiating agreements and settling grievances with Western Airlines. Respondents—the national union, its board of adjustment, and three locals—concede that the statutory authorization of the union shop does not permit the use of petitioners' contributions for union political or ideological activities, *see Machinists v. Street, supra,* and have adopted a rebate program covering such expenditures. The parties disagree about the adequacy of the rebate scheme, and about the legality of burdening objecting employees with six specific union expenses that fall between the extremes identified in *Hanson* and *Street:* the quadrennial Grand Lodge convention, litigation not involving the negotiation of agreements or agreements of settlement of grievances, union publications, social activities, death benefits for employees, and general organizing efforts.

The District Court for the Southern District of California granted summary judgment to petitioners on the question of liability. Relying entirely on *Street,* it found that the six expenses at issue here, among others, were all "non-collective bargaining activities" that could not be supported by dues collected from protesting employees. After a trial on damages, the court concluded that with regard to political and ideological activities, the union's existing rebate program, under which objecting employees were ultimately reimbursed for their share of union expenditures on behalf of political and charitable causes, was a good faith effort to comply with legal requirements and adequately protected employees' rights. Relying on exhibits presented by respondents, the court ordered refunds of approximately 40% of dues paid for the expenditures at issue here. It also required that protesting employees' annual dues thereafter be reduced by the amount spent on activities not chargeable to them during the prior year. The court seems to have envisioned that this scheme would supplant the already-existing rebate scheme, for it included political expenditures among those to be figured into the dues reduction.

The Court of Appeals for the Ninth Circuit affirmed in part and reversed in part. 685 F.2d 1065 (1982). It held that the union's rebate plan was adequate even though it allowed the union to collect the full amount of a protesting employee's dues, use part of the dues for objectionable purposes, and only pay the rebate a year later. It found suggestions in this Court's cases that such a method would be acceptable, and had itself approved the rebate approach in an earlier case. The opinion did not address the dues reduction scheme imposed by the District Court. *Id.,* at 1069-1070. Turning to the question of permissible expenditures, the Court of Appeals framed "the relevant inquiry [a]s whether a particular challenged expenditure is germane to the union's work in the realm of collective bargaining.... [That is, whether it] can be seen to promote, support or maintain the union as an effective collective bargaining agent." *Id.,* at 1072, 1074-1075. The court found that each of the challenged activities strengthened the union as a whole and helped it to run more smoothly, thus making it better able to negotiate and administer agreements. Because the six activities ultimately benefited the union's collective bargaining efforts, the union was free to finance them with dues collected from objecting employees. One judge dissented, arguing that these were all "institutional expenses" that objecting employees cannot be forced to pay. *Id.,* at 1075-1076.

Petitioners sought review of the Court of Appeals' ruling on permissible expenses and the adequacy of the rebate scheme. We granted certiorari. We hold that the union's rebate scheme was inadequate and that the Court of Appeals erred in finding that the RLA authorizes a union to spend compelled dues for its general litigation and organizing efforts.

II

... As the Court of Appeals pointed out, there is language in this Court's cases to support the validity of a rebate program. *Street* suggested "restitution to each individual employee of that portion of his money which the union expended, despite his notification, for the political causes to which he had advised the union he was opposed." 367 U.S., at 775. *See also Abood v. Detroit Board of Education,* 431 U.S. 209, 238 (1977). On the other hand, we suggested a more precise advance reduction scheme in *Railway Clerks v. Allen,* 373 U.S. 113, 122 (1963), where we described a "practical decree" comprising a refund of exacted funds in the proportion that union political expenditures bore to total union expenditures and the reduction of future exactions by the same proportion. Those opinions did not, nor did they purport to, pass upon the statutory or constitutional adequacy of the suggested remedies. Doing so now, we hold that the pure rebate approach is inadequate.

By exacting and using full dues, then refunding months later the portion that it was not allowed to exact in the first place, the union effectively charges the employees for activities that are outside the scope of the statutory authorization. The cost to the employee is, of course, much less than if the money was never returned, but this is a difference of degree only. The harm would be reduced were the union to pay interest on the amount refunded, but respondents did not do so. Even then the union obtains an involuntary loan for purposes to which the employee objects.

The only justification for this union borrowing would be administrative convenience. But there are readily available alternatives, such as advance reduction of dues and/or interest-bearing escrow accounts, that place only the slightest additional burden, if any on the union. Given the existence of acceptable alternatives, the union cannot be allowed to commit dissenters' funds to improper uses even temporarily. A rebate scheme reduces but does not eliminate the statutory violation.

III

Petitioners' primary submission is that the use of their fees to finance the challenged activities violated the First Amendment. This argument assumes that the Act allows these allegedly unconstitutional exactions. When the constitutionality of a statute is challenged, this Court first ascertains whether the statute can be reasonably construed to avoid the constitutional difficulty. *E.g., Califano v. Yamasaki,* 442 U.S. 682, 692-693 (1979); *Ashwander v. TVA,* 297 U.S. 288, 347 (1936) (concurring opinion); *Crowell v. Benson,* 285 U.S. 22, 62 (1932)....

IV

Section 2, Eleventh contains only one explicit limitation to the scope of the union shop agreement: objecting employees may not be required to tender "fines and penalties" normally required of union members. 45 U.S.C. § 152, Eleventh. If there were nothing else, an inference could be drawn from this limited exception that all other payments obtained from voluntary members can also be required of those whose membership is forced upon them. Indeed, several witnesses appearing before the congressional committees objected to the absence of any explicit limitation on the scope or amount of fees or dues that could be compelled. That Congress enacted the provision over these objections arguably indicates that it was willing to tolerate broad exactions from objecting employees.

Furthermore, Congress was well aware of the broad scope of traditional union activities. The hearing witnesses referred in general terms to the costs of "[a]ctivities of labor organizations resulting in the procurement of employee benefits," Hearings on H.R. 7789 before the House Committee on Interstate and Foreign Commerce, 81st Cong., 2d Sess., 10 (1950) (testimony of George Harrison), and the "policies and activities of labor unions," *id.,* at 50 (testimony of George Weaver). Indeed, it was pointed out that not only was the "securing and maintaining of a collective bargaining agreement ... an expensive undertaking ..., there are many other programs of a union" that require the financial and moral support of the workers. *Id.,* at 275; Hearings on S. 3295 before a Subcommittee of the Senate Committee on Labor and Public Welfare, 81st Cong., 2d Sess., 236 (1950) (statement of Theodore Brown). In short, Congress was adequately informed about the broad scope of union activities aimed at benefiting union members, and, in light of the absence of express limitations in § 2, Eleventh it could be plausibly argued that Congress purported to authorize the collection from involuntary members of the same dues paid by regular members. This view, however, was squarely rejected in *Street,* over the dissents of three Justices, and the cases that followed it.

In *Street,* the Court observed that the purpose of § 2, Eleventh was to make it possible to require all members of a bargaining unit to pay their fair share of the costs of performing the function of exclusive bargaining agent. The union shop would eliminate "free riders," employees who obtained the benefit of the union's participation in the machinery of the Act without financially supporting the union. That purpose, the Court held, Congress intended to be achieved without "vesting the unions with unlimited power to spend exacted money." 367 U.S., at 768. Undoubtedly, the union could collect from all employees what it needed to defray the expenses entailed in negotiating and administering a collective agreement and in adjusting grievances and disputes. The Court had so held in *Railway Employes Department v. Hanson,* 351 U.S. 225 (1936). But the authority to impose dues and fees was restricted at least to the "extent of denying the union the right, over the employee's objection, to use his money to support political causes which he opposes," 367 U.S., at 768, even though Congress was well aware that unions had historically expended funds in support of political candidates and issues. Employees could be required to become "members" of the union, but those who objected could not be burdened with any part of the union's expenditures in support of political or ideological causes. The Court expressed no view on other union expenses not directly involved in negotiating and administering the contract and in settling grievances.

Railway Clerks v. Allen, 373 U.S. 113 (1963), reaffirmed the approach taken in *Street,* and described the union expenditures that could fairly be charged to all employees as those "germane to collective bargaining." *Id.,* at 121, 122. Still later, in *Abood v. Board of Education,* 431 U.S. 209 (1977), we found no constitutional barrier to an agency shop agreement between a municipality and a teachers' union insofar as the agreement required every employee in the unit to pay a service fee to defray the costs of collective bargaining, contract administration, and grievance adjustment. The union, however, could not, consistently with the Constitution, collect from dissenting employees any sums for the support of ideological causes not germane to its duties as collective-bargaining agent. In neither *Allen* nor *Abood,* however, did the Court find it necessary further to define the line between union expenditures that all employees must help defray and those that are not sufficiently related to collective bargaining to justify their being imposed on dissenters.

We remain convinced that Congress' essential justification for authorizing the union shop was the desire to eliminate free riders—employees in the bargaining unit on whose behalf the union was obliged to perform its statutory functions, but who refused to contribute to the cost thereof. Only a union that is certified as the exclusive bargaining agent is authorized to negotiate a contract requiring all employees to become members of or to make contributions to the union. Until such a contract is executed, no dues or fees may be collected from objecting employees who are not members of the union; and by the same token, any obligatory payments required by a contract authorized by § 2, Eleventh terminate if the union ceases to be the exclusive bargaining agent. Hence, when employees such as petitioners object to being burdened with particular union expenditures, the test must be whether the challenged expenditures are necessarily or reasonably incurred for the purpose of performing the duties of an exclusive representative of the employees in dealing with the employer on labor-management issues. Under this standard, objecting employees may be compelled to pay their fair share of not only the direct costs of negotiating and administering a collective-bargaining contract and of settling grievances and disputes, but also the expenses of activities or undertakings normally or reasonably employed to implement or effectuate the duties of the union as exclusive representative of the employees in the bargaining unit.

With these considerations in mind, we turn to the particular expenditures for which petitioners insist they may not be charged.

V

Core member must support conventions

1. *Conventions.* Every four years, BRAC holds a national convention at which the members elect officers, establish bargaining goals and priorities, and formulate overall union policy. We have very little trouble in holding that petitioners must help defray the costs of these conventions. Surely if a union is to perform its statutory functions, it must maintain its corporate or associational existence, must elect officers to manage and carry on its affairs, and may consult its members about overall bargaining goals and policy. Conventions such as those at issue here are normal events about which Congress was thoroughly informed and seem to us to be essential to the union's discharge of its duties as bargaining agent. As the Court of Appeals pointed out, convention "activities guide the union's approach to collective bargaining and are directly related to its effectiveness in negotiating labor agreements." 685 F.2d at 1073. In fact, like all national unions, BRAC is required to hold either a referendum or a convention at least every five years for the election of officers. 29 U.S.C. § 481(a). We cannot fault it for choosing to elect its officers at a convention rather than by referendum.

2. *Social Activities.* Approximately .7% of Grand Lodge expenditures go toward purchasing refreshments for union business meetings and occasional social activities. 685 F.2d, at 1074. These activities are formally open to nonmember employees. Petitioners insist that these expenditures are entirely unrelated to the union's function as collective-bargaining representative and therefore could not be charged to them. While these affairs are not central to collective bargaining, they are sufficiently related to it to be charged to all employees. As the Court of Appeals noted, "[t]hese small expenditures are important to the union's members because they bring about harmonious working relationships, promote closer ties among employees, and create a more pleasant environment for union meetings." *Ibid.*

We cannot say that these *de minimis* expenses are beyond the scope of the Act. Like conventions, social activities at union meetings are a standard feature of union operations. In a revealing statement, Senator Thomas, Chairman of the Senate Subcommittee, made clear his disinclination to have Congress define precisely what normal, minor union expenses could be charged to objectors; he did not want the bill to say "that the unions ... must not have any of the ... kinds of little dues that they take up for giving a party, or something of that nature." Senate Hearings, *supra,* at 173-174. There is no indication that other Members of

Congress were any more inclined to scrutinize the minor incidental expenses incurred by the union in running its operations.

3. *Publications.* The Grand Lodge puts out a monthly magazine, the *Railway Clerk/interchange,* paid for out of the union treasury. The magazine's contents are varied and include articles about negotiations, contract demands, strikes, unemployment and health benefits, proposed or recently enacted legislation, general news, products the union is boycotting, and recreational and social activities. See 685 F.2d at 1074.... The Court of Appeals found that the magazine "is the union's primary means of communicating information concerning collective bargaining, contract administration, and employees' rights to employees represented by BRAC." 685 F.2d, at 1074. Under the union's rebate policy, objecting employees are not charged for that portion of the magazine devoted to "political causes." The rebate is figured by calculating the number of lines that are devoted to political issues as a proportion of the total number of lines.

The union must have a channel for communicating with the employees, including the objecting ones, about its activities. Congress can be assumed to have known that union funds go toward union publications; it is an accepted and basic union activity. The costs of "worker education" were specifically mentioned during the hearings. House Hearings, *supra,* at 275; Senate Hearings, *supra,* at 236. The magazine is important to the union in carrying out its representational obligations and a reasonable way of reporting to its constituents.

Respondents' limitation on the publication costs charged objecting employees is an important one, however. If the union cannot spend dissenters' funds for a particular activity, it has no justification for spending their funds for writing about that activity.[11]

By the same token, the Act surely allows it to charge objecting employees for reporting to them about those activities it can charge them for doing.

4. *Organizing.* The Court of Appeals found that organizing expenses could be charged to objecting employees because organizing efforts are aimed toward a stronger union, which in turn would be more successful at the bargaining table. Despite this attenuated connection with collective bargaining, we think such expenditures are outside Congress' authorization. Several considerations support this conclusion.

First, the notion that § 2, Eleventh would be a tool for the expansion of overall union power appears nowhere in the legislative history. To the contrary, BRAC's president expressly disclaimed that the union shop was sought in order to strengthen the bargaining power of unions. "Nor was any claim seriously advanced that the union shop was necessary to hold or increase union membership." *Street,* 367 U.S., at 763. Thus, organizational efforts were not what Congress aimed to enhance by authorizing the union shop.

---

[11] Given our holding that objecting employees cannot be charged for union organizing or litigation, they cannot be charged for the expense of reporting those activities to the membership.

Second, where a union shop provision is in place and enforced, all employees in the relevant unit are already organized. By definition, therefore, organizing expenses are spent on employees outside the collective-bargaining unit already represented. Using dues exacted from an objecting employee to recruit members among workers outside the bargaining unit can afford only the most attenuated benefits to collective bargaining on behalf of the dues payer.

Third, the free-rider rationale does not extend this far. The image of the smug, self-satisfied nonmember, stirring up resentment by enjoying benefits earned through other employees' time and money, is completely out of place when it comes to the union's overall organizing efforts. If one accepts that what is good for the union is good for the employees, a proposition petitioners would strenuously deny, then it may be that employees will ultimately ride for free on the union's organizing efforts outside the bargaining unit. But the free rider Congress had in mind was the employee the union was required to represent and from whom it could not withhold benefits obtained for its members. Non-bargaining unit organizing is not directed at that employee. Organizing money is spent on people who are not union members, and only in the most distant way works to the benefit of those already paying dues. Any free-rider problem here is roughly comparable to that resulting from union contributions to pro-labor political candidates. As we observed in *Street,* that is a far cry from the free-rider problem with which Congress was concerned.

5. *Litigation.* The expenses of litigation incident to negotiating and administering the contract or to settling grievances and disputes arising in the bargaining unit are clearly chargeable to petitioners as a normal incident of the duties of the exclusive representative. The same is true of fair representation litigation arising within the unit, of jurisdictional disputes with other unions, and of any other litigation before agencies or in the courts that concerns bargaining unit employees and is normally conducted by the exclusive representative. The expenses of litigation not having such a connection with the bargaining unit are not to be charged to objecting employees. Contrary to the view of the Court of Appeals, therefore, unless the Western Airlines bargaining unit is directly concerned, objecting employees need not share the costs of the union's challenge to the legality of the airline industry mutual aid pact; of litigation seeking to protect the rights of airline employees generally during bankruptcy proceedings; or of defending suits alleging violation of the non-discrimination requirements of Title VII.

6. *Death benefits.* BRAC pays from its general funds a $300 death benefit to the designated beneficiary of any member or nonmember required to pay dues to the union. In *Street,* the Court did not adjudicate the legality under § 2, Eleventh of compelled participation in a death benefit program, citing it as an example of an expenditure in the area between the costs which led directly to the complaint as to "free riders," and the expenditures to support union political activities. 367 U.S., at 769-770 and n. 18. In *Allen,* the state trial court, like the District Court in this case, found that compelled payments to support BRAC's death benefit sys-

tem were not reasonably necessary or related to collective bargaining and could not be charged to objecting employees. *See* 373 U.S., at 117. We found it unnecessary to reach the correctness of that conclusion.

Here, the Court of Appeals said that death benefits have historically played an important role in labor organizations, that insurance benefits are a mandatory subject of bargaining, and that by providing such benefits itself rather than seeking them from the employer, BRAC is in a better position to negotiate for additional benefits or higher wages. The court added that "the provision of a death benefits plan, which tends to strengthen the employee's ties to the union, is germane to the work of the union within the realm of collective bargaining." 685 F.2d, at 1074....

We find it unnecessary to rule on this question. Because the union is no longer the exclusive bargaining agent and petitioners are no longer involved in the death benefits system, the only issue is whether petitioners are entitled to a refund of their past contributions. We think that they are not so entitled, even if they had the right to an injunction to prevent future collections from them for death benefits. Although they objected to the use of their funds to support the benefits plan, they remained entitled to the benefits of the plan as long as they paid their dues; they thus enjoyed a form of insurance for which the union collected a premium. We doubt that the equities call for a refund of those payments.

VI

Petitioners' primary argument is that for the union to compel their financial support of these six activities violates the First Amendment. We need only address this contention with regard to the three activities for which, we have held, the RLA allows the union to use their contributions. We perceive no constitutional barrier.

The First Amendment does limit the uses to which the union can put funds obtained from dissenting employees. *See generally Abood,* 431 U.S. 209. But by allowing the union shop at all, we have already countenanced a significant impingement on First Amendment rights. The dissenting employee is forced to support financially an organization with whose principles and demands he may disagree. "To be required to help finance the union as a collective bargaining agent might well be thought ... to interfere in some way with the employee's freedom to associate for the advancement of ideas, or to refrain from doing so, as he sees fit." *Id.,* at 222. It has long been settled that such interference with First Amendment rights is justified by the governmental interest in industrial peace. *Ibid.; Street,* 367 U.S., at 776, 778 (Douglas, J., concurring); *Hanson,* 351 U.S., at 238. At a minimum, the union may constitutionally "expend uniform exactions under the union-shop agreement in support of activities germane to collective bargaining." *Railway Clerks v. Allen,* 373 U.S., at 122. The issue is whether these expenses involve additional interference with the First Amendment interests of objecting employees, and, if so, whether they are nonetheless adequately supported by a governmental interest.

Petitioners do not explicitly contend that union social activities implicate serious First Amendment interests. We need not determine whether contributing money to such affairs is an act triggering First Amendment protection. To the extent it is, the communicative content is not inherent in the act, but stems from the union's involvement in it. The objection is that these are *union* social hours. Therefore, the fact that the employee is forced to contribute does not increase the infringement of his First Amendment rights already resulting from the compelled contribution to the union. Petitioners may feel that their money is not being well-spent, but that does not mean they have a First Amendment complaint.

The First Amendment concerns with regard to publications and conventions are more serious; both have direct communicative content and involve the expression of ideas. Nonetheless, we perceive little additional infringement of First Amendment rights beyond that already accepted, and none that is not justified by the governmental interests behind the union shop itself. As the discussion of these expenses indicated, they "relat[e] to the work of the union in the realm of collective bargaining." *Hanson,* 351 U.S., at 235. The very nature of the free-rider problem and the governmental interest in overcoming it require that the union have a certain flexibility in its use of compelled funds. "The furtherance of the common cause leaves some leeway for the leadership of the group." *Abood,* 431 U.S., at 222, quoting *Street,* 367 U.S., at 778 (Douglas, J., concurring). These expenses are well within the acceptable range.

VII

The Court of Appeals erred in holding that respondents were entitled to charge petitioners for their pro rata share of the union's organizing and litigating expenses, and that the former rebate scheme adequately protected the objecting employees from the misuse of their contributions. The decision of the Court of Appeals is affirmed in part and reversed in part and the case remanded for further proceedings consistent with this opinion.

It is so ordered.

JUSTICE POWELL, concurring in part and dissenting in part.

I am in accord with Parts I, II, III and IV of the Court's opinion, and with all of Part V except for Subsection 1, which addresses the "convention" issue. I also do not agree with the Court's analysis in Part VI in which petitioners' First Amendment arguments are disposed of summarily.

... I agree that conventions are necessary to elect officers, to determine union policy with respect to major issues of collective bargaining, and generally to enable the national union to perform its essential functions as the exclusive bargaining representative of employees. But, it is not seriously questioned that conventions also afford opportunities—that often are fully exploited—to further political objectives of unions generally and of the particular union in convention.

The District Court's findings in this case were based on the record with respect to the 25th quadrennial convention of BRAC. Its cost to the Union was approximately $1,802,000. The minutes of the convention indicate that a number of major addresses were made by prominent politicians, including Senators Humphrey, Kennedy, Hartke, and Schweiker, the Mayor of Washington, D. C., and four congressmen. The Union has not shown how this major participation of politicians contributed even remotely to collective bargaining. Before a union may compel dissenting employees to defray the cost of union expenses, it must meet its burden of showing that those expenses were "necessarily or reasonably incurred for the purpose of performing the duties of an exclusive [collective-bargaining] representative." *See Railway Clerks v. Allen,* 373 U.S., at 122. Apparently no effort was made by the Union in this case to identify expenses fairly attributable to these and other political activities, and to make appropriate deductions from the dues of objecting employees. I do not suggest that such an allocation can be made with mathematical exactitude. But reasonable estimates surely could have been made. See *id.* The Union properly felt a responsibility to allocate expenses where political material was carried in union publications.

In view of the foregoing, I do not understand how the Court can make the judgment today that all the expenses of the 25th quadrennial meeting of BRAC qualify under the Court's new standard as "necessarily or reasonably incurred for the purpose of performing the duties of an exclusive [collective-bargaining] representative." ...

... I have expressed my disagreement with the Court's apparent determination that the Railway Labor Act permits the use of compulsory dues to help defray the costs of political activities incurred at the quadrennial conventions. Under that interpretation of the Act, it would be unnecessary to reach the constitutional question in this case. Even if Congress had intended the Act to permit such use of compulsory dues, it is clear that the First Amendment would not. Where funds are used to further political causes with which non-members may disagree, the decisions of this Court are explicit that non-member employees may not be compelled to bear such expenditures. The Court's conclusory disposition of petitioners' argument ignores the force of these decisions. See *Abood,* 431 U.S., at 234; *Street,* 376 U.S., at 777-778 (Douglas, J., concurring)....

NOTES

1. In *Lehnert v. Ferris Faculty Ass'n,* 500 U.S. 507 (1991), the Supreme Court again addressed the right of labor organizations to expend dues money received from individuals who object to the use of their contributions for activities not related to collective bargaining. In this public sector case involving a teachers union, the Court formulated a three-part test to determine which union activities are constitutionally chargeable to dissenting employees. To be chargeable, the activities must: (1) be "germane" to collective bargaining activity; (2) be justified by the government's vital interest in labor peace and avoiding "free riders" who benefit from union efforts without paying for union services; and (3) not significantly add to the burdening of free speech inherent in the allowance of an agency or union shop.

The majority found that a local bargaining representative may charge objecting employees for their pro rata share of the costs associated with otherwise chargeable activities carried out by its state and national affiliates, even if those activities are not performed for the direct benefit of the objecting workers' bargaining unit. The Court recognized that the essence of an affiliation relationship involves the notion that the parent entity will bring to bear its often considerable economic, political, and informational resources when local unions are in need of them. As a result, that portion of a local's affiliation fee that contributes to the pool of resources potentially available to it is assessed for the protection of a bargaining unit, even if it is not actually expended on that unit in any particular membership year. This rule does not provide local unions with complete discretion regarding this issue, since there must be some indication that the payment to the state or national affiliate is for services that may ultimately inure to the benefit of the local members by virtue of their membership in the parent organization, and the majority stressed that the union bears the burden of demonstrating the proportion of chargeable expenses to total expenses. The majority rejected a "statutory duties" test proposed by Justice Scalia and three other Justices that would have only permitted the use of dissenter dues money for costs associated with the union's performance of duties statutorily imposed on exclusive bargaining agents. The majority found this test too restrictive.

The Court held that the following expenditures were properly chargeable to dissenting employees: (1) national union "program expenditures" destined for other states and the expenses of a national publication used to disseminate information germane to collective bargaining, even though the challenged activities did not directly benefit persons in the dissenters' own bargaining unit, due to the affiliation relationship involved; (2) information services concerning professional development, unemployment rights, job opportunities, and other miscellaneous matters that were neither political nor public in nature and that did benefit all teachers, even though they might not directly concern members of the dissenters' bargaining unit; (3) participation by local union delegates in state and national union meetings at which bargaining strategies and representational policies are developed; and (4) expenses incident to preparation for a strike, even one that would contravene the state public sector bargaining law, since preparation for such a job action would be inextricably intertwined with the collective bargaining function. Expenses incurred in connection with the conducting of an unlawful work stoppage would not be chargeable, however, since it would not advance any governmental interest to compel dissenting employees to subsidize activity a state has proscribed.

The Supreme Court also concluded that unions could not charge dissenters for lobbying, electoral, or other political activities beyond the limited context of contract negotiation or implementation, due to the free speech implications of such conduct. It would be rare for a private sector labor organization to be able to establish that lobbying activities are chargeable to dissenting unit personnel. The Court reiterated the view that litigation expenses are not chargeable, except when they concern the dissenters' own bargaining unit, because extra-unit litigation is akin to lobbying and is unrelated to the union's duties as bargaining representative. The Court finally indicated that public relations efforts designed to enhance the reputation of the teaching profession generally were not chargeable, due to the absence of any direct connection with the collective bargaining function. *Compare Reese v. City of Columbus*, 71 F.3d 619 (6th Cir. 1995), *cert. denied*, 519 U.S. 964 (1996), holding that a local union representing city employees could constitutionally include in "fair share" fee assessed against nonmembers its international union's expenses in publicly advertising union's positions on the negotiation and implementation of bargaining agreements, even though that benefited other bargaining units, since this practice could ultimately inure to the benefit of local employees.

A closely-divided Fourth Circuit has held that the Air Line Pilots Association could use nonmember agency fees to support work stoppages conducted by pilots employed by other carriers, due to the relatively direct impact of those negotiations on the wages and benefits enjoyed by all ALPA pilots. *Crawford v. ALPA*, 992 F.2d 1295 (4th Cir.) (*en banc*), *cert. denied*, 510 U.S. 869 (1993).

2. A court of appeals ruled that voluntary union members, as distinguished from nonmembers who are contractually required to pay agency shop fees, have no right under either the Railway Labor Act or the First Amendment to refuse to pay the costs of legitimate union activities even though they are unrelated to collective bargaining. *Kidwell v. Transportation Commun. Union,* 946 F.2d 283 (4th Cir. 1991), *cert. denied*, 503 U.S. 1005 (1992). Another court found no First Amendment violation when a union insisted that nonmember employees who failed to respond within 30 days to two written notices informing them of their right to object to paying for the union's nonrepresentational activities had to pay an agency shop fee equal to full union dues. *Mitchell v. Los Angeles Unified Sch. Dist.,* 963 F.2d 258 (9th Cir.), *cert. denied*, 506 U.S. 940 (1992).

3. The Railway Labor Act's union security authorization provision presented a potential constitutional question because of the governmental action involved in the overriding of contrary state laws. Unlike the RLA, the NLRA contains an anti-preemption provision in § 14(b), allowing state "right-to-work" laws to prohibit union security agreements despite the federal authorization for them. Thus, unions argued that the Supreme Court "need not strain to avoid the plain meaning" of the NLRA, which imposes no express restrictions on the spending of dues money. Nevertheless, in *Communications Workers v. Beck*, 487 U.S. 735 (1988), the Court held (5-3) that § 8(a)(3) of the NLRA, like § 2, Eleventh of the RLA, should be interpreted as forbidding union use of compulsory fees collected from objecting nonmember employees to fund activities unrelated to collective bargaining. Although the Court declared that the NLRB had primary jurisdiction over the § 8(a)(3) claim, it concluded a federal court could decide the merits of that claim insofar as it was necessary to resolve the employees' further challenge that the union had breached its duty of fair representation by its expenditures. The Court observed that the "same concern over the resentment spawned by 'free riders' in the railroad industry prompted Congress, four years after the passage of the Taft-Hartley Act, to amend the RLA," and that, in those circumstances, "Congress intended the same language to have the same meaning in both statutes." *See* Dau-Schmidt, *Union Security Agreements Under the National Labor Relations Act: The Statute, the Constitution, and the Court's Opinion in Beck*, 27 Harv. J. Legis. 51 (1990).

4. *Chicago Teachers Union, Local 1 v. Hudson*, 475 U.S. 292 (1986), concerned the constitutional validity of the procedures adopted by the school district and the union to permit employees required by an agency shop provision to provide financial support to the labor organization to challenge that portion of their payments being expended for political or ideological causes unrelated to collective bargaining. The Court found the established procedures to be inadequate, since they were entirely controlled by the union itself and they included an impermissible rebate scheme.

> The procedure that was initially adopted by the Union ... contained three fundamental flaws. First, as in *Ellis v. Railway Clerks*, 466 U.S. 435 (1984), a remedy which merely offers dissenters the possibility of a rebate does not avoid the risk that dissenters' funds may be used temporarily for an improper purpose.... The amount at stake for each individual dissenter does not diminish this concern. For, whatever the amount, the quality of respondents' interest in not being compelled to subsidize the propagation of political or ideological views that they oppose is clear.... A forced exaction followed by a rebate equal to the amount improperly expended is ... not a permissible response to the nonunion employees' objections.
>
> Second, the "advance reduction of dues" was inadequate because it provided nonmembers with inadequate information about the basis for the proportionate share. In *Abood*, we reiterated that the nonunion employee has the burden of raising an objection, but that the union retains the burden of proof.... Basic considerations of fairness, as well as concern for the First Amendment rights at stake, also dictate that the potential objectors be given sufficient information to gauge the propriety of the union's fee....
>
> Finally, the original Union procedure was also defective because it did not provide for a reasonably prompt decision by an impartial decisionmaker.

> Although we have not so specified in the past, we now conclude that such a requirement is necessary. The nonunion employee, whose First Amendment rights are affected by the agency shop itself and who bears the burden of objecting, is entitled to have his objections addressed in an expeditious, fair, and objective manner.

The Court went on to indicate that "a full-dress administrative hearing, with evidentiary safeguards, is [not] part of the 'constitutional minimum.' ... [A]n expeditious arbitration might satisfy the requirement of a reasonably prompt decision by an impartial decisionmaker, so long as the arbitrator's selection did not represent the Union's unrestricted choice."

In *Air Line Pilots Assn. v. Miller*, 523 U.S. 866 (1998), the Supreme Court held that a labor organization may not unilaterally impose union-created arbitral procedures on nonunion employees who object to the amount of service fees assessed to "financial core members," because those procedures would impermissibly deprive the objecting individuals of access to other forums. The court concluded that *Chicago Teachers v. Hudson* did not authorize unions to require nonmembers to resolve agency fee disputes through union-established procedures, but merely authorized labor organizations to make such procedures available to objecting unit members.

5. A labor organization may not normally require agency-fee objectors to renew their objections to inappropriate union expenditures on an annual basis because their initial objections are presumed to continue from year to year. *See Shea v. Machinists Union*, 154 F.3d 508 (5th Cir. 1998).

6. A labor organization has to supply agency-fee payers with sufficient financial data to enable them to decide whether to object to any portion of their dues being expended for inappropriate purposes. Although one court has ruled that a union may reasonably assume for accounting purposes that the allocation between chargeable and nonchargeable expenditures for the international organization is equal to the allocation for each local union [*Price v. Automobile Workers*, 927 F.2d 88 (2d Cir. 1991)], another court has held that agency-fee payers are entitled to the disclosure of sufficient information to apprise them of the actual use being made by the international entity of their dues money [*Tierney v. City of Toledo*, 917 F.2d 927 (6th Cir. 1990)]. In *Teamsters Local 443 (Conn. Limousine Serv.)*, 324 N.L.R.B. No. 105, 156 L.R.R.M. 1129 (1997), the Board held that a union did not breach its duty of fair representation when it provided objectors with financial information that broke down union expenditures into thirteen categories from its annual LM-2 report and another seven categories and listed separate "chargeable" and "nonchargeable" amounts for each category. *See also Finerty v. NLRB*, 113 F.3d 1288 (D.C. Cir.), *cert. denied*, 118 S. Ct. 558 (1997) (international union with 2400 different bargaining units allowed to allocate chargeable fees for objecting members on nationwide, rather than unit-by-unit, basis).

Must a labor organization provide nonmember objectors with financial information that has been verified by an independent auditor or may they rely on their own internal auditors? *Compare IAM v. NLRB (California Saw & Knife Works)*, 133 F.3d 1012 (7th Cir. 1998) (internal union auditor sufficient) *with Ferriso v. NLRB*, 125 F.3d 865 (D.C. Cir. 1997) (requiring independent auditor).

7. *See generally* Hartley, *Constitutional Values and the Adjudication of Taft-Hartley Act Dues Objector Cases*, 41 Hastings L.J. 1 (1989); Cloke, *Mandatory Political Contributions and Union Democracy,* 4 Indus. Rel. L.J. 527 (1981); Gaebler, *Union Political Activity or Collective Bargaining? First Amendment Limitations on the Use of Union Shop Funds,* 14 U.C. Davis L. Rev. 591 (1981); Henkel & Wood, *Limitations on the Use of Union Shop Funds After Ellis: What Activities Are "Germane" to Collective Bargaining?* 35 Lab. L.J. 736 (1984); Rehmus & Kerner, *The Agency Shop After Abood: No Free Ride but What's the Fare?,* 34 Indus. & Lab. Rel. Rev. 90 (1980); Wellington, *Machinists v. Street: Statutory Interpretation and the Avoidance of Constitutional Issues,* 1961 Sup. Ct. Rev. 49; Comment, *Collective Bargaining v. The First Amendment: Court-Ordered Remedies for the Political Use of Mandatory Union Fees,* 18 U.C. Davis L. Rev. 555 (1985).

c. State "Right-to-Work" Legislation

STATUTORY REFERENCE

NLRA § 14(b)

Twenty-one states (Alabama, Arizona, Arkansas, Florida, Georgia, Idaho, Iowa, Kansas, Louisiana, Mississippi, Nebraska, Nevada, North Carolina, North Dakota, South Carolina, South Dakota, Tennessee, Texas, Utah, Virginia, and Wyoming, Lab. Rel. Rep. LRX 730:319) have "right-to-work" laws, which consist of constitutional or statutory prohibitions of union security arrangements. These laws take a variety of forms. Some merely forbid making union "membership" (or "nonmembership") a condition of employment. Such narrowly worded laws have invariably been interpreted by state courts or state attorneys general as reaching the agency shop as well as the union shop. Other statutes expressly prohibit conditioning employment on the payment of "dues, fees, or other charges of any kind" to a union. Several right-to-work laws go further, proscribing any "employment monopoly," or sanctioning individual bargaining despite the presence of a majority union. Enforcement provisions also vary widely. Most laws allow damages to persons injured by a violation, and many authorize injunctions. About half prescribe criminal penalties.

RETAIL CLERKS, LOCAL 1625 v. SCHERMERHORN

Supreme Court of the United States
373 U.S. 746, 83 S. Ct. 1461, 10 L. Ed. 2d 678 (1963)

[A collective bargaining agreement provided that employees who chose not to join the union would be required, as a condition of employment, to pay "service fees" to the union equal to the regular initiation fee and membership dues. Four nonunion employees sued to enjoin enforcement of this so-called agency shop clause on the ground it violated Florida's right-to-work law, which forbade denying a person the right to work on account of "membership or nonmembership" in a labor union. The Florida Supreme Court held its state law valid and applicable.]

MR. JUSTICE WHITE delivered the opinion of the Court....

... As is immediately apparent from its language, § 14(b) was designed to prevent other sections of the Act from completely extinguishing state power over certain union-security arrangements. And it was the proviso to § 8(a)(3), expressly permitting agreements conditioning employment upon membership in a labor union, which Congress feared might have this result. It was desired to "make certain" that § 8(a)(3) could not "be said to authorize arrangements of this sort in States where such arrangements were contrary to the State policy." H.R. Conf. Rep. No. 510, 80th Cong., 1st Sess. 60, 1 Leg. Hist. L.M.R.A. 564.

The connection between the § 8(a)(3) proviso and § 14(b) is clear. Whether they are perfectly coincident, we need not now decide, but unquestionably they overlap to some extent. At the very least, the agreements requiring "membership" in a labor union which are expressly permitted by the proviso are the same "membership" agreements expressly placed within the reach of state law by § 14(b). It follows that the *General Motors* case rules this one, for we there held that the "agency shop" arrangement involved here—which imposes on employees the only membership obligation enforceable under § 8(a) (3) by discharge, namely, the obligation to pay initiation fees and regular dues—is the "practical equivalent" of an "agreement requiring membership in a labor organization as a condition of employment." Whatever may be the status of less stringent union-security arrangements, the agency shop is within § 14(b). At least to that extent did Congress intend § 8(a)(3) and § 14(b) to coincide.

Petitioners, belatedly, would now distinguish the contract involved here from the agency shop contract dealt with in the *General Motors* case on the basis of allegedly distinctive features which are said to require a different result. Article 19 provides for nonmember payments to the union "for the purpose of aiding the Union in defraying costs in connection with its legal obligations and responsibilities as the exclusive bargaining agent of the employees in the appropriate bargaining unit," a provision which petitioners say confines the use of nonmember payments to collective bargaining purposes alone and forbids their use by the union for institutional purposes unrelated to its exclusive agency functions, all in sharp contrast, it is argued, to the *General Motors* situation where the nonmember contributions are available to the union without restriction.

We are wholly unpersuaded. There is before us little more than a complaint with its exhibits. The agency shop clause of the contract is, at best, ambiguous on its face and it should not, in the present posture of the case, be construed against respondent to raise a substantial difference between this and the *General Motors* case. There is no ironclad restriction imposed upon the use of nonmember fees, for the clause merely describes the payments as being for "the purpose of aiding the Union" in meeting collective bargaining expenses. The alleged restriction would not be breached if the service fee was used for both collective bargaining and other expenses, for the union would be "aided" in meeting its agency obligations, not only by the part spent for bargaining purposes but also by the part spent for institutional items, since an equivalent amount of other union income would thereby be freed to pay the costs of bargaining agency functions.

But even if all collections from nonmembers must be directly committed to paying bargaining costs, this fact is of bookkeeping significance only rather than a matter of real substance. It must be remembered that the service fee is admittedly the exact equal of membership initiation fees and monthly dues, ... and that, as the union says in its brief, dues collected from members may be used for a "variety of purposes, in addition to meeting the union's costs of collective bargaining." Unions "rather typically" use their membership dues "to do those things which the members authorize the union to do in their interest and on their behalf." If the union's total budget is divided between collective bargaining and institutional expenses and if nonmember payments, equal to those of a member, go entirely for collective bargaining costs, the nonmember will pay more of these expenses than his pro rata share. The member will pay less and to that extent a portion of his fees and dues is available to pay institutional expenses. The union's budget is balanced. By paying a larger share of collective bargaining costs the nonmember subsidizes the union's institutional activities. In over-all effect, economically, and we think for the purposes of § 14(b), the contract here is the same as the *General Motors* agency shop arrangement. Petitioners' argument, if accepted, would lead to the anomalous result of permitting Florida to invalidate the agency shop but forbidding it to ban the present service fee arrangement under which collective bargaining services cost the nonmember more than the member....

NOTES

1. Could a state prohibit a requirement that nonunion employees pay a "service fee" to cover the pro rata share of the union's expenses in negotiating and administering the collective-bargaining agreement? A divided panel of the D.C. Circuit held that a union violated § 8(b)(3) of the NLRA when it insisted to impasse on a provision requiring nonunion employees to pay a "representation fee," covering the union's pro rata costs of "enforcing and servicing" its collective bargaining agreement once it was in effect, in a state whose right-to-work law prohibited the requirement of such fees. *Plumbers Local 141 v. NLRB,* 675 F.2d 1257 (D.C. Cir. 1982), *cert. denied,* 459 U.S. 1171 (1983). *See* Spielmans, *Bargaining Fee Versus Union Shop,* 10 Ind. & Lab. Rel. Rev. 609 (1957). *Cf. Machinists Local 697 (Canfield Rubber Co.),* 223 N.L.R.B. 832 (1976) (costs of grievance handling). What about a fairly apportioned "registration fee" for non-union job applicants using a lawful hiring hall that serves as employers' exclusive source of employees? *See J. J. Hagerty, Inc.,* 153 N.L.R.B. 1375 (1965), *enforced,* 385 F.2d 874 (2d Cir. 1967), *cert. denied,* 391 U.S. 904 (1968) (permissible fee). What about a checkoff? *See Seapak Div., W.R. Grace Corp. v. NMU,* 300 F. Supp. 1197 (S.D. Ga. 1969), *aff'd,* 423 F.2d 1229 (5th Cir. 1970), *aff'd,* 400 U.S. 985 (1971) (not subject to state regulation).

2. Some right-to-work laws, by their terms or through interpretation, purport to outlaw the exclusive hiring hall. *See, e.g.,* Wyo. Laws c. 39, § 5; *Kaiser v. Price-Fewell, Inc.,* 235 Ark. 295, 359 S.W.2d 449 (1962), *cert. denied,* 371 U.S. 955 (1963). The NLRB, however, holds that nondiscriminatory hiring halls are not a form of union security subject to state regulation under § 14(b). *Houston Chapter, Associated Gen. Contractors,* 143 N.L.R.B. 409 (1963), *enforced,* 349 F.2d 449 (5th Cir. 1965).

3. In *Algoma Plywood & Veneer Co. v. WERB,* 336 U.S. 301 (1949), the Supreme Court upheld a state statute which did not absolutely prohibit union security agreements, but which regulated them by requiring a two-thirds employee vote for authorization.

4. *See generally* Henderson, *The Confrontation of Federal Preemption and State Right to Work Laws,* 1967 Duke L.J. 1079; Hopfl, *The Agency Shop Question,* 49 Cornell L.Q. 478 (1964).

––––––––––

Retail Clerks, Local 1625 v. Schermerhorn, 375 U.S. 96, 84 S. Ct. 219, 11 L. Ed. 2d 179 (1963). On reargument, it was held that § 14(b) allows the states not only to prohibit the execution and application of union security agreements, but also to enforce their laws by appropriate sanctions. "On the other hand, picketing in order to get an employer to execute an agreement to hire all-union labor in violation of a state union-security statute lies exclusively in the federal domain ... because state power, recognized by § 14(b), begins *only with the actual negotiation and execution of the type of agreement described by § 14(b)."* (Emphasis in the original.)

NOTES

1. An employer does not violate § 8(a)(5) in refusing to bargain over a proposal in conflict with a valid state right-to-work provision. *Fort Industry Co.,* 77 N.L.R.B. 1287 (1948).

2. The right-to-work controversy continues to generate much heat, at both the federal and state levels. Both sides in the dispute traditionally invoke hallowed moral and ethical principles, and act as if weighty economic interests depended on the outcome of the struggle. Yet there is respectable support for the view that right-to-work laws have little real impact in actual operation, and that their existence is more a symptom than a cause of union weakness in the South and parts of the West. *See generally* F. Myers, "Right to Work" in Practice (1959); P. Sultan, Right-to-Work Laws (1958); Grodin & Beeson, *State Right-to-Work Laws and Federal Labor Policy,* 52 Calif. L. Rev. 95 (1964); Pollitt, *Right to Work Law Issues: An Evidentiary Approach,* 37 N.C.L. Rev. 233 (1959). *But cf.* Kuhn, *Right-to-Work Laws—Symbols or Substance?* 14 Ind. & Lab. Rel. Rev. 587 (1961).

3. PROTECTED CONCERTED ACTIVITIES AND EMPLOYER RESPONSE

> To support a finding that § 8(a)(3) has been violated, the record in the case must show that the complaining employees were in fact discriminated against because of activities protected by § 7 of the Act and that the discrimination tended to encourage or discourage union membership. Section 7 of the Act protects the right of employees to organize for collective bargaining purposes, and to engage in other concerted activities for the purpose of collective bargaining or other mutual aid or protection. [NLRB, Twenty-Third Annual Report 63-64 (1959)].

Some concerted activities such as striking for higher wages are obviously protected by § 7 against employer reprisal. (*See* the *Mackay Radio* case in this section). But even informal action without union organization may be protected, as long as it is "concerted" and "for mutual aid and protection." For example, in *NLRB v. Washington Aluminum* Co., 370 U.S. 9 (1962), the action of seven employees who walked off their jobs to protest cold working conditions was found protected, and in *Ohio Oil Co.,* 92 N.L.R.B. 1597 (1951), an informal protest against the elimination of overtime work was held protected, although the participating employees had no authorization from other workers. *See Atlantic-Pacific Constr. Co. v. NLRB*, 52 F.3d 260 (9th Cir. 1995) (group letter protesting selection of unpopular co-worker as new supervisor protected); *Bob Evans Farms v. NLRB,* ___ F.3d ___ (7th Cir. 1998) (walkout to protest discharge of supervisor protected when employees believed supervisor's termination would adversely affect their working conditions). In *Root-Carlin, Inc.,* 92 N.L.R.B. 1313 (1951), the Board said, where "one employee discusses with another the need for union organization, their action is 'concerted' ... for it involves more than one employee, even though one be in the role of speaker and the other of listener." Similarly, concerted activity may take place where only one person seeks to induce action by others. *See, e.g., Medeco Security Locks v. NLRB*, 142 F.3d 733 (4th Cir. 1998) (employee talking to coworkers about his own test scores to enlist their support regarding matter of common interest); *Salt River Valley Water Users' Ass'n v. NLRB*, 206 F.2d 325 (9th Cir. 1953) (circulating a petition for back wages).

KBO Inc., 315 N.L.R.B. 570 (1994), *enforced by order*, 153 L.R.R.M. 2512 (6th Cir. 1996), involved an employee who was suspended for telling other workers about an alleged tape recording on which the employer's operations manager supposedly said that the employer was "taking money out of the employees' profit sharing accounts to pay the lawyers to fight the union." Even though the tape recording may not have existed, the fact that the employee honestly believed the story rendered his conduct protected.

On the other hand, in *Joanna Cotton Mills Co. v. NLRB*, 176 F.2d 749 (4th Cir. 1949), the court held that circulating a petition for removal of a supervisor was not protected when a particular individual was nursing a grudge against a specific supervisor and the petition was not truly being circulated "for mutual aid and protection." In *NLRB v. Office Towel Supply Co.*, 201 F.2d 838 (2d Cir. 1953), the court held that mere griping ("This is a hell of a place to work. They expect one girl to do the work of five and a girl doesn't get time to go to the ladies' room") is too inchoate a form of concerted activity to be protected, where the employer had no knowledge that the employee had also discussed with other employees the need for a union. *Compare Gatliff Coal Co. v. NLRB*, 953 F.2d 247 (6th Cir. 1992) (joint protest by two female employees regarding rumor started by coworkers concerning their alleged extramarital conduct with male employee protected, since the issue affected their working conditions).

NLRB v. CITY DISPOSAL SYSTEMS

Supreme Court of the United States
465 U.S. 822, 104 76 S. Ct. 1505, 79 L. Ed. 2d 839 (1984)

JUSTICE BRENNAN delivered the opinion of the Court.

James Brown, a truck driver employed by respondent, was discharged when he refused to drive a truck that he honestly and reasonably believed to be unsafe because of faulty brakes. Article XXI of the collective-bargaining agreement between respondent and Local 247 of the International Brotherhood of Teamsters, Chauffeurs, Warehousemen and Helpers of America, which covered Brown, provides:

> [t]he Employer shall not require employees to take out on the streets or
> highways any vehicle that is not in safe operating condition or equipped

with safety appliances prescribed by law. It shall not be a violation of the Agreement where employees refuse to operate such equipment unless such refusal is unjustified.

The question to be decided is whether Brown's honest and reasonable assertion of his right to be free of the obligation to drive unsafe trucks constituted "concerted activit[y]" within the meaning of § 7 of the National Labor Relations Act (NLRA or Act), 29 U.S.C. § 157. The National Labor Relations Board (NLRB or Board) held that Brown's refusal was concerted activity within § 7, and that his discharge was, therefore, an unfair labor practice under § 8(a)(1) of the Act, 29 U.S.C. 158(a). 256 N.L.R.B. 451 (1981). The Court of Appeals disagreed and declined enforcement. 683 F.2d 1005 (CA6 (1982)....

I

The facts are not in dispute in the current posture of this case. Respondent, City Disposal System, Inc. (City Disposal), hauls garbage for the City of Detroit....

James Brown was assigned to truck No. 245. On Saturday, May 12, 1979, Brown observed that a fellow driver had difficulty with the brakes of another truck, truck No. 244. As a result of the brake problem, truck No. 244 nearly collided with Brown's truck. After unloading their garbage at the land fill, Brown and the driver of truck No. 244 brought No. 244 to respondent's truck-repair facility, where they were told that the brakes would be repaired either over the weekend or in the morning of Monday, May 14.

Early in the morning of Monday, May 14, while transporting a load of garbage to the land fill, Brown experienced difficulty with one of the wheels of his own truck—No. 245—and brought that truck in for repair. At the repair facility, Brown was told that, because of a backlog at the facility, No. 245 could not be repaired that day. Brown reported the situation to his supervisor, Otto Jasmund, who ordered Brown to punch out and go home. Before Brown could leave, however, Jasmund changed his mind and asked Brown to drive truck No. 244 instead. Brown refused, explaining that "there's something wrong with that truck.... [S]omething was wrong with the brakes ... there was a grease seal or something leaking causing it to be affecting the brakes." Brown did not, however, explicitly refer to Article XXI of the collective-bargaining agreement or to the agreement in general. In response to Brown's refusal to drive truck No. 244, Jasmund angrily told Brown to go home. At that point, an argument ensued and Robert Madary, another supervisor, intervened, repeating Jasmund's request that Brown drive truck No. 244. Again, Brown refused, explaining that No. 244 "has got problems and I don't want to drive it." Madary replied that half the trucks had problems and that if respondent tried to fix all of them it would be unable to do business. He went on to tell Brown that "[w]e've got all this garbage out here to haul and you tell me about you don't want to drive." Brown responded, "Bob, what you going to do, put the garbage ahead of the safety of the men?" Finally, Madary went to his office and Brown went home. Later that day, Brown received word that he had been discharged. He immediately returned to work in an attempt to gain reinstatement but was unsuccessful.

On May 15, the day after the discharge, Brown filed a written grievance, pursuant to the collective-bargaining agreement, asserting that truck No. 244 was defective, that it had been improper for him to have been ordered to drive the truck, and that his discharge was therefore also improper. The union, however, found no objective merit in the grievance and declined to process it.

On September 7, 1979, Brown filed an unfair labor practice charge with the NLRB, challenging his discharge....

II

Section 7 of the NLRA provides that "[e]mployees shall have the right to ... join or assist labor organizations, to bargain collectively through representatives of their own choosing, and to engage in other concerted activities for the purpose of collective bargaining or other mutual aid or protection." 29 U.S.C. § 157 (emphasis added). The NLRB's decision in this case applied the Board's longstanding "*Interboro* doctrine," under which an individual's assertion of a right grounded in a collective-bargaining agreement is recognized as "concerted activit[y]" and therefore accorded the protection of § 7. *See Interboro Contractors, Inc.,* 157 N.L.R.B. 1295, 1298 (1966), enforced, 388 F.2d 495 (CA2 1967); *Bunney Bros. Construction Co.,* 139 N.L.R.B. 1516, 1519 (1962). The Board has relied on two justifications for the doctrine: First, the assertion of a right contained in a collective-bargaining agreement is an extension of the concerted action that produced the agreement, *Bunney Bros. Construction, supra,* at 1519; and second, the assertion of such a right affects the rights of all employees covered by the collective-bargaining agreement. *Interboro Contractors, supra,* at 1298 ....

Neither the Court of Appeals nor respondent appears to question that an employee's invocation of a right derived from a collective-bargaining agreement meets § 7's requirement that an employee's action be taken "for purposes of collective bargaining or other mutual aid or protection." As the Board first explained in the *Interboro* case, a single employee's invocation of such rights affects all the employees that are covered by the collective-bargaining agreement. *Interboro Contractors, Inc., supra,* at 1298. This type of generalized effect, as our cases have demonstrated, is sufficient to bring the actions of an individual employee within the "mutual aid or protection" standard, regardless of whether the employee has his own interests most immediately in mind. *See, e.g., Weingarten v. NLRB,* 420 U.S. 251, 260-261 (1974).

The term "concerted activit[y]" is not defined in the Act but it clearly enough embraces the activities of employees who have joined together in order to achieve common goals....

Although one could interpret the phrase, "to engage in concerted activities," to refer to a situation in which two or more employees are working together at the same time and the same place toward a common goal, the language of § 7 does not confine itself to such a narrow meaning. In fact, § 7 itself defines both joining and assisting labor organizations—activities in which a single employee can engage—as concerted activities. Indeed, even the courts that have rejected the *Interboro* doctrine recognize the possibility that an individual employee may be engaged in concerted activity when he acts alone. They have limited their recognition of this type of concerted activity, however, to two situations: (1) that in which the lone employee intends to induce group activity, and (2) that in which the employee acts as a representative of at least one other employee. *See, e.g., Aro, Inc. v. NLRB,* 596 F.2d, at 713, 717 (CA6 1979); *NLRB v. Northern Metal Co.,* 440 F.2d 881, 884 (CA3 1971)....

The invocation of a right rooted in a collective-bargaining agreement is unquestionably an integral part of the process that gave rise to the agreement. That process—beginning with the organization of a union, continuing into the negotiation of a collective-bargaining agreement, and extending through the enforcement of the agreement—is a single, collective activity. Obviously, an employee could not invoke a right grounded in a collective-bargaining agreement were it not for the prior negotiating activities of his fellow employees. Nor would it make sense for a union to negotiate a collective-bargaining agreement if individual employees could not invoke the rights thereby created against their employer. Moreover, when an employee invokes a right grounded in the collective-bargaining agreement, he does not stand alone. Instead, he brings to bear on his employer the power and resolve of all his fellow employees. When, for instance, James Brown refused to drive a truck he believed to be unsafe, he was in effect reminding his employer that he and his fellow employees, at the time their collective-bargaining agreement was signed, had extracted a promise from City Disposal that they would not be asked to drive unsafe trucks. He was also reminding his employer that if it persisted in ordering him to drive an unsafe truck, he could reharness the power of that group to ensure the enforcement of that promise. It was just as though James Brown was reassembling his fellow union members to reenact their decision not to drive unsafe trucks. A lone employee's invocation of a right grounded in his collective-bargaining agreement is, therefore, a concerted activity in a very real sense.

Furthermore, the acts of joining and assisting a labor organization, which § 7 explicitly recognizes as concerted, are related to collective action in essentially the same way that the invocation of a collectively bargained right is related to collective action. When an employee joins or assists a labor organization, his actions may be divorced in time, and in location as well, from the actions of fellow employees. Because of the integral relationship among the employees' actions, however, Congress viewed each employee as engaged in concerted activity. The lone employee could not join or assist a labor organization were it not for the related organizing activities of his fellow employees. Conversely, there would be limited utility in forming a labor organization if other employees could not join or assist the organization once it is formed. Thus, the formation of a labor organization is integrally related to the activity of joining or assisting such an organization in the same sense that the negotiation of a collective-bargaining agreement is integrally related to the invocation of a right provided for in the agreement. In each case, neither the individual activity nor the group activity would be complete without the other.[10]... [I]t is evident that, in enacting § 7 of the NLRA, Congress sought generally to equalize the bargaining power of the employee with that of his employer by allowing employees to band together in confronting an employer regarding the terms and conditions of their employment. There is no indication that Congress intended to limit this protection to situations in which an employee's activity and that of his fellow employees combine with one another in any particular way. Nor, more specifically, does it appear that Congress intended to have this general protection withdrawn in situations in which a single employee, acting alone, participates in an integral aspect of a collective process. Instead, what emerges from the general background of § 7—and what is consistent with the Act's statement of purpose—is a congressional intent to create an equality in bargaining power between the employee and the employer throughout the entire process of labor organizing, collective bargaining, and enforcement of collective-bargaining agreements.

The Board's *Interboro* doctrine, based on a recognition that the potential inequality in the relationship between the employee and the employer continues beyond the point at which a collective-bargaining agreement is signed, mitigates that inequality throughout the duration of the employment relationship, and is, therefore, fully consistent with congressional intent. Moreover, by applying § 7 to the actions of individual employees invoking their rights under a collective–bargaining agreement, the *Interboro* doctrine preserves the integrity of the entire collective-bargaining process; for by invoking a right grounded in a collective-

---

[10] Of course, at some point an individual employee's actions may become so remotely related to the activities of fellow employees that it cannot reasonably be said that the employee is engaged in concerted activity. For instance, the Board has held that if an employer were to discharge an employee for purely personal "griping," the employee could not claim the protection of § 7. *See, e.g., Capital Ornamental Concrete Specialities, Inc.,* 248 N.L.R.B. 851 (1980).

In addition, although the Board relies entirely on its interpretation of § 7 as support for the *Interboro* doctrine, it bears noting that under § 8(a)(1), an employer commits an unfair labor practice if he or she "interfere[s] with, [or] restrain[s]" concerted activity. It is possible, therefore, for an employer to commit an unfair labor practice by discharging an employee who is not himself involved in concerted activity, but whose actions are related to other employees' concerted activities in such a manner as to render his discharge an interference or restraint on those activities. In the context of the *Interboro* doctrine, for instance, even if an individual's invocation of rights provided for in a collective-bargaining agreement, for some reason, were not concerted activity, the discharge of that individual would still be an unfair labor practice if the result were to restrain or interfere with the concerted activity of negotiating or enforcing a collective-bargaining agreement.

bargaining agreement, the employee makes that right a reality, and breathes life, not only into the promises contained in the collective-bargaining agreement, but also into the entire process envisioned by Congress as the means by which to achieve industrial peace.

To be sure, the principal tool by which an employee invokes the rights granted him in a collective-bargaining agreement is the processing of a grievance according to whatever procedures his collective-bargaining agreement establishes. No one doubts that the processing of a grievance in such a manner is concerted activity within the meaning of § 7. *See, e.g., NLRB v. Ford Motor Co.,* 683 F.2d 156, 159 (CA6 1982); *Crown Central Petroleum Corp. v. NLRB,* 430 F.2d 724, 729 (CA5 1970). Indeed, it would make little sense for § 7 to cover an employee's conduct while negotiating a collective-bargaining agreement, including a grievance mechanism by which to protect the rights created by the agreement, but not to cover an employee's attempt to utilize that mechanism to enforce the agreement....

[A]n employee's initial statement to an employer to the effect that he believes a collectively bargained right is being violated, or the employee's initial refusal to do that which he believes he is not obligated to do, might serve as both a natural prelude to, and an efficient substitute for, the filing of a formal grievance. As long as the employee's statement or action is based on a reasonable and honest belief that he is being, or has been, asked to perform a task that he is not required to perform under his collective-bargaining agreement, and the statement or action is reasonably directed toward the enforcement of a collectively bargained right, there is no justification for overturning the Board's judgment that the employee is engaged in concerted activity, just as he would have been had he filed a formal grievance.

The fact that an activity is concerted, however, does not necessarily mean that an employee can engage in the activity with impunity. An employee may engage in concerted activity in such an abusive manner that he loses the protection of § 7. *See, e.g., Crown Central Petroleum Corp. v. NLRB,* 430 F.2d 724, 729 (CA5 1970); *Yellow Freight System, Inc.,* 247 N.L.R.B. 177, 181 (1980). *Cf. Eastex, Inc. v. NLRB,* 437 U.S. 556 (1978) (finding concerted activity nonetheless unprotected); *NLRB v. Babcock & Wilcox Co.,* 351 U.S. 105 (1956) (same). Furthermore, if an employer does not wish to tolerate certain methods by which employees invoke their collectively bargained rights, he is free to negotiate a provision in his collective-bargaining agreement that limits the availability of such methods. No-strike provisions, for instance, are a common mechanism by which employers and employees agree that the latter will not invoke their rights by refusing to work. In general, if an employee violates such a provision, his activity is unprotected even though it may be concerted. *Mastro Plastics Corp. v. NLRB,* 350 U.S. 270 (1956). Whether Brown's action in this case was unprotected, however, is not before us....

III

... Respondent argues that Brown's action was not concerted because he did not explicitly refer to the collective-bargaining agreement as a basis for his refusal to drive the truck. The Board, however, has never held that an employee must make such an explicit reference for his actions to be covered by the *Interboro* doctrine, and we find that position reasonable. We have often recognized the importance of "the Board's special function of applying the general provisions of the Act to the complexities of industrial life." *NLRB v. Erie Resistor Corp.*, 373 U.S. 221, 236 (1963). As long as the nature of the employee's complaint is reasonably clear to the person to whom it is communicated, and the complaint does, in fact, refer to a reasonably perceived violation of the collective-bargaining agreement, the complaining employee is engaged in the process of enforcing that agreement. In the context of a workplace dispute, where the participants are likely to be unsophisticated in collective-bargaining matters, a requirement that the employee explicitly refer to the collective-bargaining agreement is likely to serve as nothing more than a trap for the unwary.

Respondent further argues that the Board erred in finding Brown's action concerted based only on Brown's reasonable and honest belief that truck No. 244 was unsafe. Respondent bases its argument on the language of the collective-bargaining agreement, which provides that an employee may refuse to drive an unsafe truck "unless such refusal is unjustified." In the view of respondent, this language allows a driver to refuse to drive a truck only if the truck is objectively unsafe. Regardless of whether respondent's interpretation of the agreement is correct, a question as to which we express no view, this argument confuses the threshold question whether Brown's conduct was concerted with the ultimate question whether that conduct was protected. The rationale of the *Interboro* doctrine compels the conclusion that an honest and reasonable invocation of a collectively bargained right constitutes concerted activity, regardless of whether the employee turns out to have been correct in his belief that his right was violated. No one would suggest, for instance, that the filing of a grievance is concerted only if the grievance turns out to be meritorious. As long as the grievance is based on an honest and reasonable belief that a right had been violated, its filing is a concerted activity because it is an integral part of the process by which the collective-bargaining agreement is enforced. The same is true of other methods by which an employee enforces the agreement. On the other hand, if the collective-bargaining agreement imposes a limitation on the means by which a right may be invoked, the concerted activity would be unprotected if it went beyond that limitation....

[The case was remanded for consideration of the contention that Brown's conduct was unprotected, even if concerted.]

JUSTICE O'CONNOR, with whom THE CHIEF JUSTICE, JUSTICE POWELL and JUSTICE REHNQUIST join, dissenting....

In my view, the fact that the right the employee asserts ultimately can be grounded in the collective bargaining agreement is not enough to make the individual's self-interested action concerted. If it could, then *every* contract claim could be the basis for an unfair labor practice complaint. But the law is clear that an employer's alleged violation of a collective agreement cannot, by itself, provide the basis for an unfair labor practice complaint. *See NLRB v. C & C Plywood,* 385 U.S. 421, 427-428 (1967).... When employees act together in expressing a mutual concern, contractual or otherwise, their action is "concerted" and the statute authorizes them to seek vindication through the Board's administrative processes. In contrast, when an employee acts alone in expressing a personal concern, contractual or otherwise, his action is not "concerted;" in such cases, the statute instructs him to seek vindication through his union, and where necessary, through the courts.... There is no evidence that employee James Brown discussed the truck's alleged safety problem with other employees, sought their support in remedying the problem, or requested their or his union's assistance in protesting to his employer. He did not seek to warn others of the problem or even initially to file a grievance through his union. He simply asserted that the truck was not safe enough for *him* to drive. James Brown was not engaging in "concerted activity" in any reasonable sense of the term ....

NOTES

1. The NLRB extended the *Interboro* "constructive concerted activity" doctrine to situations in which no collective bargaining contract existed. Thus the Board found that an employee was engaged in concerted activity when he filed a safety complaint under a state statute, even though he acted alone and his co-workers showed no support for his efforts. Absent any indication that the co-workers disavowed the employee's efforts, the Board found that the consent of the co-workers was "implied." *Alleluia Cushion Co.,* 221 N.L.R.B. 999 (1975). However, in *Meyers Indus.,* 268 N.L.R.B. 493 (1984), the Board, while distinguishing *Interboro,* overruled *Alleluia Cushion* and held that a truck driver employed in a nonunion plant not covered by any bargaining agreement who refused to drive his vehicle and who complained to a state regulatory agency about allegedly unsafe brakes was not engaged in concerted activity.

In *Prill v. NLRB,* 755 F.2d 941 (D.C. Cir.), *cert. denied,* 474 U.S. 971 (1985), the court remanded *Meyers Indus.* to the NLRB for further consideration, since the court concluded that the Board had erroneously based its initial decision upon the belief that its narrow interpretation of § 7 was "mandated by the statute itself." The court noted that the Labor Board possesses substantial interpretative discretion in this area, and it directed it to reconsider the matter. On remand, the Board affirmed the definition of "concerted activities" contained in *Meyers I.* *Meyers Indus.,* 281 N.L.R.B. 882 (1986).

In *Meyers I,* the Board adopted the following definition of the term "concerted activities": "In general, to find an employee's activity to be 'concerted,' we shall require that it be engaged in with or on the authority of other employees, and not solely by and on behalf of the employee himself." The *Meyers I* definition expressly distinguishes between an employee's activities engaged in "with or on the authority of other employees" (concerted) and an employee's activities engaged in "solely by and on behalf of the employee himself" (not concerted). There is nothing in the *Meyers I* definition which states that conduct engaged in by a single employee at one point in time can *never* constitute concerted activity within the meaning of Section 7. On the contrary, the *Meyers I* definition, in part, attempts to define *when* the act of a single employee is or is not "concerted."...

In *Lloyd A. Fry* [651 F.2d 442 (6th Cir. 1981)], where concerted activity was established, the record was replete with instances in which the discharged employee (Varney) acted on a collective basis with other employees preceding his discharge. Thus, as found by the Sixth Circuit, Varney engaged in "numerous discussions" with his fellow drivers regarding the safety of the employer's trucks and Varney and a fellow employee (Wade) collectively met with management representatives specifically to discuss solutions to truck maintenance problems that had engendered numerous complaints by other employees. In the instant case, there is no record evidence whatsoever that employee Prill at any relevant time or in any manner joined forces with any other employee, or by his activities intended to enlist the support of other employees in a common endeavor....

[I]n previous Board cases, concerted activity was found where an individual, not a designated spokesman, brought a group complaint to the attention of management.... *Meyers I* recognizes that the question of whether an employee has engaged in concerted activity is a factual one based on the totality of the record evidence. When the record evidence demonstrates group activities, whether "specifically authorized" in a formal agency sense, or otherwise, we shall find the conduct to be concerted....

[W]e intended that *Meyers I* be read as fully embracing the view of concertedness exemplified by the *Mushroom Transportation* [330 F.2d 683 (3d Cir. 1964)] line of cases. We reiterate, our definition of concerted activity in *Meyers I* encompasses those circumstances where individual employees seek to initiate or to induce or to prepare for group action, as well as individual employees bringing truly group complaints to the attention of management....

Finally, because the *Alleluia Cushion* doctrine at its origin and its most appealing form concerns a single employee's invocation of a statute enacted for the protection of employees generally, we must consider whether any linkages to concerted activity may be discerned in such an individual employee act or whether overall public policy considerations should move us to protect even purely individual activity that is aimed at securing employer compliance with other statutes that benefit employees....

Can an employee's invocation of a statute be regarded as the extension of "concerted activity" in any realistic sense? Certainly the activity of the legislators themselves cannot be said to be concerted activity within the contemplation of the Wagner Act. And while there may be concerted activity in the lobbying process preceding the passage of such legislation, the linkage is attenuated; any such activity is far removed from the particular workplace, and the critical link between lobbying and enforcement of the law is the legislative process itself, which is not a part of any ongoing employee-generated process such as the negotiation and administration of collective-bargaining agreements....

In short, in construing Section 7 we are not holding that employee contract rights are more appropriate subjects for joint employee action than are rights granted by Federal and state legislation concerning such matters as employee safety. We merely find that invocation of employee contract rights is a continuation of an ongoing process of employee concerted activity, whereas employee invocation of statutory rights is not. We believe that we best effectuate the policies of the Act when we focus our resources on the protection of actions taken pursuant to that process.

Meyers II was affirmed in *Prill v. NLRB,* 835 F.2d 1481 (D.C. Cir. 1987), *cert. denied,* 487 U.S. 1205 (1988). *Accord, Ewing v. NLRB,* 861 F.2d 353 (2d Cir. 1988).

2. In *Mike Yurosek & Sons,* 310 N.L.R.B. 831 (1993), *affirmed,* 53 F.3d 261 (9th Cir. 1995), the Labor Board found that employees who individually declined overtime work were acting in concert, since their refusals were the "logical outgrowth" of concerns expressed earlier by a group of employees. *See also Every Woman's Place, Inc.,* 282 N.L.R.B. 413 (1986), *enforced,* 833 F.2d 1012 (6th Cir. 1987), holding that an employer unlawfully fired an employee for calling the U.S. Department of Labor to inquire about holiday pay requirements. Since the employee and two coworkers had repeatedly complained about overtime compensation to the employer, without a response, it was "immaterial that she was not following express instructions from the other employees" in telephoning. *Compare Manimark Corp. v. NLRB,* 7 F.3d 547 (6th Cir. 1993), wherein the court held that the focus of an individual employee on issues of group concern was not sufficient to generate NLRA protection, absent evidence the worker was acting on behalf of other employees. *See also NLRB v. Portland Limousine Co.,* ___ F.3d ___, 160 L.R.R.M. 2085 (1st Cir. 1998) (driver's refusal to drive truck after he complained to co-worker that he had smelled exhaust fumes unprotected where court found his complaint "mere griping, not an inducement or call to group action").

3. In *NLRB v. PIE Nationwide*, 923 F.2d 506 (7th Cir. 1991), the court held that an employer acted unlawfully when it discharged a truck driver who refused to accept a short-distance assignment. The "constructive concerted activity" doctrine applied to this driver's refusal, even though it was not based on an express term in the collective contract. The court found that an oral agreement between the union and the employer pertaining to short-distance assignments was sufficient to provide the worker with protection under the rationale of *City Disposal Sys.*

4. In *Whirlpool Corp. v. Marshall*, 445 U.S. 1 (1980), the Supreme Court held proper the promulgation and enforcement by the Secretary of Labor of OSHA regulations permitting employee refusals to perform unsafe work if their fear of serious injury or death is objectively reasonable. The court in *Modern Carpet Indus. v. NLRB*, 611 F.2d 811 (10th Cir. 1979), agreed with the NLRB that § 7 protects employee declinations to perform work under unsafe conditions if their fear of harm is genuine, thus obviating the need for an objective assessment.

5. On the problem of constructive concerted action, *see* Fischl, *Self, Others, and Section 7: Mutualism and Protected Protest Activities Under the National Labor Relations Act*, 89 Colum. L. Rev. 789 (1989); Morris, *NLRB Protection in the Nonunion Workplace: A Glimpse at a General Theory of Section 7 Conduct*, 137 U. Pa. L. Rev. 1673 (1989); George, *Divided We Stand: Concerted Activity and the Maturing of the NLRA*, 56 Geo. Wash. L. Rev. 509 (1988); Bethel, *Constructive Concerted Activity Under the NLRA: Conflicting Signals From the Court and the Board*, 59 Ind. L.J. 583 (1984); Dolin, *Interboro Doctrine and Courts: A History of Judicial Pronouncements on the Protected Status of Individual Assertions of Collective Rights*, 31 Am. U.L. Rev. 551-90 (1982); Gorman & Finkin, *Individual and the Requirement of "Concert" Under the National Labor Relations Act*, 130 U. Pa. L. Rev. 286-359 (1981); Note, *National Labor Relations Act Section 7: Protecting Employee Activity Through Implied Concert of Action*, 76 Nw. U.L. Rev. 813-36 (1982); Note, *Protection of Individual Action as "Concerted Activity" Under the NLRA*, 68 Cornell L. Rev. 369-93 (1983).

———————

NLRB v. Weingarten, Inc., 420 U.S. 251, 95 S. Ct. 959, 43 L. Ed. 171 (1975). A store manager and a "loss prevention specialist" summoned an employee to an interview to question her about a report from a fellow employee that she had purchased a box of chicken that sold for $2.98, but had only placed $1.00 in the cash register at the lunch counter where she worked. The store manager denied the employee's requests that a union representative be called to the interview. Although the interview revealed that the employee was innocent of the act alleged, the employee did "blurt out" that "the only thing she had ever gotten from the store without paying for it was her free lunch." Free lunches at the store were against company policy and the employee was informed that she owed the store approximately $160 for lunches.

The Supreme Court held that the employer's denial of the employee's request that her union representative be present at the investigatory interview which the employee reasonably believed might result in disciplinary action violated § 8(a)(1) of the NLRA because it interfered with the rights of the employee under § 7 of the Act. The Court agreed with the NLRB that the right to union representation at such interviews falls within the guarantee in § 7 of the right of employees to act in concert for mutual aid and protection. It viewed the request for representation as concerted activity because the union representative would safeguard the interests of all unit employees against unjust disciplinary procedures and his presence would assure all employees that they could also have his assistance if called to an investigatory interview. Mr. Justice Powell, dissenting, thought that this was not concerted activity within the meaning of the Act and that the matter is better left to collective bargaining.

NOTES

1. The NLRB declared that in deciding whether a *Weingarten* right exists at a meeting, "what is determinative is whether discipline reasonably can be expected to follow." *Northwest Eng'g Co.*, 265 N.L.R.B. 190 (1982). *See, e.g., Safeway Stores*, 303 N.L.R.B. 989 (1991), recognizing the right of an employee to union representation when directed by a supervisor to take a drug test following a series of continued absences, since the procedure could result in discipline.

A deeply divided Board accepted the Ninth Circuit's holding in *NLRB v. Certified Grocers of Cal., Ltd.*, 587 F.2d 449 (1978), that no *Weingarten* right arises if the employer intends merely to communicate a disciplinary decision previously made. *Baton Rouge Water Works Co.*, 246 N.L.R.B. 995 (1979). Concurring member Murphy suggested that the right would arise if, during the discussion, the employer sought an affirmance of its decision, such as an admission or release of a workmen's compensation claim. Chairman Fanning dissented, stating that, in practice, neither employer nor employee can know whether an intended communication will become an investigation.

2. In *Amax, Inc., Climax Molybdenum Co. Div.*, 227 N.L.R.B. 1189 (1977), a Board majority held that the right to engage in concerted activity for mutual aid or protection guarantees an employee a right to consult with his representative prior to the investigatory interview. The Tenth Circuit, however, denied enforcement of the Board's order. 584 F.2d 360 (1978). In *Pacific Tel. & Tel. Co.*, 262 N.L.R.B. 1048 (1982), *enforced*, 711 F.2d 134 (9th Cir. 1983), a majority held that the right to prior consultation includes a right to be informed as to the subject of the interview as well. *See also U.S. Postal Serv. v. NLRB*, 969 F.2d 1064 (D.C. Cir. 1992) (sustaining right of employees to consult union stewards prior to disciplinary interviews.)

An employer is not obliged to inform an employee suspected of misconduct of his right to union representation during an investigatory interview. Even where a prospective interviewee is frightened and confused, no right to union representation attaches unless he requests such assistance. *See Montgomery Ward,* 269 N.L.R.B. 904 (1984).

3. The Board also held that, although employees may not be forced to remain in an investigatory interview once their right to representation is denied, they must obey an initial order to leave the plant floor and enter an office. *Roadway Express, Inc.,* 246 N.L.R.B. 1127 (1979). The same case held that an employee may not decline to attend because his or her preferred representative is not available if some other designated representative is. Further, it is the union's obligation to keep employees informed of all available representatives.

4. Although the Labor Board ruled in *Materials Research Corp.,* 262 N.L.R.B. 1010 (1982), that nonunion employees are entitled to have co-workers present at management interviews they reasonably believe may result in discipline, it subsequently overruled *Materials Research* and held that the *Weingarten* right to be represented during investigatory interviews is an organizational right that is not available to nonunion employees. *Sears, Roebuck & Co.,* 274 N.L.R.B. 230 (1985). *See Slaughter v. NLRB,* 876 F.2d 11 (3d Cir. 1989). *See generally* Note, *Limiting the Weingarten Right in the Nonunion Setting: The Implications of Sears, Roebuck and Co.,* 35 Cath. U. L. Rev. 1033 (1986); Note, *Extending Weingarten Rights to Nonunion Employees,* 86 Colum. L. Rev. 618 (1986).

5. In *New Jersey Bell Tel. Co.,* 308 N.L.R.B. 277 (1992), the Board held that a union steward forfeited his statutory protection when he persistently sought to prevent a company official from asking the same questions of an employee suspected of misconduct. Since the employee's answers were not responsive, the Board concluded that the repeated questions did not constitute management harassment or intimidation.

6. When an employer impermissibly refuses to grant employee requests for representation during investigatory interviews, the Board will automatically issue a cease and desist order to rectify the violation. If individuals are terminated because of their invocation of their *Weingarten* right, reinstatement and backpay will also be provided. If, however, the employer's basis for the employee's discharge is unrelated to the denial of the worker's *Weingarten* right, the Board will not order reinstatement or backpay. *See Taracorp Indus.,* 273 N.L.R.B. 221 (1984). The *Taracorp* doctrine was judicially approved in *Communications Workers, Local 5008 v. NLRB,* 784 F.2d 847 (7th Cir. 1986).

7. Under what circumstances and standards, if any, might a union waive employees' rights under *Weingarten*? *See Prudential Ins. Co.,* 275 N.L.R.B. 208 (1985). *See generally* Craver, *The Inquisitorial Process in Private Employment,* 63 Cornell L. Rev. 1 (1977).

Assuming that the activity is "concerted" and that it is for "the purpose of collective bargaining or other mutual aid or protection," it still may not be protected against employer interference (§ 8(a)(1)) and discrimination (§ 8(a)(3)). Not all concerted activities are protected by § 7. The problem is how to draw the line. In general, the activities must have a lawful objective and must be carried on in a lawful manner. But what is meant by the term "lawful" in this connection?

Fairly clear are the cases in which the concerted activities are for an objective which is outlawed by the Taft-Hartley Act itself as a union unfair labor practice. It would not effectuate the policies of the act to afford relief against employer reprisal to employees who were themselves violating the act. "For example, the act expressly prohibits jurisdictional strikes, secondary boycotts, and strikes for recognition in defiance of a certified union." *See Local 1229, Electrical Workers v. NLRB,* 202 F.2d 186, 187 (D.C. Cir. 1952). Employees who engage in recognition picketing in violation of § 8(b)(7) lose their protected status under the Act, and an employer may lawfully refuse to reinstate them. *Claremont Polychemical Corp.,* 196 N.L.R.B. 613 (1972).

Other forms of concerted activity which are unprotected because the objective is illegal include:

a. A strike to force the employer to grant a wage increase in violation of a wartime wage stabilization statute, requiring approval by the War Labor Board of all wage increases. *NLRB v. Indiana Desk Co.,* 149 F.2d 987 (7th Cir. 1945); *American News Co.,* 55 N.L.R.B. 1302 (1944).

b. A strike or a boycott to compel an employer to commit an employer unfair labor practice. *Hoover Co. v. NLRB,* 191 F.2d 380 (6th Cir. 1951); *Thompson Prod., Inc.,* 72 N.L.R.B. 886 (1947).

Even though the objective is legal, the protection of the NLRA is withdrawn if the concerted activity is tortious or criminal in nature. For example, action involving sitdown strikes (forcible seizure of property) [*NLRB v. Fansteel Metallurgical Corp.,* 306 U.S. 240 (1939)] or mutiny in violation of the federal criminal code [*Southern S.S. Co. v. NLRB,* 316 U.S. 31 (1942)].

The most difficult cases concern concerted activities that are not clearly unlawful but which are thought to be inconsistent with public policy considerations, including regard for the basic rights of employers. When concerted activity appears to be inappropriate and not the sort of conduct which the members of Congress, had they thought about it, would have intended to insulate against employer reprisals, § 7 protection will be lost. *See, e.g., Carolina Freight Carriers Corp.,* 295 N.L.R.B. 1080 (1989) (persistent refusal to carry out supervisor's direct order); *NLRB v. Brookshire Grocery Co.,* 919 F.2d 359 (5th Cir. 1990) (improper obtaining of information from confidential personnel files for dissemination to other workers). *Compare Vemco, Inc. v. NLRB,* 79 F.3d 526 (6th Cir. 1996) (employees who left worksite without permission unprotected where they did not act to protest any company policy) *with Magic Finishing Co.,* 323

[handwritten margin note: Types of activities that are unprotected due to illegal or tortious behavior]

N.L.R.B. No. 28, 154 L.R.R.M. 1230 (1997) (walkout to protest excessive heat protected).

ELK LUMBER CO.

National Labor Relations Board
91 N.L.R.B. 333 (1950)

[The General Counsel's complaint alleged that the respondent Elk Lumber Company had violated §§ 8(a)(1) and 8(a)(3) of the act by discharging five employees because they engaged in protected concerted activity to protest a change in the method of wage payment.]

The Respondent contends, and the Trial Examiner apparently found, that the five carloaders were discharged, not for having engaged in concerted activities, as alleged in the complaint, but because their production was not satisfactory. It is clear, however, that their failure to produce was the result of an agreement to slow down. In our opinion, therefore, the only question presented is whether this conduct was a form of concerted activity protected by the act. We believe, contrary to the contention of the General Counsel, that it was not.

Section 7 of the act guarantees to employees the right to engage in concerted activities for the purpose of collective bargaining or other mutual aid or protection. However, both the Board and the courts have recognized that not every form of activity that falls within the letter of this provision is protected. The test, as laid down by the Board in the *Harnischfeger Corporation* case, and referred to with apparent approval by the Supreme Court in the recent *Wisconsin* case [UAWA-AFL v. WERB, 336 U.S. 245], is whether the particular activity involved is so indefensible as to warrant the employer in discharging the participating employees. Either an unlawful objective or the adoption of improper means of achieving it may deprive employees engaged in concerted activities of the protection of the act.

Here, the objective of the carloaders' concerted activity—to induce the Respondent to increase their hourly rate of pay or to return to the piecework rate—was a lawful one. To achieve this objective, however, they adopted the plan of decreasing their production to the amount they considered adequate for the pay they were then receiving. In effect, this constituted a refusal on their part to accept the terms of employment set by their employer without engaging in a stoppage, but to continue rather to work on their own terms. The courts, in somewhat similar situations, have held that such conduct is justifiable cause for discharge. Thus, in the *Conn* case [108 F.2d 390], the Court of Appeals for the Seventh Circuit found that the employer was justified in discharging employees who refused to work overtime, saying:

> We are aware of no law or logic that gives the employee the right to work upon terms prescribed solely by him. That is plainly what was sought to be done in this instance. It is not a situation in which employees ceased work in

protest against conditions imposed by the employer, but one in which the employees sought and intended to work upon their own notion of the terms which should prevail. If they had a right to fix the hours of their employment, it would follow that a similar right existed by which they could prescribe all conditions and regulations affecting their employment.

And in the *Montgomery Ward* case [157 F.2d 486], in which employees at one of the employer's plants refused to process orders from another plant where a strike was in progress, the Court of Appeals for the Eighth Circuit said:

> It was implied in the contract of hiring that these employees would do the work assigned to them in a careful and workmanlike manner; that they would comply with all reasonable orders and conduct themselves so as not to work injury to the employer's business; that they would serve faithfully and be regardful of the interests of the employer during the term of their service, and carefully discharge their duties to the extent reasonably required.... Any employee may, of course, be lawfully discharged for disobedience of the employer's directions in breach of his contract.... While these employees had the undoubted right to go on a strike and quit their employment, they could not continue to work and remain at their positions, accept the wages paid them, and at the same time select what part of their allotted tasks they cared to perform of their own volition, or refuse openly or secretly to the employer's damage, to do other work.

We believe that the principle of these decisions is applicable to the situation before us, and that, under the circumstances, the carloaders' conduct justified their discharge.

The General Counsel contends, however, that "if such activity [a slowdown] is to be condemned by the Board, it should only be done after there has been a deliberate refusal to do the Employer's bidding," and that here, "at the time of discharge there still had been no failure to comply with any command of management." In support of this contention, he asserts that "after the outset of this slowdown, the Employer obviously acquiesced in it and made no protest"; that it "did not set a definite rate [of production], nor did it make any statement as to what rate of production was considered accurate"; and that it discharged the men "without any warning or reason being given."

On the record before us, however, we find no convincing evidence that the Respondent at any time acquiesced in the slowdown....

Furthermore, although the Respondent admittedly did not tell the carloaders how many cars a day they were expected to load, and, so far as the present record shows, did not warn them that they would be discharged if they did not increase their production, it is clear that the men knew that the rate they had adopted was not satisfactory. Despite this knowledge, they continued to load fewer cars a day than they could have loaded, or than they would have loaded for more money.

Under these particular circumstances, we regard it as immaterial that the Respondent had given them no express order as to the amount of work required, or any warning that they would be discharged if they failed to meet the requirement.

We therefore find that the Respondent did not violate the act by discharging the five carloaders named in the complaint. As no other unfair labor practices are alleged, we affirm and adopt the Trial Examiner's ruling dismissing the complaint in its entirety....

NOTES

1. "Partial" strikes of various kinds have been found to constitute unprotected conduct. *See, e.g., Honolulu Rapid Transit Co.,* 110 N.L.R.B. 1806 (1954) (weekend and intermittent strikes); *Pacific Tel. & Tel. Co.,* 107 N.L.R.B. 1547 (1954) ("hit-and-run" unannounced work stoppages); *Valley City Furn. Co.,* 110 N.L.R.B. 1589 (1954), *enforced,* 230 F.2d 947 (6th Cir. 1956) (one-hour a day strikes). *Compare Cambro Mfg. Co.,* 312 N.L.R.B. 634 (1993) (continued refusal of in-plant strikers to return to work or leave plant unprotected conduct) *with Molon Motor & Coil Corp. v. NLRB,* 965 F.2d 523 (7th Cir. 1992) (employees engaged in protected activity when they remained for several hours in breakroom and refused to return to work or leave plant until they received pay raise). *See also NLRB v. Federal Security Inc.,* 154 F.3d 751 (7th Cir. 1998) (spontaneous walkout by private security guards at extremely dangerous public housing project unprotected since guards left complex unattended and endangered lives of residents).

In an effort to enhance their economic clout without the need to resort to formal strikes, some unions are effectively creating slow-downs by having employees strictly conform to inefficient employer work rules. *See* Doll & Kosanovich, *Workplace Job Action: An Effort to Reshape the Balance of Power,* 9 Lab. Law. 149 (1993); Block & Moorman, *Working to Rule and Other Alternate Job Actions,* 9 Lab. Law. 169 (1993). Would such tactics cause a loss of NLRA protection under the *Elk Lumber* approach? *See also* Becker, *"Better than a Strike": Protecting New Forms of Collective Work Stoppages Under the National Labor Relations Act,* 61 U. Chi. L. Rev. 351 (1994).

2. In *Hoover Co. v. NLRB,* 191 F.2d 380, 389-90 (6th Cir. 1951), the court indicated that efforts by nonstriking employees to generate a consumer boycott was unprotected:

> It is held that the right to strike requires that strikers who exercise it must thereby cease to work and draw their pay. *NLRB v. Montgomery Ward & Co., Inc.,* 8 Cir., 157 F.2d 486. An employee cannot work and strike at the same time. He cannot continue in his employment and openly or secretly refuse to do his work. He cannot collect wages for his employment, and, at the same time, engage in activities to injure or destroy his employer's business....

... It is a wrong done to the company for employees, while being employed and paid wages by a company, to engage in a boycott to prevent others from purchasing what their employer is engaged in selling and which is the very thing their employer is paying them to produce. An employer is not required, under the Act, to finance a boycott against himself.

See also George A. Hormel & Co. v. NLRB, 962 F.2d 1061 (D.C. Cir. 1992) (employee who participated in rally advocating consumer boycott of employer's products when no labor dispute existed could be discharged for unprotected "disloyalty").

3. During the course of a collective bargaining dispute, the TV technicians, while remaining on the job, distributed handbills in their off-hours to the public criticizing their TV station for failing to purchase the equipment needed to present live programs and suggesting that the company was treating "Charlotte as a second-class city" by putting on only programs which were on film. The handbills made no reference to the union, to a labor controversy or to collective bargaining. The Court found that this "sharp, public disparaging attack upon the quality of the Company's product and its business policies, in a manner reasonably calculated to harm the Company's reputation and reduce its income," was a demonstration of such detrimental disloyalty as to provide cause for the company's refusal to continue in its employ the perpetrators of the attack. *NLRB v. IBEW Local 1229 (Jefferson Sd. Broadcasting Co.),* 346 U.S. 464 (1953). (Justices Frankfurter, Black, and Douglas dissented.)

4. Suppose that (a) the handbill, in the *Local 1229* case, had been distributed while the employees were on strike, and (b) the handbill had stated an appeal for public support in the union's current labor dispute with the company? *Cf. Patterson-Sargent Co.,* 115 N.L.R.B. 1627 (1956), where several employees were discharged for distributing the following handbill to consumers during a strike at a paint company:

Beware Paint Substitute

The employees of the Patterson-Sargent Company in Cleveland who manufacture paint under the brand of B.P.S., were forced on strike by the Company. As a result, there is not being manufactured any paint at the Patterson-Sargent Company in Cleveland by the well-trained, experienced employees who have made the paint you have always bought.

This is a warning that you should make certain that any B.P.S. paint you buy is made by the regular employees who know the formulas and the exact amount of ingredients to put into paint. If you should happen to get paint which is made by any other than the regular, well-trained experienced workers, it might not do for you what you want it to do. It could peel, crack, blister, scale or any one of many undesirable things that would cause you inconvenience, lost time and money.

Stop! Think! Is it worth your while to risk spending your good money for a product which might not be what you are accustomed to using? You will be informed when you can again buy B.P.S. paint which is made by the regular employees in Cleveland.

The NLRB split 3-2, the majority finding this conduct disloyal disparagement of the employer's product and hence unprotected under the principles of *Local 1229*. They indicated that even if the handbill claims had been truthful, the disparagement of the employer's product would have still rendered the conduct unprotected. The dissenters argued that since the handbill was distributed during a strike and its contents showed a direct relation to a current labor dispute, its distribution should have been considered protected concerted activity.

Compare Sierra Pub'g Co. v. NLRB, 889 F.2d 210 (9th Cir. 1989), which involved four members of the union negotiating committee who, while trying to negotiate a new labor contract with a newspaper, wrote a letter to some of the paper's advertisers stating "circulation has plummeted, good employees have left for better jobs, advertising has suffered." This was held not to be such product disparagement or "disloyalty" to justify their discharge.

5. Employees have resorted to sarcastic communications and even colorful "body language" to express dissatisfaction with employer actions. Their conduct has evoked diverse reactions from the Labor Board and the courts. Protection has been accorded to rolled eyes and folded arms [*Health Care Corp. & Retirement Corp. of Am.*, 306 N.L.R.B. 63 (1992), *enforcement denied on other grounds*, 987 F.2d 1256 (6th Cir. 1993)] and a cartoon T-shirt depicting a manager as a person of low intelligence [*Reef Indus. v. NLRB*, 952 F.2d 830, 839 (5th Cir. 1991)], but not a letter mocking an employer's gift of ice cream cones [*New River Indus. v. NLRB*, 945 F.2d 1290 (4th Cir. 1991)].

6. Concerted activities that contravene basic policies of the National Labor Relations Act, such as the promotion of stable collective bargaining relationships and the sanctity of collective agreements, have also been held to be unprotected. Examples include "wildcat" strikes in derogation of the authority of the recognized collective bargaining representative. *See NLRB v. Sunbeam Lighting Co.*, 318 F.2d 661 (7th Cir. 1963); *Harnischfeger Corp. v. NLRB*, 207 F.2d 575 (7th Cir. 1953); *NLRB v. Draper Corp.*, 145 F.2d 199 (4th Cir. 1944). *See generally* Gould, *The Status of Unauthorized and "Wildcat" Strikes Under the National Labor Relations Act*, 52 Cornell L.Q. 672 (1967). *See also Emporium Capwell Co. v. Western Addition Community Org.*, 420 U.S. 50 (1975), set forth *infra*.

MASTRO PLASTICS CORP. v. NLRB

Supreme Court of the United States
350 U.S. 270, 76 S. Ct. 349, 100 L. Ed. 309 (1956)

[The petitioners were in the plastics manufacturing business in New York, and were working under a one-year collective bargaining agreement with the Carpenters Union governing wages, hours, and working conditions. The agreement provided for arbitration of disputes and contained a clause outlawing strikes. The agreement was due to expire on November 30, 1950. The Carpenters Union gave notice of a desire to negotiate new conditions of employment on October 10, 1950. Therefore, the 60-day "cooling-off" period prescribed in § 8(d)(4) would end on December 8, 1950.

[During the life of this agreement the Wholesale and Warehouse Workers Union sought to displace the Carpenters as the bargaining representative of petitioner's employees. In an effort to keep the Warehouse Workers out of their plant, petitioners, not believing the Carpenters strong enough for the task, enlisted the aid of a third union, the Pulp, Sulphite and Paper Mill Workers. Petitioners unlawfully assisted the Pulp, Sulphite and Paper Mill Workers in its organizational activities, causing the Carpenters to file unfair labor practice charges with the Board. Some members of the incumbent Carpenters Union tried to counteract the influence of petitioners upon the employees, and one of these, Ciccone, was discharged for his activities on November 10.

[The discharge of Ciccone, in conjunction with the antecedent employer unfair labor practices, precipitated a plant-wide strike accompanied by peaceful picketing, although neither the contract nor the 60-day waiting period had expired. The strikers made no demands relating to contract negotiations but offered to return to work if Ciccone were reinstated. The request was rejected by petitioner who notified the strikers of their discharge.

[In the ensuing unfair labor practice proceedings petitioner opposed reinstatement of the strikers upon two grounds: (1) because they had struck in breach of contract; and (2) because they lost their status as employees when they struck during the 60-day waiting period required by § 8(d) of the Taft-Hartley Act.]

MR. JUSTICE BURTON delivered the opinion of the Court:

... In the absence of some contractual or statutory provision to the contrary, petitioners' unfair labor practices provide adequate ground for the orderly strike that occurred here. Under those circumstances, the striking employees do not lose their status and are entitled to reinstatement with back pay, even if replacements for them have been made. Failure of the Board to enjoin petitioners' illegal conduct or failure of the Board to sustain the right to strike against that conduct would seriously undermine the primary objectives of the Labor Act. *See NLRB v. [International] Rice Milling Co.,* 341 U.S. 665, 673. While we assume that the employees, by explicit contractual provision, could have waived their right to strike against such unfair labor practices and that Congress, by explicit statutory provision, could have deprived strikers, under the circumstances of this case, of their status as employees, the questions before us are whether or not such a waiver was made by the Carpenters in their 1949-1950 contract and whether or not such a deprivation of status was enacted by Congress in § 8(d) of the act, as amended in 1947.

I

Does the collective-bargaining contract waive the employees' right to strike against the unfair labor practices committed by their employers? The answer turns upon the proper interpretation of the particular contract before us. Like other contracts, it must be read as a whole and in the light of the law relating to it when made....

On the premise of fair representation, collective-bargaining contracts frequently have included certain waivers of the employees' right to strike and of the employers' right to lockout to enforce their respective economic demands during the term of those contracts. *Provided the selection of the bargaining representative remains free,* such waivers contribute to the normal flow of commerce and to the maintenance of regular production schedules. Individuals violating such clauses appropriately lose their status as employees.

The waiver in the contract before us, upon which petitioners rely, is as follows:

> 5. The Union agrees that during the term of this agreement, there shall be no interference of any kind with the operations of the Employers, or any interruptions or slackening of production of work by any of its members. The Union further agrees to refrain from engaging in any strike or work stoppage during the term of this agreement.

That clause expresses concern for the continued operation of the plant and has a natural application to strikes and work stoppages involving the subject matter of the contract....

Petitioners argue that the words "any strike" leave no room for interpretation and necessarily include all strikes, even those against unlawful practices destructive of the foundation on which collective bargaining must rest. We disagree. We believe that the contract, taken as a whole, deals solely with the economic relationship between the employers and their employees. It is a typical collective-bargaining contract dealing with terms of employment and the normal operations of the plant. It is for one year and assumes the existence of a lawfully designated bargaining representative. Its strike and lockout clauses are natural adjuncts of an operating policy aimed at avoiding interruptions of production prompted by efforts to change existing economic relationships. The main function of arbitration under the contract is to provide a mechanism for avoiding similar stoppages due to disputes over the meaning and application of the various contractual provisions.

To adopt petitioners' all-inclusive interpretation of the clause is quite a different matter. That interpretation would eliminate, for the whole year, the employees' right to strike, even if petitioners, by coercion, ousted the employees' lawful bargaining representative and, by threats of discharge, caused the employees to sign membership cards in a new union. Whatever may be said of the legality of such a waiver when explicitly stated, there is no adequate basis for implying its existence without a more compelling expression of it than appears in § 5 of this contract....

II

Does § 8(d) of the National Labor Relations Act, as amended, deprive individuals of their status as employees if, within the waiting period prescribed by § 8(d)(4), they engage in a strike solely against unfair labor practices of their employers?....

The language in § 8(d) especially relied upon by petitioners is as follows:

> Any employee who engages in a strike within the sixty-day period specified in this subsection shall lose his status as an employee of the employer engaged in the particular labor dispute, for the purposes of §§ 8, 9, and 10 of this Act, as amended....

Petitioners contend that the above words must be so read that employees who engage in any strike, regardless of its purpose, within the 60-day waiting period, thereby lose their status as employees. That interpretation would deprive Ciccone and his fellow strikers of their rights to reinstatement and would require the reversal of the judgment of the Court of Appeals. If the above words are read in complete isolation from their context in the Act, such an interpretation is possible. However, "In expounding a statute, we must not be guided by a single sentence or member of a sentence, but look to the provisions of the whole law, and its object and policy." *United States v. Boisdore's Heirs,* 8 How. 113, 122....

Reading the clause in conjunction with the rest of § 8, the Board points out that "the sixty-day period" referred to is the period mentioned in paragraph (4) of § 8(d). That paragraph requires the party giving notice of a desire to *"terminate or modify"* such a contract, as part of its obligation to bargain under § 8(a)(5) or § 8(b)(3), to continue "in full force and effect, without resorting to strike or lockout, all the terms and conditions of the existing contract for a period of sixty days after such notice is given or until the expiration date of such contract, whichever occurs later." Section 8(d) thus seeks, during this natural renegotiation period, to relieve the parties from the economic pressure of a strike or lockout in relation to the subjects of negotiation. The final clause of § 8(d) also warns employees that, if they join a proscribed strike, they shall thereby lose their status as employees and, consequently, their right to reinstatement.

The Board reasons that the words which provide the key to a proper interpretation of § 8(d) with respect to this problem are "termination or modification." Since the Board expressly found that the instant strike was *not to terminate or modify* the contract, but was designed instead to protest the unfair labor practices of petitioners, the loss-of-status provision of § 8(d) is not applicable. We sustain that interpretation. Petitioners' construction would produce incongruous results. It concedes that prior to the 60-day negotiating period, employees have a right to strike against unfair labor practices designed to oust the employees' bargaining representative, yet petitioners' interpretation of § 8(d) means that if the employees give the 60-day notice of their desire to modify the contract, they are penalized for exercising that right to strike. This would deprive them of their most effective weapon at a time when their need for it is obvious. Although the employees' request to modify the contract would demonstrate their need for the services of their freely chosen representative, petitioners' interpretation would have the incongruous effect of cutting off the employees' freedom to strike against unfair labor practices aimed at that representative. This would relegate the employees to filing charges under a procedure too slow to be effective. The result would unduly favor the employers and handicap the employees during negotiation periods contrary to the purpose of the act. There also is inherent inequity in any interpretation that penalizes one party to a contract for conduct induced solely by the unlawful conduct of the other, thus giving advantage to the wrongdoer.

Petitioners contend that, unless the loss-of-status clause is applicable to unfair labor practice strikes, as well as to economic strikes, it adds nothing to the existing law relating to loss of status. Assuming that to be so, the clause is justifiable as a clarification of the law and as a warning to employees against engaging in economic strikes during the statutory waiting period. Moreover, in the face of the affirmative emphasis that is placed by the act upon freedom of concerted action and freedom of choice of representatives, any limitation on the employees' right to strike against violations of §§ 7 and 8(a), protecting those freedoms, must be more explicit and clear than it is here in order to restrict them at the very time they may be most needed....

As neither the collective-bargaining contract nor § 8(d) of the National Labor Relations Act, as amended, stands in the way, the judgment of the Court of Appeals is

Affirmed.

MR. JUSTICE FRANKFURTER, whom MR. JUSTICE MINTON and MR. JUSTICE HARLAN join, dissenting.

... The Board and the Court of Appeals rightly held that the "no-strike" clause in the contract does not cover a work stoppage provoked by the petitioners' unfair labor practices.... Petitioners contend that the discharged workers lost their status as employees by reason of the 60-day "cooling-off" period provided by § 8(d) of the act....

... Section 8 of the Wagner Act was amended [by the Taft-Hartley Act] and duties were placed upon unions. Collective action which violates any of these duties is, of course, activity unprotected by § 7. See Cox, The Right to Engage in Concerted Activities, 26 Ind. L.J. 319, 325-333 (1951). One of these new union duties, and an important one, is contained in § 8(d): unions may not strike to enforce their demands during the 60-day "cooling-off" period.

By reason of this new enactment, participating workers would not be engaged in a protected activity under § 7 by striking for the most legitimate economic reasons during the 60-day period. The strike would be in violation of the provision of that section which says that during the period there shall be no resort to a strike. The employer could discharge such strikers without violating § 8. This would be so if § 8 were without the loss-of-status provision. The Board would be powerless to order reinstatement under § 10. The loss-of-status provision in § 8(d) does not curtail the Board's power, since it did not have power to order reinstatement where a strike is resorted to for economic reasons before the 60-day period has expired. In such a situation the striker has no rights under §§ 8 and 10. Yet the Board would have us construe the loss-of-status provision as applicable only to the economic striker and qualifying a power which the Board does not have.

It is with respect to the unfair-labor-practice striker that the provision serves a purpose. This becomes clear if we assume that there were no such provision and examine the consequences of its absence. On such an assumption, a strike based on an unfair labor practice by the employer during the 60-day period may or may not be a protected activity under § 7. If it is, obviously discharged strikers would be entitled to reinstatement. The strike would not be a § 7 activity, however, if, for example, it were in breach of a no-strike clause in the contract which extends to a work stoppage provoked by an employer unfair labor practice, *cf. NLRB v. Sands Mfg. Co.,* 306 U.S. 332, 344 (1939), or if the no-strike clause in § 8(d)(4) (not to be confused with the loss-of-status provision) extends to such a work stoppage. However, even if the strike is not a § 7 activity, the Board in the unfair-labor-practice strike situation as distinguished from the economic strike situation, may in its discretion order the discharged participants reinstated. This is so because of the antecedent employer unfair practice which caused the strike, and which gave employees rights under § 8. If the Board finds that reinstatement of such strikers is a remedy that would effectuate the policies of the act, it has the power under § 10(c) to issue the necessary order.

This would not be the case, however, if the loss-of-status provision were held applicable to unfair-labor-practice strikes, because participating workers would lose their rights as "employees" for the purposes of §§ 8 and 10. Under the act only "employees" are eligible for reinstatement. The unfair-labor-practice strike, then, is the one situation where loss of status for the purposes of §§ 8 and 10 is of significance. At any rate, we have not been advised of any other situation to which the provision would apply.

We are therefore confronted with the demonstrable fact that if the provision stripping strikers of their status as employees during the 60-day period is to have any usefulness at all and not be an idle collection of words, the fact that a strike during that period is induced by the employer's unfair labor practice is immaterial.[1] Even though this might on first impression seem an undesirable result, it is so only by rejecting the important considerations in promoting peaceful industrial relations which might well have determined the action of Congress. In the first place, the Congress may have set a very high value on peaceful adjustments, *i.e.,* the absence of strikes. One may take judicial notice of the fact that this consideration was at the very forefront of the thinking and feeling of the Eightieth Congress. And there is another consideration not unrelated to this. While in a particular case the cause of a strike may be clear, and in a particular case there may be no controversy regarding the circumstances which prove that an employer committed an unfair labor practice, as a matter of experience that is not always true, indeed often it is not true. One of the sharpest controversies, one of the issues most difficult of determination, is the very question of what precipitated a work stoppage. This is especially true where a new contract is being negotiated. It is not at all unreasonable, therefore, to find a congressional desire to preclude litigation over what all too often is a contentious subject and to deter all strikes during the crucial period of negotiation....

... Since the loss-of-status provision has an effect only in an unfair-labor-practice strike, the judgment of the Court of Appeals should be reversed.

NOTES

1. *Mastro Plastics* holds that a general no-strike clause does not waive the employees' right to strike in response to unfair labor practices committed by the employer. Does this mean that a strike in protest of *any* unfair labor practice is immune from a general no-strike clause? In *Arlan's Dep't Store,* 133 N.L.R.B. 802 (1961), a majority of a Board panel held that only strikes in protest against *serious* unfair labor practices should be held immune from general no-strike clauses. Member Fanning dissented, taking the position that all unfair labor prac-

---

[1] It may be noted that the opponents of the Taft-Hartley Act objected to the loss-of-status provision for just this reason:

> [T]he section is silent as to the Board's authority to accommodate conflicting issues such as provocation on the part of the employer. Under this section an employer desirous of ridding himself either of the employees or their representative can engage in the most provocative conduct without fear of redress except by way of a lengthy hearing before the Board and a subsequent admonition to thereafter "cease and desist" from such practices. In striking contrast to the relatively delicate treatment provided for such action by an employer, employees unwilling idly to countenance abuse, who resort to self-help under the circumstances are removed from the protection of the statute and lose "employee" status. An employer is at liberty under such circumstances freely to replace any employee bold enough to insist upon justice. The provision denies to the Board the exercise of any discretion to accommodate the equitable doctrine of "clean hands." The provisions of the section are conclusive—the employee is subject to summary dismissal irrespective of the employer's conduct.

S. Rep. No. 105 (Minority), Part 2, 80th Cong., 1st Sess. 21-22 (1947).

tices are serious. *See also Dow Chem. Co.,* 244 N.L.R.B. 1060 (1979), *enforcement denied,* 636 F.2d 1352 (3d Cir. 1980), *cert. denied,* 454 U.S. 818 (1981).

2. *Disparate Discipline of Union Officers.* Following a work stoppage in violation of a no-strike provision, an employer may punish the strikers universally, randomly, or in proportion to guilt. Thus, it may discipline only the union steward if the steward instigated the stoppage. *Midwest Precision Castings Co.,* 244 N.L.R.B. 597 (1979). Should an employer be permitted to impose a more severe sanction on a union official who, while not instigating the work stoppage, makes no attempt to enforce a no-strike clause? In *Metropolitan Edison Co. v. NLRB,* 460 U.S. 693 (1983), the Supreme Court held unanimously that in the absence of an explicit contractual duty imposed on union officials, an employer's disparate disciplining of them more severely than other employees for merely participating in a work stoppage in breach of a no-strike clause would violate § 8(a)(3) of the NLRA. The Court noted expressly that the union officials had not taken a leadership role in the unlawful strike. The Court went on to state that a union could make a "clear and unmistakable" waiver of the officials' statutory right, but concluded that the union's silence in the face of two adverse arbitration decisions under a prior labor agreement did not constitute such a waiver.

Where a collective contract requires the union to take steps to terminate any unlawful work stoppage, an employer may discipline union officials who participate in an impermissible strike more severely than other strike participants. *See Indiana & Mich. Elec. Co.,* 273 N.L.R.B. 1540 (1985), *aff'd,* 786 F.2d 733 (6th Cir. 1986). *See* Note, *Selective Discipline of Union Officials after Metropolitan Edison v. NLRB,* 63 B.U.L. Rev. 473 (1983).

3. *Bethenergy Mines,* 308 N.L.R.B. 1242 (1992), involved five employees who were discharged because of their participation in unprotected strike conduct. The union induced the employer to reinstate them, but agreed to a provision that prevented them from holding any union office that dealt directly with management during the remaining term of the existing bargaining agreement. The Board found no unlawful discrimination against their union activity, since the reinstated individuals had voluntarily and knowingly waived their § 7 rights.

NLRB v. MACKAY RADIO & TELEGRAPH CO.

Supreme Court of the United States
304 U.S. 333, 58 S. Ct. 904, 82 L. Ed. 1381 (1938)

[The Mackay Company, which was engaged in the communication business, maintained an office in San Francisco, where it employed some sixty supervisors, operators, and clerks, many of whom were members of Local No. 3 of the American Radio Telegraphists Association. In an attempt to force the company to enter into a collective agreement covering marine and point-to-point operators the ARTA called a strike on October 4, 1935, in which Local No. 3 participated. In order to maintain service, the company brought employees from its Los Angeles and Chicago offices to fill the San Francisco strikers' places. The strike was unsuccessful, and on October 7 overtures to return to work were made in San Francisco. Company representatives advised the strikers that they could return to work, but subject to the qualification that eleven of the replacements had been promised permanent employment in San Francisco if they so desired. Accordingly, the strikers were told that they could return to work in a body, with the exception of eleven men who were told they would have to file applications for reinstatement, to be passed upon by a New York executive of the company. Thereafter, it appeared that only five of the replacements desired to remain with the company in San Francisco, and six of the eleven strikers who had been told to file formal applications for reinstatement were allowed to return to their jobs, along with the other strikers. The five strikers who were denied reinstatement were prominent in the activities of the union, and filed charges with the NLRB that the company had violated §§ 8(1) and 8(3) of the original NLRA in denying them reinstatement. An NLRB complaint issued, and in due course the NLRB held the company guilty as charged, and issued a cease and desist order, and an order requiring the company to offer the five men immediate and full reinstatement. After refusal by the circuit court of appeals to enforce this order, the case was taken by the Supreme Court on certiorari. *Held,* reversed and remanded. The strikers remained "employees" under § 2(3) of the act. While there was no unfair labor practice by the company prior to or during the strike, the Board's finding of discrimination in excluding the five strikers from reinstatement was supported by the evidence.]

MR. JUSTICE ROBERTS delivered the opinion of the Court.

... Nor was it an unfair labor practice to replace the striking employees with others in an effort to carry on the business. Although § 13 provides, "Nothing in this Act shall be construed so as to interfere with or impede or diminish in any way the right to strike," it does not follow that an employer, guilty of no act denounced by the statute, has lost the right to protect and continue his business by supplying places left vacant by strikers. And he is not bound to discharge those hired to fill the places of strikers, upon the election of the latter to resume their employment, in order to create places for them. The assurance by respondent to those who accepted employment during the strike that if they so desired their places might be permanent was not an unfair labor practice nor was it such to reinstate only so many of the strikers as there were vacant places to be filled. But the claim put forward is that the unfair labor practice indulged by the respondent was discrimination in reinstating striking employees by keeping out certain of them for the sole reason that they had been active in the union. As we have said, the strikers retained, under the Act, the status of employees. Any such discrimination in putting them back to work is, therefore, prohibited by § 8....

As we have said, the respondent was not bound to displace men hired to take the strikers' places in order to provide positions for them. It might have refused reinstatement on the grounds of skill or ability, but the Board found that it did not do so. It might have resorted to any one of a number of methods of determining which of its striking employees would have to wait because five men had taken permanent positions during the strike, but it is found that the preparation and use of the list [*i.e.,* the list of the names of the eleven men originally selected for exclusion], and the action taken by the respondent, were with the purpose to discriminate against those most active in the union. There is evidence to support these findings.

NOTES

1. *Economic Strikes.* Since the decision in the principal case, it has been recognized that where the employer is "guilty of no act denounced by the statute," it has a right, in order to keep its plant in operation, to hire permanent replacements for strikers, and thus to deprive the replaced strikers of an immediate right of reinstatement. "If employees go out on strike for economic reasons and not because of any unfair labor practices on the part of their employer, the latter may replace them in order to keep his business running, and the strikers thereafter have no absolute right of reinstatement to their old jobs. After the termination of a strike, however, an employer may not discriminatorily refuse to reinstate or reemploy the strikers merely because of their union membership or concerted activity." NLRB, Eighth Annual Report 32 (1943). In order to take advantage of their reinstatement rights, unreplaced economic strikers must make an unconditional application for reinstatement, either personally or through their union.

In *NLRB v. International Van Lines,* 409 U.S. 48 (1972), the Supreme Court held that an employer had to offer unconditional reinstatement to striking employees whom it had discharged *before* it hired permanent replacements, since the termination of economic strikers constitutes a *per se* unfair labor practice. *Compare Chromalloy Am. Corp. v. NLRB,* 873 F.2d 1150 (8th Cir. 1989), wherein the court disagreed with the Labor Board and held that an employer was merely informing striking employees of their permanent replacement, not their impermissible discharge, when it wrote them: "As of this date we have hired a permanent replacement for your job classification.... You are no longer employed." *See also Noel Foods v. NLRB*, 82 F.3d 1113 (D.C. Cir. 1996), which concerned an employer that made a pre-strike statement that it would permanently replace any employee who went on strike and that hired permanent replacements for the striking employees as soon as the work stoppage commenced. The court rejected the Labor Board's conclusion that the firm had illegally discharged the employees before the strike had begun, and held that it had lawfully exercised its *Mackay Radio* right to hire permanent replacements once the stoppage had begun.

In *Pirelli Cable Corp. v. NLRB,* 141 F.3d 503 (4th Cir. 1998), the court rejected the Board finding that an employer had illegally threatened employees when it gave them a pre-strike letter explaining its right to hire permanent replacements for striking employees.

In *Laidlaw Corp.*, 171 N.L.R.B. 1366 (1968), the Labor Board declared that "economic strikers who unconditionally apply for reinstatement at a time when their positions are filled by permanent replacements: (1) remain employees; (2) are entitled to full reinstatement upon the departure of replacements unless they have in the meantime acquired regular and substantially equivalent employment, or the employer can sustain his burden of proof that the failure to offer full reinstatement was for legitimate and substantial business reasons." *Laidlaw* was enforced in 414 F.2d 99 (7th Cir. 1969), *cert. denied,* 397 U.S. 920 (1970). The Board recognized in *Rose Printing Co.*, 304 N.L.R.B. 1076 (1991), that an employer need not offer former economic strikers reinstatement to jobs that are not the same or substantially equivalent to their old jobs, even when the workers are qualified to fill them. On the other hand, an employer may not refuse to reinstate economic strikers because of its belief that replacement workers may be hostile to the returning strikers. *Diamond Walnut Growers*, 316 N.L.R.B. 36 (1995), *enforced in relevant part*, 113 F.3d 1259 (D.C. Cir. 1997) (*en banc*), *cert. denied*, 118 S. Ct. 1299 (1998).

In *NLRB v. Oregon Steel Mills*, 47 F.3d 1536 (9th Cir. 1995), the court held that an employer violated § 8(a)(3) when it bypassed qualified strikers on a preferential rehire list in favor of temporary workers obtained through outside employment agencies. The court rejected the employer's contention that the duty to rehire strikers only applies when the firm hires new employees onto its own payroll.

In *Brooks Research & Mfg., Inc.*, 202 N.L.R.B. 634 (1973), the NLRB held that there is no time limit on an employer's obligation to reinstate economic strikers who have made an unconditional application for reinstatement. An employer may not unilaterally terminate their seniority and recall rights without bargaining with the union. An employer may, however, require unreinstated strikers to periodically indicate their continued interest in reemployment. *See Aqua-Chem, Inc.*, 288 N.L.R.B. 1108 (1988), *enforced,* 910 F.2d 1487 (7th Cir. 1990); *NLRB v. Penn Corp.*, 630 F.2d 561 (8th Cir. 1979).

Could a union and an employer, as part of a strike settlement, place time limits on the reinstatement rights of economic strikers? What are the factors that should be considered in evaluating such an agreement? In *United Aircraft Corp.*, 192 N.L.R.B. 382 (1971), *enforced in part sub nom. Machinists Lodges 743 & 1746 v. United Aircraft Corp.*, 534 F.2d 422 (2d Cir. 1975), the Labor Board indicated that it would accept a strike settlement agreement as determining the reinstatement rights of economic strikers, if the period fixed by the agreement for reinstatement of the strikers (1) is not unreasonably short, (2) is not intended to be discriminatory, or misused by either party with the intent of accomplishing a discriminatory objective, (3) was not insisted upon by the employer to undermine the status of the union, and (4) was the result of good-faith bargaining. On remand, the Board concluded that any breach by the employer of a strike settlement agreement governing the rehire of strikers is *ipso facto* a violation of § 8(a)(3). *United Aircraft Corp.,* 247 N.L.R.B. 1042 (1980), *enforced by order,* 661 F.2d 909 (2d Cir. 1981), *cert. denied,* 455 U.S. 1001 (1982). Regarding the general rights accorded economic strikers, *see* LeRoy, *Regulating Employer Use of Permanent Striker Replacements: Empirical Analysis of NLRA and RLA Strikes 1935-1991,* 16 Berkeley J. Empl. & Lab. L. 169 (1995); Estreicher, *Strikers and Replacements,* 38 Lab. L.J. 287 (1987).

(handwritten margin note: No permanent replacement)

2. *Unfair Labor Practice Strikes.* It is well established that when a strike has been called because of the employer's unfair labor practices (e.g., a refusal to bargain with a certified union), the employer is not legally free to hire permanent replacements and is obligated to reinstate the strikers upon their request. *Collins & Aikman Corp.,* 165 N.L.R.B. 678 (1967), *enforced,* 395 F.2d 277 (4th Cir. 1968).

In *Northern Wire Corp. v. NLRB,* 887 F.2d 1313 (7th Cir. 1989), the court held that union members were unfair labor practice strikers entitled to reinstatement and backpay despite their employer's contention that even without the unfair labor practices they would have struck over economic demands. It was sufficient that the stoppage was at least partially motivated by the employer's unfair labor practices. *But see California Acrylic Indus. v. NLRB,* 150 F.3d 1095 (9th Cir. 1998) (strike motivated primarily by economic issues is economic strike despite accompanying employer unfair labor practices).

3. *Economic Strikes Converted into Unfair Labor Practice Strikes.* If the employer first commits unfair labor practices *during* the course of an on-going economic strike, thereby prolonging it, the strike at that point becomes an unfair practice strike, and strikers who are replaced after that point are entitled to reinstatement upon request. *NLRB v. Pecheur Lozenge Co.,* 209 F.2d 393 (2d Cir. 1953), *cert. denied,* 347 U.S. 953 (1954); *American Cyanamid Co. v. NLRB,* 592 F.2d 356 (7th Cir. 1979). To convert an economic strike into an unfair labor practice strike, the employer's unlawful conduct must actually be found to have prolonged or intensified the work stoppage. *See F.L. Thorpe & Co. v. NLRB,* 71 F.3d 282 (8th Cir. 1995) (strikers' testimony showed continuing economic motivation despite "consternation" caused by unlawful supervisory statements); *NLRB v. Harding Glass Co.,* 80 F.3d 7 (1st Cir. 1996) (Board erroneously presumed that employer's unlawful implementation of wage proposal necessarily prolonged strike). *Compare Distillery Workers Local 42 v. NLRB,* 951 F.2d 1308 (D.C. Cir. 1991), wherein the court held that an unfair labor practice strike became an economic strike when the employees continued striking for reasons that were unrelated to the unfair labor practice, even though the employer had not fully "cured" the latter. *See generally* Comment, *Reconversion of Unfair Labor Practice Strikes to Economic Strikes,* 64 Geo. L.J. 1143 (1976).

(handwritten margin note: Employer Must have prolonged the Strike)

4. *Sympathy Strikes.* In the absence of an applicable no-strike obligation, the prevailing view is that an employer may not terminate employees who honor a primary picket line at another employer's premises. Such individuals are normally treated as economic strikers. Their employer may not discipline them, but it may hire permanent replacements for them in order to maintain efficient business operations by retaining other persons who will cross the picket line. *See, e.g., Redwing Carriers, Inc.,* 137 N.L.R.B. 1545 (1962), *enforced,* 325 F.2d 1011 (D.C. Cir. 1963), *cert. denied,* 377 U.S. 905 (1964). *But see NLRB v. L.G. Everist, Inc.,* 334 F.2d 312 (8th Cir. 1964) (holding that sympathy strikers are not engaged in protected activity). *See also Business Servs. by Manpower v. NLRB,* 784 F.2d 442 (2d Cir. 1986), in which the court ruled that the Board should not apply a per se approach to terminations involving sympathy strikers but should instead balance "the right of the employee to express his union sympathies and the right of the employer to conduct his business." *See generally* Brod, *Through the Window of Legislative History: A View of the Employees' Statutory Right to Honor a Stranger Picket Line,* 35 Kan. L. Rev. 9 (1986); Haggard, *Picket Line Observance as a Protected Concerted Activity,* 53 N.C.L. Rev. 43 (1974).

In *Indianapolis Power & Light Co.,* 273 N.L.R.B. 1715 (1985), the Labor Board overruled established precedent and held that a general no-strike clause must be read as precluding all work stoppages, including sympathy strikes. It thus sustained the right of an employer to suspend a worker who had refused to cross the picket line at the premises of another company where the applicable bargaining agreement prohibited "any strike, picketing, ... or other curtailment of work." In *IBEW Local 387 v. NLRB (Arizona Pub. Serv. Co.),* 788 F.2d 1412 (9th Cir. 1986), however, the court held that the per se application of the Board's *Indianapolis Power & Light* doctrine was inappropriate. The Board had to consider the actual intent of the contracting parties from such evidence as their bargaining history, their past practice, and the state of the law with respect to this issue at the time they negotiated their general no-strike clause. The D.C. Circuit essentially agreed with the Ninth Circuit's view in *IBEW Local 1395 v. NLRB,* 797 F.2d 280 (1986), and remanded *Indianapolis Power & Light* for further proceedings. On remand, the Board reaffirmed the views expressed in *Indianapolis Power & Light I,* but indicated that extrinsic evidence may be used to show that the contracting parties did not intend a general no-strike clause to cover sympathy strikes. *Indianapolis Power & Light Co.,* 291 N.L.R.B. 1039 (1988), *enforced,* 898 F.2d 524 (7th Cir. 1980).

TRANS WORLD AIRLINES, INC. v. INDEPENDENT FEDERATION OF FLIGHT ATTENDANTS

Supreme Court of the United States
489 U.S. 426, 109 S. Ct. 1225, 103 L. Ed. 2d 456 (1989)

JUSTICE O'CONNOR delivered the opinion of the Court.

We decide today whether, at the end of a strike, an employer is required by the Railway Labor Act (RLA or Act), 44 Stat. 577, as amended, 45 U.S.C. § 151 *et seq.,* to displace employees who worked during the strike in order to reinstate striking employees with greater seniority.

I

In March 1984, Trans World Airlines, Inc. (TWA) and the Independent Federation of Flight Attendants (IFFA or Union) began negotiations pursuant to § 6 of the RLA, 45 U.S.C. § 156, on a new collective bargaining agreement to replace their prior agreement due to expire on July 31, 1984. The existing collective bargaining agreement created a complex system of bidding the general effect of which was to insure that those flight attendants with the greatest seniority would have the best opportunity to obtain their preferred job assignments, flight schedules, and bases of operation as vacancies appeared, and to insure that senior flight attendants would be least affected by the periodic furloughs endemic to the airline industry. Thus, for example, should a job vacancy appear at the highly desirable Los Angeles or San Francisco bases of operation or "domiciles," the most senior qualified flight attendant who bid on such a vacancy would be entitled to it. Conversely, should a reduction in force eliminate a position in the Los Angeles domicile, the furloughed flight attendant could opt to displace the most junior attendant of equal rank in the entire system or the most junior attendant of lower rank either at the same domicile or in the entire system. 1981-1984 TWA/IFFA Collective Bargaining Agreement, Arts. 12-13, 18-A, 18-B.

For two years TWA and the Union unsuccessfully bargained over wages and working conditions not including the seniority bidding system. They pursued all the required dispute resolution mechanisms of the RLA, including direct negotiation, 45 U.S.C. § 152 Second, mediation, 45 U.S.C. § 155 First, and the final 30-day "cooling off" period. *Ibid.* By early 1986 a strike seemed imminent and on March 7, 1986, the Union went out on strike.

TWA informed its flight attendants before and during the strike that it would continue operations by hiring permanent replacements for striking flight attendants, by continuing to employ any flight attendant who chose not to strike, and by rehiring any striker who abandoned the strike and made an unconditional offer to return to any available vacancies. TWA also informed its flight attendants that any vacancies created as a result of the strike would be filled by application of the seniority bidding system to all working flight attendants and that such job and domicile assignments would remain effective after the strike ended. Thus, at the conclusion of the strike, senior full-term strikers would not be permitted to displace permanent replacements or junior nonstriking flight attendants and could be left without an opportunity to return to work. TWA's promise not to displace working flight attendants after the strike created two incentives specifically linked to the seniority bidding system: it gave senior flight attendants an incentive to remain at or return to work in order to retain their prior jobs and domicile assignments; it gave junior flight attendants an incentive to remain at or return to work in order to obtain job and domicile assignments that were previously occupied by more senior, striking flight attendants.

As promised, TWA continued its operations during the 72-day strike by utilizing approximately 1,280 flight attendants who either did not strike or returned to work before the end of the strike and by hiring and fully training approximately 2,350 new flight attendants, some 1,220 of whom were hired during the first few days of the strike. On May 17, 1986, the Union made an unconditional offer to TWA on behalf of the approximately 5,000 flight attendants who had remained on strike to return to work. TWA accepted the offer but refused the Union's May 27th demand that TWA displace those prestrike employees who were working as of May 17 ("crossover" employees). Accordingly, TWA initially recalled only the 197 most senior full-term strikers to fill available job and domicile vacancies. By the terms of a poststrike arbitral agreement, these strikers and all subsequently reinstated full-term strikers returned to work as vacancies arose and with precisely the seniority they would have had if no strike had occurred. In May 1988, more than 1,100 full-term strikers had been reinstated with full seniority.

In an effort to reinstate all the full-term strikers by displacing the newly hired flight attendants and less senior crossover employees, the Union proceeded on two fronts. First, it brought an injunction action alleging that the full-term strikers were not "economic strikers" but "unfair labor practice strikers" entitled to reinstatement by application of principles this Court has developed in interpreting the National Labor Relations Act (NLRA). 29 U.S.C. § 151 *et seq. See Mastro Plastics Corp. v. NLRB,* 350 U.S. 270 (1956). The District Court ultimately ruled against the Union on this claim. *Independent Federation of Flight Attendants v. Trans World Airlines, Inc.,* 682 F. Supp. 1003 (WD Mo. 1988), appeal pending, No. 88-1984M (CA8). At the same time, the Union filed the instant action contending that, even assuming the strike was economic, the full-term strikers were entitled to reinstatement either under the terms of the prestrike collective bargaining agreement or under the RLA itself. On cross motions for partial summary judgment, the District Court held that the full-term strikers were not entitled to displace either the junior crossovers or the 1,220 new hires employed by TWA immediately after the strike commenced. (The motions did not require the District Court to rule on the status of the remaining new hires.) The District Court also held that 463 new hires not fully trained by the end of the strike could be displaced by full-term strikers. *Independent Federation of Flight Attendants v. Trans World Airlines, Inc.,* 643 F. Supp. 470 (WD Mo. 1986)....

... The Court of Appeals ... affirmed the District Court's ruling that full-term strikers could not displace the 1,220 fully trained new hires but could displace the 463 untrained new hires. *Independent Federation of Flight Attendants v. Trans World Airlines, Inc.,* 819 F.2d 839 (CA8 1987). The Court of Appeals, however, reversed the District Court's ruling that more senior full-term strikers could not displace junior crossovers....

... Today, we reverse the Court of Appeals and hold that an employer is not required by the RLA to lay off junior crossovers in order to reinstate more senior full-term strikers at the conclusion of the strike.

II

We have observed in the past that carefully drawn analogies from the federal common labor law developed under the NLRA may be helpful in deciding cases under the RLA. *Trainmen v. Jacksonville Terminal Co.,* 394 U.S. 369, 377 (1969). Thus, as in this case, those lower courts that have examined the reinstatement rights of strikers under the RLA have turned to NLRA precedents for guidance. *E.g., Air Line Pilots Ass'n International v. United Air Lines, Inc.,* 614 F. Supp. 1020, 1041, 1045-1046 (ND Ill. 1985), aff'd in part and rev'd in part on other grounds, 802 F.2d 886 (CA7 1986), cert. denied, 480 U.S. 946 (1987); *National Airlines, Inc. v. International Assn. of Machinists & Aerospace Workers,* 416 F.2d 998, 1004-1006 (CA5 1969).

We first considered the reinstatement rights of strikers under the NLRA in *NLRB v. Mackay Radio & Telegraph Co.,* 304 U.S. 333 (1938). In *Mackay Radio,* radio and telegraph operators working in the San Francisco offices of a national telecommunications firm went on strike. In order to continue operations, the employer brought employees from its other offices to fill the strikers' places. At the conclusion of the strike, the striking operators sought to displace their replacements in order to return to work. We held that it was not an unfair labor practice under § 8 of the NLRA for the employer to have replaced the striking employees with others "in an effort to carry on the business," or to have refused to discharge the replacements in order to make room for the strikers at the conclusion of the strike. *Id.,* at 345-346. As we there observed, "[t]he assurance by [the employer] to those who accepted employment during the strike that if they so desired their places might be permanent was not an unfair labor practice nor was it such to reinstate only so many of the strikers as there were vacant places to be filled." *Id.,* at 346. On various occasions we have reaffirmed the holding of *Mackay Radio. See NLRB v. Erie Resistor Corp.,* 373 U.S. 221, 232 (1963). ("We have no intention of questioning the continuing vitality of the *Mackay* rule ..."); *NLRB V. Fleetwood Trailer Co.,* 389 U.S. 375, 379 (1967) (Employers have "'legitimate and substantial business justifications' for refusing to reinstate employees who engaged in an economic strike ... when the jobs claimed by the strikers are occupied by workers hired as permanent replacements during the strike in order to continue operations"); *Belknap, Inc. v. Hale,* 463 U.S. 491, 504, n. 8 (1983) ("The refusal to fire permanent replacements because of commitments made to them in the course of an economic strike satisfies the requirement ... that the employer have a 'legitimate and substantial justification' for its refusal to reinstate strikers").

TWA asks us to apply this line of cases decided under the NLRA to determine the status under the RLA of those prestrike flight attendants who were working at the conclusion of the strike. TWA argues that it would be completely anomalous to hold that full-term strikers may displace junior crossovers when, as the Union has conceded, they may not displace newly hired permanent replacements under either statute. The union, by contrast, argues that the rule of *Mackay Radio* is inapplicable to junior crossovers because of differences between the RLA and the NLRA and because, even under the NLRA, junior crossovers would be treated differently than newly hired permanent replacements.

The Union relies on *Erie Resistor, supra,* to distinguish junior cross-overs from new hires under the NLRA. In *Erie Resistor* we struck down an employer's award of 20 years' super-seniority to new hires and crossovers as an unfair labor practice within the meaning of § 8(a)(1) and § 8(a)(3) of the NLRA. 29 U.S.C. §§ 158(a)(1), 158(a)(3). We observed:

> ... Super-seniority affects the tenure of all strikers whereas permanent replacement, proper under *Mackay,* affects only those who are, in actuality, replaced. It is one thing to say that a striker is subject to loss of his job at the strike's end but quite another to hold that in addition to the threat of replacement, all strikers will at best return to their jobs with seniority inferior to that of the replacements and of those who left the strike.
>
> ...
>
> Unlike the replacement granted in Mackay which ceases to be an issue once the strike is over, the [super-seniority] plan here creates a cleavage in the plant continuing long after the strike is ended. Employees are henceforth divided into two camps: those who stayed with the union and those who returned before the end of the strike and thereby gained extra seniority. This breach is reemphasized with each subsequent layoff and stands as an ever-present reminder of the dangers connected with striking and with union activities in general. [373 U.S., at 230-231].

The Union does not and cannot contend that reinstated full-term strikers have less seniority relative to new hires and junior crossovers than they would have had if they had not remained on strike. It is clear that reinstated full-term strikers lost no seniority either in absolute or relative terms. Thus, unlike the situation in *Erie Resistor,* any future reductions in force at TWA will permit reinstated full-term strikers to displace junior flight attendants exactly as would have been the case in the absence of any strike. Similarly, should any vacancies develop in desirable job assignments or domiciles, reinstated full-term strikers who have bid on those vacancies will maintain their priority over junior flight attendants, whether they are new hires, crossovers, or full-term strikers. In the same vein, periodic bids on job scheduling will find senior reinstated full-term strikers maintaining their priority over all their junior colleagues. In short, once reinstated, the seniority of full-term strikers is in no way affected by their decision to strike.

Nevertheless, IFFA argues that TWA's refusal to displace junior crossovers will create a "cleavage" between junior crossovers and reinstated full-term strikers at TWA "long after the strike is ended." *Id.,* at 231. This is the case because desirable job assignments and domiciles that would have been occupied by the most senior flight attendants had there been no strike will continue to be held by those who did not see the strike through to its conclusion. For example, the senior full-term striker who worked in the Los Angeles domicile before the strike may have been replaced by a junior crossover. As poststrike vacancies develop in TWA's workforce, permitting reinstatement of full-term strikers, they are not likely to occur in the most desirable domiciles. Thus, it is unlikely that the senior full-term striker would be reinstated back to her preferred domicile. Resentful rifts among employees will also persist after the strike, the Union argues, because TWA's prestrike assurance of nondisplacement to junior crossovers unlike the same assurance to new hires, "set up a competition *among* those individuals who participated in the original decision to strike, and thereby undermined the group's ability to take the collective action that it is the very purpose of the [RLA] to protect."

We reject this effort to expand *Erie Resistor.* Both the RLA and the NLRA protect an employee's right to choose not to strike. 45 U.S.C. § 152 Fourth; 29 U.S.C. § 157, and, thereby, protect employees' rights to the "the benefit of their individual decisions not to strike ...." *Post,* n. 4 (BRENNAN, J., dissenting). Accordingly, in virtually every strike situation there will be some employees who disagree with their union's decision to strike and who cannot be required to abide by that decision. It is the inevitable effect of an employer's use of the economic weapons available during a period of self-help that these differences will be exacerbated and that poststrike resentments may be created. Thus, for example, the employer's right to hire permanent replacements in order to continue operations will inevitably also have the effect of dividing striking employees between those who, fearful of permanently losing their jobs, return to work and those who remain stalwart in the strike. In such a situation, apart from the "pressure on the strikers *as a group* to abandon the strike," to which the dissent refers, *post,* (BRENNAN, J., dissenting), a "competition" may arise *among* the striking employees to return to work in order to avoid being displaced by a permanent replacement. Similarly, employee awareness that an employer may decide to transfer working employees to necessary positions previously occupied by more senior striking employees will isolate employees fearful of losing those positions and employees coveting those positions from employees more committed to the strike. Conversely, a policy such as TWA employed here, in creating the incentive for individual strikers to return to work, also "puts pressure on the strikers *as a group* to abandon the strike," *ibid.,* in the same manner that the hiring of permanent replacements does.

None of these scenarios, however, present the prospect of a continuing diminution of seniority upon reinstatement at the end of the strike that was central to our decision in *Erie Resistor*. All that has occurred is that the employer has filled vacancies created by striking employees. Some of these vacancies will be filled by newly hired employees, others by doubtless more experienced and therefore more needed employees who either refused to strike or abandoned the strike. The dissent's observation that, "at the conclusion of the strike" discrimination in the filling of "available positions" based on union activity is impermissible, is beside the point. See *post,* (BRENNAN, J., dissenting). The positions occupied by newly hired replacements, employees who refused to strike, and employees who abandoned the strike, are simply not "available positions" to be filled. As noted above, those positions that were available at the conclusion of the strike were filled "according to some principle, such as seniority, that is neutral ..." *Post,* (BRENNAN, J., dissenting). That the prospect of a reduction in available positions may divide employees and create incentives among them to remain at work or abandon a strike before its conclusion is a secondary effect fairly within the arsenal of economic weapons available to employers during a period of self-help.

To distinguish crossovers from new hires in the manner IFFA proposes would have the effect of penalizing those who decided not to strike in order to benefit those who did. Because permanent replacements need not be discharged at the conclusion of a strike in which the union has been unsuccessful, a certain number of prestrike employees will find themselves without work. We see no reason why those employees who chose not to gamble on the success of the strike should suffer the consequences when the gamble proves unsuccessful. Requiring junior crossovers, who cannot themselves displace the newly hired permanent replacements, "who rank lowest in seniority," *post,* (BRENNAN, J., dissenting), to be displaced by more senior full-term strikers is precisely to visit the consequences of the lost gamble on those who refused to take the risk. While the employer and union in many circumstances may reach a back-to-work agreement that would displace crossovers and new hires or an employer may unilaterally decide to permit such displacement, nothing in the NLRA or the federal common law we have developed under that statute requires such a result. That such agreements are typically one mark of a successful strike is yet another indication that crossovers opted not to gamble; if the strike was successful the advantage gained by declining to strike disappears.

III

The Union argues, however, that whether or not the NLRA prohibits a crossover policy such as TWA's, the statutory framework of the RLA forbids such a policy....

[The Court went on to hold that § 2, Fourth of the RLA, 45 U.S.C. § 152, Fourth, which provides that "No carrier ... shall deny or in any way question the right of its employees to join, organize, or assist in organizing the labor organization of their choice, ... to interfere in any way with the organization of its employees ... or to influence or coerce employees in an effort to induce them to join or remain or not to join or remain members of any labor organization" was primarily intended to protect precertification organizing rights. That provision was not designed to regulate the forms of self-help available to carriers during a work stoppage.]

IV

Neither the RLA itself nor any analogies to the NLRA indicate that the crossover policy adopted by TWA during the period of self-help was unlawful. Rather, the decision to guarantee to crossovers the same protections lawfully applied to new hires was simple decision to apply the preexisting seniority terms of the collective bargaining agreement uniformly to all working employees. That this decision had the effect of encouraging prestrike workers to remain on the job during the strike or to abandon the strike and return to work before all vacancies were filled was an effect of the exercise of TWA's peaceful economic power, a power that the company was legally free to deploy once the parties had exhausted the private dispute resolution mechanisms of the RLA. Accordingly, the judgment of the Court of Appeals is

Reversed.

JUSTICE BRENNAN, with whom JUSTICE MARSHALL joins, dissenting.

The issue in this case is whether under the Railway Labor Act (RLA) an employer, in allocating available jobs among members of a bargaining unit at the conclusion of a strike, may discriminate against full-term strikers by giving preference to employees who crossed the picket line to return to work before the strike was over. Because I conclude that such discrimination on the basis of union activity is "inherently destructive" of the right to strike, as guaranteed by both the RLA and the National Labor Relations Act (NLRA), I dissent.

I

... The key to this case is a fundamental command of the RLA and the NLRA alike, which in the case of the RLA is textually anchored in § 2 Fourth: the employer may not engage in discrimination among its employees—whether at the precertification stage, the bargaining stage, or during or after a strike—on the basis of their degree of involvement in protected union activity such as a strike.[1]
...

---

[1]We have noted that § 2 Fourth is "comparable" to § 7 of the NLRA, which protects the right to engage in concerted activities. *Railroad Trainmen v. Jacksonville Terminal Co.,* 394 U.S. 369, 385, n. 20 (1969).

II

A.... The Court's conception of this case is most clearly expressed in a key paragraph that summarizes its discussion of the NLRA caselaw:

> To distinguish crossovers from new hires in the manner IFFA proposes would have the effect of penalizing those who decided not to strike in order to benefit those who did.... We see no reason why those employees who chose not to gamble on the success of the strike should suffer the consequences when the gamble proves unsuccessful. Requiring junior crossovers ... to be displaced by more senior full-term strikers is precisely to visit the consequences of the lost gamble on those who refused to take the risk.

This understanding of the Union's position contains a factual and a legal error, both of which infect the Court's analysis of the case.

In the first place, refusing to discriminate in favor of crossovers is not to visit the consequences of the lost strike on "those who refused to take the risk," but rather on those who rank lowest in seniority. Whether a given flight attendant chose to take the risk of the strike or not is wholly immaterial. Rather—as is virtually universally the case when work-force reductions are necessary for whatever reason in a unionized enterprise—it is the most junior employees, whether strikers or crossovers, who are most vulnerable. This is precisely the point of seniority.

More fundamental, I fear, is the legal mistake inherent in the Court's objection to "penalizing those who decided not to strike in order to benefit those who did." The Court, of course, does precisely the opposite: it allows TWA to single out for penalty precisely those employees who were faithful to the strike until the end, in order to benefit those who abandoned it. What is unarticulated is the Court's basis for choosing one position over the other. If indeed one group or the other is to be "penalized," what basis does the Court have for determining that it should be those who remained on strike rather than those who returned to work? I see none, unless it is perhaps an unarticulated hostility toward strikes. In any case the NLRA *does* provide a basis for resolving this question. It requires simply that in making poststrike reinstatements an employer may not discriminate among its employees on account of their union activity. That, in fact is the *holding* of *NLRB v. Mackay Radio, supra,* at 346—the more familiar teaching as to the employer's right to hire permanent replacements having been dictum. If an employer may not discriminate—in either direction—on the basis of the employee's strike activity, then it follows that the employer must make decisions about which employees to reinstate on the basis of some neutral criterion, such as seniority. That is precisely what the Union asks.[4]

---

[4] That some crossovers, like some strikers—in both cases the most junior members of the work force—may lose their jobs because of the collective decision to strike is simply a reflection of the employer's right to hire "permanent replacements," or perhaps of a downturn in business due to the

B. We have recognized only a narrow exception to the general principle prohibiting discrimination against employees for exercising their right to strike. Since *Mackay Radio* it has been accepted that an employer may hire "permanent replacements" in order to maintain operations during a strike, and that these replacements need not be displaced to make room for returning strikers. The question here is whether the *Mackay* exception should be expanded to cover the present case, involving as it does members of the striking bargaining unit who have crossed the picket lines, rather than new hires from outside the bargaining unit. Despite the superficial similarity between the two situations, strong reasons counsel against applying the *Mackay* rule to crossover employees.

The employer's promise to members of the bargaining unit that they will not be displaced at the end of a strike if they cross the picket lines addresses a far different incentive to the bargaining-unit members than does the employer's promise of permanence to new hires. The employer's threat to hire permanent replacements from outside the existing work force puts pressure on the strikers *as a group* to abandon the strike before their positions are filled by others. But the employer's promise to members of the striking bargaining unit that if they abandon the strike (or refuse to join it at the outset) they will retain their jobs at strike's end in preference to more senior workers who remain on strike produces an additional dynamic: now there is also an incentive for *individual* workers to seek to save (or improve) their own positions at the expense of other members of the striking bargaining unit. We have previously observed that offers of "individual benefits to the strikers to induce them to abandon the strike ... could be expected to undermine the strikers' mutual interest and place the entire strike effort in jeopardy." *NLRB v. Erie Resistor Corp.,* 373 U.S. 221, 230-231 (1963). Such a "divide and conquer" tactic thus "strike[s] a fundamental blow to union ... activity and the collective bargaining process itself."

In *Erie Resistor* we found the employer's offer of superseniority to new hires and crossovers to be "inherently destructive" of the right to strike and therefore in contravention of §§ 8(a)(1) and (a)(3) of the NLRA. 373 U.S., at 231-232. In my view the same conclusion should apply here. Beyond its specific holding outlawing superseniority, I read *Erie Resistor* to stand for the principle that there

---

strike or other factors. The Court's argument that the crossovers should not be "penalized" rests on its apparent belief that they should not be denied the benefit of their individual decisions not to strike (although it should be noted that the Court apparently objects to "penalizing" even those crossovers who voted *for* the strike, as long as they repented of that decision before the strike ended). But "[u]nion activity, by its very nature, is group activity," *NLRB v. Textile Workers,* 409 U.S. 213, 221 (1972) (BLACKMUN, J., dissenting), and inherent in the system of exclusive bargaining representatives, which is a fundament of our labor law, is the principle of majority decision—even where such decisions may impose costs on the dissenting minority. The contrary rule, moreover, would allow the employee who abandons the collectively taken decision to strike to become a free rider, enjoying the benefit of any gains won by the strike, but without sharing in its risk. See *Pattern Makers' League v. NLRB,* 473 U.S. 95, 129 (1985) (BLACKMUN, J., dissenting).

are certain tools an employer may not use, even in the interest of continued operations during a strike, and that the permissibility of discriminatory measures taken for that purpose must be evaluated by weighing the "necessity" of the employer's action (*i.e.,* its interest in maintaining operations during the strike) against its prejudice to the employees' right to strike. It seems clear to me that in this case the result of such an analysis should be to forbid the employer from giving preferential treatment to crossovers, because of the destructive impact of such an action on the strikers' mutual interest. Thus, when an employer recalls workers to fill the available positions at the conclusion of a strike, it may not discriminate against either the strikers or the crossovers. Rather it must proceed according to some principle, such as seniority, that is neutral as between them. That TWA failed to do.[7]

Precedent under the NLRA clearly forbids an employer from burdening the right to strike in the manner TWA has done in this case, and I see no reason why that conclusion should not apply equally under the RLA.

In a case like this it is not difficult to conjure up a parade of horribles to support either position. Forbidding an employer to discriminate in favor of crossovers, as I would do, makes it impossible for a junior employee who does not want to strike, and who is unable to persuade a majority of her colleagues to adopt that stance, to be sure that she can save her job. But that employee is in the same position she would be in if a layoff were necessary for other reasons beyond her control, such as an economic downturn. The principle of seniority is based on the notion that it is those employees who have worked longest in an enterprise and therefore have most at stake whose jobs should be most protected. Permitting the employer to give preference to crossovers, as the Court today does, will mean that an employee of only six months' experience, who abandoned the strike one day before it ended, could displace a 20-year veteran who chose to remain faithful to the decision made collectively with her fellow workers until the group as a whole decided to end the strike. Unfortunately there will be individual injustices whichever rule we adopt. I would favor—and I believe Congress has provided for—the rule that errs on the side of preferring solidarity

---

[7] The NLRB, in an *amicus* brief, argues that the employer not only may, but must, accord preferential treatment to crossovers, on the ground that once the crossovers have resumed work—which they have a right to do if jobs are available—the positions they occupy are not "vacant" at the end of the strike. This argument simply begs the question. If the employer is prohibited from discriminating among members of the bargaining unit on the basis of strike activity in allocating poststrike jobs, then the employer may not promise certain bargaining-unit members that the jobs will be theirs permanently, merely because those members returned to work during the strike. Whether or not employer may do this is precisely the question this case presents, and the answer to that question cannot be assumed by stating it as a premise. Neither *NLRB v. Fleetwood Trailer Co.,* 389 U.S. 375 (1967), nor *Laidlaw Corp.,* 171 N.L.R.B. 1366 (1968), dealt with the conflicting rights of crossovers and full-term strikers....

and seniority, rather than a rule that would permit the employer to discriminate on the basis of protected union activity.

JUSTICE BLACKMUN, with whom JUSTICE BRENNAN joins as to Parts I and II, dissenting.

The central question in this Railway Labor Act (RLA) case is whether it is unlawful for a carrier to refuse to reinstate employees who support a strike until its end ("full-term strikers") solely because the carrier chooses to retain in its active workforce employees who returned to work before the strike's conclusion ("crossovers").

The Court today answers that question in the negative, concluding that such conduct never violates the RLA, regardless of whether business necessity dictated the carrier's course of action. In dissent, JUSTICE BRENNAN takes the diametrically opposite view, in agreement with the Court of Appeals. JUSTICE BRENNAN finds such conduct "inherently destructive," *ante,* of the right to strike and violative of the RLA regardless of any proffered business justification. In my view, neither of these positions accurately captures the delicate balance our RLA precedents have attempted to achieve between the public's dual interests in the maintenance of transportation service during labor disputes and in the long-term stability of labor relations in the rail and airline industries.

My differences with JUSTICE BRENNAN are limited in scope. Concisely stated, I give greater weight than he does to the RLA's policy in favor of continued operations, and accordingly conclude that this case should be remanded to permit TWA to make a factual showing that its crossover policy truly was necessary for that purpose. The Court's opinion presents far greater concerns, as much because of the false assumptions that underlie the Court's analysis as because of its erroneous result.

I

....

III

A

At the conclusion of the strike, TWA refused to reinstate full-term strikers to positions then occupied by crossovers. In analyzing the lawfulness of TWA's conduct, certain NLRA principles provide a useful starting point. This Court has recognized under the NLRA that an employer's refusal to reinstate striking employees discourages employees from exercising their right to organize and to strike, *NLRB v. Fleetwood Trailer Co.,* 389 U.S., at 378, and violates the statutory prohibition against discrimination "unless the employer ... can show that his action was due to 'legitimate and substantial business justifications'." *Ibid.,* quoting *NLRB v. Great Dane Trailers, Inc.,* 388 U.S. 26, 34 (1967). If the employer fails to meet this burden, the inquiry is at an end. Furthermore, in certain circumstances, "the Board can find an unfair labor practice even if the employer introduces evidence that the conduct was motivated by business considerations," *id.,* at 34, by striking "the proper balance between the asserted business justifications and the invasion of employee rights." *Metropolitan Edison Co. v. NLRB,* 460 U.S. 693, 703 (1983), quoting *Great Dane,* 388 U.S., at 33-34....

B

In his dissent, JUSTICE BRENNAN does not reach the question whether a carrier who offers permanence to replacements and crossovers is entitled to a presumption of business necessity. Indeed, he would not even *permit* TWA to make a case-specific showing that its crossover policy was necessary for its continued operation during the strike. Here, our positions differ: I would require the carrier to prove the business necessity of offering permanence to replacements and crossovers in the facts of each case....

NOTES

1. In *NLRB v. Erie Resistor Corp.,* 373 U.S. 221, 235-36 (1963), the Supreme Court had emphasized the need for courts to give substantial deference to the views of the NLRB when deciding how to balance competing interests under the NLRA:

> [I]n view of the deference paid the strike weapon by the federal labor laws and the devastating consequences upon it which the Board found was and would be precipitated by respondent's inherently discriminatory superseniority plan, we cannot say the Board erred in the balance which it struck here... The matter before the Board lay well within the mainstream of its duties. It was attempting to deal with an issue which Congress had placed in its hands and "where Congress has in the statute given the Board a question to answer, the courts will give respect to that answer." *Labor Board v. Insurance Agents,* 361 U.S. 477, 499. Here, as in other cases, we must recognize the Board's special function of applying the general provisions of the Act to the complexities of industrial life. *Republic Aviation Corp. v. Labor Board,* 324 U.S. 793, 798; *Phelps Dodge Corp. v. Labor Board,* 313 U.S. 177, 194, and of "[appraising] carefully the interests of both sides of any labor-management controversy in the diverse circumstances of particular cases" from its special understanding of "the actualities of industrial relations." *Labor Board v. United Steelworkers,* 357 U.S. 357, 362-363. "The ultimate problem is the balancing of the conflicting legitimate interests. The function of striking that balance to effectuate national labor policy is often a difficult and delicate responsibility, which the Congress committed primar-

ily to the National Labor Relations Board, subject to limited judicial review." *Labor Board v. Truck Drivers Union,* 353 U.S. 87, 96.

In footnote 7 of his *TWA* dissenting opinion, Justice Brennan noted that the Labor Board had filed an *amicus* brief supporting the TWA interpretation of the NLRA. Why do you think the majority opinion did not rely upon the NLRB's views when it discussed applicable NLRA doctrines? If the Labor Board had balanced the competing interests and decided that returning strikers should have been permitted to displace "crossovers," might the Supreme Court have reached a different conclusion?

2. In *Mike Yurosek & Son,* 295 N.L.R.B. 304 (1989), a seasonal employer was permitted to recall permanent strike replacements laid off at the end of the preceding season ahead of unreinstated strikers. The Board found that the replacements had a reasonable expectation of recall, thus their seasonal layoffs did not create vacant positions. In *Delta-Macon Brick & Tile Co.,* 297 N.L.R.B. 1044 (1990), however, the Board held that an employer unlawfully recalled strike replacements who had been laid off for over a year ahead of unreinstated economic strikers, because the lengthy layoff of the replacements had created vacancies to which the strikers were entitled to be recalled. Nonetheless, the Fifth Circuit denied enforcement of the Board order, since it found that the replacement workers still had a "reasonable expectancy" of recall and thus had continuing recall priority over the unreinstated strikers. *NLRB v. Delta-Macon Brick & Tile Co.,* 943 F.2d 567 (5th Cir. 1991). *See Aqua-Chem, Inc. v. NLRB,* 910 F.2d 1487 (7th Cir. 1990), *reh'g denied,* 922 F.2d 403 (7th Cir.), *cert. denied,* 501 U.S. 1238 (1991) (adopting "reasonable expectation of recall" approach to determine when laid-off replacements may be recalled ahead of unreinstated strikers). *See also Waterbury Hosp. v. NLRB,* 950 F.2d 849 (2d Cir. 1991), wherein the court affirmed the Board's conclusion that nonstrikers could not be considered "permanent replacements" if they were given post-strike positions different from those they occupied during the strike, unless they were in training for the positions and the positions were open during the work stoppage. When laid-off replacement workers are recalled ahead of unreinstated strikers, are the replacements effectively being granted "super seniority" similar to that prohibited in *Erie Resistor?*

3. Although an employer that reinstates economic strikers will generally violate the NLRA if it fails to return them to their former positions on the seniority list [*NLRB v. Bingham-Williamette Co.,* 857 F.2d 661 (9th Cir. 1988)], a labor organization may expressly waive its right to undiluted seniority in exchange for an end to the work stoppage. For example, in *Gem City Ready Mix,* 270 N.L.R.B. 1260 (1984), the Board sustained the validity of a strike settlement agreement that unequivocally placed the three employees who had continued to work during the strike at the top of the seniority list. Since the waiver provision was unambiguous and the returning strikers understood its application, the NLRB upheld its

propriety, even though the strikers had apparently not been apprised of the specific statutory right being relinquished.

4. Organized labor has sought on various occasions over the past several decades to obtain legislation precluding or at least limiting the right of employers to hire replacement workers for economic strikers, but it has been unable to induce Congress to enact such restrictions. In March, 1995, President Clinton issued Executive Order 12,954 which disqualified for federal contracts in excess of $100,000 employers who hired permanent replacement workers during lawful strikes. In *Chamber of Commerce v. Reich*, 74 F.3d 1322 (D.C. Cir.), *rehearing en banc denied*, 83 F.3d 442 (D.C. Cir. 1996), the court held the Executive Order preempted by the NLRA which guarantees employers the right to hire permanent striker replacements.

5. *See generally* Estreicher, *"Collective Bargaining" or "Collective Begging"? Reflections on Antistrikebreaker Legislation*, 93 Mich. L. Rev. 577 (1994); Finkin, *Labor Policy and the Enervation of the Economic Strike*, 1990 U. Ill. L. Rev. 547 (1990); Note, *One Strike and You're Out? Creating an Efficient Permanent Replacement Doctrine*, 106 Harv. L. Rev. 669 (1993).

4. LOCKOUTS, PLANT CLOSINGS, AND "RUNAWAY SHOPS"

NLRB v. TRUCK DRIVERS, LOCAL 449, INTERNATIONAL BROTHERHOOD OF TEAMSTERS [BUFFALO LINEN CASE]

Supreme Court of the United States
353 U.S. 87, 77 S. Ct. 643, 1 L. Ed. 2d 676 (1957)

[The union, engaged in collective bargaining on a multiemployer basis with an employers association representing eight linen supply companies in Buffalo, put into effect a "whipsaw" plan by striking one of the companies. The other seven employers locked out their employees and ceased operating. Multiemployer negotiations continued, and, after one week, a new contract was signed and employees returned to work. The union charged the seven employers with violations of §§ 8(a)(1) and (3). The NLRB held no violation, since the lockout was defensive. The court of appeals found a violation, holding the lockout not privileged in the absence of unusual economic hardship.]

MR. JUSTICE BRENNAN delivered the opinion of the Court.

... We are not concerned here with the cases in which the lockout has been held unlawful because designed to frustrate organizational efforts, to destroy or undermine bargaining representation, or to evade the duty to bargain. Nor are we called upon to define the limits of the legitimate use of the lockout.[19] The narrow question to be decided is whether a temporary lockout may lawfully be used

---

[19] We thus find it unnecessary to pass upon the question whether, as a general proposition, the employer lockout is the corollary of the employees' statutory right to strike.

as a defense to a union strike tactic which threatens the destruction of the employers' interest in bargaining on a group basis....

Although the act protects the right of the employees to strike in support of their demands, this protection is not so absolute as to deny self-help by employers when legitimate interests of employees and employers collide. Conflict may arise, for example, between the right to strike and the interest of small employers in preserving multiemployer bargaining as a means of bargaining on an equal basis with a large union and avoiding the competitive disadvantages resulting from nonuniform contractual terms. The ultimate problem is the balancing of the conflicting legitimate interests. The function of striking that balance to effectuate national labor policy is often a difficult and delicate responsibility, which the Congress committed primarily to the National Labor Relations Board, subject to limited judicial review.

The Court of Appeals recognized that the National Labor Relations Board has legitimately balanced conflicting interests by permitting lockouts where economic hardship was shown. The court erred, however, in too narrowly confining the exercise of Board discretion to the cases of economic hardship. We hold that in the circumstances of the case the Board correctly balanced the conflicting interests in deciding that a temporary lockout to preserve the multiemployer bargaining basis from the disintegration threatened by the Union's strike action was lawful.

Reversed.

NLRB v. BROWN

Supreme Court of the United States
380 U.S. 278, 85 S. Ct. 980, 13 L. Ed. 2d 839 (1965)

[The union, engaged in collective bargaining on a multiemployer basis with a group of six retail food stores in Carlsbad, New Mexico, put into effect a "whipsaw" plan by striking one of the stores, Food Jet. Food Jet continued operations with management personnel and their relatives and with a few temporary replacements. The other five stores laid off their union employees, regarding "the strike against one as a strike against all." However, in contrast to the *Buffalo Linen* situation, the five stores continued operations with management personnel, relatives, and temporary replacements, who were told that their employment would end when the "whipsaw" strike ended. Group bargaining continued; an agreement was reached after about a month; and the employers immediately released the temporary employees and recalled the strikers and locked-out employees. The NLRB (3-2) found a violation of §§ 8(a)(1) and (3), inferring that the employers acted not merely to protect the integrity of their multiemployer unit, but for the purpose of inhibiting a lawful strike. The court of appeals refused to enforce the Board's order.]

Mr. Justice Brennan delivered the opinion of the Court.

... The Board's decision does not rest upon independent evidence that the respondents acted either out of hostility toward the Local or in reprisal for the whipsaw strike. It rests upon the Board's appraisal that the respondents' conduct carried its own indicia of unlawful intent, thereby establishing, without more, that the conduct constituted an unfair labor practice. It was disagreement with this appraisal, which we share, that led the Court of Appeals to refuse to enforce the Board's order....

In the circumstances of this case, we do not see how the continued operations of respondents and their use of temporary replacements any more implies hostile motivation, nor how it is inherently more destructive of employee rights, than the lockout itself. Rather, the compelling inference is that this was all part and parcel of respondents' defensive measure to preserve the multiemployer group in the face of the whipsaw strike. Since Food Jet legitimately continued business operations, it is only reasonable to regard respondents' action as evincing concern that the integrity of the employer group was threatened unless they also managed to stay open for business during the lockout. For with Food Jet open for business and respondents' stores closed, the prospect that the whipsaw strike would succeed in breaking up the employer association was not at all fanciful. The retail food industry is very competitive and repetitive patronage is highly important. Faced with the prospect of a loss of patronage to Food Jet, it is logical that respondents should have been concerned that one or more of their number might bolt the group and come to terms with the Local, thus destroying the common front essential to multiemployer bargaining. The Court of Appeals correctly pictured the respondents' dilemma in saying, "If ... the struck employer does choose to operate with replacements and the other employers cannot replace after lockout, the economic advantage passes to the struck member, the non-struck members are deterred in exercising the defensive lockout, and the whipsaw strike ... enjoys an almost inescapable prospect of success." 319 F.2d, at 11. Clearly respondents' continued operations with the use of temporary replacements following the lockout was wholly consistent with a legitimate business purpose.

Nor are we persuaded by the Board's argument that justification for the inference of hostile motivation appears in the respondents' use of temporary employees rather than some of the regular employees. It is not common sense, we think, to say that the regular employees were "willing to work at the employers' terms." 137 N.L.R.B., at 76. It seems probable that this "willingness" was motivated as much by their understandable desire to further the objective of the whipsaw strike—to break through the employers' united front by forcing Food Jet to accept the Local's terms—as it was by a desire to work for the employers under the existing unacceptable terms. As the Board's dissenting members put it, "These employees are willing only to receive wages while their brethren in the rest of the association-wide unit are exerting whipsaw pressure on one employer to gain benefits that will ultimately accrue to all employees in the association-wide unit, including those here locked out." 137 N.L.R.B., at 78. Moreover, the course of action to which the Board would limit the respondents would force them into the position of aiding and abetting the success of the whipsaw strike and consequently would render "largely illusory," 137 N.L.R.B., at 78-79, the right of lockout recognized by *Buffalo Linen;* the right would be meaningless if barred to nonstruck stores that find it necessary to operate because the struck store does so.

The Board's finding of a § 8(a)(1) violation emphasized the impact of respondents' conduct upon the effectiveness of the whipsaw strike. It is no doubt true that the collective strength of the stores to resist that strike is maintained, and even increased, when all stores stay open with temporary replacements. The pressures on the employees are necessarily greater when none of the union employees is working and the stores remain open. But these pressures are no more than the result of the Local's inability to make effective use of the whipsaw tactic. Moreover, these effects are no different from those that result from the legitimate use of any economic weapon by an employer. Continued operations with the use of temporary replacements may result in the failure of the whipsaw strike, but this does not mean that the employers' conduct is demonstrably so destructive of employee rights or so devoid of significant service to any legitimate business end that it cannot be tolerated consistently with the act. Certainly then, in the absence of evidentiary findings of hostile motive, there is no support for the conclusion that respondents violated § 8(a)(1)....

We recognize that, analogous to the determination of unfair practices under § 8(a)(1), when an employer practice is inherently destructive of employee rights and is not justified by the service of important business ends, no specific evidence of intent to discourage union membership is necessary to establish a violation of § 8(a)(3). This principle, we have said, is "but an application of the common-law rule that a man is held to intend the foreseeable consequences of his conduct." *Radio Officers Union v. NLRB, supra,* 347 U.S. at 45 (1954). For example, in *NLRB v. Erie Resistor Corp., supra,* we held that an employer's action in awarding superseniority to employees who worked during a strike was discriminatory conduct that carried with it its own indicia of improper intent. The only reasonable inference that could be drawn by the Board from the award of superseniority—balancing the prejudicial effect upon the employees against any asserted business purpose—was that it was directed against the striking employees because of their union membership; conduct so inherently destructive of employee interests could not be saved from illegality by an asserted overriding business purpose pursued in good faith. But where, as here, the tendency to discourage union membership is comparatively slight, and the employer's conduct is reasonably adapted to achieve legitimate business ends or to deal with business exigencies, we enter into an area where the improper motivation of the employer must be established by independent evidence. When so established, antiunion motivation will convert an otherwise ordinary business act into an unfair labor practice. *NLRB v. Erie Resistor Corp., supra,* 373 U.S. at 227 (1963), and cases there cited.

We agree with the Court of Appeals that respondents' conduct here clearly fits into the latter category, where actual subjective intent is determinative, and where the Board must find from evidence independent of the mere conduct involved that the conduct was primarily motivated by an antiunion animus. While the use of temporary nonunion personnel in preference to the locked-out union members is discriminatory, we think that any resulting tendency to discourage union membership is comparatively remote, and that this use of temporary personnel constitutes a measure reasonably adapted to the effectuation of a legitimate business end. Here discontent on the part of the Local's membership in all likelihood is attributable largely to the fact that the membership was locked out as a result of the Local's whipsaw stratagem. But the lockout itself is concededly within the rule of *Buffalo Linen.* We think that the added dissatisfaction and resultant pressure on membership attributable to the fact that the nonstruck employers remain in business with temporary replacements is comparatively insubstantial. First, the replacements were expressly used for the duration of the labor dispute only; thus, the displaced employees could not have looked upon the replacements as threatening their jobs. At most the union would be forced to capitulate and return its members to work on terms which, while not as desirable as hoped for, were still better than under the old contract. Second, the membership, through its control of union policy, could end the dispute and terminate the lockout at any time simply by agreeing to the employers' terms and returning to work on a regular basis. Third, in light of the union-shop provision that had been carried forward into the new contract from the old collective agreement, it would appear that a union member would have nothing to gain, and much to lose, by quitting the union. Under all these circumstances, we cannot say that the employers' conduct had any great tendency to discourage union membership. Not only was the prospect of discouragement of membership comparatively remote, but the respondents' attempt to remain open for business with the help of temporary replacements was a measure reasonably adapted to the achievement of a legitimate end—preserving the integrity of the multiemployer bargaining unit....

It is argued, finally, that the Board's decision is within the area of its expert judgment and that, in setting it aside, the Courts of Appeals exceeded the authorized scope of judicial review. This proposition rests upon our statement in *Buffalo Linen* that in reconciling the conflicting interests of labor and management the Board's determination is to be subjected to "limited judicial review." 353 U.S., at 96. When we used the phrase "limited judicial review" we did not mean that the balance struck by the Board is immune from judicial examination and reversal in proper cases. Courts are expressly empowered to enforce, modify or set aside, in whole or in part, the Board's orders, except that the findings of the Board with respect to questions of fact, if supported by substantial evidence on the record considered as a whole, shall be conclusive.... Reviewing courts are not obliged to stand aside and rubber-stamp their affirmance of administrative decisions that they deem inconsistent with a statutory mandate or that frustrate the congressional policy underlying a statute. Not only is such review always properly within the judicial province, but courts would abdicate their responsibility if they did not fully review such administrative decisions. Of course, due deference is to be rendered to agency determinations of fact, so long as there is substantial evidence to be found in the record as a whole. But where, as here, the review is not of a question of fact, but of a judgment as to the proper balance to be struck between conflicting interests, "[t]he deference owed to an expert tribunal cannot be allowed to slip into a judicial inertia which results in the unauthorized assumption by an agency of major policy decisions properly made by Congress." *American Ship Building Co. v. NLRB,* 380 U.S. at 318 (1965).

Courts must, of course, set aside Board decisions which rest on "an erroneous legal foundation." *NLRB v. Babcock & Wilcox, supra,* 351 U.S. at 112-113. Congress has not given the Board untrammeled authority to catalogue which economic devices shall be deemed freighted with indicia of unlawful intent. *NLRB v. Insurance Agents, supra,* 361 U.S. at 498. In determining here that the respondents' conduct carried its own badge of improper motive, the Board's decision, for the reasons stated, misapplied the criteria governing the application of §§ 8(a)(1) and (3). Since the order therefore rested on "an erroneous legal foundation," the Court of Appeals properly refused to enforce it.[6]

Affirmed.

MR. JUSTICE GOLDBERG, whom THE CHIEF JUSTICE joins, concurring.

... There would be grave doubts as to whether locking out and hiring permanent replacements is justified by any legitimate interest of the nonstruck employers, for *Buffalo Linen* makes clear that the test in such a situation is not whether parity is achieved between struck and nonstruck employers, but, rather, whether the nonstruck employer's actions are necessary to counteract the whipsaw effects of the strike and to preserve the employer bargaining unit. Since in this case the nonstruck employers did nothing more than hire temporary replacements, an activity necessary to counter whipsawing by the union and to preserve the bargaining unit, I agree that, applying *Buffalo Linen,* the judgment of the Court of Appeals should be affirmed.

MR. JUSTICE WHITE, dissenting.

... This decision represents a departure from the many decisions in this Court holding that the Board has primary responsibility to weigh the interest of em-

---

[6] We do not here decide whether the case would be the same had the struck employer exercised its prerogative to hire permanent replacements for the strikers under our rule in *NLRB v. Mackay Radio & Tel. Co.,* 304 U.S. 333 (1938), and the nonstruck employers had then hired permanent replacements for their locked-out employees.

ployees in concerted activities against that of the employer in operating his business....

The Court reasons that *Buffalo Linen* gave the nonstruck employer in a multiemployer unit a "right" to lockout whenever a member of the unit is struck so that a parity of economic advantage or disadvantage between the struck and nonstruck employers can be maintained. In order to maintain parity where the struck employer hires replacements, the nonstruck employers must also be free to hire replacements, lest the right to lockout to protect the unit be illusory. And they need not offer these jobs to the locked-out employees desiring to work, lest the parity between the struck and nonstruck employers be lost and the right to lockout be meaningless. If this reasoning is sound, the nonstruck employers can not only lock out employees who belong to the union because of their union membership but also hire permanent as well as temporary nonunion replacements whenever the struck employer hires such replacements, for parity may well so require. But I cannot accept this reasoning.

One, *Buffalo Linen* established no unqualified "right" of employers in a multiemployer unit to lockout....

Two, the threat to the integrity of the multiemployer unit, the consideration that was decisive in *Buffalo Linen,* is obviously very different where the struck employer continues operations with replacements; it certainly cannot be assumed that the struck employer operating with replacements is at the same disadvantage vis-à-vis the nonstruck employers as the employer in *Buffalo Linen* whose operations were totally shut down by the union. Indeed, there was no showing here that the struck employer was substantially disadvantaged at all, and the Board found that there was "no economic necessity for the other members shutting down...."

Three, the disparity between the struck employer who resumes operations and the nonstruck employers who choose to lockout to maintain a united front is caused by the unilateral action of one of the employer members of the unit and not by the union's whipsawing tactic. The integrity of the multiemployer unit may be important, but surely that consideration cannot justify employer tandem action destructive of concerted activity.

Four, the Court asserts that the right of nonstruck employers to hire temporary replacements, and to refuse to hire union men, is but a concomitant of the right to lockout to preserve the multiemployer group. This sanctification of the multiemployer unit ignores the fundamental rule that an employer may not displace union members with nonunion members solely on account of union membership, the prototype of discrimination under § 8(a)(3), *NLRB v. Mackay Radio & Telegraph Co.,* 304 U.S. 333 (1938), and may not maintain operations and refuse to retain or hire nonstriking union members, notwithstanding that most of the union members and most of the workers at that very plant are on strike. The struck employer need not continue operations, but if he does, he may not give a preference to employees not affiliated with the striking union, no more than he may do so after the strike, for § 7 explicitly and unequivocally protects the right of employees to engage and not to engage in a concerted activity and § 8(a)(3) clearly prohibits discrimination which discourages union membership....

Finally, I cannot agree with the Court's fundamental premise on which its balance of rights is founded: that a lockout followed by the hiring of nonunion men to operate the plant has but a "slight" tendency to discourage union membership, which includes participation in union activities, *Radio Officers' Union v. NLRB,* 347 U.S. 17 (1954), and to impinge on concerted activity generally. This proposition overturns the Board's longheld views on the effect of lockouts and dismissal of union members. Moreover, it is difficult to fathom the logic or industrial experience which on the one hand dictates that a guarantee to strike replacements that they will not be laid off after a strike is "inherently destructive of employee interests," although based on a legitimate and important business justification, *Erie Resistor,* 373 U.S. 221 (1963), and yet at the same time dictates that the dismissal of and refusal to hire nonstriking union members who desire to work because other union members working for a different employer have struck have but a slight unimportant inhibiting effect on affiliation with the union and on concerted activities. I think the Board's finding that this activity substantially burdens concerted activities and discourages union membership is far more consistent with *Erie Resistor* and industrial realities....

NOTE

When a union strikes some members of a multiemployer bargaining unit, the other employers lockout under *Buffalo Linen,* and some employees ask to work during the lockout, may their employer tell them they can do so if they are no longer union members? In *NLRB v. Martin A. Gleason, Inc.,* 534 F.2d 466 (2d Cir. 1976), the court held yes, so long as the employer does not solicit or encourage their union resignations. The court relied on language in *Brown* indicating that an employer could use "temporary *nonunion* personnel" during a lockout. Was the *Brown* Court equating "nonunion" with "non-unit," since all bargaining unit personnel were union members pursuant to a union security clause? Does the *Martin A. Gleason* decision authorize overt anti-union discrimination in a manner that contravenes § 8(a)(3)?

AMERICAN SHIP BUILDING CO. v. NLRB

Supreme Court of the United States
380 U.S. 300, 85 S. Ct. 955, 13 L. Ed. 2d 855 (1965)

[After two months of negotiating sessions, the American Ship Building Co. and a group of eight unions bargaining jointly reached an impasse on August 9, 1961. The company had made five previous contracts with the unions since 1952, each one preceded by a strike. The company operated four shipyards on the Great Lakes, most of their work coming in the winter months when the lakes are icebound. What limited business was obtained in the summer months was frequently such that speed of execution was of the utmost importance to minimize immobilization of the ships. Despite union protestations to the contrary, the company feared a strike would be called as soon as a ship should enter the Chicago yard or that there would be a delay in negotiations into the winter to increase strike leverage. In light of the failure to reach agreement and the lack of available work, the company gradually laid off almost all employees, sending each one a notice, "Because of the labor dispute which has been unresolved ... you are laid off until further notice." Negotiations resumed; an agreement was signed October 27; and employees were recalled the following day.

[The trial examiner found that the employer could reasonably anticipate a strike in spite of the unions' assurances to the contrary, and concluded that the employer was economically motivated and justified in laying off its employees when it did. The Board (3-2) rejected the trial examiner's conclusions and found that the layoff was motivated solely by a desire to bring economic pressure and secure settlement of the dispute on favorable terms. It was agreed that the layoff had not occurred until after a bargaining impasse had been reached.]

MR. JUSTICE STEWART delivered the opinion of the Court.

... The difference between the Board and the trial examiner is thus a narrow one turning on their differing assessments of the circumstances which the employer claims gave him reason to anticipate a strike. Both the Board and the examiner assumed, within the established pattern of Board analysis, that if the employer had shut down his yard and laid off his workers solely for the purpose of bringing to bear economic pressure to break an impasse and secure more favorable contract terms, an unfair labor practice would be made out....

The Board has, however, exempted certain classes of lockouts from proscription. "Accordingly, it has held that lockouts are permissible to safeguard against loss where there is reasonable ground for believing that a strike was threatened or imminent." [*Quaker State Oil Refining Co.,* 121 N.L.R.B. 334, 337.] Developing this distinction in its rulings, the Board has approved lockouts designed to prevent seizure of a plant by a sitdown strike, *Link-Belt Co.,* 26 N.L.R.B. 227; to forestall repetitive disruptions of an integrated operation by quickie strikes, *International Shoe Co.,* 93 N.L.R.B. 907; to avoid spoilage of materials which would result from a sudden work stoppage, *Duluth Bottling Ass'n,* 48 N.L.R.B. 1335; and to avert the immobilization of automobiles brought in for repair, *Betts Cadillac-Olds,* 96 N.L.R.B. 268....

In analyzing the status of the bargaining lockout under §§ 8(a)(1) and 8(a)(3) of the National Labor Relations Act, it is important that the practice with which we are here concerned be distinguished from other forms of temporary separation from employment. No one would deny that an employer is free to shut down his enterprise temporarily for reasons of renovation or lack of profitable work unrelated to his collective bargaining situation. Similarly, we put to one side cases where the Board has concluded on the basis of substantial evidence that the employer has used a lockout as a means to injure a labor organization or to evade his duty to bargain collectively. *Hopwood Retinning Co.,* 4 N.L.R.B. 922; *Scott Paper Box Co.,* 81 N.L.R.B. 535. What we are here concerned with is the use of a temporary layoff of employees solely as a means to bring economic pressure to bear in support of the employer's bargaining position, after an impasse has been reached. This is the only issue before us, and all that we decide.[8]

To establish that this practice is a violation of § 8(a)(1), it must be shown that the employer has interfered with, restrained, or coerced employees in the exercise of some right protected by § 7 of the act. The Board's position is premised on the view that the lockout interferes with two of the rights guaranteed by § 7: the right to bargain collectively and the right to strike. In the Board's view, the use of the lockout "punishes" employees for the presentation of and adherence to demands made by their bargaining representatives and so coerces them in the exercise of their right to bargain collectively. It is important to note that there is here no allegation that the employer used the lockout in the service of designs inimical to the process of collective bargaining. There was no evidence and no finding that the employer was hostile to his employees banding together for collective bargaining or that the lockout was designed to discipline them for doing so. It is therefore inaccurate to say that the employer's intention was to destroy or frustrate the process of collective bargaining. What can be said is that he intended to resist the demands made of him in the negotiations and to secure modification of these demands. We cannot see that this intention is in any way inconsistent with the employees' rights to bargain collectively.

Moreover, there is no indication, either as a general matter or in this specific case, that the lockout will necessarily destroy the unions' capacity for effective and responsible representation. The unions here involved have vigorously represented the employees since 1952, and there is nothing to show that their ability to do so has been impaired by the lockout. Nor is the lockout one of those acts which is demonstrably so destructive of collective bargaining that the Board need not inquire into employer motivation, as might be the case, for example, if an employer permanently discharged his unionized staff and replaced them with employees known to be possessed of a violent antiunion animus. *Cf. NLRB v. Erie Resistor Corp.,* 373 U.S. 221 (1963). The lockout may well dissuade employees from adhering to the position which they initially adopted in the bargaining, but the right to bargain collectively does not entail any "right" to insist on one's position free from economic disadvantage. Proper analysis of the problem demands that the simple intention to support the employer's bargaining position as to compensation and the like be distinguished from a hostility to the

---

[8]Contrary to the view expressed in a concurring opinion filed in this case, we intimate no view whatever as to the consequences which would follow had the employer replaced his employees with permanent replacements or even temporary help. *Cf. NLRB v. Mackay Radio & Telegraph Co.,* 304 U.S. 333 (1938).

process of collective bargaining which could suffice to render a lockout unlawful. *See NLRB v. Brown* [380 U.S. 278 (1965)].

The Board has taken the complementary view that the lockout interferes with the right to strike protected under §§ 7 and 13 of the act in that it allows the employer to pre-empt the possibility of a strike and thus leave the union with "nothing to strike against." Insofar as this means that once employees are locked out, they are deprived of their right to call a strike against the employer because he is already shut down, the argument is wholly specious, for the work stoppage which would have been the object of the strike has in fact occurred. It is true that recognition of the lockout deprives the union of exclusive control of the timing and duration of work stoppages calculated to influence the result of collective bargaining negotiations, but there is nothing in the statute which would imply that the right to strike "carries with it" the right exclusively to determine the timing and duration of all work stoppages. The right to strike as commonly understood is the right to cease work—nothing more. No doubt a union's bargaining power would be enhanced if it possessed not only the simple right to strike but also the power exclusively to determine when work stoppages shall occur, but the act's provisions are not indefinitely elastic, content-free forms to be shaped in whatever manner the Board might think best conforms to the proper balance of bargaining power.

Thus, we cannot see that the employer's use of a lockout solely in support of a legitimate bargaining position is in any way inconsistent with the right to bargain collectively or with the right to strike. Accordingly, we conclude that on the basis of the findings made by the Board in this case, there has been no violation of § 8(a)(1).

Section 8(a)(3) prohibits discrimination in regard to tenure or other conditions of employment to discourage union membership. Under the words of the statute there must be both discrimination and a resulting discouragement of union membership. It has long been established that a finding of violation under this section will normally turn on the employer's motivation....

This is not to deny that there are some practices which are inherently so prejudicial to union interests and so devoid of significant economic justification that no specific evidence of intent to discourage union membership or other antiunion animus is required. In some cases, it may be that the employer's conduct carries with it an inference of unlawful intention so compelling that it is justifiable to disbelieve the employer's protestations of innocent purpose. *Radio Officers' Union v. NLRB, supra,* 347 U.S. at 44-45; *NLRB v. Erie Resistor Corp., supra.* Thus where many have broken a shop rule, but only union leaders have been discharged, the Board need not listen too long to the plea that shop discipline was simply being enforced. In other situations, we have described the process as the "far more delicate task ... of weighing the interests of employees in concerted activity against the interest of the employer in operating his business in a particular manner...." *NLRB v. Erie Resistor Corp., supra,* 373 U.S. at 229 (1965).

But this lockout does not fall into that category of cases arising under § 8(a)(3) in which the Board may truncate its inquiry into employer motivation. As this case well shows, use of the lockout does not carry with it any necessary implication that the employer acted to discourage union membership or otherwise discriminate against union members as such. The purpose and effect of the lockout was only to bring pressure upon the union to modify its demands. Similarly, it does not appear that the natural tendency of the lockout is severely to discourage union membership while serving no significant employer interest. In fact, it is difficult to understand what tendency to discourage union membership or otherwise discriminate against union members was perceived by the Board. There is no claim that the employer locked out only union members, or locked out any employee simply because he was a union member; nor is it alleged that the employer conditioned rehiring upon resignation from the union. It is true that the employees suffered economic disadvantage because of their union's insistence on demands unacceptable to the employer, but this is also true of many steps which an employer may take during a bargaining conflict, and the existence of an arguable possibility that someone may feel himself discouraged in his union membership or discriminated against by reason of that membership cannot suffice to label them violations of § 8(a)(3) absent some unlawful intention. The employer's permanent replacement of strikers (*NLRB v. Mackay Radio & Telegraph Co., supra*), his unilateral imposition of terms (*Labor Board v. Tex-Tan, Inc.,* 318 F.2d 472, 479-482), or his simple refusal to make a concession which would terminate a strike—all impose economic disadvantage during a bargaining conflict, but none is necessarily a violation of § 8(a)(3).

To find a violation of § 8(a)(3) then, the Board must find that the employer acted for a proscribed purpose. Indeed, the Board itself has always recognized that certain "operative" or "economic" purposes would justify a lockout. But the Board has erred in ruling that only these purposes will remove a lockout from the ambit of § 8(a)(3), for that section requires an intention to discourage union membership or otherwise discriminate against the union. There was not the slightest evidence and there was no finding, that the employer was actuated by a desire to discourage membership in the union as distinguished from a desire to affect the outcome of the particular negotiations in which he was involved. We recognize that the "union membership" which is not to be discouraged refers to more than the payment of dues and that measures taken to discourage participation in protected union activities may be found to come within the proscription. *Radio Officers' Union v. NLRB, supra,* 347 U.S. at 39-40. However, there is nothing in the act which gives employees the right to insist on their contract demands, free from the sort of economic disadvantage which frequently attends bargaining disputes. Therefore, we conclude that where the intention proven is merely to bring about a settlement of a labor dispute on favorable terms, no violation of § 8(a)(3) is shown.

The conclusions which we draw from analysis of §§ 8(a)(1) and 8(a)(3) are consonant with what little of relevance can be drawn from the balance of the statute and its legislative history. In the original version of the act, the predecessor of § 8(a)(1) declared it an unfair labor practice "[t]o attempt, by interference, influence, restraint, favor, coercion, or lockout, or by any other means, to impair the right of employees guaranteed in section 4."[11] Prominent in the criticism leveled at the bill in the Senate Committee hearings was the charge that it did not accord evenhanded treatment to employers and employees because it prohibited the lockout while protecting the strike. In the face of such criticism, the Committee added a provision prohibiting employee interference with employer bargaining activities[13] and deleted the reference to the lockout.[14] A plausible inference to be drawn from this history is that the language was defeated to nullify those who saw in the bill an inequitable denial of resort to the lockout, and to remove any language which might give rise to fears that the lockout was being proscribed *per se*. It is in any event clear that the Committee was concerned with the status of the lockout and that the bill, as reported and as finally enacted, contained no prohibition on the use of the lockout as such.

Although neither § 8(a)(1) nor § 8(a)(3) refers specifically to the lockout, various other provisions of the Labor Management Relations Act do refer to the lockout, and these references can be interpreted as a recognition of the legitimacy of the device as a means of applying economic pressure in support of bargaining positions. Thus 29 U.S.C. § 158(d)(4) (1958 ed.) prohibits the use of strike or lockout unless requisite notice procedures have been complied with; 29 U.S.C. § 173(c) (1958 ed.) directs the Federal Mediation and Conciliation Service to

---

[11] 1 Legislative History of the Labor Management Relations Act, 1935, 3 (hereafter L.M.R.A.). Section 4 of the bill provided:

> Employees shall have the right to organize and join labor organizations, and to engage in concerted activities, either in labor organizations or otherwise, for the purposes of organizing and bargaining collectively through representatives of their own choosing or for other purposes of mutual aid or protection.

Ibid.

[13] S. 2926, § 3 (2):

> It shall be an unfair labor practice [f]or employees to attempt, by interference or coercion, to impair the exercise by employers of the right to join or form employer organizations and to designate representatives of their own choosing for the purpose of collective bargaining.

1 L.M.R.A. 1087.

[14] S. 2926, § 3 (1):

> It shall be an unfair labor practice [f]or an employer to attempt, by interference or coercion, to impair the exercise by employees of the right to form or join labor organizations, to designate representatives of their own choosing, and to engage in concerted activities for the purpose of collective bargaining or other mutual aid or protection.

1 L.M.R.A. 1087.

seek voluntary resolution of labor disputes without resort to strikes or lockouts; and 29 U.S.C. §§ 176, 178 (1958 ed.), authorize procedures whereby the President can institute a board of inquiry to forestall certain strikes or lockouts. The correlative use of the terms "strike" and "lockout" in these sections contemplates that lockouts will be used in the bargaining process in some fashion. This is not to say that these provisions serve to define the permissible scope of a lockout by an employer. That, in the context of the present case, is a question ultimately to be resolved by analysis of §§ 8(a)(1) and 8(a)(3).

The Board has justified its ruling in this case and its general approach to the legality of lockouts on the basis of its special competence to weigh the competing interests of employers and employees and to accommodate these interests according to its expert judgment. "The Board has reasonably concluded that the availability of such a weapon would so substantially tip the scales in the employer's favor as to defeat the Congressional purpose of placing employees on a par with their adversaries at the bargaining table." To buttress its decision as to the balance struck in this particular case, the Board points out that the employer has been given other weapons to counterbalance the employees' power of strike. The employer may permanently replace workers who have gone out on strike, or by stockpiling and subcontracting, maintain his commercial operations while the strikers bear the economic brunt of the work stoppage. Similarly, the employer can institute unilaterally the working conditions which he desires once his contract with the union has expired. Given these economic weapons, it is argued, the employer has been adequately equipped with tools of economic self-help.

There is, of course, no question that the Board is entitled to the greatest deference in recognition of its special competence in dealing with labor problems. In many areas its evaluation of the competing interests of employer and employee should unquestionably be given conclusive effect in determining the application of §§ 8(a)(1), (a)(3), and (a)(5). However, we think that the Board construes its functions too expansively when it claims general authority to define national labor policy by balancing the competing interests of labor and management.

While a primary purpose of the National Labor Relations Act was to redress the perceived imbalance of economic power between labor and management, it sought to accomplish that result by conferring certain affirmative rights on employees and by placing certain enumerated restrictions on the activities of employers.... Having protected employee organization in countervailance to the employers' bargaining power, and having established a system of collective bargaining whereby the newly coequal adversaries might resolve their disputes, the act also contemplated resort to economic weapons should more peaceful measures not avail. Sections 8(a)(1) and 8(a)(3) do not give the Board a general authority to assess the relative economic power of the adversaries in the bargaining process and to deny weapons to one party or the other because of its assessment of that party's bargaining power. *NLRB v. Brown* [380 U.S. 278 (1965)]. In this case the Board has, in essence, denied the use of the bargaining lockout to the employer because of its conviction that use of this device would give the employer "too much power." In so doing, the Board has stretched §§ 8(a)(1) and 8(a)(3) far beyond their functions of protecting the rights of employee organization and collective bargaining. What we have recently said in a closely related context is equally applicable here:

> [W]hen the Board moves in this area ... it is functioning as an arbiter of the sort of economic weapons the parties can use in seeking to gain acceptance of their bargaining demands. It has sought to introduce some standard of properly "balanced" bargaining power, or some new distinction of justifiable and unjustifiable, proper and "abusive" economic weapons into ... the Act.... We have expressed our belief that this amounts to the Board's entrance into the substantive aspect of the bargaining process to an extent Congress has not countenanced.

NLRB v. Insurance Agents' Int'l Union, 361 U.S. 477, 497-498 (1960).

We are unable to find that any fair construction of the provisions relied on by the Board in this case can support its finding of an unfair labor practice. Indeed, the role assumed by the Board in this area is fundamentally inconsistent with the structure of the act and the function of the sections relied upon. The deference owed to an expert tribunal cannot be allowed to slip into a judicial inertia which results in the unauthorized assumption by an agency of major policy decisions properly made by Congress. Accordingly, we hold that an employer violates neither § 8(a)(1) nor § 8(a)(3) when, after a bargaining impasse has been reached, he temporarily shuts down his plant and lays off his employees for the sole purpose of bringing economic pressure to bear in support of his legitimate bargaining position.

Reversed.

MR. JUSTICE WHITE, concurring in the result.

... In my view the issue posed in this case is whether an employer who in fact anticipates a strike may inform customers of this belief to protect his commercial relationship with customers and to safeguard their property, thereby discouraging business, and then lay off employees for whom there is no available work. I, like the trial examiner, think he may, and do not think this conduct can be impeached under §§ 8(a)(1) and 8(a)(3) by merely asserting that the employer and his customers were erroneous in believing a strike was imminent....

... Since I think an employer's decision to lay off employees because of lack of work is not ordinarily barred by the act, and since neither the Board nor the Court properly can ignore this claim, I would reverse the Board's order, but without reaching out to decide an issue not at all presented by this case....

MR. JUSTICE GOLDBERG, with whom THE CHIEF JUSTICE joins, concurring in the result.

I concur in the Court's conclusion that the employer's lockout in this case was not a violation of either § 8(a)(1) or § 8(a)(3) of the National Labor Relations Act, 49 Stat. 453, as amended, 29 U.S.C. §§ 158(a)(1) and (3) (1958 ed.), and I therefore join in the judgment reversing the Court of Appeals. I reach this result not for the Court's reasons, but because, from the plain facts revealed by the record, it is crystal clear that the employer's lockout here was justified. The very facts recited by the Court in its opinion show that this employer locked out his employees in the face of a threatened strike under circumstances where, had the choice of timing been left solely to the unions, the employer and his customers would have been subject to economic injury over and beyond the loss of business normally incident to a strike upon the termination of the collective bargaining agreement. A lockout under these circumstances has been recognized by the Board itself to be justifiable and not a violation of the labor statutes. *Betts Cadillac-Olds, Inc.,* 96 N.L.R.B. 268....

My view of this case would make it unnecessary to deal with the broad question of whether an employer may lock out his employees solely to bring economic pressure to bear in support of his bargaining position. The question of which types of lockout are compatible with the labor statute is a complex one as this decision and the other cases decided today illustrate. *See Textile Workers Union v. Darlington Mfg. Co.,* [380 U.S.] at 263; *NLRB v. Brown,* [380 U.S.] at 278. This Court has said that the problem of the legality of certain types of strike activity must be "revealed by unfolding variant situations" and requires "an evolutionary process for its rational response, not a quick, definitive formula as a comprehensive answer." *Electrical Workers, Local 761 v. NLRB,* 366 U.S. 667, 674 (1961); *see also NLRB v. Steelworkers, supra,* 357 U.S. 362-363 (1958). The same is true of lockouts.

The types of situation in which an employer might seek to lock out his employees differ considerably one from the other. This case presents the situation of an employer with a long history of union recognition and collective bargaining, confronted with a history of past strikes, who locks out only after considerable good-faith negotiation involving agreement and compromise on numerous issues, after a bargaining impasse has been reached, more than a week after the prior contract has expired, and when faced with the threat of a strike at a time when he and the property of his customers can suffer unusual harm. Other cases in which the Board has held a lockout illegal have presented far different situations. For example, in *Quaker State Oil Refining Corp., supra,* an employer locked out his employees the day after his contract with the union expired although no impasse had been reached in the bargaining still in progress, no strike had been threatened by the unions, which had never called a sudden strike during the 13 years they had bargained with the employer, and the unions had offered to resubmit the employer's proposals to his employees for a vote. *See also Utah Plumbing and Heating Contractors Ass'n,* 126 N.L.R.B. 973. These decisions of the Labor Board properly take into account, in determining the legality of lockouts under the labor statutes, such factors as the length, character, and history of the collective bargaining relation between the union and the employer, as well as whether a bargaining impasse has been reached. Indeed, the Court itself seems to recognize that there is a difference between locking out before a bargaining impasse has been reached and locking out after collective bargaining has been exhausted, for it limits its holding to lockouts in the latter type of situation without deciding the question of the legality of locking out before bargaining is exhausted. Since the examples of different lockout situations could be multiplied, the logic of the Court's limitation of its holding should lead it to recognize that the problem of lockouts requires "an evolutionary process," not "a quick, definitive formula," for its answer.

The Court should be chary of sweeping generalizations in this complex area. When we deal with the lockout and the strike, we are dealing with weapons of industrial warfare. While the parties generally have their choice of economic weapons, see *NLRB v. Insurance Agents,* 361 U.S. 477 (1960), this choice, both with respect to the strike and the lockout, is not unrestricted. While we have recognized "the deference paid the strike weapon by the federal labor laws," *NLRB v. Erie Resistor, supra* at 235, not all forms of economically motivated strikes are protected nor even permissible under the labor statutes or the prior decisions of this Court. Moreover, a lockout prompted by an antiunion motive is plainly illegal under the National Labor Relations Act, though no similar restrictions as to motive operate to limit the legality of a strike. See *NLRB v. Somerset Shoe Co.,* 111 F.2d 681 (1st Cir. 1940); *NLRB v. Stremel,* 141 F.2d 317 (10th Cir. 1944); *NLRB v. Somerset Classics, Inc.,* 193 F.2d 613 (2d Cir. 1952). The varieties of restriction imposed upon strikes and lockouts reflect the complexities presented by variant factual situations.

The Court not only overlooks the factual diversity among different types of lockout, but its statement of the rules governing unfair labor practices under §§ 8(a)(1) and (3) does not give proper recognition to the fact that "[t]he ultimate problem [in this area] is the balancing of the conflicting legitimate interests." *NLRB v. Truck Drivers Union,* 353 U.S. 87, 96 (1957). The Court states that employer conduct, not actually motivated by antiunion bias, does not violate §§ 8(a)(1) or (3) unless it is "demonstrably so destructive of collective bargaining," or "so prejudicial to union interests and so devoid of significant economic justification," that no antiunion animus need be shown. This rule departs substantially from both the letter and the spirit of numerous prior decisions of the Court. See, e.g., *NLRB v. Truck Drivers Union, supra,* 353 U.S. at 96; *Republic Aviation Corp. v. NLRB,* 324 U.S. 793 (1945); *NLRB v. Babcock & Wilcox Co.,* 351 U.S. 105 (1956); *NLRB v. Burnup & Sims, Inc.,* 379 U.S. 21 (1964).

These decisions demonstrate that the correct test for determining whether § 8(a)(1) has been violated in cases not involving an employer antiunion motive is whether the business justification for the employer's action outweighs the interference with § 7 rights involved. In *Republic Aviation Corp. v. NLRB, supra,* for example, the Court affirmed a Board holding that a company "no-solicitation" rule was invalid as applied to prevent solicitation of employees on company property during periods when employees were free to do as they pleased, not because such a rule was "demonstrably ... destructive of collective bargaining," but simply because there was no significant employer justification for the rule and there was a showing of union interest, though far short of a necessity, in its abolition. See also, NLRB v. Burnup & Sims, Inc., supra.

A similar test is applicable in § 8(a)(3) cases where no antiunion motive is shown. The Court misreads Radio Officers' Union v. NLRB, 347 U.S. 17, and NLRB v. Erie Resistor Corp., supra, in stating that the test in such cases under § 8(a)(3) is whether practices "are inherently so prejudicial to union interests and so devoid of significant economic justification that no specific evidence of intent to discourage union membership or other antiunion animus is required." Supra, at pp. 863, 864. Radio Officers did not restrict the application of § 8(a)(3) in cases devoid of antiunion motive to the extreme situations encompassed by the Court's test. Rather, in holding applicable the common-law rule that a man is presumed to intend the foreseeable consequences of his own actions, the Court extended the reach of § 8(a)(3) to all cases in which a significant antiunion effect is foreseeable regardless of the employer's motive. In such cases the Court, in Erie Resistor Corp., held that conduct might be determined by the Board to violate § 8(a)(3) where the Board's determination resulted from a reasonable "weighing [of] the interests of employees in concerted activity against the interests of the employer in operating his business in a particular manner and ... [from] balancing in the light of the Act and its policy the intended consequences upon employee rights against the business ends to be served by the employer's conduct." 373 U.S. at 229.

These cases show that the tests as to whether an employer's conduct violates § 8(a)(1) or violates § 8(a)(3) without a showing of antiunion motive come down to substantially the same thing: whether the legitimate economic interests of the employer justify his interference with the rights of his employees—a test involving "the balancing of the conflicting legitimate interests." NLRB v. Truck Drivers Union, supra, 353 U.S. at 96. As the prior decisions of this Court have held, "[t]he function of striking ... [such a] balance, ... often a difficult and delicate responsibility, ... Congress committed primarily to the National Labor Relations Board, subject to limited judicial review." Ibid.

This, of course, does not mean that reviewing courts are to abdicate their function of determining whether, giving due deference to the Board, the Board has struck the balance consistently with the language and policy of the act. See NLRB v. Brown, supra; NLRB v. Truck Drivers Union, supra. Nor does it mean that reviewing courts are to rubberstamp decisions of the Board where the application of principles in a particular case is irrational or not supported by substantial evidence on the record as a whole. Applying these principles to the factual situation here presented, I would accept the Board's carefully limited rule, fashioned by the Board after weighing the "conflicting legitimate interests" of employers and unions, that a lockout does not violate the act where used to "safeguard against unusual operational problems or hazards or economic loss where there is reasonable ground for believing that a strike [is] ... threatened or imminent." *Quaker State Oil Refining Corp., supra* at 337. This rule is consistent with the policies of the act and based upon the actualities of industrial relations. I would, however, reject the determination of the Board refusing to apply this rule to this case, for the undisputed facts revealed by the record bring this case clearly within the rule.

In view of the necessity for, and the desirability of, weighing the legitimate conflicting interests in variant lockout situations, there is not and cannot be any simple formula which readily demarks the permissible from the impermissible lockout. This being so, I would not reach out in this case to announce principles which are determinative of the legality of all economically motivated lockouts whether before or after a bargaining impasse has been reached. In my view both the Court and the Board, in reaching their opposite conclusions, have inadvisably and unnecessarily done so here. Rather, I would confine our decision to the simple holding, supported both by the record and the actualities of industrial relations, that the employer's fear of a strike was reasonable, and therefore, under the settled decisions of the Board, which I would approve, the lockout of his employees was justified.

NOTES

1. Suppose six employers are bargaining jointly with a union, although they do not have a formally established multiemployer unit. An impasse is reached in the bargaining, and the union strikes two of the employers, advising its members that this would be the most effective way to obtain an industry-wide settlement. May the other four employers lock out without committing an unfair labor practice? *Weyerhaeuser Co.,* 166 N.L.R.B. 299 (1967) *(Held:* Yes), *enforcement denied,* 398 F.2d 770 (D.C. Cir. 1968).

Suppose two Detroit newspapers have bargained on a multiemployer basis with most of the fourteen unions that represent various groups of their employees, but have each bargained separately with the Teamsters regarding their distribution workers. During negotiations with the Teamsters, the two papers conferred on three common issues, and the News agreed that if the Teamsters struck the Free Press on these issues, the News would not publish. The Free Press is struck and the News locks out. Teamsters President Hoffa had said that he regarded the News' latest proposal as a final offer, and had threatened the News with a strike. Is the News' lockout lawful? *Evening News Ass'n,* 166 N.L.R.B. 219 (1967), *affirmed,* 404 F.2d 1159 (6th Cir. 1968), *cert. denied,* 395 U.S. 923 (1969) *(Held:* Yes). The Board said: "There is no question but that the Supreme Court's American Ship decision has obliterated, as a matter of law, the line previously drawn by the Board between offensive and defensive lockouts.... The

Court stated that the test of a lockout's legality, assuming no motive to discourage union activity or to evade bargaining exists, is whether the lockout 'is inherently so prejudicial to union interest and so devoid of significant economic justification' that no evidence of intent is necessary. That test affords the basis for our determination here."

2. A preimpasse lockout to support an employer's bargaining position and to forestall a strike during its busy shipping season was held lawful in *Darling & Co.,* 171 N.L.R.B. 801 (1968). The Board stated that the absence of an impasse did not render the *American Ship* tests per se inapplicable, although "the finding of an impasse in negotiations may be a factor supporting the determination that a particular lockout is lawful." The determination must be made on a case-by-case basis. Here there had been extensive good faith bargaining on all subjects and accord on many issues, but continuing disagreement on certain key items, including a work assignment clause. Strikes had occurred during the parties' twenty-year relationship, and work assignments were a major issue in a crippling strike about four years earlier. *Darling & Co.* was affirmed *sub nom. Lane v. NLRB,* 418 F.2d 1208 (D.C. Cir. 1969).

3. Even though three employers could lawfully lock out their employees following the expiration of their separate collective bargaining agreements with a union, the hiring of temporary replacements was ruled a violation of § 8(a)(1) and (3) by the Labor Board in the absence of a showing of a substantial business justification for the employers' conduct. *Inland Trucking Co.,* 179 N.L.R.B. 350 (1969). In enforcing the Board's order, the Seventh Circuit observed that the use of replacements by an employer during an offensive, as distinguished from a defensive, lockout "would not merely pit the employer's ability to withstand a shut down of its business against the employees' ability to endure cessation of their jobs, but would permit the employer to impose on his employees the pressure of being out of work while obtaining for himself the returns of continued operation. Employees would be forced, at the initiative of the employer, not only to forego their job earnings, but, in addition, to watch other workers enjoy the earning opportunities over which the locked-out employees were endeavoring to bargain." *Inland Trucking Co. v. NLRB,* 440 F.2d 562 (7th Cir.), *cert. denied,* 404 U.S. 858 (1971). Nonetheless, in *Ottawa Silica Co.,* 197 N.L.R.B. 449 (1972), *aff'd,* 482 F.2d 945 (6th Cir. 1973), and *Inter-Collegiate Press,* 199 N.L.R.B. 177 (1972), *aff'd,* 486 F.2d 837 (8th Cir. 1973), *cert. denied,* 416 U.S. 938 (1974), the Board majority found no violation where the employer showed legitimate and substantial business justification for using temporary replacements during an otherwise lawful lockout and there was no wrongful motivation.

In *Harter Equip.,* 280 N.L.R.B. 597 (1986), *review denied,* 829 F.2d 458 (3d Cir. 1987), the Labor Board reviewed the *Inland Trucking* and *Ottawa Silica* decisions and concluded that "an employer does not violate § 8(a)(3) and (1), absent specific proof of antiunion motivation, by using temporary employees in order to engage in business operations during an otherwise lawful lockout, including a lockout initiated for the sole purpose of bringing economic pressure to bear in support of a legitimate bargaining position." The 3-1 majority found that the temporary replacement measure was "reasonably adapted to the achievement of a legitimate employer interest" and had "only a comparatively slight adverse effect on protected employee rights."

In *Ancor Concepts, Inc.*, 323 N.L.R.B. No. 134, 155 L.R.R.M. 1102 (1997), the Labor Board held that the hiring of *permanent* replacements is inconsistent with a lawful lockout and violative of § 8(a)(3). Since the Second Circuit found no factual basis for the conclusion that *permanent* replacements had in fact been hired, it denied enforcement of the Board's decision. *NLRB v. Ancor Concepts, Inc.*, ___ F.3d ___ (2d Cir. 1999). *Compare Johns-Manville Prods. v. NLRB*, 557 F.2d 1126 (5th Cir. 1977) (sabotage by employees during contract negotiations constituted in-plant "strike" that justified their lockout and subsequent *permanent* replacement).

4. *International Paper Co. v. NLRB*, 115 F.3d 1045 (D.C. Cir. 1997), involved an employer that locked out its production and maintenance workers during a bargaining dispute. The employer temporarily subcontracted the maintenance work to an outside firm. It then solicited a permanent subcontracting proposal for the maintenance work and asked the union at the bargaining table for the right to retain an outside maintenance firm on a permanent basis. When the union rejected the company's subcontracting proposal, it entered into a permanent subcontract which each party could terminate on thirty days notice. The Labor Board found that any permanent subcontracting of the work of locked out personnel was "inherently destructive" of employee rights and thus a violation of § 8(a)(3). On appeal, the D.C. Circuit rejected the Board's analysis. It found that the employer had merely entered into a temporary subcontractual relationship when the lockout began. It then sought union permission to convert the temporary subcontracting arrangement into a permanent one. Only after bargaining over the matter to impasse did the employer establish a permanent subcontracting relationship. The court thus found no "inherently destructive" behavior, and it went on to hold that the creation of a permanent subcontracting arrangement during a lockout after good faith negotiations with the union did not contravene the NLRA.

5. *See* Baird, *Lockout Law: The Supreme Court and the NLRB,* 38 Geo. Wash. L. Rev. 396 (1970); Bernhardt, *Lockouts: An Analysis of Board and Court Decisions Since Brown and American Ship,* 57 Cornell L. Rev. 211 (1972); Feldesman & Koretz, *Lockouts,* 46 Boston U.L. Rev. 329 (1966); Oberer, *Lockouts and the Law: The Impact of American Ship Building and Brown Food,* 51 Cornell L.Q. 193 (1966); Note, *An Employer Who Locks Out His Employees Solely as a Means of Applying Economic Pressure May Not Hire Temporary Replacements,* 23 Syracuse L. Rev. 179 (1972).

Proof of Motive in Cases Involving Violations of §§ 8(a)(3) and (1)

In *NLRB v. Great Dane Trailers Inc.,* 388 U.S. 26 (1967), the Supreme Court further explored the extent to which *scienter* must be proved to find a violation of § 8(a)(3). In that case, an employer was held by the NLRB to have violated § 8(a)(3) when it refused to pay striking employees vacation benefits that had accrued under a terminated bargaining agreement while announcing an intent to pay such benefits to those individuals who had worked on a certain day during the strike. The court of appeals [363 F.2d 130 (5th Cir. 1966)] refused enforcement, because it found no affirmative showing of an unlawful employer motivation to discourage union membership.

The Supreme Court overturned the appeals court decision. It divided employer conduct into two categories: (1) extreme action that is "inherently destructive" of employee rights, and (2) behavior that has a "comparatively slight" effect on those rights. In both situations, "once it had been proved that the employer engaged in discriminatory conduct which could have adversely affected employee rights to some extent, the burden is upon the employer to establish that it was motivated by legitimate objectives...." The court held that a violation of § 8(a)(3) can be found without proof of improper motive in unusual instances in which "inherently destructive" conduct is present even though the employer offers evidence of justification. With respect to conduct that has a "comparatively slight" effect, if the employer comes forward with exculpatory evidence that outweighs the interference with employee § 7 rights, a violation can be found only if antiunion motivation is proved.

NOTES

1. Although the Supreme Court had found in *Great Dane Trailers* that an employer's refusal to pay striking employees their accrued vacation benefits constituted an unfair labor practice, the Seventh Circuit found no such violation when a company rescheduled vacations due to commence during an impending strike for all plant personnel until the end of the work stoppage. The court noted that the employer had not discriminated between striking and nonstriking employees, no antiunion animus was found, the employer had a valid business reason for postponing the vacations of all workers until the strike was over, and the employer's action was not found to be "inherently destructive" of employee rights. *See Stokeley-Van Camp v. NLRB,* 722 F.2d 1324 (7th Cir. 1983). *See also Forest Prods. Co. v. NLRB,* 888 F.2d 72 (10th Cir. 1989), wherein the court held that an employer's failure to distribute matching contributions under a Christmas savings program to permanently replaced strikers did not violate § 8(a)(3), where the program required participants to be employed on the distribution date and the employer had previously treated persons as ineligible when they were on leave or layoff on the distribution date.

2. For contrasting applications of the *Great Dane* test by the Labor Board, *compare Texaco, Inc.,* 285 N.L.R.B. 241 (1987) (unlawful to suspend accident and sick benefits to three disabled employees who were receiving benefits when strike began) *with Amoco Oil Co.,* 285 N.L.R.B. 918 (1987) (lawful to suspend disability benefits to locked-out employees when plan had nondiscriminatory dual requirement that claimants be disabled *and* otherwise scheduled to work).

3. In *Summa Corp.,* 282 N.L.R.B. 667 (1987), the Labor Board held that a hotel violated § 8(a)(3) when it gave a one-time $4000 party for employees who had not struck or who had abandoned a strike, some three months after the strike had ended. The employer unsuccessfully tried to demonstrate as business justification that it wished to show its appreciation for "consistent loyalty" and wanted to "cool" down the "great deal of animosity" continuing between invitees and former strikers. *See also Rubatex Corp.,* 235 N.L.R.B. 833 (1978), *enforced,* 601 F.2d 147 (4th Cir.), *cert. denied,* 444 U.S. 928 (1979) (post-strike cash bonuses to people who worked during strike not supported by valid business justification). What if at the beginning of a strike an employer offered cash bonuses to individuals who worked for the duration of the work stoppage?

4. In *NLRB v. Burnup & Sims, Inc.,* 379 U.S. 21 (1964), the Supreme Court held that an employer violated § 8(a)(1) when it discharged two employees who were engaged in protected organizing activities, even though it had no wrongful motive. In this case, the employer terminated the two employees when it was informed they were planning to use violence during the union's organizing campaign; the information later proved to be untrue. The Court held that the policy behind § 8(a)(1) dictated the reinstatement of the employees, "Otherwise, the protected activity would lose some of its immunity, since the example of employees who are discharged on false charges would or might have a deterrent effect on other employees." Employer good faith in the discharges was deemed irrelevant, because the false charges were inextricably intertwined with the employees' protected organizing activities.

5. *See* Christensen & Svanoe, *Motive and Intent in the Commission of Unfair Labor Practices,* 77 Yale L.J. 1269 (1968); Getman, *Section 8(a)(3) of the NLRA and the Effort to Insulate Free Employee Choice,* 32 U. Chi. L. Rev. 735 (1965); Oberer, *The Scienter Factor in Sections 8(a)(1) and (3) of the Labor Act: Of Balancing, Hostile Motive, Dogs and Tails,* 52 Cornell L.Q. 491 (1967); Shieber, *Section 8(a)(1) of the NLRA: A Rationale, Part I, Discrimination,* 29 La. L. Rev. 46 (1968); Shieber and Moore, *Part II, Encouragement and Discouragement of Membership in Any Labor Organization and the Significance of Employer Motive,* 33 La. L. Rev. 1 (1972); Note, *Employer Motive and § 8(a)(3) Violations,* 48 B.U. L. Rev. 142 (1968); Note, *Intent, Effect, Purpose and Motive as Applicable Elements to §§ 8(a)(1) and (3) Violations of the NLRA,* 7 Wake Forest L. Rev. 616 (1971); Cox, *Reexamination of the Role of Employer Motive under §§ 8(a)(1) and 8(a)(3) of the NLRA,* 5 U. Puget Sound L. Rev. 161 (1982).

TEXTILE WORKERS UNION v. DARLINGTON MFG. CO.

Supreme Court of the United States
380 U.S. 263, 85 S. Ct. 994, 13 L. Ed. 2d 827 (1965)

MR. JUSTICE HARLAN delivered the opinion of the Court.

We here review judgments of the Court of Appeals setting aside and refusing to enforce an order of the National Labor Relations Board which found respondent Darlington guilty of an unfair labor practice by reason of having permanently closed its plant following petitioner union's election as the bargaining representative of Darlington's employees.

Darlington Manufacturing Company was a South Carolina corporation operating one textile mill. A majority of Darlington's stock was held by Deering Milliken, a New York "selling house" marketing textiles produced by others.[1] Deering Milliken in turn was controlled by Roger Milliken, president of Darlington, and by other members of the Milliken family.[2] The National Labor Relations Board found that the Milliken family, through Deering Milliken, operated 17 textile manufacturers, including Darlington, whose products, manufactured in 27 different mills, were marketed through Deering Milliken.

In March 1956 petitioner Textile Workers Union initiated an organizational campaign at Darlington which the company resisted vigorously in various ways, including threats to close the mill if the union won a representation election.[3] On September 6, 1956, the union won an election by a narrow margin. When Roger Milliken was advised of the union victory, he decided to call a meeting of the Darlington board of directors to consider closing the mill. Milliken testified before the Labor Board:

> I felt that as a result of the campaign that had been conducted and the promises and statements made in these letters that had been distributed [favoring unionization], that if before we had had some hope, possible hope of achieving competitive [costs] ... by taking advantage of new machinery that was being put in, that this hope had diminished as a result of the election because a majority of the employees had voted in favor of the union.... [R. 457].

---

[1] Deering Milliken & Co. owned 41% of the Darlington stock. Cotwool Manufacturing Co., another textile manufacturer, owned 18% of the stock. In 1960 Deering Milliken & Co. was merged into Cotwool, the survivor being named Deering Milliken, Inc.

[2] The Milliken family owned only 6% of the Darlington stock, but held a majority stock interest in both Deering Milliken & Co. and Cotwool, see note 1, *supra*.

[3] The Board found that Darlington had interrogated employees and threatened to close the mill if the union won the election. After the decision to liquidate was made (see *infra*), Darlington employees were told that the decision to close was caused by the election, and they were encouraged to sign a petition disavowing the union. These practices were held to violate § 8(a)(1) of the National Labor Relations Act, and that part of the Board decision is not challenged here.

The board of directors met on September 12 and voted to liquidate the corporation, action which was approved by the stockholders on October 17. The plant ceased operations entirely in November, and all plant machinery and equipment was sold piecemeal at auction in December.

The union filed charges with the Labor Board claiming that Darlington had violated §§ 8(a)(1) and 8(a)(3) of the National Labor Relations Act by closing its plant, and § 8(a)(5) by refusing to bargain with the union after the election.[5] The Board, by a divided vote, found that Darlington had been closed because of the antiunion animus of Roger Milliken, and held that to be a violation of § 8(a)(3).[6] The Board also found Darlington to be part of a single integrated employer group controlled by the Milliken family through Deering Milliken; therefore Deering Milliken could be held liable for the unfair labor practices of Darlington.[7] Alternatively, since Darlington was a part of the Deering Milliken enterprise, Deering Milliken had violated the Act by closing part of its business for a discriminatory purpose. The Board ordered back pay for all Darlington employees until they obtained substantially equivalent work or were put on preferential hiring lists at the other Deering Milliken mills. Respondent Deering Milliken was ordered to bargain with the union in regard to details of compliance with the Board order. 139 N.L.R.B. 241.

On review, the Court of Appeals sitting *en banc,* set aside the order and denied enforcement by a divided vote. 325 F.2d 682. The Court of Appeals held that even accepting arguendo the Board's determination that Deering Milliken had the status of a single employer, a company has the absolute right to close out a part or all of its business regardless of antiunion motives. The court therefore did not review the Board's finding that Deering Milliken was a single integrated employer.... We hold that so far as the Labor Act is concerned, an employer has the absolute right to terminate his entire business for any reason he pleases, but disagree with the Court of Appeals that such right includes the ability to close part of a business no matter what the reason. We conclude that the cause must be remanded to the Board for further proceedings.

---

[5] The union asked for a bargaining conference on September 12, 1956 (the day that the board of directors voted to liquidate), but was told to await certification by the Board. The union was certified on October 24, and did meet with Darlington officials in November, but no actual bargaining took place. The Board found this to be a violation of § 8(a)(5). Such a finding was in part based on the determination that the plant closing was an unfair labor practice, and no argument is made that § 8(a)(5) requires an employer to bargain concerning a purely business decision to terminate his enterprise. *Cf. Fibreboard Paper Prod. Corp. v. NLRB,* 379 U.S. 203 (1964).

[6] Since the closing was held to be illegal, the Board found that the gradual discharges of all employees during November and December constituted § 8(a)(1) violations. The propriety of this determination depends entirely on whether the decision to close the plant violated § 8(a)(3).

[7] Members Leedom and Rodgers agreed with the trial examiner that Deering Milliken was not a single employer. Member Rodgers dissented in arguing that Darlington had not violated § 8(a)(3) by closing.

Preliminarily it should be observed that both petitioners argue that the Darlington closing violated § 8(a)(1) as well as § 8(a)(3) of the Act. We think, however, that the Board was correct in treating the closing only under § 8(a)(3).[8] Section 8(a)(1) provides that it is an unfair labor practice for an employer "to interfere with, restrain, or coerce employees in the exercise of" § 7 rights. Naturally, certain business decisions will, to some degree, interfere with concerted activities by employees. But it is only when the interference with § 7 rights outweighs the business justification for the employer's action that § 8(a)(1) is violated. *See e.g., NLRB v. Steelworkers,* 357 U.S. 357 (1958); *Republic Aviation Corp. v. NLRB,* 324 U.S. 793 (1945). A violation of § 8(a)(1) alone therefore presupposes an act which is unlawful even absent a discriminatory motive. Whatever may be the limits of § 8(a)(1), some employer decisions are so peculiarly matters of management prerogative that they would never constitute violations of § 8(a)(1), whether or not they involved sound business judgment, unless they also violated § 8(a)(3). Thus it is not questioned in this case that an employer has the right to terminate his business, whatever the impact of such action on concerted activities, if the decision to close is motivated by other than discriminatory reasons.[10] But such action, if discriminatorily motivated, is encompassed within the literal language of § 8(a)(3). We therefore deal with the Darlington closing under that section.

I

We consider first the argument, advanced by the petitioner union but not by the Board, and rejected by the Court of Appeals, that an employer may not go completely out of business without running afoul of the Labor Act if such action is prompted by a desire to avoid unionization.[11] Given the Board's findings on the issue of motive, acceptance of this contention would carry the day for the Board's conclusion that the closing of this plant was an unfair labor practice, even on the assumption that Darlington is to be regarded as an independent unrelated employer. A proposition that a single businessman cannot choose to go out of business if he wants to would represent such a startling innovation that it

---

[8] The Board did find that Darlington's discharge of employees following the decision to close violated § 8(a)(1). See note 6, *supra.*

[10] It is also clear that the ambiguous act of closing a plant following the election of a union is not, absent an inquiry into the employer's motive, inherently discriminatory. We are thus not confronted with a situation where the employer "must be held to intend the very consequences which foreseeably and inescapably flow from his actions...." (*NLRB v. Erie Resistor Corp.,* 373 U.S. 221, 228 (1963)), in which the Board could find a violation of § 8(a)(3) without an examination into motive. *See Radio Officers v. NLRB,* 347 U.S. 17, 42-43 (1954); *Teamsters Local v. NLRB,* 365 U.S. 667, 674-676 (1961).

[11] The Board predicates its argument on the finding that Deering Milliken was an integrated enterprise, and does not consider it necessary to argue that an employer may not go completely out of business for antiunion reasons. Brief for National Labor Relations Board, at 3, n. 2.

should not be entertained without the clearest manifestation of legislative intent or unequivocal judicial precedent so construing the Labor Act. We find neither.

So far as legislative manifestation is concerned, it is sufficient to say that there is not the slightest indication in the history of the Wagner Act or of the Taft-Hartley Act that Congress envisaged any such result under either statute.

As for judicial precedent, the Board recognized that "[t]here is no decided case directly dispositive of Darlington's claim that it had an absolute right to close its mill, irrespective of motive." 139 N.L.R.B., at 250. The only language by this Court in any way adverting to this problem is found in *Southport Petroleum Co. v. NLRB*, 315 U.S. 100, 106 (1942), where it was stated:

> Whether there was a bona fide discontinuance and a true change of own-ership—which would terminate the duty of reinstatement created by the Board's order—or merely a disguised continuance of the old employer, does not clearly appear....

The courts of appeals have generally assumed that a complete cessation of business will remove an employer from future coverage by the Act. Thus the Court of Appeals said in these cases: The Act "does not compel a person to become or remain an employee. It does not compel one to become or remain an employer. Either may withdraw from that status with immunity, so long as the obligations of an employment contract have been met." 325 F.2d, at 685. The Eighth Circuit, in *NLRB v. New Madrid Mfg. Co.*, 215 F.2d 908, 914 (8th Cir. 1954), was equally explicit:

> But none of this can be taken to mean that an employer does not have the absolute right, at all times, to permanently close and go out of business ... for whatever reason he may choose, whether union animosity or anything else, and without his being thereby left subject to a remedial liability under the Labor Management Relations Act for such unfair labor practices as he may have committed in the enterprise, except up to the time that such actual and permanent closing ... has occurred.[12]

The AFL-CIO suggests in its *amicus* brief that Darlington's action was similar to a discriminatory lockout, which is prohibited "'because designed to frustrate organizational efforts, to destroy or undermine bargaining representation, or to evade the duty to bargain.'" One of the purposes of the Labor Act is to prohibit the discriminatory use of the economic weapons in an effort to obtain future benefits. The discriminatory lockout designed to destroy a union like a "runaway shop," is a lever which has been used to discourage collective employee activities in the future. But a complete liquidation of a business yields no such future bene-

---

[12] In *New Madrid* the business was transferred to a new employer, which was held liable for the unfair labor practices committed by its predecessor before closing. The closing itself was not found to be an unfair labor practice.

fit for the employer, if the termination is bona fide.[14] It may be motivated more by spite against the union than by business reasons, but it is not the type of discrimination which is prohibited by the Act. The personal satisfaction that such an employer may derive from standing on his beliefs or the mere possibility that other employers will follow his example are surely too remote to be considered dangers at which the labor statutes were aimed.[15] Although employees may be prohibited from engaging in a strike under certain conditions, no one would consider it a violation of the Act for the same employees to quit their employment *en masse,* even if motivated by a desire to ruin the employer. The very permanence of such action would negate any future economic benefit to the employees. The employer's right to go out of business is no different.

We are not presented here with the case of a "runaway shop,"[16] whereby Darlington would transfer its work to another plant or open a new plant in another locality to replace its closed plant.[17] Nor are we concerned with a shutdown where the employees, by renouncing the union, could cause the plant to reopen.[18] Such cases would involve discriminatory employer action for the purpose of obtaining some benefit from the employees in the future.[19] We hold here

---

[14] The Darlington property and equipment could not be sold as a unit, and were eventually auctioned off piecemeal. We therefore are not confronted with a sale of a going concern, which might present different considerations under §§ 8(a)(3) and 8(a)(5). *Cf. John Wiley & Sons v. Livingston,* 376 U.S. 543 (1964); *NLRB v. Deena Artware, Inc.,* 361 U.S. 398 (1960).

[15] *Cf.* NLRB § 8(c), 29 U.S.C. § 158(c) (1958 ed.). Different considerations would arise were it made to appear that the closing employer was acting pursuant to some arrangement or understanding with other employers to discourage employee organizational activities in their businesses.

[16] *E.g., NLRB v. Preston Feed Corp.,* 309 F.2d 346 (4th Cir. 1962); *NLRB v. Wallick,* 198 F.2d 477 (3d Cir. 1952). An analogous problem is presented where a department is closed for antiunion reasons but the work is continued by independent contractors. *See, e.g., NLRB v. Kelly & Picerne, Inc.,* 298 F.2d 895 (1st Cir. 1962); *Jays Foods, Inc. v. NLRB,* 292 F.2d 317 (7th Cir. 1961); *NLRB v. R. C. Mahon Co.,* 269 F.2d 44 (6th Cir. 1959); *NLRB v. Bank of Am.,* 130 F.2d 624 (9th Cir. 1942); *Williams Motor Co. v. NLRB,* 128 F.2d 960 (8th Cir. 1942).

[17] After the decision to close the plant, Darlington accepted no new orders, and merely continued operations for a time to fill pending orders. 139 N.L.R.B., at 244.

[18] *E.g., NLRB v. Norma Mining Corp.,* 206 F.2d 38 (4th Cir. 1963). Similarly, if all employees are discharged but the work continues with new personnel, the effect is to discourage any future union activities. *See NLRB v. Waterman S.S. Corp.,* 309 U.S. 206 (1940); *NLRB v. National Garment Co.,* 166 F.2d 233 (8th Cir. 1948); *NLRB v. Stremel,* 141 F.2d 317 (10th Cir. 1944).

[19] All of the cases to which we have been cited involved closings found to have been motivated, at least in part, by the expectation of achieving future benefits. See cases cited notes 16, 18 *supra.* The two cases which are urged as indistinguishable from *Darlington* are *NLRB v. Savoy Laundry,* 327 F.2d 370 (9th Cir. 1956), and *NLRB v. Missouri Transit Co.,* 250 F.2d 261 (8th Cir. 1957). In *Savoy Laundry* the employer operated one laundry plant where he processed both retail laundry pickups and wholesale laundering. Once that laundry was marked, all of it was processed together. After some of the employees organized, the employer discontinued most of the wholesale service, and thereafter discharged some of his employees. There was no separate wholesale department, and the discriminatory motive was obviously to discourage unionization in the entire plant. *Missouri Transit* presents a similar situation. A bus company operated an interstate line and intrastate shuttle

only that when an employer closes his entire business, even if the liquidation is motivated by vindictiveness toward the union, such action is not an unfair labor practice.[20]

II

While we thus agree with the Court of Appeals that viewing Darlington as an independent employer the liquidation of its business was not an unfair labor practice, we cannot accept the lower court's view that the same conclusion necessarily follows if Darlington is regarded as an integral part of the Deering Milliken enterprise.

The closing of an entire business, even though discriminatory, ends the employer-employee relationship; the force of such a closing is entirely spent as to that business when termination of the enterprise takes place. On the other hand, a discriminatory partial closing may have repercussions on what remains of the business, affording employer leverage for discouraging the free exercise of § 7 rights among remaining employees of much the same kind as that found to exist in the "runaway shop" and "temporary closing" cases. Moreover, a possible remedy open to the Board in such a case, like the remedies available in the "runaway shop" and "temporary closing" cases, is to order reinstatement of the discharged employees in the other parts of the business. No such remedy is available when an entire business has been terminated. By analogy to those cases involving a continuing enterprise we are constrained to hold, in disagreement with the Court of Appeals, that a partial closing is an unfair labor practice under § 8(a)(3) if motivated by a purpose to chill unionism in any of the remaining plants of the single

---

service connecting a military base with the interstate terminal. When the union attempted to organize all of the drivers, the shuttle service was sold and the shuttle drivers discharged. Although the two services were treated as separate departments, it is clear from the facts of the case that the union was attempting to organize all of the drivers, and the discriminatory motive of the employer was to discourage unionization in the interstate service as well as the shuttle service.

[20] Nothing we have said in this opinion would justify an employer interfering with employee organizational activities by threatening to close his plant, as distinguished from announcing a decision to close already reached by the board of directors or other management authority empowered to make such a decision. We recognize that this safeguard does not wholly remove the possibility that our holding may result in some deterrent effect on organizational activities independent of that arising for the closing itself. An employer may be encouraged to make a definite decision to close on the theory that its mere announcement before a representation election will discourage the employees from voting for the union, and thus his decision may not have to be implemented. Such a possibility is not likely to occur, however, except in a marginal business; a solidly successful employer is not apt to hazard the possibility that the employees will call his bluff by voting to organize. We see no practical way of eliminating this possible consequence of our holding short of allowing the Board to order an employer who chooses so to gamble with his employees not to carry out his announced intention to close. We do not consider the matter of sufficient significance in the over-all labor-management relations picture to require or justify a decision different from the one we have made.

employer and if the employer may reasonably have foreseen that such closing will likely have that effect.

While we have spoken in terms of a "partial closing" in the context of the Board's finding that Darlington was part of a larger single enterprise controlled by the Milliken family, we do not mean to suggest that an organizational integration of plants or corporations is a necessary prerequisite to the establishment of such a violation of § 8(a)(3). If the persons exercising control over a plant that is being closed for antiunion reasons (1) have an interest in another business, whether or not affiliated with or engaged in the same line of commercial activity as the closed plant, of sufficient substantiality to give promise of their reaping a benefit from the discouragement of unionization in that business; (2) act to close their plant with the purpose of producing such a result; and (3) occupy a relationship to the other business which makes it realistically foreseeable that its employees will fear that such business will also be closed down if they persist in organizational activities, we think that an unfair labor practice has been made out.

Although the Board's single employer finding necessarily embraced findings as to Roger Milliken and the Milliken family which, if sustained by the Court of Appeals, would satisfy the elements of "interest" and "relationship" with respect to other parts of the Deering Milliken enterprise, that and the other Board findings fall short of establishing the factors of "purpose" and "effect" which are vital requisites of the general principles that govern a case of this kind.

Thus, the Board's findings as to the purpose and foreseeable effect of the Darlington closing pertained *only* to its impact on the Darlington employees. No findings were made as to the purpose and effect of the closing with respect to the employees in the other plants comprising the Deering Milliken group. It does not suffice to establish the unfair labor practice charged here to argue that the Darlington closing necessarily had an adverse impact upon unionization in such other plants. We have heretofore observed that employer action which has a foreseeable consequence of discouraging concerted activities generally does not amount to a violation of § 8(a)(3) in the absence of a showing of motivation which is aimed at achieving the prohibited effect. *See Teamsters Local v. NLRB,* 365 U.S. 667 (1961), and the concurring opinion therein, at 677. In an area which trenches so closely upon otherwise legitimate employer prerogatives, we consider the absence of Board findings on this score a fatal defect in its decision. The Court of Appeals for its part did not deal with the question of purpose and effect at all, since it concluded that an employer's right to close down his entire business because of distaste for unionism, also embraced a partial closing so motivated.

Apart from this, the Board's holding should not be accepted or rejected without court review of its single employer finding, judged, however, in accordance with the general principles set forth above. Review of that finding, which the lower court found unnecessary on its view of the cause, now becomes necessary in light of our holding in this part of our opinion, and is a task that devolves upon the Court of Appeals in the first instance. *Universal Camera Corp. v. NLRB*, 340 U.S. 474 (1951).

In these circumstances, we think the proper disposition of this cause is to require that it be remanded to the Board so as to afford the Board the opportunity to make further findings on the issue of purpose and effect. *See, e.g., NLRB v. Virginia Elec. & Power Co.*, 314 U.S. 469, 479-480 (1941). This is particularly appropriate here since the case involve issues of first impression. If such findings are made, the cases will then be in a posture for further review by the Court of Appeals on all issues. Accordingly, without intimating any view as to how any of these matters should eventuate, we vacate the judgments of the Court of Appeals and remand the cases to that court with instructions to remand them to the Board for further proceedings consistent with this opinion.

It is so ordered.

MR. JUSTICE STEWART took no part in the decision of these cases.

MR. JUSTICE GOLDBERG took no part in the consideration or decision of these cases.

NOTES

1. On remand, the Trial Examiner concluded that there was insufficient evidence to show a purpose to chill unionism at the other plants or a foreseeable chilling effect. The NLRB, however, disagreed and concluded that the record indicated, at least in part, an illegal "purpose" and "foreseeable effect." *Darlington Mfg. Co.*, 165 N.L.R.B. 1074 (1967), *enforced*, 397 F.2d 760 (4th Cir.), *cert. denied*, 393 U.S. 1023 (1968).

Evidence the Board found telling included the following:

(a) Roger Milliken made speeches to South Carolina government and business leaders before the Darlington organization drive, indicating his intense concern with what he regarded as a threat to the Southern industrial community posed by unionism and the need to preserve "cooperation between management and labor ... at all costs." Section 8(c) does not preclude the Board from using such speeches as evidence of motivation, the Board said, because "this Section left unrestricted the Board's right to consider employer statements for purposes for which they would be admissible in courts of law."

(b) Milliken sent officials of all other Deering Milliken mills reprints of a trade magazine article headlined, "Darlington Situation Becomes Object Lesson to All Concerned," urging the other mill officials to undertake a "public relations" program to make the community leaders understand the consequences of unionization. "The only way the community leaders could make use of this information would be by impressing upon employees the risks of unionism."

(c) The dispatch with which Milliken closed the plant and auctioned off the machinery led the Board to infer that "he saw the opportunity to convey to all his employees an object lesson of the folly of selecting the Union."

(d) There was evidence that news of the Darlington closing spread rapidly to other Deering Milliken plants and was much discussed, frequently in terms of "Mr. Milliken would not operate a plant under a union." From such evidence, the Board inferred a "foreseeable chilling effect." Proof of actual effect, according to the NLRB, is not an essential element.

2. *NLRB v. O'Neill,* 965 F.2d 1522 (9th Cir. 1992), *cert. denied,* 509 U.S. 904 (1993), involved an employer that closed and abruptly reopened a meat processing plant under the auspices of new corporations controlled by the same person. Since the principal actor fraudulently concealed the operative facts from the representative union, the court sustained the right of the Labor Board to toll the six-month statute of limitations until the union obtained knowledge of the relevant circumstances.

3. For an example of the "runaway shop," which the Supreme Court mentioned in *Darlington* at note 16, as an unfair labor practice, *see Garwin Corp.,* 153 N.L.R.B. 664 (1965), *enforced in part,* 374 F.2d 295 (D.C. Cir. 1967). In this case, the employer's motivation for the move was found to be antiunion hostility—not economic necessity. However, when the employer offers sufficient economic reasons for the plant removal, it may be difficult to establish wrongful purpose. *NLRB v. Rapid Bindery, Inc.,* 293 F.2d 170 (2d Cir. 1961); *NLRB v. Adkins Transfer Co.,* 226 F.2d 324 (6th Cir. 1955).

When a "runaway shop" violation is found, the Board often finds it difficult to formulate an adequate remedy. In determining the appropriateness of ordering restoration of a discriminatorily relocated operation, the Board has decided to abandon the standard of whether restoration would jeopardize the "continued viability" of the business and inquire only whether restoration would be "unduly burdensome." *Lear Siegler, Inc.,* 295 N.L.R.B. 857 (1989). *See Coronet Foods, Inc. v. NLRB,* 981 F.2d 1284 (D.C. Cir. 1993); *Mid-South Bottling Co. v. NLRB,* 876 F.2d 458 (5th Cir. 1989) (finding orders directing reopening of discriminatorily closed facilities not unduly burdensome). *Compare Electronic Data Sys. Corp. v. NLRB,* 985 F.2d 801 (5th Cir. 1993), wherein the court refused to enforce an NLRB order directing a company that consolidated operations to thwart unionization of one facility to revoke the consolidation arrangement, since it found that a less restrictive remedy granting the affected workers back pay and reinstatement at the consolidated firm would adequately protect their rights. When restoration of eliminated operations is not feasible, the Board may order back pay, reinstatement at either the old or the new location, and, reimbursement for necessary moving expenses. *Industrial Fabricating, Inc.,* 119 N.L.R.B. 162 (1957), *enforced,* 272 F.2d 184 (6th Cir. 1959); *Rome Prod. Co.,* 77 N.L.R.B. 1217 (1948). *See generally* Note, *Applicable Remedies When an Employer*

Transfers to a New Location to Avoid Dealing With a Union, 53 Mich. L. Rev. 627 (1955).

4. The question whether the employer can be ordered to bargain with the old union at the new location will be discussed in Part Four, *infra.*

5. REMEDIAL PROBLEMS

CLEAR PINE MOULDINGS, INC.

National Labor Relations Board
268 N.L.R.B. 1044 (1984), *enforced,* 765 F.2d 148 (9th Cir. 1985),
cert. denied, 474 U.S. 1105 (1986)

[In a previous decision, the Labor Board found Clear Pine Mouldings to have violated § 8(a)(1) through the improper interrogation of employees regarding their protected activities, § 8(a)(3) through the reprimanding of a worker because of his membership on a Union committee, and § 8(a)(5) through both surface bargaining and the unilateral substitution of a new health plan for the existing program following the expiration of the bargaining agreement. 238 N.L.R.B. 69 (1978), *enf'd,* 632 F.2d 721 (9th Cir. 1980). In this supplemental proceeding, the Board had to decide whether two of the employees who had participated in an unfair labor practice strike in response to the Company's unlawful conduct had forfeited their right to backpay and reinstatement.]

A. The Facts. 1. Rodney Sittser. One week prior to the strike Sittser and two other employees "cornered" employee Johnny Webb against a wall at work and told Webb he would have to go on strike as voted by the other employees. When Webb said that he had been on vacation when the strike vote was taken, the employees began shoving Webb, and Sittser stated that Webb should watch out because they might burn his house or garage or something. Webb testified that Sittser repeated his threat to him over the telephone on several other occasions.

Sittser also had a prestrike encounter with employee Don Clark at Clark's home. According to Clark, as the two men discussed the strike and the possibility of employees dropping out of the Union, Sittser became progressively angrier. Clark heard Sittser make a phone call to Union Business Agent Phillip Douglass during which Sittser suggested that a group of union members visit an employee named Cecil Barber to "straighten him out." Sittser also told Clark that the hands of certain knife-grinding personnel should be broken. Clark testified that his experience with Sittser made him so nervous that he put his house up for sale in anticipation of getting a job elsewhere.

The final incident involving Sittser also involved Helen Wright, who had resigned from the Union at the start of the strike. Shortly after the strike began, Wright was leaving work at the end of her shift when Sittser flagged down her car and told her that she was taking her life in her hands by crossing the picket line and would live to regret it. Wright testified that she took alternate routes to work after this conversation because Sittser's remarks frightened her.

2. Robert Anderson. When the night shift ended at 1 a.m. on 6 August 1977, there were 40 to 50 pickets outside the plant who were carrying baseball bats, tire irons, and ax handles and were accompanied by dogs. Nonstriking employee Don Close testified that picketers stopped a truck belonging to nonstriker Ron Reese, jerked open the doors, and broke the windows. Close identified striker Robert Anderson as using a 2-foot-long club to beat on the truck. Night-Shift Superintendent Jerry Payne testified that he saw the doors of Reese's truck open with people hanging on the doors trying to pull Reese out. In addition, Payne saw nonstriking employee Jerry Sherrer try to leave the plant on a motorcycle when a person Payne later identified as Anderson swung at Sherrer with a club.

As Close proceeded out of the plant, picketers called him names and beat on his truck, causing a dent near a window. Close became so nervous at the prospect of being blocked in by the picketers ahead of him that he backed his truck up, knocking over Anderson in the process, and exited in another direction. Nonstriking employee Tom Tucker testified that Anderson hit Close's truck with a club, was knocked over when Close's truck rolled back, and then looked up from his position on the ground to threaten Tucker with the words, "I am going to kill you, you son-of-a-bitch."[5] Nonstriker Steve Hardt testified that, as he attempted to drive through the picket line, Anderson hit his car with a club, leaving a one-quarter-inch-deep dent in the rain gutter on the passenger side.

B. The Administrative Law Judge's Decision. The judge specifically discredited Rodney Sittser's denials and credited the testimony of Webb, Clark, and Wright that Sittser made verbal threats of violence. The judge also credited the testimony of Close, Payne, Tucker, and Hardt, and specifically found that on 6 August 1977 Robert Anderson carried a clublike object with him which he used to hammer on vehicles leaving the plant. Of particular note is the judge's inference, based on all the credited testimony, that Anderson went to the picket line "equipped and ready to engage in pugnacious behavior."

Despite these findings, the judge concluded that Sittser's strike-related threats and Anderson's picket line misconduct were not sufficiently serious to disqualify the two strikers from reinstatement. The judge observed that Sittser's verbal threats were not accompanied by any further actions and occurred only during a short period near the beginning of a 4-month strike. The judge also noted that Anderson's threatening conduct on the picket line was limited to a single incident during the first week of the strike. The judge concluded that these were minor, isolated acts of the type that the Board has excused as trivial misconduct not egregious enough to deprive strikers of the Act's protection.

Section 7 of the Act gives employees the right to peacefully strike, picket, and engage in other concerted activities for the purpose of collective bargaining or

---

[5] Anderson was still carrying the club when he threatened Tucker, even though he had been knocked to the ground.

other mutual aid or protection. Section 7 also grants employees the equivalent right to "refrain from" these activities.

Previously, the Board has held that "not every impropriety committed in the course of a strike deprives an employee of the protective mantle of the Act" and that "minor acts of misconduct must have been in the contemplation of Congress when it provided for the right to strike...."[6] However, the Board has also acknowledged that "serious acts of misconduct which occur in the course of a strike may disqualify a striker from the protection of the Act."

The difficulty lies in deciding whether particular strike misconduct results in the loss of statutory protection the employees otherwise would have. In the past, the Board has held that verbal threats by strikers, "not accompanied by any physical acts or gestures that would provide added emphasis or meaning to [the] words," do not constitute serious strike misconduct warranting an employer's refusal to reinstate the strikers. On the other hand, the Board has held that verbal threats which are accompanied by physical movements or contacts, such as hitting cars, do constitute serious strike misconduct. The Board summarized its standard for finding strike misconduct based on verbal threats in *Coronet Casuals,* where it stated that "absent violence ... a picket is not disqualified from reinstatement despite ... making abusive threats against nonstrikers...."

We disagree with this standard because actions such as the making of abusive threats against nonstriking employees equate to "restraint and coercion" prohibited elsewhere in the Act and are not privileged by Section 8(c) of the Act. Although we agree that the presence of physical gestures accompanying a verbal threat may increase the gravity of verbal conduct, we reject the per se rule that words alone can never warrant a denial of reinstatement in the absence of physical acts. Rather, we agree with the United States Court of Appeals for the First Circuit that "[a] serious threat may draw its credibility from the surrounding circumstances and not from the physical gestures of the speaker."[11] We also agree with the United States Court of Appeals for the Third Circuit that an employer need not "countenance conduct that amounts to intimidation and threats of bodily harm."[12] In *McQuaide,* the Third Circuit applied the following objective test for determining whether verbal threats by strikers directed at fellow employees justify an employer's refusal to reinstate: "'whether the misconduct is such that, under the circumstances existing, it may reasonably tend to coerce or intimidate

---

[6] *Coronet Casuals,* 207 NLRB 304, 305 (1973).

[11] *Associated Grocers of New England v. NLRB,* 562 F.2d 1333, 1336 (1st Cir. 1977), denying enf. in part to 227 NLRB 1200.

[12] *NLRB v. W.C. McQuaide, Inc.,* 552 F.2d 519, 527 (3d Cir. 1977), denying enf. in part to 220 NLRB 593 (1975). We read the *McQuaide* standard to essentially adopt a "reasonably tends to restrain and coerce" measure for the loss of reinstatement rights.

employees in the exercise of rights protected under the Act.'" We believe this is the correct standard and we adopt it.[14]

The legislative history of the Labor Management Relations Act supports the adoption of such a standard. Although the Act specifically recognizes the right to strike, and although any strike which involves picketing may have a coercive aspect, it is clear that Congress never intended to afford special protection to all picket line conduct, whatever the circumstances.[16] The legislative history of the Labor Management Relations Act clearly indicates that Congress intended to impose limits on the types of employee strike conduct that would be considered protected....

We believe it is appropriate, at this point, to state our view that the existence of a "strike" in which some employees elect to voluntarily withhold their services does not in any way privilege those employees to engage in other than peaceful picketing and persuasion. They have no right, for example, to threaten those employees who, for whatever reason, have decided to work during the strike, to block access to the employer's premises, and certainly no right to carry or use weapons or other objects of intimidation. As we view the statute, the only activity the statute privileges in this context, other than peaceful patrolling, is the nonthreatening expression of opinion, verbally or through signs and pamphleteering, similar to that found in Section 8(c).[23]

In deciding whether reinstatement should be ordered after an unfair labor practice strike, the Board has in the past balanced the severity of the employer's unfair labor practices that provoked the strike against the gravity of the striker's misconduct. We do not agree with this test. There is nothing in the statute to support the notion that striking employees are free to engage in or escalate violence of misconduct in proportion to their individual estimates of the degree or seriousness of an employer's unfair labor practices. Rather, it is for the Board to fashion

---

[14] Previous Board decisions that failed to apply this standard are overruled to the extent they are inconsistent with our decision today....

We would also apply an analogous standard to the assessment of strikers' verbal and nonverbal conduct directed against persons who do not enjoy the protection of Sec. 7 of the Act.

[16] See generally H.R. Conf. Rep. No. 510 on H.R. 3020, 80th Cong., 1st Sess., reprinted in Legislative History of the Labor Management Relations Act, 1947 at 542-544. "It is apparent that many forms and varieties of concerted activities which the Board, particularly in its early days, regarded as protected by the Act will no longer be treated as having that protection, since obviously persons who engage in or support unfair labor practices will not enjoy immunity under the Act." Id. at 544. "[I]n section 10(c) of the amended act ... it is specifically provided that no order of the Board shall require the reinstatement of any individual or the payment to him of back pay if such individual was suspended or discharged for cause, and this, of course, applies with equal force whether or not the acts constituting the cause for discharging were committed in connection with a concerted activity." Id. at 543.

[23] This of course does not prevent a union from advising its members of the possible consequences crossing a picket line may have under lawful provisions of the union's constitution and bylaws.

remedies and policies which will discourage unfair labor practices and the resort to violence and unlawful coercion by employers and employees alike. In cases of picket line and strike misconduct, we will do this by denying reinstatement and backpay to employees who exceed the bounds of peaceful and reasoned conduct.[25]

Accordingly, we find that the Respondent's denial of reinstatement to Robert Anderson and Rodney Sittser did not violate the Act.

Applying the above standard to the present case, the acts of striker Anderson, in carrying a 2-foot-long club, using it to swing at a nonstriking employee motorcyclist, and using it to beat on vehicles of nonstriking employees, are each sufficient to warrant denial of reinstatement, for each of these acts reasonably tended, under the circumstances, "to coerce or intimidate employees in the exercise of rights protected under the Act." The circumstances clearly indicate that violence or instilling a fear of bodily harm was the reasonably intended use of the club where strikers, at the time, were also carrying tire irons, baseball bats, and ax handles, and were accompanied by dogs. Such conduct is inherently coercive and intimidating with respect to the exercise of employees' Section 7 right to refrain from engaging in protected activities. Likewise, Anderson's verbal threat to kill nonstriking employee Tucker was also unprotected since it was similarly coercive and intimidating with respect to Tucker's exercise of his Section 7 rights. This is particularly true here where Anderson was equipped with a weapon and had in fact been using it. Finally, Anderson's conduct in striking Close's truck with a club, an act of property damage, tended to coerce or intimidate employees in the exercise of their protected right to refrain from striking.

We also find that the conduct of striking employee Sittser was unprotected. His threat to nonstriking employee Wright to the effect that she was taking her life in her own hands by crossing the picket line, and would live to regret it, clearly had a reasonable tendency to coerce and intimidate her with respect to the exercise of her rights under the Act. Similarly, Sittser's repeated threats to employee Webb, which included threats to burn Webb's house, are egregious examples of statements which reasonably tend to coerce and intimidate employees in

---

[25] Balancing the misconduct of strikers against the seriousness of the employer's unfair labor practice is inappropriate because it condones misconduct on the part of employees as a response to the employer's unfair labor practice and indeed makes it part of the remedy protected by the Act. Retaliation breeds retaliation and, in the emotion-charged strike atmosphere, retaliation will likely initiate an escalation of misconduct culminating in the violent coercive actions we condemn. It would be virtually impossible for all practical purposes for employees to know what is expected of them during a strike because balancing remains illusive and would be applied only long after the operative events have occurred. Likewise we believe that the unclear and permissive standards previously employed by the Board have failed to adequately protect employee rights. Rather, it is our purpose to discourage any belief that misconduct is ever a proper element of labor relations. Only in this way can we honor the Act's commitment to the peaceful settlement of labor disputes without resort to coercion, intimidation, and violence. Therefore, we refuse to adopt a standard which will allow the illegal acts of one party to justify the wrongful acts of another.

the exercise of statutory rights. Sittser's statement to employee Clark to the effect that the hands of certain knife-grinding personnel should be broken is coercive, because, although ostensibly it referred to employees other than Clark, it reasonably tended to coerce and intimidate Clark in the free exercise of his Section 7 rights. In this context, we also find that Sittser's less specific threat made in Clark's presence to "straighten ... out" another employee likewise reasonably tended to coerce and intimidate Clark....

MEMBERS ZIMMERMAN and DENNIS, concurring:

We join our colleagues in adopting the *McQuaide* test as the appropriate standard for determining whether strike misconduct warrants denial of reinstatement. In so doing, we reject the previous Board rule that a verbal threat could never justify denial of reinstatement in the absence of physical gestures.[2] Furthermore, we agree that the *McQuaide* standard applies not only to misconduct directed at nonstriking employees but also, by analogy, to strikers' retaliation against non-employees such as supervisors. As the First Circuit held in *Associated Grocers,* the common question is whether the particular strike misconduct "in the circumstances reasonably tends to coerce or intimidate." ...

NOTES

1. Contrast the Board's opinion with the view expressed in *Local 833, UAW v. NLRB,* 300 F.2d 699, 702-03 (D.C. Cir.), *cert. denied,* 370 U.S. 911 (1962):

[W]here an employer who has committed unfair labor practices discharges employees for unprotected acts of misconduct, the Board must consider both the seriousness of the employer's unlawful acts and the seriousness of the

---

[2] Member Dennis joins her colleagues in overruling past Board decisions that are inconsistent with the new standard.

Member Zimmerman participated in the decision in *Georgia Kraft Co.,* 258 NLRB 908 (1981). On further consideration, he believes that, to the extent the Board's test there was described as precluding a denial of reinstatement solely because physical gestures or violence did not accompany the statements under consideration, the test was too narrow. In his view, the absence of physical gestures or violence, though a consideration in such cases, is not dispositive of whether reinstatement of an employee is an appropriate exercise of the Board's responsibility to remedy unfair labor practices. He believes that in adopting a standard that encompasses threats that are wholly verbal, however, the Board must take care not to condemn statements which are not reasonably likely to instill fear of physical harm. Under common law and statute, threats unaccompanied by acts ordinarily are not illegal or actionable. The first amendment protects pure speech from governmental restraint, even protecting a threat to kill where the circumstances show it to be hyberbole. *Watts v. United States,* 394 U.S. 705 (1969). The Board's application of the *McQuaide* test of coercive tendency must be informed by the knowledge that picket line actions often include tense, angry, and hostile confrontations in which emotions run high and threats are hurled that cannot reasonably be interpreted as auguries of violence. The Board must take care not to impose on industrial disputes a code of ethics alien to the realities of confrontational strikes and picket lines and contrary to our national tradition of free speech. *See NLRB v. W.C. McQuaide, Inc.,* 552 F.2d at 528.

employees' misconduct in determining whether reinstatement would effectuate the policies of the Act. Those policies inevitably come into conflict when both labor and management are at fault. To hold that employee "misconduct" automatically precludes compulsory reinstatement ignores two considerations which we think important. First, the employer's antecedent unfair labor practices may have been so blatant that they provoked employees to resort to unprotected action. Second, reinstatement is the only sanction which prevents an employer from benefiting from his unfair labor practices through discharges which may weaken or destroy a union.

Even when it balanced the misconduct of unfair labor practice strikers against the seriousness of the prior employer misconduct, the Board would not reinstate strikers who were guilty of violent intimidation of nonstrikers. *Oneita Knitting Mills v. NLRB,* 375 F.2d 385 (4th Cir. 1967); *Kayser-Roth Hosiery Co.,* 187 N.L.R.B. 562 (1970), *modified,* 447 F.2d 396 (6th Cir. 1971).

In *Caterpillar, Inc.,* 322 N.L.R.B. 674 (1996), the Board held that a union official had been illegally discharged, even though during a grievance interview the employee had used obscene language toward a supervisor and struck the supervisor with his finger, because the employer's "unjust and discriminatory" treatment had provoked the alleged insubordination.

2. For a good discussion of the distinction between strike conduct that reasonably tends to coerce or intimidate employees and that which does not under the reinstatement test adopted in *Clear Pine Mouldings, see Newport News Shipbuilding Co. v. NLRB,* 738 F.2d 1404 (4th Cir. 1984). *Compare NMC Finishing v. NLRB,* 101 F.3d 528 (8th Cir. 1996) (offensive, obscene picket sign singling out specific nonstriker for vilification justified employer's refusal to reinstate striker carrying sign) *with Catalytic, Inc.,* 275 N.L.R.B. 97 (1985) (striker who anonymously telephoned residence of nonstriker and called nonstriker's wife a "God damned bitch" did not engage in coercive conduct, since no threat involved).

3. When an employer refuses to reinstate economic strikers based upon the honest belief that they have engaged in unprotected misconduct, their terminations will be sustained, unless the General Counsel can demonstrate that the suspected strike misconduct did not actually occur or was insufficient to warrant discharge. *See Schreiber Mfr. v. NLRB,* 725 F.2d 413 (6th Cir. 1984). Even when it is found that an employer violated the NLRA by discharging strikers for misconduct in which they were not involved, reinstatement and backpay will still be denied if the evidence shows that the strikers had engaged in other egregious misconduct. *See Teamsters Local 162 v. NLRB,* 782 F.2d 839 (9th Cir. 1986).

If an employer discharges an employee in response to that worker's exercise of protected rights but the discriminatee gives false testimony in the subsequent Labor Board proceeding, should the normal reinstatement order be denied? In *ABF Freight Sys. v. NLRB,* 510 U.S. 317 (1994), the Court sustained the power of the

Board to order reinstatement where it weighed the severity of the employee's later misconduct against the severity of the employer's antecedent unfair labor practice and ruled in favor of the employee.

4. What if the misconduct occurred during an economic strike instead of a strike caused by the employer's unfair labor practices? In the leading case of *NLRB v. Thayer Co.*, 213 F.2d 748, 752-53 (1st Cir.), *cert. denied,* 348 U.S. 883 (1954), Judge Magruder said:

> If an economic strike as conducted is not concerted activity within the protection of § 7, then the employer is free to discharge the participating employees for the strike activity and the Board is powerless to order their reinstatement.... This is so because, if the particular collective action is not a protected § 7 activity, the employer commits no unfair labor practice by thus terminating the employment relation. He has not interfered with, restrained or coerced employees in the exercise of their rights guaranteed in § 7.... Therefore, since the power of the Board to order reinstatement under § 10(c) is dependent upon its finding that an unfair labor practice has been committed, and since by hypothesis the economic strike was not caused by an unfair labor practice, it becomes crucial to the question of reinstatement of an economic striker to inquire whether the strike as conducted constituted concerted activity within the protection of § 7. On the other hand, where, as in the instant case, the strike was caused by an unfair labor practice, the power of the Board to order reinstatement is not necessarily dependent upon a determination that the strike activity was a "concerted activity" within the protection of § 7. Even if it was not, the National Labor Relations Board has power under § 10(c) to order reinstatement if the discharges were not "for cause" and if such an order would effectuate the policies of the Act.

5. *See generally* Cox, *The Right to Engage in Concerted Activities,* 26 Ind. L.J. (1951); Lipton, *Misconduct in Concerted Activities,* 8 Labor L.J. 299 (1957); Schatzki, *Some Observations and Suggestions Concerning a Misnomer—"Protected" Concerted Activities,* 47 Texas L. Rev. 378 (1969); Note, *Strike Misconduct as Grounds for Denial of Reinstatement,* 32 N.Y.U.L. Rev. 839 (1957).

Phelps Dodge Corp. v. NLRB, 313 U.S. 177, 61 S. Ct. 845, 85 L. Ed. 1271 (1941). In this landmark case, the Supreme Court interpreted the National Labor Relations Act as giving the Board broad and flexible powers to fashion remedies to effectuate the purposes of the act. The Court held that the Board has the power to order the hiring of applicants for employment who were discriminated against because of their union membership. Would you have any problems with this, in the light of the language of § 10(c)—"affirmative action, including reinstatement of employees with or without back pay"? The Court also indicated that the Board may order reinstatement of employees who have been discriminated against, even though they have obtained substantially equivalent employment. Would you have any difficulty with this, in the light of the language in § 2(3) of the act? Finally, the Court held that, in calculating back pay, a deduction should be made, not only for actual interim earnings, but also for amounts the worker failed without excuse to earn. The Court further recognized the discretion possessed by the Board when it is formulating appropriate remedies:

> A statute expressive of such large public policy as that on which the National Labor Relations Board is based must be broadly phrased and necessarily carries with it the task of administrative application. There is an area plainly covered by the language of the act and an area no less plainly without it. But in the nature of things Congress could not catalogue all the devices or stratagems for circumventing the policies of the act. Nor could it define the whole gamut of remedies to effectuate these policies in an infinite variety of specific situations. Congress met these difficulties by leaving the adaptation of means to end to the empiric process of administration. The exercise of the process was committed to the Board, subject to limited judicial review. Because the relation of remedy to policy is peculiarly a matter for administrative competence, courts must not enter the allowable area of the Board's discretion and must guard against the danger of sliding unconsciously from the narrow confines of law into the more spacious domain of policy. On the other hand, the power with which Congress invested the Board implies responsibility—the responsibility of exercising its judgment in employing the statutory powers. The act does not create rights for individuals which must be vindicated according to a rigid scheme of remedies. It entrusts to an expert agency the maintenance and promotion of industrial peace. [313 U.S. at 194.]

NOTES

1. In *Tubari, Ltd. v. NLRB,* 959 F.2d 451 (3d Cir. 1992), the court reversed the Labor Board determination and held that no back pay was due unlawfully discharged employees who had obtained interim jobs picketing for their union at lower pay, since they had not fulfilled their duty to mitigate damages.

2. Unemployment compensation benefits are not deducted from back pay. *See NLRB v. Gullett Gin Co.,* 340 U.S. 361 (1951). Does this make the employee "more than whole"? *See also NLRB v. Illinois Dep't of Employment Sec.,* 988 F.2d 735 (7th Cir. 1993) (NLRB may enjoin state effort to recoup unemployment compensation from individuals granted back pay awards under the NLRA).

A court may not refuse to enforce a back-pay order merely because of an inordinate Board delay in formulating a back-pay specification. *NLRB v. Ironworkers, Local 480,* 466 U.S. 720 (1984).

Discriminatees who willfully conceal interim earnings forfeit back pay for all calendar quarters in which they were engaged in the concealment. *American Nav. Co.,* 268 N.L.R.B. 426 (1983).

3. *Period of computation.* In *F.W. Woolworth Co.,* 90 N.L.R.B. 289 (1950), the Board significantly revised its policy with respect to the manner of computation of back-pay awards to take account of interim earnings of discharged employees. Prior thereto the practice was to compute such awards "by calculating the difference between what an employee would have earned, during the whole period of discrimination, absent discrimination against him, and what he actually earned in other employment during this period." NLRB, Fifteenth Annual Report 155-56 (1950). In *Woolworth,* the policy adopted was to compute the difference between "(1) the earnings the employee would have received in each separate calendar quarter or portion thereof, but for the employer's discrimination against him and (2) the quarterly earnings from other employment in each quarter during the period of discrimination," so that "earnings of one particular quarter shall have no effect upon the back-pay liability for any other quarter." *Id.* at 156. This method of quarterly computation was approved by the Supreme Court in *NLRB v. Seven-Up Bottling Co.,* 344 U.S. 344 (1953).

4. In 1962, the NLRB commenced the practice of requiring the payment of six percent interest on back pay due to discriminatorily discharged employees. *Isis Plumbing & Heating Co.,* 138 N.L.R.B. 716 (1962). The practice was approved in *Philip Carey Mfg. Co. v. NLRB,* 331 F.2d 720 (6th Cir.), *cert. denied,* 379 U.S. 888 (1964). In *New Horizons for Retarded,* 283 N.L.R.B. 1173 (1987), the Board decided to follow the "short-term federal rate" charged by the Internal Revenue Service for underpaid federal taxes.

5. *Sure-Tan, Inc. v. NLRB,* 467 U.S. 883 (1984), concerned an employer that reported undocumented aliens to the Immigration and Naturalization Service in retaliation for their union activities. The aliens thereafter agreed to leave the country voluntarily. The Supreme Court agreed with the Labor Board that such illegal aliens constitute "employees" within the meaning of the NLRA, and it thus found that the employer's retaliatory action had violated the Act. Recognizing the unusual nature of undocumented aliens, the Supreme Court made the Board's reinstatement and back-pay order conditional on the discriminatees' legal re-entry into the United States. This limitation was based upon the fact that employees "must be deemed unavailable for work (and the accrual of backpay therefore tolled) during any period when the employees were not lawfully entitled to be present and employed in the United States." *See Sure-Tan, Inc.,* 277 N.L.R.B. 302 (1985).

In *NLRB v. A.P.R.A. Fuel Oil Buyers Group*, 134 F.3d 50 (2d Cir. 1997), the court sustained the authority of the Labor Board to order the reinstatement of undocumented aliens—conditioned on the discriminatees' verification of their lawful right to work in the U.S. The Court also upheld the Board's backpay order covering the period from their terminations until either their reinstatement or the expiration of a reasonable time allowed for them to comply with the Immigration Reform and Control Act requirements for individuals who wish to remain in the country. *Compare Garment Workers Local 12 v. NLRB [Felbro, Inc.],* 795 F.2d 705 (9th Cir. 1986) (reading *Sure-Tan* as barring from reinstatement and back pay only those undocumented aliens who are outside the country without entry papers and finding wrongfully terminated undocumented aliens still residing in the U.S. and not subject to deportation proceedings entitled to normal back-pay remedy) *with Del Rey Tortilleria, Inc. v. NLRB,* 976 F.2d 1115 (7th Cir. 1992) (holding that illegally terminated undocumented aliens who have not yet been deported are not entitled to back pay since they have no right to be employed within the U.S.). *See* Comment, 134 U. Pa. L. Rev. 703 (1986).

6. In cases in which the Board finds "massive" unfair labor practices, it often orders novel remedies. Among these are the remedies used in the numerous cases involving J.P. Stevens & Co. The Board has ordered, and the courts have upheld, the following remedies: requiring the employer to post notice of the Board's order not only in the plant in which the unfair labor practice occurred, but in all forty-three company plants, and requiring the employer to mail the order to each of the employees in the forty-three plants (380 F.2d 292 (2d Cir. 1967)); requiring that the employer give the union, upon request, reasonable access to plant bulletin boards for a period of one year, and requiring the Board order to be read to employees during working time (441 F.2d 514 (5th Cir. 1971); 461 F.2d 490 (4th Cir. 1972)); requiring the employer to give a list of the names and addresses of all the employees in all its plants to the union (406 F.2d 1017 (4th Cir. 1968); 417 F.2d 533 (5th Cir. 1969)). In finding J.P. Stevens to be in civil contempt, the court in 464 F.2d 1326 (2d Cir. 1972), *cert. denied,* 410 U.S. 926 (1973) ordered the company to pay to the NLRB all costs and expenses, including counsel fees and salaries, incurred by the Board as a result of the contempt proceedings. The Board accepted one circuit court's offer to consider more drastic remedies against J.P. Stevens by ordering the company to pay the Amalgamated Clothing and Textile Workers Union's litigation and organizing expenses at the Wallace, N.C. plant. 244 N.L.R.B. 407 (1979), *enforced,* 668 F.2d 767 (4th Cir. 1982), *vacated and remanded for further consideration in light of Summit Valley Indus. v. Carpenters,* 476 U.S. 717 (1982).

In *Unbelievable, Inc. v. NLRB*, 118 F.3d 795 (D.C. Cir. 1997), a divided court held that the Labor Board lacks the authority to order an employer to reimburse the charging party or the Board for litigation expenses incurred in connection with the prosecution of unfair labor practice charges. The court majority found that such an order was contrary to *Alyeska Pipeline Service Co. v. Wilderness Society*, 421 U.S. 240 (1975), in which the Supreme Court held that under the American rule each party must bear its own legal expenses in the absence of a clear congressional mandate to the contrary.

7. The Labor Board has held that the corporate veil may be pierced and personal liability imposed when: (1) shareholders and officers have failed to maintain separate identities, with corporate and individual assets being indistinct, and (2) adherence to corporate form would sanction fraud, promote injustice, or lead to the evasion of legal obligations. *White Oak Coal Co.*, 318 N.L.R.B. 732 (1995), *enforced*, 152 L.R.R.M. 2128 (4th Cir. 1996).

Suppose an employer that has been found guilty of discriminatory discharges sells its business to a bona fide purchaser (not just an alter ego of the employer) that has knowledge of the unfair labor practices? The Supreme Court concluded that such a purchaser who continues to operate the business without significant change may be held jointly and severally liable with the seller for remedying the antecedent unfair labor practices. *Golden State Bottling Co. v. NLRB*, 414 U.S. 168 (1973). *See also NLRB v. Laborers*, 882 F.2d 949 (5th Cir. 1989); *NLRB v. Metallic Lathers, Local 46*, 727 F.2d 234 (2d Cir. 1984) (applying same rule to successor unions). *Compare Peters v. NLRB*, 153 F.3d 289 (6th Cir. 1998) (refusing to apply *Golden State Bottling* to party that purchased bankrupt firm through receivership sale because of inability of purchaser to negotiate indemnification provision or reduced sales price with predecessor entity).

SECTION II. Representation Questions

A. ESTABLISHING REPRESENTATIVE STATUS THROUGH NLRB ELECTIONS

STATUTORY REFERENCES

RLA § 2, Fourth and Ninth; NLRA § 9

FOREWORD

Problems with respect to the representation of employees arise at the moment the process of organization begins, and continue until a given union achieves a secure position as bargaining representative. The labor relations acts have accented these problems by according a special status to the union that succeeds in organizing a "majority" of the employees in a defined group. At the same time, the statutes have provided procedures that may be used to determine whether a given union has achieved this status. In this section we are concerned with these procedures and the questions that arise in connection with their use. Problems with respect to the use by unions of collective action for organizational purposes are to be treated in Part Three. Presumptively, the availability and use of the labor relations act procedures have tended to reduce the resort to self-help.

The procedure in representation cases has been summarized by the NLRB in its "Statements of Procedure, Subpart C—Representation Cases Under Section 9(c) of the Act." This statement is reproduced in *Selected Federal Statutes* and should be read at this point.

NLRB, TWENTY-SIXTH ANNUAL REPORT 3, 4 (1961)

In fiscal 1961, the National Labor Relations Board delegated its decisional powers with respect to employee collective bargaining election cases to its 28 regional directors. This was a new procedural step—and one of the most important in Board history—made possible by the 1959 amendments to the Act. The principal effect of this delegation was to permit regional directors to decide in their regions election cases that before the 1959 amendments had been ruled on only by the five-man Board in Washington.

This delegation includes decisions as to whether a question concerning representation exists, determination of appropriate bargaining unit, directions of elections to determine whether employees wish union representation for collective-bargaining purposes, and rulings on other matters such as challenged ballots and objections to elections.

Announcing the delegation, Chairman McCulloch said:

> This delegation of decision making and other powers by the Board to its regional directors promises to be one of the most far-reaching steps the Board has ever taken with respect to its election cases. It should provide a major speed up in NLRB case handling in line with the policy of President Kennedy for the independent regulatory agencies.

Actions taken by regional directors under the delegation are final, subject to discretionary review by the Board in Washington on restricted grounds. The Board's delegation covers not only employee petitions to select collective-bargaining representatives, but also employer petitions questioning representation, employee petitions to decertify unions, and petitions to rescind union-security authorizations.

In the delegation the Board provided that review of regional directors' decisions could be sought on these four grounds:

1. Where a substantial question of law or policy is raised because of (a) the absence of, or (b) the departure from, officially reported precedent.

2. Where a regional director's decision on a substantial factual issue is clearly erroneous, and such error prejudicially affects the rights of a party.

3. Where the conduct of the hearing in an election case or any ruling made in connection with the proceeding has resulted in prejudicial error.

4. Where there are compelling reasons for reconsideration of an important Board rule or policy.

NLRB, FORTY-SIXTH ANNUAL REPORT 31 (1981)

The Act requires that an employer bargain with the representative designated by a majority of his employees in a unit appropriate for collective bargaining. But it does not require that the representative be designated by any particular procedure as long as the representative is clearly the choice of a majority of the employees. As one method for employees to select a majority representative, the Act authorizes the Board to conduct representation elections. The Board may conduct such an election after a petition has been filed by or on behalf of the employees, or by an employer who has been confronted with a claim for recognition from an individual or a labor organization. Incident to its authority to conduct elections, the Board has the power to determine the unit of employees appropriate for collective bargaining, and formally to certify a collective-bargaining representative upon the basis of the results of the election. Once certified by the Board, the bargaining agent is the exclusive representative of all employees in the appropriate unit for collective bargaining in respect to rates of pay, wages, hours of employment, or other conditions of employment. The Act also empowers the Board to conduct elections to decertify incumbent bargaining agents which have been previously certified, or which are being currently recognized by the employer. Decertification petitions may be filed by employees, or individuals other than management representatives, or by labor organizations acting on behalf of employees.

NOTES

1. Employees are eligible to vote in Board representation elections if they were employed on the "voter eligibility date" (usually the payday immediately preceding the election) *and* were employed on the date of the election. Individuals on sick leave remain eligible, as do laid off personnel who have a reasonable expectation of recall in the foreseeable future. *Red Arrow Freight Lines*, 278 N.L.R.B. 965 (1986).

2. In deciding whether temporary employees are eligible to vote, the Board has applied two different tests. Under the "reasonable expectation" test, temporary workers with a reasonable expectation of continued employment are allowed to vote, while under the "date certain" test, temporary employees whose terms of employment remain uncertain are permitted to vote. In *NLRB v. S.R.D.C., Inc.*, 45 F.3d 328 (9th Cir. 1995), the court decided that the "date certain" approach should generally be used to determine the voting eligibility of temporary personnel.

1. BARS TO CONDUCTING AN ELECTION

NLRB, THIRTY-SEVENTH ANNUAL REPORT 50-52 (1972)

In certain situations the Board, in the interest of promoting the stability of labor relations, will conclude that circumstances appropriately preclude the raising of a question concerning representation. Thus, under the Board's contract-bar rules, a present election among employees currently covered by a valid collective-bargaining agreement may, with certain exceptions, be barred by an outstanding contract. Generally, these rules require that to operate as a bar, the contract must be in writing, properly executed, and binding on the parties; it must be of definite duration and in effect for no more than 3 years; and it must also contain substantive terms and conditions of employment which in turn must be consistent with the policies of the Act.

The period during the contract term when a petition may be timely filed is ordinarily calculated from the expiration date of the agreement. A petition is timely when filed not more than 90 nor less than 60 days before the terminal date of an outstanding contract. Thus, a petition which is filed during the last 60 days of a valid contract will be considered untimely and will be dismissed. During this 60-day "insulated" period, the parties to the existing contract are free to execute a new or amended agreement without the intrusion of a rival petition, but if no agreement is reached or if the agreement which is reached does not constitute a bar itself, then a petition filed after the expiration of the old valid contract will be timely and entertained. In addition, the Board's contract-bar rules do not permit the parties to an existing collective-bargaining relationship to avoid this filing period by executing an amendment or new contract term which prematurely extends the date of expiration of that contract. In the event of such premature extension, the new contract ordinarily will not bar an election.

NOTES

1. The statutory objective of stability in labor relations is also promoted by the longstanding, judicially approved Board practice under which the certification of a representative by the Board ordinarily will be held binding for at least 1 year, barring all representation petitions filed within the 1-year period. Under some circumstances where the employer frustrates the union's bargaining efforts for a significant portion of the certification year, however, the Board may extend the period for a commensurate time.

2. In *Seton Med. Ctr.*, 317 N.L.R.B. 87 (1995), the Board held that employee ratification of an unsigned document summarizing a tentative agreement on some, but not all, issues was insufficient to establish a contract bar.

"The Board has decided to adopt the rule that a contract does not bar an election if executed (1) before any employees had been hired or (2) prior to a substantial increase in personnel. When the question of a substantial increase in personnel is in issue, a contract will bar an election only if at least 30 percent of the complement employed at the time of the hearing had been employed at the time the contract was executed, *and* 50 percent of the job classifications in existence at the time of the hearing were in existence at the time the contract was executed." *General Extrusion Co.,* 121 N.L.R.B. 1165 (1958).

3. In *Shen-Valley Meat Packers, Inc.*, 261 N.L.R.B. 958 (1982), a union and an employer had a five-year contract which provided for a general reopening at the end of the second year. After the second year, the parties amended their agreement to "reaffirm" its provisions through the remainder of the original five-year period. This contract was held to be a bar to a rival petition filed after the third anniversary date of the initial long-term agreement. The contract, however, would not have barred a rival petition filed within the "open period," 60 to 90 days before the third anniversary. Also, the Board stated that if the parties had not reaffirmed their agreement by the third anniversary, the contract would no longer have been a bar. For a discussion of the "premature extension doctrine," *see Deluxe Metal Furn.,* 121 N.L.R.B. 995 (1958).

4. In *Paragon Prod. Corp.,* 134 N.L.R.B. 662, 666 (1961), the Board said: "[W]e now hold that only those contracts containing a union-security provision which is clearly unlawful on its face, or which has been found to be unlawful in an unfair labor practice proceeding, may not bar a representation petition. A clearly unlawful union-security provision for this purpose is one which by its express terms clearly and unequivocally goes beyond the limited form of union-security permitted by § 8(a)(3) of the act, and is therefore incapable of a lawful interpretation. Such unlawful provisions include (1) those which expressly and unambiguously require the employer to give preference to union members (a) in hiring, (b) in laying off, or (c) for purpose of seniority; (2) those which specifically withhold from incumbent nonmembers and/or new employees the statutory 30-day grace period; and (3) those which expressly require as a condition of continued employment the payment of sums of money other than periodic dues and initiation fees uniformly required."

5. In *Food Haulers, Inc.,* 136 N.L.R.B. 394 (1962), the NLRB held that a contract stands as a bar to an election, even though it contains an illegal "hot-cargo" clause. The majority reasoned that the clause, though unlawful, does not interfere with the employees' choice of bargaining representative or with any other objective of contract-bar rules, and the setting aside of the entire contract as an election bar on a finding of an unlawful hot-cargo clause constitutes a more drastic sanction in the representation proceeding than is permitted under the statute in unfair labor practice proceedings. *See* § 8(e) and the material in Part Three on "hot-cargo" contracts.

6. *Pioneer Bus Co.,* 140 N.L.R.B. 54 (1962), involved an employer that met separately with representatives of white and black workers and executed separate contracts with each. Although the contractual terms were substantially the same, the Board held that this separate representational treatment along racial lines prevented the contracts from standing as a bar to a new election. The Board stated, "Consistent with clear court decisions in other contexts which condemn government sanctioning of racially separate groupings as inherently discriminatory, the Board will not permit its contract bar rules to be utilized to shield contracts such as those here involved from the challenge of otherwise appropriate election petitions."

7. If a union is defunct, its contract will not be a bar. A union is defunct if it is unable or unwilling to represent the employees. However, loss of all members in the unit does not constitute defunctness if the representative otherwise continues in existence and is willing and able to represent the employees. *Hershey Choco-late Corp.,* 121 N.L.R.B. 901 (1958).

The *Hershey* case also dealt with the situation where a schism develops in the union that made the contract. The Board held that the contract will not bar an election where a local union has voted in open meeting after notice to disaffiliate from its parent union because of a basic intra-union conflict over policy existing at the highest level of the parent union. On the other hand, the Board will not find a schism where there is only a local faction fight. The schism doctrine was very important in two periods of labor history; (1) when the CIO expelled a number of unions on grounds of alleged Communist domination, setting up rival unions to compete for their members, and (2) when the AFL-CIO expelled a number of unions on charges of corruption and misuse of members' funds, again setting up rival unions to attempt to take their place.

8. *NLRB v. Financial Inst. Emps.,* 475 U.S. 192 (1986), involved a local labor organization that had been certified as the bargaining representative of the employees at the Seattle-First National Bank. When that organization decided to affiliate with an international union, it conducted an affiliation election in which only union members were eligible to vote. Since non-union employees in the affected bargaining unit were not permitted to vote in the affiliation election, the Labor Board refused to amend the organization's certification to reflect the new affiliation. The Supreme Court ruled that the local union had the right to limit voter eligibility to actual members, since the affiliation election concerned a matter of internal union affairs which was not regulated by the NLRA.

2. DEFINING THE APPROPRIATE UNIT

NLRB, THIRTEENTH ANNUAL REPORT 35-36 (1948)

Under § 9(a) of the amended act, as before, the collective bargaining representative designated by the majority of the employees *in an appropriate unit,* is the exclusive representative of all the employees in that unit, "for the purposes of collective bargaining in respect to rates of pay, wages, hours of employment, or other conditions of employment." And it is the Board's responsibility under § 9(b) of the act to "decide in each case whether, in order to assure to employees the fullest freedom in exercising the rights guaranteed by this act, the unit appropriate for the purposes of collective bargaining shall be the employer unit, craft unit, plant unit, or subdivision thereof...." Guided by this general statement of statutory purposes and standards, the opening part of which was slightly rephrased but not substantially changed by the amendments, the Board, over a period of years, has formulated certain criteria which are applicable to the determination of all questions concerning the appropriate bargaining unit. Except in the particular and important situations discussed below, the 1947 amendments of the act have left unchanged these familiar basic tests of appropriateness. Chief among them is the rule, restated by the Board this year in *Matter of Chrysler*

Corp. [76 N.L.R.B. 55] that "employees with similar interests shall be placed in the same bargaining unit." This factor of mutuality of interest, together with the history of collective bargaining in the particular plant or industry involved, is given great weight by the Board in deciding any unit controversy, whether the dispute concerns the geographical scope of the proper bargaining unit, or its general character (for example, whether craft or industrial), or questions as to the inclusion of particular occupational categories of employees.

In deciding each case on its own facts, as it must do, the Board is vested with broad discretion, but its discretion in certain instances is now limited by provisions of the amended act. In brief outline, the innovations are as follows: "Professional employees," "guards," and "supervisors," respectively, are now defined in the statute; and supervisors, as well as "independent contractors" are expressly excluded from the definition of "employees" covered by the act. Two new provisos added to § 9(b) dictate conditions affecting the unit placement of professional employees and guards. Another proviso, § 9(b)(2), affects the Board's consideration of certain cases involving the familiar controversy over craft versus industrial units. Finally, § 9(c)(5) prescribes that the extent of employee organization shall not be "controlling" in unit determinations.

NOTES

1. *Professional Employees. See Leedom v. Kyne, infra.*

2. Section 9(b)(3) provides that no labor organization shall be certified as the representative of employees in a bargaining unit of guards if it admits to membership, or is affiliated with any organization that admits to membership, employees other than guards. Although the Labor Board previously permitted such a mixed organization to intervene in a representation proceeding and be on the ballot with an all-guard petitioning union, it has rejected this approach and no longer allows a mixed organization to intervene in an election proceeding pertaining to a guard unit. *See University of Chicago,* 272 N.L.R.B. 873 (1984). In *Wells Fargo Armored Serv.,* 270 N.L.R.B. 787 (1984), *aff'd,* 755 F.2d 5 (2d Cir. 1985), the Board similarly ruled that an employer that has voluntarily recognized a mixed union as the representative of an all-guard unit does not commit an unfair labor practice when it subsequently withdraws recognition from that entity. *Compare Velez v. Puerto Rico Marine Mgt.,* 957 F.2d 933 (1st Cir. 1992) (finding that collective contract covering unit containing guard and nonguard personnel may be enforced in § 301 suit).

Although armored car drivers who carry valuable customer goods and are trained to protect those goods with weapons they are authorized to carry are considered "guards" under § 9(b)(3), unarmed courier-guards who merely transport customer property and who receive minimal training with respect to the protection of that property do not constitute statutory "guards." *Purolator Courier Corp.,* 300 N.L.R.B. 812 (1990).

3. The Supreme Court has sustained the power of the Labor Board to exclude from bargaining units the close relatives of management without the need for a demonstration that such relatives enjoy special job-related privileges. When the Board finds that the familial ties of employees are sufficient to align their interests with management, they may be excluded from the proposed unit. *See NLRB v. Action Automotive, Inc.,* 469 U.S. 490 (1985).

4. *Extent of Organization.* Although § 9(c)(5) states that "the extent to which the employees have organized shall not be controlling," this does not prevent the Board from determining a unit that coincides with the extent of union organizing, if that unit is found to be appropriate when other factors are considered. It only prohibits reliance on the extent of organization as the *controlling factor. NLRB v. Morganton Full Fashioned Hosiery Co.,* 241 F.2d 913 (4th Cir. 1957); *Westinghouse Elec. Corp. v. NLRB,* 236 F.2d 939 (3d Cir. 1956).

In *Overnite Transp. Co.,* 322 N.L.R.B. 723 (1996), the Board considered the unit placement appropriate at different terminals of the same trucking firm, even though the result was the inclusion of mechanics when the union wanted them and their exclusion when the union did not want them. *But cf. NLRB v. Lundy Packing Co.,* 68 F.3d 1577 (4th Cir. 1995), *cert. denied,* 518 U.S. 1019 (1996) (finding Board unit determination in contravention of § 9(c)(5)).

5. *Railway Labor Act.* What is the nature of the National Mediation Board's authority under § 2, Fourth and Ninth, of the RLA to define the "craft or class" for bargaining purposes? *Compare* § 9(b) of the NLRA. Is the mediation board's task that of merely *identifying* existing crafts and classes? Is there a difference between the process of identification and that of determining what is an "appropriate" bargaining unit of employees? Why does the RLA stress the "craft or class" as the unit for bargaining purposes?

See generally Krislov, *Representation Disputes in the Railroad and Airline Industries,* 7 Lab. L.J. 98 (1956); Northrup, *The Appropriate Bargaining Unit Question Under the Railway Labor Act,* 60 Quarterly J. Econ. 250 (1946); Eischen, *Representation Disputes and Their Resolution in the Railroad and Airline Industries,* in The Railway Labor Act at Fifty (1976).

a. Craft and Industrial Units

Globe Machine & Stamping Co., 3 N.L.R.B. 294 (1937). Three AFL unions—the Metal Polishers Union (claiming to represent the polishers and buffers), the Machinists Union (claiming to represent the punch press operators) and Federal Labor Union No. 18788 (claiming to represent the rest of the production and maintenance workers in the plant)—filed representation petitions with the NLRB. The UAW-CIO intervened, claiming to represent *all* the production and maintenance workers. For some years, prior to 1937, most of the employees involved had belonged to some one of the AFL unions, or its predecessor. The UAW had undertaken a strenuous organizational campaign in 1937, and claimed that it had organized most of the plant. There was some evidence that there had been a swing back to the AFL unions in some of the skilled groups, but the membership rolls of the four unions were in such confusion that no accurate finding was possible as to the preference of the various contended-for-groups. The Board found that the polishing and the punch press work at the plant was done in separate, clearly defined areas, and was differentiated as to skill from other classifications, but that the actual production at the plant was highly integrated. It further found that the history of bargaining in the plant was inconclusive to show any clear pattern of preference or clear appropriateness of either plant-wide or separate units. The Board decided to permit the employee vote to define the appropriate unit or units:

> In view of the facts described above, it appears that the Company's production workers can be considered either as a single unit appropriate for the purposes of collective bargaining, as claimed by the UAWA, or as three such units, as claimed by the petitioning unions. The history of successful separate negotiations at the Company's plant, and also the essential separateness of polishing and punch press work at that plant, and the existence of a requirement of a certain amount of skill for that work, are proof of the feasibility of the latter approach. The successful negotiation of a plant-wide agreement on May 20, 1937, as well as the interrelation and interdependence of the various departments at the Company's plant, are proof of the feasibility of the former.
>
> In such a case where the considerations are so evenly balanced, the determining factor is the desire of the men themselves. On this point, the record affords no help. There has been a swing toward the UAW and then away from it. The only documentary proof is completely contradictory. We will therefore order elections to be held separately for the men engaged in polishing and those engaged in punch press work. We will also order an election for the employees of the Company engaged in production and maintenance, exclusive of the polishers and punch press workers and of clerical and supervisory employees. [3 N.L.R.B. at 299-300]
>
> On the results of these elections will depend the determination of the appropriate unit for the purposes of collective bargaining. Such of the groups as do not choose the UAWA will constitute separate and distinct appropriate units, and such as do choose the UAWA will, together, constitute a single appropriate unit.

NOTE

The Board's "*Globe*" election approach was upheld in *NLRB v. Underwood Mach. Co.,* 179 F.2d 118 (1st Cir. 1949), against the employer's claim that the Board had improperly delegated to the employees themselves the determination of what should be the appropriate unit. The Board, having made a determination that either a single unit or several units in the plant would be "appropriate," could properly come to the conclusion that the single factor that would tip the scales was the preference of the employees.

MALLINCKRODT CHEMICAL WORKS

National Labor Relations Board
162 N.L.R.B. 387 (1966)

[The petitioner (IBEW) sought a separate unit composed of certain skilled instrument mechanics in a chemical plant.]

Reconsideration of the American Potash Doctrine

Petitioner, relying on its showing that the instrument mechanics are craftsmen and on its claim that it qualifies as a traditional representative of such craftsmen, contends it has met the requirements set forth in the *American Potash* decision[4] for obtaining a craft severance election. On the other hand, the Employer, though not receding from its contention that the instrument mechanics are not true craftsmen and that the Petitioner is not, in any event, the traditional representative of such mechanics, argues that the *American Potash* decision improperly makes the question of severance turn solely on affirmative findings with respect to the above issues, ignoring many other relevant and weighty considerations. In this latter respect, the Employer places particular emphasis on the fact that the *American Potash* decision precludes, for all practical purposes, consideration of the duration and character of the representation which craft employees have received while being represented in a more inclusive unit, and completely rules out any consideration of the effect that integration of the functions of the craft employees involved in the proceeding with the overall production processes of the employer may have on the Board's unit determination. With respect to both points, the Employer urges that to the extent the *American Potash* decision forbids realistic consideration of bargaining history and integration of the craft employees' functions in the production process unless the case involves one of the so-called *National Tube* industries,[5] it is plainly discriminatory in application and requires reversal.

We believe there is much force to the Employer's arguments and contentions, and we have undertaken in this and other cases a review of our present policies regarding severance elections.

At the outset, it is appropriate to set forth the nature of the issue confronting the Board in making unit determinations in severance cases. Underlying such

---

[4] *American Potash & Chemical Corp.*, 107 N.L.R.B. 1418.

[5] *National Tube Co.*, 76 N.L.R.B. 1199; *Permanente Metals Co.*, 89 N.L.R.B. 804; *Corn Prod. Ref. Co.*, 80 N.L.R.B. 362; *Weyerhaeuser Timber Co.*, 87 N.L.R.B. 1076. See also, *American Potash & Chemical Corp.*, supra at 1422.

determinations is the need to balance the interest of the employer and the total employee complement in maintaining the industrial stability and resulting benefits of an historical plant-wide bargaining unit as against the interest of a portion of such complement in having an opportunity to break away from the historical unit by a vote for separate representation. The Board does not exercise its judgment lightly in these difficult areas. Each such case involves a resolution of "what would best serve the working man in his effort to bargain collectively with his employer, and what would best serve the interest of the country as a whole."[6] It is within the context of this declared legislative purpose that Congress has delegated to the Board the obligation to determine appropriate bargaining units. We do not believe that the Board can properly, or perhaps even lawfully, discharge its statutory duties by delegating the performance of so important a function to a segment of the affected employee body. Thus, we accept the Court's view in *Pittsburgh Plate Glass* that "the Board was not authorized by ... [the act] to surrender to anyone else its statutory duty to determine in each case the appropriate unit or collective bargaining." *(Ibid.)*

The cohesiveness and special interest of a craft or departmental group seeking severance may indicate the appropriateness of a bargaining unit limited to that group. However, the interests of all employees in continuing to bargain together in order to maintain their collective strength, as well as the public interest and the interests of the employer and the plant union in maintaining overall plant stability in labor relations and uninterrupted operation of integrated industrial or commercial facilities, may favor adherence to the established patterns of bargaining.

The problem of striking a balance has been the subject of Board and Congressional concern since the early days in the administration of the Wagner Act. In the *American Can* decision,[7] the Board refused to allow craft severance in the face of a bargaining history on a broader basis. This so-called *American Can* doctrine was not, however, rigidly applied to rule out all opportunities for craft severance.[8] Nevertheless, when Congress amended the Wagner Act in 1947 by enactment of the Taft-Hartley Act, it added a proviso to § 9(b), stating in pertinent part:

> The Board shall ... not decide that any craft unit is inappropriate on the ground that a different unit has been established by a prior Board determi-

---

[6] *NLRB v. Pittsburgh Plate Glass Co.*, 270 F.2d 167, 173 (4th Cir. 1959), *cert. denied*, 361 U.S. 943.

[7] *American Can Co.*, 13 N.L.R.B. 1252. *See also, Pressed Steel Car Co.*, 69 N.L.R.B. 629.

[8] *See*, for example, *Bendix Aviation Corp.*, 39 N.L.R.B. 81; *Aluminum Corp. of America*, 42 N.L.R.B. 772; *General Elec. Co., Lynn River Works & Everett Plant*, 58 N.L.R.B. 57; *Remington Rand, Inc.*, 62 N.L.R.B. 1419; *United States Potash Co.*, 63 N.L.R.B. 1379; *International Minerals & Chemical Corp.*, 71 N.L.R.B. 878; *Food Machinery Corp.*, 72 N.L.R.B. 918. Sometimes severance was denied because of bargaining history and other factors. *See*, for example, *Packard Motor Car Co.*, 63 N.L.R.B. 317; *Tamiami Trail Tours, Inc.*, 74 N.L.R.B. 918.

nation, unless a majority of the employees in the proposed craft unit vote against separate representation.

Though the legislative history indicates that this proviso grew out of Congressional concern that the *American Can* doctrine unduly restricted the rights of craft employees to seek a separate representation, it is equally clear that Congress did not intend to take away the Board's discretionary authority to find craft units to be inappropriate for collective-bargaining purposes if a review of *all* the facts, both *pro* and *con* severance, led to such result. Thus, as stated in *Senate Report No. 105 on S. 1126,* submitted by Senator Taft:

> Since the decision in the *American Can* case (13 N.L.R.B. 1252), where the Board refused to permit craft units to be "carved out" from a broader bargaining unit already established, the Board, except under unusual circumstances, has virtually compelled skilled artisans to remain part of a comprehensive plant unit. The committee regards the application of this doctrine as inequitable. *Our bill still leaves to the Board discretion to review all the facts in determining the appropriate unit,* but it may not decide that any craft unit is inappropriate on the ground that a different unit has been established by a prior Board determination.[9] [Emphasis supplied.]

This conclusion is further buttressed by the fact that the House Bill provisions[10] making the granting of severance mandatory were rejected by Congress in favor of the present provision which, as Senator Taft described it above, requires the Board to exercise its "discretion to review all the facts."

Shortly after the enactment of § 9(b)(2), the Board, in the *National Tube* case, dismissed a craft severance petition filed on behalf of a group of bricklayer craftsmen who were employed in the basic steel industry. After an exhaustive analysis of the section and its legislative history, the Board concluded that: "(1) the only restriction imposed by § 9(b)(2) is that a prior Board determination cannot be the basis for denying separate representation to a craft group; (2) under the language of the statute there is nothing to bar the Board from considering either a prior determination or the bargaining history of a particular employer as a factor, even if not controlling, in determining the appropriateness of a proposed craft unit; (3) there is nothing in either statute or legislative history to preclude the

---

[9] Leg. Hist. 417-418. A statement by Senator Taft on the floor of the Senate is to the same effect: "In effect I think it (§ 9(b)(2)) gives greater power to the craft units to organize separately. It does not go the full way of giving them the absolute right in every case; it simply provides that the Board shall have discretion and shall not bind itself by previous decision, but that the subject shall always be open for further consideration." 93 Cong. Rec. 3952; 2 Leg. Hist. 1009.

[10] See H.R. 3020, § 9(f)(2), 1 Leg. Hist. 188-9. See, also, Hearings before the Senate Committee on S. 55, 80th Cong., 1st Sess., 1007 et seq. (1947), for a proposal by the President of the American Federation of Labor which would have made the establishment of craft units mandatory unless the craft employees rejected separate representation.

Board from considering or giving such weight as it deems necessary to the factors of bargaining history in an industry, the basic nature of the duties performed by the craft employees in relation to those of the production employees, the integration of craft functions with the overall production processes of the employer, and many other circumstances upon which the Board has customarily based its determination as to the appropriateness or inappropriateness of a proposed unit." The bricklayer unit was there found to be inappropriate because of the existence of such a pattern and history of bargaining in the basic steel industry and because the functions of the craft bricklayers were intimately connected with the basic steel production process which was highly integrated in nature.[11] In subsequent cases,[12] the same grounds were relied upon for denying the formation of craft units in the wet milling, basic aluminum, and lumbering industries.

In the *American Potash* decision, the Board, in effect, reversed the *National Tube* decision as to both the proper construction of § 9(b)(2) and the propriety of denying craft severance on the basis of integrated production processes in an industry where the prevailing pattern of bargaining is industrial in character.

As to the first, the Board stated:

... [W]e find that the intent of Congress will best be effectuated by a finding, and we so find, that a craft group will be appropriate for severance purposes in cases where a true craft group is sought and where, in addition, the union is one which traditionally represents that craft.

... All that we are considering here is whether true craft groups should have an opportunity to decide the issue for themselves. We conclude that we *must* afford them that choice in order to give effect to the statute. [Emphasis supplied.]

As to the second, the Board stated:

... [W]e feel that the right of separate representation should not be denied members of a craft group merely because they are employed in an industry which involves highly integrated production processes and in which the prevailing pattern of bargaining is industrial in character. We shall, therefore, not extend the practice of denying craft severance on an industry-wide basis.

It is apparent that the decision in *American Potash* was predicated in substantial part on the view that § 9(b)(2) virtually forecloses discretion and compels the

---

[11]This decision was basically an affirmation of earlier decisions in *Geneva Steel Co.*, 57 N.L.R.B. 50; 67 N.L.R.B. 1159, and *Tennessee Coal, Iron & R.R.*, 39 N.L.R.B. 617. Similarly, the *Corn Products Refining* decision reaffirmed an earlier decision involving the same company, reported at 60 N.L.R.B. 92. Thus, the doctrine known as the *National Tube* doctrine had its origin in decisions decided prior to the amendments. The doctrine applies to new plants as well as old plants in the industries involved, and precludes the initial establishment of craft units as well as the severance of such units. *See Kaiser Aluminum & Chemical Corp.*, 119 N.L.R.B. 695.

[12]*See* cases cited in note 5.

board to grant craft severance. This view represented an almost diametrically opposite construction of the statute from that adopted by the Board in *National Tube*. On the basis of what has already been indicated herein respecting the legislative history of the section, we believe the revised construction of the statute adopted in *American Potash* was erroneous, a belief apparently shared by the Court of Appeals for the Fourth Circuit:[13]

> The Board was right ... [in the *National Tube* decision] in reaching the conclusion that the addition of subsection 2 of § 9(b) created no ambiguity. As amended, § 9(b) does not strip the Board of its original power and duty to decide in each case what bargaining unit is most appropriate.... In effect it frees the Board from the domination of its past decisions and directs it to re-examine each case on its merits and leaves it free to select that unit which it deems best suited to accomplish the statutory purposes.... Congress clearly did not command the Board, as it could have done, to establish a craft bargaining unit whenever requested by a qualified craft union, or relieve the Board of its duty to consider the interests of the plant unions and wishes of the employees who desire to bargain on a plantwide basis. The amended section expressly requires the Board to decide *in each case* what unit would be most appropriate to effectuate the overall purpose of the Act to preserve industrial peace.

Rejecting, as we do, the statutory interpretation on which the *American Potash* decision is premised, and recognizing that *American Potash* itself constituted a change in the applicable criteria, we now consider whether the tests laid down in the *American Potash* case nevertheless permit a satisfactory resolution of the issues posed in severance cases. We find that they do not. *American Potash* established two basic tests: (1) the employees involved must constitute a true craft or departmental group, and (2) the union seeking to carve out a craft or departmental unit must be one which has traditionally devoted itself to the special problems of the group involved. These tests do serve to identify and define those employee groups which normally have the necessary cohesiveness and special interests to distinguish them from the generality of production and maintenance employees, and place in the scales of judgment the interests of the craft employees. However, they do not consider the interests of the other employees and thus do not permit a weighing of the craft group against the competing interests favoring continuance of the established relationship. Thus, by confining consideration solely to the interests favoring severance, the *American Potash* tests preclude the Board from discharging its statutory responsibility to make its unit determinations on the basis of all relevant factors, including those factors which weigh against severance. In short, application of these mechanistic tests leads always to the conclusion that the interests of craft employees always prevail. It does this, moreover, without

---

[13] *NLRB v. Pittsburgh Plate Glass Co.*, 270 F.2d 167, 172-73 (4th Cir. 1959).

affording a voice in the decision to the other employees, whose unity of association is broken and whose collective strength is weakened by the success of the craft or departmental group in pressing its own special interests.

Furthermore, the *American Potash* decision makes arbitrary distinctions between industries by forbidding the application of the *National Tube* doctrine to other industries whose operations are as highly integrated, and whose plantwide bargaining patterns are as well established, as is the case in the so-called *"National Tube"* industries. In fact, the *American Potash* decision is inherently inconsistent in asserting that "... it is not the province of this Board to dictate the course and pattern of labor organization in our vast industrial complex," while, at the same time, establishing rules which have that very effect. Thus, *American Potash* clearly "dictate[s] the course and pattern of labor organization" by establishing rigid qualifications for unions seeking craft units and by automatically precluding severance of all such units in *National Tube* industries.

It is patent, from the foregoing, that the *American Potash* tests do not effectuate the policies of the act. We shall, therefore, no longer allow our inquiry to be limited by them. Rather, we shall, as the Board did prior to *American Potash*, broaden our inquiry to permit evaluation of all considerations relevant to an informed decision in this area. The following areas of inquiry are illustrative of those we deem relevant:

1. Whether or not the proposed unit consists of a distinct and homogeneous group of skilled journeymen craftsmen performing the functions of their craft on a nonrepetitive basis, or of employees constituting a functionally distinct department, working in trades or occupations for which a tradition of separate representation exists.[14]

2. The history of collective bargaining of the employees sought and at the plant involved, and at other plants of the employer, with emphasis on whether the existing patterns of bargaining are productive of stability in labor relations, and whether such stability will be unduly disrupted by the destruction of the existing patterns of representation.

3. The extent to which the employees in the proposed unit have established and maintained their separate identity during the period of inclusion in a broader unit, and the extent of their participation or lack of participation in the establishment and maintenance of the existing pattern of representation and the prior opportunities, if any, afforded them to obtain separate representation.

4. The history and pattern of collective bargaining in the industry involved.

---

[14] We are not in disagreement with the emphasis the *American Potash* decision placed on the importance of limiting severance to true craft or traditional departmental groups, nor do we disagree with the admonitions contained in that decision as to the need for strict adherence to these requirements. Our dissatisfaction with the Board's existing policy in this area stems not only from the overriding importance given to a finding that a proposed unit is composed of such employees, but also to the loose definition of a true craft or traditional department which may be derived from the decisions directing severance elections pursuant to the *American Potash* decision.

5. The degree of integration of the employer's production processes, including the extent to which the continued normal operation of the production processes is dependent upon the performance of the assigned functions of the employees in the proposed unit.

6. The qualifications of the union seeking to "carve out" a separate unit, including that union's experience in representing employees like those involved in the severance action.[15]

In view of the nature of the issue posed by a petition for severance, the foregoing should not be taken as a hard and fast definition or an inclusive or exclusive listing of the various considerations involved in making unit determinations in this area. No doubt other factors worthy of consideration will appear in the course of litigation.[16] We emphasize the foregoing to demonstrate our intention to free ourselves from the restrictive effect of rigid and inflexible rules in making our unit determinations. Our determinations will be made only after a weighing of all relevant factors on a case-by-case basis, and we will apply the same principles and standards to all industries.[17]

Turning to the facts of this case, we conclude that it will not effectuate the policies of the act to permit the disruption of the production and maintenance unit by permitting Petitioner to "carve out" a unit of instrument mechanics. Our conclusion is predicated on the following considerations.

The Employer is engaged in the production of uranium metal. It is the only enterprise in the country which is engaged in all phases of such production. All of its finished product is sold to the Atomic Energy Commission. Continued stability in labor relations at such facilities is vital to our national defense.

---

[15] With respect to this factor, we shall no longer require, as a *sine qua non* for severance, that the petitioning union qualify as a "traditional representative" in the *American Potash* sense. The fact that a union may or may not have devoted itself to representing the special interests of a particular craft or traditional departmental group of employees is a factor which will be considered in making our unit determinations in this area.

[16] We are in a period of industrial progress and change which so profoundly affect the product, process, operational technology, and organization of industry that a concomitant upheaval is reflected in the types and standards of skills, the working arrangements, job requirements, and community of interests of employees. Through modern technological development, a merging and overlapping of old crafts is taking place and new crafts are emerging. Highly skilled workers are, in some situations, required to devote those skills wholly to the production process itself, so that old departmental lines no longer reflect a homogeneous grouping of employees.

[17] To the extent that *American Potash* forecloses inquiry into all relevant factors, and to the extent that it limits consideration of the factors of industry bargaining history and integration of operations to cases arising in the so-called *National Tube* industries, it is overruled. To the extent that the decisions in *National Tube Company, supra, Permanente Metals Co., supra, Corn Products Refining Company, supra, Weyerhaeuser Timber Company, supra,* and decisions relying thereon, may be read as automatically foreclosing craft or departmental severance or the initial formation of such units in unorganized plants in the industries involved, they are hereby overruled.

The Employer produces uranium metal by means of a highly integrated continuous flow production system which the record herein shows is beyond doubt as highly integrated as are the production processes of the basic steel, basic aluminum, wet milling, and lumbering industries. The process itself is largely dependent upon the proper functioning of a wide variety of instrument controls which channel the raw materials through the closed pipe system and regulate the speed of flow of the materials as well as the temperatures within different parts of the system. These controls are an integral part of the production system. The instrument mechanics' work on such controls is therefore intimately related to the production process itself. Indeed, in performing such work, they must do so in tandem with the operators of the controls to insure that the system continues to function while new controls are installed, and existing controls are calibrated, maintained, and repaired.

The instrument mechanics have been represented as part of a production and maintenance unit for the last 25 years. The record does not demonstrate that their interests have been neglected by their bargaining representative. In fact, the record shows that their pay rates are comparable to those received by the skilled electricians who are currently represented by the Petitioner, and that such rates are among the highest in the plant. The instrument mechanics have their own seniority system for purposes of transfer, layoff, and recall. Viewing this long lack of concern for maintaining and preserving a separate group identity for bargaining purposes, together with the fact that Petitioner has not traditionally represented the instrument mechanic craft, we find that the interests served by maintenance of stability in the existing bargaining unit of approximately 280 production and maintenance employees outweigh the interests served by affording the 12 instrument mechanics an opportunity to change their mode of representation.

We conclude that the foregoing circumstances present a compelling argument in support of the continued appropriateness of the existing production and maintenance unit for purposes of collective bargaining, and against the appropriateness of a separate unit of instrument mechanics. In reaching this conclusion, we have not overlooked the fact that the instrument mechanics do constitute an identifiable group of skilled journeymen mechanics, similar to groups the Board heretofore has found entitled to severance from an overall unit. However, it appears that the separate community of interests which these employees enjoy by reason of their skills and training has been largely submerged in the broader community of interests which they share with other employees by reason of long and uninterrupted association in the existing bargaining unit, the high degree of integration of the employer's production processes, and the intimate connection of the work of these employees with the actual uranium metal-making process itself. We find, accordingly, that the unit sought by the Petitioner is inappropriate for the purposes of collective bargaining. We shall, therefore, dismiss the petition.

MEMBER FANNING dissented.

NOTES

1. In *General Motors Corp.,* 120 N.L.R.B. 1215 (1958), several organizations of skilled workers in the automobile industry petitioned for craft severance elections. The NLRB, in a rather unusual proceeding, heard oral argument in Detroit. The UAW, intervening, argued that these organizations did not meet the "traditional" craft representative test of the *American Potash* case and that the Board ought not to establish any craft or "smaller-than-plant-wide" bargaining units in the automobile industry generally. The Board did not find it necessary to rule on these important issues, dismissing the petition on the ground that the units requested were not appropriate in that they were not coextensive with the existing bargaining unit. The Board found that although originally the UAW was certified by the Board as bargaining representative in each GM plant as a separate bargaining unit, there now exists a single company-wide bargaining unit as a result of a long multiplant bargaining history in which national agreements were negotiated. Since the organizations of skilled craft workers had requested single-plant elections, the requested units were inappropriate because they were not coextensive with the existing company-wide bargaining unit.

See Cohen, *Two Years Under Mallinckrodt: A Review of the Board's Latest Craft Unit Policy,* 20 Lab. L.J. 195 (1969); Sharp, *Craft Certification: New Expansion of an Old Concept,* 33 Ohio St. L.J. 102 (1972); Note, *Unit Determination and the Problem of Craft Severance,* 19 Case W. Res. L. Rev. 327 (1968).

2. House and Senate Reports pertaining to the 1974 Health Care Amendment to the NLRA cautioned the Board not to allow the number of hospital bargaining units to proliferate unduly. The Board initially construed this admonition to proscribe only the myriad of craft units peculiar to the printing and construction industries, and it adopted the industrial community-of-interests standards set forth in *American Cyanamid Co.,* 131 N.L.R.B. 909 (1961). Several courts of appeals concluded that the legislative history of the 1974 Amendment indicated that more stringent unit determination standards were intended. *See, e.g., St. Vincent's Hosp. v. NLRB,* 567 F.2d 588 (3d Cir. 1977); *NLRB v. Frederick Mem. Hosp.,* 691 F.2d 191 (4th Cir. 1982).

The Labor Board thereafter replaced the traditional community-of-interests standards with more stringent "disparity-of-interests" criteria. *St. Francis Hosp.,* 271 N.L.R.B. 948 (1984). A proposed health care unit would be judged in terms of traditional criteria, but "sharper than usual differences" between the wages, hours, and working conditions of the employees in the proposed unit and those in an "overall professional or nonprofessional unit" had to be demonstrated before a separate, less inclusive unit would be found appropriate.

In May of 1987, a 3-2 Board majority finally decided on the "historic" step of using a rulemaking procedure to define appropriate units in the health-care industry. 125 Lab. Rel. Rep. 81 (June 8, 1987). Effective May 22, 1989, Board rules provided for the following eight separate bargaining units in "acute care" hospitals: (1) registered nurses, (2) physicians, (3) all other professionals, (4) technical employees, (5) skilled maintenance employees, (6) clerical employees, (7) guards, and (8) all other nonprofessional employees. 29 C.F.R. § 103.30. In *American Hosp. Ass'n v. NLRB,* 499 U.S. 606 (1991), the Supreme Court sustained this exercise of the Board's rulemaking power. Although § 9(b) requires the NLRB to determine the appropriate bargaining unit "in each case," the Court found that this language did not preclude the promulgation of general standards that will be applied in relevant cases. Hospitals challenging the propriety of these presumptively appropriate units must demonstrate the existence of "extraordinary circumstances" warranting the establishment of different units. *St. Margaret Mem. Hosp. v. NLRB,* 991 F.2d 1146 (3d Cir. 1993). In appropriate cases, the Labor Board continues to permit broader hospital units, including "wall-to-wall" units. *Dominican Santa Cruz Hosp.,* 307 N.L.R.B. 506 (1992). In *Fair Oaks Anesthesia Ass'n v. NLRB,* 975 F.2d 1068 (4th Cir. 1992), the court sustained a hospital unit consisting of registered nurse anesthetists employed by a professional corporation that provided anesthesia services under a contract with an acute-care hospital.

When skilled maintenance workers seek severance from an established unit at an acute care hospital, the Board continues to apply the traditional *Mallinckrodt Chem.* standards. *See Kaiser Found. Hosps.,* 312 N.L.R.B. 933 (1993).

In *Park Manor Care Ctr.,* 305 N.L.R.B. 872 (1991), the Board confirmed its decision to proceed on a case-by-case basis when determining appropriate units in nursing homes and other non-acute care facilities, applying what it said might be termed a "pragmatic or empirical community of interests" test.

See generally Grunewald, *The NLRB's First Rulemaking: An Exercise in Pragmatism,* 41 Duke L.J. 274 (1991); Bumpass, *Appropriate Bargaining Units in Health Care Institutions: An Analysis of Congressional Intent and Its Implementation by the National Labor Relations Board,* 20 B.C.L. Rev. 867 (1979); Note, *Appropriate Bargaining Units in Non-Profit Hospitals,* 37 Wash. & Lee L. Rev. 1221 (1980).

3. In 1977, the NLRB amended its rules to establish a "vote and impound" procedure that provides for the holding of a scheduled representation election and the impounding of the ballots pending review of unit determination issues by the Labor Board. In *NLRB v. Lorimar Prods.,* 771 F.2d 1294 (9th Cir. 1985), the court found that application of the "vote and impound" procedure while alternative unit formulations were being considered by the Board was improper. If the Board wants to conduct elections on an expedited basis while unit determination issues are still being litigated, it must provide eligible voters with two different ballots—to permit them to indicate their sentiments depending upon the composition of the unit ultimately approved by the Board. The Board must recognize that employees who might vote in favor of representation if the unit were defined in one way might vote against representation if it were defined differently.

b. Multiple Plant Units

NLRB, SEVENTEENTH ANNUAL REPORT 68-69 (1952)

When dealing with employees of companies which operate more than one plant, the Board must frequently determine whether an employer-wide unit, or a less comprehensive one, is appropriate. In making such determinations, the Board must take into consideration all relevant factors, but it is precluded by the act from determining the scope of the unit solely on the basis of the extent to which the company's employees have organized. This statutory limitation sometimes is invoked in opposition to a less than company-wide unit. On this point, the Board has repeatedly held that it is precluded only from giving *controlling* weight to extent of organization, but not from taking the present extent of the employees' organization into consideration together with other pertinent circumstances. In cases where extent of organization was the only basis for the proposed unit, the Board has consistently rejected the unit.

Principal factors considered in cases where multiplant units are proposed include: (1) bargaining history, (2) the extent of interchange and contacts between employees in the various plants, (3) the extent of functional integration of operations between the plants, (4) differences in the products of the plants or in the skills and types of work required, (5) the centralization, or lack of centralization, of management and supervision, particularly in regard to labor relations and the power to hire and discharge, and (6) the physical or geographical location of the plants in relation to each other.

In most cases, several of these factors are present—some pointing to the appropriateness of a multiplant unit, others pointing to the appropriateness of a narrower unit. In each case, the Board must weigh all the factors present, one against the other, in deciding the proper scope of the unit. However, in certain industries, company-wide or multiplant units are generally favored. Foremost among such industries are public utilities, such as power, telephone, and gas companies, where it has long been the Board's policy to establish system-wide or multiplant units whenever feasible. This policy is based upon the highly integrated and interdependent character of public utility operations and the high degree of coordination among the employees required by the type of service rendered.

The Board similarly favors system-wide and division-wide units of employees in the transportation industry.

NOTES

1. Over the years the Board has developed a presumption in favor of single-plant or single-store units in many industries. The presumption will be relied on absent "a functional integration so severe as to negate the identity" of the one-unit facility. *NLRB v. Living & Learning Ctrs.,* 652 F.2d 209 (5th Cir. 1981). *See also NLRB v. Cell Agrl. Mfg. Co.,* 41 F.3d 389 (8th Cir. 1994) (case where single facility presumption rebutted).

Despite a longstanding rule favoring system-wide bargaining units in public utilities, the Board ordered separate elections for craft and technical employees and for production and maintenance employees in two autonomous administrative segments that a power company created to meet the "radical cultural change" in the industry generated by deregulation. *PECO Energy Co.,* 322 N.L.R.B. 1074 (1997).

2. *Borden, Inc. v. NLRB,* 19 F.3d 502 (10th Cir.), *cert. denied,* 513 U.S. 927 (1994), concerned an employer that consolidated operations of an old plant and a newly acquired facility. Although the same union represented the employees at both locations, the different plants were covered by separate bargaining agreements. The court sustained the Board's decision to require the employer to continue to apply the old plant agreement to old plant employees transferred to the new facility until a new collective contract could be negotiated covering all of the personnel at the new location.

3. When an employer transfers a portion of an organized workforce to a new location, the new facility is normally regarded as a separate unit. *Gitano Group,* 308 N.L.R.B. 1172 (1992). If a majority of the employees in the new unit are transferees from the existing bargaining unit, the Board presumes that these individuals continue to support the union and requires the employer to recognize the union at the new facility.

4. *Chain Stores.* In *Sav-On Drugs,* 138 N.L.R.B. 1032 (1962), the Board modified its bargaining unit policy with regard to chain store operations so that the same unit criteria applied to multiplant operations are determinative of the appropriate bargaining unit for chain stores. Here the Board allowed a single store in the chain to be an appropriate bargaining unit where there was: (1) geographical separation of the store in question, (2) substantial authority of store manager, (3) minimal interchange of employees between this store and other stores, (4) absence of bargaining history for any employees in the division, and (5) fact that no union was seeking to represent employees on a broader basis.

Although a single retail store is presumptively an appropriate unit, separate units of employees working at each of an employer's ten stores in one state were held not appropriate where: (1) the manager of each store lacked autonomy; (2) most administrative and personnel functions were centralized at the main office; (3) the main office established labor relations policy; (4) all ten stores were located in shopping malls with at least one other company-owned store not the subject of an election petition; and (5) there was substantial interchange of employees on a temporary basis, and permanent transfers of 10 percent to 15 percent of the employee complement. *Petrie Stores Corp.,* 266 N.L.R.B. 75 (1983).

5. *See* Note, *The Board and § 9(c)(5): Multi-Location and Single-Location Bargaining Units in the Insurance and Retail Industries,* 79 Harv. L. Rev. 811 (1966); Note, *Effects of the NLRB's Unit Policies in the Retail Chain Store Industry,* 23 Lab. L.J. 80 (1972); Vladek, *Nixon Board and Retail Bargaining Units,* 61 Cornell L. Rev. 416 (1976).

c. Multiple Employer Units

NLRB, TWENTY-THIRD ANNUAL REPORT 36-37 (1958)

In dealing with requests for multi-employer units, the Board is primarily guided by the rule that a single-employer unit is presumptively appropriate and that to establish a contested claim for a broader unit a controlling history of collective bargaining on such a basis by the employers and the union involved must be shown. But no controlling weight was given to multi-employer bargaining which was preceded by a long history of single-employer bargaining, was of brief duration, did not result in a written contract of substantial duration, and was not based on any Board unit finding.

The existence of a controlling multi-employer bargaining history may also depend on whether the employer group has in fact bargained jointly or on an individual basis. Generally, the Board will find that joint bargaining is established where the employers involved have for a substantial period directly participated in joint bargaining or delegated the power to bind them in collective bargaining to a joint agent, have executed the resulting contract, and have not negotiated on an individual basis. Execution of the contract by each employer separately does not preclude a finding of a multi-employer bargaining history where the employers are clearly shown to have participated in a pattern of joint bargaining.

(1) Scope of Multi-Employer Unit

A multi-employer unit may include only employers who have participated in and are bound by joint negotiations. The mere adoption of a group contract by an employer who has not participated in joint bargaining directly or through an agent, or has indicated his intention not to be bound by future group negotiations, is insufficient to permit his inclusion in a proposed multi-employer unit.

(2) Withdrawal from Multi-Employer Unit

A petition for a single-employer unit, in the face of a multi-employer bargaining history, will be granted if it appears that the employer involved has effectively withdrawn from the multi-employer group and has abandoned group bargaining. In order for withdrawal from multi-employer bargaining to be effective, the withdrawing party must unequivocally indicate at an appropriate time that it desires to abandon such bargaining. Pointing out in one case that the necessary stability in bargaining relations requires reasonable limits on the time and manner for withdrawal from an established multi-employer bargaining unit, the Board held that—

> The decision to withdraw must contemplate a sincere abandonment, with relative permanency, of the multi-employer unit and the embracement of a different course of bargaining on an individual-employer basis. The element of good faith is a necessary requirement in any such decision to withdraw, because of the unstabilizing and disrupting effect on multi-employer collective bargaining which would result if such withdrawal were permitted to be lightly made.

A majority of the Board also believed that the issues raised in this case justified establishment of "specific ground rules" governing the withdrawal from multi-employer bargaining units in future cases. Noting particularly that insurance of stability in multi-employer bargaining relationships requires limitations on the timing of withdrawals, the majority announced that hereafter—

> [The Board] would ... refuse to permit the withdrawal of an employer or a union from a duly established multi-employer bargaining unit, except upon adequate written notice given prior to the date set by the contract for modification, or to the agreed-upon date to begin the multi-employer negotiations. Where actual bargaining negotiations based on the existing multi-employer unit have begun, we would not permit, except on mutual consent, an abandonment of the unit upon which each side has committed itself to the other, absent unusual circumstances. [*Retail Associates, Inc.,* 120 N.L.R.B. 388 (1958).]

Charles D. Bonanno Linen Service v. NLRB, 454 U.S. 404, 102 S. Ct. 720, 70 L. Ed. 2d 656 (1982). Bonanno Linen Service, Inc., was a member of a linen supply association, consisting of 10 employers, that negotiated as a multi-employer unit with Teamsters Local No. 25. The union and the Association held 10 bargaining sessions during March and April 1975, attempting to come to terms on a new contract. After the union membership rejected a contract agreed to by the Association and the union, negotiations reached an impasse over the issue of the method of compensation (the union demanded the drivers be paid on commission, while the Association insisted on continuing payment at an hourly rate). When subsequent meetings failed to break the impasse, the union began a selective strike against one member of the multi-employer unit, Bonanno. The Association responded with a lockout, and Bonanno then hired permanent replacements for its strikers and gave notice to the Association and union that it was withdrawing from the multi-employer unit. When the Association and the union reached agreement, Bonanno refused to sign the contract and denied that it was bound by its terms. The union, which had not consented to Bonanno's withdrawal from the bargaining unit, filed unfair labor practice charges. The Board, adhering to its position first enunciated in *Hi-Way Billboards, Inc.,* 206 N.L.R.B. 22 (1973), that an impasse is not such an "unusual circumstance" as to justify unilateral withdrawal from the bargaining unit, ordered Bonanno to sign and implement the contract retroactively.

The Supreme Court, expressing its view that multi-employer bargaining is beneficial for industrial harmony, adopted the Board's analysis that "an impasse is not sufficiently destructive of group bargaining to justify unilateral withdrawal," since an impasse is merely a "temporary deadlock or hiatus in negotiations which in almost all cases is eventually broken either through a change of mind or the application of economic force." Speaking for the Court, Justice White observed that "several courts of appeals have rejected *Hi-Way Billboards* on the grounds that impasse may precipitate a strike against one or all members of the unit and that upon impasse the Board permits the union to execute interim agreements with individual employers." After emphasizing the NLRB's primary responsibility for "the balancing of the conflicting legitimate interests," Justice White declared:

> The Board's reasons for adhering to its *Hi-Way Billboards* position are telling. They are surely adequate to survive judicial review. First, it is said that strikes and interim agreements often occur in the course of negotiations prior to impasse and that neither tactic is necessarily associated with impasse. Second, it is "vital" to understand that the Board distinguishes "between interim agreements which contemplate adherence to a final unitwide contract and are thus not antithetical to group bargaining and individual agreements which are clearly inconsistent with, and destructive of, group bargaining." 243 N.L.R.B. at 1096....
>
> On the other hand, where the union, not content with interim agreements that expire with the execution of a unit-wide contract, executes separate agreements that will survive unit negotiations, the union has so "effectively fragmented and destroyed the integrity of the bargaining unit," *id.,* as to create an "unusual circumstance" under *Retail Associates* rules. Furthermore, the Board has held that the execution of separate agreements that would permit either the union or the employer to escape the binding effect of an agreement resulting from group bargaining is a refusal to bargain and an unfair labor practice on the part of both the union and any employer executing such an agreement. *Teamsters Union Local No. 378 (Olympia Automobile Dealers Assn.),* 243 N.L.R.B. 1086 (1979). The remaining members of the unit thus can insist that parties remain subject to unit negotiations in accordance with their original understanding.

Chief Justice Burger and Justice Rehnquist dissented in *Bonnano,* insisting the Board had struck the wrong balance in this case. They pointed out that there was no more temporary impasse at the time of the employer's withdrawal: "[T]he negotiations had been stalemated for more than six months, a selective strike and unit-wide lockout had kept employees away from their jobs for five months, and there were no signs that the parties would return to the bargaining table.... Thus, with all of the members of a multiemployer group closed down or crippled by a strike or a lockout, the union is permitted to 'divide and conquer' by coming to terms with some of the employers, allowing them to resume operations with a full staff." These Justices would authorize employer withdrawal upon impasse. Justice O'Connor and Justice Powell also dissented, wishing to avoid "the absolute positions adopted both by the majority and by the dissent." They would examine the circumstances of each case to determine whether an employer's withdrawal from multiemployer bargaining should be permitted. They would allow it when there is "a complete breakdown in negotiations, not a temporary impasse," and when "an agreement, interim or final, operates to fragment a bargaining unit."

NOTES

1. The courts of appeals have approved the Board's "specific ground rules" governing employer withdrawals from multi-employer associations. *See Universal Insulation Corp. v. NLRB,* 361 F.2d 406 (6th Cir. 1966); *NLRB v. Unelko Corp.,* 478 F.2d 1404 (7th Cir. 1973). *Compare Plumbers Local 669 (Lexington Fire Protection Group),* 318 N.L.R.B. 347 (1995) (omission of employer's name from 25 to 30 page list of some 300 companies for which a multiemployer association was bargaining adequately informed the union that this employer had withdrawn from the multiemployer unit).

Rules governing employer withdrawal are equally applicable to unions. Since the multi-employer unit depends for its existence on the continued consent of both parties, if either party indicates in a timely and unequivocal fashion a preference for bargaining on a single-employer basis, the Board gives effect to that preference. *Detroit Newspaper Pub'rs Ass'n v. NLRB,* 372 F.2d 569 (6th Cir. 1967); *Publishers Ass'n of New York City v. NLRB,* 364 F.2d 293 (2d Cir.), *cert. denied,* 385 U.S. 971 (1966). Nonetheless, the Board does allow a union to withdraw from multi-employer unit with respect to some of the employers, while continuing multi-employer bargaining with the others. *Pacific Coast Ass'n of Pulp & Paper Mfrs.,* 163 N.L.R.B. 892 (1967). The Board noted that if the employer had made a timely bid to withdraw, it would be allowed to do so, and the union may be allowed no less a right to withdraw.

When an employer that has sent timely notice of its withdrawal from a multi-employer association engages in subsequent conduct that is inconsistent with its stated intent to abandon group bargaining, it may find itself bound by the newly negotiated multi-employer agreement. *See NLRB v. Dependable Tile Co.,* 774 F.2d 1376 (9th Cir. 1985).

2. What are the advantages and disadvantages of multi-employer bargaining from (1) the employers' point of view, (2) the union's point of view, (3) the point of view of the general public? *See* C. Rehmus, Multiemployer Bargaining (1965); Leslie, *Multiemployer Bargaining Rules,* 75 Va. L. Rev. 241 (1989); Freidin, *The Taft-Hartley Act and Multi-Employer Bargaining,* and Pollock, *Social Implications of Industry-Wide Bargaining,* in Industry-wide Collective Bargaining Series, Labor Relations Council, Wharton School of Finance and Commerce (1948-1949).

3. THE CONDUCT OF REPRESENTATION ELECTIONS

NLRB, THIRTY-FIRST ANNUAL REPORT 59, 61-65 (1966)

Section 9(c)(1) of the act provides that if, upon a petition filed, a question of representation exists, the Board must resolve it through an election by secret ballot. The election details are left to the Board. Such matters as voting eligibility, timing of elections, and standards of election conduct are subject to rules laid down in the Board's Rules and Regulations and in its decisions. Board elections are conducted in accordance with strict standards designed to assure that the participating employees have an opportunity to determine, and to register a free and untrammeled choice in the selection of, a bargaining representative. Any party to an election who believes that the standards have not been met may file timely objections to the election with the regional director under whose supervision it was held. In that event, the regional director may, as the situation warrants, either make an administrative investigation of the objections or hold a formal hearing to develop a record as the basis for decision. If the election was held pursuant to a consent-election agreement authorizing a determination by the regional director, the regional director will then issue a decision on the objections which is final. If the election was held pursuant to a consent agreement authorizing a determination by the Board, the regional director will then issue a report on objections which is then subject to exceptions by the parties and decision by the Board. However, if the election was one directed by the Board, the regional director may (1) either make a report on the objections, subject to exceptions with the decision to be made by the Board, or (2) dispose of the issues by issuing a decision, which is then subject to limited review by the Board.

Disclosure of Names and Addresses of Eligible Employees

In fulfillment of "the Board's function to conduct elections in which employees have the opportunity to cast their ballots for or against representation under circumstances that are free not only from interference, restraint, or coercion violative of the act, but also from other elements that prevent or impede a free and reasoned choice," the Board, in the *Excelsior Underwear* case,[67] promulgated an employee name and address disclosure rule designed to facilitate campaign communications with the eligible voters and thereby assure an informed electorate. It established as a requirement applicable prospectively to all election cases[68] that within 7 days after the election has been directed or agreed upon, "the employer must file with the Regional Director an election eligibility list, containing the names and addresses of all the eligible voters. The Regional Director, in turn, shall make this information available to all parties in the case. Failure to comply with this requirement shall be grounds for setting aside the election whenever proper objections are filed." ...

In rejecting the contention that disclosure could only be required if the union would otherwise be unable to reach the employees with its message, the Board distinguished court cases[69] which limit a union's access to employer's premises to those situations where alternative channels of communication are unavailable. It viewed those decisions as being predicated upon protection of property rights, a significant employer interest, whereas in the situation presented the employer has no such significant interest in the secrecy of employee names and addresses.

NOTES

1. Could the Labor Board adopt a rule requiring employers that give "captive audience" speeches to provide unions with the chance to reply? Consider the Board's reasoning in *Excelsior Underwear, Inc.,* 156 N.L.R.B. 1236, 1244-46 (1966):

> The argument is also made ... that under the decisions of the Supreme Court in *Babcock & Wilcox* and [*NuTone*] ..., the Board may not require employer disclosure of employee names and addresses unless, in the particular case involved the union would otherwise be unable to reach the employees with its message. We disagree.... [B]oth *Babcock* and *NuTone* dealt with the circumstances under which the Board might find an employer to have committed an unfair labor practice in violation of § 8 of the Act, whereas the instant cases pose the substantially distinguishable issue of the circumstances under which the Board may set aside an election. "[T]he test of conduct which may interfere with the 'laboratory conditions' for an election is considerably more restrictive than the test of conduct which amounts

---

[67] 156 N.L.R.B. 1236 (1966).

[68] The requirement not only applies to petitions for certification or decertification of representatives under § 9(c)(1) of the act, but also to deauthorization elections under § 9(e)(1). Due to the expedited procedure it does not apply to elections conducted pursuant to § 8(b)(7)(C). It became applicable only to elections directed or consented to subsequent to 30 days from the date of the *Excelsior* decision.

[69] *NLRB v. Babcock & Wilcox Co.,* 351 U.S. 105 (1956); *NLRB v. United Steelworkers (NuTone, Inc.),* 357 U.S. 357 (1958).

to interference, restraint, or coercion which violates § 8(a)(1)". *Dal-Tex Optical Co.,* 137 N.L.R.B. 1782 (1962). Whether or not an employer's refusal to disclose employee names and addresses after an election is directed would constitute "interference, restraint, or coercion" within the meaning of § 8(a)(1) of the Act, despite the existence of alternative channels of communication open to the union, is a question on which we express no view because it is not before us. However, we are persuaded, for the reasons previously stated, that disclosure is one of the "safeguards necessary to insure the fair and free choice of bargaining representative by employees" and that an employer's refusal to disclose, regardless of the existence of alternative channels of communication, tends to interfere with a fair and free election. Thus *Babcock* and *NuTone,* which dealt with the substantially different issue of whether the employers' conduct violated § 8(a)(1), are, for this reason also, inapposite.

2. In *North American Health Care Facility,* 315 N.L.R.B. 359 (1994), the Board indicated that it will set aside representation elections won by employers that have failed to provide unions with *Excelsior* lists containing the full first and last names of unit employees. Companies may no longer simply include the last names and first initials of workers.

3. In *Bear Truss Inc.,* 325 N.L.R.B. No. 216, 159 L.R.R.M. 1199 (1998), the Board refused to set aside an election despite ten inaccurate addresses on an *Excelsior* list of 142 eligible voters, where the employer had prepared the list in good faith and the errors were due to the failure of employees to notify the employer of changed addresses as they were supposed to do.

4. The validity of the *Excelsior Underwear* "names-and-addresses" rule was sustained by the Supreme Court in *NLRB v. Wyman-Gordon Co.,* 394 U.S. 759 (1969). *See* White, *Union Representation Election Reform: Equal Access and the Excelsior Rule,* 67 Ind. L.J. 129 (1991); Note, *The Judicial Role in the Enforcement of the "Excelsior" Rule,* 66 Mich. L. Rev. 1292 (1968).

NLRB, THIRTY-FIRST ANNUAL REPORT 66-68 (1966)

Conduct Affecting Elections—Election Propaganda

Threats of adverse economic consequences as well as appeals to racism were alleged as a basis for objections to the election in the *Universal Mfg. Corp.* case.[80] There, the Board was called upon to evaluate the impact of antiunion election campaign propaganda originating with community groups which injected themselves into the campaign. The community members and groups, not shown to be acting as agents of the employer, were responsible for newspaper editorials, advertisements, and handbills containing appeals to racist sentiment,

---

[80] 156 N.L.R.B. 1459 (1966).

charges of Communist control over unions and the civil rights movement, and warnings of economic disaster to the community in the event of unionization of the plant. Applying its established standards[81] that racial propaganda will not be tolerated unless the statements are "truthful, temperate, and germane to a party's position," and do not "deliberately seek to overstress and exacerbate racial feelings by irrelevant, inflammatory appeals," the Board found that permissible bounds had been exceeded by handbills, cartoons, and newspaper editorials concerning actions and attitudes of union leaders and supporters. The matters commented on were, at best, irrelevant to the campaign and inflammatory in nature and intent. In some instances the handbills were distributed by methods which also established that "the sponsoring parties intended, not to educate or inform the employees about an issue germane to the election, but to prompt them to vote against the union 'on racial grounds alone.'"

The newspaper editorials, full-page advertisements, and handbills reiterated the themes that success of the union might cause the plant to close and would squelch any chance for industrial expansion in the area, thereby impairing employment opportunities and causing higher taxes, and in general could spell out economic hardship for employees, their families, and neighbors. The newspaper communications also contained threats of blacklisting, along with statements which linked unions, civil rights, and communism as if they were aspects of a single pernicious entity, implying that union dues would end up in Communist Party coffers. The Board found that "By appealing to the employees' sentiments as civic minded individuals, injecting the fear of personal economic loss, and playing on racial prejudice, the full-page ads, the editorials, the cartoon, and the handbill were calculated to convince the employees that a vote for the union meant the betrayal of the community's best interests. Faced with pressures of this sort, the employees in our opinion were inhibited from freely exercising their choice in the election." The election was therefore set aside.

Employer Talks to Employee Groups

In determining whether preelection propaganda has interfered with the holding of a free election, the Board looks not only to the content of the propaganda but also at the circumstances under which it was disseminated. One means of dissemination which may overstep permissible bounds is employer talks to groups of employees brought together in some "locus of final authority in the plant,"[82] such as a supervisor's office, under circumstances where statements made may be expected to have greater impact. In one case,[83] decided during the year, the Board overruled an objection to an election based upon the fact that the employer had held a series of meetings in the plant cafeteria attended by groups of from 10

---

[81] *Sewell Mfg. Co.,* 138 N.L.R.B. 66, Twenty-Eighth Annual Report 58-59 (1963).

[82] *General Shoe Corp.,* 97 N.L.R.B. 499.

[83] *Dempster Brothers, Inc.,* 154 N.L.R.B. 688.

to 14 employees to propagandize against union representation. The meetings, all held more than 24 hours before the election, were addressed by the company president and its attorney with comments limited to legitimate campaign propaganda. The Board noted that the plant cafeteria had been used for other employee meetings and activities in the past and that about 90 percent of the 400 unit employees, eligible and ineligible, were at different times called to the meetings in question. Under these circumstances, it found "insufficient basis for concluding that the Employer's action in holding group meetings constituted an isolation of a few from among the many at a locus of managerial authority in order to create an aura of special treatment to individuals, as distinguished from employees as a whole, so as to bring ... [that] conduct within the prohibition of the *General Shoe* doctrine."

Another limitation upon the circumstances under which propaganda is disseminated is the *Peerless Plywood*[84] rule prohibiting either party from making election speeches on company time to massed assemblies of employees within 24 hours before the election, even though such speeches may not be otherwise objectionable.

NOTES

1. In *Dal-Tex Optical Co.*, 137 N.L.R.B. 1782 (1962), the employer delivered speeches to employees that were found to be grounds for setting aside the election. The Board held that conduct that is violative of § 8(a)(1) automatically interferes with the exercise of a free election "because the test of conduct which may interfere with the 'laboratory conditions' for an election is considerably more restrictive than the test of conduct which amounts to interference, restraint, or coercion which violates § 8(a)(1)." The Board found that "Congress specifically limited § 8(c) to the adversary proceedings involved in unfair labor practice cases and it has no application to representation cases.... The strictures of the first amendment, to be sure, must be considered in all cases." *See also Trane Co.*, 137 N.L.R.B. 1506 (1962); *Lord Baltimore Press,* 142 N.L.R.B. 308 (1963); *Oak Mfg. Co.*, 141 N.L.R.B. 1323 (1963).

Although conduct violative of § 8(a)(1) presumptively interferes with employee free choice, the Board occasionally declines to set an election aside when the unfair labor practice was isolated and too minimal to have affected the results of the election. *Caron Int'l, Inc.*, 246 N.L.R.B. 1120 (1979).

2. In *Barton Nelson Inc.*, 318 N.L.R.B. 712 (1995), supervisor distribution of antiunion hats directly to employees was held to warrant setting aside an election, even though there was no evidence of a listing of who did or did not take the hats. *See also Circuit City Stores*, 324 N.L.R.B. No. 19, 156 L.R.R.M. 1001 (1997) (store manager interfered with election when he approached individual

---

[84] *Peerless Plywood Co.,* 107 N.L.R.B. 427, Nineteenth Annual Report 65 (1954).

employees prior to election and gave them coffee mugs bearing the slogans "Vote No" and "Just Vote No").

In *Sunrise Rehabilitation Hosp.*, 320 N.L.R.B. 212 (1995), the Board held that an employer interfered with an election by offering employees who were not scheduled to work two hours of pay to come in to vote, since those employees may have felt obliged to return the employer's favor by voting against the union.

3. In *Flex Prods., Inc.*, 280 N.L.R.B. 1117 (1986), the Labor Board held an employer did not interfere with an election when its president met individually with about 120 of its 164 employees in the plant manager's office during the twenty-four hours preceding the election. The president had previously met with employees in the manager's office; the president periodically walked around the plant and greeted employees, who called him by his first name; and his remarks at the individual meetings were temperate and noncoercive. In *Industrial Acoustics Co. v. NLRB*, 912 F.2d 717 (4th Cir. 1990), however, the court ruled that a union's election-eve and election-day campaign broadcasts to employees from a soundcar parked 25 to 30 yards from the main plant entrance contravened the *Peerless Plywood* twenty-four-hour "captive audience" rule and invalidated the union's election victory. *Accord, Bro-Tech Corp. v. NLRB*, 105 F.3d 890 (3d Cir. 1997). *Compare Overnite Transp. Co. v. NLRB*, 104 F.3d 109 (7th Cir. 1997) (boisterous, party-like behavior, including sign carrying, horn blowing, and flag waving, outside a truck terminal in which NLRB election was being held did not invalidate election).

4. *Comet Elec.*, 314 N.L.R.B. 1215 (1994), involved an employer that required employee attendance at an antiunion, captive audience meeting scheduled after the conclusion of the work day. The employees could not obtain their paychecks until the meeting was over. The Board found that the employer had interfered with employee free choice, since the employees were effectively punished for exercising their right to organize.

5. Just before Board elections, some employers present employees with split pay checks—one containing the amount of periodic union dues and the other containing the remainder of their take-home pay—to remind them of the cost of unionization. In *Kalin Constr. Co.*, 321 N.L.R.B. 649 (1996), the Board established a strict rule prohibiting employers from altering the usual paycheck process during the twenty-four hours prior to the scheduled opening of the polls. Employers wishing to issue split pay checks must now do so more than twenty-four hours before elections commence.

6. *Misleading Statements.* The NLRB has vacillated in recent years regarding its treatment of pre-election misrepresentations. In 1962, the Board indicated that it would set aside an election whenever it appeared that: (1) there had been a material misrepresentation of fact, (2) this misrepresentation came from a party who had special knowledge or was in an authoritative position to know the true facts, and (3) no other party had sufficient opportunity to correct the misrepresentations before the election. *Hollywood Ceramics Co.,* 140 N.L.R.B. 221 (1962).

In *Shopping Kart Food Mkt.,* 228 N.L.R.B. 1311 (1977), a 3-2 Board majority abandoned the *Hollywood Ceramics* test and stated that the Board would no longer set elections aside on the basis of misleading statements. Elections would only be set aside when a party has engaged in coercive tactics, such as threats of reprisal, or deceptive practices, such as the use of forged documents, but the Board would no longer probe the truth or falsity of campaign statements. The majority asserted that Board rules "must be based on a view of employees as mature individuals who are capable of recognizing campaign propaganda for what it is and discounting it." Although the Board briefly returned to the *Hollywood Ceramics* approach in *General Knit of Cal., Inc.,* 239 N.L.R.B. 619 (1978), it quickly overruled *General Knit* and returned to the "sound rule" of *Shopping Kart. See Midland Nat'l Life Ins. Co.,* 263 N.L.R.B. 127 (1982). As a result, the Board no longer evaluates the veracity of campaign representations. Appellate courts have accepted the Board's *Midland Nat'l Life Ins.* approach. *See, e.g., United States Ecology v. NLRB,* 772 F.2d 1478 (9th Cir. 1985); *NLRB v. Affiliated Midwest Hosp.,* 789 F.2d 524 (7th Cir. 1986). *Compare Dayton Hudson Dep't Store v. NLRB,* 79 F.3d 546 (6th Cir.), *cert. denied,* 519 U.S. 819 (1996) (union's pre-election letter that grossly exaggerated employer's profitability did not invalidate union's election victory) *with NLRB v. Hub Plastics,* 52 F.3d 608 (6th Cir. 1995) (union statements prior to election indicating that the NLRB had found the company guilty of unfair labor practice violations, when the Board had only issued a complaint against that firm, may provide a basis for setting aside the union's election victory).

Until recently, the Labor Board distinguished use of official NLRB election documents during organizing campaigns. While altered documents that clearly identified the party responsible for the additional markings would not serve as the basis to set aside elections, the circulation of altered Board documents that did not indicate the party responsible for the changes would warrant the voiding of elections. *See, e.g., Archer Servs.,* 298 N.L.R.B. 312 (1990). After the NLRB revised its Notice of Election form to specifically disavow Board involvement in any defacement or alteration of Board documents and to assert NLRB neutrality in the election process, the Labor Board decided that it would no longer permit modified Board documents to provide the basis for new elections, even when it is not clear which party changed the documents in question. *See Irvington Nursing Care Serv.,* 312 N.L.R.B. No. 101, 144 L.R.R.M. 1142 (1993).

See generally Getman & Goldberg, *The Behavioral Assumptions Underlying NLRB Regulation of Campaign Misrepresentations: An Empirical Evaluation,* 28 Stan. L. Rev. 263 (1976); J. Getman, S. Goldberg & J. Herman, Union Representation Elections: Law and Reality (1976); Becker, *Democracy in the Workplace: Union Representation Elections and Federal Labor Law,* 77 Minn. L. Rev. 495 (1993); Lachman, *Freedom of Speech in a Union Representative Elec-*

tion: Employer Campaigning and Employee Response, 1982 Am. Bar. Found. Res. J. 755; Note, *A Look at the Revolving NLRB Policies Governing Union Representation Election Campaigns,* 19 Wake Forest L. Rev. 417 (1983). *Compare* Dickens, *The Effects of Company Campaigns on Certification Elections: Law and Reality Once Again,* 36 Indus. & Lab. Rel. Rev. 560 (1983) *with* Goldberg, Getman & Brett, *The Relationship Between Free Choice and Labor Board Doctrine: Differing Empirical Approaches,* 79 Nw. U.L. Rev. 721 (1984),\ *and* Cooper, *Authorization Cards and Union Representation Election Outcome: An Empirical Assessment of the Assumption Underlying the Supreme Court's Gessel Decision,* 79 Nw. U.L. Rev. 87 (1984). *See generally* Getman, *Ruminations on Union Organizing in the Private Sector,* 53 U. Chi. L. Rev. 45 (1986).

7. *Larson Tool & Stamping Co.,* 296 N.L.R.B. 895 (1989), involved employer letters to employees that stated: "During [an economic] strike, you could LOSE YOUR JOB TO A PERMANENT REPLACEMENT." The Board found that the employer's unqualified statement about job loss could "fairly be understood as a threat of reprisal." *Fred Wilkinson Assocs.,* 297 N.L.R.B. 737 (1990), concerned a firm that informed employees: "The only thing [the union] can guarantee is a strike. In fact, the only thing [the union] can do to try to get the Company to agree to its demands is to call a strike." The Board found that these statements "created an atmosphere of fear" by suggesting that a strike was inevitable in any effort to obtain concessions from the employer. *Compare Fiber-Lam, Inc.,* 301 N.L.R.B. 94 (1991), wherein the Board found that an employer's statement that economic strikers could lose their jobs since a company is free to replace them did not cross the "narrow line" between the permissible warning of employees regarding the possible adverse consequences of a strike and the impermissible threat of job losses if workers elected to unionize. *See also SPX Corp.,* 320 N.L.R.B. 219 (1995) (employer's predictions, unsupported by objective facts, that union victory would mean loss of customers invalidated election). *Compare Custom Window Extrusions,* 314 N.L.R.B. 850 (1994) (employer did not violate Act when it sent employees letter stating that "only the Company can raise wages. All a union can do is call a strike in an attempt to force the Company to do something," since this communication did not convey to employees the futility of selecting a union as their bargaining agent).

8. For contrasting treatment of racial and ethnic slurs voiced by union supporters, *compare M & M Supermarkets v. NLRB,* 818 F.2d 1567 (11th Cir. 1987) (anti-Semitic remarks against employer's owners by black employees so derogatory and inflammatory that they destroyed laboratory conditions necessary for a free and fair election) *and Ki (USA) Corp. v. NLRB,* 35 F.3d 256 (6th Cir. 1994) (union appeals to racial and national origin prejudice sufficiently inflammatory to invalidate election results) *with Catherine's Inc.,* 316 N.L.R.B. 186 (1995) (union comments concerning Jewish law firm representing employer and fact the few white employees in workforce would likely vote against union insufficient to warrant setting aside election) *and NLRB v. Herbert Halperin Distrib.*

Corp., 826 F.2d 287 (4th Cir. 1987) (comments such as "those goddam white boys—they won't support the blacks" did not indicate an atmosphere so inflamed by racial prejudice as to invalidate the election).

9. For concise summaries of NLRB rules regarding pre-election propaganda, *see* Becker, *Democracy in the Workplace: Union Representation Elections and Federal Labor Law,* 77 Minn. L. Rev. 495 (1993); S. Schlossberg & J. Scott, *Organizing and the Law* (4th ed. 1991); K. McGuiness, How to Take a Case Before the NLRB (5th ed. 1986); Bok, *The Regulation of Campaign Tactics in Representation Elections Under the NLRA,* 78 Harv. L. Rev. 38 (1964); Pollitt, *The National Labor Relations Board and Race Hate Propaganda in Union Organization Drives,* 17 Stan. L. Rev. 373 (1965); Note, *Labor Representation Elections and the Constitutional Right to Campaign Vigorously—The Use of Racial Propaganda,* 23 S.C.L.Q. 400 (1971); Symposium: *Four Perspectives on Union Representation Elections: Law and Reality, The Getman, Goldberg and Herman Questions,* 28 Stan. L. Rev. 1161 (1976); Roomkin & Abrams, *Using Behavioral Evidence in NLRB Regulation: A Proposal,* 90 Harv. L. Rev. 1441 (1977); King, *Pre-election Conduct, Expanding Employer Rights and Some New and Renewed Perspectives,* 2 Ind. Rel. L.J. 185 (1977).

10. In *NLRB v. Savair Mfg. Co.,* 414 U.S. 27 (1973), the Court held that an election had to be set aside where a union offered to waive the initiation fee, if the union won the election, for all employees who executed pre-election authorization cards. This practice allowed the union to "buy" authorization card signatures from employees seeking to avoid having to pay the initiation fee and may have caused some card signers to feel obliged to vote for the union in the Board election. In *NLRB v. VSA Inc.,* 24 F.3d 588 (4th Cir.), *cert. denied,* 513 U.S. 1041 (1994), the court held that a union did not act improperly when it offered to waive initiation fees for all employees if it won the election. *Savair Mfg. Co.* was distinguished, since the waiver in that case was limited to employees who signed authorization cards prior to the election.

Does a labor organization impermissibly influence election results when it provides prospective bargaining unit employees with free legal services in a class action wage or civil rights suit filed prior to the election? *Compare Nestle Ice Cream Co. v. NLRB,* 46 F.3d 578 (6th Cir. 1995) (yes) *with Novotel New York,* 321 N.L.R.B. 624 (1996) (no). *See also NLRB v. Dickinson Press,* 153 F.3d 282 (6th Cir. 1998) (pre-election distribution of T-shirts containing pro-union message did not warrant overturning of election due to inexpensive nature of T-shirts).

11. *What Constitutes a Majority Choice?* It has been held that the outcome of an NLRB election depends on "a majority of those voting in the election" rather than "a majority of those eligible to vote." *R.C.A. Mfg. Co.,* 2 N.L.R.B. 168 (1936). *See also Lee-Mark Mfg. Co.,* 85 N.L.R.B. 1299 (1949) (tie vote in decertification election results in decertification of incumbent union due to lack of continued majority support).

The Labor Board will not invalidate an election as "unrepresentative" because less than a "substantial" number of eligible voters participate. Results will be certified if there is "adequate notice and opportunity to vote and employees are not prevented from voting by the conduct of a party or by unfairness in the scheduling or mechanics of the election." *Lemco Constr., Inc.,* 283 N.L.R.B. 459 (1987).

Eligible employees must usually vote in person, with mail ballots only being used when voters are scattered over a wide geographic area, employee schedules vary so greatly that they are not at a common location at common times, or a strike or lockout is in progress. *San Diego Gas & Elec.,* 325 N.L.R.B. No. 218, 158 L.R.R.M. 1257 (1998).

12. *Runoff Elections.* When two or more unions are competing for certification, and no union or the "no representation" choice receives a majority of the votes cast, § 9(c)(3) requires that "a run-off shall be conducted, the ballot providing for a selection between the two choices receiving the largest number of valid votes cast in the election." Thus, if 100 employees vote in the original election as follows: 45 for Union A, 30 for No Union, and 25 for Union B, the runoff will be between Union A and No Union.

13. *Eligibility to Vote During a Strike.* During the Wagner Act period, strikers were allowed to vote, but a Taft-Hartley amendment deprived replaced economic strikers of the right to vote. Experience demonstrated that this could be used as a "union-busting" device, so Congress modified § 9(c)(3) in 1959 to provide that "employees engaged in an economic strike who are not entitled to reinstatement shall be eligible to vote under such regulations as the Board shall find are consistent with the purposes and provisions of the National Labor Relations Act, as amended, in any election conducted within twelve months after the commencement of the strike."

In *Pacific Tile & Porcelain Co.,* 137 N.L.R.B. 1358 (1962), the NLRB clarified its rules concerning the voting eligibility of strikers and replacements. To challenge an economic striker's vote, the challenger must affirmatively show that the striker has "no further interest in his struck job." To challenge a replacement's vote, the challenger had to show that the individual was not employed on a permanent basis. In *O.E. Butterfield Inc.,* 319 N.L.R.B. 1004 (1995), however, the Board modified the *Pacific Tile & Porcelain Co.* rules when it held that in representation cases, as in unfair labor practice cases, the burden is on the employer to demonstrate that strike replacements are permanent employees and thus qualified to vote in an election.

In *Gulf States Paper Corp.,* 219 N.L.R.B. 806 (1975), the Board held that economic strikers who have been on strike for more than one year and have been permanently replaced are ineligible to vote in an NLRB election. However, unreplaced economic strikers are eligible to vote if their jobs have not been permanently eliminated, they have not found permanent employment elsewhere, and the employer has not refused to reinstate them for misconduct rendering them unsuitable for reemployment.

Harter Equip., 293 N.L.R.B. 647 (1989), concerned the voting rights of locked out employees and their replacements. The Board held that the five employees who had been locked out and replaced were the only persons eligible to vote on a decertification petition filed about two years after the lockout began, even though seventeen employees were currently working in bargaining unit positions. The locked out employees had not abandoned their jobs and could not be permanently replaced. Regardless of their number, the replacements were all temporaries, since the employer had directed the lockout at the bargaining unit itself, not merely the employees who comprised it when the lockout commenced.

14. In *NLRB v. Mansion House Ctr. Mgt. Corp.*, 473 F.2d 471 (1973), the Eighth Circuit held that racial discrimination by the interested union may preclude issuance of an NLRB bargaining order. The Court said that "the remedial machinery of the National Labor Relations Act cannot be made available to a union which is unwilling to correct past practices of racial discrimination. Federal complicity through recognition of a discriminating union serves not only to condone the discrimination, but in effect legitimizes and perpetuates such invidious practices. Certainly such a degree of federal participation in the maintenance of racially discriminatory practices violates basic constitutional tenets."

In response to the *Mansion House* case, the Board announced in *Bekins Moving & Storage Co.*, 211 N.L.R.B. 138 (1974), that it would consider claims of invidious discrimination by a union in a representation proceeding, but only after the union has won the election. In *Handy Andy, Inc.*, 228 N.L.R.B. 447 (1977), however, the Board reversed *Bekins,* and concluded that neither the Fifth Amendment nor the NLRA requires the Board to resolve such questions before certifying a union. "Indeed, it appears to us that the contrary is true; namely, that the Board is not authorized to withhold certification of a labor organization duly selected by a majority of the unit employees." The Board stated that claims of invidious discrimination will be considered in appropriate unfair labor practice proceedings, particularly when charges claim that the union is failing to carry out its duty of fair representation.

See generally, Axelrod and Kaufman, *Mansion House—Bekins—Handy Andy: The National Labor Relations Board's Role in Racial Discrimination Cases,* 45 Geo. Wash. L. Rev. 675 (1977).

4. COURT REVIEW OF REPRESENTATION PROCEEDINGS

LEEDOM v. KYNE

Supreme Court of the United States
358 U.S. 184, 79 S. Ct. 180, 3 L. Ed. 2d 210 (1958)

MR. JUSTICE WHITTAKER delivered the opinion of the Court.

Section 9(b)(1) of the National Labor Relations Act, § 9, 49 Stat. 453, 61 Stat. 143, 29 U.S.C. § 159(b)(1), provides that, in determining the unit appropriate for collective bargaining purposes, "the Board shall not (1) decide that any unit is appropriate for such purposes if such unit includes both professional employees and employees who are not professional employees unless a majority of such professional employees vote for inclusion in such unit." The Board, after refusing to take a vote among the professional employees to determine whether a majority of them would "vote for inclusion in such unit," included both professional and nonprofessional employees in the bargaining unit that it found appropriate. The sole and narrow question presented is whether a Federal District Court has jurisdiction of an original suit to vacate that determination of the Board because made in excess of its powers.

The facts are undisputed. Buffalo Section, Westinghouse Engineers Association, Engineers and Scientists of America, a voluntary unincorporated labor organization, hereafter called the Association, was created for the purpose of promoting the economic and professional status of the nonsupervisory professional employees of Westinghouse Electric Corporation at its plant in Cheektowaga, New York, through collective bargaining with their employer. In October, 1955, the Association petitioned the National Labor Relations Board for certification as the exclusive collective bargaining agent of all nonsupervisory professional employees, being then 233 in number, of the Westinghouse Company at its Cheektowaga plant, pursuant to the provisions of § 9 of the act, 29 U.S.C. § 159. A hearing was held by the board upon that petition. A competing labor organization was permitted by the Board to intervene. It asked the Board to expand the unit to include employees in five other categories who performed technical work and were thought by it to be "professional employees" within the meaning of § 2(12) of the act, 29 U.S.C. § 152(12). The Board found that they were not professional employees within the meaning of the act. However, it found that nine employees in three of those categories should nevertheless be included in the unit because they "share a close community of employment interests with [the professional employees, and their inclusion would not] destroy the predominantly professional character of such a unit." The Board, after denying the Association's request to take a vote among the professional employees to determine whether a majority of them favored "inclusion in such unit," included the 233 professional employees and the nine nonprofessional employees in the unit and directed an election to determine whether they desired to be represented by the Association, by the other labor organization, or by neither. The Association moved the Board to stay the election and to amend its decision by excluding the nonprofessional employees from the unit. The Board denied that motion and went ahead with the election at which the Association received a majority of the valid votes cast and was thereafter certified by the Board as the collective bargaining agent for the unit.

Thereafter respondent, individually, and as president of the Association, brought this suit in the District Court against the members of the Board, alleging the foregoing facts and asserting that the Board had exceeded its statutory power in including the professional employees, without their consent, in a unit with nonprofessional employees in violation of § 9(b)(1) which commands that the Board "shall not" do so, and praying, among other things, that the Board's action be set aside. The defendants, members of the Board, moved to dismiss for want of jurisdiction and, in the alternative, for a summary judgment. The plaintiff also moved for summary judgment. The trial court found that the Board had disobeyed the express command of § 9(b)(1) in including nonprofessional employees and professional employees in the same unit without the latter's consent, and in doing so had acted in excess of its powers to the injury of the professional employees, and that the court had jurisdiction to grant the relief prayed. It accordingly denied the Board's motion and granted the plaintiff's motion and entered judgment setting aside the Board's determination of the bargaining unit and also the election and the Board's certification.

On the Board's appeal it did not contest the trial court's conclusion that the Board, in commingling professional with nonprofessional employees in the unit, had acted in excess of its powers and had thereby worked injury to the statutory rights of the professional employees. Instead, it contended only that the District Court lacked jurisdiction to entertain the suit. The Court of Appeals held that the District Court did have jurisdiction and affirmed the judgment. 101 App. D.C. 398, 249 F.2d 490....

Petitioners, members of the Board, concede here that the District Court had jurisdiction of the suit under § 24(8) of the Judicial Code, 28 U.S.C. § 1337, unless the review provisions of the National Labor Relations Act destroyed it. In *American Federation of Labor v. NLRB,* 308 U.S. 401 (1940), this Court held that a Board order in certification proceedings under § 9 is not "a final order" and therefore is not subject to judicial review except as it may be drawn in question by a petition for enforcement or review of an order, made under § 10(c) of the act, restraining an unfair labor practice. But the Court was at pains to point out in that case "[t]he question [there presented was] distinct from ... whether petitioners are precluded by the provisions of the Wagner Act from maintaining an independent suit in a district court to set aside the Board's action because contrary to the statute...." *Id.* at 404. The Board argued there, as it does here, that the provisions of the act, particularly § 9(d), have foreclosed review of its action by an original suit in a District Court. This Court said: "But that question is not presented for decision by the record before us. Its answer involves a determination whether the Wagner Act, in so far as it has given legally enforceable rights, has deprived the district courts of some portion of their original jurisdiction conferred by § 24 of the Judicial Code. It can be appropriately answered only upon a showing in such a suit that unlawful action of the Board has inflicted an injury on the petitioners for which the law, *apart from the review provisions of the Wagner Act,* affords a remedy. This question can be properly and adequately considered only when it is brought to us for review upon a suitable record." *Id.* at 412. (Emphasis added.)

The record in this case squarely presents the question found not to have been presented by the record in American Federation of Labor v. NLRB, *supra.* This case, in its posture before us, involves "unlawful action of the Board [which] has inflicted an injury on the [respondent]." Does the law, "apart from the review provisions of the ... act," afford a remedy? We think the answer surely must be yes. This suit is not one to "review," in the sense of that term as used in the act, a decision of the Board made within its jurisdiction. Rather it is one to strike down an order of the Board made in excess of its delegated powers and contrary to a specific prohibition in the act. Section 9(b)(1) is clear and mandatory. It says that, in determining the unit appropriate for the purposes of collective bargaining, "the Board *shall not* (1) decide that any unit is appropriate for such purposes if such unit includes both professional employees and employees who are not professional employees unless a majority of such professional employees vote for inclusion in such unit." (Emphasis added.) Yet, the Board included in the unit employees whom it found were not professional employees, after refusing to determine whether a majority of the professional employees would "vote for inclusion in such unit." Plainly, this was an attempted exercise of power that had been specifically withheld. It deprived the professional employees of a "right" assured to them by Congress. Surely, in these circumstances, a Federal District Court has jurisdiction of an original suit to prevent deprivation of a right so given.

In *Texas & New Orleans R. Co. v. Railway Clerks,* 281 U.S. 548 (1930), it was contended that, because no remedy had been expressly given for redress of the congressionally created right in suit, the act conferred "merely an abstract right which was not intended to be enforced by legal proceedings." *Id.* at 558. This Court rejected that contention. It said: "While an affirmative declaration of duty contained in a legislative enactment may be of imperfect obligation because not enforceable in terms, a definite statutory prohibition of conduct which would thwart the declared purpose of the legislation cannot be disregarded.... If Congress intended that the prohibition, as thus construed, should be enforced, the courts would encounter no difficulty in fulfilling its purpose.... The definite prohibition which Congress inserted in the act cannot therefore be overridden in the view that Congress intended it to be ignored. As the prohibition was appropriate to the aim of Congress, and is capable of enforcement, the conclusion must be that enforcement was contemplated." *Id.* at 568, 569. And compare *Virginian R. Co. v. System Federation,* 300 U.S. 515.

In *Switchmen's Union v. National Mediation Board,* 320 U.S. 297, this Court held that the District Court did not have jurisdiction of an original suit to review an order of the National Mediation Board determining that all yardmen of the rail lines operated by the New York Central system constituted an appropriate bargaining unit, because the Railway Labor Board had acted within its delegated powers. But in the course of that opinion the Court announced principles that are controlling here. "If the absence of jurisdiction of the federal courts meant a sacrifice or obliteration of a right which Congress had created, the inference would be strong that Congress intended the statutory provisions governing the general jurisdiction of those courts to control. That was the purport of the decisions of this Court in *Texas & New Orleans R. Co. v. Brotherhood of Clerks,* 281 U.S. 548 (1930), and *Virginian R. Co. v. System Federation,* 300 U.S. 515 (1937). In those cases it was apparent that but for the general jurisdiction of the federal courts there would be no remedy to enforce the statutory commands which Congress had written into the Railway Labor Act. The result would have been that the 'right' of collective bargaining was unsupported by any legal sanction. That would have robbed the act of its vitality and thwarted its purpose." *Id.* at 300.

Here, differently from *Switchmen's* case, "absence of jurisdiction of the federal courts" would mean "a sacrifice or obliteration of a right which Congress" has given professional employees, for there is no other means within their control (*American Federation of Labor v. NLRB, supra*), to protect and enforce that right. And "the inference [is] strong that Congress intended the statutory provisions governing the general jurisdiction of those courts to control." 320 U.S. at 300. This Court cannot lightly infer that Congress does not intend judicial protection of rights it confers against agency action taken in excess of delegated powers. *Cf. Harmon v. Brucker,* 355 U.S. 579 (1958); *Stark v. Wickard,* 321 U.S. 288 (1944); *School of Magnetic Healing v. McAnnulty,* 187 U.S. 94 (1902).

Where, as here, Congress has given a "right" to the professional employees it must be held that it intended that right to be enforced, and the "courts ... encounter no difficulty in fulfilling its purpose." *Texas & New Orleans R. Co. v. Railway Clerks, supra* at 568.

The Court of Appeals was right in holding, in the circumstances of this case, that the District Court had jurisdiction of this suit, and its judgment is

Affirmed.

MR. JUSTICE BRENNAN, whom MR. JUSTICE FRANKFURTER joins, dissenting.

The legislative history of the Wagner Act, and of the Taft-Hartley amendments, shows a considered congressional purpose to restrict judicial review of National Labor Relations Board representation certifications to review in the Courts of Appeals in the circumstances specified in § 9(d), 29 U.S.C. § 159(d). The question was extensively debated when both acts were being considered, and on both occasions Congress concluded that, unless drastically limited, time-consuming court procedures would seriously threaten to frustrate the basic national policy of preventing industrial strife and achieving industrial peace by promoting collective bargaining....

The Court today opens a gaping hole in this congressional wall against direct resort to the courts. The Court holds that a party alleging that the Board was guilty of "unlawful action" in making an investigation and certification of representatives need not await judicial review until the situation specified in § 9(d)

arises, but has a case immediately cognizable by a District Court under the
"original jurisdiction" granted by 28 U.S.C. § 1337 of "any civil action or proceeding arising under any Act of Congress regulating commerce." The Court,
borrowing a statement from *Switchmen's Union v. National Mediation Board,*
320 U.S. 297, 300 (1943), finds that, in such case "the inference [is] strong that
Congress intended the statutory provisions governing the general jurisdiction of
those [District] courts to control." ...

I daresay that the ingenuity of counsel will, after today's decision, be entirely
adequate to the task of finding some alleged "unlawful action," whether in statutory interpretation or otherwise, sufficient to get a foot in a District Court door
under 28 U.S.C. § 1337. Even when the Board wins such a case on the merits, ...
while the case is dragging through the courts the threat will be ever present of the
industrial strife sought to be averted by Congress in providing only drastically
limited judicial review under § 9(d). Both union and management will be able to
use the tactic of litigation to delay the initiation of collective bargaining when it
suits their purposes....

It is no support for the Court's decision that the respondent union may suffer
hardship if review under 28 U.S.C. § 1337 is not open to it. The Congress was
fully aware of the disadvantages and possible unfairness which could result from
the limitation on judicial review enacted in § 9(d). The House proposal for direct
review of Board certifications in the Taft-Hartley amendments was based in part
upon the fact that, under the Wagner Act, the operation of § 9(d) was "unfair to
... the union that loses, which has no appeal at all no matter how wrong the certification may be; [and to] the employees, who have no appeal...." Congress nevertheless continued the limited judicial review provided by § 9(d) because Congress believed the disadvantages of broader review to be more serious than the
difficulties which limited review posed for the parties. Furthermore, Congress
felt that the Board procedures and the limited review provided in § 9(d) were
adequate to protect the parties....

I would reverse and remand the case to the District Court with instructions to
dismiss the complaint for lack of jurisdiction of the subject matter.

NOTES

1. What kinds of alleged errors by the NLRB in representation proceedings
may be challenged by direct suit in equity in the district courts under the doctrine
of *Leedom v. Kyne? See generally* Harper, *The Case for Limiting Judicial Review
of Labor Board Certification Decisions,* 55 Geo. Wash. L. Rev. 262 (1987);
Goldberg, *District Court Review of NLRB Representation Proceedings,* 42 Ind.
L.J. 455 (1967).

2. A district court may enjoin the NLRB from holding an election among seamen on foreign-flag ships even though the Board did not violate any specific
prohibition in the NLRA, since the Board's assertion of power to determine rep-

resentation of foreign seamen aboard foreign flag vessels had aroused vigorous protests from foreign governments and created international problems for the United States, the presence of which was a uniquely compelling justification for prompt judicial resolution of the controversy. *McCulloch v. Sociedad Nacional de Marineros de Honduras,* 372 U.S. 10 (1963).

Fay v. Douds, 172 F.2d 720 (2d Cir. 1949), indicated that direct district court intervention would be appropriate in cases involving a clear deprivation of a constitutional right that could not be adequately remedied through regular Labor Board representation procedures.

3. In *Boire v. Greyhound Corp.,* 376 U.S. 473 (1964), the Court held that a federal district court erred when it enjoined the Board from conducting an election among maintenance and service workers at a bus company's terminals. The district court had found that the NLRB had misapplied the act in holding the bus company and the maintenance company to be joint employers.

> [W]hether Greyhound possessed sufficient indicia of control to be an "employer" is essentially a factual issue, unlike the question in *Kyne,* which depended solely upon construction of the statute. The *Kyne,* exception is a narrow one, not to be extended to permit plenary district court review of Board orders in certification proceedings whenever it can be said that an erroneous assessment of the particular facts before the Board has led it to a conclusion which does not comport with the law. Judicial review in such a situation has been limited by Congress to the courts of appeals, and then only under the conditions explicitly laid down in § 9(d) of the Act.

4. How does an employer normally obtain judicial review of an NLRB representation ruling? *See, e.g., NLRB v. Pittsburgh Plate Glass Co.,* 270 F.2d 167 (4th Cir. 1959), *cert. denied,* 361 U.S. 943 (1960). How would a union do it? *See* discussion of this question in *Physicians Nat'l House Staff Ass'n v. Murphy,* 100 L.R.R.M. 3055 (D.C. Cir. 1979), *vacated, Physicians Nat'l House Staff Ass'n v. Fanning,* 642 F.2d 492 (D.C. Cir. 1980), *cert. denied,* 450 U.S. 917 (1981).

B. ESTABLISHING REPRESENTATIVE STATUS THROUGH UNFAIR LABOR PRACTICE PROCEEDINGS

We have thus far been concerned with formal representation proceedings that result, if the union wins the secret ballot election, in certification of the union as exclusive bargaining representative. It has historically been common for collective bargaining relationships to be established simply by unions showing employers that they represent a majority of their employees, usually by "card checks" of authorization cards signed by the employees, and by voluntary employer recognition of the bargaining rights of those labor organizations.

If the employer refuses to recognize the union, another procedure by which the union can get the NLRB to order the employer to bargain with it and thus establish representative status, is to bring unfair labor practice proceedings.

NLRB v. GISSEL PACKING CO.

Supreme Court of the United States
395 U.S. 575, 89 S. Ct. 1918, 23 L. Ed. 2d 547 (1969)

MR. CHIEF JUSTICE WARREN delivered the opinion of the Court.

These cases involve the extent of an employer's duty under the National Labor Relations Act to recognize a union that bases its claim to representative status solely on the possession of union authorization cards, and the steps an employer may take, particularly with regard to the scope and content of statements he may make, in legitimately resisting such card-based recognition. The specific questions facing us here are whether the duty to bargain can arise without a Board election under the Act; whether union authorization cards, if obtained from a majority of employees without misrepresentation or coercion, are reliable enough generally to provide a valid, alternate route to majority status; whether a bargaining order is an appropriate and authorized remedy where an employer rejects a card majority while at the same time committing unfair labor practices that tend to undermine the union's majority and make a fair election an unlikely possibility; and whether certain specific statements made by an employer to his employees constituted such an election-voiding unfair labor practice and thus fell outside the protection of the First Amendment and § 8(c) of the Act. For reasons given below, we answer each of these questions in the affirmative.

I

... In each of the cases from the Fourth Circuit, the course of action followed by the Union and the employer and the Board's response were similar. In each case, the union waged an organizational campaign, obtained authorization cards from a majority of employees in the appropriate bargaining unit, and then on the basis of the cards, demanded recognition by the employer. All three employers refused to bargain on the ground that authorization cards were inherently unreliable indicators of employee desires; and they either embarked on, or continued, vigorous antiunion campaigns that gave rise to numerous unfair labor practice charges. In *Gissel,* where the employer's campaign began almost at the outset of the Union's organizational drive, the Union (petitioner in No. 691), did not seek an election, but instead filed three unfair labor practice charges against the employer, for refusing to bargain in violation of § 8(a)(5), for coercion and intimidation of employees in violation of § 8(a)(1), and for discharge of union adherents in violation of § 8(a)(3). In *Heck's* an election sought by the Union was never held because of nearly identical unfair labor practice charges later filed by the Union as a result of the employer's antiunion campaign, initiated after the

Union's recognition demand. And in *General Steel,* an election petitioned for by the Union and won by the employer was set aside by the Board because of the unfair labor practices committed by the employer in the pre-election period.

In each case, the Board's primary response was an order to bargain directed at the employers, despite the absence of an election in *Gissel* and *Heck's* and the employer's victory in *General Steel.* More specifically the Board found in each case that (1) the union had obtained valid authorization cards[4] from a majority of the employees in the bargaining unit and was thus entitled to represent the employees for collective bargaining purposes; and (2) that the employers' refusal to bargain with the unions in violation of § 8(a)(5) was motivated not by a "good faith" doubt of the unions' majority status, but by a desire to gain time to dissipate that status. The Board based its conclusion as to the lack of good faith doubt on the fact that the employers had committed substantial unfair labor practices during their antiunion campaign efforts to resist recognition. Thus, the Board found that all three employers had engaged in restraint and coercion of employees in violation of § 8(a)(1)—in *Gissel,* for coercively interrogating employees about union activities, threatening them with discharge and promising them benefits; in *Heck's,* for coercively interrogating employees, threatening reprisals, creating the appearance of surveillance, and offering benefits for opposing the Union; and in *General Steel,* for coercive interrogation and threats of reprisals, including discharge. In addition, the Board found that the employers in *Gissel* and *Heck's* had wrongfully discharged employees for engaging in union activities in violation of § 8(a)(3). And, because the employers had rejected the card-based bargaining demand in bad faith, the Board found that all three had refused to recognize the unions in violation of § 8(a)(5).

Only in *General Steel* was there any objection by an employer to the validity of the cards and the manner in which they had been solicited, and the doubt raised by the evidence was resolved in the following manner. The customary approach of the Board in dealing with allegations of misrepresentation by the union and misunderstanding by the employees of the purpose for which the cards were being solicited has been set out in *Cumberland Shoe Corp.,* 144 N.L.R.B. 1268 (1964), and reaffirmed in *Levi Strauss & Co.,* 172 N.L.R.B. No. 57, 68 L.R.R.M. 1338 (1968). Under the *Cumberland Shoe* doctrine, if the card itself is unambi-

---

[4] The cards used in all four campaigns in Nos. 573 and 691 and in the one drive in No. 585 unambiguously authorized the Union to represent the signing employee for collective bargaining purposes; there was no reference to elections. Typical of the cards was the one used in the Charleston campaign in *Heck's,* and it stated in relevant part:

> Desiring to become a member of the above Union of the International Brotherhood of Teamsters, Chauffeurs, Warehousemen and Helpers of America, I hereby make application for admission to membership. I hereby authorize you, or your agents or representatives to act for me as collective bargaining agent on all matters pertaining to rates of pay, hours or any other condition of employment.

guous (*i.e.,* states on its face that the signer authorizes the union to represent the employee for collective bargaining purposes and not to seek an election), it will be counted unless it is proved that the employee was told that the card was to be used *solely* for the purpose of obtaining an election. In *General Steel,* the trial examiner considered the allegations of misrepresentation at length and, applying the Board's customary analysis, rejected the claims with findings that were adopted by the Board and are reprinted in the margin.

Consequently, the Board ordered the companies to cease and desist from their unfair labor practices, to offer reinstatement and back pay to the employees who had been discriminatorily discharged, to bargain with the Union on request, and to post the appropriate notices.

On appeal, the Court of Appeals for the Fourth Circuit, in *per curiam* opinions in each of the three cases (398 F.2d 336, 337, 339), sustained the Board's findings as to the §§ 8(a)(1) and (3) violations, but rejected the Board's findings that the employers' refusal to bargain violated § 8(a)(5) and declined to enforce those portions of the Board's orders directing the respondent companies to bargain in good faith. The court based its § 8(a)(5) rulings on its 1967 decisions raising the same fundamental issues, *Crawford Mfg. Co. v. NLRB,* 386 F.2d 367 (C.A. 4th Cir. 1967), *cert. denied,* 390 U.S. 1028 (1968); *NLRB v. Logan Packing Co.,* 386 F.2d 562 (C.A. 4th Cir. 1967); *NLRB v. Sehon Stevenson & Co., Inc.,* 386 F.2d 551 (C.A. 4th Cir. 1967). The court in those cases held that the 1947 Taft-Hartley amendments to the Act, which permitted the Board to resolve representation disputes by certification under § 9(c) only by secret ballot election, withdrew from the Board the authority to order an employer to bargain under § 8(a)(5) on the basis of cards, in the absence of NLRB certification, unless the employer knows independently of the cards that there is in fact no representation dispute. The court held that the cards themselves were so inherently unreliable that their use gave an employer virtually an automatic, good faith claim that such a dispute existed, for which a secret election was necessary. Thus, these rulings established that a company could not be ordered to bargain unless (1) there was no question about a union's majority status (either because the employer agreed the cards were valid or had conducted his own poll so indicating), or (2) the employer's §§ 8(a)(1) and (3) unfair labor practices committed during the representation campaign were so extensive and pervasive that a bargaining order was the only available Board remedy irrespective of a card majority....

II

In urging us to reverse the Fourth Circuit and to affirm the First Circuit, the National Labor Relations Board contends that we should approve its interpretation and administration of the duties and obligations imposed by the Act in authorization card cases. The Board argues (1) that unions have never been limited under § 9(c) of either the Wagner Act or the 1947 amendments to certified elections as the sole route to attaining representative status. Unions may, the Board contends, impose a duty to bargain on the employer under § 8(a)(5) by reliance on other evidence of majority employee support, such as authorization cards. Contrary to the Fourth Circuit's holding, the Board asserts, the 1947 amendments did not eliminate the alternative routes to majority status. The Board contends (2) that the cards themselves, when solicited in accordance with Board standards which adequately insure against union misrepresentation, are sufficiently reliable indicators of employee desires to support a bargaining order against an employer who refuses to recognize a card majority in violation of § 8(a)(5). The Board argues (3) that a bargaining order is the appropriate remedy for the § 8(a)(5) violation, where the employer commits other unfair labor practices that tend to undermine union support and render a fair election improbable.

Relying on these three assertions, the Board asks us to approve its current practice, which is briefly as follows. When confronted by a recognition demand based on possession of cards allegedly signed by a majority of his employees, an employer need not grant recognition immediately, but may, unless he has knowledge independently of the cards that the union has a majority, decline the union's request and insist on an election, either by requesting the union to file an election petition or by filing such a petition himself under § 9(c)(1)(B). If, however, the employer commits independent and substantial unfair labor practices disruptive of election conditions, the Board may withhold the election or set it aside, and issue instead a bargaining order as a remedy for the various violations. A bargaining order will not issue, of course, if the union obtained the cards through misrepresentation or coercion or if the employer's unfair labor practices are unrelated generally to the representation campaign. Conversely, the employers in these cases urge us to adopt the views of the Fourth Circuit....

The traditional approach utilized by the Board for many years has been known as the *Joy Silk* doctrine. *Joy Silk Mills, Inc. v. NLRB,* 85 N.L.R.B. 1263 (1949), *enforced* 87 U.S. App. D.C. 360, 185 F.2d 732 (C.A.D.C. Cir. 1950). Under that rule, an employer could lawfully refuse to bargain with a union claiming representative status through possession of authorization cards if he had a "good faith doubt" as to the union's majority status; instead of bargaining, he could insist that the union seek an election in order to test out his doubts. The Board, then, could find a lack of good faith doubt and enter a bargaining order in one of two ways. It could find (1) that the employer's independent unfair labor practices were evidence of bad faith, showing that the employer was seeking time to dissipate the union's majority. Or the Board could find (2) that the employer had come forward with no reasons for entertaining any doubt and therefore that he must have rejected the bargaining demand in bad faith. An example of the second category was *Snow & Sons,* 134 N.L.R.B. 709 (1961), *enforced* 308 F.2d 687 (C.A. 9th Cir. 1962), where the employer reneged on his agreement to bargain after a third party checked the validity of the card signatures and insisted on an election because he doubted that the employees truly desired representation. The Board entered a bargaining order with very broad language to the effect that an employer could not refuse a bargaining demand and seek an election instead "without valid ground therefor," 134 N.L.R.B. at 710-711. *See also Dixon Ford Shoe Co., Inc.,* 150 N.L.R.B. 861 (1965); *Kellogg Mills,* 147 N.L.R.B. 342, 346 (1964), *enforced* 347 F.2d 219 (C.A. 9th Cir. 1965).

The leading case codifying modifications to the *Joy Silk* doctrine was *Aaron Brothers,* 158 N.L.R.B. 1077 (1966). There the Board made it clear that it had shifted the burden to the General Counsel to show bad faith and that an employer "will not be held to have violated his bargaining obligation ... simply because he refuses to rely on cards, rather than an election, as the method for determining the union's majority." 158 N.L.R.B., at 1078. Two significant consequences were emphasized. The Board noted (1) that not every unfair labor practice would automatically result in a finding of bad faith and therefore a bargaining order; the Board implied that it would find bad faith only if the unfair labor practice was serious enough to have the tendency to dissipate the union's majority. The Board noted (2) that an employer no longer needed to come forward with reasons for rejecting a bargaining demand. The Board pointed out, however, that a bargaining order would issue if it could prove that an employer's "course of conduct" gave indications as to the employer's bad faith. As examples of such a "course of conduct," the Board cited *Snow & Sons, supra; Dixon Ford Shoe Co., Inc., supra,* and *Kellogg Mills, supra,* thereby reaffirming *John P. Serpa, Inc.,* 155 N.L.R.B. No. 12 (1965), where the Board had limited *Snow & Sons* to its facts.

Although the Board's brief before this Court generally followed the approach as set out in *Aaron Brothers, supra,* the Board announced at oral argument that it had virtually abandoned the *Joy Silk* doctrine altogether. Under the Board's current practice, an employer's good faith doubt is largely irrelevant, and the key to the issuance of a bargaining order is the commission of serious unfair labor practices that interfere with the election processes and tend to preclude the holding of a fair election. Thus, an employer can insist that a union go to an election, regardless of his subjective motivation, so long as he is not guilty of misconduct; he need give no affirmative reasons for rejecting a recognition request, and he can demand an election with a simple "no comment" to the union. The Board pointed out, however, (1) that an employer could not refuse to bargain if he *knew,* through a personal poll for instance, that a majority of his employees supported the union, and (2) that an employer could not refuse recognition initially because of questions as to the appropriateness of the unit and then later claim, as an afterthought, that he doubted the union's strength.

The union argues here that an employer's right to insist on an election in the absence of unfair labor practices should be more circumscribed, and a union's right to rely on cards correspondingly more expanded, than the Board would have us rule. The union's contention is that an employer, when confronted with a card-based bargaining demand, can insist on an election only by filing the election petition himself immediately under § 9(c)(1)(B) and not by insisting that the union file the election petition, whereby the election can be subjected to considerable delay. If the employer does not himself petition for an election, the union argues, he must recognize the union regardless of his good or bad faith and regardless of his other unfair labor practices, and should be ordered to bargain if the cards were in fact validly obtained. And if this Court should continue to utilize the good faith doubt rule, the union contends that at the least we should put the burden on the employer to make an affirmative showing of his reasons for entertaining such doubt.

Because the employers' refusal to bargain in each of these cases was accompanied in each instance by independent unfair labor practices which tend to preclude the holding of a fair election, we need not decide whether a bargaining order is ever appropriate in cases where there is no interference with the election processes....

III

A. The first issue facing us is whether a union can establish a bargaining obligation by means other than a Board election and whether the validity of alternate routes to majority status, such as cards, was affected by the 1947 Taft-Hartley amendments. The most commonly traveled route for a union to obtain recognition as the exclusive bargaining representative of an unorganized group of employees is through the Board's election and certification procedures under § 9(c) of the Act (29 U.S.C. § 159(c) (1964 ed.)); it is also, from the Board's point of view, the preferred route. A union is not limited to a Board election, however, for, in addition to § 9, the present Act provides in § 8(a)(5) ..., as did the Wagner Act in § 8(5), that "it shall be an unfair labor practice for an employer ... to refuse to bargain collectively with the representatives of his employees, subject to the provisions of section 9(a)." Since § 9(a), in both the Wagner Act and the present Act, refers to the representative as the one "designated or selected" by a majority of the employees without specifying precisely how that representative is to be chosen, it was early recognized that an employer had a duty to bargain whenever the union representative presented "convincing evidence of majority support." Almost from the inception of the Act, then, it was recognized that a union did not have to be certified as the winner of a Board election to invoke a bargaining obligation; it could establish majority status by other means under the unfair labor practice provision of § 8(a)(5)—by showing convincing support, for instance, by a union-called strike or strike vote, or, as here, by possession of cards signed by a majority of the employees authorizing the union to represent them for collective bargaining purposes....

... Indeed, the 1947 amendments weaken rather than strengthen the position taken by the employers here and the Fourth Circuit below. An early version of the bill in the House would have amended § 8(5) of the Wagner Act to permit the Board to find a refusal to bargain violation only where an employer had failed to bargain with a union "currently recognized by the employer or certified as such [through an election] under section 9." Section 8(a)(5) of H.R. 3020, 80th Cong., 1st Sess. (1947). The proposed change, which would have eliminated the use of cards, was rejected in Conference (H.R. Conf. Rep. No. 510, 80th Cong., 1st Sess., 41 (1947)), however, and we cannot make a similar change in the Act simply because, as the employers assert, Congress did not expressly approve the use of cards in rejecting the House amendment. Nor can we accept the Fourth Circuit's conclusion that the change was wrought when Congress amended § 9(c) to make election the sole basis for *certification* by eliminating the phrase "any other suitable method to ascertain such representatives," under which the Board had occasionally used cards as a certification basis. A certified union has the benefit of numerous special privileges which are not accorded unions recognized voluntarily or under a bargaining order and which, Congress could determine, should not be dispensed unless a union has survived the crucible of a secret ballot election.

The employers rely finally on the addition to § 9(c) of subparagraph (B), which allows an employer to petition for an election whenever "one or more individuals or labor organizations have presented to him a claim to be recognized as the representative defined in section 9(a)." That provision was not added, as the employers assert, to give them an absolute right to an election at any time; rather, it was intended, as the legislative history indicates, to allow them, after asked to bargain, to test out their doubts as to a union's majority in a secret election which they would then presumably not cause to be set aside by illegal antiunion activity. We agree with the Board's assertion here that there is no suggestion that Congress intended § 9(c)(1)(B) to relieve any employer of his § 8(a)(5) bargaining obligation where, without good faith, he engaged in unfair labor practices disruptive of the Board's election machinery. And we agree that the policies reflected in § 9(c)(1)(B) fully support the Board's present administration of the Act ...; for an employer can insist on a secret ballot election, unless, in the words of the Board, he engages "in contemporaneous unfair labor practices likely to destroy the union's majority and seriously impede the election." ...

In short, we hold that the 1947 amendments did not restrict an employer's duty to bargain under § 8(a)(5) solely to those unions whose representative status is certified after a Board election.

B. We next consider the question whether authorization cards are such inherently unreliable indicators of employee desires that whatever the validity of other alternate routes to representative status, the cards themselves may never be used to determine a union's majority and to support an order to bargain. In this context, the employers urge us to take the step the 1947 amendments and their legislative history indicate Congress did not take, namely, to rule out completely the use of cards in the bargaining arena. Even if we do not unhesitatingly accept the Fourth Circuit's view in the matter, the employers argue, at the very least we should overrule the *Cumberland Shoe* doctrine ... and establish stricter controls over the solicitation of the cards by union representatives....

That the cards, though admittedly inferior to the election process, can adequately reflect employee sentiment when that process has been impeded, needs no extended discussion, for the employers' contentions cannot withstand close examination. The employers argue that their employees cannot make an informed choice because the card drive will be over before the employer has had a chance to present his side of the unionization issues. Normally, however, the union will inform the employer of its organization drive early in order to subject the employer to the unfair labor practice provisions of the Act; the union must be able to show the employer's awareness of the drive in order to prove that his contemporaneous conduct constituted unfair labor practices on which a bargaining order can be based if the drive is ultimately successful. *See, e.g., Hunt Oil Co.,* 157 N.L.R.B. 282 (1966); *Don Swart Trucking Co.,* 154 N.L.R.B. 1345 (1965). Thus, in all of the cases here but the Charleston campaign in *Heck's* the employer, whether informed by the union or not, was aware of the union's organizing drive almost at the outset and began his antiunion campaign at that time; and even in the *Heck's-Charleston* case, where the recognition demand came about a week after the solicitation began, the employer was able to deliver a speech before the union obtained a majority. Further, the employers argue that without a secret ballot an employee may, in a card drive, succumb to group pressures or sign simply to get the union "off his back" and then be unable to change his mind as he would be free to do once inside a voting booth. But the same pressures are likely to be equally present in an election, for election cases arise most often with small bargaining units where virtually every voter's sentiments can be carefully and individually canvassed. And no voter, of course, can change his mind after casting a ballot in an election even though he may think better of his choice shortly thereafter.

The employer's second complaint, that the cards are too often obtained through misrepresentation and coercion, must be rejected also in view of the Board's present rules for controlling card solicitation, which we view as adequate to the task where the cards involved state their purpose clearly and unambiguously on their face. We would be closing our eyes to obvious difficulties, of course, if we did not recognize that there have been abuses, primarily arising out of misrepresentations by union organizers as to whether the effect of signing a card was to designate the union to represent the employee for collective bargaining purposes or merely to authorize it to seek an election to determine that issue. And we would be equally blind if we did not recognize that various courts of appeals and commentators have differed significantly as to the effectiveness of the Board's *Cumberland Shoe* doctrine ... to cure such abuses....

We need make no decision as to the conflicting approaches used with regard to dual-purpose cards, for in each of the five organization campaigns in the four cases before us the cards used were single-purpose cards, stating clearly and unambiguously on their face that the signer designated the union as his representative. And even the view forcefully voiced by the Fourth Circuit below that unambiguous cards as well present too many opportunities for misrepresentation comes before us somewhat weakened in view of the fact that there were no allegations of irregularities in four of those five campaigns *(Gissel,* the two *Heck's* campaigns, and *Sinclair)*. Only in *General Steel* did the employer challenge the cards on the basis of misrepresentations. There, the trial examiner, after hearing testimony from over 100 employees and applying the traditional Board approach ... concluded that "all of these employees not only intended, but were fully aware that they were designating the union as their representative." Thus, the sole question before us, raised in only one of the four cases here, is whether the *Cumberland Shoe* doctrine is an adequate rule under the Act for assuring employee free choice.

In resolving the conflict among the circuits in favor of approving the Board's *Cumberland* rule, we think it sufficient to point out that employees should be bound by the clear language of what they sign unless that language is deliberately and clearly canceled by a union adherent with words calculated to direct the signer to disregard and forget the language above his signature. There is nothing inconsistent in handing an employee a card that says the signer authorizes the union to represent him and then telling him that the card will probably be used first to get an election. Elections have been, after all, and will continue to be, held in the vast majority of cases; the union will still have to have the signatures of 30% of the employees when an employer rejects a bargaining demand and insists that the union seek an election. We cannot agree with the employers here that employees as a rule are too unsophisticated to be bound by what they sign unless expressly told that their act of signing represents something else. In addition to approving the use of cards, of course, Congress has expressly authorized reliance on employee signatures alone in other areas of labor relations, even where criminal sanctions hang in the balance, and we should not act hastily in disregarding congressional judgments that employees can be counted on to take responsibility for their acts.

We agree, however, with the Board's own warnings in *Levi Strauss,* 172 N.L.R.B. No. 57, 68 L.R.R.M. 1338, 1341, and n.7 (1968), that in hearing testimony concerning a card challenge, trial examiners should not neglect their obligation to ensure employee free choice by a too easy mechanical application of the *Cumberland* rule. We also accept the observation that employees are more likely than not, many months after a card drive and in response to questions by company counsel, to give testimony damaging to the union, particularly where company officials have previously threatened reprisals for union activity in violation of § 8(a)(1). We therefore reject any rule that requires a probe of an employee's subjective motivations as involving an endless and unreliable inquiry....

C. Remaining before us is the propriety of a bargaining order as a remedy for a § 8(a)(5) refusal to bargain where an employer has committed independent unfair labor practices which have made the holding of a fair election unlikely or which have in fact undermined a union's majority and caused an election to be set aside. We have long held that the Board is not limited to a cease-and-desist order in such cases, but has the authority to issue a bargaining order without first requiring the union to show that it has been able to maintain its majority status. *See NLRB v. Katz,* 369 U.S. 736, 748, n.16 (1962); *NLRB v. P. Lorillard Co.,* 314 U.S. 512 (1942). And we have held that the Board has the same authority even where it is clear that the union, which once had possession of cards from a majority of the employees, represents only a minority when the bargaining order is entered. *Franks Bros. Co. v. NLRB,* 321 U.S. 702 (1943). We see no reason now to withdraw this authority from the Board. If the Board could enter only a cease-and-desist order and direct an election or a rerun, it would in effect be rewarding the employer and allowing him "to profit from [his] own wrongful refusal to bargain." *Franks Bros., supra,* at 704, while at the same time severely curtailing the employees' right freely to determine whether they desire a representative. The employer could continue to delay or disrupt the election processes and put off indefinitely his obligation to bargain; and any election held under these circumstances would not be likely to demonstrate the employees' true, undistorted desires....

Before considering whether the bargaining orders were appropriately entered in these cases, we should summarize the factors that go into such a determination. Despite our reversal of the Fourth Circuit below in Nos. 573 and 691 on all major issues, the actual area of disagreement between our position here and that of the Fourth Circuit is not large as a practical matter. While refusing to validate the general use of a bargaining order in reliance on cards, the Fourth Circuit nevertheless left open the possibility of imposing a bargaining order, without need of inquiry into majority status on the basis of cards or otherwise, in "exceptional" cases marked by "outrageous" and "pervasive" unfair labor practices. Such an order would be an appropriate remedy for those practices, the court noted, if they are of "such a nature that their coercive effects cannot be eliminated by the application of traditional remedies, with the result that a fair and reliable election cannot be had." *NLRB v. Logan Packing Co.,* 386 F.2d 562, 570 (C.A. 4th Cir. 1967); *see also NLRB v. Heck's supra,* 308 F.2d, at 338. The Board itself, we should add, has long had a similar policy of issuing a bargaining order, in the absence of a § 8(a)(5) violation or even a bargaining demand, when that was the only available, effective remedy for substantial unfair labor practices....

The only effect of our holding here is to approve the Board's use of the bargaining order in less extraordinary cases marked by less pervasive practices which nonetheless still have the tendency to undermine majority strength and impede the election processes. The Board's authority to issue such an order on a lesser showing of employer misconduct is appropriate, we should reemphasize, where there is also a showing that at one point the union had a majority; in such a case, of course, effectuating ascertainable employee free choice becomes as important a goal as deterring employer misbehaviour. In fashioning a remedy in the exercise of its discretion, then, the Board can properly take into consideration the extensiveness of an employer's unfair practices in terms of their past effect on election conditions and the likelihood of their recurrence in the future. If the Board finds that the possibility of erasing the effects of past practices and of ensuring a fair election (or a fair rerun) by the use of traditional remedies, though present, is slight and that employee sentiment once expressed through cards would, on balance, be better protected by a bargaining order, then such an order should issue....

We emphasize that under the Board's remedial power there is still a third category of minor or less extensive unfair labor practices, which, because of their minimal impact on the election machinery, will not sustain a bargaining order. There is, the Board says, no *per se* rule that the commission of any unfair practice will automatically result in a § 8(a)(5) violation and the issuance of an order to bargain. *See Aaron Brothers, supra.*

With these considerations in mind, we turn to an examination of the orders in these cases. In *Sinclair,* No. 585, the Board made a finding, left undisturbed by the First Circuit, that the employer's threats of reprisal were so coercive that, even in the absence of a § 8(a)(5) violation, a bargaining order would have been necessary to repair the unlawful effect of those threats. The Board therefore did not have to make the determination called for in the intermediate situation above that the risks that a fair rerun election might not be possible were too great to disregard the desires of the employees already expressed through the cards....

In the three cases in Nos. 573 and 691 from the Fourth Circuit, on the other hand, the Board did not make a similar finding that a bargaining order would have been necessary in the absence of an unlawful refusal to bargain. Nor did it make a finding that, even though traditional remedies might be able to ensure a fair election, there was insufficient indication that an election (or a rerun in *General Steel)* would definitely be a more reliable test of the employees' desires than the card count taken before the unfair labor practices occurred. The employees [employers] argue that such findings would not be warranted, and the court below ruled in *General Steel* that available remedies short of a bargaining order could guarantee a fair election.... We think it possible that the requisite findings were implicit in the Board's decisions below to issue bargaining orders (and to set aside the election in *General Steel);* and we think it clearly inappropriate for the court below to make any contrary finding on its own.... Because the Board's current practice at the time required it to phrase its findings in terms of an employer's good- or bad-faith doubts (see Part II, *supra),* however, the precise analysis the Board now puts forth was not employed below, and we therefore remand these cases to the Board for proper findings....

NOTES

1. On remand in *Gissel,* the Board upheld issuance of a bargaining order, since it found that the employer's unfair labor practices, both before and after the denial of the union's request for recognition on the basis of authorization cards, were sufficiently pervasive to preclude the holding of a fair election. *Gissel Packing Co.,* 180 N.L.R.B. 54 (1969), *enforced,* 76 L.R.R.M. 2175 (4th Cir. 1970). Does this suggest that in most post-*Gissel* decisions, the same types of unfair labor practices which formerly were used to show the employer's lack of a "good faith doubt" under the *Joy Silk* doctrine will now be used to demonstrate the unlikelihood of holding a fair and reliable election? *See, e.g., Garland Knitting Mills,* 178 N.L.R.B. 396 (1969), *enforced,* 72 L.R.R.M. 2686 (D.C. Cir. 1969); *J.H. Rutter-Rex Mfg. Co.,* 180 N.L.R.B. 878, *enforced,* 434 F.2d 1318 (6th Cir. 1970).

2. Remedial bargaining orders are most frequently issued in cases involving § 8(a)(3) discharges of union activists, threats to layoff union supporters or to close unionized facilities, and similar "hallmark" violations. In recent years, the NLRB and courts have suggested that extraordinary bargaining orders should be reserved for extreme cases. For example, in *Almet, Inc.,* 305 N.L.R.B. 626 (1991), *affirmed,* 987 F.2d 445 (7th Cir. 1993), the Board held that an employer's threats to close the plant and to discharge union supporters and its suspension of one union activist were not "sufficiently egregious" to warrant a bargaining order, since the conduct took place two months before the election and the employer subsequently "ameliorated" the effects of its unlawful conduct by assuring employees that it would stay open and by compensating the suspended employee for his lost time. *See also Kinney Drugs, Inc. v. NLRB,* 74 F.3d 1419 (2d Cir. 1996) (single hallmark violation—employer threat to discharge two union supporters unless they called meeting to discourage co-workers from voting for union—insufficient to support bargaining order).

The *Gissel* tests apply even when the union possessed a "bare majority" of authorization cards. *NLRB v. Empire Corp.,* 518 F.2d 860 (6th Cir. 1975). *Compare NLRB v. Village IX, Inc.,* 723 F.2d 1360 (7th Cir. 1983) (indicating that when a union loses a representation election, tainted by employer unfair labor practices, by a substantial margin, a remedial bargaining order should not be issued, even in favor of a union possessing a card majority, unless the continuing impact of the prior unfair labor practices is truly significant).

3. The Labor Board believes that *Gissel* "contemplated that the propriety of a bargaining order would be judged as of the time of the commission of the unfair labor practices and not in the light of subsequent events." Otherwise, an employer could profit from its wrongdoing by preventing a union whose majority has been undermined from securing a bargaining order. *Gibson Prods.,* 185 N.L.R.B. 362 (1970), *supplemented,* 199 N.L.R.B. 794 (1972), *enforcement denied,* 494 F.2d 762 (5th Cir. 1974). *Accord: New Alaska Dev. Corp. v. NLRB,*

441 F.2d 491 (7th Cir. 1971) (bargaining order valid even though turnover of employees and their lack of knowledge of threats had changed situation so that fair election could now be had); *NLRB v. L.B. Foster Co.,* 418 F.2d 1 (9th Cir. 1969) (court cannot set aside bargaining order merely because there was possibility that not one employee remained who had been at plant during the original election). The Fifth Circuit disagreed, declaring that no bargaining order should issue unless *at the time such an order is directed* the Board "finds the electoral atmosphere unlikely to produce a fair election." *NLRB v. American Cable Sys.,* 427 F.2d 446 (5th Cir.), *cert. denied,* 400 U.S. 957 (1970). *Accord: General Steel Prods. v. NLRB,* 445 F.2d 1350 (4th Cir. 1971).

4. Courts continue to differ with respect to the impact of elapsed time on the enforceability of remedial bargaining orders. *Compare America's Best Quality Coatings v. NLRB,* 44 F.3d 516 (7th Cir.), *cert. denied,* 515 U.S. 1158 (1995) (bargaining order sustained despite delay of three-four years and alleged unit turnover) *and NLRB v. Wallkill Valley Gen. Hosp.,* 866 F.2d 632 (3d Cir. 1989) (enforcing bargaining order based on nine-year-old violations) *with DTR Indus. v. NLRB,* 39 F.3d 106 (6th Cir. 1994) (bargaining order invalid due to failure of Board to give adequate consideration to five-year delay since underlying unfair labor practices and possibility that fair rerun election could now be held) *and Impact Indus. v. NLRB,* 847 F.2d 379 (7th Cir. 1988) (no enforcement of bargaining order when Board failed to adequately consider impact of seven year lapse of time since union's loss of election). *See also NLRB v. Windsor Indus.,* 730 F.2d 860 (2d Cir. 1984) (even highly coercive "hallmark" violations during organizing campaign do not ipso facto support issuance of bargaining order, without adequate consideration of passage of time and employee turnover). *See generally* Note, *"After All, Tomorrow is Another Day": Should Subsequent Events Affect the Validity of Bargaining Orders?* 31 Stan. L. Rev. 505 (1979).

5. Appellate courts occasionally remand bargaining order cases for more detailed explanations regarding the reasons the Board believes that the effects of employer unfair labor practices cannot be ameliorated through more conventional remedial orders and thus warrant the unusual issuance of bargaining directives. *See, e.g., NLRB v. Armcor Indus.,* 535 F.2d 239 (3d Cir. 1976); *NLRB v. Jamaica Towing, Inc.,* 632 F.2d 208 (2d Cir. 1980) (stating its strong preference for an election over a bargaining order). *See also Quazite Div. of Morrison Molded Fiberglass Co. v. NLRB,* 87 F.3d 493 (D.C. Cir. 1996).

6. In *J.P. Stevens Co. v. NLRB,* 441 F.2d 514 (5th Cir.), *cert. denied,* 404 U.S. 830 (1971), the court interpreted *Gissel* as authorizing the issuance of a bargaining order to a union that has never established its majority status, where an employer's unfair labor practices are so "outrageous" and "pervasive" that their coercive effects cannot be overcome by traditional remedies. Although the *Stevens* court found that the union at one point actually did represent a majority of the loyees, the court said that the employer's "full scale war against unioniza" made it unnecessary for the union to demonstrate its majority status. The company had discharged three leading union adherents and had engaged in a campaign of blatant surveillance, interrogation, and threats. *Accord, United Dairy Farmers Co-Op Ass'n v. NLRB,* 633 F.2d 1054 (3d Cir. 1980).

Encouraged by *United Dairy Farmers,* the NLRB, for the first time, found an employer's unfair labor practices sufficiently "outrageous" and "pervasive" to justify the issuance of an original bargaining order in favor of a union that had never established its majority status. *Conair Corp.,* 261 N.L.R.B. 1189 (1982). The violations of the Act were enumerated as follows:

> Numerous threats of plant closure, discharge, and loss of benefits; numerous promises of increased or new benefits; coercive interrogation of employees; numerous acts of soliciting employee grievance with promises to remedy the same; grants of numerous benefits to employees; creating the impression of surveillance; the failure to give timely reinstatement to 36 unfair labor practice strikers; and the outright discharge and refusal to reinstate 16 other unfair labor practice strikers.

A panel of the D.C. Circuit denied enforcement of the Board's *Conair* bargaining order, 721 F.2d 1355 (1983), *cert. denied,* 467 U.S. 1241 (1984). Although agreeing that the employer's unfair labor practices were outrageous and pervasive, the majority concluded that any departure from the principle of majority rule should be left to Congress. Judge Wald dissented on the ground that the bargaining order was the only way to remedy the employer's "massive and unrelenting coercive conduct." In *Gourmet Foods, Inc.,* 270 N.L.R.B. 578 (1984), the Board indicated that it would no longer issue bargaining orders in favor of unions that have not established majority support. *See* Note, *Nonmajority Bargaining Orders: The Only Effective Remedy for Pervasive Employer Unfair Labor Practices During Union Organizing Campaigns,* 20 U. Mich. J.L. Ref. 617 (1987); Lankford, *Nonmajority Bargaining Orders: A Study in Indecision,* 46 Alb. L.J. 363 (1982).

Under the Board's "dual card" doctrine, authorization cards that are signed by employees for two competing unions will not be counted when determining the majority status of either labor organization. *Human Dev. Ass'n v. NLRB,* 937 F.2d 657 (D.C. Cir. 1991), *cert. denied,* 503 U.S. 950 (1992).

7. In *Seeler v. Trading Port, Inc.,* 517 F.2d 33 (2d Cir. 1975), the court held that in *Gissel*-type cases, a regional director may obtain a preliminary bargaining order against an employer under § 10(j) of the NLRA, pending a final determination by the Board concerning the union's bargaining status. *Accord, Levine v. C. & W. Mining Co.,* 610 F.2d 432 (6th Cir. 1979). A § 10(j) injunction was denied in *Boire v. Pilot Freight Carriers,* 515 F.2d 1185 (5th Cir. 1977). *See* Pettibone, *Section 10(j) Bargaining Order in Gissel-Type Cases,* 27 Lab. L.J. 648 (1976); Comment, *The Use of Section 10(j)* of the *Labor-Management Relations Act in Employer Refusal to Bargain Cases,* 1976 U. Ill. L.F. 845; Note, *The Propriety of*

Section 10(j) Bargaining Orders in Gissel Situations, 82 Mich. L. Rev. 112 (1983).

8. An employer that conducts a poll and verifies that a majority of its employees wants union representation forfeits its right to an election and subjects itself to issuance of a § 8(a)(5) bargaining order, regardless of whether the poll was lawfully conducted. *NLRB v. English Bros. Pattern & Foundry,* 679 F.2d 787 (9th Cir. 1982). *Compare Georgetown Hotel v. NLRB,* 835 F.2d 1467 (D.C. Cir. 1987) (employer could lawfully decline to recognize union after it reneged on agreement to conduct private election, since there was never any actual verification of union's majority status).

Although § 9(c)(3) prohibits the holding of more than one valid election within twelve months, it does not preclude issuance of an otherwise appropriate Board bargaining order within one year of a valid election. *Camvac Int'l, Inc.,* 297 N.L.R.B. 853 (1990); *Conren, Inc.,* 156 N.L.R.B. 592 (1966), *enforced,* 368 F.2d 173 (7th Cir. 1966), *cert. denied,* 386 U.S. 974 (1967).

9. In *Marie Phillips, Inc.,* 178 N.L.R.B. 340 (1969), *enforced,* 443 F.2d 667 (D.C. Cir. 1970), the Board rejected an employer's contention that 26 unequivocal authorization cards which helped establish a union's majority were invalid because the union had solicited them by misrepresenting that a majority of the employees had already signed. The Board indicated that an objective standard must be used to determine the impact of misrepresentations on the validity of authorization cards: "Where the objective facts, as evidenced by events contemporaneous with the signing, clearly demonstrate that the misrepresentation was the decisive factor in causing an employee to sign a card, we shall not count such a card in determining a union's majority. However,... where the only indication of reliance is a signer's subsequent testimony as to his subjective state of mind when signing the card, such showing is insufficient to invalidate the card."

10. Authorization cards that are either ambiguous as to their effect, or are "dual purpose" cards (authorizing the union to represent the employees and to obtain an election) have often been denied validity in representation matters, particularly if their purpose is not made clear to signers. *Dayco Corp. v. NLRB,* 382 F.2d 577 (6th Cir. 1967); *NLRB v. Peterson Bros.,* 342 F.2d 221 (5th Cir. 1965).

11. After a union has lost a representation election, the Board will only issue a bargaining order to remedy pre-election unfair labor practices if the labor organization files both unfair labor practice charges *and* timely election objections. "We will not grant [a bargaining order] ... unless the election be set aside on the basis of meritorious objections filed in the representation case." *Irving Air Chute Co.,* 149 N.L.R.B. 627 (1964), *enforced,* 350 F.2d 176 (2d Cir. 1965). *See also Photobell Co.,* 158 N.L.R.B. 738 (1966) ("The basic premise underlying this type of case is that there is no outstanding valid election. If there is a valid election outstanding, no bargaining order can issue.").

12. In *Trading Port, Inc.,* 219 N.L.R.B. 298 (1975), the Board indicated that "an employer's obligation under a bargaining order remedy should commence as of the time the employer has embarked on a clear course of unlawful conduct or has engaged in sufficient unfair labor practices to undermine the union's majority status." What is the significance of a retroactive bargaining order to the affected labor organization?

13. For pre-*Gissel* discussions, *see* Bok, Phillips & St. Antoine, *Seminar on Free Speech and Preelection Conduct,* in Southwestern Legal Foundation, Labor Law Developments, Proceedings of 11th Annual Institute on Labor Law 239 (1964); Lesnick, *Establishment of Collective Bargaining Rights Without an Election,* 65 Mich. L. Rev. 851 (1967); Lewis, *The Use and Abuse of Authorization Cards in Determining Union Majority,* 16 Lab. L.J. 434 (1965); Rains, *Authorization Cards as an Indefensible Basis for Board Directed Union Representation Status: Fact and Fancy,* 18 Lab. L.J. 226 (1967); Note, *Refusal-to-Recognize Charges Under § 8(a)(5) of the NLRA: Card Checks and Employee Free Choice,* 33 U. Chi. L. Rev. 389 (1966); Note, *Union Authorization Cards,* 75 Yale L.J. 805 (1966).

Post-*Gissel* discussions include Bethel & Melfi, *The Failure of Gissel Bargaining Orders,* 14 Hofstra Lab. L.J. 423 (1997); Christensen & Christensen, *Gissel Packing and "Good Faith Doubt": The Gestalt of Required Recognition of Unions Under the NLRA,* 37 U. Chi. L. Rev. 411 (1970); Cooper, *Authorization Cards and Union Representation Election Outcome: An Empirical Assessment of the Assumption Underlying The Supreme Court's Gissel Decision,* 79 Nw. U.L. Rev. 87 (1984); Bethel & Melfi, *Judicial Enforcement of NLRB Bargaining Orders: What Influences the Courts?,* 22 U. Cal. Davis L. Rev. 138 (1988); Lewis, *Gissel Packing: Was the Supreme Court Right?,* 56 A.B.A.J. 877 (1970); Platt, *Supreme Court Looks at Bargaining Orders Based on Authorization Cards,* 4 Ga. L. Rev. 779 (1970); Pogrebin, *NLRB Bargaining Orders Since Gissel: Wanderings From a Landmark,* 46 St. John's L. Rev. 193 (1971); Note, *NLRB v. Gissel Packing: Bargaining Orders and Employee Free Choice,* 45 N.Y.U.L. Rev. 318 (1970).

LINDEN LUMBER DIVISION, SUMMER & CO. v. NLRB

Supreme Court of the United States
419 U.S. 301, 95 S. Ct. 429, 42 L. Ed. 2d 465 (1974)

MR. JUSTICE DOUGLAS delivered the opinion of the Court.

These cases present a question expressly reserved in *National Labor Relations Board v. Gissel Packing Co.,* 395 U.S. 575, 595, 601, n. 18 (1969).

In *Linden* respondent union obtained authorization cards from a majority of petitioner's employees and demanded that it be recognized as the collective-bargaining representative of those employees. Linden said it doubted the union's claimed majority status and suggested the union petition the Board for an election. The union filed such a petition with the Board but later withdrew it when Linden declined to enter a consent election agreement or abide by an election on the ground that respondent union's organizational campaign had been improperly assisted by company supervisors. Respondent union thereupon renewed its demand for collective bargaining; and again Linden declined, saying that the union's claimed membership had been improperly influenced by supervisors. Thereupon respondent union struck for recognition as the bargaining representative and shortly filed a charge of unfair labor practice against Linden based on its refusal to bargain.

There is no charge that Linden engaged in an unfair labor practice apart from its refusal to bargain. The Board held that Linden should not be guilty of an unfair labor practice solely on the basis "of its refusal to accept evidence of majority status other than the results of a Board election." ...

In *Wilder* there apparently were 30 employees in the plant and the union with 11 signed and two unsigned authorization cards requested recognition as the bargaining agent for the company's production and maintenance employees. Of the 30 employees 18 were in the production and maintenance unit which the Board found to be appropriate for collective bargaining. No answer was given by Wilder, and recognitional picketing began. The request was renewed when the two unsigned cards were signed, but Wilder denied recognition. Thereupon the union filed unfair labor practice charges against Wilder. A series of Board decisions and judicial decisions, not necessary to recapitulate here, consumed about seven years until the present decision by the Court of Appeals. The Board made the same ruling as respects Wilder as it did in Linden's case.... On petitions for review of the Court of Appeals reversed. 487 F.2d 1099 (1973). We reverse the Court of Appeals.

In *Gissel* we held that an employer who engages in "unfair" labor practices "likely to destroy the union's majority and seriously impede the election" may not insist that before it bargains the union get a secret ballot election. 395 U.S. at 600. There were no such unfair labor practices here, nor had the employer in either case agreed to a voluntary settlement of the dispute and then reneged. As noted, we reserved in *Gissel* the questions "whether, absent election interference by an employer's unfair labor practices, he may obtain an election only if he petitions for one himself; whether, if he does not, he must bargain with a card majority if the union chooses not to seek an election; and whether, in the latter situation, he is bound by the Board's ultimate determination of the card results regardless of his earlier good faith doubts, or whether he can still insist on a Union-sought election if he makes an affirmative showing of his positive reasons for believing there is a representation dispute." *Id.* at 601, n. 18.

We recognized in *Gissel* that while the election process had acknowledged superiority in ascertaining whether a union has majority support, cards may "adequately reflect employee sentiment." *Id.* at 603.

Generalizations are difficult; and it is urged by the unions that only the precise facts should dispose of concrete cases. As we said, however, in *Gissel,* the Board had largely abandoned its earlier test that the employer's refusal to bargain was warranted, if he had a good-faith doubt that the union represented a majority....

In the present cases the Board found that the employers "should not be found guilty of a violation of Section 8(a)(5) solely upon the basis of [their] refusal to accept evidence of majority status other than the results of a Board election." ... The question whether the employers had good reasons or poor reasons was not deemed relevant to the inquiry. The Court of Appeals concluded that if the employer had doubts as to a union's majority status, it could and should test out its doubts by petitioning for an election....

To take the Board's position is not to say that authorization cards are wholly unreliable as an indication of employee support of the union. An employer concededly may have valid objections to recognizing a union on that basis. His objection to cards may, of course, mask his opposition to unions. On the other hand he may have rational, good-faith grounds for distrusting authorization cards in a given situation. He may be convinced that the fact that a majority of the employees strike and picket does not necessarily establish that they desire the particular union as their representative. Fear may indeed prevent some from crossing a picket line; or sympathy for strikers, not the desire to have the particular union in the saddle, may influence others. These factors make difficult an examination of the employer's motive to ascertain whether it was in good faith. To enter that domain is to reject the approval by *Gissel* of the retreat which the Board took from its "good faith" inquiries.

The union which is faced with an unwilling employer has two alternative remedies under the Board's decision in the instant case. It can file for an election; or it can press unfair labor practices against the employer under *Gissel.* The latter alternative promises to consume much time. In *Linden* the time between filing the charge and the Board's ruling was about 4½ years; in *Wilder,* about 6½ years. The Board's experience indicates that the median time in a contested case is 388 days. *Gissel*, 395 U.S. at 611, n. 30. On the other hand the median time between the filing of the petition for an election and the decision of the regional director is about 45 days. In terms of getting on with the problems of inaugurating regimes of industrial peace, the policy of encouraging secret elections under the Act is favored. The question remains—should the burden be on the union to ask for an election or should it be the responsibility of the employer?

The Court of Appeals concluded that since Congress in 1947 authorized employers to file their own representation petitions by enacting § 9(c)(1)(B), the burden was on them. But the history of that provision indicates it was aimed at eliminating the discrimination against employers which had previously existed under the Board's prior rules, permitting employers to petition for an election only when confronted with claims by two or more unions. There is no suggestion that Congress wanted to place the burden of getting a secret election on the employer.

Today an employer is faced with this situation. A man comes into his office and says, "I represent your employees. Sign this agreement or we strike tomorrow." Such instances have occurred all over the United States. The employer has no way in which to determine whether this man really does represent his employees or does not. The bill gives him the right to go to the Board under those circumstances, and say, "I want an election. I want to know who is the bargaining agent for my employees."

93 Cong. Rec. 3838 (1947) (remarks of Senator Taft).

Our problem is not one of picking favorites but of trying to find the congressional purpose by examining the statutory and administrative interpretations that squint one way or another. Large issues ride on who takes the initiative. A common issue is, what should be the representative unit? In *Wilder* the employer at first took the position that the unit should be one of 30 employees. If it were 18, as the union claimed (or even 25 as the employer later argued), the union with its 13 authorization cards (assuming them to be valid) would have a majority. If the unit were 30, the union would be out of business.

Section 9(c)(1)(B) visualizes an employer faced with a claim by individuals or unions "to be recognized as the representative defined in § 9(a)." That question of representation is raised only by a claim that the applicant represents a majority of employees, "in a unit appropriate for such purposes." § 9(a). If there is a significant discrepancy between the unit which the employer wants and the unit for which the union asked recognition, the Board will dismiss the employer's petition. [Citing cases.] In that event the union, if it desired the smaller unit, would have to file its own petition, leaving the employer free to contest the appropriateness of that unit. The Court of Appeals thought that if the employer were required to petition the Board for an election, the litigable issues would be reduced. The recurring conflict over what should be the appropriate bargaining unit coupled with the fact that if the employer asks for a unit which the union opposes, his election petition is dismissed is answer enough.

The Board has at least some expertise in these matters and its judgment is that an employer's petition for an election, though permissible, is not the required course. It points out in its brief here that an employer wanting to gain delay can draw a petition to elicit protests by the union, and the thought that an employer petition would obviate litigation over the sufficiency of the union's showing of interest is in its purview apparently not well taken. A union petition to be sure must be backed by a 30% showing of employee interest. But the sufficiency of such a showing is not litigable by the parties.

In light of the statutory scheme and the practical administrative procedural questions involved, we cannot say that the Board's decision that the union should go forward and ask for an election on the employer's refusal to recognize the authorization cards was arbitrary and capricious or an abuse of discretion.

In sum, we sustain the Board in holding that, unless an employer has engaged in an unfair labor practice that impairs the electoral process, a union with authorization cards purporting to represent a majority of the employees, which is refused recognition, has the burden of taking the next step in invoking the Board's election procedure.

Reversed.

MR. JUSTICE STEWART, with whom MR. JUSTICE WHITE, MR. JUSTICE MARSHALL, and MR. JUSTICE POWELL join, dissenting.

....

Section 9(a) expressly provides that the employees' exclusive bargaining representative shall be the union "designated or selected" by a majority of the employees in an appropriate unit. Neither § 9(a) nor § 8(a)(5), which makes it an unfair labor practice for an employer to refuse to bargain with the representative of his employees, specifies how that representative is to be chosen. The language of the Act thus seems purposefully designed to impose a duty upon an employer to bargain whenever the union representative presents convincing evidence of majority support, regardless of the method by which that support is demonstrated. And both the Board and this Court have in the past consistently interpreted §§ 8(a)(5) and 9(a) to mean exactly that....

As the Court recognized in *Gissel,* the 1947 Taft-Hartley amendments strengthen this interpretation of the Act. One early version of the House bill would have amended the Act to permit the Board to find an employer unfair labor practice for refusing to bargain with a union only if the union was "currently recognized by the employer or certified as such [through an election] under section 9." Section 8(a)(5) of H. R. 3020, 80th Cong., 1st Sess. The proposed change, which would have eliminated any method of requiring employer recognition of a union other than a Board-supervised election, was rejected in Conference. H. R. Conf. Rep. No. 510, 80th Cong., 1st Sess., 41. After rejection of the proposed House amendment, the House Conference Report explicitly stated that § 8(a)(5) was intended to follow the provisions of "existing law." *Ibid.* And "existing law" unequivocally recognized that a union could establish majority status and thereby impose a bargaining obligation on an unwilling employer by means other than petitioning for and winning a Board-supervised election. *NLRB v. Gissel Packing Co., supra,* at 596-598.

The 1947 amendments, however, did provide an alternative to immediate union recognition for an employer faced with a union demand to bargain on behalf of his employees. Section 9(c)(1)(B), added to the Act in 1947, provides that an employer, alleging that one or more individuals or labor organizations have presented a claim to be recognized as the exclusive representative of his employees, may file a petition for a Board-supervised representation election.

This section, together with §§ 8(a)(5) and 9(a), provides clear congressional direction as to the proper approach to the situation before us. When an employer is faced with a demand for recognition by a union that has presented convincing evidence of majority support, he may elect to follow one of four alternatives. First, he is free to recognize the union and thereby satisfy his § 8(a)(5) obligation to bargain with the representatives "designated or selected" by his employees. Second, he may petition for a Board-supervised election, pursuant to § 9(c)(1)(B). *NLRB v. Gissel Packing Co., supra,* at 599. Third, rather than file his own election petition, the employer can agree to be bound by the results of an expedited consent election ordered after the filing of a union election petition. See 29 CFR § 102.62. Finally, the employer can refuse to recognize the union, despite its convincing evidence of majority support, and also refuse either to petition for an election or to consent to a union-requested election. In this event, however, the Act clearly provides that the union may charge the employer with an unfair labor practice under § 8(a)(5) for refusing to bargain collectively with the representatives of his employees. If the General Counsel issues a complaint and the Board determines that the union in fact represents a majority of the employees, the Board must issue an order directing the employer to bargain with the union. *See, e.g., NLRB v. Dahlstrom Metallic Door Co.,* 112 F.2d 756; cf. *NLRB v. Gissel Packing Co.,* 395 U.S., at 595-600.

The Court offers two justifications for its approval of the new Board practice which, disregarding the clear language of §§ 8(a)(5) and 9(a), requires an employer to bargain only with a union certified as bargaining representative after a Board-supervised election conducted upon the petition of the union.

First, it is suggested that to require the Board under some circumstances to find a § 8(a)(5) violation when an employer refuses to bargain with the noncertified union supported by a majority of his employees would compel the Board to reenter the domain of subjective "good faith" inquiries. *Ante,* at slip op. 5. This fear is unwarranted....

Within broad limits imposed by the Act itself, the Board may use its understanding of the policies and practical considerations of the Act's administration to determine the circumstances under which an employer must take evidence of majority support as "convincing." *Cf. NLRB v. Insurance Agents' International Union,* 361 U.S. 477, 499; *NLRB v. Local 449, Teamsters,* 353 U.S. 87, 96. The Act in no way requires the Board to define "convincing evidence" in a manner that reintroduces a subjective test of the employer's good faith in refusing to bargain with the union. If the Board continues to believe, as it has in the recent past, that it is unworkable to adopt any standard for determining when an employer has breached his duty to bargain that incorporates a subjective element, *see NLRB v. Gissel Packing Co.,* 395 U.S. at 592-594, it may define "convincing evidence of majority support" solely by reference to objective criteria—for example, by reference to "a union-called strike or strike vote, or, as here, by possession of cards signed by a majority of the employees...." *Id.* at 597.

Even with adoption of such an objective standard for measuring "convincing evidence of majority support," the employer's "subjective" doubts would be adequately safeguarded by § 9(c)(1)(B)'s assurance of the right to file his own petition for an election. Despite the Board's broad discretion in this area, however, the Act simply does not permit the Board to adopt a rule that avoids *subjective* inquiries by eliminating entirely *all* inquiries into an employer's obligation to bargain with a noncertified union selected by a majority of his employees.

The second ground upon which the Court justifies its approval of the Board's new practice is that it serves to remove from the employer the burden of obtaining a Board-supervised election.... Although I agree with the Court that it would be improper to impose such an obligation on an employer, the Board's new policy is not necessary to eliminate such a burden.

The only employer obligation relevant to this case, apart from the requirement that the employer not commit independent unfair labor practices that would prejudice the holding of a fair election, is the one imposed by §§ 8(a)(5) and 9(a) of the Act: an employer has a duty to bargain collectively with the representative designated or selected by his employees. When an employer is confronted with "convincing evidence of majority support," he has the *option* of petitioning for an election or consenting to an expedited union-petitioned election. As the Court explains, § 9(c)(1)(B) does not require the employer to exercise this option. If he does not, however, and if he does not voluntarily recognize the union, he must take the risk that his conduct will be found by the Board to constitute a violation of his § 8(a)(5) duty to bargain. In short, petitioning for an election is not an employer obligation; it is a device created by Congress for the employer's self-protection, much as Congress gave unions the right to petition for elections to establish their majority status but deliberately chose not to require a union to seek an election before it could impose a bargaining obligation on an unwilling employer. *NLRB v. Gissel Packing Co.,* 395 U.S. at 598-599.

The language and history of the Act clearly indicate that Congress intended to impose upon an employer the duty to bargain with a union that has presented convincing evidence of majority support, even though the union has not petitioned for and won a Board-supervised election. "It is not necessary for us to justify the policy of Congress. It is enough that we find it in the statute. That policy cannot be defeated by the Board's policy." *Colgate-Palmolive-Peet Co. v. NLRB,* 388 U.S. 355, 363. Accordingly, I would affirm the judgment of the Court of Appeals remanding the case to the Board, but for further proceedings consistent with the views expressed in this opinion.

NOTE

In *Retail Clerks Local 455 v. NLRB (Kroger Co.),* 510 F.2d 802 (D.C. Cir. 1975), the court held, contrary to the NLRB, that an employer could waive its right to petition for an election by signing a so-called "additional store clause," under which the employer agreed to recognize the union as bargaining agent for the employees in any store added to the original unit. In this particular case, the union had also proffered concededly valid authorization cards from a majority of the employees in the store in dispute.

C. DURATION OF THE DUTY TO BARGAIN

BROOKS v. NLRB

Supreme Court of the United States
348 U.S. 96, 75 S. Ct. 176, 99 L. Ed. 125 (1954)

MR. JUSTICE FRANKFURTER delivered the opinion of the Court.

The National Labor Relations Board conducted a representation election in petitioner's Chrysler-Plymouth agency on April 12, 1951. District Lodge No. 727, International Association of Machinists, won by a vote of eight to five, and the Labor Board certified it as the exclusive bargaining representative on April 20. A week after the election and the day before the certification, petitioner received a handwritten letter signed by nine of the 13 employees in the bargaining unit stating: "We, the undersigned majority of the employees ... are not in favor of being represented by Union Local No. 727 as a bargaining agent."

Relying on this letter and the decision of the Court of Appeals for the Sixth Circuit in *NLRB v. Vulcan Forging Co.,* 188 F.2d 927 (6th Cir. 1951), petitioner refused to bargain with the union. The Labor Board found, 98 N.L.R.B. 976, that petitioner had thereby committed an unfair labor practice in violation of §§ 8(a)(1) and 8(a)(5) of the amended National Labor Relations Act, 61 Stat. 140-141, 29 U.S.C. §§ 158(a)(1), (a)(5), and the Court of Appeals for the Ninth Circuit enforced the Board's order to bargain, 204 F.2d 899 (9th Cir. 1953). In view of the conflict between the Circuits, we granted certiorari, 347 U.S. 916 (1954).

The issue before us is the duty of an employer toward a duly certified bargaining agent, if, shortly after the election which resulted in the certification, the union has lost, without the employer's fault, a majority of the employees from its membership.

Under the original Wagner Act, the Labor Board was given the power to certify a union as the exclusive representative of the employees in a bargaining unit when it had determined, by election or "any other suitable method," that the union commanded majority support. Section 9(c), 49 Stat. 453. In exercising this authority the Board evolved a number of working rules of which the following are relevant to our purpose:

> (a) A certification, if based on a Board-conducted election, must be honored for a "reasonable" period, ordinarily "one year," in the absence of "unusual circumstances."
>
> (b) "Unusual circumstances" were found in at least three situations: (1) The certified union dissolved or became defunct; (2) as a result of a schism, substantially all the members and officers of the certified union transferred

their affiliation to a new local or international; (3) the size of the bargaining unit fluctuated radically within a short time.

(c) Loss of majority support after the "reasonable" period could be questioned in two ways: (1) employer's refusal to bargain, or (2) petition by a rival union for a new election.

(d) If the initial election resulted in a majority for "no union," the election—unlike a certification—did not bar a second election within a year.

The Board uniformly found an unfair labor practice where, during the so-called "certification year," an employer refused to bargain on the ground that the certified union no longer possessed a majority. While the courts in the main enforced the Board's decisions, they did not commit themselves to one year as the determinate content of reasonableness. The Board and the courts proceeded along this line of reasoning:

(a) In the political and business spheres, the choice of the voters in an election binds them for a fixed time. This promotes a sense of responsibility in the electorate and needed coherence in administration. These considerations are equally relevant to healthy labor relations.

(b) Since an election is a solemn and costly occasion, conducted under safeguards to voluntary choice, revocation of authority should occur by a procedure no less solemn than that of the initial designation. A petition or a public meeting—in which those voting for and against unionism are disclosed to management, and in which the influences of mass psychology are present—is not comparable to the privacy and independence of the voting booth.

(c) A union should be given ample time for carrying out its mandate on behalf of its members, and should not be under exigent pressure to produce hot-house results or be turned out.

(d) It is scarcely conducive to bargaining in good faith for an employer to know that, if he dillydallies or subtly undermines, union strength may erode and thereby relieve him of his statutory duties at any time, while if he works conscientiously toward agreement, the rank and file may, at the last moment, repudiate their agent.

(e) In these situations, not wholly rare, where unions are competing, raiding and strife will be minimized if elections are not at the hazard of informal and short-term recall.

Certain aspects of the Labor Board's representation procedures came under scrutiny in the Congress that enacted the Taft-Hartley Act in 1947, 61 Stat. 136. Congress was mindful that, once employees had chosen a union, they could not vote to revoke its authority and refrain from union activities, while if they voted against having a union in the first place, the union could begin at once to agitate for a new election. The National Labor Relations Act was amended to provide that (a) employees could petition the Board for a decertification election, at which they would have an opportunity to choose no longer to be represented by a union, 61 Stat. 144, 29 U.S.C. § 159(c)(1)(A)(ii); (b) an employer, if in doubt as to the majority claimed by a union without formal election or beset by the conflicting claims of rival unions, could likewise petition the Board for an election, 61 Stat. 144, 29 U.S.C. § 159(c)(1)(B); (c) after a valid certification or decertification election had been conducted, the Board could not hold a second election in the same bargaining unit until a year had elapsed, 61 Stat. 144, 29 U.S.C. § 159(c)(3); (d) Board certification could only be granted as the result of an election, 61 Stat. 144, 29 U.S.C. § 159(c)(1), though an employer would presumably still be under a duty to bargain with an uncertified union that had a clear majority, *see NLRB v. Kobritz,* 193 F.2d 8 (1st Cir. 1951).

The Board continued to apply its "one-year certification" rule after the Taft-Hartley Act came into force, except that even "unusual circumstances" no longer left the Board free to order an election where one had taken place within the preceding 12 months. Conflicting views became manifest in the Court of Appeals when the Board sought to enforce orders based on a refusal to bargain in violation of its rule. Some Circuits sanctioned the Board's position. The Court of Appeals for the Sixth Circuit denied enforcement. The Court of Appeals for the Third Circuit held that a "reasonable" period depended on the facts of the particular case.

The issue is open here. No case touching the problem has directly presented it. In *Franks Bros. Co. v. NLRB,* 321 U.S. 702 (1944), we held that where a union's majority was dissipated after an employer's unfair labor practice in refusing to bargain, the Board could appropriately find that such conduct had undermined the prestige of the union and require the employer to bargain with it for a reasonable period despite the loss of majority. And in *NLRB v. Mexia Textile Mills, Inc.,* 339 U.S. 563 (1950), we held that a claim of an intervening loss of majority was no defense to a proceeding for enforcement of an order to cease and desist from certain unfair labor practices.

Petitioner contends that whenever an employer is presented with evidence that his employees have deserted their certified union, he may forthwith refuse to bargain. In effect, he seeks to vindicate the rights of his employees to select their bargaining representative. If the employees are dissatisfied with their chosen union, they may submit their own grievance to the Board. If an employer has doubts about his duty to continue bargaining, it is his responsibility to petition the Board for relief, while continuing to bargain in good faith at least until the Board has given some indication that his claim has merit. Although the Board may, if the facts warrant, revoke a certification or agree not to pursue a charge of unfair labor practice, these are matters for the Board; they do not justify the employer self-help or judicial intervention. The underlying purpose of this statute is industrial peace. To allow employers to rely on employees' rights in refusing to bargain with the formally designated union is not conducive to that end, it is inimical to it. Congress has devised a formal mode for selection and rejection of bargaining agents and has fixed the spacing of elections, with a view of furthering industrial stability and with due regard to administrative prudence.

We find wanting the arguments against these controlling considerations. In placing a nonconsenting minority under the bargaining responsibility of an agency selected by a majority of the workers, Congress has discarded common-law doctrines of agency. It is contended that since a bargaining agency may be ascertained by methods less formal than a supervised election, informal repudiation should also be sanctioned where decertification by another election is precluded. This is to make situations that are different appear the same. Finally, it is not within the power of this Court to require the Board, as is suggested, to relieve a small employer, like the one involved in this case, of the duty that may be exacted from an enterprise with many employees.

To be sure, what we have said has special pertinence only to the period during which a second election is impossible. But the Board's view that the one-year period should run from the date of certification rather than the date of election seems within the allowable area of the Board's discretion in carrying out congressional policy. *See Phelps Dodge Corp. v. NLRB,* 313 U.S. 177, 192-197 (1941); *NLRB v. Seven-Up Bottling Co.,* 344 U.S. 344 (1953). Otherwise, encouragement would be given to management or a rival union to delay certification by spurious objections to the conduct of an election and thereby diminish the duration of the duty to bargain. Furthermore, the Board has ruled that one year after certification the employer can ask for an election or, if he has fair doubts about the union's continuing majority, he may refuse to bargain further with it. This, too, is a matter appropriately determined by the Board's administrative authority.

We concluded that the judgment of the Court of Appeals enforcing the Board's order must be

Affirmed.

NOTES

1. Mere inaction during the certification year will not constitute a waiver of a union's bargaining rights. *See Airport Shuttle—Cincinnati, Inc. v. NLRB,* 703 F.2d 220 (6th Cir. 1983) (union did not contact employer for seven months after certification and was completely dormant during that period).

In *Americare-New Lexington Health Care,* 316 N.L.R.B. 1226 (1995), *enforced,* 124 F.3d 753 (6th Cir. 1997), the Board refused to limit the certification year presumption of majority support to the year following the initial certification of unions. It held that the certification year presumption also applies to the twelve-month period following election victories by incumbent unions in *decertification* elections.

2. In *Mar-Jac Poultry Co.,* 136 N.L.R.B. 785 (1962), the Board held that when an employer agrees to bargain in good faith in settlement of a certified union's refusal-to-bargain charge, an election petition by the employer will be denied for twelve months following the settlement agreement. The union was said to be entitled to at least one year of actual bargaining from the date of the settlement. *Accord, Van Dorn Co.,* 300 N.L.R.B. 278 (1990), *enforced,* 939 F.2d 402 (6th Cir. 1991).

In *Bryant & Stratton Business Inst. v. NLRB,* 140 F.3d 169 (2d Cir. 1998), the court sustained a Board order requiring the employer to bargain as if the union's initial certification had been extended for an additional year, despite the fact the parties had engaged in bargaining during the initial certification year, where the Board found that the employer had tainted the earlier negotiations through unfair labor practices designed to undermine union support.

3. An uncertified union that has been lawfully recognized on the basis of a "card check" or the settlement of refusal-to-bargain charges is entitled to retain bargaining rights for a "reasonable period of time." The NLRB will not entertain a decertification petition filed during this period, and the filing of such a petition does not constitute sufficient grounds for the employer to refuse to bargain with the union. *Universal Gear Serv. Corp.,* 157 N.L.R.B. 1169 (1966), *enforced,* 394 F.2d 396 (6th Cir. 1968); *NLRB v. Montgomery Ward & Co.,* 399 F.2d 409 (7th Cir. 1968). How long is "reasonable"? What factors should be considered? *Compare Brennan's Cadillac, Inc.,* 231 N.L.R.B. 225 (1977) (3 months adequate; two members dissenting), *with Vantran Elec. Corp.,* 231 N.L.R.B. 1021 (1977) (4½ months inadequate; one member dissenting), *enforcement denied,* 580 F.2d 921 (7th Cir. 1978).

In *Exxel/Atmos v. NLRB,* 28 F.3d 1243 (D.C. Cir. 1994), the court agreed with the Board that an employer violated § 8(a)(5) when it withdrew recognition from a union it had voluntarily recognized eight months earlier and demanded a representation election. Although the company had some evidence that union support had declined, an employer is not entitled to an election after voluntary recognition until the passage of a "reasonable period of time," which is generally one year. *Compare NLRB v. Albany Steel Co.,* 17 F.3d 564 (2d Cir. 1994), wherein the court concluded that while the employer had unlawfully withdrawn recognition from an incumbent union, it had the right to insist on a secret ballot election before resuming recognition due to the "significant evidence placing the union's majority status in doubt."

4. An employer is also bound to bargain for the period during which an existing labor contract is a bar to a Board election, despite good-faith doubts about the union's continuing majority. This is so whether the union has been certified [*Hexton Furn. Co.,* 111 N.L.R.B. 342 (1955)], or has been recognized voluntarily without an election [*Shamrock Dairy, Inc.,* 119 N.L.R.B. 998 (1957)]. *See also NLRB v. Cornerstone Bldrs.,* 963 F.2d 1075 (8th Cir. 1992) (even unsigned bargaining agreement that would not bar election may prevent employer's unilateral withdrawal of recognition). *See generally* Neary, *The Union's Loss of Majority Status and the Employer's Obligation to Bargain,* 36 Tex. L. Rev. 878 (1958); Weeks, *The Union's Mid-Contract Loss of Majority Support: A Wavering Presumption,* 20 Wake Forest L. Rev. 883 (1984).

5. Although a majority of the employees had signed documents indicating lack of support for the union, withdrawal of recognition was found by the Board to be unlawful when the employer had provided more than ministerial aid to the employees' decertification efforts by getting them an attorney, providing support staff, and correcting the wording of the opposition document. *Vic Koenig Chevrolet, Inc.,* 321 N.L.R.B. 1255 (1996). The Seventh Circuit, however, denied enforcement of the Board order, because it found the NLRB's evaluative criteria unclear and disagreed with the Board's finding of excessive employer involvement. *Vic Koenig Chevrolet v. NLRB,* 126 F.3d 947 (7th Cir. 1997).

AUCIELLO IRON WORKS, INC. v. NLRB

Supreme Court of the United States
517 U.S. 781, 116 S. Ct. 1754, 135 L. Ed. 2d 64 (1996)

JUSTICE SOUTER delivered the opinion of the Court.

The question here is whether an employer may disavow a collective-bargaining agreement because of a good-faith doubt about a union's majority status at the time the contract was made, when the doubt arises from facts known to the employer before its contract offer had been accepted by the union. We hold that the National Labor Relations Board reasonably concluded that an employer challenging an agreement under these circumstances commits an unfair labor practice in violation of §§ 8(a)(1) and (5) of the National Labor Relations Act....

I

Petitioner Auciello Iron Works of Hudson, Massachusetts, had 23 production and maintenance employees during the period in question. After a union election in 1977, the NLRB certified Shopmen's Local No. 501, a/w International Association of Bridge, Structural, and Ornamental Iron Workers, AFL-CIO, as the collective-bargaining representative of Auciello's employees. Over the following years, the company and the Union were able to negotiate a series of collective-bargaining agreements, one of which expired on September 25, 1988. Negotiations for a new one were unsuccessful throughout September and October 1988, however, and when Auciello and the Union had not made a new contract by October 14, 1988, the employees went on strike. Negotiations continued, nonetheless, and, on November 17, 1988, Auciello presented the Union with a complete contract proposal. On November 18, 1988, the picketing stopped, and nine days later, on a Sunday evening, the Union telegraphed its acceptance of the outstanding offer. The very next day, however, Auciello told the Union that it doubted that a majority of the bargaining unit's employees supported the Union, and for that reason disavowed the collective-bargaining agreement and denied it had any duty to continue negotiating. Auciello traced its doubt to knowledge acquired before the Union accepted the contract offer, including the facts that 9 employees had crossed the picket line, that 13 employees had given it signed forms indicating their resignation from the Union, and that 16 had expressed dissatisfaction with the Union.

In January 1989, the Board's General Counsel issued an administrative complaint charging Auciello with violation of §§ 8(a)(1) and (5) of the NLRA. An administrative law judge found that a contract existed between the parties and that Auciello's withdrawal from it violated the Act.... The Board affirmed the administrative law judge's decision;[2] it treated Auciello's claim of good-faith doubt as irrelevant and ordered Auciello to reduce the collective-bargaining agreement to a formal written instrument.... But when the Board applied to the Court of Appeals for the First Circuit for enforcement of its order, the Court of Appeals declined on the ground that the Board had not adequately explained its refusal to consider Auciello's defense of good-faith doubt about the Union's majority status.... On remand, the Board issued a supplemental opinion to justify its position, ... and the Court of Appeals thereafter enforced the order as resting on a "policy choice [both] ... reasonable and ... quite persuasive." 60 F.3d 24, 27 (C.A.1 1995). We granted certiorari, ... and now affirm.

II

A

The object of the National Labor Relations Act is industrial peace and stability, fostered by collective-bargaining agreements providing for the orderly reso-

---

[2] The Board has developed a number of criteria to assess whether a collective-bargaining contract has been formed, see, *e.g., Appalachian Shale Products Co.,* 121 N.L.R.B. 1160 (1958), which may not always coincide with those that would govern in the general area of contract law, see *Ben Franklin Nat. Bank,* 278 N.L.R.B. 986, 993-994 (1986). We accept, for purposes of deciding this case the Board's conclusion that a contract was formed here within the meaning of the Act. Our review of this case is thus limited to the narrow question whether an employer may withdraw from a collective-bargaining contract once formed when it possessed enough evidence to assert a good-faith doubt about the union's majority status at the time of formation.

Auciello has suggested that the contract itself was invalid *ab initio* because the union in fact lacked majority support at the time of acceptance. Because the substantiation required to make this showing is greater than that required to assert a good-faith doubt, see *NLRB v. Curtin Matheson Scientific, Inc.,* 494 U.S. 775, 788, n. 8, the Board has not taken a position on whether such a claim could excuse an employer's decision to repudiate an otherwise valid contract and disavow its duty to bargain with the union. Auciello concedes that it failed to advance this claim in its answer to the General Counsel's complaint, the Board never considered this question, and Auciello sought certiorari review only of the question whether an employer is bound by a union's acceptance in this context when "the Employer had a reasonable basis for a good faith doubt." Pet. for Cert. i. Accordingly, we conclude that this question is not properly before us and decline to address it.

lution of labor disputes between workers and employees.... *Fall River Dyeing & Finishing Corp. v. NLRB*, 482 U.S. 27, 38 (1987). To such ends, the Board has adopted various presumptions about the existence of majority support for a union within a bargaining unit, the precondition for service as its exclusive representative. Cf. *id.*, at 37-39. The first two are conclusive presumptions. A union "usually is entitled to a conclusive presumption of majority status for one year following" Board certification as such a representative. *Id.*, at 37. A union is likewise entitled under Board precedent to a conclusive presumption of majority status during the term of any collective-bargaining agreement, up to three years. See *NLRB v. Burns Int'l Security Services, Inc.*, 406 U.S. 272, 290, n. 12 (1972)....

There is a third presumption, though not a conclusive one. At the end of the certification year or upon expiration of the collective-bargaining agreement, the presumption of majority status becomes a rebuttable one. See *NLRB v. Curtin Matheson Scientific, Inc.*, 494 U.S. 775, 778 (1990); see n. 6, *infra*. Then, an employer may overcome the presumption (when, for example, defending against an unfair labor practice charge) "by showing that, at the time of [its] refusal to bargain, either (1) the union did not *in fact* enjoy majority support, or (2) the employer had a 'good-faith' doubt, founded on a sufficient objective basis, of the union's majority support." *Curtin Matheson, supra,* at 778 (emphasis in original). Auciello asks this Court to hold that it may raise the latter defense even after a collective-bargaining contract period has apparently begun to run upon a union's acceptance of an employer's outstanding offer.

B

The same need for repose that first prompted the Board to adopt the rule presuming the union's majority status during the term of a collective-bargaining agreement also led the Board to rule out an exception for the benefit of an employer with doubts arising from facts antedating the contract. The Board said that such an exception would allow an employer to control the timing of its assertion of good-faith doubt and thus to "'sit' on that doubt and ... raise it after the offer is accepted." 317 N.L.R.B., at 370. The Board thought that the risks associated with giving employers such "unilatera[l] control [over] a vital part of the collective-bargaining process," *ibid.*, would undermine the stability of the collective-bargaining relationship, *id.*, at 374, and thus outweigh any benefit that might in theory follow from vindicating a doubt that ultimately proved to be sound.

The Board's judgment in the matter is entitled to prevail. To affirm its rule of decision in this case, indeed, there is no need to invoke the full measure of the "considerable deference" that the Board is due, *NLRB v. Curtin Matheson Scientific, Inc., supra*, at 786, by virtue of its charge to develop national labor policy ... It might be tempting to think that Auciello's doubt was expressed so soon after the apparent contract formation that little would be lost by vindicating that doubt and wiping the contractual slate clean, if in fact the company can make a convincing case for the doubt it claims. On this view, the loss of repose would be slight. But if doubts about the union's majority status would justify repudiating a contract one day after its ostensible formation, why should the same doubt not serve as well a year into the contract's term? Auciello implicitly agrees on the need to provide some cutoff, but argues that the limit should be expressed as a "reasonable time" to repudiate the contract. That is, it seeks case-by-case determinations of the appropriate time for asserting a good-faith doubt in place of the Board's bright-line rule cutting off the opportunity at the moment of apparent contract formation. Auciello's desire is natural, but its argument fails to point up anything unreasonable in the Board's position.

The Board's approach generally allows companies an adequate chance to act on their preacceptance doubts before contract formation, just as Auciello could have acted effectively under the Board's rule in this case. Auciello knew that the picket line had been crossed and that a number of its employees had expressed dissatisfaction with the Union at least nine days before the contract's acceptance, and all of the resignation forms Auciello received were dated at least five days before the acceptance date. During the week preceding the apparent formation of the contract, Auciello had at least three alternatives to doing nothing. It could have withdrawn the outstanding offer and then, like its employees, petitioned for a representation election. See 29 U.S.C. § 159(c)(1)(A)(ii) (employee petitions); § 159(c)(1)(B) (employer petitions); *NLRB v. Financial Institution Employees,* 475 U.S. 192, 198 (1986). "[I]f the Board determines, after investigation and hearing, that a question of representation exists, it directs an election by secret ballot and certifies the result." *Ibid.* Following withdrawal, it could also have refused to bargain further on the basis of its good-faith doubt, leaving it to the Union to charge an unfair labor practice, against which it could defend on the basis of the doubt. Cf. *Curtin Matheson,* 494 U.S., at 778. And, of course, it could have withdrawn its offer to allow it time to investigate while it continued to fulfil its duty to bargain in good faith with the Union. The company thus had generous opportunities to avoid the presumption before the moment of acceptance.

There may, to be sure, be cases where the opportunity requires prompt action,[6] but labor negotiators are not the least nimble, and the Board could reasonably have thought the price of making more time for the sluggish was too high, since it would encourage bad-faith bargaining. As Auciello would have it, any employer with genuine doubt about a union's hold on its employees would be invited to go right on bargaining, with the prospect of locking in a favorable contract that it could, if it wished, then challenge. Here, for example, if Auciello had acted before the Union's telegram by withdrawing its offer and declining

---

[6] We note that in the unusual circumstance in which evidence leading the employer to harbor such a doubt arises at the same time the union accepts the offer, the Board has agreed to examine such occurrences on a case-by-case basis. 317 N.L.R.B. 364, 374-375 (1995).

further negotiation based on its doubt (or petitioning for decertification), flames would have been fanned, and if it ultimately had been obliged to bargain further, a favorable agreement would have been more difficult to obtain. But by saving its challenge until after a contract had apparently been formed, it could not end up with a worse agreement than the one it had. The Board could reasonably say that giving employers some flexibility in raising their scruples would not be worth skewing bargaining relationships by such one-sided leverage, and the fact that any collective-bargaining agreement might be vulnerable to such a postformation challenge would hardly serve the Act's goal of achieving industrial peace by promoting stable collective-bargaining relationships. Cf. *Fall River Dyeing*, 482 U.S., at 38-39; *Franks Bros. Co. v. NLRB,* 321 U.S. 702, 705 (1944).

Nor do we find anything compelling in Auciello's contention that its employees' statutory right "to bargain collectively through representatives of their own choosing" and to refrain from doing so, 29 U.S.C. § 157, compels us to reject the Board's position. Although we take seriously the Act's command to respect "the free choice of employees" as well as to "promot[e] stability in collective-bargaining relationships," *Fall River Dyeing, supra,* at 38 (internal quotation marks omitted), we have rejected the position that employers may refuse to bargain whenever presented with evidence that their employees no longer support their certified union. "To allow employers to rely on employees' rights in refusing to bargain with the formally designated union is not conducive to [industrial peace], it is inimical to it." *Brooks v. NLRB*, 348 U.S. 96, 103 (1954). The Board is accordingly entitled to suspicion when faced with an employer's benevolence as its workers' champion against their certified union, which is subject to a decertification petition from the workers if they want to file one. There is nothing unreasonable in giving a short leash to the employer as vindicator of its employees' organizational freedom.

C

Merits aside, Auciello also claims that the precedent of *Garment Workers v. NLRB*, 366 U.S. 731 (1961), compels reversal, but it does not. In *Garment Workers*, we held that a bona fide but mistaken belief in a union's majority status cannot support an employer's agreement purporting to recognize a union newly organized but as yet uncertified. We upheld the Board's rule out of concern that an employer and a union could make a deal giving the union "'a marked advantage over any other [union] in securing the adherence of employees,'" *id.,* at 738 (quoting *NLRB v. Pennsylvania Greyhound Lines, Inc.,* 303 U.S. 261, 267 (1938)), thereby distorting the process by which employees elect the bargaining agent of their choice. 366 U.S., at 738-739. Here, in contrast, the Union continued to enjoy a rebuttable presumption of majority support, and the bargaining unit employees had ample opportunity to initiate decertification of the Union but apparently chose not to do so. With entire consistency, the Board may deny employers the power gained from recognizing a union, even when it flows from a good-faith but mistaken belief in a newly organized union's majority status, and at the same time deny them the power to disturb collective-bargaining agreements based on a doubt (without more) that its employees' bargaining agent has retained majority status. Good-faith belief can neither force a union's precipitate recognition nor destroy a recognized union's contracting authority after the fact by intentional delay. There is, indeed, a symmetry in the two positions.

* * *

We hold that the Board reasonably found an employer's precontractual, good-faith doubt inadequate to support an exception to the conclusive presumption arising at the moment a collective-bargaining contract offer has been accepted. We accordingly affirm the judgment of the Court of Appeals for the First Circuit.

It is so ordered.

NLRB v. CURTIN MATHESON SCIENTIFIC, INC.

Supreme Court of the United States
494 U.S. 775, 110 S. Ct. 1542, 108 L. Ed. 2d 801 (1990)

JUSTICE MARSHALL delivered the opinion of the Court.

This case presents the question whether the National Labor Relations Board, in evaluating an employer's claim that it had a reasonable basis for doubting a union's majority support, must presume that striker replacements oppose the union. We hold that the Board acted within its discretion in refusing to adopt a presumption of replacement opposition to the union and therefore reverse the judgment of the Court of Appeals.

I

Upon certification by the NLRB as the exclusive bargaining agent for a unit of employees, a union enjoys an irrebuttable presumption of majority support for one year. *Fall River Dyeing & Finishing Corp. v. NLRB,* 482 U.S. 27, 37 (1987). During that time, an employer's refusal to bargain with the union is per se an unfair labor practice under §§ 8(a)(1) and 8(a)(5) of the National Labor Relations Act.... See *Celanese Corp. of America,* 95 N.L.R.B. 664, 672 (1951); R. Gorman, Labor Law, Unionization and Collective Bargaining 109 (1976). After the first year, the presumption continues but is rebuttable. *Fall River, supra,* at 38. Under the Board's longstanding approach, an employer may rebut that presumption by showing that, at the time of the refusal to bargain, either (1) the union did not *in fact* enjoy majority support, or (2) the employer had a "good faith" doubt, founded on a sufficient objective basis, of the union's majority support. *Station KKHI,* 284 N.L.R.B. 1339 (1987), enf'd, 891 F.2d 230 (CA9 1989). The question presented in this case is whether the Board must, in determining whether an employer has presented sufficient objective evidence of a good-faith doubt, presume that striker replacements oppose the union.

The Board has long presumed that new employees hired in nonstrike circumstances support the incumbent union in the same proportion as the employees they replace. See, e.g., *National Plastic Products Co.,* 78 N.L.R.B. 699, 706 (1948). The Board's approach to evaluating the union sentiments of employees hired to replace strikers, however, has not been so consistent. Initially, the Board appeared to assume that replacements did not support the union. See, e.g., *Stoner Rubber Co.,* 123 N.L.R.B. 1440, 1444 (1959) ....

A 1974 decision, *Peoples Gas System, Inc.,* 214 N.L.R.B. 944 (1974), rev'd and remanded on other grounds *sub nom. Teamsters Local Union 769 v. NLRB,* 174 U.S. App. D.C. 310, 316, 532 F.2d 1385, 1391 (1976), signalled a shift in the Board's approach. The Board recognized that "it is of course possible that the replacements, who had chosen not to engage in the strike activity, might nevertheless have favored union representation." 214 N.L.R.B., at 947. Still, the Board held that "it was not unreasonable for [the employer] to infer that the degree of union support among these employees who had chosen to ignore a Union-sponsored picket line might well be somewhat weaker than the support offered by those who had vigorously engaged in concerted activity on behalf on [*sic*] Union-sponsored objectives." *Ibid.*

A year later, in *Cutten Supermarket,* 220 N.L.R.B. 507 (1975), the Board reversed course completely, stating that striker replacements, like new employees generally, are presumed to support the union in the same ratio as the strikers they replaced. *Id.,* at 509. The Board's initial adherence to this new approach, however, was equivocal. In *Arkay Packaging Corp.,* 227 N.L.R.B. 397 (1976), review denied *sub nom. New York Printing Pressmen & Offset Workers Union, No. 51 v. NLRB,* 575 F.2d 1045 (CA2 1978), the Board stated that "it would be wholly unwarranted and unrealistic to presume as a matter of law that, when hired, the replacements for the union employees who had gone out on strike favored representation by the Unions to the same extent as the strikers." 227 N.L.R.B., at 397-398.... Finally, in 1980, the Board reiterated that the presumption that new employees support the union applies equally to striker replacements. *Pennco, Inc.,* 250 N.L.R.B. 716, 717-718 (1980), enf'd, 684 F.2d 340 (CA6), cert. denied, 459 U.S. 994 (1982).

In 1987, after several Courts of Appeals rejected the Board's approach, the Board determined that no universal generalizations could be made about replacements' union sentiments that would justify a presumption either of support for or of opposition to the union. *Station KKHI,* 284 N.L.R.B. 1339 (1987). On the one hand, the Board found that the prounion presumption lacked empirical foundation because "incumbent unions and strikers sometimes have shown hostility toward the permanent replacements" and "replacements are typically aware of the union's primary concern for the striker's welfare, rather than that of the replacements." *Id.,* at 1344. On the other hand, the Board found that an antiunion presumption was "equally unsupportable" factually. *Ibid.* The Board observed that a striker replacement "may be forced to work for financial reasons, or may disapprove of the strike in question but still desire union representation and would support other union initiatives." *Ibid.* Moreover, the Board found as a matter of policy that adoption of an antiunion presumption would "substantially impair the employees' right to strike by adding to the risk of replacement the risk of loss of the bargaining representative as soon as replacements equal in number to the strikers are willing to cross the picket line." *Ibid.* Accordingly, the Board held that it would not apply any presumption regarding striker replacements' union sentiments, but would determine their views on a case-by-case basis. 284 N.L.R.B., at 1344-1345.

II

We now turn to the Board's application of its *Station KKHI* no-presumption approach in this case. Respondent Curtin Matheson Scientific, Inc., buys and sells laboratory instruments and supplies. In 1970, the Board certified Teamsters Local 968, General Drivers, Warehousemen and Helpers as the collective-bargaining agent for respondent's production and maintenance employees. On May 21, 1979, the most recent bargaining agreement between respondent and the Union expired. Respondent made its final offer for a new agreement on May 25, but the Union rejected that offer. Respondent then locked out the 27 bargaining-unit employees. On June 12, respondent renewed its May 25 offer, but the Union again rejected it. The Union then commenced an economic strike. The record contains no evidence of any strike-related violence or threats of violence.

Five employees immediately crossed the picket line and reported for work. On June 25, while the strike was still in effect, respondent hired 29 permanent replacement employees to replace the 22 strikers. The Union ended its strike on July 16, offering to accept unconditionally respondent's May 25 contract offer. On July 20, respondent informed the Union that the May 25 offer was no longer available. In addition, respondent withdrew recognition from the Union and refused to bargain further, stating that it doubted that the Union was supported by a majority of the employees in the unit. Respondent subsequently refused to provide the Union with information it had requested concerning the total number of bargaining-unit employees on the payroll, and the job classification and seniority of each employee. As of July 20, the bargaining unit consisted of 19 strikers, 25 permanent replacements, and the 5 employees who had crossed the picket line at the strike's inception.

On July 30, the Union filed an unfair labor practice charge with the Board. Following an investigation, the General Counsel issued a complaint, alleging that respondent's withdrawal of recognition, refusal to execute a contract embodying the terms of the May 25 offer, and failure to provide the requested information violated §§ 8(a)(1) and 8(a)(5) of the NLRA.... In its defense to the charge, respondent claimed that it had a reasonably based, good-faith doubt of the Union's majority status. The Administrative Law Judge agreed with respondent and dismissed the complaint. The Board, however, reversed, holding that respondent lacked sufficient objective basis to doubt the Union's majority support. 287 N.L.R.B. No. 35 (1987).

First, the Board noted that the crossover of 5 of the original 27 employees did not in itself support an inference that the 5 had repudiated the Union, because their failure to join the strike may have "indicate[d] their economic concerns rather than a lack of support for the union.".... Second, the Board found that the resignation from their jobs of two of the original bargaining-unit employees, including the chief shop steward, after the commencement of the strike did not indicate opposition to the Union, but merely served to reduce the size of the bargaining unit as of the date of respondent's withdrawal of recognition.... Third, the Board discounted statements made by six employees to a representative of respondent during the strike. Although some of these statements may have indicated rejection of the Union as the bargaining representative, the Board noted, others "appear[ed] ambiguous at best.".... Moreover, the Board stated, "[e]ven attributing to them the meaning most favorable to the Respondent, it would merely signify that 6 employees of a total bargaining unit of approximately 50 did not desire to keep the Union as the collective-bargaining representative."....

Finally, regarding respondent's hiring of striker replacements, the Board stated that, in accordance with the *Station KKHI* approach, it would "not use any presumptions with respect to [the replacements'] union sentiments," but would instead "take a case-by-case approach [and] require additional evidence of a lack of union support on the replacements' part in evaluating the significance of this factor in the employer's showing of good faith doubt.".... The Board noted that respondent's only evidence of the replacements' attitudes toward the Union was its employee relations director's account of a conversation with one of the replacements. The replacement employee reportedly told her that he had worked in union and nonunion workplaces and did not see any need for a union as long as the company treated him well; in addition, he said that he did not think the Union in this case represented the employees.... The Board did not determine whether this statement indicated the replacement employee's repudiation of the Union, but found that the statement was, in any event, an insufficient basis for "inferring the union sentiments of the replacement employees as a group."....

The Board therefore concluded that "the evidence [was] insufficient to rebut the presumption of the Union's continuing majority status.".... Accordingly, the Board held that respondent had violated §§ 8(a)(1) and 8(a)(5) by withdrawing recognition from the Union, failing to furnish the requested information, and refusing to execute a contract embodying the terms respondent had offered on May 25, 1979. The Board ordered respondent to bargain with the Union on request, provide the requisite information, execute an agreement, and make the bargaining-unit employees whole for whatever losses they had suffered from respondent's failure to execute a contract.

The Court of Appeals, in a divided opinion, refused to enforce the Board's order, holding that respondent was justified in doubting the Union's majority support. 859 F.2d 362 (CA5 1988). Specifically, the court rejected the Board's decision not to apply any presumption in evaluating striker replacements' union sentiments and endorsed the so-called "Gorman presumption" that striker replacements oppose the union. We granted certiorari ... to resolve a circuit split on the question whether the Board must presume that striker replacements oppose the union.

III

A

This Court has emphasized often that the NLRB has the primary responsibility for developing and applying national labor policy.... This Court therefore has accorded Board rules considerable deference.... We will uphold a Board rule as long as it is rational and consistent with the Act, ... even if we would have formulated a different rule had we sat on the Board.... Furthermore, a Board rule is entitled to deference even if it represents a departure from the Board's prior policy. See *NLRB v. J. Weingarten, Inc.*, 420 U.S. 251, 265-266 (1975) ("The use by an administrative agency of the evolutional approach is particularly fitting. To hold that the Board's earlier decisions froze the development of this important aspect of the national labor law would misconceive the nature of administrative decisionmaking")....

B

Before assessing the Board's justification for rejecting the antiunion presumption, we will make clear precisely how that presumption would differ in operation from the Board's current approach. As noted above, ... the starting point for the Board's analysis is the basic presumption that the union is supported by a majority of bargaining-unit employees. The employer bears the burden of rebutting that presumption, after the certification year, either by showing that the union in fact lacks majority support or by demonstrating a sufficient objective basis for doubting the union's majority status. Respondent here urges that in evaluating an employer's claim of a good-faith doubt, the Board must adopt a second, subsidiary presumption—that replacement employees oppose the union. Under this approach, if a majority of employees in the bargaining unit were striker replacements, the employer would not need to offer any objective evidence of the employees' union sentiments to rebut the presumption of the union's continuing majority status. The presumption of the replacements' opposition to the union would, in effect, override the presumption of continuing majority status. In contrast, under its no-presumption approach the Board "take[s] into account the particular circumstances surrounding each strike and the hiring of replacements, while retaining the long-standing requirement that the employer must come forth with some objective evidence to substantiate his doubt of continuing majority status." 859 F.2d, at 370 (Williams, J., dissenting).[8]

C

We find the Board's no-presumption approach rational as an empirical matter. Presumptions normally arise when proof of one fact renders the existence of another fact "so probable that it is sensible and timesaving to assume the truth of [the inferred] fact ... until the adversary disproves it." E. Cleary, McCormick on Evidence § 343, p. 969 (3d ed. 1984). Although replacements often may not favor the incumbent union, the Board reasonably concluded, in light of its long experience in addressing these issues, that replacements may in some circumstances desire union representation despite their willingness to cross the picket line. Economic concerns, for instance, may force a replacement employee to work for a struck employer even though he otherwise supports the union and wants the benefits of union representation. In this sense the replacement worker is no different from a striker who, feeling the financial heat of the strike on herself and her family, is forced to abandon the picket line and go back to work. Cf. *Lyng v. Automobile Workers,* 485 U.S. 360, 371 (1988) (recognizing that "a striking individual faces an immediate and often total drop in income during a strike"). In addition, a replacement, like a nonstriker or a strike crossover, may disagree with the purpose or strategy of the particular strike and refuse to support that strike, while still wanting that union's representation at the bargaining table.

Respondent insists that the interests of strikers and replacements are diametrically opposed and that unions inevitably side with the strikers. For instance, respondent argues, picket-line violence often stems directly from the hiring of replacements. Furthermore, unions often negotiate with employers for strike settlements that would return the strikers to their jobs, thereby displacing some or all of the replacements. Respondent asserts that replacements, aware of the union's loyalty to the strikers, most likely would not support the union. In a related argument, respondent contends that the Board's no-presumption approach is irreconcilable with the Board's decisions holding that employers have no duty to bargain with a striking union over replacements' employment terms because the "inherent conflict" between strikers and replacements renders the union incapa-

---

[8]Contrary to respondent's assertion, the Board's no-presumption approach does not constitute an unexplained abandonment of the good-faith doubt defense to a refusal to bargain charge.... This Court has never expressly considered the validity of the good-faith doubt standard.... We decline to address that issue here, as both parties assume the validity of the standard, and resolution of the issue is not necessary to our decision....

ble of "bargain[ing] simultaneously in the best interests of both strikers and their replacements." *Service Electric Co.,* 281 N.L.R.B. 633, 641 (1986)....

These arguments do not persuade us that the Board's position is irrational. Unions do not inevitably demand displacement of all strike replacements....

The extent to which a union demands displacement of permanent replacement workers logically will depend on the union's bargaining power. Under this Court's decision in *NLRB v. Mackay Radio & Telegraph Co.,* 304 U.S. 333 (1938), an employer is not required to discharge permanent replacements at the conclusion of an economic strike to make room for returning strikers; rather, the employer must only reinstate strikers as vacancies arise. The strikers' only chance for immediate reinstatement, then, lies in the union's ability to force the employer to discharge the replacements as a condition for the union's ending the strike. Unions' leverage to compel such a strike settlement will vary greatly from strike to strike. If, for example, the jobs at issue do not require highly trained workers and the replacements perform as well as the strikers did, the employer will have little incentive to hire back the strikers and fire the replacements; consequently, the union will have little bargaining power. Consumers' reaction to a strike will also determine the union's bargaining position. If the employer's customers have no reluctance to cross the picket line and deal with the employer, the union will be in a poor position to bargain for a favorable settlement. Thus, a union's demands will inevitably turn on the strength of the union's hand in negotiations. A union with little bargaining leverage is unlikely to press the employer—at least not very forcefully or for very long—to discharge the replacements and reinstate all the strikers. Cognizant of the union's weak position, many if not all of the replacements justifiably may not fear that they will lose their jobs at the end of the strike. They may still want the union's representation after the strike, though, despite the union's lack of bargaining strength during the strike, because of the union's role in processing grievances, monitoring the employer's actions, and performing other non-strike roles. Because the circumstances of each strike and the leverage of each union will vary greatly, it was not irrational for the Board to reject the antiunion presumption and adopt a case-by-case approach in determining replacements' union sentiments.

Moreover, even if the interests of strikers and replacements conflict during the strike, those interests may converge after the strike, once job rights have been resolved. Thus, while the strike continues, a replacement worker whose job appears relatively secure might well want the union to continue to represent the unit regardless of the union's bargaining posture during the strike....

Furthermore, the Board has not deemed picket-line violence or a union's demand that replacements be terminated irrelevant to its evaluation of replacements' attitudes toward the union. The Board's position, rather, is that "the hiring of permanent replacements who cross a picket line, *in itself,* does not support an inference that the replacements repudiate the union as collective-bargaining representative." *Station KKHI,* 284 N.L.R.B., at 1344 (emphasis added). In both

Station KKHI and this case, the Board noted that the picket line was peaceful, *id.,* at 1345; *Curtin Matheson Scientific,* 287 N.L.R.B., at 352; and in neither case did the employer present evidence that the union was actively negotiating for ouster of the replacements. To the extent that the Board regards evidence of these factors relevant to its evaluation of replacements' union sentiments, then, respondent's contentions ring hollow....

In sum, the Board recognized that the circumstances surrounding each strike and replacements' reasons for crossing a picket line vary greatly. Even if replacements often do not support the union, then, it was not irrational for the Board to conclude that the probability of replacement opposition to the union is insufficient to justify an antiunion presumption.

D

The Board's refusal to adopt an antiunion presumption is also consistent with the Act's "overriding policy" of achieving "'industrial peace.'" *Fall River,* 482 U.S., at 38 (quoting *Brooks v. NLRB,* 348 U.S. 96, 103 (1954)).[12] In *Fall River,* the Court held that the presumption of continuing majority support for a union "further[s] this policy by 'promot[ing] stability in collective-bargaining relationships, without impairing the free choice of employees.'" *Ibid....* The Court reasoned that this presumption "enable[s] a union to concentrate on obtaining and fairly administering a collective-bargaining agreement without worrying that, unless it produces immediate results, it will lose majority support." *Ibid.* (citing *Brooks v. NLRB, supra,* at 100). In addition, this presumption "remove[s] any temptation on the part of the employer to avoid good-faith bargaining in the hope that, by delaying, it will undermine the union's support among the employees." 482 U.S., at 38.

The Board's approach to determining the union views of strike replacements is directed at this same goal because it limits employers' ability to oust a union without adducing any evidence of the employees' union sentiments and encourages negotiated solutions to strikes. It was reasonable for the Board to conclude that the antiunion presumption, in contrast, could allow an employer to eliminate the union merely by hiring a sufficient number of replacement employees. That rule thus might encourage the employer to avoid good-faith bargaining over a strike settlement, and instead to use the strike as a means of removing the union altogether.... Restricting an employer's ability to use a strike as a means of terminating the bargaining relationship serves the policies of promoting industrial stability and negotiated settlements....

Furthermore, it was reasonable for the Board to decide that the antiunion presumption might chill employees' exercise of their statutory right to engage in

---

[12] We do not mean to imply that adoption of the antiunion presumption would be inconsistent with the Act's policy. That question is not before us.

"concerted activities," including the right to strike. If an employer could remove a union merely by hiring a sufficient number of replacements, employees considering a strike would face not only the prospect of being permanently replaced, but also a greater risk that they would lose their bargaining representative, thereby diminishing their chance of obtaining reinstatement through a strike settlement. It was rational for the Board to conclude, then, that adoption of the anti-union presumption could chill employees' exercise of their right to strike.

Although the Board generally may not act "as an arbiter of the sort of economic weapons the parties can use," *NLRB v. Insurance Agents,* 361 U.S. 477, 497 (1960), it may adopt rules restricting conduct that threatens to destroy the collective-bargaining relationship or that may impair employees' rights to engage in concerted activity.... The Board's no-presumption approach is rationally directed at protecting the bargaining process and preserving employees' right to engage in concerted activity. We therefore find, in light of the considerable deference we accord Board rules, ... that the Board's approach is consistent with the Act.

IV

We hold that the Board's refusal to adopt a presumption that striker replacements oppose the union is rational and consistent with the Act. We therefore reverse the judgment of the Court of Appeals and remand for further proceedings consistent with this opinion.

It is so ordered.

[The concurring opinion of CHIEF JUSTICE REHNQUIST and the dissenting opinion of JUSTICE BRENNAN are omitted.]

JUSTICE SCALIA, with whom JUSTICE O'CONNOR and JUSTICE KENNEDY join, dissenting.

The Court makes heavy weather out of what is, under well-established principles of administrative law, a straightforward case. The National Labor Relations Board ... has established as one of the central factual determinations to be made in § 8(a)(5) unfair-labor-practice adjudications, whether the employer had a reasonable, good-faith doubt concerning the majority status of the union at the time it requested to bargain. The Board held in the present case that such a doubt was not established by a record showing that at the time of the union's request a majority of the bargaining unit were strike replacements, and containing no affirmative evidence that any of those replacements supported the union. The question presented is whether that factual finding is supported by substantial evidence. Since the principal employment-related interest of strike replacements (to retain their jobs) is almost invariably opposed to the principal interest of the striking union (to replace them with its striking members) it seems to me impossible to conclude on this record that the employer did not have a reasonable, good-faith doubt regarding the union's majority status. The Board's factual finding being unsupported by substantial evidence, it cannot stand. I therefore dissent from the judgment reversing the Fifth Circuit's refusal to enforce the Board's order....

[O]f the 49 employees in the bargaining unit at the time of respondent's refusal to bargain, a majority (25) were strike replacements, and another 5 were former employees who had crossed the union's picket line. It may well be doubtful whether the latter group could be thought to support the union, but it suffices to focus upon the 25 strike replacements, who must be thought to oppose the union if the Board's own policies are to be believed. There was a deep and inherent conflict between the interests of these employees and the interests of the union....

The respondent in this case, therefore, had an employee bargaining unit a majority of whose members (1) were not entitled to have their best interests considered by the complainant union, (2) would have been foolish to expect their best interests to be considered by that union, and indeed (3) in light of their status as breakers of that union's strike, would have been foolish not to expect their best interests to be subverted by that union wherever possible. There was, moreover, not a shred of affirmative evidence that any strike replacement supported, or had reason to support, the union. On those facts, any reasonable factfinder must conclude that the respondent possessed, not necessarily a certainty, but at least a reasonable, good-faith doubt, that the union did not have majority support....

Also embarrassingly wide of the mark is the Court's observation that "[u]nions do not inevitably demand displacement of all strike replacements."... It is not necessary to believe that unions inevitably demand displacement of all strike replacements in order to doubt (as any reasonable person must) that strike replacements support a union that is under no obligation to take their employment interests into account, and that is almost certain to demand displacement of as many strike replacements as is necessary to reinstate former employees....

It is the proper business of the Board, as of most agencies, to deal in both presumptions (i.e., presumptions of law) and inferences (presumptions of fact). The former it may create and apply *in the teeth of the facts,* as means of implementing authorized law or policy in the course of adjudication. An example is the virtually irrebuttable presumption of majority support for the union during the year following the union's certification by the Board, *Station KKHI,* 284 N.L.R.B., at 1340. The latter, however—inferences (or presumptions of fact)—are not creatures of the Board but its masters, representing the dictates of reason and logic that must be applied in making adjudicatory factual determinations. Whenever an agency's action is reversed in court for lack of "substantial evidence," the reason is that the agency has ignored inferences that reasonably must be drawn, or has drawn inferences that reasonably cannot be. As I have discussed above, that is what happened here....

Of course the Board may choose to implement authorized law or policy in adjudication by *forbidding* a *rational* inference, just as it may do so by *requiring* a *nonrational* one (which is what a presumption of law is). And perhaps it could lawfully have reached the outcome it did here in that fashion—saying that *even though* it must reasonably be inferred that an employer has good-faith doubt of majority status when more than half of the bargaining unit are strike replacements whose job rights have not been resolved, we will not permit that inference to be made. (This would produce an effect close to a rule of law eliminating the good-faith doubt defense except for cases in which the employer can demonstrate, by employee statements, lack of support for the union.) But that is not what the agency did here. It relied on the reasoning of *Station KKHI,* which rested upon the conclusion that, as a matter of logic and reasoning, "the hiring of permanent replacements who cross a picket line, in itself, does not support an inference that the replacements repudiate the union as collective-bargaining representative."... That is simply false. It is bad factfinding, and must be reversed under the "substantial evidence" test....

Stoner Rubber Co., 123 N.L.R.B. 1440 (1959). A union was certified after winning a representation election by a vote of 32 to 27. Contract negotiations broke down and the union struck. Five months after the strike began and fourteen months after the election, the employer was operating with a complement of eighteen permanent replacements and eighteen former strikers who had abandoned the strike. At this point the employer, believing the union no longer represented a majority of the employees, granted a wage increase without consulting the union. The Board held, 3 to 2, there was no violation of § 8(a)(5). Two members reasoned that after the expiration of the certification year, a certification creates only a presumption of continued majority which may be rebutted by employer evidence sufficient to cast serious doubt on the union's status. Thereafter the NLRB General Counsel, to establish a violation, would have to produce proof that on the refusal to bargain date the union in fact represented a majority of the employees. A third member maintained that an employer should not have to act thus at its peril, and that there should be no violation when an employer takes unilateral action after the certification year, so long as it has a reasonable, good-faith belief the union no longer represents a majority. Two members of the Board, dissenting, argued that after the certification year an employer may withdraw recognition if it has a good-faith doubt of continued majority standing, but that it may not take unilateral action without affording the union an opportunity to protect its established position as bargaining representative.

NOTES

1. The NLRB revised the *Stoner Rubber* rules in *Pioneer Flour Mills,* 174 N.L.R.B. 1202 (1969), *enforced,* 427 F.2d 983 (5th Cir.), *cert. denied,* 400 U.S. 942 (1970), to take account of the 1959 amendment to § 9(c)(3) of the NLRA. Since the amendment provides that replaced economic strikers are entitled to vote in any election conducted within twelve months of the commencement of the strike, the Board held that economic strikers must be counted as members of the bargaining unit for the first twelve months of the strike for the purposes of determining the union's majority status in a § 8(a)(5) case.

2. The "serious doubt" that is sufficient to rebut the presumption of a union's continuing majority following expiration of the certification year has two components: (1) a reasonable basis in fact, and (2) good faith. *Johns-Manville Sales Corp. v. NLRB,* 906 F.2d 1428 (10th Cir. 1990), involved a bitter and violent work stoppage that began on April 12. By May 10 there were 509 "employees"— 230 strikers, 267 permanent replacements, and 12 cross-overs who decided to work during the strike. After a decertification petition containing the names of 211 individuals was filed with the Labor Board, the employer withdrew recognition from the incumbent union. The Labor Board found a § 8(a)(5) violation, since the company failed to provide objective evidence to indicate that a majority of the "employees" had rejected union representation. The Tenth Circuit ruled that the Board erred in requiring proof of antiunion sentiment expressed by a majority of employees on an individual basis. It concluded that "objective manifestations of lack of majority support" justifying the employer's withdrawal of recognition could be found in six factors: (1) the hiring of 267 replacement workers; (2) the pervasive strike violence; (3) the decertification petition containing 211 names; (4) numerous comments to plant managers by replacement workers disparaging the union and rejecting union representation; (5) union resignations by seven nonstrikers; and (6) the union's sole remaining contract demand for striker reinstatement and its failure to attempt to organize the replacement workers. *Compare Liquid Carriers Corp.,* 319 N.L.R.B. 317 (1995), *enforced,* 101 F.3d 691 (3d Cir. 1996), wherein the Board held that an employer did not have an objective basis for a good-faith doubt concerning a striking union's continued majority status, even though the union had expressed animosity toward the strike replacements and had never abandoned its demand for their removal and the reinstatement of the strikers.

The filing of a decertification petition is generally not sufficient to establish a bona fide doubt regarding an incumbent union's presumed continuing majority support—even when accompanied by some inactivity at the bargaining table. *NLRB v. Flex Plastics,* 726 F.2d 272 (6th Cir. 1984).

NLRB v. New Assocs., 35 F.3d 828 (3d Cir. 1994), involved an employer that had withdrawn recognition from an incumbent union following the filing of a decertification petition with the NLRB. Since the Board had declined to disclose the fact that a majority of unit employees had signed the decertification petition, the court held that the employer had a sufficient basis for withdrawing recognition. The court indicated that an employer may withdraw recognition whenever it *or* the Labor Board is aware of the fact that a majority of unit members have signed a decertification petition.

3. A significant change in the identity of the incumbent union due to affiliation with a new international labor organization may generate sufficient confusion regarding that union's continued majority status to support an employer's recognition withdrawal. *United Elec. Workers v. NLRB (Newell Porcelain Co.),* 986 F.2d 70 (4th Cir. 1993). *Compare Sullivan Bros. Printers,* 317 N.L.R.B. 561 (1995), *affirmed,* 99 F.3d 1217 (1st Cir. 1996) (merger of two sister locals not significant enough change to relieve employer of duty to bargain with resulting entity).

See generally LeRoy, *Strike Crossovers and Striker Replacements: An Empirical Test of the NLRB's No-Presumption Policy,* 33 Ariz. L. Rev. 291 (1991); Flynn, *The Economic Strike Bar: Looking Beyond the "Union Sentiments" of Permanent Replacements,* 61 Temple L. Rev. 691 (1988); Ray, *Industrial Stability and Decertification Elections: Need for Reform,* 1984 Ariz. St. L.J. 257; Comment, *Application of the Good-Faith-Doubt Test to the Presumption of Continued Majority Status of Incumbent Unions,* 1981 Duke L.J. 718; Note, *Employee Postcertification Polls to Determine Union Support,* 84 Mich. L. Rev. 1770 (1986).

4. When an employer decides to conduct a *Struksnes* poll to determine whether an incumbent representative continues to enjoy majority support, the company must be able to demonstrate that objective considerations provide it with a "reasonable doubt" concerning the union's current majority status—the same burden applicable to cases in which an employer simply withdraws recognition. *Allentown Mack Sales & Service v. NLRB,* 118 S. Ct. 818 (1998).

5. In *Midwest Piping & Supply Co.,* 63 N.L.R.B. 1060 (1945), the Board ruled an employer violated § 8(1) (§ 8(a)(1)) by negotiating a contract with one of two rival unions whose representation petitions were pending before the Board. Extensions of the *Midwest Piping* doctrine were cut back in *Bruckner Nursing Home,* 262 N.L.R.B. 955 (1982), which held that an employer may lawfully recognize and contract with a labor organization that represents an uncoerced majority in a rival-union, initial organizing situation, so long as no valid election petition has been filed with the Board. *See also Dresser Indus.,* 264 N.L.R.B. 1088 (1982) (decertification petition). In *RCA Del Caribe, Inc.,* 262 N.L.R.B. 963 (1982), the Labor Board held that the mere filing of a representation petition by an outside union will no longer prevent an employer from bargaining or contracting with an incumbent union. Under the new rule, an employer would violate § 8(a)(5) of the Act by withdrawing from negotiations solely because of the rival union's pending petition. *See* Estreicher & Telsey, *A Recast Midwest Piping Doctrine: The Case for Judicial Acceptance,* 36 Lab. L.J. 14 (1985).

6. In *John Deklewa & Sons,* 282 N.L.R.B. 1375 (1987), *enforced,* 843 F.2d 770 (3d Cir.), *cert. denied,* 488 U.S. 889 (1988), the Board overruled *R.J. Smith Constr. Co.,* 191 N.L.R.B. 693 (1971), and announced that henceforth it would apply the following principles to § 8(f) "prehire contracts" in the construction industry:

(1) a collective-bargaining agreement permitted by Section 8(f) shall be enforceable through the mechanisms of Section 8(a)(5) and Section 8(b)(3); (2) such agreements will not bar the processing of valid petitions filed pursuant to Section 9(c) and Section 9(e); (3) in processing such petitions, the appropriate unit normally will be the single employer's employees covered by the agreement; and (4) upon the expiration of such agreements, the signatory union will enjoy no presumption of majority status, and either party may repudiate the 8(f) bargaining relationship.

The Board's *Deklewa* principles have been accepted by appellate courts. *See, e.g., NLRB v. Bufco Corp.,* 899 F.2d 608 (7th Cir. 1990); *Mesa Verde Constr. Co. v. Northern Cal. Dist. Council of Laborers,* 861 F.2d 1124 (9th Cir. 1988) (*en banc*).

Since a union demand for a prehire agreement does not constitute a claim of majority support, such a request does not provide the basis for the filing of a representation petition by the target employer. *PSM Steel Constr.,* 309 N.L.R.B. 1302 (1992).

A construction union may enforce a prehire contract under § 301 of the LMRA against corporate entities related to the signatory employer, regardless of proof of majority status in a Board-determined appropriate unit. *IBEW Local 613 v. Fowler Indus.,* 884 F.2d 551 (11th Cir. 1989), *cert. denied,* 494 U.S. 1066 (1990).

AMERICAN SEATING CO.

National Labor Relations Board
106 N.L.R.B. 250 (1953)

....

The facts in the case are undisputed. On September 20, 1949, following an election, the Board certified International Union, Automobile, Aircraft and Agricultural Implement Workers of America (UAW-CIO), and its Local No. 135, herein called the UAW-CIO, as bargaining representative of the Respondent's production and maintenance employees. On July 1, 1950, the Respondent and the UAW-CIO entered into a three-year collective bargaining contract covering all employees in the certified unit. Shortly before the expiration of two years from the date of signing of the contract, Pattern Makers' Association of Grand Rapids, Pattern Makers' League of North America, AFL, herein called the Union, filed a representation petition seeking to sever a craft unit of patternmakers from the existing production and maintenance unit. Both the Respondent and the UAW-CIO opposed the petition, contending that their three-year contract which would not expire until July 1, 1953, was a bar. In a decision issued on September 4, 1952, the Board rejected this contention. It held that, as the contract had been in existence for two years, and as the contracting parties had failed to establish that contracts for three-year terms were customary in the seating industry, the contract was not a bar during the third year of its term. Accordingly, the Board directed an election in a unit of patternmakers, which the Union won.

On October 6, 1952, the Board certified the Union as bargaining representative of the Respondent's patternmakers. Approximately ten days later, the Union submitted to the Respondent a proposed collective bargaining agreement covering terms and conditions of employment for patternmakers to be effective immediately. The Respondent replied that it recognized the Union as bargaining representative of the patternmakers and that it was willing to negotiate or discuss subjects properly open for discussion, but that the existing contract with the UAW-CIO was still in full force and effect and remained binding upon all employees, including patternmakers, until its July 1, 1953, expiration date.

... The Respondent contends that the certification of the Pattern Makers merely resulted in the substitution of a new bargaining representative for patternmakers in place of the old representative, with the substantive terms of the contract remaining unchanged. In support of this position, the Respondent argues that the UAW-CIO was the agent of the patternmakers when it entered into the 1950 agreement with that organization, and that the patternmakers, as principals, are bound by that contract to the expiration date thereof, notwithstanding that they have changed their agent. The General Counsel, on the other hand, contends that the certification of the Pattern Makers resulted in making the existing contract with the UAW-CIO inoperative as to the employees in the unit of patternmakers.

The Respondent's principal-agent argument assumes that common-law principles of agency control the relationship of exclusive bargaining representative to employees in an appropriate unit. We think that this assumption is unwarranted and overlooks the unique character of that relationship under the National Labor Relations Act.

... A duly selected statutory representative is the representative of a shifting group of employees in an appropriate unit which includes not only those employees who approve such relationship, but also those who disapprove and those who have never had an opportunity to express their choice. Under agency principles, a principal has the power to terminate the authority of his agent at any time. Not so in the case of a statutory bargaining representative. Thus, in its most important aspects the relationship of statutory bargaining representative to employees in an appropriate unit resembles a political rather than a private law relationship. In any event, because of the unique character of the statutory representative, a solution for the problem presented in this case must be sought in the light of that special relationship rather than by the device of pinning labels on the various parties involved and applying without change principles of law evolved to govern entirely different situations.

... One of the problems in this connection arises from the claim that a collective bargaining contract of fixed term should bar a new election during the entire term of such contract. In solving this problem, the Board has had to balance two separate interests: The interest of employees and society in the stability that is essential to the effective encouragement of collective bargaining, and the some-times conflicting interest of employees in being free to change their representa-tives at will. Reconciling these two interests in the early days of the Act, the Board decided that it would not consider a contract of unreasonable duration a bar to an election to determine a new bargaining representative. The Board fur-ther decided that a contract of more than one year was of unreasonable duration and that it would direct an election after the first year of the existence of such a contract. In 1947, in the further interest of stability, the Board extended from one to two years the period during which a valid collective bargaining contract would be considered a bar to a new determination of representatives.

... If the Respondent's contention is sound, a certified bargaining representa-tive might be deprived of effective statutory power as to the most important sub-jects of collective bargaining for an unlimited number of years as the result of an agreement negotiated by an unwanted and repudiated bargaining representative. There is no provision in the statute for this kind of emasculated certified bar-gaining representative. Moreover, the rule urged by the Respondent seems hardly calculated to reduce "industrial strife" by encouraging the "practice and proce-dure of collective bargaining," the declared purpose of the National Labor Rela-tions Act, as amended.

The purpose of the Board's rule holding a contract of unreasonable duration not a bar to a new determination of representatives is the democratic one of in-suring to employees the right at reasonable intervals of reappraising and chang-ing, if they so desire, their union representation. Bargaining representatives are thereby kept responsive to the needs and desires of their constituents; and em-ployees dissatisfied with their representative know that they will have the op-portunity of changing them by peaceful means at an election conducted by an impartial Government agency. Strikes for a change of representatives are thereby reduced and effects of employee dissatisfaction with their representatives are mitigated. But, if a newly chosen representative is to be hobbled in the way pro-posed by the Respondent, a great part of the benefit to be derived from the no-bar rule will be dissipated. There is little point in selecting a new bargaining repre-sentative which is unable to negotiate new terms and conditions of employment for an extended period of time.

We hold that, for the reasons which led the Board to adopt the rule that a con-tract of unreasonable duration is not a bar to a new determination of representa-tives, such a contract may not bar full statutory collective bargaining, including the reduction to writing of any agreement reached, as to any group of employees in an appropriate unit covered by such contract, upon the certification of a new collective bargaining representative for them. Accordingly, we find that by re-fusing on and after October 16, 1952, to bargain with the Pattern Makers con-cerning wages, hours, and other working conditions for employees in the unit of patternmakers, the Respondent violated §§ 8(a)(5) and (1) of the Act....

NOTES

1. Would the newly certified union in the principal case be free to strike for changes in contract terms? *Compare* § 8(d)(4) of the NLRA. Should the employer as well as the union be entitled to demand bargaining for a new contract?

2. *See generally* Cox, *The Legal Nature of Collective Bargaining Agreements,* 57 Mich. L. Rev. 1, 7-14 (1958); Freidin, *The Board, "The Bar," and the Bargain,* 59 Colum. L. Rev. 61, 82 (1959); Comment, *Union Affiliations and Collective Bargaining,* 128 U. Pa. L. Rev. 430 (1979).

———————

Garment Workers Local 57 v. NLRB [Garwin Corp.], 374 F.2d 295 (D.C. Cir.), *cert. denied,* 387 U.S. 942 (1967). The employer, without consulting the union about its decision, closed its plant in New York City, discharged its employees, and moved its operations to Miami, Florida. The NLRB found the move was motivated by antiunion sentiment, not economic necessity, and held the employer in violation of § 8(a)(5), (3), and (1) of the Act. In addition to ordering reinstatement and back pay for the workers, the Board ordered the "runaway" employer to bargain with the union either at the New York plant or the new Florida location, regardless of whether the union had majority status. The court of appeals refused enforcement of the bargaining portion of the Board's order, saying "the remedy fashioned by the Board in this case imposes on the Florida workers a bargaining representative without reference to their choice." Removing the benefits of the employer's wrongdoing, "standing alone and without relationship to redressing grievances of the New York workers, who suffered the violation of their statutory rights," was not enough "to justify infringing fundamental rights of comparable magnitude vested by law in the Florida workers." A dissenting judge stated: "That the Board, in striking a balance between the need to protect a collective bargaining relationship and the interests of new employees in being free to select their own bargaining agent, has determined to give precedence to the former is, in my view, a judgment consistent with its statutory responsibilities." [On remand, the Board ordered bargaining upon proof of a union majority in Florida. 169 N.L.R.B. 1030 (1968), *enforced,* 70 L.R.R.M. 2465 (D.C. Cir.), *cert. denied,* 395 U.S. 980 (1969).]

NOTES

1. A widespread phenomenon of recent years, especially in construction, has been the formation by unionized firms of nonunion subsidiaries to permit more competitive bidding for work in the nonunion sector of an industry. What doctrines and policies studied to date are relevant in determining the legal status of these "double-breasted" operations? *Compare South Prairie Constr. Co. v. Operating Eng'rs Local 627,* 425 U.S. 800 (1976) *with Appalachian Constr., Inc.,* 235

N.L.R.B. 685 (1978). *See generally* Bornstein, *The Emerging Law of the "Double Breasted" Operation in the Construction Industry,* 28 Lab. L.J. 77 (1977); Befort, *Labor Law and the Double-Breasted Employer: A Critique of the Single Employer and Alter Ego Doctrines and a Proposed Reformulation,* 1987 Wis. L. Rev. 67.

2. Special problems arise when one employer succeeds to the status of another, whether by purchase, merger, or otherwise, and the predecessor's employees are represented by a union and covered by an outstanding collective bargaining agreement. The bargaining rights and duties of the successor employer in such circumstances, the propriety of unilateral action on its part, and the possible survival of contractual obligations, will be treated together in Part Four, Section III.E, *infra.*

PART THREE

UNION COLLECTIVE ACTION

SELIG PERLMAN, A THEORY OF THE LABOR MOVEMENT 238-42 (1928)

In an economic community, there is a separation between those who prefer a secure, though modest return—that is to say, a mere livelihood—and those who play for big stakes and are willing to assume risk in proportion. The first compose the great bulk of manual workers of every description ... while the latter are, of course, the entrepreneurs and the big business men. The limited or unlimited purpose is, in either case, the product of a simple survey of accessible economic opportunity and of a psychic self-appraisal. The manual worker is convinced by experience that he is living in a world of limited opportunity. He sees, to be sure, how others, for instance business men, are finding the same world a storehouse of apparently unlimited opportunity. Yet he decisively discounts that, so far as he is himself concerned. The business man, on the contrary, is an eternal optimist. To him the world is brimful of opportunities that are only waiting to be made his own....

The economic pessimism of the manual group is at the bottom of its characteristic manner of adjusting the relation of the individual to the whole group. It prompts also the attitude of exclusion which manual groups assume towards those regarded as "outsiders." Again the manualist's psychology can best be brought out by contrast with that of the fully developed business man. Basically the business man is an economic individualist, a competitor *par excellence.* If opportunity is plentiful, if the enterprising person can create his own opportunity, what sane object can there be in collectively controlling the extent of the individual's appropriation of opportunity, or in drastically excluding those from other localities? Nor will this type of individual submit to group control, for he is confident of his ability to make good bargains for himself. If, on the contrary, opportunity is believed to be limited, as in the experience of the manual worker, it then becomes the duty of the group to prevent the individual from appropriating more than his rightful share, while at the same time protecting him against oppressive bargains. *The group then asserts its collective ownership over the whole amount of opportunity,* and, having determined who are entitled to claim a share in that opportunity, undertakes to parcel it out fairly, directly or indirectly, among its recognized members, permitting them to avail themselves of such opportunities, job or market, only on the basis of a "common rule." Free competition becomes a sin against one's fellows, anti-social, like a self-indulgent consumption of the stores of a beleaguered city, and obviously detrimental to the individual as

353

well. A collective disposal of opportunity, including the power to keep out unde-sirables, and a "common rule" in making bargains are as natural to the manual group as *"laissez-faire"* is to the business man.

NEIL W. CHAMBERLAIN, THE PHILOSOPHY OF AMERICAN MANAGEMENT TOWARD LABOR, in LABOR IN A CHANGING AMERICA 181-82 (W. Haber ed. 1966)*

When a businessman strives for cost reduction, quality control, an improved rate of output, he is simply conforming to the institutional role which has been written for him by the society of which he is a part. But inescapably, that role brings him into conflict with organized labor, whose own institutional role is bound up with preserving the income continuity of its members, protecting the value of their learned skills, relaxing disciplinary and production pressures. It is not a matter of one of these groups being right and the other wrong, or of one being narrowly preoccupied with money values and the other more broadly con-cerned with human values. It is simply that American society has written differ-ent scripts for these two sets of economic performers, and the roles in which they are respectively cast *call* for a clash of objectives on the economic stage....

... The consequence of this continuing encounter is readily predictable. In terms of management's philosophical disposition toward organized labor, it leads to a state of mind where unions are identified with efforts to interfere with that efficient performance which society expects of business—to interfere by such tactics as fighting for the retention of outworn work rules and customs, opposing new technologies, insisting on rewards for long service rather than ability. One can hardly expect managers to look benignly on those who are impeding it in doing its job, however sincere or well motivated they may be.

LLOYD G. REYNOLDS, STANLEY H. MASTERS & COLLETTA H. MOSER, LABOR ECONOMICS AND LABOR RELATIONS 495, 497, 512 (9th ed. 1986)**

In an average year, about 2 million workers are involved in strikes. This is about 10 percent of union members, and 2.5 percent of all employed workers. The average length of strikes is about four weeks. The amount of time lost through strikes, as a proportion of total working time in the economy, averages about 0.20 percent.... There has been no significant uptrend or downtrend in strike activity over the past 30 years. In only three years has the proportion of working time lost exceeded 0.25 percent....

To discover [what] was responsible for a particular strike requires careful analysis of the circumstances. The union normally makes the first overt move, and the public therefore tends to regard it as the aggressor. The employer can cause a strike by doing nothing; the union has to take the positive step of calling out the workers. But all one can conclude from the fact of a strike is that there was a failure to reach agreement. The reasons for the failure can be learned from an inside knowledge of the people and issues involved....

As regards economic cost, one must distinguish between private and social cost, between cost to the parties and cost to the economy. The striking workers lose some wages and the company loses some profit. These are losses that the parties consider it worthwhile to bear rather than settle on adverse terms. The loss to the economy consists in a reduced output of goods and services available for consumption or investment.

A strike may not involve any loss in national output. In a seasonal industry, a strike may simply change the location of the slack season. A strike in men's clothing factories early in the spring season means only that the factories will have to work longer at the end of the season to make up for lost time. In this case there is not even a loss of income to the parties, merely a postponement of income to a later date....

SECTION I. Introduction

It is apparent that labor organizations are not mere fraternal societies conducting polite social functions. They are militant groups formed for the primary purpose of advancing what are conceived to be the economic interests of their members, and they have not been content to rely exclusively on the art of persuasion through exhortation either in gaining members or in wresting concessions from employers. From the beginning they have also made use also of economic and political action to gain their ends. Economic action has typically taken the form of the strike, the picket line, and the boycott.

A. COLLECTIVE ACTION AT COMMON LAW

Part One contained a brief treatment of the early antecedents of American labor law and an outline of the principles that courts have used, or purportedly used, when deciding cases involving collective action by labor groups. It was suggested that the concept most frequently found in the cases was that union activities that inflict injury had to be tested by the propriety of the objective being sought and the means being used. This is the general principle which, in 1938, was articulated by Professor Shulman and his assisting experts in the *Torts Restatement* of the law of labor disputes. The rules stated in the *Restatement* were by no means universally accepted by the courts, and there is a real question whether anything purporting to be an actual "restatement" could reasonably be attempted.

We have come a long way from the views represented in the early nineteenth century criminal conspiracy cases. The right of individuals to quit their jobs is considered to be inviolate, at least as against injunctive or other official restraint, and the peaceful strike is privileged at common law, at least as long as the objective is "proper" and it does not go beyond the "proper" area for economic action. Picketing has had more difficulty in gaining recognition as an accepted method of collective action, because, it has carried in the minds of some judges connotations of violence regardless of its actual physical characteristics. Many courts have been quick to seize upon the slightest manifestation of violence or abuse (e.g., numbers of picketers, minor breaches of peace, rough and tumble and frequently "unnice" language) as a pretext for granting relief despite lip service to the doctrine, now generally established, that peaceful and nonfraudulent picketing for a proper objective is lawful. The boycott has fared least well, particularly when it has been found to be "secondary."

Labor law with respect to union collective action can be thought of as consisting of four layers. The common law, which we have been discussing, is the underlying layer. It is essentially tort law, and most of the cases involved the equitable injunctive remedy. When union activity would be characterized as tortious, either because of its wrongful objective or its wrongful means, the next question to be considered by a court would be whether there is an anti-injunction statute which prevents issuance of the decree. This may be thought of as the second layer of labor law.

B. ANTI-INJUNCTION STATUTES

An attempt was made in 1914 to get the federal courts out of the business of issuing injunctions in labor disputes by the passage of the Clayton Act. However, this legislative effort was not fully effective. One frequent basis for an injunction in the federal courts was the Sherman Antitrust Act. During the decade of the 1920s, in such cases as *Duplex Printing Press Co. v. Deering,* 254 U.S. 443 (1921), and *Bedford Cut Stone Co. v. Journeymen Stone Cutters' Ass'n,* 274 U.S. 37 (1927), the federal courts continued to issue injunctions against secondary boycotts as violations of the antitrust laws.

Public dissatisfaction with the labor injunction grew in the late 1920s and early 1930s, with agitation for reform coming not only from representatives of the labor movement, but also from persons in the legal profession who were concerned about the reputation of the judicial system. The particularized evils of the labor injunction that were highly publicized at this time are set forth in the historical introduction (Part One, *supra*). *See generally* F. Frankfurter & N. Greene, The Labor Injunction (1930).

The Norris-La Guardia Act, enacted in 1932, operates as a restriction upon the equity jurisdiction of the federal courts in cases involving or growing out of *labor disputes* (*see* § 13). The act is set out in *Selected Federal Statutes*. Its incidence is twofold: (1) it lays down certain definite requirements of procedure and proof (which we shall refer to as "procedural" requirements) that must be met before an injunction may issue (*see* §§ 6, 7, 8, 9, 10, 11 and 12); and (2) it removes from the federal courts all "jurisdiction" to restrain certain specified kinds of acts, even though the procedural requirements are met (*see* § 4). The validity of the Norris-La Guardia Act was sustained in *Lauf v. E.G. Shinner & Co.,* 303 U.S. 323 (1938).

The Norris Act has now been substantially duplicated by state legislation in a number of states, in some instances with variations designed to meet specific problems considered important. Another substantial group of states have statutes more limited in scope, some of which are of the Clayton Act variety. For a summary of the legislative pattern, *see* Smith & Delancey, *The State Legislatures and Unionism,* 38 Mich. L. Rev. 987, 1013-20 (1940). For the current status of anti-injunction acts in particular states, *see* the state labor law volume of one of the loose-leaf labor law services. The constitutionality of the Wisconsin anti-injunction act was sustained in *Senn v. Tile Layers Protection Union,* 301 U.S. 468 (1937).

MARINE COOKS & STEWARDS v. PANAMA STEAMSHIP CO.

Supreme Court of the United States
362 U.S. 365, 80 S. Ct. 779, 4 L. Ed. 2d 797 (1960)

MR. JUSTICE BLACK delivered the opinion of the Court.

The respondents, who are the owner, time charterer, and master of the Liberian registered vessel, S.S. Nikolos, brought this action in a United States District Court against the petitioner union and its members praying for temporary and permanent injunctions to restrain, and for damages allegedly suffered from, the union's peaceful picketing of the ship in American waters and its threats to picket shore consignees of the ship's cargo should they accept delivery. The union's sole contention was that the District Court was without jurisdiction to restrain the picketing because of the Norris-La Guardia Act which states in § 1:

> That no court of the United States, as herein defined, shall have jurisdiction to issue any restraining order or temporary or permanent injunction in a case involving or growing out of a labor dispute, except in a strict conformity with the provisions of this Act; nor shall any such restraining order or temporary or permanent injunction be issued contrary to the public policy declared in this Act.

Section 4 of that same law specifically denies jurisdiction to District Courts to issue any restraining order or temporary or permanent injunction to prohibit unions from:

> (e) Giving publicity to the existence of, or the facts involved in, any labor dispute, whether by advertising, speaking, patrolling, or by any other method not involving fraud or violence; ...

Notwithstanding these provisions of the Norris-La Guardia Act and despite an express finding that the union and its members had not been guilty of fraud, or threatened or committed any acts of physical violence to any person or any property, the District Court issued a temporary injunction to restrain the picketing. The injunction prohibited picketing by the petitioner union of "the S.S. 'Nikolos' or any other vessel registered under a foreign flag and manned by an alien crew and owned, operated or chartered by" respondents, in the Puget Sound area. This action of the court was based on its conclusions that (a) the case did not involve or grow out of any labor dispute within the meaning of the Norris-La Guardia Act and (b) even if there were a labor dispute within the meaning of that Act, the court had jurisdiction to restrain the picketing because it interfered in the internal economy of a vessel registered under the flag of a friendly foreign power and amounted to "an unlawful interference with foreign commerce." The court's conclusion rested on the following facts, about which there was no substantial dispute.

The petitioner and other national labor organizations act as bargaining representatives for most of the unlicensed personnel of vessels that fly the American flag on the Pacific Coast. Petitioner alone, pursuant to National Labor Relations Board certification, represents employees of the stewards department on a large majority of those vessels. The S.S. Nikolos is owned by a Liberian corporation, was time-chartered for this trip by another Liberian corporation, and all members of its crew were aliens working under employment contracts made outside this country. There was no labor dispute between the ship's employees and the ship. The Nikolos picked up a cargo of salt in Mexico and carried it to the harbor of the port of Tacoma, Washington, for delivery to an American consignee there. After the ship entered the Tacoma harbor it was met by the union's boat which began to circle around the Nikolos displaying signs marked "PICKET BOAT." Later an additional sign was put on the boat reading: "AFL-CIO seamen protest loss of their livelihood to foreign flag ships with sub-standard wages or sub-standard conditions." The union threatened to extend its picketing to the consignee of the salt should an attempt be made to berth and unload that cargo. Although the picketing was peaceful and there was no fraud, the result was that the ship could not deliver its cargo.

On appeal from the temporary injunction to the Court of Appeals the petitioner argued that the injunction granted by the District Court was beyond the jurisdiction of that court because of the provisions of § 4 of the Norris-La Guardia Act,

but the Court of Appeals rejected that contention and upheld the injunction....
Certiorari was granted to consider the question of the applicability of the Norris-
La Guardia Act here.

That Act's language is broad. The language is broad because Congress was
intent upon taking the federal courts out of the labor injunction business except in
the very limited circumstances left open for federal jurisdiction under the Norris-
La Guardia Act. The history and background that led Congress to take this view
have been adverted to in a number of prior opinions of this Court in which we
refused to give the Act narrow interpretations that would have restored many labor dispute controversies to the courts.[7]

It is difficult to see how this controversy could be thought to spring from anything except one "concerning terms or conditions of employment," and hence a
labor dispute within the meaning of the Norris-La Guardia Act. The protest stated
by the pickets concerned "sub-standard wages or sub-standard conditions." The
controversy does involve, as the Act requires, "persons who are engaged in the
same industry, trade, craft or occupation." And it is immaterial under the Act that
the unions and the ship and the consignees did not "stand in a proximate relation
of employer and employee." This case clearly does grow out of a labor dispute
within the meaning of the Norris-La Guardia Act.

The District Court held, however, that even if this case involved a labor dispute under the Norris-La Guardia Act the court had jurisdiction to issue the injunction because the picketing was an "unlawful interference with foreign commerce" and interfered "in the internal economy of a vessel registered under the
flag of a friendly foreign power" and prevented "such a vessel from lawfully
loading or discharging cargo at ports in the United States." The Court of Appeals
adopted this position, but cited no authority for its statement that the picketing
was "unlawful," nor have the respondents in this Court pointed to any statute or
persuasive authority proving that petitioner's conduct was unlawful. Compare
§ 20 of the Clayton Act, 15 U.S.C. § 20. And even if unlawful, it would not follow that the federal court would have jurisdiction to enjoin the particular conduct
which § 4 of the Norris-La Guardia Act declared shall not be enjoined. Nor does
the language of the Norris-La Guardia Act leave room to hold that jurisdiction it
denies a District Court to issue a particular type of restraining order can be restored to it by a finding that the nonenjoinable conduct may "interfere in the internal economy of a vessel registered under the flag of a friendly foreign power."

---

[7] ... "The underlying aim of the Norris-La Guardia Act was to restore the broad purpose which
Congress thought it had formulated in the Clayton Act but which was frustrated, so Congress believed, by unduly restrictive judicial construction." *United States v. Hutcheson*, 312 U.S. 219, 236.

This congressional purpose, as is well known, was prompted by a desire to protect the rights of
laboring men to organize and bargain collectively and to withdraw federal courts from a type of
controversy for which many believed they were ill-suited and from participation in which, it was
feared, judicial prestige might suffer. *See* Frankfurter and Greene, The Labor Injunction (1930), at
200; Gregory, Labor and the Law (1958), at 184-199.

Congress passed the Norris-La Guardia Act to curtail and regulate the jurisdiction of courts, not, as they passed the Taft-Hartley Act, to regulate the conduct of people engaged in labor disputes.... [T]he ship that voluntarily enters the territorial limits of this country subjects itself to our laws and jurisdiction as they exist. The fact that a foreign ship enters a United States court as a plaintiff cannot enlarge the jurisdiction of that court. There is not presented to us here, and we do not decide, whether the picketing of petitioner was tortious under state or federal law. All we decide is that the Norris-La Guardia Act deprives the United States court of jurisdiction to issue the injunction it did under the circumstances shown.

The judgment of the Court of Appeals is reversed and the case is remanded to the District Court with directions to dismiss the petition for injunction.

It is so ordered.

NOTES

1. In *New Negro Alliance v. Sanitary Grocery Co.,* 303 U.S. 552 (1938), the Supreme Court reversed the granting of an injunction against the New Negro Alliance, an incorporated association (not a labor union) that was boycotting and picketing a grocery store, demanding that the store hire blacks. The Supreme Court applied the Norris-La Guardia Act, reasoning that the parties in a labor dispute need not have the relationship of employer and employee, and that the Alliance had a direct interest in the labor dispute. The Court also emphasized that the Act is not concerned with the motives for the dispute.

Emphasizing that the term "labor dispute" in § 4 of the Norris-La Guardia Act must not be narrowly construed, the Supreme Court held that a politically motivated refusal by longshoremen to load vessels with cargo bound for the Soviet Union could not be enjoined by the federal courts. *Jacksonville Bulk Terms., Inc. v. ILA,* 457 U.S. 702 (1982). Since an employer and the union representing its employees had a dispute over the interpretation of the no-strike clause of their labor contract, the employer-employee relationship was the "matrix" of the controversy. The union's noneconomic motives did not take the dispute out of the reach of Norris-La Guardia.

2. In *San Antonio Comm. Hosp. v. Southern Cal. Dist. Council of Carpenters,* 125 F.3d 1230 (9th Cir. 1997), the Ninth Circuit upheld an injunction against union picketing of a hospital's maternity entrance with a banner reading, "THIS MEDICAL FACILITY IS FULL OF RATS." The union insisted the "rats" referred to a construction contractor that was not paying prevailing union wages. The court concluded that the banner fell within the "fraud" exception to Norris-LaGuardia's anti-injunction ban, since it could deceive the public into believing the hospital was infested with rodents.

3. Under § 10(j) and (*l*) of the National Labor Relations Act, the NLRB is empowered, and in the case of some union unfair labor practices, directed, to petition a federal district court for a temporary restraining order. Also, in order to enforce its orders, the NLRB is authorized under § 10(e) to petition a federal court of appeals for an enforcement order.

Accordingly, § 10(h) of the Act provides:

> (h) When granting appropriate temporary relief or a restraining order, or making and entering a decree enforcing, modifying, and enforcing as so modified, or setting aside in whole or in part an order of the Board, as provided in this section, the jurisdiction of courts sitting in equity shall not be limited by the Act entitled "An Act to amend the Judicial Code and to define and limit the jurisdiction of courts sitting in equity, and for other purposes," approved March 23, 1932 (29 U.S.C. §§ 101-15) [Norris-La Guardia Act].

Thus the Norris-La Guardia Act does not preclude injunctions against unfair labor practices when they are sought by the NLRB. But this does not mean that private parties are permitted to obtain injunctions against unfair labor practices. "The short answer to the argument that the Labor Management Relations Act of 1947 ... has removed the limitations of the Norris-La Guardia Act upon the power to issue injunctions against what are known as secondary boycotts is that the law has been changed only where an injunction is sought by the National Labor Relations Board, not where proceedings are instituted by a private party." *Bakery Sales Drivers, Local 33 v. Wagshal*, 333 U.S. 437, 442 (1948). The statutory scheme, as shown by the legislative history, is to vest paramount authority in the NLRB.

4. The Ninth Circuit has indicated that district courts must consider traditional equitable doctrines when deciding whether to issue § 10(j) injunctions sought by Labor Board attorneys. Despite the NLRB's weighing of public interest factors when deciding whether to request § 10(j) relief, courts must still evaluate: (1) the likelihood the plaintiff will ultimately prevail on the merits; (2) the possibility the plaintiff will be irreparably injured if temporary relief is not granted; (3) the extent to which the balance of hardships favors one party or the other; and (4) whether the public interest will be advanced by the granting of the preliminary relief being sought. *Miller v. California Pac. Med. Ctr.*, 991 F.2d 536 (9th Cir. 1993). *See also Arlook v. S. Lichtenberg & Co.*, 952 F.2d 367 (11th Cir. 1992) (when considering issuance of § 10(j) injunctions, courts should focus on Board's "reasonable cause" determinations, not the actual merits of the underlying disputes).

5. The power to initiate or maintain injunctive actions under § 10(*l*) is restricted to the NLRB. Thus, charging parties have been denied permission even to intervene in proceedings brought by a Board regional director against a union under § 10(*l*). *Solien v. Miscellaneous Drivers & Helpers Union, Local 610 [Sears, Roebuck & Co.]*, 440 F.2d 124 (8th Cir.), *cert. denied*, 403 U.S. 905 (1971). At the same time, regional director discretion under the mandatory injunction provisions of § 10(*l*) is limited, and an employer charging a union with an unlawful secondary boycott may to go into federal district court for a mandamus order compelling the regional director to seek a temporary injunction against the union's activity. *Terminal Freight Handling Co. v. Solien,* 444 F.2d 699 (8th Cir. 1971), *cert. denied,* 405 U.S. 996 (1972).

Unions and individuals charged with criminal contempt for violating § 10(*l*) injunctions are not entitled to jury trials under 18 U.S.C. § 3692. *Muniz v. Hoffman,* 422 U.S. 454 (1975).

6. In *Brotherhood of R.R. Trainmen v. Atlantic Coast Line R.R.,* 362 F.2d 649, *aff'd by equally divided Court,* 385 U.S. 20 (1966), the Fifth Circuit held that the Norris-La Guardia Act required the vacating of an injunction issued against striking employees of the Florida East Coast Railroad who picketed the premises of the Jacksonville Terminal Co. to get its employees to cease performing certain essential services for FEC trains coming into the terminal. Any "unlawfulness under nonlabor legislation such as the Interstate Commerce Act did not remove the restrictions of the Norris-La Guardia Act upon the jurisdiction of federal courts."

7. The applicability of the Norris-La Guardia Act will be considered further in a number of other cases involving its relationship to the antitrust laws, the Railway Labor Act, and the Taft-Hartley Act. These include *Boys Mkts., Inc. v. Retail Clerks Local 770,* 398 U.S. 235 (1970) (federal courts may enjoin certain strikes in breach of contract in action under § 301 of LMRA), *infra; Order of R.R. Telegraphers v. Chicago & N.W.R.R.,* 362 U.S. 330 (1960) (strike to prevent elimination of railroad stations and certain jobs therein nonenjoinable "labor dispute"), *infra; Brotherhood of R.R. Trainmen v. Chicago River & Ind. R.R.,* 353 U.S. 30 (1957) (strike over grievances arising under existing collective agreement enjoinable when disputes are subject to final and binding arbitration before the National Railroad Adjustment Board); *Textile Workers v. Lincoln Mills,* 353 U.S. 448 (1957) (federal court may decree specific performance of agreement to arbitrate under § 301 of LMRA), *infra; United States v. Hutcheson,* 312 U.S. 219 (1941) (union conduct nonenjoinable under Norris-La Guardia, also immune to Sherman Act prosecution), *infra; Steele v. Louisville & Nashville R.R.,* 323 U.S. 192 (1944) (federal court may issue injunction to enforce union's fair representation duty), *infra.*

8. *Compare Windward Shipping Ltd. v. American Radio Ass'n,* 415 U.S. 104 (1974) *and American Radio Ass'n v. Mobile S.S. Ass'n,* 419 U.S. 215 (1974), in which the Supreme Court upheld the power of *state* courts to enjoin picketing of foreign flag ships.

C. LABOR RELATIONS ACTS AND OTHER STATUTES

A third layer of law, overlaying the common law and interacting with the anti-injunction legislation, is now to be found in federal and state labor relations statutes and other miscellaneous regulations of labor union collective action. Undoubtedly the most important development in this field was the proscription of union unfair labor practices in the Taft-Hartley Act of 1947, with the additions and refinements made in the Landrum-Griffin Act of 1959.

Most of Part Three of this book will be devoted to a detailed consideration of how this modern labor legislation regulates the most important and controversial aspects of union collective action, such as organizational and recognition picketing, secondary boycotts, hot cargo agreements, jurisdictional strikes and featherbedding.

But first we shall take a brief look at the fourth and highest layer of law—constitutional protection. This primarily concerns free speech rights under the First and Fourteenth Amendments. However, to the extent that Congress has either outlawed or protected certain collective action by unions, the federal law has taken on additional importance because of the doctrine of federal preemption. This federal-state problem will be examined in detail in the last section of Part Three. The materials in this next section dealing with state regulation of various union practices must all be read, as far as industries affecting interstate commerce are concerned, with the qualification that some of the state action discussed is now precluded under the federal preemption doctrine.

SECTION II. Constitutional Protection

INTERNATIONAL BROTHERHOOD OF TEAMSTERS, LOCAL 695, A.F.L. v. VOGT, INC.

Supreme Court of the United States
354 U.S. 284, 77 S. Ct. 1166, 1 L. Ed. 2d 1347 (1957)

MR. JUSTICE FRANKFURTER delivered the opinion of the Court.

This is one more in the long series of cases in which this Court has been required to consider the limits imposed by the Fourteenth Amendment on the power of a State to enjoin picketing. The case was heard below on the pleadings and affidavits, the parties stipulating that the record contained "all of the facts and evidence that would be adduced upon a trial on the merits...." Respondent owns and operates a gravel pit in Oconomowoc, Wisconsin, where it employs 15 to 20 men. Petitioner unions sought unsuccessfully to induce some of respondent's employees to join the unions and commenced to picket the entrance to respondent's business with signs reading, "The men on this job are not 100% affiliated with the AFL." "In consequence," drivers of several trucking companies refused to deliver and haul goods to and from respondent's plant, causing substantial damage to respondent. Respondent thereupon sought an injunction to restrain the picketing.

The trial court did not make the finding, requested by respondent, "That the picketing of plaintiff's premises has been engaged in for the purpose of coercing, intimidating and inducing the employer to force, compel, or induce its employees to become members of defendant labor organizations, and for the purpose of injuring the plaintiff in its business because of its refusal to in any way interfere with the rights of its employees to join or not to join a labor organization." It nevertheless held that by virtue of Wis. Stat. § 103.535, prohibiting picketing in the absence of a "labor dispute," the petitioners must be enjoined from maintaining any pickets near respondent's place of business, from displaying at any place near respondent's place of business signs indicating that there was a labor dispute between respondent and its employees or between respondent and any of the petitioners, and from inducing others to decline to transport goods to and from respondent's business establishment.

On appeal, the Wisconsin Supreme Court at first reversed, relying largely on *AFL v. Swing,* 312 U.S. 321 (1941), to hold § 103.535 unconstitutional, on the ground that picketing could not constitutionally be enjoined merely because of the absence of a "labor dispute." 270 Wis. 315, 71 N.W.2d 359 (1955).

Upon reargument [270 Wis. 321A, 74 N.W.2d 749, 753 (1956)], however, the court withdrew its original opinion. Although the trial court had refused to make the finding requested by respondent, the Supreme Court, noting that the facts as to which the request was made were undisputed, drew the inference from the undisputed facts and itself made the finding. It canvassed the whole circumstances surrounding the picketing and held that "One would be credulous indeed to believe under the circumstances that the Union had no thought of coercing the employer to interfere with its employees in their right to join or refuse to join the defendant union." Such picketing, the court held, was for "an unlawful purpose," since Wis. Stat. § 111.06(2)(b) made it an unfair labor practice for an employee individually or in concert with others to "coerce, intimidate or induce any employer to interfere with any of his employes in the enjoyment of their legal rights ... or to engage in any practice with regard to his employees which would constitute an unfair labor practice if undertaken by him on his own initiative." Relying on *Building Service Employees v. Gazzam,* 339 U.S. 532 (1950), and *Pappas v. Stacey,* 151 Me. 36, 116 A.2d 497 (1955), the Wisconsin Supreme Court therefore affirmed the granting of the injunction on this different ground. 270 Wis. 315, 74 N.W.2d 749 (1956)....

It is inherent in the concept embodied in the Due Process Clause that its scope be determined by a "gradual process of judicial inclusion and exclusion," *Davidson v. New Orleans,* 96 U.S. 97, 104 (1878). Inevitably, therefore, the doctrine of a particular case "is not allowed to end with its enunciation, and ... an expression in an opinion yields later to the impact of facts unforeseen." *Jaybird Mining Co. v. Weir,* 271 U.S. 609, 619 (1926) (Brandeis, J., dissenting). It is not too surprising that the response of States—legislative and judicial—to use of the injunction in labor controversies should have given rise to a series of adjudications in this Court relating to the limitations on state action contained in the provisions of the Due Process Clause of the Fourteenth Amendment. It is also not too surprising that examination of these adjudications should disclose an evolving, not a static, course of decision.

The series begins with *Truax v. Corrigan,* 257 U.S. 312 (1921), in which a closely divided Court found it to be violative of the Equal Protection Clause—not of the Due Process Clause—for a State to deny use of the injunction in the special class of cases arising out of the labor conflicts. The considerations that underlay that case soon had to yield, through legislation and later through litigation, to the persuasiveness of undermining facts. Thus, to remedy the abusive use of the injunction in the federal courts (*see* Frankfurter and Greene, The Labor Injunction), the Norris-La Guardia Act, 47 Stat. 70, 29 U.S.C. § 101, withdrew, subject to qualifications, jurisdiction from the federal courts to issue injunctions in labor disputes to prohibit certain acts. Its example was widely followed by state enactments.

Apart from remedying the abuses of the injunction in this general type of litigation, legislatures and courts began to find in one of the aims of picketing an aspect of communication. This view came to the fore in *Senn v. Tile Layers Union,* 301 U.S. 468 (1937), where the Court held that the Fourteenth Amendment did not prohibit Wisconsin from authorizing peaceful stranger picketing by a union that was attempting to unionize a shop and to induce an employer to refrain from working in his business as a laborer.

Although the Court had been closely divided in the *Senn* case, three years later, in passing on a restrictive instead of a permissive state statute, the Court made sweeping pronouncements about the right to picket in holding unconstitutional a statute that had been applied to ban all picketing, with "no exceptions based upon either the number of persons engaged in the proscribed activity, the peaceful character of their demeanor, the nature of their dispute with an employer, or the restrained character and the accurateness of the terminology used in notifying the public of the facts of the dispute." *Thornhill v. Alabama,* 310 U.S. 88, 99 (1940). As the statute dealt at large with all picketing, so the Court broadly assimilated peaceful picketing in general to freedom of speech, and as such protected against abridgement by the Fourteenth Amendment.

These principles were applied by the Court in *AFL v. Swing,* 312 U.S. 321 (1941), to hold unconstitutional an injunction against peaceful picketing, based on a State's common-law policy against picketing when there was no immediate dispute between employer and employee. On the same day, however, the Court upheld a generalized injunction against picketing where there had been violence because "it could justifiably be concluded that the momentum of fear generated by past violence would survive even though future picketing might be wholly peaceful." *Milk Wagon Drivers Union v. Meadowmoor Dairies,* 312 U.S. 287, 294 (1941).

Soon, however, the Court came to realize that the broad pronouncements, but not the specific holding, of *Thornhill* had to yield "to the impact of facts unforeseen," or at least not sufficiently appreciated. *Cf. People v. Charles Schweinler Press,* 214 N.Y. 395, 108 N.E. 639 (1915), 28 Harv. L. Rev. 790. Cases reached the Court in which a State had designed a remedy to meet a specific situation or to accomplish a particular social policy. These cases made manifest that picketing, even though "peaceful," involved more than just communication of ideas and could not be immune from all state regulation. "Picketing by an organized group is more than free speech, since it involves patrol of a particular locality and since the very presence of a picket line may induce action of one kind or another, quite irrespective of the nature of the ideas which are being disseminated." *Bakery and Pastry Drivers Local v. Wohl,* 315 U.S. 769, 776 (1942) (concurring opinion); *see Carpenters and Joiners Union v. Ritter's Cafe,* 315 U.S. 722, 725-728 (1942).

These latter two cases required the Court to review a choice made by two States between the competing interests of unions, employers, their employees, and the public at large. In the *Ritter's Cafe* case, Texas had enjoined as a violation of its antitrust law picketing of a restaurant by unions to bring pressure on its owner with respect to the use of nonunion labor by a contractor of the restaurant owner in the construction of a building having nothing to do with the restaurant. The Court held that Texas could, consistent with the Fourteenth Amendment, insulate from the dispute a neutral establishment that industrially had no connection with it. This type of picketing certainly involved little, if any, "communication."

In *Bakery and Pastry Drivers Local v. Wohl,* 315 U.S. 769 (1942), in a very narrowly restricted decision, the Court held that because of the impossibility of otherwise publicizing a legitimate grievance and because of the slight effect on "strangers" to the dispute, a State could not constitutionally prohibit a union from picketing bakeries in its efforts to have independent peddlers, buying from bakers and selling to small stores, conform to certain union requests. Although the Court in *Ritter's Cafe* and *Wohl* did not question the holding of *Thornhill,* the strong reliance on the particular facts in each case demonstrated a growing awareness that these cases involved not so much questions of free speech as review of the balance struck by a State between picketing that involved more than "publicity" and competing interests of state policy. (*See also Cafeteria Employees Union v. Angelos,* 320 U.S. 293 (1943), where the Court reviewed a New York injunction against picketing by a union of a restaurant that was run by the owners without employees. The New York court appeared to have justified an injunction on the alternate grounds that there was no "labor dispute" under the New York statute or that use of untruthful placards justified the injunction. We held, in a brief opinion, that the abuses alleged did not justify an injunction against all picketing and that *AFL v. Swing* governed the alternate ground for decision.)

The implied reassessments of the broad language of the *Thornhill* case were finally generalized in a series of cases sustaining injunctions against peaceful picketing, even when arising in the course of a labor controversy, when such picketing was counter to valid state policy in a domain open to state regulation. The decisive reconsideration comes in *Giboney v. Empire Storage & Ice Co.,* 336 U.S. 490 (1949). A union, seeking to organize peddlers, picketed a wholesale dealer to induce it to refrain from selling to nonunion peddlers. The state courts, finding that such an agreement would constitute a conspiracy in restraint of trade in violation of the state antitrust laws, enjoined the picketing. This Court affirmed unanimously.... The Court ... concluded that it was "clear that appellants were doing more than exercising a right of free speech or press.... They were exercising their economic power together with that of their allies to compel Empire to abide by union rather than by state regulation of trade." *Id.* 336 U.S. at page 503.

The following Term, the Court decided a group of cases applying and elaborating on the theory of *Giboney.* In *Hughes v. Superior Court,* 339 U.S. 460 (1950), the Court held that the Fourteenth Amendment did not bar use of the injunction to prohibit picketing of a place of business solely to secure compliance with a demand that its employees be hired in percentage to the racial origin of its customers. "We cannot construe the Due Process Clause as prohibiting California from securing respect for its policy against involuntary employment on racial lines by prohibiting systematic picketing that would subvert such policy." *Id.* 339 U.S. at page 466. The Court also found it immaterial that the state policy had been expressed by the judiciary rather than by the legislature.

On the same day, the Court decided *International Brotherhood of Teamsters Union v. Hanke,* 339 U.S. 470 (1950), holding that a State was not restrained by the Fourteenth Amendment from enjoining picketing of a business, conducted by the owner himself without employees, in order to secure compliance with a demand to become a union shop. Although there was no one opinion for the Court, its decision was another instance of the affirmance of an injunction against picketing because directed against a valid public policy of the State.

A third case, *Building Service Employees v. Gazzam,* 339 U.S. 532 (1950), was decided the same day. Following an unsuccessful attempt at unionization of a small hotel and refusal by the owner to sign a contract with the union as bargaining agent, the union began to picket the hotel with signs stating that the owner was unfair to organized labor. The State, finding that the object of the picketing was in violation of its statutory policy against employer coercion of employees' choice of bargaining representative, enjoined picketing for such purpose. This Court affirmed, rejecting the argument that "the *Swing* case, *supra,* is controlling.... In that case this Court struck down the State's restraint of picketing based solely on the absence of an employer-employee relationship. An adequate basis for the instant decree is the unlawful objective of the picketing, namely, coercion by the employer of the employees' selection of a bargaining representative. Peaceful picketing for any lawful purpose is not prohibited by the decree under review." *Id.* 339 U.S. at page 539.

A similar problem was involved in *Plumbers Union, Local 10 v. Graham,* 345 U.S. 192 (1953), where a state court had enjoined, as a violation of its "Right to Work" law, picketing that advertised that nonunion men were being employed on a building job. This Court found that there was evidence in the record supporting a conclusion that a substantial purpose of the picketing was to put pressure on the general contractor to eliminate nonunion men from the job and, on the reasoning of the cases that we have just discussed, held that the injunction was not in conflict with the Fourteenth Amendment.

This series of cases, then, established a broad field in which a State, in enforcing some public policy, whether of its criminal or its civil law, and whether announced by its legislature or its courts, could constitutionally enjoin peaceful picketing aimed at preventing effectuation of that policy.

In the light of this background, the Maine Supreme Judicial Court in 1955 decided, on an agreed statement of facts, the case of *Pappas v. Stacey,* 151 Me. 36, 116 A.2d 497, 498 (1955). From the statement, it appeared that three union employees went on strike, and picketed a restaurant peacefully "for the sole purpose of seeking to organize other employees of the Plaintiff, ultimately to have the Plaintiff enter into collective bargaining and negotiations with the Union...." Maine had a statute providing that workers should have full liberty of self-organization, free from restraint by employers or other persons. [R.S. 1954, ch. 30, § 15]. The Maine Supreme Judicial Court drew the inference from the agreed statement of facts that "there is a steady and exacting pressure upon the employer to interfere with the free choice of the employees in the matter of organization. To say that the picketing is not designed to bring about such action is to forget an obvious purpose of the picketing—to cause economic loss to the business during noncompliance by the employees with the requests of the union." 151 Me. at 42, 116 A.2d at 500. It therefore enjoined the picketing, and an appeal was taken to this Court.

The whole series of cases discussed above allowing, as they did, wide discretion to a State in the formulation of domestic policy, and not involving a curtailment of free speech in its obvious and accepted scope, led this Court without the need of further argument, to grant appellee's motion to dismiss the appeal in that it no longer presented a substantial federal question. 350 U.S. 870.

The *Stacey* case is this case. As in *Stacey,* the present case was tried without oral testimony. As in *Stacey,* the highest state court drew the inference from the facts that the picketing was to coerce the employer to put pressure on his employees to join the union, in violation of the declared policy of the State. (For a declaration of similar congressional policy, see § 8 of the Taft-Hartley Act, 61 Stat. 140, 29 U.S.C. § 158). The cases discussed above all hold that, consistent with the Fourteenth Amendment, a State may enjoin such conduct.

Of course, the mere fact that there is "picketing" does not automatically justify its restraint without an investigation into its conduct and purposes. State courts, no more than state legislatures, can enact blanket prohibitions against picketing. *Thornhill v. Alabama* and *AFL v. Swing, supra.* The series of cases following *Thornhill* and *Swing* demonstrate that the policy of Wisconsin enforced by the prohibition of this picketing is a valid one. In this case, the circumstances set forth in the opinion of the Wisconsin Supreme Court afford a rational basis for the inference it drew concerning the purpose of the picketing. No question was raised here concerning the breadth of the injunction, but of course its terms must be read in the light of the opinion of the Wisconsin Supreme Court, which justified it on the ground that the picketing was for the purpose of coercing the employer to coerce his employees. "If astuteness may discover argumentative excess in the scope of the [injunction] beyond what we constitutionally justify by this opinion, it will be open to petitioners to raise the matter, which they have not raised here, when the [case] on remand [reaches] the [Wisconsin] court." *Teamsters Union v. Hanke,* 399 U.S. at 480-481.

Therefore, having deemed it appropriate to elaborate on the issues in the case, we affirm.

Affirmed.

MR. JUSTICE WHITTAKER took no part in the consideration or decision of this case.

MR. JUSTICE DOUGLAS, with whom THE CHIEF JUSTICE and MR. JUSTICE BLACK concur, dissenting.

The Court has now come full circle. In *Thornhill v. Alabama,* 310 U.S. 88, 102 (1940), we struck down a state ban on picketing on the ground that "the dissemination of information concerning the facts of a labor dispute must be regarded as within that area of free discussion that is guaranteed by the Constitution." Less than one year later, we held that the First Amendment protected organizational picketing on a factual record which cannot be distinguished from the one now before us. *AFL v. Swing,* 312 U.S. 321 (1941). Of course, we have always recognized that picketing has aspects which make it more than speech. *Bakery Drivers Local v. Wohl,* 315 U.S. 769, 776-777 (1942) (concurring opinion). That difference underlies our decision in *Giboney v. Empire Storage & Ice Co.,* 336 U.S. 490 (1949). There, picketing was an essential part of "a single and integrated course of conduct, which was in violation of Missouri's valid law." *Id.* 336 U.S. at page 498. And *see NLRB v. Virginia Power Co.,* 314 U.S. 469, 477-478 (1941). We emphasized that "there was clear danger, imminent and immediate, that unless restrained, appellants would succeed in making [the state] policy a dead letter...." 336 U.S. at page 503. Speech there was enjoined because it was an inseparable part of conduct which the State constitutionally could and did regulate.

But where, as here, there is no rioting, no mass picketing, no violence, no disorder, no fisticuffs, no coercion—indeed nothing but speech—the principles announced in *Thornhill* and *Swing* should give the advocacy of one side of a dispute First Amendment protection.

The retreat began when, in *Teamsters Union v. Hanke,* 339 U.S. 470 (1950), four members of the Court announced that all picketing could be prohibited if a state court decided that that picketing violated the State's public policy. The retreat became a rout in *Plumbers Union, Local 10 v. Graham,* 345 U.S. 192

(1953). It was only the "purpose" of the picketing which was relevant. The state court's characterization of the picketers' "purpose" had been made well-nigh conclusive. Considerations of the proximity of picketing to conduct which the State could control or prevent were abandoned, and no longer was it necessary for the state court's decree to be narrowly drawn to prescribe a specific evil. *Id.* 345 U.S. at pages 201-205 (dissenting opinion).

Today, the Court signs the formal surrender. State courts and state legislatures cannot fashion blanket prohibitions on all picketing. But, for practical purposes, the situation now is as it was when *Senn v. Tile Layers Union,* 301 U.S. 468 (1937), was decided. State courts and state legislatures are free to decide whether to permit or suppress any particular picket line for any reason other than a blanket policy against all picketing. I would adhere to the principle announced in *Thornhill.* I would adhere to the result reached in *Swing.* I would return to the test enunciated in *Giboney*—that this form of expression can be regulated or prohibited only to the extent that it forms an essential part of a course of conduct which the State can regulate or prohibit. I would reverse the judgment below.

NOTES

1. For discussions of the *Vogt* case and its predecessors, *see* Cox, *Strikes, Picketing, and the Constitution,* 4 Vand. L. Rev. 574 (1951); Gregory, *Peaceful Picketing and Freedom of Speech,* 26 A.B.A.J. 709 (1940); Farmer & Williamson, *Picketing and the Injunctive Power of State Courts—From Thornhill to Vogt,* 35 U. Det. L.J. 431 (1958); Samoff, *Picketing and the First Amendment: "Full Circle" and "Formal Surrender,"* 9 Lab. L.J. 889 (1958); Note, *Stranger Picketing and the Vogt Case,* 1958 Wis. L. Rev. 154. For two excellent but contradictory analyses of the problem of picketing and free speech, *see* Gregory, *Constitutional Limitations on the Regulation of Union and Employer Conduct,* 49 Mich. L. Rev. 191 (1950); and Jones, *Free Speech: Pickets on the Grass, Alas!, Amidst Confusion, a Consistent Principle,* 29 S. Cal. L. Rev. 137 (1956).

2. It should be emphasized that, although the Supreme Court made sweeping pronouncements about the right to picket in the landmark *Thornhill* case, the holding was a narrow one. The Alabama courts had made it clear that they would apply their criminal statute to prohibit a single individual from walking slowly back and forth on the public sidewalk in front of the premises of an employer, without speaking to anyone, carrying a sign or placard on a staff above his head, stating only the fact that the employer did not employ union men. Since the statute, as authoritatively construed and applied, left no room for exceptions, the Court held it to be invalid on its face. *See Nash v. Chandler,* 848 F.2d 567 (5th Cir. 1988), striking down Texas statute prohibiting "mass picketing" which was impermissibly defined to cover more than two pickets within fifty feet of any entrance to the premises being picketed or within fifty feet of other picketers.

3. *Giant Eagle Mkts. Co. v. UFCW Local 23,* 539 Pa. 411, 652 A.2d 1286 (1995), involved mass picketing by striking employees at store entrances. The court indicated that non-coercive labor picketing enjoys First Amendment protection and that isolated incidents of picket-line misconduct would not warrant injunctive relief. Nonetheless, when striking employees blocked store entrances, swarmed around customers, and engaged in other acts of intimidation, their conduct constituted a "seizure" subject to injunctive proscription.

4. *The Constitutional Status of Strikes.* The Supreme Court has never held state or federal regulation of strikes unconstitutional on "civil rights" grounds. Yet, it can hardly be doubted that in the union hierarchy of values the "right" to strike ranks higher than the "right" to picket.

In *UAW-AFL, Local 232 v. WERB,* 336 U.S. 245 (1949), the Supreme Court upheld a state order against intermittent, unannounced work stoppages (quickie strikes) against constitutional challenge under the fourteenth amendment. Mr. Justice Jackson in discussing § 13 of the NLRA, commented:

> This Court less than a decade earlier [than the Wagner Act] had stated that law to be that the state constitutionally could prohibit strikes and make a violation criminal. It had unanimously adopted the language of Mr. Justice Brandeis that "Neither the common law, nor the Fourteenth Amendment, confers the absolute right to strike," *Dorchy v. Kansas,* 272 U.S. 306, 311. Dissenting views most favorable to labor in other cases had conceded the right of the state legislature to mark the limits of tolerable industrial conflict in the public interest. *Duplex Co. v. Deering,* 254 U.S. 443, 488. This court has adhered to that view. *Thornhill v. Alabama,* 310 U.S. 88, 103. The right to strike, because of its more serious impact upon the public interest, is more vulnerable to regulation than the right to organize and select representatives for lawful purposes of collective bargaining which this Court has characterized as a "fundamental right." [336 U.S. at 259].

In *Postal Clerks v. Blount,* 325 F. Supp. 879 (D.D.C. 1971), a three-judge federal court said:

> At common law no employee, whether public or private, had a constitutional right to strike in concert with his fellow workers. Indeed, such collective action on the part of employees was often held to be a conspiracy. When the right of private employees to strike finally received full protection, it was by statute, Section 7 of the National Labor Relations Act, which "took this conspiracy weapon away from the employer in employment relations which affect interstate commerce" and guaranteed to employees in the private sector the right to engage in concerted activities for the purpose of collective bargaining.... It seems clear that public employees stand on no stronger footing in this regard than private employees and that in the absence of a statute, they too do not possess the right to strike.... Given the fact

that there is no constitutional right to strike, it is not irrational or arbitrary for the Government to ... prohibit strikes by those in public employment....

Judge J. Skelly Wright concurred in the result. However, he stated that the question is a very difficult one and that:

> [I]t is by no means clear to me that the right to strike is not fundamental. The right to strike seems intimately related to the right to form labor organizations, a right which the majority recognizes as fundamental and which, more importantly, is generally thought to be constitutionally protected under the First Amendment—even for public employees.... If the inherent purpose of a labor organization is to bring the workers' interests to bear on management, the right to strike is, historically and practically, an important means of effectuating that purpose. A union that never strikes, or which can make no credible threat to strike, may wither away in ineffectiveness. That fact is not irrelevant to the constitutional calculations.... I do believe that the right to strike is, at least, within constitutional concern....

The Supreme Court affirmed the decision and upheld a ban on strikes by federal employees without hearing argument or writing an opinion. 404 U.S. 802 (1971). Mr. Justice Douglas thought the case should be set for oral argument.

5. Would an injunction or a statute outlawing strikes run afoul of the Thirteenth Amendment which prohibits involuntary servitude? The Supreme Court considered this question in the *UAW-AFL* case above, saying:

> The Union contends that the statute, as thus applied, violates the Thirteenth Amendment in that it imposes a form of compulsory service or involuntary servitude. However, nothing in the statute or the order makes it a crime to abandon work individually (*Compare Pollock v. Williams,* 322 U.S. 4), or collectively. Nor does either undertake to prohibit or restrict any employee from leaving the service of the employer, either for reason or without reason, either with or without notice. The facts afford no foundation for the contention that any action of the State has the purpose or effect of imposing any form of involuntary servitude." [336 U.S. at 251].

HUDGENS v. NLRB

Supreme Court of the United States
424 U.S. 507, 96 S. Ct. 1029, 47 L. Ed. 2d 128 (1976)

MR. JUSTICE STEWART delivered the opinion of the Court.

A group of labor union members who engaged in peaceful primary picketing within the confines of a privately owned shopping center were threatened by an agent of the owner with arrest for criminal trespass if they did not depart. The question presented is whether this threat violated the National Labor Relations Act, as amended 61 Stat. 136, 29 U.S.C. § 151 *et seq.* The National Labor Relations Board concluded that it did, 205 N.L.R.B. 628, and the Court of Appeals for the Fifth Circuit agreed. 501 F.2d 161. We granted certiorari because of the seemingly important questions of federal law presented. 420 U.S. 971.

I

The petitioner, Scott Hudgens, is the owner of the North DeKalb Shopping Center, located in suburban Atlanta, Ga. The center consists of a single large building with an enclosed mall. Surrounding the building is a parking area which can accommodate 2,640 automobiles. The shopping center houses 60 retail stores leased to various businesses. One of the lessees is the Butler Shoe Company. Most of the stores, including Butler's, can be entered only from the interior mall.

In January 1971, warehouse employees of the Butler Shoe Company went on strike to protest the company's failure to agree to demands made by their union in contract negotiations.[1] The strikers decided to picket not only Butler's warehouse but its nine retail stores in the Atlanta area as well, including the store in the North DeKalb Shopping Center. On January 22, 1971, four of the striking warehouse employees entered the center's enclosed mall carrying placards which read, "Butler Shoe Warehouse on Strike, AFL-CIO, Local 315." The general manager of the shopping center informed the employees that they could not picket within the mall or on the parking lot and threatened them with arrest if they did not leave. The employees departed but returned a short time later and began picketing in an area of the mall immediately adjacent to the entrances of the Butler store. After the picketing had continued for approximately 30 minutes, the shopping center manager again informed the picketers that if they did not leave they would be arrested for trespassing. The picketers departed.

The union subsequently filed with the Board an unfair labor practice charge against Hudgens, alleging interference with rights protected by § 7 of the Act, 29 U.S.C. § 157. Relying on this Court's decision in *Amalgamated Food Employees Union, Local 590 v. Logan Valley Plaza, Inc.,* 391 U.S. 308, the Board entered a cease-and-desist order against Hudgens, reasoning that because the warehouse employees enjoyed a First Amendment right to picket on the shopping center property, the owner's threat of arrest violated § 8(a)(1) of the Act.[3] Hudgens filed a petition for review in the Court of Appeals for the Fifth Circuit. Soon thereafter this Court decided *Lloyd Corp. v. Tanner,* 407 U.S. 551, and *Central*

---

[1]The Butler warehouse was not located within the North DeKalb Shopping Center.

[3]*Hudgens v. Local 315, Retail, Wholesale and Department Store Union,* 192 N.L.R.B. 671 (1971).... While Hudgens was not the employer of the employees involved in this case, it seems to be undisputed that he was an employer engaged in commerce within the meaning of § 2(6) and (7) of the Act. The Board has held that a statutory "employer" may violate § 8(a)(1) with respect to employees other than his own. *See Austin Co.,* 101 N.L.R.B. 1257, 1258-1259. *See also* § 2(13) of the Act.

Hardware Co. v. NLRB, 407 U.S. 539, and the Court of Appeals remanded the case to the Board for reconsideration in the light of those two decisions.

The Board, in turn, remanded to an administrative law judge, who made findings of fact, recommendations and conclusions to the effect that Hudgens had committed an unfair labor practice by excluding the picketers. This result was ostensibly reached under the statutory criteria set forth in *NLRB v. Babcock & Wilcox Co.,* 351 U.S. 105, a case which held that union organizers who seek to solicit for union membership may intrude on an employer's private property if no alternative means exist for communicating with the employees. But the administrative law judge's opinion also relied on this Court's constitutional decision in *Logan Valley* for a "realistic view of the facts." The Board agreed with the findings and recommendation of the administrative law judge, but departed somewhat from his reasoning. It concluded that the picketers were within the scope of Hudgens' invitation to members of the public to do business at the shopping center, and that it was, therefore, immaterial whether or not there existed an alternative means of communicating with the customers and employees of the Butler store.[4]

Hudgens again petitioned for review in the Court of Appeals for the Fifth Circuit, and there the Board changed its tack and urged that the case was controlled not by *Babcock & Wilcox,* but by *Republic Aviation Corp. v. NLRB,* 324 U.S. 793, a case which held that an employer commits an unfair labor practice if he enforces a no-solicitation rule against employees on his premises who are also union organizers, unless he can prove that the rule is necessitated by special circumstances. The Court of Appeals enforced the Board's cease-and-desist order but on the basis of yet another theory. While acknowledging that the source of the picketers' rights was § 7 of the Act, the Court of Appeals held that the competing constitutional and property right considerations discussed in *Lloyd Corp. v. Tanner, supra,* "burde[n] the General Counsel with the duty to prove that other locations less intrusive upon Hudgens' property rights than picketing inside the mall were either unavailable or ineffective," 501 F.2d, at 169, and that the Board's General Counsel had met that burden in this case.

In this Court the petitioner Hudgens continues to urge that *Babcock & Wilcox Co.* is the controlling precedent, and that under the criteria of that case the judgment of the Court of Appeals should be reversed. The respondent union agrees that a statutory standard governs, but insists that, since the § 7 activity here was not organizational as in *Babcock* but picketing in support of a lawful economic strike, an appropriate accommodation of the competing interests must lead to an affirmance of the Court of Appeals' judgment. The respondent Board now contends that the conflict between employee picketing rights and employer property rights in a case like this must be measured in accord with the commands of the

---

[4] *Hudgens v. Local 315, Retail, Wholesale and Department Store Union,* 205 N.L.R.B. 628 (1973).

First Amendment, pursuant to the Board's asserted understanding of *Lloyd Corp. v. Tanner, supra,* and that the judgment of the Court of Appeals should be affirmed on the basis of that standard.

II

As the above recital discloses, the history of this litigation has been a history of shifting positions on the part of the litigants, the Board, and the Court of Appeals. It has been a history, in short, of considerable confusion, engendered at least in part by decisions of this Court that intervened during the course of the litigation. In the present posture of the case the most basic question is whether the respective rights and liabilities of the parties are to be decided under the criteria of the National Labor Relations Act alone, under a First Amendment standard, or under some combination of the two. It is to that question, accordingly, that we now turn.

It is, of course, a commonplace that the constitutional guarantee of free speech is a guarantee only against abridgment by government, federal or state. *See Columbia Broadcasting System, Inc. v. Democratic National Committee,* 412 U.S. 94. Thus, while statutory or common law may in some situations extend protection or provide redress against a private corporation or person who seeks to abridge the free expression of others, no such protection or redress is provided by the Constitution itself.

This elementary proposition is little more than a truism. But even truisms are not always unexceptionably true, and an exception to this one was recognized almost 30 years ago in the case *Marsh v. Alabama,* 326 U.S. 501. In *Marsh,* a Jehovah's Witness who had distributed literature without a license on a sidewalk in Chickasaw, Ala., was convicted of criminal trespass. Chickasaw was a so-called company town, wholly owned by the Gulf Shipbuilding Corporation. It was described in the Court's opinion as follows:

> Except for [ownership by a private corporation] it has all the characteristics of any American town. The property consists of residential buildings, streets, a system of sewers, a sewage disposal plant and a "business block" on which business places are situated. A deputy of the Mobile County Sheriff, paid by the company, serves as the town's policeman. Merchants and service establishments have rented the stores and business places on the business block and the United States uses one of the places as a post office from which six carriers deliver mail to the people of Chickasaw and the adjacent area. The town and the surrounding neighborhood, which can not be distinguished from the Gulf property by anyone not familiar with the property lines, are thickly settled, and according to all indications the residents use the business block as their regular shopping center. To do so, they now, as they have for many years, make use of a company-owned paved street and sidewalk located alongside the store fronts in order to enter and leave

the stores and the post office. Intersecting company-owned roads at each end of the business block lead into a four-lane public highway which runs parallel to the business block at a distance of thirty feet. There is nothing to stop highway traffic from coming onto the business block and upon arrival a traveler may make free use of the facilities available there. In short the town and its shopping district are accessible to and freely used by the public in general and there is nothing to distinguish them from any other town and shopping center except the fact that the title to the property belongs to a private corporation. [326 U.S., at 502-503.]

The Court pointed out that if the "title" to Chickasaw had "belonged not to a private but to a municipal corporation and had appellant been arrested for violating a municipal ordinance rather than a ruling by those appointed by the corporation to manage a company town it would have been clear that appellant's conviction must be reversed." 326 U.S., at 504. Concluding that Gulf's "property interests" should not be allowed to lead to a different result in Chickasaw, which did "not function differently from any other town," 326 U.S., at 506-508, the Court invoked the First and Fourteenth Amendments to reverse the appellant's conviction.

It was the *Marsh* case that in 1968 provided the foundation for the Court's decision in *Amalgamated Food Employees Union Local 590 v. Logan Valley Plaza, Inc.,* 391 U.S. 308. That case involved peaceful picketing within a large shopping center near Altoona, Pa. One of the tenants of the shopping center was a retail store that employed a wholly nonunion staff. Members of a local union picketed the store, carrying signs proclaiming that it was nonunion and that its employees were not receiving union wages or other union benefits. The picketing took place on the shopping center's property in the immediate vicinity of the store. A Pennsylvania court issued an injunction that required all picketing to be confined to public areas outside the shopping center, and the Supreme Court of Pennsylvania affirmed the issuance of this injunction. This Court held that the doctrine of the *Marsh* case required reversal of that judgment.

The Court's opinion pointed out that the First and Fourteenth Amendments would clearly have protected the picketing if it had taken place on a public sidewalk:

It is clear that if the shopping center premises were not privately owned but instead constituted the business area of a municipality, which they to a large extent resemble, petitioners could not be barred from exercising their First Amendment rights there on the sole ground that title to the property was in the municipality. *Lovell v. Griffin,* 303 U.S. 444 (1938); *Hague v. CIO,* 307 U.S. 496 (1939); *Schneider v. State,* 308 U.S. 147 (1939); *Jamison v. Texas,* 318 U.S. 413 (1943). The essence of those opinions is that streets, sidewalks, parks, and other similar public places are so historically associated with the exercise of First Amendment rights that access to them for the purpose of exercising such rights cannot constitutionally be denied broadly and absolutely. [391 U.S., at 315.]

The Court's opinion then reviewed the *Marsh* case in detail, emphasized the similarities between the business block in Chickasaw, Ala., and the Logan Valley shopping center, and unambiguously concluded:

> The shopping center here is clearly the functional equivalent of the business district of Chickasaw involved in *Marsh.* [391 U.S., at 318.]

Upon the basis of that conclusion, the Court held that the First and Fourteenth Amendments required reversal of the judgment of the Pennsylvania Supreme Court.

There were three dissenting opinions in the *Logan Valley* case, one of them by the author of the Court's opinion in *Marsh,* Mr. Justice Black. His disagreement with the Court's reasoning was total:

> In affirming petitioners' contentions the majority opinion relies on *Marsh v. Alabama, supra,* and holds that respondents' property has been transformed to some type of public property. But *Marsh* was never intended to apply to this kind of situation. *Marsh* dealt with the very special situation of a company-owned town, complete with streets, alleys, sewers, stores, residences, and everything else that goes to make a town.... I can find very little resemblance between the shopping center involved in this case and Chickasaw, Alabama. There are no homes, there is no sewage disposal plant, there is not even a post office on this private property which the Court now considers the equivalent of a "town". [391 U.S., at 330-331 (footnote omitted).]
>
> ....
>
> The question is, Under what circumstances can private property be treated as though it were public? The answer that *Marsh* gives is when that property has taken on *all* the attributes of a town, *i.e.,* "residential buildings, streets, a system of sewers, a sewage disposal plant and a 'business block' on which business places are situated." [326 U.S., at 502.] I can find nothing in *Marsh* which indicates that if one of these features is present, *e.g.,* a business district, this is sufficient for the Court to confiscate a part of an owner's private property and give its use to people who want to picket on it. [391 U.S., at 332.]
>
> ....
>
> To hold that store owners are compelled by law to supply picketing areas for pickets to drive store customers away is to create a court-made law wholly disregarding the constitutional basis on which private ownership of property rests in this country.... [391 U.S., at 332-33.]

Four years later the Court had occasion to reconsider the *Logan Valley* doctrine in *Lloyd Corp. v. Tanner,* 407 U.S. 551. That case involved a shopping center covering some 50 acres in downtown Portland, Ore. On a November day in 1968 five young people entered the mall of the shopping center and distributed handbills protesting the then ongoing American military operations in Vietnam. Security guards told them to leave, and they did so, "to avoid arrest." 407 U.S., at 556. They subsequently brought suit in a federal district court, seeking declaratory and injunctive relief. The trial court ruled in their favor, holding that the distribution of handbills on the shopping center's property was protected by the First and Fourteenth Amendments. The Court of Appeals for the Ninth Circuit affirmed the judgment, 446 F.2d 545, expressly relying on this Court's *Marsh* and *Logan Valley* decisions. This Court reversed the judgment of the Court of Appeals.

The Court in its *Lloyd* opinion did not say that it was overruling the *Logan Valley* decision. Indeed, a substantial portion of the Court's opinion in *Lloyd* was devoted to pointing out the differences between the two cases, noting particularly that, in contrast to the handbilling in *Lloyd,* the picketing in *Logan Valley* had been specifically directed to a store in the shopping center and the picketers had had no other reasonable opportunity to reach their intended audience. 407 U.S., at 561-567. But the fact is that the reasoning of the Court's opinion in *Lloyd* cannot be squared with the reasoning of the Court's opinion in *Logan Valley.*

It matters not that some members of the Court may continue to believe that the *Logan Valley* case was rightly decided. Our institutional duty is to follow until changed the law as it now is, not as some members of the Court might wish it to be. And in the performance of that duty *we make clear now,* if it was not clear before, *that the rationale of Logan Valley did not survive the Court's decision in the Lloyd case.* Not only did the *Lloyd* opinion incorporate lengthy excerpts from two of the dissenting opinions in *Logan Valley,* 407 U.S., at 562-563, 565; the ultimate holding in *Lloyd* amounted to a total rejection of the holding in *Logan Valley:*

> The basic issue in this case is whether respondents, in the exercise of asserted First Amendment rights, may distribute handbills on Lloyd's private property contrary to its wishes and contrary to a policy enforced against *all* handbilling. In addressing this issue, it must be remembered that the First and Fourteenth Amendments safeguard the rights of free speech and assembly by limitations on *state* action, not on action by the owner of private property used nondiscriminatorily for private purposes only.... [407 U.S., at 567.]
>
> ....
>
> Respondents contend ... that the property of a large shopping center is "open to the public," serves the same purposes as a "business district" of a municipality, and therefore has been dedicated to certain types of public use. The argument is that such a center has sidewalks, streets, and parking areas which are functionally similar to facilities customarily provided by munici-

palities. It is then asserted that all members of the public, whether invited as customers or not, have the same right of free speech as they would have on the similar public facilities in the streets of a city or town.

The argument reaches too far. The Constitution by no means requires such an attenuated doctrine of dedication of private property to public use. The closest decision in theory, *Marsh v. Alabama, supra,* involved the assumption by a private enterprise of all of the attributes of a state-created municipality and the exercise by that enterprise of semi-official municipal functions as a delegate of the State. In effect, the owner of the company town was performing the full spectrum of municipal powers and stood in the shoes of the State. In the instant case there is no comparable assumption or exercise of municipal functions or power. [407 U.S., at 568-569 (footnote omitted).]

....

We hold that there has been no such dedication of Lloyd's privately owned and operated shopping center to public use as to entitle respondents to exercise therein the asserted First Amendment rights.... [407 U.S., at 570.]

If a large self-contained shopping center *is* the functional equivalent of a municipality, as *Logan Valley* held, then the First and Fourteenth Amendments would not permit control of speech within such a center to depend upon the speech's content. For while a municipality may constitutionally impose reasonable time, place, and manner regulations on the use of its streets and sidewalks for First Amendment purposes, *see Cox v. New Hampshire,* 312 U.S. 569; *Poulos v. New Hampshire,* 345 U.S. 395, and may even forbid altogether such use of some of its facilities, *see Adderley v. Florida,* 385 U.S. 39, what a municipality may *not* do under the First and Fourteenth Amendments is to discriminate in the regulation of expression on the basis of the content of that expression. *Erznoznik v. City of Jacksonville,* 422 U.S. 205. "[A]bove all else, the First Amendment means that government has no power to restrict expression because of its message, its ideas, its subject matter, or its content." *Police Department of Chicago v. Mosley,* 408 U.S. 92, 95. It conversely follows, therefore, that if the respondents in the *Lloyd* case did not have a First Amendment right to enter that shopping center to distribute handbills concerning Vietnam, then the respondents in the present case did not have a First Amendment right to enter this shopping center for the purpose of advertising their strike against the Butler Shoe Company.

We conclude, in short, that under the present state of the law the constitutional guarantee of free expression has no part to play in a case such as this.

III

From what has been said it follows that the rights and liabilities of the parties in this case are dependent exclusively upon the National Labor Relations Act.

Under the Act the task of the Board, subject to review by the courts, is to resolve conflicts between § 7 rights and private property rights, "and to seek a proper accommodation between the two." *Central Hardware Co. v. NLRB,* 407 U.S. 539, 543. What is "a proper accommodation" in any situation may largely depend upon the content and the context of the § 7 rights being asserted. The task of the Board and the reviewing courts under the Act, therefore, stands in conspicuous contrast to the duty of a court in applying the standards of the First Amendment, which requires "above all else" that expression must not be restricted by government "because of its message, its ideas, its subject matter, or its content."

In the *Central Hardware* case, and earlier in the case of *NLRB v. Babcock & Wilcox Co.,* 351 U.S. 105, the Court considered the nature of the Board's task in this area under the Act. Accommodation between employees' § 7 rights and employers' property rights, the Court said in *Babcock & Wilcox,* "must be obtained with as little destruction of one as is consistent with the maintenance of the other." 351 U.S., at 112.

Both *Central Hardware* and *Babcock & Wilcox* involved organizational activity carried on by nonemployees on the employers' property.[10] The context of the § 7 activity in the present case was different in several respects which may or may not be relevant in striking the proper balance. First, it involved lawful economic strike activity rather than organizational activity. *See United Steelworkers v. NLRB (Carrier Corp.),* 376 U.S. 492, 499; *Bus Employees v. Missouri,* 374 U.S. 74, 82; *NLRB v. Erie Resistor Corp.,* 373 U.S. 221, 234. *Cf. Houston Insulation Contractors Assn. v. NLRB,* 386 U.S. 664, 668-669. Second, the § 7 activity here was carried on by Butler's employees (albeit not employees of its shopping center store), not by outsiders. *See NLRB v. Babcock & Wilcox Co.,* 351 U.S., at 111-113. Third, the property interests impinged upon in this case were not those of the employer against whom the § 7 activity was directed, but of another.

The *Babcock & Wilcox* opinion established the basic objective under the Act: accommodation of § 7 rights and private property rights "with as little destruction of one as is consistent with the maintenance of the other." The locus of that accommodation, however, may fall at differing points along the spectrum depending on the nature and strength of the respective § 7 rights and private property rights asserted in any given context. In each generic situation, the primary responsibility for making this accommodation must rest with the Board in the first instance. *See NLRB v. Babcock & Wilcox,* 351 U.S., at 112; *cf. NLRB v. Erie Resistor Corp.,* 373 U.S. 221, 235-236; *NLRB v. Truckdrivers Union,* 353 U.S. 87,

---

[10] A wholly different balance was struck when the organizational activity was carried on by employees already rightfully on the employer's property, since the employer's management interests rather than his property interests were there involved. *Republic Aviation Corp. v. NLRB,* 324 U.S. 793. This difference is "one of substance." *NLRB v. Babcock & Wilcox Co.,* 351 U.S., at 113.

97. "The responsibility to adapt the Act to changing patterns of industrial life is entrusted to the Board." *NLRB v. Weingarten, Inc.,* 420 U.S. 251, 266.

For the reasons stated in this opinion, the judgment is vacated and the case is remanded to the Court of Appeals with directions to remand to the National Labor Relations Board, so that the case may be there considered under the statutory criteria of the National Labor Relations Act alone.

It is so ordered.

MR. JUSTICE STEVENS took no part in the consideration or decision of this case.

MR. JUSTICE POWELL, with whom THE CHIEF JUSTICE joins, concurring.

Although I agree with MR. JUSTICE WHITE's concurring view that *Lloyd Corp. v. Tanner,* 407 U.S. 551 (1972), did not overrule *Amalgamated Food Employees Union v. Logan Valley Plaza,* 391 U.S. 308 (1968), and that the present case can be distinguished narrowly from *Logan Valley,* I nevertheless have joined the opinion of the Court today.

The law in this area, particularly with respect to whether First Amendment or labor law principles are applicable, has been less than clear since *Logan Valley* analogized a shopping center to the "company town" in *Marsh v. Alabama,* 326 U.S. 501 (1946). Mr. Justice Black, the author of the Court's opinion in *Marsh,* thought the decisions were irreconcilable. I now agree with Mr. Justice Black that the opinions in these cases cannot be harmonized in a principled way. Upon more mature thought, I have concluded that we would have been wiser in *Lloyd Corp.* to have confronted this disharmony rather than draw distinctions based upon rather attenuated factual differences.

The Court's opinion today clarifies the confusion engendered by these cases by accepting Mr. Justice Black's reading of *Marsh* and by recognizing more sharply the distinction between the First Amendment and labor law issues that may arise in cases of this kind. It seems to me that this clarification of the law is desirable.

MR. JUSTICE WHITE, concurring in the judgment.

While I concur in the result reached by the Court, I find it unnecessary to inter *Amalgamated Food Employees Union Local 590 v. Logan Valley Plaza, Inc.,* 391 U.S. 308 (1968), and therefore do not join the Court's opinion. I agree that "the constitutional guarantee of free expression has no part to play in a case such as this," *ante,* p. 13; but *Lloyd Corp. v. Tanner,* 407 U.S. 551 (1972), did not overrule *Logan Valley,* either expressly or implicitly, and I would not, somewhat after the fact, say that it did.

One need go no further than *Logan Valley* itself, for the First Amendment protection established by *Logan Valley* was expressly limited to the picketing of a specific store for the purpose of conveying information with respect to the operation in the shopping center of *that* store:

The picketing carried on by petitioners was directed specifically at patrons of the Weis Market located within the shopping center and the message sought to be conveyed to the public concerned the manner in which that particular market was being operated. We are, therefore, not called upon to consider whether respondents' property rights could, consistently with the First Amendment, justify a bar on picketing which was not thus directly related in its purpose to the use to which the shopping center property was being put. [391 U.S., at 320 n. 9.]

On its face, *Logan Valley* does not cover the facts of this case. The pickets of the Butler Shoe Company store in the North DeKalb Shopping Center were not purporting to convey information about the "manner in which that particular [store] was being operated" but rather about the operation of a warehouse not located on the Center's premises. The picketing was thus not "directly related in its purpose to the use to which the shopping center property was being put."

The First Amendment question in this case was left open in *Logan Valley*. I dissented in *Logan Valley,* 391 U.S., at 337, and I see no reason to extend it further. Without such extension, the First Amendment provides no protection for the picketing here in issue and the Court need say no more. *Lloyd v. Tanner* is wholly consistent with this view. There is no need belatedly to overrule *Logan Valley,* only to follow it as is.

MR. JUSTICE MARSHALL, with whom MR. JUSTICE BRENNAN joins, dissenting.

The Court today holds that the First Amendment poses no bar to a shopping center owner's prohibiting speech within his shopping center. After deciding this far-reaching constitutional question, and overruling *Food Employees Local 590 v. Logan Valley,* 391 U.S. 308 (1968), in the process, the Court proceeds to remand for consideration of the statutory question whether the shopping center owner in this case unlawfully interfered with the Butler Shoe Company employees' rights under § 7 of the National Labor Relations Act, 29 U.S.C. § 157.

In explaining why it addresses any constitutional issue at all, the Court observes simply that the history of the litigation has been one of "shifting positions on the part of the litigants, the Board, and the Court of Appeals," *ante,* at 5, as to whether relief was being sought, or granted, under the First Amendment, under § 7 of the Act, or under some combination of the two. On my reading, the Court of Appeals' decision and, even more clearly, the Board's decision here for review, were based solely on § 7, not on the First Amendment; and this Court ought initially consider the statutory question without reference to the First Amendment—the question on which the Court remands. But even under the Court's reading of the opinions of the Board and the Court of Appeals, the statutory question on which it remands is now before the Court. By bypassing that question and reaching out to overrule a constitutionally based decision, the Court surely departs from traditional modes of adjudication.

I would affirm the judgment of the Court of Appeals on purely statutory grounds. And on the merits of the only question that the Court decides, I dissent from the overruling of *Logan Valley*.

....

II

On the merits of the purely statutory question that I believe is presented to the Court, I would affirm the judgment of the Court of Appeals. To do so, one need not consider whether consumer picketing by employees is subject to a more permissive test under § 7 than the test articulated in *Babcock & Wilcox* for organizational activity by nonemployees. In *Babcock & Wilcox* we stated that an employer "must allow the union to approach his employees on his property"[5] if the employees are "beyond the reach of reasonable efforts to communicate with them," 351 U.S., at 113—that is, if "other means" of communication are not "readily available." *Id.,* at 114. Thus the general standard that emerges from *Babcock & Wilcox* is the ready availability of reasonably effective alternative means of communication with the intended audience.

In *Babcock & Wilcox* itself, the intended audience was the employees of a particular employer, a limited identifiable group; and it was thought that such an audience could be reached effectively by means other than entrance onto the employer's property—for example, personal contact at the employees' living quarters, which were "in reasonable reach." *Id.,* at 113. In this case, of course, the intended audience was different, and what constitutes reasonably effective alternative means of communication also differs. As the Court of Appeals noted, the intended audience in this case "was only identifiable as part of the citizenry of greater Atlanta until it approached the store, and thus for the picketing to be effective, the location chosen was crucial unless the audience could be known and reached by other means." 501 F.2d, at 168. Petitioner contends that the employees could have utilized the newspapers, radio, television, direct mail, handbills, and billboards to reach the citizenry of Atlanta. But none of those means is likely to be as effective as on-location picketing: the initial impact of communication by those means would likely be less dramatic, and the potential for dilution of impact significantly greater. As this Court has observed:

> Publication in a newspaper, or by distribution of circulars, may convey the same information or make the same charge as do those patrolling a picket line. But the very purpose of a picket line is to exert influences, and it produces consequences, different from other modes of communication. The loyalties and responses evoked and exacted by picket lines are unlike those

---

[5] It is irrelevant, in my view, that the property in this case was owned by the shopping center owner rather than by the employer. The nature of the property interest is the same in either case.

flowing from appeals by printed word. [*Hughes v. Superior Court,* 339 U.S. 460, 465 (1950).]

In addition, all of the alternatives suggested by petitioner are considerably more expensive than on-site picketing. Certainly *Babcock & Wilcox* did not require resort to the mass media,[6] or to more individualized efforts on a scale comparable to that which would be required to reach the intended audience in this case.

Petitioner also contends that the employees could have picketed on the public rights-of-way, where vehicles entered the shopping center. Quite apart from considerations of safety, that alternative was clearly inadequate: prospective customers would have had to read the picketers' placards while driving by in their vehicles—a difficult task indeed. Moreover, as both the Board and the Court of Appeals recognized, picketing at an entrance used by customers of all retail establishments in the shopping center, rather than simply customers of the Butler Shoe Company store, may well have invited undesirable secondary effects.

In short, I believe the Court of Appeals was clearly correct in concluding that "alternatives to picketing inside the mall were either unavailable or inadequate." 501 F.2d, at 169. Under *Babcock & Wilcox,* then, the picketing in this case was protected by § 7. I would affirm the judgment of the Court of Appeals on that basis.

III

Turning to the constitutional issue resolved by the Court, I cannot escape the feeling that *Logan Valley* has been laid to rest without ever having been accorded a proper burial. The Court today announces that "the ultimate holding in *Lloyd* amounted to a total rejection of the holding in *Logan Valley.*" *Ante,* at 11. To be sure, some Members of the Court, myself included, believed that *Logan Valley* called for a different result in *Lloyd* and alluded in dissent to the possibility that "it is *Logan Valley* itself that the Court finds bothersome." 407 U.S., at 570, 584 (MARSHALL, J., dissenting). But the fact remains that *Logan Valley* explicitly reserved the question later decided in *Lloyd,* and *Lloyd* carefully preserved the holding of *Logan Valley.* And upon reflection, I am of the view that the two decisions are reconcilable.

....

It is inescapable that after *Lloyd, Logan Valley* remained "good law," binding on the state and federal courts. Our institutional duty in this case, if we consider the constitutional question at all, is to examine whether *Lloyd* and *Logan Valley* can continue to stand side-by-side, and, if they cannot, to decide which one must fall. I continue to believe that the First Amendment principles underlying *Logan*

---

[6] The only alternative means of communication referred to in *Babcock & Wilcox* were "personal contacts on streets or at home, telephones, letters or advertised meetings to get in touch with the employees." 351 U.S., at 111.

Valley are sound, and were unduly limited in *Lloyd.* But accepting *Lloyd,* I am not convinced that *Logan Valley* must be overruled.

The foundation of *Logan Valley* consisted of this Court's decisions recognizing a right of access to streets, sidewalks, parks, and other public places historically associated with the exercise of First Amendment rights. *E.g., Hague v. CIO,* 307 U.S. 496, 515-516 (1939); *Schneider v. State,* 308 U.S. 147 (1939); *Cantwell v. Connecticut,* 310 U.S. 296, 308 (1940); *Cox v. New Hampshire,* 312 U.S. 569, 574 (1941); *Jamison v. Texas,* 318 U.S. 413 (1943); *Saia v. New York,* 334 U.S. 558 (1948). Thus, the Court in *Logan Valley* observed that access to such forums "cannot constitutionally be denied broadly and absolutely." 391 U.S., at 315. The importance of access to such places for speech-related purposes is clear, for they are often the only places for effective speech and assembly.

Marsh v. Alabama, 326 U.S. 501 (1946), which the Court purports to leave untouched, made clear that in applying those cases granting a right of access to streets, sidewalks and other public places, courts ought not let the formalities of title put an end to analysis. The Court in *Marsh* observed that "the town and its shopping district are accessible to and freely used by the public in general and there is nothing to distinguish them from any other town and shopping center except the fact that the title to the property belongs to a private corporation." *Id.,* at 503. That distinction was not determinative:

> Ownership does not always mean absolute dominion. The more an owner, for his advantage, opens up his property for use by the public in general, the more do his rights become circumscribed by the statutory and constitutional rights of those who use it. [*Id.,* at 506.]

Regardless of who owned or possessed the town in *Marsh,* the Court noted, "the public ... has an identical interest in the functioning of the community in such manner that the channels of communication remain free," *id.,* at 507, and that interest was held to prevail.

The Court adopts the view that *Marsh* has no bearing on this case because the privately owned property in *Marsh* involved all the characteristics of a typical town. But there is nothing in *Marsh* to suggest that its general approach was limited to the particular facts of that case. The underlying concern in *Marsh* was that traditional public channels of communication remain free, regardless of the incidence of ownership. Given that concern, the crucial fact in *Marsh* was that the company owned the traditional forums essential for effective communications; it was immaterial that the company also owned a sewer system and that its property in other respects resembled a town.

In *Logan Valley* we recognized what the Court today refuses to recognize— that the owner of the modern shopping center complex, by dedicating his property to public use as a business district, to some extent displaces the "state" from control of historical First Amendment forums, and may acquire a virtual monopoly of places suitable for effective communication. The roadways, parking lots and walkways of the modern shopping center may be as essential for walkways of the modern shopping center may be as essential for effective speech as the streets and sidewalks in the municipal or company-owned town. I simply cannot reconcile the Court's denial of any role for the First Amendment in the shopping center with *Marsh's* recognition of a full role for the First Amendment on the streets and sidewalks of the company-owned town.

My reading of *Marsh* admittedly carried me farther than the Court in *Lloyd*, but the *Lloyd* Court remained responsive in its own way to the concerns underlying *Marsh*. *Lloyd* retained the availability of First Amendment protection when the picketing is related to the function of the shopping center, and when there is no other reasonable opportunity to convey the message to the intended audience. Preserving *Logan Valley* subject to *Lloyd's* two related criteria guaranteed that the First Amendment would have application in those situations in which the shopping center owner had most clearly monopolized the forums essential for effective communication. This result, although not the optimal one in my view, *Lloyd Corp. v. Tanner,* 407 U.S. 551, 570, 579-583 (MARSHALL, J., dissenting), is nonetheless defensible.

In *Marsh,* the private entity had displaced the "state" from control of all the places to which the public had historically enjoyed access for First Amendment purposes, and the First Amendment was accordingly held fully applicable to the private entity's conduct. The shopping center owner, on the other hand, controls only a portion of such places, leaving other traditional public forums available to the citizen. But the shopping center owner may nevertheless control all places essential for the effective undertaking of some speech-related activities—namely, those related to the activities of the shopping center. As for those activities, then, the First Amendment ought to have application under the reasoning of *Marsh,* and that was precisely the state of the law after *Lloyd.*

The Court's only apparent objection to this analysis is that it makes the applicability of the First Amendment turn to some degree on the subject matter of the speech. But that in itself is no objection, and the cases cited by the Court to the effect that government may not "restrict expression because of its message, its ideas, its subject matter, or its content," *Police Department of Chicago v. Mosley,* 408 U.S. 92, 95 (1972), are simply inapposite. In those cases, it was clearly the government that was acting, and the First Amendment's bar against infringing speech was unquestionably applicable; the Court simply held that the government, faced with a general command to permit speech, cannot choose to forbid some speech because of its message. The shopping center cases are quite different; in these cases the primary regulator is a private entity whose property has "assume[d] to some significant degree the functional attributes of public property devoted to public use." *Central Hardware Co. v. NLRB, supra,* 407 U.S. at 547. The very question in these cases is whether, and under what circumstances, the First Amendment has any application at all. The answer to that question, under the view of *Marsh* described above, depends to some extent on the subject of the speech the private entity seeks to regulate, because the degree to which the private entity monopolizes the effective channels of communication may depend upon what subject is involved. This limited reference to the subject matter of the speech poses none of the dangers of government suppression or censorship that lay at the heart of the cases cited by the Court. *See, e.g., Police Department of Chicago v. Mosley,* 408 U.S. 92, 95-96 (1972). It is indeed ironic that those cases, whose obvious concern was the promotion of free speech, are cited today to require its surrender.

In the final analysis, the Court's rejection of any role for the First Amendment in the privately owned shopping center complex stems, I believe, from an overly formalistic view of the relationship between the institution of private ownership of property and the First Amendment's guarantee of freedom of speech. No one would seriously question the legitimacy of the values of privacy and individual autonomy traditionally associated with privately owned property. But property that is privately owned is not always held for private use, and when a property owner opens his property to public use the force of those values diminishes. A degree of privacy is necessarily surrendered; thus, the privacy interest that petitioner retains when he leases space to 60 retail businesses and invites the public onto his land for the transaction of business and other members of the public is small indeed. *Cf. Paris Adult Theatre I v. Slaton,* 413 U.S. 49, 65-67 (1973). And while the owner of property open to public use may not automatically surrender any of his autonomy interest in managing the property as he sees fit, there is nothing new about the notion that that autonomy interest must be accommodated with the interests of the public. As this Court noted some time ago, albeit in another context:

> Property does become clothed with a public interest when used in a manner to make it of public consequence, and affect the community at large. When, therefore, one devotes his property to a use in which the public has an interest, he, in effect, grants to the public an interest in that use, and must submit to be controlled by the public for the common good, to the extent of the interest he has thus created. [*Munn v. Illinois,* 94 U.S. 113, 126 (1876).]

The interest of members of the public in communicating with one another on subjects relating to the businesses that occupy a modern shopping center is substantial. Not only employees with a labor dispute, but also consumers with complaints against business establishments, may look to the location of a retail store as the only reasonable avenue for effective communication with the public. As far as these groups are concerned, the shopping center owner has assumed the traditional role of the state in its control of historical First Amendment forums. *Lloyd* and *Logan Valley* recognized the vital role the First Amendment has to play in such cases, and I believe that this Court errs when it holds otherwise.

NOTES

1. On remand, pursuant to the decision of the Supreme Court, the Board reaffirmed its conclusion that the owner of the mall violated the NLRA by threatening to cause the arrest of the retail store's warehouse employees who picketed the retail store located within the owner's enclosed shopping mall. *Scott Hudgens,* 230 N.L.R.B. 414 (1977).

2. In a case involving area standards picketing in a shopping center, the Board held that a peaceful demand by the employer store owner (against whom the union was picketing) that pickets leave the shopping center property violated § 8(a)(1). *Giant Food Mkts.,* 241 N.L.R.B. 727 (1979). The Sixth Circuit denied enforcement, finding insufficient evidence in the record to support the Board conclusion that trespass on private property was permissible to prevent "dilution" of the "area standards" message carried by the picketers. 633 F.2d 18 (1980). *See also United Supermarkets,* 283 N.L.R.B. 814 (1987).

3. A panel of the Ninth Circuit found conduct by picketing economic strikers lawful in *Seattle-First Nat'l Bank v. NLRB,* 651 F.2d 1272 (1980). The employer, a restaurant, was located on the forty-sixth floor of a bank building. Striking employees stationed themselves both at the ground level and in the foyer of the restaurant. In finding a state court action preempted by the unfair labor practice filing, the court found restriction to the ground floor likely to cause "substantial dilution" of the picketers' message. On remand, the Board was only left to decide upon guidelines for noninterruptive picketing on both levels.

4. *See generally* Etelson, *Picketing and Freedom of Speech: Comes the Evolution,* 10 John Marshall J. of Prac. & Proc. 1 (1976); Comment, *Hudgens v. NLRB: A Final Definition of the Public Forum?* 13 Wake Forest L. Rev. 139 (1977).

SECTION III. Picketing and Union Discipline

A. REGULATION OF COERCIVE METHODS IN PICKETING

Picketing and its attendant representations and verbal onslaughts have presented courts and legislators with difficult problems. The general shift to a test of physical coercion gradually led most courts to give at least lip service to the doctrine that "peaceful" and noncoercive picketing for a lawful purpose is privileged, but it was frequently easy to discover nonpeaceful and coercive incidents with which to characterize the entire situation. Courts then had to decide whether to enjoin all of the picketing or only the discrete acts of coercion. Very often picketing has been accompanied by bitter invective of, and courts have pondered whether and to what extent to have regard for the sensibilities of others by holding the picketers to certain minimum standards of propriety with respect to their use of language. Frequently the publications of picketers have contained misrepresentations of fact, and the question has been whether to require minimal veracity.

VEGELAHN v. GUNTNER

Supreme Judicial Court of Massachusetts
167 Mass. 92, 44 N.E. 1077 (1896)

[Read the case again as reproduced *supra.*]

NOTES

1. Judicial attitudes toward picketing, usually finding expression in cases where injunctions were sought, have varied considerably since the *Vegelahn* case. At one end of the spectrum are such statements as that of McPherson, J., in *Atchison, Topeka & Santa Fe Ry. v. Gee,* 139 F. 582, 584 (S.D. Ia. 1905): "There is and can be no such thing as peaceful picketing, any more than there can be chaste vulgarity, or peaceful mobbing or lawful lynching." *See also Pierce v. Stablemen's, Local 8760,* 156 Cal. 70, 103 P. 324 (1909). Hardly more sympathetic toward picketing was the approach of Berry, V.C. in *Gevas v. Greek Restaurant Worker's Club,* 99 N.J. Eq. 770, 134 A. 309, 313 (1926): "Obviously, the line of demarcation between peaceful picketing, if there is any such thing, and that which is threatening, intimidating, and coercive, is so finely drawn as to be imperceptible." On the other hand, some judges came to adopt the approach of Holmes, J. in the *Vegelahn* case, that only the abuses of picketing should be enjoined—violence, threats, obstruction of entrances, fraud, and misrepresentation. This was the view taken by the drafters of the Restatement of Torts §§ 775, 798-99 (1939).

2. Assuming that violence has already occurred in the course of picketing, and that the court will enjoin future violence, should the court issue a broad injunction against all further picketing, as a matter of practical policy? If the picketing is for a proper objective, but violence has occurred would a broad injunction against all further picketing violate the Federal Constitution?

MILK WAGON DRIVERS, LOCAL 753 v. MEADOWMOOR DAIRIES, INC.

Supreme Court of the United States
312 U.S. 287, 61 S. Ct. 552, 85 L. Ed. 836 (1941)

MR. JUSTICE FRANKFURTER delivered the opinion of the Court.

The supreme court of Illinois sustained an injunction against the Milk Wagon Drivers Union over the latter's claim that it involved an infringement of the freedom of speech guaranteed by the Fourteenth Amendment.... The present respondent, Meadowmoor Dairies, Inc., brought suit against the Union and its officials to stop interference with the distribution of its products. A preliminary injunction restraining all union conduct, violent and peaceful, promptly issued, and the case was referred to a master for report. Besides peaceful picketing of the stores handling Meadowmoor's products, the master found that there had been violence on a considerable scale.... In the light of his findings, the master recommended that all picketing, and not merely violent acts, should be enjoined. The trial court, however, accepted the recommendations only as to acts of violence and permitted peaceful picketing. The reversal of this ruling by the supreme court, 371 Ill. 377, 21 N.E.2d 308, directing a permanent injunction as recommended by the master, is now before us.

The question, which thus emerges, is whether a state can choose to authorize its courts to enjoin acts of picketing in themselves peaceful when they are enmeshed with contemporaneously violent conduct, which is concededly outlawed....

In this case, the master found "intimidation of the customers of the plaintiff's vendors by the commission of the acts of violence," and the supreme court justified its decision because picketing, "in connection with or following a series of assaults or destruction of property, could not help but have the effect of intimidating the persons in front of whose premises such picketing occurred, and of causing them to believe that non-compliance would possibly be followed by acts of an unlawful character." It is not for us to make an independent valuation of the testimony before the master. We have not only his findings but his findings authenticated by the state of Illinois speaking through her supreme court. We can reject such a determination only if we can say that it is so without warrant as to be a palpable evasion of the constitutional guarantee here invoked. The place to resolve conflicts in the testimony and in its interpretation was in the Illinois courts and not here. To substitute our judgment for that of the state court is to transcend the limits of our authority. And to do so, in the name of the Fourteenth Amendment in a matter peculiarly touching the local policy of a state regarding violence, tends to discredit the great immunities of the Bill of Rights. No one will doubt that Illinois can protect its storekeepers from being coerced by fear of window-smashings or burnings or bombings. And acts which, in isolation, are peaceful may be part of a coercive thrust when entangled with acts of violence. The picketing in this case was set in a background of violence. In such a setting it could justifiably be concluded that the momentum of fear generated by past violence would survive even though future picketing might be wholly peaceful. So the supreme court of Illinois found. We cannot say that such a finding so contradicted experience as to warrant our rejection. Nor can we say that it was written into the Fourteenth Amendment that a state, through its courts, cannot base protection against future coercion on an inference of the continuing threat of past misconduct....

NOTES

1. What findings must the trial court make, to issue a broad injunction under the *Meadowmoor* case? In *Youngdahl v. Rainfair,* 355 U.S. 131, 139 (1957), the Supreme Court held:

> The picketing proper, as contrasted with the activities around the headquarters, was peaceful. There was little, if any, conduct designed to exclude those who desired to return to work. Nor can we say that a pattern of violence was established which would inevitably reappear in the event picketing were later resumed. *Cf. Milk Wagon Drivers Union v. Meadowmoor Dairies, Inc.,* 312 U.S. 287. What violence there was was scattered in time and much of it was unconnected with the picketing. There is nothing in the record to indicate that an injunction against such conduct would be ineffective if picketing were resumed. Accordingly, insofar as the injunction before us prohibits petitioners and others cooperating with them from threatening violence against, or provoking violence on the part of, any of the officers, agents or employees of respondent and prohibits them from obstructing or attempting to obstruct the free use of the streets adjacent to respondent's place of business, and the free ingress and egress to and from that property, it is affirmed. On the other hand, to the extent the injunction prohibits all other picketing and patrolling of respondent's premises and in particular prohibits peaceful picketing, it is set aside.

2. *Mass Picketing.* Even where no actual violence has occurred, the courts have enjoined that form of picketing in which the pickets march so closely together as to block free ingress and egress. As the New Jersey court put it, "a picket fence is not the legitimate child of a picket line." *Westinghouse Elec. Corp. v. UE, Local 410,* 139 N.J. Eq. 97, 49 A.2d 896 (1946).

Is it simply *mass* picketing that is enjoinable, despite constitutional doctrine and the anti-injunction acts, or is it mass picketing that *in fact* denies access to the plant or blocks the use of the streets? And what *is* "mass" picketing—200, 100, or ten pickets? *Cf. American Steel Foundries v. Tri-City Central Trades Council,* 257 U.S. 184 (1921) (violence found; injunction limited pickets to one at each gate and all others enjoined from congregating nearby); *Westinghouse Elec. Corp. v. UE, Local 107,* 383 Pa. 297, 118 A.2d 180 (1955) (no violence found, but mass picketing enjoined; pickets limited to three at each gate, spaced not less than ten feet apart, and others enjoined from congregating in large numbers nearby). Should the assemblage of large numbers of strikers near the struck plant be privileged in order to demonstrate solidarity and maintain morale, even if such acts are likely to lead to a breach of the peace?

3. *Standards Applied to Language Used by Pickets.* The courts have traditionally enjoined the use of language that constitutes fraud, libel, misrepresentation, or inciting to a breach of the peace. Consider, however, some of the problems involved in the application of such general standards.

a. Does the statement, "Employer is unfair to organized labor," constitute misrepresentation or fraud, when it has no labor dispute *with its employees*? Does "employer unfair" wrongfully imply that its workers are on strike—or does it simply mean that its place of business is nonunion? *Cf. Cafeteria Employees, Local 302 v. Angelos,* 320 U.S. 293 (1943) ("To use loose language or undefined slogans that are part of the conventional give and take of our political and economic controversies—like 'unfair' and 'Fascist'—is not to falsify fact"); *Paducah Newspapers, Inc. v. Wise,* 247 S.W.2d 989 (Ky. 1951), *cert. denied,* 343 U.S. 942 (1952) (libel).

b. May pickets be enjoined from calling persons working during a strike "scabs"? *Compare United States v. Taliaferro,* 290 F. 214, 218 (W.D. Va. 1922) *with Walter A. Wood Mowing & Repairing Mach. Co. v. Toohey,* 114 Misc. 185, 190, 191, 186 N.Y.S. 95, 99 (1921) *and Youngdahl v. Rainfair,* 355 U.S. 131, 134-35 (1957).

c. What about "silent" forms of alleged intimidation, such as the visible writing down of license numbers of automobiles entering a place of business being picketed? In *Wallace Co. v. Machinists, Local 1005,* 155 Ore. 652, 63 P.2d 1090 (1936), the court said, "We disapprove of taking the license numbers of automobiles belonging to customers of the plaintiffs, as it may reasonably be interpreted by such customers as an implied threat to do them injury and thereby interfere with the right of the plaintiffs to transact business." But in *Loder Bros. Co. v. Machinists, Local 1506,* 209 Ore. 305, 306 P.2d 411 (1957), where the union followed the taking of license numbers with a letter to the car owners moderately stating the issues in the labor dispute and requesting support, the court refused an injunction. *See* Jones, *The Loder Letter—Have Union Picketers Finally Found the Formula?* 4 U.C.L.A. L. Rev. 370 (1957).

TEAMSTERS, LOCAL 901 [LOCK JOINT PIPE & CO.]

National Labor Relations Board
202 N.L.R.B. 399 (1973)

[During a strike, three officials of the union, designated as being agents of the union, threatened nonstriking employees with physical harm and damaged some cars. They also threatened truck drivers who handled the employer's product with physical harm to themselves and their trucks, and attempted to wreck one truck while it was being driven. The Administrative Law Judge found that the union was guilty of restraint and coercion within § 8(b)(1) and recommended as a remedy, in addition to the usual cease and desist order and mailing of the Board order to all employees, that the union be ordered to give backpay to the employees who were unable to work because of the union's unfair labor practices.]

We agree with the Administrative Law Judge that Respondent Union violated Section 8(b)(1)(A) by engaging in threats and picket line violence at the Lock Joint Plant in Puerto Rico beginning on August 9, 1971.

We do not, however, agree with his further recommendation that the proper remedy in this case, contrary to Board precedent, is an order directing the Union to give backpay to all employees who did not work as a result of these unfair labor practices. From the very earliest days of the Taft-Hartley Act the desirability of such a remedy has been argued to the Board. In each case the Board has refused to enlarge the scope of its traditional remedies for picket line misconduct. The latest Board decision, *Long Construction Company*, 145 NLRB 554, involved physical injury to employees attempting to cross the picket line. The Board reiterated its view that a backpay order was not appropriate where the union's unfair labor practices involved solely interference with an employee's right of ingress to his place of employment.

These important decisions have stood the test of 24 years of court litigation and Congressional scrutiny. They have not been reversed or nullified and we do not believe the time has come for the Board itself to take that step. *National Cash Register Co., et al. v. N.L.R.B.*, 466 F.2d 945, on which our dissenting colleagues rely, stands only for the well-established principle that where an employer unlawfully prevents an employee from working at the insistence of a union both are jointly and severally liable for the employee's loss of pay.[4]

In exercising its broad discretionary powers under Section 10(c) of the Act the Board has always been careful to balance the effectiveness of a particular remedy against its consequences. Thus, the Board has refrained from directing an otherwise appropriate remedy where practical and economic considerations dictated a lesser deterrent.... The extension of backpay liability to a situation where, as here, only picket line misconduct has occurred involves important considerations going to the heart of the right to strike under Sections 7 and 13 of the Act. Those sections of the Act have been called the safety valves of labor management relations. Emotions run high among those for and those against the union. Regrettably, sometimes there is violence and the threat of violence. This we deplore and in no way condone. However, adequate remedies under the Act other than backpay exist to prevent the occurrence of violence without interfering with the right to strike.[5] Where union agents, including pickets, engage in conduct violative of

---

[4] *See also Stuart Wilson, Inc.*, 200 NLRB No. 83, 82 LRRM 1165, which is likewise distinguishable as there the employer discriminated against the employees by sending them home because of the union's unlawful threats and violence.

[5] As we noted in *Long, supra,* the lack of a Board order awarding backpay to employees unable to work because of injuries resulting from a union's unlawful conduct will not leave such employees without redress against those responsible for their injuries. These individuals will still have available those private remedies traditionally used to process claims resulting from another's tortious conduct. In fact they may be better served by pursuing such remedies as the employee's pay

Section 8(b)(1)(A) the Board enjoins the continuation of such conduct and may, if warranted seek an immediate court injunction under Section 10(j) of the Act. If such judicially directed injunctive relief is ignored effective contempt action is available. Finally, when a union resorts to or encourages the use of violent tactics to enforce its representation rights the Board may decline to issue a bargaining order to remedy an employer's unfair labor practices and instead may direct an election to determine whether or not the union is the recognized representative.

To do more, in our opinion, runs the risk of inhibiting the right of employees to strike to such an extent as to substantially diminish that right. For the misconduct of a few pickets may be sufficient to find the union in violation of Section 8(b)(1)(A) and enough to intimidate many employees. The Board would then be required, under the logic of our dissenting colleagues, to seek backpay for all intimidated employees. Faced with this financial responsibility, few unions would be in a position to establish a picket line. In our opinion, union misconduct of this nature, while serious, does not warrant the adoption of a remedy so severe as to risk the diminution of the right to strike, a fundamental right guaranteed by Sections 7 and 13 of the Act. Rather, we believe, the availability to the General Counsel of Section 10(j) of the Act, implemented by contempt action, if necessary, as well as the withholding of an otherwise appropriate bargaining order and the direction of an election are the preferred methods of deterring picket line misconduct violative of Section 8(b)(1)(A).

MILLER, CHAIRMAN, and KENNEDY, MEMBER, dissenting in part:

We agree with our colleagues that by engaging in acts of violence against non-striking employees, by damaging the property of nonstriking employees, and by threatening injury to other employees, the Union has, in violation of Section 8(b)(1)(A), engaged in coercive activity designed to prevent nonstriking employees from working and to deter striking employees from returning to work. However, we dissent from our colleagues' refusal to adopt the Administrative Law Judge's recommended remedy to make the employees whole for the loss of wages suffered when they were prevented from working by the Union's unlawful conduct.

We are unable to perceive the basis of our colleagues' conclusion that backpay remedy herein would unnecessarily "risk the diminution of the right to strike," and their reliance on the existence of "adequate remedies ... other than backpay ... to prevent the occurrence of violence without interfering with the right to strike." Section 10(c)'s concern is not with preventing or deterring violence but with eliminating and remedying the effects of that violence. Hence, any incidental deterrent or penal effect of backpay is irrelevant in our determination of an adequate remedy for the violation found herein. Indeed, it is difficult to comprehend

---

may be only a small part of the total required to make him whole, such as medical expenses as well as compensation for physical injury and pain and suffering.

how making an employee whole for loss of wages suffered because of the union's unlawful activity in preventing employees from working is any less remedial or any more punitive or deterrent in effect than making an employee whole for loss of wages suffered when the employer would not allow him to work because of the union's unlawful activity.

In our view, a backpay order herein is no more penal or deterring in effect than any other backpay order issued by the Board. Indeed, a backpay remedy in the instant case is necessary to remove the effect of the Union's unlawful conduct and thereby effectuate the policies of the Act.

NOTES

1. *Iron Workers Local 111 (Northern States Steel),* 298 N.L.R.B. 930 (1990), *enforced,* 946 F.2d 1264 (7th Cir. 1991), involved two "travelers" from another geographical area who had taken jobs in Local 111's jurisdiction. Local 111 coerced them into quitting their jobs in violation of § 8(b)(1)(A). Although Local 111 argued that the rationale of *Lock Joint Pipe* precluded an award of back pay, the Labor Board carefully distinguished between § 8(b)(1)(A) conduct associated with work stoppages or picket line activity and behavior not intertwined with such protected conduct. It indicated that it would normally award back pay to employees prevented from working because of union coercion unconnected with strike or picketing activity.

> [W]here ... the union, ... without the use of strike or picketing misconduct, causes a severance or interference in an employee's tenure or terms of employment, no ... Board concerns about the right to strike come into play. Moreover, merely ordering the offending union to cease and desist from its unlawful conduct will neither remove the chilling effect on the victimized employees' willingness to exercise their statutory rights nor restore the status quo ante. Only a backpay remedy can accomplish those ends.

2. The NLRA, as amended in 1947, prohibits unions and their agents from restraining and coercing employees in the exercise of § 7 rights, which include the right to refrain from concerted activities. "The legislative history of the act shows that, by this particular section, Congress primarily intended to proscribe the *coercive conduct* which sometimes accompanies a strike, but not the strike itself. By § 8(b)(1)(A), Congress sought to fix the rules of the game, to insure that strikes and other organizational activities of employees were conducted peaceably by persuasion and propaganda and not by physical force, or threats of force, or of economic reprisal. In that section, Congress was aiming at means, not at ends." *Perry Norvell Co.,* 80 N.L.R.B. 225, 239 (1948). *See also National Maritime Union,* 78 N.L.R.B. 971 (1948). *See generally* Haggard, *Labor Union Violence as an Unfair Labor Practice,* 34 S.C. L. Rev. 273 (1982). *See also NLRB v. Driv-*

ers, Chauffeurs, Helpers, Local 639, 362 U.S. 274 (1960), *infra,* (peaceful organizational picketing not § 8(b)(1)(A) violation).

3. In *International Longshoremen's & Warehousemen's Union, CIO, Local 6 (Sunset Line & Twine Co.),* 79 N.L.R.B. 1487 (1948), the NLRB discussed the responsibility of a union for the acts of individuals:

> [T]he Board has a clear statutory mandate to apply the "ordinary law of agency." The act, as amended, envisages that the Board shall now hold labor organizations responsible for conduct of their agents which is proscribed by § 8(b) of the statute, just as it has always held employers responsible for the acts of their agents which were violative of § 8(a). For this purpose we are to treat labor organizations as legal entities, like corporations, which act, and can only act, through their duly appointed agents, as distinguished from their individual members.[41] Hence, our task of determining the responsibility of unions in cases arising under § 8(b) of the act is not essentially new, for the Board has been deciding similar questions in cases involving corporate employers, ever since the statute was enacted in 1935. The fact patterns in § 8(b) cases, however, are a novel study in the administration of the act. We have rarely had occasion to examine the relationships between a labor organization and its officers or other persons allegedly representing it, especially for the purpose of deciding whether or not the officer or other person was acting, in a particular instance, as the agent of the labor organization. Because this is a case of first impression in that sense, we shall set forth, in abstract, those fundamental rules of the law of agency which we believe must control our decision of the issue of responsibility in this and similar cases:
>
> 1. The burden of proof is on the party asserting an agency relationship, both as to the existence of the relationship and as to the nature and extent of the agent's authority. In this case, for example, it was incumbent upon the General Counsel to prove, not only that the acts of restraint and coercion alleged in the complaint were committed, but also that those acts were committed by agents of the Respondent Unions, acting in their representative capacity. The Respondents' failure to introduce evidence *negating* the imputations in the complaint did not relieve the General Counsel of that burden.
>
> 2. Agency is a *contractual relationship,* deriving from the mutual consent of principal and agent that the agent shall act for the principal. But the principal's consent, technically called authorization or ratification,

[41] Proponents of the 1947 Amendments stated emphatically, in the Senate debates, that a member of a labor union is not *per se* an agent of the union. *See* 93 Cong. Rec. 4561 (May 2, 1947); *Id.* 4142 (April 25, 1947). *See also, United States v. White,* 322 U.S. 694, 702 (1944); *Hill v. Eagle Glass & Mfg. Co.,* 219 F. 719 (4th Cir. 1915), *rev'd on other grounds,* 245 U.S. 275 (1917).

may be manifested by conduct, sometimes even passive acquiescence, as well as by words. Authority to act as agent in a given manner will be implied whenever the conduct of the principal is such as to show that he actually intended to confer that authority.

3. A principal may be responsible for the act of his agent within the scope of the agent's general authority, or the "scope of his employment" if the agent is a servant, even though the principal has not specifically authorized or indeed may have specifically forbidden the act in question. It is enough if the principal empowered the agent to represent him in the general area within which the agent acted.

Under what circumstances, "according to the ordinary law of agency," should a union be held to have committed an unfair labor practice because of violence by a picket who is not a union officer or business agent? *See International Woodworkers (W.T. Smith Lumber Co.),* 116 N.L.R.B. 507 (1956), *enforced,* 243 F.2d 745 (5th Cir. 1957). When would the International Union, as well as the Local Union, be held liable under § 8(b)(1)(A) for picket line threats and violence?

B. UNION FINES AND DISCIPLINE AS COERCION

NLRB v. ALLIS-CHALMERS MFG. CO.

Supreme Court of the United States
388 U.S. 175, 87 S. Ct. 2001, 18 L. Ed. 2d 1123 (1967)

MR. JUSTICE BRENNAN delivered the opinion of the Court.

The question here is whether a union which threatened and imposed fines [of $20 to $100] and brought suit for their collection, against members who crossed the union's picket line and went to work during an authorized strike against their employer, committed the unfair labor practice under § 8(b)(1)(A) of the National Labor Relations Act of engaging in conduct "to restrain or coerce" employees in the exercise of their right guaranteed by § 7 to "refrain from" concerted activities....

I

... It is highly unrealistic to regard § 8(b)(1), and particularly its words "restrain or coerce," as precisely and unambiguously covering the union conduct involved in this case. On its face court enforcement of fines imposed on members for violation of membership obligations is no more conduct to "restrain or coerce" satisfaction of such obligations than court enforcement of penalties imposed on citizens for violation of their obligations as citizens to pay income taxes, or court awards of damages against a contracting party for nonperformance of a contractual obligation voluntarily undertaken. But even if the inherent imprecision of the words "restrain or coerce" may be overlooked, recourse to legislative history to determine the sense in which Congress used the words is not foreclosed....

To say that Congress meant in 1947 by the § 7 amendments and § 8(b)(1)(A) to strip unions of the power to fine members for strikebreaking, however lawful the strike vote, and however fair the disciplinary procedures and penalty, is to say that Congress preceded the Landrum-Griffin amendments with an even more pervasive regulation of the internal affairs of unions. It is also to attribute to Congress an intent at war with the understanding of the union-membership relation which has been at the heart of its effort "to fashion a coherent labor policy" and which has been a predicate underlying action by this Court and the state courts. More importantly, it is to say that Congress limited unions in the powers necessary to the discharge of their role as exclusive statutory bargaining agents by impairing the usefulness of labor's cherished strike weapon. It is no answer that the proviso to § 8(b)(1)(A) preserves to the union the power to expel the offending member. Where the union is strong and membership therefore valuable, to require expulsion of the member visits a far more severe penalty upon the member than a reasonable fine. Where the union is weak, and membership therefore of little value, the union faced with further depletion of its ranks may have no real choice except to condone the member's disobedience. Yet it is just such weak unions for which the power to execute union decisions taken for the benefit of all employees is most critical to effective discharge of its statutory function.

Congressional meaning is of course ordinarily to be discerned in the words Congress uses. But when the literal application of the imprecise words "restrain or coerce" Congress employed in § 8(b)(1)(A) produce the extraordinary results we have mentioned we should determine whether this meaning is confirmed in the legislative history of the section.

II

The explicit wording of § 8(b)(2), which is concerned with union powers to affect a member's employment, is in sharp contrast with the imprecise words of § 8(b)(1)(A).... Senator Taft, in answer to protestations by Senator Pepper that § 8(b)(2) would intervene into the union's internal affairs and "deny it the right to protect itself against a man in the union who betrays the objectives of the union ...," stated:

> *The pending measure does not propose any limitation with respect to the internal affairs of unions.* They still will be able to fire any members they wish to fire, *and they still will be able to try any of their members.* All that they will not be able to do, after the enactment of this bill, is this: If they fire a member for some reason other than nonpayment of dues they cannot make

his employer discharge him from his job and throw him out of work. That is the only result of the provision under discussion.[13] ...

What legislative materials there are dealing with § 8(b)(1)(A) contain not a single word referring to the application of its prohibitions to traditional internal union discipline in general, or disciplinary fines in particular. On the contrary there are a number of assurances by its sponsors that the section was not meant to regulate the internal affairs of unions....

It is true that there are references in the Senate debate on § 8(b)(1)(A) to an intent to impose the same prohibitions on unions that applied to employers as regards restraint and coercion of employees in their exercise of § 7 rights. However apposite this parallel might be when applied to organizational tactics, it clearly is inapplicable to the relationship of a union member to his own union. Union membership allows the member a part in choosing the very course of action to which he refuses to adhere, but he has of course no role in employer conduct, and nonunion employees have no voice in the affairs of the union.

Cogent support for an interpretation of the body of § 8(b)(1) as not reaching the imposition of fines and attempts at court enforcement is the proviso to § 8(b)(1).... Senator Holland offered the proviso during debate and Senator Ball immediately accepted it, stating that it was not the intent of the sponsors in any way to regulate the internal affairs of unions. At the very least it can be said that the proviso preserves the rights of unions to impose fines, as a lesser penalty than expulsion, and to impose fines which carry the explicit or implicit threat of expulsion for nonpayment. Therefore, under the proviso the rule in the UAW constitution governing fines is valid and the fines themselves and expulsion for nonpayment would not be an unfair labor practice. Assuming that the proviso cannot also be read to authorize court enforcement of fines, a question we need not reach, the fact remains that to interpret the body of § 8(b)(1) to apply to the imposition and collection of fines would be to impute to Congress a concern with the permissible *means* of enforcement of union fines and to attribute to Congress a narrow and discrete interest in banning court enforcement of such fines. Yet there is not one word of the legislative history evidencing any such congressional concern. And as we have pointed out, a distinction between court enforcement and expulsion would have been anomalous for several reasons. First, Congress was operating within the context of the "contract theory" of the union-member relationship which widely prevailed at that time. The efficacy of a contract is precisely its legal enforceability. A lawsuit is and has been the ordinary way by which performance of private money obligations is compelled. Second, as we have noted, such a distinction would visit upon the member of a strong union a potentially more severe punishment than court enforcement of fines, while im-

---

[13]93 Cong. Rec. 4193, II Legislative History of the Labor Management Relations Act of 1947, 1097 (hereafter, Leg. Hist.).

pairing the bargaining facility of the weak union by requiring it either to condone misconduct or deplete its ranks.

There may be concern that court enforcement may permit the collection of unreasonably large fines. However, even were there evidence that Congress shared this concern, this would not justify reading the Act also to bar court enforcement of reasonable fines.

The 1959 Landrum-Griffin amendments, thought to be the first comprehensive regulation by Congress of the conduct of internal union affairs,[33] also negate the reach given § 8(b)(1)(A) by the majority *en banc* below.... In 1959 Congress did seek to protect union members in their relationship to the union by adopting measures to insure the provision of democratic processes in the conduct of union affairs and procedural due process to members subjected to discipline. Even then, some Senators emphasized that "[I]n establishing and enforcing statutory standards great care should be taken not to undermine union self-government or weaken unions in their role as collective-bargaining agents." S. Rep. No. 187, 86th Cong., 1st Sess., 7. The Eighty-sixth Congress was thus plainly of the view that union self-government was not regulated in 1947. Indeed, that Congress expressly recognized that a union member may be "fined, suspended, expelled, or otherwise disciplined," and enacted only procedural requirements to be observed. 29 U.S.C. § 411(a)(5). Moreover, Congress added a proviso to the guarantee of freedom of speech and assembly disclaiming any intent "to impair the right of a labor organization to adopt and enforce reasonable rules as to the responsibility of every member toward the organization as an institution...." 29 U.S.C. § 411(a)(2)....

Thus this history of congressional action does not support a conclusion that the Taft-Hartley prohibitions against restraint or coercion of an employee to refrain from concerted activities included a prohibition against the imposition of fines on members who decline to honor an authorized strike and attempts to collect such fines. Rather, the contrary inference is more justified in light of the repeated refrain throughout the debates on § 8(b)(1)(A) and other sections that Congress did not propose any limitations with respect to the internal affairs of unions, aside from barring enforcement of a union's internal regulations to affect a member's employment status.

III

... The collective bargaining agreements with the locals incorporate union security clauses. Full union membership is not compelled by the clauses: an employee is required only to become and remain "a member of the union to the ex-

---

[33] In 1957, in *Machinists v. Gonzales,* 356 U.S. 617, 620, we said: "[T]he protection of union members in their rights as members from arbitrary conduct by unions and union officers has not been undertaken by federal law, and indeed the assertion of any such power has been expressly denied."

tent of paying his monthly dues...." The majority *en banc* below nevertheless regarded full membership to be "the result not of individual voluntary choice but of the insertion of [this] union security provision in the contract under which a substantial minority of the employees may have been forced into membership." 358 F.2d at 660. But the relevant inquiry here is not what motivated a member's full membership but whether the Taft-Hartley amendments prohibited disciplinary measures against a full member who crossed his union's picket line. It is clear that the fined employees involved in these cases enjoyed full union membership. Each executed the pledge of allegiance to the UAW constitution and took the oath of full membership. Moreover, the record of the Milwaukee County Court case against Benjamin Natzke discloses that two disciplined employees testified that they had fully participated in the proceedings leading to the strike. They attended the meetings at which the secret strike vote and the renewed strike vote were taken. It was upon this and similar evidence that the Milwaukee County Court found that Natzke "had by his actions become a member of the union for all purposes...." Allis-Chalmers offered no evidence in this proceeding that any of the fined employees enjoyed other than full union membership. We will not presume the contrary. *Cf. Machinists v. Street,* 367 U.S. 740, 774. Indeed, it is and has been Allis-Chalmers' position that the Taft-Hartley prohibitions apply whatever the nature of the membership. Whether those prohibitions would apply if the locals had imposed fines on members whose membership was in fact limited to the obligation of paying monthly dues is a question not before us and upon which we intimate no view.

The judgment of the Court of Appeals is

Reversed.

MR. JUSTICE WHITE, concurring.

It is true that § 8(b)(1)(A) makes it an unfair labor practice for a union to restrain or coerce any employees in the exercise of § 7 rights, but the proviso permits the union to make its own rules with respect to acquisition and retention of membership. Hence, a union may expel to enforce its own internal rules, even though a particular rule limits the § 7 rights of its members and even though expulsion to enforce it would be a clear and serious brand of "coercion" imposed in derogation of those § 7 rights. Such restraint and coercion Congress permitted by adding the proviso to § 8(b)(1)(A). Thus, neither the majority nor the dissent in this case questions the validity of the union rule against its members crossing picket lines during a properly called strike, nor the propriety of expulsion to enforce the rule. Section 8(b)(1)(A), therefore, does not bar *all* restraint and coercion by a union to prevent the exercise by its members of their § 7 rights. "Coercive" union rules are enforceable at least by expulsion.

The dissenting opinion in this case, although not questioning the enforceability of coercive rules by expulsion from membership, questions whether fines for violating such rules are enforceable at all, by expulsion or otherwise. The dissent would at least hold court collection of fines to be an unfair labor practice, apparently for the reason that fines collectible in court may be more coercive than fines enforceable by expulsion. My Brother BRENNAN, for the Court, takes a different view, reasoning that since expulsion would in many cases—certainly in this one involving a strong union—be a far more coercive technique for enforcing a union rule and for collecting a reasonable fine than the threat of court enforcement, there is no basis for thinking that Congress, having accepted expulsion as a permissible technique to enforce a rule in derogation of § 7 rights, nevertheless intended to bar enforcement by another method which may be far less coercive.

I do not mean to indicate, and I do not read the majority opinion otherwise, that every conceivable internal union rule which impinges upon the § 7 rights of union members is valid and enforceable by expulsion and court action. There may well be some internal union rules which on their face are wholly invalid and unenforceable. But the Court seems unanimous in upholding the rule against crossing picket lines during a strike and its enforceability by expulsion from membership. On this premise I think the opinion written for the Court is the more persuasive and sensible construction of the statute and I therefore join it, although I am doubtful about the implications of some of its generalized statements.

MR. JUSTICE BLACK, whom MR. JUSTICE DOUGLAS, MR. JUSTICE HARLAN, and MR. JUSTICE STEWART join, dissenting....

I

In determining what the Court here holds, it is helpful to note what it does not hold. Since the union resorted to the courts to enforce its fines instead of relying on its own internal sanctions such as expulsion from membership, the Court correctly assumes that the proviso to § 8(b)(1)(A) cannot be read to authorize its holding. Neither does the Court attempt to sustain its holding by reference to § 7 which gives employees the right to refrain from engaging in concerted activities. To be sure, the Court in characterizing the union-member relationship as "contractual" and in emphasizing that its holding is limited to situations where the employee is a "full member" of the union, implies that by joining a union an employee gives up or waives some of his § 7 rights. But the Court does not say that a union member is without the § 7 right to refrain from participating in such concerted activity as an economic strike called by his union....

With no reliance on the proviso to § 8(b)(1)(A) or on the meaning of § 7, the Court's holding boils down to this: a court-enforced reasonable fine for nonparticipation in a strike does not "restrain or coerce" an employee in the exercise of his right not to participate in the strike. In holding as it does, the Court interprets the words "restrain or coerce" in a way directly opposed to their literal meaning, for the Court admits that fines are as coercive as penalties imposed on citizens for the nonpayment of taxes. Though Senator Taft, in answer to charges that these words were ambiguous, said their meaning "is perfectly clear," 93 Cong. Rec. 4021, II Leg. Hist. 1025, and though any union official with sufficient intelligence and learning to be chosen as such could hardly fail to comprehend the meaning of these plain, simple English words, the Court insists on finding an "inherent imprecision" in these words. And that characterization then allows the Court to resort to "what legislative materials there are."

... The real reason for the Court's decision is its policy judgment that unions, especially weak ones, need the power to impose fines on strikebreakers and to enforce those fines in court. It is not enough, says the Court, that the unions have the power to expel those members who refuse to participate in a strike or who fail to pay fines imposed on them for such failure to participate; it is essential that weak unions have the choice between expulsion and court-enforced fines, simply because the latter are more effective in the sense of being more punitive. Though the entire mood of Congress in 1947 was to curtail the power of unions, as it had previously curtailed the power of employers, in order to equalize the power of the two, the Court is unwilling to believe that Congress intended to impair "the usefulness of labor's cherished strike weapon." I cannot agree with this conclusion or subscribe to the Court's unarticulated premise that the Court has power to add a new weapon to the union's economic arsenal whenever the Court believes that the union needs that weapon. That is a job for Congress, not this Court.

II

... Contrary to the Court, I am not at all certain that a union's right under the proviso to prescribe rules for the retention of membership includes the right to restrain a member from working by trying him on the vague charge of "conduct unbecoming a union member" and fining him for exercising his § 7 right of refusing to participate in a strike, even though the fine is only enforceable by expulsion from membership. It is one thing to say that Congress did not wish to interfere with the union's power, similar to that of any other kind of voluntary association, to prescribe specific conditions of membership. It is quite another thing to say that Congress intended to leave unions free to exercise a court-like power to try and punish members with a direct economic sanction for exercising their right to work. Just because a union might be free, under the proviso, to expel a member for crossing a picket line does not mean that Congress left unions free to threaten their members with fines. Even though a member may later discover that the threatened fine is only enforceable by expulsion, and in that sense a "lesser penalty," the direct threat of a fine, to a member normally unaware of the method the union might resort to for compelling its payment, would often be more coercive than a threat of expulsion.

Even on the assumption that § 8(b)(1)(A) permits a union to fine a member as long as the fine is only enforceable by expulsion, the fundamental error of the Court's opinion is its failure to recognize the practical and theoretical difference between a court-enforced fine, as here, and a fine enforced by expulsion or less drastic intra-union means. As the Court recognizes, expulsion for nonpayment of a fine may, especially in the case of a strong union, be more severe than judicial collection of the fine. But, if the union membership has little value and if the fine is great, then court-enforcement of the fine may be more effective punishment, and that is precisely why the Court desires to provide weak unions with this alternative to expulsion, an alternative which is similar to a criminal court's power to imprison defendants who fail to pay fines....

The Court disposes of this tremendous practical difference between court-enforced and union-enforced fines by suggesting that Congress was not concerned with "the permissible means of enforcement of union fines" and that court-enforcement of fines is a necessary consequence of the "contract theory" of the union-member relationship. And then the Court cautions that its holding may only apply to court enforcement of "reasonable fines." Apparently the Court believes that these considerations somehow bring reasonable court-enforced fines within the ambit of "internal union affairs." There is no basis either historically or logically for this conclusion or the considerations upon which it is based. First, the Court says that disciplinary fines were commonplace at the time the Taft-Hartley Act was passed, and thus Congress could not have meant to prohibit these "traditional internal discipline" measures without saying so. Yet there is not one word in the authorities cited by the Court that indicates that court enforcement of fines was commonplace or traditional in 1947, and, to the contrary, until recently unions rarely resorted to court enforcement of union fines. Second, Congress' unfamiliarity in 1947 with this recent innovation and consequent failure to make any distinction between union-enforced and court-enforced fines cannot support the conclusion that Congress was unconcerned with the "means" a union uses to enforce its fines. Congress was expressly concerned with enacting "rules of the game" for unions to abide by. 93 Cong. Rec. 4436, II Leg. Hist. 1206....

V

... The union here had a union security clause in its contract with Chalmers. That clause made it necessary for all employees, including the ones involved here, to pay dues and fees to the union. But § 8(a)(3) and § 8(b)(2) make it clear that "Congress intended to prevent utilization of union security agreements for any purpose other than to compel payment of union dues and fees." *Radio Officers' Union v. Labor Board,* 347 U.S. 17, 41. If the union uses the union security clause to compel employees to pay dues, characterizes such employees as members, and then uses such membership as a basis for imposing court-enforced fines upon those employees unwilling to participate in a union strike, then the union security clause is being used for a purpose other than "to compel payment of union dues and fees." It is being used to coerce employees to join in union activity in violation of § 8(b)(2).

The Court suggests that this problem is not present here, because the fined employees failed to prove they enjoyed other than full union membership, that their role in the union was not in fact limited to the obligation of paying dues. For several reasons, I am unable to agree with the Court's approach. Few employees forced to become "members" of the union by virtue of the union security clause will be aware of the fact that they must somehow "limit" their membership to avoid the union's court-enforced fines. Even those who are brash enough to attempt to do so may be unfamiliar with how to do it. Must they refrain from doing anything but paying dues, or will signing the routine union pledge still leave them with less than full membership? And finally, it is clear that what restrains the employee from going to work during a union strike is the union's threat that it will fine him and collect those fines from him in court. How many employees in a union shop whose names appear on the union's membership rolls will be willing to ignore that threat in the hope that they will later be able to convince the Labor Board or the state court that they were not full members of the union?

NOTES

1. Union discipline that frustrates an overriding federal labor policy will be held to violate § 8(b)(1)(A). For example, a labor organization may not fine members who refuse to participate in a work stoppage that contravenes a contractual no-strike clause. *Laborers Local 135 (Bechtel Power Corp.)*, 271 N.L.R.B. 777 (1984), *enforced,* 782 F.2d 1030 (3d Cir. 1986). Nor may it discipline members who refuse to honor a picket line established by a sister union, when such action would violate contractual prohibitions against sympathy strikes. *District 50, Local 12419 (Nat'l Grinding Wheel Co.),* 176 N.L.R.B. 628 (1969); *Food & Commercial Workers, Local 1439 (Rosauer's Supermarkets),* 275 N.L.R.B. 30 (1985). *See also Plumbers, Local 444 (Hanson Plumbing)*, 277 N.L.R.B. 1231 (1985), *enforced,* 827 F.2d 579 (9th Cir. 1987) (union violated § 8(b)(1)(A) when it fined members who refused to honor primary picket line at a common situs construction project, since union impermissibly sought to exert pressure against the primary general contractor through secondary subcontractor).

In *Laborers Local 324 (AGC of California)*, 318 N.L.R.B. 589 (1995), a divided Board held that a union violated § 8(b)(1)(A) when it adopted a no-solicitation/no-distribution rule at its hiring halls because a member had strongly criticized the union leadership in his newsletter, and when the union subsequently threatened his arrest and removal for distributing dissident literature in a hiring hall parking lot. Dissenting Members Browing and Truesdale argued that the mere passing of a facially lawful rule relating to purely internal union conduct did not violate § 8(b)(1)(A), and that the majority had engaged in "an unprecedented and unjustifiable intrusion into internal union affairs." The Ninth Circuit denied enforcement, declaring that the NLRB had improperly focused on the union's animus toward a particular member and that the Board could not make the union's motivation the determining factor in assessing the legality of a facially valid rule. *Laborers Local 324 v. NLRB*, 123 F.3d 1176 (9th Cir. 1997).

2. When a union and an employer included a "two-way" amnesty provision in their strike settlement agreement, the union violated § 8(b)(1)(A) by disciplining members for working during the strike. The policy favoring collective bargaining overrode the right of the union to regulate its internal affairs. *Operating Eng'rs, Local 39 (San Jose Hosp.)*, 240 N.L.R.B. 1122 (1979).

3. If union discipline does not "restrain or coerce" employees within the meaning of § 8(b)(1)(A) in the circumstances of the principal case, does it make any difference *why* the penalty is imposed? In *Scofield v. NLRB*, 394 U.S. 423 (1969), the Supreme Court found no violation of § 8(b)(1)(A) when a union sued in state court to collect fines levied against members who had breached a union rule forbidding the receipt of pay for production that exceeded a set ceiling. *See also Distillery Workers Local 186 (E & J Gallo Winery)*, 296 N.L.R.B. 519 (1989) (union could lawfully fine member who announced she would defy strike call and argued for ouster of union, since this was more than expression of dissenting opinion and justified union's action to maintain membership strike solidarity); *Paperworkers Local 5 (Int'l Paper Co.)*, 294 N.L.R.B. 1168 (1989) (union could fine members who defied ban on performance of work outside bargaining unit).

In *NLRB v. Marine & Shipbuilding Workers*, 391 U.S. 418 (1968), the Court held that a union violated § 8(b)(1)(A) by expelling a member for filing an unfair labor practice charge with the Board without first having exhausted internal union remedies. Declared the Court: "... § 8(b)(1)(A) assures a union freedom of self-regulation where its legitimate internal affairs are concerned. But where a union rule penalizes a member for filing an unfair labor practice charge with the Board other considerations of public policy come into play."

4. Should it make any difference whether a union penalizes a member who files a decertification petition through a fine or expulsion? *See Molders Local 125 (Blackhawk Tanning Co.)*, 178 N.L.R.B. 208 (1969), *enforced*, 442 F.2d 92 (7th Cir. 1971) (fine is punitive and forbidden, while expulsion is defensive and allowable). *See also Tri-Rivers Marine Eng'rs (U.S. Steel Corp.)*, 189 N.L.R.B. 838 (1971) (union may threaten to expel member who solicits authorization cards for rival union, but may not fine that person).

5. *Compare NLRB v. IUE Local 745*, 759 F.2d 533 (6th Cir. 1985) (union violated § 8(b)(1)(A) when steward threatened to fine member $1000 if he testified in favor of employer at arbitral hearing pertaining to fellow member's discharge grievance) *with Graphic Commun. Union (Georgia Pac. Corp.)*, 300 N.L.R.B. 1072 (1990) (union may discipline member who gave perjured testimony at arbitral hearing, but only if member's perjury was first established before external forum, rather than in internal union proceeding).

6. When labor organizations discipline employee-members because of their opposition to union practices or heated discussions regarding contractual rights that do not transcend the bounds of robust debate, they will generally be found in violation of § 8(b)(1)(A). *See Operating Eng'rs Local 139 (AGC of Am.),* 273 N.L.R.B. 992 (1984); *Combustion Eng'g,* 272 N.L.R.B. 957 (1984). The Seventh Circuit found no § 8(b)(1)(A) violation in *Operating Eng'rs Local 139,* since the union fine imposed on a member who had published a dissident newspaper did not affect that person's employment relationship. 796 F.2d 985 (1986).

7. Union discipline imposed on supervisor-members in response to their performance of certain job functions may be found to coerce the affected employer with respect to its selection of grievance adjustment or bargaining representatives, and thus contravene § 8(b)(1)(B). *Compare Florida Power & Light Co. v. IBEW Local 641,* 417 U.S. 790 (1974) (union may fine supervisor-members who perform rank-and-file work during strike) *with American Broadcasting Cos. v. Writers Guild of Am., West, Inc.,* 437 U.S. 411 (1978) (union may not fine supervisor-members for performing customary supervisory functions, including grievance adjustment) *and Dallas Mailers Union (Dow Jones Co.),* 181 N.L.R.B. 286 (1970), *enforced on other grounds,* 445 F.2d 730 (D.C. Cir. 1971) (union may not discipline supervisor-members because of way in which they administer labor contract). *See generally* Grissom, *Union Discipline of Supervisor-Members: Drawing the Line After Florida Power,* 27 Ala. L. Rev. 575 (1975).

In *NLRB v. IBEW Local 340,* 481 U.S. 573 (1987), the Supreme Court held that a union did not violate § 8(b)(1)(B) by fining two supervisor-members who had breached the union constitution by working for employers that did not have contracts with the union, since those supervisors did not engage in collective bargaining or grievance adjustment. The Court expressly rejected the Board's "reservoir doctrine," under which all persons defined as § 2(11) "supervisors" were considered part of a "reservoir" of workers available for future employer selection as bargaining representatives or grievance adjusters. The Court ruled that § 8(b)(1)(B) only protects those supervisors who currently possess bargaining or grievance adjustment authority.

8. *See generally* Hartley, *National Labor Relations Board Control of Union Discipline and the Myth of Nonintervention,* 16 Vt. L. Rev. 11 (1991); Atleson, *Union Fines and Picket Lines: The NLRA and Union Disciplinary Power,* 17 U.C.L.A. L. Rev. 681 (1970); Gould, *Some Limitations Upon Union Discipline Under the National Labor Relations Act: the Radiations of Allis-Chalmers,* 1970 (Duke L.J. 1067; Silard, *Labor Board Regulation of Union Discipline After Allis-Chalmers, Marine Workers, and Scofield,* 38 Geo. Wash. L. Rev. 187 (1969).

NLRB v. Boeing Co., 412 U.S. 67, 93 S. Ct. 1952, 36 L. Ed. 2d 752 (1973). During an 18-day economic strike, certain union members crossed the picket line and returned to work. Although the weekly earnings of the workers ranged from $95 to $145, the returning members were each fined $450. After the union filed state court actions to collect the unpaid fines, charges were filed with the NLRB under § 8(b)(1)(A) claiming that the excessive nature of the fines coerced and restrained the disciplined members. The Labor Board held that "Congress did not intend to give [it] authority to regulate the size of union fines or to establish standards with respect to a fine's reasonableness." The Supreme Court sustained this conclusion.

> [I]n both [*NLRB v. Allis-Chalmers Mfg. Co.,* 388 U.S. 175 (1967)] and in [*Scofield v. NLRB,* 394 U.S. 423 (1969)], the reasonableness of the fines was assumed. Being squarely presented with the issue in this case, we recede from the implications of the dicta in these earlier cases. While "unreasonable" fines may be more coercive than "reasonable" fines, all fines are coercive to a greater or lesser degree. The underlying basis for the holdings of *Allis-Chalmers* and Scofield was not that reasonable fines were noncoercive under the language of § 8(b)(1)(A) of the Act, but was instead that those provisions were not intended by Congress to apply to the imposition by the union of fines not affecting the employer-employee relationship and not otherwise prohibited by the Act. The reason for this determination, in turn, was that Congress had not intended by enacting this section to regulate the internal affairs of unions to the extent that would be required in order to base unfair labor practice charges on the levying of such fines....

> Issues as to the reasonableness or unreasonableness of such fines must be decided upon the basis of the law of contracts, voluntary associations, or such other principles of law as may be applied in a forum competent to adjudicate the issue. Under our holding, state courts will be wholly free to apply state law to such issues ....

NOTES

1. The NLRB has concluded that it is not to assess the fairness of the internal union procedures by which fines are imposed. *UE Local 1012 (General Elec. Co.),* 187 N.L.R.B. 375 (1970). Procedural due process, said the Board, is irrelevant in determining the legality of fines under the NLRA. *See also Carpenters Local 720 v. NLRB (UMC of Louisiana),* 798 F.2d 781 (5th Cir. 1986).

2. *See generally* Archer, *Allis-Chalmers Recycled: A Current View of a Union's Right to Fine Employees for Crossing a Picket Line,* 7 Ind. L. Rev. 498 (1974); Craver, *The Boeing Decision: A Blow to Federalism, Individual Rights and Stare Decisis,* 122 U. Pa. L. Rev. 556 (1974).

PATTERN MAKERS' LEAGUE OF NORTH AMERICA v. NLRB

Supreme Court of the United States
473 U.S. 95, 105 S. Ct. 3064, 87 L. Ed. 2d 68 (1985)

JUSTICE POWELL delivered the opinion of the Court.

The Pattern Makers' League of North America, AFL-CIO (the League), a labor union, provides in its constitution that resignations are not permitted during a strike or when a strike is imminent. The League fined 10 of its members who, in violation of this provision, resigned during a strike and returned to work. The National Labor Relations Board held that these fines were imposed in violation of § 8(b)(1)(A) of the National Labor Relations Act, 29 U.S.C. § 158(b)(1)(A). We granted a petition for a writ of certiorari in order to decide whether § 8(b)(1)(A) reasonably may be construed by the Board as prohibiting a union from fining members who have tendered resignations invalid under the union constitution.

I

The League is a national union composed of local associations (locals). In May 1976, its constitution was amended to provide that:

> No resignation or withdrawal from an Association, or from the League, shall be accepted during a strike or lockout, or at a time when a strike or lockout appears imminent.

This amendment, known as League Law 13, became effective in October 1976, after being ratified by the League's locals. On May 5, 1977, when a collective-bargaining agreement expired, two locals began an economic strike against several manufacturing companies in Rockford, Illinois and Beloit, Wisconsin, Forty-three of the two locals' members participated. In early September 1977, after the locals formally rejected a contract offer, a striking union member submitted a letter of resignation to the Beloit association. He returned to work the following day. During the next three months, 10 more union members resigned from the Rockford and Beloit locals and returned to work. On December 19, 1977, the strike ended when the parties signed a new collective-bargaining agreement. The locals notified 10 employees who had resigned that their resignations had been rejected as violative of League Law 13.[2] The locals further informed the em-

---

[2] Kohl, the other employee who returned to work, was expelled from the union. On January 14, 1978, the Beloit local notified Kohl's employer that because he was no longer a union member, he should be discharged pursuant to the "union shop" agreement. Two weeks later, the Beloit local informed Kohl that he could gain readmission to the union, and thus remain employed, if he paid back dues, a readmission fee, and $4,200 in "damages ... for deserting the strike by returning to work." *Pattern Makers' League of North America,* 265 N.L.R.B. 1332, 1337 (1982) (decision of G. Wacknov, ALJ). Kohl was denied readmission to the union because he refused to pay the amounts allegedly due. Nevertheless, he was not discharged by his employer. *Ibid.*

ployees that, as union members, they were subject to sanctions for returning to work. Each was fined approximately the equivalent of his earnings during the strike.

The Rockford-Beloit Pattern Jobbers' Association (the Association) had represented the employers throughout the collective-bargaining process. It filed charges with the Board against the League and its two locals, the petitioners. Relying on § 8(b)(1)(A), the Association claimed that levying fines against employees who had resigned was an unfair labor practice. Following a hearing, an Administrative Law Judge found that the petitioners had violated § 8(b)(1)(A) by fining employees for returning to work after tendering resignations. *Pattern Makers' League of North America,* 265 N.L.R.B. 1332, 1339 (1982) (decision of G. Wacknov, ALJ). The Board agreed that § 8(b)(1)(A) prohibited the union from imposing sanctions on the 10 employees. *Pattern Makers' League of North America, supra.* In holding that League Law 13 did not justify the imposition of fines on the members who attempted to resign, the Board relied on its earlier decision in *Machinists Local 1327 (Dalmo Victor II),* 263 N.L.R.B. 984 (1982), *enf. denied,* 725 F.2d 1212 (CA9 1984).[5]

The United States Court of Appeals for the Seventh Circuit enforced the Board's order. 724 F.2d 57 (1983). The Court of Appeals stated that by restricting the union members' freedom to resign, League Law 13 "frustrate[d] the overriding policy of labor law that employees be free to choose whether to engage in concerted activities." *Id.,* at 60. Noting that the "mutual reliance" theory was given little weight in *NLRB v. Textile Workers,* 409 U.S. 213 (1972), the court rejected petitioners' argument that their members, by participating in the strike vote, had "waived their Section 7 right to abandon the strike." 724 F.2d, at 60-61.

---

[5] In *Machinists Local 1327 (Dalmo Victor II),* 263 N.L.R.B. 984 (1982), *enf. denied,* 725 F.2d 1212 (CA9 1984), several employees resigned from a union and returned to work during a strike. The union constitution prohibited resignations during, or within 14 days preceding, strikes. As in this case, the employees' resignations were not accepted, and they were fined for aiding and abetting the employer. The Board held that fining these employees for returning to work after tendering resignations violated § 8(b)(1)(A).

Chairman Van de Water and Member Hunter stated that no restriction on the right to resign was permissible under the Act; they reasoned that such a rule allowed the union to exercise control over "external matters." Moreover, these Board members thought that restrictions on resignation impaired the congressional policy, embodied in § 8(a)(3), of voluntary unionism. Therefore, they concluded that any discipline premised on such a rule violates Section 8(b)(1)(A). 263 N.L.R.B., at 988.

Members Fanning and Zimmerman asserted that a rule legitimately could restrict the right to resign for a period of 30 days. Because the rule in question restricted the right to resign indefinitely, however, they agreed that the union had violated § 8(b)(1)(A), 29 U.S.C. § 158(b)(1)(A). *Id.,* at 987.

Member Jenkins, the lone dissenter, contended that the union's restriction on resignation was protected by the proviso to § 8(b)(1)(A), which states that a union may "prescribe its own rules with respect to the acquisition or retention of membership therein." *Id.,* at 993.

Finally, the Court of Appeals reasoned that under *Scofield v. NLRB,* 394 U.S. 423 (1969), labor organizations may impose disciplinary fines against members only if they are "free to leave the union and escape the rule[s]." 724 F.2d, at 61.

We granted a petition for a writ of certiorari, 469 U.S. — (1984), to resolve the conflict between the Courts of Appeals over the validity of restrictions on union members' right to resign. The Board has held that such restrictions are invalid and do not justify imposing sanctions on employees who have attempted to resign from the union. Because of the Board's "special competence" in the field of labor relations, its interpretation of the Act is accorded substantial deference. *NLRB v. Weingarten, Inc.,* 420 U.S. 251, 266 (1975). The question for decision today is thus narrowed to whether the Board's construction of § 8(b)(1)(A) is reasonable. *NLRB v. City Disposal Systems, Inc.,* 465 U.S. 822, 830 (1984). We believe that § 8(b)(1)(A) properly may be construed as prohibiting the fining of employees who have tendered resignations ineffective under a restriction in the union constitution. We therefore affirm the judgment of the Court of Appeals enforcing the Board's order.

II

A. Section 7 of the Act, 29 U.S.C. § 157, grants employees the right to "refrain from any or all [concerted] ... activities ...." This general right is implemented by § 8(b)(1)(A). The latter section provides that a union commits an unfair labor practice if it "restrain[s] or coerce[s] employees in the exercise" of their § 7 rights. When employee members of a union refuse to support a strike (whether or not a rule prohibits returning to work during a strike), they are refraining from "concerted activity." Therefore, imposing fines on these employees for returning to work "restrain[s]" the exercise of their § 7 rights. Indeed, if the terms "refrain" and "restrain or coerce" are interpreted literally, fining employees to enforce compliance with any union rule or policy would violate the Act.

Despite this language from the Act, the Court in *NLRB v. Allis-Chalmers,* 388 U.S. 175 (1967), held that § 8(b)(1)(A) does not prohibit labor organizations from fining current members. In *NLRB v. Textile Workers, supra,* and *Machinists & Aerospace Workers v. NLRB,* 412 U.S. 84 (1973) (per curiam), the Court found as a corollary that unions may not fine former members who have resigned lawfully. Neither *Textile Workers, supra,* nor *Machinists, supra,* however, involved a provision like League Law 13, restricting the members' right to resign. We decide today whether a union is precluded from fining employees who have attempted to resign when resignations are prohibited by the union's constitution.

B. The Court's reasoning in *Allis-Chalmers, supra,* supports the Board's conclusion that petitioners in this case violated § 8(b)(1)(A). In *Allis-Chalmers,* the Court held that imposing court-enforceable fines against current union members does not "restrain or coerce" the workers in the exercise of their § 7 rights.[10] In so concluding, the Court relied on the legislative history of the Taft-Hartley Act. It noted that the sponsor of § 8(b)(1)(A) never intended for that provision "'to interfere with the internal affairs or organization of unions,'" 388 U.S., at 187, quoting 93 Cong. Rec. 4272 (1947) (statement of Sen. Ball), and that other proponents of the measure likewise disclaimed an intent to interfere with unions' "internal affairs." 388 U.S., at 187-190. From the legislative history, the Court reasoned that Congress did not intend to prohibit unions from fining present members, as this was an internal matter. The Court has emphasized that the crux of *Allis-Chalmers'* holding was the distinction between "internal and external enforcement of union rules ...." *Scofield v. NLRB*, 394 U.S., at 428. *See also NLRB v. Boeing Co.*, 412 U.S. 67, 73 (1973).

The Congressional purpose to preserve unions' control over their own "internal affairs" does not suggest an intent to authorize restrictions on the right to resign. Traditionally, union members were free to resign and escape union discipline. In 1947, union constitutional provisions restricting the right to resign were uncommon, if not unknown. Therefore, allowing unions to "extend an employee's membership obligation through restrictions on resignation" would "expan[d] the definition of internal action" beyond the contours envisioned by the Taft-Hartley Congress. *International Ass'n of Machinists, Local 1414 (Neufeld Porsche-Audi, Inc.)*, 270 N.L.R.B. No. 209, p. 11 (1984).[13]

C. Language and reasoning from other opinions of this Court confirm that the Board's construction of § 8(b)(1)(A) is reasonable. In *Scofield v. NLRB*, 394 U.S. 423 (1969), the Court upheld a union rule setting a ceiling on the daily wages that members working on an incentive basis could earn. The union members' freedom to resign was critical to the Court's decision that the union rule did not "restrain or coerce" the employees within the meaning of § 8(b)(1)(A). It stated that the rule was "reasonably enforced against union members who [were] free to leave the union and escape the rule." *Id.*, at 430. The Court deemed it important that if members were unable to take full advantage of their contractual right to earn ad-

---

[10] The proviso to § 8(b)(1)(A), 29 U.S.C. § 158(b)(1)(A) states that nothing in the section shall "impair the right of a labor organization to prescribe its own rules with respect to the acquisition or retention of membership therein." The Court in *Allis-Chalmers* assumed that the proviso could not be read to authorize the imposition of court-enforceable fines. 388 U.S., at 192. *See NLRB v. Boeing Co.*, 412 U.S. 67, 71, n. 5 (1973) ("This Court ..., in holding that court enforcement of union fines was not an unfair labor practice in *NLRB v. Allis-Chalmers Mfg. Co.*, relied on congressional intent only with respect to the first part of this section") (citation omitted).

[13] An *International Assn. of Machinists, Local 1414 (Neufeld Porsche-Audi, Inc.)*, 270 N.L.R.B. No. 209 (1984), a majority of the Board held that *any* restriction on the right to resign violates the Act. This was the position taken by Chairman Van de Water and Member Hunter in *Machinists Local 1327, Dalmo Victor II*, 263 N.L.R.B. 984 (1982), *enf. denied*, 725 F.2d 1212 (CA9 1984). *See* n. 5, *supra.*

ditional pay, it was because they had "chosen to become *and remain* union members." *Id.,* at 435 (emphasis added).

The decision in *NLRB v. Textile Workers,* 409 U.S. 213 (1972), also supports the Board's view that § 8(b)(1)(A) prohibits unions from punishing members not free to resign. There, 31 employees resigned their union membership and resumed working during a strike. We held that fining these former members "restrained or coerced" them, within the meaning of § 8(b)(1)(A). In reaching this conclusion, we said that "the vitality of § 7 requires that the member be free to refrain in November from the actions he endorsed in May." *Id.,* at 217-218. Restrictions on the right to resign curtail the freedom that the *Textile Workers* Court deemed so important. *See also Machinists, supra.*

III

Section 8(b)(1)(A) allows unions to enforce only those rules that "impai[r] no policy Congress has imbedded in the labor laws ...." *Scofield, supra,* at 430. The Board has found union restrictions on the right to resign to be inconsistent with the policy of voluntary unionism implicit in § 8(a)(3). *See Neufeld Porsche-Audi,* 270 N.L.R.B. No. 209 (1984); *Machinists Local 1327 (Dalmo Victor II),* 263 N.L.R.B., at 992 (Chairman Van de Water and Member Hunter, concurring), *enf. denied,* 725 F.2d 1212 (1984). We believe that the inconsistency between union restrictions on the right to resign and the policy of voluntary unionism supports the Board's conclusion that League Law 13 is invalid.

Closed shop agreements, legalized by the Wagner Act in 1935, became quite common in the early 1940s. Under these agreements, employers could hire and retain in their employ only union members in good standing. R. Gorman, *Labor Law,* ch. 28, § 1, p. 639 (1976). Full union membership was thus compulsory in a closed shop; in order to keep their jobs, employees were required to attend union meetings, support union leaders, and otherwise adhere to union rules. Because of mounting objections to the closed shop, in 1947—after hearings and full consideration—Congress enacted the Taft-Harley Act. Section 8(a)(3) of that Act effectively eliminated compulsory union membership by outlawing the closed shop. The union security agreements permitted by § 8(a)(3) require employees to pay dues, but an employee cannot be discharged for failing to abide by union rules or policies with which he disagrees.[16]

---

[16] Under § 8(a)(3), the only aspect of union membership that can be required pursuant to a union shop agreement is the payment of dues. *See Radio Officers v. NLRB,* 347 U.S. 17, 41 (1954) (union security agreements cannot be used for "any purpose other than to compel payment of union dues and fees"). "'Membership,' as a condition of employment, is whittled down to its financial core." *NLRB v. General Motors Corp.,* 373 U.S. 734, 742 (1963). *See also Ellis v. Railway Clerks,* 466 U.S. — (1984) (under the Railway Labor Act, employees in a "union shop" cannot be compelled to pay dues to support certain union activities). Therefore, an employee required by a union

Full union membership thus no longer can be a requirement of employment. If a new employee refuses formally to join a union and subject himself to its discipline, he cannot be fired. Moreover, no employee can be discharged if he initially joins a union, and subsequently resigns. We think it noteworthy that § 8(a)(3) protects the employment rights of the dissatisfied member, as well as those of the worker who never assumed full union membership. By allowing employees to resign from a union at any time, § 8(a)(3) protects the employee whose views come to diverge from those of his union.

League Law 13 curtails this freedom to resign from full union membership. Nevertheless, the petitioners contend that League Law 13 does not contravene the policy of voluntary unionism imbedded in the Act. They assert that this provision does not interfere with workers' employment rights because offending members are not discharged, but only fined. We find this argument unpersuasive, for a union has not left a "worker's employment rights inviolate when it exacts [his entire] paycheck in satisfaction of a fine imposed for working." Wellington, *Union Fines and Workers' Rights,* 85 Yale L.J. 1022, 1023 (1976). Congress in 1947 sought to eliminate completely any requirement that the employee maintain full union membership. Therefore, the Board was justified in concluding that by restricting the right of employees to resign, League Law 13 impairs the policy of voluntary unionism.

IV

We now consider specifically three arguments advanced by petitioners: (i) union rules restricting the right to resign are protected by the proviso to § 8(b)(1)(A); (ii) the legislative history of the Act shows that Congress did not intend to protect the right of union members to resign; and (iii) labor unions should be allowed to restrict the right to resign because other voluntary associations are permitted to do so.[18]

---

security agreement to assume financial "membership" is not subject to union discipline. Such an employee is a "member" of the union only in the most limited sense.

[18] The dissent suggests that the Board's decision is inconsistent with 29 U.S.C. § 163, which provides that nothing in the Act "shall be construed so as ... to interfere with or impede or diminish in any way the right to strike." The Board does not believe, and neither do we, that its interpretation of § 8(b)(1)(A) impedes the "right to strike." "It [will] not outlaw anybody striking who want[s] to strike. It [will] not prevent anyone using the strike in a legitimate way .... All it [will] do [is] ... outlaw such restraint and coercion as would prevent people from going to work if they wished to go to work." 93 Cong. Rec. 4436 (1947) (remarks of Sen. Taft).

Moreover, we do not believe that the effectiveness of strikes will be unduly hampered by the Board's decision. An employee who voluntarily has joined a union will be reluctant to give up his membership. As Dean Wellington has said:

"In making his resignation decision, the dissident must remember that the union whose policies he finds distasteful will continue to hold substantial economic power over him as exclusive bargaining agent. By resigning, the worker surrenders his right to vote for union officials, to express himself at union meetings, and even participate in determining the amount or use of dues he may be

A. Petitioners first argue that the proviso to § 8(b)(1)(A) expressly allows unions to place restrictions on the right to resign. The proviso states that nothing in § 8(b)(1)(A) shall "impair the right of a labor organization to prescribe its own rules with respect to the acquisition or retention of membership therein." 29 U.S.C. § 158(b)(1)(A). Petitioners contend that because League Law 13 places restrictions on the right to withdraw from the union, it is a "rul[e] with respect to the ... retention of membership," within the meaning of the proviso.

Neither the Board nor this Court has ever interpreted the proviso as allowing unions to make rules restricting the right to resign. Rather, the Court has assumed that "rules with respect to the ... retention of membership" are those that provide for the expulsion of employees from the union. The legislative history of the Taft-Hartley Act is consistent with this interpretation. Senator Holland, the proviso's sponsor, stated that § 8(b)(1)(A) should not outlaw union rules "which ha[ve] to do with the admission *or the expulsion* of members." 93 Cong. Rec. 4271 (1947) (emphasis added). Senator Taft accepted the proviso, for he likewise believed that a union should be free to "refuse [a] man admission to the union, or *expel him from the union."* Id., at 4272 (emphasis added). Furthermore, the legislative history of the Labor-Management Reporting and Disclosure Act of 1959, 29 U.S.C. § 401 *et seq.,* confirms that the proviso was intended to protect union rules involving admission and expulsion. Accordingly, we find no basis for refusing to defer to the Board's conclusion that League Law 13 is not a "rule with respect to the retention of membership," within the meaning of the proviso.

B. The petitioners next argue that the legislative history of the Taft-Hartley Act shows that Congress made a considered decision not to protect union members' right to resign. Section 8(c) of the House bill contained a detailed "bill of rights" for labor union members. H.R. 3020, § 8(c), 80th Cong., 1st Sess., at pp. 22-26 (1947). Included was a provision making it an unfair labor practice to "deny to any [union] member the right to resign from the organization at any time." H.R. 3020, *supra,* § 8(c)(4), at 23. The Senate bill, on the other hand, did not set forth specific employee rights, but stated more generally that it was an unfair labor practice to "restrain or coerce" employees in the exercise of their § 7 rights. H.R. 3020, 80th Cong., 1st Sess., § 8(b)(1)(A), p. 81 (1947) (as passed Senate). The Taft-Hartley Act contains the Senate bill's general language rather than the more specific House prohibitions. *See* 29 U.S.C. § 158(b)(1)(A). The petitioners contend that the omission of the House provision shows that Congress expressly decided not to protect the "right to resign."

The legislative history does not support this contention. The "right to resign" apparently was included in the original House bill to protect workers unable to resign because of "closed shop" agreements. Union constitutions limiting the right to resign were uncommon in 1947; closed shop agreements, however, often

---

forced to pay under a union security clause." Wellington, *Union Fines and Workers' Rights,* 85 Yale L.J. 1022, 1046 (1976).

impeded union resignations. The House Report, H.R. Rep. No. 245, 80th Cong., 1st Sess. (1947), confirms that closed shop agreements provided the impetus for the inclusion of a right to resign in the House bill. The report simply states that even under the proposed legislation, employees could be required to pay dues pursuant to union security agreements. *Id.,* at 32. Because the closed shop was outlawed by the Taft-Hartley Act, *see* § 8(a)(3), 29 U.S.C. § 158(a)(3), it is not surprising that Congress though it unnecessarily explicitly to preserve the right to resign....

C. In *Textile Workers,* 409 U.S., at 216, and *Machinists,* 412 U.S., at 88 (per curiam) the Court stated that when a union constitution does not purport to restrict the right to resign, the "law which normally is reflected in our free institutions" is applicable. Relying on this quoted language, petitioners argue that League Law 13 is valid. They assert that because the common law does not prohibit restrictions on resignation, such provisions are not violative of § 8(b)(1)(A) of the Act. We find no merit in this argument. *Textile Workers, supra,* and *Machinists, supra,* held only that in the absence of restrictions on the right to resign, members are free to leave the union at any time. Although the Court noted that its decisions were consistent with the common-law rule, it did not state that the validity of restrictions on the right to resign should be determined with reference to common law.

The Court's decision in *NLRB v. Marine & Shipbuilding Workers,* 391 U.S. 418 (1968), demonstrates that many union rules, although valid under the common law of associations, run afoul of § 8(b)(1)(A) of the Act. There the union expelled a member who failed to comply with a rule requiring the "exhaust[ion of] all remedies and appeals within the Union ... before ... resort to any court or other tribunal outside of the Union." *Id.,* at 421. Under the common law, associations may require their members to exhaust all internal remedies. *See, e.g., Medical Soc. of Mobile Cty. v. Walker,* 245 Ala. 135, 16 So. 2d 321 (1944). Nevertheless, the *Marine Workers* Court held that "considerations of public policy" mandated a holding that the union rule requiring exhaustion violated § 8(b)(1)(A), 29 U.S.C. § 158(b)(1)(A). 391 U.S., at 424; *see also Scofield v. NLRB,* 394 U.S., at 430 (union rule is invalid under § 8(b)(1)(A) if it "impairs [a] policy Congress has imbedded in the labor laws").

The Board reasonably has concluded that League Law 13 "restrains or coerces" employees, *see* § 8(b)(1)(A), and is inconsistent with the congressional policy of voluntary unionism. Therefore, whatever may have been the common law, the Board's interpretation of the Act merits our deference.

V

The Board has the primary responsibility for applying "'the general provisions of the Act to the complexities of industrial life.'" *Ford Motor Co. v. NLRB,* 441 U.S. 488, 496 (1979), quoting *NLRB v. Erie Resistor Corp.,* 373 U.S. 221, 236

(1963), quoting, *NLRB v. Steelworkers,* 357 U.S. 357, 362-363 (1958). Where the Board's construction of the Act is reasonable, it should not be rejected "merely because the courts might prefer another view of the statute." *Ford Motor Co. v. NLRB, supra,* at 497. In this case, two factors suggest that we should be particularly reluctant to hold that the Board's interpretation of the Act is impermissible. First, in related cases this Court invariably has yielded to Board decisions on whether fines imposed by a union "restrain or coerce" employees. Second, the Board consistently has construed § 8(b)(1)(A) as prohibiting the imposition of fines on employees who have tendered resignations invalid under a union constitution.[28] Therefore, we conclude that the Board's decision here is entitled to our deference.

VI

The Board found that by fining employees who had tendered resignations, the petitioners violated § 8(b)(1)(A) of the Act, even though League Law 13 purported to render the resignations ineffective. We defer to the Board's interpretation of the Act and so affirm the judgment of the Court of Appeals enforcing the Board's order.

It is so ordered.

JUSTICE WHITE, concurring.

I agree with the Court that the Board's construction of §§ 7 and 8(b)(1)(A) is a permissible one and should be upheld. The employee's rights under § 7 include, among others, the right to refrain from joining or assisting a labor organization and from engaging in concerted activities for mutual aid or protection. The right to join or not to join a labor union includes the right to resign, and § 8(b)(1)(A) forbids unions to interfere with that right except to the extent, if any, that such interference is permitted by the proviso to that section, which preserves the union's right to prescribe its own rules with respect to the acquisition or retention of membership. The proviso might be read as permitting restrictions on resignation

---

[28] In *United Automobile, Aerospace & Agricultural Implement Workers, Local 647 (General Electric Co.),* 197 N.L.R.B. 608 (1972), the Board held that § 8(b)(1)(A) prohibits a union from fining employees who have resigned, even when a provision in the union constitution purports to make the resignations invalid. There two employees resigned during a strike and returned to work. Their resignations were ineffective under a union constitutional provision permitting resignations only during the last ten days of the union's fiscal year. The Board nevertheless held that the employees could not be fined for crossing the picket line. It noted that imposing fines on these employees was inconsistent with *Scofield v. NLRB,* 394 U.S. 423 (1969), for they effectively were denied "a voluntary method of severing their relationship with the Union." 197 N.L.R.B., at 609. The Board reached the same conclusion in *United Automobile, Aerospace & Agricultural Implement Workers, Local 469 (Master Lock Co.),* 221 N.L.R.B. 748 (1975). *See also Local 1384, United Automobile, Aerospace & Agricultural Implement Workers (Ex-Cell-O Corp.),* 219 N.L.R.B. 729 (1975).

during a strike, since they would seem to relate to the "retention" of membership. But it can also be sensibly read to refer only to the union's right to determine who shall be allowed to join and to remain in the union. The latter is the Board's interpretation. Under that view, restrictions on resignations are not saved by the proviso, and the rule at issue in this case may not be enforced....

JUSTICE BLACKMUN, with whom JUSTICE BRENNAN and JUSTICE MARSHALL join, dissenting....

I

A. Having determined that the individual worker standing alone lacked sufficient bargaining power to achieve a fair agreement with his employer over the terms and conditions of his employment, Congress passed the NLRA in order to protect employees' rights to join together and act collectively. *See* 29 U.S.C. § 151. Thus, the heart of the Act is the protection of workers' § 7 rights to self-organization and to free collective bargaining, which are in turn protected by § 8 of the Act. 29 U.S.C. §§ 157 and 158.

Because the employees' power protected in the NLRA is the power to act collectively, it has long been settled that the collective has a right to promulgate rules binding on its members, so long as the employee's decision to become a member is a voluntary one and the rules are democratically adopted. When these requirements of free association are met, the union has the right to enforce such rules "through reasonable discipline," including fines. *See NLRB v. Allis-Chalmers Mfg. Co.,* 388 U.S. 175, 181 (1967). Unless internal rules can be enforced, the union's status as bargaining representative will be eroded, and the rights of the members to act collectively will be jeopardized. *Ibid.* "Union activity, by its very nature, is group activity, and is grounded on the notion that strength can be garnered from unity, solidarity, and mutual commitment. This concept is of particular force during a strike, where the individual members of the union draw strength from the commitments of fellow members, and where the activities carried on by the union rest fundamentally on the mutual reliance that inheres in the 'pact.'" *NLRB v. Textile Workers,* 409 U.S. 213, 221 (1973) (dissenting opinion); *see Allis-Chalmers, supra,* at 181.

It is in the proviso to § 8(b)(1)(A), 29 U.S.C. § 158(b)(1)(A), that Congress preserved for the union the right to establish "the contractual relationship between union and member." *Textile Workers, supra,* at 217. Recognizing "the law which normally is reflected in our free institutions," *id.,* at 216, Congress in the proviso preserved a union's status as a voluntary association free to define its own membership....

League Law 13 is an internal union rule, a "rule with respect to the acquisition or retention of membership" protected by the proviso to § 8(b)(1)(A). It requires that employees who freely choose to join the union promise to remain members during a strike or lockout, as well as during the time when a strike or lockout appears imminent. In other words, the rule imposes a condition upon members of the bargaining unit who would like to acquire membership rights. The rule stands for the proposition that to become a union member one must be willing to incur a certain obligation upon which others may rely; as such, it is a rule literally involving the acquisition and retention of membership. Conversely, League Law 13 does not in any way affect the relationship between the employee and the employer. An employee who violates the rule does not risk losing his job, and the union cannot seek an employer's coercive assistance in collecting any fine that is imposed. The rule neither coerces a worker to become a union member against his will, nor affects an employee's status as an employee under the Act. Thus, it clearly falls within the powers of any voluntary association to enact and enforce "the requirements and standards of membership itself," so as to permit the association effectively to pursue collective goals. 93 Cong. Rec. 4433 (1947) (remarks of Sen. Ball).

B....

Moreover, Congress explicitly has rejected the Court's interpretation of §§ 7 and 8(b)(1)(A). The "right to refrain" language upon which the Court relies was contained in § 7(a) of the House version of the Act, H.R. 3020, 80th Cong., 1st Sess. (1947) (House bill). Section 7 of the House bill was divided into subsection (a), granting "employees" the right to refrain from concerted activity, and subsection (b), granting "members of any labor organization" rights concerning the "affairs of the organization." Corresponding to these provisions were § 8(b), which made it an unfair labor practice for anyone to interfere with an employee's § 7(a) rights, and § 8(c), which made it an unfair labor practice to interfere with an employee's § 7(b) rights. In particular, § 8(c) created a bill of rights for union members in their dealings with their union, establishing 10 unfair labor practices which regulated the major facets of the member-union relationship. Among these specifically enumerated rights was § 8(c)(4), which made it an unfair labor practice "to deny to any member the right to resign from the organization at any time."

Thus, the House regarded the "right to refrain" of § 7(a) as the right not to join in union activity, making it illegal for "representatives and their partisans and adherents to harass or abuse employees into joining labor organizations." H.R. Rep. No. 245, 80th Cong., 1st Sess., 30 (1947). And the House believed that § 7(b) and § 8(c) of its bill, which included a proscription of internal rules concerning a member's right to resign, regulated the member-union relationship. There is no suggestion that the House considered the right to refrain to include the right to abandon an agreed-upon undertaking at will, nor to relate to the rights against the union protected by §§ 7(b) and 8(c) of the House bill, including the right to resign at will. Rather, these distinct rights arose from separate sections of the House bill.

It is critical to an understanding of the Taft-Hartley bill, therefore, to recognize that the Senate explicitly *rejected* the House bill's §§ 7(b) and 8(c). It did so not, as the Court intimates, because it considered the specific provisions of §§ 7(b) and 8(c) to encompass the "right to refrain" language adopted from § 7(a), but because it decided that "the formulation of a code of rights for individual members of trade unions ... should receive more extended study by a special joint congressional committee." S. Rep. No. 105, 80th Cong., 1st Sess., 2 (1947)....

The Court also attempts to justify its result by suggesting that League Law 13 impairs a federal labor policy mandating "voluntary unionism" implicit in § 8(a)(3) of the Act, and thus is unenforceable under § 8(a)(1) of the Act. *See ante,* quoting *Scofield,* 394 U.S., at 430. Thus, the Court says, for the same reason that Congress determined that the closed shop should be prohibited as a violation of an employee's right to refrain from concerted activity, a promise not to leave the union during a strike should not be enforceable. Both rules, the Court intimates, "protec[t] the employment rights of the dissatisfied member."

The Court, however, again ignores the distinction between internal and external rules fashioned in its prior cases, and so misunderstands the concept of "voluntary unionism" implicated by the Act. The purpose of the union unfair labor practice provisions added to § 8(a)(3) was to "preven[t] the union from inducing the employer to use the emoluments of the job to enforce the union's rules." *Scofield,* 394 U.S., at 429. By outlawing the closed shop and the union shop Congress ensured that a union's disciplinary rules can have no effect on the employment rights of the member, and so cannot impinge upon the policy of voluntary unionism protected by § 8(a)(3) of the Act.

The proviso serves a fundamentally different purpose—to make manifest that § 8 did not grant the Board the authority to impair the basic right of all membership associations to establish their own reasonable membership rules. League Law 13 is such a rule. It binds members to a reciprocal promise not to resign and return to work during a strike. It does not involve use of the employer's power or affect an individual's employment status, and so does not implicate § 8(a)(3). A member who violates the union rule may be fined, or even expelled from the union, but his employment status remains unaffected. Despite the Court's suggestions to the contrary, "voluntary unionism" does not require that an employee who has freely chosen to join a union and retain his membership therein, in full knowledge that by those decisions he has accepted specified obligations to other members, nevertheless has a federally protected right to disregard those obligations at will, regardless of the acts of others taken in reliance on them....

II

Congress' decision not to intervene in the internal affairs of a union reflects Congress' understanding that membership in a union—if not a precondition for one's right to employment—is a freely chosen membership in a voluntary association. The Court therefore has looked to "the law which normally is reflected in our free institutions" to determine whether any given membership rule is lawful.

NLRB v. Textile Workers, 409 U.S., at 216. And the common law of associations establishes that an association may place reasonable restrictions on its members' right to resign where such restrictions are designed to further a basic purpose for which the association was formed—here, where the restriction "reflects a legitimate union interest." *Scofield,* 394 U.S., at 430. The Pattern Makers evidently promulgated League Law 13 to protect the common interest in maintaining a united front during an economic strike. Such a rule protects individual union members' decisions to place their own and their families' welfare at risk in reliance on the reciprocal decisions of their fellow workers, and furthers the union's ability to bargain with the employer on equal terms, as envisioned by the Act. As such, the rule comports with the broader goals of federal labor policy, which guarantees workers the right to collective action and, in particular, the right to strike.

Specifically, Congress has mandated that nothing in the Act, including the "right to refrain" relied upon by the Court today, "shall be construed so as either to interfere with or impede or diminish in any way the right to strike, or to affect the limitations or qualifications on that right." 29 U.S.C. § 163. The strike or the threat to strike is the workers' most effective means of pressuring employers, and so lies at the center of the collective activity protected by the Act. "The economic strike against the employer is the ultimate weapon in labor's arsenal for achieving agreement upon its terms." *Allis-Chalmers,* 388 U.S., at 181. Consequently, the Court has recognized that "'[t]he power to fine or expel strike-breakers is essential if the union is to be an effective bargaining agent.'" *Ibid.,* quoting Summers, *Legal Limitations on Union Discipline,* 64 Harv. L. Rev. 1049, 1049 (1951).

To be effective, the decision to strike, like the decision to bargain collectively, must be respected by the minority until democratically revoked. The employees' collective decision to strike is not taken lightly, and entails considerable costs. *See NLRB v. Mackay Radio & Tel. Co.,* 304 U.S. 333, 345 (1938) (employer has right permanently to replace workers on economic strike). Before workers undertake such a course, it is reasonable that they have some assurance that collectively they will have the means to withstand the pressures the employer is able lawfully to impose on them. A voluntarily and democratically adopted rule prohibiting resignations during a strike is one such means. By ensuring solidarity during a strike, it enforces the union's "legitimate interest in presenting a united front ... and in not seeing its strength dissipated and its stature denigrated by subgroups within the unit separately pursuing what they see as separate interests." *Emporium Capwell Co. v. Western Addition Community Organization,* 420 U.S. 50, 70 (1975)....

Enforcement of a promise not to resign during a strike, then, is not a limitation of a § 7 right, but is a vindication of that right to act collectively and engage in collective bargaining, so long as the promise is voluntarily made. It is a way to effectuate "[t]he majority-rule concept [that] is today unquestionably at the center of our federal labor policy." *Allis-Chalmers,* 388 U.S., at 180, quoting Welling-ton, *Union Democracy and Fair Representation; Federal Responsibility in a Federal System,* 67 Yale L.J. 1327, 1333 (1958). As such, League Law 13 is a condition on union membership that a union might reasonably impose to advance its legitimate ends, and so is an internal union rule protected by the proviso pre-serving a union's right to enact reasonable rules defining the conditions of union membership....

If the dissenting members disagreed either with the decision to enact League Law 13, or with the decision to strike, they were free to try to influence their colleagues to their view. If they did not agree with the enactment of League Law 13, they were free as well to resign from the union when the rule was promul-gated over their objection. Once the strike had begun, if they believed that the union officers were no longer acting in their best interest, they were free to try to convince their colleagues to end the strike, to replace their leaders, or even to decertify their union. *See Allis-Chalmers,* 388 U.S., at 191. Having failed to per-suade the majority to their view, they should not be free to break their promise to their fellow workers....

JUSTICE STEVENS, dissenting.

The legislative history of the Labor-Management Relations Act of 1947 dis-cussed in Part I-B of JUSTICE BLACKMUN's dissenting opinion, coupled with the plain language in the proviso to § 8(b)(1)(A) persuades me that the "right to re-frain" protected by § 7 of the Act does not encompass the "right to resign." Ac-cordingly, I respectfully dissent.

NOTES

1. In *Typographical Union (Register Pub'g Co.),* 270 N.L.R.B. 1386 (1984), the Labor Board held that unions that refuse to give effect to valid member resig-nations violate § 8(b)(1)(A). In *Carpenters, Local 470 (Tacoma Boatbuilding),* 277 N.L.R.B. 513 (1985), the Board held that a labor organization could not fine members who crossed a picket line after they sent letters to the union changing their membership status "from that of a 'full' member to that of a 'financial core' member," since "financial core" members are not subject to union disciplinary authority. *See also Teamsters Local 670 v. NLRB,* 856 F.2d 1250 (9th Cir. 1988) (§ 8(b)(1)(A) violation when union retaliated against "financial core" members for their strike-related activities by refusing to issue them work-registration cer-tificates and by denying them access to union pharmacy and clinics).

2. A labor organization may fine employees who return to work on the same day they mail letters of resignation to their union, where they are found to still be union members at the time they cross the picket line. *See CWA, Local 9201 (Pa-cific Northwest Bell),* 275 N.L.R.B. 1529 (1985). *But cf. NLRB v. Teamsters Lo-cal 438,* 837 F.2d 888 (9th Cir. 1988) (resignation placed in union's after-hours deposit box on night before member crossed picket line was effective when deposited).

Although the Labor Board had previously recognized that mailed resignations took effect on the day after they were mailed or whenever the union could establish it actually received those communications, it has adopted a uniform rule presuming that all mailed resignations become effective at 12:01 a.m. local time on the day following their postmarks. *Pattern & Model Makers Ass'n (Michigan Model Mfg.),* 310 N.L.R.B. 929 (1993).

3. The Seventh Circuit upheld the Labor Board extension of *Pattern Makers* to prohibit union rules preventing resignations in anticipation of or during the pendency of disciplinary proceedings. The court remarked that this interpretation of § 8(b)(1)(A) would not affect unions' "most potent sanctions—expulsion and suspension for cause," and would also leave available certain "secondary penalties" for preresignation conduct, such as conditions upon reinstatement. *NLRB v. Sheet Metal Workers Local 73,* 840 F.2d 501 (7th Cir. 1988). *Accord, UAW Local 449 v. NLRB,* 865 F.2d 791 (6th Cir.), *cert. denied,* 493 U.S. 818 (1989); *NLRB v. Sheet Metal Workers Local 16,* 873 F.2d 236 (9th Cir. 1989).

4. Although labor organizations cannot fine individuals who resign before they return to work during a strike, the Labor Board has held (3-2) that they can expel or suspend such persons. Such a distinction between fines and membership revocation respects the right of unions under the proviso to § 8(b)(1)(A) "to prescribe [their] own rules with respect to the acquisition or retention of membership therein." *Meat Cutters, Local 81 (MacDonald Meat Co.),* 284 N.L.R.B. 1084 (1987).

5. *See generally* Abraham, *Individual Autonomy and Collective Empowerment in Labor Law: Union Membership Resignations and Strikebreaking in the New Economy,* 63 N.Y.U. L. Rev. 1268 (1988); Note, *A Union's Right to Control Strike-Period Resignations,* 85 Colum. L. Rev. 339 (1985); Comment, *Union Restrictions on the Right to Resign: A Proposal for a New Reasonableness Test,* 22 Harv. J. Leg. 551 (1985); Comment, *Section 8(b)(1)(A) from Allis-Chalmers to Pattern Makers' League: A Case Study in Judicial Legislation,* 74 Calif. L. Rev. 1409 (1986); Note, *Union Power to Discipline Members Who Resign,* 86 Harv. L. Rev. 1536 (1973).

C. ORGANIZATIONAL AND RECOGNITION PICKETING

NLRB v. DRIVERS, CHAUFFEURS, HELPERS, LOCAL 639 [CURTIS BROS.]

Supreme Court of the United States
362 U.S. 274, 80 S. Ct. 706, 4 L. Ed. 2d 710 (1960)

[The union was certified by the Board in 1953 as the exclusive bargaining representative of Curtis Brothers' drivers, helpers, warehousemen, and furniture finishers. An impasse was reached in the resultant bargaining and the union started picketing the company's premises early in 1954. This picketing continued for about two years, during which time the company replaced the strikers.

[On February 1, 1955, the company filed a representation petition, in which it questioned the union's continued majority status and asked for an election. About two weeks later, on February 16, 1955, the union filed a statement purportedly disavowing any current intention to represent the employees in their dealings with the company. Before such disclaimer, the union's picket signs read: "CURTIS BROTHERS ON STRIKE. UNFAIR TO ORGANIZED LABOR. DRIVERS, HELPERS, AND WAREHOUSEMEN OF LOCAL 639 (AF of L)." Thereafter, they read on one side "CURTIS BROS. EMPLOYS Non-Union drivers, helpers, warehousemen, etc. Unfair to Teamsters Union No. 639 AFL," and on the other side "Teamsters Union No. 639 AFL wants employees of Curtis Bros. to join them to gain union wages, hours and working conditions."

[In September 1955, the Board directed an election in the representation case, finding that the union was still seeking to win immediate recognition by the company. The Board reasoned:

["[T]hat the Union's current picketing activities cannot be reconciled with its disclaimer of interest in representing the employees in question. In the light of all the material facts of this case, including the certification of the Petitioner, the circumstances preceding the strike, the nature of the first signs carried by the pickets, the brief discontinuance of picketing, and its early resumption, we are convinced that the current picketing is not for the sole purpose of getting employees to join the Union, as the more recent picket signs indicate, but is tantamount to a present demand that the Employer enter into a contract with the Union without regard to the question of its majority status among the employees concerned. [Citing cases.]"

[Twenty-eight employees voted against Local 639, and only one for it. As stated, the union never altered its picketing activities. It is conceded that at no time after February, 1955, did the union represent a majority of the employees.

[The NLRB held that the picketing violated § 8(b)(1)(A). The court of appeals set the Board's order aside.]

MR. JUSTICE BRENNAN delivered the opinion of the Court.

The question in this case is whether peaceful picketing by a union, which does not represent a majority of the employees, to compel immediate recognition as the employees' exclusive bargaining agent, is conduct of the union "to restrain or coerce" the employees in the exercise of rights guaranteed in § 7, and thus an unfair labor practice under § 8(b)(1)(A) of the Taft-Hartley Act....

After we granted certiorari, the Congress enacted the Labor-Management Reporting and Disclosure Act of 1959, which, among other things, adds a new § 8(b)(7) to the National Labor Relations Act. It was stated by the Board on oral argument that if this case arose under the 1959 Act, the Board might have proceeded against the Local under § 8(b)(7). This does not, however, relegate this litigation to the status of an unimportant controversy over the meaning of a statute which has been significantly changed. For the Board contends that new § 8(b)(7) does not displace § 8(b)(1)(A) but merely "supplements the power already conferred by § 8(b)(1)(A)." It argues that the Board may proceed against peaceful "recognitional" picketing conducted by a minority union in more situations than are specified in § 8(b)(7) and without regard to the limitations of § 8(b)(7)(C)....

We conclude that the Board's interpretation of § 8(b)(1)(A) finds support neither in the way Congress structured § 8(b) nor in the legislative history of § 8(b)(1)(A). Rather it seems clear, and we hold, that Congress in the Taft-Hartley Act authorized the Board to regulate peaceful "recognitional" picketing only when it is employed to accomplish objectives specified in § 8(b)(4); and that § 8(b)(1)(A) is a grant of power to the Board limited to authority to proceed against union tactics involving violence, intimidation, and reprisal or threats thereof—conduct involving more than the general pressures upon persons employed by the affected employers implicit in economic strikes.

The Board's own interpretation for nearly a decade after the passage of the Taft-Hartley Act gave § 8(b)(1)(A) this limited application....

We are confirmed in our view by the action of Congress in passing the Labor-Management Reporting and Disclosure Act of 1959. That act goes beyond the Taft-Hartley Act to legislate a comprehensive code governing organizational strikes and picketing and draws no distinction between "organizational" and "recognitional" picketing. While proscribing peaceful organizational strikes in many situations, it also establishes safeguards against the Board's interference with legitimate picketing activity. See § 8(b)(7)(C). Were § 8(b)(1)(A) to have the sweep contended for by the Board, the Board might proceed against peaceful picketing in disregard of these safeguards. To be sure, what Congress did in 1959 does not establish what it meant in 1947. However, as another major step in an evolving pattern of regulation of union conduct, the 1959 Act is a relevant consideration. Courts may properly take into account the later act when asked to extend the reach of the earlier act's vague language to the limits which, read literally, the words might permit. We avoid the incongruous result implicit in the Board's construction, by reading § 8(b)(1)(A) which is only one of many interwoven sections in a complex act mindful of the manifest purpose of the Congress to fashion a coherent national labor policy.

Affirmed.

NOTE

Provisions of the Labor-Management Reporting and Disclosure Act of 1959 dealing with organizational and recognition picketing. As can readily be observed in the *Curtis Bros.* case, there was considerable confusion in 1958 and 1959 as to the applicability of § 8(b)(1) of the NLRA to organizational and recognition picketing. During the same period, the McClellan Committee hearings were revealing instances in which certain unions, particularly the Teamsters, were employing such economic weapons under circumstances that were widely regarded as abusive. President Eisenhower, in his radio-television appeal for "an effective labor reform law" dramatized the problem in this manner:

> Chief among the abuses from which Americans need protection are the oppressive practices of coercion.
>
> Take a company in the average American town—your town. A union official comes into the office, presents the company with a proposed labor contract, and demands that the company either sign or be picketed. The company refuses, because its employees don't want to join that union.
>
> And remember, the law definitely gives employees the right to have or not to have a union—clearly a basic American right of choice.
>
> Now what happens? The union official carries out the threat and puts a picket line outside the plant, to drive away customers, to cut off deliveries. In short, to force the employees into a union they do not want. This is one example of what has been called blackmail picketing. It is unfair and unjust. This could force the company out of business and result in the loss of all the jobs in the plant.
>
> I want that sort of thing stopped. So does America. [N.Y. Times, Aug. 7, 1959, at 8, col. 6].

Congressman Griffin, in explaining the Landrum-Griffin bill to the House, similarly described the need for legislation:

> It is intended to prohibit blackmail recognition picketing by unions which do not represent the employees. Under the National Labor Relations Act elaborate election machinery is provided for ascertaining the wishes of employees in selecting or rejecting bargaining representatives. The act contains provisions for giving employees an opportunity to vote by secret ballot. In recent years the safeguards intended by these election provisions have been thwarted by unions which have lost elections and unions which do not have enough employee support to petition for an election but yet insist upon compelling employers to sign contracts with them—irrespective of the sentiment of the employees.
>
> The customary method employed to force employers to do this is to place picket lines around their plants or shops. Such picketing, even when peaceful, will frequently cause small employers to capitulate. The picket line is a signal for truckers not to pick up or deliver goods to employees of maintenance contractors. Pickets also deter many customers from entering retail or

service establishments. In the face of such tactics employees whose jobs are in jeopardy as they see their employer's business choked off are soon coerced into joining the picketing union—even though they might prefer another union. In many such cases their employer forces them in a particular union by signing a compulsory membership agreement with the picketing union.

The NLRB has attempted to give some relief to employers and employees victimized in such situations by holding it an unfair labor practice for a union to picket for recognition after it has lost an election. While such relief seems called for, nevertheless the courts of appeal are in conflict as to whether the Board has even this limited power. [105 Cong. Rec. 14347 (1959)].

AFL-CIO President George Meany argued, however, that the Landrum-Griffin bill would "prohibit any union from advertising to the public that an employer is unfair to labor, pays substandard wages or operates a sweatshop." N.Y. Times, Aug. 7, 1959, at 8, col. 6.

The House of Representatives passed the Landrum-Griffin bill, embodying essentially the administration's proposals. The final enactment drafted by the conference committee of the House and Senate followed the Landrum-Griffin bill in general as to organizational and recognition picketing, but with certain mitigating modifications exacted by Senator Kennedy and others.

INTERNATIONAL HOD CARRIERS LOCAL 840
(BLINNE CONSTRUCTION CO.)

National Labor Relations Board
135 N.L.R.B. 1153 (1962)

Supplemental Decision and Order

On February 20, 1961, the Board (Member Fanning dissenting) issued a Decision and Order in this case finding that Respondent Union had engaged in unfair labor practices in violation of Section 8(b)(7)(C) of the Act. Thereafter, on or about April 3, 1961, Respondent Union filed with the Board a motion for reconsideration and for dismissal of the complaint ....

I

....

As indicated by its text, the thrust of Section 8(b)(7) is to deal with recognition and organization picketing, a matter not dealt with directly in the Taft-Hartley Act except to the limited extent provided in Section 8(b)(4)(C) of that Act....

Even a cursory examination of the legislative history of the provisions here in issue reveals that, like the so-called "secondary boycott" provisions of the Taft-Hartley Act, Section 8(b)(7) was also "to a marked degree, the result of conflict and compromise between strong contending forces and deeply held views on the role of organized labor in the free economic life of the Nation and the appropriate balance to be struck between the uncontrolled power of management and labor to further their respective interests." *Local 1976, United Brotherhood of Carpenters and Joiners of America, AFL, et al. (Sand Door & Plywood Co.) v. N.L.R.B.,* 357 U.S. 93, 99-100....

II

Before proceeding to determine the application of Section 8(b)(7)(C) to the facts of the instant case, it is essential to note the interplay of the several subsections of Section 8(b)(7), of which subparagraph (C) is only a constituent part.

The section as a whole, as is apparent from its opening phrases, prescribes limitations only on picketing for an object of "recognition" or "bargaining" (both of which terms will hereinafter be subsumed under the single term "recognition") or for an object of organization. Picketing for other objects is not proscribed by this section. Moreover, not all picketing for recognition or organization is proscribed. A "currently certified" union may picket for recognition or organization of employees for whom it is certified. And even a union which is not certified is barred from recognition or organization picketing only in three general areas. The first area, defined in subparagraph (A) of Section 8(b)(7), relates to situations where another union has been lawfully recognized and a question concerning representation cannot appropriately be raised. The second area, defined in subparagraph (B), relates to situations where, within the preceding 12 months, a "valid election" has been held.

The intent of subparagraphs (A) and (B) is fairly clear. Congress concluded that where a union has been lawfully recognized and a question concerning representation cannot appropriately be raised, or where the employees within the preceding 12 months have made known their views concerning representation, both the employer and employees are entitled to immunity from recognition or organization picketing for prescribed periods.

Congress did not stop there, however. Deeply concerned with other abuses, most particularly "blackmail" picketing, Congress concluded that it would be salutary to impose even further limitations on picketing for recognition or organization. Accordingly, subparagraph (C) provides that even where such picketing is not barred by the provisions of (A) or (B) so that picketing for recognition or organization would otherwise be permissible, such picketing is limited to a reasonable period not to exceed 30 days unless a representation petition is filed prior to the expiration of that period. Absent the filing of such a timely petition, continuation of the picketing beyond the reasonable period becomes an unfair labor practice. On the other hand, the filing of a timely petition stays the limitation and picketing may continue pending the processing of the petition. Even here, however, Congress by the addition of the first proviso to subparagraph (C) made it possible to foreshorten the period of permissible picketing by directing the holding of an expedited election pursuant to the representation petition.

The expedited election procedure is applicable, of course, only in a Section 8(b)(7)(C) proceeding, i.e., where an 8(b)(7)(C) unfair labor practice charge has been filed. Congress rejected efforts to amend the provisions of Section 9(c) of the Act so as to dispense generally with preelection hearings. Thus, in the absence of an 8(b)(7)(C) unfair labor practice charge, a union will not be enabled to obtain an expedited election by the mere device of engaging in recognition or organization picketing and filing a representation petition.[10] And on the other hand, a picketing union which files a representation petition pursuant to the mandate of Section 8(b)(7)(C) and to avoid its sanctions will not be propelled into an expedited election, which it may not desire, merely because it has filed such a petition. In both the above situations, the normal representation procedures are applicable; the showing of a substantial interest will be required, and the preelection hearing directed in Section 9(c)(1) will be held.

This, in our considered judgment, puts the expedited election procedure prescribed in the first proviso to subparagraph (C) in its proper and intended focus. That procedure was devised to shield aggrieved employers and employees from the adverse effects of prolonged recognition or organization picketing. Absent such a grievance, it was not designed either to benefit or to handicap picketing activity. As District Judge Thornton aptly stated in *Reed v. Roumell,* 185 F. Supp. 4 (D.C., E. Mich.), "If [the first proviso] were intended to confer a primary or independent right to an expedited election entirely separated from the statutory scheme, it would seem that such intention would have manifested itself in a more forthright manner, rather than in the shy seclusion of Section 8(b)(7)(C)."

Subparagraphs (B) and (C) serve different purposes. But it is especially significant to note their interrelationship. Congress was particularly concerned, even where picketing for recognition or organization was otherwise permissible, that the question concerning representation which gave rise to the picketing be resolved as quickly as possible. It was for this reason that it provided for the filing of a petition pursuant to which the Board could direct an expedited election in which the employees could freely indicate their desires as to representation. If, in the free exercise of their choice, they designate the picketing union as their bargaining representative, that union will be certified and it will by the express terms of Section 8(b)(7) be exonerated from the strictures of that section. If, conversely, the employees reject the picketing union, that union will be barred from picketing for 12 months thereafter under the provisions of subparagraph (B).

---

[10] Congress plainly did not intend such a result. See Congressman Barden's statement (105 Daily Cong. Rec., A8062, September 2, 1959; 2 Legis. Hist. 1813). And the Board has ruled further that a charge filed by a picketing union or a person "fronting" for it may not be utilized to invoke an expedited election. *Claussen Baking Company,* Case No. 11-RC-1329, May 5, 1960 (not published in NLRB volumes). *See also Reed v. Roumell,* cited *infra.*

The scheme which Congress thus devised represents what that legislative body deemed a practical accommodation between the right of a union to engage in legitimate picketing for recognition or organization and abuse of that right. One caveat must be noted in that regard. The congressional scheme is, perforce, based on the premise that the election to be conducted under the first proviso to subparagraph (C) represents the free and uncoerced choice of the employee electorate. Absent such a free and uncoerced choice, the underlying question concerning representation is not resolved and, more particularly, subparagraph (B) which turns on the holding of a "valid election" does not become operative.

There remains to be considered only the second proviso to subparagraph (C). In sum, that proviso removes the time limitation imposed upon, and preserves the legality of, recognition or organization picketing falling within the ambit of subparagraph (C), where that picketing merely advises the public that an employer does not employ members of, or have a contract with, a union unless an effect of such picketing is to halt pickups or deliveries, or the performance of services. Needless to add, picketing which meets the requirements of the proviso also renders the expedited election procedure inapplicable.

Except for the final clause in Section 8(b)(7) which provides that nothing in that section shall be construed to permit any act otherwise proscribed under Section 8(b) of the Act, the foregoing sums up the limitations imposed upon recognition or organization picketing by the Landrum-Griffin amendments. However, at the risk of laboring the obvious, it is important to note that structurally, as well as grammatically, subparagraphs (A), (B), and (C) are subordinate to and controlled by the opening phrases of Section 8(b)(7). In other words, the thrust of all the Section 8(b)(7) provisions is only upon picketing for an object of recognition or organization, and not upon picketing for other objects. Similarly, both structurally and grammatically, the two provisos in subparagraphs (C) appertain only to the situation defined in the principal clause of that subparagraph.

III

Having outlined, in concededly broad strokes, the statutory framework of Section 8(b)(7) and particularly subparagraph (C) thereof, we may appropriately turn to a consideration of the instant case which presents issues going to the heart of that legislation.

The relevant facts may be briefly stated. On February 2, 1960, all three common laborers employed by Blinne at the Fort Leonard Wood jobsite signed cards designating the Union to represent them for purposes of collective bargaining. The next day the Union demanded that Blinne recognize the Union as the bargaining agent for the three laborers. Blinne not only refused recognition but told the Union it would transfer one of the laborers, Wann, in order to destroy the

Union's majority.[13] Blinne carried out this threat and transferred Wann 5 days later, on February 8. Following this refusal to recognize the Union and the transfer of Wann the Union started picketing at Fort Wood. The picketing, which began on February 8, immediately following the transfer of Wann, had three announced objectives: (1) recognition of the Union; (2) payment of the Davis-Bacon scale of wages; and (3) protest against Blinne's unfair labor practices in refusing to recognize the Union and in threatening to transfer and transferring Wann.

The picketing continued, with interruptions due to bad weather, until at least March 11, 1960, a period of more than 30 days from the date the picketing commenced. The picketing was peaceful, only one picket was on duty, and the picket sign he carried read "C.A. Blinne Construction Company, unfair." The three laborers on the job (one was the replacement for Wann) struck when the picketing started.

The Union, of course, was not the certified bargaining representative of the employees. Moreover, no representation petition was filed during the more than 30 days in which picketing was taking place. On March 1, however, about 3 weeks after the picketing commenced and well within the statutory 30-day period, the Union filed unfair labor practice charges against Blinne, alleging violations of Section 8(a)(1), (2), (3), and (5). On March 22, the Regional Director dismissed the 8(a)(2) and (5) charges, whereupon the Union forthwith filed a representation petition under Section 9(c) of the Act. Subsequently, on April 20, the Regional Director approved a unilateral settlement agreement with Blinne with respect to the Section 8(a)(1) and (3) charges which had not been dismissed. In the settlement agreement, Blinne neither admitted nor denied that it had committed unfair labor practices.

General Counsel argues that a violation of Section 8(b)(7)(C) has occurred within the literal terms of that provision because (1) the Union's picketing was concededly for an object of obtaining recognition; (2) the Union was not currently certified as the representative of the employees involved; and (3) no petition for representation was filed within 30 days of the commencement of the picketing. Inasmuch as the Union made no contention that its recognition picketing was "informational" within the meaning of the second proviso to subparagraph (C) or that it otherwise comported with the strictures of that proviso, General Counsel contends that a finding of unfair labor practice is required.

Respondent Union, for its part, points to the manifest inequity of such a finding and argues that Congress could not have intended so incongruous a result. In essence, its position is that it was entitled to recognition because it represented all the employees in the appropriate unit, that Blinne by a series of unfair labor practices deprived the Union and the employees it sought to represent of funda-

---

[13]Blinne's assumption that this transfer would destroy the Union's majority was in error. However, that error has no significance in this case.

mental rights guaranteed by the Act, and that the impact of a finding adverse to the Union would be to punish the innocent and reward the wrongdoer. More specifically, Respondent argues that Section 8(b)(7)(C) was not intended to apply to picketing by a majority union and that, in any event, Blinne's unfair labor practices exonerated it from the statutory requirement of filing a timely representation petition....

IV

....

A. *The contention that Section 8(b)(7)(C) does not proscribe picketing for recognition or organization by a majority union*

Respondent, urging the self-evident proposition that a statute should be read as a whole, argues that Section 8(b)(7)(C) was not designed to prohibit picketing for recognition by a union enjoying majority status in an appropriate unit. Such picketing is for a lawful purpose inasmuch as Sections 8(a)(5) and 9(a) of the Act specifically impose upon an employer the duty to recognize and bargain with a union which enjoys that status. Accordingly, Respondent contends, absent express language requiring such a result, Section 8(b)(7)(C) should not be read in derogation of the duty so imposed....

[W]e find [this contention] to be without merit. To be sure, the legislative history is replete with references that Congress in framing the 1959 amendments was primarily concerned with "blackmail" picketing where the picketing union represented none or few of the employees whose allegiance it sought. Legislative references susceptible to an interpretation that Congress was concerned with the evils of majority picketing are sparse. Yet it cannot be gainsaid that Section 8(b)(7) by its explicit language exempts only "currently certified" unions from its proscriptions. Cautious as we should be to avoid a mechanical reading of statutory terms in involved legislative enactments, it is difficult to avoid giving the quoted words, essentially words of art, their natural construction. Moreover, such a construction is consonant with the underlying statutory scheme which is to resolve disputed issues of majority status, whenever possible, by the machinery of a Board election. Absent unfair labor practices or preelection misconduct warranting the setting aside of the election, majority unions will presumably not be prejudiced by such resolution. On the other hand, the admitted difficulties of determining majority status without such an election are obviated by this construction....

B. *The contention that employer unfair labor practices are a defense to a charge of a Section 8(b)(7)(C) violation*

We turn now to the second issue, namely, whether employer unfair labor practices are a defense to an 8(b)(7)(C) violation. As set forth in the original Decision and Order, the Union argues that Blinne was engaged in unfair labor practices within the meaning of Section 8(a)(1) and (3) of the Act; that it filed appropriate unfair labor practice charges against Blinne within a reasonable period of time after the commencement of the picketing; that it filed a representation petition as soon as the 8(a)(2) and (5) allegations of the charges were dismissed; that the 8(a)(1) and (3) allegations were in effect sustained and a settlement agreement was subsequently entered into with the approval of the Board; and that, therefore, this sequence of events should satisfy the requirements of Section 8(b)(7)(C).

The majority of the Board in the original Decision and Order rejected this argument. Pointing out that the representation petition was concededly filed more than 30 days after the commencement of the picketing, the majority concluded that the clear terms of Section 8(b)(4)(C) had been violated.

The majority also addressed itself specifically to the Union's contention that Section 8(b)(7)(C) could not have been intended by Congress to apply where an employer unfair labor practice had occurred. Its opinion alludes to the fact that the then Senator, now President, Kennedy had proposed statutory language to the effect that any employer unfair labor practice would be a defense to a charge of an 8(b)(7) violation both with respect to an application to the courts for a temporary restraining order and with respect to the unfair labor practice proceeding itself. The majority noted that the Congress did not adopt this proposal but instead limited itself merely to the insertion of a proviso in Section 10(*l*) prohibiting the application for a restraining order under Section 8(b)(7)(C) if there was reason to believe that a Section 8(a)(2) violation existed. Accordingly, the majority concluded that Congress had specifically rejected the very contention which Respondent urged....

It seems fair to say that Congress was unwilling to write an exemption into Section 8(b)(7)(C) dispensing with the necessity for filing a representation petition wherever employer unfair labor practices were alleged. The fact that the bill as ultimately enacted by the Congress did not contain the amendment to Section 10(*l*) which the Senate had adopted in S. 1555 cogently establishes that this reluctance was not due to oversight. On the other hand, it strains credulity to believe that Congress proposed to make the rights of union and employees turn upon the results of an election which, because of the existence of unremedied unfair labor practices, is unlikely to reflect the true wishes of the employees.

We do not find ourselves impaled on the horns of this dilemma. Upon careful reappraisal of the statutory scheme we are satisfied that Congress meant to require, and did require, in an 8(b)(7)(C) situation, that a representation petition be filed within a reasonable period, not to exceed 30 days. By this device machinery can quickly be set in motion to resolve by a free and fair election the underlying question concerning representation out of which the picketing arises. This is the normal situation, and the situation which the statute is basically designed to serve.

There is legitimate concern, however, with the abnormal situation, that is, the situation where because of unremedied unfair labor practices a free and fair election cannot be held. We believe Congress anticipated this contingency also. Thus, we find no mandate in the legislative scheme to compel the holding of an election pursuant to a representation petition where, because of unremedied unfair labor practices or for other valid reason, a free and uncoerced election cannot be held. On the contrary, the interrelated provisions of subparagraphs (B) and (C), by their respective references to a "valid election" and to a "certif[ication of] results" presuppose that Congress contemplated only a fair and free election. Only after such an election could the Board certify the results and only after such an election could the salutary provisions of subparagraph (B) become operative.

In our view, therefore, Congress intended that, except to the limited extent set forth in the first proviso, the Board in 8(b)(7)(C) cases follow the tried and familiar procedures it typically follows in representation cases where unfair labor practice charges are filed. That procedure, as already set forth, is to hold the representation case in abeyance and refrain from holding an election pending the resolution of the unfair labor practice charges. Thus, the fears that the statutory requirement for filing a timely petition will compel a union which has been the victim of unfair labor practices to undergo a coerced election are groundless. No action will be taken on that petition while unfair labor practice charges are pending, and until a valid election is held pursuant to that petition, the union's right to picket under the statutory scheme is unimpaired.

On the other side of the coin, it may safely be assumed that groundless unfair labor practice charges in this area, because of the statutory priority accorded Section 8(b)(7) violations, will be quickly dismissed. Following such dismissal an election can be directed forthwith upon the subsisting petition, thereby effectuating the congressional purpose. Moreover, the fact that a timely petition is on file will protect the innocent union, which through a mistake of fact or law has filed a groundless unfair labor practice charge, from a finding of an 8(b)(7)(C) violation. Thus, the policy of the entire Act is effectuated and all rights guaranteed by its several provisions are appropriately safeguarded. *See Mastro Plastics Corp. v. N.L.R.B.,* 350 U.S. 270, 285.

The facts of the instant case may be utilized to demonstrate the practical operation of the legislative scheme. Here the union had filed unfair labor practice charges alleging violations by the employer of Section 8(a)(1), (2), (3), and (5) of the Act. General Counsel found the allegations of 8(a)(2) and (5) violations groundless. Hence had these allegations stood alone and had a timely petition been on file, an election could have been directed forthwith and the underlying question concerning representation out of which the picketing arose could have

been resolved pursuant to the statutory scheme. The failure to file a timely petition frustrated that scheme.[24]

On the other hand, the Section 8(a)(1) and (3) charges were found meritorious.
Under these circumstances, and again consistent with uniform practice, no election would have been directed notwithstanding the currency of a timely petition;
the petition would be held in abeyance pending a satisfactory resolution of the
unfair labor practice charges. The aggrieved union's right to picket would not be
abated in the interim and the sole prejudice to the employer would be the delay
engendered by its own unfair labor practices. The absence of a timely petition,
however, precludes disposition of the underlying question concerning representation which thus remains unresolved even after the Section 8(a)(1) and (3)
charges are satisfactorily disposed of. Accordingly, to condone the refusal to file
a timely petition in such situations would be to condone the flouting of a legislative judgment. Moreover, and most important, to impose a lesser requirement
would fly in the face of the public interest which prompted that judgment.

Conclusion

Because we read Section 8(b)(7)(C) as requiring in the instant case the filing
of a timely petition and because such a petition was admittedly not filed until
more than 30 days after the commencement of the picketing, we find that Respondent violated Section 8(b)(7)(C) of the Act. As previously noted, it is undisputed that "an object" of the picketing was for recognition. It affords Respondent

---

[24] We would, however, have had a much different case here if the Section 8(a)(5) charge had
been found meritorious so as to warrant issuance of a complaint. A representation petition assumes
an unresolved question concerning representation. A Section 8(a)(5) charge, on the other hand,
presupposes that no such question exists and that the employer is wrongfully refusing to recognize
or bargain with a statutory bargaining representative. Because of this basic inconsistency, the Board
has over the years uniformly refused to entertain representation petitions where a meritorious
charge of refusal to bargain has been filed and, indeed, has dismissed any representation petition
which may already have been on file. The same considerations apply where a meritorious Section
8(a)(5) charge is filed in a Section 8(b)(7)(C) context. Congressional acquiescence in the Board's
long-standing practice prior to the enactment of Section 8(b)(7)(C) imports, in our view, congressional approval of a continuation of that practice thereafter. *Cf. Gullett Gin Co. v. N.L.R.B.,* 340
U.S. 361, 366. Accordingly, where a meritorious 8(a)(5) charge was filed in an 8(b)(7)(C) situation,
the Board dismissed the representation petition. *See Robert P. Scott, Inc. v. Rothman,* 46 LRRM
2793 (D.C.D.C.); *Colony Materials, Inc. v. Rothman,* 46 LRRM 2794 (D.C.D.C.). So here, if a
meritorious 8(a)(5) charge had been filed, a petition for representation would not have been required....
[T]he filing of a representation petition will not be required of a union when it has filed a meritorious 8(a)(5) charge, but will be required where it has filed other 8(a) charges. The point of the
distinction—a point which our colleagues inexplicably ignore—is simply this: a meritorious 8(a)(5)
case moots the question concerning representation which the petition is designed to resolve; other
8(a) charges merely delay the time when that unresolved question can be submitted to a free election by the employees....

no comfort that its picketing was also in protest against the discriminatory transfer of an employee and against payment of wages at a rate lower than that prescribed by law. Had Respondent confined its picketing to these objectives rather than, as it did, include a demand for recognition, we believe none of the provisions of Section 8(b)(7) would be applicable.[29] Under the circumstances here, however, Section 8(b)(7)(C) is applicable.

Accordingly, having concluded as in the original decision herein that a violation of Section 8(b)(7)(C) has occurred, albeit for differing reasons, we reaffirm the Order entered therein.

[The "separate opinion" of MEMBERS ROGERS and LEEDOM and the "concurring and dissenting" opinion of MEMBER FANNING are omitted.]

SMITLEY, d/b/a CROWN CAFETERIA v. NLRB

United States Court of Appeals, Ninth Circuit
327 F.2d 351 (1964)

[The NLRB dismissed a complaint that the union had engaged in unlawful recognition picketing under § 8(b)(7)(C).]

DUNIWAY, Circuit Judge.... The findings of the Board as to the facts are not attacked. It found, in substance, that the unions picketed the cafeteria for more than thirty days before filing a representation petition under § 9(c) of the act (29 U.S.C. § 159(c)), that an object of the picketing was to secure recognition, that the purpose of the picketing was truthfully to advise the public that petitioners employed nonunion employees or had no contract with the unions, and that the picketing did not have the effect of inducing any stoppage of deliveries or services to the cafeteria by employees of any other employer. The matter was twice heard by the Board, which first concluded, by a majority of 3 to 2, that the picketing did violate the statute in question (130 N.L.R.B. 570), and then held, following a change in its membership, and by a majority of 3 to 2, that the picketing did not violate the statute (135 N.L.R.B. 1183). We conclude that the views of the Board, as stated after its second consideration of the matter, are correct, and that the statute has not been violated.

---

[29] As noted at the outset, Section 8(b)(7) is directed only at recognition and organization picketing and not at picketing for other objects including so-called protest picketing against unfair labor practices. There is ample legislative history to substantiate the proposition that Congress did not intend to outlaw picketing against unfair labor practices as such. *See,* for example, 105 Daily Cong. Rec. 5756, 5766, 15121, 15907, 16400, 16541; 2 Legis. Hist. 1361, 1384, 1429, 1714. Absent other evidence (such as is present in this case) of an organizational, recognition, or bargaining objective it is clear that Congress did not consider picketing against unfair labor practices as such to be also for proscribed objectives and, hence, outlawed. Parenthetically, it follows that cease-and-desist order issued against picketing in violation of Section 8(b)(7) will enjoin only picketing for recognition, bargaining, or organization and will not be a bar to protest picketing against unfair labor practices....

The Board states its interpretation of the section, including the proviso quoted above, as follows:

> Congress framed a general rule covering all organizational or recognitional picketing carried on for more than 30 days without the filing of a representation petition. Then, Congress excepted from that rule picketing which, although it had an organizational or recognitional objective, was addressed primarily to the public, was truthful in nature, and did not interfere to any significant extent with deliveries or the rendition of services by the employees of any other employer.

We think that this is the correct interpretation. It will be noted that subdivision (7) of subsection (b), § 8, quoted above, starts with the general prohibition of picketing "where an object thereof is forcing or requiring an employer to recognize or bargain with a labor organization" (This is often called recognitional picketing) "... or forcing or requiring the employees of an employer to accept or select such labor organization...." (This is often called organizational picketing), "... unless such labor organization is currently certified as the representative of such employees:...." This is followed by three subparagraphs, (A), (B) and (C). Each begins with the same word, "where." (A) deals with the situation "where" the employer has lawfully recognized another labor organization and a question of representation cannot be raised under § 9(c). (B) refers to the situation "where," within the preceding 12 months, a valid election under § 9(c) has been conducted. (C), with which we are concerned, refers to a situation "where" there has been no petition for an election under § 9(c) filed within a reasonable period of time, not to exceed thirty days, from the commencement of the picketing. Thus, § 8(b)(7) does not purport to prohibit all picketing having the named "object" of recognitional or organizational picketing. It limits the prohibition of such picketing to three specific situations.

There are no exceptions or provisos in subparagraphs (A) and (B), which describe two of those situations. There are, however, two provisos in subparagraph (C). The first sets up a special procedure for an expedited election under § 9(c). The second is the one with which we are concerned. It is an exception to the prohibition of "such picketing," *i.e.,* recognitional or organizational picketing, being a proviso to a prohibition of such picketing "where" certain conditions exist. It can only mean, indeed, it says, that "such picketing," which otherwise falls within subparagraph (C), is not prohibited if it falls within the terms of the proviso. That proviso says that subparagraph (C) is not to be construed to prohibit "any picketing" for "the purpose" of truthfully advising the public (including consumers) that an employer does not employ members of, or have a contract with, a labor organization. To this exception there is an exception, stated in the last "unless" clause, namely, that "such picketing," *i.e.,* picketing where "an object" is recognitional or organizational, but which has "the" excepting "purpose," would still be illegal if an effect were to induce any individual employee of other persons not to pick up, deliver, or transport any goods, or not to perform any services. Admittedly, the picketing here does not fall within the "unless" clause in the second proviso to subparagraph (C). It does, however, fall within the proviso, since it does have "the purpose" that brings it within the proviso. It also has "an object" that brings it within the first sentence of subsection (b) and the first clause of subdivision (7), and within the circumstances stated in the opening clause of subparagraph (C). If it did not have "an object" bringing it within subdivision (7), it would not be prohibited at all. Moreover, if it did have that "object," it still would not be prohibited at all, unless it occurred in circumstances described in subparagraph (A), (B) or (C). Here, neither (A) or (B) applies; (C) does. But, unlike (A) or (B), it has an excepting proviso. Unless that proviso refers to picketing having as "an object" either recognition or organization, it can have no meaning, for it would not be an exception or proviso to anything. It would be referring to conduct not prohibited in § 8(b) at all.

Petitioners urge that if the picketing has "an object" recognition or organization, then it is still illegal, even though it has "the purpose" of truthfully advising the public, etc., within the meaning of the second proviso to subparagraph (C). It seems to us, as it did to the Board, that to so construe the statute would make the proviso meaningless. The hard realities of union-employer relations are such that it is difficult, indeed almost impossible, for us to conceive of picketing falling within the terms of the proviso that did not also have as "an object" obtaining a contract with the employer. This is normally the ultimate objective of any union in relation to an employer who has employees whose jobs fall within the categories of employment that are within the jurisdiction of the union, which is admittedly the situation here.

We note that the Court of Appeals for the Second Circuit has reached a similar conclusion. In *NLRB v. Local 3, International Bhd. of Electrical Workers,* 317 F.2d 193 (2d Cir. 1963), that court considered the section at some length, and said:

> It seems, however, much more realistic to suppose that Congress framed a general rule covering the field of recognitional and organizational picketing, conducted under alternate sets of circumstances described in subparagraphs (A), (B), and (C), and then excepted from the operation of the rule, as it applied to the circumstances set forth in subparagraph (C), a comparatively innocuous species of picketing having the immediate purpose of informing or advising the public, even though its ultimate object was success in recognition and organization....
>
> One of the principal difficulties in construing and applying subparagraph (C) is that § 8(b)(7) contains the partially synonymous words, "object" and "purpose," used in two distinct contexts but to which much of the same evidence is relevant. These are: "where an object thereof is forcing or requiring an employer to recognize or bargain ..." and "for the purpose of truthfully

advising the public...." It does not necessarily follow that, where an object of the picketing is forcing or requiring an employer to recognize or bargain, the purpose of the picketing, in the context of the second proviso, is not truthfully to advise the public, etc. The union may legitimately have a long range or strategic objective of getting the employer to bargain with or recognize the union and still the picketing may be permissive. This proviso gives the union freedom to appeal to the unorganized public for spontaneous popular pressure upon an employer; it is intended, however, to exclude the invocation of pressure by organized labor groups or members of unions, as such.

The permissible picketing is, therefore, that which through the dissemination of certain allowed representations, is designed to influence members of the unorganized public, as individuals, because the impact upon the employer by way of such individuals is weaker, more indirect and less coercive.

We agree. *See also Getreu v. Bartenders and Hotel & Restaurant Employees Union Local 58,* 181 F. Supp. 738 (N.D. Ind. 1960).

Both sides have reviewed legislative history. We think this unnecessary, because we think that the meaning of the statute is clear. We also find the history inconclusive, but it seems to us to point somewhat more strongly toward the view that we here adopt than to the contrary view. Petitioners rely on language used by Senator Kennedy, who was one of the sponsors of the bill in the Senate and one of the Senate Conferees, in which he referred to the second proviso as permitting "purely informational" picketing. Counsel for petitioners frankly conceded, however, at oral argument, that most of the legislative history is against the view that he urged, and we agree. A discussion of legislative history appears in the dissent to the Board's first opinion (130 N.L.R.B. 576-77) and we therefore do not repeat it here. We think that even Senator Kennedy's comment, upon which petitioners most heavily rely, taken in context, was not intended to have the limiting effect which petitioners would give it. Senator Kennedy was more concerned, on the one hand, with the economic pressure involved in recognitional and organizational picketing, and on the other hand, with the right of labor truthfully to advise the public that the employer was nonunion, or that the employer did not have a contract with the union, than he was with whether or not, in addition to having an informational purpose described in the proviso, there was also a recognitional or organizational object. See 105 Cong. Rec. 17898 (1959). *See also* Cox, *The Landrum-Griffin Amendments to the National Labor Relations Act,* 44 Minn. L. Rev. 257, 267. Mr. Cox, now the Solicitor General, was then Senator Kennedy's chief advisor on the bill.

We think that, in substance, the effect of the second proviso to subparagraph (C) is to allow recognitional or organizational picketing to continue if it meets two important restrictions: (1) it must be addressed to the public and be truthful and (2) it must not induce other unions to stop deliveries or services. The picketing here met those criteria.

NOTES

1. In other decisions interpreting § 8(b)(7), the NLRB and the courts have declared:

a. Picketing solely to protest an employee's discharge and not for union recognition does not violate § 8(b)(7)(C). *UAW, Local 259 (Fanelli Ford Sales, Inc.),* 133 N.L.R.B. 1468 (1961).

b. Picketing by the incumbent union to compel the employer to comply with an existing bargaining agreement is not unlawful recognition picketing within the meaning of § 8(b)(7)(C) of the NLRA. *Building & Constr. Trades Council (Sullivan Elec. Co.),* 146 N.L.R.B. 1086 (1964). *Compare Teamsters Local 812 v. NLRB,* 937 F.2d 684 (D.C. Cir. 1991) (recognition picketing by incumbent union after it lost representation election violated § 8(b)(7)(B) since within twelve months of valid election).

c. Employees who engage in recognition picketing in violation of § 8(b)(7) lose their protected status under the Act, and an employer may lawfully refuse to reinstate them. *Claremont Polychemical Corp.,* 196 N.L.R.B. 613 (1972).

d. In *NLRB v. Iron Workers Local 103,* 434 U.S. 335 (1978), the Supreme Court held that it was a violation of § 8(b)(7)(C) for an uncertified union, not representing a majority of construction employees, to engage in extended picketing to enforce a § 8(f) prehire agreement, since such picketing was legally equivalent to picketing for organizational purposes. *Cf. Laborers Local 1184 (NVE Constr.),* 296 N.L.R.B. 1325 (1989), *affirmed,* 934 F.2d 1084 (9th Cir. 1991) (union may picket construction industry employer for the reasonable time period specified in § 8(b)(7)(C), when it is seeking recognition through § 8(f) prehire agreement).

e. Although § 8(b)(7)(C) refers to "picketing" that "has been conducted," *threats to picket* are proscribed by the same provision. While an unretracted union threat to engage in picketing if an employer does not grant union recognition does not contravene § 8(b)(7)(C) if the threatening union may lawfully seek to represent the employees in question, a similar threat by a labor organization that is barred from being certified as a collective bargaining representative of the target employees constitutes an immediate § 8(b)(7)(C) violation since such a disqualified union cannot file a valid representation petition. *Service Employees, Local 73 (A-1 Security Serv. Co.),* 224 N.L.R.B. 434 (1976), *enforced,* 578 F.2d 361 (D.C. Cir. 1978).

2. In defining the term "effect" in the proviso to § 8(b)(7)(C), the Board has looked to the "actual impact" on the employer's business, rather than to a quantitative test based solely on the number of deliveries not made or services not performed, when determining whether to remove informational picketing from the proviso's protection. The presence or absence of a violation depends on whether the picketing actually disrupted, interfered with or curtailed employer business. For example, in *Retail Clerks, Local 324 (Barker Bros. Corp. & Golds, Inc.)*, 138 N.L.R.B. 478 (1962), enforced, 328 F.2d 431 (9th Cir. 1964), where the union picketed eighteen stores over a period of twelve weeks, taking active measures to insure no interruption of service, the Board held that three delivery stoppages, two work delays, and several delivery delays were insufficient to constitute the "effect" contemplated by the proviso.

HOUSTON BUILDING & CONSTRUCTION TRADES COUNCIL [CLAUDE EVERETT CONSTRUCTION CO.]

National Labor Relations Board
136 N.L.R.B. 321 (1962)

... The Respondent, a council of local unions in the building and construction industry in the Houston, Texas, area, inquired on March 8, 1961, about the wage rates of Claude Everett Construction Company, a general construction contractor in that area. The Respondent's representative was told by Wilson, the Company's construction superintendent, that it operated an "open shop," and that its wage rates were lower than those negotiated in the area by the local unions which were members of the Respondent. On March 10, 1961, the Respondent wrote to the Company protesting its "substandard" wages and threatening to picket its construction site on March 13, unless "prevailing" rates were paid. When this letter had not been answered by March 16, the Respondent began picketing the Company's jobsite with a sign which read as follows:

> Houston Building and Construction Trades Council, AFL-CIO protests substandard wages and conditions being paid on this job by Claude Everett Company. Houston Building and Construction Trades Council does not intend by this picket line to induce or encourage the employees of any other employer to engage in a strike or a concerted refusal to work.

Such picketing continued for more than 30 days without the filing of a petition under § 9(c) of the act. The Respondent has never been certified as the representative of the Company's employees. The parties stipulated at the hearing that the picketing interfered with deliveries and services by inducing individuals employed by suppliers, service companies, and common carriers not to make pick-ups or deliveries or to perform services for the Company.

The Trial Examiner found that the Respondent picketed the Company to require it to conform its wage rates to those paid by employers having union contracts. Relying on the original Board decision in the *Calumet Contractors* case,[2] he concluded that such picketing violated § 8(b)(7)(C) of the act. Subsequent to

---

[2] *Hod Carriers, Local 41 (Calumet Contractors Ass'n)*, 130 N.L.R.B. 78.

the issuance of his Intermediate Report, however, the Board, having reconsidered the *Calumet Contractors* case,[3] found the picketing there involved not unlawful, and stated that:

> ... Respondent's admitted objective to require the Association ... to conform standards of employment to those prevailing in the area, is not tantamount to, nor does it have an objective of, recognition or bargaining. A union may legitimately be concerned that a particular employer is undermining area standards of employment by maintaining lower standards. It may be willing to forego recognition and bargaining provided subnormal working conditions are eliminated from area considerations.

While the *Calumet Contractors* case arose under § 8(b)(4)(C) of the act, which prohibits only recognitional picketing, whereas the instant case arose under § 8(b)(7)(C), which proscribes both recognitional and organizational picketing, the language of both subsections is similar, and the rationale in that case is equally applicable herein. The Respondent in the present case did not, in its conversation with the Company, its letter to the Company, or its picket sign, claim to represent the Company's employees, request recognition by the Company, or solicit employees of the Company to become members of any of the locals which are members of the Respondent. Moreover, the undisputed testimony of Executive Secretary Graham reveals that the Respondent Union has on numerous occasions in the past made similar protests against substandard wages paid by other employers without ever requesting recognition as the bargaining representative of their employees. Thus, it is clear, from the entire record, that the objective of the Respondent's picketing was to induce the Company to raise its wage rates to the union scale prevailing in the area. We cannot, as do our dissenting colleagues, equate this attempt to maintain area wage standards with conduct "forcing or requiring an employer to recognize or bargain with a labor organization as the representative of his employees, or forcing or requiring the employees ... to accept or select such labor organization as their collective bargaining representative," the conduct proscribed by § 8(b)(7).

Nor do we agree with our dissenting colleagues that the fact that the picketing interfered with deliveries and services in itself constitutes a violation of § 8(b)(7)(C). To determine the effect of § 8(b)(7)(C), we must look at the section in its entirety, in accord with the long-established principle of statutory construction that a legislative enactment is to be read in its entirety, not in bits and pieces. It is clear that this section, read as a whole, declares picketing by an uncertified union unlawful if it has a recognitional or organizational objective and if a petition has not been filed within a reasonable time, and that the interruption-of-deliveries clause does not enter into the picture unless the picketing can first be

---

[3] *Hod Carriers, Local 41 (Calumet Contractors Ass'n),* 133 N.L.R.B. 512 (Members Rodgers and Leedom dissenting).

shown to have such a prohibited objective. As we stated in the *Blinne* case [135 N.L.R.B. 1153]:

> [S]tructurally, as well as grammatically, subparagraphs (A), (B), and (C) are subordinate to and controlled by the opening phrases of § 8(b)(7). In other words, the thrust of all the § 8(b)(7) provisions is only upon picketing for an object of recognition or organization, and not upon picketing for other objects. Similarly, both structurally and grammatically, the two provisos in subparagraph (C) appertain only to the situation defined in the principal clause of that subparagraph.

Our dissenting colleagues interpret the second proviso of subparagraph (C) as though it creates a completely independent unfair labor practice, without reference to the fact that it is a subsidiary clause in a section which initially prohibits picketing with a recognitional or organizational objective. Such a reading would remove the proviso from its statutory setting, an interpretive result we feel constrained to avoid.

Accordingly, on the basis of the facts in the present case and of "the thrust of all the § 8(b)(7) provisions," we find that the Respondent's picketing did not have a recognitional or organizational objective, and, therefore, that it did not violate the act even though the picketing interfered with deliveries and services. Accordingly, we shall dismiss the complaint.

[The Board dismissed the complaint.]

[MEMBERS RODGERS and LEEDOM dissented.]

NOTES

1. *Compare Centralia Bldg. Trades Council (Pacific Sign & Steel Bldg. Co.) v. NLRB*, 363 F.2d 699 (D.C. Cir. 1966), wherein the Board and the court held that the union's picketing was not "area standards" picketing but rather recognition picketing, when the union, without inquiring whether Pacific's wages were in fact substandard, demanded that it sign an agreement to pay its employees "wages and fringe benefits equal to such allowances then being received by comparable employees working under the Union Agreement. If [the Union's] industry agreements were so negotiated as to provide increases or decreases, Pacific's total 'economic package' was to be increased or decreased by an equivalent amount." The union also demanded that its accountants be permitted to make monthly inspection of Pacific's records as to the economic benefits being paid to its employees. It was held that the net effect of this would be to establish the union as negotiator of Pacific's wages and benefits, tantamount to recognition, despite the union's disclaimers to the contrary. *See also Retail Clerks, Local 899 (State-Mart, Inc.),* 166 N.L.R.B. 818 (1967), *enforced,* 404 F.2d 855 (9th Cir. 1968) (although a union may picket for "area standards" by demanding that the nonunion employer pay its employees an economic package equal in total cost to what unionized employers pay, the picketing becomes unlawful "recognition" picketing, when the union insists that the package include specific benefits, such as a welfare and pension plan).

2. The Sixth Circuit has held that area standards picketing by nonemployees is only protected conduct when the union can demonstrate that is has meaningful evidence indicating that the target firm actually provides its employees with substandard wages and benefits. *NLRB v. Great Scott,* 39 F.3d 678 (6th Cir. 1994). *See also O'Neil's Markets v. NLRB,* 95 F.3d 733 (8th Cir. 1996) (union wishing to have nonemployees engage in area standards picketing must demonstrate bona fide attempt to ascertain if employer is actually paying less than area standards wage).

3. *See* Rosen, *Area Standards Picketing,* 23 Lab. L.J. 67 (1972); Note, *Picketing for Area Standards: An Exception to Section 8(b)(7),* 1968 Duke L.J. 767.

SECTION IV. Secondary Pressure

No problem of labor law is more complex or confusing than the attempt to restrict, within "legitimate" areas, the use by unions of the power they may exert through strikes, picketing, and boycotts. The difficulty arises from the fact that, even when conducted peacefully, these methods involve economic coercion. A strike by employees to force their employer to accede to some demand is the simplest example. We are not concerned here with this kind of coercion, however, since, subject to the propriety of the object being sought and to such statutory prerequisites as may be applicable, the legal privilege to engage in such a primary strike is no longer questioned. Nor is it doubted any longer that picketing in support of such a strike is permissible so long as it is peaceable. But when such picketing goes beyond the bounds of "fair persuasion," to use the language of the *Restatement of Torts,* in the sense that it involves an attempt to induce, by economic threats, non-dealing with the employer, or when the strike is sought to be supported by "secondary" or "sympathetic" action by other labor groups or is itself secondary or sympathetic, or when the strikers or their union agents seek to enlist the support of consumers or others against their employer, the problem with which we are here concerned arises. The basic question is how far and on what principle Congress should intervene to limit such use of economic force.

NOTES

1. Should a distinction be drawn between the situation in which an embattled union simply *asks* for the support (by boycott) of other unions and of the consuming public without being able to *command* such support and that in which the union is able, by virtue of binding obligations, as through a central trades council, to command a labor boycott? If either procedure is thought to be undesirable, what is the legal remedy—to enjoin the request for the public support, in the first case, and the request for the aid of affiliates in the second? What if the action of affiliates is unsolicited, and comes automatically whenever a member union itself resorts to collective action? It is well known that many unions, either by formulated policy or by custom, "respect" picket lines established by other unions, even non-affiliated unions. The result is that, in some cases, an employer embroiled in a dispute with its own union suddenly finds, for example, that it cannot get supplies because members of a teamsters' or drivers' union will not deliver goods across the picket line.

2. In 1947, the LMRA proscribed certain types of secondary activity. The Supreme Court recognized, however, that Congress had not prohibited all forms of secondary conduct:

> Whatever may have been said in Congress preceding the passage of the Taft-Hartley Act concerning the evil of all forms of "secondary boycotts" and the desirability of outlawing them, it is clear that no such sweeping prohibition was in fact enacted in § 8(b)(4)(A). The section does not speak generally of secondary boycotts. It describes and condemns specific union conduct directed to specific objectives.

Local 1976, United Bhd. of Carpenters & Joiners v. NLRB, 357 U.S. 93, 98 (1958).

As a result of a widespread feeling that there were "loopholes" in the provisions of the LMRA dealing with secondary boycotts, and particularly as the result of the McClellan Committee's dramatization of the power of James R. Hoffa and the Teamsters Union, Congress acted in the Labor-Management Reporting and Disclosure Act amendments to tighten up the secondary boycott provisions. Some cases decided under the Taft-Hartley Act have been retained in this edition to show the background of the 1959 legislation. The charts on the following two pages may be of assistance in analyzing § 8(b)(4)(A) and (B) before and after the 1959 amendments. When reading cases decided before the 1959 amendments, it should be noted that the language that was previously set forth in § 8(b)(4)(A) became § 8(b)(4)(B).

3. For helpful general discussions of secondary boycotts under the federal statutes, *see* Farmer, *Secondary Boycotts—Loopholes Closed or Reopened?,* Geo. L.J. 392 (1964); Goetz, *Secondary Boycotts and the LMRA: A Path Through the Swamp,* 19 Kan. L. Rev. 651 (1971); Koretz, *Federal Regulation of Secondary Strikes and Boycotts—Another Chapter,* 59 Colum. L. Rev. 125 (1959); Lesnick, *Job Security and Secondary Boycotts: The Reach of NLRA §§ 8(b)(4) and 8(e),* 113 U. Pa. L. Rev. 1000 (1965); Lesnick, *The Gravamen of the Secondary Boycott,* 62 Colum. L. Rev. 1363 (1962); Ross, *Assessment of the Landrum-Griffin Act's Secondary Boycott Amendments to the Taft-Hartley Act,* 22 Lab. L.J. 675 (1971); St. Antoine, *What Makes Secondary Boycotts Secondary?,* Southwestern Legal Foundation, Labor Law Developments, Proceedings of the Eleventh An-

ANALYSIS OF §§ 8(b)(4)(A) and (B) PRIOR TO
1959 AMENDMENTS
§ 8(b)(4)

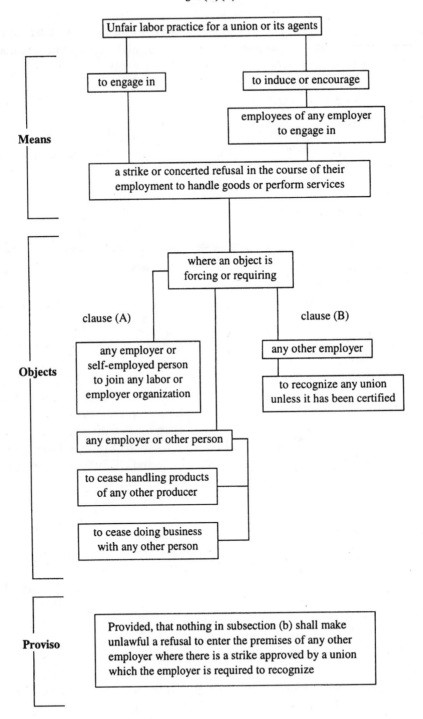

ANALYSIS OF §§ 8(b)(4)(A) and (B) AS AMENDED IN 1959
§ 8(b)(4)

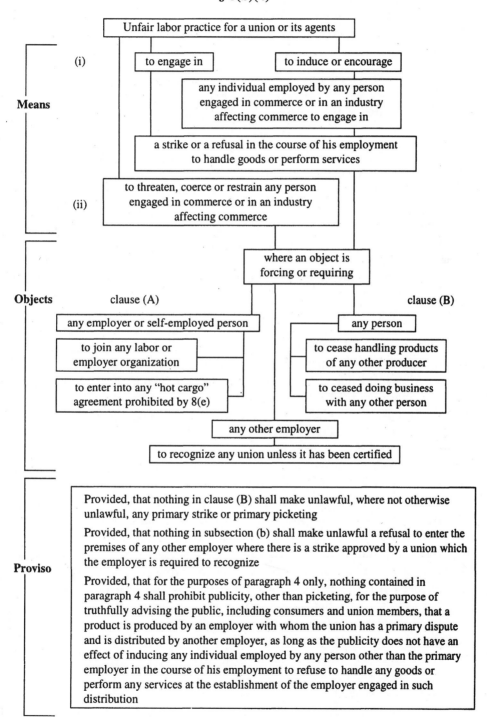

Unfair labor practice for a union or its agents

Means

(i)

to engage in

to induce or encourage

any individual employed by any person engaged in commerce or in an industry affecting commerce to engage in

a strike or a refusal in the course of his employment to handle goods or perform services

(ii)

to threaten, coerce or restrain any person engaged in commerce or in an industry affecting commerce

where an object is forcing or requiring

Objects

clause (A)

any employer or self-employed person

to join any labor or employer organization

to enter into any "hot cargo" agreement prohibited by 8(e)

clause (B)

any person

to cease handling products of any other producer

to ceased doing business with any other person

any other employer

to recognize any union unless it has been certified

Proviso

Provided, that nothing in clause (B) shall make unlawful, where not otherwise unlawful, any primary strike or primary picketing

Provided, that nothing in subsection (b) shall make unlawful a refusal to enter the premises of any other employer where there is a strike approved by a union which the employer is required to recognize

Provided, that for the purposes of paragraph 4 only, nothing contained in paragraph 4 shall prohibit publicity, other than picketing, for the purpose of truthfully advising the public, including consumers and union members, that a product is produced by an employer with whom the union has a primary dispute and is distributed by another employer, as long as the publicity does not have an effect of inducing any individual employed by any person other than the primary employer in the course of his employment to refuse to handle any goods or perform any services at the establishment of the employer engaged in such distribution

nual Institute on Labor Law 5 (1965); St. Antoine, *Secondary Boycotts and Hot Cargo: A Study in Balance of Power,* 40 U. Det. L.J. 189 (1962); Shalov, *The Landrum-Griffin Amendments: Labor's Use of the Secondary Boycott,* 45 Cornell L.Q. 724 (1960).

A. PRIMARY-SECONDARY DISTINCTION

NLRB v. INTERNATIONAL RICE MILLING CO.

Supreme Court of the United States
341 U.S. 665, 71 S. Ct. 961, 95 L. Ed. 1277 (1951)

MR. JUSTICE BURTON delivered the opinion of the Court.

The question presented is whether a union violated § 8(b)(4) of the National Labor Relations Act, 49 Stat. 449, 29 U.S.C. § 151, as amended by the Labor Management Relations Act, 1947, under the following circumstances: Although not certified or recognized as the representative of the employees of a certain mill engaged in interstate commerce, the agents of the union picketed the mill with the object of securing recognition of the union as the collective bargaining representative of the mill employees. In the course of their picketing, the agents sought to influence, or in the language of the statute they "encouraged," two men in charge of a truck of a neutral customer of the mill to refuse, in the course of their employment, to go to the mill for an order of goods. For the reasons hereinafter stated, we hold that such conduct did not violate § 8(b)(4)....

This review is confined to the single incident described in the complaint issued by the Acting Regional Director of the National Labor Relations Board against the International Brotherhood of Teamsters, Chauffeurs, Warehousemen and Helpers of America, Local 201, AFL, herein called the union. The complaint originally was based upon four charges made against the union by several rice mills engaged in interstate commerce near the center of the Louisiana rice industry. The mills included the International Rice Milling Company, Inc., which gives its name to this proceeding, and the Kaplan Rice Mills, Inc., a Louisiana corporation, which operated the mill at Kaplan, Louisiana, where the incident now before us occurred. The complaint charged that the union or its agents, by their conduct toward two employees of a neutral customer of the Kaplan Rice Mills, engaged in an unfair labor practice contrary to § 8(b)(4). The Board, with one member not participating, adopted the findings and conclusions of its trial examiner as to the facts but disagreed with his recommendation that those facts constituted a violation of § 8(b)(4)(A) or (B). The Board dismissed the complaint but attached the trial examiner's intermediate reports to its decision. 84 N.L.R.B. 360. The court of appeals set aside the dismissal and remanded the case for further proceedings. 183 F.2d 21....

The findings adopted by the Board show that the incident before us occurred at the union's picket line near the Kaplan Mill, October, 1947. The pickets generally carried signs, one being "This job is unfair to" the union. The goal of the pickets was recognition of the union as the collective bargaining representative of the mill employees, but none of those employees took part in the picketing. Late one afternoon two employees of The Sales and Services House, which was a customer of the mill, came in a truck to the Kaplan Mill to obtain rice or bran for their employer. The union had no grievance against the customer and the latter was a neutral in the dispute between the union and the mill. The pickets formed a line across the road and walked toward the truck. When the truck stopped, the pickets told its occupants there was a strike on and that the truck would have to go back. Those on the truck agreed, went back to the highway and stopped. There one got out and went to the mill across the street. At that time a vice president of the Kaplan Mill came out and asked whether the truck was on its way to the mill and whether its occupants wanted to get the order they came for. The man on the truck explained that he was not the driver and that he would have to see the driver. On the driver's return, the truck proceeded, with the vice president, to the mill by a short detour. The pickets ran toward the truck and threw stones at it. The truck entered the mill, but the findings do not disclose whether the articles sought there were obtained. The Board adopted the finding that "the stopping of the Sales House truck drivers and the use of force in connection with the stoppage were within the 'scope of the employment' of the pickets as agents of the respondent [union] and that such activities are attributable to the respondent." 84 N.L.R.B. 360, 372.

The most that can be concluded from the foregoing, to establish a violation of § 8(b)(4), is that the union, in the course of picketing the Kaplan Mill, did encourage two employees of a neutral customer to turn back from an intended trip to the mill and thus to refuse, in the course of their employment, to transport articles or perform certain services for their employer. We may assume, without the necessity of adopting the Board's findings to that effect, that the objects of such conduct on the part of the union and its agents were (1) to force Kaplan's customer to cease handling transporting or otherwise dealing in products of the mill or to cease doing business with Kaplan, at that time and place, and (2) to add to the pressure on Kaplan to recognize the union as the bargaining representative of the mill employees.

A sufficient answer to this claimed violation of the section is that the union's picketing and its encouragement of the men on the truck did not amount to such an inducement or encouragement to "concerted" activity as the section proscribes. While each case must be considered in the light of its surrounding circumstances, yet the applicable proscriptions of § 8(b)(4) are expressly limited to the inducement or encouragement of *concerted* conduct by the employees of the neutral employer. That language contemplates inducement or encouragement to some concert of action greater than is evidenced by the pickets' request to a driver of a single truck to discontinue a pending trip to a picketed mill. There was no attempt by the union to induce any action by the employees of the neutral customer which would be more widespread than that already described. There were no inducements or encouragements applied elsewhere than on the picket line. The limitation of the complaint to an incident in the geographically restricted area near the mill is significant, although not necessarily conclusive. The picketing was directed at the Kaplan employees and at their employer in a manner traditional in labor disputes. Clearly, that, in itself, was not proscribed by § 8(b)(4). Insofar as the union's efforts were directed beyond that and toward the employees of anyone other than Kaplan, there is no suggestion that the union sought *concerted* conduct by such other employees. Such efforts also fall short of the proscriptions in § 8(b)(4). In this case, therefore, we need not determine the specific objects toward which a union's encouragement of concerted conduct must be directed in order to amount to an unfair labor practice under subsection (A) or (B) of § 8(b)(4). A union's inducements or encouragements reaching individual employees of neutral employers only as they happen to approach the picketed place of business generally are not aimed at concerted, as distinguished from individual, conduct by such employees. Generally, therefore, such actions do not come within the proscription of § 8(b)(4), and they do not here.

In the instant case the violence on the picket line is not material. The complaint was not based upon that violence, as such. To reach it, the complaint more properly would have relied upon § 8(b)(1)(A) or would have addressed itself to local authorities. The substitution of violent coercion in place of peaceful persuasion would not in itself bring the complained-of conduct into conflict with § 8(b)(4). It is the object of union encouragement that is proscribed by that section, rather than the means adopted to make it felt.

That Congress did not seek, by § 8(b)(4), to interfere with the ordinary strike has been indicated recently by this Court. This is emphasized in § 13 as follows:

"Nothing in this Act, except as specifically provided for herein, shall be construed so as either to interfere with or impede or diminish in any way the right to strike, or to affect the limitations or qualifications on that right." 61 Stat. 151, 29 U.S.C. (Supp. III) § 163.

By § 13, Congress has made it clear that § 8(b)(4), and all other parts of the act which otherwise might be read so as to interfere with, impede or diminish the union's traditional right to strike, may be so read only if such interference, impediment or diminution is "specifically provided for" in the act. No such specific provision in § 8(b)(4) reaches the incident here. The material legislative history supports this view.

On the single issue before us, we sustain the action of the Board and the judgment of the court of appeals, accordingly is

Reversed.

NOTES

1. *Inducement of "concerted" activity.* The 1959 amendments removed the requirement for inducement of a "concerted" refusal to work on the part of employees of secondary employers. Congressman Griffin, in his analysis of this provision of the Landrum-Griffin bill, explained it as follows:

> As the present act forbids inducing "employees" to engage in a strike or "concerted" refusal to do their work, the courts have held that unions may induce employees one at a time to engage in secondary boycotts (citing *NLRB v. International Rice Milling Co.,* 341 U.S. 665). By changing "employees" to "any individual" and omitting the word "concerted," the proposed revision ... closes this loophole. [105 Cong. Rec. 14347 (1959)].

2. *"Primary" Picketing.* Was the fundamental basis for the decision in the *Rice Milling* case the fact that the picketing was "primary" in the sense that it was done at the primary employer's premises?

Consider the following quotation from *Local 618, Automotive, Petr. & Allied Indus. Employees Union, AFL-CIO v. NLRB,* 249 F.2d 332, 334 (8th Cir. 1957):

> In *National Labor Relations Board v. International Rice Milling Co.,* 341 U.S. 665 (1951), the Court found picketing at the primary employer's premises did not exceed conduct, traditional and permissible in a primary strike, and hence that the picketing there involved did not constitute an unfair labor practice violative of 8(b)(4)(A).

When the 1959 amendments to the LMRA were passed, the conference committee inserted a new proviso to the secondary boycott provisions of the Landrum-Griffin bill: "[N]othing contained in clause (B) of this paragraph (4) shall be construed to make unlawful, where not otherwise unlawful, any primary strike or primary picketing." The House managers explained:

> The purpose of this provision is to make it clear that the changes in § 8(b)(4) do not overrule or qualify the present rules of law permitting picketing at the site of a primary labor dispute. This provision does not eliminate, restrict, or modify the limitations on picketing at the site of a primary labor dispute that are in existing law. See for example, *NLRB v. Denver Building & Construction Trades Council* (341 U.S. 675 (1951)); *Brotherhood of Painters, Decorators, & Paper Hangers, and Pittsburgh Plate Glass Co.,* (110 N.L.R.B. 455 (1954)); *Moore Dry Dock Co.,* (81 N.L.R.B. 1108); *Washington Coca-Cola Bottling Works, Inc.,* (107 N.L.R.B. [229] (1953)). [H.R. Rep. No. 1147, 86th Cong., 1st Sess. 38 (1959)].

3. In *Landgrebe Motor Transp. v. IAM Dist. 72,* 763 F.2d 241 (7th Cir. 1985), the court held that the fact that union members who were picketing at the premises of the primary employer utilized violence to prevent a trucking company employee from entering the primary employer's facility to pick up a load did not negate the primary nature of the picketing or deprive it of the protection afforded by the primary picketing proviso to § 8(b)(4)(B). *See also Production Workers Local 707 v. NLRB (Checker Taxi Co.),* 793 F.2d 323 (D.C. Cir. 1986), holding that picketing at the premises of the primary employer is not subject to the secondary picketing proscription of § 8(b)(4)(B) merely because the labor organization is picketing on behalf of independent contractors, instead of employees.

4. *Compare Dowd v. ILA,* 975 F.2d 779 (11th Cir. 1992) (American labor organization that induced foreign union to exert pressure against secondary party to assist American union with primary dispute in U.S. violated § 8(b)(4)(B)) *with International Longshoremen's Ass'n v. NLRB [Canaveral Port Auth.],* 56 F.3d 205 (D.C. Cir. 1995), *cert. denied,* 516 U.S. 1158 (1996) (since ILA and Japanese unions are independent entities and there was no evidence the Japanese unions were acting as agents for ILA when they threatened to boycott Florida grapefruit shipped by nonunion firms, the Labor Board could not impose § 8(b)(4)(B) liability on ILA based on the secondary threats by the Japanese unions).

5. The Supreme Court has held that the Railway Labor Act contains no express or implied ban on secondary activity. As a result, the Norris-La Guardia Act's broad prohibition against injunctions in "labor disputes" prevents a district court from enjoining picketing by a railroad workers' union even against railroads not "substantially aligned" with the railroad involved in the primary dispute. The Court noted that the union and the primary employer had exhausted the "major dispute" procedures of the RLA, and that therefore the parties were entitled to resort to self-help. *Burlington N.R.R. v. Maintenance of Way Employees,* 481 U.S. 429 (1987).

B. COMMON SITUS PROBLEMS

SAILORS' UNION OF THE PACIFIC & MOORE DRY DOCK CO.

National Labor Relations Board
92 N.L.R.B. 547 (1950)

[Samsoc, a Greek-owned shipping company made a contract with Kaiser Gypsum to carry gypsum from Mexico in the Samsoc ship *Phopho*. This meant replacement of an American crew for the Greek ship with a Greek crew. To convert the *Phopho* for this job, it was placed in the Moore Dry Dock Co. shipyard. Moore Dry Dock agreed that two weeks before completion Samsoc could put its crew on board for training purposes. In January, 1950, while the boat was in the shipyard, the union learned of the arrangement. It demanded bargaining rights on the ship, but on February 16, this demand was refused. On the next day it placed pickets at the entrance to the shipyard. The union also informed the bargaining representatives of Moore's employees that the *Phopho* was "hot" and requested cooperation. On February 21, all of Moore's employees refused to work on the *Phopho,* but continued on other work.]

Section 8(b)(4)(A) is aimed at secondary boycotts and secondary strike activities. It was not intended to proscribe primary action by a union having a legitimate labor dispute with an employer. Picketing at the premises of a primary employer is traditionally recognized as primary action, even though it is "necessarily designed to induce and encourage third persons to cease doing business with the picketed employer...."[3]

Hence, if Samsoc, the owner of the *S.S. Phopho,* had had a dock of its own in California to which the *Phopho* had been tied up while undergoing conversion by Moore Dry Dock employees, picketing by the Respondent at the dock site would unquestionably have constituted *primary* action even though the Respondent might have expected that the picketing would be more effective in persuading Moore employees not to work on the ship than to persuade the seamen aboard the *Phopho* to quit that vessel. The difficulty in the present case arises therefore, not because of any difference in picketing objectives,[5] but from the fact that the *Phopho* was not tied up at its own dock, but at that of Moore, while the picketing was going on in front of the Moore premises.

In the usual case, the *situs* of a labor dispute is the premises of the primary employer. Picketing of the premises is also picketing of the *situs*; the test of legality of picketing is that enunciated by the Board in the *Pure Oil*[7] and *Ryan Construction*[8] cases. But in some cases the *situs* of the dispute may not be limited to a fixed location; it may be ambulatory. Thus, in the *Schultz*[9] case, a majority of the Board held that the truck upon which a truck driver worked was the *situs* of a labor dispute between him and the owner of the truck. Similarly, we hold in the present case that, as the *Phopho* was the place of employment of the seamen, it was the *situs* of the dispute between Samsoc and the Respondent over working conditions aboard the vessel.

When the *situs* is ambulatory, it may come to rest temporarily at the premises of another employer. The perplexing question is: Does the right to picket follow the *situs* while it is stationed at the premises of a secondary employer, when the only way to picket that *situs* is in front of the secondary employer's premises? Admittedly, no easy answer is possible. Essentially the problem is one of balancing the right of a union to picket at the site of its dispute as against the right of

---

[3] *Oil Workers Local 346 (Pure Oil Co.)* [84 N.L.R.B. 315, 318].

[5] "Plainly, the object of all picketing at all times is to influence third persons to withhold their business or services from the struck employer. In this respect there is no distinction between lawful primary picketing and unlawful secondary picketing proscribed by § 8(b)(4)(A)." *Teamsters Local 807 (Schultz Refrigerated Service, Inc.)* [87 N.L.R.B. 502].

[7] [*Supra* note 3.]

[8] [United Electrical, Radio & Machine Workers (Ryan Constr. Co.), 85 N.L.R.B. 417.]

[9] [*Supra* note 5.]

a secondary employer to be free from picketing in a controversy in which it is not directly involved.

When a secondary employer is harboring the *situs* of a dispute between a union and a primary employer, the right of neither the union to picket nor of the secondary employer to be free from picketing can be absolute. The enmeshing of premises and *situs* qualifies both rights. In the kind of situation that exists in this case, we believe that picketing of the premises of a secondary employer is primary if it meets the following conditions: (a) The picketing is strictly limited to times when the *situs* of dispute is located on the secondary employer's premises; (b) at the time of the picketing the primary employer is engaged in its normal business at the *situs;* (c) the picketing is limited to places reasonably close to the location of the *situs;* (d) the picketing discloses clearly that the dispute is with the primary employer. All these conditions were met in the present case.

(a) During the entire period of the picketing the *Phopho* was tied up at a dock in the Moore shipyard.

(b) Under its contract with Samsoc, Moore agreed to permit the former to put a crew on board the *Phopho* for training purposes during the last two weeks before the vessel's delivery to Samsoc. At the time the picketing started on February 17, 1950, 90 per cent of the conversion job had been completed, practically the entire crew had been hired, the ship's oil bunkers had been filled and other stores were shortly to be put aboard. The various members of the crew commenced work as soon as they reported aboard the *Phopho*. Those in the deck compartment did painting and cleaning up; those in the steward's department, cooking and cleaning up; and those in the engine department, oiling and cleaning up. The crew were thus getting the ship ready for sea. They were on board to serve the purposes of Samsoc, the *Phopho*'s owners, and not Moore. The normal business of a ship does not only begin with its departure on the scheduled voyage. The multitudinous steps of preparation, including hiring and training a crew and putting stores aboard, are as much a part of the normal business of a ship as the voyage itself. We find, therefore, that the *Phopho* was engaged in its normal business.

(c) Before placing its pickets outside the entrance to the Moore shipyard, the Respondent Union asked, but was refused, permission to place its pickets at the dock where the *Phopho* was tied up. The respondent, therefore, posted its pickets at the yard entrance which, as the parties stipulated, was as close to the *Phopho* as they could get under the circumstances.

(d) Finally, by its picketing and other conduct the Respondent was scrupulously careful to indicate that its dispute was solely with the primary employer, the owners of the *Phopho*. Thus the signs carried by the pickets said only that the *Phopho* was unfair to the Respondent. The *Phopho* and not Moore was declared "hot." Similarly, in asking co-operation of other unions, the Respondent clearly revealed that its dispute was with the *Phopho*. Finally, Moore's own witnesses admitted that no attempt was made to interfere with other work in progress in the Moore yard.

We believe that our dissenting colleagues' expressions of alarm are based on a misunderstanding of our decision. We are not holding, as the dissenters seem to think, that a union which has a dispute with a shipowner over working conditions of seamen aboard a ship may lawfully picket the premises of an independent shipyard to which the shipowner has delivered his vessel for overhaul and repair. We are only holding that, if a shipyard permits the owner of a vessel to use its dock for the purpose of readying and training a crew and putting stores aboard a ship, a union representing seamen may then, within the careful limitations laid down in this decision, lawfully picket the front of the shipyard premises to advertise its dispute with the shipowner....

NOTES

1. If the shipping company (primary employer with whom union had its dispute) removed all of its employees from the ship while it was in dry dock undergoing repairs, continued union picketing would usually contravene § 8(b)(4)(B). The ongoing union presence would indicate that the labor organization was endeavoring to enmesh secondary parties in its dispute with the primary employer. On the other hand, if the shipping company removed its nonsupervisory employees but kept supervisory personnel on the ship to oversee the repairs, the union would probably still be allowed to picket the dry dock, so long as its signs clearly stated that the dispute was solely with the shipping company. The continued presence of the supervisors on the ship would establish that the primary employer was still located on the dry dock premises and was engaged in normal operations. *See Seafarers Int'l Union v. NLRB,* 265 F.2d 585 (D.C. Cir. 1959). In response to the argument that "an object" of the union's continued picketing must have been to induce employees of the dry dock company to refuse to work on the ship, the court found that since the picketing was "primary," such inducement of dry dock employees was an "incidental" effect of lawful primary picketing.

Compare Plumbers Local 519 v. NLRB (H. L. Robertson & Assocs.), 416 F.2d 1120 (D.C. Cir. 1969), in which a nonunion subcontractor responded to union picketing by arranging with the general contractor to work only on weekends and after 4:30 P.M. on weekdays, and the union was duly notified of this change. The court held that it was unlawful for the union to continue to picket the construction site during regular weekday hours, since the primary subcontractor was no longer located at that site during those hours.

2. *Electrical Workers Local 501 v. NLRB,* 756 F.2d 888 (D.C. Cir. 1985), involved a union engaged in an area standards dispute with a nonunion subcontractor working on a multi-employer construction project. The court indicated that the labor organization may not have violated § 8(b)(4)(B) when it picketed a gate reserved for neutral parties, since the gate designated for the exclusive use of the primary subcontractor and its employees was "effectively hidden from public view." The court directed the Labor Board to determine whether a site existed where the union could reasonably have conveyed its message to the public without involving secondary parties in its dispute. "In view of its protected interest in communicating its area standards dispute with [the primary employer] to the general public, we believe that [the union's] refusal to confine its picketing to a back entrance hidden from virtually all public view does not by itself imply an unlawful intent to enmesh neutrals." *Compare Carpenters Local 33 (CB Constr. Co.)*, 289 N.L.R.B. 528 (1988), *affirmed*, 873 F.2d 316 (D.C. Cir. 1989).

3. Even though a union complied with the *Moore Dry Dock* standards for common situs picketing (including picketing only at the gate reserved for the primary nonunion subcontractor), and used signs stating that the subcontractor was not paying area wage rates, the evidence established that the union's real purpose was to force the general contractor to replace the subcontractor. As a result, the court found that the picketing violated § 8(b)(4)(B) of the NLRA. The damaging evidence included the union's lack of concern about the subcontractor's actual compliance or noncompliance with area standards, instructions to pickets not to tell persons whether they should cross the lines, and the temporary removal of the pickets in the mistaken belief that the general contractor had replaced the nonunion sub with a union sub. *IBEW Local 480 v. NLRB*, 413 F.2d 1085 (D.C. Cir. 1969). *See also Teamsters Local 126 (Ready Mixed Concrete, Inc.)*, 200 N.L.R.B. 253 (1972).

4. Suppose the primary employer has a place of business at which the union could publicize the dispute by picketing, but the employer also sends delivery trucks to the premises of secondary employers. Could the union legally picket the trucks while they are at the secondary premises, if the four *Moore Dry Dock* tests are met? Although the NLRB once held that the existence of a primary place of business at which adequate publicity of the dispute could be given to the *primary employees* was strong evidence that an object of the picketing while the trucks were at the secondary employer's premises was to induce refusal to work by secondary employees and thus violate the Act [*See Brewery & Beverage Drivers Local 67 (Washington Coca-Cola Bottling Works)*, 107 N.L.R.B. 299 (1953), *enforced*, 220 F.2d 380 (D.C. Cir. 1955)], it subsequently reversed this position and currently believes that the fact a struck employer has a separate place of business at which the union can picket is merely one of the circumstances to be considered in determining the legality of ambulatory picketing at a common situs. *IBEW, Local 861 (Plauche Elec., Inc.)*, 135 N.L.R.B. 250 (1962). The Board also said that the *Moore Dry Dock* standards "are not to be applied on an indiscriminate 'per se' basis, but are to be regarded merely as aids in determining the underlying question of statutory violation."

NLRB v. DENVER BUILDING & CONSTRUCTION TRADES COUNCIL

Supreme Court of the United States
341 U.S. 675, 71 S. Ct. 943, 95 L. Ed. 1284 (1951)

MR. JUSTICE BURTON delivered the opinion of the Court.

The principal question here is whether a labor organization committed an unfair labor practice, within the meaning of § 8(b)(4)(A) of the National Labor Relations Act,... as amended by the Labor Management Relations Act, 1947, by engaging in a strike, an object of which was to force the general contractor on a construction project to terminate its contract with a certain subcontractor on that project. For the reasons hereafter stated, we hold that such an unfair labor practice was committed.

In September, 1947, Doose & Lintner was the general contractor for the construction of a commercial building in Denver, Colorado. It awarded a subcontract for electrical work on the building, in an estimated amount of $2,300, to Gould & Preisner, a firm which for 20 years had employed nonunion workmen on construction work in that city. The latter's employees proved to be the only nonunion workmen on the project. Those of the general contractor and of the other subcontractors were members of unions affiliated with the respondent Denver Building and Construction Trades Council (here called the Council). In November a representative of one of those unions told Gould that he did not see how the job could progress with Gould's nonunion men on it. Gould insisted that they would complete the electrical work unless bodily put off. The representative replied that the situation would be difficult for both Gould & Preisner and Doose & Lintner.

January 8, 1948, the Council's Board of Business Agents instructed the Council's representative "to place a picket on the job stating that the job was unfair" to it. In keeping with the Council's practice, each affiliate was notified of that decision. That notice was a signal in the nature of an order to the members of the affiliated unions to leave the job and remain away until otherwise ordered. Representatives of the Council and each of the respondent unions visited the project and reminded the contractor that Gould & Preisner employed nonunion workmen and said that union men could not work on the job with nonunion men. They further advised that if Gould & Preisner's men did work on the job, the Council and its affiliates would put a picket on it to notify their members that nonunion men were working on it and that the job was unfair. All parties stood their ground.

January 9, the Council posted a picket at the project carrying a placard stating "This Job Unfair to Denver Building and Construction Trades Council." He was paid by the Council and his picketing continued from January 9 through January 22. During that time the only persons who reported for work were the nonunion electricians of Gould & Preisner. January 22, before Gould & Preisner had completed its subcontract, the general contractor notified it to get off the job so that Doose & Lintner could continue with the project. January 23, the Council removed its picket and shortly thereafter the union employees resumed work on the project. Gould & Preisner protested this treatment but its workmen were denied entrance to the job.

On charges filed by Gould & Preisner, the Regional Director of the National Labor Relations Board issued the complaint in this case against the Council and the respondent unions. It alleged that they had engaged in a strike or had caused strike action to be taken on the project by employees of the general contractor and of other subcontractors, an object of which was to force the general contractor to cease doing business with Gould & Preisner on that project.

Between the Board's receipt of the charges and the filing of the complaint based upon them, the Regional Director of the Board petitioned the United States District Court for the District of Colorado for injunctive relief. That petition was dismissed on the jurisdictional ground that the activities complained of did not affect interstate commerce. *Sperry v. Denver Building Trades Council,* 77 F. Supp. 321 (1958). Such action will be discussed later under the heading of *res judicata.* Hearings were held by the Board's trial examiner on the merits of the complaint. The Board adopted its examiner's findings, conclusions and recommendations, with minor additions and modifications not here material. It attached the examiner's intermediate report to its decision and ordered respondents to cease and desist from engaging in the activities charged. 82 N.L.R.B. 1195. Respondents petitioned the United States Court of Appeals for the District of Columbia Circuit for a review under § 10(f). The Board answered and asked for enforcement of its order. That court held, with one judge dissenting, that the conduct complained of affected interstate commerce sufficiently to give the Board jurisdiction over it, but the court unanimously set aside the order of the Board and said: "Convinced that the action in the circumstances of this case is primary and not secondary we are obliged to refuse to enforce the order based on § 8(b)(4)(A)." 87 App. D.C. 293, 304, 186 F.2d 326, 337....

III

The Secondary Boycott.—We now reach the merits. They require a study of the objectives of the strike and a determination whether the strike came within the definition of an unfair labor practice stated in § 8(b)(4)(A).

The language of that section which is here essential is as follows:

> (b) It shall be an unfair labor practice for a labor organization....
>
> (4) to engage in ... a strike ... where an object thereof is: (A) forcing or requiring ... any employer or other person ... to cease doing business with any other person; ....

While § 8(b)(4) does not expressly mention "primary" or "secondary" disputes, strikes or boycotts, that section often is referred to in the act's legislative history as one of the act's "secondary boycott sections." The other is § 303, 61 Stat. 158, 29 U.S.C. (Supp. III) § 187, which uses the same language in defining the basis for private actions for damages caused by these proscribed activities.

Senator Taft, who was the sponsor of the bill in the Senate and was the Chairman of the Senate Committee on Labor and Public Welfare in charge of the bill, said, in discussing this section:

> ... [U]nder the provisions of the Norris-La Guardia Act, it became impossible to stop a secondary boycott or any other kind of a strike, no matter how unlawful it may have been at common law. All this provision of the bill does is to reverse the effect of the law as to secondary boycotts. It has been set forth that there are good secondary boycotts and bad secondary boycotts. Our committee heard evidence for weeks and never succeeded in having anyone tell us any difference between different kinds of secondary boycotts. So we have so broadened the provision dealing with secondary boycotts as to make them an unfair labor practice. [93 Cong. Rec. 4198].

The Conference Report to the House of Representatives said:

> Under clause (A) [of § 8(b)(4)] strikes or boycotts, or attempts to induce or encourage such action, were made unfair labor practices if the purpose was to force an employer or other person to cease using, selling, handling, transporting, or otherwise dealing in the products of another, or to cease doing business with any other person. Thus it was made an unfair labor practice for a union to engage in a strike against employer A for the purpose of forcing that employer to cease doing business with employer B. Similarly it would not be lawful for a union to boycott employer A because employer A uses or otherwise deals in the goods of, or does business with, employer B. [H.R. Rep. No. 510, 80th Cong., 1st Sess. 43].

At the same time that §§ 7 and 13 safeguard collective bargaining, concerted activities and strikes between the primary parties to a labor dispute, § 8(b)(4) restricts a labor organization and its agents in the use of economic pressure where an object of it is to force an employer or other person to boycott someone else.

A. We must first determine whether the strike in this case had a proscribed object. The conduct which the Board here condemned is readily distinguishable from that which it declined to condemn in the *Rice Milling* case, *supra* at 665. There the accused union sought merely to obtain its own recognition by the operator of a mill, and the union's pickets near the mill sought to influence two employees of a customer of the mill not to cross the picket line. In that case we supported the Board in its conclusion that such conduct was no more than was traditional and permissible in a primary strike. The union did not engage in a strike against the customer. It did not encourage concerted action by the customer's employees to force the customer to boycott the mill. It did not commit any unfair labor practice proscribed by § 8(b)(4).

In the background of the instant case there was a long-standing labor dispute between the Council and Gould & Preisner due to the latter's practice of employing nonunion workmen on construction jobs in Denver. The respondent labor organizations contend that they engaged in a primary dispute with Doose & Lintner alone, and that they sought simply to force Doose & Lintner to make the project an all-union job. If there had been no contract between Doose & Lintner and Gould & Preisner there might be substance in their contention that the dispute involved no boycott. If, for example, Doose & Lintner had been doing all the electrical work on this project through its own nonunion employees, it could have replaced them with union men and thus disposed of the dispute. However, the existence of the Gould & Preisner subcontract presented a materially different situation. The nonunion employees were employees of Gould & Preisner. The only way that respondents could attain their purpose was to force Gould & Preisner itself off the job. This, in turn, could be done only through Doose & Lintner's termination of Gould & Preisner's subcontract. The result is that the Council's strike, in order to attain its ultimate purpose, must have included among its objects that of forcing Doose & Lintner to terminate that subcontract. On that point, the Board adopted the following finding:

> That *an* object, if not the only object, of what transpired with respect to ... Doose & Lintner was to force or require them to cease doing business with Gould & Preisner seems scarcely open to question, in view of all of the facts. And it is clear, at least as to Doose & Lintner, that that purpose was achieved. [(Emphasis supplied.) 82 N.L.R.B. at 1212].

We accept this crucial finding. It was an object of the strike to force the contractor to terminate Gould & Preisner's subcontract.

B. We hold also that a strike with such an object was an unfair labor practice within the meaning of § 8(b)(4)(A).

It is not necessary to find that the *sole* object of the strike was that of forcing the contractor to terminate the subcontractor's contract. This is emphasized in the legislative history of the section. *See also, NLRB v. Wine, Liquor & Distillery Workers Union,* 178 F.2d 584, 586 (2d Cir. 1949).

We agree with the Board also in its conclusion that the fact that the contractor and subcontractor were engaged on the same construction project, and that the contractor had some supervision over the subcontractor's work, did not eliminate the status of each as an independent contractor or make the employees of one the employees of the other. The business relationship between independent contractors is too well established in the law to be overridden without clear language doing so. The Board found that the relationship between Doose & Lintner and Gould & Preisner was one of "doing business" and we find no adequate reason for upsetting that conclusion.

Finally, § 8(c) safeguarding freedom of speech has no significant application to the picket's placard in this case. Section 8(c) does not apply to a mere signal by a labor organization to its members, or to the members of its affiliates, to engage in an unfair labor practice such as a strike proscribed by § 8(b)(4)(A). That the placard was merely such a signal, tantamount to a direction to strike, was found by the Board.

> ... [T]he issues in this case turn upon acts by labor organizations which are tantamount to directions and instructions to their members to engage in strike action. The protection afforded by § 8(c) of the Act to the expression of 'any views, arguments or opinion' does not pertain where, as here, the issues raised under § 8(b)(4)(A) turn on official directions or instructions to a union's own members. [82 N.L.R.B. at 1213].

The further conclusion that § 8(c) does not immunize action against the specific provisions of § 8(b)(4)(A) has been announced in other cases. *See IBEW, Local 108 v. NLRB, infra* at 694.

Not only are the findings of the Board conclusive with respect to questions of fact in this field when supported by substantial evidence on the record as a whole, but the Board's interpretation of the act and the Board's application of it in doubtful situations are entitled to weight. In the views of the Board as applied to this case we find conformity with the dual congressional objectives of preserving the right of labor organizations to bring pressure to bear on offending employers in primary labor disputes and of shielding unoffending employers and others from pressures in controversies not their own.

For these reasons we conclude that the conduct of respondents constituted an unfair labor practice within the meaning of § 8(b)(4)(A). The judgment of the Court of Appeals accordingly is reversed and the case is remanded to it for procedure not inconsistent with this opinion.

It is so ordered.

MR. JUSTICE JACKSON would affirm the judgment of the Court of Appeals.

MR. JUSTICE DOUGLAS, with whom MR. JUSTICE REED joins, dissenting.

The employment of union and nonunion men on the same job is a basic protest in trade union history. That was the protest here. The union was not out to destroy the contractor because of his antiunion attitude. The union was not pursuing the contractor to other jobs. All the union asked was that union men not be compelled to work alongside nonunion men on the same job. As Judge Rifkind stated in an analogous case, "the union was not extending its activity to a front remote from the immediate dispute but to one intimately and indeed inextricably united to it."

The picketing would undoubtedly have been legal if there had been no subcontractor involved—if the general contractor had put nonunion men on the job.

The presence of a subcontractor does not alter one whit the realities of the situation; the protest of the union is precisely the same. In each the union was trying to protect the job on which union men were employed. If that is forbidden, the Taft-Hartley Act makes the right to strike, guaranteed by § 13, dependent on fortuitous business arrangements that have no significance so far as the evils of the secondary boycott are concerned. I would give scope to both § 8(b)(4) and § 13 by reading the restrictions of § 8(b)(4) to reach the case where an industrial dispute spreads from the job to another front.

NOTES

1. There may be unusual circumstances under which a general contractor on a construction project assumes such substantial control over subcontractor employees that it would no longer be regarded as a neutral, but instead as a primary employer along with the subcontractors, and thus be subject to subcontractor union picketing without recourse under § 8(b)(4)(B). *See Teamsters Local 363 (Roslyn Americana Corp.),* 214 N.L.R.B. 868 (1974).

2. In *Plumbers Local 32 v. NLRB (Ramada, Inc.),* 912 F.2d 1108 (9th Cir. 1990), the court held that the Labor Board erred when it found that a union violated § 8(b)(4)(ii)(B) when it threatened to picket a construction project after the general contractor subcontracted work to a nonunion firm, since there was no evidence to indicate that the threat was intended to include the unlawful picketing of secondary parties located at the job site.

INTERNATIONAL UNION OF ELECTRICAL, RADIO & MACHINE WORKERS, LOCAL 761, AFL-CIO v. NLRB [GENERAL ELECTRIC CO.]

Supreme Court of the United States
366 U.S. 667, 81 S. Ct. 1285, 6 L. Ed. 2d 592 (1961)

MR. JUSTICE FRANKFURTER delivered the opinion of the Court.

Local 761 of International Union of Electrical, Radio and Machine Workers, AFL-CIO was charged with a violation of § 8(b)(4)(A) of the National Labor Relations Act, as amended by the Taft-Hartley Act, 61 Stat. 136, 141, upon the following facts.

General Electric Corporation operates a plant outside of Louisville, Kentucky, where it manufactures washers, dryers, and other electrical household appliances. The square-shaped, thousand-acre, unfenced plant is known as Appliance Park. A large drainage ditch makes ingress and egress impossible except over five roadways across culverts, designated as gates.

Since 1954, General Electric sought to confine the employees of independent contractors, described hereafter, who work on the premises of the Park, to the use of Gate 3-A and confine its use to them. The undisputed reason for doing so was to insulate General Electric employees from the frequent labor disputes in which the contractors were involved. Gate 3-A is 550 feet away from the nearest entrance available for General Electric employees, suppliers, and deliverymen. Although anyone can pass the gate without challenge, the roadway leads to a guardhouse where identification must be presented. Vehicle stickers of various shapes and colors enable a guard to check on sight whether a vehicle is authorized to use Gate 3-A. Since January 1958, a prominent sign has been posted at the gate which states: "GATE 3-A FOR EMPLOYEES OF CONTRACTORS ONLY—G. E. EMPLOYEES USE OTHER GATES." On rare occasions, it appears, a General Electric employee was allowed to pass the guardhouse, but such occurrence was in violation of company instructions. There was no proof of any unauthorized attempts to pass the gate during the strike in question.

The independent contractors are utilized for a great variety of tasks on the Appliance Park premises. Some do construction work on new buildings; some install and repair ventilation and heating equipment; some engage in retooling and rearranging operations necessary to the manufacture of new models; others do "general maintenance work." These services are contracted to outside employers either because the company's employees lack the necessary skill or manpower, or because the work can be done more economically by independent contractors. The latter reason determined the contracting of maintenance work for which the Central Maintenance department of the company bid competitively with the contractors. While some of the work done by these contractors had on occasion been previously performed by Central Maintenance, the findings do not disclose the number of employees of independent contractors who were performing these routine maintenance services, as compared with those who were doing specialized work of a capital-improvement nature.

The Union, petitioner here, is the certified bargaining representative for the production and maintenance workers who constitute approximately 7,600 of the 10,500 employees of General Electric at Appliance Park. On July 27, 1958, the Union called a strike because of 24 unsettled grievances with the company. Picketing occurred at all gates, including Gate 3-A, and continued until August 9 when an injunction was issued by a Federal District Court. The signs carried by the pickets at all gates read: "LOCAL 761 ON STRIKE G.E. UNFAIR." Because of the picketing, almost all of the employees of independent contractors refused to enter the company premises.

Neither the legality of the strike or of the picketing at any of the gates except 3-A is in dispute, nor that the picketing was other than peaceful in nature. The sole claim was that the picketing before the gate exclusively used by employees of independent contractors was conduct proscribed by § 8(b)(4)(A).

The Trial Examiner recommended that the Board dismiss the complaint. He concluded that the limitations on picketing which the Board had prescribed in so-called "common situs" cases were not applicable to the situation before him, in that the picketing at Gate 3-A represented traditional primary action which necessarily had a secondary effect of inconveniencing those who did business with the struck employer. He reasoned that if a primary employer could limit the area of picketing around his own premises by constructing a separate gate for employees of independent contractors, such a device could also be used to isolate employees of his suppliers and customers, and that such action could not relevantly be distinguished from oral appeals made to secondary employees not to cross a picket line where only a single gate existed.

The Board rejected the Trial Examiner's conclusion, 123 N.L.R.B. 1547. It held that since only the employees of the independent contractors were allowed to use Gate 3-A, the Union's object in picketing there was "to enmesh these employees of the neutral employers in its dispute with the Company" thereby constituting a violation of § 8(b)(4)(A) because the independent employees were encouraged to engage in a concerted refusal to work "with an object of forcing the independent contractors to cease doing business with the Company."

The Court of Appeals for the District of Columbia granted enforcement of the Board's order, 107 App. D.C. 402, 278 F.2d 282. Although noting that a fine line was being drawn, it concluded that the Board was correct in finding that the objective of the Gate 3-A picketing was to encourage the independent-contractor employees to engage in a concerted refusal to perform services for their employers in order to bring pressure on General Electric....

I

Section 8(b)(4)(A) ... could not be literally construed; otherwise it would ban most strikes historically considered to be lawful, so-called primary activity. "While § 8(b)(4) does not expressly mention 'primary' or 'secondary' disputes, strikes or boycotts, that section often is referred to in the Act's legislative history as one of the Act's 'secondary boycott sections.'" *NLRB v. Denver Bldg. & Constr. Trades Council,* 341 U.S. 675, 686 (1951). "Congress did not seek by § 8(b)(4), to interfere with the ordinary strike...." *NLRB v. International Rice Milling Co.,* 341 U.S. 665, 672 (1951). The impact of the section was directed toward what is known as the secondary boycott whose "sanctions bear, not upon the employer who alone is a party to the dispute, but upon some third party who has no concern in it." *IBEW, Local 501 v. NLRB,* 181 F.2d 34, 37 (2d Cir. 1950). Thus the section "left a striking labor organization free to use persuasion, including picketing, not only on the primary employer and his employees but on numerous others. Among these were secondary employers who were customers or suppliers of the primary employer and persons dealing with them ... and even employees of secondary employers so long as the labor organization did not ... 'induce or encourage the employees of any employer to engage, in a strike or a concerted refusal in the course of their employment'...." *NLRB v. Teamsters Local 294,* 284 F.2d 887, 889 (2d Cir. 1960).

But not all so-called secondary boycotts were outlawed in § 8(b)(4)(A). "The section does not speak generally of secondary boycotts. It describes and condemns specific union conduct directed to specific objectives.... Employees must be induced; they must be induced to engage in a strike or concerted refusal; an object must be to force or require their employer or another person to cease doing business with a third person. Thus, much that might argumentatively be found to fall within the broad and somewhat vague concept of secondary boycott is not in terms prohibited." *Local 1976, United Brotherhood of Carpenters & Joiners v. NLRB,* 357 U.S. 93, 98 (1958). *See also United Bhd. of Carpenters (Wadsworth Bldg. Co.),* 81 N.L.R.B. 802, 805.

Important as is the distinction between legitimate "primary activity" and banned "secondary activity," it does not present a glaringly bright line. The objectives of any picketing include a desire to influence others from withholding from the employer their services or trade. *See Sailors' Union of the Pacific (Moore Dry Dock),* 92 N.L.R.B. 547. "[I]ntended or not, sought for or not, aimed for or not, employees of neutral employers do take action sympathetic with strikers and do put pressure on their own employers." *Seafarers Int'l Union v. NLRB,* 105 App. D.C. 211, 265 F.2d 585, 590 (1959). "It is clear that, when a union pickets an employer with whom it has a dispute, it hopes, even if it does not intend, that all persons will honor the picket line, and that hope encompasses the employees of neutral employers who may in the course of their employment (deliverymen and the like) have to enter the premises." *Id.* at page 591. "Almost all picketing, even at the situs of the primary employer and surely at that of the secondary, hopes to achieve the forbidden objective, whatever other motives there may be and however small the chances of success." Local 294, *supra,* 284 F.2d at 890. But picketing which induces secondary employees to respect a picket line is not the equivalent of picketing which has an object of inducing those employees to engage in concerted conduct against their employer in order to force him to refuse to deal with the struck employer. *NLRB v. International Rice Milling Co., supra.*

However difficult the drawing of lines more nice than obvious, the statute compels the task. Accordingly, the Board and the courts have attempted to devise reasonable criteria drawing heavily upon the means to which a union resorts in promoting its cause. Although "[n]o rigid rule which would make ... [a] few factors conclusive is contained in or deducible from the statute," *Sales Drivers v. NLRB,* 97 App. D.C. 173, 229 F.2d 514, 517 (1955), "[I]n the absence of admissions by the union of an illegal intent, the nature of acts performed shows the intent." *Seafarers Int'l Union, supra* at 591.

The nature of the problem, as revealed by unfolding variant situations, inevitably involves an evolutionary process for its rational response, not a quick, definitive formula as a comprehensive answer. And so, it is not surprising that the Board has more or less felt its way during the fourteen years in which it has had to apply § 8(b)(4)(A), and has modified and reformed its standards on the basis of accumulating experience....

II

The early decisions of the Board following the Taft-Hartley amendments involved activity which took place around the secondary employer's premises. For example, in *Wadsworth Building Co., supra,* the union set up a picket line around the situs of a builder who had contracted to purchase prefabricated houses from the primary employer. The Board found this to be illegal secondary activity. *See also Printing Specialties Union (Sealbright Pacific),* 82 N.L.R.B. 271. In contrast, when picketing took place around the premises of the primary employer, the Board regarded this as valid primary activity....

In *United Electrical Workers (Ryan Constr. Corp.),* 85 N.L.R.B. 417, Ryan had contracted to perform construction work on a building adjacent to the Bucyrus plant and inside its fence. A separate gate was cut through the fence for Ryan's employees which no employee of Bucyrus ever used. The Board concluded that the union—on strike against Bucyrus—could picket the Ryan gate, even though an object of the picketing was to enlist the aid of Ryan employees, since Congress did not intend to outlaw primary picketing....

However, the impact of the new situations made the Board conscious of the complexity of the problem by reason of the protean forms in which it appeared. This became clear in the "common situs" cases—situations where two employers were performing separate tasks on common premises. The *Moore Dry Dock* case, *supra,* laid out the Board's new standards in this area....

In *Local 55 (PBM),* 108 N.L.R.B. 363, the Board for the first time applied the *Dry Dock* test although the picketing occurred at premises owned by the primary employer. There, an insurance company owned a tract of land that it was developing, and also served as the general contractor. A neutral subcontractor was also doing work at the site. The union, engaged in a strike against the insurance company, picketed the entire premises, characterizing the entire job as unfair, and the employees of the subcontractor walked off. The Court of Appeals for the Tenth Circuit enforced the Board's order which found the picketing to be illegal on the ground that the picket signs did not measure up to the *Dry Dock* standard that they clearly disclose that the picketing was directed against the struck employer only. 218 F.2d 226.

The Board's application of the *Dry Dock* standards to picketing at the premises of the struck employer was made more explicit in *Retail Fruit & Vegetable Clerks (Crystal Palace Market),* 116 N.L.R.B. 856. The owner of a large common market operated some of the shops within, and leased out others to independent sellers. The union, although given permission to picket the owner's individual stands, chose to picket outside the entire market. The Board held that this action was violative of § 8(b)(4)(A) in that the union did not attempt to minimize the effect of its picketing, as required in a common-situs case, on the operations of the neutral employers utilizing the market. "We believe ... that the foregoing principles should apply to all common situs picketing, including cases where, as here, the picketed premises are owned by the primary employer." 116 N.L.R.B., at 859. The *Ryan* case, *supra,* was overruled to the extent it implied the contrary. The Court of Appeals for the Ninth Circuit, in enforcing the Board's order, specifically approved its disavowance of an ownership test. 249 F.2d 591. The Board made clear that its decision did not affect situations where picketing which had effects on neutral third parties who dealt with the employer occurred at premises occupied solely by him. "In such cases, we adhere to the rule established by the Board ... that more latitude be given to picketing at such separate primary premises than at premises occupied in part (or entirely) by secondary employers." 116 N.L.R.B., at 860, n. 10.

In rejecting the ownership test in situations where two employers were performing work upon a common site, the Board was naturally guided by this Court's opinion in *Rice Milling,* in which we indicated that the location of the picketing at the primary employer's premises was "not necessarily conclusive" of its legality. 341 U.S. at 671. Where the work done by the secondary employees is unrelated to the normal operations of the primary employer, it is difficult to perceive how the pressure of picketing the entire situs is any less on the neutral employer merely because the picketing takes place at property owned by the struck employer. The application of the *Dry Dock* tests to limit the picketing effects to the employees of the employer against whom the dispute is directed carries out the "dual congressional objectives of preserving the right of labor organizations to bring pressure to bear on offending employers in primary labor disputes and of shielding unoffending employers and others from pressures in controversies not their own." *NLRB v. Denver Bldg. & Constr. Trades Council, supra,* 341 U.S. at 692 (1951).

III

From this necessary survey of the course of the Board's treatment of our problem, the precise nature of the issue before us emerges. With due regard to the relation between the Board's function and the scope of judicial review of its ruling, the question is whether the Board may apply the *Dry Dock* criteria so as to make unlawful picketing at a gate utilized exclusively by employees of independent contractors who work on the struck employers' premises. The effect of such a holding would not bar the union from picketing at all gates used by the employees, suppliers, and customers of the struck employer. Of course an employer may not, by removing all his employees from the situs of the strike, bar the union from publicizing its cause, *see Automotive, Petroleum, Local 618 v. NLRB,* 249 F.2d 332 (8th Cir. 1957). The basis of the Board's decision in this case would not remotely have that effect, nor any such tendency for the future.

The Union claims that if the Board's ruling is upheld, employers will be free to erect separate gates for deliveries, customers, and replacement workers which will be immunized from picketing. This fear is baseless. The key to the problem is found in the type of work that is being performed by those who use the separate gate. It is significant that the Board has since applied its rationale, first stated in the present case, only to situations where the independent workers were performing tasks unconnected to the normal operations of the struck employer— usually construction work on his buildings. In such situations, the indicated limitations on picketing activity respect the balance of competing interests that Congress has required the Board to enforce. On the other hand, if a separate gate were devised for regular plant deliveries, the barring of picketing at that location would make a clear invasion on traditional primary activity of appealing to neutral employees whose tasks aid the employer's everyday operations....

In a case similar to the one now before us, the Court of Appeals for the Second Circuit sustained the Board in its application of § 8(b)(4)(A) to a separate-gate situation. "There must be a separate gate marked and set apart from other gates; the work done by the men who use the gate must be unrelated to the normal operations of the employer, and the work must be of a kind that would not, if done when the plant were engaged in its regular operations, necessitate curtailing those operations." *United Steelworkers v. NLRB,* 289 F.2d 591, 595 (2d Cir. 1961). These seem to us controlling considerations.

IV

The foregoing course of reasoning would require that the judgment below sustaining the Board's order be affirmed but for one consideration, even though this consideration may turn out not to affect the result. The legal path by which the Board and the Court of Appeals reached their decisions did not take into account that if Gate 3-A was in fact used by employees of independent contractors who performed conventional maintenance work necessary to the normal operations of General Electric, the use of the gate would have been a mingled one outside the bar of § 8(b)(4)(A). In short, such mixed use of this portion of the struck employer's premises would not bar picketing rights of the striking employees. While the record shows some such mingled use, it sheds no light on its extent. It may well turn out to be that the instances of these maintenance tasks were so insubstantial as to be treated by the Board as *de minimis.* We cannot here guess at the quantitative aspects of this problem. It calls for Board determination. For determination of the questions thus raised, the case must be remanded by the Court of Appeals to the Board.

Reversed.

THE CHIEF JUSTICE and MR. JUSTICE BLACK concur in the result.

MR. JUSTICE DOUGLAS.

I did not vote to grant certiorari in this case because it seemed to me that the problem presented was in the keeping of the Courts of Appeals within the meaning of *Universal Camera Corp. v. NLRB,* 340 U.S. 474, 490 (1951). Since the

Court of Appeals followed the guidelines of that case (*see* 278 F.2d 282, 286), I would leave the decision with it. I cannot say it made any egregious error, though I might have decided the case differently had I sat on the Labor Board or on the Court of Appeals.

NOTES

1. In *United Steelworkers v. NLRB (Carrier Corp.),* 376 U.S. 492 (1964), the Supreme Court unanimously upheld a union's picketing of a gate through which a railroad entered a fenced-in area alongside the primary employer's plant, the right-of-way being owned by the railroad. The Court stated that its decision was grounded on the doctrine enunciated in the 1961 *General Elec.* reserved-gate picketing case, *i.e.,* if the duties of the secondary employees were connected with the normal operations of the struck plant, then the picketing would be primary activity within the protection of the primary-picketing proviso to § 8(b)(4)(B). In noting that "the location of the picketing is an important but not decisive factor," the Court said that in the instant case the "railroad gate adjoined company property and was in fact the railroad entrance gate to the Carrier plant." Therefore, "for the purposes of § 8(b)(4) picketing at a situs so proximate and related to the employer's day-to-day operations is no more illegal than if it had occurred at a gate owned by Carrier." Moreover, the Court held that "under § 8(b)(4) the distinction between primary and secondary picketing carried on at a separate gate maintained on the premises of the primary employer does not rest upon the peaceful or violent nature of the conduct, but upon the type of work being done by the picketed secondary employees." However, the Court cautioned that this did not mean that violent primary picketing is in all respects legal but only that it is not forbidden by the secondary boycott provisions.

2. Anchortank is in the business of unloading chemicals from ships and storing them until ready for further shipment. The union struck Anchortank (primary) and picketed a public dock abutting Anchortank's property where ships were unloaded. Part of the picketing was done by means of a small motorboat carrying a sign, "To the public—Union on strike against Anchortank. Union does not have a dispute with any other employer." As a result of this picketing, pilots (who are required to assist ships to and from the dock to sea) refused to handle the vessels arriving for Anchortank unloading or departing from Anchortank handling. The court sustained the Board's finding that this activity accomplished no more than traditional primary picketing. *Anchortank, Inc. v. NLRB,* 601 F.2d 233 (3d Cir. 1979).

3. Santa Fe operates a rail terminal at Richmond, California. Approximately 40 percent of the rail freight traffic at that terminal is intermodal freight transported to and from the rail terminal in truck trailers and containers. Santa Fe awarded Piggyback a subcontract to ramp and deramp the trailers and containers at the rail terminal. This work had previously been performed by union members for a wholly owned subsidiary of Santa Fe. When Piggyback, a nonunion firm, allegedly reneged on a promise to hire the former union workers, the union began to picket and handbill Santa Fe's Richmond terminal. To insulate itself from the dispute between the union and Piggyback, Santa Fe designated Gate 1 as the sole entrance for employees, customers, and suppliers of Piggyback, with four other "neutral" gates being reserved for the exclusive use of Santa Fe employees, customers, and suppliers. Although Piggyback employees, customers, and suppliers only used Gate 1 and the union admitted that it had no labor dispute with Santa Fe, it picketed and handbilled all four neutral gates urging employees and customers entering the Santa Fe terminal either to honor the picket line or to cease all work related to Piggyback's operations. Union-represented drivers of UPS and other Santa Fe customers honored the picket line by refusing to deliver intermodal freight to the Richmond terminal. The Board and the court rejected a union request to apply the *General Electric* "related work" doctrine, because the picketing occurred at premises that were neither owned by the primary employer (Piggyback) nor proximate to the primary employer's premises. They instead applied the *Moore Dry Dock* common situs standards, and found a § 8(b)(4)(B) violation due to the union's impermissible picketing of neutral gates that were not used by employees of the primary employer. *NLRB v. General Truck Drivers Local 315 (Atchison, Topeka & Santa Fe Ry.)*, 20 F.3d 1017 (9th Cir.), *cert. denied*, 513 U.S. 946 (1994).

Operating Eng'rs Local 150 v. NLRB (Heckett Multiserv Div.), 47 F.3d 218 (7th Cir. 1995), concerned the legality of picketing by a labor organization that struck a firm that had a subcontract to process and dispose of slag from a steel mill. The court held that the union violated § 8(b)(4)(B) when it picketed at gates reserved for the employees and suppliers of the steel mill and a neutral subcontractor, since the union deliberately sought to enmesh those neutral parties in its dispute with the struck subcontractor.

4. If a union struck a manufacturer and picketed the single gate used by both primary employees and contractor personnel who were performing unrelated construction work on the manufacturer's premises, could the pickets appeal to the contractor employees? *See Teamsters Local 901 v. NLRB*, 293 F.2d 881 (D.C. Cir. 1961) (finding *General Electric* "related work" doctrine limited to separate gate situations, even when picketing union could easily distinguish between primary and secondary employees).

5. *See generally* Cantor, *Separate Gates, Related Work, and Secondary Boycotts,* 27 Rutgers L. Rev. 613 (1974).

BUILDING & CONSTRUCTION TRADES COUNCIL OF NEW ORLEANS [MARKWELL & HARTZ, INC.]

National Labor Relations Board
155 N.L.R.B. 319 (1965),
enforced, 387 F.2d 79 (5th Cir. 1967), *cert. denied,* 391 U.S. 914 (1968)

A. The Facts

In the period covered by the complaint, M & H was the general contractor on a project for expansion of a filtration plant on the premises of the East Jefferson Water Works, District No. 1, in Jefferson Parish, Louisiana. M & H decided to perform about 80 percent of the project with its own employees while subcontracting the balance. Included in the work contracted out was the piledriving awarded to Binnings, and the electrical work awarded to Barnes. Both Binnings and Barnes employ members of craft unions affiliated with Respondent.

The East Jefferson Water Works is surrounded by a chain-link fence, with two vehicular gates on Jefferson Highway which bounds the property on the north, and two additional gates on Arnoult Road, bounding the premises on the east. The gate on Jefferson Highway closest to Arnoult Road is the principal gate insofar as the construction project is concerned, and is called the main gate. On Arnoult Road the northern-most gate is the warehouse gate while the southern-most shall be referred to as the rear gate.

At all times material, Respondent has been engaged in a primary labor dispute with M & H, and has had no dispute with either Binnings or Barnes.

On October 17 [1963], in connection with its dispute with M & H, Respondent commenced picketing the gates leading to the jobsite. The picketing took place during normal workhours, with the number of pickets varying from one to three individuals. The picket sign listed both the rates that should be paid on the job and carried the following message:

MARKWELL AND HARTZ
GENERAL CONTRACTOR
DOES NOT HAVE A SIGNED AGREEMENT WITH THE
BUILDING AND CONSTRUCTION TRADES COUNCIL
OF NEW ORLEANS
AFL-CIO

The picketing continued until enjoined in the ... 10 (*l*) proceeding on January 16, 1964. At no time during the picketing did employees of Binnings or Barnes cross the picket line to perform work in connection with their employers' subcontract.

The validity of Respondent's picketing prior to October 23 is not in issue. However, on that date M & H posted the two gates on Jefferson Highway and the warehouse gate on Arnoult Road, reserving them for use of subcontractors and persons making deliveries to the project, and prohibiting their use by M & H's employees. The rear gate on Arnoult Road was designated for exclusive use of the latter.

That morning, when Respondent's picket encountered the newly marked gates, he moved to the rear gate which was reserved for M & H's employees. As a result, piledriving crews employed by Binnings entered the main gate and began working. About an hour and a half later the picket returned to the main gate, and Binnings' employees walked off. M & H then decided to remove its employees, with the exception of the superintendent and project engineer, in the hope that Binnings would then be able to complete the piledriving work. By 10 o'clock that morning its employees were off the site. Though Respondent was notified of the absence of the primary employees, the picketing continued. When Binnings' crew again honored the picket line, M & H recalled its employees. They reported to work on October 24 at 10 a.m. to complete the piledriving work themselves.

On November 14, M & H changed the signs on the Jefferson Highway gates to indicate that these entrances were not to be used by employees of M & H or carriers and suppliers making deliveries to M & H, and that such persons were to use the rear gate on Arnoult Road. M & H informed Respondent of these changes and notified suppliers to use the rear gate only. Identical changes were made at the warehouse gate on November 16, and on December 6 the rear gate was marked as reserved for use of employees of M & H and suppliers and carriers making deliveries to M & H.

The record does not show that the gates were at any time used in a manner inconsistent with the postings. Excepting a brief period on October 23, and the period between December 16 and 20, Respondent picketed the gates which were posted for exclusive use of subcontractors and which were not used by M & H's employees and suppliers.[3]

B. Discussion

On these facts, we are asked to decide whether a union, in furtherance of a primary dispute with a general contractor in the construction industry, may lawfully engage in jobsite picketing at gates reserved and set apart for exclusive use of neutral subcontractors....

Without passing upon whether the subcontractor gates involved herein were established and maintained in accordance with the *General Electric* requirements, we are of the opinion that the principles expressed in that case are inapposite in determining whether a union may lawfully extend its dispute with a general contractor on a construction site by picketing gates reserved for exclusive use of subcontractors also engaged on that project. Rather, we believe that this

---

[3] Because M & H, Binnings, Barnes, and suppliers and carriers making deliveries to M & H are the only persons identified as using the four gates, it is assumed that, after November 16, Binnings and Barnes and their employees had exclusive use of all gates save the "rear gate" set aside for M & H, its employees, and persons making deliveries to it.

issue must be resolved in the light of the *Moore Dry Dock* standards, traditionally applied by the Board in determining whether picketing at a common situs is protected primary activity.

Unlike *General Electric* and *Carrier Corp.,* both of which involved picketing *at the premises of a struck manufacturer,* the picketing in the instant case occurred at a construction project on which M & H, the primary employer, was but one of several employers operating on premises owned and operated by a third party, the Jefferson Parish Water Works. Picketing of neutral and primary contractors under such conditions, has been traditionally viewed as presenting a "common situs" problem.[9]

Over the years, the distinction between common situs picketing and that which occurs at premises occupied solely by the struck employer has been a guiding consideration in Board efforts to strike a balance between the competing interests underlying the boycott provisions of the act. Mindful of the fact that "Congress did not seek, by § 8(b)(4), to interfere with the ordinary strike,"[11] the Board has given wide latitude to picketing and related conduct confined to the sole premises of the primary employer. On the other hand, in the interest of shielding "unoffending employers" from disputes not their own, the Board has taken a more restrictive view of common situs picketing, requiring that it be conducted so as "to minimize its impact on neutral employees insofar as this can be done without substantial impairment of the effectiveness of the picketing in reaching the primary employees."[13]

In accordance with the foregoing, the Board, in determining whether a labor organization, when picketing a common situs, has taken all reasonable precaution to prevent enmeshment of neutrals, traditionally applies the limitations set forth in the *Moore Dry Dock* case. In our opinion application of these standards to all common situs situations, including those, which like the instant case, involve picketing of gates reserved exclusively for neutral contractors on a construction project, serves the "dual congressional objectives" underlying the boycott provisions of the act.

---

[9] *See ... Carpenters, Local 55 (Professional & Business Men's Life Ins. Co.),* 108 N.L.R.B. 363, *enforced,* 218 F.2d 226 (10th Cir. 1954). The Board, in the *PBM* case, rejected a contention that, where the union's dispute is with the general contractor, the entire project must be viewed as the primary situs, stating at 366, that:

> [T]he Supreme Court has rejected the view that prime contractors and subcontractors working on a construction project constitute for present purposes a single integrated operation. The Supreme Court has agreed with the Board "in its conclusion that the fact that the contractor and subcontractor were engaged in the same construction project, and that the contractor had some supervision over the subcontractor's work, did not eliminate the status of each as an independent contractor or make the employees of one the employees of the other."

NLRB v. Denver Bldg. Council, 341 U.S. 675, at 689-690 (1951).

[11] *International Rice Milling Co. v. NLRB,* 341 U.S. 665, 672 (1951).

[13] *Crystal Palace Market, supra* at 859.

The instant facts, when considered in the light of the legislative history and decisional precedent, do not warrant a departure from our long-established policy with respect to common situs picketing. Quite to the contrary, our continued adherence to the *Moore Dry Dock* standards in such cases comports with the clear expression of Congress, in enacting the "primary strike and picketing" proviso, that said proviso "... does not eliminate, restrict, or modify the limitations on picketing at the site of a primary dispute that are in existing law."[14] Nor do the Supreme Court's decisions in *General Electric* and *Carrier* detract from our conclusions in this regard; for, the mere fact that picketing of a neutral gate *at premises of a struck employer,* may in proper circumstances be lawful primary action, does not require a like finding when a labor organization applies *direct* pressure upon secondary employers engaged on a common situs.[15] That the Supreme Court had no intention of overriding this historic distinction is evidenced by its express approval of the *Moore Dry Dock* standards,[16] and its observation that the *General Electric* case did not present a common situs situation to which the *Moore Dry Dock* standards should apply.[17] It is plain, therefore, that the Court did not seek to interfere with the Board's traditional approach to common situs problems;[18] rather, the Court's decisions in *General Electric* and *Carrier Corp.,* merely represent an implementation of the concomitant policy that lenient treat-

---

[14] As indicated by the following statement on the part of the House conferees, the enactment of specific language protecting primary activity was accompanied by express preservation of the *Denver Building Trades* and *Moore Dry Dock* cases:

> [T]he amendment adopted by the committee of conference contains a provision "that nothing contained in clause (B) of this paragraph (4) shall be construed to make unlawful, where not otherwise unlawful, any primary strike or primary picketing." The purpose of this provision is to make it clear that the changes in § 8(b)(4) do not overrule or qualify the present rules of law permitting picketing at the site of a primary labor dispute. This provision does not eliminate, restrict, or modify the limitations on picketing at the site of a primary labor dispute that are in existing law. *See,* for example, *NLRB v. Denver Building and Construction Trades Council, et al.* (341 U.S. 675 (1951)); ... *Moore Dry Dock Co.* (81 N.L.R.B. 1108) *[sic];* ... [1 Leg. Hist. 942 (1959)].

[15] The diverse inferences to be drawn from economic pressures applied to neutrals at the premises of a struck employer and that applied at a common situs were recognized in early decisions of the Supreme Court interpreting § 8(b)(4). Thus in *NLRB v. Carpenters, Local 74 (Ira A. Watson Co., d/b/a Watson's Specialty Store),* 341 U.S. 707 (1951), in finding a union's inducement of work stoppages at a common situs to be secondary and unlawful, the Court distinguished *International Rice Milling Co., supra,* pointing out at 712, that picketing at the premises of the struck employer was not involved.

[16] *IUE, Local 761 (General Electric Co.) v. NLRB,* 366 U.S. 667, 679 (1961).

[17] *Steelworkers (Carrier Corp.) v. NLRB,* 376 U.S. 492, 497 (1964).

[18] As stated by the Supreme Court in *Denver Bldg. & Const. Trades Council, supra,* 692: "the Board's interpretation of the Act and ... application of it in doubtful situations are entitled to weight."

ment be given to strike action taking place at the separate premises of a struck employer.

Applying the *Moore Dry Dock* standards to the instant case requires the timing and location of the picketing and the legends on the picket signs to be tailored to reach the employees of the primary employer, rather than those of the neutral employer, and deviations from these requirements establish the secondary object of the picketing and render it unlawful. Indeed, our dissenting colleagues do not disagree with this principle, but cite the *PBM* decision[20] with apparent approval. If the mere failure, as in *PBM*, to name the general contractor on the picket signs as the sole disputant suffices to demonstrate that a union is seeking to induce employees of the subcontractors not to work, it is self-evident that picketing a gate used solely by the neutral subcontractors demonstrates the same purpose. And if it is unlawful to induce such employees in the indirect, and more subtle, fashion represented by the facts in *PBM*, it is *a fortiori* unlawful in the direct inducement of such employees at a separate gate. *PBM*, in short, stands for the proposition that the relationship of a subcontractor to a general contractor does not make the former's employees fair game in connection with a union's dispute with the latter. The sole difference between *PBM* and the instant case lies in the means used to convey the union's respective messages to the employees of the neutral subcontractors. That this is an irrelevant difference is established by the Supreme Court's holding in *IBEW, Local 501 (Samuel Langer) v. NLRB*,[21] that "The words 'induce and encourage' are broad enough to include in them every form of influence and persuasion." Since Respondent's picketing at the neutral gates of Binnings and Barnes continued after November 16, we find, in agreement with the General Counsel, that the picketing after that date[22] failed to comply with

---

[20] *Supra* note 9.

[21] 341 U.S. 694, 701-702 (1951).

[22] We do not regard, as unlawful, Respondent's picketing prior to November 16, as it was on that date that the respective neutral gates were first marked to preclude use by persons making deliveries to M & H. Although a common situs problem is presented where a gate is reserved for both neutral subcontractors and persons making deliveries to a struck contractor, a balance of the competing interests underlying § 8(b)(4)(B) requires our respecting the traditional right of labor organizations to appeal to such deliverymen as a lawful incident of legitimate strike action against the primary employer.

In so finding, we note that, on October 23, M & H withdrew its employees for a 24-hour period in an attempt to prevent any legitimate picketing of the project. It is apparent that the primary employees were removed from the project though work was then available for them, that they could have been recalled at any time, that M & H's superintendent and project engineer remained on the job at all times, and that M & H otherwise continued its duties as general contractor during the 24-hour absence of its employees. In the circumstances, we are satisfied that despite the removal of its workers, M & H was then engaged in its normal business on the project, and that Respondent's continued picketing during this period fully complied with *Moore Dry Dock*, and did not evidence a departure from what at that time constituted lawful primary action. *IBEW, Local 3 (New Power Wire & Elec. Corp.)*, 144 N.L.R.B. 1089; *IBEW, Local 861 (Brownfield Electric, Inc.)*, 145

the *Moore Dry Dock* requirement that such action take place reasonably close to the situs of Respondent's dispute with M & H. We are completely satisfied that Respondent's picketing at the subcontractor gates was to induce strike action by employees of subcontractors with whom Respondent had no dispute. By such conduct, Respondent unlawfully sought to disrupt the operations of the neutral subcontractors and their employees and to enmesh them in the primary dispute in a manner which could not be condoned as an unavoidable by-product of legitimate primary picketing.

The dissent does not persuade us otherwise. The dissent's analysis, although well-stated and on first reading not unreasonable as an application of *General Electric* standards in a construction industry setting, nevertheless runs counter to firmly established principles governing common situs picketing in that industry. Simply because the work of the neutral subcontractors in one sense is "related to M & H's normal operations," our dissenting colleagues would exonerate the pickets' appeals to the secondary employees to honor the picket line aimed at M & H. And notwithstanding their suggestion (in footnote 35) that they would apply the "related work" standard only where the dispute is with a general contractor, the plain logic of their position is equally applicable where the primary dispute is with a building construction *sub* contractor whose employees are working closely with employees of other subcontractors or those of the general contractors. Given the close relation—which is not only characteristic of but almost inevitable at many stages of a building construction project—of the work duties of the various other employees with those of the primary subcontractor, the principle of the dissent would also permit picket line appeals to the employees of the neutral general contractor and other subcontractors whatever the situation as to common or separate gates.

But it was precisely this claim, that the *close* working relations of various building construction contractors on a common situs involved them in a common undertaking which destroyed the neutrality and thus the immunity of secondary employers and employees to picket line appeals, that the Supreme Court rejected in *Denver Building Trades.* And there is not the slightest intimation by the Court in *General Electric* or *Carrier* that it was reversing or revising the rule in *Denver.* Although our dissenting colleagues disclaim such a purpose, by applying the "close relation to normal operations" test of *General Electric,* the theory of the dissent, if logically extended, is one that would in effect reverse *Denver* not only where the overarching general contractor on the building site is the primary employer, but also, where the intertwined work of a construction *sub* contractor is the primary target....

For the reasons stated, we conclude that Respondent violated § 8(b)(4)(i) and (ii)(B) of the act by inducing employees of Binnings and Barnes to engage in

---

N.L.R.B. 1163; and *Seafarers' Int'l Union (Salt Dome Production Co.) v. NLRB,* 265 F.2d 585 (D.C. Cir. 1959).

work stoppages, and by restraining and coercing said Employers, for an object of forcing or requiring them to cease doing business with M & H....

MEMBERS FANNING and JENKINS, dissenting:

We dissent from the majority's conclusion that Respondent violated § 8(b)(4)(B) of the act by picketing, in the course of its primary dispute with Markwell & Hartz, gates reserved for employees of the subcontractors M & H had engaged to aid it in performing the construction work it was obligated to complete. In our view, the majority has inferred that Respondent's picketing was for an unlawful object simply from the fact that the reserved gates were used only by secondary employees, without inquiry into the question of whether the appeals to such employees, were, in the circumstances of this case, permissible primary activity, an inquiry which we believe is required by the Supreme Court's decisions in *General Electric* and *Carrier Corp.* As we believe, for reasons stated below, that the Court in those decisions applied principles of general application, we dissent from the majority's conclusion that the tests announced in *General Electric* for determining whether appeals to employees of neutral contractors constitute legitimate primary activity are not applicable to the building and construction industry....

The *General Electric* case involved appeals to employees of neutral subcontractors and the Court, noting that "the key to the problem is found in the type of work that is being performed by those who use the separate gate," held that, before such appeals may be ruled unlawful under § 8(b)(4)(B),

> There must be a separate gate, marked and set apart from other gates; the work done by the men who use the [separate] gate must be unrelated to the normal operations of the employer, and the work must be of a kind that would not, if done when the plant were engaged in its regular operations, necessitate curtailing those operations.

The crucial consideration regarding this holding is not, as the majority apparently views it, that it was made with respect to conduct occurring in connection with a strike at an industrial plant, but that it held that appeals to respect a picket line made to employees of secondary employers whose operations do not meet the tests stated above constitute legitimate primary activity just as do similar appeals to employees of neutral suppliers and deliverers.

In view of the foregoing, we find, contrary to the majority opinion, that the principles set forth in the *General Electric* decision, and the tests there enunciated by the Court for the application of those principles, govern picketing in the construction industry as well as in other industries. In our view, neither the fact that the Court expressly approved the *Moore Dry Dock* standards, nor its holding that the *General Electric* case did not present a common situs situation to which those standards should be applied, requires a different conclusion. The *Moore Dry Dock* standards were not designed to restrict primary activity at common situs disputes, but rather to assure that banned secondary activity would not be permitted.... Furthermore, it is clear that, had the Board concluded in its decision on remand in the *General Electric* case[31] that the work of the neutral contractors was not directly related to General Electric's normal operations, the application of the *Moore Dry Dock* tests to the picketing of the reserved gate in that case would be permissible.

Significantly, Congress has not seen fit to distinguish between industries, by adopting a more narrow definition of the lawful scope of picketing in the construction industry than is permitted in other industries. Certainly, the economic pressure sustained by neutral subcontractors as a consequence of reserved gate picketing on a construction job is no different from that imposed by like conduct upon neutral subcontractors performing work on premises occupied by a struck manufacturer. Nor is it any different from the pressures sustained by neutral suppliers making deliveries to the struck primary employer whether he be a manufacturer or a general contractor in the building and construction industry. Accordingly, it is only by determining the legality of reserved gate picketing by standards generally applicable to all industries that the dual congressional objectives are served and the competing interests of picketing unions and secondary employers protected.

Nor do we regard the Court's decision in *Denver Bldg. & Constr. Trades Council* as precluding application of *General Electric* to the instant case. In *Denver,* the Court held that despite their close relationship, the several contractors on a construction job were not allies or a single employer for purposes of the boycott provisions of the act.[35]

---

[31] 137 N.L.R.B. 1684. In this connection, the Board found that construction operations performed by contractors for General Electric, whose employees also were engaged in similar construction work, were "directly related" to General Electric's operations, thus giving the union engaged in a primary dispute with General Electric the right to make direct appeals to employees of the neutral contractors to honor its picket line. It is ironical, to say the least, for the majority now to hold that the undisputed direct relationship which does exist between the operations of general contractors and their subcontractors in the building and construction industry goes for nought in determining whether a striking union's picket line publication of its primary dispute with the general contractor, with consequent appeals to neutral employees to respect the picket line, constitutes legitimate primary activity.

[35] [341 U.S. 675], 680-690. In *Denver,* the conduct evidencing the union's objective of enmeshing the neutral employer was its demand that the neutral general contractor remove a nonunion subcontractor from the project, which demand was accompanied by picketing which failed to disclose that the Respondent Council's primary dispute was only with a nonunion subcontractor. These facts plus the other factors supporting the finding that the picketing constituted a "signal in the nature of an order to the members of the affiliated unions to leave the job and remain away until otherwise ordered" demonstrated the secondary objectives of the picketing, and distinguishes that case from the instant case. Here, in contrast, the Respondent's primary dispute is with the general contractor and the picketing clearly discloses this fact.... We have no quarrel with the requirement that a union's picketing at a common situs must clearly disclose that its dispute is with the primary employer. We in fact insist upon observance of that requirement but, when it and the other *Moore*

The Supreme Court in *General Electric* affirmed the rule stated in *Denver* and, accepting the separate legal status of *General Electric* and its contractors, addressed itself to the question whether the picketing involved had an unlawful secondary objective. Here, too, we accept the proposition that the various contractors at a construction job are separate employers and concern ourselves only with the circumstances under which the Board, absent direct proof or admission, may properly infer that the picketing involved had an unlawful secondary objective.

In applying the *General Electric* standards to the instant case, we find that the work of Binnings and Barnes was related to the normal operations of M & H, the general contractor. In this connection it is relevant that employees of the named subcontractors were scheduled to work during the picketing period together with the employees of M & H in completing the filtration plant expansion job.[38] In addition, during this period, M & H's project engineer and superintendent were to work with the subcontractors to insure that M & H's commitment to the owner was performed in compliance with project specifications. We find that M & H's portion of the work on this job was part of its normal operations, as was completion of the entire project, and that the work of the subcontractors was related to both M & H's work on the job and its responsibility to complete the project itself, and hence related to M & H's normal operations.[39] We, accordingly, hold that the work of the subcontractors failed to meet the "unrelated work" condition[40]

Dry Dock requirements are observed, we believe that there is no warrant for inferring that the picketing is for an object other than to induce employees to honor the picket line. In view of the *General Electric* decision, we believe that the *Moore Dry Dock* tests cannot be applied in a manner which will bar primary appeals to employees of employers whose operations are directly related to the normal operations of the struck employer. In so finding, we do not imply that simply because a union has a dispute with one subcontractor on a construction project, appeals to employees of other subcontractors using different gates constitute primary appeals within the meaning of the *General Electric* decision.... In such situations, the work of the employees of the neutral general contractor and subcontractors, though obviously bearing a close relationship to the work of the primary employees, is nevertheless not work which the primary subcontractor has obligated himself to perform or which lies within his power to control or to assign to whomsoever he sees fit. It is therefore not "related to the normal operations of the [primary] employer" nor does it "otherwise contribut[e] to the operations which the strike is endeavoring to halt" within the meaning of the *General Electric* and *Carrier* decisions....

[38] M & H undertook to perform about 80 percent of the project with its own employees, while subcontracting the balance. It also appears that M & H in certain instances could not work until completion of a subcontractor's phase of the job, while in others subcontractors would have to hold up while M & H was performing.

[39] In so finding, we reject the General Counsel's view that the "unrelated work" condition is met unless the work is "identical or substantially similar" to that of the primary employer. The work of those using the reserved gate may be related to the normal operations of the primary employer though not "identical or substantially similar" to that normally performed by the latter....

and, on this basis, we find that Respondent had the right to appeal to the employees of the subcontractor to honor its picket line around M & H's operations.

This being the case, the fact that such appeals were addressed to those employees at gates reserved for their exclusive use by M & H furnishes no basis for the majority's conclusion that the picketing after November 16 "failed to comply with the *Moore Dry Dock* requirement that such action take place reasonably close to the situs of Respondent's dispute with M & H." As the Supreme Court indicated in the *General Electric* decision, the barring of picketing through the device of a gate reserved for the exclusive use of secondary employees whose tasks aid the struck employer's every day operations constitutes a clear invasion of traditional primary activity. Furthermore, the *Moore Dry Dock* tests are utilized by the Board to aid it in determining whether certain kinds of picketing constitute proscribed secondary or protected primary activity whereas the *General Electric* tests are designed to aid in determining whether a union has the right to appeal directly to the secondary employees using a reserved gate. Accordingly, it seems obvious that the former tests must be applied in a manner which will give full effect to the latter tests. As we find that Respondent had the right to appeal to the employees of the neutral subcontractor, we find that the picketing at the reserved gates constituted compliance with the requirement that its picketing be limited to places reasonably close to the situs of Respondent's dispute with M & H. Accordingly, as the picketing also conformed to the other *Moore Dry Dock* tests, we perceive no basis on which to conclude that Respondent's object in picketing the reserved gates was to induce the employees of M & H's subcontractors to engage in a refusal to perform services with the object of forcing their employers to cease dealing with M & H.

Accordingly, we would find that Respondent's picketing did not violate § 8(b)(4)(B), and we would dismiss the complaint.

NOTES

1. The *Markwell & Hartz* approach was subsequently applied even where the general contractor was engaged in building an apartment complex on land that it owned. *Carpenters, Local 470 (Mueller-Anderson, Inc.),* 224 N.L.R.B. 315 (1976), *affirmed,* 564 F.2d 1360 (9th Cir. 1977).

2. Where electrical fixtures to be used by Hoff, a nonunion electrical subcontractor with whom the IBEW had a dispute, were delivered through a "neutral gate" at a construction project, the union's picketing of that gate did not violate § 8(b)(4) of the Act. The fact that the fixtures were ordered and owned by the project's owner made no difference. Since they were to be used and installed by Hoff, the union was free to picket the gate where its supplies were delivered. *J.F.*

---

[40] Having found that the work of those using the reserved gate was directly related to the normal operations of M & H, we need not decide whether, or under what circumstances, the "interruption of operations" test applies to reserved gate picketing in the construction industry.

Hoff Elec. Co. v. NLRB, 642 F.2d 1266 (1980), *cert. denied,* 451 U.S. 918 (1981).

In *Electrical Workers Local 76 v. NLRB,* 742 F.2d 498 (9th Cir. 1984), the court sustained a § 8(b)(4)(B) determination based upon the union's picketing of a neutral gate reserved for neutral construction contractor employees even though the guard had permitted a municipal garbage truck to enter through that gate to service the trash dumpster used by both the primary employer television station and the secondary construction contractor. The court noted that this incident did not irrevocably destroy the neutrality of the reserved gate, since the incident in question had occurred without the fault of the television station and was followed by immediate corrective action. *See also OCWA Local 3-689 (Martin Marietta),* 307 N.L.R.B. 1031 (1992) (use of neutral gate on several occasions by geologist employed by service contractor of primary employer insufficient to cause loss of gate's neutral status).

3. In *NLRB v. Operating Eng'rs Local 825 (Burns & Roe, Inc.),* 400 U.S. 297 (1971), Burns, a general contractor, subcontracted all construction work on a project to three companies, White, Chicago Bridge, and Poirier. All three employed members of an operating engineers union, but White, unlike Chicago Bridge and Poirier, did not have a collective bargaining agreement with the union. White installed an electric welding machine and assigned its operation to members of an ironworkers union. The engineers demanded this work and informed Burns, the general contractor, that they would strike the job unless Burns signed a contract, which would bind all three subcontractors as well as Burns, giving the engineers jurisdiction over the welding equipment. When White and Burns refused to accede to these demands, the engineers struck the project. The NLRB found the union guilty of violating both §§ 8(b)(4)(B) and 8(b)(4)(D) (the latter being the "jurisdictional dispute" provision). A court of appeals approved the 8(b)(4)(D) finding but disapproved the 8(b)(4)(B) finding. On a review limited to the 8(b)(4)(B) issue, the Supreme Court reversed the court of appeals:

> The more difficult task is to determine whether one of Local 825's objectives was to force Burns and the other neutrals to "cease doing business" with White as § 8(b)(4)(B) requires. The Court of Appeals concluded that the union's objective was to force Burns "to use its influence with the subcontractor to change the subcontractor's conduct, not to terminate their relationship" and that this was not enough. That court read the statute as requiring that the union demand nothing short of a complete termination of the business relationship between the neutral and the primary employer. Such a reading is too narrow.

> Some disruption of business relationships is the necessary consequence of the purest form of primary activity. These foreseeable disruptions are, however, clearly protected. *Steelworkers (Carrier),* 376 U.S. at 492; *Electrical Workers (General Electric),* 366 U.S. at 682. Likewise, secondary activity

could have such a limited goal and the foreseeable result of the conduct could be, while disruptive, so slight that the "cease doing business" requirement is not met.

Local 825's goal was not so limited nor were the foreseeable consequences of its secondary pressure slight. The operating engineers sought to force Burns to bind all the subcontractors on the project to a particular form of job assignments. The clear implication of the demands was that Burns would be required either to force a change in White's policy or to terminate White's contract. The strikes shut down the whole project. If Burns was unable to obtain White's consent, Local 825 was apparently willing to continue disruptive conduct that would bring all the employers to their knees.

Certainly, the union would have preferred to have the employers capitulate to its demands; it wanted to take the job of operating the welding machines away from the Ironworkers. It was willing, however, to try to obtain this capitulation by forcing neutrals to compel White to meet union demands. To hold that this flagrant secondary conduct with these most serious disruptive effects was not prohibited by § 8(b)(4)(B) would be largely to ignore the original congressional concern....

C. THE ALLY DOCTRINE

NLRB v. BUSINESS MACHINE & OFFICE APPLIANCE MECHANICS CONFERENCE BOARD, IUE, LOCAL 459 [ROYAL TYPEWRITER CO.]

United States Court of Appeals, Second Circuit
228 F.2d 553 (1955), *cert. denied*, 351 U.S. 962 (1956)

LUMBARD, Circuit Judge. This case arose out of a labor dispute between the Royal Typewriter Company and the Business Machine and Office Appliance Mechanics Conference Board, Local 459, IUE-CIO, the certified bargaining agent of Royal's typewriter mechanics and other service personnel. The National Labor Relations Board now seeks enforcement of an order directing the Union to cease and desist from certain picketing and to post appropriate notices.

The findings of the Board, adequately supported by the record, disclose the following facts, about which there is no significant dispute. On about March 23, 1954, the Union, being unable to reach agreement with Royal on the terms of a contract, called the Royal service personnel out on strike. The service employees customarily repair typewriters either at Royal's branch offices or at its customers' premises. Royal has several arrangements under which it is obligated to render service to its customers. First, Royal's warranty on each new machine obligates it to provide free inspection and repair for one year. Second, for a fixed periodic fee Royal contracts to service machines not under warranty. Finally, Royal is committed to repairing typewriters rented from it or loaned by it to replace machines undergoing repair. Of course, in addition Royal provides repair service on call by non-contract users.

During the strike Royal differentiated between calls from customers to whom it owed a repair obligation and others. Royal's office personnel were instructed to tell the latter to call some independent repair company listed in the telephone directory. Contract customers, however, were advised to select such an independent from the directory, to have the repair made, and to send a receipted invoice to Royal for reimbursement for reasonable repairs within their agreement with Royal. Consequently many of Royal's contract customers had repair services performed by various independent repair companies. In most instances the customer sent Royal the unpaid repair bill and Royal paid the independent company directly. Among the independent companies paid directly by Royal for repairs made for such customers were Typewriter Maintenance and Sales Company and Tytell Typewriter Company....

During May, 1954, the Union picketed four independent typewriter repair companies who had been doing work covered by Royal's contracts pursuant to the arrangement described above. The Board found this picketing unlawful with respect to Typewriter Maintenance and Tytell. Typewriter Maintenance was picketed for about three days and Tytell for several hours on one day. In each instance the picketing, which was peaceful and orderly, took place before entrances used in common by employees, deliverymen and the general public. The signs read substantially as follows (with the appropriate repair company name inserted):

Notice to the Public Only
Employees of Royal Typewriter Company
on Strike
Tytell Typewriter Company Employees
Are Being Used as Strikebreakers

————

Business Machine & Office Appliance
Mechanics Union, Local 459, IUE-CIO

Both before and after this picketing, which took place in mid-May, Tytell and Typewriter Maintenance did work on Royal accounts and received payment directly from Royal. Royal's records show that Typewriter Maintenance's first voucher was passed for payment by Royal on April 20, 1954, and Tytell's first voucher was passed for payment on May 3, 1954. After these dates each independent serviced various of Royal's customers on numerous occasions and received payment directly from Royal....

On the above facts the Trial Examiner and the Board found that ... the repair company picketing violated § 8(b)(4) of the National Labor Relations Act, 29 U.S.C. § 158(b)(4)....

We are of the opinion that the Board's finding with respect to the repair company picketing cannot be sustained. The independent repair companies were so allied with Royal that the Union's picketing of their premises was not prohibited by § 8(b)(4)(A).

We approve the "ally" doctrine which had its origin in a well reasoned opinion by Judge Rifkind in the *Ebasco* case, *Douds v. Architects, Engineers, Chemists & Technicians, Local 231,* 75 F. Supp. 672 (S.D.N.Y. 1948). Ebasco, a corporation engaged in the business of providing engineering services, had a close business relationship with Project, a firm providing similar services. Ebasco subcontracted some of its work to Project and when it did so Ebasco supervised the work of Project's employees and paid Project for the time spent by Project's employees on Ebasco's work plus a factor for overhead and profit. When Ebasco's employees went on strike, Ebasco transferred a greater percentage of its work to Project, including some jobs that had already been started by Ebasco's employees. When Project refused to heed the Union's requests to stop doing Ebasco's work, the Union picketed Project and induced some of Project's employees to cease work. On these facts Judge Rifkind found that Project was not "doing business" with Ebasco within the meaning of § 8(b)(4)(A) and that the Union had therefore not committed an unfair labor practice under that Section. He reached this result by looking to the legislative history of the Taft-Hartley Act and to the history of the secondary boycotts which it sought to outlaw. He determined that Project was not a person "wholly unconcerned in the disagreement between an employer and his employees" such as § 8(b)(4)(A) was designed to protect. The result has been described as a proper interpretation of the Act by its principal sponsor, Senator Taft, 95 Cong. Rec. 8709 (1949), and President Eisenhower in his January, 1954, recommendations to Congress for revision of the Act included a suggestion which would make this rule explicit.

Here there was evidence of only one instance where Royal contacted an independent (Manhattan Typewriter Service, not named in the complaint) to see whether it could handle some of Royal's calls. Apart from that incident there is no evidence that Royal made any arrangement with an independent directly. It is obvious, however, that what the independents did would inevitably tend to break the strike. As Judge Rifkind pointed out in the *Ebasco* case:

> The economic effect on Ebasco's employees was precisely that which would flow from Ebasco's hiring strikebreakers to work on its own premises.

And at 95 Cong. Rec. 8709 (1949) Senator Taft said:

> The spirit of the Act is not intended to protect a man who in the last case I mentioned is cooperating with a primary employer and taking his work and doing the work which he is unable to do because of the strike.

President Eisenhower's recommendation referred to above was to make it explicit "that concerted action against (1) an employer who is performing 'farmed-out' work for the account of another employer whose employees are on strike ... will not be treated as a secondary boycott." Text of President's Message to Congress on Taft-Hartley Amendments, January 11, 1954. At least one commentator has suggested that the enactment of this change would add nothing to existing law. Cushman, Secondary Boycotts and the Taft-Hartley Law, 6 Syracuse L. Rev. 109, 121 (1954). Moreover, there is evidence that the secondary strikes and boycotts sought to be outlawed by § 8(b)(4)(A) were only those which had been unlawful at common law. 93 Cong. Rec. 3950, 4323 (1947) (Senator Taft), 2 Legislative History of Labor Management Relations Act, 1947, 1006, 1106. And although secondary boycotts were generally unlawful, it has been held that the common law does not proscribe union activity designed to prevent employers from doing the farmed-out work of a struck employer. *Iron Moulders Union v. Allis-Chalmers Co.,* 166 Fed. 45, 51 (7th Cir. 1908). Thus the picketing of the independent typewriter companies was not the kind of secondary activity which § 8(b)(4)(A) of the Taft-Hartley Act was designed to outlaw. Where an employer is attempting to avoid the economic impact of a strike by securing the services of others to do his work, the striking union obviously has a great interest, and we think a proper interest, in preventing those services from being rendered. This interest is more fundamental than the interest in bringing pressure on customers of the primary employer. Nor are those who render such services completely uninvolved in the primary strike. By doing the work of the primary employer they secure benefits themselves at the same time that they aid the primary employer. The ally employer may easily extricate himself from the dispute and insulate himself from picketing by refusing to do that work. A case may arise where the ally employer is unable to determine that the work he is doing is "farmed-out." We need not decide whether the picketing of such an employer would be lawful, for that is not the situation here. The existence of the strike, the receipt of checks from Royal, and the picketing itself certainly put the independents on notice that some of the work they were doing might be work farmed-out by Royal. Wherever they worked on new Royal machines they were probably aware that such machines were covered by a Royal warranty. But in any event, before working on a Royal machine they could have inquired of the customer whether it was covered by a Royal contract and refused to work on it if it was. There is no indication that they made any effort to avoid doing Royal's work. The Union was justified in picketing them in order to induce them to make such an effort. We therefore hold that an employer is not within the protection of § 8(b)(4)(A) when he knowingly does work which would otherwise be done by the striking employees of the primary employer and where this work is paid for by the primary employer pursuant to an arrangement devised and originated by him to enable him to meet his contractual obligations. The result must be the same whether or not the primary employer makes any direct arrangement with the employers providing the services....

Enforcement of the Board's order is therefore in all respects denied.

NOTES

1. In *Graphic Arts Union, Local 277 (S & M Rotogravure Serv.)*, 222 N.L.R.B. 280 (1976), the Board held that the ally doctrine applied, despite the announcement by the struck employer that it had decided to discontinue that part of the business (engraving rotogravure cylinders) which the union had struck and which it had subcontracted out during the strike, since there was no "clear and convincing proof" that the subcontracting arrangement was really "permanent." Also, the fact that the struck employer had the customer contract for the ally's services did not prevent it from being an ally, where the struck employer "orchestrated" the arrangements and the ally knew it was doing struck work. *See also* later decisions in this case, 225 N.L.R.B. 1253 (1976), *affirmed*, 545 F.2d 1079 (7th Cir. 1976).

2. In *Teamsters Local 563 (Fox Valley Material Suppliers Ass'n)*, 176 N.L.R.B. 386 (1969), *enforced*, 76 L.R.R.M. 3002 (7th Cir.), *cert. denied*, 404 U.S. 912 (1971), the Labor Board indicated that a contractor could become an ally of a primary employer by "unknowingly" performing struck work for it. An employer has "the burden of determining whether or not it is engaged in neutral or ally type work." Here, the contractor was hired directly by the primary employer, and had reason to know the latter was involved in a strike.

3. Where the jobsite of a supplier of building stone which usually delivered its stone f.o.b. was struck and customers arranged with independent truckers to go get the stone and deliver it, the truckers became allies, subject to picketing while the trucks were unloading. The customers deducted the delivery cost from the contract price of the stone. The court of appeals said, "it is not important how the ally gets that work ... it makes no difference who makes the telephone call which brings into the dispute those who do the struck work." *Laborers Int'l Union Local 859 v. NLRB*, 446 F.2d 1319 (D.C. Cir. 1971). *Compare Teamsters Local 959 v. NLRB*, 743 F.2d 734 (9th Cir. 1984).

4. Under what circumstances will common ownership and control bring two businesses within the "ally doctrine"? In *Miami Newspaper Pressmen's Local 46 v. NLRB*, 322 F.2d 405 (D.C. Cir. 1963), the court enforced a Board order holding that common ownership of two newspapers, each, however, owned by a different corporation, was not alone sufficient to deprive either of them of its neutral status in a labor dispute involving the other. The court emphasized that the two papers were independently managed and transacted only a negligible amount of business between each other. *See also Television & Radio Artists v. NLRB*, 462 F.2d 887 (D.C. Cir. 1972).

In *Teamsters, Local 391 v. NLRB (Vulcan Materials Co.)*, 543 F.2d 1373 (D.C. Cir. 1976), *cert. denied*, 430 U.S. 967 (1977), the union had a labor dispute with the Mideast division of Vulcan. It then picketed the Chattanooga division of Vulcan, inducing its employees to strike in furtherance of the union's dispute with the Mideast division. The Board found, and the Court of Appeals agreed, that Chattanooga and Mideast were separate "persons" within the meaning of § 8(b)(4), since the divisions were operated as autonomous enterprises; thus the union's picketing was illegal. *See also Teamsters, Local 456 (Carvel Corp.)*, 273 N.L.R.B. 516 (1984).

5. When an ally relationship is found, employees of the secondary employer may be induced to stop work entirely and not to cease working on "hot" products destined to or from the primary employer, since that party is considered an extension of the primary employer. *See Shopmen's Local 501 (Oliver Whyte Co.)*, 120 N.L.R.B. 856 (1958).

6. *See generally* Levin, *"Wholly Unconcerned": The Scope and Meaning of the Ally Doctrine Under Section 8(b)(4) of the NLRA*, 119 U. Pa. L. Rev. 283 (1970); Irving, *Struck Work Ally Doctrine: Some Issues and Answers*, 9 Ga. L. Rev. 303 (1976).

D. CONSUMER PICKETING

NLRB v. RETAIL CLERKS, LOCAL 1001
[SAFECO TITLE INSURANCE CO.]

Supreme Court of the United States
447 U.S. 607, 100 S. Ct. 2372, 65 L. Ed. 2d 377 (1980)

MR. JUSTICE POWELL delivered the opinion of the Court.

The question is whether § 8(b)(4)(ii)(B) of the National Labor Relations Act, 29 U.S.C. § 158(b)(4)(ii)(B), forbids secondary picketing against a struck product when such picketing predictably encourages consumers to boycott a neutral party's business.

I

Safeco Title Insurance Co. underwrites real estate title insurance in the State of Washington. It maintains close business relationships with five local title companies. The companies search land titles, perform escrow services, and sell title insurance. Over 90% of their gross incomes derives from the sale of Safeco insurance. Safeco has substantial stockholdings in each title company, and at least one Safeco officer serves on each company's board of directors. Safeco, however, has no control over the companies' daily operations. It does not direct their personnel policies, and it never exchanges employees with them.

Local 1001 of the Retail Store Employees Union became the certified bargaining representative for certain Safeco employees in 1974. When contract negotiations between Safeco and the Union reached an impasse, the employees went on strike. The Union did not confine picketing to Safeco's office in Seattle. The Union also picketed each of the five local title companies. The pickets carried signs declaring that Safeco had no contract with the Union, and they distributed handbills asking consumers to support the strike by cancelling their Safeco policies.

Safeco and one of the title companies filed complaints with the National Labor Relations Board. They charged that the Union had engaged in an unfair labor practice by picketing in order to promote a secondary boycott against the title companies. The Board agreed. 226 N.L.R.B. 754 (1976). It found the title companies to be neutral in the dispute between Safeco and the Union. The Board then concluded that the Union's picketing violated § 8(b)(4)(ii)(B) of the National Labor Relations Act. The Union had directed its appeal against Safeco insurance policies. But since the sale of those policies accounted for substantially all of the title companies' business, the Board found that the Union's action was "reasonably calculated to induce customers not to patronize the neutral parties at all." The Board therefore rejected the Union's reliance upon *NLRB v. Fruit Packers (Tree Fruits)*, 377 U.S. 58 (1964), which held that § 8(b)(4)(ii)(B) allows secondary picketing against a struck product. It ordered the Union to cease picketing and to take limited corrective action.

The United States Court of Appeals for the District of Columbia Circuit set aside the Board's order. 194 U.S. App. D.C. 400, 600 F.2d 280 (1979) (en banc). The court agreed that the title companies were neutral parties entitled to the benefit of § 8(b)(4)(ii)(B). It held, however, that *Tree Fruits* leaves neutrals susceptible to whatever consequences may flow from secondary picketing against the consumption of products produced by an employer involved in a labor dispute. Even when product picketing predictably encourages consumers to boycott a neutral altogether, the court concluded, § 8(b)(4)(ii)(B) provides no protection.

We granted a writ of certiorari to consider whether the Court of Appeals correctly understood § 8(b)(4)(ii)(B) as interpreted in *Tree Fruits*. Having concluded that the Court of Appeals misapplied the statute, we now reverse and remand for enforcement of the Board's order.

II

In *Tree Fruits,* the Court held that § 8(b)(4)(ii)(B) does not prohibit all peaceful picketing at secondary sites. There, a union striking certain Washington fruit packers picketed large supermarkets in order to persuade consumers not to buy Washington apples. Concerned that a broad ban against such picketing might run afoul of the First Amendment, the Court found the statute directed to an "'isolated evil.'" The evil was use of secondary picketing "to persuade the customers of the secondary employer to cease trading with him in order to force him to cease dealing with, or to put pressure upon, the primary employer." Congress intended to protect secondary parties from pressures that might embroil them in the labor disputes of others, but not to shield them from business losses caused by a campaign that successfully persuades consumers "to boycott the primary employer's goods." Thus, the Court drew a distinction between picketing "to shut off all trade with the secondary employer unless he aids the union in its dispute with the primary employer" and picketing that "only persuades his customers not to buy the struck product." The picketing in that case, which "merely follow[ed] the struck product," did not "'threaten, coerce, or restrain'" the secondary party within the meaning of § 8(b)(4)(ii)(B).

Although *Tree Fruits* suggested that secondary picketing against a struck product and secondary picketing against a neutral party were "poles apart," the courts soon discovered that product picketing could have the same effect as an illegal secondary boycott. In *Hoffman ex rel. NLRB v. Cement Masons Local 337*, 468 F.2d 1187 (CA9 1972), *cert. denied*, 411 U.S. 986 (1973), for example, a union embroiled with a general contractor picketed the housing subdivision that he had constructed for a real estate developer. Pickets sought to persuade prospective purchasers not to buy the contractor's houses. The picketing was held illegal because purchasers "could reasonably expect that they were being asked not to transact any business whatsoever" with the neutral developer. "[W]hen a union's interest in picketing a primary employer at a 'one product' site [directly conflicts] with the need to protect ... neutral employers from the labor disputes of others," Congress has determined that the neutrals' interests should prevail.[7]

Cement Masons highlights the critical difference between the picketing in this case and the picketing at issue in *Tree Fruits*. The product picketed in *Tree Fruits* was but one item among the many that made up the retailer's trade. If the appeal against such a product succeeds, the Court observed, it simply induces the neutral retailer to reduce his orders for the product or "to drop the item as a poor seller." The decline in sales attributable to consumer rejection of the struck product puts pressure upon the primary employer, and the marginal injury to the neutral retailer is purely incidental to the product boycott. The neutral therefore has little reason to become involved in the labor dispute. In this case, on the other hand, the title companies sell only the primary employer's product and perform the services associated with it. Secondary picketing against consumption of the primary product leaves responsive consumers no realistic option other than to boycott the title companies altogether. If the appeal succeeds, each company "stops buying the struck product, not because of a falling demand, but in response to

---

[7]The so-called merged product cases also involve situations where an attempt to follow the struck product inevitably encourages an illegal boycott of the neutral party. *See K & K Construction Co. v. NLRB*, 592 F.2d 1228, 1231-1234 (CA3 1979); *American Bread Co. v. NLRB*, 411 F.2d 147, 154-155 (CA6 1969); *Honolulu Typographical Union No. 37 v. NLRB*, 401 F.2d 952, 954-955 (1968); Note, *Consumer Picketing and the Single-Product Secondary Employer*, 47 U. Chi. L. Rev. 112, 132-136 (1979).

pressure designed to inflict injury on [its] business generally." Thus, "the union does more than merely follow the struck product; it creates a separate dispute with the secondary employer." Such an expansion of labor discord was one of the evils that Congress intended § 8(b)(4)(ii)(B) to prevent.

As long as secondary picketing only discourages consumption of a struck product, incidental injury to the neutral is a natural consequence of an effective primary boycott. But the Union's secondary appeal against the central product sold by the title companies in this case is "reasonably calculated to induce customers not to patronize the neutrals at all." 226 N.L.R.B., at 757.[8] The resulting injury to their businesses is distinctly different from the injury that the Court considered in *Tree Fruits.* Product picketing that reasonably can be expected to threaten neutral parties with ruin or substantial loss simply does not square with the language or the purpose of § 8(b)(4)(ii)(B).[10] Since successful secondary picketing would put the title companies to a choice between their survival and the severance of their ties with Safeco, the picketing plainly violates the statutory

---

[8] *See Local 14055, United Steelworkers (Dow Chemical Co.),* 211 N.L.R.B. 649, 651-652 (1974), enforcement denied, 173 U.S. App. D.C. 229, 524 F.2d 853 (1975), vacated and remanded, 429 U.S. 807 (1976), complaint dismissed, 229 N.L.R.B. 302 (1977).

We do not disagree with Mr. Justice Brennan's dissenting view that successful secondary product picketing may have no greater effect upon a neutral than a legal primary boycott. But when the neutral's business depends upon the products of a particular primary employer, secondary product picketing can produce injury almost identical to the harm resulting from an illegal secondary boycott. *See generally* Duerr, *Developing a Standard for Secondary Consumer Picketing,* 26 Lab. L.J. 585 (1975). Congress intended § 8(b)(4)(ii)(B) to protect neutrals from that type of coercion. Mr. Justice Brennan's view that the legality of secondary picketing should depend upon whether the pickets "urge only a boycott of the primary employer's product," would provide little or no protection. No well-advised union would allow secondary pickets to carry placards urging anything other than a product boycott. Section 8(b)(4)(ii)(B) cannot bear a construction so inconsistent with the congressional intention to prevent neutrals from becoming innocent victims in contests between others.

[10] Representative Griffin, a sponsor of the Landrum-Griffin amendments that brought § 8(b)(4)(ii)(B) into law, emphasized to the Congress that the statute would outlaw secondary picketing likely to coerce the neutral party. "If the purpose of the picketing," he said, "is to coerce or to restrain the employer of that second establishment, to get him not to do business with the manufacturer—then such a boycott could be stopped." 105 Cong. Rec. 15,673 (1959), reprinted in 2 NLRB, Legislative History of the Labor-Management Reporting and Disclosure Act of 1959, at 1615 (1959).

Senator McClellan, who offered a bill quite similar to the statute actually adopted, noted that secondary picketing is particularly likely to coerce neutrals who have based their businesses upon one manufacturer's products. He pointed out that

> [W]e have cases of merchants who for 20 years, 10 years, or for a long period of time, may have been handling a particular brand of product. A merchant may have built his business around the product, such as the John Deere plows or some kind of machinery from some other company. The merchant may have built up his trade entirely on that product.

Id., at 6667, reprinted in 2 Legislative History, *supra,* at 1194.

ban on the coercion of neutrals with the object of "forcing or requiring [them] to cease ... dealing in the [primary] produc[t] ... or to cease doing business with" the primary employer. § 8(b)(4)(ii)(B); *see Tree Fruits,* 377 U.S., at 68.[11]

III

The Court of Appeals suggested that application of § 8(b)(4)(ii)(B) to the picketing in this case might violate the First Amendment. We think not. Although the Court recognized in *Tree Fruits* that the Constitution might not permit "a broad ban against peaceful picketing," the Court left no doubt that Congress may prohibit secondary picketing calculated "to persuade the customers of the secondary employer to cease trading with him in order to force him to cease dealing with, or to put pressure upon, the primary employer." Such picketing spreads labor discord by coercing a neutral party to join the fray. In *Electrical Workers v. NLRB,* 341 U.S. 694, 705 (1951), this Court expressly held that a prohibition on "picketing in furtherance of [such] unlawful objectives" did not offend the First Amendment. *See American Radio Ass'n v. Mobile S.S. Ass'n,* 419 U.S. 215, 229-231 (1974); *Teamsters Union v. Vogt, Inc.,* 354 U.S. 284 (1957). We perceive no reason to depart from that well-established understanding. As applied to picketing that predictably encourages consumers to boycott a secondary business, § 8(b)(4)(ii)(B) imposes no impermissible restrictions upon constitutionally protected speech.

Accordingly, the judgment of the Court of Appeals is reversed and the case is remanded with directions to enforce the National Labor Relations Board's order.

So ordered.

MR. JUSTICE BLACKMUN, concurring in part and concurring in the result.

I join Parts I and II of the Court's opinion, but not Part III. The Court's cursory discussion of what for me are difficult First Amendment issues presented by this case fails to take account of the effect of this Court's decision in *Police Department of Chicago v. Mosley,* 408 U.S. 92 (1972), on the question whether the National Labor Relations Act's content-based ban on peaceful picketing of secondary employers is constitutional. The failure to take *Mosley* into account is particularly ironic given that the Court today reaffirms and extends the principles of that case in *Carey v. Brown, ante.*

---

[11]The picketing in *Tree Fruits* and the picketing in this case are relatively extreme examples of the spectrum of conduct that the Board and the courts will encounter in complaints charging violations of § 8(b)(4)(ii)(B). If secondary picketing were directed against a product representing a major portion of a neutral's business, but significantly less than that represented by a single dominant product, neither *Tree Fruits* nor today's decision necessarily would control. The critical question would be whether, by encouraging customers to reject the struck product, the secondary appeal is reasonably likely to threaten the neutral party with ruin or substantial loss. Resolution of the question in each case will be entrusted to the Board's expertise.

In *NLRB v. Fruit Packers,* 377 U.S. 58, 76 (1964), Mr. Justice Black wrote a concurring opinion in which he concluded that § 8(b)(4)(ii)(B) of the National Labor Relations Act "abridges freedom of speech and press in violation of the First Amendment." He said:

> In short, we have neither a case in which picketing is banned because the picketers are asking others to do something unlawful nor a case in which *all* picketing is, for reasons of public order, banned. Instead, we have a case in which picketing, otherwise lawful, is banned only when the picketers express particular views. The result is an abridgement of the freedom of these picketers to tell a part of the public their side of a labor controversy, a subject the free discussion of which is protected by the First Amendment. [*Id.,* at 79. (Emphasis in original)].

These views, central to Mr. Justice Black's vision of the First Amendment, were, one would have supposed until today, "accepted" by the Court in *Mosley. See* 408 U.S., at 98.

I have never been fully comfortable with *Mosley*'s equating all content selectivity in affording access to picketers with censorship. *See Mosley,* 408 U.S., at 102 (concurring statement). For this reason, I join today in Mr. Justice Rehnquist's dissenting opinion in *Carey v. Brown.* I concur in the result in this case, however, only because I am reluctant to hold unconstitutional Congress' striking of the delicate balance between union freedom of expression and the ability of neutral employers, employees, and consumers to remain free from coerced participation in industrial strife. My vote should not be read as foreclosing an opposite conclusion where another statutory ban on peaceful picketing, unsupported by equally substantial governmental interests, is at issue.

MR. JUSTICE STEVENS, concurring in part and concurring in the result.

For the reasons stated by Mr. Justice Harlan and Mr. Justice Black in their separate opinions in *Tree Fruits,* 377 U.S. 58, 76, 80, I am persuaded that Congress intended to prohibit this secondary picketing, and for the reasons stated by Mr. Justice Powell, I agree that this case is not governed by *Tree Fruits.* I therefore join Parts I and II of the Court's opinion.

The constitutional issue, however, is not quite as easy as the Court would make it seem because, as Mr. Justice Black pointed out in *Tree Fruits,* "we have a case in which picketing, otherwise lawful, is banned only when the picketers express particular views." In other words, this is another situation in which regulation of the means of expression is predicated squarely on its content. *See Consolidated Edison Co. v. Public Service Commission,* 447 U.S. 530, 546 (Stevens, J., concurring). I agree with the Court that this content-based restriction is permissible but not simply because it is in furtherance of objectives deemed unlawful by Congress. That a statute proscribes the otherwise lawful expression of views in a particular manner and at a particular location cannot in itself totally justify the restriction. Otherwise the First Amendment would place no limit on Congress' power. In my judgment, it is our responsibility to determine whether the method or manner of expression, considered in context, justifies the particular restriction.

I have little difficulty in concluding that the restriction at issue in this case is constitutional. Like so many other kinds of expression, picketing is a mixture of conduct and communication. In the labor context, it is the conduct element rather than the particular idea being expressed that often provides the most persuasive deterrent to third persons about to enter a business establishment. In his concurring opinion in *Bakery Drivers Local v. Wohl,* 315 U.S. 769, 776-777, Mr. Justice Douglas stated:

> Picketing by an organized group is more than free speech, since it involves patrol of a particular locality and since the very presence of a picket line may induce action of one kind or another, quite irrespective of the nature of the ideas which are being disseminated. Hence those aspects of picketing make it the subject of restrictive regulation.

Indeed, no doubt the principal reason why handbills containing the same message are so much less effective than labor picketing is that the former depend entirely on the persuasive force of the idea.

The statutory ban in this case affects only that aspect of the union's effort to communicate its views that calls for an automatic response to a signal, rather than a reasoned response to an idea. And the restriction on picketing is limited in geographical scope to sites of neutrals in the labor dispute. Because I believe that such restrictions on conduct are sufficiently justified by the purpose to avoid embroiling neutrals in a third party's labor dispute, I agree that the statute is consistent with the First Amendment.

MR. JUSTICE BRENNAN, with whom MR. JUSTICE WHITE and MR. JUSTICE MARSHALL join, dissenting.

NLRB v. Fruit Packers, 377 U.S. 58 (1964) (*Tree Fruits*), held that it was permissible under § 8(b)(4)(ii)(B) of the National Labor Relations Act (NLRA) for a union involved in a labor dispute with a primary employer to conduct peaceful picketing at a secondary site with the object of persuading consumers to boycott the primary employer's product. Today's decision stunts *Tree Fruits* by declaring that secondary site picketing is illegal when the primary employer's product at which it is aimed happens to be the only product which the secondary retailer distributes. I dissent.

The NLRA does not place the secondary site off limits to all consumer picketing over the dispute with the primary employer. The Act only forbids a labor union from picketing to "coerce" a secondary firm into joining the union's struggle against the primary employer. § 8(b)(4)(ii)(B). But inasmuch as the secondary retailer is, by definition, at least partially dependent upon the sale of the primary employer's goods, the secondary firm will necessarily feel the pressure of labor activity pointed at the primary enterprise. Thus, the pivotal problem in secondary site picketing cases is determining when the pressure imposed by consumer picketing is illegitimate, and therefore deemed to "coerce" the secondary retailer.

Tree Fruits addressed this problem by focusing upon whether picketing at the secondary site is directed at the primary employer's product, or whether it more broadly exhorts customers to withhold patronage from the full range of goods carried by the secondary retailer, *including those goods originating from nonprimary sources*. The *Tree Fruits* test reflects the distinction between economic damage sustained by the secondary firm solely by virtue of its dependence upon the primary employer's goods, and injuries inflicted upon interests of the secondary firm that are unrelated to the primary dispute—injuries that are calculated to influence the secondary retailer's conduct with respect to the primary dispute.

The former sort of harm is simply the result of union success in its conflict with the primary employer. The secondary firm is hurt only insofar as it entwines its economic fate with that of the primary employer by carrying the latter's goods. To be sure, the secondary site may be a battleground; but the secondary retailer, in its own right, is not enlisted as a combatant.

The latter kind of economic harm to the secondary firm, however, does not involve merely the necessary commercial fallout from the primary dispute. Appeals to boycott nonprimary goods sold by a secondary retailer place more at stake for the retailer than the risk it has assumed by handling the primary employer's product. Four considerations indicate that this broader pressure is highly undesirable from the standpoint of labor policy. First, nonprimary product boycotts distort the strength of consumer response to the primary dispute; the secondary retailer's decision to continue purchasing the primary employer's line becomes a function of consumer reaction to the primary conflict *amplified* by the impact of the boycott upon nonprimary goods. Second, although it seems proper to compel the producer or retailer of an individual primary product to internalize the costs of labor conflict engendered in the course of the item's production, a nonprimary product boycott may unfairly impose multiple costs upon the secondary retailer who does not wish to terminate his relationship with the primary employer. Third, nonprimary product boycotts attack interests of the secondary firm that are not derivative of the interests of the primary enterprise; because the retailer thereby becomes an independent disputant, the primary labor controversy may be aggravated and complicated. Finally, by affecting the sales on nonprimary goods handled by the secondary firm, the disruptive effect of the primary dispute is felt even by those businesses that manufacture and sell nonprimary products to the secondary retailer.

These sound reasons support *Tree Fruits'* conclusion that the legality of secondary site picketing should turn upon whether the union pickets urge only a boycott of the primary employer's product.[2] Concomitantly, *Tree Fruits* expressly rejected the notion that the coerciveness of picketing should depend upon the extent of loss suffered by the secondary firm through diminished purchases of the primary product. Nevertheless, the Court has now apparently abandoned the *Tree Fruits* approach, choosing instead to identify coerciveness with the percentage of the secondary firm's business made up by the primary product.

The conceptual underpinnings of this new standard are seriously flawed. The type of economic pressure exerted upon the secondary retailer by a primary product boycott is the same whatever the percentage of its business the primary product composes—in each case, a decline in sales at the secondary outlet may well lead either to a decrease in purchases from the primary employer or to product substitution. To be sure, the damaging effect of this pressure upon individual secondary firms will vary, but it is far from clear that the harmfulness of a primary product boycott is necessarily correlated with the percentage of the secondary firm's business the product constitutes. For example, a marginally profitable large retailer may handle a multiplicity of products, yet find the decrease in sales of a single, very profitable, primary product ruinous. A small healthy single product secondary retailer, on the other hand, might be able to sustain losses during a boycott, or substitute a comparable product.

Moreover, it is odd to treat the NLRA's prohibition against coercion of neutral secondary parties as a means of protecting single product secondary firms from the effects of a successful primary product boycott. A single product retailer will always suffer a degree of harm incident to a successful primary product boycott, whether or not the retailer becomes the focus of union activity. Thus, a ban on coercion of neutral businesses is mismatched to the goal of averting that harm. Far more sensible would be to read the statutory ban on coercion of neutral parties as shielding secondary firms from the injuries that ensue precisely because of union conduct aimed at them. Nonprimary product boycotts fall within this category because they are specifically targeted at the secondary retailer.

Unlike the *Tree Fruits* rule, the test formulated by the Court in this case is not rooted in the policy of maintaining secondary firm neutrality with respect to the primary dispute. There is no ground to believe that a single product secondary retailer is more prone than a multiproduct retailer to react to a primary product boycott by joining the union in its struggle against the primary employer. On the contrary, the single product secondary firm is likely to be the primary employer's

---

[2]Because a "merged product" consists in part of nonprimary products, the prohibition of "merged product" boycotts follows as a matter of logic and of policy from *Tree Fruits'* primary product boycott test. Thus, "merged product" cases, *see, e.g., American Bread Co. v. NLRB*, 411 F.2d 147, 154 (CA6 1969), do not support the Court's view that certain purely primary product boycotts are proscribed by the National Labor Relations Act. In fact, "merged product" boycotts are wholly different than primary product boycotts against single product retailers. "Merged product" boycotts need not entail a total withholding of patronage from the secondary retailer, which may carry other, nonmerged, products.

strongest ally because of the alignment of their respective economic interests. Nor is it especially unfair to subject the single product retailer to a primary product boycott. Whatever the percentage of a retailer's business that is constituted by a given item, the retailer necessarily assumes the risks of interrupted supply of declining sales that follow when labor conflict embroils the manufacturer of the item.

By shifting its focus from the nature of the product boycotted to the composition of the secondary firm's business, today's decision substitutes a confusing and unsteady standard for *Tree Fruits'* clear approach to secondary site picketing. Labor unions will no longer be able to assure that their secondary site picketing is lawful by restricting advocacy of a boycott to the primary product, as ordained by *Tree Fruits.* Instead, picketers will be compelled to guess whether the primary product makes up a sufficient proportion of the retailer's business to trigger the displeasure of the courts or the Labor Relations Board. Indeed, the Court's general disapproval of "[p]roduct picketing that reasonably can be expected to threaten neutral parties with ruin or substantial loss ...," *ante,* at 614, leaves one wondering whether unions will also have to inspect balance sheets to determine whether the primary product they wish to picket is too profitable for the secondary firm.

I continue to "disagree ... that the test of 'to threaten, coerce, or restrain' ... is whether [the secondary retailer] ... suffered or was likely to suffer economic loss." *Tree Fruits, supra,* at 72. I would adhere to the primary product test. Accordingly, I dissent.

NOTES

1. May a union engage in consumer picketing of nonunion bread served in a restaurant or nonunion paper bags used by a grocery store? Is the restaurant or grocery store distributing a primary product, or has that product lost its identity and become fully integrated into the "products" of the secondary retailers? *Compare Teamsters Local 327 (American Bread Co.),* 170 N.L.R.B. 91 (1968), *enforced,* 411 F.2d 147 (6th Cir. 1969) (bread sold to restaurant "merged" into secondary meals and thus not subject to consumer picketing) *with Paperworkers Local 832 (Duro Paper Bag Mfg. Co.),* 236 N.L.R.B. 1525 (1978) (paper bags used by grocery store not "merged" into secondary retail products and thus subject to consumer appeals). The Sixth Circuit set aside the Board's *Duro Paper Bag* finding, since the court viewed the bags as being "merged" into the "products" of the secondary grocery store). *Kroger Co. v. NLRB,* 647 F.2d 634 (6th Cir. 1981). *See also Honolulu Typographical Union v. NLRB,* 401 F.2d 952 (D.C. Cir. 1968).

2. The Board is not prohibited from looking behind the facade of "consumer picketing" to determine whether the true purpose of the union's action is to appeal to secondary employees. For example, in *NLRB v. Millmen & Cabinet Mak-*

ers, Local 550, 367 F.2d 953 (9th Cir. 1966), the court affirmed the Board's finding that union picketing at a construction site to protest the builder's use of a particular lumber company's products was unlawful despite picket signs stating "Consumer picket" and "Directed to Consumers only." The picketing union did not inform the builder or its employees of the intended purpose of the picketing, the signs did not explain that there was no dispute with the builder, and the signs did not request any specific consumer action.

3. *See generally* Lewis, *Consumer Picketing and the Court—The Questionable Yield of Tree Fruits,* 49 Minn. L. Rev. 479 (1965); St. Antoine, *Free Speech or Economic Weapon? The Persisting Problem of Picketing,* 16 Suffolk L. Rev. 883 (1982); Note, *Secondary Boycotts and the First Amendment,* 51 U. Chi. L. Rev. 811 (1984); Note, *Consumer Picketing, Statutory Interpretation and the First Amendment,* 81 Mich. L. Rev. 1817 (1983).

E. THREATS AND COERCION OF SECONDARY EMPLOYERS

NLRB v. Servette, Inc., 377 U.S. 46, 84 S. Ct. 1098, 12 L. Ed. 2d 121 (1964). During a strike against Servette, a wholesale food distributor, the union requested managers of retail chain stores not to handle goods from Servette and threatened to pass out handbills asking the public not to buy named items distributed by Servette. The Supreme Court held that this conduct did not contravene § 8(b)(4)(i), since the union did not seek to induce the managers to cease work. It instead sought to have them make a managerial decision not to handle goods from Servette. The Court further found that the union's behavior did not "threaten, restrain, or coerce" the retailers within the meaning of § 8(b)(4)(ii). The handbilling would be a form of publicity protected by the proviso, and a union may threaten to do that which it may legally do. Even though a wholesaler like Servette does not make anything, it is a "producer," within the meaning of the publicity proviso to § 8(b)(4). If the manager "agreed" with the union not to handle the struck products, would their accord constitute a "hot cargo" contract under § 8(e)?

NOTES

1. Senator John F. Kennedy, reporting to the Senate from the conference committee on the 1959 amendments, said:

> [T]he union shall be free to conduct informational activity short of picketing. In other words, the union can hand out handbills at the shop, can place advertisements in the newspapers, can make announcements over the radio, and can carry on all publicity short of having ambulatory picketing in front of the secondary site. [105 Cong. Rec. 17,899 (1959)].

In *Tree Fruits*, the Supreme Court relied upon such legislative comments as it carefully distinguished between consumer *picketing* and consumer *handbilling*:

> Peaceful consumer picketing to shut off all trade with the secondary employer unless he aids the union in its dispute with the primary employer, is poles apart from such picketing which only persuades his customers not to buy the struck product. The proviso indicates no more than that the Senate conferees' constitutional doubts led Congress to authorize publicity other than picketing which persuades the customers of a secondary employer to stop all trading with him, but not such publicity which has the effect of cutting off his deliveries or inducing his employees to cease work. On the other hand, picketing which persuades the customers of a secondary employer to stop all trading with him was also to be barred.

Is there a fundamental difference between picketing and handbilling? *See generally*, Note, *Picketing and Publicity Under Section 8(b)(4) of the LMRA*, 73 Yale L.J. 1265 (1964).

2. Since picketing was expressly excluded from the protection of the publicity proviso to § 8(b)(4), problems have arisen as to whether or not certain union activities should be characterized as picketing. The *William J. Burns* case *(Service & Maint. Employees, Local 399)*, 136 N.L.R.B. 431 (1962), illustrates the difficulties the Board sometimes encounters. Members Rodgers and Leedom were convinced that patrolling by twenty to seventy union members in an elliptical path in front of the main entrance to a sports arena constituted "picketing" and thus violated § 8(b)(4)(ii)(B), even though the patrollers distributed handbills but carried no placards. Members Brown and Fanning held that even if the patrolling did not constitute picketing, it did exceed the limits of allowable publicity since the patrollers, by virtue of their numbers and close-knit formation, imposed some element of physical restraint upon patrons of the arena. Chairman McCulloch voted to dismiss the complaint. *Cf. United Furn. Workers (Jamestown Sterling Corp.)*, 146 N.L.R.B. 474 (1964), *remanded*, 337 F.2d 936 (2d Cir. 1964) (conduct of union representatives in nailing picket signs to poles and trees in front of an employer's premises and watching signs from their cars across the street was "picketing" within the meaning of § 8(b)(7)).

Carrying of placards is not necessarily "picketing." An essential element of picketing, the Board has said, is some form of confrontation between the pickets and employees, customers or suppliers who are trying to enter the picketed premises. Union members patrolling shopping centers and the entrances to public buildings with signs advertising a labor dispute were found to be conducting "publicity other than picketing." *Chicago Typographical Union, Local 16*, 151 N.L.R.B. 1666 (1965).

EDWARD J. DeBARTOLO CORP. v. FLORIDA GULF COAST BUILDING TRADES COUNCIL

Supreme Court of the United States
485 U.S. 568, 108 S. Ct. 1392, 99 L.Ed.2d 645 (1988)

JUSTICE WHITE delivered the opinion of the Court.

This case centers around the respondent union's peaceful handbilling of the businesses operating in a shopping mall in Tampa, Florida, owned by petitioner, the Edward J. DeBartolo Corporation (DeBartolo). The union's primary labor dispute was with H. J. High Construction Company (High) over alleged substandard wages and fringe benefits. High was retained by the H. J. Wilson Company (Wilson) to construct a department store in the mall, and neither DeBartolo nor any of the other 85 or so mall tenants had any contractual right to influence the selection of contractors.

The union, however, sought to obtain their influence upon Wilson and High by distributing handbills asking mall customers not to shop at any of the stores in the mall "until the Mall's owner publicly promises that all construction at the Mall will be done using contractors who pay their employees fair wages and fringe benefits."[1] The handbills' message was that "[t]he payment of substandard

---

[1] The handbill read:

PLEASE *DON'T SHOP AT EAST LAKE SQUARE MALL* PLEASE

The FLA. GULF COAST BUILDING TRADES COUNCIL, AFL-CIO is requesting that you do not shop at the stores in the East Lake Square Mall because of The Mall ownership's contribution to substandard wages.

The Wilson's Department Store under construction on these premises is being built by contractors who pay substandard wages and fringe benefits. In the past, the Mall's owner, The Edward J. DeBartolo Corporation, has supported labor and our local economy by insuring that the Mall and its stores be built by contractors who pay fair wages and fringe benefits. Now, however, and for no apparent reason, the Mall owners have taken a giant step backwards by permitting our standards to be torn down. The payment of substandard wages not only diminishes the working person's ability to purchase with earned, rather than borrowed, dollars, but it also undercuts the wage standard of the entire community. Since low construction wages at this time of inflation means decreased purchasing power, do the owners of East Lake Mall intend to compensate for the decreased purchasing power of workers of the community by encouraging the stores in East Lake Mall to cut their prices and lower their profits? CUT-RATE WAGES ARE NOT FAIR UNLESS MERCHANDISE PRICES ARE ALSO CUT-RATE.

We ask for your support in our protest against substandard wages. Please do not patronize the stores in the East Lake Square Mall until the Mall's owner publicly promises that all construction at the Mall will be done using contractors who pay their employees fair wages and fringe benefits. IF YOU MUST ENTER THE MALL TO DO BUSINESS, please express to the store managers your concern over substandard wages and your support of our efforts.

We are appealing only to the public—the consumer. We are not seeking to induce any person to cease work or to refuse to make deliveries.

wages not only diminishes the working person's ability to purchase with earned, rather than borrowed, dollars, but it also undercuts the wage standard of the entire community." The handbills made clear that the union was seeking only a consumer boycott against the other mall tenants, not a secondary strike by their employees. At all four entrances to the mall for about three weeks in December 1979, the union peacefully distributed the handbills without any accompanying picketing or patrolling.

After DeBartolo failed to convince the union to alter the language of the handbills to state that its dispute did not involve DeBartolo or the mall lessees other than Wilson and to limit its distribution to the immediate vicinity of Wilson's construction site, it filed a complaint with the National Labor Relations Board (Board), charging the union with engaging in unfair labor practices under § 8(b)(4) of the National Labor Relations Act.... The Board's General Counsel issued a complaint, but the Board eventually dismissed it, concluding that the handbilling was protected by the publicity proviso of § 8(b)(4). *Florida Gulf Coast Bldg. & Constr. Trades Council,* 252 N.L.R.B. 702 (1980). The Court of Appeals for the Fourth Circuit affirmed the Board, 662 F.2d 264 (1981), but this Court reversed in *Edward J. DeBartolo Corp. v. NLRB,* 463 U.S. 147 (1983). There, we concluded that the handbilling did not fall within the proviso's limited scope of exempting "publicity intended to inform the public that the primary employer's product is 'distributed by' the secondary employer" because DeBartolo and the other tenants, as opposed to Wilson, did not distribute products of High. *Id.,* at 155-157. Since there had not been a determination below whether the union's handbilling fell within the prohibition of § 8(b)(4), and, if so, whether it was protected by the First Amendment, we remanded the case.

On remand, the Board held that the union's handbilling was proscribed by § 8(b)(4)(ii)(B). 273 N.L.R.B. 1431 (1985). It stated that under its prior cases "handbilling and other activity urging a consumer boycott constituted coercion." *Id.,* at 1432. The Board reasoned that "[a]ppealing to the public not to patronize secondary employers is an attempt to inflict economic harm on the secondary employers by causing them to lose business," and "such appeals constitute 'economic retaliation' and are therefore a form of coercion." *Id.,* at 1432, n. 6. It viewed the object of the handbilling as attempting "to force the mall tenants to cease doing business with DeBartolo in order to force DeBartolo and/or Wilson's not to do business with High." *Id.,* at 1432. The Board observed that it need not inquire whether the prohibition of this handbilling raised serious questions under the First Amendment, for "the statute's literal language and the applicable case law require[d]" a finding of a violation. *Ibid.* Finally, it reiterated its longstanding position that "as a congressionally created administrative agency, we will presume the constitutionality of the Act we administer." *Ibid....*

We agree with the Court of Appeals and respondents that this case calls for the invocation of the *Catholic Bishop* rule, for the Board's construction of the statute, as applied in this case, poses serious questions of the validity of § 8(b)(4) under the First Amendment. The handbills involved here truthfully revealed the existence of a labor dispute and urged potential customers of the mall to follow a wholly legal course of action, namely, not to patronize the retailers doing business in the mall. The handbilling was peaceful. No picketing or patrolling was involved. On its face, this was expressive activity arguing that substandard wages should be opposed by abstaining from shopping in a mall where such wages were paid. Had the union simply been leafletting the public generally, including those entering every shopping mall in town, pursuant to an annual educational effort against substandard pay, there is little doubt that legislative proscription of such leaflets would pose a substantial issue of validity under the First Amendment. The same may well be true in this case, although here the handbills called attention to a specific situation in the mall allegedly involving the payment of unacceptably low wages by a construction contractor.

That a labor union is the leafletter and that a labor dispute was involved does not foreclose this analysis. We do not suggest that communications by labor unions are never of the commercial speech variety and thereby entitled to a lesser degree of constitutional protection. The handbills involved here, however, do not appear to be typical commercial speech such as advertising the price of a product or arguing its merits, for they pressed the benefits of unionism to the community and the dangers of inadequate wages to the economy and the standard of living of the populace. Of course, commercial speech itself is protected by the First Amendment, *Virginia Pharmacy Bd. v. Virginia Citizens Consumer Council, Inc.,* 425 U.S. 748, 762 (1976), and however these handbills are to be classified, the Court of Appeals was plainly correct in holding that the Board's construction would require deciding serious constitutional issues....

The Board was urged to construe the statute in light of the asserted constitutional considerations, but thought that it was constrained by its own prior authority and cases in the courts of appeals, as well as by the express language of the Act, to hold that § 8(b)(4) must be construed to forbid the handbilling involved here. Even if this construction of the Act were thought to be a permissible one, we are quite sure that in light of the traditional rule followed in *Catholic Bishop,* we must independently inquire whether there is another interpretation, not raising these serious constitutional concerns, that may fairly be ascribed to § 8(b)(4)(ii). This the Court has done in several cases....

We follow this course here and conclude, as did the Court of Appeals, that the section is open to a construction that obviates deciding whether a congressional prohibition of handbilling on the facts of this case would violate the First Amendment.

The case turns on whether handbilling such as involved here must be held to "threaten, coerce, or restrain any person" to cease doing business with another, within the meaning of § 8(b)(4)(ii)(B). We note first that "induc[ing] or encourag[ing]" employees of the secondary employer to strike is proscribed by § 8(b)(4)(i). But more than mere persuasion is necessary to prove a violation of

§ 8(b)(4)(ii): that section requires a showing of threats, coercion, or restraints. Those words, we have said, are "nonspecific, indeed vague," and should be interpreted with "caution" and not given a "broad sweep." *Drivers, supra,* at 290; and in applying § 8(b)(1)(A) they were not to be construed to reach peaceful recognitional picketing. Neither is there any necessity to construe such language to reach the handbills involved in this case. There is no suggestion that the leaflets had any coercive effect on customers of the mall. There was no violence, picketing, or patrolling and only an attempt to persuade customers not to shop in the mall.

The Board nevertheless found that the handbilling "coerced" mall tenants and explained in a footnote that "[a]ppealing to the public not to patronize secondary employers is an attempt to inflict economic harm on the secondary employers by causing them to lose business. As the case law makes clear, such appeals constitute 'economic retaliation' and are therefore a form of coercion." 273 N.L.R.B., at 1432, n. 6. Our decision in *Tree Fruits,* however, makes untenable the notion that *any* kind of handbilling, picketing, or other appeals to a secondary employer to cease doing business with the employer involved in the labor dispute is "coercion" within the meaning of § 8(b)(4)(ii)(B) if it has some economic impact on the neutral. In that case, the union picketed a secondary employer, a retailer, asking the public not to buy a product produced by the primary employer. We held that the impact of this picketing was not coercion within the meaning of § 8(b)(4) even though, if the appeal succeeded, the retailer would lose revenue.

NLRB v. Retail Store Employees, 447 U.S. 607 (1980) (*Safeco*), in turn, held that consumer picketing urging a general boycott of a secondary employer aimed at causing him to sever relations with the union's real antagonist was coercive and forbidden by § 8(b)(4). It is urged that *Safeco* rules this case because the union sought a general boycott of all tenants in the mall. But "picketing is qualitatively 'different from other modes of communication,'" *Babbitt v. Farm Workers,* 442 U.S. 289, 311, n. 17 (1979) (quoting *Hughes v. Superior Court,* 339 U.S. 460, 465 (1950)), and *Safeco* noted that the picketing there actually threatened the neutral with ruin or substantial loss. As JUSTICE STEVENS pointed out in his concurrence in *Safeco, supra,* at 619, picketing is "a mixture of conduct and communication" and the conduct element "often provides the most persuasive deterrent to third persons about to enter a business establishment." Handbills containing the same message, he observed, are "much less effective than labor picketing" because they "depend entirely on the persuasive force of the idea." *Ibid....*

In *Tree Fruits,* we could not discern with the "requisite clarity" that Congress intended to proscribe all peaceful consumer picketing at secondary sites. There is even less reason to find in the language of § 8(b)(4)(ii), standing alone, any clear indication that handbilling, without picketing, "coerces" secondary employers. The loss of customers because they read a handbill urging them not to patronize a business, and not because they are intimidated by a line of picketers, is the result of mere persuasion, and the neutral who reacts is doing no more than what its customers honestly want it to do.

The Board argues that our first *DeBartolo* case goes far to dispose of this case because there we said that the only nonpicketing publicity "exempted from the prohibition is publicity intended to inform the public that the primary employer's product is 'distributed by' the secondary employer." 463 U.S., at 155. We also indicated that if the handbilling were protected by the proviso, the distribution requirement would be without substantial practical effect. *Id.,* at 157. But we obviously did not there conclude or indicate that the handbills were covered by § 8(b)(4)(ii), for we remanded the case on this very issue. *Id.,* at 157-158.

It is nevertheless argued that the second proviso to § 8(b)(4) makes clear that that section, as amended in 1959, was intended to proscribe nonpicketing appeals such as handbilling urging a consumer boycott of a neutral employer.... By its terms, the proviso protects nonpicketing communications directed at customers of a distributor of goods produced by an employer with whom the union has a labor dispute. Because handbilling and other consumer appeals not involving such a distributor are not within the proviso, the argument goes, those appeals must be considered coercive within the meaning of § 8(b)(4)(ii). Otherwise, it is said, the proviso is meaningless, for if handbilling and like communications are never coercive and within the reach of the section, there would have been no need whatsoever for the proviso.

This approach treats the proviso as establishing an exception to a prohibition that would otherwise reach the conduct excepted. But this proviso has a different ring to it. It states that § 8(b)(4) "shall not be construed" to forbid certain described nonpicketing publicity. That language need not be read as an exception. It may indicate only that without the proviso, the particular nonpicketing communication the proviso protects might have been considered to be coercive, even if other forms of publicity would not be. Section 8(b)(4), with its proviso, may thus be read as not covering nonpicketing publicity, including appeals to customers of a retailer as they approach the store, urging a complete boycott of the retailer because he handles products produced by nonunion shops.

The Board's reading of § 8(b)(4) would make an unfair labor practice out of any kind of publicity or communication to the public urging a consumer boycott of employers other than those the proviso specifically deals with. On the facts of this case, newspaper, radio, and television appeals not to patronize the mall would be prohibited; and it would be an unfair labor practice for unions in their own meetings to urge their members not to shop in the mall. Nor could a union's handbills simply urge not shopping at a department store because it is using a nonunion contractor, although the union could safely ask the store's customers not to buy there because it is selling mattresses not carrying the union label. It is difficult, to say the least, to fathom why Congress would consider appeals urging a boycott of a distributor of a nonunion product to be more deserving of protection than nonpicketing persuasion of customers of other neutral employers such as that involved in this case.

Neither do we find any clear indication in the relevant legislative history that Congress intended § 8(b)(4)(ii) to proscribe peaceful handbilling, unaccompanied by picketing, urging a consumer boycott of a neutral employer. That section was one of several amendments to the NLRA enacted in 1959 and aimed at closing what were thought to be loopholes in the protections to which secondary employers were entitled. We recounted the legislative history in *Tree Fruits* and *NLRB v. Servette, Inc.*, 377 U.S. 46 (1964), and the Court of Appeals carefully reexamined it in this case and found "no affirmative intention of Congress clearly expressed to prohibit nonpicketing labor publicity." 796 F.2d, at 1346. For the following reasons, for the most part expressed by the Court of Appeals, we agree with that conclusion.

First, among the concerns of the proponents of the provision barring threats, coercion, or restraints aimed at secondary employers was consumer boycotts of neutral employers carried out by picketing. At no time did they suggest that merely handbilling the customers of the neutral employer was one of the evils at which their proposals were aimed. Had they wanted to bar any and all nonpicketing appeals, through newspapers, radio, television, handbills or otherwise, the debates and discussions would surely have reflected this intention. Instead, when asked, Congressman Griffin, co-sponsor of the bill that passed the House, stated that the bill covered boycotts carried out by picketing neutrals but would not interfere with the constitutional right of free speech. 105 Cong. Rec. 15673, 2 Leg. Hist. 1615.

Second, the only suggestions that the ban against coercing secondary employers would forbid peaceful persuasion of customers by means other than picketing came from the opponents of any proposals to close the perceived loopholes in § 8(b)(4). Among their arguments in both the House and the Senate was that picketing and handbilling a neutral employer to force him to cease dealing in the products of an employer engaged in labor disputes, appeals which were then said to be legal, would be forbidden by the proposal that became § 8(b)(4)(ii). The prohibition, it was said, "reaches not only picketing but leaflets, radio broadcasts, and newspaper advertisements, thereby interfering with freedom of speech." 105 Cong. Rec. 15540, 2 Leg. Hist. 1576. The views of opponents of a bill with respect to its meaning, however, are not persuasive....

Third, § 8(b)(4)(ii) was one of the amendments agreed upon by a House-Senate Conference on the House's Landrum-Griffin bill and the Senate's Kennedy-Ervin bill. An analysis of the Conference bill was presented in the House by Representative Griffin and in the Senate by Senator Goldwater. With respect to appeals to consumers, the summary said that the House provision prohibiting secondary consumer picketing was adopted but "with clarification that other forms of publicity are not prohibited." 105 Cong. Rec. 18706, Leg. Hist. 1454 (Sen. Goldwater); 105 Cong. Rec. 18022, Leg. Hist. 1712 (Rep. Griffin). The clarification referred to was the second proviso to § 8(b)(4). See *supra*. The Court of Appeals held that although the proviso was itself confined to advising the customers of an employer that the latter was distributing a product of another employer with whom the union had a labor dispute, the legislative history did not foreclose understanding the proviso as a clarification of the meaning of § 8(b)(4) rather than an exception to a general ban on consumer publicity. We agree with this view.

In addition to the summary presented by Senator Goldwater and Congressman Griffin, Senator Kennedy, the Chairman of the Conference Committee, in presenting the Conference Report on the Senate floor, 105 Cong. Rec. 17898-17899, 2 Leg. Hist. 1431-1432, stated that under the amendments as reported by the Conference Committee, a "union can hand out handbills at the shop, can place advertisements in newspapers, can make announcements over the radio, and can carry on all publicity short of having ambulatory picketing in front of a secondary site." And he assured Senator Goldwater that union buy-America campaigns—that is, publicity requesting that consumers not buy foreign-made products, even though there is no ongoing labor dispute with the actual producer—would not be prohibited by the section.

Senator Kennedy included in his statement, however, the following:

> Under the Landrum-Griffin Bill it would have been impossible for a union to inform the customers of a secondary employer that that employer or store was selling goods which were made under racket conditions or sweatshop conditions, or in a plant where an economic strike was in progress. We were not able to persuade the House conferees to permit picketing in front of that secondary shop, but we were able to persuade them to agree that the union shall be free to conduct informational activity short of picketing. [105 Cong. Rec. 17898-17899, 2 Leg. Hist. 1432].

The Board relies on this part of the Senator's exposition as an authoritative interpretation of the words "threaten, coerce, or restrain" and argues that except as saved by the express language of the proviso, informational appeals to customers not to deal with secondary employers are unfair labor practices. The Senator's remarks about the meaning of § 8(b)(4)(ii) echoed his views, and that of others, expressed in opposing and defeating in the Senate any attempts to give more protection to secondary employers from consumer boycotts, whether carried out by picketing or nonpicketing means. And if the proviso added in conference were an exception rather than a clarification, it surely would not follow, as the Senator said, that under the Conference bill, unions would be free to "conduct informational activity short of picketing" and could handbill, advertise in newspapers, and carry out all publicity short of ambulatory picketing in front of a secondary site. Nor would buy-America appeals be permissible, for they do not fall within the proviso's terms. At the very least, the Kennedy-Goldwater colloquy falls far short of revealing a clear intent that all nonpicketing appeals to customers urging a secondary boycott were unfair practices unless protected by the express words of the proviso. Nor does that exchange together with the other bits of legislative history relied on by the Board rise to that level.

In our view, interpreting § 8(b)(4) as not reaching the handbilling involved in this case is not foreclosed either by the language of the section or its legislative history. That construction makes unnecessary passing on the serious constitutional questions that would be raised by the Board's understanding of the statute. Accordingly, the judgment of the Court of Appeals is

Affirmed.

JUSTICE O'CONNOR and JUSTICE SCALIA concur in the judgment.

JUSTICE KENNEDY took no part in the consideration or decision of this case.

NOTES

1. Under what circumstances, if any, would peaceful consumer handbilling be "coercive" within the meaning of § 8(b)(4)(ii)? What if it successfully induced substantial numbers of people to withhold their patronage of a large mall?

If secondary union handbilling is accompanied by picketing or involves other confrontational tactics, § 8(b)(4)(ii)(B) liability is likely to be found. *See Boxhorn's Big Muskego Gun Club v. Electrical Workers,* 798 F.2d 1016 (7th Cir. 1986).

2. The *DeBartolo II* decision has significantly expanded the publicity tactics available to labor organizations. *Compare Steelworkers (Pet, Inc.),* 288 N.L.R.B. 1190 (1988) (*DeBartolo II* permits union striking one subsidiary within diversified corporation to seek consumer boycott of all products of parent corporation, even though subsidiary did not "produce products" for parent corporation or even "work on" them) *with Pet, Inc. v. NLRB,* 641 F.2d 545 (8th Cir. 1981) (pre-*DeBartolo II* refusal to permit such conduct). *See also Brown & Root v. Louisiana State AFL-CIO,* 10 F.3d 316 (5th Cir. 1994). *See* Kohler, *Setting the Conditions for Self-Rule: Unions, Associations, Our First Amendment Discourse and the Problem of De Bartolo,* 1990 Wis. L. Rev. 149 (1990); Pope, *Labor-Community Coalitions and Boycotts: The Old Labor Law, the New Unionism, and the Living Constitution,* 69 Tex. L. Rev. 889 (1991).

3. In *Service Employees Local 399 (Delta Air Lines),* 263 N.L.R.B. 996 (1982), *affirmed,* 743 F.2d 1417 (9th Cir. 1984), the Board recognized that a union's distribution of handbills urging consumers to boycott the secondary party, an airline, was not "for the purpose of truthfully advising the public" within the meaning of the publicity proviso, when it only provided information about the airline's allegedly poor safety and customer satisfaction record and did not mention the primary party, a nonunion janitorial firm serving the airline's offices.

4. A variety of union activities other than traditional picketing and handbilling have been labeled "coercion" under § 8(b)(4)(ii)(B). These have included "shop-ins" in which union members "descended in droves" on secondary retailers to immobilize them with numerous purchases of small, inexpensive items, paid for with large denomination bills (*Pye v. Teamsters Local 122*, 61 F.3d 1013 (1st Cir. 1995)), and a union demand for arbitration of a dispute over a realty company's choice of a cleaning subcontractor (*Service Employees Local 32B-32J v. NLRB (Nevins Realty Corp.)*, 68 F.3d 490 (D.C. Cir. 1995)). In the latter case, the union contended the employer had breached its obligation to make the subcontractor retain its predecessor's employees. The court concluded, however, that since bargaining unit members had never done the cleaning work, the union's arbitration claim was not aimed at work preservation but was instead a "classic secondary boycott."

F. HOT CARGO AGREEMENTS

UNITED BROTHERHOOD OF CARPENTERS & JOINERS, LOCAL 1976 v. NLRB [SAND DOOR]

Supreme Court of the United States
357 U.S. 93, 78 S. Ct. 1011, 2 L. Ed. 2d 1186 (1958)

MR. JUSTICE FRANKFURTER delivered the opinion of the Court.

....

[This case] arises out of a labor dispute between carpenter unions and an employer engaged in the building construction trade in Southern California. The Sand Door and Plywood Company is the exclusive distributor in Southern California of doors manufactured by the Paine Lumber Company of Oshkosh, Wisconsin. Watson and Dreps are millwork contractors who purchase doors from Sand. Havstad and Jensen are the general contractors who were at the time of the dispute involved, engaged in the construction of a hospital in Los Angeles. Havstad and Jensen are parties to a master labor agreement negotiated with the United Brotherhood of Carpenters and Joiners of America on behalf of its affiliated district councils and locals including petitioner unions. This agreement, comprehensively regulating the labor relations of Havstad and Jensen and its carpenter employees, includes a provision that, "workmen shall not be required to handle nonunion material."

In August, 1954, doors manufactured by Paine and purchased by Sand were delivered to the hospital construction site by Watson and Dreps. On the morning of August 17, Fleisher, business agent of petitioner Local 1976, came to the construction site and notified Steinert, Havstad and Jensen's foreman, that the doors were nonunion and could not be hung. Steinert therefore ordered employees to cease handling the doors. When Nicholson, Havstad, and Jensen's general superintendent, appeared on the job and asked Fleisher why the workers had been prevented from handling the doors, he stated that they had been stopped until it could be determined whether the doors were union or nonunion. Subsequent negotiations between officers of Sand and the Union failed to produce an agreement that would permit the doors to be installed....

... The employees' action may be described as a "strike or concerted refusal," and there is a "forcing or requiring" of the employer, even though there is a hot cargo provision. The realities of coercion are not altered simply because it is said that the employer is forced to carry out a prior engagement rather than forced now to cease doing business with another. A more important consideration, and one peculiarly within the cognizance of the Board because of its closeness to and familiarity with the practicalities of the collective bargaining process, is the possibility that the contractual provision itself may well not have been the result of choice on the employer's part free from the kind of coercion Congress has condemned. It may have been forced upon him by strikes that, if used to bring about a boycott when the union is engaged in a dispute with some primary employer, would clearly be prohibited by the act. Thus, to allow the union to invoke the provision to justify conduct that in the absence of such a provision would be a violation of the statute might give it the means to transmit to the moment of boycott, through the contract, the very pressures from which Congress has determined to relieve secondary employers.

Thus inducements of employees that are prohibited under § 8(b)(4)(A) in the absence of a hot cargo provision are likewise prohibited when there is such a provision. The Board has concluded that a union may not, on the assumption that the employer will respect his contractual obligation, order its members to cease handling goods, and that any direct appeal to the employees to engage in a strike or concerted refusal to handle goods is proscribed. This conclusion was reached only after considerable experience with the difficulty of determining whether an employer has in fact acquiesced in a boycott, whether he did or did not order his employees to handle the goods, and the significance of an employer's silence. Of course if an employer does intend to observe the contract, and does truly sanction and support the boycott, there is no violation of § 8(b)(4)(A). A voluntary employer boycott does not become prohibited activity simply because a hot cargo clause exists. But there remains the question whether the employer has in fact truly sanctioned and supported the boycott, and whether he has exercised the choice contemplated by the statute. The potentiality of coercion in a situation where the union is free to approach the employees and induce them to enforce their contractual rights by self-help is very great. Faced with a concerted work stoppage already in progress, an employer may find it substantially more difficult than he otherwise would to decide that business should go on as usual and that his employees must handle the goods. His "acquiescence" in the boycott may be anything but free. In order to give effect to the statutory policy, it is not unreasonable to insist, as the Board has done, that even when there is a contractual provision the union must not appeal to the employees or induce them not to handle the goods. Such a rule expresses practical judgment on the effect of union conduct in the framework of actual labor disputes and what is necessary to preserve to the employer the freedom of choice that Congress has decreed. On such a matter the judgment of the Board must be given great weight, and we ought not set against it our estimate of the relevant factors.

There is no occasion to consider the invalidity of hot cargo provisions as such. The sole concern of the Board in the present cases was whether the contractual provision could be used by the unions as a defense to a charge of inducing employees to strike or refuse to handle goods for objectives proscribed by § 8(b)(4)(A). As we have said, it cannot be so used. But the Board has no general commission to police collective bargaining agreements and strike down contractual provisions in which there is no element of an unfair labor practice. Certainly the voluntary observance of a hot cargo provision by an employer does not constitute a violation of § 8(b)(4)(A), and its mere execution is not, contrary to the suggestion of two members of the Board in the *Genuine Parts* case, Truck Drivers, 119 N.L.R.B. No. 53, *prima facie* evidence of prohibited inducement of employees. It does not necessarily follow from the fact that the unions cannot invoke the contractual provision in the manner in which they sought to do so in the present cases that it may not, in some totally different context not now before the Court still have legal radiations affecting the relations between the parties. All we need now say is that the contract cannot be enforced by the means specifically prohibited in § 8(b)(4)(A).

MR. JUSTICE DOUGLAS, with whom THE CHIEF JUSTICE and MR. JUSTICE BLACK concur, dissenting....

The provision of the collective bargaining agreement in the *Carpenters* case is typical of those in issue here:

> Workmen shall not be required to handle non-union material.

That provision was bargained for like every other claim in the collective agreement. It was agreed to by the employer. How important it may have been to the parties—how high or low in their scale of values—we do not know. But on these records it was the product of bargaining, not of coercion. The Court concedes that its inclusion in the contracts may not be called "forcing or requiring" the employer to cease handling other products within the meaning of the act. Enforcing the collective bargaining agreement—standing by its terms—is not one of the coercive practices at which the act was aimed. Enforcement of these agreements is conducive to peace. Disregard of collective agreements—the flouting of them—is disruptive. That was the philosophy of the *Conway's Express* decision of the Labor Board, 87 N.L.R.B. 972, *aff'd sub nom. Rabouin v. NLRB,* 195 F.2d 906 (2d Cir. 1952), and I think it squares with the act.

The present decision is capricious. The boycott is lawful if the employer agrees to abide by this collective bargaining agreement. It is unlawful if the employer reneges.

The hostile attitude of labor against patronizing or handling "unfair" goods goes deep into our history. It is not peculiarly American, though it has found expression in various forms in our history from the refusal of Americans to buy British tea, to the refusal of Abolitionists to buy slave-made products, to the refusal of unions to work on convict-made or on other nonunion goods. Unions have adhered to the practice because of their principle of mutual aid and protection. Section 7 of the act, indeed, recognizes that principle in its guarantee that "Employees shall have the right ... to engage in ... concerted activities for the purpose of collective bargaining or other mutual aid or protection." We noticed in *Apex Hosiery Co. v. Leader,* 310 U.S. 469, 503 (1940), that the elimination of "competition from non-union made goods" was a legitimate labor objective.

The reason an employer may also agree to that phase of union policies, the reason he may acquiesce in the inclusion of such a clause in a particular collective agreement, may only be surmised. Perhaps he sees eye to eye with the union. Perhaps he receives important concessions in exchange for his assistance to the union.

Certain it is that where he voluntarily agrees to the "unfair" goods clause he is not forced or coerced in the statutory sense....

We act today more like a Committee of the Congress than the Court. We strain to outlaw bargaining contracts long accepted, long used. Perhaps these particular provisions have evils in them that should be declared contrary to the public interest. They are, however, so much a part of the very fabric of collective bargaining that we should leave this policy-making to Congress and not rush in to undo what a century or more of experience has imbedded into labor-management agreements. I have not found a word of legislative history which even intimates that these "unfair" goods provisions of collective bargaining agreements are unlawful.

NOTES

1. Congress took drastic action with respect to "hot cargo" agreements in the amendments to the LMRA included in the Labor-Management Reporting and Disclosure Act of 1959. The House members of the conference committee made the following explanation:

> The Senate bill amends § 8 of the National Labor Relations Act, as amended, by adding at the end thereof a new subsection (e) which makes it an unfair labor practice for any labor organization and any employer who is a common carrier subject to part II of the Interstate Commerce Act to enter into any contract or agreement, express or implied, whereby such employer ceases or refrains or agrees to cease or refrain from handling, using, or

transporting any of the products of any other employer, or to cease doing business with the same.

The House amendment amends § 8 of the National Labor Relations Act, as amended, by adding at the end thereof a new subsection (e) to make it an unfair labor practice for any labor organization and any employer to enter into any contract or agreement, express or implied, whereby such employer ceases or refrains or agrees to cease or refrain from handling, using, selling, transporting or otherwise dealing in any of the products of any other employer, or to cease doing business with any other person. The House amendment also makes any such agreement heretofore or hereafter executed unenforcible and void.

The committee of conference adopted the House amendment but added three provisos. The first proviso specifies—

> that nothing in this subsection (e) shall apply to an agreement between a labor organization and an employer in the construction industry relating to the contracting or subcontracting of work to be done at the site of the construction, alteration, painting, or repair of a building, structure, or other work.

It should be particularly noted that the proviso relates only and exclusively to the contracting or subcontracting of work to be done at the site of the construction. The proviso does not exempt from § 8(e) agreements relating to supplies or other products or materials shipped or otherwise transported to and delivered on the site of the construction. The committee of conference does not intend that this proviso should be construed so as to change the present state of the law with respect to the validity of this specific type of agreement relating to work to be done at the site of the construction project or to remove the limitations which the present law imposes with respect to such agreements. Picketing to enforce such contracts would be illegal under the *Sand Door* case, *Carpenters, Local 1976, AFL v. NLRB*, 357 U.S. 93 (1958). To the extent that such agreements are legal today under § 8(b)(4) of the National Labor Relations Act, as amended, the proviso would prevent such legality from being affected by § 8(e). The proviso applies only to § 8(e) and therefore leaves unaffected the law developed under § 8(b)(4). The *Denver Building Trades* case and the *Moore Dry Dock* cases would remain in full force and effect. The proviso is not intended to limit, change, or modify the present state of the law with respect to picketing at the site of a construction project. Restrictions and limitations imposed upon such picketing under present law as interpreted, for example, in the U. S. Supreme Court decision in the *Denver Building Trades* case would remain in full force and effect. It is not intended that the proviso change the existing law with respect to judicial enforcement of these contracts or with respect to the legality of a strike to obtain such a contract.

The second proviso specifies that for the purposes of this subsection (e) and § 8(b)(4) the terms "any employer," "any person engaged in commerce or an industry affecting commerce," and "any person" when used in relation to the terms "any other producer, processor, or manufacturer," "any other employer," or "any other person" shall not include persons in the relation of a jobber, manufacturer, contractor, or subcontractor working on the goods or premises of a jobber or manufacturer or performing parts of an integrated process of production in the apparel and clothing industry. This proviso grants a limited exemption in three specific situations in the apparel and clothing industry, but in no other industry regardless of whether similar integrated processes of production may exist between jobbers, manufacturers, contractors, and subcontractors.

The third proviso applies solely to the apparel and clothing industry. [H.R. Rep. No. 1147, 86th Cong., 1st Sess. 39-40 (1959)].

2. Under the 1959 amendments to § 8(b)(4)(A), a strike to obtain a "hot cargo" clause prohibited by § 8(e) was made a union unfair labor practice. Likewise, union threats or coercion designed to induce an employer to enter into such an agreement was also prohibited.

Since the construction industry *proviso* excepts agreements "relating to the contracting or subcontracting of work to be done at the site of the construction," a construction union may picket or strike *to obtain* such a contractual restriction without violating § 8(b)(4)(A)—*i.e.*, it is not seeking an agreement prohibited by § 8(e). *Laborers Local 383 v. NLRB,* 323 F.2d 422 (9th Cir. 1963); *Essex County & Vicinity Dist. Council of Carpenters v. NLRB,* 332 F.2d 636 (3d Cir. 1964). As the *Sand Door* decision recognized, however, a union could not employ such coercive tactics *to enforce* such a clause, due to the absence of any exemption from § 8(b)(4)(B). *Compare R.M. Perlman v. Local 89-22-1, ILGWU,* 33 F.3d 145 (2d Cir. 1994) (explaining the broader exemption from § 8(e) *and* § 8(b)(4)(B) granted to garment industry labor organizations).

3. In *Connell Constr. Co. v. Plumbers Local 100,* 421 U.S. 616 (1975) (set forth *infra*), the union contended in an antitrust case that an agreement, which it had made with a general building contractor, that it would subcontract plumbing work to be done at its job sites only to firms having contracts with Local 100, was explicitly allowed by the construction industry proviso to § 8(e) of the NLRA. The Supreme Court held that the agreement was not protected by the proviso. Connell employed no plumbers itself and Local 100 had no collective bargaining relationship with it. The Court said, "We think [the § 8(e) proviso's] authorization extends only to agreements in the context of collective bargaining relationships and, in light of congressional references to the *Denver Building Trades* problems, possibly to common-situs relationships on particular jobsites as well."

In *Woelke & Romero Framing, Inc. v. NLRB,* 456 U.S. 645 (1982), the Supreme Court held that the construction industry proviso to § 8(e) protects union signatory subcontracting clauses sought or negotiated in the context of a collective bargaining relationship, thus resolving an issue left open in *Connell Constr. Co.* The decision involved two cases in which employers with established collective bargaining relationships challenged clauses that required them to subcontract work only to subcontractors who had agreements with a particular union. The employers contended that the proviso protected only subcontracting agreements that applied to sites and times at which union employees were working, and did not protect agreements requiring subcontractors to have agreements with particular unions. In rejecting this contention, the Court found that the proviso was added because Congress wanted to preserve the status quo regarding agreements in the construction industry. It stated: "Congress believed that broad subcontracting clauses similar to those at issue here were part of the pattern of collective-bargaining prior to 1959, and that the Board and the Courts had found them to be lawful. This perception was apparently accurate. Thus, endorsing the clauses at issue here is fully consistent with the legislative history of § 8(e) and the construction industry proviso." *Compare Iron Workers Dist. Council v. NLRB (Hoffman Constr. Co.),* 913 F.2d 1470 (9th Cir. 1990) (union violated § 8(b)(4)(A) when it picketed general contractor seeking clause limiting subcontracting to union firms, when bargaining relationship between union and general contractor had terminated prior to time of picketing).

4. The Supreme Court has sustained the NLRB's rule that, in the absence of a § 8(b)(4)(B) violation, it is inappropriate to reimburse sums such as union dues and fees paid pursuant to an agreement that is invalid under § 8(e). *Shepard v. NLRB,* 459 U.S. 344 (1983).

TRUCK DRIVERS, LOCAL 413 v. NLRB

United States Court of Appeals, District of Columbia Circuit
334 F.2d 539 (1964), *cert. denied,* 379 U.S. 916 (1964)

J. SKELLY WRIGHT, Circuit Judge. The National Labor Relations Board has found certain Picket Line, Struck Goods, Subcontracting, and Hazardous Work clauses in the collective bargaining agreements of petitioner unions void under § 8(e) of the Labor Act. In their Petition to Review and Set Aside, the unions contend that these provisions are outside the prohibitions of § 8(e) because their aim is benefit to the employees of the bargaining unit, not control of, or interference with, the contracting employer's third-party relationships. The Board cross-petitions for enforcement.

A preliminary issue is whether it is the *object,* the *effect,* or the express or implied *terms* of the challenged clauses which are relevant to the § 8(e) charge. The unions suggest an object test, by parity of reasoning with § 8(b)(4)(B)'s secondary boycott provisions. The Trial Examiner, in one of these companion cases,

No. 17,663, considered the effect of the clauses to be relevant to their validity under § 8(e), and took extensive evidence of their effect. The Board, however, at the instance of its General Counsel, held that the implementation of a contract was not relevant to its validity under § 8(e), that extrinsic evidence of object alone was not determinative, and that the contract must be tested by its terms, express or implied. *See Mary Feifer, d/b/a American Feed Co.,* 133 N.L.R.B. 214 (1961). We agree.

The Picket Line Clause

A key provision in the union contracts protects the right of individual employees to refuse to cross picket lines by immunizing them against employer discipline. This picket line clause is broadly worded to achieve maximum application permitted by the law. The Board held that under § 8(e) of the act the clause may validly apply only to certain types of picket lines; the union apparently would apply it to all.

The clause provides:

> It shall not be a violation of this Agreement and it shall not be cause for discharge or disciplinary action in the event an employee refuses to enter upon any property involved in a labor dispute or refuses to go through or work behind any picket line, including the picket line of Unions party to this Agreement and including picket lines at the Employer's place or places of business.

The Board concedes that the contract clause may permissibly operate to protect refusals to cross a picket line where the line is in connection with a *primary* dispute at the *contracting* employer's *own premises*. This seems clearly correct. Employees who refuse to cross such a line are entitled to the same protection as strikers under §§ 7 and 13 of the act. *See N.L.R.B. v. John S. Swift Co.,* 277 F.2d 641, 646 (7th Cir. 1960). The refusal to cross being a protected activity, the union and the employer may provide by contract that such refusal shall not be grounds for discharge. *See NLRB v. Rockaway News Co.,* 345 U.S. 71, 80 (1953).

A different result must be reached where the picket line at the contracting employer's own premises is itself in promotion of a *secondary* strike or boycott. Refusal to cross that line would itself be secondary activity. To the extent that the clause would protect such refusal to cross, it would then be authorizing a secondary strike, and would *pro tanto* be void under § 8(e) of the act. There is no merit to the unions' suggestion that this clause is outside the reach of § 8(e) because it protects *individual* refusals, not *union*-induced refusals. We read our own cases as having rejected this argument. *See Los Angeles Mailers Union No. 9 v. NLRB,* 114 App. D.C. 72, 311 F.2d 121 (1962).

The Board also held that the clause may validly protect refusals to cross a picket line at the premises of *another* employer if that picket line meets the conditions expressed in the *proviso* to § 8(b)(4) of the act. Clearly this is the law. *See NLRB v. Rockaway News Co., supra....*

The remaining question concerns refusals to cross a picket line at another employer's premises where that line does *not* meet the conditions of the § 8(b)(4) *proviso.* The unions maintain that refusal to cross any lawful primary picket line is primary activity under the act and that protection thereof in the bargaining agreement falls outside the ambit of § 8(e). The Board held that refusal to cross a non-*proviso* picket line constitutes secondary activity, and that contractual protection of such activity violates § 8(e).

A useful approach to this question is through the legislative history of the 1959 amendments which incorporated § 8(e) into the act. The House Labor Committee report stated: "It is settled law that the National Labor Relations Act does not require a truck driver to cross a primary picket line.... [T]he employer could agree that he would not require the driver to enter the strikebound plant." House Committee Report, 1 Legislative History of the Labor-Management Reporting and Disclosure Act of 1959 at 779 (1959). It is also clear "that the right to refuse to cross a primary picket line would not be affected by" the hot cargo ban in the bill passed by the Senate. Kennedy-Thompson analysis, 2 *id.* 1708 (2-3). "However, in order to set at rest false apprehensions on this score, the [House] committee appended the disclaimer proviso" which appears in the bill as reported by the House Committee. This disclaimer explicitly protected the right of refusal to cross primary picket lines, and the right to sign contracts immunizing such refusals from employer discipline. The entire House Committee bill, however, including this disclaimer, was replaced by the Landrum-Griffin substitute on the floor of the House. But the Landrum-Griffin substitute was unacceptable to the Senate conferees because: "[T]he House [Landrum-Griffin] bill apparently destroys the right to picket a plant and to honor a picket line even in a strike for higher wages. This change in the present law is entirely unacceptable." 2 *id.* 1708(3). It seems clear that, at least on this point, the Senate viewpoint was adopted in conference, modifying the Landrum-Griffin version. The Senate conferees secured the insertion of the following broad and all-encompassing declaration of congressional policy in the bill: *"Provided,* That nothing contained in this clause (B) shall be construed to make unlawful, where not otherwise unlawful, any primary strike or primary picketing." § 8(b)(4)(B).

The then Senator Kennedy explained the effects of this new provision to the Senate:

> ... The secondary boycott provisions of the House bill would have curtailed legitimate union activities. Accordingly, the Senate conferees insisted that the report secure the following rights:
>
> (a) The right to engage in primary strikes and primary picketing even though the employees of other employers refused to cross the picket line.

The fact of the matter is that there is some question under the Landrum-Griffin bill whether employees of another employer could have properly refused not [sic] to cross a picket line in a primary strike. That has been clarified in the conference report.

2 Legislative History of the Labor-Management Reporting and Disclosure Act of 1959 at 1432-1433.

Senator Kennedy further stated in a report to the Senate on the Conference: "We have protected the right of employees of a secondary employer, in the case of a primary strike, to refuse to cross a primary strike picket line." 2 *id.* 1389(1). This stated effect of the Senate-House Conference action seems to have been generally accepted....

In addition, Professor Cox, now the Solicitor General, who was one of the principal architects of the legislation, has confirmed that the intendment of the act is that "section 8(e) would not prohibit agreements sanctioning refusal to cross a lawful primary picket line."

It would seem that even without this legislative history, a similar conclusion would be demanded by the case law. It has been clear since *Rockaway News* that whenever refusal to cross a picket line is a protected activity, unions and employers may sign contracts providing that the refusal shall not be ground for discharge. In *Rockaway News* the activity in question was within the § 8(b)(4) *proviso*, but the Court did not limit the principle there announced to *proviso* activity. The Board itself recently held in the *Redwing* and *Everist* cases that refusal to cross a primary picket line was indeed a protected activity, without even considering whether the picket lines met the terms of the § 8(b)(4) *proviso*. And, in *Redwing*, we affirmed the Board's holding "that the employees had in fact engaged in *protected* concerted activity when they refused to cross the picket line," also without regard to whether the *proviso* was satisfied. *Sub nom. Teamsters Local 79 v. NLRB*, 117 App. D.C. 84, 325 F.2d 1011, 1012 (1963). In fact, we are aware of no case which limits protection of refusal to cross a primary picket line to § 8(b)(4) *proviso* situations.

Similar conclusions are suggested by *NLRB v. International Rice Milling Co., supra,* and *Electrical Workers Local 761 v. National Labor Relations Board*, 366 U.S. 667 (1961). Since "appealing to neutral employees whose tasks aid the employer's everyday operations" is a "traditional primary activity," *id.* at 681 of 366 U.S., primary picketing retains its primary characteristic even though it induces deliverymen to refuse to cross the line. Thus it seems clear that refusal to cross a lawful primary picket line, absent demonstrated secondary intent, is itself primary, and as such falls outside the act's proscriptions against secondary activity. *Teamsters, Local 79 v. NLRB, supra. Compare Seafarers Int'l Union v. NLRB*, 105 App. D.C. 211, 216, 265 F.2d 585, 590 (1959). Since § 8(e) is limited to secondary activity, a provision in the bargaining agreement immunizing the exercise of this protected right against employer discipline does not violate it. *See NLRB v. Rockaway News Co., supra.*

The Struck Goods Clause

A second section of the collective bargaining agreement which is in dispute concerns Struck Goods. It reads:

Recognizing that many individual employees covered by this contract may have personal convictions against aiding the adversary of other workers, and recognizing the propriety of individual determination by an individual workman as to whether he shall perform work, labor or service which he deems contrary to his best interest, the parties recognize and agree that:

[(a)] It shall not be a violation of this Agreement and it shall not be a cause for discharge or disciplinary action if any employee refuses to perform any service which, but for the existence of a controversy between a labor union and any other person (whether party to this Agreement or not), would be performed by the employees of such person.

[(b)] Likewise, it shall not be a violation of the Agreement and it shall not be a cause for discharge or disciplinary action if any employee refuses to handle any goods or equipment transported, interchanged, handled or used by any carrier or other person, whether a party to this Agreement or not, at any of whose terminals or places of business there is a controversy between such carrier, or person, or its employees on the one hand and a labor union on the other hand; and such rights may be exercised where such goods or equipment are being transported, handled or used by the originating, interchanging or succeeding carriers or persons, whether parties to this agreement or not.

[(c)] The Employer agrees that it will not cease or refrain from handling, using, transporting, or otherwise dealing in any of the products of any other employer or cease doing business with any other person, or fail in any obligation imposed by the Motor Carriers' Act or other applicable law, as a result of individual employees exercising their rights under this Agreement or under law, but the Employer shall, notwithstanding any other provision in this Agreement, when necessary, handle, use, transport or otherwise deal in such products and continue doing such business by use of other employees (including management and representatives), other carriers, or by any other method it deems appropriate or proper.

In considering clause (a) of this section, the Board acknowledged that it may lawfully apply where the relationship between the contracting employer and the employer with a labor dispute is so close as to render them "allies." The present state of the struck work-ally doctrine is outlined in *Douds v. Federation of Architects,* 75 F. Supp. 672 (S.D.N.Y. 1948), and *NLRB v. Business Machine &*

Office Appliance Mechanics, 228 F.2d 553 (2d Cir. 1955), *cert. denied,* 351 U.S. 962 (1956). These cases are specifically cited in the conference report on the 1959 amendments, as representing the existing law which Congress did not intend to supersede. 1 Legislative History of the Labor-Management Reporting and Disclosure Act of 1959 at 942. Under these decisions, an employer is characterized as an "ally" of the struck firm "when he knowingly does work which would otherwise be done by the striking employees of the primary employer and where this work is paid for by the primary employer pursuant to an arrangement devised and originated by him to enable him to meet his contractual obligations. The result must be the same whether or not the primary employer makes any direct arrangement with the employers providing the services." *NLRB v. Business Machine & Office Appliance Mechanics, supra* at 559 of 228 F.2d. As Judge Learned Hand phrased the test: "One does not make oneself a party to the dispute with a primary employer by taking over the business that the strike has prevented him from doing. On the other hand if a secondary employer, knowing of the strike, not only accepts the customer of the primary employer but takes his pay, not from the customer but from the primary employer ... [then he has] made common cause with the primary employer." Concurring opinion, *id.* at 562. This court has adopted the ally doctrine in *New York Mailers' Union No. 6 v. NLRB,* 114 App. D.C. 370, 371, 316 F.2d 371, 372 (1963).

The Trial Examiner found clause (a) to be limited in scope to the "ally" doctrine, and therefore valid. But the Board read the clause as impermissibly broad, in that under it employees of the contracting employer might refuse to perform services which met the *first* test of *Business Machine, supra* ("otherwise done by the striking employees"), even if the *second* test of that rule were not met ("pursuant to an arrangement"). *But cf. NLRB v. Amalgamated Lithographers,* 309 F.2d 31, 37-38 (9th Cir. 1962), *cert. denied,* 372 U.S. 943 (1963).

We agree with the Board that to the extent clause (a) protects refusals to work beyond the scope of the ally doctrine, it authorizes a secondary boycott, and so is *pro tanto* void under § 8(e) of the Labor Act. We refrain from defining the exact limits of the ally doctrine, however, and do not decide whether *Business Machine* tests are adequate for all variations in factual situations. Such spelling out is best left for the elucidating process of gradual inclusion and exclusion provided by specific cases.

Clause (b) of the Struck Goods section, set out above, seems to be a typical hot cargo clause, prohibited by § 8(e) of the act. The unions contend, however, that this clause—like others in the contract—is immune from § 8(e)'s prohibition because it protects the freedom of decision of the individual laborer, rather than creates a power of decision in the union itself. Since few workers will exercise their rights under these clauses, the unions argue, there will be no substantial interference with the business of the employer, particularly in view of the provisions of clause (c). The short answer to this contention is that it has already been rejected by this court. *See Los Angeles Mailers Union No. 9 v. NLRB, supra....*

Moreover, the legislative history of the 1959 amendments equates these "employee-rights" clauses with other hot cargo clauses. It is clear that § 8(e) was aimed, among other targets, at provisions in contracts under which an employer agrees: he cannot "require his employees to handle any [goods] which ... came from an employer engaged in a labor dispute," 1 Legislative History of the Labor-Management Reporting and Disclosure Act of 1959 at 779 (House Report); he cannot "require his employees to handle goods or provide other services for the benefit of an employer who is involved in a labor dispute," 2 *id.* at 1007 (Senator McClellan); "that his employees do not have to handle goods which the union labels as 'hot,'" 2 *id.* at 1197 (Senator Curtis); "his employees do not have to handle or work on goods produced or handled by another employer who happens to be in disfavor with the union," 2 *id.* at 1079 (Senator Goldwater); he will "not ... carry the goods and not ... require his employees to handle them," 2 *id.* at 1708 (Kennedy-Thompson analysis).

We must conclude, therefore, as did the Board, that this clause (b) is void under § 8(e) of the act and that clause (c) does not save it.

The Subcontracting Clause

The third major challenged provision of the collective bargaining agreements here concerns Subcontracting:

> The Employer agrees to refrain from using the services of any person who does not observe the wages, hours and conditions of employment established by labor unions having jurisdiction over the type of services performed.[13]

The Board found this clause was secondary, and therefore void under § 8(e) of the act. It reasoned:

> Like the typical hot cargo clause itself, a subcontractor clause is secondary where it limits, *not the fact of subcontracting*—either prohibiting it outright or conditioning it upon, *e.g.,* current full employment in the unit—but the *persons with whom* the signatory employer may subcontract.

This Board position groups together, as secondary, contract clauses which impose boycotts on subcontractors not signatory to union agreements, and those which merely require subcontractors to meet the equivalent of union standards in order to protect the work standards of the employees of the contracting employer. But the distinction between these two types of clauses is vital. Union-signatory subcontracting clauses are secondary, and therefore within the scope of § 8(e), while union-standards subcontracting clauses are primary as to the contracting

---

[13] Since this clause is entitled "Subcontracting," we assume—in the absence of any indication to the contrary—that its scope is limited to the contracting out of work which otherwise would be performed by members of the bargaining unit.

employer. We so held in *Building & Construction Trades Council v. NLRB,* 117 App. D.C. 239, 328 F.2d 540 (1964)....

This clause would be a union-signatory clause if it required subcontractors to have collective bargaining agreements with petitioner unions or their affiliates, or with unions generally. We interpret it, however, as merely requiring that subcontractors observe the equivalent of union wages, hours, and the like. Since we find that this clause only requires union standards, and not union recognition, we follow the line of cases in this court cited above to rule it primary, and thus outside § 8(e)'s prohibitions....

We therefore conclude that a decree should be drafted condemning the challenged contract clauses only to the extent found unlawful by this court.

Enforced in part and set aside in part.

NOTES

1. In *Sheet Metal Workers Local 91 (Schebler Co.),* 294 N.L.R.B. 766 (1989), *enforced in part and remanded,* 905 F.2d 417 (D.C. Cir. 1990), the Board found an "integrity clause," under which a local union retained the right to rescind a bargaining agreement if the employer had "ownership interests" in another business whose employees' "wage package, hours, and working conditions are inferior" to those in the local's contract, a "hot cargo" provision violative of § 8(e), since its purpose was not to protect unit work but "to satisfy union objectives elsewhere." *See Sheet Metal Workers Local 91 (Schebler Co.),* 305 N.L.R.B. 1055 (1991) (on remand).

2. *See generally* St. Antoine, *Secondary Boycotts and Hot Cargo: A Study in Balance of Power,* 40 U. Det. L.J. 189 (1962); Victor, *Hot Cargo Clauses: An Examination of Developments Under Section 8(e) of the LMRDA of 1959,* 15 Lab. L.J. 269 (1964); Note, *Hot Cargo Agreements Under the National Labor Relations Act: An Analysis of Section 8(e),* 38 N.Y.U. L. Rev. 97 (1963); Note, *Hot Cargo Clauses: The Scope of Section 8(e),* 71 Yale L.J. 158 (1961). *See also* Carney & Florsheim, *Treatment of Refusals to Cross Picket Lines: "By-paths and Crookt Ways,"* 55 Cornell L.Q. 940 (1970).

NATIONAL WOODWORK MANUFACTURERS ASS'N v. NLRB

Supreme Court of the United States
386 U.S. 612, 87 S. Ct. 1250, 18 L. Ed. 357 (1967)

MR. JUSTICE BRENNAN delivered the opinion of the Court.

Under the Landrum-Griffin Act amendments enacted in 1959, § 8(b)(4)(A) of the National Labor Relations Act became § 8(b)(4)(B) and § 8(e) was added. The questions here are whether, in the circumstances of these cases, the Metropolitan District Council of Philadelphia and Vicinity of the United Brotherhood of Carpenters and Joiners of America, AFL-CIO (hereafter the Union), committed the unfair labor practices prohibited by §§ 8(e) and 8(b)(4)(B).

Frouge Corporation, a Bridgeport, Connecticut, concern, was the general contractor on a housing project in Philadelphia. Frouge had a collective bargaining agreement with the Carpenters' International Union under which Frouge agreed to be bound by the rules and regulations agreed upon by local unions with contractors in areas in which Frouge had jobs. Frouge was therefore subject to the provisions of a collective bargaining agreement between the Union and an organization of Philadelphia contractors, the General Building Contractors Association, Inc. A sentence in a provision of that agreement entitled Rule 17 provides that "... No member of this District Council will handle ... any doors ... which have been fitted prior to being furnished on the job ...."[2] Frouge's Philadelphia project called for 3,600 doors. Customarily, before the doors could be hung on such projects, "blank" or "blind" doors would be mortised for the knob, routed for the hinges, and beveled to make them fit between jambs. These are tasks traditionally performed in the Philadelphia area by the carpenters employed on the jobsite. However, precut and prefitted doors ready to hang may be purchased from door manufacturers. Although Frouge's contract and job specifications did not call for premachined doors, and "blank" or "blind" doors could have been ordered, Frouge contracted for the purchase of premachined doors from a Pennsylvania door manufacturer which is a member of the National Woodwork Manufacturers Association, petitioner in No. 110 and respondent in No. 111. The Union ordered its carpenter members not to hang the doors when they arrived at the jobsite. Frouge thereupon withdrew the prefabricated doors and substituted "blank" doors which were fitted and cut by its carpenters on the jobsite.

The National Woodwork Manufacturers Association and another filed charges with the National Labor Relations Board against the Union alleging that by including the "will not handle" sentence of Rule 17 in the collective bargaining agreement the Union committed the unfair labor practice under § 8(e) of entering into an "agreement ... whereby [the] employer ... agrees to cease or refrain from handling ... any of the products of any other employer ...," and alleging further that in enforcing the sentence against Frouge, the Union committed the unfair labor practice under § 8(b)(4)(B) of "forcing or requiring any person to cease

---

[2] The full text of Rule 17 is as follows:

> No employee shall work on any job on which cabinet work, fixtures, millwork, sash, doors, trim or other detailed millwork is used unless the same is Union-made and bears the Union Label of the United Brotherhood of Carpenters and Joiners of America. No member of this District Council will handle material coming from a mill where cutting out and fitting has been done for butts, locks, letter plates, or hardware of any description, nor any doors or transoms which have been fitted prior to being furnished on job, including base, chair, rail, picture moulding, which has been previously fitted. This section to exempt partition work furnished in sections.

The National Labor Relations Board determined that the first sentence violated § 8 (e), 149 N.L.R.B. 646, 655-656, and the Union did not seek judicial review of that determination.

using ... the products of any other ... manufacturer ...." The National Labor Relations Board dismissed the charges, 149 N.L.R.B. 646.[3] The Board adopted the findings of the Trial Examiner that the "will not handle" sentence in Rule 17 was language used by the parties to protect and preserve cutting out and fitting as unit work to be performed by the jobsite carpenters. The Board also adopted the holding of the Trial Examiner that both the sentence of Rule 17 itself and its maintenance against Frouge were therefore "primary" activity outside the prohibitions of §§ 8(e) and 8(b)(4)(B)....

The Court of Appeals for the Seventh Circuit reversed the Board in this respect. 354 F.2d 594, 599 (1965). The court held that the "will not handle" agreement violated § 8(e) without regard to any "primary" or "secondary" objective, and remanded to the Board with instructions to enter an order accordingly....

The Court of Appeals sustained, however, the dismissal of the § 8(b)(4)(B) charge. The court agreed with the Board that the Union's conduct as to Frouge involved only a primary dispute with it and held that the conduct was therefore not prohibited by that section but expressly protected by the proviso "that nothing contained in this clause (B) shall be construed to make unlawful, where not otherwise unlawful, any primary strike or primary picketing ...." 354 F.2d, at 597.

We granted certiorari on the petition of the Woodwork Manufacturers Association in No. 110 and on the petition of the Board in No. 111. 384 U.S. 968. We affirm in No. 110 and reverse in No. 111.

I

Even on the doubtful premise that the words of § 8(e) unambiguously embrace the sentence of Rule 17,[4] this does not end inquiry into Congress' purpose in

---

[3] There were also charges of violation of §§ 8(e) and 8(b)(4)(B) arising from the enforcement of the Rule 17 provision against three other contractors whose contracts with the owners of the construction projects involved specified that the contractors should furnish and install precut and prefinished doors. The Union refused to permit its members to hang these doors. The Board held that this refusal violated § 8(b)(4)(B). The Board reasoned that, since these contractors (in contrast to Frouge) did not have "control" over the work that the Union sought to preserve for its members, the Union's objective was secondary—to compel the project owners to stop specifying precut doors in their contracts with the employer-contractors. 149 N.L.R.B., at 658. The Union petitioned the Court of Appeals to set aside the remedial order issued by the Board on this finding, but the court sustained the Board. 354 F.2d 594, 597 (1965). The Union did not seek review of the question here. Not before us, therefore, is the issue argued by the AFL-CIO in its brief *amicus curiae*, namely, whether the Board's "right-to-control doctrine—that employees can never strike against their own employer about a matter over which he lacks the legal power to grant their demand"—is an incorrect rule of law inconsistent with the Court's decision in *Labor Board v. Insurance Agents' International Union*, 361 U.S. 477, 497-498 (1960).

[4] The statutory language of § 8(e) is far from unambiguous. It prohibits agreements to "cease ... from handling ... any of the products *of any other employer*...." (Emphasis supplied.) Since both the product and its source are mentioned, the provision might be read not to prohibit an agreement relating solely to the nature of the product itself, such as a work-preservation agreement, but only to

enacting the section. It is a "familiar rule, that a thing may be within the letter of the statute and yet not within the statute, because not within its spirit, nor within the intention of its makers." *Holy Trinity Church v. United States,* 143 U.S. 457, 459 (1892). That principle has particular application in the construction of labor legislation which is "to a marked degree, the result of conflict and compromise between strong contending forces and deeply held views on the role of organized labor in the free economic life of the Nation and the appropriate balance to be struck between the uncontrolled power of management and labor to further their respective interests." *Carpenters, Local 1976 v. NLRB (Sand Door),* 357 U.S. 93, 99-100 (1958)....

Strongly held opposing views have invariably marked controversy over labor's use of the boycott to further its aims by involving an employer in disputes not his own. But congressional action to deal with such conduct has stopped short of proscribing identical activity having the object of pressuring the employer for agreements regulating relations between him and his own employees. That Congress meant §§ 8(e) and 8(b)(4)(B) to prohibit only "secondary" objectives clearly appears from an examination of the history of congressional action on the subject....

[The Court reviewed the legislative history regarding the treatment of secondary boycotts under the Sherman Act, Clayton Act, Norris-La Guardia Act, and Taft-Hartley Act.]

Judicial decisions interpreting the broad language of § 8(b)(4)(A) of the Taft-Hartley Act uniformly limited its application to such "secondary" situations.[16] This limitation was in "conformity with the dual congressional objectives of preserving the right of labor organizations to bring pressure to bear on offending employers in primary labor disputes and of shielding unoffending employers and others from pressures in controversies not their own." *NLRB v. Denver Bldg. Trades Council,* 341 U.S. 675, 692 (1951). This Court accordingly refused to read § 8(b)(4)(A) to ban traditional primary strikes and picketing having an im-

---

prohibit one arising from an objection to the other employers or a definable group of employers who are the source of the product, for example, their nonunion status.

[16] [Citations] An oft-cited definition of the conduct banned by § 8(b)(4)(A) was that of Judge Learned Hand in *I.B.E.W. v. NLRB,* 181 F.2d 34, 37 (2d Cir. 1950): "The gravamen of a secondary boycott is that its sanctions bear, not upon the employer who alone is a party to the dispute, but upon some third party who has no concern in it. Its aim is to compel him to stop business with the employer in the hope that this will induce the employer to give in to his employees' demands." For the scholarly acceptance of this primary-secondary dichotomy in the scope of § 8(b)(4)(A), see Koretz, *Federal Regulation of Secondary Strikes and Boycotts—A New Chapter,* 37 Cornell L. Q. 235 (1952); Tower, *A Perspective on Secondary Boycotts,* 2 Lab. L.J. 727 (1951); Cushman, *Secondary Boycotts and the Taft-Hartley Law,* 6 Syracuse L. Rev. 109 (1954); Lesnick, *The Gravamen of the Secondary Boycott,* 62 Col. L. Rev. 1363 (1962); Cox, *The Landrum-Griffin Amendments to the National Labor Relations Act,* 44 Minn. L. Rev. 257, 271 (1959); Aaron, *The Labor-Management Reporting and Disclosure Act of 1959,* 73 Harv. L. Rev. 1086, 1112 (1960). For the NLRB's vacillations during the period, see Lesnick, *supra,* 62 Col. L. Rev., at 1366-1392.

pact on neutral employers even though the activity fell within its sweeping terms. *NLRB v. Int'l Rice Milling Co.*, 341 U.S. 665 (1951); see *IUE, Local 761 v. NLRB*, 366 U.S. 667 (1961). Thus, however severe the impact of primary activity on neutral employers, it was not thereby transformed into activity with a secondary objective.

The literal terms of § 8(b)(4)(A) also were not applied in the so-called "ally doctrine" cases, in which the union's pressure was aimed toward employers performing the work of the primary employer's striking employees. The rationale, again, was the inapplicability of the provision's central theme, the protection of neutrals against secondary pressure, where the secondary employer against whom the union's pressure is directed has entangled himself in the vortex of the primary dispute. "The union was not extending its activity to a front remote from the immediate dispute but to one intimately and indeed inextricably united to it." *Douds v. Metropolitan Federation of Architects*, 75 F.Supp. 672, 677 (S.D.N.Y. 1948); see *NLRB v. Business Machine & Office Appliance Mechanics*, 228 F.2d 553 (2d Cir. 1955). We summarized our reading of § 8(b)(4)(A) just a year before enactment of § 8(e):

> It aimed to restrict the area of industrial conflict insofar as this could be achieved by prohibiting the most obvious, widespread, and, as Congress evidently judged, dangerous practice of unions to widen that conflict: the coercion of neutral employers, themselves not concerned with a primary labor dispute, through the inducement of their employees to engage in strikes or concerted refusals to handle goods.

Carpenters, Local 1976 v. NLRB (Sand Door), 357 U.S. 93, 100 (1958)....

In effect Congress, in enacting § 8(b)(4)(A) of the Act, returned to the regime of *Duplex Printing Press Co. v. Deering*, 254 U.S. 443 (1921), and *Bedford Cut Stone Co. v. Stone Cutters' Ass'n*, 274 U.S. 37 (1927), and barred as a secondary boycott union activity directed against a neutral employer, including the immediate employer when in fact the activity directed against him was carried on for its effect elsewhere.

Indeed, Congress in rewriting § 8(b)(4)(A) as § 8(b)(4)(B) took pains to confirm the limited application of the section to such "secondary" conduct. The word "concerted" in former § 8(b)(4) was deleted to reach secondary conduct directed to only one individual. This was in response to the Court's holding in *NLRB v. Int'l Rice Milling Co.*, 341 U.S. 665 (1951), that "concerted" required proof of inducement of two or more employees. But to make clear that the deletion was not to be read as supporting a construction of the statute as prohibiting the incidental effects of traditional primary activity, Congress added the proviso that nothing in the amended section "shall be construed to make unlawful, where not otherwise unlawful, any primary strike or primary picketing." Many statements and examples proffered in the 1959 debates confirm this congressional acceptance of the distinction between primary and secondary activity.

II

The Landrum-Griffin Act amendments in 1959 were adopted only to close various loopholes in the application of § 8(b)(4)(A) which had been exposed in Board and court decisions. We discussed some of these loopholes, and the particular amendments adopted to close them, in *NLRB v. Servette, Inc.*, 377 U.S. 46, 51-54 (1964)....

Section 8(e) simply closed still another loophole.[22] In *Carpenters, Local 1976 v. NLRB (Sand Door)*, 357 U.S. 93 (1958), the Court held that it was no defense to an unfair labor practice charge under § 8(b)(4)(A) that the struck employer had agreed, in a contract with the union, not to handle nonunion material. However, the Court emphasized that the mere execution of such a contract provision (known as a "hot cargo" clause because of its prevalence in Teamsters Union contracts), or its voluntary observance by the employer, was not unlawful under § 8(b)(4)(A). Section 8(e) was designed to plug this gap in the legislation by making the "hot cargo" clause itself unlawful. The *Sand Door* decision was believed by Congress not only to create the possibility of damage actions against employers for breaches of "hot cargo" clauses, but also to create a situation in which such clauses might be employed to exert subtle pressures upon employers to engage in "voluntary" boycotts. Hearings in late 1958 before the Senate Select Committee explored seven cases of "hot cargo" clauses in Teamsters Union contracts, the use of which the Committee found conscripted neutral employers in Teamsters organizational campaigns.[24]

This loophole-closing measure likewise did not expand the type of conduct which § 8(b)(4)(A) condemned. Although the language of § 8(e) is sweeping, it closely tracks that of § 8(b)(4)(A), and just as the latter and its successor § 8(b)(4)(B) did not reach employees' activity to pressure their employer to preserve for themselves work traditionally done by them, § 8(e) does not prohibit agreements made and maintained for that purpose.

The legislative history of § 8(e) confirms this conclusion....

The only mention of a broader reach for § 8(e) appears in isolated statements by opponents of that provision, expressing fears that work preservation agreements would be banned. These statements have scant probative value against the

[22] Throughout the committee reports and debates on § 8(e), it was referred to as a measure designed to close a loophole in § 8(b)(4)(A) of the 1947 Act. See, e.g., S. Rep. No. 187, 86th Cong., 1st Sess., 78-79, I 1959 Leg. Hist. 474-475 (1959) (Minority Views); H.R. Rep. No. 741, 86th Cong., 1st Sess., 20-21, I 1959 Leg. Hist. 778-779.

[24] See Final Report of the Senate Select Committee on Improper Activities in the Labor or Management Field, S. Rep. No. 1139, 86th Cong., 2d Sess., 3 (1960). The Final Report, ordered to be printed after enactment of the Landrum-Griffin Act, defined a "hot cargo" clause as "an agreement between a union and a unionized employer that his employees shall not be required to work on or handle 'hot goods' or 'hot cargo' being manufactured or transferred by another employer with whom the union has a labor dispute or whom the union considers and labels as being unfair to organized labor." *Ibid.*

backdrop of the strong evidence to the contrary. Too, "we have often cautioned against the danger, when interpreting a statute, of reliance upon the views of its legislative opponents. In their zeal to defeat a bill, they understandably tend to overstate its reach." *NLRB v. Fruit & Vegetable Packers*, 377 U.S. 58, 66 (1964). "It is the sponsors that we look to when the meaning of the statutory words is in doubt." *Schwegmann Bros. v. Calvert Distillers Corp.*, 341 U.S. 384, 394-395 (1951)....

In addition to all else, "the silence of the sponsors of [the] amendments is pregnant with significance...." *NLRB v. Fruit & Vegetable Packers, supra*, at 66. Before we may say that Congress meant to strike from workers' hands the economic weapons traditionally used against their employers' efforts to abolish their jobs, that meaning should plainly appear. "In this era of automation and onrushing technological change, no problems in the domestic economy are of greater concern than those involving job security and employment stability. Because of the potentially cruel impact upon the lives and fortunes of the working men and women of the Nation, these problems have understandably engaged the solicitous attention of government, of responsible private business, and particularly of organized labor." *Fibreboard Paper Prods. Corp. v. NLRB*, 379 U.S. 203, 225 (concurring opinion of Stewart, J.). We would expect that legislation curtailing the ability of management and labor voluntarily to negotiate for solutions to these significant and difficult problems would be preceded by extensive congressional study and debate, and consideration of voluminous economic, scientific, and statistical data.... It would ... be incongruous to interpret § 8(e) to invalidate clauses over which the parties may be mandated to bargain and which have been successfully incorporated through collective bargaining in many of this Nation's major labor agreements.

Finally, important parts of the historic accommodation by Congress of the powers of labor and management are §§ 7 and 13 of the National Labor Relations Act, passed as part of the Wagner Act in 1935 and amended in 1947. The former section assures to labor "the right ... to bargain collectively through representatives of their own choosing, and to engage in other concerted activities for the purpose of collective bargaining or other mutual aid or protection ...." Section 13 preserves the right to strike, of which the boycott is a form, except as specifically provided in the Act. In the absence of clear indicia of congressional intent to the contrary, these provisions caution against reading statutory prohibitions as embracing employee activities to pressure their own employers into improving the employees' wages, hours, and working conditions....

The Woodwork Manufacturers Association and amici who support its position advance several reasons, grounded in economic and technological factors, why "will not handle" clauses should be invalid in all circumstances. Those arguments are addressed to the wrong branch of government. It may be "that the time has come for a re-evaluation of the basic content of collective bargaining as contemplated by the federal legislation. But that is for Congress. Congress has demonstrated its capacity to adjust the Nation's labor legislation to what, in its legislative judgment, constitutes the statutory pattern appropriate to the developing state of labor relations in the country. Major revisions of the basic statute were enacted in 1947 and 1959. To be sure, then, Congress might be of opinion that greater stress should be put on ... eliminating more and more economic weapons from the ... [Union's] grasp.... But Congress' policy has not yet moved to this point ...." *NLRB v. Insurance Agents' Int'l Union,* 361 U.S. 477, 500 (1960).

III

The determination whether the "will not handle" sentence of Rule 17 and its enforcement violated § 8(e) and § 8(b)(4)(B) cannot be made without an inquiry into whether, under all the surrounding circumstances,[38] the Union's objective was preservation of work for Frouge's employees, or whether the agreements and boycott were tactically calculated to satisfy union objectives elsewhere. Were the latter the case, Frouge, the boycotting employer, would be a neutral bystander, and the agreement or boycott would, within the intent of Congress, become secondary. There need not be an actual dispute with the boycotted employer, here the door manufacturer, for the activity to fall within this category, so long as the tactical object of the agreement and its maintenance is that employer, or benefits to other than the boycotting employees or other employees of the primary employer thus making the agreement or boycott secondary in its aim. The touchstone is whether the agreement or its maintenance is addressed to the labor relations of the contracting employer vis-à-vis his own employees. This will not always be a simple test to apply. But "however difficult the drawing of lines more nice than obvious, the statute compels the task." *IUE, Local 761 v. NLRB,* 366 U.S. 667, 674 (1961).

That the "will not handle" provision was not an unfair labor practice in these cases is clear. The finding of the Trial Examiner, adopted by the Board, was that the objective of the sentence was preservation of work traditionally performed by the jobsite carpenters. This finding is supported by substantial evidence, and therefore the Union's making of the "will not handle" agreement was not a violation of § 8(e).

Similarly, the Union's maintenance of the provision was not a violation of § 8(b)(4)(B). The Union refused to hang prefabricated doors whether or not they bore a union label, and even refused to install prefabricated doors manufactured off the jobsite by members of the Union. This and other substantial evidence supported the finding that the conduct of the Union on the Frouge jobsite related solely to preservation of the traditional tasks of the jobsite carpenters.

---

[38] As a general proposition, such circumstances might include the remoteness of the threat of displacement by the banned product or services, the history of labor relations between the union and the employers who would be boycotted, and the economic personality of the industry. See Comment, 62 Mich. L. Rev. 1176, 1185 et seq. (1964).

The judgment is affirmed in No. 110, and reversed in No. 111.

It is so ordered.

Memorandum of MR. JUSTICE HARLAN.

In joining the Court's opinion, I am constrained to add these few words by way of underscoring the salient factors which, in my judgment, make for the decision that has been reached in these difficult cases.

1. The facts as found by the Board and the Court of Appeals show that the contractual restrictive-product rule in question, and the boycott in support of its enforcement, had as their sole objective the protection of union members from a diminution of work flowing from changes in technology. Union members traditionally had performed the task of fitting doors on the jobsite, and there is no evidence of any motive for this contract provision and its companion boycott other than the preservation of that work. This, then, is not a case of a union seeking to restrict by contract or boycott an employer with respect to the products he uses, for the purpose of acquiring for its members work that had not previously been theirs.

2. The only question thus to be decided, and which is decided, is whether Congress meant, in enacting §§ 8(b)(4)(B) and 8(e) of the National Labor Relations Act, to prevent this kind of labor-management arrangement designed to forestall possible adverse effects upon workers arising from changing technology.

3. Because of the possibly profound impacts that the answer to this question may have upon labor-management relations and upon other aspects of the economy, both sides of today's division in the Court agree that we must be especially careful to eschew a resolution of the issue according to our own economic ideas and to find one in what Congress has done. It is further agreed that in pursuing the search for the true intent of Congress we should not stop with the language of the statute itself, but must look beneath its surface to the legislative history.

4. It is recognized by court and counsel on both sides that the legislative history of § 8(b)(4)(B), with which § 8(e), it is agreed, is to be taken *pari passu,* contains only the most tangential references to problems connected with changing technology. Also, a circumspect reading of the legislative record evincing Congress' belief that the statutory provisions in question prohibited agreements and conduct of the kind involved in *Allen Bradley Co. v. IBEW Local 3*, 325 U.S. 797 (1945), will not support a confident assertion that Congress also had in mind the sort of union-management activity before us here. And although it is arguable that Congress, in the temper of the times, would have readily accepted a proposal to outlaw work-preservation agreements and boycotts, even, as here, in their most limited sense, such a surmise can hardly serve as a basis for the construction of an existing statute.

5. We are thus left with a legislative history which, on the precise point at issue, is essentially negative, which shows with fair conclusiveness only that Congress was not squarely faced with the problem these cases present. In view of

Congress' deep commitment to the resolution of matters of vital importance to management and labor through the collective bargaining process, and its recognition of the boycott as a legitimate weapon in that process, it would be unfortunate were this Court to attribute to Congress, on the basis of such an opaque legislative record, a purpose to outlaw the kind of collective bargaining and conduct involved in these cases. Especially at a time when Congress is continuing to explore methods for meeting the economic problems increasingly arising in this technological age from scientific advances, this Court should not take such a step until Congress has made unmistakably clear that it wishes wholly to exclude collective bargaining as one avenue of approach to solutions in this elusive aspect of our economy.

MR. JUSTICE STEWART, whom MR. JUSTICE BLACK, MR. JUSTICE DOUGLAS, and MR. JUSTICE CLARK join, dissenting....

The Court undertakes a protracted review of legislative and decisional history in an effort to show that the clear words of the statute should be disregarded in these cases. But the fact is that the relevant history fully confirms that Congress meant what it said, and I therefore dissent.

The Court concludes that the Union's conduct in these cases falls outside the ambit of § 8(b)(4) because it had an ultimate purpose that the Court characterizes as "primary" in nature—the preservation of work for union members. But § 8(b)(4) is not limited to boycotts that have as their only purpose the forcing of any person to cease using the products of another; it is sufficient if that result is "an object" of the boycott. Legitimate union objectives may not be accomplished through means proscribed by the statute. See *NLRB v. Denver Bldg. Trades Council,* 341 U.S. 675, 688-689. Without question, preventing Frouge from using prefitted doors was "an object" of the Union's conduct here.

It is, of course, true that courts have distinguished "primary" and "secondary" activities, and have found the former permitted despite the literal applicability of the statutory language. See *IBEW, Local 761 v. NLRB,* 366 U.S. 667. But the Court errs in concluding that the product boycott conducted by the Union in these cases was protected primary activity. As the Court points out, a typical form of secondary boycott is the visitation of sanctions on Employer A, with whom the union has no dispute, in order to force him to cease doing business with Employer B, with whom the union does have a dispute. But this is not the only form of secondary boycott that § 8(b)(4) was intended to reach. The Court overlooks the fact that a product boycott for work preservation purposes has consistently been regarded by the courts, and by the Congress that passed the Taft-Hartley Act, as a proscribed "secondary boycott." [citing *Allen Bradley* and earlier labor antitrust decisions]....

Although it was deeply concerned with the extensive restraints on trade caused by product boycotts, the 80th Congress specifically declined to amend the antitrust laws to reach the *Allen Bradley* type of secondary boycott because it correctly understood that such practices were already directly covered by § 8(b)(4) of the 1947 Act....

The Court seeks to avoid the thrust of this legislative history stemming from *Allen Bradley* by suggesting that in the present cases, the product boycott was used to preserve work opportunities traditionally performed by the Union, whereas in *Allen Bradley* the boycott was originally designed to create new job opportunities. But it is misleading to state that the union in *Allen Bradley* used the product boycott as a "sword." The record in that case establishes that the boycott was undertaken for the defensive purpose of restoring job opportunities lost in the depression. Moreover, the Court is unable to cite anything in *Allen Bradley,* or in the Taft-Hartley Act and its legislative history, to support a distinction in the applicability of § 8(b)(4) based on the origin of the job opportunities sought to be preserved by a product boycott. The Court creates its sword and shield distinction out of thin air; nothing could more clearly indicate that the Court is simply substituting its own concepts of desirable labor policy for the scheme enacted by Congress....

———————

   NLRB v. International Longshoremen's Ass'n, 447 U.S. 490, 100 S. Ct. 2305, 65 L. Ed. 2d 289 (1980). Prior to the introduction of containerization, trucks carried loose, or break-bulk, cargo to and from piers, and that cargo was transferred piece-by-piece from truck tailgates to ship holds and from ship holds to trucks by longshore workers. During the 1960s, shipping companies introduced containers ranging in length from 20 to 40 feet. These were filled by producers, warehousers, or shippers, transported to the piers on trucks, and loaded onto ships by large cranes container-by-container. Incoming vessels were unloaded in a similar manner. In an effort to preserve member jobs, the ILA negotiated bargaining agreement provisions that required all containers owned or leased by shipping companies that were to be stripped (unloaded) or stuffed (loaded) within a 50-mile radius of the port to be restripped and restuffed by longshore employees on the piers before they could be loaded onto or unloaded from ships. Shipping firms claimed that these contractual provisions violated § 8(e) and that ILA efforts to enforce these rules contravened § 8(b)(4)(B). Since the Labor Board found that ILA workers had not engaged in such stripping or stuffing prior to containerization, it concluded that the challenged provisions constituted secondary "work acquisition" rather than primary "work preservation." The Supreme Court, however, rejected the Board's "simplistic" approach and directed it to engage in a more searching evaluation.

   Section 8(b)(4)(B) of the Act prohibits unions and their agents from engaging in secondary activities whose object is to force one employer to cease doing business with another. Section 8(e) makes unlawful those collective-bargaining agreements in which the employer agrees to cease doing

business with any other person. Although § 8(e) does not in terms distinguish between primary and secondary activity, we have held that, as in
§ 8(b)(4)(B), Congress intended to reach only agreements with secondary
objectives. See *NLRB v. Pipefitters,* 429 U.S. 507, 517 (1977) (hereinafter
Pipefitters); *National Woodwork Mfgrs. Ass'n v. NLRB,* 386 U.S. 612, 620,
635 (1967) (hereinafter *National Woodwork*).

Among the primary purposes protected by the Act is "the purpose of preserving for the contracting employees themselves work traditionally done by them."
Pipefitters, supra, at 517. Whether an agreement is a lawful work preservation
agreement depends on "whether, under the surrounding circumstances, the Union's objective was preservation of work for [bargaining unit] employees, or
whether the [agreement was] tactically calculated to satisfy union objectives
elsewhere.... The touchstone is whether the agreement or its maintenance is addressed to the labor relations of the contracting employer vis-à-vis his own employees." *National Woodwork, supra,* at 644-645 (footnotes omitted). Under this
approach, a lawful work preservation agreement must pass two tests: First, it
must have as its objective the preservation of work traditionally performed by
employees represented by the union. Second, the contracting employer must have
the power to give the employees the work in question—the so-called "right of
control" test of *Pipefitters, supra.* The rationale of the second test is that if the
contracting employer has no power to assign the work, it is reasonable to infer
that the agreement has a secondary objective, that is, to influence whoever does
have such power over the work. "Were the latter the case, [the contracting em-
ployer] would be a neutral bystander, and the agreement or boycott would, within
the intent of Congress, become secondary." *National Woodwork, supra,* at
644-645.

In applying the work preservation doctrine, the first and most basic question is: What is the "work" that the agreement allegedly seeks to preserve?
... [I]n many cases it is not so easy to find the starting point of the analysis.
Work preservation agreements typically come into being when employees'
traditional work is displaced, or threatened with displacement, by technological innovation. The national labor policy expresses a preference for addressing "the threats to workers posed by increased technology and automation" by means of "labor-management agreements to ease these effects
through collective bargaining on this most vital problem created by advanced technology." *National Woodwork, supra,* at 641, 642. In many instances, technological innovation may change the method of doing the work,
instead of merely shifting the same work to a different location. One way to
preserve the work of the employees represented by the union in the face of
such a change is simply to insist that the innovation not be adopted and that
the work continue to be done in the traditional way. The union in *National
Woodwork* followed this tactic and negotiated an agreement in which the

employer agreed not to use prefabricated materials. We held that agreement was lawful under §§ 8(e) and 8(b)(4)(B). But the protection Congress afforded to work preservation agreements cannot be limited solely to employees who respond to change with intransigence....

The Board's approach reflects a fundamental misconception of the work preservation doctrine as it has been applied in our previous cases. Identification of the work at issue in a complex case of technological displacement requires a careful analysis of the traditional work patterns that the parties are allegedly seeking to preserve, and of how the agreement seeks to accomplish that result under the changed circumstances created by the technological advance. The analysis must take into account "all the surrounding circumstances," *National Woodwork,* 386 U.S., at 644, including the nature of the work both before and after the innovation. In a relatively simple case, such as *National Woodwork* or *Pipefitters,* the inquiry may be of rather limited scope. Other, more complex cases will require a broader view, taking into account the transformation of several interrelated industries or types of work; this is such a case. Whatever its scope, however, the inquiry must be carefully focused: to determine whether an agreement seeks no more than to preserve the work of bargaining unit members, the Board must focus on the work of the bargaining unit employees, not on the work of other employees who may be doing the same or similar work, and examine the relationship between the work as it existed before the innovation and as the agreement proposes to preserve it....

Thus the Board's determination that the work of longshoremen has historically been the loading and unloading of ships should be only the beginning of the analysis. The next step is to look at how the contracting parties sought to preserve that work, to the extent possible, in the face of a massive technological change that largely eliminated the need for cargo handling at intermediate stages of the intermodal transportation of goods, and to evaluate the relationship between traditional longshore work and the work which the Rules attempt to assign to ILA members. This case presents a much more difficult problem than either *National Woodwork* or *Pipefitters* because the union did not simply insist on doing the work as it had always been done and try to prevent the employers from using container ships at all .... Instead, ILA permitted the great majority of containers to pass over the piers intact, reserving the right to stuff and strip only those containers that would otherwise have been stuffed or stripped locally by anyone except the beneficial owner's employees. The legality of the agreement turns, as an initial matter, on whether the historical and functional relationship between this retained work and traditional longshore work can support the conclusion that the objective of the agreement was work preservation rather than the satisfaction of union goals elsewhere.... [I]n judging the legality of a thoroughly bargained and apparently reasonable accommodation to technological change, the question is not whether the Rules represent the most rational or efficient response to innovation, but whether they are a legally permissible effort to preserve jobs.

NOTES

1. On remand, the Labor Board generally sustained the validity of the ILA Rules on Containers. They were found to have a lawful work preservation objective, since they were functionally related to the traditional loading and unloading work performed by longshore workers. On the other hand, the practice of "short-stopping" (the loading and unloading of full shippers' loads) and certain warehousing practices were found to have an unlawful work acquisition objective, since these particular steps in the cargo-handling process no longer existed and the new container technology made the work of the longshore personnel wholly duplicative of the tasks performed by truckers and warehousers. *Longshoremen (ILA) (N.Y. Shipping Ass'n)*, 266 N.L.R.B. 230 (1983). On appeal, the Fourth Circuit rejected the Board's finding of any work acquisition objective with respect to these functions and sustained the ILA rules in their entirety. The Supreme Court affirmed the court's decision. *NLRB v. International Longshoremen's Ass'n*, 473 U.S. 61 (1985).

In *New York Shipping Ass'n v. FMC*, 854 F.2d 1338 (D.C. Cir. 1988), *cert. denied*, 488 U.S. 1041 (1989), the court sustained the authority of the Federal Maritime Commission to exclude labor policy considerations when it concluded that the "Rules on Containers" preserving the work of ILA members contravened shipping laws as being unreasonable and unjustly discriminatory vis-à-vis certain classes of shippers.

2. In *American Boiler Mfrs. Ass'n v. NLRB*, 404 F.2d 547 (8th Cir. 1968), *cert. denied*, 398 U.S. 960 (1970), *National Woodwork* was read as sustaining a "work re acquisition" clause. The employer argued unsuccessfully that the allowable preservation of "traditional work" encompassed only work that is "currently, continuously and exclusively performed by unit employees." *Compare Carrier Air Conditioning Co. v. NLRB*, 547 F.2d 1178 (2d Cir. 1976), *cert. denied*, 431 U.S. 974 (1977).

3. *Maui Trucking v. Operating Eng'rs Local 3*, 37 F.3d 436 (9th Cir. 1994), considered the legality of a contractual provision in an agreement between Local 3 and a general contractor association that specified the minimum wages and benefits that had to be paid to nonunion subcontractor employees performing off-site hauling work. The court indicated that this restriction would constitute a lawful primary work preservation clause if it was designed to protect the employment opportunities of general contractor employees, but would be an unlawful secondary provision if it preserved almost no general contractor jobs and was effectively designed to regulate the employment conditions of the nonunion subcontractors. *Compare Painters Dist. Council 51 (Manganaro Corp.)*, 321

N.L.R.B. 158 (1996) (anti-dual-shop or anti-double-breasting clause had work preservation as its objective, thus union could demand it in contract with drywall contractor whose parent had a nonunion subsidiary without violating hot-cargo ban of § 8(e)).

In *Marrowbone Dev. Co. v. Dist. 17*, 147 F.3d 296 (4th Cir. 1998), the court refused to enforce an arbitral award that required a coal mine operator to cease using subcontractors to transport and deliver materials at a mining complex, because that work had not been traditionally performed by bargaining unit members at the specific coal complex involved. As a result, the Court found that the national coal agreement provision being enforced constituted an illegal hot cargo clause as applied to this particular complex, because it was effectively designed to acquire—not to preserve—work for members of the bargaining unit that was directly affected.

4. *Application of Pipefitters' "Right to Control" Test.* In *Carpenters Local 742 (J.L. Simmons Co.),* 237 N.L.R.B. 564 (1978), on remand following the *Pipefitters* case, the Board held that a union whose members refused to install premachined doors in a hospital violated § 8(b)(4). Their employer did not have the right to control use of the doors, since they were provided for in the hospital's specifications. As a result, this work stoppage was not primary, but was designed to influence the hospital. Does it make any difference that the union's attorney suggested that the dispute might be resolved by the negotiation of a wage premium for each precut door installed? The Board held no; that is merely the substitution of one form of economic pressure for another for the same wrongful, secondary objective—to influence the hospital. Could the union legally demand, in the *next* collective bargaining agreement, that if the employer violates the work-preservation agreement, it will pay a premium in return for the union members handling the precut doors? Chairman Fanning added a caveat stating that he does not understand the *Simmons* case to decide that question. *See also Chamber of Commerce v. NLRB,* 574 F.2d 457 (9th Cir.), *cert. denied,* 439 U.S. 981 (1978).

United Scenic Artists, Local 829 v. NLRB, 762 F.2d 1027 (D.C. Cir. 1985), involved a dispute concerning the painting of scenery and props. Theatre Techniques, Inc. (TTI), which supplies theatrical settings for Broadway shows, had a subcontractual arrangement with Nolan Scenery Studios under which Nolan was to paint scenery and props provided by TTI. Nolan had a bargaining agreement with Local 829 which gave that union jurisdiction over the sculpting and painting of props. When some props arrived from TTI which had already been fabricated, Nolan employees refused to paint them. Although they ultimately agreed to paint those props, they charged Nolan a premium rate. Nolan never informed Local 829 that TTI had contractual control over the disputed work. The NLRB found a § 8(b)(4)(B) violation, even though the union's economic pressure had been directed at Nolan, since the Board presumed that a labor organization has an unlawful secondary objective whenever its conduct affects a neutral employer and it fails to demonstrate a "good faith belief" that the primary employer controls the disputed work. The D.C. Circuit reversed. It rejected the NLRB's presumption of unlawful motivation under such circumstances, holding instead that there must be proof to establish that the labor organization actually possessed the "specific intent" to coerce a neutral party before a § 8(b)(4)(B) violation can be sustained.

5. *See generally* Feldacker, *Subcontracting Restrictions and the Scope of § 8(b)(4)(A) and (B) and of § 8(e) of the NLRA,* 17 Lab. L.J. 170 (1966); Hickey, *Subcontracting Clauses Under § 8(e) of the NLRA,* 40 Notre Dame Law. 377 (1965); Lesnick, *Job Security and Secondary Boycotts: The Reach of NLRA §§ 8(b)(4) and 8(e),* 113 U. Pa. L. Rev. 1000 (1965); Comment, *Subcontracting Clauses and § 8(e) of the National Labor Relations Act,* 62 Mich. L. Rev. 1176 (1964); Comment, *Automation and the Work Preservation Doctrine: Accommodating Productivity and Job Security Interests,* 32 U.C.L.A. L. Rev. 135 (1984); Note, *Rational Approach to Secondary Boycotts and Work Preservation,* 57 Va. L. Rev. 1280 (1971); Leslie, *Right to Control: A Study in Secondary Boycotts and Labor Antitrust,* 89 Harv. L. Rev. 904 (1976).

G. DAMAGES FOR UNLAWFUL SECONDARY ACTIVITY

UNITED MINE WORKERS, DISTRICT 28 v. PATTON

United States Court of Appeals, Fourth Circuit
211 F.2d 742 (1954), *cert. denied,* 348 U.S. 824 (1954)

[Plaintiff was a partner in a mining operation in the coal fields of Western Virginia. The basis of the action was that the defendants by a strike at the mines of the Clinchfield Coal Corp. caused that corporation to cease doing business with plaintiff, resulting in the destruction of the partnership business. A jury in the trial court below awarded the partnership actual damages in the sum of $150,000 and punitive damages in the sum of $75,000 under the provisions of § 303 of the LMRA.]

PARKER, CHIEF JUDGE.... The chief argument of the defendants ... is that there is no evidence that they authorized or ratified the strikes upon which plaintiffs rely for recovery. It is true that there is no evidence of any resolution of either the United Mine Workers or District 28 authorizing or ratifying the strikes. There is evidence, however, that the strikes were called by the Field Representative of the United Mine Workers, who was employed by District 28, and that he was engaged in the organization work that was being carried on by the international union through District 28, which was a mere division of the international union....

Section 301(b) of the Labor Management Relations Act, 29 U.S.C. § 185 (b) expressly provides:

(b) Any labor organization which represents employees in an industry affecting commerce as defined in this chapter and any employer whose activities affect commerce as defined in this chapter shall be bound by the acts of its agents....

[S]ection 301(e), 61 Stat. 156, 157, 29 U.S.C. § 185(e) ... provides:

> For the purposes of this section, in determining whether any person is acting as an "agent" of another person so as to make such other person responsible for his acts, the question of whether the specific acts performed were actually authorized or subsequently ratified shall not be controlling....

In his analysis of the bill Senator Taft had the following to say, 93 Cong. Record, p. 7001, Legislative History of Labor Management Relations Act, Vol. 2, p. 1622:

> Section 2(2), 2(13), and 301(e):
>
> The conference agreement in defining the term employer struck out the vague phrase in the Wagner Act "anyone acting in the interest of an employer" and inserted in lieu thereof the word "agent." The term agent is defined in § 2(13) and § 301(e), since it is used throughout the unfair labor practice sections of title I and in §§ 301 and 303 of title III. In defining the term the conference amendment reads "the question of whether the specific acts performed were actually authorized or subsequently ratified shall not be controlling." This restores the law of agency as it has been developed at common law....

[W]e think there was error in allowing the jury to award punitive damages. This is not a case brought under the diversity jurisdiction of the federal courts to enforce a common law liability, where we are governed by state decisions and would be bound on the question of punitive damages by the decision of the Supreme Court of Appeals of Virginia in *United Constr. Workers v. Laburnum Constr. Corp., supra,* 194 Va. 872, 75 S.E.2d 694 (1953). There is no diversity of citizenship and the plaintiffs are entitled to invoke the jurisdiction of the federal courts only because they sue on a cause of action created by a federal statute, *i.e.,* on the cause of action created by § 303(b) of the Labor Management Relations Act, 29 U.S.C. § 187(b), heretofore quoted. That section makes no provision for the recovery of punitive damages; but on the contrary provides expressly that the aggrieved party "shall recover *the damages by him sustained* and the cost of the suit." (Italics supplied.) "Punitive damages are damages beyond and above the amount which a plaintiff has really suffered, and they are awarded upon the theory that they are a punishment to the defendant, and not a mere matter of compensation for injuries sustained by plaintiff." *Washington Gas Light Co. v. Lansden,* 172 U.S. 534, 553 (1899)....

In the absence of anything in the act itself or in its history indicating an intention on the part of Congress to authorize the recovery of punitive damages by this highly controversial legislation, the courts would not be justified, we think, in construing it to permit such recovery....

NOTES

1. *Punitive damages.* As indicated in the principal case, punitive damages cannot be awarded under § 303, but such damages may be granted under applicable state law. In *Teamsters Local 20 v. Morton,* 377 U.S. 252 (1964), however, the Court unanimously held that "state law has been displaced by § 303 in private damage actions based on peaceful union secondary activity." Consequently, the Court declared that "the district court was without authority to award punitive damages," or "damages proximately caused by unlawful, primary activities, even though the petitioner may have contemporaneously engaged in unlawful acts elsewhere."

UMW v. Gibbs, 383 U.S. 715 (1966), involved a mine superintendent who filed suit in federal district court seeking compensatory damages under § 303 and compensatory and punitive damages under a state common law claim. The district court found no violation of the Taft-Hartley Act, but, having taken "pendent" jurisdiction over the state law claim, awarded compensatory and punitive damages. The Supreme Court reversed. The state claim was not preempted, as it had been in *Morton,* because *Gibbs* involved violence, and federal labor law does not preempt state laws regulating violence. The district court properly exercised "pendent" jurisdiction over the state claim in the § 303 suit. Nonetheless, § 6 of the Norris-La Guardia Act applied to the suit in federal court on the state claim, and, under § 6, there was not clear proof of actual participation, authorization, or ratification of violence by the international union.

2. *Parties plaintiff under § 303.* Either primary or secondary employers may sue for damages under § 303. *United Brick & Clay Workers v. Deena Artware,* 198 F.2d 637 (6th Cir.), *cert. denied,* 344 U.S. 897 (1952) (primary); *ILA v. Allied Int'l, Inc.,* 456 U.S. 212 (1982) (secondary). In the *Allied* case, the plaintiff was an importer of timber whose business was totally disrupted when the ILA refused to unload a shipload of timber coming from the Soviet Union in order to protest the Russian invasion of Afghanistan. The Supreme Court held that the union had violated § 8(b)(4)(B) of the NLRA, which was aimed precisely at the sort of activity alleged. The union had no labor dispute with the importer, the shipper, or the stevedoring firm, all of which were neutral parties, and there is no exemption from § 8(b)(4)(B) for "political" boycotts.

Although the literal language of § 303(b) would appear to permit anyone even remotely injured by reason of an unlawful secondary boycott to sue for damages, courts have generally extended standing only to those parties foreseeably injured in a manner intended by the labor organization involved. "[T]here must have been some action by the defendant union against the plaintiff (or immediately affecting the plaintiff's property), which caused reasonably foreseeable injury to the plaintiff, and was a means by which the defendant sought to achieve an unlawful end." *Charvet v. Longshoremen's Ass'n,* 736 F.2d 1572 (D.C. Cir. 1984). Since there was no evidence to suggest that the boycotting union sought to injure the employees of the neutral company whose ships its members refused to unload, the court found that an employee of that employer lacked standing to sue the union for the economic losses she suffered when her boycotted employer abolished her job. *See also Fulton v. Plumbers & Steamfitters,* 695 F.2d 402 (9th Cir. 1982), *cert. denied,* 464 U.S. 913 (1983).

3. *Nature of the remedy.* Under § 303 a union may be sued for damages by a private party in federal district court for engaging in any of the kinds of activity defined in § 8(b)(4). This does not mean that the filing of a damage suit must await a final NLRB order stating that § 8(b)(4) was violated. An action may be brought under § 303 regardless of whether unfair practice charges are filed with the NLRB; or, if unfair practice charges have been filed with the NLRB, a damage suit may be brought at the same time. *Longshoremen's Union v. Juneau Spruce Corp.,* 342 U.S. 237 (1952). Damages have been awarded even though there has been a finding that no unfair labor practice was committed. *See United Brick & Clay Workers v. Deena Artware, supra.* However, in several cases, a final decision of the NLRB as to an unfair labor practice under § 8(b)(4) has been treated as res judicata or collateral estoppel in a subsequent § 303 action. *Paramount Transp. Sys. v. Teamsters Local 150,* 436 F.2d 1064 (9th Cir. 1971); *International Wire v. IBEW Local 38,* 475 F.2d 1078 (6th Cir.), *cert. denied,* 414 U.S. 867 (1973). *See* Note, *The Applicability of Res Judicata and Collateral Estoppel to Actions Brought Under Section 8(b)(4) of the National Labor Relations Act,* 67 Mich. L. Rev. 824 (1969).

In accordance with the standard American rule, § 303 does not authorize the awarding of attorney's fees to the winning party in § 8(b)(4) proceedings before the NLRB. *Summit Valley Indus. v. Carpenters Local 112,* 456 U.S. 717 (1982).

4. When meritorious § 8(b)(4) charges are filed with the NLRB, it is obliged to seek preliminary injunctive relief under § 10(1).

SECTION V. Jurisdictional Disputes

NLRB, THIRTY-SEVENTH ANNUAL REPORT 121 (1972)

Section 8(b)(4)(D) prohibits a labor organization from engaging in or inducing strike action for the purpose of forcing any employer to assign particular work to "employees in a particular labor organization or in a particular trade, craft, or class rather than to employees in another labor organization or in another trade, craft, or class, unless such employer is failing to conform to an order or certification of the Board determining the bargaining representative for employees performing such work."

An unfair labor practice charge under this section, however, must be handled differently from a charge alleging any other type of unfair labor practice. Section 10(k) requires that parties to a jurisdictional dispute be given 10 days, after notice of the filing of the charges with the Board, to adjust their dispute. If at the end of that time they are unable to "submit to the Board satisfactory evidence that they have adjusted, or agreed upon methods for the voluntary adjustment of the dispute," the Board is empowered to hear the dispute and make an affirmative assignment of the disputed work.

Section 10(k) further provides that pending 8(b)(4)(D) charges shall be dismissed where the Board's determination of the underlying dispute has been complied with, or the parties have voluntarily adjusted the dispute. An 8(b)(4)(D) complaint issues if the party charged fails to comply with the Board's determination. A complaint may be also issued by the General Counsel in the event recourse to the method agreed upon to adjust the dispute fails to result in an adjustment.

NLRB v. RADIO & TELEVISION BROADCAST ENGINEERS, LOCAL 1212 [CBS]

Supreme Court of the United States
364 U.S. 573, 81 S. Ct. 330, 5 L. Ed. 2d 302 (1961)

MR. JUSTICE BLACK delivered the opinion of the Court.

This case, in which the Court of Appeals refused to enforce a cease-and-desist order of the National Labor Relations Board, grew out of a "jurisdictional dispute" over work assignments between the respondent union, composed of television "technicians," and another union, composed of "stage employees." Both of these unions had collective bargaining agreements in force with the Columbia Broadcasting System and the respondent union was the certified bargaining agent for its members, but neither the certification nor the agreements clearly apportioned between the employees represented by the two unions the work of providing electric lighting for television shows. This led to constant disputes, extending over a number of years, as to the proper assignment of this work, disputes that were particularly acrimonious with reference to "remote lighting" that is, lighting for telecasts away from the home studio. Each union repeatedly urged Columbia to amend its bargaining agreement so as specifically to allocate remote lighting to its members rather than to members of the other union. But, as the Board found, Columbia refused to make such an agreement with either union because "the rival locals failed to agree on the resolution of this jurisdictional dispute over remote lighting." Thus feeling itself caught "between the devil and the deep blue," Columbia chose to divide the disputed work between the two unions according to criteria improvised apparently for the sole purpose of maintaining peace between the two. But, in trying to satisfy both of the unions, Columbia has apparently not succeeded in satisfying either. During the recent years, it has been forced to contend with work stoppages by each of the two unions when a particular assignment was made in favor of the other.

The precise occasion for the present controversy was the decision of Columbia to assign the lighting work for a major telecast from the Waldorf-Astoria Hotel in New York City to the stage employees. When the technicians' protest of this assignment proved unavailing, they refused to operate the cameras for the program and thus forced its cancellation. This caused Columbia to file the unfair labor practice charge which started these proceedings, claiming a violation of § 8(b)(4)(D) of the National Labor Relations Act. That section clearly makes it an unfair labor practice for a labor union to induce a strike or a concerted refusal to work in order to compel an employer to assign particular work to employees represented by it rather than to employees represented by another union, unless the employer's assignment is in violation of "an order or certification of the Board determining the bargaining representative for employees performing such work...." Obviously, if § 8(b)(4)(D) stood alone, what this union did in the absence of a Board order or certification entitling its members to be assigned to these particular jobs would be enough to support a finding of an unfair labor practice in a normal proceeding under § 10(c) of the act. But when Congress created this new type of unfair labor practice by enacting § 8(b)(4)(D) as part of the Taft-Hartley Act in 1947, it also added § 10(k) to the act. Section 10(k), set out below, quite plainly emphasizes the belief of Congress that it is more important to industrial peace that jurisdictional disputes be settled permanently than it is that unfair labor practice sanctions for jurisdictional strikes be imposed upon unions. Accordingly, § 10(k) offers strong inducements to quarrelling unions to settle their differences by directing dismissal of unfair labor practice charges upon voluntary adjustment of jurisdictional disputes. And even where no voluntary adjustment is made, "the Board is empowered and directed," by § 10(k), "to hear and determine the dispute out of which such unfair labor practice shall have arisen," and upon compliance by the disputants with the Board's decision the unfair labor practice charges must be dismissed.

In this case respondent failed to reach a voluntary agreement with the stage employees union so the Board held the § 10(k) hearing as required to "determine the dispute." The result of this hearing was a decision that the respondent union was not entitled to have the work assigned to its members because it had no right to it under either an outstanding Board order or certification, as provided in § 8(b)(4)(D), or a collective bargaining agreement.[12] The Board refused to con-

---

[12] This latter consideration was made necessary because the Board has adopted the position that jurisdictional strikes in support of contract rights do not constitute violations of § 8(b)(4)(D) despite the fact that the language of that section contains no provision for special treatment of such strikes. *See Fur Workers, Local 26,* 90 N.L.R.B. 1379. The Board has explained this position as resting upon the principle that "to fail to hold as controlling ... the contractual preemption of the work in dispute would be to encourage disregard for observance of binding obligations under collective

sider other criteria, such as the employer's prior practices and the custom of the industry, and also refused to make an affirmative award of the work between the employees represented by the two competing unions. The respondent union refused to comply with this decision, contending that the Board's conception of its duty to "determine the dispute" was too narrow in that this duty is not at all limited, as the Board would have it, to strictly legal considerations growing out of prior Board orders, certifications or collective bargaining agreements. It urged, instead, that the Board's duty was to make a final determination, binding on both unions, as to which of the two unions' members were entitled to do the remote lighting work, basing its determination on factors deemed important in arbitration proceedings, such as the nature of the work, the practices and customs of this and other companies and of these and other unions, and upon other factors deemed relevant by the Board in the light of its experience in the field of labor relations. On the basis of its decision in the § 10(k) proceeding and the union's challenge to the validity of that decision, the Board issued an order under § 10(c) directing the union to cease and desist from striking to compel Columbia to assign remote lighting work to its members. The Court of Appeals for the Second Circuit refused to enforce the cease-and-desist order, accepting the respondent's contention that the Board had failed to make the kind of determination that § 10(k) requires. The Third and Seventh Circuits have construed § 10(k) the same way, while the Fifth Circuit has agreed with the Board's narrower conception of its duties. Because of this conflict and the importance of this problem, we granted certiorari.

We agree with the Second, Third and Seventh Circuits that § 10(k) requires the Board to decide jurisdictional disputes on their merits and conclude that in this case that requirement means that the board should affirmatively have decided whether the technicians or the stage employees were entitled to the disputed work. The language of § 10(k), supplementing § 8(b)(4)(D) as it does, sets up a method adopted by Congress to try to get jurisdictional disputes settled. The words "hear and determine the dispute" convey not only the idea of hearing but also the idea of deciding a controversy. And the clause "the dispute out of which such unfair labor practice shall have arisen" can have no other meaning except a jurisdictional dispute under § 8(b)(4)(D) which is a dispute between two or more groups of employees over which is entitled to do certain work for an employer. To determine or settle the dispute as between them would normally require a decision that one or the other is entitled to do the work in dispute. Any decision short of that would obviously not be conducive to quieting a quarrel between two groups which, here as in most instances, is of so little interest to the employer that he seems perfectly willing to assign work to either if the other will just let him alone. This language also indicates a congressional purpose to have the Board do something more than merely look at prior Board orders and certifica-

---

bargaining agreements and invite the very jurisdictional disputes § 8(b)(4)(D) is intended to prevent." *National Ass'n of Broadcast Engineers* [105 N.L.R.B. 355], at 364.

tions or a collective bargaining contract to determine whether one or the other union has a clearly defined statutory or contractual right to have the employees it represents perform certain work tasks. For, in the vast majority of cases, such a narrow determination would leave the broader problem of work assignments in the hands of the employer, exactly where it was before the enactment of § 10(k)—with the same old basic jurisdictional dispute likely continuing to vex him, and the rival unions, short of striking, would still be free to adopt other forms of pressure upon the employer. The § 10(k) hearing would therefore accomplish little but a restoration of the pre-existing situation, a situation already found intolerable by Congress and by all parties concerned. If this newly granted Board power to hear and determine jurisdictional disputes had meant no more than that, Congress certainly would have achieved very little to solve the knotty problem of wasteful work stoppages due to such disputes.

This conclusion reached on the basis of the language of § 10(k) and § 8(b)(4)(D) is reinforced by reference to the history of those provisions. Prior to the enactment of the Taft-Hartley Act, labor, business and the public in general had for a long time joined in hopeful efforts to escape the disruptive consequences of jurisdictional disputes and resulting work stoppages. To this end unions had established union tribunals, employers had established employer tribunals, and both had set up joint tribunals to arbitrate such disputes. Each of these efforts had helped some but none had achieved complete success. The result was a continuing and widely expressed dissatisfaction with jurisdictional strikes. As one of the forerunners to these very provisions of the act, President Truman told the Congress in 1947 that disputes "involving the question which labor union is entitled to perform a particular task" should be settled, and that if the "rival unions are unable to settle such disputes themselves, provision must be made for peaceful and binding determination of the issues."[19] And the House Committee report on one of the proposals out of which these sections came recognized the necessity of enacting legislation to protect employers from being "the helpless victims of quarrels that do not concern them at all."[20]

The Taft-Hartley Act as originally offered contained only a section making jurisdictional strikes an unfair labor practice. Section 10(k) came into the measure as the result of an amendment offered by Senator Morse which, in its original form, proposed to supplement this blanket proscription by empowering and directing the Board either "to hear and determine the dispute out of which such unfair labor practice shall have arisen or to appoint an arbitrator to hear and determine such dispute...." That the purpose of this amendment was to set up machinery by which the underlying jurisdictional dispute would be settled is clear and, indeed, even the Board concedes this much. The authority to appoint an ar-

---

[19] 93 Cong. Rec. 136.
[20] H.R. Rep. No 245, 80th Cong., 1st Sess. 23, I Legislative History of the Labor Management Relations Act, 1947, at 314 (hereinafter cited as Leg. Hist.).

bitrator passed the Senate but was eliminated in conference, leaving it to the Board alone "to hear and determine" the underlying jurisdictional dispute. The Board's position is that this change can be interpreted as an indication that Congress decided against providing for the compulsory determination of jurisdictional disputes. We find this argument unpersuasive, to say the very least. The obvious effect of this change was simply to place the responsibility for compulsory determination of the dispute entirely on the Board, not to eliminate the requirement that there be such a compulsory determination. The Board's view of its powers thus has no more support in the history of § 10(k) than it has in the language of that section. Both show that the section was designed to provide precisely what the Board has disclaimed the power to provide—an effective compulsory method of getting rid of what were deemed to be the bad consequences of jurisdictional disputes.

The Board contends, however, that this interpretation of § 10(k) should be rejected, despite the language and history of that section. In support of this contention, it first points out that § 10(k) sets forth no standards to guide it in determining jurisdictional disputes on their merits. From this fact, the Board argues that § 8(b)(4)(D) makes the employer's assignment decisive unless he is at the time acting in violation of a Board order or certification and that the proper interpretation of § 10(k) must take account of this right of the employer. It is true, of course, that employers normally select and assign their own individual employees according to their best judgment. But here, as in most situations where jurisdictional strikes occur, the employer has contracted with two unions, both of which represent employees capable of doing the particular tasks involved. The result is that the employer has been placed in a situation where he finds it impossible to secure the benefits of stability from either of these contracts, not because he refuses to satisfy the unions, but because the situation is such that he cannot satisfy them. Thus, it is the employer here, probably more than anyone else, who has been and will be damaged by a failure of the Board to make the binding decision that the employer has not been able to make. We therefore are not impressed by the Board's solicitude for the employer's right to do that which he has not been, and most likely will not be, able to do. It is true that this forces the Board to exercise under § 10(k) powers which are broad and lacking in rigid standards to govern their application. But administrative agencies are frequently given rather loosely defined powers to cope with problems as difficult as those posed by jurisdictional disputes and strikes. It might have been better, as some persuasively argued in Congress, to intrust this matter to arbitrators. But Congress, after discussion and consideration, decided to intrust this decision to the Board. It has had long experience in hearing and disposing of similar labor problems. With this experience and a knowledge of the standards generally used by arbitrators, unions, employers, joint boards and others in wrestling with this problem, we are confident that the Board need not disclaim the power given it for lack of standards. Experience and common sense will supply the grounds for the perform-ance of this job which Congress has assigned the Board.

The Board also contends that respondent's interpretation of § 10(k) should be avoided because that interpretation completely vitiates the purpose of Congress to encourage the private settlement of jurisdictional disputes. This contention proceeds on the assumption that the parties to a dispute will have no incentive to reach a private settlement if they are permitted to adhere to their respective views until the matter is brought before the Board and then given the same opportunity to prevail which they would have had in a private settlement. Respondent dis-agrees with this contention and attacks the Board's assumption. We find it un-necessary to resolve this controversy for it turns upon the sort of policy determi-nation that must be regarded as implicitly settled by Congress when it chose to enact § 10(k). Even if Congress has chosen the wrong way to accomplish its aim, that choice is binding both upon the Board and upon this Court.

The Board's next contention is that respondent's interpretation of § 10(k) should be rejected because it is inconsistent with other provisions of the Taft-Hartley Act. The first such inconsistency urged is with §§ 8(a)(3) and 8(b)(2) of the act on the ground that the determination of jurisdictional disputes on their merits by the Board might somehow enable unions to compel employers to dis-criminate in regard to employment in order to encourage union membership. The argument here, which is based upon the fact that § 10(k), like § 8(b)(4)(D), ex-tends to jurisdictional disputes between unions and unorganized groups as well as to disputes between two or more unions, appears to be that groups represented by unions would almost always prevail over non-union groups in such a determina-tion because their claim to the work would probably have more basis in custom and tradition than that of unorganized groups. No such danger is present here, however, for both groups of employees are represented by unions. Moreover, we feel entirely confident that the Board, with its many years of experience in guarding against and redressing violations of §§ 8(a)(3) and 8(b)(2), will devise means of discharging its duties under § 10(k) in a manner entirely harmonious with those sections. A second inconsistency is urged with § 303(a)(4) of the Taft-Hartley Act, which authorizes suits for damages suffered because of jurisdic-tional strikes. The argument here is that since § 303(a)(4) does not permit a union to establish, as a defense to an action for damages under that section, that it is entitled to the work struck for on the basis of such factors as practice or custom, a similar result is required here in order to preserve "the substantive symmetry" between § 303(a)(4) on the one hand and §§ 8(b)(4)(D) and 10(k) on the other. This argument ignores the fact that this court has recognized the separate and distinct nature of these two approaches to the problem of handling jurisdictional strikes.[26] Since we do not require a "substantive symmetry" between the two, we

---

[26] *International Longshoremen v. Juneau Spruce Corp.*, 342 U.S. 237 (1957).

need not and do not decide what effect a decision of the Board under § 10(k) might have on actions under § 303(a)(4)....

We conclude therefore that the Board's interpretation of its duty under § 10(k) is wrong and that under that section it is the Board's responsibility and duty to decide which of two or more employee groups claiming the right to perform certain work tasks is right and then specifically to award such tasks in accordance with its decision. Having failed to meet that responsibility in this case, the Board could not properly proceed under § 10(c) to adjudicate the unfair labor practice charge. The Court of Appeals was therefore correct in refusing to enforce the order which resulted from that proceeding.

Affirmed.

NOTES

1. In *Transportation-Commun. Employees Union v. Union Pac. R.R.,* 385 U.S. 157 (1966), the Supreme Court directed the National Railroad Adjustment Board to resolve railroad work-assignment disputes on the merits. The TCEU (representing the telegraphers) complained to the NRAB that the railroad had given certain automated jobs to the clerks, claiming that the telegraphers were entitled to the work under their contract. The clerks' union, given notice, declined to participate, indicating their readiness to file another proceeding under their contract if the railroad took away their jobs. Without considering the clerks' contract, the NRAB held that the telegraphers were entitled to the work. The Supreme Court held that the NRAB must exercise its exclusive jurisdiction to settle the entire work-assignment dispute between the competing unions in one proceeding, considering both contracts and "usage, practice and custom." Mr. Justice Fortas and Chief Justice Warren dissented, urging that Congress had not assigned this function to the NRAB, as it had to the NLRB under § 10(k) of the Taft-Hartley Act, which has no counterpart in the Railway Labor Act.

2. The essence of a "jurisdictional dispute" within the meaning of §§ 8(b)(4)(D) and 10(k) is the existence of "a dispute between two or more groups of employees over which is entitled to do certain work for an employer." When one of two potentially competing labor organizations expressly disclaims interest in the work at issue, no jurisdictional dispute exists, and the Labor Board lacks the authority to conduct a § 10(k) proceeding or to find a § 8(b)(4)(D) violation. *See ILWU Local 62-B v. NLRB,* 781 F.2d 919 (D.C. Cir. 1986).

A jurisdictional dispute need not involve two competing unions. A union thus violated § 8(b)(4)(D) when it picketed an employer for assigning wood-chip loading work to its own nonunion employees rather than to union employees who had performed loading work for a separate company with which the employer was no longer dealing. *ILWU Local 14 v. NLRB,* 85 F.3d 646 (D.C. Cir. 1996).

3. A union that wins a § 10(k) award may use economic pressure to compel the employer's compliance without running afoul of § 8(b)(4)(D), but the union may not rely on § 8(a)(3) even if the employer succumbs to pressure from another union and discharges the winning union's members in order to assign their work to the other union's members. The Labor Board says it cannot "implement our 10(k) determinations via the 8(a)(3) route." *Brady-Hamilton Stevedore Co.,* 198 N.L.R.B. 147 (1972), *affirmed,* 504 F.2d 1222 (9th Cir. 1974).

4. In *ILWU Local 32 v. Pacific Maritime Ass'n,* 773 F.2d 1012 (9th Cir. 1985), *cert. denied,* 476 U.S. 1158 (1986), the court found that a union violated § 8(b)(4)(D) when, after it had lost a § 10(k) proceeding to another labor organization, it filed a § 301 suit seeking to enforce an arbitral award directing the employer to make "time-in-lieu" payments for the work it had lost, since such action was without merit in light of the NLRB's § 10(k) determination and constituted "coercion" within the meaning of § 8(b)(4)(D). *See also Longshoremen v. NLRB,* 884 F.2d 1407 (D.C. Cir. 1989) (filing of grievance contrary to prior § 10(k) award constitutes "coercion" under § 8(b)(4)(D)).

Compare the *ILWU Local 32* and *Longshoremen* decisions *with Miron Constr. Co. v. Operating Eng'rs Local 139,* 44 F.3d 558 (7th Cir.), *cert. denied,* 514 U.S. 1096 (1995), wherein the court indicated that the Operating Engineers Union that had lost a § 10(k) proceeding to the Laborers Union could lawfully seek arbitration of its claim that the employer had violated its collective contract with the Operating Engineers when it subcontracted work to a firm that had a contract with the Laborers Union. The court said that an arbitral award of back pay to the Operating Engineers Union would not be inconsistent with the NLRB's prior § 10(k) determination. *See also Laborers Dist. Council of Indiana (Capitol Drilling Supplies),* 318 N.L.R.B. 809 (1995), holding that a construction union's grievance alleging that a general contractor's subcontracting of certain work breached a lawful union-signatory subcontracting clause did not constitute a claim to the *subcontractor* for the work and was thus not a violation of § 8(b)(4)(D) in the absence of any strike, picketing, or other coercive action.

5. The Supreme Court held in *NLRB v. Plasterers Local 79,* 404 U.S. 116 (1971), that employers with substantial financial stakes in the outcome of § 10(k) proceedings are "parties to the dispute" within the meaning of the section. The NLRB is thus empowered to determine jurisdictional disputes under § 10(k), when only the competing unions, and not the interested employers, have agreed on a voluntary method of adjustment.

6. The factors the Board considers relevant in determining who is entitled to disputed work include: "the skills and work involved, certifications by the Board, company and industry practice, agreements between unions and between employers and unions, awards of arbitrators, joint boards, and the AFL-CIO in the same or related cases, the assignment made by the employer, and the efficient operation of the employer's business." *Machinists Lodge 1743 (J.A. Jones Constr. Co.),* 135 N.L.R.B. 1402, 1410-1411 (1962).

7. *See generally* Cohen, *The NLRB and Section 10(k): A Study of the Reluctant Dragon,* 14 Lab. L.J. 905 (1963); Hickey, *Government Regulation of Inter-Union*

Work Assignment Disputes, 16 S.C.L. Rev. 333 (1964); Leslie, *The Role of the NLRB and the Courts in Resolving Union Jurisdictional Disputes,* 75 Colum. L. Rev. 1470 (1975); O'Donoghue, *Jurisdictional Disputes in the Construction Industry Since "CBS,"* 52 Geo. L.J. 314 (1964); Player, *Work Assignment Disputes Under Section 10(k): Putting the Substantive Cart Before the Procedural Horse,* 52 Tex. L. Rev. 417 (1974); Sussman, *Section 10(k): Mandate for Change,* 47 B.U.L. Rev. 201 (1967).

SECTION VI. "Featherbedding"

AMERICAN NEWSPAPER PUBLISHERS ASS'N v. NLRB

Supreme Court of the United States
345 U.S. 100, 73 S. Ct. 552, 97 L. Ed: 852 (1953)

MR. JUSTICE BURTON delivered the opinion of the Court.

The question here is whether a labor organization engages in an unfair labor practice within the meaning of § 8(b)(6) of the National Labor Relations Act, as amended by the Labor Management Relations Act, 1947, when it insists that newspaper publishers pay printers for reproducing advertising matter for which the publishers ordinarily have no use. For the reasons hereafter stated, we hold that it does not....

When a newspaper advertisement was set up in type, it was impressed on a cardboard matrix, or "mat." These mats were used by their makers and also were reproduced and distributed, at little or no cost, to other publishers who used them as molds for metal castings from which to print the same advertisement. This procedure by-passed all compositors except those who made up the original form. Facing this loss of work, ITU secured the agreement of newspaper publishers to permit their respective compositors, at convenient times, to set up duplicate forms for all local advertisements in precisely the same manner as though the mat had not been used. For this reproduction work the printers received their regular pay. The doing of this "made work" came to be known in the trade as "setting bogus." It was a wasteful procedure. Nevertheless, it has become a recognized idiosyncrasy of the trade and a customary feature of the wage structure and work schedule of newspaper printers.... On rare occasions the reproduced compositions are used to print the advertisements when rerun, but, ordinarily, they are promptly consigned to the "hell box" and melted down.

However desirable the elimination of all industrial featherbedding practices may have appeared to Congress, the legislative history of the Taft-Hartley Act demonstrates that when the legislation was put in final form Congress decided to limit the practice but little by law.

A restraining influence throughout this congressional consideration of featherbedding was the fact that the constitutionality of the Lea Act penalizing featherbedding in the broadcasting industry was in litigation.... The case was pending here on appeal throughout the debate on the Taft-Hartley bill. Not until June 23, 1947, on the day of the passage of the Taft-Hartley bill over the President's veto, was the constitutionality of the Lea Act upheld. *United States v. Petrillo,* 332 U.S. 1 (1947).

The purpose of the sponsors of the Taft-Hartley bill to avoid the controversial features of the Lea Act is made clear in the written statement which Senator Taft, cosponsor of the bill and Chairman of the Senate Committee on Labor and Public Welfare, caused to be incorporated in the proceedings of the Senate, June 5, 1947. Referring to the substitution of § 8(b)(6) in place of the detailed featherbedding provisions of the House bill, that statement said:

> The provisions in the Lea Act from which the House language was taken are now awaiting determination by the Supreme Court, partly because of the problem arising from the term "in excess of the number of employees reasonably required." Therefore, the conferees were of the opinion that general legislation on the subject of featherbedding was not warranted at least until the joint study committee proposed by this bill could give full consideration to the matter. [93 Cong. Rec. 6443].

On the same day this was amplified in the Senator's oral statement on the floor of the Senate:

> There is one further provision which may possibly be of interest which was not in the Senate bill. The House had rather elaborate provisions prohibiting so-called featherbedding practices and making them unlawful labor practices. The Senate conferees, while not approving of featherbedding practices, felt that it was impracticable to give to a board or a court the power to say that so many men are all right, and so many men are too many. It would require a practical application of the law by the courts in hundreds of different industries, and a determination of facts which it seemed to me would be almost impossible. So we declined to adopt the provisions which are now in the Petrillo Act. After all, that statute applies to only one industry. Those provisions are now the subject of court procedure. Their constitutionality has been questioned. We thought that probably we had better wait and see what happened, in any event, even though we are in favor of prohibiting all featherbedding practices. However, we did accept one provision which makes it an unlawful labor practice for a union to accept money for people who do not work. That seemed to be a fairly clear case, easy to determine, and we accepted that additional unfair labor practice on the part of unions, which was not in the Senate bill.

93 Cong. Rec. 6441. *See also,* his supplementary analysis inserted in the Record June 12, 1947. 93 Cong. Rec. 6859.

As indicated above, the Taft-Hartley bill, H.R. 3020, when it passed in the House, April 17, 1947, contained in §§ 2(17) and 12(a)(3)(B) an explicit condemnation of featherbedding. Its definition of featherbedding was based upon that in the Lea Act. For example, it condemned practices which required an employer to employ "persons in excess of the number of employees reasonably required by such employer to perform actual services," as well as practices which required an employer to pay "for services ... which are not to be performed."

The substitution of the present § 8(b)(6) for that definition compels the conclusion that § 8(b)(6) means what the court below has said it means. The Act now limits it condemnation to instances where a labor organization or its agents exact pay from an employer in return for services not performed or not to be performed. Thus, where work is done by an employee, with the employer's consent, a labor organization's demand that the employee be compensated for time spent in doing the disputed work does not become an unfair labor practice. The transaction simply does not fall within the kind of featherbedding defined in the statute.... Section 8(b)(6) leaves to collective bargaining the determination of what, if any, work, including bona fide "made work," shall be included as compensable services and what rate of compensation shall be paid for it.

Accordingly, the judgment of the Court of Appeals sustaining dismissal of the complaint, insofar as it was based upon § 8(b)(6), is

Affirmed.

[The dissenting opinions of MR. JUSTICE DOUGLAS and MR. JUSTICE CLARK, with whom THE CHIEF JUSTICE joined, are omitted.]

————

NLRB v. Gamble Enterprises, 345 U.S. 117, 73 S. Ct. 560, 97 L. Ed. 864 (1953). The Musicians' Union refused to permit out-of-town orchestras to appear in respondent's theater unless it agreed to employ local musicians for a number of independent performances having a relation to the number of travelling band appearances. This and similar union proposals were declined by respondent on the ground that the local orchestra was neither necessary nor desired. Respondent sought a Board order based on § 8(b)(6). *Held:* "Since we and the Board treat the union's proposals as in good faith contemplating the performance of actual services, we agree that the union has not, on this record, engaged in a practice proscribed by § 8(b)(6). It has remained for respondent to accept or reject the union's offers on their merits in the light of all material circumstances. We do not find it necessary to determine also whether such offers were 'in the nature of an exaction.' We are not dealing here with offers of mere 'token' or nominal services. The proposals before us were appropriately treated by the Board as offers in good faith of substantial performances by competent musicians. There is no reason to think that sham can be substituted for substance under § 8(b)(6) any more than under any other statute. Payments for 'standing-by,' or for the substantial equivalent of 'standing-by,' are not payments for services performed, but when an employer receives a bona fide offer of competent performance of relevant services, it remains for the employer, through free and fair negotiation, to determine whether such offer shall be accepted and what compensation shall be paid for the work done." 345 U.S. at 123-24.

NOTES

1. What language would you devise to effectuate an appropriate public policy with respect to "featherbedding" in light of the experience under § 8(b)(6)?

2. For discussions of the "featherbedding" question, *see* Aaron, *Governmental Restraints of Featherbedding,* 5 Stan. L. Rev. 680 (1953); Daykin, *Featherbedding,* 7 Lab. L.J. 699 (1956); Edelman & Kovarsky, *Featherbedding: Law and Arbitration,* 10 Lab. L.J. 233 (1959); Van de Water, *A Fresh Look at Featherbedding,* 7 Baylor L. Rev. 138 (1955); Wood, *Wisdom of Outlawing Featherbedding,* 6 Lab. L.J. 821 (1955); Note, *Featherbedding and Taft-Hartley,* 52 Colum. L. Rev. 1020 (1952); Note, *Technological Change: Management Prerogative vs. Job Security,* 31 Ind. L.J. 389 (1956). *See also* Countryman, *The Organized Musicians,* 16 U. Chi. L. Rev. 56 (1948), 239 (1949).

SECTION VII. Emergency Disputes

A. INTRODUCTION

A basic tenet of national labor policy is that most disputes over the terms and conditions of employment should be settled through free collective bargaining. The possibility of a work stoppage encourages the parties to seek a mutually acceptable agreement. Such shutdowns as do occur—and the worker-days lost through strikes are always an extremely small percentage of total days worked—are generally regarded in peacetime as a reasonable price to pay for the advantages of industrial self-regulation.

The provision of mediation services is an important part of the national labor policy, the objective of mediation being to assist parties to achieve their own negotiated settlements.

There are some situations (not easily defined) in which the external impact of a work stoppage may be so great that further steps are considered necessary to protect the public interest. The dilemma is that these steps must be formulated in a way that preserves—not weakens—the basic social institution of collective bargaining.

The following material briefly describes our present laws governing such emergency disputes and various proposals that have been made to improve them.

B. NATIONAL EMERGENCY STRIKES UNDER THE LMRA

STATUTORY REFERENCES

LMRA §§ 206-10

Whenever in the opinion of the President there is an actual or threatened strike or lockout affecting all or a substantial part of an entire industry engaged in commerce which, if permitted to occur or continue, will constitute a threat to the national health or safety, the President may invoke the national emergency strike procedures contained in §§ 206 through 210 of the LMRA. In order to delay or suspend such strikes, the President may:

(i) appoint a board of inquiry to report without recommendation on the facts of the dispute;

(ii) on receipt of the board's report, order the Attorney General to seek a federal district court injunction restraining the strike;

(iii) if an injunction is issued, reconvene the board of inquiry which shall report on the current positions of the parties in the eventuality they do not reach an agreement within 60 days;

(iv) publish the board's second report, including the efforts that have been made toward settlement and the employer's last offer;

(v) within 15 days after publication of the board's second report, require the NLRB to conduct a strike vote to determine if the employees will accept the employer's last offer of settlement; and

(vi) if the strike vote rejects the employer's offer, the Attorney General must move to discharge the injunction within five days.

KLEILER, A LEGISLATIVE HISTORY OF THE NATIONAL EMERGENCY PROVISIONS, in EMERGENCY DISPUTES AND NATIONAL POLICY 91, 106-08 (I. Bernstein, H. Enarson & R. Fleming eds. 1955)*

The important fact about the legislative history is that the emergency provisions survived the Senate Committee and the Senate-House conference in almost the exact form that Senator Taft wanted. In his own committee and in the conference he made numerous compromises in other parts of the bill to gain support, but the emergency section of the law is almost pure Taft. To the extent that it provided for injunctions against strikes, this part of the bill was popular with an overwhelming majority in Congress; but the Taft concept of how to handle emergency disputes was far more sophisticated than that of the average injunction-minded legislator.

Senator Taft recognized that the injunctive process does not deal with the main causes of labor trouble. He regarded injunctions only as a device for enforced delay to give mediation, fact-finding, and energized public opinion an opportunity to produce a settlement. He wanted no recommendations from the fact-finding board simply because he believed that government boards with power to recommend settlements come dangerously close to compulsory arbitration. He opposed compulsory arbitration as vigorously as he opposed seizure. If compulsory arbitration were available as a routine remedy, Taft contended, there would always be pressure to resort to it by whichever party thought it would receive better treatment through such a process than it would receive in collective bargaining. If a national emergency dispute could not be settled during the delay process, Taft believed, then no authority lower than the Congress should deal with it. He felt strongly that if the safety and health of the people were finally threatened, an emergency law should be designed to deal with the particular emergency....

The record-breaking wave of large strikes created the need. The imminent expiration of wartime legislation made the need more imperative. The antilabor sentiment found in the 1946 election returns fixed the attitude. The distrust in Congress of the President eliminated any possibility of increasing the chief executive's authority to handle labor disputes.

Uniquely designed to emphasize the paramountcy of Congress over the President in emergencies while simultaneously providing a method for prompt government action to delay strikes, the virtues of the Taft bill were readily apparent. Not even the supporters of the Hartley bill were much dismayed when the House conferees went along with the Senate on the emergency provisions. As a product of its times, Senator Taft's proposal for handling the troublesome strike problem looked good enough to Congress, and Congress did not want to take the time to shop for anything better.

NOTES

1. The constitutionality of the Taft-Hartley Act national emergency dispute provisions was sustained by the Supreme Court in *United Steelworkers v. United States,* 361 U.S. 39 (1959).

For thorough critical examinations of the operation of the Taft-Hartley procedures, *see* Jones, *The National Emergency Disputes Provisions of the Taft-Hartley Act: A View From a Legislative Draftsman's Desk,* 17 Case W. Res. L. Rev. 133 (1965); Jones, *Toward a Definition of "National Emergency Dispute,"* 1971 Wis. L. Rev. 700; Rehmus, *The Operation of the National Emergency Provisions of the LMRA of 1947,* 62 Yale L.J. 1047 (1953).

2. Some use has been made of extra-statutory procedures. For example, President Truman used a fact-finding board that made recommendations in the steel dispute of 1949. Also, in the steel dispute of 1952, President Truman did not use the Taft-Hartley procedures, resorting instead to the use of the Wage Stabilization Board for recommendations, and ultimately to seizure. However, the Supreme Court held that the President had exceeded his powers in seizing the steel mills in the absence of legislative authorization. *Youngstown Sheet & Tube Co. v. Sawyer,* 343 U.S. 579 (1952).

3. Before issuing an injunction, the court must find that all or a substantial part of an industry engaged in commerce will be affected, and that the strike if permitted to occur or continue will endanger the national health or safety. It is not necessary, however, that there be a finding that the strike is industry-wide. *United States v. United Steelworkers,* 202 F.2d 132 (2d Cir.), *cert. denied,* 344 U.S. 915 (1953). In fact, a strike at a single plant that manufactures vital equipment for the atomic energy industry may threaten national health or safety. *United States v. American Locomotive Co.,* 109 F. Supp. 78 (W.D.N.Y. 1952), *affirmed,* 202 F.2d 132 (2d Cir. 1953).

4. Some of the criticisms that have been made regarding the Taft-Hartley emergency dispute procedures include the following: (a) the burden of the 80-day injunction falls too heavily on the workers, since they must continue to work under the existing working conditions; (b) the 80-day injunction merely delays the strike deadline date, and it is difficult to get the parties to engage in serious bargaining during this time period; (c) the ballot on the employer's last offer has proved to be futile, since the employees invariably vote to support their union's position, and this vote actually constitutes an obstacle to genuine bargaining near the end of the period; and (d) the board of inquiry, not being empowered to make recommendations, fails to serve its potentially most useful function—focusing public attention on and rallying public opinion pressure behind a basis for settlement. With respect to the last point, however, it may be observed that the emergency boards under the Railway Labor Act do make recommendations, and experience with them in recent years has not been particularly successful.

C. EMERGENCY RAILROAD AND AIRLINE DISPUTES

STATUTORY REFERENCES

RLA §§ 5, 6, 10

Under the Railway Labor Act (which applies to railroads and airlines) the procedure is as follows: (1) the parties are required to give 30 days' notice of an intended change in the existing agreement; (2) the National Mediation Board attempts to mediate the dispute; (3) if mediation fails, the NMB suggests voluntary arbitration; (4) if arbitration is declined, the NMB gives notice that its efforts have failed, and for 30 days thereafter no change may be made in rates of pay, rules, or working conditions; (5) if the NMB believes that the dispute "threatens substantially to interrupt interstate commerce to a degree such as to deprive any section of the country of essential transportation service," it notifies the President, who may appoint a board to investigate and report—with recommended settlement terms—within 30 days; and (6) after the creation of such a board and for 30 days after it has made its report to the President, no change may be made in existing conditions.

For many years, the Railway Labor Act procedures appeared to function quite effectively. Since World War II, however, the situation has progressively deteriorated. In the words of an emergency board in 1952: "[D]irect collective bargaining failed to settle a growing number of cases. More and more cases came to the Mediation Board. Mediation itself came to be increasingly difficult, except in the smaller cases. More and more Emergency Boards had to be appointed, mainly for the big national cases involving over-all wage rate, hours, and rules.... The term 'emergency,' in the sense of limitation to rare cases, was becoming outmoded. Nor were the recommendations of these Boards being accepted, if distasteful to the organization.... The post-recommendation strikes led to further government intervention—White House conferences...."

In 1963, 1967, 1970, 1971, 1991, and 1992 certain railroad labor disputes proved so intractable that the President found it necessary to request Congressional intervention through the enactment of special legislation that disposed of the particular disputes through binding determinations.

For an overall assessment of experience in the railroad and airline industries, *see* Cullen, *Emergency Boards Under the Railway Labor Act* and *Strike Experience Under the Railway Labor Act,* in The Railway Labor Act at Fifty (C. Rehmus, ed. 1976).

D. STATE EMERGENCY DISPUTE LEGISLATION

A number of states have enacted legislation placing limitations on strikes in public utilities or other essential industries. Those statutes prohibiting strikes and providing for systems of compulsory arbitration with respect to employers and employees subject to the National Labor Relations Act were invalidated on the ground of federal preemption in *Street, Elec. Ry. & Motor Coach Employees Div. 998 v. WERB,* 340 U.S. 383 (1951). *See also Street, Elec. Ry. & Motor Coach Employees, Div. 1287 v. Missouri,* 374 U.S. 74 (1963).

E. ALTERNATIVE APPROACHES AND PROPOSALS

WILLIAMS, SETTLEMENT OF LABOR DISPUTES IN INDUSTRIES AFFECTED WITH A NATIONAL INTEREST, 49 A.B.A. J. 862, 867-68 (1963)*

Critical labor disputes differ. Each has its own stumbling-blocks to settlement. The impact upon the public differs. Sometimes the public can tolerate a work stoppage for quite a while, even though in a critical industry. At other times a strike for one minute, as in the case of electric power, could be disastrous. These

---

considerations indicate that there should be a choice of procedures for use in resolving critical work stoppages.

There might well be concern that the choice-of-procedures approach leaves too much to the discretion of the President. But power must be lodged somewhere, and it cannot be lodged in a more responsible place than in the executive. To have these procedures available is not to give the President a bludgeon consisting of threats of many different kinds of procedures. The power should be given to the President, instead, because of the need for flexibility, since the disputes differ so much in their attributes.

Variety of Procedures Should Be Available

The remaining issue, is the nature of the procedures which should be available in handling critical labor disputes. Properly, the most usually recommended procedure is the development and refinement of the process of fact finding by an independent board, coupled with the additional power of that board to suggest terms of settlement. The theory is that there will be strong pressures upon the parties to settle in close conformity to the recommendations, if the recommendations are reasonable. Public opinion, reacting to a sensible proposal for settlement, could make it quite difficult for the parties to refuse to accept it.

One serious need is for the fact-finding boards to be activated before the emergency develops. The investigation should be made and the recommendation should be ready before the strike occurs. Earlier governmental intervention is receiving increasing acceptance, as is shown through its approval by the President's Labor-Management Committee. We should experiment with the operation of fact-finding boards, and the details need not be explored here.

From time to time the government has used the device of seizing businesses to bring about the end of critical strikes. But seizure as the sole governmental intervention disregards the rights of employees. It takes away the source of bargaining strength, the right to strike, and gives nothing to take its place. Seizure should be used only as an enforcement device to aid in effectively carrying out other procedures, such as fact finding with recommendations. Seizure was used merely as an enforcing device during World War II.

It is necessary to accept the need to have available additional means for governmental intervention more stringent than fact finding. There are some work stoppages in which, because of the nature of the goods withdrawn from the market, the public automatically opposes those who strike, regardless of the merits of the dispute. In these situations employers would be enabled effectively to hold out against any board-recommended settlement properly favorable to the workers. It follows that when necessary the government should have the power to introduce a fact-finding board's recommendations as the work conditions actually to be used for a temporary period. It is true this device would tend strongly to establish the recommended settlement as the final settlement of the dispute, since the parties would be forced to operate under these conditions for a time. Yet where the strike cannot be tolerated, some such procedure is justified. It must be stressed again that in this kind of situation collective bargaining in the usual sense cannot exist. Since it cannot, wages and working conditions must ultimately be established in another way if the parties fail to reach agreement under the threat of governmental intervention.

Compulsory Arbitration May Be Justified

Even the final step, so bitterly opposed both by management and labor, is justified by the analysis here set forth. The compulsory arbitration of wages and working conditions to settle a dispute in an industry in which a work stoppage would be disastrous to the national interest is a proper procedure to have available. We used compulsory arbitration in wartime because we could not tolerate strikes. It needs to be an available ultimate weapon in those instances in which the right to strike simply cannot exist.

Compulsory settlement procedures should not ever be the only available procedures in a given industry, no matter how critical. Often mechanisms short of compulsory settlement could bring the parties to a resolution of the labor dispute. It must be frankly realized that the availability and use of compulsory arbitration tends seriously to weaken bargaining; the party most likely to benefit from a forced settlement may negotiate only perfunctorily. But the premise here stated is that at least sometimes there cannot be a right to strike. When this is so, bargaining is not available as the ultimate solution to the dispute, and the fact that compulsory settlement seriously weakens the bargaining does not outweigh the necessity that a means of settlement without stoppage must be ready for use, although only in the most extreme situations. If the right to strike is gone, something else must take its place.

The most common objection stated both to compulsory arbitration and to fact finding with recommendations is that they put the government in the business of fixing wages, leading inevitably to a managed economy. We already have enough experience to show that this is not necessarily so. We have had a number of past instances of fact finding with recommendations forming the basis of settlement. There is a clear distinction to be made. The wage settlement proposed with regularity by a government agency is a far greater intrusion by the government than is the recommendation of an *ad hoc* fact-finding board or board of arbitration which has been chosen to bring about settlement of one particular dispute. Insofar as the independent board can approximate the settlement that the parties themselves would have reached if the strike had been allowed to run its course, the settlement has no more effect upon the economy than would the settlement of the parties themselves. Of course, just what the settlement of the parties would have been can never be known exactly. But there is enough experience with collective bargaining settlements and voluntary arbitrations of wage disputes to know that, given the facts, the economic pattern which should be followed can be ascertained.

Collective Bargaining Is Absolute Requisite

The key to the resolution of the emergency dispute problem is therefore revealed. The matter of pressure in settlements by governmental intervention through emergency-dispute processes will not disrupt the role of collective bargaining so long as the settlements brought about follow collective bargaining patterns rather than establish them. The maintaining and strengthening of effective collective bargaining then becomes the absolute requisite to the keeping of emergency procedures in narrow bounds. If the basic labor-cost decisions in the American economy are made by collective bargaining, we have little to fear from the occasional emergency settlement dictated by *ad hoc* governmental intervention. The dictated settlements can follow the pattern established by bargaining.

So it is that the newly awakened emphasis on improving collective bargaining is as significant a part of the solution to the emergency strike problem as are the techniques for dealing with such strikes. Governmental intervention in emergency work stoppages need not bring about governmental management of the economic bargains in our society if collective bargaining is strengthened to maintain its proper role in making these economic decisions.

We must endeavor to reach this balanced approach. Realistically speaking, we cannot continue to hold a false belief that the right to strike is unlimited. We cannot insist that all bargains must be made through the collective bargaining process. We can and must make every effort to hone the keen edge of collective bargaining so that it is an effective tool in all but the very hardest of cases. But we must be courageous enough to handle the hardest cases another way.

The alternative is facing the resolution of each crisis after the crisis occurs. Drastic measures which will destroy the process of collective bargaining seem the inevitable outgrowth of such a passive approach when the spectrum of the kinds of crises which can arise is viewed. Advance preparation for emergencies by creating the structures to meet them is needed to preserve our economic freedom. Freedom does not flourish in chaos, but in enlightened order.

NOTES

1. For other expositions of the "choice of procedures" or "arsenal of weapons" approach, *see* A. Cox, Law and the National Labor Policy (1960); Fleming, *Emergency Strikes and National Policy,* 11 Lab. L.J. 267, 336 (1960); Wirtz, *The "Choice of Procedures" Approach to National Emergency Disputes,* in Emergency Disputes and National Policy (I. Bernstein, H. Enarson & R. Fleming eds. 1955).

Problems attendant upon seizure are discussed in Cox, *Seizure in Emergency Disputes,* in Emergency Disputes and National Policy, *supra,* and in Teller, *Government Seizure in Labor Disputes,* 60 Harv. L. Rev. 1017 (1947).

Compulsory arbitration is analyzed in Jones, Farmer & Feller, *Compulsory Arbitration: Three Views,* 51 Va. L. Rev. 369, 396, 410 (1965) (three separate papers). *See also* Aaron, Landis & Katz, *Emergency Dispute Settlement,* in Southwestern Legal Foundation, Labor Law Developments 1967, Proceedings of the 13th Annual Institute on Labor Law 185, 209, 223 (1967) (three separate papers).

New approaches to "creative bargaining" are summarized by Wirtz, *The Challenge to Free Collective Bargaining,* in Labor Arbitration and Industrial Change, Proceedings of the 16th Annual Meeting, National Academy of Arbitrators 297 (1963).

2. Would it be possible to establish a "non-stoppage strike" alternative during which operations would continue as usual? Once such a job action has been declared, workers would have their wages reduced by a set amount, and their employer would have its gross earnings reduced by a similar amount, until the impasse was resolved. It might also be possible to create a "graduated strike" during which employees would only cease to work certain portions of the week. *See generally* Marceau & Musgrave, *Strikes in Essential Industries: A Way Out,* 27 Harv. Bus. Rev. 287 (1949); Goble, *The Non-Stoppage Strike,* 2 Lab. L.J. 105 (1951); McCalmont, *The Semi-Strike,* 15 Ind. & Lab. Rel. Rev. 191 (1962); Marshall & Marshall, *Nonstoppage Strike Proposals—A Critique,* 7 Lab. L.J. 299 (1956). *See also* Bernstein, *Alternatives to the Strike in Public Labor Relations,* 85 Harv. L. Rev. 459 (1971).

SECTION VIII. National Labor Relations Act Preemption

To what extent does federal labor legislation "preempt" the regulatory power of the states? This perplexing and persistent question has produced numerous decisions by the United States Supreme Court since 1945.

All of the following materials on federal preemption are concerned with industries "affecting commerce." In those small and local trades in which there is no direct or indirect connection with interstate commerce, state power remains unaffected by the federal preemption doctrine.

Ever since its original enactment, the National Labor Relations Act has provided in § 10(a) that the NLRB may, by agreement, cede to a state agency jurisdiction over labor disputes affecting commerce unless the applicable state statute "is inconsistent with the corresponding provision of this act or has received a construction inconsistent therewith." No cession agreements are currently in effect.

The "No-Man's-Land" and the 1959 Amendments. The Supreme Court in *Guss v. Utah Labor Relations Bd.,* 353 U.S. 1 (1957), created a legal "no-man's-land" by holding that the states were preempted from acting with respect to parties that "affected" commerce but over which the NLRB declined to exercise jurisdiction. Although the NLRB expanded its jurisdictional standards in 1958, this was only a partial solution, since about four-fifths of the cases previously consigned to the "no-man's-land" still remained there.

Congress considered several alternative proposals during its deliberations on the 1959 amendments to the NLRA. Section 14(c), which was enacted, permits states to assert jurisdiction when the Labor Board declines. It also provides, however, that the NLRB may not narrow its jurisdiction beyond the point set by the discretionary standards in effect on August 1, 1959. The bill did not say whether the states were to apply federal or state law, but Senator Kennedy, the conference chairman, was more explicit: "It was the opinion of the Senate that the Federal law should prevail with respect to interstate commerce, and, in order to compromise that feature, it was agreed that State law could prevail, but only in those areas in which the National Labor Relations Board does not now assume jurisdiction." 105 Cong. Rec. 17720 (1959). State courts have generally assumed that local law is applicable. *See, e.g., Cooper v. Nutley Sun Printing Co.,* 36 N.J. 189, 175 A.2d 639 (1961); *Kempf v. Carpenters Local 1273,* 229 Or. 337, 367 P.2d 436 (1961).

SAN DIEGO BUILDING TRADES COUNCIL v. GARMON

Supreme Court of the United States
359 U.S. 236, 79 S. Ct. 773, 3 L. Ed. 2d 775 (1959)

[In the *Garmon* case, which has become the leading case setting out the general principles of federal preemption, the issue on certiorari was whether the State of California had jurisdiction to award damages for a tort under state law against a union for engaging in peaceful picketing. The purpose of the picketing was in dispute, the union claiming that the only purpose was to educate the workers and persuade them to become members and the employer claiming that the sole purpose was to compel the employer to execute a union shop agreement.]

MR. JUSTICE FRANKFURTER delivered the opinion of the Court ....

Administration is more than a means of regulation; administration is regulation. We have been concerned with conflict in its broadest sense; conflict with a complex and interrelated federal scheme of law, remedy, and administration. Thus, judicial concern has necessarily focused on the nature of the activities which the States have sought to regulate, rather than on the method of regulation adopted. When the exercise of state power over a particular area of activity threatened interference with the clearly indicated policy of industrial relations, it has been judicially necessary to preclude the States from acting. However, due regard for the presuppositions of our embracing federal system, including the principle of diffusion of power not as a matter of doctrinaire localism but as a promoter of democracy, has required us not to find withdrawal from the States of power to regulate where the activity regulated was a merely peripheral concern of the Labor Management Relations Act. *See IAM v. Gonzales,* 356 U.S. 617 (1958). Or where the regulated conduct touched interests so deeply rooted in local feeling and responsibility that, in the absence of compelling congressional direction, we could not infer that Congress had deprived the States of the power to act.

When it is clear or may fairly be assumed that the activities which a State purports to regulate are protected by § 7 of the Taft-Hartley Act, or constitute an unfair labor practice under § 8, due regard for the federal enactment requires that state jurisdiction must yield. To leave the States free to regulate conduct so plainly within the central aim of federal regulation involves too great a danger of conflict between power asserted by Congress and requirements imposed by state law. Nor has it mattered whether the States have acted through laws of broad general application rather than laws specifically directed towards the governance of industrial relations. Regardless of the mode adopted, to allow the States to control conduct which is the subject of national regulation would create potential frustration of national purposes.

At times it has not been clear whether the particular activity regulated by the states was governed by § 7 or § 8 or was, perhaps, outside both these sections. But courts are not primary tribunals to adjudicate such issues. It is essential to the administration of the Act that these determinations be left in the first instance to the National Labor Relations Board. What is outside the scope of this Court's authority cannot remain within a State's power and state jurisdiction too must yield to the exclusive primary competence of the Board. *See, e.g., Garner v. Teamsters,* 346 U.S. 485 (1953), especially at 489-491; *Weber v. Anheuser-Busch, Inc.,* 348 U.S. 468 (1955).

The case before us is such a case. The adjudication in California has throughout been based on the assumption that the behavior of the petitioning unions constituted an unfair labor practice. This conclusion was derived by the California courts from the facts as well as from their view of the Act. It is not for us to decide whether the National Labor Relations Board would have, or should have, decided these questions in the same manner. When an activity is arguably subject to § 7 or § 8 of the Act, the States as well as the federal courts must defer to the exclusive competence of the National Labor Relations Board if the danger of state interference with national policy is to be averted.

To require the States to yield to the primary jurisdiction of the National Board does not ensure Board adjudication of the status of a disputed activity. If the Board decides, subject to appropriate federal judicial review, that conduct is protected by § 7, or prohibited by § 8, then the matter is at an end, and the States are ousted of all jurisdiction. Or the Board may decide that an activity is neither protected nor prohibited, and thereby raise the question whether such activity may be regulated by the States[4] .... In the absence of the Board's clear determination that an activity is neither protected nor prohibited or of compelling precedent applied to essentially undisputed facts, it is not for this Court to decide whether such activities are subject to state jurisdiction....The governing consideration is that to allow the States to control activities that are potentially subject to federal regulation involves too great a danger of conflict with national labor policy.[5]

In the light of these principles the case before us is clear. Since the National Labor Relations Board has not adjudicated the status of the conduct for which the State of California seeks to give a remedy in damages, and since such activity is arguably within the compass of § 7 or § 8 of the Act, the State's jurisdiction is displaced.

Nor is it significant that California asserted its power to give damages rather than to enjoin what the Board may restrain though it could not compensate. Our concern is with delimiting areas of conduct which must be free from state regulation if national policy is to be left unhampered. Such regulation can be as effectively exerted through an award of damages as through some form of preventive relief. The obligation to pay compensation can be, indeed is designed to be, a potent method of governing conduct and controlling policy. Even the States' salutary effort to redress private wrongs or grant compensation for past harm cannot be exerted to regulate activities that are potentially subject to the exclusive federal regulatory scheme. *See Garner v. Teamsters,* 346 U.S. 485, 492-497 (1953). It may be that an award of damages in a particular situation will not, in fact, conflict with the active assertion of federal authority. The same may be true of the incidence of a particular state injunction. To sanction either involves a conflict with federal policy in that it involves allowing two law-making sources to govern. In fact, since remedies form an ingredient of any integrated scheme of regulation, to allow the State to grant a remedy here which has been withheld from the National Labor Relations Board only accentuates the danger of conflict.

It is true that we have allowed the States to grant compensation for the consequences, as defined by the traditional law of torts, of conduct marked by violence and imminent threats to the public order. *UAW v. Russell,* 356 U.S. 634 (1958); *United Constr. Workers v. Laburnum,* 347 U.S. 656 (1954). We have also allowed the States to enjoin such conduct. *Youngdahl v. Rainfair,* 355 U.S. 131 (1957); *UAW v. WERB,* 351 U.S. 266 (1956). State jurisdiction has prevailed in these situations because the compelling state interest, in the scheme of our feder-

---

[4] *See UAW v. WERB,* 336 U.S. 245 (1949). The approach taken in that case, in which the Court undertook for itself to determine the status of the disputed activity, has not been followed in later decisions, and is no longer of general application.

[5] "When Congress has taken the particular subject matter in hand coincidence is as ineffective as opposition ...." *Charleston & West. Carolina R. Co. v. Varnville Furniture Co.,* 237 U.S. 597, 601 (1915).

alism, in the maintenance of domestic peace is not overridden in the absence of clearly expressed congressional direction. We recognize that the opinion in *United Constr. Workers v. Laburnum*, 347 U.S. 656 (1954), found support in the fact that the state remedy had no federal counterpart. But that decision was determined, as is demonstrated by the question to which review was restricted by the "type of conduct" involved, *i.e.*, "intimidation and threats of violence." In the present case there is no such compelling state interest.

[The concurring opinion of MR. JUSTICE HARLAN, with whom JUSTICES CLARK, WHITTAKER, and STEWART joined, is omitted.]

NOTES

1. Under the "federal supremacy" clause of Article VI of the U.S. Constitution, it is clear that a state prohibition or limitation that is in conflict with a federally protected right is preempted. For example, the Supreme Court has struck down a number of state laws limiting the right to strike on the part of the employees of privately owned utilities. *UAW v. O'Brien*, 339 U.S. 454 (1950); *Street, Elec. Ry. & Motor Coach Emps., Div. 998 v. WERB*, 340 U.S. 383 (1951); *Street Elec. Ry. & Motor Coach Emps., Div. 1287 v. Missouri*, 374 U.S. 74 (1963) (statute forbidding strikes after seizure by the state).

2. Employees of a state-owned railroad enjoy the right to strike under the federal Railway Labor Act, despite a state law prohibiting strikes by public employees. Operation of a railroad, declared the Supreme Court, is not one of the traditional functions of state governments that are generally immune from federal regulation by virtue of the tenth amendment. "Federal regulation of state-owned railroads simply does not impair a state's ability to function as a state." *United Transp. Union v. Long Island R.R.*, 455 U.S. 678, 686 (1982).

3. *Scope and Review of State Court Injunctions.* In *Youngdahl v. Rainfair, Inc.*, 355 U.S. 131 (1957), the Supreme Court held that a state may enjoin threats of violence, obstruction of the streets and of entrances to a plant, and massed namecalling, calculated to provoke violence, but the state may not simultaneously enjoin other picketing at the plant, because regulation of peaceful picketing is within the exclusive domain of the NLRB.

When a state court issues an injunction against union collective action that appears to be within the exclusive jurisdiction of NLRB, a federal court will not entertain a union petition to enjoin enforcement of that state court injunction, since under 28 U.S.C. § 2283, "a court of the United States may not grant an injunction to stay proceedings in a State court except as expressly authorized by Act of Congress, or where necessary in aid of its jurisdiction, or to protect or effectuate its judgments." *Amalgamated Clothing Workers v. Richman Bros.*, 348 U.S. 511 (1955). The union must ordinarily appeal the injunctive order to the highest state court and then to the United States Supreme Court. A union's burden in contesting a state court injunction has been considerably eased, however, by Supreme Court decisions modifying the general rule as follows:

a. If an unfair labor practice charge has been filed with the NLRB and the Board has sought a federal court injunction, the federal court, "in aid of its jurisdiction," may enjoin the enforcement of the state court injunction. *Capital Serv. v. NLRB,* 347 U.S. 501 (1954). Even in the absence of unfair labor practice charges, the NLRB may seek federal injunctive relief against preempted state court action. In *NLRB v. Nash-Finch Co.,* 404 U.S. 138 (1971), the Supreme Court sustained the power of the Board to ask a federal court to enjoin a state court injunction against peaceful picketing, despite the prohibition of 28 U.S.C. § 2283 against federal injunctions to stay state court proceedings and the failure of the affected company to file § 8(b)(4) or § 8(b)(7) charges against the union. Since the Board had no basis for requesting a § 10(j) or § 10(*l*) injunction, the express exception in § 2283 permitting a federal court to enjoin state proceedings "in aid of its jurisdiction" was not applicable. But in order "to prevent frustration of the policies of the Act," the Board was found to have "implied authority," as a federal agency, "to enjoin state action where its federal power preempts the field."

b. The United States Supreme Court has jurisdiction to review a state supreme court's authorization of a *temporary* injunction in a controversy within the exclusive competence of the NLRB, even though the Supreme Court's jurisdiction is limited to the review of "final" judgments of state courts under 28 U.S.C. § 1257. *Construction & Gen. Laborers, Local 438 v. Curry,* 371 U.S. 542 (1963). "The truth is that authorizing the issuance of a temporary injunction, as is frequently true of temporary injunctions in labor disputes, may effectively dispose of petitioner's rights and render entirely illusory his right to review here as well as his right to a hearing before the Labor Board."

c. *ILA v. Davis,* 476 U.S. 380 (1986), held that since a preemption claim challenges the actual power of a state court to hear a particular case, that jurisdictional question must be resolved according to federal—not state—law. The Court thus rejected a state court attempt to treat a preemption issue as an "affirmative defense" that could be waived if not raised in a timely fashion.

d. The Supreme Court is not bound by a state court's ruling that a case has been rendered moot by the completion of the job that was the object of the picketing, since "the question of mootness is itself a question of federal law upon which we must pronounce final judgment." *Liner v. Jafco, Inc.,* 375 U.S. 301 (1964). *See also Allee v. Medrano,* 416 U.S. 802 (U.S. 1974).

e. A state court has no power to hold a person in contempt for violating an injunction entered by a court lacking jurisdiction because of federal preemption. It is a denial of due process to convict someone of contempt without giving the person an opportunity to establish that the state court was trenching on exclusive federal domain. *In re Green,* 369 U.S. 689 (1962). *See also Ex parte George,* 371 U.S. 72 (1962). *Compare United States v. United Mine Workers,* 330 U.S. 258

(1947) (a state court may issue a temporary injunctive order that must be obeyed while it determines whether it possesses jurisdiction over the underlying controversy).

AMALGAMATED ASS'N OF STREET, ELECTRIC RAILWAY & MOTOR COACH EMPLOYEES OF AMERICA v. LOCKRIDGE

Supreme Court of the United States
403 U.S. 274, 91 S. Ct. 1909, 29 L. Ed. 2d 473 (1971)

[Lockridge was employed by Greyhound Lines under a collective contract that contained a union security clause. The union constitution had conflicting provisions regarding the status of members who failed to tender their dues in a timely manner. One stated that members one month behind were debarred from benefits, with persons two months in arrears being suspended from membership. Another provision said that members working in shops covered by union security clauses shall be suspended from membership and terminated from employment if they fell one month behind. The union had not previously sought the discharge of delinquent members until they were two months in arrears. Nonetheless, after Lockridge fell one month behind, the union sought and obtained his termination. He then sued the union in state court, claiming that it had violated an implied promise not to seek the termination of members who were only one month in arrears. Lockridge obtained a judgment for $32,678.56 against the union on a breach of contract theory. The question whether the union had properly sought his job termination involved interpretation of both the union constitution and the collective bargaining agreement. The Supreme Court reversed the judgment on the basis of federal preemption, and the Court's opinion explains more fully the rationale of *Garmon.*]

MR. JUSTICE HARLAN delivered the opinion of the Court....

II

A.... [I]n *San Diego Building Trades Council v. Garmon,* 359 U.S. 236, 245 (1959), we held that the National Labor Relations Act preempts the jurisdiction of state and federal courts to regulate conduct "arguably subject to § 7 or § 8 of the Act." On their face, [§§ 8(b)(2), 8(b)(1)(A), and 8(a)(3)] of the Act at least arguably either permit or forbid the union conduct dealt with by the judgment below. For the evident thrust of this aspect of the federal statutory scheme is to permit the enforcement of union security clauses, by dismissal from employment, only for failure to pay dues. Whatever other sanctions may be employed to exact compliance with those internal union rules unrelated to dues payment, the Act seems generally to exclude dismissal from employment. *See Radio Officers' Union v. National Labor Relations Bd.,* 347 U.S. 17 (1954). Indeed, in the course of rejecting petitioner's preemption argument, the Idaho Supreme Court stated that, in its opinion, the Union "did most certainly violate 8(b)(1)(A), did most certainly violate 8(b)(2) ... and probably caused the employer to violate 8(a)(3)." 93 Idaho at 299, 460 P.2d at 724. Thus, given the broad preemption principle enunciated in *Garmon,* the want of state court power to resolve Lockridge's complaint might well seem to follow as a matter of course.

The Idaho Supreme Court, however, concluded that it nevertheless possessed jurisdiction in these circumstances. That determination, as we understand it, rested upon three separate propositions; all of which are urged here by respondent. The first is that the Union's conduct was not only an unfair labor practice, but a breach of its contract with Lockridge as well. "Preemption is not established simply by showing that the same facts will establish two different legal wrongs." 93 Idaho at 300, 460 P.2d at 725. In other words *Garmon,* the state court and respondent assert, states a principle applicable only where the state law invoked is designed specifically to regulate labor relations; it has no force where the State applies its general common law of contracts to resolve disputes between a union and its members. Secondly, it is urged that the facts that might be shown to vindicate Lockridge's claim in the Idaho state courts differ from those relevant to proceedings governed by the National Labor Relations Act. It is said that the conduct regulated by the Act is union and employer discrimination; general contract law takes into account only the correctness of competing interpretations of the language embodied in agreements. 93 Idaho at 303-304, 460 P.2d at 728-729. Finally, there recurs throughout the state court opinion, and the arguments of respondent here, the theme that the facts of the instant case render it virtually indistinguishable from *Association of Machinists v. Gonzales,* 356 U.S. 617 (1959), where this Court upheld the exercise of state court jurisdiction in an opinion written only one Term prior to *Garmon* by the author of *Garmon* and which was approvingly cited in the *Garmon* opinion itself.

We do not believe that any of these arguments suffice to overcome the plain purport of *Garmon* as applied to the facts of this case. However, we have determined to treat these considerations at some length because of the understandable confusion, perhaps in a measure attributable to the previous opinions of this Court, they reflect over the jurisprudential bases upon which the *Garmon* doctrine rests.

B. The constitutional principles of preemption, in whatever particular field of law they operate, are designed with a common end in view: to avoid conflicting regulation of conduct by various official bodies which might have some authority over the subject matter. A full understanding of the particular preemption rule set forth in *Garmon* especially requires, we think, appreciation of the precise nature and extent of the potential for injurious conflict that would inhere in a system unaffected by such a doctrine, and also the setting in which the general problem of accommodating conflicting claims of competence to resolve disputes touching upon labor relations has been presented to this Court....

The rationale for preemption, then, rests in large measure upon our determination that when it set down a federal labor policy Congress plainly meant to do more than simply to alter the then prevailing substantive law. It sought as well to restructure fundamentally the processes for effectuating that policy, deliberately placing the responsibility for applying and developing this comprehensive legal system in the hands of an expert administrative body rather than the federalized judicial system. Thus, that a local court, while adjudicating a labor dispute also within the jurisdiction of the NLRB, may purport to apply legal rules identical to those prescribed in the federal Act or may eschew the authority to define or apply principles specifically developed to regulate labor relations does not mean that all relevant potential for debilitating conflict is absent.

A second factor that has played an important role in our shaping of the preemption doctrine has been the necessity to act without specific congressional direction. The precise extent to which state law must be displaced to achieve those unifying ends sought by the national legislature has never been determined by the Congress. This has, quite frankly, left the Court with few available options. We cannot declare preempted all local regulation that touches or concerns in any way the complex interrelationships between employees, employers, and unions; obviously, much of this is left to the States. Nor can we proceed on a case-by-case basis to determine whether each particular final judicial pronouncement does, or might reasonably be thought to, conflict in some relevant manner with federal labor policy. This Court is ill-equipped to play such a role and the federal system dictates that this problem be solved with a rule capable of relatively easy application, so that lower courts may largely police themselves in this regard. Equally important, such a principle would fail to take account of the fact, as discussed above, that simple congruity of legal rules does not, in this area, prove the absence of untenable conflict. Further, it is surely not possible for this Court to treat the National Labor Relations Act section by section, committing enforcement of some of its provisions wholly to the NLRB and others to the concurrent domain of local law. Nothing in the language or underlying purposes of the Act suggests any basis for such distinctions. Finally, treating differently judicial power to deal with conduct protected by the Act from that prohibited by it would likewise be unsatisfactory. Both areas equally involve conduct whose legality is governed by federal law, the application of which Congress committed to the Board, not courts.

This is not to say, however, that these inherent limitations on this Court's ability to state a workable rule that comports reasonably with apparent congressional objectives are necessarily self-evident. In fact, varying approaches were taken by the Court in initially grappling with this preemption problem. Thus, for example, some early cases suggested the true distinction lay between judicial application of general common law, which was permissible, as opposed to state rules specifically designed to regulate labor relations, which were preempted. *See, e.g., Automobile Workers v. Russell,* 356 U.S. 634, 645 (1958). Others made preemption turn on whether the States purported to apply a remedy not provided for by the federal scheme, *e.g., Weber v. Anheuser-Busch, Inc.,* 348 U.S. 468, 479-480 (1955), while in still others the Court undertook a thorough scrutiny of the federal Act to ascertain whether the state courts had, in fact, arrived at conclusions inconsistent with its provisions, *e.g., Automobile Workers v. Wisconsin Employment Relations Bd.,* 336 U.S. 245 (1949). For the reasons outlined above none of these approaches proved satisfactory, however, and each was ultimately abandoned. It was, in short, experience—not pure logic—which initially taught that each of these methods sacrificed important federal interests in a uniform law of labor relations centrally administered by an expert agency without yielding anything in return by way of predictability or ease of judicial application.

The failure of alternative analyses and the interplay of the foregoing policy considerations, then, led this Court to hold in *Garmon,* 359 U.S. at 244·

> When it is clear or may fairly be assumed that the activities which a State purports to regulate are protected by § 7 of the National Labor Relations Act, or constitute an unfair labor practice under § 8, due regard for the federal enactment requires that state jurisdiction must yield. To leave the States free to regulate conduct so plainly within the central aim of federal regulation involves too great a danger of conflict between power asserted by Congress and requirements imposed by state law.

C. Upon these premises, we think that *Garmon* rather clearly dictates reversal of the judgment below. None of the propositions asserted to support that judgment can withstand an application, in light of those factors that compelled its promulgation, of the *Garmon* rule.

Assuredly the proposition that Lockridge's complaint was not subject to the exclusive jurisdiction of the NLRB because it charged a breach of contract rather than an unfair labor practice is not tenable. Preemption, as shown above, is designed to shield the system from conflicting regulation of conduct. It is the conduct being regulated, not the formal description of governing legal standards, that is the proper focus of concern. Indeed, the notion that a relevant distinction exists for such purposes between particularized and generalized labor law was explicitly rejected in *Garmon* itself. 359 U.S. at 244.

The second argument, closely related to the first, is that the state courts in resolving this controversy, did deal with different conduct, *i.e.,* interpretation of contractual terms, than would the NLRB which would be required to decide whether the Union discriminated against Lockridge. At bottom, of course, the Union's action in procuring Lockridge's dismissal from employment is the conduct which Idaho courts have sought to regulate. Thus, this second point demonstrates at best that Idaho defines differently what sorts of such union conduct may permissibly be proscribed. This is to say either that the regulatory schemes, state and federal, conflict (in which case preemption is clearly called for) or that Idaho is dealing with conduct to which the federal Act does not speak. If the latter assertion was intended, it is not accurate. As pointed out in Part II A, *supra,* the relevant portions of the Act operate to prohibit a union from causing or attempting to cause an employer to discriminate against an employee because his membership in the union has been terminated "on some ground other than" his failure to pay those dues requisite to membership. This has led the Board routinely and frequently to inquire into the proper construction of union regulations in order to ascertain whether the union properly found an employee to have been derelict in his dues-paying responsibilities, where his discharge was procured on the asserted grounds of nonmembership in the union.... That a union may in good faith have misconstrued its own rules has not been treated by the Board as a defense to a claimed violation of § 8(b)(2). In the Board's view, it is the fact of misapplication by a union of its rules, not the motivation for that discrimination, that constitutes an unfair labor practice....

From the foregoing, then, it would seem that this case indeed represents one of the clearest instances where the *Garmon* principle, properly understood, should operate to oust state court jurisdiction. There being no doubt that the conduct here involved was arguably protected by § 7 or prohibited by § 8 of the Act, the full range of very substantial interests the preemption doctrine seeks to protect are directly implicated here.

However, a final strand of analysis underlies the opinion of the Idaho Supreme Court, and the position of respondent, in this case. Our decision in *Association of Machinists v. Gonzales,* 356 U.S. 617 (1958), it is argued, fully survived the subsequent reorientation of preemption doctrine effected by the *Garmon* decision, providing, in effect, an express exception for the exercise of judicial jurisdiction in cases such as this....

Although it was decided only one Term subsequent to *Gonzales, Garmon* clearly did not fully embrace the technique of the prior case. It was precisely the realization that disparities in remedies and administration could produce substantial conflict, in the practical sense of the term, between the relevant state and federal regulatory schemes and that this Court could not effectively and responsibly superintend on a case-by-case basis the exertion of state power over matters arguably governed by the National Labor Relations Act that impelled the somewhat broader formulation of the preemption doctrine in *Garmon.* It seems evident that the full-blown rationale of *Gonzales* could not survive the rule of *Garmon.* Nevertheless, *Garmon* did not cast doubt upon the result reached in *Gonzales,* but cited it approvingly as an example of the fact that state court jurisdiction is not preempted "where the activity regulated was a merely peripheral concern of the ... Act." 359 U.S. at 243.

Against this background, we attempted to define more precisely the reach of *Gonzales* within the more comprehensive framework *Garmon* provided in the companion cases of *Plumbers Union v. Borden,* 373 U.S. 690 (1963), and *Iron Workers v. Perko,* 373 U.S. 701 (1963).

Borden had sued his union in state courts, alleging that the union had arbitrarily refused to refer him to a particular job which he had lined up. He recovered damages, based on lost wages, on the grounds that this conduct constituted both tortious interference with his right to contract for employment and a breach of promise, implicit in his membership arrangement with the union, not to discriminate unfairly against any member or deny him the right to work. Perko had obtained a large money judgment in the Ohio courts on proof that the union had conspired, without cause, to deprive him of employment as a foreman by demanding his discharge from one such position he had held and representing to others that his foreman's rights had been suspended. We held both Perko's and Borden's judgments inconsistent with the *Garmon* rule essentially for the same reasons we have concluded that Lockridge could not, consistently with the *Garmon* decision, maintain his lawsuit in the state courts. We further held there was no necessity to "consider the present vitality of [the *Gonzales*] rationale in the light of more recent decisions," because in those cases, unlike *Gonzales*, "the crux of the action[s] ... concerned alleged interference with the plaintiff's existing or prospective employment relations and was not directed to internal union matters." Because no specific claim for restoration of membership rights had been advanced, "there was no permissible state remedy to which the award of consequential damages for loss of earnings might be subordinated." *Perko*, 373 U.S. at 705. *See also Borden*, 373 U.S. at 697.

In sum, what distinguished *Gonzales* from *Borden* and *Perko* was that the former lawsuit "was focused on purely internal union matters," *Borden, supra,* at 697, a subject the National Labor Relations Act leaves principally to other processes of law. The possibility that, in defining the scope of the union's duty to Gonzales, the state courts would directly and consciously implicate principles of federal law was at best tangential and remote. In the instant case, however, this possibility was real and immediate. To assess the legality of his union's conduct toward Gonzales the California courts needed only to focus upon the union's constitution and by-laws. Here, however, Lockridge's entire case turned upon the construction of the applicable union security clause, a matter as to which, as shown above, federal concern is pervasive and its regulation complex. The reasons for Gonzales' deprivation of union membership had nothing to do with matters of employment, while Lockridge's cause of action and claim for damages was based solely upon the procurement of his discharge from employment. It cannot plausibly be argued, in any meaningful sense, that Lockridge's lawsuit "was focused upon purely internal matters." Although nothing said in *Garmon* necessarily suggests that States cannot regulate the general conditions which unions may impose on their membership, it surely makes crystal clear that *Gonzales* does not stand for the proposition that the resolution of any union-member conflict is within state competence so long as one of the remedies provided is restoration of union membership. This much was settled by *Borden* and *Perko*, and it is only upon such an unwarrantably broad interpretation of *Gonzales* that the judgment below could be sustained.

III

The preemption doctrine we apply today is, like any other purposefully administered legal principle, not without exception. Those same considerations that underlie *Garmon* have led this Court to permit the exercise of judicial power over conduct arguably protected or prohibited by the Act where Congress has affirmatively indicated that such power should exist, *Smith v. Evening News,* 371 U.S. 195 (1962); *Teamsters v. Morton,* 377 U.S. 252 (1964), where this Court cannot, in spite of the force of the policies *Garmon* seeks to promote, conscientiously presume that Congress meant to intrude so deeply into areas traditionally left to local law, *e.g., Linn v. Plant Guard Workers,* 383 U.S. 53 (1966); *Automobile Workers v. Russell,* 356 U.S. 634 (1958), and where the particular rule of law sought to be invoked before another tribunal is so structured and administered that, in virtually all instances, it is safe to presume that judicial supervision will not disserve the interests promoted by the federal labor statutes, *Vaca v. Sipes,* 386 U.S. 171 (1967).

In his brief before this Court, respondent has argued for the first time since this lawsuit was started that two of these exceptions to the *Garmon* principle independently justify the Idaho courts' exercise of jurisdiction over this controversy. First, Lockridge contends that his action, properly viewed, is one to enforce a collective bargaining agreement. Alternatively, he asserts the suit, in essence, was one to redress petitioner's breach of its duty of fair representation. As will be seen, these contentions are somewhat intertwined.

In § 301 of the Taft-Hartley Act, Congress authorized federal courts to exercise jurisdiction over suits brought to enforce collective bargaining agreements. We have held that such actions are judicially cognizable, even where the conduct alleged was arguably protected or prohibited by the National Labor Relations Act because the history of the enactment of § 301 reveals that "Congress deliberately chose to leave the enforcement of collective agreements 'to the usual processes of law.'" *Charles Dowd Box Co. v. Courtney,* 368 U.S. 502, 513 (1962). It is firmly established, further, that state courts retain concurrent jurisdiction to adjudicate such claims, *Charles Dowd Box Co., supra,* and that individual employees have standing to protect rights conferred upon them by such agreements, *Smith v. Evening News, supra; Humphrey v. Moore,* 375 U.S. 335 (1964).

Our cases also clearly establish that individual union members may sue their employers under § 301 for breach of a promise embedded in the collective bargaining agreement that was intended to confer a benefit upon the individual. *Smith v. Evening News, supra.* Plainly, however, this is not such a lawsuit. Lockridge specifically dropped Greyhound as a named party from his initial complaint and has never reasserted a right to redress from his former employer.

This Court has further held in *Humphrey v. Moore,* 375 U.S. 335 (1964), that § 301 will support, regardless of otherwise applicable preemption considerations, a suit in the state courts by a union member against his union that seeks to redress union interference with rights conferred on individual employees by the employer's promises in the collective-bargaining agreement, where it is proved that such interference constituted a breach of the duty of fair representation. Indeed, in *Vaca v. Sipes,* 386 U.S. 171 (1967), we held that an action seeking damages for injury inflicted by a breach of a union's duty of fair representation was judicially cognizable in any event, that is, even if the conduct complained of was arguably protected or prohibited by the National Labor Relations Act and whether or not the lawsuit was bottomed on a collective agreement. Perhaps Count One of Lockridge's second amended complaint could be construed to assert either or both of these theories of recovery. However, it is unnecessary to pass upon the extent to which *Garmon* would be inapplicable if it were shown that in these circumstances petitioner not only breached its contractual obligations to respondent, but did so in a manner that constituted a breach of the duty of fair representation. For such a claim to be made out, Lockridge must have proved "arbitrary or bad faith conduct on the part of the union." *Vaca v. Sipes, supra,* at 193. There must be "substantial evidence of fraud, deceitful action or dishonest conduct." *Humphrey v. Moore, supra,* at 348. Whether these requisite elements have been proved is a matter of federal law. Quite obviously, they were not even asserted to be relevant in the proceedings below. As the Idaho Supreme Court stated in affirming the verdict for Lockridge, "[t]his was a misinterpretation of a contract. Whatever the underlying motive for expulsion might have been, this case has been submitted and tried on the interpretation of the contract, not on a theory of discrimination." Thus, the trial judge's conclusion of law in sustaining Lockridge's claim specifically incorporates the assumption that the Union's "acts ... were predicated solely upon the ground that [Lockridge] had failed to tender periodic dues in conformance with the requirements of the union Constitution and employment contract as they interpreted [it] ...." App., 66. Further, the trial court excluded as irrelevant petitioner's proffer of evidence designed to show that the Union's interpretation of the contract was reasonably based upon its understanding of prior collective bargaining agreements negotiated with Greyhound. Transcript of Trial, at 259-260....

For the reasons stated above, the judgment below is

Reversed.

MR. JUSTICE WHITE, with whom THE CHIEF JUSTICE joins, dissenting.

... I cannot agree with the opinion of the Court because it reaffirms the *Garmon* doctrine as applied to conduct arguably protected under § 7, as well as to that arguably prohibited under § 8. The essential difference, for present purposes, between activity which is arguably prohibited and that which is arguably protected is that a hearing on the latter activity is virtually impossible unless one deliberately commits an unfair labor practice. In a typical unfair practice case, by alleging conduct arguably prohibited by § 8 the charging party can at least present the General Counsel with the facts, and if the General Counsel issues a complaint, the charging party can present the Board with the facts and arguments to support the claim. But for activity which is arguably protected, there is no provision for an authoritative decision by the Board in the first instance; yet the *Garmon* rule blindly preempts other tribunals....

Though the most natural arena for this conflict occurs when picketers trespass on private property, *see Taggart v. Weinacker's, Inc.,* 397 U.S. 223, 227 (1970) (Burger, C.J., concurring), ... other instances include "quickie" strikes or slowdowns, *see NLRB v. Holcombe,* 325 F.2d 508 (5th Cir. 1963), or employees' inaccurate complaints to state officials about sanitary conditions in the plant, *Walls Mfg. Co. v. NLRB,* 116 U.S. App. D.C. 140, 321 F.2d 753 (1963), or collective activity designed to persuade the employer to hire Negroes, *NLRB v. Tanner Motor Livery, Ltd.,* 349 F.2d 1 (9th Cir. 1965), or failure to participate in a union check-off, *Radio Officers' Union v. NLRB,* 347 U.S. 17, 24-28 (1954).

There seems little point in a doctrine which, in the name of national policy, encourages the commission of unfair labor practices, the evils which above all else were the object of the Act. Surely the policy of seeking uniformity in the regulation of labor practices must be given closer scrutiny when it leads to the alternative "solutions" of denying the aggrieved party a hearing or encouraging the commission of a putative unfair labor practice as the price of that hearing....

Congress found the no-man's land created by *Guss* unacceptable precisely because there was no way to have rights determined. In terms of congressional intention I find it unsupportable to hold that one threatened by conduct illegal under state law may not proceed against it because it is arguably protected by federal law when he has absolutely no lawful method for determining whether that is actually, as well as arguably, the case. Particularly is this true where the dispute is between a union and its members and the latter are asserting claims under state law based on the union constitution. I would permit the state court to entertain the action and if the union defends on the ground that its conduct is protected by federal law, to pass on that claim at the outset of the proceeding. If the federal law immunizes the challenged union action, the case is terminated; but if not, the case is adjudicated under state law.

[The dissenting opinion of MR. JUSTICE DOUGLAS and the dissenting statement of MR. JUSTICE BLACKMUN are omitted.]

NOTES

1. When is an employed person excluded from NLRA coverage and subject to state jurisdiction? In *Iron Workers, Local 207 v. Perko,* 373 U.S. 701 (1963), cited in *Lockridge,* a state damage action was brought against a union for allegedly conspiring to deprive a member of his job as a "foreman." The plaintiff argued against preemption on the ground he was a "supervisor" and thus outside the NLRA's definition of "employee." The Supreme Court held that the plaintiff's duties made him at least arguably an "employee" within the meaning of the act, thereby precluding state jurisdiction. Similarly, in *Marine Eng'rs Beneficial Ass'n v. Interlake S.S. Co.*, 370 U.S. 173 (1962), the Supreme Court ruled that since a union of marine engineers was arguably a "labor organization" as defined by the federal act, even though it was allegedly composed entirely of supervisors, the NLRB had exclusive primary jurisdiction to determine the union's status. As a result, a state court could not enjoin MEBA's picketing of a ship employing nonunion marine engineers.

In *Operating Eng'rs Local 926 v. Jones*, 460 U.S. 669 (1983), a "supervisor" sued a union in state court for tortious interference with his employment contract because it had allegedly procured his discharge on the ground he was not a union member. The Supreme Court held the state action preempted by federal law. The union had arguably violated § 8(b)(1)(A) of the NLRA by coercing an "employee," since low-level construction industry supervisors such as the complainant often fluctuate between supervisory and nonsupervisory positions. The union had also arguably violated § 8(b)(1)(B) of the NLRA by coercing the employer in its choice of a collective bargaining representative.

On the other hand, a state is not foreclosed from acting once the NLRB has concluded, through the dismissal of a representation petition or unfair labor practice charges, that there is no federal jurisdiction because the union consists exclusively of supervisors. In such circumstances a state court may enjoin peaceful organizational picketing by the supervisors' union. *Hanna Mining Co. v. District 2, Marine Eng'rs*, 382 U.S. 181 (1965).

2. A state may assume jurisdiction over organizational picketing or "area standards" picketing by an American labor organization aimed at foreign seamen on vessels of foreign registry, since the maritime operations of foreign flag ships employing alien seamen are not in "commerce" within the meaning of the NLRA. *Incres S.S. Co. v. International Maritime Workers*, 372 U.S. 24 (1963); *Windward Shipping, Ltd. v. American Radio Ass'n*, 415 U.S. 104 (U.S. 1974). *See also American Radio Ass'n v. Mobile S.S. Ass'n*, 419 U.S. 215 (1974).

3. *See generally* Silverstein, *Against Preemption in Labor Law*, 24 Conn. L. Rev. 1 (1991); Come, *Federal Preemption of Labor-Management Relations: Current Problems with the Application of Garmon*, 56 Va. L. Rev. 1435 (1970); Cox, *Labor Law Preemption Revisited*, 85 Harv. L. Rev. 1337 (1972); Lesnick, *Preemption Reconsidered: The Apparent Reaffirmation of Garmon*, 72 Colum. L. Rev. 469 (1972). *See also* Bryson, *A Matter of Wooden Logic: Labor Law Preemption and Individual Rights*, 51 Texas L. Rev. 1037 (1973).

Teamsters Local 24 v. Oliver, 358 U.S. 283, 79 S. Ct. 297, 3 L. Ed. 2d 312 (1959). Teamster locals entered into a collective bargaining agreement with motor carriers operating in twelve midwestern states, including Ohio. The contract included a provision prescribing the minimum rental fee and other terms of the lease when a motor vehicle was leased to a carrier by an owner who drove his own vehicle for the carrier. At the suit of one owner driver, the Ohio courts enjoined a local and several carriers from giving effect to this provision, on the ground it violated the Ohio antitrust law as a form of price-fixing. The United States Supreme Court held that the provision in dispute dealt with a subject matter within the scope of "collective bargaining" under federal law, and that the Ohio antitrust law could not be applied to prevent the parties from carrying out their agreement on a matter "as to which federal law directs them to bargain." The Court reasoned that the purpose of the questioned clause was to protect the negotiated wage scale for employees driving carrier-owned vehicles. If owner-drivers accepted inadequate rentals for their trucks, they would have to make up the excess operating costs from their compensation as drivers. This in effect would undercut the union's wage scale, and might invite a progressive curtailment of jobs through the gradual withdrawal of carrier-owned vehicles from service. Concluded the Court: "Of course, the paramount force of federal law remains even though it is expressed in the details of a contract federal law empowers the parties to make, rather than in terms of an enactment of Congress.... Clearly it is immaterial that the conflict is between federal labor law and the application of what the State characterizes as an anti-trust law.... [T]he conflict here is between the federally sanctioned agreement and state policy which seeks specifically to adjust relationships in the world of commerce."

NOTE

In *Weber v. Anheuser-Busch, Inc.,* 348 U.S. 468 (1955), the Supreme Court set aside a state court injunction against a strike to force an employer to agree to assign certain repair work to machinists rather than carpenters. The strike had been found to violate Missouri's restraint of trade statute, after the NLRB had ruled it did not violate § 8(b)(4)(D) of the National Labor Relations Act. The Board had not passed on possible violations of subsections (A) or (B). The Supreme Court commented that if the union conduct did not fall within the prohibition of § 8 of the NLRA, it might fall within the protection of § 7, and rejected the employer's attempt to distinguish the *Garner* preemption decision on the ground that there the state was trying to regulate "labor relations as such." *See generally* Cox, *Federalism in the Law of Labor Relations,* 67 Harv. L. Rev. 1297, 1324-31 (1954); Meltzer, *The Supreme Court, Congress, and State Jurisdiction Over Labor Relations,* 59 Colum. L. Rev. 6, 47-55 (1959).

Machinists, Lodge 76 v. Wisconsin Employment Relations Commission, 427 U.S. 132, 96 S. Ct. 2548, 49 L. Ed. 2d 396 (1976). As a bargaining tactic during negotiations for renewal of an expired collective agreement, the union refused to work overtime. The employer filed an unfair labor practice charge against the union, claiming a violation of the union's duty to bargain under § 8(b)(3) of the NLRA; but the Regional Director of the Board dismissed the charge on the ground that the conduct was not prohibited by the Act. The employer then filed a complaint before the Wisconsin Employment Relations Commission charging that the refusal to work overtime was an unfair labor practice under state law. Finding a state law violation, the WERC issued a cease and desist order, which was sustained by the Wisconsin Supreme Court.

The U.S. Supreme Court reversed on the ground of federal preemption, expressly overruling its earlier case of *UAW v. WERB*, 336 U.S. 245 (1949), which had held that states could regulate union conduct (intermittent, unannounced work stoppages) that Congress had neither prohibited nor protected. The Court now held that an inquiry must be made as to whether Congress intended that the conduct involved be unregulated and left to be controlled by the free play of economic forces. Stating that the use of economic pressure by the parties to a labor dispute is not a grudging exception under the NLRA but is part and parcel of the process of collective bargaining, the Court found that Wisconsin had entered into the substantive aspects of collective bargaining to an extent that Congress had not countenanced.

NOTES

1. In *New York Tel. Co. v. New York State Dep't of Labor,* 440 U.S. 519 (1979), the Supreme Court held that the federal preemption doctrine did not invalidate the New York unemployment compensation statute, which gives benefits to strikers after eight weeks. Dissenting Justice Powell, joined by Chief Justice Burger and Justice Stewart, thought that such payments were preempted because they substantially altered the economic balance of free collective bargaining, contrary to the policy of the national labor laws. However, the majority found that the legislative history of the NLRA and the Social Security Act showed that Congress intended that the states be free to authorize or prohibit the payment of unemployment benefits to strikers.

2. The Michigan Employment Security Act specifically disqualifies from unemployment compensation employees who have provided "financing" by means other than the payment of regular union dues for any strike which causes their unemployment. Employees who had contributed "emergency dues" to augment the UAW strike fund were laid off by General Motors as a result of UAW-financed strikes at other GM plants. The Michigan Supreme Court found that the laid off individuals were ineligible for unemployment benefits due to their special strike fund contributions. Although such financing of local work stoppages constitutes protected activity under § 7, the Supreme Court held in *Baker v. General Motors Corp.,* 478 U.S. 621 (1986), that this state disqualification determination was not preempted by the NLRA. In Title IX of the Social Security Act, Congress expressly provided states with broad discretion to decide the particular type of unemployment program they wished to establish, and no employer action impaired the § 7 rights of the affected employees. *Compare Steelworkers v. Johnson,* 830 F.2d 924 (8th Cir. 1987) (NLRA preempted South Dakota unemployment compensation statute provision denying benefits to union employees while granting them to nonunion employees during lockouts).

A section of the Illinois Unemployment Insurance Act provides that whenever employers issue checks satisfying government-mandated backpay awards covering weeks for which unemployment benefits were paid, the checks must be made payable jointly to the interested employees and to the Unemployment Director to ensure the recoupment of previously paid benefits. In *NLRB v. Illinois Dep't of Emp. Sec.,* 988 F.2d 735 (7th Cir. 1993), the court found that application of this provision to NLRB backpay awards was preempted, because it impermissibly interfered with the Labor Board's exclusive remedial authority.

3. The New Jersey Casino Control Act disqualifies individuals connected with organized crime from serving as officials and business agents of unions representing employees at Atlantic City casinos. It also provides that a labor organization may be prohibited from receiving union dues from casino employees and from administering any pension or welfare fund if any officer is a disqualified person. In *Brown v. Hotel & Restaurant Employees Local 54,* 468 U.S. 491 (1984), a closely divided Supreme Court held that the provision preventing organized crime figures from serving as union officials was not preempted, because it does not conflict with § 7 of the NLRA—which neither contains express preemptive language nor otherwise indicates a congressional intent to usurp the entire field of labor management relations. *Hill v. Florida,* 325 U.S. 538 (1945), which had struck down a Florida statute which provided for the licensing of union business agents and precluded the licensing of anyone who had not been a citizen for at least ten years, who had been convicted of a felony, or who was not of "good moral character," on the ground it impermissibly interfered with the § 7 freedom of employees to select bargaining representatives of their own choosing, was distinguished. Section 504(a) of the subsequently enacted LMRDA specifically disqualifies from union office individuals convicted of certain crimes, and the 4-3 *Brown* majority concluded that this indicated that Congress no longer views the freedom of employees to select union officers to be an unfettered right. Furthermore, § 603(a) of the LMRDA explicitly disclaims any congressional intent to preempt state laws regulating the responsibility of union officials, so long as such statutes do not conflict with LMRDA provisions. The *Brown* majority thus found that Congress no longer intended to preclude all state regulations governing the qualifications of labor leaders. The Court finally noted that the New Jersey provision was designed to vindicate a legitimate and compelling state interest, and it emphasized the fact that the law "does not implicate the employees' express § 7 right to select a particular labor union as their collective-bargaining representative, but only their subsidiary right to select the officials of that union organization." Due to a procedural matter, the *Brown* majority declined to rule upon the validity of the Casino Control Act's dues collection prohibition provision. It did, however, instruct the district court to consider on remand whether the imposition of such a dues collection ban would so incapacitate appellee union as to prevent it from performing its functions as the employees' chosen bargaining agent. Since the New Jersey Commission had not tried to prevent appellee union from administering pension and welfare funds, the Court refused to assess the propriety of that statutory authorization. *See also Hotel Employees v. Nevada Gaming Comm'n,* 984 F.2d 1507 (9th Cir. 1993) (neither NLRA nor LMRDA preempts Nevada gaming control statutes and regulations governing "suitability" of persons associated with gaming establishments).

Metropolitan Life Ins. Co. v. Massachusetts, 471 U.S. 724, 105 S. Ct. 2380, 85 L. Ed. 2d 728 (1985). The Supreme Court was asked to decide whether a state law which requires certain minimum mental health care benefits to be provided in general health insurance polices and employee health care plans which cover hospital and surgical expenses was preempted by federal law. After first determining that the Massachusetts provision was protected by an express anti-preemption section contained in ERISA which authorizes states to regulate insurance, the unanimous Supreme Court went on to find that such state-established minimum standards are not preempted by the NLRA:

> The NLRA is concerned primarily with establishing an equitable process for determining terms and conditions of employment, and not with particular substantive terms of the bargain that is struck when the parties are negotiating from relatively equal positions. The NLRA's declared purpose is to remedy "[t]he inequality of bargaining power between employees who do not possess full freedom of association or actual liberty of contract, and employers who are organized in the corporate or other forms of ownership association."...
>
> One of the ultimate goals of the Act was the resolution of the problem of "depress[ed] wage rates and the purchasing power of wage earners in industry," 29 U.S.C. § 151, and "the widening gap between wages and profits," 79 Cong. Rec. 2371 (1935) (remarks of Sen. Wagner), thought to be the cause of economic decline and depression. Congress hoped to accomplish this by establishing procedures for more equitable private bargaining.
>
> The evil Congress was addressing thus was entirely unrelated to local or federal regulation establishing minimum terms of employment. Neither inequality of bargaining power nor the resultant depressed wage rates were

thought to result from the choice between having terms of employment set by public law or having them set by private agreement. No incompatibility exists, therefore, between federal rules designed to restore the equality of bargaining power, and state or federal legislation that imposes minimal substantive requirements on contract terms negotiated between parties to labor agreements, at least so long as the purpose of the state legislation is not incompatible with these general goals of the NLRA.

Accordingly, it never has been argued successfully that minimal labor standards imposed by other *federal* laws were not to apply to unionized employers and employees. *See, e.g., Barrentine v. Arkansas-Best Freight System, Inc.,* 450 U.S. 728, 737, 739 (1981). Nor has Congress ever seen fit to exclude unionized workers and employers from laws establishing federal minimal employment standards. We see no reason to believe that for this purpose Congress intended state minimum labor standards to be treated differently from minimum federal standards.

Minimum state labor standards affect union and nonunion employees equally, and neither encourage nor discourage the collective-bargaining processes that are the subject of the NLRA. Nor do they have any but the most indirect effect on the right of self-organization established in the Act. Unlike the NLRA, mandated-benefit laws are not laws designed to encourage or discourage employees in the promotion of their interests collectively; rather, they are in part "designed to give specific minimum protections to *individual* workers and to ensure that *each* employee covered by the Act would receive" the mandated health insurance coverage. *Barrentine,* 450 U.S., at 739 (emphasis in original). Nor do these laws even inadvertently affect these interests implicated in the NLRA. Rather, they are minimum standards "independent of the collective-bargaining process [that] devolve on [employees] as individual workers, not as members of a collective organization." *Id.* at 745.

NOTE

A closely divided Supreme Court held that a Maine statute requiring a one-time severance payment for employees in the event of a plant closing was not preempted by either ERISA or the NLRA. *Fort Halifax Packing Co. v. Coyne,* 482 U.S. 1 (1987). The majority first concluded that ERISA's preemption provision applies only to "employee benefit *plans,"* and that the Maine statute neither established, fostered, hindered, nor regulated such a plan. Second, the statute, like that in *Metropolitan Life,* simply created a minimum substantive labor standard that did not undercut the collective bargaining promoted by the NLRA. The four dissenting Justices believed that the statutory requirement of severance payments by employers was itself enough to fall within ERISA's preemption of all state laws that "relate to any employee benefit plan." *See generally* Note,

NLRA Preemption of State and Local Plant Relocation Laws, 86 Colum. L. Rev. 407 (1986).

Sears, Roebuck & Co. v. San Diego County Dist. Council of Carpenters, 436 U.S. 180, 98 S. Ct. 1745, 56 L. Ed. 2d 209 (1978). Two Carpenters Union representatives visited the Chula Vista, California Sears store to protest the fact that carpentry work was being performed by individuals who had not been dispatched from the union hiring hall. When the Sears store manager failed to engage a contractor that used hiring hall workers, the union established a picket line on Sears property. They picketed on privately owned walkways adjacent to the store and on the privately owned parking lot. The Sears manager demanded that the union remove the pickets from Sears property, but the union refused. Sears filed a state court action seeking an injunction against the continuing trespass. The state trial court enjoined the trespassory picketing, and the court of appeals affirmed on the ground the trespass laws fell within the longstanding preemption exception for matters of deep and traditional state concern. The California Supreme Court, however, reversed, finding that state court jurisdiction was preempted by conduct that was arguably protected by § 7 of the NLRA.

On appeal, the U.S. Supreme Court rejected the union's preemption claim. It could have followed the court of appeal's logic and held that trespass laws fall within the exception for matters of deep and traditional state concern, but it elected to engage in a more searching analysis that involved an examination of both the arguably prohibited and arguably protected preemption concepts enunciated in *San Diego Building Trades Council v. Garmon,* 359 U.S. 236 (1959), *supra.*

With respect to the arguably prohibited question, the Court noted that the focus of the state court trespass action was significantly different from NLRA concerns under §§ 8(b)(4)(D) and 8(b)(7):

> We start from the premise that the Union's picketing on Sears' property after the request to leave was continuing trespass in violation of state law. We note, however, that the scope of the controversy in the state court was limited. Sears asserted no claim that the picketing itself violated any state or federal law. It sought simply to remove the pickets from its property to the public walkways, and the injunction issued by the state court was strictly confined to the relief sought. Thus, as a matter of state law, the location of the picketing was illegal but the picketing itself was unobjectionable....
>
> If an object of the picketing was to force Sears into assigning the carpentry work away from its employees to Union members dispatched from the hiring hall, the picketing may have been prohibited by 8(b)(4)(D). Alternatively, if an object of the picketing was to coerce Sears into signing a prehire or members-only type agreement with the Union, the picketing was at least

arguably subject to the prohibition on recognitional picketing contained in
§ 8(b)(7)(C). Hence, if Sears had filed an unfair labor practice charge
against the Union, the Board's concern would have been limited to the
question whether the Union's picketing had an objective proscribed by the
Act; the location of the picketing would have been irrelevant.

The Court thus rejected preemption under the arguably prohibited concept.

The Supreme Court then evaluated the arguably protected theory to determine
whether there was any real likelihood that application of state trespass laws
would undermine federal labor policies contained in § 7. It first noted that Sears
had expressly demanded that the union pickets leave its premises, providing the
union with the opportunity to file a § 8(a)(1) charge with the NLRB and have that
agency decide whether the trespassory picketing was protected conduct due to
the absence of alternative means of communication:

> The primary jurisdiction rationale unquestionably requires that when the
> same controversy may be presented to the state court or the NLRB, it must
> be presented to the Board. But that rationale does not extend to cases in
> which an employer has no acceptable method of invoking, or inducing the
> Union to invoke, the jurisdiction of the Board. We are therefore persuaded
> that the primary jurisdiction rationale does not provide a *sufficient* justifica-
> tion for preempting state jurisdiction over arguably protected conduct when
> the party who could have presented the protection issue to the Board has not
> done so and the other party to the dispute has no acceptable means of doing
> so....
>   In *NLRB v. Babcock & Wilcox,* 351 U.S. 105, ... the Court recognized that
> in certain circumstances nonemployee union organizers may have a limited
> right of access to an employer's premises for the purpose of engaging in or-
> ganization solicitation. And the Court has indicated that *Babock* extends to
> § 7 rights other than organizational activity, though the "locus" of the "ac-
> commodation of § 7 rights and the private property rights ... may fall at dif-
> fering points along the spectrum depending on the nature and strength of the
> respective § 7 rights and private property rights asserted in any given con-
> text." *Hudgens v. NLRB,* 424 U.S. 507.
>   For purpose of analysis we must assume that the Union could have
> proved that its picketing was, at least in the absence of a trespass, protected
> by § 7. The remaining question is whether under *Babcock* the trespassory
> nature of the picketing caused it to forfeit its protected status. Since it cannot
> be said with certainty that, if the Union had filed an unfair labor practice
> charge against Sears, the Board would have fixed the locus of the accom-
> modation at the unprotected end of the spectrum, it is indeed "arguable" that
> the Union's peaceful picketing, though trespassory, was protected. Never-
> theless, permitting state courts to evaluate the merits of an argument that
> certain trespassory activity is protected does not create an unacceptable risk

of interference with conduct which the Board, and a court reviewing the board's decision, would find protected. For while there are unquestionably examples of trespassory union activity in which the question whether it is protected is fairly debatable, experience under the Act teaches that such situations are rare and that a trespass is far more likely to be unprotected than protected.

The Court thus found an absence of preemption under the arguably protected concept.

NOTES

1. On remand, the California Supreme Court found the picketing lawful under state law, and held that a state anti-injunction statute required vacating the injunction. *Sears, Roebuck v. Carpenters,* 25 Cal.3d 317, 599 P.2d 676 (1979), *cert. denied,* 447 U.S. 935 (1980).

2. *Riesbeck Food Mkts. v. UFCW, Local 23,* 185 W. Va. 12, 404 S.E.2d 404, *cert. denied,* 502 U.S. 856 (1991), concerned peaceful, informational labor picketing on the premises of a nonunion supermarket. The supermarket sought an injunction against the trespassory picketing, and the union filed a § 8(a)(1) charge that resulted in an NLRB complaint. The West Virginia Supreme Court concluded that the filing of the unfair labor practice charge and the issuance of the Board complaint preempted state court jurisdiction over the peaceful trespassory picketing, since such action indicated that the union activity was "arguably protected" under the NLRA.

3. In *Farmer v. Carpenters,* 430 U.S. 290 (1977), the Supreme Court held that the NLRA does not preempt a state court tort action by a union member against the union and its officials seeking damages for the intentional infliction of emotional distress through "frequent public ridicule" and "incessant verbal abuse." But a verdict could not be based on evidence of discriminatory job referrals, except where such discrimination is accomplished through a "particularly abusive manner" involving outrageous conduct.

4. In *Linn v. Plant Guard Workers,* 383 U.S. 53 (1966), the Supreme Court held that state libel suits based on defamatory statements made in the course of a union organizing campaign are not preempted. The Court noted the compelling state interest involved—a matter so deeply rooted in local feeling and responsibility that it cannot be assumed that Congress had deprived the states of the power to act. However, the Court limited the availability of state remedies for libel to those instances in which complainants can show that the defamatory statements were circulated with malice and caused them actual damage. "The standards enunciated in *New York Times v. Sullivan,* 376 U.S. 254 (1964), are adopted by analogy rather than by constitutional compulsion. We apply the malice test to effectuate the statutory design with respect to preemption. Construing the Act to permit recovery of damages in a state cause of action only for defamatory statements published with knowledge of their falsity or with reckless disregard of whether they were true or false guards against abuse of libel actions and unwarranted intrusion upon free discussion envisioned by the Act."

In *Letter Carriers Branch 496 v. Austin,* 418 U.S. 264 (1974), decided under E.O. 11491, then applicable to federal employees, the Supreme Court held that the *Linn* partial preemption doctrine requires a state court to instruct on "malice" in terms of the reckless-or-knowing falsehood test of *New York Times* rather than in common-law terms. The Court concluded that a union was protected by the federal labor laws in listing plaintiffs as scabs under a heading containing Jack London's colorful definition of "The Scab," which includes such epithets as "tumor of rotten principles" and "traitor."

Would the *Linn* standards apply to libel committed during collective bargaining sessions or grievance-adjustment meetings, or should union and employer statements in such circumstances be considered "unqualifiedly privileged"? *Compare General Motors Corp. v. Mendicki,* 367 F.2d 66 (10th Cir. 1966) ("unqualifiedly privileged") *with Thompson v. Public Serv. Co.,* 800 P.2d 1299 (Colo. Sup. Ct. 1990), *cert. denied,* 502 U.S. 973 (1991) (only "qualifiedly privileged"). *See generally* Currier, *Defamation in Labor Disputes: Preemption and the New Federal Common Law,* 53 Va. L. Rev. 1 (1967).

5. *Beverly Hills Foodland v. UFCW Local 655,* 39 F.3d 191 (8th Cir. 1994), concerned the propriety of an employer's defamation and tortious interference suit against a labor organization that had engaged in a publicity and consumer boycott campaign against a nonunion store that focused on the store's alleged treatment of black employees. Handbills and picket signs characterized the store owners as "racist," accused them of being unfair to black employees, and asked whether the store engaged in discriminatory practices. The court noted the expansive protection afforded to speech during labor disputes and held that the union's conduct did not transcend the bounds of acceptable behavior under the standard enunciated in *Linn.*

6. In addition to the *Farmer* and *Linn* exceptions to preemption, the Supreme Court has held that the Railway Labor Act did not prevent the enforcement of a state law prohibiting racial discrimination in employment. *Colorado Anti-Discrimination Comm'n v. Continental Air Lines,* 372 U.S. 714 (1963). *Compare Chaulk Servs. v. Massachusetts Comm'n Against Discrimination,* 70 F.3d 1361 (1st Cir. 1995) (NLRB's primary jurisdiction preempted claim before a state agency that an employer had harassed a female employee about her activity as a union organizer because of her gender).

In *Hume v. American Disposal Co.,* 124 Wash.2d 656, 880 P.2d 988 (1994), *cert. denied,* 513 U.S. 1112 (1995), the court held that the Labor Board's exclusive jurisdiction over unfair labor practices did not preempt claims under Washington law that prohibited employer retaliation against employees who assert wage claims and harassment claims under state law, because of the deep and traditional state interest associated with these claims.

BELKNAP, INC. v. HALE

Supreme Court of the United States
463 U.S. 491, 103 S. Ct. 3172, 77 L. Ed. 2d 798 (1983)

JUSTICE WHITE delivered the opinion of the Court....

I

Petitioner Belknap, Inc., is a corporation engaged in the sale of hardware products and certain building materials. A bargaining unit consisting of all of Belknap's warehouse and maintenance employees selected International Brotherhood of Teamsters Local No. 89 (Union) as their collective bargaining representative. In 1975, the Union and Belknap entered into an agreement which was to expire on January 31, 1978. The two opened negotiations for a new contract shortly before the expiration of the 1975 agreement, but reached an impasse. On February 1, 1978, approximately 400 Belknap employees represented by Local 89 went out on strike. Belknap then granted a wage increase, effective February 1, for union employees who stayed on the job.

Shortly after the strike began, Belknap placed an advertisement in a local newspaper seeking applicants to "permanently replace striking warehouse and maintenance employees." A large number of people responded to the offer and were hired. After each replacement was hired, Belknap presented to the replacement the following statement for his signature:

> I, the undersigned, acknowledge and agree that I as of this date have been employed by Belknap, Inc. at its Louisville, Kentucky, facility as a regular full time permanent replacement to permanently replace _____ in the job classification of _____.

On March 7, Local 89 filed unfair labor practice charges against petitioner Belknap. The charge was based on the unilateral wage increase granted by Belknap. Belknap countered with charges of its own. On April 4, the company distributed a letter which said, in relevant part:

To All Permanent Replacement Employees

We recognize that many of you continue to be concerned about your status as an employee. The company's position on this matter has not changed nor do we expect it to change. You will continue to be permanent replacement employees so long as you conduct yourselves in accordance with the policies and practices that are in effect here at Belknap.

We continue to meet and negotiate in good faith with the Union. It is our hope and desire that a mutually acceptable agreement can be reached in the near future. However, we have made it clear to the Union that we have no intention of getting rid of the permanent replacement employees just in order to provide jobs for the replaced strikers if and when the Union calls off the strike.

On April 27, the Regional Director issued a complaint against Belknap, asserting that the unilateral increase violated §§ 8(a)(1), 8(a)(3), and 8(a)(5) of the Act. Three days later, on April 7, the company again addressed the strike replacements:

> We want to make it perfectly clear, once again, that there will be no change in your employment status as a result of the charge by the National Labor Relations Board, which has been reported in this week's newspapers.

> We do not believe there is any substance to the charge and we feel confident we can prove in the court's satisfaction that our intent and actions are completely within the law.

A hearing on the unfair labor practice charges was scheduled for July 19. The Regional Director convened a settlement conference shortly before the hearing was to take place. He explained that if a strike settlement could be reached, he would agree to the withdrawal and dismissal of the unfair labor practice charges and complaints against both the Company and the Union. During these discussions the parties made various concessions, leaving one major issue unresolved, the recall of the striking workers. The parties finally agreed that the Company would, at a minimum, reinstate 35 strikers per week. The settlement agreement was then reduced to writing. Petitioner laid off the replacements, including the twelve respondents, in order to make room for the returning strikers.

Respondents sued Belknap in the Jefferson County, Kentucky, Circuit Court for misrepresentation and breach of contract. Belknap, they alleged, had proclaimed that it was hiring permanent employees, knowing both that the assertion was false and that respondents would detrimentally rely on it. The alternative claim was that Belknap was liable for breaching its contracts with respondents by firing them as a result of its agreement with Local 89. Each respondent asked for $250,000 in compensatory damages, and an equal amount in punitive damages.

[Belknap claimed the replacements' causes of action were preempted by the NLRA, but a Kentucky appellate court disagreed.]

II

Our cases have announced two doctrines for determining whether state regulations or causes of action are preempted by the NLRA. Under the first, set out in *San Diego Building Trades Council v. Garmon*, 359 U.S. 236 (1959), state regulations and causes of action are presumptively preempted if they concern conduct that is actually or arguably either prohibited or protected by the Act. *Id.* at 245. The state regulation or cause of action may, however, be sustained if the behavior to be regulated is behavior that is of only peripheral concern to the federal law or touches interests deeply rooted in local feeling and responsibility. *Id.* at 243-244; *Sears, Roebuck & Co. v. Carpenters,* 436 U.S. 180, 200 (1978); *Farmer v. Carpenters,* 430 U.S. 290, 296-297 (1977). In such cases, the state's interest in controlling or remedying the effects of the conduct is balanced against both the interference with the Board's ability to adjudicate controversies committed to it by the Act, *Farmer v. Carpenters, supra* at 297; *Sears, Roebuck & Co. v. Carpenters, supra* at 200, and the risk that the state will sanction conduct that the Act protects. *Id.* at 205. The second preemption doctrine, set out in *Machinists v. Wisconsin Employment Relations Commission,* 427 U.S. 132 (1976), proscribes state regulation and state-law causes of action concerning conduct that Congress intended to be unregulated, *id.* at 140, conduct that was to remain a part of the self-help remedies left to the combatants in labor disputes, *id.* at 147-148.

Petitioner argues that the action was preempted under both *Garmon* and *Machinists.* The Board and the AFL-CIO, in *amicus* briefs, place major emphasis on *Machinists;* they argue that the Kentucky courts are attempting to impose Kentucky law with respect to areas or subjects that Congress intended to be unregulated. We address first the *Machinists* and then the *Garmon* submissions.

III

It is asserted that Congress intended the respective conduct of the Union and Belknap during the strike beginning on February 1 "'to be controlled by the free play of economic forces,'" *Machinists v. Wisconsin Employment Relations Commission, supra* at 140, *quoting NLRB v. Nash-Finch,* 404 U.S. 138, 144 (1971), and that entertaining the action against Belknap was an impermissible attempt by the Kentucky courts to regulate and burden one of the employer's primary weapons during an economic strike, that is, the right to hire permanent replacements. To permit the suit filed in this case to proceed would upset the delicate balance of forces established by the federal law. Subjecting the employer to costly suits for damages under state law for entering into settlements calling for the return of strikers would also conflict with the federal labor policy favoring the settlement of labor disputes. These arguments, it is urged, are valid whether or not a strike is an economic strike.

We are unpersuaded. It is true that the federal law permits, but does not require, the employer to hire replacements during a strike, replacements that it need not discharge in order to reinstate strikers if it hires the replacements on a "permanent" basis within the meaning of the federal labor law. But when an employer attempts to exercise this very privilege by promising the replacements that they will not be discharged to make room for returning strikers, it surely does not follow that the employer's otherwise valid promises of permanent employment are nullified by federal law and its otherwise actionable misrepresentations may not be pursued. *See, J. I. Case, Co. v. NLRB,* 321 U.S. 332 (1944); *see infra....* We find unacceptable the notion that the federal law on the one hand insists on promises of permanent employment if the employer anticipates keeping the replacements in preference to returning strikers, but on the other hand forecloses damage suits for the employer's breach of these very promises. Even more mystifying is the suggestion that the federal law shields the employer from damages suits for misrepresentations that are made during the process of securing permanent replacements and are actionable under state law.

Arguments that entertaining suits by innocent third parties for breach of contract or for misrepresentation will "burden" the employer's right to hire permanent replacements are no more than arguments that "this is war", that "anything goes", and that promises of permanent employment that under federal law the employer is free to keep, if it so chooses, are essentially meaningless. It is one thing to hold that the federal law intended to leave the employer and the union free to use their economic weapons against one another, but is quite another to hold that either the employer or the union is also free to injure innocent third parties without regard to the normal rules of law governing those relationships. We cannot agree with the dissent that Congress intended such a lawless regime.

The argument that entertaining suits like this will interfere with the asserted policy of the federal law favoring settlement of labor disputes fares no better. This is just another way of asserting that the employer need not answer for its repeated assurances of permanent employment or for its otherwise actionable misrepresentations to secure permanent replacements. We do not think that the normal contractual rights and other usual legal interests of the replacements can be so easily disposed of by broad-brush assertions that no legal rights may accrue to them during a strike because the federal law has privileged the "permanent" hiring of replacements and encourages settlement.

In defense of this position, Belknap, supported by the Board in an amicus brief, urges that permitting the state suit where employers may, after the beginning of a strike, either be ordered to reinstate strikers or find it advisable to sign agreements providing for reinstatement of strikers, will deter employers from making permanent offers of employment or at the very least force them to condition their offer by stating the circumstances under which replacements must be fired. This would considerably weaken the employer's position during the strike, it is said, because without assuring permanent employment, it would be difficult to secure sufficient replacements to keep the business operating. Indeed, as the Board interprets the law, the employer must reinstate strikers at the conclusion of even a purely economic strike unless it has hired "permanent" replacements, that is, hired in a manner that would "show that the men [and women] who replaced the strikers were regarded by themselves and the [employer] as having received their jobs on a permanent basis." *Georgia Highway Express, Inc.*, 165 NLRB 514, 516 (1967), *aff'd sub nom. Truck Drivers and Helpers Local No. 728 v. NLRB*, 403 F.2d 921 (CADC), *cert. denied*, 393 U.S. 935 (1968).

We remain unconvinced. If serious detriment will result to the employer from conditioning offers so as to avoid a breach of contract if the employer is forced by Board order to reinstate strikers or if the employer settles on terms requiring such reinstatement, much the same result would follow from Belknap's and the Board's construction of the Act. Their view is that, as a matter of federal law, an employer may terminate replacements, without liability to them, in the event of settlement or Board decision that the strike is an unfair labor practice strike. Any offer of permanent employment to replacements is thus necessarily conditional and nonpermanent. This view of the law would inevitably become widely known and would deter honest employers from making promises that they know they are not legally obligated to keep. Also, many putative replacements would know that the proffered job is, in important respects, non-permanent and may not accept employment for that reason. It is doubtful, with respect to the employer's ability to hire, that there would be a substantial difference between the effect of the Board's preferred rule and a rule that would subject the employer to damages liability unless it suitably conditions its offers of employment made to replacements.

Belknap counters that conditioning offers in such manner will render replacements non-permanent employees subject to discharge to make way for strikers at the conclusion or settlement of a purely economic strike, which would not be the case if replacements had been hired on a "permanent" basis as the Board now understands that term. The balance of power would thus be distorted if the employer is forced to condition its offers for its own protection. Under Belknap's submission, however, which is to some extent supported by the Board, Belknap's promises, although in form assuring permanent employment, would as a matter of law be non-permanent to the same extent as they would be if expressly conditioned on the eventuality of settlement requiring reinstatement of strikers and on its obligation to reinstate unfair labor practice strikers. As we have said, we cannot believe that Congress determined that the employer must be free to deceive by promising permanent employment knowing that it may choose to reinstate strikers or may be forced to do so by the Board.

An employment contract with a replacement promising permanent employment, subject only to settlement with its employees' union and to a Board unfair labor practice order directing reinstatement of strikers, would not in itself render the replacement a temporary employee subject to displacement by a striker over the employer's objection during or at the end of what is proved to be a purely economic strike. The Board suggests that such a conditional offer "might" render the replacements only temporary hires that the employer would be required to discharge at the conclusion of a purely economic strike. Br. at 17. But the permanent-hiring requirement is designed to protect the strikers, who retain their employee status and are entitled to reinstatement unless they have been permanently replaced. That protection is unnecessary if the employer is ordered to reinstate them because of the commission of unfair labor practices. It is also meaningless if the employer settles with the union and agrees to reinstate strikers. But the protection is of great moment if the employer is not found guilty of unfair practices, does not settle with the union, or settles without a promise to reinstate. In that eventuality, the employer, although he has prevailed in the strike, may refuse reinstatement only if he has hired replacements on a permanent basis. If he has promised to keep the replacements on in such a situation, discharging them to make way for selected strikers whom he deems more experienced or more efficient would breach his contract with the replacements. Those contracts, it seems to us, create a sufficiently permanent arrangement to permit the prevailing employer to abide by its promises.[8]

We perceive no substantial impact on the availability of settlement of economic or unfair labor practice strikes if the employer is careful to protect itself against suits like this in the course of contracting with strike replacements. Its risk of liability if it discharges replacements pursuant to a settlement or to a Board order would then be minimal. We fail to understand why in such circumstances the employer would be any less willing to settle the strike than it would be under the regime proposed by Belknap and the Board, which as a matter of law, would permit it to settle without liability for misrepresentation or for breach of contract.

Belknap and its supporters, the Board and the AFL-CIO, offer no substantial case authority for the proposition that the *Machinists* rationale forecloses this suit. Surely *Machinists* did not deal with solemn promises of permanent employment, made to innocent replacements, that the employer was free to make

---

[8]The refusal to fire permanent replacements because of commitments made to them in the course of an economic strike satisfies the requirement of *NLRB v. Fleetwood Trailer Co.,* 389 U.S. 375, 380 (1967), that the employer have a "legitimate and substantial justification" for his refusal to reinstate strikers. That the offer and promise of permanent employment are conditional does not render the hiring any less permanent if the conditions do not come to pass. All hirings are to some extent conditional. As the Board recognizes, Brief of the National Labor Relations Board as *Amicus Curiae* 16-17 (NLRB Br.), although respondents were hired on a permanent basis, they were subject to discharge in the event of a business slowdown. Had Belknap not settled and no unfair practices been filed, surely it would have been free to retain respondents and obligated to do so by the terms of its promises to them. The result should be the same if Belknap had promised to retain them if it did not settle with the union and if it were not ordered to reinstate strikers.

The dissent and the concurrence make much of conditional offers of employment, asserting that they prevent replacements from being permanent employees. As indicated in the text, however, the Board's position is that even unconditional contracts of permanent employment are as a matter of law defeasible, first, if the strike turns out to be an unfair labor practice strike, and second, if the employer chooses to settle with the union and reinstate the strikers. If these implied conditions, including those dependent on the volitional act of settlement, do not prevent the replacements from being permanent employees, neither should express conditions which do no more than inform replacements what their legal status is in any event.

The dissent and the concurrence suggest that if offers of permanent employment are not necessary to secure the manpower to keep the business operating, returning strikers must be given preference over replacements who have been hired on a permanent basis. That issue is not posed in this case, but we note that the Board has held to the contrary.... *Hot Shoppes, Inc.,* 146 N.L.R.B. 802, 804 (1964)....

and keep under federal law. *J. I. Case, Co. v. NLRB,* 321 U.S. 332 (1944), suggests that individual contracts of employment must give way to otherwise valid provisions of the collective bargaining contract, *id.* at 336-339 but it was careful to say that the Board "has no power to adjudicate the validity or effect of such contracts except as to their effect on matters within its jurisdiction," *id.* at 340. There, the cease-and-desist order, as modified, stated that the discontinuance of the individual contracts was "without prejudice to the assertion of any legal rights the employee may have acquired under such contract or to any defenses thereto by the employer." *Id.* at 342 (emphasis deleted); see *supra....*

There is still another variant or refinement of the argument that the employer and the Union should be privileged to settle their dispute and provide for striker reinstatement free of burdensome law suits such as this. It is said that respondent replacements are employees within the bargaining unit, that the Union is the bargaining representative of petitioner's employees, and the replacements are thus bound by the terms of the settlement negotiated between the employer and "their" representative. The argument is not only that as a matter of federal law the employer cannot be foreclosed from discharging the replacements pursuant to a contract with a bargaining agent, but also that by virtue of the agreement with the Union it is relieved from responding in damages for its knowing breach of contract—that is, that the contracts are not only not specifically enforceable but also may be breached free from liability for damages. We need not address the former issue—the issue of specific performance—since the respondents ask only damages. As to the damages issue, as we have said above, such an argument was rejected in *J. I. Case.*

If federal law forecloses this suit, more specific and persuasive reasons than those based on *Machinists* must be identified to support any such result. Belknap insists that the rationale of the *Garmon* decision, properly construed and applied, furnishes these reasons.

IV

The complaint issued by the Regional Director alleged that on or about February 1, Belknap unilaterally put into effect a 5-per-hour wage increase, that such action constituted unfair labor practices under §§ 8(a)(1), 8(a)(3) and 8(a)(5), and that the strike was prolonged by these violations. If these allegations could have been sustained, the strike would have been an unfair labor practice strike almost from the very start. From that time forward, Belknap's advertised offers of permanent employment to replacements would arguably have been unfair labor practices since they could be viewed as threats to refuse to reinstate unfair labor practice strikers. *See NLRB v. Laredo Coca Cola Bottling Co.,* 613 F.2d 1338, 1341 (CA5), *cert. denied,* 449 U.S. 889 (1980). Furthermore, if the strike had been an unfair labor practice strike, Belknap would have been forced to reinstate the strikers rather than keep replacements on the job. *Mastro Plastics Corp. v.*

NLRB, 350 U.S. 270, 278 (1956). Belknap submits that its offers of permanent employment to respondents were therefore arguably unfair labor practices, the adjudication of which were within the exclusive jurisdiction of the Board, and that discharging respondents to make way for strikers was protected activity since it was no more than the federal law required in the event the unfair labor practices were proved.

Respondents do not dispute that it was the Board's exclusive business to determine, one, whether Belknap's unilateral wage increase was an unfair labor practice, which would have converted the strike into an unfair labor practice strike that [would] require the reinstatement of strikers, and, two, whether Belknap also committed unfair labor practices by offering permanent employment to respondents. They submit, however, that under our cases, properly read, their actions for fraud and breach of contract, are not preempted. We agree with respondents.

Under *Garmon,* a state may regulate conduct that is of only peripheral concern to the Act or which is so deeply rooted in local law that the courts should not assume that Congress intended to preempt the application of state law. In *Linn v. Plant Guard Workers,* 383 U.S. 53 (1966), we held that false and malicious statements in the course of a labor dispute were actionable under state law if injurious to reputation, even though such statements were in themselves unfair labor practices adjudicable by the Board. Likewise, in *Farmer v. Carpenters,* 430 U.S. 290 (1977), we held that the Act did not preempt a state action for intentionally inflicting emotional distress, even though a major part of the cause of action consisted of conduct that was arguably an unfair labor practice. Finally in *Sears, Roebuck & Co. v. Carpenters,* 436 U.S. 180 (1978), we held that a state trespass action was permissible and not preempted, since the action concerned only the location of the picketing while the arguable unfair labor practice would focus on the object of the picketing. In that case, we emphasized that a critical inquiry in applying the *Garmon* rules, where the conduct at issue in the state litigation is said to be arguably prohibited by the Act and hence within the exclusive jurisdiction of the NLRB, is whether the controversy presented to the state court is identical with that which could be presented to the Board. There the state court and Board controversies could not fairly be called identical. This is also the case here.

Belknap contends that the misrepresentation suit is preempted because it related to the offers and contracts for permanent employment, conduct that was part and a parcel of an arguable unfair labor practice. It is true that whether the strike was an unfair labor practice strike and whether the offer to replacements was the kind of offer forbidden during such a dispute were matters for the Board. The focus of these determinations, however, would be on whether the rights of strikers were being infringed. Neither controversy would have anything in common with the question whether Belknap made misrepresentations to replacements that were actionable under state law. The Board would be concerned with the impact on strikers[,] not with whether the employer deceived replacements. As in *Linn v. Plant Guard Workers, supra,* "the Board [will] not be ignored since its sanctions alone can adjust the equilibrium disturbed by an unfair labor practice." *Id.* at 66. The strikers cannot secure reinstatement, or indeed any relief, by suing for misrepresentation in state court. The state courts in no way offer them an alternative forum for obtaining relief that the Board can provide. The same was true in *Sears* and *Farmer.* Hence, it appears to us that maintaining the misrepresentation action would not interfere with the Board's determination of matters within its jurisdiction and that such an action is of no more than peripheral concern to the Board and the federal law. At the same time, Kentucky surely has a substantial interest in protecting its citizens from misrepresentations that have caused them grievous harm. It is no less true here than it was in *Linn v. Plant Guard Workers, supra* at 63, that "[t]he injury" remedied by the state law "has no relevance to the Board's function" and that "[t]he Board can award no damages, impose no penalty, or give any other relief" to the plaintiffs in this case. The state interests involved in this case clearly outweigh any possible interference with the Board's function that may result from permitting the action for misrepresentation to proceed.

Neither can we accept the assertion that the breach of contract claim is preempted. The claimed breach is the discharge of respondents to make way for strikers, an action allegedly contrary to promises that were binding under state law. As we have said, respondents do not deny that had the strike been adjudicated an unfair labor practice strike Belknap would have been required to reinstate the strikers, an obligation that the state could not negate.[13] But respondents do assert that such an adjudication has not been made, that Belknap prevented such an adjudication by settling with the Union and voluntarily agreeing to reinstate strikers, and that, in any event, the reinstatement of strikers, even if ordered by the Board, would only prevent the specific performance of Belknap's promises to respondents, not immunize Belknap from responding in damages from its breach of its otherwise enforceable contracts.

For the most part, we agree with respondents. We have already concluded that the federal law does not expressly or impliedly privilege an employer, as part of a settlement with a union, to discharge replacements in breach of its promises of permanent employment. Also, even had there been no settlement and the Board had ordered reinstatement of what it held to be unfair labor practice strikers, the suit for damages for breach of contract could still be maintained without in any way prejudicing the jurisdiction of the Board or the interest of the federal law in insuring the replacement of strikers. The interests of the Board and the NLRA, on

---

[13] Kentucky may not mandate specific performance of the contract between Belknap and respondents nor may it enter an injunction requiring the reinstatement of respondents as a remedy for fraud if either action necessitates the firing of a striker entitled to reinstatement. To do so would be to deprive returning strikers of jobs committed to them by the national labor laws....

the one hand, and the interest of the state in providing a remedy to its citizens for breach of contract, on the other, are "discrete" concerns, cf. *Farmer v. Carpenters, supra,* at 304. We see no basis for holding that permitting the contract cause of action will conflict with the rights of either the strikers or the employer or would frustrate any policy of the federal labor laws.

V

Because neither the misrepresentation nor the breach-of-contract cause of action is preempted under *Garmon* or *Machinists,* the decision of the Kentucky Court of Appeals is

Affirmed.

[The opinion of JUSTICE BLACKMUN, concurring in the judgment, is omitted.]

JUSTICE BRENNAN, with whom JUSTICE MARSHALL and JUSTICE POWELL join, dissenting....

Despite the conceded difficulty of this case, I cannot agree with the Court's conclusion that neither respondents' breach of contract claim nor their misrepresentation claim is preempted by federal law. In my view these claims go to the core of federal labor policy. If respondents are allowed to pursue their claims in state court, employers will be subject to potentially conflicting state and federal regulation of their activities; the efficient administration of the National Labor Relations Act will be threatened; and the structure of the economic weapons Congress has provided to parties to a labor dispute will be altered. In short, the purposes and policies of federal law will be frustrated. I, therefore, respectfully dissent....

Respondents' breach of contract claim is based on the allegation that petitioner breached his contracts with them by entering into a settlement agreement with the union that called for the gradual reinstatement of the strikers respondents had replaced.... The strike involved in this case, however, arguably was converted into an unfair labor practice strike almost immediately after it started.... If the strike was converted into an unfair labor practice strike, the striking employees were entitled to reinstatement irrespective of petitioner's decision to hire permanent replacements.... Under these circumstances, federal law would have required petitioner to reinstate the striking employees and to discharge the replacements. In this light, it is clear that petitioner's decision to breach its contracts with respondents was arguably *required* by federal law....

In my view ... basic principles compel a conclusion that respondents' breach of contract claim is preempted. The potential for conflicting regulation clearly exists in this case. Respondents' breach of contract claim seeks to regulate activity that may well have been required by federal law. Petitioner may have to answer in damages for taking such an action. This sort of conflicting regulation is intolerable. As the Court stated in *Motor Coach Employees v. Lockridge, supra,* if "the regulatory schemes, state and federal, conflict ... pre-emption is clearly called for...." 403 U.S. at 292....

Prohibiting specific enforcement, but permitting a damages award, does nothing to eliminate the conflict between state and federal law in this context. The Court fails to recognize that "regulation can be as effectively exerted through an award of damages as through some form of preventive relief." *Garmon,* 359 U.S. at 247. "The obligation to pay compensation can be, indeed is designed to be, a potent method of governing conduct and controlling policy." *Ibid.* The force of these observations is apparent in this case. If an employer is confronted with potential liability for discharging workers he has hired to replace striking employees, he is likely to be much less willing to enter into a settlement agreement calling for the dismissal of unfair labor practice charges and for the reinstatement of strikers. Instead, he is much more likely to refuse to settle and to litigate the charges at issue while retaining the replacements. Such developments would frustrate the strong federal interest in ending strikes and in settling labor disputes. In addition, the National Labor Relations Board has suggested that any impediment to the settlement of unfair labor practice charges would have a serious adverse effect on the Board's administration of the Act. Finally, any obstacle to strike settlement agreements clearly affects adversely the interest of striking employees in returning to work, to say nothing of the public interest in ending labor strife. Consideration of these factors leads to the clear conclusion that respondents' breach of contract claim must be preempted....

Respondents' misrepresentation claim stands on a somewhat different footing than their breach of contract claim. There is no sense in which it can be said that federal law required petitioner to misrepresent to respondents the terms on which they were hired. Permitting respondents to pursue their misrepresentation claim in state court, therefore, does not present the same potential for directly conflicting regulation of employer activity as permitting respondents to pursue their breach of contract claim. Nor can it be said that petitioner's alleged misrepresentation was "arguably protected" under *Garmon.* While it is arguable that petitioner's alleged offers of permanent employment were prohibited by the Act and therefore preempted under *Garmon,* ... careful analysis yields the conclusion that this is not a sufficient ground for preempting respondents' misrepresentation claim. In my view, however, respondents' misrepresentation claim is preempted under the analysis articulated principally in *Machinists v. Wisconsin Emp. Rel. Comm'n,* 427 U.S. 132 (1976)....

Machinists relied on *Garner* and *Morton* in expressly articulating a branch of labor law preemption analysis distinct from the *Garmon* line of cases. The Court in *Machinists* described this branch as "focusing upon the crucial inquiry whether Congress intended that the conduct involved be unregulated because left 'to be controlled by the free play of economic forces.'" 427 U.S. at 140 (citation omitted). While earlier cases had addressed this question within the context of union and employee activities, see *id.,* at 147, the Court noted that "self-help is ... also the prerogative of the employer because he, too, may properly employ economic weapons Congress meant to be unregulable." *Ibid.* The Court stated: "Whether self-help economic activities are employed by employer or union, the crucial inquiry regarding preemption is the same: whether 'the exercise of plenary state authority to curtail or entirely prohibit self-help would frustrate effective implementation of the Act's processes.'" *Id.* at 147-148 (citation omitted).

As noted, ... employers have the right to hire replacements for striking employees. This is an economic weapon that the employer may use to combat pressure brought to bear by the union. Permitting the use of this weapon is part of the balance struck by the Act between labor and management. There is no doubt that respondents' misrepresentation claim, involving as it does the potential for substantial employer liability, burdens an employer's right to resort to this weapon. This is especially apparent when one considers the fact that the character of a strike is often unclear. A strike that starts as an economic strike, during which an employer is entitled to hire permanent replacements that he need not discharge to make way for returning strikers, may be converted into an unfair labor practice strike, in which case the employer loses his right to hire permanent replacements subsequent to the date of the conversion....

Based on this analysis, it is clear that permitting respondents to pursue their misrepresentation claim in state court would limit and substantially burden an employer's resort to an economic weapon available to him under federal law. This would have the inevitable effect of distorting the delicate balance struck by the Act between the rights of labor and management in labor disputes. For these reasons, respondents' misrepresentation claim must be preempted....

NOTES

1. In *Wisconsin Dep't of Indus., Labor & Human Relations v. Gould, Inc.,* 475 U.S. 282 (1986), the Supreme Court held that the NLRA preempted a Wisconsin statute debarring any firm violating the NLRA three times within five years from doing business with the state. To the state's argument that its scheme should escape preemption as an exercise of the spending power rather than the regulatory power, the Court responded: "But that seems to us a distinction without a difference, at least in this case, because on its face the debarment statute serves plainly as a means of enforcing the NLRA." The Court also said: "Because Wisconsin's debarment law functions unambiguously as a supplemental sanction for violations of the NLRA, it conflicts with the Board's comprehensive regulation of industrial relations in precisely the same way as would a state statute preventing repeat labor law violators from doing any business with private parties within the State." *See also Employers Ass'n v. United Steelworkers,* 32 F.3d 1297 (8th Cir. 1994) and *Midwest Motor Express v. Teamsters Local 120,* 512 N.W.2d 881 (Minn. Sup. Ct. 1994) (Minn. Striker Replacement Act proscribing hiring of permanent striker replacements preempted by NLRA); *Rum Creek Coal Sales v.*

Caperton, 971 F.2d 1148 (4th Cir. 1992) (W. Va. Neutrality Statute forbidding state police from aiding either party in labor dispute preempted by NLRA to extent it bars police from preventing illegal conduct by striking workers).

2. In 1980, when the Golden State Transit Corporation applied for a renewal of its taxicab license, the City of Los Angeles conditioned renewal upon Golden State's settlement of its existing bargaining dispute by a certain date. When the dispute was not resolved by that date, Los Angeles refused to renew Golden State's taxicab license. The Supreme Court was asked to determine whether the actions of Los Angeles were preempted by the NLRA.

> Congress' decision to prohibit certain forms of economic pressure while leaving others unregulated represents an intentional balance "between the uncontrolled power of management and labor to further their respective interests." *Machinists v. Wisconsin Empl. Rels. Comm.,* 427 U.S. 132, 146 (1976). States are therefore prohibited from imposing additional restrictions on economic weapons of self-help, such as strikes or lockouts, unless such restrictions presumably were contemplated by Congress. "Whether self-help economic activities are employed by employer or union, the crucial inquiry regarding pre-emption is the same: whether the exercise of plenary state authority to curtail or entirely prohibit self-help would frustrate effective implementation of the Act's processes." *Id.* at 147-48.... The parties' resort to economic pressure was a legitimate part of their collective-bargaining process. But the bargaining process was thwarted when the city in effect imposed a positive durational limit on the exercise of self-help.

Since the Court found that Los Angeles had "[entered] into the substantive aspects of the bargaining process to an extent Congress has not countenanced," it concluded that its actions were preempted. *Golden State Transit Corp. v. City of Los Angeles,* 475 U.S. 608 (1986). *See also Golden State Transit Corp. v. City of Los Angeles,* 493 U.S. 103 (1989) (holding that Golden State Transit had federal court damage remedy under 42 U.S.C. § 1983 against Los Angeles for violation of its LMRA rights).

The Illinois Burial Rights Act requires cemeteries and gravediggers to bargain for the creation of a labor pool that will perform religiously required interments during labor disputes. In *Cannon v. Edgar,* 33 F.3d 880 (7th Cir. 1994), the court found this provision preempted by the NLRA, since it constituted a direct intrusion by the state into the collective bargaining process.

3. The Supreme Court has sustained a Massachusetts Water Resources Authority bidding specification requiring contractors wishing to work on the $6 billion Boston Harbor cleanup project to comply with the terms of a master labor agreement, since the Court concluded that such a lawful prehire agreement requirement may be imposed by a state acting as the owner of a construction project, as opposed to a state acting in a regulatory capacity. *Building & Constr. Trades Council v. Associated Bldrs. & Contractors,* 507 U.S. 218 (1993). *See* *also Associated Bldrs. & Contractors v. City of Seward,* 966 F.2d 492 (9th Cir. 1992), *cert. denied,* 507 U.S. 984 (1993) (city acting pursuant to work-preservation clause in own bargaining agreement not preempted from requiring private bidders on municipal project to enter into labor contract with union representing city employees who normally perform work involved).

4. Some of the leading articles on federal-state relations in labor law include Gottesman, *Rethinking Labor Law Preemption: State Laws Facilitating Unionization,* 7 Yale J. Reg. 355 (1990); Cox, *Federalism in the Law of Labor Relations,* 67 Harv. L. Rev. 1297 (1954); Cox, *Labor Law Preemption Revisited,* 85 Harv. L. Rev. 1337 (1972); Kirby, *Constitutional Issues in Labor Law: Federal Preemption in Labor Relations,* 63 Nw. U.L. Rev. 1 (1968); Lesnick, *Preemption Reconsidered: The Apparent Reaffirmation of Garmon,* 72 Colum. L. Rev. 469 (1972); Meltzer, *The Supreme Court, Congress, and State Jurisdiction Over Labor Relations* (pts. 1 & 2), 59 Colum. L. Rev. 6, 269 (1959); Michelman, *State Power to Govern Concerted Employee Activities,* 74 Harv. L. Rev. 641 (1961); Smith & Clark, *Reappraisal of the Role of the States in Shaping Labor Relations Law,* 1965 Wis. L. Rev. 411; Updegraff, *Preemption, Predictability and Progress in Labor Law,* 17 Hastings L.J. 473 (1966); Wellington, *Labor and the Federal System,* 26 U. Chi. L. Rev. 542 (1959); Cox, *Recent Developments in Federal Labor Law Preemption,* 41 Ohio St. L.J. 277 (1980).

5. A separate preemption doctrine arising under § 301 of the LMRA with respect to state causes of action that would necessitate the interpretation or application of terms contained in bargaining agreements is discussed in Part Four, Section III.D, *infra.*

PART FOUR

COLLECTIVE BARGAINING

ALBERT REES, THE ECONOMICS OF TRADE UNIONS 74, 89-90, 186-87 (2d ed. 1977)*

My own best guess of the average effects of all American unions on the wages of their members in recent years would lie somewhere between 15 and 20 per cent....

Many people view trade unions as a device for increasing the worker's share in the distribution of income at the expense of capital; that is, at the expense of the receivers of rent, interest, and profits. Attempts to test this view, which is often expressed by the unions themselves, have led to a number of studies of the effect of unions on labor's share. The studies to date must be regarded as highly inconclusive; no union effect on labor's share can be discovered with any consistency....

It may seem very strange that statistical studies can find a considerable effect of unions on wages and none on labor's share. On further consideration, however, this result is quite reasonable.... [A] successful union will not necessarily raise labor's share even in its own industry. The wage bill will rise following a wage increase if the demand for labor is inelastic (that is, if the percentage reduction in employment is smaller than the percentage increase in wages) and this will raise labor's share in the short run. But as time passes the employer will tend to substitute capital for labor.... In extreme cases, total wage payments may fall as employment contracts so that they are smaller than they were before the wage increase.... It is thus entirely possible for a union simultaneously to raise the relative wages of its members and to reduce their aggregate share of income arising in their industry....

If the union is viewed solely in terms of its effect on the economy, it must in my opinion be considered an obstacle to the optimum performance of our economic system. It alters the wage structure in a way that impedes the growth of employment in sectors of the economy where productivity and income are naturally high and that leaves too much labor in low-income sectors of the economy like southern agriculture and the least skilled service trades. It benefits most those workers who would in any case be relatively well off, and while some of this gain may be at the expense of the owners of capital, most of it must be at the expense of consumers and the lower-paid workers. Unions interfere blatantly with the use of the most productive techniques in some industries, and this effect

---

*Reprinted with the permission of the University of Chicago Press.

is probably not offset by the stimulus to higher productivity furnished by some other unions.

Many of my fellow economists would stop at this point and conclude that unions are harmful and that their power should be curbed. I do not agree that one can judge the value of a complex institution from so narrow a point of view. Other aspects of unions must also be considered. The protection against the abuse of managerial authority given by seniority systems and grievance procedures seems to me to be a union accomplishment of the greatest importance. So too is the organized representation in public affairs given the worker by the political activities of unions.... If the job rights won for workers by unions are not conceded by the rest of society simply because they are just, they should be conceded because they help to protect the minimum consensus that keeps our society stable. In my judgment, the economic losses imposed by unions are not too high a price to pay for their successful performance of this role.

NOTE

For other views, *see* R. Lester, Economics of Labor 292-330, 597-602 (2d ed. 1964); L. Reynolds, S. Masters & C. Moser, Labor Economics and Labor Relations 257-60, 541-62 (10th ed. 1991); S. Slichter, J. Healey & E. Livernash, The Impact of Collective Bargaining on Management 954-61 (1960).

FREEMAN & MEDOFF, THE TWO FACES OF UNIONISM, in THE PUBLIC INTEREST 69, 76, 78-82, 85, 86 (Fall 1979)*

Since, in fact, unions have both monopoly and collective-voice/institutional-response components, the key question for understanding unionism in the United States relates to the relative importance of these two faces. Are unions primarily monopolistic institutions, or are they primarily voice institutions that induce socially beneficial responses?

Most of the econometric analysis of unions has focused on the question of central concern to the monopoly view: How large is the union wage effect? In his important book, Unionism and Relative Wages, H. Gregg Lewis summarized results of this analysis through the early 1960's, concluding that, while differing over time and across settings, the union wage effect averages on the order of 10 to 15 percent.

As predicted by the monopoly wage model, the capital-labor ratio and average "quality" of labor both appear to be somewhat greater than "optimal" in union settings. However, the total loss in output due to this misallocation of resources appears to be minuscule; an analysis done by Albert Rees suggests that the loss is less than 0.3 percent of the gross national product.

One of the central tenets of the collective-voice/institutional-response model is that among workers receiving the same pay, unions reduce employee turnover and its associated costs by offering "voice" as an alternative to exit. Our own research shows that, with diverse factors (including wages) held constant, unionized workers do have significantly lower quit rates than nonunion workers who are comparable in other respects.

Our analyses of newly available data on unionism and output per worker in many establishments or sectors suggests that the monopoly view of unions as a major deterrent to productivity is erroneous. In some settings, unionism leads to *higher* productivity, not only because of the greater capital intensity and higher labor quality, but also because of what can best be termed institutional-response factors.

In manufacturing, productivity in the organized sector appears to be substantially higher than in the unorganized sector, by an amount that could roughly offset the increase in total costs attributable to higher union wages.

There is limited tentative evidence that, on average, net profits are reduced somewhat by unionism, particularly in oligopolistic industries, though there are notable exceptions. At present, there is no definitive accounting of what proportion of the union wage effect comes at the expense of capital, other labor, or consumers, and what portion is offset by previously unexploited possibilities for productivity improvements.

Finally, it is important to note that despite what some critics of unions might claim, strikes do not seem to cost society a substantial amount of goods and services. For the economy as a whole, the percentage of total working time lost directly to strikes during the past two decades has never been greater than 0.5 percent and has averaged about 0.2 percent.

Under the monopoly view, the exit and entry of workers permits each individual to find a firm offering the mix of employee benefits and personnel policies that he or she prefers. In the voice view, a union provides management with information at the bargaining table concerning policies affecting its entire membership (e.g., the mix of the employee-compensation package or the firm's employment practices during a downturn) which can be expected to be different from that derived from the movements of marginal workers.

Data on the remuneration of individual workers and on the expenditures for employees by firms show that the proportion of compensation allotted to fringe benefits is markedly higher for organized blue-collar workers than for similar nonunion workers. Within most industries, important fringes such as pensions, and life, accident, and health insurance are much more likely to be found in unionized establishments.

According to the monopoly model, the workers displaced from unionized firms as a result of union wage gains raise the supply of labor to nonunion firms, which can therefore be expected to reduce wages. Thus in the monopoly view unionized workers are likely to be made better off at the expense of nonunion workers. The fact that organized blue-collar workers would tend to be more skilled and higher paid than other blue-collar workers even in the absence of unionism implies further that unionism benefits "labor's elite" at the expense of those with less skill and earning power.

In fact, the collective-voice/institutional-response model suggests very different effects on equality than does the monopoly view. Given that union decisions are based on a political process, and given that the majority of union members are likely to have earnings below the mean (including white-collar workers) in any workplace, unions can be expected to seek to reduce wage inequality. Union members are also likely to favor a less-dispersed distribution of earnings for reasons of ideology and organizational solidarity. Finally, by its nature, collective bargaining reduces managerial discretion in the wage-setting process, and this should also reduce differences among similarly situated workers.

Our empirical estimates, based on new data, show that standardization policies have substantially reduced wage inequality, and that this effect dominates the monopoly wage effect. When, for instance, the distribution of earnings for male blue-collar workers is graphed, the results for unionized workers in both the manufacturing and nonmanufacturing sectors show a much narrower distribution, compressed at the extremes and radically peaked in the middle. For nonunion workers, by contrast, the graphs show a much more dispersed pattern of earnings.

In addition to reducing earnings inequality among blue-collar workers, union wage policies contribute to the equalization of wages by decreasing the differential between covered blue-collar workers and uncovered white-collar workers. In manufacturing, though white-collar workers earn an average of 49 percent more than blue-collar workers, our estimates indicate that in unionized enterprises this premium is only 32 percent; in the nonmanufacturing sector, where white-collar workers average 31 percent more in earnings than blue-collar workers, the estimated differential is only 19 percent where there are unions.

NOTE

For other wide-ranging discussions of the economic impact of unions and collective bargaining, with proposals for future legal approaches, *see* Barenberg, *The Political Economy of the Wagner Act: Power, Symbol, and Workplace Cooperation*, 106 Harv. L. Rev. 1381 (1993): Dau-Schmidt, *A Bargaining Analysis of American Labor Law and the Search for Bargaining Equity and Industrial Peace*, 91 Mich. L. Rev. 419 (1992); Estreicher, *Freedom of Contract and Labor Law Reform: Opening Up the Possibilities for Value-Added Unionism*, 71 N.Y.U. L. Rev. 827 (1996); Getman & Marshall, *Industrial Relations in Transition: The Paper Industry Example*, 102 Yale L.J. 1803 (1993); Gould, *Reflections on Workers' Participation, Influence, and Powersharing: The Future of Industrial Relations*, 58 U. Cinn. L. Rev. 381 (1989); Hiatt & Jackson, *Union Survival Strategies for the Twenty-First Century*, 12 Lab. Lawyer 165 (1996); Hyde, *A

Theory of Labor Legislation, 38 Buffalo L. Rev. 383 (1990); Hylton, *Efficiency and Labor Law*, 87 NW. U. L. Rev. 471 (1993); Stone, *The Legacy of Industrial Pluralism: The Tension Between Individual Employment Rights and the New Deal Collective Bargaining System*, 59 U. Chi. L. Rev. 575 (1992); Weiler & Mundlak, *New Directions for the Law of the Workplace*, 102 Yale L.J. 1907 (1993).

SECTION I. The Duty to Bargain Collectively

A. EXCLUSIVE REPRESENTATION AND MAJORITY RULE

J.I. CASE CO. v. NLRB

Supreme Court of the United States
321 U.S. 332, 64 S. Ct. 576, 88 L. Ed. 762 (1944)

MR. JUSTICE JACKSON delivered the opinion of the Court.

This cause was heard by the National Labor Relations Board on stipulated facts which so far as concern present issues are as follows:

The petitioner, J.I. Case Company, at its Rock Island, Illinois, plant, from 1937 offered each employee an individual contract of employment. The contracts were uniform and for a term of one year. The Company agreed to furnish employment as steadily as conditions permitted, to pay a specified rate, which the Company might redetermine if the job changed, and to maintain certain hospital facilities. The employee agreed to accept the provisions, to serve faithfully and honestly for the term, to comply with factory rules, and that defective work should not be paid for. About 75% of the employees accepted and worked under these agreements....

While the individual contracts executed August 1, 1941, were in effect, a CIO union petitioned the Board for certification as the exclusive bargaining representative of the production and maintenance employees. On December 17, 1941, a hearing was held, at which the Company urged the individual contracts as a bar to representation proceedings. The Board, however, directed an election, which was won by the union. The union was thereupon certified as the exclusive bargaining representative of the employees in question in respect to wages, hours, and other conditions of employment.

The union then asked the Company to bargain. It refused, declaring that it could not deal with the union in any manner affecting rights and obligations under the individual contracts while they remained in effect. It offered to negotiate on matters which did not affect rights under the individual contracts, and said that upon the expiration of the contracts it would bargain as to all matters. Twice the Company sent circulars to its employees asserting the validity of the individual contracts and stating the position that it took before the Board in reference to them.

The Board held that the Company had refused to bargain collectively, in violation of § 8(5) of the National Labor Relations Act....

Individual contracts, no matter what the circumstances that justify their execution or what their terms, may not be availed of to defeat or delay the procedures prescribed by the National Labor Relations Act looking to collective bargaining, nor to exclude the contracting employee from a duly ascertained bargaining unit; nor may they be used to forestall bargaining or to limit or condition the terms of the collective agreement. "The Board asserts a public right vested in it as a public body, charged in the public interest with the duty of preventing unfair labor practices." *National Licorice Co. v. NLRB,* 309 U.S. 350, 364 (1940). Wherever private contracts conflict with its functions, they obviously must yield or the Act would be reduced to a futility.

It is equally clear since the collective trade agreement is to serve the purpose contemplated by the Act, the individual contract cannot be effective as a waiver of any benefit to which the employee otherwise would be entitled under the trade agreement. The very purpose of providing by statute for the collective agreement is to supersede the terms of separate agreements of employees with terms which reflect the strength and bargaining power and serve the welfare of the group. Its benefits and advantages are open to every employee of the represented unit, whatever the type or terms of his pre-existing contract of employment.

But it is urged that some employees may lose by the collective agreement, that an individual workman may sometimes have, or be capable of getting, better terms than those obtainable by the group and that his freedom of contract must be respected on that account. We are not called upon to say that under no circumstances can an individual enforce an agreement more advantageous than a collective agreement, but we find the mere possibility that such agreements might be made no ground for holding generally that individual contracts may survive or surmount collective ones. The practice and philosophy of collective bargaining looks with suspicion on such individual advantages. Of course, where there is a great variation in circumstances of employment or capacity of employees, it is possible for the collective bargain to prescribe only minimum rates or maximum hours or expressly to leave certain areas open to individual bargaining. But except as so provided, advantages to individuals may prove as disruptive of industrial peace as disadvantages. They are a fruitful way of interfering with organization and choice of representative; increased compensation, if individually deserved, is often earned at the cost of breaking down some other standard thought to be for the welfare of the group, and always creates the suspicion of being paid at the long-range expense of the group as a whole. Such discriminations not infrequently amount to unfair labor practices. The workman is free, if he values his own bargaining position more than that of the group, to vote against representation; but the majority rules, and if it collectivizes the employment bargain, individual advantages or favors will generally in practice go in as a contribution to the collective result. We cannot except individual contracts generally from the operation of collective ones because some may be more individually advantageous. Individual contracts cannot subtract from collective ones, and whether under some circumstances they may add to them in matters covered by the collective bargain, we leave to be determined by appropriate forums under the laws of contracts applicable, and to the Labor Board if they constitute unfair labor practices.

It also is urged that such individual contracts may embody matters that are not necessarily included within the statutory scope of collective bargaining, such as stock purchase, group insurance, hospitalization, or medical attention. We know of nothing to prevent the employee's, because he is an employee, making any contract provided it is not inconsistent with a collective agreement or does not amount to or result from or is not part of an unfair labor practice. But in so doing the employer may not incidentally exact or obtain any diminution of his own obligation or any increase of those of employees in the matters covered by collective agreement. Hence we find that the contentions of the Company that the individual contracts precluded a choice of representatives and warranted refusal to bargain during their duration were properly overruled. It follows that representation to the employees by circular letter that they had such legal effect was improper and could properly be prohibited by the Board....

NOTES

1. In *Order of R.R. Telegraphers v. Railway Express Agency,* 321 U.S. 342 (1944), the Supreme Court held that individual contracts made after the collective agreement did not supersede the collective provisions. Under the collective agreement, unexpectedly high rates were payable to a few specially situated station agents. To correct this situation, the company made individual contracts with those agents, but without getting the union's approval or modifying the collective agreement. Under the principle of exclusive representation, the Court held that the union was entitled to be consulted about "the exceptional as well as the routine rates, rules and working conditions."

2. In *Caterpillar Inc. v. Williams,* 482 U.S. 386, 396 (1987), the Supreme Court stated:

> *J.I. Case* does not stand for the proposition that all individual employment contracts are subsumed into, or eliminated by, the collective-bargaining agreement .... Thus, individual employment contracts are not inevitably superseded by any subsequent collective agreement covering an individual employee, and claims based upon them may arise under state law. [A] plaintiff covered by a collective-bargaining agreement is permitted to assert legal rights *independent* of that agreement, including state-law contract rights, so long as the contract relied upon is *not* a collective-bargaining agreement.

3. The power of exclusive representation enables unions to bind dissenters, within certain limits, on the wages they will receive, the hours they will work, and nearly every other facet of their industrial existence. Is this a far more significant encroachment on "individual rights" than the union shop, under which employees may be required to contribute to the financial support of their bargaining representative? Should the doctrine of majority rule be the proper target of those concerned about excessive union power and denial of individual employee voice? Or is exclusive representation indispensable to the effective functioning of collective bargaining? *See generally* Carlson, *The Origin and Future of Exclusive Representation in American Labor Law*, 30 Duq. L. Rev. 779 (1992); Schatzki, *Majority Rule, Exclusive Representation, and the Interests of Individual Workers: Should Exclusivity Be Abolished?* 123 U. Pa. L. Rev. 897 (1975); Schreiber, *The Origin of the Majority Rule and Simultaneous Development of Institutions to Protect the Minority: A Chapter in Early American Labor Law,* 25 Rutgers L. Rev. 237 (1971); Strauss, *Is the New Deal Collapsing? With What Might It Be Replaced?*, 34 Indus. Rel. L. Rev. 329 (1995); Weyand, *Majority Rule in Collective Bargaining,* 45 Colum. L. Rev. 556 (1945). For consideration of exclusivity and majority rule in a broader context, *see* Bok, *Reflections on the Distinctive Character of American Labor Laws,* 84 Harv. L. Rev. 1394, 1426-27 (1971). *See also* Summers, *Unions without Majority—A Black Hole?,* 66 Chi.-Kent L. Rev. 531 (1990).

4. Exclusivity is unique to American and Canadian labor law regimes; other forms of worker organization and collective representation prevail in most economically advanced democracies. *See generally* Blaupain & Engel (eds.), Comparative Labour Law and Industrial Relations in Industrialized Market Economies (1993). For example, Japanese law requires employers to bargain with any union representing at least two people; multiple unionism is common. *See* Hajime Matsuzaki, *Enterprise Unions in Japan*, 34 Indus. Rel. 617 (1992).

On the other hand, in many of these countries the detailed administration of the work place is the prerogative of a paternalistic management. There is little connection between the plant level and the industry level of workers' organizations, and their functions tend to be more social and political than economic. Does this experience shed any light on the problem of exclusive representation?

Is it coincidental that union density is lower in the United States and Canada than it is in industrialized countries that have rejected majority rule and exclusivity?

EMPORIUM CAPWELL CO. v. WESTERN ADDITION COMMUNITY ORGANIZATION

Supreme Court of the United States
420 U.S. 50, 95 S. Ct. 977, 43 L. Ed. 2d 12 (1975)

Opinion of the Court by MR. JUSTICE MARSHALL....

This litigation presents the question whether, in light of the national policy against racial discrimination in employment, the National Labor Relations Act protects concerted activity by a group of minority employees to bargain with their employer over issues of employment discrimination. The National Labor Relations Board held that the employees could not circumvent their elected representative to engage in such bargaining. The Court of Appeals for the District of Columbia Circuit reversed and remanded, holding that in certain circumstances the activity would be protected.... We now reverse.

I

The Emporium Capwell Co. (Company) operates a department store in San Francisco. At all times relevant to this litigation it was a party to the collective bargaining agreement negotiated by the San Francisco Retailer's Council, of which it was a member, and the Department Store Employees Union (Union) which represented all stock and marking area employees of the Company. The agreement, in which the Union was recognized as the sole collective bargaining agency for all covered employees, prohibited employment discrimination by reason of race, color, creed, national origin, age, or sex, as well as union activity. It had a no-strike or lockout clause, and it established grievance and arbitration machinery for processing any claimed violation of the contract, including a violation of the antidiscrimination clause.

On April 3, 1968, a group of Company employees covered by the agreement met with the Secretary-Treasurer of the Union, Walter Johnson, to present a list of grievances including a claim that the Company was discriminating on the basis of race in making assignments and promotions. The union official agreed to take certain of the grievances and to investigate the charge of racial discrimination. He appointed an investigating committee and prepared a report on the employees' grievances, which he submitted to the Retailer's Council and which the Council in turn referred to the Company. The report described "the possibility of racial discrimination" as perhaps the most important issue raised by the employees and termed the situation at the Company as potentially explosive if corrective action were not taken....

Shortly after receiving the report, the Company's labor relations director met with Union representatives and agreed to "look into the matter" of discrimination and see what needed to be done. Apparently unsatisfied with these representations, the Union held a meeting in September attended by Union officials, Company employees, and representatives of the California Fair Employment Practices Committee (FEPC) and the local antipoverty agency. The Secretary-Treasurer of the Union announced that the Union had concluded that the Company was discriminating, and that it would process every such grievance through to arbitration if necessary. Testimony about the Company's practices was taken and transcribed by a court reporter, and the next day the Union notified the Company of its formal charge and demanded that the joint union-management Adjustment Board be convened "to hear the entire case."

At the September meeting some of the Company's employees had expressed their view that the contract procedures were inadequate to handle a systemic grievance of this sort; they suggested that the Union instead begin picketing the store in protest. Johnson explained that the collective agreement bound the Union to its processes and expressed his view that successful grievants would be helping not only themselves but all others who might be the victims of invidious discrimination as well. The FEPC and antipoverty agency representatives offered the same advice. Nonetheless, when the Adjustment Board meeting convened on October 16, James Joseph Hollins, Tom Hawkins, and two other employees whose testimony the Union had intended to elicit refused to participate in the grievance procedure. Instead, Hollins read a statement objecting to reliance on correction of individual inequities as an approach to the problem of discrimination at the store and demanding that the president of the Company meet with the four protestants to work out a broader agreement for dealing with the issue as they saw it. The four employees then walked out of the hearing.

Hollins attempted to discuss the question of racial discrimination with the Company president shortly after the incidents of October 16. The president refused to be drawn into such a discussion but suggested to Hollins that he see the personnel director about the matter. Hollins, who had spoken to the personnel director before, made no effort to do so again. Rather, he and Hawkins and several other dissident employees held a press conference on October 22 at which they denounced the store's employment policy as racist, reiterated their desire to deal directly with "the top management" of the Company over minority employment conditions, and announced their intention to picket and institute a boycott of the store. On Saturday, November 2, Hollins, Hawkins, and at least two other employees picketed the store throughout the day and distributed at the entrance handbills urging consumers not to patronize the store.[2] Johnson encountered the

---

[2] The full text of the handbill read:

* * BEWARE * * * * BEWARE * * * * BEWARE * *
EMPORIUM SHOPPERS
"Boycott Is On" "Boycott Is On" "Boycott Is On"

For years at The Emporium black, brown, yellow and red people have worked at the lowest jobs at the lowest levels. Time and time again we have seen intelligent, hard working brothers and sisters denied promotions and respect.

The Emporium is a 20th Century colonial plantation. The brothers and sisters are being treated the same way as our brothers are being treated in the slave mines of Africa.

Whenever the racist pig at The Emporium injures or harms a black sister or brother, they injure and insult all black people. THE EMPORIUM MUST PAY FOR THESE INSULTS. Therefore, we encourage all of our people to take their money out of this racist store, until black people have full employment and are promoted justly through out The Emporium.

picketing employees, again urged them to rely on the grievance process, and warned that they might be fired for their activities. The picketers, however, were not dissuaded, and they continued to press their demand to deal directly with the Company president.

On November 7, Hollins and Hawkins were given written warnings that a repetition of the picketing or public statements about the Company could lead to their discharge. When the conduct was repeated the following Saturday, the two employees were fired.

Respondent Western Addition Community Organization, a local civil rights association of which Hollins and Hawkins were members, filed a charge against the Company with the National Labor Relations Board. The Board's General Counsel subsequently issued a complaint alleging that in discharging the two the Company had violated § 8 (a)(1) of the National Labor Relations Act.... After a hearing the NLRB Trial Examiner found that the discharged employees had believed in good faith that the Company was discriminating against minority employees, and that they had resorted to concerted activity on the basis of that belief. He concluded, however, that their activity was not protected by § 7 of the Act and that their discharges did not, therefore, violate § 8 (a)(1).

The Board, after oral argument, adopted the findings and conclusions of its Trial Examiner and dismissed the complaint. 192 N.L.R.B. 173. Among the findings adopted by the Board was that the discharged employees' course of conduct

> was no mere presentation of a grievance, but nothing short of a demand that the [Company] bargain with the picketing employees for the entire group of minority employees.

The Board concluded that protection of such an attempt to bargain would undermine the statutory system of bargaining through an exclusive, elected representative, impede elected unions' efforts at bettering the working conditions of minority employees "and place on the Employer an unreasonable burden of attempting to placate self-designated representatives of minority groups while abiding by the terms of a valid bargaining agreement and attempting in good faith to meet whatever demands the bargaining representative put forth under that agreement."

On respondent's petition for review the Court of Appeals reversed and remanded. The court was of the view that concerted activity directed against racial discrimination enjoys a "unique status" by virtue of the national labor policy against discrimination, as expressed in both the NLRA, *see United Packinghouse Workers Union v. NLRB,* 416 F.2d 1126, *cert. denied,* 396 U.S. 903 (1969), and in Title VII of the Civil Rights Act of 1964, 42 U.S.C. § 2000e *et seq.,* and that

---

We welcome the support of our brothers and sisters from the churches, unions, sororities, fraternities, social clubs, Afro-American Institute, Black Panther Party, W. A. C. O. and the Poor Peoples Institute.

the Board had not adequately taken account of the necessity to accommodate the exclusive bargaining principle of the NLRA to the national policy of protecting action taken in opposition to discrimination from employer retaliation. The court recognized that protection of the minority group concerted activity involved in this case would interfere to some extent with the orderly collective bargaining process, but it considered the disruptive effect on that process to be outweighed where protection of minority activity is necessary to full and immediate realization of the policy against discrimination. In formulating a standard for distinguishing between protected and unprotected activity, the majority held that the "Board should inquire, in cases such as this, whether the union was actually remedying the discrimination to the *fullest extent possible by the most expedient and efficacious means.* Where the union's efforts fall short of this high standard, the minority group's concerted activity cannot lose its section 7 protection." Accordingly, the court remanded the case for the Board to make this determination and, if it found in favor of the employees, to consider whether their particular tactics were so disloyal to their employer as to deprive them of § 7 protection under our decision in *NLRB v. Local Union No. 1229,* 346 U.S. 464 (1953).

II

Before turning to the central question of labor policy raised by this case, it is important to have firmly in mind the character of the underlying conduct to which we apply them. As stated, the Trial Examiner and the Board found that the employees were discharged for attempting to bargain with the Company over the terms and conditions of employment as they affected racial minorities. Although the Court of Appeals expressly declined to set aside this finding, respondent has devoted considerable effort to attacking it in this Court, on the theory that the employees were attempting only to present a grievance to their employer within the meaning of the first proviso to § 9(a). We see no occasion to disturb the finding of the Board. *Universal Camera Corp. v. NLRB,* 340 U.S. 474, 491 (1951). The issue, then, is whether such attempts to engage in separate bargaining are protected by § 7 of the Act or proscribed by § 9(a).

A.... Central to the policy of fostering collective bargaining, where the employees elect that course, is the principle of majority rule. *See NLRB v. Jones & Laughlin Steel Corp.,* 301 U.S. 1 (1937). If the majority of a unit chooses union representation, the NLRA permits them to bargain with their employer to make union membership a condition of employment, thereby imposing their choice upon the minority.... In establishing a regime of majority rule, Congress sought to secure to all members of the unit the benefits of their collective strength and bargaining power, in full awareness that the superior strength of some individuals or groups might be subordinated to the interest of the majority.... As a result, "[t]he complete satisfaction of all who are represented is hardly to be expected." *Ford Motor Co. v. Huffman,* 345 U.S. 330, 338 (1953)....

In vesting the representatives of the majority with this broad power Congress did not, of course, authorize a tyranny of the majority over minority interests. First, it confined the exercise of these powers to the context of a "unit appropriate for the purposes of collective bargaining," *i.e.,* a group of employees with a sufficient commonality of circumstances to ensure against the submergence of a minority with distinctively different interests in the terms and conditions of their employment. *See Allied Chemical Workers v. Pittsburgh Plate Glass Co.,* 404 U.S. 157, 171 (1971). Second, it undertook in the 1959 Landrum-Griffin amendments, 73 Stat. 519, to assure that minority voices are heard as they are in the functioning of a democratic institution. Third, we have held, by the very nature of the exclusive bargaining representative's status as representative of *all* unit employees, Congress implicitly imposed upon it a duty fairly and in good faith to represent the interests of minorities within the unit. *Vaca v. Sipes, supra; Wallace Corp. v. NLRB,* 323 U.S. 248 (1948); *cf. Steele v. Louisville & N. R. Co.,* 323 U.S. 192 (1944). And the Board has taken the position that a union's refusal to process grievances against racial discrimination, in violation of that duty, is an unfair labor practice. *Hughes Tool Co.,* 147 N.L.R.B. 1573 (1964); *see Miranda Fuel Co.,* 140 N.L.R.B. 181 (1962), *enforcement denied,* 326 F.2d 172 (2d Cir. 1962). Indeed, the Board has ordered a union implicated by a collective bargaining agreement in discrimination with an employer to propose specific contractual provisions to prohibit racial discrimination. *See Local Union No. 12, United Rubber Workers of America v. NLRB,* 368 F.2d 12 (5th Cir. 1966) (enforcement granted).

B. Against this background of long and consistent adherence to the principle of exclusive representation tempered by safeguards for the protection of minority interests, respondent urges this Court to fashion a limited exception to that principle: employees who seek to bargain separately with their employer as to the elimination of racially discriminatory employment practices peculiarly affecting them, should be free from the constraints of the exclusivity principle of § 9 (a). Essentially because established procedures under Title VII or, as in this case, a grievance machinery, are too time-consuming, the national labor policy against discrimination requires this exception, respondent argues, and its adoption would not unduly compromise the legitimate interests of either unions or employers.

Plainly, national labor policy embodies the principles of nondiscrimination as a matter of highest priority, *Alexander v. Gardner-Denver Co.,* 415 U.S. 36, 47 (1974), and it is a common-place that we must construe the NLRA in light of the broad national labor policy of which it is a part. *See Textile Workers v. Lincoln Mills,* 353 U.S. 448, 456-458 (1958). These general principles do not aid respondent, however, as it is far from clear that separate bargaining is necessary to help eliminate discrimination. Indeed, as the facts of this case demonstrate, the proposed remedy might have just the opposite effect. The collective bargaining agreement in this case prohibited without qualification all manner of invidious discrimination and made any claimed violation a grievable issue. The grievance procedure is directed precisely at determining whether discrimination has occurred. That orderly determination, if affirmative, could lead to an arbitral award enforceable in court. Nor is there any reason to believe that the processing of grievances is inherently limited to the correction of individual cases of discrimination. Quite apart from the essentially contractual question of whether the Union could grieve against a "pattern or practice" it deems inconsistent with the nondiscrimination clause of the contract, one would hardly expect an employer to continue in effect an employment practice that routinely results in adverse arbitral decisions.

The decision by a handful of employees to bypass the grievance procedure in favor of attempting to bargain with their employer, by contrast, may or may not be predicated upon the actual existence of discrimination. An employer confronted with bargaining demands from each of several minority groups would not necessarily, or even probably, be able to agree to remedial steps satisfactory to all at once. Competing claims on the employer's ability to accommodate each group's demands, *e.g.,* for reassignments and promotions to a limited number of positions, could only set one group against the other even if it is not the employer's intention to divide and overcome them. Having divided themselves, the minority employees will not be in position to advance their cause unless it be by recourse *seriatim* to economic coercion, which can only have the effect of further dividing them along racial or other lines. Nor is the situation materially different where, as apparently happened here, self-designated representatives purport to speak for all groups that might consider themselves to be victims of discrimination. Even if in actual bargaining the various groups did not perceive their interests as divergent and further subdivide themselves, the employer would be bound to bargain with them in a field largely preempted by the current collective bargaining agreement with the elected bargaining representatives....

What has been said here in evaluating respondent's claim that the policy against discrimination requires § 7 protection for concerted efforts at minority bargaining has obvious implications for the related claim that legitimate employer and union interests would not be unduly compromised thereby. The court below minimized the impact on the Union in this case by noting that it was not working at cross-purposes with the dissidents, and that indeed it could not do so consistent with its duty of fair representation and perhaps its obligations under Title VII. As to the Company, its obligations under Title VII are cited for the proposition that it could have no legitimate objection to bargaining with the dissidents in order to achieve full compliance with that law.

This argument confuses the employees' substantive right to be free of racial discrimination with the procedures available under the NLRA for securing these rights. Whether they are thought to depend upon Title VII or have an independent source in the NLRA, they cannot be pursued at the expense of the orderly collective bargaining process contemplated by the NLRA. The elimination of discrimination and its vestiges is an appropriate subject of bargaining, and an employer may have no objection to incorporating into a collective agreement the substance of his obligation not to discriminate in personnel decisions; the Company here has done as much, making any claimed dereliction a matter subject to the grievance-arbitration machinery as well as to the processes of Title VII. But that does not mean that he may not have strong and legitimate objections to bargaining on several fronts over the implementation of the right to be free of discrimination for some of the reasons set forth above. Similarly, while a union cannot lawfully bargain for the establishment or continuation of discriminatory practices, *see Steele v. Louisville & N. R. Co., supra,* 42 U.S.C. § 2000-2(c)(3), it has legitimate interest in presenting a united front on this as on other issues and in not seeing its strength dissipated and its stature denigrated by subgroups within the unit separately pursuing what they see as separate interests. When union and employer are not responsive to their legal obligations, the bargain they have struck must yield *pro tanto* to the law, whether by means of conciliation through the offices of the EEOC, or by means of federal court enforcement at the instance of either that agency or the party claiming to be aggrieved.

Accordingly, we think neither aspect of respondent's contention in support of a right to short-circuit orderly, established processes for eliminating discrimination in employment is well-founded. The policy of industrial self-determination as expressed in § 7 does not require fragmentation of the bargaining unit along racial or other lines in order to consist with the national labor policy against discrimination. And in the face of such fragmentation, whatever its effect on discriminatory practices, the bargaining process that the principle of exclusive representation is meant to lubricate could not endure unhampered.

III

... Even assuming that § 704(a) [of Title VII] protects employees' picketing and instituting a consumer boycott of their employer, the same conduct is not necessarily entitled to affirmative protection from the NLRA. Under the scheme of that Act, conduct which is not protected concerted activity may lawfully form the basis for the participants' discharge. That does not mean that the discharge is immune from attack on other statutory grounds in an appropriate case....

Reversed.

[The dissenting opinion of MR. JUSTICE DOUGLAS is omitted.]

NOTES

1. What was the critical factor in *Emporium Capwell*? Would it have been different if there had been no collective bargaining agreement, even though one was about to be concluded? Or if the employees had walked out without union authorization to protest employer action but had made no effort to take negotiations into their own hands? *See East Chicago Rehabilitation Ctr. v. NLRB,* 710

F.2d 397 (7th Cir. 1983), *cert. denied,* 465 U.S. 1065 (1984). Is a dissident employee protected if he insists his employer discuss replacing the incumbent union with an outside rival? *Cf. NLRB v. Chelsea Labs.,* 825 F.2d 680 (2d Cir. 1987), *cert. denied,* 484 U.S. 1026 (1988), *noted,* 55 Brooklyn L. Rev. 721 (1989). *See also* Cantor, *Dissident Worker Action, After The Emporium,* 29 Rutgers L. Rev. 35 (1975); Craver, *Minority Action Versus Union Exclusivity: The Need to Harmonize NLRA and Title VII Policies,* 26 Hastings L.J. 1 (1974); Silverstein, *Union Decisions on Collective Bargaining Goals: A Proposal for Interest Group Participation,* 77 Mich. L. Rev. 1485 (1979).

2. Justice Marshall suggests two justifications for exclusivity/majority rule. The first is that exclusivity is more efficient, more workable, than a system of individual bargaining or multiple representation, which would likely complicate bargaining and create leapfrogging and whipsawing problems between competing factions of employees. The second is that exclusivity shores up union strength by allowing employees to present a united front in their dealings with the employer, avoiding problems of internecine competition among workers which would ultimately undermine the collective effort. How persuasive are these justifications? *See* Finkin, *The Road Not Taken: Some Thoughts on Non-majority Employee Representation,* 69 Chi.-Kent L. Rev. 195 (1993).

3. The principles of exclusivity and majority rule inevitably deny voice to dissident workers in unionized workplaces. Does this raise particular problems in an increasingly diverse workforce? Is the Court correct that separate bargaining would only further divide employees along racial or gender lines? Or does the fact pattern of *Emporium Capwell* itself provide evidence that competing subgroups, once constituted by employer discrimination, will endure? Does withholding § 7 protection for the actions of the dissident employees resolve these divisions? If not, what does it accomplish? Would women and minorities enjoy more or less protection for concerted activity to oppose employer discrimination in a nonunion workplace? *See* Elizabeth M. Iglesias, *Structures of Subordination: Women of Color at the Intersection of Title VII and the NLRA. NOT!,* 28 Harv. C.R.-C.L. L. Rev. 395 (1993).

4. For reform proposals designed to address the tension between a system predicated on majority rule and exclusivity, and the identity-based interests of a race- and gender-diverse workforce, *see* Cobble, *The Next Unionism: Structural Innovations for a Revitalized Labor Movement,* 48 Lab. L.J. 439 (1997); Crain, *Women, Labor Unions and Hostile Work Environment Sexual Harassment: The Untold Story,* 4 Tex. J. Women & L. 9 (1995); German, *Safeguarding Employee Rights in a Post-Union World: A New Conception of Employee Communities,* 30 Colum. J. L. & Soc. Probs. 369 (1997); Hyde, *Employee Identity Caucuses in Silicon Valley: Can They Transcend the Boundaries of the Firm?,* 48 Lab. L.J. 491 (1997); McUsic & Selmi, *Postmodern Unions: Identity Politics in the Workplace,* 82 Iowa L. Rev. 1339 (1997).

B. THE NATURE OF THE DUTY TO BARGAIN

The obligation to "bargain collectively" is generally, though not universally, included in federal and state labor relations acts. The original NLRA imposed the duty on the employer as a means of implementing the right to organize and to bargain collectively which was declared in § 7. The "Wagner Act" type of statute exacted no requirements of unions. The later "Taft-Hartley" type of statute made the bargaining obligation mutual.

The legal duty which the original NLRA and the RLA created was not defined by Congress. Section 2, First, of the RLA requires that the parties exert "every reasonable effort to make and maintain agreements concerning rates of pay, rules, and working conditions," and § 2, Ninth, obligates the carrier to "treat with" the duly certified employee representative. These provisions, together with the duty "to bargain collectively" specified in the Wagner Act, and corresponding provisions of state acts, had to be given meaning by the courts and the enforcement agencies. *See generally* C. Rehmus, The Railway Labor Act at Fifty (1976); Thoms & Dooley, *Collective Bargaining Under the Railway Labor Act*, 20 Transp. L.J. 275 (1992).

In the first case to come before the Supreme Court under the RLA, it was declared that the statute "does not undertake to compel agreement between the employer and employees, but it does command those preliminary steps without which no agreement can be reached," including "reasonable efforts to compose differences." *Virginian Ry. v. System Fed'n No. 40,* 300 U.S. 515, 548 (1937). Even prior to this decision there had been some development of the concept of bargaining by the National Labor Board and the old National Labor Relations Board, which had been given advisory adjudicative responsibility regarding § 7a of the National Industrial Recovery Act of 1933. In the much cited *Houde Eng'g Corp.* case, 1 N.L.R.B. (Old) 35 (1934), the old NLRB interpreted the decisions of the NLB as having established the "incontestably sound principle that the employer is obligated by the statute to negotiate in good faith with his employees' representatives; to match their proposals, if unacceptable, with counter-proposals; and to make every reasonable effort to reach an agreement." In applying § 8(5) of the NLRA of 1935, the NLRB adopted this principle with the full support of the courts. The duty to bargain encompassed an obligation to enter into negotiations with "an open and fair mind" and "a sincere purpose to find a basis of agreement." *See, e.g., NLRB v. Boss Mfg. Co.,* 118 F.2d 187, 189 (7th Cir. 1941); *Globe Cotton Mills v. NLRB,* 103 F.2d 91, 94 (5th Cir. 1939); *Highland Park Mfg. Co.,* 12 N.L.R.B. 1238, 1248-49 (1939), *enforced,* 110 F.2d 632 (4th Cir. 1940).

Section 8(5) of the NLRA had its origin in a Senate bill (S. 2926) introduced by Senator Wagner in March 1934. One provision, obviously patterned on the Railway Labor Act counterpart, read as follows:

> It shall be an unfair labor practice ... to refuse to recognize and/or deal with representatives of his [the employer's] employees, or to fail to exert every reasonable effort to make and maintain agreements with such representatives concerning wages, hours, and other conditions of employment.

At the committee hearings on the bill Dr. Slichter of Harvard argued for deletion of the requirement of a "reasonable effort to make and maintain agreements," and so forth, as merely the expression of a pious wish: "You cannot make it a definite duty of a man to try to agree.... You might almost enact that the lions and lambs shall not fail to exert every reasonable effort to lie down together." Dr. Leiserson, then Chairman of the Petroleum Labor Policy Board, disagreed: "Now, I think it is exceedingly important that it should stay in the bill. It should not be thrown out on the theory, 'Well, you cannot enforce that anyway.' If we can say, ... to an employer, 'Now, you really haven't tried to agree with them, so that we will avoid a strike. They have elected their representatives. Now sit down and make an earnest effort, the way the law says.' You will avoid many disputes in that way." Smith, *The Evolution of the "Duty to Bargain" Concept in American Law,* 39 Mich. L. Rev. 1065, 1083-84 (1941).

The Senate Committee on Education and Labor, reporting in 1935 on the Wagner-Connery Bill, said regarding § 8(5):

> The committee wishes to dispel any possible false impression that this bill is designed to compel the making of agreements or to permit governmental supervision of their terms. It must be stressed that the duty to bargain collectively does not carry with it the duty to reach an agreement, because the essence of collective bargaining is that either party shall be free to decide whether proposals made to it are satisfactory.

Id. at 1085.

Senator Walsh, Chairman of the Committee on Education and Labor, summed up one prominent legislative attitude in these terms:

> The bill indicates the method and manner in which employees may organize, the method and manner of selecting their representatives or spokesmen, and leads them to the office door of their employer with the legal authority to negotiate for their fellow employees. The bill does not go beyond the office door. It leaves the discussion between the employer and the employee, and the agreements which they may or may not make, voluntary and with that sacredness and solemnity to a voluntary agreement with which both parties to an agreement should be enshrouded.

Id. at 1087. *See also* Latham, *Legislative Purpose and Administrative Policy Under the National Labor Relations Act,* 4 Geo. Wash. L. Rev. 433 (1936). For contrasting views, *see* W. Spencer, The National Labor Relations Act 24 (1935); Rheinstein, *Methods of Wage Policy,* 6 U. Chi. L. Rev. 552, 576 (1939).

When Congress passed the LMRA in 1947, § 8(d) was written into the law, spelling out to some extent the duty to bargain collectively.

The Senate bill (S. 1126), in its proposed amendment of the NLRA, included a § 8(d) substantially similar to this section as eventually enacted, but lacking its final paragraph. The Senate Committee on Labor and Public Welfare stated, S. Rep. No. 105, 80th Cong., 1st Sess. 24 (1947):

> Section 8(d) contains a definition of the duty to bargain collectively and, consequently, relates both to the duties of employers to bargain and labor organizations to bargain under Sections 8(a)(5) and 8(b)(3), respectively. The definition makes it clear that the duty to bargain collectively does not require either party to agree to a particular demand or to make a concession. It should be noted that the word "concession" was used rather than "counterproposal" to meet an objection raised by the Chairman of the Board to a corresponding provision in one of the early drafts of the bill.

The Conference Committee reported concerning the version of § 8(d) as finally enacted, H.R. Rep. No. 510, 80th Cong., 1st Sess. 34 (1947):

> This mutual obligation was not to compel either party to agree to a proposal or require the making of any concession. Hence, the Senate amendment, while it did not prescribe a purely objective test of what constituted collective bargaining, as did the House bill, had, to a very substantial extent, the same effect as the House bill in this regard, since it rejected, as a factor in determining good faith, the test of making a concession and thus prevented the Board from determining the merits of the positions of the parties.

1. GOOD FAITH

LABOR STUDY GROUP,* THE PUBLIC INTEREST IN NATIONAL LABOR POLICY 82 (Committee for Economic Development 1961)

Parties have been told that they must bargain in good faith, and elaborate tests have been devised in an attempt to determine "objectively" whether the proper subjective attitude prevails. The limitations and artificiality of such tests are apparent, and the possibilities of evasion are almost limitless.... Basically, it is unrealistic to expect that, by legislation, "good faith" can be brought to the bargaining table. Indeed, the provisions designed to bring "good faith" have become a tactical weapon used in many situations as a means of harassment.

---

*The members of the Study Group were Clark Kerr, Douglass V. Brown, David L. Cole, John T. Dunlop, William Y. Elliott, Albert Rees, Robert M. Solow, Philip Taft, and George W. Taylor.

GENERAL ELECTRIC CO.

National Labor Relations Board
150 N.L.R.B. 192 (1964)

....

The Trial Examiner found that Respondent had not bargained in good faith with the Union, thereby violating § 8(a)(5) and (1) of the Act, as evidenced by:

(a) Its failure timely to furnish certain information requested by the Union during contract negotiations.

(b) Its attempts, while engaged in national negotiations with the Union, to deal separately with Locals on matters which were properly the subject of national negotiations, and its solicitations of Locals separately to abandon or refrain from supporting the strike.

(c) Its presentation of its personal accident insurance proposal to the Union on a take-it-or-leave-it basis.[3]

(d) Its over-all approach to and conduct of bargaining.

We agree with these findings of the Trial Examiner. Because Respondent's defense of its bargaining conduct raises a fundamental question as to the requirements of the statutory bargaining obligation, we have stated for more particular emphasis the reasons why we agree with the Trial Examiner that Respondent did not bargain in good faith with the Union.

In challenging the Trial Examiner's finding that it violated § 8(a)(5), Respondent argues that an employer cannot be found guilty of having violated its statutory bargaining duty where it is desirous of entering into a collective bargaining agreement, where it has met and conferred with the bargaining representative on all required subjects of bargaining as prescribed by statute and has not taken unlawful unilateral action, and where it has not demanded the inclusion in the collective bargaining contract of any illegal clauses or insisted to an impasse upon any nonmandatory bargaining provisions. Given compliance with the above, Respondent further argues that an employer's technique of bargaining is not subject to approval or disapproval by the Board.

Respondent reads the statutory requirements for bargaining collectively too narrowly. It is true that an employer does violate § 8(a)(5) where it enters into bargaining negotiations with a desire not to reach an agreement with the union, or has taken unilateral action with respect to a term or condition of employment, or has adamantly demanded the inclusion of illegal or nonmandatory clauses in the collective bargaining contract. But, having refrained from any of the foregoing

---

[3] For the reasons set forth in his dissent in *Equitable Life Ins. Co.,* 133 N.L.R.B. 1675, 1677, Member Fanning would not find that Respondent's refusal to bargain in regard to the insurance plan was unlawful. However, he believes that Respondent's take-it-or-leave-it position on June 13 can be properly considered in gauging its over-all good faith in negotiations.

conduct, an employer may still have failed to discharge its statutory obligation to bargain in good faith. As the Supreme Court has said:[8]

> ... the Board is authorized to order the cessation of behavior which is in effect a refusal to negotiate, *or* which directly obstructs or inhibits the actual process of discussion, *or* which reflects a cast of mind against reaching agreement. [Emphasis supplied.]

Thus, a party who enters into bargaining negotiations with a "take-it-or-leave-it" attitude violates its duty to bargain although it goes through the forms of bargaining, does not insist on any illegal or nonmandatory bargaining proposals, and wants to sign an agreement.[9] For good-faith bargaining means more than "going through the motions of negotiating."[10] "... [T]he essential thing is rather the serious intent to adjust differences and to reach an acceptable common ground...."[11]

Good-faith bargaining thus involves both a procedure for meeting and negotiating, which may be called the externals of collecting bargaining, and a bona fide intention, the presence or absence of which must be discerned from the record. It requires recognition by both parties, not merely formal but real, that "collective bargaining" is a shared process in which each party, labor union and employer, has the right to play an active role. On the part of the employer, it requires at a minimum recognition that the statutory representative is the one with whom it must deal in conducting bargaining negotiations, and that it can no longer bargain directly or indirectly with the employees. It is inconsistent with this obligation for an employer to mount a campaign, as Respondent did, both before and during negotiations, for the purpose of disparaging and discrediting the statutory representative in the eyes of its employee constituents, to seek to persuade the employees to exert pressure on the representative to submit to the will of the employer, and to create the impression that the employer rather than the union is the true protector of the employees' interests. As the Trial Examiner phrased it, the employer's statutory obligation is to deal with the employees through the union, and not with the union through the employees.

We do not rely solely on Respondent's campaign among its employees for our finding that it did not deal in good faith with the Union. Respondent's policy of disparaging the Union by means of the communications campaign as fully detailed in the Trial Examiner's Intermediate Report, was implemented and furthered by its conduct at the bargaining table. Thus, the negotiations themselves, although maintaining the form of "collective bargaining," fell short, in a realistic

---

[8] *NLRB v. Bennie Katz, etc., d/b/a Williamsburg Steel Prod. Co., supra* [369 U.S. 736] at 747 (1962).

[9] *NLRB v. Insurance Agents' Union, AFL-CIO (Prudential Ins. Co.),* 361 U.S. 477, 487 (1960).

[10] *NLRB v. Truitt Mfg. Co.,* 351 U.S. 149, 155 (1956) (Frankfurter, J.).

[11] First Annual Report of the National Labor Relations Board, at 85, quoted with approval by the Supreme Court in *NLRB v. Insurance Agents' Union, AFL-CIO (Prudential Ins. Co.), supra* at 485.

sense, of the concept of meaningful and fruitful "negotiation" envisaged by the Act. As the record in the case reflects, Respondent regards itself as a sort of administrative body which has the unilateral responsibility for determining wages and working conditions for employees, and it regards the union's role as merely that of a kind of advisor for an interested group—the employees. Thus, according to its professed philosophy of "bargaining," Respondent on the basis of its own research and evaluation of union demands, determines what is "right" for its employees, and then makes a "fair and firm offer" to the unions without holding anything back for later trading or compromising. It professes a willingness to make prompt adjustments in its offer, but only if new information or a change in facts indicates that its initial offer is no longer "right." It believes that if its research has been done properly there will be no need to change its offer unless something entirely unforeseen has developed in the meantime. Simultaneously, Respondent emphasizes, especially to employees, that as a matter of policy it will not be induced by a strike or a threat of a strike to make any change in its proposals which it believes to be "wrong." This "bargaining" approach undoubtedly eliminates the "ask-and-bid" or "auction" form of bargaining, but in the process devitalizes negotiations and collective bargaining and robs them of their commonly accepted meaning. "Collective bargaining" as thus practiced is tantamount to mere formality and serves to transform the role of the statutory representative from a joint participant in the bargaining process to that of an advisor. In practical effect, Respondent's "bargaining" position is akin to that of a party who enters into negotiations "with a predetermined resolve not to budge from an initial position," an attitude inconsistent with good-faith bargaining. In fact Respondent here went even further. It consciously placed itself in a position where it could not give unfettered consideration to the merits of any proposals the Union might offer. Thus, Respondent pointed out to the Union, after Respondent's communications to the employees and its "fair and firm offer" to the Union, that "everything we think we should do is in the proposal and we told our employees that, and we would look ridiculous if we changed now."

In short, both major facets of Respondent's 1960 "bargaining" technique, its campaign among the employees and its conduct at the bargaining table, complementing each other, were calculated to disparage the Union and to impose without substantial alteration Respondent's "fair and firm" proposal, rather than to satisfy the true standards of good-faith collective bargaining required by the statute. A course of conduct whose major purpose is so directed scarcely evinces a sincere desire to resolve differences and reach a common ground. For the above reasons, as well as those elaborated at greater length by the Trial Examiner in his Intermediate Report, we adopt his conclusion that Respondent did not bargain in good faith with the Union, thereby violating § 8(a)(5) and (1) of the Act.

Our concurring colleague, Member Jenkins, who joins us in finding certain conduct of the Respondent inconsistent with its bargaining obligation under the statute, misreads the majority opinion, and the Trial Examiner's Intermediate

Report which we affirm, in asserting that our decision is not based on an assessment of Respondent's conduct, but only on its approach to or techniques in bargaining.

On the contrary our determination is based upon our review of the Respondent's entire course of conduct, its failure to furnish relevant information, its attempts to deal separately with locals and to bypass the national bargaining representative, the manner of its presentation of the accident insurance proposal, the disparagement of the Union as bargaining representative by the communication program, its conduct of the negotiations themselves, and its attitude or approach as revealed by all these factors.

Nothing in our decision bans fact-gathering or any specific methods of formulating proposals. We prescribe no time-table for negotiators. We lay down no rules as to any required substance or content of agreements. Our decision rests rather upon a consideration of the totality of Respondent's conduct.

In one central point of our colleague's comment, with all respect we believe he is in error. His strictures in relation to our interpretation of the law's restraints on "take-it-or-leave-it" bargaining were decisively answered by the Supreme Court in its review of the nature of the bargaining obligation in *Insurance Agents:*[18]

> ... The legislative history [of Taft-Hartley] makes it plain that Congress was wary of the position of some unions, and wanted to ensure that they would approach the bargaining table with the same attitude of willingness to reach an agreement as had been enjoined on management earlier. It intended to prevent employee representatives from putting forth the same "take it or leave it" attitude that had been condemned in management.

And in JUSTICE FRANKFURTER's opinion in *Truitt*[19] ... the Justice also wrote:

> ... [I]t [good faith] is inconsistent with a predetermined resolve not to budge from an initial position.

While we share his objective and that of our dissenting colleague of encouraging a maximum of freedom and experimentation in collective bargaining, when questions are raised under the law as construed by the courts and the Board concerning the conformity of a specific respondent's course of conduct with the requirements of the law, the Board must apply the law to the totality of that conduct in the interest of preserving and fostering collective bargaining itself. That is what we have sought to do here....

MEMBER LEEDOM, dissenting in part:

My colleagues have found that the Respondent failed to bargain in good faith with the Union in the 1960 negotiations, both in certain specific respects and

---

[18] *NLRB v. Insurance Agents' Union, AFL-CIO, supra* at 487.
[19] *NLRB v. Truitt Mfg. Co., supra* at 154.

generally. Although I agree with the specific violations found, I cannot justify the bad-faith finding with respect to the Respondent's overall bargaining conduct.

On the issue as to Respondent's overall good or bad faith it should be conceded that there are various approaches to, and tactics in, negotiations that are wholly consistent with the bargaining obligation imposed by the Act; and it seems to me that both management and labor should not be discouraged from seeking new techniques in dealing with the constantly evolving problems with which they are faced across the bargaining table. Consequently we should take care not to create the impression that we view with suspicion novel approaches to, and techniques of, collective bargaining....

No matter how much we may disclaim any intent to compel bargaining to proceed in some set form, the fact that we closely scrutinize what goes on at the bargaining table will necessarily have the effect of directing bargaining into channels which we have in the past approved, for in such channels will lie security in bargaining, if not success. Whether the substitution of our judgment as to the proper forms and content of bargaining be made directly or indirectly is a difference of no consequence insofar as it interferes with free bargaining and tends to discourage innovation both in tactics and proposals which, as I believe, could be of benefit not only to the parties but to the public as well. Consequently, good policy suggests that we leave the parties to their own devices at the bargaining table unless some compelling facts force us into the area of bargaining ....

I do not mean to suggest that the issue of good or bad faith has any clear cut answer here. My position is not dictated so much by strong conviction as by uncertainty. I am not persuaded by the reasons that the majority state for their finding of bad-faith bargaining; and the finding itself and the supporting rationale leave me in the dark as to their practical efficacy. But I am particularly disturbed by the treatment accorded Respondent's communications. Surely the Respondent can lawfully communicate with its employees. Yet here, although the communications are held to be some evidence of bad faith, the majority neither in its decision nor in adopting the Trial Examiner's Recommended Order provides the Respondent with any guides by which it can with reasonable certainty determine what it can lawfully say to its employees. In areas such as this bordering on § 8(c) of the Act and free speech, I believe that the Respondent is entitled to something more by way of clarification than the vague proscription implied in the general bargaining order. But I doubt if the facts and findings indicate what specific limitations can properly be laid down. In any event, the situation with respect to the bad-faith finding is at best ambiguous, and I would, therefore, find that the General Counsel has failed to prove by a preponderance of the evidence that the Respondent did not bargain in good faith during the 1960 negotiations with the Union.

[The concurring opinion of MEMBER JENKINS is omitted.]

NOTE

The bargaining technique employed by General Electric in the 1960 negotiations is commonly known as "Boulwareism," after Lemuel R. Boulware, a former GE vice-president who first devised it in the late 1940s. It is discussed in detail by its leading academic exponent in H. Northrup, Boulwareism (1964). *See also* Cooper, *Boulwareism and the Duty to Bargain in Good Faith,* 20 Rutgers L. Rev. 653 (1966); Gross, Cullen & Hanslowe, *Good Faith in Labor Negotiations: Tests and Remedies,* 53 Cornell L. Rev. 1009 (1968); Note, *Boulwareism and Good Faith Collective Bargaining,* 63 Mich. L. Rev. 1473 (1965).

————

"Almost ten years after the events that gave rise to this controversy," as the court put it, the Second Circuit in a 2-to-1 decision sustained the Labor Board's condemnation of "Boulewareism." Three judges wrote opinions totaling some forty pages. Reproduced below are severely edited excerpts from the majority and minority opinions, with the emphasis on those portions dealing with General Electric's "overall approach to bargaining."

NLRB v. GENERAL ELECTRIC CO.

United States Court of Appeals, Second Circuit
418 F.2d 736 (1969), *cert. denied,* 397 U.S. 965 (1970)

IRVING R. KAUFMAN, Circuit Judge....

The new plan ["Boulewareism"] was threefold. GE began by soliciting comments from its local management personnel on the desires of the work force, and the type and level of benefits that they expected. These were then translated into specific proposals, and their cost and effectiveness researched, in order to formulate a "product" that would be attractive to the employees, and within the Company's means. The last step was the most important, most innovative, and most often criticized. GE took its "product"—now a series of fully-formed bargaining proposals—and "sold" it to its employees and the general public. Through a veritable avalanche of publicity, reaching awesome proportions prior to and during negotiations, GE sought to tell its side of the issues to its employees. It described its proposals as a "fair, firm offer," characteristic of its desire to "do right voluntarily," without the need for any union pressure or strike. In negotiations, GE announced that it would have nothing to do with the "blood-and-threat-and-thunder" approach, in which each side presented patently unreasonable demands, and finally chose a middle ground that both knew would be the probable outcome even before the beginning of the bargaining. The Company believed that such tactics diminished the company's credibility in the eyes of its employees, and at the same time appeared to give the union credit for wringing from the Company what it had been willing to offer all along. Henceforth GE would hold nothing back when it made its offer to the Union; it would take all the facts into consideration, and make that offer it thought right under all the circumstances. Though willing to accept Union suggestions based on facts the Company might have overlooked, once the basic outlines of the proposal had been set, the mere fact that the Union disagreed would be no ground for change. When GE said firm, it meant firm, and it denounced the traditional give and take of the so-called auction bargaining as "flea bitten eastern type of cunning and dishonest but pointless haggling."

To bring its position home to its employees, GE utilized a vast network of plant newspapers, bulletins, letters, television and radio announcements, and personal contacts through management personnel....

We now approach the most troublesome and most vigorously contested of the charges. In addition to the three specific unfair labor practices, GE is also charged with an overall failure to bargain in good faith, compounded like a mosaic of many pieces, but depending not on any one alone. They are together to be understood to comprise the "totality of the circumstances."...

Specifically, the Board found that GE's bargaining stance and conduct, considered as a whole, were designed to derogate the Union in the eyes of its members and the public at large. This plan had two major facets: first, a take-it-or-leave-it approach ("firm, fair offer") to negotiations in general which emphasized both the powerlessness and uselessness of the Union to its members, and second, a communications program that pictured the Company as the true defender of the employees' interests, further denigrating the Union, and sharply curbing the Company's ability to change its own position.

The Board relies both on the unfair labor practices already discussed and on several other specific instances to show that GE had developed a pattern of conduct inconsistent with good faith bargaining. It points to GE's proposed personal accident insurance proposal on a take-it-or-leave-it basis as an example of an attempt to bypass the Union, and an attempt to disparage its importance and usefulness in the eyes of its members....

[A]cts not in themselves unfair labor practices may support an inference that a party is acting in bad faith. *See NLRB v. Insurance Agents' Union,* 361 U.S. 477, 506 (1960) (Frankfurter, J., concurring). While GE may have believed that it was acting within its "rights" in offering a take-it-or-leave-it proposal, doing so may still be some evidence of lack of good faith. Here there was no substantial justification offered for refusing to discuss the matter, other than a niggling—and incorrect—view of the contract and the statute. *Cf. NLRB v. Reed & Prince Mfg. Co.,* 205 F.2d 131 (1st Cir.) (Magruder, J.) ("must make *some* reasonable effort in *some* direction") *cert. denied,* 346 U.S. 887 (1953). Given the effects of take-it-or-leave-it proposals on the Union, ... the Board could appropriately infer the presence of anti-Union animus, and in conjunction with other similar conduct could reasonably discern a pattern of illegal activity designed primarily to subvert the Union.

We have already discussed at length the Company's failure to furnish information. As in the instance of the personal accident insurance proposal, GE's attitude on information was characterized by a pettifogging insistence on doing not one whit more than the law absolutely required, an insistence that eventually strayed over into doing considerably less. GE's conduct, as the Board's opinion points out, was all of a piece. It negotiated, to the greatest possible extent, by ignoring the legitimacy and relevance of the Union's position as statutory representative of its members. Thus it is hardly surprising that IUE requests for information were met (at least once negotiations had begun) with less than enthusiasm, for they reflect the Union's contrary belief that it had to know the worth of the Company proposals in order to evaluate them for its members....

When the last act was virtually played out and it had become apparent that the Union would have to end its abortive strike and concede to GE's terms, the Company continued to display a stiff and unbending patriarchal posture hardly consistent with "common willingness among the parties to discuss freely and fully their respective claims and demands and, when these are opposed, to justify them on reason." *NLRB v. George P. Pilling & Son Co.,* 119 F.2d 32, 37 (3d Cir. 1941). With the Union, as it were, "on the ropes," the Company insisted that IUE choose the options that it preferred, and assent to the contract unconditionally, without ever seeing the final contract language. When the Union protested that the memorandum proposed for its signature was too vague, the Company refused to submit more definite language. Four days later, the Union capitulated completely and signed the short form memorandum, still without having seen the final contract to which it was agreeing....

The Company's stand, however, would be utterly inexplicable without the background of its publicity program. Only when viewed in that context does it become meaningful. We have already indicated that one of the central tenets of "the Boulware approach" is that the "product" or "firm, fair offer" must be marketed vigorously to the "consumers" or employees, to convince them that the Company, and not the Union, is their true representative. GE, the Trial Examiner found, chose to rely "entirely" on its communications program to the virtual exclusion of genuine negotiations, which it sought to evade by any means possible. Bypassing the national negotiators in favor of direct settlement dealings with employees and local officials forms another consistent thread in this pattern. The aim, in a word, was to deal with the Union through the employees, rather than with the employees through the Union.

The Company's refusal to withhold publicizing its offer until the Union had had an opportunity to propose suggested modifications is indicative of this attitude. Here two interests diverged. The command of the Boulware approach was clear: employees and the general public must be barraged with communications that emphasized the generosity of the offer, and restated the firmness of GE's position. A genuine desire to reach a mutual accommodation might, on the other hand, have called for GE to await Union comments before taking a stand from which it would be difficult to retreat. GE hardly hesitated. It released the offer the next day without waiting for Union comments on the specific portions.

The most telling effect of GE's marketing campaign was not on the Union, but on GE itself. Having told its employees that it had made a "firm, fair offer," that there was "nothing more to come," and that it would not change its position in the face of "threats" of a strike, GE had in effect rested all on the expectation that it could institute its offer without significant modification. Properly viewed, then, its communications approach determined its take-it-or-leave-it bargaining strategy. Each was the natural complement of the other; if either were substantially changed, the other would in all probability have to be modified as well....

The Company, having created a view of the bargaining process that admitted of no compromise, was trapped by its own creation. It could no longer seek peace without total victory, for it had by its own words and actions branded any compromise a defeat.

GE urges that § 8(c) ... prohibits the Board from considering its publicity efforts in passing on the legality of its bargaining conduct.... GE would have us read that section as a bar to the Board's use of any communications, in any manner, unless the communication itself contained a threat or a promise of benefit. The legislative history, past decisions, and the logic of the statutory framework, however, indicate a contrary conclusion.

The bald prohibition of § 8(c) invited comment when it was enacted, as well as later. Senator Taft replied to some of the criticism of the bill that bears his name:

> It should be noted that this subsection is limited to "views, arguments, or opinions" and does not cover instructions, directions, or other statements that would ordinarily be deemed relevant and admissible in courts of law.

I Legislative History of the LMRA 1947, at 1541. The key word is "relevant." The evil at which the section was aimed was the alleged practice of the Board in inferring the existence of an unfair labor practice from a totally unrelated speech or opinion delivered by an employer. Senator Taft later indicated, for example, in the context of a § 8(a)(3) discriminatory firing, that prior statements of the employer would have to be shown to "tie in" with the specific unfair labor practice. I Legislative History of the LMRA 1947, at 1545. Later references to the section described the barred statements as those which were "severable or unrelated," and "irrelevant or immaterial." II Legislative History of the LMRA 1947, at 429 (Senate Report), 549 (House Conference Report). The objective of § 8(c) then, was to impose a rule of relevancy on the Board in evaluating the legality of statements by parties to a labor dispute. Its purpose was hardly to eliminate all communications from the Board's purview, for to do so would be to emasculate a statute whose structure depends heavily on evaluation of motive and intent....

While it is clear that the Board is not to control the substantive terms of a collective bargaining contract, nonetheless the parties must do more than meet. Our brother Friendly makes much of the point that General Electric did bargain and reach an "agreement" with the Union.... The statute does not say that any "agreement" reached will validate whatever tactics have been employed to exact it. To imply such a Congressional purpose would be to encourage parties to make their violation so blatant that it would be impossible for the other side to continue to exist without signing. Instead the statute clearly contemplates that to the end of encouraging productive bargaining, the parties must make "a serious attempt to resolve differences and reach a common ground," *NLRB v. Insurance Agents' Int'l Union,* 361 U.S. 477, 486, 487, 488 (1960), an effort inconsistent with a "predetermined resolve not to budge from an initial position." *NLRB v. Truitt Mfg. Co.,* 351 U.S. 149, 154-155 (1956) (Frankfurter, J., concurring)....

The Company and the dissenting opinion seem to take the novel position that the holding in *Insurance Agents'*—that the Board might not forbid a partial strike during bargaining—ousts the Board's control over bargaining tactics. But in *NLRB v. Katz,* 369 U.S. 736 (1962), the Court held that at least one tactic—instituting unilateral changes during bargaining—was forbidden, for it put a bargainable topic outside the reach of the bargaining process. GE had done no less; it has, if anything, done more. By its communications and bargaining strategy it in effect painted itself into a corner on *all* bargainable matters....

We do not today hold that an employer may not communicate with his employees during negotiations. Nor are we deciding that the "best offer first" bargaining technique is forbidden. Moreover, we do not require an employer to engage in "auction bargaining," or, as the dissent seems to suggest, compel him to make concessions, "minor" or otherwise....

We hold that an employer may not so combine "take-it-or-leave-it" bargaining methods with a widely publicized stance of unbending firmness that he is himself unable to alter a position once taken. It is this specific conduct that GE must avoid in order to comply with the Board's order, and not a carbon copy of every underlying event relied upon by the Board to support its findings. Such conduct, we find, constitutes a refusal to bargain "in fact." *NLRB v. Katz,* 369 U.S. 736, 743 (1962). It also constitutes, as the facts of this action demonstrate, an absence of subjective good faith, for it implies that the Company can deliberately bargain and communicate as though the Union did not exist, in clear derogation of the Union's status as exclusive representative of its members under § 9(a)....

FRIENDLY, Circuit Judge (concurring and dissenting)....

The danger of collision with § 8(c) or (d) arises only when the Board makes a finding of violation although the parties have sat down with each other and have not engaged in any proscribed tactic. Still I have no difficulty with the Board's making a finding of bad faith based on an entire course of conduct so long as the standard of bad faith is, in Judge Magruder's well-known phrase, a "desire not to reach an agreement with the Union." *NLRB v. Reed & Prince Mfg. Co.,* 205 F.2d 131, 134 (1st Cir.), *cert. denied,* 346 U.S. 887 (1953)....

While the lead opinion makes much use of the "take-it-or-leave-it" phrase, it never defines this. I should suppose it meant a resolve to adhere to a position without even listening to and considering the views of the other side. To go further and say that a party, whether employer or union, who, after listening to and considering such proposals, violates § 8(a)(5) if he rejects them because of confidence in his own bargaining power, would ignore the explicit command of § 8(d)....

It surely cannot be, for example, that a union intent on imposing area standards violates § 8(b)(3) if it refuses to heed the well-documented presentation of an employer who insists that acceptance of them will drive him out of business. Neither can it be that a union violates § 8(b)(3) if it insists on its demands because it knows the employer simply cannot stand a strike. It must be equally true that an employer is not to be condemned for "take-it-or-leave-it" bargaining when, after discussing the union's proposals and supporting arguments, he formulates what he considers a sufficiently attractive offer and refuses to alter it unless convinced an alteration is "right."...

Once we rid ourselves of the prejudice inevitably engendered by this catch-phrase, we reach the argument that a party violates § 8(a)(5) if he gets himself into a situation where he is "unable to alter a position once taken," even though he would otherwise be willing to do so.

While this sounds fair enough, as does the Board's somewhat similar remark about the continuing duty to give "unfettered consideration," it would seemingly outlaw practices that no one has considered illegal up to this time. A union that has won a favorable contract from one employer and has broadcast that it will take no less from others seems to me to be quite as "unable to alter a position once taken" as GE was here, yet I should not have supposed this violated the Act. So also with an employer who has negotiated a contract with one union and has proclaimed that he will do no better for others. To say that taking such positions violates § 8(b)(3) or 8(a)(5) is steering a collision course with § 8(d)....

An essential element to the Board's conclusion of GE's offending was the Company's publicity campaign. "The disparagement of the Union as bargaining representative" is item (5) in the Board's bill of particulars...

I find no warrant for such a holding in the language of the statute, its legislative history or decisions construing it. GE's communications fit snugly under the phrase "views, argument, or opinion" in § 8(c). The very archetypes of what Congress had in mind were communications by an employer to his workers designed to influence their decisions contrary to union views, and communications by unions to workers designed to influence their decisions contrary to employer views. The statute draws no distinctions between communications by an employer in an effort to head off organization and communications after organization intended to show that he is doing right by his employees and will do no more under the threat of a strike. Congress had enough faith in the common sense of the American working man to believe he did not need—or want—to be shielded by a government agency from hearing whatever arguments employers or unions desired to make to him. Freedom of choice by employees after hearing all relevant arguments is the cornerstone of the National Labor Relations Act....

The Examiner coined a phrase, echoed both by the Board and in the lead opinion, ... namely, that GE's communications program was an attempt "to deal with the Union through the employees rather than with the employees through the Union." ... Picturesque characterizations of this sort, at such sharp variance with the record, scarcely aid the quest for a right result. Members of Congress would probably be surprised to learn that being "exclusive representatives" means that interested parties may not go to constituents in an endeavor to influence the representatives to depart from positions they have taken. There can be nothing wrong in an employer's urging employees to communicate with their representatives simply because the communication is one the representatives do not want to hear. I thus find it impossible to accept the proposition that, by exercising its § 8(c) right to persuade the employees and by encouraging them to exercise their right to persuade their representatives, GE was somehow "ignoring the legitimacy and relevance of the Union's position as statutory representative of its members." ...

NOTES

1. "Hard bargaining" by an employer is not in itself unlawful. *Dierks Forests, Inc.,* 148 N.L.R.B. 923 (1964); *American Thread Co.,* 274 N.L.R.B. 1112 (1985). At some juncture in the negotiations an employer clearly may make a firm and final offer. In *Philip Carey Mfg. Co.,* 140 N.L.R.B. 1103 (1963), *enforced in part,* 331 F.2d 720 (6th Cir.), *cert. denied,* 379 U.S. 888 (1964), the Board held that an employer did not violate § 8(a)(5) when it made a final offer at the eleventh meeting in a series of give-and-take bargaining sessions. The Board and the courts do not always see eye-to-eye, however, on the legality of particular instances of hard bargaining. *See, e.g.,* Brown, *Hard Bargaining: The Board Says No, the Court Says Yes,* 8 Employee Rel. L.J. 37 (1982).

Occasionally, an employer's substantive proposals have been treated as evidence of bad faith, especially when combined with other conduct such as delaying tactics. So classified were an insistence on an "open shop" and absolute employer control over wage rates, *NLRB v. Wright Motors, Inc.,* 603 F.2d 604 (7th Cir. 1979), an offer of little or no wage increase during a period of double-digit inflation, *K-Mart Corp. v. NLRB,* 626 F.2d 704 (9th Cir. 1980), and an uncompromising management rights proposal that was "obviously unpalatable" to the union, *Sparks Nugget v. NLRB,* 968 F.2d 991 (9th Cir. 1992). *See also Bartlett-Collins Co.,* 237 N.L.R.B. 770 (1978), *enforced,* 639 F.2d 652 (10th Cir.), *cert. denied,* 452 U.S. 961 (1981) (employer insisted on presence of court reporter as precondition to contract negotiations). In the latter case, the Board apparently applied a *per se* theory of illegality, an approach that was sharply criticized in

Modjeska, *Guess Who's Coming to the Bargaining Table?*, 39 Ohio St. L.J. 415 (1978).

Nevertheless, regressive proposals are not necessarily indicative of bad faith. According to the Board, the good faith/bad faith line is drawn where the cumulative effect of the employer's proposals effectively negates the union's ability to act as representative of the employees. So, for example, if the employer's proposals require the waiver of statutory rights without making any economic concessions or offering to accept limits on employer rights, thus leaving the union or the employees in a worse position than they were prior to bargaining, bad faith is shown. *See Hydrotherm, Inc.*, 302 N.L.R.B. 990 (1991). However, proposals to reduce the status quo by eliminating a union security clause, reducing wages and benefits, and insisting on at-will employment are not indicative of bad faith bargaining if the employer has a legitimate business reason for its proposal. *See Goldsmith Motors Corp.*, 310 N.L.R.B. 1279 (1993) (employer in "difficult financial straits" did not show bad faith by making regressive proposals); *Optica Lee Borinquen, Inc.*, 307 N.L.R.B. 705 (1992), *enforced,* 991 F.2d 786 (1st Cir. 1993) (deep reductions sought in allegedly noncompetitive existing benefits not evidence of bad faith); *S & F Enters.*, 312 N.L.R.B. 770 (1993) (employer's rigidity on at-will employment and refusal to agree to arbitration was justified by its "undisputedly precarious financial condition"); *AMF Bowling Co.*, 314 N.L.R.B. 969 (1994), *enforcement denied on other grounds,* 63 F.3d 1293 (4th Cir. 1995) (regressive economic position which included request to eliminate union security clause was not evidence of bad faith where motivated by economic considerations and the employer's concerns about remaining competitive).

In a few instances a finding of bad faith has been predicated in part on the employer's rejection of proposals submitted by the union. The proposals at issue included a clause embodying a right guaranteed employees by the labor relations statute, *Montgomery Ward & Co.*, 37 N.L.R.B. 100 (1941), *enforced,* 133 F.2d 676 (9th Cir. 1943); permission for the union to use the company bulletin board, an accepted practice in the industry, *Reed & Prince Mfg. Co.*, 96 N.L.R.B. 850 (1951), *enforced,* 205 F.2d 131 (1st Cir.), *cert. denied,* 346 U.S. 887 (1953); and a checkoff provision, *H.K. Porter Co.*, 153 N.L.R.B. 1370 (1965), *enforced,* 363 F.2d 272 (D.C. Cir.), *cert. denied,* 385 U.S. 851 (1966), and *Roanoke Iron & Bridge Works, Inc.*, 160 N.L.R.B. 175 (1966), *enforced,* 390 F.2d 846 (D.C. Cir. 1967), *cert. denied,* 391 U.S. 904 (1968) (employer intransigent for purpose of undermining union, not for "legitimate" business reasons).

2. Ordinarily, the good faith of the employer is to be judged by the NLRB on the basis of all the circumstances. The test is whether the "totality of the employer's conduct ... manifests a mindset at odds with reaching an agreement." *South Carolina Baptist Ministries,* 310 N.L.R.B. 156 (1993). An employer's preelection speeches concerning its intentions in negotiations may be evidence of unlawful "surface bargaining." *NLRB v. Overnite Transp. Co.,* 938 F.2d 815 (7th Cir. 1991). Similarly, an employer's statements at the bargaining table that it "would not mind" if its proposals prompted a strike, and that the General Manager "wanted a strike so that he could replace the employees and get rid of the unions," combined with "regressive and confrontational proposals" (wage reduction, elimination of the pension plan and institution of an inferior health plan) evidenced egregious surface bargaining and a desire to frustrate agreement. *Unbelievable, Inc., dba Frontier Hotel & Casino*, 318 N.L.R.B. 857 (1995), *enforced in part*, 118 F.3d 795 (D.C. Cir. 1997).

How much of this inquiry is based on the form that bargaining takes rather than its substance? In *NLRB v. Montgomery Ward & Co.*, 133 F.2d 676, 687 (9th Cir. 1943), the court said: "Wards was not bound to offer a counterproposal ... but when one is asked for, it ought to be made, although not indispensable. [I]t is not incumbent upon the employees continually to present new contracts until ultimately one meets the approval of the company." Could one say there is a duty to make counterproposals but no duty to make concessions? What would that mean? *See* Marcus, *The Employer's Duty to Bargain: Counterproposal v. Concession*, 17 Lab. L.J. 541 (1966).

3. The Labor Board has indicated that an employer has a fundamental First Amendment right under the NLRA to communicate directly with employees to publicize its bargaining position, so long as it does not endeavor to deal directly with the employees or to bypass the workers' chosen bargaining agent, and the communication is accomplished in a noncoercive manner. *See United Technologies*, 274 N.L.R.B. 1069 (1985), *enforced*, 789 F.2d 121 (2d Cir. 1986). There is no requirement that the union be given a meaningful opportunity to consider a proposal before the employer disseminates information to employees. *Americare Pine Lodge Nursing and Rehabilitation Center v. NLRB*, 160 L.R.R.M. 2201 (4th Cir. 1999). *See also General Store No. Two*, 273 N.L.R.B. 415 (1984), which permitted an employer to directly inform bargaining unit members that their failure to accept immediate mid-term concessions similar to those recently given by their representative labor organization to a competing company might result in dire consequences, since the union president had authorized the employer to express its concerns to the employees in an effort to "condition" them for the concessions that would ultimately be required.

4. On good faith bargaining in general, *see* Cox, *The Duty to Bargain in Good Faith*, 71 Harv. L. Rev. 1401 (1958); Duvin, *The Duty to Bargain: Law in Search of Policy*, 64 Colum. L. Rev. 248 (1964); Feinsinger, *The National Labor Relations Act and Collective Bargaining*, 57 Mich. L. Rev. 807 (1959); Fick, *Negotiation Theory and the Law of Collective Bargaining*, 38 Kan. L. Rev. 81 (1989); Fleming, *New Challenges for Collective Bargaining*, 1964 Wis. L. Rev. 426; Murphy, *Impasse and the Duty to Bargain in Good Faith*, 39 U. Pitt. L. Rev. 1 (1977); Norton, *Bargaining and the Ethic of Process*, 64 N.Y.U. L. Rev. 493 (1989).

NLRB v. AMERICAN NATIONAL INSURANCE CO.

Supreme Court of the United States
343 U.S. 395, 72 S. Ct. 824, 96 L. Ed. 1027 (1952)

MR. CHIEF JUSTICE VINSON delivered the opinion of the Court.

This case arises out of a complaint that respondent refused to bargain collectively with the representatives of its employees as required under the National Labor Relations Act, as amended.

The Office Employees International Union, AFL, Local No. 27, certified by the National Labor Relations Board as the exclusive bargaining representative of respondent's office employees, requested a meeting with respondent for the purpose of negotiating an agreement governing employment relations. At the first meetings, beginning on November 30, 1948, the Union submitted a proposed contract covering wages, hours, promotions, vacations and other provisions commonly found in collective bargaining agreements, including a clause establishing a procedure for settling grievances arising under the contract by successive appeals to management with ultimate resort to an arbitrator.

On January 10, 1949, following a recess for study of the Union's contract proposals, respondent objected to the provisions calling for unlimited arbitration. To meet this objection, respondent proposed a so-called management functions clause listing matters such as promotions, discipline and work scheduling as the responsibility of management and excluding such matters from arbitration. The Union's representative took the position "as soon as [he] heard [the proposed clause]" that the Union would not agree to such a clause so long as it covered matters subject to the duty to bargain collectively under the Labor Act.

Several further bargaining sessions were held without reaching agreement on the Union's proposal or respondent's counter-proposal to unlimited arbitration. As a result, the management functions clause was "by-passed" for bargaining on other terms of the Union's contract proposal. On January 17, 1949, respondent stated in writing its agreement with some of the terms proposed by the Union and, where there was disagreement, respondent offered counterproposals, including a clause entitled "Functions and Prerogatives of Management" along the lines suggested at the meeting of January 10th. The Union objected to the portion of the clause providing:

> The right to select and hire, to promote to a better position, to discharge, demote or discipline for cause, and to maintain discipline and efficiency of employees and to determine the schedules of work is recognized by both union and company as the proper responsibility and prerogative of management to be held and exercised by the company, and while it is agreed that an employee feeling himself to have been aggrieved by any decision of the company in respect to such matters, or the union in his behalf, shall have the right to have such decision reviewed by top management officials of the company under the grievance machinery hereinafter set forth, it is further

agreed that the final decision of the company made by such top management officials shall not be further reviewable by arbitration.

At this stage of the negotiations, the National Labor Relations Board filed a complaint against respondent based on the Union's charge that respondent had refused to bargain as required by the Labor Act and was thereby guilty of interfering with the rights of its employees guaranteed by § 7 of the Act and of unfair labor practices under §§ 8(a)(1) and 8(a)(5) of the Act. While the proceeding was pending, negotiations between the Union and respondent continued with the management functions clause remaining an obstacle to agreement....

On May 19, 1949, a Union representative offered a second contract proposal which included a management functions clause containing much of the language found in respondent's second counterproposal, quoted above, with the vital difference that questions arising under the Union's proposed clause would be subject to arbitration as in the case of other grievances. Finally, on January 13, 1950, after the Trial Examiner had issued his report but before decision by the Board, an agreement between the Union and respondent was signed. The agreement contained a management functions clause that rendered nonarbitrable matters of discipline, work schedules and other matters covered by the clause. The subject of promotions and demotions was deleted from the clause and made the subject of a special clause establishing a union-management committee to pass upon promotion matters.

While these negotiations were in progress, the Board's Trial Examiner conducted hearings on the Union's complaint. The Examiner held that respondent had a right to bargain for inclusion of a management functions clause in a contract. However, upon review of the entire negotiations, including respondent's unilateral action in changing working conditions during the bargaining, the Examiner found that from and after November 30, 1948, respondent had refused to bargain in a good faith effort to reach agreement. The Examiner recommended that respondent be ordered in general terms to bargain collectively with the Union.

The Board agreed with the Trial Examiner that respondent had not bargained in a good faith effort to reach an agreement with the Union. But the Board rejected the Examiner's views on an employer's right to bargain for a management functions clause and held that respondent's action in bargaining for inclusion of any such clause "constituted, quite [apart from] Respondent's demonstrated bad faith, per se violations of § 8(a)(5) and (1)." Accordingly, the Board not only ordered respondent in general terms to bargain collectively with the Union (par. 2 (a)), but also included in its order a paragraph designed to prohibit bargaining for any management functions clause covering a condition of employment. (Par. 1(a).) 89 N.L.R.B. 185....

First. The National Labor Relations Act is designed to promote industrial peace by encouraging the making of voluntary agreements governing relations between unions and employers. The Act does not compel any agreement whatsoever between employees and employers. Nor does the Act regulate the substantive terms governing wages, hours and working conditions which are incorporated in an agreement. The theory of the Act is that the making of voluntary labor agreements is encouraged by protecting employees' rights to organize for collective bargaining and by imposing on labor and management the mutual obligation to bargain collectively.

Enforcement of the obligation to bargain collectively is crucial to the statutory scheme. And, as has long been recognized, performance of the duty to bargain requires more than a willingness to enter upon a sterile discussion of union-management differences. Before the enactment of the National Labor Relations Act, it was held that the duty of an employer to bargain collectively required the employer "to negotiate in good faith with his employees' representatives; to match their proposals, if unacceptable, with counterproposals; and to make every reasonable effort to reach an agreement." The duty to bargain collectively, implicit in the Wagner Act as introduced in Congress, was made express by the insertion of the fifth employer unfair labor practice accompanied by an explanation of the purpose and meaning of the phrase "bargain collectively in a good faith effort to reach an agreement." This understanding of the duty to bargain collectively has been accepted and applied throughout the administration of the Wagner Act by the National Labor Relations Board and the Courts of Appeal.

In 1947, the fear was expressed in Congress that the Board "has gone very far, in the guise of determining whether or not employers had bargained in good faith, in setting itself up as the judge of what concessions an employer must make and of the proposals and counterproposals that he may or may not make." Accordingly, the Hartley Bill, passed by the House, eliminated the good faith test and expressly provided that the duty to bargain collectively did not require submission of counterproposals. As amended in the Senate and passed as the Taft-Hartley Act, the good faith test of bargaining was retained and written into § 8(d) of the National Labor Relations Act. That section contains the express provision that the obligation to bargain collectively does not compel either party to agree to a proposal or require the making of a concession.

Thus it is now apparent from the statute itself that the Act does not encourage a party to engage in fruitless marathon discussions at the expense of frank statement and support of his position. And it is equally clear that the Board may not, either directly or indirectly, compel concessions or otherwise sit in judgment upon the substantive terms of collective bargaining agreements.

Second. The Board offers in support of the portion of its order before this Court a theory quite apart from the test of good faith bargaining prescribed in § 8(d) of the Act, a theory that respondent's bargaining for a management functions clause as a counterproposal to the Union's demand for unlimited arbitration was, *"per se,"* a violation of the Act.

Counsel for the Board do not contend that a management functions clause covering some conditions of employment is an illegal contract term. As a matter of fact, a review of typical contract clauses collected for convenience in drafting labor agreements shows that management functions clauses similar in essential detail to the clause proposed by respondent have been included in contracts negotiated by national unions with many employers. The National War Labor Board, empowered during the last war "[t]o decide the dispute, and provide by order the wages and hours and all other terms and conditions (customarily included in collective bargaining agreements)," ordered management functions clauses included in a number of agreements. Several such clauses ordered by the War Labor Board provided for arbitration in case of union dissatisfaction with the exercise of management functions, while others, as in the clause proposed by respondent in this case, provided that management decisions would be final. Without intimating any opinion as to the form of management function clause proposed by respondent in this case or the desirability of including any such clause in a labor agreement, it is manifest that bargaining for management functions clauses is common collective bargaining practice.

If the Board is correct, an employer violates the Act by bargaining for a management functions clause touching any condition of employment without regard to the traditions of bargaining in the particular industry or such other evidence of good faith as the fact in this case that respondent's clause was offered as a counterproposal to the Union's demand for unlimited arbitration. The Board's argument is a technical one for it is conceded that respondent would not be guilty of an unfair labor practice if, instead of proposing a clause that removed some matters from arbitration, it simply refused in good faith to agree to the Union proposal for unlimited arbitration. The argument starts with a finding, not challenged by the court below or by respondent, that at least some of the matters covered by the management functions clause proposed by respondent are "conditions of employment" which are appropriate subjects of collective bargaining under §§ 8(a)(5), 8(d) and 9(a) of the Act. The Board considers that employer bargaining for a clause under which management retains initial responsibility for work scheduling, a "condition of employment," for the duration of the contract is an unfair labor practice because it is "in derogation of" employees' statutory rights to bargain collectively as to conditions of employment.[22]

Conceding that there is nothing unlawful in including a management functions clause in a labor agreement, the Board would permit an employer to "propose"

---

[22] The Board's argument would seem to prevent an employer from bargaining for a "no-strike" clause, commonly found in labor agreements, requiring a union to forego for the duration of the contract the right to strike expressly granted by § 7 of the Act. However, the Board has permitted an employer to bargain in good faith for such a clause. *Shell Oil Co.,* 77 N.L.R.B. 1306 (1948). This result is explained by referring to the "salutary objective" of such a clause. *Bethlehem Steel Co.,* 89 N.L.R.B. 341, 345 (1950).

such a clause. But the Board would forbid bargaining for any such clause when the Union declines to accept the proposal, even where the clause is offered as a counterproposal to a Union demand for unlimited arbitration. Ignoring the nature of the Union's demand in this case, the board takes the position that employers subject to the Act must agree to include in any labor agreement provisions establishing fixed standards for work schedules or any other condition of employment. An employer would be permitted to bargain as to the content of the standard so long as he agrees to freeze a standard into a contract. Bargaining for more flexible treatment of such matters would be denied employers even though the result may be contrary to common collective bargaining practice in the industry. The Board was not empowered so to disrupt collective bargaining practices. On the contrary, the term "bargain collectively" as used in the Act "has been considered to absorb and give statutory approval to the philosophy of bargaining as worked out in the labor movement in the United States." *Order of Railroad Telegraphers v. Railway Express Agency,* 321 U.S. 342 (1944).

Congress provided expressly that the Board should not pass upon the desirability of the substantive terms of labor agreements. Whether a contract should contain a clause fixing standards for such matters as work scheduling or should provide for more flexible treatment of such matters is an issue for determination across the bargaining table, not by the Board. If the latter approach is agreed upon, the extent of union and management participation in the administration of such matters is itself a condition of employment to be settled by bargaining.

Accordingly, we reject the Board's holding that bargaining for the management functions clause proposed by respondent was, *per se,* an unfair labor practice. Any fears the Board may entertain that use of management functions clauses will lead to evasion of an employer's duty to bargain collectively as to "rates of pay, wages, hours and conditions of employment" do not justify condemning all bargaining for management functions clauses covering any "condition of employment" as *per se* violations of the Act. The duty to bargain collectively is to be enforced by application of the good faith bargaining standards of § 8(d) to the facts of each case rather than by prohibiting all employers in every industry from bargaining for management functions clauses altogether....

Accepting as we do the finding of the Court below that respondent bargained in good faith for the management functions clause proposed by it, we hold that respondent was not in that respect guilty of refusing to bargain collectively as required by the National Labor Relations Act. Accordingly, enforcement of paragraph 1(a) of the Board's order was properly denied.

Affirmed.

MR. JUSTICE MINTON, with whom MR. JUSTICE BLACK and MR. JUSTICE DOUGLAS join, dissenting:

I do not see how this case is solved by telling the National Labor Relations Board that since *some* "management functions" clauses are valid (which the

Board freely admits), respondent was not guilty of an unfair labor practice *in this case*. The record is replete with evidence that respondent insisted on a clause which would classify the control over certain conditions of employment as a management prerogative, and that the insistence took the form of a refusal to reach a settlement unless the union accepted the clause. The Court of Appeals agreed that the respondent was "steadfast" in this demand. Therefore, *this case* is one where the employer came into the bargaining room with a demand that certain topics upon which it had a duty to bargain were to be removed from the agenda—that was the price the union had to pay to gain a contract. There is all the difference between the hypothetical "management functions" clauses envisioned by the majority and this "management functions" clause as there is between waiver and coercion. No one suggests that an employer is guilty of an unfair labor practice when it proposes that it be given unilateral control over certain working conditions and the union accepts the proposal in return for various other benefits. But where, as here, the employer tells the union that the only way to obtain a contract as to wages is to agree not to bargain about certain other working conditions, the employer has refused to bargain about those other working conditions. There is more than a semantic difference between a proposal that the union waive certain rights and a demand that the union give up those rights as a condition precedent to enjoying other rights.

I need not and do not take issue with the Court of Appeals' conclusion that there was no absence of good faith. Where there is a refusal to bargain, the Act does not require an inquiry as to whether that refusal was in good faith or bad faith. The duty to bargain about certain subjects is made absolute by the Act. The majority seems to suggest that an employer could be found guilty of bad faith if it used a "management functions" clause to close off bargaining about all topics of discussion. Whether the employer closes off all bargaining or, as in this case, only a certain area of bargaining, he has refused to bargain as to whatever he has closed off, and any discussion of his good faith is pointless.

That portion of § 8(d) of the Act which declares that an employer need not agree to a proposal or make concessions does not dispose of this case. Certainly the Board lacks power to compel concessions as to the substantive terms of labor agreements. But the Board in this case was seeking to compel the employer to bargain about subjects properly within the scope of collective bargaining. That the employer has such a duty to bargain and that the Board is empowered to enforce the duty is clear.

An employer may not stake out an area which is a proper subject for bargaining and say, "As to this we will not bargain." To do so is a plain refusal to bargain in violation of § 8(a)(5) of the Act. If employees' bargaining rights can be cut away so easily, they are indeed illusory. I would reverse.

NOTES

1. Does *American Nat'l Ins. Co.* justify an employer's insistence on a management functions clause reserving unilateral control over virtually all aspects of the employment relationship, leaving the employees hardly better off than they would be without any agreement? *Compare White v. NLRB*, 255 F.2d 564 (5th Cir. 1958) ("Yes") *and Gulf States Mfrs. v. NLRB*, 579 F.2d 1298 (5th Cir. 1978), 598 F.2d 896 (5th Cir. 1979) (en banc) *with NLRB v. Reed & Prince Mfg. Co.*, 205 F.2d 131 (1st Cir. 1953), *cert. denied*, 346 U.S. 887 (1953) *and NLRB v. A-1 King Size Sandwiches*, 732 F.2d 872 (11th Cir.), *cert. denied*, 469 U.S. 1035 (1984). For a sharply different perspective on the appropriate governance of the workplace under the NLRA, *see* J. Atleson, Values and Assumptions in American Labor Law 111-35 (1983); Klare, *Judicial Deradicalization of the Wagner Act and the Origins of Modern Legal Consciousness*, 1937-41, 62 Minn. L. Rev. 265 (1978); Comment, *The Radical Potential of the Wagner Act: The Duty to Bargain Collectively*, 129 U. Pa. L. Rev. 1392 (1981); Note, *Subjects of Bargaining Under the NLRA and the Limits of Liberal Political Imagination*, 97 Harv. L. Rev. 475 (1983).

2. According to the NLRB, an employer did not engage in bad-faith bargaining when it proposed a strong management rights clause, a no-strike clause making union officials responsible for encouraging wildcat strikers to return to work, and a binding arbitration provision limited to matters of discharge or discipline. The Board concluded that both sides bargained hard, that the employer's proposals were not unduly harsh, vindictive, or unreasonable, and that apart from the contract proposals themselves, other evidence indicated the employer had bargained in good faith. *Chevron Chem. Co.*, 261 N.L.R.B. 44 (1982), *enforced*, 701 F.2d 172 (5th Cir. 1983). Similarly, an employer that insisted on broad management rights, at-will employment, no arbitration provision, and authority to award merit increases engaged in hard bargaining but did not violate § 8(a)(5), in part because it did not insist that the union waive its right to strike. *Coastal Elec. Coop.*, 311 N.L.R.B. 1126 (1993).

3. Suppose instead that the employer insists on incorporating into the collective agreement its pre-election employee handbook, which establishes basic terms and conditions of employment and is unilaterally modifiable by the employer at any time. Would this violate § 8(a)(5)? *See Radisson Plaza Minneapolis*, 307 N.L.R.B. 94 (1992), *enforced*, 987 F.2d 1376 (8th Cir. 1993).

––––––––––

NLRB v. Insurance Agents' Int'l Union, 361 U.S. 477, 80 S. Ct. 419, 4 L. Ed. 2d 454 (1960). In order to put economic pressure on an employer to yield to bargaining demands, a union of insurance agents engaged in concerted on-the-job activities designed to harass the company. These included refusal for a time to solicit new business, refusal to follow reporting procedures, late arrival at work and early departure, failure to attend meetings, and picketing of company offices. Although the union continued to negotiate with the employer in an effort to reach agreement on a new contract, the National Labor Relations Board held that its harassing tactics constituted a refusal to bargain in good faith as required by § 8(b)(3) of the NLRA. The Supreme Court disagreed. Pointing out that Congress did not intend the NLRB to regulate the substantive terms of labor agreements, the Court stated: "[I]f the Board could regulate the choice of economic weapons that may be used as part of collective bargaining, it would be in a position to exercise considerable influence upon the substantive terms on which the parties contract." Even on the assumption the employees' conduct was unprotected, and they could have been discharged for it, it was not inconsistent with good faith bargaining.

General Electric Co. v. NLRB, 412 F.2d 512 (2d Cir. 1969). The IUE and seven other unions representing General Electric workers, concerned over the company's technique of presenting a separate "fair, firm offer" to each union almost simultaneously and then whipsawing one against the other, formed a Committee on Collective Bargaining (CCB) to coordinate bargaining in 1966 with GE and its major competitor, Westinghouse. After GE rejected the CCB's request for informal joint discussions, the company and the IUE set a date to begin individual negotiations. But the GE representatives walked out when they discovered that the IUE bargaining committee had been enlarged by one person from each of the other seven unions comprising the CCB, even though the IUE insisted the seven new committee members had no vote and were present only to assist the IUE and not to represent their own unions. The NLRB found the company had violated § 8(a)(5) in its refusal to confer and the Second Circuit agreed. The court observed that the right of both employees and employers "to choose whomever they wish to represent them in formal labor negotiations is fundamental to the statutory scheme." The rare exceptions to the rule of free choice of representatives are situations where personal ill will or conflicts of interest create a "clear and present" danger to the collective bargaining process. Furthermore, there was no showing that the CCB was attempting to use the augmented negotiating committee to impose joint bargaining on the company or that the IUE was committed not to accept any GE offer unless the other unions agreed. The company was therefore obligated to test the IUE's good faith.

NOTES

1. Was the IUE's introduction of "coordinated bargaining" in the 1966 negotiations a predictable escalation of the combat following GE's resort to Boulwareism in 1960? Does it seem like an effective technique? *See generally* Northrup, *Boulwareism v. Coalitionism—The 1966 GE Negotiations,* Management of Personnel Quarterly, Summer 1966, at 2; Anker, *Pattern Bargaining,*

Antitrust Laws and the National Labor Relations Act, in N.Y.U. Nineteenth Annual Conference on Labor 81 (1967); Goldberg, *Coordinated Bargaining Tactics of Unions,* 54 Cornell L. Rev. 897 (1969).

2. Should labor organizations representing different bargaining units of the same employer ever be entitled to insist upon joint negotiations? If so, when? In *AFL-CIO Joint Negotiating Comm. (Phelps Dodge Corp.),* 184 N.L.R.B. 754 (1970), the Labor Board held that a group of unions violated § 8(b)(3) by insisting in effect on company-wide bargaining. The unions demanded the simultaneous and satisfactory settlement of contracts in other bargaining units of the company, and struck in support of their demands. The Board said that the integrity of a bargaining unit, whether established by certification or by voluntary agreement of the parties, may not be unilaterally attacked. Enforcement was denied in *AFL-CIO Joint Negotiating Comm. v. NLRB,* 459 F.2d 374 (3d Cir.), *cert. denied,* 409 U.S. 1059 (1972). The court of appeals pointed out that all the union demands were mandatory subjects of bargaining, and that the parallel action of the units in going to impasse was not evidence of an attempt to merge the bargaining of separate units. "The fact a demand may have extra-unit effects does not alter its status as a mandatory subject of bargaining." *But cf. Paperworkers Local 620,* 309 N.L.R.B. 44 (1992) (union demand for pooled voting among all units in ratifying agreement was unlawful; agreement in one unit may not be conditioned upon the satisfactory conclusion of negotiations for another unit); *see* Getman & Marshall, *Industrial Relations in Transition: The Paper Industry Example*, 102 Yale L.J. 1803 (1993) (criticizing *Paperworkers* decision and doctrine).

3. An employer may not insist upon joint negotiations with two unions representing separate units of the company's employees. To carry such a demand to impasse is a violation of § 8(a)(5), since only the employees or their representatives have the right to select the members of the union's bargaining team. *F. W. Woolworth Co.,* 179 N.L.R.B. 748 (1969).

———————

Charles D. Bonanno Linen Service v. NLRB, 454 U.S. 404, 102 S. Ct. 720, 70 L. Ed. 2d 656 (1982). For several years Bonanno was a member of the Linen Supply Association, a group of ten employers formed to negotiate with a Teamsters local as a multiemployer unit. In February 1975, Bonanno authorized the Association to represent it in the forthcoming negotiations. The union and the Association held ten bargaining sessions during March and April. On April 30 the negotiators reached a tentative agreement but the union members rejected it. By May 15 bargaining had come to an impasse over the method of compensation. On June 23 the union selectively struck Bonanno and in response most other Association members locked out their drivers. The stalemate continued over the summer despite sporadic meetings. Bonanno permanently replaced all its striking drivers and on November 21 announced its withdrawal from the Association because of the "ongoing impasse." Shortly thereafter, the Association ended its lockout and resumed negotiations, without Bonanno. A new contract was agreed upon in April 1976 but Bonanno refused to be bound by its terms. The Supreme Court accepted the NLRB's recognition of the voluntary nature of multiemployer bargaining, and the notion that both unions and employers may withdraw by giving timely, unequivocal notice prior to negotiations. Absent unusual circumstances, however, the policy of promoting labor peace supports the rule that no party can unilaterally withdraw during negotiations. A 5-4 majority of the Court concluded that it should defer to the Board's judgment that an impasse, standing alone, was not such an unusual circumstance or so destructive of group bargaining as to justify a unilateral withdrawal. Even the possibility that a union might sign interim agreements with certain employers, pending the execution of a unit-wide contract, would not destroy the integrity of the multiemployer unit.

NOTES

1. Chief Justice Burger and Justice Rehnquist dissented in *Bonanno,* arguing that the Court's majority was too deferential to the NLRB's flat rule that an impasse does not justify an employer's withdrawal from multiemployer bargaining, regardless of the severity and length of the impasse and the presence of interim agreements with some employers. Those dissenters contended that a rule permitting unilateral withdrawal upon impasse was more consistent with the goal of industrial peace and less likely to force the parties into "escalated economic warfare." Justices O'Connor and Powell, dissenting, would avoid the "absolute positions" of both the majority and the Chief Justice. Instead, they would require an examination into the particular circumstances of any impasse. For example, when there is a "complete breakdown in negotiations," not just a "temporary impasse," they would allow an employer to withdraw. What are the respective merits or deficiencies of these various per se and ad hoc approaches? Is "industrial peace" a valid criterion for appraising this type of case? For a thought-provoking analysis of *Bonanno, see* Leslie, *Multiemployer Bargaining Rules,* 75 Va. L. Rev. 241 (1989).

2. Withdrawal from multiemployer bargaining is always permissible upon the "mutual consent" of the union and the association. *Retail Assocs.,* 120 N.L.R.B. 388 (1958). An employer may withdraw during bargaining if negotiations were initiated prematurely. *Action Elec. Co. v. IBEW Local 292,* 856 F.2d 1062 (8th Cir. 1988). But an interest-arbitration clause in a multiemployer association's new contract was held binding on a company that made an untimely attempt to withdraw. *Sheet Metal Workers Local 104 v. Simpson Sheet Metal,* 954 F.2d 554 (9th Cir. 1992). If impasse alone does not justify unilateral withdrawal after multiemployer negotiations have begun, what circumstances would? What about a sharp decline in a company's business—would this constitute "unusual circumstances," permitting a unilateral withdrawal from multiemployer negotiations?

See Serv-All Co., 199 N.L.R.B. 1131 (1972), *enforcement denied,* 491 F.2d 1273 (10th Cir. 1974). *See generally* Bock, *Multiemployer Bargaining and Withdrawing From the Association After Bargaining Has Begun: 38 Years of "Unusual Circumstances" Under Retail Associates,* 13 Hofstra Lab. L.J. 519 (1996).

3. The rules for post-impasse withdrawal from a multiemployer bargaining group enunciated in *Retail Associates* do not apply to pre-hire bargaining relationships established by construction industry parties under § 8(f). As a result, a continuing obligation to participate in negotiations for a new agreement does not apply to employers with § 8(f) relationships. *Luterbach Constr.,* 315 N.L.R.B. 976 (1994).

4. Uniformity of labor standards in an industry or geographical area is a traditional goal of many unions. After a union has come to terms with the principal employer association in a given area, is it an unlawful refusal to bargain for the union to require an identical contract with every independent employer? Is there any difference between the union's "take-it-or-leave-it" attitude in such circumstances and GE's in the 1960 negotiations with the IUE? Even if the union engaged in the usual give-and-take bargaining with the employer association, what good is this to an independent confronted by a peremptory demand to sign the standard labor agreement?

2. BARGAINING REMEDIES

H.K. PORTER CO. v. NLRB

Supreme Court of the United States
397 U.S. 99, 90 S. Ct. 821, 26 L. Ed. 2d 146 (1970)

MR. JUSTICE BLACK delivered the opinion of the Court.

After an election respondent United Steelworkers Union was, on October 5, 1961, certified by the National Labor Relations Board as the bargaining agent for the employees at the Danville, Virginia, plant of the petitioner, H.K. Porter Co. Thereafter negotiations commenced for a collective bargaining agreement. Since that time the controversy has seesawed between the Board, the Court of Appeals for the District of Columbia Circuit, and this Court. This delay of over eight years is not because the case is exceedingly complex, but appears to have occurred chiefly because of the skill of the company's negotiators in taking advantage of every opportunity for delay in an Act more noticeable for its generality than for its precise prescriptions. The entire lengthy dispute mainly revolves around the union's desire to have the company agree to "check off" the dues owed to the union by its members, that is, to deduct those dues periodically from the company's wage payments to the employees. The record shows, as the Board found, that the company's objection to a checkoff was not due to any general principle or policy against making deductions from employees' wages. The company does deduct charges for things like insurance, taxes, and contributions to charities, and at some other plants it has a checkoff arrangement for union dues.

The evidence shows, and the court below found, that the company's objection was not because of inconvenience, but solely on the ground that the company was "not going to aid and comfort the union." Efforts by the union to obtain some kind of compromise on the checkoff request were all met with the same staccato response to the effect that the collection of union dues was the "union's business" and the company was not going to provide any assistance. Based on this and other evidence the Board found, and the Court of Appeals approved the finding, that the refusal of the company to bargain about the checkoff was not made in good faith, but was done solely to frustrate the making of any collective bargaining agreement. In May 1966, the Court of Appeals upheld the Board's order requiring the company to cease and desist from refusing to bargain in good faith and directing it to engage in further collective bargaining, if requested by the union to do so, over the checkoff. *United Steelworkers v. NLRB,* 363 F.2d 272, *cert. denied,* 385 U.S. 851.

In the course of that opinion, the Court of Appeals intimated that the Board conceivably might have required petitioner to agree to a checkoff provision as a remedy for the prior bad-faith bargaining, although the order enforced at that time did not contain any such provision. 363 F.2d at 275-276, n. 16. In the ensuing negotiations the company offered to discuss alternative arrangements for collecting the union's dues, but the union insisted that the company was required to agree to the checkoff proposal without modification. Because of this disagreement over the proper interpretation of the court's opinion, the union, in February 1967, filed a motion for clarification of the 1966 opinion. The motion was denied by the court on March 22, 1967, in an order suggesting that contempt proceedings before the Board would be the proper avenue for testing the employer's compliance with the original order. A request for the institution of such proceedings was made by the union, and in June 1967, the Regional Director of the Board declined to prosecute a contempt charge, finding that the employer had "satisfactorily complied with the affirmative requirements of the Order." ... The union then filed in the Court of Appeals a motion for reconsideration of the earlier motion to clarify the 1966 opinion. The court granted that motion and issued a new opinion in which it held that in certain circumstances a "checkoff may be imposed as a remedy for bad-faith bargaining." *United Steelworkers v. NLRB,* 389 F.2d 295, 298 (1967). The case was then remanded to the Board and on July 3, 1968, the Board issued a supplemental order requiring the petitioner to "[g]rant to the Union a contract clause providing for the checkoff of union dues." 172 N.L.R.B. No. 72. The Court of Appeals affirmed this order, *H.K. Porter Co. v. NLRB,* 414 F.2d 1123 (1969). We granted certiorari to consider whether the Board in these circumstances had the power to remedy the unfair labor practice by requiring the company to agree to check off the dues of the workers.... For reasons to be stated we hold that while the Board does have power under the Labor Management Relations Act ... to require employers and employees to negotiate, it is without power to compel a company or a union to agree to any substantive contractual provision of a collective bargaining agreement.

Since 1935 the story of labor relations in this country has largely been a history of governmental regulation of the process of collective bargaining. In that year Congress decided that disturbances in the area of labor relations led to undesirable burdens on and obstructions of interstate commerce, and passed the National Labor Relations Act.... Without spelling out the details, the Act provided that it was an unfair labor practice for an employer to refuse to bargain. Thus a general process was established which would ensure that employees as a group could express their opinions and exert their combined influence over the terms and conditions of their employment. The Board would act to see that the process worked.

The object of this Act was not to allow governmental regulation of the terms and conditions of employment, but rather to ensure that employers and their employees could work together to establish mutually satisfactory conditions. The basic theme of the Act was that through collective bargaining the passions, arguments, and struggles of prior years would be channeled into constructive, open discussions leading, hopefully, to mutual agreement. But it was recognized from the beginning that agreement might in some cases be impossible, and it was never intended that the Government would in such cases step in, become a party to the negotiations and impose its own views of a desirable settlement. This fundamental limitation was made abundantly clear in the legislative reports accompanying the 1935 Act.... The discussions on the floor of Congress consistently reflect this same understanding.

The Act was passed at a time in our Nation's history when there was considerable legal debate over the constitutionality of any law that required employers to conform their business behavior to any governmentally imposed standards. It was seriously contended that Congress could not constitutionally compel an employer to recognize a union and allow his employees to participate in setting the terms and conditions of employment. In *NLRB v. Jones & Laughlin Steel Corp.,* 301 U.S. 1 (1937), this Court, in a 5-to-4 decision, held that Congress was within the limits of its constitutional powers in passing the Act. In the course of that decision the Court said:

> The Act does not compel agreements between employers and employees. It does not compel any agreement whatever.... The theory of the Act is that free opportunity for negotiation with accredited representatives of employees is likely to promote industrial peace and may bring about the adjustments and agreements which the Act in itself does not attempt to compel.

Id. at 45.

In 1947 Congress reviewed the experience under the Act and concluded that certain amendments were in order. In the House committee report accompanying what eventually became the Labor Management Relations Act of 1947, the committee referred to the above quoted language in *Jones & Laughlin* and said:

> "Notwithstanding this language of the Court, the present Board has gone very far, in the guise of determining whether or not employers had bargained in good faith, in setting itself up as the judge of what concessions an employer must make and of the proposals and counterproposals that he may or may not make.
>
> ....
>
> "[U]nless Congress writes into the law guides for the Board to follow, the Board may attempt to carry this process still further and seek to control more and more the terms of collective bargaining agreements."[3]

Accordingly Congress amended the provisions defining unfair labor practices and said in § 8(d) that: "... *such obligation [to bargain collectively] does not compel either party to agree to a proposal or require the making of a concession.*"

In discussing the effect of that amendment, this Court said it is "clear that the Board may not, either directly or indirectly, compel concessions or otherwise sit in judgment upon the substantive terms of collective bargaining agreements." *NLRB v. American Ins. Co.,* 343 U.S. 395, 404 (1952). Later this Court affirmed that view stating that "it remains clear that § 8(d) was an attempt by Congress to prevent the Board from controlling the settling of the terms of collective bargaining agreements." *NLRB v. Insurance Agents,* 361 U.S. 477, 487 (1960). The parties to the instant case are agreed that this is the first time in the 35-year history of the Act that the Board has ordered either an employer or a union to agree to a substantive term of a collective bargaining agreement.

Recognizing the fundamental principle "that the National Labor Relations Act is grounded on the premise of freedom of contract," 389 F.2d at 300, the Court of Appeals in this case concluded that nevertheless in the circumstances presented here the Board could properly compel the employer to agree to a proposed checkoff clause. The Board had found that the refusal was based on a desire to frustrate agreement and not on any legitimate business reason. On the basis of that finding the Court of Appeals approved the further finding that the employer had not bargained in good faith, and the validity of that finding is not now before us. Where the record thus revealed repeated refusals by the employer to bargain in good faith on this issue, the Court of Appeals concluded that ordering agreement to the checkoff clause "may be the only means of assuring the Board, and the court, that [the employer] no longer harbors an illegal intent." 389 F.2d at 299.

In reaching this conclusion the Court of Appeals held that § 8(d) did not forbid the Board from compelling agreement. That court felt that "[s]ection 8(d) defines

---

[3] H.R. Rep. No. 245, 80th Cong., 1st Sess. 19-20 (1947).

collective bargaining and relates to a determination of *whether* a ... violation has occurred and not to the *scope* of the remedy which may be necessary to cure violations which have already occurred." 389 F.2d at 299. We may agree with the Court of Appeals that as a matter of strict, literal interpretation of that section it refers only to deciding when a violation has occurred, but we do not agree that that observation justifies the conclusion that the remedial powers of the Board are not also limited by the same considerations that led Congress to enact § 8(d). It is implicit in the entire structure of the Act that the Board acts to oversee and referee the process of collective bargaining, leaving the results of the contest to the bargaining strengths of the parties. It would be anomalous indeed to hold that while § 8(d) prohibits the Board from relying on a refusal to agree as the sole evidence of bad faith bargaining, the Act permits the Board to compel agreement in that same dispute. The Board's remedial powers under § 10 of the Act are broad, but they are limited to carrying out the policies of the Act itself. One of these fundamental policies is freedom of contract. While the parties' freedom of contract is not absolute under the Act, allowing the Board to compel agreement when the parties themselves are unable to do so would violate the fundamental premise on which the Act is based—private bargaining under governmental supervision of the procedure alone, without any official compulsion over the actual terms of the contract.

In reaching its decision the Court of Appeals relied extensively on the equally important policy of the Act that workers' rights to collective bargaining are to be secured. In this case the Court apparently felt that the employer was trying effectively to destroy the union by refusing to agree to what the union may have considered its most important demand. Perhaps the court, fearing that the parties might resort to economic combat, was also trying to maintain the industrial peace which the Act is designed to further. But the Act as presently drawn does not contemplate that unions will always be secure and able to achieve agreement even when their economic position is weak, nor that strikes and lockouts will never result from a bargaining to impasse. It cannot be said that the Act forbids an employer or a union to rely ultimately on its economic strength to try to secure what it cannot obtain through bargaining. It may well be true, as the Court of Appeals felt, that the present remedial powers of the Board are insufficiently broad to cope with important labor problems. But it is the job of Congress, not the Board or the courts, to decide when and if it is necessary to allow governmental review of proposals for collective bargaining agreements and compulsory submission to one side's demands. The present Act does not envision such a process.

The judgment is reversed and the case is remanded to the Court of Appeals for further action consistent with this opinion.

Reversed and remanded.

MR. JUSTICE WHITE took no part in the decision of this case.

MR. JUSTICE MARSHALL took no part in the consideration or decision of this case.

[The concurring opinion of MR. JUSTICE HARLAN and the dissenting opinion of MR. JUSTICE DOUGLAS, in which MR. JUSTICE STEWART concurred, are omitted.]

NOTES

1. Does *H.K. Porter* undercut the anti-Boulwareism stance of the NLRB and the Second Circuit in the *General Elec.* decisions, *supra*? The Board has ruled that even where an employer signals a refusal to compromise, makes no effort to reach agreement, and offers a status quo proposal which amounts to bad faith bargaining in violation of § 8(a)(5), the employer cannot be ordered to cease and desist from making such a proposal because "no party can be required to agree to any particular substantive bargaining provision." *See J & C Towing Co.,* 307 N.L.R.B. 198 (1992); *see also* Goldstein, *When and Where Should Be the Limits of NLRB Intervention?* in N.Y.U. Twenty-Third Annual Conference on Labor 55 (1970). *See generally* Comment, *The H.K. Porter Experiment in Bargaining Remedies: A Study in Black and Wright,* 56 Va. L. Rev. 530 (1970).

2. An employer granted a pay increase to unrepresented workers on the same day it started bargaining with a union representing a unit of unskilled workers. Eventually, the union and the employer agreed on a similar wage increase for the represented workers, but the employer refused to make the raise retroactive to the date the unrepresented workers got it. The NLRB found violations of both § 8(a)(1) and (a)(5), and ordered the employer to grant the pay increase retroactively. The Fourth Circuit denied enforcement of the retroactivity portion of the Board's order, declaring the Board has no authority to order agreement on mandatory subjects of bargaining, including the issue of retroactivity being negotiated by the parties. *Clearwater Finishing Co. v. NLRB,* 670 F.2d 464 (4th Cir. 1982).

On the other hand, *Invaldi v. NLRB,* 48 F.3d 444 (9th Cir. 1995), involved an employer that refused to execute a collective contract with a union that had accepted the firm's "last, best and final offer" four months after the offer had been made. Although the employer argued that its offer had lapsed when the union failed to accept it within a reasonable period of time, the Labor Board found no indication that the offer had been withdrawn before union acceptance. The court affirmed the Board's finding that the employer's refusal to execute the accepted agreement contravened § 8(a)(5) and enforced the remedial order directing the company to execute that contract.

3. To remedy an employer's two unlawful refusals to bargain with a certified union, the Labor Board ordered a six-month extension of the union's certification year in *Colfor, Inc.,* 282 N.L.R.B. 1173 (1987), *enforced,* 838 F.2d 164 (6th Cir. 1988). But the Board, with judicial approval, held that *H.K. Porter* precluded it from extending the term of a three-year collective bargaining agreement that a union had unlawfully refused to execute. *Hyatt Mgt. Corp. v. NLRB,* 817 F.2d 140 (D.C. Cir. 1987).

EX-CELL-O CORP.

National Labor Relations Board
185 N.L.R.B. 107 (1970)

This case began with the UAW's request for recognition on August 3, 1964. Ex-Cell-O refused the Union's request on August 10, 1964, and the Union immediately filed a petition for Certification of Representative. After a hearing the Regional Director ordered an election, which was held on October 22, 1964, and a majority of the employees voted for the Union. The Company, however, filed objections to the conduct of the election, alleging that the Union made certain misrepresentations which assertedly interfered therewith, but the Acting Regional Director, in a Supplemental Decision of December 29, 1964, overruled them. The Company then requested review of that decision, which the Board granted, and a hearing was held on May 18 and 19, 1965. The Hearing Officer issued his Report on Objections on July 15, 1965, and recommended that the objections be overruled. The Company filed exceptions thereto, but on October 28, 1965, the Board adopted the Hearing Officer's findings and recommendations and affirmed the Regional Director's certification of the Union.

The day after the Board's certification was issued, the Company advised the Union that it would refuse to bargain in order to secure a court review of the Board's action and later reiterated this position after receiving the Union's request for a bargaining meeting. The Union thereupon filed the 8(a)(1) and (5) charge in this case and the complaint was issued on November 23, 1965. The Respondent's answer admitted the factual allegations of the complaint but denied the violation on the ground that the Board's certification was invalid. The hearing herein, originally scheduled for February 15, 1966, commenced on June 1, 1966; it was adjourned until June 29, 1966, to permit the Union to offer evidence supporting its request for a compensatory remedy for the alleged refusal to bargain; the hearing was postponed again until July 28, 1966. The Company also petitioned the United States District Court for an injunction against the Regional Director and the Trial Examiner to restrain the latter from closing the hearing until the Regional Director had produced the investigative records in the representation case. The court issued a summary judgment denying the injunction on December 13, 1966, and on December 21, 1966, the Trial Examiner formally closed his hearing. On March 2, 1967, the Trial Examiner issued his Decision, finding that the Company had unlawfully refused to bargain in violation of Section 8(a)(5) and (1) of the Act and recommended the standard bargaining order as a remedy. In addition the Trial Examiner ordered the Company to compensate its employees for monetary losses incurred as a result of its unlawful conduct.

It is not disputed that Respondent refused to bargain with the Union, and we hereby affirm the Trial Examiner's conclusion that Respondent thereby violated Section 8(a)(1) and (5) of the Act. The compensatory remedy which he recommends, however, raises important issues concerning the Board's powers and duties to fashion appropriate remedies in its efforts to effectuate the policies of the National Labor Relations Act.

It is argued that such a remedy exceeds the Board's general statutory powers. In addition, it is contended that it cannot be granted because the amount of employee loss, if any, is so speculative that an order to make employees whole would amount to the imposition of a penalty. And the position is advanced that the adoption of this remedy would amount to the writing of a contract for the parties, which is prohibited by Section 8(d).

We have given most serious consideration to the Trial Examiner's recommended financial reparations order, and are in complete agreement with his finding that current remedies of the Board designed to cure violations of Section 8(a)(5) are inadequate. A mere affirmative order that an employer bargain upon request does not eradicate the effects of an unlawful delay of 2 or more years in the fulfillment of a statutory bargaining obligation. It does not put the employees in the position of bargaining strength they would have enjoyed if their employer had immediately recognized and bargained with their chosen representative. It does not dissolve the inevitable employee frustration or protect the Union from a loss of employee support attributable to such delay. The inadequacy of the remedy is all the more egregious where, as in the recent *NLRB v. Tiidee Products*[6] case, the court found that the employer had raised "frivolous" issues in order to postpone or avoid its lawful obligation to bargain. We have weighed these considerations most carefully. For the reasons stated below, however, we have reluctantly concluded that we cannot approve the Trial Examiner's Recommended Order that Respondent compensate its employees for monetary losses incurred as a consequence of Respondent's determination to refuse to bargain until it had tested in court the validity of the Board's certification.

Section 10(c) of the Act directs the Board to order a person found to have committed an unfair labor practice to cease and desist and "to take such affirmative action including reinstatement of employees with or without back pay, as will effectuate the policies of this Act." This authority, as our colleagues note with full documentation, is extremely broad and was so intended by Congress. It is not so broad, however, as to permit the punishment of a particular respondent or a class of respondents. Nor is the statutory direction to the Board so compelling that the Board is without discretion in exercising the full sweep of its power, for it would defeat the purposes of the Act if the Board imposed an otherwise proper remedy that resulted in irreparable harm to a particular respondent and hampered rather than promoted meaningful collective bargaining. Moreover, as

---

[6] 426 F.2d 1243 (D.C. Cir. 1970), [*cert. denied*, 400 U.S. 950 (1970)].

the Supreme Court recently emphasized, the Board's grant of power does not extend to compelling agreement. (*H.K. Porter Co., Inc. v. NLRB*, 397 U.S. 99.) It is with respect to these three limitations upon the Board's power to remedy a violation of Section 8(a)(5) that we examine the UAW's requested remedy in this case.

The Trial Examiner concluded that the proposed remedy was not punitive, that it merely made the employees partially whole for losses occasioned by the Respondent's refusal to bargain, and was much less harsh than a backpay order for discharged employees, which might require the Respondent to pay wages to these employees as well as their replacements. Viewed solely in the context of an assumption of employee monetary losses resulting directly from the Respondent's violation of Section 8(a)(5), as finally determined in court, the Trial Examiner's conclusion appears reasonable. There are, however, other factors in this case which provide counter weights to that rationale. In the first place, there is no contention that this Respondent acted in a manner flagrantly in defiance of the statutory policy. On the contrary, the record indicates that this Respondent responsibly fulfills its legally established collective bargaining obligations. It is clear that Respondent merely sought judicial affirmance of the Board's decision that the election of October 22, 1964, should not be set aside on the Respondent's objections. In the past whenever an employer has sought court intervention in a representation proceeding the Board has argued forcefully that court intervention would be premature, that the employer had an unquestioned right under the statute to seek court review of any Board order before its bargaining obligation became final. Should this procedural right in 8(a)(5) cases be tempered by a large monetary liability in the event the employer's position in the representation case is ultimately found to be without merit? Of course, an employer or a union, which engages in conduct later found in violation of the Act, does so at the peril of ultimate conviction and responsibility for a make-whole remedy.

But the validity of a particular Board election tried in an unfair labor practice case is not, in our opinion, an issue on the same plane as the discharge of employees for union activity or other conduct in flagrant disregard of employee rights. There are wrongdoers and wrongdoers. Where the wrong in refusing to bargain is, at most, a debatable question, though ultimately found a wrong, the imposition of a large financial obligation on such a respondent may come close to a form of punishment for having elected to pursue a representation question beyond the Board and to the courts. The desirability of a compensatory remedy in a case remarkably similar to the instant case was recently considered by the Court of Appeals for the District of Columbia in *United Steelworkers [Quality Rubber Manufacturing Company, Inc.] v. NLRB*, [430 F.2d 519] (July 10, 1970). There the court, distinguishing *Tiidee Products, supra*, indicated that the Board was warranted in refusing to grant such a remedy in an 8(a)(5) case where the employer "desired only to obtain an authoritative determination of the validity of the Board's decision." It is not clear whether the court was of the opinion that the requested remedy was within the Board's discretion or whether it would have struck down such a remedy as punitive in view of the technical nature of the respondent's unfair labor practice. In any event, we find ourselves in disagreement with the Trial Examiner's view that a compensatory remedy as applied to the Respondent in the instant case is not punitive "in any sense of the word."

In *Tiidee Products* the court suggested that the Board need not follow a uniform policy in the application of a compensatory remedy in 8(a)(5) cases. Indeed, the court noted that such uniformity in this area of the law would be unfair when applied "to unlike cases." The court was of the opinion that the remedy was proper where the employer had engaged in a "manifestly unjustifiable refusal to bargain" and where its position was "palpably without merit." As in *Quality Rubber,* the court in *Tiidee Products* distinguished those cases in which the employer's failure to bargain rested on a "debatable question." With due respect for the opinion of the Court of Appeals for the District of Columbia, we cannot agree that the application of a compensatory remedy in 8(a)(5) cases can be fashioned on the subjective determination that the position of one respondent is "debatable" while that of another is "frivolous." What is debatable to the Board may appear frivolous to a court, and vice versa. Thus, the debatability of the employer's position in an 8(a)(5) case would itself become a matter of intense litigation.

We do not believe that the critical question of the employer's motivation in delaying bargaining should depend so largely on the expertise of counsel, the accident of circumstances, and the exigencies of the moment.

In our opinion, however, the crucial question to be determined in this case relates to the policies which the requested order would effectuate. The statutory policy as embodied in Section 8(a)(5) and (d) of the Act was considered at some length by the Supreme Court in *H.K. Porter Co., Inc. v. NLRB, supra....*

It is argued that the instant case is distinguishable from *H.K. Porter* in that here the requested remedy merely would require an employer to compensate employees for losses they incurred as a consequence of their employer's failure to agree to a contract he would have agreed to if he had bargained in good faith. In our view, the distinction is more illusory than real. The remedy in *H.K. Porter* operates prospectively to bind an employer to a specific contractual term. The remedy in the instant case operates retroactively to impose financial liability upon an employer flowing from a presumed contractual agreement. The Board infers that the latter contract, though it never existed and does not and need not exist, was denied existence by the employer because of his refusal to bargain. In either case the employer has not agreed to the contractual provision for which he must accept full responsibility as though he had agreed to it. Our colleagues contend that a compensatory remedy is not the "writing of a contract" because it does not "specify new or continuing terms of employment and does not prohibit changes in existing terms and conditions." But there is no basis for such a remedy unless the Board finds, as a matter of fact, that a contract would have resulted from bargaining. The fact that the contract, so to speak, is "written in the air" does not diminish its financial impact upon the recalcitrant employer who, willy-nilly, is forced to accede to terms never mutually established by the parties. Despite the admonition of the Supreme Court that Section 8(d) was intended to mean what it says, *i.e.,* that the obligation to bargain "does not compel either party to agree to a proposal or require the making of a concession," one of the parties under this remedy is forced by the Government to submit to the other side's demands.

It does not help to argue that the remedy could not be applied unless there was substantial evidence that the employer would have yielded to these demands during bargaining negotiations. Who is to say in a specific case how much an employer is prepared to give and how much a union is willing to take? Who is to say that a favorable contract would, in any event, result from the negotiations? And it is only the employer of such good will as to whom the Board might conclude that he, at least, would have given his employees a fair increase, who can be made subject to a financial reparations order; should such an employer be singled out for the imposition of such an order? To answer these questions the Board would be required to engage in the most general, if not entirely speculative, inferences to reach the conclusion that employees were deprived of specific benefits as a consequence of their employer's refusal to bargain.

Much as we appreciate the need for more adequate remedies in 8(a)(5) cases, we believe that, as the law now stands, the proposed remedy is a matter for Congress, not the Board. In our opinion, however, substantial relief may be obtained immediately through procedural reform, giving the highest possible priority to 8(a)(5) cases combined with full resort to the injunctive relief provisions of Section 10(j) and (e) of the Act.

MEMBERS MCCULLOCH and BROWN, dissenting in part: Although concurring in all other respects in the Decision and Order of the Board, we part company with our colleagues on the majority in that we would grant the compensatory remedy recommended by the Trial Examiner. Unlike our colleagues, we believe that the Board has the statutory authority to direct such relief and that it would effectuate the policies of the Act to do so in this case.

Section 10(c) of the Act directs the Board to remedy unfair labor practices by ordering the persons committing them to cease and desist from their unlawful conduct "and to take such affirmative action including reinstatement of employees with or without back pay, as will effectuate the policies of this Act...." The phrase "affirmative action" is nowhere qualified in the statute, except that such action must "effectuate the policies of this Act," and indicates the intent of Congress to vest the Board with remedial powers coextensive with the underlying policies of the law which is to be enforced. The provision "did not pass the Wagner Act Congress without objection to the uncontrolled breadth of this power."

But the broad language survived the challenge....

Deprivation of an employee's statutory rights is often accompanied by serious financial injury to him. Where this is so, an order which only guarantees the exercise of his rights in the future often falls far short of expunging the effects of the unlawful conduct involved. Therefore, one of the Board's most effective and well-established affirmative remedies for unlawful conduct is an order to make employees financially whole for losses resulting from violations of the Act. Various types of compensatory orders have been upheld by the Supreme Court in the belief that "Making the workers whole for losses suffered on account of an unfair practice is part of the vindication of the public policy which the Board enforces." The most familiar of these is the backpay order used to remedy the effect of employee discharges found to be in violation of Section 8(a)(3) of the Act....

It is clear from the Act that the Board's compensatory remedies need not be limited to the above situations, and the courts have always interpreted the phrase "with or without back pay" as being merely an illustrative example of the general grant of power to award affirmative relief....

The Board has already recognized in certain refusal-to-bargain situations that the usual bargaining order is not sufficient to expunge the effects of an employer's unlawful and protracted denial of its employees' right to bargain. Though the bargaining order serves to remedy the loss of the legal right and protect its exercise in the future, it does not remedy the financial injury which may also have been suffered. In a number of situations the Board has ordered the employer who unlawfully refused to bargain to compensate its employees for their resultant financial losses. Thus, some employers unlawfully refuse to sign after an agreement. The Board has in these cases ordered the employer to execute the agreement previously reached and, according to its terms, to make whole the employees for the monetary losses suffered because of the unlawful delay in its effectuation....

The question now before us is whether a reimbursement order is an appropriate remedy for other types of unlawful refusals to bargain. On the basis of the foregoing analysis regarding Section 10(c), we believe that the Board has the power to order this type of relief. Further, for the reasons set forth herein, we are of the view that the compensatory remedy is appropriate and necessary in this case to effectuate the policies of the Act....

The present remedies for unlawful refusals to bargain often fall short, as in the present case, of adequately protecting the employees' right to bargain. Recent court decisions, congressional investigations, and scholarly studies have concluded that, in the present remedial framework, justice delayed is often justice denied.

In *NLRB v. Tiidee Products, Inc.,* the Court of Appeals for the District of Columbia Circuit recently stated that:

> While the Board's usual bargaining remedy may provide some bargaining from the date of the order's enforcement, it operates in a real sense so as to

be counterproductive, and actually to reward an employer's refusal to bargain during the critical period following a union's organization of his plant. The obligation of collective bargaining is the core of the Act, and the primary means fashioned by Congress for securing industrial peace....

... Employee interest in a union can wane quickly as working conditions remain apparently unaffected by the union or collective bargaining. When the company is finally ordered to bargain with the union some years later, the union may find that it represents only a small fraction of the employees.... Thus the employer may reap a second benefit from his original refusal to comply with the law: He may continue to enjoy lower labor expenses after the order to bargain either because the union is gone or because it is too weak to bargain effectively....

The present case is but another example of a situation where a bargaining order by itself is not really adequate to remedy the effects of an unlawful refusal to bargain. The Union herein requested recognition on August 3, 1964, and proved that it represented a majority of employees 2½ months later in a Board-conducted election. Nonetheless, since October 1965 the employer, by unlawfully refusing to bargain with the Union, had deprived its employees of their legal right to collective bargaining through their certified bargaining representative. While a bargaining order at this time, operating prospectively, may insure the exercise of that right in the future, it clearly does not repair the injury to the employees here, caused by the Respondent's denial of their rights during the past 5 years.

In these refusal-to-bargain cases there is at least a legal injury.... [W]here the legal injury is accompanied by financial loss, the employees should be compensated for it. The compensatory period would normally run from the date of the employer's unlawful refusal to bargain until it commences to negotiate in good faith, or upon the failure of the Union to commence negotiations within 5 days of the receipt of the Respondent's notice of its desire to bargain with the Union, although here a later starting date could be used because this remedy would be a substantial departure from past practices. Further, the Board could follow its usual procedure of providing a general reimbursement order with the amount, if any, to be determined as part of the compliance procedure.

This type of compensatory remedy is in no way forbidden by section 8(d). It would be designed to compensate employees for injuries incurred by them by virtue of the unfair labor practices and would not require the employer to accept the measure of compensation as a term of any contract which might result from subsequent collective bargaining. The remedy contemplated in no way "writes a contract" between the employer and the union, for it would not specify new or continuing terms of employment and would not prohibit changes in existing terms and conditions. All of these would be left to the outcome of bargaining, the commencement of which would terminate Respondent's liability.

Furthermore, this compensatory remedy is not a punitive measure. It would be designed to do no more than reimburse the employees for the loss occasioned by the deprivation of their right to be represented by their collective bargaining agent during the period of the violation. The amount to be awarded would be only that which would reasonably reflect and be measured by the loss caused by the unlawful denial of the opportunity for collective bargaining. Thus, employees would be compensated for the injury suffered as a result of their employer's unlawful refusal to bargain, and the employer would thereby be prohibited from enjoying the fruits of its forbidden conduct to the end, as embodied in the Act, that collective bargaining be encouraged and the rights of injured employees be protected.... [W]here the defendant's wrongful act prevents exact determination of the amount of damage, he cannot plead such uncertainty in order to deny relief to the injured person, but rather must bear the risk of the uncertainty which was created by his own wrong. The Board is often faced with the task of determining the precise amount of a make-whole order where the criteria are less than ideal, and has successfully resolved the questions presented....

A showing at the compliance stage by the General Counsel or Charging Party by acceptable and demonstrable means that the employees could have reasonably expected to gain a certain amount of compensation by bargaining would establish a prima facie loss, and the Respondent would then be afforded an opportunity to rebut such a showing. This might be accomplished, for example by adducing evidence to show that a contract would probably not have been reached, or that there would have been less or no increase in compensation as a result of any contract which might have been signed.

Accordingly, uncertainty as to the amount of loss does not preclude a make-whole order proposed here, and some reasonable method or basis of computation can be worked out as part of the compliance procedure.... Thus, if the particular employer and union involved have contracts covering other plants of the employer, possibly in the same or a relevant area, the terms of such agreements may serve to show what the employees could probably have obtained by bargaining. The parties could also make comparisons with compensation patterns achieved through collective bargaining by other employees in the same geographic area and industry. Or the parties might employ the national average percentage changes in straight time hourly wages computed by the Bureau of Labor Statistics....

NOTES

1. Was the Board majority in *Ex-Cell-O* primarily influenced by theoretical or by practical considerations? Did *H.K. Porter* preclude the "make-whole" remedy sought by the union?

2. The conventional Board remedy for an employer violation of § 8(a)(5) is a cease-and-desist order and an affirmative order for the employer to bargain collectively with the majority representative of its employees. Since the Board cannot compel agreement, is an order to bargain anything more than a pious exhortation? Empirical studies indicate that it is. Thus, one survey revealed that successful bargaining relationships were eventually established in seventy-five percent of the cases sampled which went through to a final Board order, and in ninety percent of the cases which were voluntarily adjusted after the issuance of a complaint. *See* P. Ross, The Government as a Source of Union Power 180-230 (1965); McCulloch, *The Development of Administrative Remedies,* 14 Lab. L.J. 339, 348 (1963). Nonetheless, doubts remain about the efficacy of the Board's traditional remedy, especially where a union is seeking recognition or is trying to negotiate its first contract. This has led to the focusing of attention on innovative Board remedies. *See, e.g.,* Bartosic & Lanoff, *Escalating the Struggle Against Taft-Hartley Contemnors,* 39 U. Chi. L. Rev. 255 (1972); J. F. Hunsicker, J. Kane & P. Walther, NLRB Remedies for Unfair Labor Practices (2d ed. 1986); Irving, *Remedies Under the NLRA: An Update,* in N.Y.U. Thirty-Second Annual Conference on Labor 73 (1979); D. McDowell & K. Huhn, NLRB Remedies for Unfair Labor Practices (1976); Morris, *The Role of the NLRB and the Courts in the Collective Bargaining Process: A Fresh Look at the Conventional Wisdom and Unconventional Remedies,* 30 Vand. L. Rev. 661 (1977); St. Antoine, *A Touchstone for Labor Board Remedies,* 14 Wayne L. Rev. 1039 (1968); Note, *The Use of Section 10(j) of the Labor-Management Relations Act in Employer Refusal to Bargain Cases,* 1976 Ill. L. F. 845.

3. Recently, the Board sought to utilize § 10(j) in order to avert the impact of an employer's violation of its bargaining obligation under § 8(a)(5). Section 10(j) affords the Board the right to petition the district court for interim judicial relief "upon the issuance of a [Board] complaint." In *NLRB v. Detroit Newspaper Agency,* 984 F. Supp. 1048 (E.D. Mich. 1997), *aff'd sub. nom Schaub v. Detroit Newspaper Agency,* 145 F.3d 1333 (6th Cir. 1998), however, the Board's petition for relief was filed after both the ALJ's resolution of the underlying § 8(a)(5) complaint and the issuance of a new complaint based on the employers' failure to comply with the ALJ's order while challenges to the ALJ's determination were still pending before the Board. The Board sought an injunction ordering the employers to reinstate striking employees, based upon the ALJ's conclusion that the employer had engaged in bad faith bargaining in violation of § 8(a)(5), prompting an unfair labor practice strike by the union and the hiring of replacement workers by the employer. The district court denied the Board's request, reasoning that the Board had failed to show reasonable cause that the newspapers had violated § 8(a)(5), and therefore that the strike was an unfair labor practice strike rather than an economic strike. According to the court, § 10(j) relief was inappropriate where there had been no final adjudication by the Board on the alleged and ongoing illegality. The court chastised the Board for waiting more than two years after the strike began to seek § 10(j) relief, pointing out that no court order could repair the erosion of union support and scattering of former strikers that had occurred in the interim.

Did the Board lose here because it produced *more* evidence than is required for issuance of § 10(j) relief (the ALJ's conclusions based on the evidence presented to him, rather than a mere complaint filed with the Board)? What is the effect of the district court's ruling on the future utility of § 10(j)? Must the Board's adjudicatory processes be completed on the question of liability before it may order relief? What, then, is the purpose of § 10(j)?

Postscript: One year later, a unanimous Board upheld the ALJ's ruling that the newspapers had violated § 8(a)(5) by unilaterally implementing proposals affecting editorial employees; and consequently that the strike was an unfair labor practice strike from its inception. *Detroit Newspapers Agency dba Detroit Newspapers, The Detroit News, Inc. and the Detroit Free Press (Detroit I)*, 326 N.L.R.B. No. 64 (1998).

4. As indicated in the *Ex-Cell-O* opinions, a court of appeals has ruled (2-1) that the usual cease-and-desist order is inadequate to remedy an employer's "clear and flagrant" violation of its bargaining duty. *IUE v. NLRB (Tiidee Prods., Inc.)*, 426 F.2d 1243 (D.C. Cir.), *cert. denied*, 400 U.S. 950 (1970) (*Tiidee I*). The case was remanded to the Board for further consideration of an appropriate remedy, which might include back pay to compensate the employees for the benefits denied them by the employer's refusal to bargain. In reaching this result, the majority stressed that the remand was limited to consideration of past damages, and not to compulsion of a future contract term, thus distinguishing the case from the Supreme Court's decision in *H.K. Porter*. The same court held that the Board had not abused its discretion in refusing to grant make-whole relief, however, where employers declined to bargain in good faith and made efforts to challenge a union's certification or other representational determinations. *United Steelworkers v. NLRB (Quality Rubber Mfg. Co.)*, 430 F.2d 519 (D.C. Cir. 1970). In keeping with this distinction, the D.C. Circuit Court of Appeals subsequently sustained the Board's decision in *Ex-Cell-O* on the ground that the company's objections to the certification there fell in the "fairly debatable" rather than the "frivolous" or "bad faith" category. *Ex-Cell-O Corp. v. NLRB*, 449 F.2d 1058 (D.C. Cir. 1971).

The "make-employees-whole" remedy was interred, at least for the foreseeable future, in *Tiidee Products, Inc.*, 194 N.L.R.B. 1234 (1972), *enforced*, 502 F.2d 349 (D.C. Cir. 1974), *cert. denied*, 421 U.S. 991 (1975) [*Tiidee II*]; *see also Betra Mfg. Co.*, 233 N.L.R.B. 1126 (1977), *enforced*, 624 F.2d 192 (9th Cir. 1980), *cert. denied*, 450 U.S. 996 (1981). On remand following *Tiidee I*, a unanimous Board rejected a reimbursement order, even where the employer's refusal to bargain was a "clear and flagrant" violation of law. Nonetheless, the Board thought such a violation did merit a remedy going beyond the customary cease and desist order. It therefore required the employer to reimburse both the NLRB and the union for their litigation expenses, to mail copies of the NLRB's notice to each employee's home, to keep the union supplied with an employee name-and-address list for one year, and to give the union reasonable access to company bulletin boards. The court of appeals enforced the award in *Tiidee II*, bowing to the Board's expertise in concluding it was incapable of calculating an appropriate make-whole remedy, but eliminated the award of litigation expenses to the Board. *Cf. Virginia Concrete Co. v. NLRB*, 75 F.3d 974 (4th Cir. 1996) (sustaining a Board order requiring an employer that had unlawfully ceased contributions to multiemployer health, welfare, and pension funds to make the funds whole for any losses, despite the company's claim this would force it to make payments greater than the benefits union employees actually received).

The struggle for remedial authority between the Board and the courts of appeals has continued, however. In *NLRB v. Food Store Emps. Local 347 (Heck's, Inc.)*, 417 U.S. 1 (1974), the Supreme Court held that a court of appeals exceeded its authority in ordering an employer guilty of "aggravated and pervasive" unfair labor practices to pay a union's litigation expenses and excess organizational costs, since the NLRB had ruled against such a remedy. The proper procedure was a remand to the Board for reconsideration in light of its 1972 *Tiidee* decision.

5. The Board has imposed a variety of extraordinary remedies in cases involving pervasive and outrageous unfair labor practices which occur during the organizing and election phase, but the courts have restricted its ability to remedy even the most flagrant violations of the duty to bargain when the remedy involves compulsion of future contract terms in any fashion. For example, when an employer had committed over 100 unfair labor practices during a union organizing campaign, a divided court of appeals sustained an extensive list of Board remedies, including union access to nonwork areas during employees' nonwork time and the opportunity to deliver a thirty-minute speech to employees on working time prior to a new election. But the court by another 2-1 vote refused to require the employer to extend to union employees a pay increase granted nonunion employees. *Fieldcrest Cannon, Inc. v. NLRB*, 97 F.3d 65 (4th Cir. 1996).

Similarly, the Fourth Circuit agreed to extend the NLRB's remedy of litigation and organizing expenses, usually awarded only when an employer raises "frivolous" defenses, to an employer's "arguably non-frivolous" but ultimately unsuccessful litigation where there was "flagrant, aggravated, persistent, and pervasive employer misconduct." *J.P. Stevens & Co. v. NLRB*, 668 F.2d 767, 777 (1982). The Supreme Court vacated and remanded on the award of attorneys' fees, however, 458 U.S. 1118 (1982), foreshadowing what was to come (*see* note 6, below).

6. The Board's remedial orders involving make-whole awards to the union and the Board have fared better than its efforts to make employees whole. An employer that persisted in a flat refusal to bargain with a newly certified union or to supply the union with relevant information was ordered to pay all the costs incurred by the union and the Board in investigating, preparing, and litigating the case against the employer. *Care Manor of Farmington,* 318 N.L.R.B. 330 (1995). An employer that resisted enforcement of a Board order on frivolous grounds, as a delaying tactic, was assessed double costs and attorneys' fees under Federal Rule of Appellate Procedure 38 and 28 U.S.C. § 1912 in *NLRB v. Catalina Yachts,* 679 F.2d 180 (9th Cir. 1982).

Awards of attorney's fees, however, can be problematic. Since 1973, the D.C. Circuit Court of Appeals had taken the position that the Board had the authority to award attorney's fees where the employer engaged in frivolous litigation. *See Food Store Employees Union Local No. 347 v. NLRB,* 476 F.2d 546 (D.C. Cir. 1973), *rev'd on other grounds,* 417 U.S. 1 (1974). In *Unbelievable, Inc. v. NLRB,* 118 F.3d 795 (D.C. Cir. 1997) the court of appeals overturned its own precedent, ruling that the Board lacks authority to award attorney's fees absent a statute clearly indicating Congressional intent to permit an exception to the traditional American rule that each side must bear its own litigation expenses.

In *Unbelievable,* the Board found that the employer had engaged in "egregious and deliberate surface bargaining" designed to frustrate agreement and provoke a strike. Accordingly, the Board ordered the employer to reimburse the unions for their negotiating expenses. Because the employer's position in litigation over the issue was frivolous—indeed, its attorney's testimony at the Board hearing was "unresponsive, aggressive, and flagrantly disrespectful," demonstrating "his intent to make a charade of this proceeding" and persuading the Board that "Unbelievable lived up to its illchosen name"—the Board also ordered the company to pay the unions' and the Board's litigation expenses, including attorneys' fees.

The D.C. Circuit upheld the award of negotiating expenses, finding that there was substantial evidence that the company's misconduct in bargaining was unusually aggravated. By a 2-1 vote, however, the court reversed the award of litigation expenses and attorneys' fees, reasoning that the Supreme Court's adherence to the American Rule that each side must bear its own litigation expenses had been clarified and strengthened in other contexts in a series of cases decided since 1975. Without clear support in the NLRA or its legislative history for the Board's authority to alter the rule, the Board lacked the power to make such an award, and the courts could not enforce it. Moreover, since it is not an unfair labor practice to present a frivolous defense to an unfair labor practice charge, the Board's award of attorney's fees exceeded its delegated authority over labor-management relations and focused instead on the conduct of litigation, a matter beyond the Board's special expertise. To the Board's argument that keeping its docket clear is part and parcel of its appropriate exercise of authority over workplace dynamics, the majority responded that the attempt to exercise this power— to deter frivolous litigation—is essentially punitive, and thus beyond the Board's delegated authority.

Judge Wald, dissenting from the portion of the opinion overturning the award of litigation expenses and attorney's fees, wrote:

In a case like this one, where an employer has flagrantly refused to collectively bargain in good faith, a union is compelled to vindicate its statutory rights in proceedings before the Board.... Wasting the union's time and depleting its resources through presentation of a frivolous defense at a Board proceeding is a tactical maneuver designed to deepen the economic wound caused by the surface bargaining.... It is merely continuation of the same bad faith recalcitrance employed at the bargaining table in a new forum. A diehard respondent can go up the chain of decisionmaking causing greater economic burdens to the union at each stage by employing dilatory tactics during the administrative adjudication by the Administrative Law Judge ("ALJ"), the Board's review of the ALJ's recommendation, and, finally, appeal of the Board's order to a United States Court of Appeals. The whole process can take years. In addition to exhausting the charging party's legal war chest, the delay often leads to employee frustration and eventual loss of employee support due to attrition or loss of confidence in a seemingly ineffectual union, and it often permits continued employer anti-union activity. *Cf. Ex-Cell-O Corp.,* 185 N.L.R.B. 107 (1970). Ironically, by the purposeful presentation of an entirely frivolous defense, an employer turns the Board's processes into an instrument of its own unlawful conduct.

....

There can be scant doubt that awarding attorney's fees to a charging party who has been subjected to surface bargaining and bad faith, frivolous litigation effectuates the policies of the NLRA by directly remedying the economic injury incurred by the party. In this regard, reimbursement for expenses of litigation is no different from compensation for the costs of bad faith negotiation, which the majority approves in this very case.

Who is correct? *Cf. Alwin Mfg. Co.,* 326 N.L.R.B. No. 63 (1998) (Board ordered employer to pay union's costs incurred in negotiations, unfair labor practice strike, litigation expenses and attorney's fees, as well as Board's litigation costs, relying on § 10(c) and Board's inherent authority to control its own proceedings through an application of the "bad-faith" exception to the American Rule; the Board cited and distinguished *Unbelievable, Inc.*).

7. Under the proposed Labor Reform Act of 1978, an employer would have been subject to a make-whole remedy in favor of its employees if it unlawfully refused to bargain with a union prior to the execution of a first contract. Would this provision have been preferable to the law as it has developed?

3. UNILATERAL ACTION

NLRB v. KATZ

Supreme Court of the United States
369 U.S. 736, 82 S. Ct. 1107, 8 L. Ed. 230 (1962)

MR. JUSTICE BRENNAN delivered the opinion of the Court.

Is it a violation of the duty "to bargain collectively" imposed by § 8(a)(5) of the National Labor Relations Act for an employer, without first consulting a union with which it is carrying on bona fide contract negotiations, to institute changes regarding matters which are subjects of mandatory bargaining under § 8(d) and which are in fact under discussion? The National Labor Relations Board answered the question affirmatively in this case, in a decision which expressly disclaimed any finding that the totality of the respondents' conduct manifested bad faith in the pending negotiations. 126 N.L.R.B. 288. A divided panel of the Court of Appeals for the Second Circuit denied enforcement of the Board's cease-and-desist order, finding in our decision in *NLRB v. Insurance Agents,* 361 U.S. 477 (1960), a broad rule that the statutory duty to bargain cannot be held to be violated, when bargaining is in fact being carried on, without a finding of the respondent's subjective bad faith in negotiating. 289 F.2d 700.... We granted certiorari, 368 U.S. 811, in order to consider whether the Board's decision and order were contrary to *Insurance Agents.* We find nothing in the Board's decision inconsistent with *Insurance Agents* and hold that the Court of Appeals erred in refusing to enforce the Board's order....

As amended and amplified at the hearing and construed by the Board, the complaint's charge of unfair labor practices particularly referred to three acts by the company: Unilaterally granting numerous merit increases in October 1956 and January 1957; unilaterally announcing a change in sick-leave policy in March 1957; and unilaterally instituting a new system of automatic wage increases during April 1957. As the ensuing litigation has developed, the company has defended against the charges along two fronts: First, it asserts that the unilateral changes occurred after a bargaining impasse had developed through the union's fault in adopting obstructive tactics. According to the Board, however, "the evidence is clear that the Respondent undertook its unilateral actions before negotiations were discontinued in May 1957, or before, as we find on the record, the existence of any possible impasse." 126 N.L.R.B. at 289-290. There is ample support in the record considered as a whole for this finding of fact, which is consistent with the Examiner's Intermediate Report, 126 N.L.R.B. at 295-296, and which the Court of Appeals did not question.

The second line of defense was that the Board could not hinge a conclusion that § 8(a)(5) had been violated on unilateral actions alone, without making a finding of the employer's subjective bad faith at the bargaining table; and that the unilateral actions were merely evidence relevant to the issue of subjective good faith. This argument prevailed in the Court of Appeals....

The duty "to bargain collectively" enjoined by § 8(a)(5) is defined by § 8(d) as the duty to "meet ... and confer in good faith with respect to wages, hours, and other terms and conditions of employment." Clearly, the duty thus defined may be violated without a general failure of subjective good faith; for there is no occasion to consider the issue of good faith if a party has refused even to negotiate *in fact*—"to meet ... and confer"—about any of the mandatory subjects. A refusal to negotiate *in fact* as to any subject which is within § 8(d), and about which the union seeks to negotiate, violates § 8(a)(5) though the employer has every desire to reach agreement with the union upon an over-all collective agreement and earnestly and in all good faith bargains to that end. We hold that an employer's unilateral change in conditions of employment under negotiation is similarly a violation of § 8(a)(5), for it is a circumvention of the duty to negotiate which frustrates the objectives of § 8(a)(5) much as does a flat refusal.[11]

The unilateral actions of the respondent illustrate the policy and practical considerations which support our conclusion.

We consider first the matter of sick leave. A sick-leave plan had been in effect since May 1956, under which employees were allowed ten paid sick-leave days annually and could accumulate half the unused days, or up to five days each year. Changes in the plan were sought and proposals and counterproposals had come up at three bargaining conferences. In March 1957, the company, without first notifying or consulting the union, announced changes in the plan, which reduced from ten to five the number of paid sick-leave days per year, but allowed accumulation of twice the unused days, thus increasing to ten the number of days which might be carried over. This action plainly frustrated the statutory objective of establishing working conditions through bargaining. Some employees might view the change to be a diminution of benefits. Others, more interested in accumulating sick-leave days, might regard the change as an improvement. If one view or the other clearly prevailed among the employees, the unilateral action

---

[11] *Compare Medo Corp. v. Labor Board,* 321 U.S. 678 (1944); *May Department Stores v. NLRB,* 326 U.S. 376 (1945); *NLRB v. Crompton-Highland Mills,* 337 U.S. 217 (1949).

In *Medo,* the Court held that the employer interfered with his employees' right to bargain collectively through a chosen representative, in violation of § 8(1), 49 Stat. 452 (now § 8(a)(1)), when it treated directly with employees and granted them a wage increase in return for their promise to repudiate the union they had designated as their representative. It further held that the employer violated the statutory duty to bargain when he refused to negotiate with the union after the employees had carried out their promise.

May held that the employer violated § 8(1) when, after having unequivocally refused to bargain with a certified union on the ground that the unit was inappropriate, it announced that it had applied to the War Labor Board for permission to grant a wage increase to all its employees except those whose wages had been fixed by "closed shop agreements."

Crompton-Highland Mills sustained the Board's conclusion that the employer's unilateral grant of a wage increase substantially greater than any it had offered to the union during negotiations which had ended in impasse clearly manifested bad faith and violated the employer's duty to bargain.

might well mean that the employer had either uselessly dissipated trading material or aggravated the sick-leave issue. On the other hand, if the employees were more evenly divided on the merits of the company's changes, the union negotiators, beset by conflicting factions, might be led to adopt a protective vagueness on the issue of sick leave, which also would inhibit the useful discussion contemplated by Congress in imposing the specific obligation to bargain collectively.

Other considerations appear from consideration of the respondents' unilateral action in increasing wages. At the April 4, 1957, meeting the employers offered, and the union rejected, a three-year contract with an immediate across-the-board increase of $7.50 per week, to be followed at the end of the first year and again at the end of the second by further increases of $5 for employees earning less than $90 at those times. Shortly thereafter, without having advised or consulted with the union, the company announced a new system of automatic wage increases whereby there would be an increase of $5 every three months up to $74.99 per week; an increase of $5 every six months between $75 and $90 per week; and a merit review every six months for employees earning over $90 per week. It is clear at a glance that the automatic wage increase system which was instituted unilaterally was considerably more generous than that which had shortly theretofore been offered to and rejected by the union. Such action conclusively manifested bad faith in the negotiations, *NLRB v. Crompton-Highland Mills,* 337 U.S. 217 (1949), and so would have violated § 8(a)(5) even on the Court of Appeals' interpretation, though no additional evidence of bad faith appeared. An employer is not required to lead with his best offer; he is free to bargain. But even after an impasse is reached he has no license to grant wage increases greater than any he has ever offered the union at the bargaining table, for such action is necessarily inconsistent with a sincere desire to conclude an agreement with the union.[12]

The respondents' third unilateral action related to merit increases, which are also a subject of mandatory bargaining. *NLRB v. Allison & Co.,* 165 F.2d 766 (6th Cir. 1948). The matter of merit increases had been raised at three of the conferences during 1956 but no final understanding had been reached. In January 1957, the company, without notice to the union, granted merit increases to 20 employees out of the approximately 50 in the unit, the increases ranging between $2 and $10. This action too must be viewed as tantamount to an outright refusal to negotiate on that subject, and therefore as a violation of § 8(a)(5), unless the fact that the January raises were in line with the company's long-standing practice of granting quarterly or semiannual merit reviews—in effect, were a mere continuation of the status quo—differentiates them from the wage increases and the changes in the sick-leave plan. We do not think it does. Whatever might be the case as to so-called "merit raises" which are in fact simply automatic in-

---

[12]Of course, there is no resemblance between this situation and one wherein an employer, after notice and consultation, "unilaterally" institutes a wage increase identical with one which the union has rejected as too low....

creases to which the employer has already committed himself, the raises here in question were in no sense automatic, but were informed by a large measure of discretion. There simply is no way in such case for a union to know whether or not there has been a substantial departure from past practice, and therefore the union may properly insist that the company negotiate as to the procedures and criteria for determining such increases.

It is apparent from what we have said why we see nothing in *Insurance Agents* contrary to the Board's decision. The union in that case had not in any way whatever foreclosed discussion of any issue, by unilateral actions or otherwise. The conduct complained of consisted of partial-strike tactics designed to put pressure on the employer to come to terms with the union negotiators. We held that Congress had not, in § 8(b)(3), the counterpart of § 8(a)(5), empowered the Board to pass judgment on the legitimacy of any particular economic weapon used in support of genuine negotiations. But the Board *is* authorized to order the cessation of behavior which is in effect a refusal to negotiate, or which directly obstructs or inhibits the actual process of discussion, or which reflects a cast of mind against reaching agreement. Unilateral action by an employer without prior discussion with the union does amount to a refusal to negotiate about the affected conditions of employment under negotiation, and must of necessity obstruct bargaining, contrary to the congressional policy. It will often disclose an unwillingness to agree with the union. It will rarely be justified by any reason of substance. It follows that the Board may hold such unilateral action to be an unfair labor practice in violation of § 8(a)(5), without also finding the employer guilty of over-all subjective bad faith. While we do not foreclose the possibility that there might be circumstances which the Board could or should accept as excusing or justifying unilateral action, no such case is presented here.

The judgment of the Court of Appeals is reversed and the case is remanded with direction to the court to enforce the Board's order.

It is so ordered.

MR. JUSTICE FRANKFURTER took no part in the decision of this case.

MR. JUSTICE WHITE took no part in the consideration or decision of this case.

NOTES

1. To what extent does *Katz* make an employer's unilateral change in working conditions a refusal to bargain per se? How does the approach differ from that in *NLRB v. Crompton-Highland Mills, Inc.,* 337 U.S. 217 (1949), cited in note 11 of the *Katz* opinion?

2. An employer's unilateral *decrease* of benefits during negotiations has also been held a violation of § 8(a)(5). *Molders Local 155 v. NLRB (United States Pipe & Foundry Co.),* 442 F.2d 742 (D.C. Cir. 1971); *Borden, Inc.,* 196 N.L.R.B. 1170 (1972). Is this consistent with the employer lockout (*American Ship*) and union "harassment" (*Insurance Agents*) decisions? *See* Schatzki, *The Employer's Unilateral Act—A Per Se Violation—Sometimes,* 44 Texas L. Rev. 470, 502-03 (1966).

3. An employer generally may not make unilateral changes in working conditions during collective bargaining until there is an overall impasse as to the agreement as a whole. Employers may declare an impasse when there is no realistic possibility that continuing negotiations would be fruitful. An employer may implement upon impasse only a final offer which (1) is a product of good faith negotiations untainted by unfair labor practices; (2) has been presented to, and rejected by, the union, and (3) is implemented in a fashion that does not disparage the union in its capacity as bargaining representative, or the collective bargaining process itself. The theory behind allowing implementation of final offers is that unilateral implementation—at least when accompanied by these safeguards—can function as an aid in breaking impasse, "a controlled escape route to put a stalemated relationship onto a new, more positive path." Dannin, *Legislative Intent and Impasse Resolution Under the National Labor Relations Act: Does Law Matter?*, 15 Hofstra Lab. & Emp. L.J. 11, 26 (1997).

Whether impasse has been reached is a difficult question. How many bargaining sessions must parties conduct on an important issue before an impasse may be declared? *See Lou Stecher's Super Mkts.,* 275 N.L.R.B. 475 (1985) (three meetings sufficient where parties had long bargaining history and both recognized importance of "boxed beef" issue for job security). *See also Triple A Maintenance Corp.,* 283 N.L.R.B. 44, 56 (1987) (five sessions). Critical of the Board's impasse findings is Turner, *Impasse in the "Real World" of Labor Relations: Where Does the Board Stand?* 10 Employee Rel. L.J. 468 (1984-85).

In *Beverly Farm Foundation Inc. v. NLRB,* 144 F.3d 1048 (7th Cir. 1998), the Seventh Circuit enforced a Board order finding that the employer had violated §§ 8(a)(1) and 8(a)(5) of the NLRA by prematurely declaring an impasse, unilaterally implementing its final offer, and withdrawing union recognition. Rejecting Beverly's contention that impasse had occurred where the parties had met nineteen times over a one-year period and were still far apart, the Board noted that the parties had only discussed economic issues on three occasions of the nineteen, the union's bargaining posture was flexible, and the union had assured the employer that no strike was likely. The Board ordered a ten-month extension on the union's certification period, dating from resumption of bargaining; the court enforced the order.

4. After an "impasse" in bargaining has been reached, an employer is usually free to initiate changes unilaterally, so long as they are not more favorable than the proposals made to the union. *NLRB v. U.S. Sonics Corp.,* 312 F.2d 610 (1st Cir. 1963); *Pacific Gamble Robinson Co. v. NLRB,* 186 F.2d 106 (6th Cir. 1950) (strike replacements were offered wages not substantially higher than those offered the union before the strike). An employer who implements *less* favorable terms following rejection by the union membership of a more favorable bargaining proposal does not violate the Act. In *Telescope Casual Furniture Inc.*, 326 N.L.R.B. No. 60 (1998), the Board ruled 2-1 that a company that utilized regressive bargaining tactics including simultaneous presentation of two proposals, one a "final offer" and the other a "less favorable alternative," did not violate § 8(a)(5). Because its alternative proposal was utilized to pressure the union to come to agreement rather than designed to frustrate the possibility of agreement, and because the company repeatedly offered to bargain over and to modify the alternative in ways calculated to be more acceptable to the union, the bargaining strategy itself was permissible. Since the less favorable alternative ultimately implemented by the employer was encompassed within the proposals presented to and rejected by the union, its unilateral implementation did not violate the Act.

5. An exception to the rule of implementation following impasse was outlined in *McClatchy Newspapers, Inc.* 321 N.L.R.B. 1386 (1996). A 2-1 majority of the NLRB held that an employer could not unilaterally change wages after bargaining to impasse on a proposal to institute a merit-pay plan that effectively gave the employer unfettered discretion over future wage increases, reasoning that such unlimited managerial authority would be "*inherently* destructive of the fundamental principles of collective bargaining." Although the D.C. Circuit found the question presented difficult, it deferred to the Board's statutory interpretation and enforced its decision, noting that the Board's holding was limited to cases in which the employer refused to state any "definable objective procedures and criteria" for determining merit. Unilateral implementation of such a merit-pay plan undermines the union's authority as the representative of the employees by depriving it of information necessary to bargain knowledgeably in subsequent sessions, thus preventing it from having any impact on the determination of wage rates. *McClatchy Newspapers, Inc. v. NLRB*, 131 F.3d 1026 (D.C. Cir. 1997), *cert. denied*, 118 S. Ct. 2341 (1998). *Cf. Colorado-Ute Electric Ass'n v. NLRB*, 939 F.2d 1392 (10th Cir. 1991), *cert. denied*, 504 U.S. 955 (1992) (holding that merit pay is a mandatory subject of bargaining upon which a party may lawfully insist to impasse; it does not amount to a proposal that the union waive its statutory right to be consulted about wage changes).

6. Even in the absence of an impasse, business necessity, such as the need to maintain operations during a strike, may enable an employer to institute unilateral changes, provided they are consistent with offers unaccepted by the union. *NLRB v. Bradley Washfountain Co.*, 192 F.2d 144 (7th Cir. 1951); *Raleigh Water Heater Mfg. Co.*, 136 N.L.R.B. 76 (1962). *But cf. International Distrib. Ctrs.*, 281 N.L.R.B. 742 (1986) ("precarious financial condition" no justification). Unilateral action is permissible while bargaining is ongoing only where a serious business emergency arises requiring prompt action. *See Master Window Cleaning, Inc., d/b/a Bottom Line Enterprises*, 302 N.L.R.B. 373 (1991), *enforced*, 15 F.3d 1087 (9th Cir. 1994). In *RBE Electronics*, 320 N.L.R.B. 80 (1995), the Board reconfirmed two aspects of a limited exception for "economic exigencies." First, an employer may be excused entirely from bargaining about certain items if there are extraordinary, unforeseen events having a major economic impact and requiring immediate company action. Second, in circumstances falling short of that, but still calling for prompt action, an employer may act unilaterally if the union waives an opportunity to bargain or the parties reach impasse on the particular matter proposed for change.

7. What types of employer actions would constitute a change in working conditions triggering an obligation to bargain? Overruling a line of cases going back over twenty years, the Board held in *Carpenters Local 1031*, 321 N.L.R.B. 30 (1996), that an employer's unilateral change of the work hours of a single employee could violate the duty to bargain.

Changes in past practice present complex issues where the past practice relates to a regularly recurring event. In *Daily News of Los Angeles*, 315 N.L.R.B. 1236 (1994), the Board divided on the test for determining the legality of an employer's unilateral discontinuance of a past practice during negotiations for a new agreement. Chair Gould and Member Browning would find that any pre-impasse modification that effectuates a change in mandatory terms and conditions is proscribed by *NLRB v. Katz*. Members Stephens and Cohen, however, would find that when the past practice concerned an annual event, such as an annual wage increase, and the event was scheduled to take effect during the current contract negotiations, the employer would satisfy its bargaining duty with respect to this year's occurrence if it gave the union reasonable advance notice and the opportunity to bargain about the scheduled event. The employer would thereafter be free to implement its final proposal with respect to this year's event even if the parties had not yet reached an impasse. On the other hand, if the employer's proposal pertained to a permanent change in an established practice that would affect future years, the employer would not be allowed to make any permanent modification in that practice without bargaining to impasse. On the facts in *Daily News*, the Board unanimously found a violation. Enforcement followed in 73 F.3d 406 (D.C. Cir. 1996), *cert. denied*, 117 S. Ct. 764 (1997) (holding 2-1 that an employer may not unilaterally discontinue during negotiations a merit-pay program fixed as to timing and criteria, and discretionary only as to amount). *See also Bonnell/Tredegar Indus. v. NLRB*, 46 F.3d 339 (4th Cir. 1995) (employer violated § 8(a)(5) when it unilaterally modified the method of calculating a contractually required Christmas bonus, even though the contract did not specify the method of calculation, because the bonus formula had become an implied term of employment that could not be unilaterally altered); *NLRB v. Plainville Ready Mix Concrete*, 44 F.3d 1320 (6th Cir.), *cert. denied*, 516 U.S. 974 (1995) (employer violated § 8(a)(5) when it dropped existing gain sharing and incentive pay from its post-impasse wage plan without implementing increases in the hourly wage rates, because the employer had consistently treated the proposed hourly wage increases as the quid pro quo for the elimination of gain sharing and incentive pay). *Cf. Acme Die Casting v. NLRB*, 93 F.3d 854 (D.C. Cir. 1996) (refusing to enforce Board order finding § 8(a)(5) violation by employer who failed to give a wage increase in the year following the employees' pro-union vote, because the Board had failed to articulate a comprehensive standard for determining whether an employer had established a settled practice of regular wage increases).

8. On the combined effect of management rights clauses and past practice, *compare Chicago Tribune Co. v. NLRB,* 974 F.2d 933 (7th Cir. 1992) (clause allowing employer to impose "reasonable rules relating to employee conduct" permitted unilateral establishment of drug-testing policy that authorized discipline for off-the-job drug-related conduct that could affect job performance or workplace safety) *with Hi-Tech Cable Corp.,* 309 N.L.R.B. 3 (1992), *enforced,* 25 F.3d 1044 (5th Cir. 1994) (provision authorizing employer to "make, change, and enforce reasonable rules for efficiency, cleanliness, safety, attendance, conduct and working conditions" did not allow unilateral establishment of no-tobacco rule).

Unilateral changes in benefits available under employee medical and pension plans have presented special problems. In *NLRB v. E-Systems,* 103 F.3d 435 (5th Cir. 1997), the Fifth Circuit ruled that unilateral alteration of medical plan benefits did not violate the Act where the employer had reserved the right to make such alterations in the labor contract. In *Grondorf, Field, Black & Co. v. NLRB,* 107 F.3d 882 (D.C. Cir. 1997), the D.C. Circuit enforced a Board order finding that the unilateral replacement of union-sponsored health and pension benefit plans with employer-sponsored plans violated the Act. However, the court refused to enforce the remedial portion of the Board's order, which would have compensated the union for all missed contributions, reasoning that the remedy was punitive in nature since the employees were covered by the employer-sponsored plan during the relevant time frame.

9. What steps should be taken by an employer, upon entering negotiations for a new contract, to ensure that it will not be precluded from extending such employment benefits as it thinks necessary to keep a satisfied work force, in the event it is unable to conclude an agreement with the union? *See generally* Stewart & Engeman, *Impasse, Collective Bargaining, and Action,* 39 U. Cinn. L. Rev. 233 (1970).

10. The expiration of an existing contract does not in itself allow an employer to take unilateral action. *Industrial Union of Marine & Shipbuilding Workers v. NLRB,* 320 F.2d 615 (3d Cir. 1963), *cert. denied,* 375 U.S. 984 (1964); *Teamsters Local 175 v. NLRB,* 788 F.2d 27 (D.C. Cir. 1986). Once a union contract has expired, should an employer's right to institute unilateral changes vary depending on the nature of the particular working conditions involved? For example, should there be different treatment of a union shop and check-off, super-seniority for union officials, hiring halls, and the grievance or arbitration procedure? *See Industrial Union of Marine & Shipbuilding Workers v. NLRB, supra; NLRB v. Cone Mills Corp.,* 373 F.2d 595 (4th Cir. 1967); *Southwestern Steel & Supply, Inc. v. NLRB,* 806 F.2d 1111 (D.C. Cir. 1986); Note, *Good Faith Grievance Handling as an Aspect of the Duty to Bargain Collectively,* 38 N.Y.U.L.

Rev. 350 (1963). What is the effect of *Nolde Bros. v. Bakery & Confectionery Workers Local 358,* 430 U.S. 243 (1977), *infra?*

In *TWA v. Independent Fed'n of Flight Attendants,* 485 U.S. 175 (1988), the Supreme Court affirmed by an equally divided Court the holding of the Eighth Circuit, 809 F.2d 483 (1987), that the union security and dues check-off provisions in a preexisting contract survived an impasse in the parties' negotiations, since the employer had not included them in its notice to the union of intended changes prior to bargaining.

11. Unilateral employer action is discussed in Bowman, *An Employer's Unilateral Action—An Unfair Labor Practice?* 9 Vand. L. Rev. 487 (1956); Cox, *The Duty to Bargain in Good Faith,* 71 Harv. L. Rev. 1401 (1958); Comment, *Impasse in Collective Bargaining,* 44 Texas L. Rev. 769 (1966).

12. Could a union violate § 8(b)(3) by unilateral action? How? *See Painters Dist. Council 9,* 186 N.L.R.B. 964 (1970), *enforced,* 453 F.2d 783 (2d Cir. 1971), *cert. denied,* 408 U.S. 930 (1972) (production ceiling). *But cf. Scofield v. NLRB,* 394 U.S. 423 (1969).

Detroit & Toledo Shore Line R.R. v. United Transportation Union, 396 U.S. 142, 90 S. Ct. 294, 24 L. Ed. 2d 325 (1969). Section 6 of the Railway Labor Act provides that "rates of pay, rules, or working conditions shall not be altered" during the period from the first notice of a proposed change in an agreement until the conclusion of any proceedings concerning a "major dispute" before the National Mediation Board. A railroad made certain "outlying work assignments" while a dispute over the issue was pending before the NMB. This meant that railroad employees had to report for work at points elsewhere than at the railroad's principal yard. The railroad contended that § 6 requires a party to preserve the status quo only in those working conditions covered by the parties' existing collective agreement, and insisted that nothing in its contract precluded the railroad from altering the location of work assignments. The Supreme Court disagreed, and upheld an injunction against the railroad's establishing new outlying assignments. According to the Court, the status quo applies to those "actual, objective working conditions and practices, broadly conceived, which were in effect prior to the time the pending dispute arose and which are involved in or related to that dispute." The Court cautioned, however, that "the mere fact that the collective agreement before us does not expressly prohibit outlying assignments would not have barred the railroad from ordering the assignments that gave rise to the present dispute if, apart from the agreement, such assignments had occurred for a sufficient period of time with the knowledge and acquiescence of the employees to become in reality a part of the actual working conditions."

4. SUPPLYING INFORMATION

NLRB v. TRUITT MANUFACTURING CO.

Supreme Court of the United States
351 U.S. 149, 76 S. Ct. 753, 100 L. Ed. 1027 (1956)

MR. JUSTICE BLACK delivered the opinion of the Court.

The National Labor Relations Act makes it an unfair labor practice for an employer to refuse to bargain in good faith with the representative of his employees. The question presented by this case is whether the National Labor Relations Board may find that an employer has not bargained in good faith where the employer claims it cannot afford to pay higher wages but refuses requests to produce information substantiating its claim.

The dispute here arose when a union representing certain of respondent's employees asked for a wage increase of 10 cents per hour. The company answered that it could not afford to pay such an increase, it was undercapitalized, had never paid dividends, and that an increase of more than 2½ cents per hour would put it out of business. The union asked the company to produce some evidence substantiating these statements, requesting permission to have a certified public accountant examine the company's books, financial data, etc. This request being denied, the union asked that the company submit "full and complete information with respect to its financial standing and profits," insisting that such information was pertinent and essential for the employees to determine whether or not they should continue to press their demand for a wage increase. A union official testified before the trial examiner that "[W]e were wanting anything relating to the Company's position, any records or what have you, books, accounting sheets, cost expenditures, what not, anything to back the Company's position that they were unable to give any more money." The company refused all the requests, relying solely on the statement that "the information ... is not pertinent to this discussion and the company declines to give you such information; You have no legal right to such."

On the basis of these facts the National Labor Relations Board found that the company had "failed to bargain in good faith with respect to wages in violation of Section 8(a)(5) of the Act." 110 N.L.R.B. 856. The Board ordered the company to supply the union with such information as would "substantiate the Respondent's position of its economic inability to pay the requested wage increase." The Court of Appeals refused to enforce the Board's order, agreeing with respondent that it could not be held guilty of an unfair labor practice because of its refusal to furnish the information requested by the union. 224 F.2d 869 (4th Cir. 1955). In *NLRB v. Jacobs Mfg. Co.*, 196 F.2d 680 (2d Cir. 1952), the Second Circuit upheld a Board finding of bad-faith bargaining based on an employer's refusal to supply financial information under circumstances similar to those here. Because of the conflict and the importance of the question we granted certiorari....

The company raised no objection to the Board's order on the ground that the scope of information required was too broad or that disclosure would put an undue burden on the company. Its major argument throughout has been that the information requested was irrelevant to the bargaining process and related to matters exclusively within the province of management. Thus we lay to one side the suggestion by the company here that the Board's order might be unduly burdensome or injurious to its business. In any event, the Board has heretofore taken the position in cases such as this that "It is sufficient if the information is made available in a manner not so burdensome or time-consuming as to impede the process of bargaining." And in this case the Board has held substantiation of the company's position requires no more than "reasonable proof."

We think that in determining whether the obligation of good-faith bargaining has been met the Board has a right to consider an employer's refusal to give information about its financial status. While Congress did not compel agreement between employers and bargaining representatives, it did require collective bargaining in the hope that agreements would result. Section 204(a)(1) of the Act admonishes both employers and employees to "exert every reasonable effort to make and maintain agreements concerning rates of pay, hours, and working conditions...." In their effort to reach an agreement here both the union and the company treated the company's ability to pay increased wages as highly relevant. The ability of an employer to increase wages without injury to his business is a commonly considered factor in wage negotiations. Claims for increased wages have sometimes been abandoned because of an employer's unsatisfactory business condition; employees have even voted to accept wage decreases because of such conditions.

Good-faith bargaining necessarily requires that claims made by either bargainer should be honest claims. This is true about an asserted inability to pay an increase in wages. If such an argument is important enough to present in the give and take of bargaining, it is important enough to require some sort of proof of its accuracy. And it would certainly not be farfetched for a trier of fact to reach the conclusion that bargaining lacks good faith when an employer mechanically repeats a claim of inability to pay without making the slightest effort to substantiate the claim. Such has been the holding of the Labor Board since shortly after the passage of the Wagner Act. In *Pioneer Pearl Button Co.,* decided in 1936, where the employer's representative relied on the company's asserted "poor financial condition," the Board said: "He did no more than take refuge in the assertion that the respondent's financial condition was poor; he refused either to prove his statement, or to permit independent verification. This is not collective bargaining." 1 N.L.R.B. 837, 842-843. This was the position of the Board when the Taft-Hartley Act was passed in 1947 and has been its position ever since. We agree with the Board that a refusal to attempt to substantiate a claim of inability to pay increased wages may support a finding of a failure to bargain in good faith.

The Board concluded that under the facts and circumstances of this case the respondent was guilty of an unfair labor practice in failing to bargain in good faith. We see no reason to disturb the findings of the Board. We do not hold, however, that in every case in which economic inability is raised as an argument against increased wages it automatically follows that the employees are entitled to substantiating evidence. Each case must turn upon its particular facts. The inquiry must always be whether or not under the circumstances of the particular case the statutory obligation to bargain in good faith has been met. Since we conclude that there is support in the record for the conclusion of the Board here that respondent did not bargain in good faith, it was error for the Court of Appeals to set aside the Board's order and deny enforcement.

Reversed.

[MR. JUSTICE FRANKFURTER, whom MR. JUSTICE CLARK and MR. JUSTICE HARLAN joined, concurred in part and dissented in part in an opinion that is omitted.]

NLRB v. Acme Industrial Co., 385 U.S. 432, 87 S. Ct. 565, 17 L. Ed. 2d 495 (1967). A collective bargaining agreement provided that if plant equipment was moved to another location, employees subject as a result to layoff or reduction in grade could transfer under certain conditions to the new location. The contract also contained a grievance procedure culminating in binding arbitration. When the union discovered that certain machinery was being removed from the employer's plant, it filed contract grievances and requested information about the dates of the move, the destination of the equipment, the amount of machinery involved, the reason for the transfer, and the new use to be made of the equipment. The employer replied it had no duty to furnish this information since no layoffs or reductions had occurred within the five-day time limit for filing grievances. The NLRB ruled the employer had refused to bargain in good faith, observing that the information sought was "necessary in order to enable the Union to evaluate intelligently the grievances filed" and pointing out that the agreement contained no "clause by which the Union waives its statutory right to such information." The Supreme Court upheld the Board's order. The "duty to bargain unquestionably extends beyond the period of contract negotiations and applies to labor-management relations during the term of an agreement." Moreover, the Board did not have to await an arbitrator's determination of the relevancy of the information before enforcing the union's statutory rights under § 8(a)(5). The Board "was not making a binding construction of the labor contract. It was only acting upon the probability that the desired information was relevant, and that it would be of use to the union in carrying out its statutory duties and responsibilities.... Thus, the assertion of jurisdiction by the Board in this case in no way threatens the power which the parties have given the arbitrator to make binding interpretations of the labor agreement."

NOTES

1. Under *Truitt* and *Acme*, is an employer's failure to supply relevant information a refusal to bargain per se? Should it be? For contrasting views, *see Woodworkers Locals 6-7 & 6-122 v. NLRB*, 263 F.2d 483 (D.C. Cir. 1959); *Taylor Forge & Pipe Works v. NLRB*, 234 F.2d 227 (7th Cir.), *cert. denied*, 352 U.S. 942 (1956). What is the relationship between *Truitt*'s honesty-in-bargaining policy, the good faith bargaining obligation, and the duty to disclose relevant information upon which bargaining positions are predicated? *See generally* Hylton, *An Economic Theory of the Duty to Bargain*, 83 Geo. L.J. 19 (1994).

2. *Wage and financial data.* An employer must furnish all information necessary and relevant to the performance of the union's collective bargaining responsibilities. This applies to the administration as well as the negotiation of the labor agreement. *J.I. Case Co. v. NLRB*, 253 F.2d 149 (7th Cir. 1958); *Columbia Univ.*, 298 N.L.R.B. 941 (1990) (interest arbitration). In determining relevance, the Labor Board and the courts have distinguished between wage data and financial data. Wage data include information concerning all the factors that enter into the computation of wages or other forms of compensation. Generally, an employer has to supply all requested wage data not obviously beyond the needs of the union. Examples of wage data that must be furnished are: job rates and classifications, *Taylor Forge & Pipe Works v. NLRB, supra;* time study data, *NLRB v. Otis Elev. Co.*, 208 F.2d 176 (2d Cir. 1953); merit increases, *Otis Elev. Co.*, 170 N.L.R.B. 395 (1968); pension information, *Union Carbide Corp.*, 197 N.L.R.B. 717 (1972); group insurance data, *Stowe-Woodward, Inc.*, 123 N.L.R.B. 287 (1959); and incentive earnings, *Dixie Mfg. Co.*, 79 N.L.R.B. 645 (1948), *enforced*, 180 F.2d 173 (6th Cir. 1950). Wage data must ordinarily be made available regardless of employer claims of "confidentiality." *General Elec. Co. v. NLRB*, 466 F.2d 1177 (6th Cir. 1972); *cf. Resorts Int'l Hotel Casino v. NLRB*, 996 F.2d 1553 (3d Cir. 1993) (complaining customers' names). *But cf. Pennsylvania Power & Light Co.*, 301 N.L.R.B. 1104 (1991) (no disclosure of names of informants about alleged drug use by employees).

Financial data include sales and production figures and other information concerning the employer's ability to meet the union's economic demands. Generally, an employer need not divulge such information unless he makes his financial position an issue in the negotiations by claiming he cannot afford to pay. *Empire Term. Warehouse Co.*, 151 N.L.R.B. 1359 (1965), *aff'd*, 355 F.2d 842 (D.C. Cir. 1966); *Caster Mold & Mach. Co.*, 148 N.L.R.B. 1614 (1964). The Board has distinguished between an employer claim of present inability to pay (which triggers the duty to supply financial information) and an "employer's projections of its future inability to compete" (which do not trigger the duty to supply financial information). *Nielsen Lithographing Co.,* 305 N.L.R.B. 697 (1991), *enforced sub nom. GCIU Local 508 v. NLRB,* 977 F.2d 1168 (7th Cir. 1992). According to the Board, the critical distinction between the two is this:

> The employer who claims a present inability to pay, or a prospective inability to pay during the life of the contract being negotiated, is claiming essentially that it *cannot* pay. By contrast, the employer who claims only economic difficulties or business losses or the prospect of layoffs is simply saying that it does not *want* to pay.

Thus, employers demanding concessions to enable them to compete more effectively are not required to honor union requests to see their financial records, since they are not claiming an inability to satisfy the existing terms. *Steelworkers Local 14534 v. NLRB,* 983 F.2d 240 (D.C. Cir. 1993).

The Board has had difficulty in drawing the line between claims of inability to pay and claims of competitive disadvantage. For example, in *ConAgra Inc. v. NLRB,* 117 F.3d 1435 (D.C. Cir. 1997), the employer sought steep wage cuts and made statements during bargaining that sales volume had declined sharply, that "we need to be competitive," and that "we want the company to continue." The Board in a 2-1 decision found these comments sufficient to trigger an obligation to provide the union with financial information. The D.C. Circuit reversed, holding that the Board's ruling was inconsistent with its *Nielsen Lithographing* doctrine. Judge Wald filed a separate concurrence suggesting that the Board review its *Nielsen Lithographing* rationale in search of an approach that would more tightly link disclosure obligations to the union's need to evaluate the accuracy of factual claims made by the employer. *See also Stroehmann Bakeries, Inc. v. NLRB,* 95 F.3d 218 (2d Cir. 1996) (reversing Board order requiring disclosure of financial information to union based on employer claim of inability to pay).

Is the difference in the treatment of wage data and financial data justified in the first place? Could anything be more "relevant" to a union in formulating its demands in preparation for collective bargaining than knowledge of the employer's capacity to pay? *See* Bloch, *The Disclosure of Profits in the Normal Course of Collective Bargaining,* 2 Lab. Law. 47 (1986); Robbins, *Rethinking Financial Information Disclosure Under the National Labor Relations Act,* 47 Vand. L. Rev. 1905 (1994). Can wages legitimately be distinguished from other relatively fixed "cost pressures" that are verifiable by reviewing third-party contracts? *See Taylor Hosp.,* 317 N.L.R.B. 991 (1995), *enforced,* 82 F.3d 406 (3rd Cir. 1996) (Board allowed union access to insurance contracts); *United States Testing Co. v. NLRB,* 160 F.3d 14 (1998) (employer required to provide union with information concerning individual claims histories of employees when it proposes cutting health benefits).

3. *Employee privacy; employer trade secrets.* The Supreme Court has declared that an employer has sufficient interest in the secrecy of psychological aptitude test questions and answers to refuse disclosure, and that disclosure of individual scores may be conditioned on the employees' consent, even though the union desires the information to prepare for an arbitration. *Detroit Edison Co. v. NLRB,* 440 U.S. 301 (1979). A union whose collective agreement contained a nondiscrimination clause was held entitled to statistical data on an employer's minority and female employment and to the corresponding work force analyses, but not to the employer's entire affirmative action plan. *IUE v. NLRB (Westinghouse Elec. Corp.),* 648 F.2d 18 (D.C. Cir. 1980). The court cited the interest of the employees in privacy as a reason for compelling the production only of compilations of complaints of discrimination, rather than copies of them. *See generally* Newman & Wilson, *Direct Disclosures to Unions of Equal Employment Opportunity Information Under the NLRA,* in N.Y.U. Thirty-Fourth Annual Conference on Labor 229 (1981).

Employers that regularly use toxic substances have been required to provide unions with information concerning their generic names, morbidity and mortality tables, toxicological studies, insurance claims, radiation levels, etc., but not the medical records of identified individuals. Bargaining was also ordered to establish appropriate safeguards to protect the employers' proprietary interests in trade secrets. *Oil, Chem. & Atomic Workers Local 6-418 v. NLRB,* 711 F.2d 348 (D.C. Cir. 1983). *See* Comments, 5 Indus. Rel. L.J. 247 (1983); 66 Iowa L. Rev. 1333 (1981). Union agents must generally be allowed to enter plant premises when necessary to monitor health and safety conditions. *NLRB v. American Nat'l Can Co.,* 924 F.2d 518 (4th Cir. 1991). Unions are also entitled to copies of environmental audits. In *Detroit Newspaper Agency,* 317 N.L.R.B. 1071 (1995), the Board ruled against an employer who refused to provide the union with an unredacted copy of an environmental audit of the workplace. Even if the employer had a legitimate claim of confidentiality, that was outweighed by the union's interest in health and safety when the audit was a routine annual report and not prepared in response to a specific health and safety problem.

However, the Third Circuit has held that an employer could lawfully refuse to turn over absence and tardiness records containing highly personal health information without the employees' written consent. *New Jersey Bell Tel. Co. v. NLRB,* 720 F.2d 789 (3d Cir. 1983). To what extent may the Federal Privacy Act serve as a defense for employers in these cases? *See, e.g., Goodyear Atomic Corp.,* 266 N.L.R.B. 890 (1983), *enforced,* 738 F.2d 155 (6th Cir. 1984).

4. How much information must the employer provide to the union in order to assist the union in serving as an effective advocate and representative of the employees? The Eighth Circuit has held that an employer is not obliged to provide a union with requested information that might be relevant to enforcement of a bargaining agreement when compliance would be burdensome and the union's predominant purpose in requesting the information is to harass the employer and force it to forego a right it has under the collective contract. *NLRB v. Wachter Constr. Co.,* 23 F.3d 1378 (8th Cir. 1994). *See also Detroit Edison Co.,* 314 N.L.R.B. 1273 (1994) (employer not required to furnish requested information that has no apparent connection to contract enforcement). On the other hand, an employer cannot refuse to supply relevant information just because the union may use it for purposes the employer finds objectionable. Thus, a company had to furnish the names, addresses, and wage rates of employees even though the union might solicit them to join an FLSA suit. *NLRB v. CJC Holdings, Inc.*, 97 F.3d 114 (5th Cir. 1996). Similarly, a divided Board held that an employer unlawfully refused to provide a union with information concerning work rules that could lead to employee discipline, despite the employer's contention that many policies were developed case by case. *Praxair, Inc.*, 317 N.L.R.B. 435 (1995). The dissenting member thought it sufficient that the employer had directed the union to the collective agreement, the company's safety manual, and posted signs around the plant. And most recently, an ALJ ordered a health care employer to provide the union with information concerning patient care quality, reasoning that the union had a legitimate purpose for its request since issues surrounding patient care were potentially mandatory subjects of bargaining. *See Kaiser Foundation Hospitals and the Permanente Medical Group, Inc.*, No. 32-CA-15728 (N.L.R.B. 1997).

Unions seeking to challenge discriminatory hiring practices may obtain employer information concerning the race, national origin, and gender of job applicants, but only if the union is able to show facts supporting a reasonable basis for a belief that discrimination is occurring and further inquiry is justified. In *Hertz Corp.*, 319 N.L.R.B. 597 (1995), the Board held that a car rental company must provide this information to the union where its labor agreement contained a no-discrimination clause, since it was relevant to the union's function as bargaining agent. The Third Circuit denied enforcement because the union had failed to communicate to Hertz any facts to support its suspicion of hiring discrimination. *Hertz Corp. v. NLRB*, 105 F.3d 868 (3d Cir. 1997).

5. An exclusive bargaining representative is entitled to a list of the names and addresses of the employees in the unit when this is necessary for the effective negotiation or administration of the collective agreement. *Prudential Ins. Co.*, 173 N.L.R.B. 792 (1968), *enforced,* 412 F.2d 77 (2d Cir.), *cert. denied,* 396 U.S. 928 (1969). *See also Florida Mach. & Foundry Co.*, 174 N.L.R.B. 1156 (1969), *rev'd and remanded on other grounds,* 441 F.2d 1005 (D.C. Cir. 1970) (names of employees working during strike). *But cf. Chicago Tribune Co. v. NLRB,* 79 F.3d 604 (7th Cir. 1996) (employer need not furnish union with the names and addresses of strike replacements when there had been violence against replacements in the past, applying a "totality of the circumstances" approach). What about information concerning unit (or non-unit) employees being trained to perform non-unit (or unit) work in the event of a strike? *See, e.g., Newspaper Guild v. NLRB,* 548 F.2d 863 (9th Cir. 1977); *NLRB v. A.S. Abell Co.,* 624 F.2d 506 (4th Cir. 1980). Concerning unionized employers' so-called "double-breasted" or open shop operations? *See NLRB v. Associated Gen. Contractors,* 633 F.2d 766 (9th Cir. 1980), *cert. denied,* 452 U.S. 915 (1981); *NLRB v. Leonard B. Hebert, Jr. &*

Co., 696 F.2d 1120 (5th Cir.), *cert. denied,* 464 U.S. 817 (1983); *NLRB v. Public Service Electric and Gas Co.,* 157 F.3d 222 (1998).

6. *Witnesses.* An employer need not provide a union with the written statements of employee witnesses prior to an arbitration. *Anheuser-Busch, Inc.,* 237 N.L.R.B. 982 (1978). What about a company's investigative report of a conversation with a complaining customer? *See NLRB v. New Jersey Bell Tel. Co.,* 936 F.2d 144 (3d Cir. 1991). *GTE California Inc.,* 324 N.L.R.B. No. 78, 156 L.R.R.M. 1113 (1997), involved a telecommunications company that discharged an employee because of a complaint from a customer with a "nonpublished/unlisted number." The firm denied a union request for the identity of the complaining customer, due to confidentiality concerns, but offered to dial the customer and allow the union to speak with that person. The Board found that the company's interest in protecting the identity of the customer was significant and that its proposed accommodation that would have allowed the union to speak with her anonymously was sufficient to enable the union to satisfy its representational duty. What about a videotape of an alleged incident of misconduct? *See Square D Elec. Co.,* 266 N.L.R.B. 795 (1983).

7. *Manner of presentation.* The employer is not obliged to supply information in the exact form requested so long as it is submitted in a manner which is not unduly burdensome to interpret. *Westinghouse Elec. Corp.,* 129 N.L.R.B. 850 (1960); *McLean-Arkansas Lumber Co.,* 109 N.L.R.B. 1022 (1954). But an employer's "no photocopy" rule was held unlawful in *Communications Workers Local 1051 v. NLRB,* 644 F.2d 923 (1st Cir. 1981). Must an employer let a union make its own technological studies of disputed operations on the plant premises? *Compare Fafnir Bearing Co. v. NLRB,* 362 F.2d 716 (2d Cir. 1966) ("Yes") *and NLRB v. Holyoke Water Power Co.,* 778 F.2d 49 (1st Cir. 1985) *with Hercules Motor Corp.,* 136 N.L.R.B. 1648 (1962). When a union requests access to company premises to conduct a time study, the Eighth Circuit has indicated that the NLRB may balance the employer's property rights against the employees' right to effective representation. *See Brown Shoe Co. v. NLRB,* 33 F.3d 1019 (8th Cir. 1994). Is this approach consistent with the doctrine articulated in *Lechmere* with respect to nonemployee access for organizing purposes?

A union's access may be conditioned on its execution of a trade secrets agreement. *Hercules, Inc. v. NLRB,* 833 F.2d 426 (2d Cir. 1987). On the need to provide access to the company's books, *compare Metlox Mfg. Co.,* 153 N.L.R.B. 1388 (1965), *enforced,* 378 F.2d 728 (9th Cir. 1967) (conclusory profit-and-loss statement inadequate) *with McLean-Arkansas Lumber Co., supra.*

8. *Union disclosure.* Unions may also have an obligation to furnish information requested by employers. *Firemen & Oilers Local 288,* 302 N.L.R.B. 1008 (1991) (employee medical records needed to support excuse from work).

9. The duty to furnish information is discussed in Bartosic & Hartley, *The Employer's Duty to Supply Information to the Union,* 58 Cornell L. Rev. 23 (1972); Fanning, *The Obligation to Furnish Information During the Contract Term,* 9

Ga. L. Rev. 375 (1975); Huston, *Furnishing Information as an Element of Employer's Good Faith Bargaining,* 35 U. Det. L.J. 471 (1958); Miller, *Employer's Duty to Furnish Economic Data to Unions—Revisited,* 17 Lab. L.J. 272 (1966); Shedlin, *Regulation of Disclosure of Economic and Financial Data and the Impact on the American System of Labor-Management Relations,* 41 Ohio St. L.J. 441 (1980).

C. THE SUBJECT MATTER OF COLLECTIVE BARGAINING

NEIL CHAMBERLAIN, THE UNION CHALLENGE TO MANAGEMENT CONTROL 8-9 (1948)

The problem is highly charged with an ethical content. Judgments are required as to the moral validity of legal relationships, the justification for economic powers and distributive shares, the degree of weight to be accorded technological efficiency, the philosophical foundations for political arrangements. Here indeed lies the final basis for decision. We should be missing the heart of the problem if we failed to realize that legal and economic arguments, technological and political considerations must give way before widely held moral convictions. What is the ethical basis of the workers' struggle for increasing participation in business decisions? On what standards of justice and rightness does management rest its defensive tactics? Such questions should not produce wry smiles from those recalling union terrorism and intimidation, and management use of *agents provocateurs,* bribery, and tear gas. Such condemned activity reveals the deep roots of ethical persuasions.

S. SLICHTER, J. HEALY & E. LIVERNASH, THE IMPACT OF COLLECTIVE BARGAINING ON MANAGEMENT 958 (1960)*

Management has moved in the direction of concessions to unions, for example, by accepting a narrowing of managerial discretion, most obviously indicated by the expanded scope of labor contracts, by agreeing to extensive reliance on seniority, and by endorsing arbitration of grievances. Managements have also furthered the process of adjustment by the development of management by policy. Unions have made important concessions to the needs of management, for example, in the acceptance of job evaluation, progressive discipline, and discipline for wildcat strikes.

Adjustment of the goals and policies of management and of unions has gone farther in the case of some issues than others. It has gone farthest in the following areas: (1) work-sharing and layoff systems, (2) formal or informal evaluation of particular job rates, (3) administration of the wide range of employee benefit

---

*Copyright © 1960. Reprinted by permission of The Brookings Institution.

plans and provisions, (4) systems of employee discipline, including the control of wildcats, (5) scheduling of work, (6) development and operation of the grievance procedure, and (7) acceptance of arbitration. Adjustment is less well developed in the following areas: (1) production standards and wage incentives, (2) promotion principles, (3) work assignment, and (4) subcontracting.

NLRB v. WOOSTER DIVISION OF BORG-WARNER CORP.

Supreme Court of the United States
356 U.S. 342, 78 S. Ct. 718, 2 L. Ed. 2d 823 (1958)

MR. JUSTICE BURTON delivered the opinion of the Court.

In these cases an employer insisted that its collective-bargaining contract with certain of its employees include: (1) a "ballot" clause calling for a prestrike secret vote of those employees (union and non-union) as to the employer's last offer, and (2) a "recognition" clause which excluded, as a party to the contract, the International Union which had been certified by the National Labor Relations Board as the employees' exclusive bargaining agent, and substituted for it the agent's uncertified local affiliate. The Board held that the employer's insistence upon either of such clauses amounted to a refusal to bargain, in violation of § 8(a)(5) of the National Labor Relations Act, as amended. The issue turns on whether either of these clauses comes within the scope of mandatory collective bargaining as defined in § 8(d) of the Act. For the reasons hereafter stated, we agree with the Board that neither clause comes within that definition. Therefore, we sustain the Board's order directing the employer to cease insisting upon either clause as a condition precedent to accepting any collective-bargaining contract....

[T]he "ballot" clause ... provided that, as to all nonarbitrable issues (which eventually included modification, amendment or termination of the contract), there would be a 30-day negotiation period after which, before the union could strike, there would have to be a secret ballot taken among all employees in the unit (union and non-union) on the company's last offer. In the event a majority of the employees rejected the company's last offer, the company would have an opportunity, within 72 hours, of making a new proposal and having a vote on it prior to any strike. The union's negotiators announced they would not accept this clause "under any conditions."

From the time that the company first proposed these clauses, the employees' representatives thus made it clear that each was wholly unacceptable. The company's representatives made it equally clear that no agreement would be entered into by it unless the agreement contained both clauses. In view of this impasse, there was little further discussion of the clauses, although the parties continued to bargain as to other matters. The company submitted a "package" proposal covering economic issues but made the offer contingent upon the satisfactory settlement of "all other issues...." The "package" included both of the controversial clauses. On March 15, 1953, the unions rejected that proposal and the membership voted to strike on March 20 unless a settlement were reached by then. None was reached and the unions struck. Negotiations, nevertheless, continued....

Read together, [§§ 8(a)(5) and 8(d)] establish the obligation of the employer and the representative of its employees to bargain with each other in good faith with respect to "wages, hours, and other terms and conditions of employment...." The duty is limited to those subjects, and within that area neither party is legally obligated to yield. *NLRB v. American National Insurance Co.,* 343 U.S. 395. As to other matters, however, each party is free to bargain or not to bargain, and to agree or not to agree.

The company's good faith has met the requirements of the statute as to the subjects of mandatory bargaining. But that good faith does not license the employer to refuse to enter into agreements on the ground that they do not include some proposal which is not a mandatory subject of bargaining. We agree with the Board that such conduct is, in substance, a refusal to bargain about the subjects that are within the scope of mandatory bargaining. This does not mean that bargaining is to be confined to the statutory subjects. Each of the two controversial clauses is lawful in itself. Each would be enforceable if agreed to by the unions. But it does not follow that, because the company may propose these clauses, it can lawfully insist upon them as a condition to any agreement.

Since it is lawful to insist upon matters within the scope of mandatory bargaining and unlawful to insist upon matters without, the issue here is whether either the "ballot" or the "recognition" clause is a subject within the phrase "wages, hours, and other terms and conditions of employment" which defines mandatory bargaining. The "ballot" clause is not within that definition. It relates only to the procedure to be followed by the employees among themselves before their representative may call a strike or refuse a final offer. It settles no term or condition of employment—it merely calls for an advisory vote of the employees. It is not a partial "no-strike" clause. A "no-strike" clause prohibits the employees from striking during the life of the contract. It regulates the relations between the employer and the employees. *See NLRB v. American National Insurance Co., supra* at 408, n.22. The "ballot" clause, on the other hand, deals only with relations between the employees and their unions. It substantially modifies the collective bargaining system provided for in the statute by weakening the independence of the "representative" chosen by the employees. It enables the employer, in effect, to deal with its employees rather than with their statutory representative. *Cf. Medo Photo Supply Corp. v. NLRB,* 321 U.S. 678 (1944).

The "recognition" clause likewise does not come within the definition of mandatory bargaining. The statute requires the company to bargain with the certified representative of its employees. It is an evasion of that duty to insist that the certified agent not be a party to the collective bargaining contract. The Act does not prohibit the voluntary addition of a party, but that does not authorize the employer to exclude the certified representative from the contract....

MR. JUSTICE FRANKFURTER joins this opinion insofar as it holds that insistence by the company on the "recognition" clause, in conflict with the provisions of the Act requiring an employer to bargain with the representative of his employees, constituted an unfair labor practice. He agrees with the views of MR. JUSTICE HARLAN regarding the "ballot" clause. The subject matter of that clause is not so clearly outside the reasonable range of industrial bargaining as to establish a refusal to bargain in good faith, and is not prohibited simply because not deemed to be within the rather vague scope of the obligatory provisions of § 8(d).

MR. JUSTICE HARLAN, whom MR. JUSTICE CLARK and MR. JUSTICE WHITTAKER join, concurring in part and dissenting in part....

The legislative history behind the Wagner and Taft-Hartley Acts persuasively indicates that the Board was never intended to have power to prevent good faith bargaining as to any subject not violative of the provisions or policies of those Acts....

[E]arly intrusions of the Board into the substantive aspects of the bargaining process became a matter of concern to Congress, and in the 1947 Taft-Hartley amendments to the Wagner Act, Congress took steps to curtail them by writing into § 8(d) the particular fields as to which it considered bargaining *should* be required....

The decision of this Court in 1952 in *NLRB v. American National Insurance Co., supra,* was fully in accord with this legislative background in holding that the Board lacked power to order an employer to cease bargaining over a particular clause because such bargaining under the Board's view, entirely apart from a showing of bad faith, constituted *per se* an unfair labor practice....

I therefore cannot escape the view that today's decision is deeply inconsistent with legislative intention and this Court's precedents. The Act sought to compel management and labor to meet and bargain in good faith as to certain topics. This is the *affirmative* requirement of § 8(d) which the Board is specifically empowered to enforce, but I see no warrant for inferring from it any power in the Board to *prohibit* bargaining in good faith as to lawful matters not included in § 8(d). The Court reasons that such conduct on the part of the employer, when carried to the point of insistence, is in substance equivalent to a refusal to bargain as to the statutory subjects, but I cannot understand how this can be said over the Trial Examiner's unequivocal finding that the employer did in fact bargain in "good faith," not only over the disputed clauses but also over the statutory subjects....

The most cursory view of decisions of the Board and the circuit courts under the National Labor Relations Act reveals the unsettled and evolving character of collective bargaining agreements. Provisions which two decades ago might have been thought to be the exclusive concern of labor or management are today commonplace in such agreements. The bargaining process should be left fluid, free from intervention of the Board leading to premature crystallization of labor agreements into any one pattern of contract provisions, so that these agreements can be adapted through collective bargaining to the changing needs of our society and to the changing concepts of the responsibilities of labor and management. What the Court does today may impede this evolutionary process. Under the facts of this case, an employer is precluded from attempting to limit the likelihood of a strike. But by the same token it would seem to follow that unions which bargain in good faith would be precluded from insisting upon contract clauses which might not be deemed statutory subjects within § 8(d).

As unqualifiedly stated in *American National Insurance Co., supra,* ... it is through the "good faith" requirement of § 8(d) that the Board is to enforce the bargaining provisions of § 8. A determination that a party bargained as to statutory or non-statutory subjects in good or bad faith must depend upon an evaluation of the total circumstances surrounding any given situation. I do not deny that there may be instances where unyielding insistence on a particular item may be a relevant consideration in the overall picture in determining "good faith," for the demands of a party might in the context of a particular industry be so extreme as to constitute some evidence of an unwillingness to bargain. But no such situation is presented in this instance by the "ballot" clause. "No strike" clauses, and other provisions analogous to the "ballot" clause limiting the right to strike, are hardly novel to labor agreements. And in any event the uncontested finding of "good faith" by the Trial Examiner forecloses that issue here.

Of course, an employer or union cannot insist upon a clause which would be illegal under the Act's provisions, *NLRB v. National Maritime Union,* 175 F.2d 686 (2d Cir. 1949), or conduct itself so as to contravene specific requirements of the Act. *Medo Photo Supply Corp. v. NLRB,* 321 U.S. 678 (1944). But here the Court recognizes, as it must, that the clause is lawful under the Act, and I think it clear that the company's insistence upon it violated no statutory duty to which it was subject....

The company's insistence on the "recognition" clause, which had the effect of excluding the International Union as a party signatory to agreement and making Local 1239 the sole contracting party on the union side, presents a different problem. In my opinion the company's action in this regard did constitute an unfair labor practice since it contravened specific requirements of the Act....

NOTES

1. Would unions or employers have benefitted the most from a decision in *Borg-Warner* that *all* lawful provisions are "mandatory" subjects, on which bargaining is required and which may be forced to an impasse? Is an employer more likely to be disadvantaged by the obligation to bargain over a "management function," or by its failure to bargain over a decision that the NLRB later rules is a mandatory subject? Does *Borg-Warner* give the Board too great a power to freeze or expand the list of topics on which unions and employers must bargain? Would it have been preferable to analyze the problem simply in terms of the parties' "good faith"? *Cf. American Nat'l Ins. Co., supra. See* Cox, *Labor Decisions of the Supreme Court at the October Term, 1957,* 44 Va. L. Rev. 1057, 1075 (1958); Fleming, *The Obligation to Bargain in Good Faith,* 16 Sw. L.J. 43 (1962); Christensen, *New Subjects and New Concepts in Collective Bargaining,* in A.B.A. Section of Labor Relations Law Proceedings 245 (1970). *Borg-Warner* is noted in 11 Stan. L. Rev. 188 (1958); 43 Minn. L. Rev. 1225 (1959). *See also* Note, *Major Operational Decisions and Free Collective Bargaining: Eliminating the Mandatory/Permissive Distinction,* 102 Harv. L. Rev. 1971 (1989); Note, *The Viability of Distinguishing Between Mandatory and Permissive Subjects of Bargaining in a Cooperative Setting,* 41 Vand. L. Rev. 577 (1988).

2. Employee compensation in a wide variety of forms has been held to be "wages" or "other conditions of employment," and thus a mandatory subject of bargaining. *See, e.g., Inland Steel Co. v. NLRB,* 170 F.2d 247 (7th Cir. 1948), *cert. denied,* 336 U.S. 960 (1949) (pensions); *NLRB v. Wonder State Mfg. Co.,* 344 F.2d 210 (8th Cir. 1965) (Christmas bonus); *Central Ill. Pub. Serv. Co.,* 139 N.L.R.B. 1407 (1962), *enforced,* 324 F.2d 916 (7th Cir. 1963) (employee discounts); *Getty Ref. & Mktg. Co.,* 279 N.L.R.B. 924 (1986) (recreation fund); *Bituminous Roadways of Colo.,* 314 N.L.R.B. 1010 (1994) (discontinuance of dental and vision care program); *Loral Defense Sys.—Akron,* 320 N.L.R.B. 755 (1996) (transfer to new delivery system for health insurance). Rental fees in company-owned housing provided for employees who want it may be a mandatory topic of bargaining, depending on such circumstances as the distance to, and the availability of, other accommodations. *American Smelting & Ref. Co. v. NLRB,* 406 F.2d 552 (9th Cir.), *cert. denied,* 395 U.S. 935 (1969). What about the prices of food in a plant's cafeteria and vending machines? *See Ford Motor Co. v. NLRB,* 441 U.S. 488 (1979).

3. In *Ford Motor Co. v. NLRB, supra,* the Supreme Court described mandatory subjects of bargaining as those which are "plainly germane to the working environment" and are "not among those managerial decisions which lie at the core of entrepreneurial control." Applying this test, the Board has found that a wide variety of employer investigatory tools or methods used to detect employee misconduct are mandatory subjects of bargaining, since they have the potential to affect the continued employment of employees through discipline up to and including discharge, and are neither entrepreneurial in character nor fundamental to the basic direction of the enterprise. *See Lockheed Shipbuilding Co.,* 273 N.L.R.B. 171 (1984) (physical examinations); *Austin-Berryhill, Inc.,* 246 N.L.R.B. 1139 (1979) (polygraph testing); *Johnson-Bateman Co.,* 295 N.L.R.B. 180 (1989) (mandatory drug testing); *W-I Forest Prods. Co.,* 304 N.L.R.B. 957 (1991) (plant-wide ban on smoking); and *Colgate-Palmolive Co.,* 323 N.L.R.B. No. 82, 155 L.R.R.M. 1034 (1997) (installation and use of hidden surveillance cameras in the workplace). But drug testing of job applicants is not a mandatory subject of bargaining. *Star Tribune,* 295 N.L.R.B. 543 (1989). *See generally* Symposium, *Drug Testing in the Workplace,* 33 Wm. & Mary L. Rev. 1 (1991); Crain, *Ex-*

panded Employee Drug-Detection Programs and the Public Good: Big Brother at the Bargaining Table, 64 N.Y.U. L. Rev. 1286 (1989).

4. Other provisions governing the employment relation that have been ruled subject to mandatory bargaining include a no-strike clause covering both union and nonunion members of the bargaining unit, *Lloyd A. Fry Roofing Co.,* 123 N.L.R.B. 647 (1959); a nondiscriminatory exclusive hiring hall arrangement in a right-to-work state, *Associated Gen. Contractors,* 143 N.L.R.B. 409 (1963), *enforced,* 349 F.2d 449 (5th Cir. 1965), *cert. denied,* 382 U.S. 1026 (1966); and a change in a union's work jurisdiction, as distinguished from the scope of the bargaining unit, *IATSE Local 666 v. NLRB,* 904 F.2d 47 (D.C. Cir. 1990).

5. On the other hand, matters considered too remote from the employment relationship, or deemed a peculiar prerogative of employer or union, are not mandatory subjects of bargaining. If lawful, such matters are permissible subjects. The parties may bargain by mutual agreement, but neither side may insist on a proposal to an impasse. Examples of nonmandatory topics are performance bonds, *NLRB v. American Compress Warehouse, Div. of Frost-Whited Co.,* 350 F.2d 365 (5th Cir. 1965), *cert. denied,* 382 U.S. 982 (1966); a narrowly tailored newspaper code of ethics, *see Peerless Publications, Inc.,* 283 N.L.R.B. 334 (1987); the *amount* of an agency shop fee charged nonmembers, as distinguished from the union security provision, *North Bay Dev. Disabilities Servs. v. NLRB,* 905 F.2d 476 (D.C. Cir. 1990), *cert. denied,* 498 U.S. 1082 (1991); a clause permitting an employer to deal directly with employees concerning job buy-outs, *Toledo Typographical Union No. 63 v. NLRB,* 907 F.2d 1220 (D.C. Cir. 1990), *cert. denied,* 498 U.S. 1053 (1991); and an interest arbitration clause, *Laidlaw Transit Inc.,* 323 N.L.R.B. No. 156, 156 L.R.R.M. 1029 (1997). How should an employer demand that a union call off a strike as a condition for further negotiations be classified? *See Gibson Greetings, Inc.,* 310 N.L.R.B. 1286 (1993), *reversed in part,* 53 F.3d 385 (D.C. Cir. 1995). What about a union demand for bargaining over the choice of the insurance carrier for an employee health plan? *See Connecticut Light & Power Co. v. NLRB,* 476 F.2d 1079 (2d Cir. 1973); *cf. Keystone Consol. Indus. v. NLRB,* 606 F.2d 171 (7th Cir. 1979).

6. A party that insists upon a non-mandatory subject for bargaining as a precondition to agreement on mandatory topics violates the duty to bargain, even if it does so in good faith. *NLRB v. Greensburg Coca-Cola Bottling,* 40 F.3d 669 (3rd Cir. 1994). Suppose a group of employers in the same industry repeatedly present identical bargaining proposals in negotiations with a union that represents all of the employees but in separate units, and which has offered individualized proposals and wishes to bargain separately with each employer? *See Don Lee Distributor Inc. (Warren) v. NLRB,* 145 F.3d 834 (6th Cir. 1998) (enforcing Board ruling that multiemployer bargaining by a group of employers that refuse to bargain separately without the union's consent violates § 8(a)(5) because it "constitutes unlawful insistence on a nonmandatory subject, namely, the expanded scope of the bargaining unit"). *Cf. Spentonbush/Red Star Cos. v. NLRB,*

106 F.3d 484 (2d Cir. 1997) (finding that repeated demands by a company concerning exclusion of tug-boat and barge captains from the bargaining unit—a nonmandatory subject—did not violate § 8(a)(5) as long as the proposal was not presented as an ultimatum).

Suppose a union accepts an employer's total package proposal with the exception of a single nonmandatory item, a grievance settlement. Would the employer's subsequent refusal to execute the agreement necessarily constitute an unlawful insistence on a permissive subject? Would the issue turn entirely on whether an impasse had been reached? *See Good GMC, Inc.,* 267 N.L.R.B. 1033 (1983). *Cf. C-E Natco,* 272 N.L.R.B. 502 (1984) (nonmandatory performance bond as "alternative" to lockout).

What if a party insists upon a mandatory subject but suggests possible leeway with respect to that topic if the other side is willing to make concessions on a nonmandatory issue?

7. National policies from outside the field of labor relations may occasionally have to be taken into account in determining the allowable scope of mandatory bargaining. For example, how should the NLRB treat a demand by a contractors' association for a so-called "most favored nation" clause, under which there would be a readjustment in the association's contract if the union subsequently granted more favorable terms to any other employer? Consider the implications of *United Mine Workers v. Pennington,* 381 U.S. 657 (1965), *infra* (anticompetitive collective bargaining agreements as antitrust violations). In *Dolly Madison Indus.,* 182 N.L.R.B. 1037 (1970), the Labor Board declared a "most favored nation" clause to be a mandatory subject of bargaining, which an employer could insist upon in the absence of a "predatory purpose." The Board distinguished *Pennington* on the ground the clause sought here did not obligate the union to impose the same standards on competitors of the employer. Is this a realistic assessment of the practicalities of the situation? Should the nature of the clause itself, or the presence of a "predatory purpose," be the critical factor in these cases?

8. Should a labor union be able to demand bargaining over employer practices adversely affecting the public interest, such as pollution of the atmosphere? *See generally* Oldham, *Organized Labor, the Environment, and the Taft-Hartley Act,* 71 Mich. L. Rev. 936 (1973); Comment, *A Case for Air Pollution as a Mandatory Bargaining Subject,* 51 Or. L. Rev. 223 (1971).

ALLIED CHEMICAL & ALKALI WORKERS LOCAL 1 v. PITTSBURGH PLATE GLASS CO.

Supreme Court of the United States
404 U.S. 157, 92 S. Ct. 383, 30 L. Ed. 2d 341 (1971)

MR. JUSTICE BRENNAN delivered the opinion of the Court....

I

Since 1949, Local 1, Allied Chemical and Alkali Workers of America, has been the exclusive bargaining representative for the employees "working" on hourly rates of pay at the Barberton, Ohio, facilities of the respondent, Pittsburgh Plate Glass Company. In 1950, the Union and the Company negotiated an employee group health insurance plan, in which, it was orally agreed, retired employees could participate by contributing the required premiums, to be deducted from their pension benefits. This program continued unchanged until 1962, except for an improvement unilaterally instituted by the Company in 1954 and another improvement negotiated in 1959.

In 1962 the Company agreed to contribute two dollars per month toward the cost of insurance premiums of employees who retired in the future and elected to participate in the medical plan. The parties also agreed at this time to make 65 the mandatory retirement age. In 1964 insurance benefits were again negotiated, and the company agreed to increase its monthly contribution from two to four dollars, applicable to employees retiring after that date and also to pensioners who had retired since the effective date of the 1962 contract. It was agreed, however, that the Company might discontinue paying the two-dollar increase if Congress enacted a national health program.

In November 1965, Medicare, a national health program, was enacted. 79 Stat. 291, 42 U.S.C. § 1395 *et. seq.* The 1964 contract was still in effect, and the Union sought mid-term bargaining to renegotiate insurance benefits for retired employees. The Company responded in March 1966 that, in its view, Medicare rendered the health insurance program useless because of a non-duplication of benefits provision in the Company's insurance policy, and stated, without negotiating any change, that it was planning to (a) reclaim the additional two-dollar monthly contribution as of the effective date of Medicare; (b) cancel the program for retirees; and (c) substitute the payment of the three-dollar monthly subscription fee for supplemental Medicare coverage for each retired employee.

The Union acknowledged that the Company had the contractual right to reduce its monthly contribution, but challenged its proposal unilaterally to substitute supplemental Medicare coverage for the negotiated health plan. The Company, as it had done during the 1959 negotiations without pressing the point, disputed the Union's right to bargain in behalf of retired employees, but advised the Union that upon further consideration it had decided not to terminate the health plan for pensioners. The Company stated instead that it would write each retired employee, offering to pay the supplemental Medicare premium if the employee would withdraw from the negotiated plan. Despite the Union's objections the Company did circulate its proposal to the retired employees, and 15 of 190 retirees elected to accept it. The Union thereupon filed unfair labor practice charges....

II

... This obligation [to bargain under §§ 1, 8(a)(5), 8(d), and 9(a)] extends only to the "terms and conditions of employment" of the employer's "employees" in the "unit appropriate for such purposes" which the union represents.... The Board found that benefits of already retired employees fell within these constraints on alternative theories. First, it held that pensioners are themselves "employees" and members of the bargaining unit, so that their benefits are a "term and condition" of their employment....

First.... In this cause we hold that the Board's decision is not supported by the law. The Act, after all, as § 1 makes clear, is concerned with the disruption to commerce that arises from interference with the organization and collective bargaining rights of "workers"—not those who have retired from the work force. The inequality of bargaining power that Congress sought to remedy was that of the "working" man, and the labor disputes that it ordered to be subjected to collective bargaining were those of employers and their active employees. Nowhere in the history of the National Labor Relations Act is there any evidence that retired workers are to be considered as within the ambit of the collective bargaining obligations of the statute.

To the contrary, the legislative history of § 2(3) itself indicates that the term "employee" is not to be stretched beyond its plain meaning embracing only those who work for another for hire.... In doubtful cases resort must still be had to economic and policy considerations to infuse § 2(3) with meaning. But, as the House comments ... demonstrate, this is not a doubtful case. The ordinary meaning of "employee" does not include retired workers; retired employees have ceased to work for another for hire.

The decisions on which the Board relied in construing § 2(3) to the contrary are wide of the mark. The Board enumerated "unfair labor practice situations where the statute has been applied to persons who have not been initially hired by an employer or whose employment has terminated." ... Yet all of these cases involved people who, unlike the pensioners here, were members of the active work force available for hire and at least in that sense could be identified as "employees." No decision under the Act is cited, and none to our knowledge exists, in which an individual who has ceased work without expectation of further employment has been held to be an "employee."...

Second. Section 9(a) of the Labor Relations Act accords representative status only to the labor organization selected or designated by the majority of employees in a "unit appropriate" "for the purposes of collective bargaining."...

In this case, in addition to holding that pensioners are not "employees" within the meaning of the collective bargaining obligations of the Act, we hold that they were not and could not be "employees" included in the bargaining unit. The unit determined by the Board to be appropriate was composed of "employees of the Employer's plant ... working on hourly rates, including group leaders who work on hourly rates of pay...." Apart from whether retirees could be considered "employees" within this language, they obviously were not employees "working" or "who work" on hourly rates of pay. Although those terms may include persons on temporary or limited absence from work, such as employees on military duty, it would utterly destroy the function of language to read them as embracing those whose work has ceased with no expectation of return....

Here, even if, as the Board found, active and retired employees have a common concern in assuring that the latter's benefits remain adequate, they plainly do not share a community of interests broad enough to justify inclusion of the retirees in the bargaining unit. Pensioners' interests extend only to retirement benefits, to the exclusion of wage rates, hours, working conditions, and all other terms of active employment. Incorporation of such a limited-purpose constituency in the bargaining unit would create the potential for severe internal conflicts which would impair the unit's ability to function and would disrupt the processes of collective bargaining. Moreover, the risk cannot be overlooked that union representatives on occasion might see fit to bargain for improved wages or other conditions favoring active employees at the expense of retirees' benefits....

Third. The Board found that bargaining over pensioners' rights has become an established industrial practice. But industrial practice cannot alter the conclusions that retirees are neither "employees" nor bargaining unit members. The parties dispute whether a practice of bargaining over pensioners' benefits exists and, if so, whether it reflects the views of labor and management that the subject is not merely a convenient but a mandatory topic of negotiation. But even if industry commonly regards retirees' benefits as a statutory subject of bargaining, that would at most, as we suggested in *Fibreboard Corp. v. NLRB,* 379 U.S. 203, 211 (1964), reflect the interests of employers and employees in the subject matter as well as its amenability to the collective bargaining process; it would not be determinative. Common practice cannot change the law and make into bargaining unit "employees" those who are not.

III

Even if pensioners are not bargaining unit "employees," are their benefits, nonetheless, a mandatory subject of collective bargaining as "terms and conditions of employment" of the active employees who remain in the unit? The Board held, alternatively, that they are, on the ground that they "vitally" affect the "terms and conditions of employment" of active employees principally by influencing the value of both their current and future benefits....

Section 8(d) of the Act, of course, does not immutably fix a list of subjects for mandatory bargaining.... But it does establish a limitation against which proposed topics must be measured. In general terms, the limitation includes only issues which settle an aspect of the relationship between the employer and employees. *See, e.g., NLRB v. Borg-Warner Corp.,* [356 U.S. 342 (1958)]. Although normally matters involving individuals outside the employment relationship do not fall within that category, they are not wholly excluded. In *Teamsters Union v. Oliver,* 358 U.S. 283 (1959), for example, an agreement had been negotiated in the trucking industry, establishing a minimum rental which carriers would pay to truck owners who drove their own vehicles in the carriers' service in place of the latter's employees. Without determining whether the owner-drivers were themselves "employees," we held that the minimum rental was a mandatory subject of bargaining, and hence immune from state antitrust laws, because the term "was integral to the establishment of a stable wage structure for clearly covered employee-drivers." *United States v. Drum,* 368 U.S. 370, 382-383, n.26 (1962). Similarly, in *Fibreboard Corp. v. NLRB, supra* at 215, we held that "the type of 'contracting out' involved in this case—the replacement of employees in the existing bargaining unit with those of an independent contractor to do the same work under similar conditions of employment—is a statutory subject of collective bargaining...." ...

The Board urges that *Oliver* and *Fibreboard* provide the principle governing this case. The Company, on the other hand, would distinguish those decisions on the ground that the unions there sought to protect employees from outside threats, not to represent the interests of third parties. We agree with the Board that the principle of *Oliver* and *Fibreboard* is relevant here; in each case the question is not whether the third-party concern is antagonistic to or compatible with the interests of bargaining unit employees, but whether it vitally affects the "terms and conditions" of their employment. But we disagree with the Board's assessment of the significance of a change in retirees' benefits to the "terms and conditions of employment" of active employees.

The benefits which active workers may reap by including retired employees under the same health insurance contract are speculative and insubstantial at best. As the Board itself acknowledges in its brief, the relationship between the inclusion of retirees and the overall insurance rate is uncertain. Adding individuals increases the group experience and thereby generally tends to lower the rate, but including pensioners, who are likely to have higher medical expenses, may more than offset that effect. In any event, the impact one way or the other on the "terms and conditions of employment" of active employees is hardly comparable to the loss of jobs threatened in *Oliver* and *Fibreboard....* The inclusion of retirees in the same insurance contract surely has even less an impact on the "terms and conditions of employment" of active employees than some of the contracting activities which we excepted from our holding in *Fibreboard.*

The mitigation of future uncertainty and the facilitation of agreement on active employees' retirement plans which the Board said would follow from the union's representation of pensioners are equally problematical.... Under the Board's theory, active employees undertake to represent pensioners in order to protect their own retirement benefits, just as if they were bargaining for, say, a cost-of-living escalation clause. But there is a crucial difference. Having once found it advantageous to bargain for improvements to pensioners' benefits, active workers are not forever thereafter bound to that view or obliged to negotiate in behalf of retirees again. To the contrary, they are free to decide, for example, that current income is preferable to greater certainty in their own retirement benefits or, indeed, to their retirement benefits altogether. By advancing pensioners' interests now, active employees, therefore, have no assurance that they will be the beneficiaries of similar representation when they retire....

We recognize that "classification of bargaining subjects as 'terms [and] conditions of employment' is a matter concerning which the Board has special expertise." *Meat Cutters v. Jewel Tea,* 381 U.S. 676, 685-686 (1965). The Board's holding in this case, however, depends on the application of law to facts, and the legal standard to be applied is ultimately for the courts to decide and enforce. We think that in holding the "terms and conditions of employment" of active employees to be *vitally* affected by pensioners' benefits, the Board here simply neglected to give the adverb its ordinary meaning. *Cf. NLRB v. Brown,* 380 U.S. 278, 292 (1965).

IV

The question remains whether the Company committed an unfair labor practice by offering retirees an exchange for their withdrawal from the already negotiated health insurance plan.... We need not resolve, however, whether there was a "modification" within the meaning of § 8(d), because we hold that even if there was, a "modification" is a prohibited unfair labor practice only when it changes a term that is a mandatory rather than a permissive subject of bargaining.

Paragraph (4) of § 8(d), of course, requires that a party proposing a modification continue "in full force and effect ... all the terms and conditions of the existing contract" until its expiration. Viewed in isolation from the rest of the provision, that language would preclude any distinction between contract obligations that are "terms and conditions of employment" and those that are not. But in construing § 8(d), "'we must not be guided by a single sentence or member of a sentence, but look to the provisions of the whole law, and to its object and policy.'" *Mastro Plastics Corp. v. NLRB,* 350 U.S. 270, 285 (1956).... Seen in that light, § 8(d) embraces only mandatory topics of bargaining. The provision begins by defining "to bargain collectively" as meeting and conferring "with respect to wages, hours, and other terms and conditions of employment." It then goes on to state that "the duty to bargain collectively shall also mean" that mid-term unilateral modifications and terminations are prohibited. Although this part of the section is introduced by a "proviso" clause,... it quite plainly is to be construed *in pari materia* with the preceding definition. Accordingly, just as § 8(d) defines the obligation to bargain to be with respect to mandatory terms alone, so it prescribes the duty to maintain only mandatory terms without unilateral modification for the duration of the collective-bargaining agreement....

The structure and language of § 8(d) point to a more specialized purpose than merely promoting general contract compliance. The conditions for a modification or termination set out in paragraphs (1) through (4) plainly are designed to regulate modifications and terminations so as to facilitate agreement in place of economic warfare....

If that is correct, the distinction that we draw between mandatory and permissive terms of bargaining fits the statutory purpose. By once bargaining and agreeing on a permissive subject, the parties, naturally, do not make the subject a mandatory topic of future bargaining. When a proposed modification is to a permissive term, therefore, the purpose of facilitating accord on the proposal is not at all in point, since the parties are not required under the statute to bargain with respect to it. The irrelevance of the purpose is demonstrated by the irrelevance of the procedures themselves of § 8(d). Paragraph (2), for example, requires an offer "to meet and confer with the other party for the purpose of negotiating a new contract or a contract containing the proposed modifications." But such an offer is meaningless if a party is statutorily free to refuse to negotiate on the proposed change to the permissive term. The notification to mediation and conciliation services referred to in paragraph (3) would be equally meaningless, if required at all. We think it would be no less beside the point to read paragraph (4) of § 8(d) as requiring continued adherence to permissive as well as mandatory terms. The remedy for a unilateral mid-term modification to a permissive term lies in an action for breach of contract,... not in an unfair-labor-practice proceeding.

As a unilateral mid-term modification of a permissive term such as retirees' benefits does not, therefore, violate § 8(d), the judgment of the Court of Appeals is

Affirmed.

MR. JUSTICE DOUGLAS dissents.

NOTES

1. Has the Supreme Court foreclosed an employer and a union from converting a permissive bargaining subject into a mandatory one, even for the life of a contract? If so, is this a sound result?

2. Do you understand the Court to be assuming, in Part IV of *Pittsburgh Plate Glass,* that there is an exact correspondence between the kind of subject matter over which an employer must bargain at the request of the union, and the kind of subject matter as to which an employer may not institute unilateral changes without prior bargaining? Is such parallelism logically necessary? Is it desirable?

3. The "vitally affects" test of the principal case only comes into play when the demand relates to persons outside the bargaining unit. This stiffer standard does not apply when the issue involves some immediate aspect of the relationship between an employer and its own unit employees. *Ford Motor Co. v. NLRB,* 441

U.S. 488 (1979) (food prices in plant concessions operated by a third party). The Board has ruled that changes in retiree benefits are mandatory subjects of bargaining if the changes would impact future benefits to current bargaining unit employees. *See Midwest Power Systems,* 323 N.L.R.B. No. 61, 155 L.R.R.M. 1001 (1997). What about an employer's change in a health insurance plan for non-bargaining unit employees which affects the spouses of employees in the bargaining unit—does this vitally affect the terms and conditions of employment of the unit employees? *See Torrington Co.,* 305 N.L.R.B. 938 (1991), *reconsideration denied,* 307 N.L.R.B. 485 (1992) (no—any adverse impact is incidental). What about child care benefits? *See* Crain, *Feminizing Unions: Challenging the Gendered Structure of Wage Labor,* 89 Mich. L. Rev. 1155, 1218-19 n.355 (1990).

4. Retirees plainly retain contract rights in pension benefits after their active employment ceases. May their former employer deal directly with them in settling disputes over their claims, without notice to or the consent of the union? *See, e.g., UAW v. Yard-Man, Inc.,* 716 F.2d 1476 (6th Cir. 1983), *cert. denied,* 465 U.S. 1007 (1984). How may retirees enforce pension and insurance rights contained in bargaining agreements? *See Anderson v. Alpha Portland Indus.,* 752 F.2d 1293 (8th Cir.), *cert. denied,* 471 U.S. 1102 (1985).

Retirees are not entitled to lifetime health insurance absent a contract to that effect, and an employer was held able to terminate a plan after a collective bargaining agreement expired in *Senn v. United Dominion Indus.,* 951 F.2d 806 (7th Cir. 1992), *cert. denied,* 509 U.S. 903 (1993). *But cf. Bidlack v. Wheelabrator Corp.,* 993 F.2d 603 (7th Cir. 1993) (parties may have intended to confer vested rights to health care upon retirees), *cert. denied,* 510 U.S. 909 (1993).

5. If retirees retain their contractually bargained-for benefits after they retire, what about employees who transfer to new jobs with the same company but in a different bargaining unit represented by a different union? The Sixth Circuit reasoned that there exists "no basis in federal labor law for treating such workers differently from retirees or other workers who have left the original bargaining unit, but who are clearly entitled to continued receipt of previously vested benefits." *Anderson v. AT&T Corp.,* 147 F.3d 467 (6th Cir. 1998), *cert. denied,* 160 L.R.R.M. 2192 (1999). Accordingly, production employees transferred from defunct plants to other plants in a nationwide downsizing were entitled to retain the wage and pension supplements which the original union had obtained for them.

6. Union-employer bargaining over employee pensions and other benefit plans has been substantially affected by the passage of the Employee Retirement Income Security Act in 1974. *See generally* Fillion & Trebilcock, *The Duty to Bargain Under ERISA,* 17 Wm. & Mary L. Rev. 251 (1975).

FIBREBOARD PAPER PRODUCTS CORP. v. NLRB

Supreme Court of the United States
379 U.S. 203, 85 S. Ct. 398, 13 L. Ed. 2d 233 (1964)

MR. CHIEF JUSTICE WARREN delivered the opinion of the Court.

This case involves the obligation of an employer and the representative of his employees under §§ 8(a)(5), 8(d) and 9(a) of the National Labor Relations Act to "confer in good faith with respect to wages, hours, and other terms and conditions of employment." The primary issue is whether the "contracting out" of work being performed by employees in the bargaining unit is a statutory subject of collective bargaining under those sections.

Petitioner, Fibreboard Paper Products Corporation (the Company), has a manufacturing plant in Emeryville, California. Since 1937 the East Bay Union Machinists, Local 1304, United Steelworkers of America, AFL-CIO (the Union) has been the exclusive bargaining representative for a unit of the Company's maintenance employees. In September 1958, the Union and the Company entered the latest of a series of collective bargaining agreements which was to expire on July 31, 1959.... On May 26, 1959, the Union gave timely notice of its desire to modify the contract and sought to arrange a bargaining session with Company representatives.... Efforts by the Union to schedule a bargaining session met with no success until July 27, four days before the expiration of the contract, when the Company notified the Union of its desire to meet....

At the July 27 meeting, the Company informed the Union that it had determined that substantial savings could be effected by contracting out the work upon expiration of its collective bargaining agreements with the various labor organizations representing its maintenance employees. The Company delivered to the Union representatives a letter which stated in pertinent part:

> For some time we have been seriously considering the question of letting out our Emeryville maintenance work to an independent contractor, and have now reached a definite decision to do so effective August 1, 1959.
>
> In these circumstances, we are sure you will realize that negotiation of a new contract would be pointless. However, if you have any questions, we will be glad to discuss them with you....

By July 30, the Company had selected Fluor Maintenance, Inc., to do the maintenance work. Fluor had assured the Company that maintenance costs could be curtailed by reducing the work force, decreasing fringe benefits and overtime payments, and by preplanning and scheduling the services to be performed. The contract provided that Fluor would: "furnish all labor, supervision and office help required for the performance of maintenance work ... at the Emeryville plant of Owner as Owner shall from time to time assign to Contractor during the period of this contract; and shall also furnish such tools, supplies and equipment in connection therewith as Owner shall order from Contractor, it being understood, however, that Owner shall ordinarily do its own purchasing of tools, supplies and equipment."

The contract further provided that the Company would pay Fluor the costs of the operation plus a fixed fee of $2,250 per month....

On July 31, the employment of the maintenance employees represented by the Union was terminated and Fluor employees took over. That evening the Union established a picket line at the Company's plant.

The Union filed unfair labor practice charges against the Company, alleging violations of §§ 8(a)(1), 8(a)(3) and 8(a)(5). After hearings were held upon a complaint issued by the National Labor Relations Board's Regional Director, the Trial Examiner filed an Intermediate Report recommending dismissal of the complaint. The Board accepted the recommendation and dismissed the complaint. 130 N.L.R.B. 1558.

Petitions for reconsideration, filed by the General Counsel and the Union, were granted. Upon reconsideration, the Board adhered to the Trial Examiner's finding that the Company's motive in contracting out its maintenance work was economic rather than antiunion but found nonetheless that the Company's "failure to negotiate with ... [the Union] concerning its decision to subcontract its maintenance work constituted a violation of Section 8(a)(5) of the Act."...

The Board ordered the Company to reinstitute the maintenance operation previously performed by the employees represented by the Union, to reinstate the employees to their former or substantially equivalent positions with back pay computed from the date of the Board's supplemental decision, and to fulfill its statutory obligation to bargain.

On appeal, the Court of Appeals for the District of Columbia Circuit granted the Board's petition for enforcement. 322 F.2d 411....

I

... Because of the limited grant of certiorari, we are concerned here only with whether the subject upon which the employer allegedly refused to bargain—contracting out of plant maintenance work previously performed by employees in the bargaining unit, which the employees were capable of continuing to perform—is covered by the phrase "terms and conditions of employment" within the meaning of § 8(d).

The subject matter of the present dispute is well within the literal meaning of the phrase "terms and conditions of employment." *See Order of Railroad Telegraphers v. Chicago & N.W.R. Co.,* 362 U.S. 330 (1960). A stipulation with respect to the contracting out of work performed by members of the bargaining unit might appropriately be called a "condition of employment." The words even more plainly cover termination of employment which, as the facts of this case indicate, necessarily results from the contracting out of work performed by members of the established bargaining unit.

The inclusion of "contracting out" within the statutory scope of collective bargaining also seems well designed to effectuate the purposes of the National Labor Relations Act. One of the primary purposes of the Act is to promote the peaceful settlement of industrial disputes by subjecting labor-management controversies to the mediatory influence of negotiation. The Act was framed with an awareness that refusals to confer and negotiate had been one of the most prolific causes of industrial strife. *NLRB v. Jones & Laughlin Steel Corp.,* 301 U.S. 1, 42-43 (1937). To hold, as the Board has done, that contracting out is a mandatory subject of collective bargaining would promote the fundamental purpose of the Act by bringing a problem of vital concern to labor and management within the framework established by Congress as most conducive to industrial peace.

The conclusion that "contracting out" is a statutory subject of collective bargaining is further reinforced by industrial practices in this country. While not determinative, it is appropriate to look to industrial bargaining practices in appraising the propriety of including a particular subject within the scope of mandatory bargaining. *NLRB v. American Nat'l Ins. Co.,* 343 U.S. 395, 408 (1952). Industrial experience is not only reflective of the interests of labor and management in the subject matter but is also indicative of the amenability of such subjects to the collective bargaining process. Experience illustrates that contracting out in one form or another has been brought, widely and successfully, within the collective bargaining framework.[6] Provisions relating to contracting out exist in numerous collective bargaining agreements,[7] and "[c]ontracting out work is the basis of many grievances; and that type of claim is grist in the mills of the arbitrators." *United Steelworkers v. Warrior & Gulf Nav. Co.,* 363 U.S. 574, 584 (1960).

The situation here is not unlike that presented in *Teamsters Union, Local 24 v. Oliver,* 358 U.S. 283 (1959), where we held that conditions imposed upon contracting out work to prevent possible curtailment of jobs and the undermining of conditions of employment for members of the bargaining unit constituted a statutory subject of collective bargaining. The issue in that case was whether state antitrust laws could be applied to a provision of a collective bargaining agreement which fixed the minimum rental to be paid by the employer motor carrier who leased vehicles to be driven by their owners rather than the carrier's employees. We held that the agreement was upon a subject matter as to which federal law directed the parties to bargain and hence that state antitrust laws could not be applied to prevent the effectuation of the agreement....

---

[6] *See* Lunden, *Subcontracting Clauses in Major Contracts,* 84 Monthly Lab. Rev. 579, 715 (1961).

[7] A Department of Labor study analyzed 1,687 collective bargaining agreements, which applied to approximately 7,500,000 workers (about one-half of the estimated work force covered by collective bargaining agreements). Among the agreements studied, approximately one-fourth (378) contained some form of a limitation on subcontracting. Lunden, *supra* at 581.

The facts of the present case illustrate the propriety of submitting the dispute to collective negotiation. The Company's decision to contract out the maintenance work did not alter the Company's basic operation. The maintenance work still had to be performed in the plant. No capital investment was contemplated; the Company merely replaced existing employees with those of an independent contractor to do the same work under similar conditions of employment. Therefore, to require the employer to bargain about the matter would not significantly abridge his freedom to manage the business.

The Company was concerned with the high cost of its maintenance operation. It was induced to contract out the work by assurances from independent contractors that economies could be derived by reducing the work force, decreasing fringe benefits, and eliminating overtime payments. These have long been regarded as matters peculiarly suitable for resolution within the collective bargaining framework, and industrial experience demonstrates that collective negotiation has been highly successful in achieving peaceful accommodation of the conflicting interests. Yet, it is contended that when an employer can effect cost savings in these respects by contracting the work out, there is no need to attempt to achieve similar economies through negotiation with existing employees or to provide them with an opportunity to negotiate a mutually acceptable alternative. The short answer is that, although it is not possible to say whether a satisfactory solution could be reached, national labor policy is founded upon the congressional determination that the chances are good enough to warrant subjecting such issues to the process of collective negotiation.

The appropriateness of the collective bargaining process for resolving such issues was apparently recognized by the Company. In explaining its decision to contract out the maintenance work, the Company pointed out that in the same plant other unions "had joined hands with management in an effort to bring about an economical and efficient operation," but "we had not been able to attain that in our discussions with this particular Local." Accordingly, based on past bargaining experience with this union, the Company unilaterally contracted out the work. While "the Act does not encourage a party to engage in fruitless marathon discussions at the expense of frank statement and support of his position," *NLRB v. American Nat'l Ins. Co.,* 343 U.S. 395, 404 (1958), it at least demands that the issue be submitted to the mediatory influence of collective negotiations. As the Court of Appeals pointed out, "it is not necessary that it be likely or probable that the union will yield or supply a feasible solution but rather that the union be afforded an opportunity to meet management's legitimate complaints that its maintenance was unduly costly."

We are thus not expanding the scope of mandatory bargaining to hold, as we do now, that the type of "contracting out" involved in this case—the replacement of employees in the existing bargaining unit with those of an independent contractor to do the same work under similar conditions of employment—is a statutory subject of collective bargaining under § 8(d). Our decision need not and does not encompass other forms of "contracting out" or "subcontracting" which arise daily in our complex economy.[8]

II

The only question remaining is whether, upon a finding that the Company had refused to bargain about a matter which is a statutory subject of collective bargaining, the Board was empowered to order the resumption of maintenance operations and reinstatement with back pay. We believe that it was so empowered....

[Section 10(c)] "charges the Board with the task of devising remedies to effectuate the policies of the Act." *NLRB v. Seven-Up Bottling Co.,* 344 U.S. 344, 346 (1953). The Board's power is a broad discretionary one, subject to limited judicial review. *Ibid.* "[T]he relation of remedy to policy is peculiarly a matter for administrative competence...." *Phelps Dodge Corp. v. NLRB,* 313 U.S. 177, 194 (1941). "In fashioning remedies to undo the effects of violations of the Act, the Board must draw on enlightenment gained from experience." *NLRB v. Seven-Up Bottling Co.,* 344 U.S. 344, 346 (1953). The Board's order will not be disturbed "unless it can be shown that the order is a patent attempt to achieve ends other than those which can fairly be said to effectuate the policies of the Act." *Virginia Elec. & Power Co. v. NLRB,* 319 U.S. 533, 540 (1943). Such a showing has not been made in this case.

There has been no showing that the Board's order restoring the status quo ante to insure meaningful bargaining is not well designed to promote the policies of the Act. Nor is there evidence which would justify disturbing the Board's conclusion that the order would not impose an undue or unfair burden on the Company.[10]

It is argued, nonetheless, that the award exceeds the Board's powers under § 10(c) in that it infringes the provision that "[n]o order of the Board shall require the reinstatement of any individual as an employee who has been suspended or discharged, or the payment to him of any back pay, if such individual was suspended or discharged for cause...." The legislative history of that provision indicates that it was designed to preclude the Board from reinstating an individual who had been discharged because of misconduct. There is no indication, how-

---

[8] As the Solicitor General points out, the terms "contracting out" and "subcontracting" have no precise meaning. They are used to describe a variety of business arrangements altogether different from that involved in this case. For a discussion of the various types of "contracting out" or "subcontracting" arrangements, see Brief for Respondent, pp. 13-17; Brief for Electronic Industries Association as *amicus curiae,* pp. 5-10.

[10] The Board stated: "We do not believe that requirement [restoring the *status quo ante*] imposes an undue or unfair burden on Respondent. The record shows that the maintenance operation is still being performed in much the same manner as it was prior to the subcontracting arrangement. Respondent has a continuing need for the services of maintenance employees; and Respondent's subcontract is terminable at any time upon 60 days' notice." 138 N.L.R.B. at 555, n. 19.

ever, that it was designed to curtail the Board's power in fashioning remedies when the loss of employment stems directly from an unfair labor practice as in the case at hand.

The judgment of the Court of Appeals is

Affirmed.

MR. JUSTICE GOLDBERG took no part in the consideration or decision of this case.

MR. JUSTICE STEWART, with whom MR. JUSTICE DOUGLAS and MR. JUSTICE HARLAN join, concurring.

....

The question posed is whether the particular decision sought to be made unilaterally by the employer in this case is a subject of mandatory collective bargaining within the statutory phrase "terms and conditions of employment." That is all the Court decides. The Court most assuredly does not decide that every managerial decision which necessarily terminates an individual's employment is subject to the duty to bargain. Nor does the Court decide that subcontracting decisions are as a general matter subject to that duty. The Court holds no more than that this employer's decision to subcontract this work, involving "the replacement of employees in the existing bargaining unit with those of an independent contractor to do the same work under similar conditions of employment" is subject to the duty to bargain collectively. Within the narrow limitations implicit in the specific facts of this case, I agree with the Court's decision....

While employment security has thus properly been recognized in various circumstances as a condition of employment, it surely does not follow that every decision which may affect job security is a subject of compulsory collective bargaining. Many decisions made by management affect the job security of employees. Decisions concerning the volume and kind of advertising expenditures, product design, the manner of financing, and of sales, all may bear upon the security of the workers' jobs. Yet it is hardly conceivable that such decisions so involve "conditions of employment" that they must be negotiated with the employees' bargaining representative.

In many of these areas the impact of a particular management decision upon job security may be extremely indirect and uncertain, and this alone may be sufficient reason to conclude that such decisions are not "with respect to ... conditions of employment." Yet there are other areas where decisions by management may quite clearly imperil job security, or indeed terminate employment entirely. An enterprise may decide to invest in labor-saving machinery. Another may resolve to liquidate its assets and go out of business. Nothing the Court holds today should be understood as imposing a duty to bargain collectively regarding such managerial decisions, which lie at the core of entrepreneurial control....

Applying these concepts to the case at hand, I do not believe that an employer's subcontracting practices are, as a general matter, in themselves conditions of employment. Upon any definition of the statutory terms short of the most expansive, such practices are not conditions—tangible or intangible—of any person's employment. The question remains whether this particular kind of subcontracting decision comes within the employer's duty to bargain. On the facts of this case, I join the Court's judgment, because all that is involved is the substitution of one group of workers for another to perform the same task in the same plant under the ultimate control of the same employer. The question whether the employer may discharge one group of workers and substitute another for them is closely analogous to many other situations within the traditional framework of collective bargaining. Compulsory retirement, layoffs according to seniority, assignment of work among potentially eligible groups within the plant—all involve similar questions of discharge and work assignment, and all have been recognized as subjects of compulsory collective bargaining....

This kind of subcontracting falls short of such larger entrepreneurial questions as what shall be produced, how capital shall be invested in fixed assets, or what the basic scope of the enterprise shall be. In my view, the Court's decision in this case has nothing to do with whether any aspects of those larger issues could under any circumstances be considered subjects of compulsory collective bargaining under the present law....

NOTES

1. Over the past three decades, the most controversial issue regarding the scope of the duty to bargain has been the extent to which employers must negotiate about managerial decisions that result in a shrinkage of employee job opportunities. The NLRB for a long time held that in the absence of antiunion animus, management did not have to bargain over decisions to subcontract, relocate operations, or introduce technological improvements, although it did have to bargain about the *effects* of such decisions on the employees displaced. Layoff schedules, severance pay, and transfer rights were thus bargainable, but the basic decision to discontinue an operation was not. *See, e.g., Brown-McLaren Mfg. Co.,* 34 N.L.R.B. 984 (1941); *Brown-Dunkin Co.,* 125 N.L.R.B. 1379 (1959), *enforced,* 287 F.2d 17 (10th Cir. 1961). Under the so-called Kennedy Board, however, a whole range of managerial decisions were reclassified as mandatory subjects of bargaining. These included decisions to terminate a department and subcontract its work, *Town & Country Mfg. Co.,* 136 N.L.R.B. 1022 (1962), *enforced,* 316 F.2d 846 (5th Cir. 1963); to consolidate operations through technological innovations, *Renton News Record,* 136 N.L.R.B. 1294 (1962); and to close one plant of a multiplant enterprise, *Ozark Trailers, Inc.,* 161 N.L.R.B. 561 (1966).

The direction and rationale of the Board during this period were indicated in *Westinghouse Elec. Corp.,* 150 N.L.R.B. 1574 (1965), when it stated that the unilateral contracting out of unit work would violate § 8(a)(5) where it "involved a departure from previously established operating practices, effected a change in conditions of employment, or resulted in a significant impairment of job tenure, employment security, or reasonably anticipated work opportunities for those in the bargaining unit."

Later, beginning in the Nixon-Ford era, the NLRB seemed to back away from some of the rulings of the Kennedy Board. This was exemplified by *Summit Tooling Co.,* 195 N.L.R.B. 479 (1972), *enforced,* 83 L.R.R.M. 2044 (7th Cir. 1973), where an employer closed the manufacturing portion of its operations without prior bargaining. Even though the shutdown could be characterized as a partial plant closing, a 2-1 Board majority held that the employer did not violate § 8(a)(5) by its failure to bargain concerning its decision to terminate the manufacturing division. To require bargaining "would significantly abridge Respondent's freedom to manage its own affairs." *See also General Motors Corp.,* 191 N.L.R.B. 951 (1971) (sale of dealership; two Board members dissenting), *aff'd sub nom. UAW Local 864 v. NLRB,* 470 F.2d 422 (D.C. Cir. 1972) (one judge dissenting). Under the Kennedy Board as well as its successors, there was uncertainty about an employer's obligation to bargain over an economically motivated decision to relocate a plant or certain operations. *See Garwin Corp.,* 153 N.L.R.B. 664, 665, 680 (1965), *enforced in part,* 374 F.2d 295 (D.C. Cir.), *cert. denied,* 387 U.S. 942 (1967); *Cooper Thermometer Co.,* 160 N.L.R.B. 1902 (1966), *enforced,* 376 F.2d 684 (2d Cir. 1967); *Westinghouse Elec. Corp.,* 174 N.L.R.B. 636 (1969). A critical factor in relocation cases may be the severity of any adverse impact on unit jobs. But apparently there is no duty to bargain about a decision to go completely out of business. *See Textile Workers v. Darlington Mfg. Co.,* 380 U.S. 263, 267 n.5 (1965).

Meanwhile, the courts of appeals had become hopelessly divided in their reaction to the Labor Board's "partial closing" doctrine, thus paving the way for the Supreme Court decision in the principal case that follows next. For a good account of these judicial meanderings, *see Brockway Motor Trucks Div. v. NLRB,* 582 F.2d 720, 727-31 (3d Cir. 1978), *noted in* 92 Harv. L. Rev. 768 (1979).

2. What remedy should the Board provide when an employer institutes job changes without fulfilling its duty to bargain? Should it always order resumption of the discontinued operations, as in *Fibreboard?* What if this will cause the employer severe financial loss, or prevent it from competing economically in the market? On the other hand, if the status quo ante is not restored, how can the union engage in meaningful bargaining even about the effects of the changes on the employees? For consideration of these questions, *see Renton News Record, supra.*

Restoration of an employer's operation was held improper under § 10(j)'s temporary injunction provision, even though the NLRB had met its "relatively insubstantial" burden of showing reasonable cause to believe the employer had unlawfully subcontracted bargaining unit work and laid off the employees, since it would impose undue hardship on the employer and was not necessary to preserve the Board's ultimate remedial authority. *Calatrello v. "Automatic" Sprinkler Corp. of Am.,* 55 F.3d 208 (6th Cir. 1995). On the other hand, the Third Circuit granted the Board's request for a § 10(j) injunction to block the sale of a unionized plant pending the Board's final resolution of unfair labor practice charges based on the employer's threat to close the plant in the event of a strike. *See Hirsch v. Dorsey Trailers, Inc.,* 147 F.3d 243 (3d Cir. 1998). Because sale of the plant would have rendered the Board powerless to order the work returned to the plant, a remedy that the ALJ hearing the case had already concluded was appropriate, any negative financial impact on the company was of its own making, and injunctive relief was justified.

If an employer unlawfully moves a plant without prior bargaining, may the Board order it to bargain at the new location despite the union's lack of a majority status there? How would this affect the rights of the employees at the new plant? *See Garwin Corp., supra.* Where an employer unlawfully failed to bargain over the effects of closing one of its plants, the NLRB ordered it to pay terminated employees their normal wages until (1) the parties bargained to agreement, (2) an impasse occurred, (3) the union failed to request bargaining within a stipulated period, or (4) the union failed to bargain in good faith. No employee was to be paid, however, beyond the date he secured equivalent employment elsewhere or beyond the date the employer went out of business entirely. *Royal Plating & Polishing Co.,* 160 N.L.R.B. 990 (1966).

3. Contemporaneous critiques of *Fibreboard* and its kin may be found in Farmer, *Good Faith Bargaining Over Subcontracting,* 51 Geo. L.J. 558 (1963); Goetz, *The Duty to Bargain About Changes in Operations,* 1964 Duke L.J. 1; Platt, *The Duty to Bargain as Applied to Management Decisions,* 19 Lab. L.J. 143 (1968); Rabin, *Fibreboard and the Termination of Bargaining Unit Work: The Search for Standards in Defining the Scope of the Duty to Bargain,* 71 Colum. L. Rev. 803 (1971); Rabin, *The Decline and Fall of Fibreboard,* in N.Y.U. Twenty-Fourth Annual Conference on Labor 237 (1972); Smith, *Subcontracting and Union-Management Legal and Contractual Relations,* 17 W. Res. L. Rev. 1278 (1966); Schwartz, *Plant Relocation or Partial Termination—The Duty to Decision-Bargain,* 39 Fordham L. Rev. 81 (1970).

FIRST NATIONAL MAINTENANCE CORP. v. NLRB

Supreme Court of the United States
452 U.S. 666, 101 S. Ct. 2573, 69 L. Ed. 2d 318 (1981)

JUSTICE BLACKMUN delivered the opinion of the Court.

Must an employer, under its duty to bargain in good faith "with respect to wages, hours, and other terms and conditions of employment," §§ 8(d) and

8(a)(5) of the National Labor Relations Act, as amended, negotiate with the certified representative of its employees over its decision to close a part of its business? In this case, the National Labor Relations Board (the Board) imposed such
a duty on petitioner with respect to its decision to terminate a contract with a
customer, and the United States Court of Appeals, although differing over the
appropriate rationale, enforced its order.

I

Petitioner, First National Maintenance Corporation (FNM), is a New York
corporation engaged in the business of providing housekeeping, cleaning, maintenance, and related services for commercial customers in the New York City
area. It supplies each of its customers, at the customer's premises, contracted-for
labor force and supervision in return for reimbursement of its labor costs (gross
salaries, FICA and FUTA taxes, and insurance) and payment of a set fee. It contracts for and hires personnel separately for each customer, and it does not transfer employees between locations.

During the Spring of 1977, petitioner was performing maintenance work for
the Greenpark Care Center, a nursing home in Brooklyn. Its written agreement
dated April 28, 1976, with Greenpark specified that Greenpark "shall furnish all
tools, equipment [sic], materials, and supplies," and would pay petitioner weekly
"the sum of five hundred dollars plus the gross weekly payroll and fringe benefits." Its weekly fee, however, had been reduced to $250 effective November 1,
1976. The contract prohibited Greenpark from hiring any of petitioner's employees during the term of the contract and for 90 days thereafter. Petitioner employed approximately 35 workers in its Greenpark operation.

Petitioner's business relationship with Greenpark, seemingly, was not very
remunerative or smooth.... On June 30, [1977], by telephone, it asked that its
weekly fee be restored at the $500 figure and, on July 6, it informed Greenpark in
writing that it would discontinue its operations there on August 1 unless the increase were granted. By telegram on July 25, petitioner gave final notice of termination.

While FNM was experiencing these difficulties, District 1199, National Union
of Hospital and Health Care Employees, Retail, Wholesale and Department Store
Union, AFL-CIO (the union), was conducting an organization campaign among
petitioner's Greenpark employees. On March 31, 1977, at a Board-conducted
election, a majority of the employees selected the union as their bargaining agent.
On July 12, the union's vice president, Edward Wecker, wrote petitioner, notifying it of the certification and of the union's right to bargain, and stating: "We
look forward to meeting with you or your representative for that purpose. Please
advise when it will be convenient." Petitioner neither responded nor sought to
consult with the union.

On July 28, petitioner notified its Greenpark employees that they would be discharged 3 days later. Wecker immediately telephoned petitioner's secretary-treasurer, Leonard Marsh, to request a delay for the purpose of bargaining. Marsh refused the offer to bargain and told Wecker that the termination of the Greenpark operation was purely a matter of money, and final, and that the 30-days' notice provision of the Greenpark contract made staying on beyond August 1 prohibitively expensive.... With nothing but perfunctory further discussion, petitioner on July 31 discontinued its Greenpark operation and discharged the employees.

The union filed an unfair labor practice charge against petitioner, alleging violations of the Act's §§ 8(a)(1) and (5). After a hearing held upon the Regional Director's complaint, the administrative law judge made findings in the union's favor. Relying on *Ozark Trailers, Inc.*, 161 N.L.R.B. 561 (1966), he ruled that petitioner had failed to satisfy its duty to bargain concerning both the decision to terminate the Greenpark contract and the effect of that change upon the unit employees.... The National Labor Relations Board adopted the administrative law judge's findings without further analysis....

The United States Court of Appeals for the Second Circuit, with one judge dissenting in part, enforced the Board's order, although it adopted an analysis different from that espoused by the Board. 627 F.2d 596 (1980). The Court of Appeals reasoned that no *per se* rule could be formulated to govern an employer's decision to close part of its business. Rather, the court said, § 8(d) creates a *presumption* in favor of mandatory bargaining over such a decision, a presumption that is rebuttable "by showing that the purposes of the statute would not be furthered by imposition of a duty to bargain," for example, by demonstrating that "bargaining over the decision would be futile," or that the decision was due to "emergency financial circumstances," or that the "custom of the industry, shown by the absence of such an obligation from typical collective bargaining agreements, is not to bargain over such decisions." *Id.*, at 601-602.

The Court of Appeals' decision in this case appears to be at odds with decisions of other Courts of Appeals, some of which decline to require bargaining over any management decision involving "a major commitment of capital investment" or a "basic operational change" in the scope or direction of an enterprise, and some of which indicate that bargaining is not mandated unless a violation of § 8(b)(3) (a partial closing motivated by antiunion animus) is involved. The Court of Appeals for the Fifth Circuit has imposed a duty to bargain over partial closing decisions. *See NLRB v. Winn-Dixie Stores, Inc.*, 361 F.2d 512, *cert. denied*, 385 U.S. 935 (1966). The Board itself has not been fully consistent in its rulings applicable to this type of management decision....

II

Although parties are free to bargain about any legal subject, Congress has limited the mandate or duty to bargain to matters of "wages, hours, and other terms and conditions of employment." A unilateral change as to a subject within this category violates the statutory duty to bargain and is subject to the Board's remedial order. *NLRB v. Katz,* 369 U.S. 736 (1962). Conversely, both employer and union may bargain to impasse over these matters and use the economic weapons at their disposal to attempt to secure their respective aims. *NLRB v. American National Ins. Co.,* 343 U.S. 395 (1952).[13] Congress deliberately left the words "wages, hours, and other terms and conditions of employment" without further definition, for it did not intend to deprive the Board of the power further to define those terms in light of specific industrial practices.[14]

Nonetheless, in establishing what issues must be submitted to the process of bargaining, Congress had no expectation that the elected union representative would become an equal partner in the running of the business enterprise in which the union's members are employed. Despite the deliberate open-endedness of the statutory language, there is an undeniable limit to the subjects about which bargaining must take place....

Some management decisions, such as choice of advertising and promotion, product type and design, and financing arrangements, have only an indirect and attenuated impact on the employment relationship. *See Fibreboard,* 379 U.S., at 223 (Stewart, J., concurring). Other management decisions, such as the order of

---

[13] A matter that is not a mandatory subject of bargaining, unless it is illegal, may be raised at the bargaining table to be discussed in good faith, and the parties may incorporate it into an enforceable collective bargaining agreement. Labor and management may not, however, insist on it to the point of impasse. *NLRB v. Borg-Warner Corp.,* 356 U.S. 342 (1958).

[14] In enacting the Labor Management Relations Act, 1947, Congress rejected a proposal in the House to limit the subjects of bargaining to "(i) [w]age rates, hours of employment, and work requirements; (ii) procedures and practices relating to discharge, suspension, lay-off, recall, seniority, and discipline, or to promotion, demotion, transfer and assignment within the bargaining unit; (iii) conditions, procedures, and practices governing safety, sanitation, and protection of health at the place of employment; (iv) vacations and leaves of absence; and (v) administrative and procedural provisions relating to the foregoing subjects." H.R. 3020 § 2(11), 80th Cong., 1st Sess. (1947).

The adoption, instead, of the general phrase now part of § 8(d) was clearly meant to preserve future interpretation by the Board. *See* H.R. Rep. No. 245, 80th Cong., 1st Sess., 71 (1947) (minority report) ("The appropriate scope of collective bargaining cannot be determined by a formula; it will inevitably depend upon the traditions of an industry, the social and political climate at any given time, the needs of employers and employees, and many related factors. What are proper subject matters for collective bargaining should be left in the first instance to employers and trade-unions, and in the second place, to any administrative agency skilled in the field and competent to devote the necessary time to a study of industrial practices and traditions in each industry or area of the country, subject to review by the courts. It cannot and should not be strait-jacketed by legislative enactment."); H.R. Conf. Rep. No. 510, 80th Cong., 1st Sess., 34-35 (1947). Specific references in the legislative history to plant closings, however, are inconclusive. See 79 Cong. Rec. 7673, 9682 (1935) (comments of Sen. Walsh and Rep. Griswold).

succession of layoffs and recalls, production quotas, and work rules, are almost exclusively "an aspect of the relationship" between employer and employee. *Chemical Workers*, 404 U.S., at 178. The present case concerns a third type of management decision, one that had a direct impact on employment, since jobs were inexorably eliminated by the termination, but had as its focus only the economic profitability of the contract with Greenpark, a concern under these facts wholly apart from the employment relationship. This decision, involving a change in the scope and direction of the enterprise, is akin to the decision whether to be in business at all, "not in [itself] primarily about conditions of employment, though the effect of the decision may be necessarily to terminate employment." *Fibreboard*, 379 U.S., at 223 (Stewart, J., concurring). *Cf. Textile Workers v. Darlington Co.*, 380 U.S. 263, 268 (1965) ("an employer has the absolute right to terminate its entire business for any reason it pleases"). At the same time, this decision touches on a matter of central and pressing concern to the union and its member employees: the possibility of continued employment and the retention of the employees' very jobs. *See Brockway Motor Trucks, Etc. v. NLRB*, 582 F.2d 720, 735-736 (CA3 1978); *Ozark Trailers, Inc.*, 161 N.L.R.B. 561, 566-568 (1966).

Petitioner contends it had no duty to bargain about its decision to terminate its operations at Greenpark. This contention requires that we determine whether the decision itself should be considered part of petitioner's retained freedom to manage its affairs unrelated to employment.[15] The aim of labeling a matter a mandatory subject of bargaining, rather than simply permitting, but not requiring, bargaining, is to "promote the fundamental purpose of the Act by bringing a problem of vital concern to labor and management within the framework established by Congress as most conducive to industrial peace," *Fibreboard*, 379 U.S., at 211. The concept of mandatory bargaining is premised on the belief that collective discussions backed by the parties' economic weapons will result in decisions that are better for both management and labor and for society as a whole. *Ford Motor Co.*, 441 U.S., at 500-501; *Borg-Warner*, 356 U.S., at 350 (condemning employer's proposal of "ballot" clause as weakening the collective-bargaining process). This will be true, however, only if the subject proposed for discussion is amenable to resolution through the bargaining process. Management must be free from the constraints of the bargaining process[17] to the extent

---

[15] There is no doubt that petitioner was under a duty to bargain about the results or effects of its decision to stop the work at Greenpark, or that it violated that duty. Petitioner consented to enforcement of the Board's order concerning bargaining over the effects of the closing and has reached agreement with the union on severance pay.

[17] The employer has no obligation to abandon its intentions or to agree with union proposals. On proper subjects, it must meet with the union, provide information necessary to the union's understanding of the problem, and in good faith consider any proposals the union advances. In concluding to reject a union's position as to a mandatory subject, however, it must face the union's possible use of strike power....

essential for the running of a profitable business. It also must have some degree of certainty beforehand as to when it may proceed to reach decisions without fear of later evaluations labeling its conduct an unfair labor practice. Congress did not explicitly state what issues of mutual concern to union and management it intended to exclude from mandatory bargaining. Nonetheless, in view of an employer's need for unencumbered decisionmaking, bargaining over management decisions that have a substantial impact on the continued availability of employment should be required only if the benefit, for labor-management relations and the collective bargaining process, outweighs the burden placed on the conduct of the business.

The Court in *Fibreboard* implicitly engaged in this analysis with regard to decision to subcontract for maintenance work previously done by unit employees. Holding the employer's decision a subject of mandatory bargaining, the Court relied not only on the "literal meaning" of the statutory words, but also reasoned:

> The Company's decision to contract out the maintenance work did not alter the Company's basic operation. The maintenance work still had to be performed in the plant. No capital investment was contemplated; the Company merely replaced existing employees with those of an independent contractor to do the same work under similar conditions of employment. Therefore, to require the employer to bargain about the matter would not significantly abridge his freedom to manage the business. 379 U.S. at 213.

The Court also emphasized that a desire to reduce labor costs, which it considered a matter "peculiarly suitable for resolution within the collective bargaining framework," was at the base of the employer's decision to subcontract. The prevalence of bargaining over "contracting out" as a matter of industrial practice generally was taken as further proof of the "amenability of such subjects to the collective bargaining process."

With this approach in mind, we turn to the specific issue at hand: an economically-motivated decision to shut down part of a business.

III

A. Both union and management regard control of the decision to shut down an operation with the utmost seriousness. As has been noted, however, the Act is not intended to serve either party's individual interest, but to foster in a neutral manner a system in which the conflict between these interests may be resolved. It seems particularly important, therefore, to consider whether requiring bargaining over this sort of decision will advance the neutral purposes of the Act.

A union's interest in participating in the decision to close a particular facility or part of an employer's operations springs from its legitimate concern over job security. The Court has observed: "The words of [§ 8(d)] ... plainly cover termination of employment which ... necessarily results" from closing an operation.

Fibreboard, 379 U.S. at 210. The union's practical purpose in participating, however, will be largely uniform: it will seek to delay or halt the closing. No doubt it will be impelled, in seeking these ends, to offer concessions, information, and alternatives that might be helpful to management or forestall or prevent the termination of jobs.[19] It is unlikely, however, that requiring bargaining over the decision itself, as well as its effects, will augment this flow of information and suggestions. There is no dispute that the union must be given a significant opportunity to bargain about these matters of job security as part of the "effects" bargaining mandated by § 8(a)(5). And, under § 8(a)(5), bargaining over the effects of a decision must be conducted in a meaningful manner and at a meaningful time, and the Board may impose sanctions to insure its adequacy. A union, by pursuing such bargaining rights, may achieve valuable concessions from an employer engaged in a partial closing. It also may secure in contract negotiations provisions implementing rights to notice, information, and fair bargaining.

Moreover, the union's legitimate interest in fair dealing is protected by § 8(a)(3) which prohibits partial closings motivated by anti-union animus, when done to gain an unfair advantage. *Textile Workers v. Darlington Co.,* 380 U.S. 263 (1965). Under § 8(a)(3) the Board may inquire into the motivations behind a partial closing. An employer may not simply shut down part of its business and mask its desire to weaken and circumvent the union by labeling its decision "purely economic."

Thus, although the union has a natural concern that a partial closing decision not be hastily or unnecessarily entered into, it has some control over the effects of the decision and indirectly may ensure that the decision itself is deliberately considered. It also has direct protection against a partial closing decision that is motivated by an intent to harm a union.

Management's interest in whether it should discuss a decision of this kind is much more complex and varies with the particular circumstances. If labor costs are an important factor in a failing operation and the decision to close, management will have an incentive to confer voluntarily with the union to seek concessions that may make continuing the business profitable. At other times, management may have great need for speed, flexibility, and secrecy in meeting business opportunities and exigencies. It may face significant tax or securities conse-

---

[19] We are aware of past instances where unions have aided employers in saving failing businesses by lending technical assistance, reducing wages and benefits or increasing production, and even loaning part of earned wages to forestall closures. *See* S. Slichter, J. Healy & E. Livernash, The Impact of Collective Bargaining on Management 845-851 (1960); C. Golden & H. Rutenberg, The Dynamics of Industrial Democracy 263-291 (1942). *See also United Steel Workers, Etc. v. U.S. Steel Corp.,* 492 F. Supp. 1 (ND Ohio), *aff'd in part and vacated in part,* 631 F.2d 1264 (CA6 1980) (union sought to purchase failing plant); 104 Lab. Rel. Rep. 239 (1980) (employee ownership plan instituted to save company); *id.,* at 267-268 (union accepted pay cuts to reduce plant's financial problems). These have come about without the intervention of the Board enforcing a statutory requirement to bargain.

quences that hinge on confidentiality, the timing of a plant closing, or a reorganization of the corporate structure. The publicity incident to the normal process of bargaining may injure the possibility of a successful transition or increase the economic damage to the business. The employer also may have no feasible alternative to the closing, and even good-faith bargaining over it may be both futile and cause the employer additional loss.

There is an important difference, also, between permitted bargaining and mandated bargaining. Labeling this type of decision mandatory could afford a union a powerful tool for achieving delay, a power that might be used to thwart management's intentions in a manner unrelated to any feasible solution the union might propose. In addition, many of the cases before the Board have involved, as this one did, not simply a refusal to bargain over the decision, but a refusal to bargain at all, often coupled with other unfair labor practices. In these cases, the employer's action gave the Board reason to order remedial relief apart from access to the decisionmaking process. It is not clear that a union would be equally dissatisfied if an employer performed all its bargaining obligations apart from the additional remedy sought here.

While evidence of current labor practice is only an indication of what is feasible through collective bargaining, and not a binding guide, *see Chemical Workers,* 404 U.S., at 176, that evidence supports the apparent imbalance weighing against mandatory bargaining. We note that provisions giving unions a right to participate in the decisionmaking process concerning alteration of the scope of an enterprise appear to be relatively rare. Provisions concerning notice and "effects" bargaining are more prevalent.

Further, the presumption analysis adopted by the court of appeals seems ill suited to advance harmonious relations between employer and employee. An employer would have difficulty determining beforehand whether it was faced with a situation requiring bargaining or one that involved economic necessity sufficiently compelling to obviate the duty to bargain. If it should decide to risk not bargaining, it might be faced ultimately with harsh remedies forcing it to pay large amounts of backpay to employees who likely would have been discharged regardless of bargaining, or even to consider reopening a failing operation. Also, labor costs may not be a crucial circumstance in a particular economically-based partial termination. And in those cases, the Board's traditional remedies may well be futile. If the employer intended to try to fulfill a court's direction to bargain, it would have difficulty determining exactly at what stage of its deliberations the duty to bargain would arise and what amount of bargaining would suffice before it could implement its decision. If an employer engaged in some discussion, but did not yield to the union's demands, the Board might conclude that the employer had engaged in "surface bargaining," a violation of its good faith. A union, too, would have difficulty determining the limits of its prerogatives, whether and when it could use its economic powers to try to alter an employer's decision, or whether, in doing so, it would trigger sanctions from the Board.

We conclude that the harm likely to be done to an employer's need to operate freely in deciding whether to shut down part of its business purely for economic reasons outweighs the incremental benefit that might be gained through the union's participation in making the decision,[22] and we hold that the decision itself is *not* part of § 8(d)'s "terms and conditions," over which Congress has mandated bargaining.[23]

B. In order to illustrate the limits of our holding, we turn again to the specific facts of this case. First, we note that when petitioner decided to terminate its Greenpark contract, it had no intention to replace the discharged employees or to move that operation elsewhere. Petitioner's sole purpose was to reduce its economic loss, and the union made no claim of anti-union animus. In addition, petitioner's dispute with Greenpark was solely over the size of the management fee Greenpark was willing to pay. The union had no control or authority over that fee. The most that the union could have offered would have been advice and concessions that Greenpark, the third party upon whom rested the success or failure of the contract, had no duty even to consider. These facts in particular distinguish this case from the subcontracting issue presented in *Fibreboard*. Further, the union was not selected as the bargaining representative or certified until well after petitioner's economic difficulties at Greenpark had begun. We thus are not faced with an employer's abrogation of ongoing negotiations or an existing bargaining agreement. Finally, while petitioner's business enterprise did not involve the investment of large amounts of capital in single locations, we do not believe that the absence of "significant investment or withdrawal of capital" is crucial. The decision to halt work at this specific location represented a significant change in petitioner's operations, a change not unlike opening a new line of business or going out of business entirely.

---

[22] In this opinion we of course intimate no view as to other types of management decisions, such as plant relocations, sales, other kinds of subcontracting, automation, etc., which are to be considered on their particular facts.

[23] Despite the contentions of *amicus* AFL-CIO our decision in *Order of Railroad Telegraphers v. Chicago & N.W.R. Co.,* 362 U.S. 330 (1960), does not require that we find bargaining over this partial closing decision mandatory. Although the Court in part relied on an expansive interpretation of § 2, first, which requires railroads to "exert every reasonable effort to make and maintain agreements concerning rates of pay, rules, and working conditions," and § 13(c) the Norris-LaGuardia Act, 29 U.S.C. § 113(c), defining "labor dispute" as "any controversy concerning terms or conditions of employment," its decision also rested on the particular aims of the Railway Labor Act and national transportation policy. *See* 362 U.S., at 336-338. The mandatory scope of bargaining under the Railway Labor Act and the extent of the prohibition against injunctive relief contained in Norris-LaGuardia are not coextensive with the National Labor Relations Act and the Board's jurisdiction over unfair labor practices. *See Chicago & N.W.R. Co. v. Transportation Union,* 402 U.S. 570, 579, n. 11 (1971) ("parallels between the duty to bargain in good faith and the duty to exert every reasonable effort, like all parallels between the NLRA and the Railway Labor Act, should be drawn with the utmost care and with full awareness of the differences between the statutory schemes").

The judgment of the court of appeals, accordingly, is reversed and the case is remanded to that court for further proceedings consistent with this opinion.

JUSTICE BRENNAN, with whom JUSTICE MARSHALL joins, dissenting.

....

I respectfully dissent.

The Court bases its decision on a balancing test. It states that "bargaining over management decisions that have a substantial impact on the continued availability of employment should be required only if the benefit, for labor-management relations and the collective-bargaining process, outweighs the burden placed on the conduct of the business." I cannot agree with this test, because it takes into account only the interests of *management;* it fails to consider the legitimate employment interests of the workers and their Union. *Cf. Brockway Motor Trucks v. NLRB,* 582 F.2d 720, 734-740 (CA3 1978) (balancing of interests of workers in retaining their jobs against interests of employers in maintaining unhindered control over corporate direction). This one-sided approach hardly serves "to foster in a neutral manner" a system for resolution of these serious, two-sided controversies.

Even if the Court's statement of the test were accurate, I could not join in its application, which is based solely on speculation. Apparently, the Court concludes that the benefit to labor-management relations and the collective-bargaining process from negotiation over partial closings is minimal, but it provides no evidence to that effect. The Court acknowledges that the Union might be able to offer concessions, information, and alternatives that might obviate or forestall the closing, but it then asserts that "[i]t is unlikely, however, that requiring bargaining over the decision ... will augment this flow of information and suggestions." Recent experience, however, suggests the contrary. Most conspicuous, perhaps, were the negotiations between Chrysler Corporation and the United Auto Workers, which led to significant adjustments in compensation and benefits, contributing to Chrysler's ability to remain afloat. Even where labor costs are not the direct cause of a company's financial difficulties, employee concessions can often enable the company to continue in operation—if the employees have the opportunity to offer such concessions.

The Court further presumes that management's need for "speed, flexibility, and secrecy" in making partial closing decisions would be frustrated by a requirement to bargain. In some cases the Court might be correct. In others, however, the decision will be made openly and deliberately, and considerations of "speed, flexibility, and secrecy" will be inapposite. Indeed, in view of management's admitted duty to bargain over the effects of a closing, it is difficult to understand why additional bargaining over the closing itself would necessarily unduly delay or publicize the decision.

I am not in a position to judge whether mandatory bargaining over partial closings *in all cases* is consistent with our national labor policy, and neither is the

Court. The primary responsibility to determine the scope of the statutory duty to bargain has been entrusted to the NLRB, which should not be reversed by the courts merely because they might prefer another view of the statute. I therefore agree with the Court of Appeals that employers presumptively have a duty to bargain over a decision to close an operation, and that this presumption can be rebutted by a showing that bargaining would be futile, that the closing as due to emergency financial circumstances, or that, for some other reason, bargaining would not further the purposes of the National Labor Relations Act.

NOTES

1. How much importance should be attached to the "limits" on its holding mentioned by the Court in Part III-B of the opinion? *First National Maintenance* was soon given a broad reading in *NLRB v. Robin Am. Corp.,* 667 F.2d 1170 (5th Cir. 1982), which limited enforcement of a bargaining order to the closing of a particular department that had been discontinued for antiunion reasons. The court of appeals understood the Supreme Court to be "overruling" previous doctrine imposing a general duty to bargain over partial closing decisions, including economically motivated closings.

2. What effect, if any, might *First National Maintenance* be expected to have on the growing movement in this country for increased worker participation in management decisionmaking through so-called "quality of work life" programs and the like? *See, e.g.,* Fischer, Shaw, Weinberg, *The Impact of Experiments in Labor-Management Cooperation on Collective Bargaining Practices,* in N.Y.U. Thirty-Fifth Annual Conference on Labor 89 (1982) (three separate papers); Harper, *Reconciling Collective Bargaining with Employee Supervision of Management,* 137 U. Pa. L. Rev. 1 (1988); St. Antoine, *Legal Barriers to Worker Participation in Management Decision Making,* 58 Tulane L. Rev. 1301 (1984); Wallace & Driscoll, *Social Issues in Collective Bargaining,* in J. Stieber, R. McKersie & D. Mills, eds., U.S. Industrial Relations 1950-1980: A Critical Assessment 238 (1981). *Cf.* Summers, *Industrial Democracy: America's Unfulfilled Promise,* 28 Clev. St. L. Rev. 29 (1979); Hyde, *In Defense of Employee Ownership,* 67 Chi.-Kent L. Rev. 159 (1991).

3. Scholarly reactions to *First National Maintenance* include Harper, *Leveling the Road from Borg-Warner to First National Maintenance: The Scope of Mandatory Bargaining,* 68 Va. L. Rev. 1447 (1982); Irving, *Closing and Sales of Businesses: A Settled Area?* 33 Lab. L.J. 218 (1982); Kohler, *Distinctions Without Differences: Effects Bargaining in Light of First National Maintenance,* 5 Indus. Rel. L.J. 402 (1983); P. Miscimarra, *The NLRB and Managerial Discretion* (1983). *See also* Heinsz, *Partial Closing Conundrum: The Duty of Employers and Unions to Bargain in Good Faith,* 1981 Duke L.J. 71; Note, *Mandatory Bargaining and the Disposition of Closed Plants,* 95 Harv. L. Rev. 1896 (1982); Note, *Leading the Horse to Water: The Employer's Duty to Bargain After First*

National Maintenance, 65 Chi.-Kent L. Rev. 555 (1989); Note, *Decision-Bargaining and the NLRA—A Plea for the Resurrection of First National Maintenance,* 68 Tex. L. Rev. 625 (1990).

Dubuque Packing Co., 303 N.L.R.B. 386 (1991), *enforced sub nom. Food & Commercial Workers Local 150-A v. NLRB,* 1 F.3d 24 (D.C. Cir. 1993), *cert. dismissed,* 511 U.S. 1138 (1994). An employer was held to have violated § 8(a)(5) by failing to bargain with the union over the relocation of its hog slaughtering operations from its home plant in Dubuque, Iowa, to a new plant in Rochelle, Illinois. In its analysis, the Labor Board noted the uncertainty created by the different tests set forth in a famous earlier plurality decision, *Otis Elev. Co.,* 269 N.L.R.B. 891 (1984), to determine when an employer must bargain about a decision to relocate work from one facility to another. A unanimous NLRB first reviewed the principles of *Fibreboard* and *First Nat'l Maint.* The Board noted that relocation decisions have a direct impact upon employment. It then indicated that such decisions are more analogous to subcontracting cases than to plant closure situations, since the employer usually plans to continue the same basic operations at the new location. Based upon these considerations, the Board formulated new standards to be applied to determine when an employer has to bargain about a relocation decision:

> Initially, the burden is on the General Counsel to establish that the employer's decision involved a relocation of unit work unaccompanied by a basic change in the nature of the employer's operation. If the General Counsel successfully carries his burden in this regard, he will have established prima facie that the employer's relocation decision is a mandatory subject of bargaining. At this juncture, the employer may produce evidence rebutting the prima facie case by establishing that the work performed at the new location varies significantly from the work performed at the former plant, establishing that the work performed at the former plant is to be discontinued entirely and not moved to the new location, or establishing that the employer's decision involves a change in the scope and direction of the enterprise. Alternatively, the employer may proffer a defense to show by a preponderance of the evidence: (1) that labor costs (direct and/or indirect) were not a factor in the decision or (2) that even if labor costs were a factor in the decision, the union would not have offered labor cost concessions that could have changed the employer's decision to relocate.

> The first prong of the employer's burden is self-explanatory. If the employer shows that labor costs were irrelevant to the decision to relocate unit work, bargaining over the decision will not be required because the decision would not be amenable to resolution through the bargaining process.

Under the second prong, an employer would have no bargaining obligation if it showed that, although labor costs were a consideration in the decision to relocate unit work, it would not remain at the present plant because, for example, the costs for modernization of equipment or environmental controls were greater than any labor cost concessions the union could offer. On the other hand, an employer would have a bargaining obligation if the union could and would offer concessions that approximate, meet, or exceed the anticipated costs or benefits that prompted the relocation decision, since the decision then would be amenable to resolution through the bargaining process....

[A]n employer would enhance its chances of establishing this defense by describing the reasons for relocating to the union, fully explaining the underlying cost or benefit considerations, and asking whether the union could offer labor cost reductions that would enable the employer to meet its profit objectives.

The Board noted that there may be unusual situations requiring an expedited employer relocation decision, and it indicated that such exigent circumstances might, in appropriate cases, relieve an employer of the duty to notify the union and provide it with an opportunity to bargain over such a decision.

NOTES

1. The *Dubuque Packing* test does not apply to subcontracting decisions in which "virtually all that is changed through the subcontracting is the identity of the employees doing the work," or to cases in which the employer consolidates jobs and lays off unit employees, continuing to do the same work with fewer employees. Such decisions continue to be governed by *Fibreboard. See Mid-State Ready Mix. Div., Torrington Indus.,* 307 N.L.R.B. 809 (1992), *supplemented by* 316 N.L.R.B. 500 (1995); *Westinghouse Elec. Corp.,* 313 N.L.R.B. 452 (1993), *enforced sub nom. Salaried Employees Ass'n of Baltimore Div., Federation of Indep. Salaried Unions v. NLRB,* 46 F.3d 1126 (4th Cir.), *cert. denied,* 514 U.S. 1037 (1995).

2. *Dubuque* also does not apply to work reassignments from the union to the nonunion side of a "double-breasted" employer. An employer who wishes to alter its established practice of dividing work assignments between union and nonunion facilities has a duty to bargain first. An employer who temporarily closed its union plant and reassigned the work to its nonunion facility as a cost-cutting measure, without prior bargaining, violated § 8(a)(5). *Geiger Ready-Mix Co. v. NLRB,* 87 F.3d 1363 (D.C. Cir. 1996). *See also Taylor Warehouse Corp. v. NLRB,* 98 F.3d 892 (6th Cir. 1996).

3. It is not always clear which cases require application of the *Dubuque* analysis. *Furniture Rentors of America v. NLRB,* 36 F.3d 1240 (3d Cir. 1994), involved an employer that was encountering serious problems with its delivery personnel. The theft of $10,000 worth of furniture resulted in the arrest and resignation of several employees. The firm experienced problems with respect to packing and handling that caused damage to furniture. Delivery teams averaged three deliveries per day compared to the industry standard of four or five. When two employees and a supervisor were apprehended as part of a plot to steal furniture, the company unilaterally decided to close its delivery department and hire a contractor to perform the required delivery work. Since the Labor Board concluded that the factors that led to the employer's subcontracting decision were amenable to resolution through the bargaining process, it found the firm's failure to bargain about this decision violative of § 8(a)(5). The Third Circuit found the Board's rote application of the *Dubuque Packing* test overly simplistic in a case involving such complex managerial considerations, and it remanded the case to the NLRB for a more searching analysis. Even if the Board were to determine that the subcontracting decision had been based on factors amenable to resolution through the bargaining process, it must then decide whether the likelihood and degree of benefit, if any, to be derived from bargaining in a situation of this kind would outweigh the employer's obvious need for prompt action. On remand, the Board applied *Fibreboard* and *First National Maintenance* and found no § 8(a)(5) violation. 318 N.L.R.B. 602 (1995).

4. In cases which do require application of the *Dubuque* analysis, the employer's motivation can sometimes be critical. An employer who subcontracted out backlogged unit work to another firm in an effort to avoid lost sales rather than to eliminate overtime work by unit personnel was not obligated to bargain with the union over its subcontracting decision. *See Dorsey Trailers Inc. v. NLRB,* 134 F.3d 125 (3d Cir. 1998); *see also NLRB v. Wehr Constructors, Inc.,* 159 F.3d 946 (6th Cir. 1998) (general contractor has no obligation to bargain over each individual decision to subcontract work to a nonunion subcontractor where imposing such a duty would severely hamper the employer's ability to conduct its business on a day-to-day basis). However, the D.C. Circuit required bargaining on the subcontracting of trucking operations done for the purpose of avoiding the liability risks of maintaining a truck fleet, despite the employer's contention that the subcontractor's labor costs were so low that the employer's own drivers would have to take a $25,000 a year pay cut and thus bargaining would be futile. *Rock-Tenn Co. v. NLRB,* 101 F.3d 1441 (D.C. Cir. 1996).

Alternatively, the duty to bargain over relocation decisions may be predicated on other factors. Expressly disavowing reliance on *Dubuque,* the Board found a trucking firm in violation of § 8(a)(5) when it failed to bargain about a decision to relocate operations from one facility to another, since this move was not severable from the employer's unlawful unilateral decision to switch from a single-driver to a team-driver system. Chairman Gould, concurring, announced his readiness to overrule *Dubuque* "to the extent that it restricts the analysis of a relocation decision to labor costs." He would have imposed a duty to bargain about such relocation decisions if they are "amenable to bargaining," whether they are triggered by labor costs or other costs, pointing out that a test which provides only for labor costs as the trigger is a "clear invitation to posturing, game-playing, and obfuscation in an attempt to conceal and deceive." *Q-I Motor Express*, 323 N.L.R.B. No. 142, 155 L.R.R.M. 1097 (1997).

5. To what extent may a management rights clause waive a union's right to bargain over an employer's decision to subcontract or relocate work? *Compare Reece Corp.*, 294 N.L.R.B. 448 (1989) *with Batavia Newspapers Corp.*, 311 N.L.R.B. 477 (1993). The D.C. Circuit draws a distinction between a union's waiver of the right to bargain and a provision that covers a particular issue, thus fixing the parties' rights and foreclosing further mandatory bargaining. *UMW 1974 Pension (Trust) v. Pittston Co.*, 984 F.2d 469 (D.C. Cir.), *cert. denied*, 509 U.S. 924 (1993).

On the other hand, to what extent might unions protect themselves by negotiating for job security mechanisms that give the union the right to obtain advance information from the employer about outsourcing decisions, the right to discuss alternatives with management, the right to compete by bringing subcontracted work in house, or establish skills training programs designed to assist displaced workers in finding other positions? The United Auto Workers' Union has successfully negotiated such provisions in its contracts with automakers, but how many other unions will have sufficient bargaining leverage to obtain them?

6. Whether or not an employer must bargain over the actual decision to relocate operations, failure to inform the union prior to beginning the move may violate the duty to bargain over the effects of the decision, since timely notice is necessary to give the union an opportunity to negotiate while it still represents employees at work and thus retains some bargaining leverage. *Metropolitan Teletronics Corp.*, 279 N.L.R.B. 957 (1986), *enforced*, 819 F.2d 1130 (2d Cir. 1987). For a consideration of what constitutes sufficient "effects bargaining" by an employer, *see Otis Elev. Co.*, 283 N.L.R.B. No. 223 (1987). In *NLRB v. Challenge-Cook Bros.*, 843 F.2d 230 (6th Cir. 1988), a management rights clause and a zipper clause were held not to be a clear and unmistakable waiver of a union's right to bargain over the effect of an employer's unilateral relocation decision.

7. Should the same or a different standard apply to an employer's duty to bargain about the effects of the sale of a business? *See NLRB v. Compact Video Services,*, 121 F.3d 478 (9th Cir. 1997) (unionized firm whose parent corporation decides to sell its assets to another company risks violating § 8(a)(5) if it fails to notify the union of the proposed sale and provide it with the opportunity to bargain over the *effects* of the transaction on unit members). *See also Reidel Int'l*, 300 N.L.R.B. 282 (1990) (union entitled to as much notice of closing as "needed for meaningful bargaining at a meaningful time"); *Providence and Mercy Hosps. v. NLRB*, 93 F.3d 1012 (1st Cir. 1996) (hospitals violated § 8(a)(5) by refusing to provide union with information about a proposed merger with a competing health care system; despite hospitals' contention that bargaining would have to await consummation of the merger, the union was entitled to information at an earlier date in order to prepare for bargaining over the effects of the merger and the structural attributes of the new system).

In a case decided under the Railway Labor Act, the Supreme Court held that a railroad had no initial obligation to bargain with the unions representing its workers about either the sale of its assets or the effect of that sale on the employees, but that the railroad did have to bargain, in response to the unions' filing of a statutory change of status notice, about the effects of the sale to the extent the seller could satisfy the unions' demands. *Pittsburgh & Lake Erie R.R. v. RLEA,* 491 U.S. 490 (1989).

8. *See generally* George, *To Bargain or Not to Bargain: A New Chapter in Work Relocation Decisions,* 69 Minn. L. Rev. 667 (1985); St. Antoine, *The Collective Bargaining Process, in American Labor Policy 215 (C. Morris ed. 1987); Comment, NLRB Narrows Duty to Bargain over Management Decisions: Otis Elevator II and Its Progeny,* 21 Wake Forest L. Rev. 725 (1986). The *Dubuque* case is noted in 93 Colum. L. Rev. 932 (1993); 43 Lab. L.J. 579 (1992); 53 Ohio St. L. J. 909 (1992).

9. The Worker Adjustment and Retraining Notification Act (1988), 29 U.S.C. § 2101, requires employers with 100 or more employees to give 60 days' advance notice of shutdowns affecting at least 50 workers and of layoffs lasting more than six months and affecting one-third of the workers at a site. Provisions in earlier bills that would have required good faith consultations with any bargaining representative regarding possible alternatives to the proposed closing or layoff were omitted in the act as passed. *See generally* Yost, *The Worker Adjustment and Retraining Act of 1988: Advance Notice Required?,* 38 Cath. U. L. Rev. 675 (1989). The Supreme Court has held unanimously that a union may sue on behalf of its members for the damages caused by an employer's violation of the WARN Act. *UFCW Local 751 v. Brown Group, Inc.,* 517 U.S. 544 (1996).

D. THE DUTY TO BARGAIN DURING A CONTRACT'S TERM

THE JACOBS MANUFACTURING CO.

National Labor Relations Board
94 N.L.R.B. 1214 (1951)

... In July 1948, the Respondent and the Union executed a two-year bargaining contract which, by its terms, could be reopened one year after its execution date for discussion of "wage rates." In July, 1949, the Union invoked the reopening clause of the 1948 contract, and thereafter gave the Respondent written notice of its "wage demands." In addition to a request for a wage increase, these demands included a request that the Respondent undertake the entire cost of an existing group insurance program, and another request for the establishment of a pension plan for the Respondent's employees. When the parties met thereafter to consider the Union's demands, the Respondent refused to discuss the Union's pension and insurance requests on the ground that they were not appropriate items of discussion under the reopening clause of the 1948 contract.

The group insurance program to which the Union alluded in its demands was established by the Respondent before 1948. It was underwritten by an insurance company, and provided life, accident, health, surgical, and hospital protection. All the Respondent's employees were eligible to participate in the program, and the employees shared its costs with the Respondent. When the 1948 contract was being negotiated, the Respondent and the Union had discussed changes in this *insurance program,* and had agreed to increase certain of the benefits as well as the costs. However, neither the changes thereby effected, nor the insurance program itself, was mentioned in the 1948 contract.

As indicated by the Union's request, there was no pension plan for the Respondent's employees in existence in 1949. The subject of *pensions,* moreover, had not been discussed during the 1948 negotiations; and, like insurance, that subject is not mentioned in the 1948 contract.

a. For the reasons stated below, Chairman Herzog and Members Huston and Styles agree with the Trial Examiner's conclusion that the Respondent violated § 8(a)(5) of the Act by refusing to discuss the matter of *pensions* with the Union....

We are satisfied ... that the 1948 contract did not in itself impose on the Respondent any obligation to discuss pensions or insurance. The reopening clause of that contract refers to *wage rates,* and thus its intention appears to have been narrowly limited to matters directly related to the amount and matter of compensation for work. For that reason, a requirement to discuss pensions or insurance cannot be predicated on the language of the contract.

On the other hand, a majority of the Board believes that, regardless of the character of the reopening clause, the Act itself imposed upon the Respondent the duty to discuss *pensions* with the Union during the period in question.

It is now established as a principle of law that the matter of pensions is a subject which falls within the area where the statute requires bargaining. And, as noted above, the 1948 contract between the Respondent and the Union was silent with respect to the subject of pensions; indeed, the matter had never been raised or discussed by the parties. The issue raised, therefore, is whether the Respondent was absolved of the obligation to discuss pensions because of the limitation contained in § 8(d) of the amended Act dealing with the duty to discuss or agree to the modification of an existing bargaining contract....

The crucial point at issue here ... is the construction to be given the phrase "terms and conditions *contained in* a contract." (Emphasis supplied.) The Board in the *Tide Water* [85 N.L.R.B. 1096] case, concluded that the pertinent portion of § 8(d) *refers to terms and conditions which have been integrated and embodied into a writing.* Conversely it does not have reference to matters relating to wages, hours and other terms and conditions of employment, which have not been reduced to writing. As to the written terms of the contract either party may refuse to bargain further about them, under the limitations set forth in the paragraph, without committing an unfair labor practice. With respect to unwritten terms dealing with wages, hours and other terms and conditions of employment, the obligation remains on both parties to bargain continuously.

Thus, as already construed by this Board in the *Tide Water* case, § 8(d) does not itself license a party to a bargaining contract to refuse, during the life of the contract, to discuss a bargainable subject unless it has been made part of the agreement itself. Applied here, therefore, the *Tide Water* construction of § 8(d) means that the Respondent was obligated to discuss the Union's pension demand.

Members Huston and Styles have carefully re-examined the Board's construction of § 8(d) in the *Tide Water* case, and are persuaded that the view the Board adopted in the *Tide Water* case best effectuates the declared policy of the Act. Chairman Herzog, while joining in the result with respect to the obligation to bargain here concerning pensions—never previously discussed by the parties— joins in the rationale herein *only* to the extent that it is consistent with his views separately recited below, concerning the insurance program.

By making mandatory the discussion of bargainable subjects not already covered by a contract, the parties to the contract are encouraged to arrive at joint decisions with respect to bargainable matters, that, at least to the party requesting discussion, appear at the time to be of some importance. The Act's policy of "encouraging the practice and procedure of collective bargaining" is consequently furthered. A different construction of § 8(d) in the circumstances—one that would permit a party to a bargaining contract to avoid discussion when it was sought on subject matters not contained in the contract—would serve, at its best, only to dissipate whatever the good will that had been engendered by the previous bargaining negotiations that led to the execution of a bargaining contract; at its worst, it could bring about the industrial strife and the production interruptions that the policy of the Act also seeks to avert.

The significance of this point cannot be overemphasized. It goes to the heart of our disagreement with our dissenting colleague, Member Reynolds. His dissent stresses the need for "contract stability," and asserts that the furtherance of sound collective bargaining requires that the collective bargaining agreement be viewed as fixing, for the term of the contract, all aspects of the employer-employee relationship, and as absolving either party of the obligation to discuss, during that term, even those matters which had never been raised, or discussed in the past. We could hardly take issue with the virtue of "contract stability," at least in the abstract, and we would certainly agree that everyone is better off when, in negotiating an agreement, the parties have been able to foresee what all the future problems may be, to discuss those problems, and either to embody a resolution of them in the contract, or to provide that they may not be raised again during the contract. But we are here concerned with the kind of case in which, for one reason or another, this has *not* been done, and the question is what best effectuates the policies of the Act in *such* a case.

In this connection we cannot ignore the fact that to say that a party to an agreement is absolved by § 8(d) of an obligation to discuss a subject not contained in a contract does not mean that the other party is prohibited from taking economic action to compel bargaining on that subject. The portion of § 8(d) we are here considering does no more than provide a *defense* to a charge of a refusal to bargain under § 8(a)(5) or § 8(b)(3) of the Act. It does not render unlawful economic action aimed at securing lawful objectives.[10] That being so, the view urged by Member Reynolds achieves "contract stability" but only at the price of industrial strife, and that is a result which now more than ever we must avoid. The basic policy of this Act to further collective bargaining is founded on the proposition—amply demonstrated by experience—that collective bargaining provides an escape valve for the pressures which otherwise result in industrial strife. With this policy in mind, we are loath to narrow the area of mandatory bargaining, except where the amended statute, in the clearest terms, requires that we do so.

The construction of § 8(d) adopted by the Board in the *Tide Water* case serves also to simplify, and thus to speed, the bargaining process. It eliminates the pressure upon the parties at the time when a contract is being negotiated to raise those subjects that may not then be of controlling importance, but which might in the future assume a more significant status. It also assures to both unions and employers that, if future conditions require some agreement as to matters about which the parties have not sought, or have not been able to obtain agreement, then some discussion of those matters will be forthcoming when necessary.

We cannot believe that Congress was unaware of the foregoing considerations when it amended the Act by inserting § 8(d), or that it sought, by the provision in question, to freeze the bargaining relationship by eliminating any mandatory discussion that might lead to the addition of new subject matter to an existing contract. What § 8(d) does do is to reject the pronouncements contained in some pre-1947 Board and court decisions—sometimes *dicta,* sometimes necessary to the holding—to the effect that the duty to bargain continues even as to those matters

---

[10] We must note, however, contrary to the assertion of Member Reynolds, that nothing in this decision is to be construed as a determination of the issue of whether a union may strike to compel bargaining on a modification of a contract which seeks to add a matter not contained in the contract without complying with the procedural requirements of § 8(d). Our decision here is limited to a construction of the language "modification of the terms and conditions *contained in* a contract." The issue raised by our dissenting colleague is not before us in this case, and we in no way pass upon it.

upon which the parties have reached agreement and which are set forth in the terms of a written contract. But we believe it does no more. Those bargainable issues which have never been discussed by the parties, and which are in no way treated in the contract, remain matters which both the union and the employer are obliged to discuss at any time.

In so holding, we emphasize that under this rule, no less than in any other circumstance, the duty to bargain implies only an obligation to *discuss* the matter in question in good faith with a sincere purpose of reaching some agreement. It does not require that either side agree, or make concessions. And if the parties originally desire to avoid later discussion with respect to matters not specifically covered in the terms of an executed contract, they need only so specify in the terms of the contract itself. Nothing in our construction of § 8(d) precludes such an agreement, entered into in good faith, from foreclosing future discussion of matters not contained in the agreement.[13]

b. Chairman Herzog, for reasons set forth in his separate opinion, believes that—unlike the pensions issue—the Respondent was under no obligation to bargain concerning the *group insurance program.*

However, Members Huston and Styles—a minority of the Board on this issue—are of the further opinion that the considerations discussed above leading to the conclusion that the Respondent was obligated to discuss the matter of pensions, also impel the conclusion that the Respondent was obligated to discuss the Union's group insurance demand. Like pensions, the matter of group insurance benefits is a subject which has been held to be within the area of compulsory bargaining; and like pensions, the Respondent's group insurance program was not mentioned in the terms of the 1948 contract. Members Huston and Styles therefore believe that so far as the controlling facts are concerned the ultimate issues presented by the Union's pension and group insurance demands are identical....

Members Huston and Styles believe, moreover, that the view adopted by Chairman Herzog on the insurance issue is subject to the same basic criticism as

---

[13]For an example of a contract in which such a provision was incorporated, see the contract between United Automobile Workers of America and General Motors Corp., set forth in *Labor Relations Manual* (BNA), vol. 26, p. 63, 91, which states:

(154) The parties acknowledge that during the negotiations which resulted in this agreement, each had the unlimited right and opportunity to make demands and proposals with respect to any subject or matter not removed by law from the area of collective bargaining, and that the understandings and agreements arrived at by the parties after the exercise of that right and opportunity are set forth in this agreement. Therefore, the Corporation and the Union, for the life of this agreement, each voluntarily and unqualifiedly waives the right, and each agrees that the other shall not be obligated, to bargain collectively with respect to any subject or matter not specifically referred to or covered in this agreement, even though such subjects or matter may not have been within the knowledge or contemplation of either or both of the parties at the time that they negotiated or signed this agreement.

is the view of Member Reynolds—it exalts "contract stability" over industrial peace; it eliminates mandatory collective bargaining on subjects about which one of the parties *now* wants discussion, and concerning which it may well be willing to take economic action if discussion is denied, solely because the matter has once been discussed in a manner which may warrant an inference that the failure to mention that subject in the contract was part of the bargain. Members Huston and Styles are constrained to reject the view of Chairman Herzog for the further reason that it would establish a rule which is administratively unworkable, and would inject dangerous uncertainty into the process of collective bargaining. Apart from the extremely difficult problems of proof—illustrated in this very case—which would constantly confront the Board in cases of this type, the parties to collective bargaining negotiations would always be faced with this question after a subject has been *discussed*—"Have we really *negotiated,* or are we under an obligation to discuss the subject further if asked to?" To this query the rule of the *Tide Water* case gives a clear and concise answer: "You are obligated to discuss any bargaining subject upon request unless you have reduced your agreement on that subject to writing or unless you have agreed in writing not to bargain about it during the term of the contract." Members Huston and Styles would apply that rule without deviation....

CHAIRMAN HERZOG, concurring in part:

I believe that this Respondent was *not* under a duty to discuss the Union's *group insurance* demand. The individual views which lead me, by a different road, to the result reached on this issue by Members Reynolds and Murdock, are as follows:

Unlike the issue of pensions, concerning which the contract is silent and the parties did not negotiate at all in 1948, the subject of group insurance was fully discussed while the Respondent and the Union were negotiating the agreement. True, that agreement is silent on the subject, so it cannot literally be said that there is a term "contained in" the 1948 contract relating to the group insurance program. The fact remains that during the negotiations which preceded its execution, the issue was consciously explored. The record reveals that the Union expressly requested that the preexisting program be changed so that the Respondent would assume its entire cost, the very proposal that was again made as part of the 1949 midterm demand which gave rise to this case. The Respondent rejected the basic proposal on this first occasion, but agreement was then reached—although outside the written contract—to increase certain benefits under the group insurance program.

In my opinion, it is only reasonable to assume that rejection of the Union's basic proposal, coupled in this particular instance with enhancement of the substantive benefits, constituted a part of the contemporaneous "bargain" which the parties made when they negotiated the entire 1948 contract. In the face of this record as to what the parties discussed and did, I believe that it would be an abuse of this Board's mandate to throw the weight of Government sanction behind the Union's attempt to disturb, in midterm, a bargain sealed when the original agreement was reached.

To hold otherwise would encourage a labor organization—or, in a § 8(b)(3) case, an employer—to come back, time without number, during the term of a contract, to demand resumed discussion of issues which, although perhaps not always incorporated in the written agreement, the other party had every good reason to believe were put at rest for a definite period. I do not think that the doctrine of the *Tide Water* case was ever intended to go so far as to extend to facts like these, or that it should be so extended. Without regard to the niceties of construing the words of § 8(d) of the amended Act, I am satisfied that it would be both inequitable and unwise to impose a statutory obligation to bargain in situations of this sort. That would serve only to stimulate uncertainty and evasion of commitments at a time when stability should be the order of the day.

MEMBER REYNOLDS, concurring separately and dissenting in part: ...

[I]t is my opinion that § 8(d) imposes no obligation on either party to a contract to bargain on any matter during the term of the contract except as the express provisions of the contract may demand. This is a result reasonably compatible with the particular § 8(d) language involved, as well as with § 8(d) as a whole. Moreover, not only does the result accord stability and dignity to collective bargaining agreements, but it also gives substance to the practice and procedure of collective bargaining.

It is well established that the function of collective bargaining agreements is to contribute stability, so essential to sound industrial relations. Contractually stabilized industrial relations enable employers, because of fixed labor costs, to engage in sound long-range production planning, and employees, because of fixed wage, seniority, promotion, and grievance provisions, to anticipate secure employment tenure. Hence when an employer and a labor organization have through the processes of collective bargaining negotiated an agreement containing the terms and conditions of employment for a definite period of time, their total rights and obligations emanating from the employer-employee relationship should remain fixed for that time. Stabilized therefore are the rights and obligations of the parties with respect to all bargainable subjects whether the subjects are or are not specifically set forth in the contract. To hold otherwise and prescribe bargaining on unmentioned subjects would result in continued alteration of the total rights and obligations under the contract, thus rendering meaningless the concept of contract stability.

That a collective bargaining agreement stabilizes all rights and conditions of employment is consonant with the generally accepted concept of the nature of such an agreement. The basic terms and conditions of employment existing at the time the collective bargaining agreement is executed, and which are not specifically altered by, or mentioned in, the agreement, are part of the *status quo* which the parties, by implication, consider as being adopted as an essential element of the agreement. This view is termed "reasonable and logical," and its widespread endorsement as sound industrial relations practice makes it a general rule followed in the arbitration of disputes arising during the term of a contract. The reasonableness of the approach is apparent upon an understanding of collective bargaining techniques. Many items are not mentioned in a collective bargaining agreement either because of concessions at the bargaining table or because one of the parties may have considered it propitious to forego raising one subject in the hope of securing a more advantageous deal on another. Subjects traded off or foregone should, under these circumstances, be as irrevocably settled as those specifically covered and settled by the agreement. To require bargaining on such subjects during midterm debases initial contract negotiations....

MEMBER MURDOCK, dissenting in part:

I am unable to agree with my colleagues of the majority that by refusing to discuss pensions and insurance with the Union under the particular circumstances of this case, the Respondent violated § 8(a)(5) of the Act.

Despite the fact that the reopening clause in the contract which the Union here invoked was limited to "wage rates," the Union included insurance and pensions in its demands thereunder in addition to a wage increase. In my view the Respondent properly took the position that the parties were meeting pursuant to the reopening provision of the contract to discuss wage rates and that pensions and insurance were not negotiable thereunder and would not be discussed at that time....

NOTES

1. The Board majority's position that pensions were a bargainable issue since neither discussed in negotiations nor embodied in the contract received judicial support in *NLRB v. Jacobs Mfg. Co.,* 196 F.2d 680 (2d Cir. 1952). The differences among the Board members in the *Jacobs* case may well have resulted from the critical comments of Professors Cox and Dunlop in *Regulation of Collective Bargaining by the National Labor Relations Board,* 63 Harv. L. Rev. 389 (1950), and *The Duty to Bargain Collectively During the Term of an Existing Agreement,* 63 Harv. L. Rev. 1097 (1950). For a vigorous defense of the Board, *see* Findling & Colby, *Regulation of Collective Bargaining by the National Labor Relations Board—Another View,* 51 Colum. L. Rev. 170 (1951).

2. What must be said during negotiations to give rise to the inference that a particular matter was intended to be left in the employer's hands for the period of the contract? How reliable is the evidence likely to be? *Compare NLRB v. Nash-Finch Co.,* 211 F.2d 622 (8th Cir. 1954) *and Speidel Corp.,* 120 N.L.R.B. 733 (1958) *with Beacon Piece Dyeing & Finishing Co.,* 121 N.L.R.B. 953 (1958), *and Cloverleaf Div. of Adams Dairy Co.,* 147 N.L.R.B. 1410 (1964). In *Proctor*

Mfg. Corp., 131 N.L.R.B. 1166, 1169 (1961), the Board declared: "The Board's rule, applicable to negotiations during the contract term with respect to a subject which has been discussed in precontract negotiations but which has not been specifically covered in the resulting contract, is that the employer violates Section 8(a)(5) if, during the contract term, he refuses to bargain or takes unilateral action with respect to the particular subject, unless it can be said from an evaluation of the prior negotiations that the matter was 'fully discussed' or 'consciously explored' and that the Union 'consciously yielded' or clearly and unmistakably waived its interest in the matter." *See also Daniel I. Burk Enters.,* 313 N.L.R.B. 1263 (1994) (no union waiver of right to bargain over economically motivated closing and termination of employees even where parties' current and past labor contracts anticipated layoffs during economic downturns).

A union can waive its bargaining rights during the term of a contract by conduct or by inaction. The union must act with due diligence and pursue its bargaining rights promptly once informed of a proposed change by the employer. *See YHA Inc. v. NLRB,* 2 F.3d 168 (6th Cir. 1993) (union waived its right to bargain where employer gave formal notice of proposed no-smoking rule eight days before implementation, and union did not request bargaining in that period); *but cf. NLRB v. Roll and Hold Warehouse and Distribution Corp.,* 162 F.3d 513 (7th Cir. 1998) (no union waiver where company unilaterally changed its attendance policy and presented the new plan directly to employees, undermining the negotiating role of the union). For contrasting rulings on the requirements for a union waiver of the right to bargain over management decisions or their effects, *compare American Diamond Tool,* 306 N.L.R.B. 570 (1992) (union waiver of bargaining rights regarding layoffs when union failed without excuse to use opportunity to request bargaining over layoffs and "signalled" willingness to permit such unilateral conduct in the future), *with Porta-King Bldg. Sys.,* 310 N.L.R.B. 539 (1993), *enforced,* 14 F.3d 1258 (8th Cir. 1994) (no waiver regarding layoffs when employer failed to notify union before laying off employees, despite employer's prior practice of unilateral layoffs at former, discontinued unionized operation).

3. Through the use of a "zipper" clause, a union may forego its right to bargain about any employment term not contained in the contract, but such a waiver must be clear and unmistakable. *See Tide Water Associated Oil Co.,* 85 N.L.R.B. 1096 (1949); *GTE Automatic Elec., Inc.,* 261 N.L.R.B. 1491 (1982). *Cf. LeRoy Mach. Co.,* 147 N.L.R.B. 1431 (1964) (waiver through management functions clause). *But cf. Stuart Radiator Core Mfg. Co.,* 173 N.L.R.B. 125 (1968) (employer violated § 8(a)(5) by rigid insistence in bargaining on broad zipper clause, broad management rights clause, and narrow arbitration clause).

An employer may not unilaterally discontinue a year-end bonus which was not mentioned in the collective agreement. Despite the presence of a "zipper" clause, no waiver will be found of the union's right to bargain on the subject. *Pepsi-Cola Distrib. Co.,* 241 N.L.R.B. 869 (1979), *enforced,* 646 F.2d 1173 (6th Cir. 1981), *cert. denied,* 456 U.S. 936 (1982). Nor did standard management rights and zip-per clauses excuse an employer from bargaining with a union before modifying a corporate-wide pension plan by adopting one of the four alternative model amendments mandated by the Internal Revenue Service—even where the collec-tive agreement provided that the union employees' plan would be maintained the "same" as plans available on a corporate basis, and the changes in the nonunit employees' plans were "unquestionably" lawful. *Bertram-Trojan Inc.,* 319 N.L.R.B. 741 (1995). Similarly, in *Elliott Turbomachinery Co.,* 320 N.L.R.B. 141 (1995) the Board ruled that a management rights clause that first listed a number of specific items over which the company had exclusive control, and then added an incomplete sentence beginning, "To decide location of its plant, and to relocate the same," was ambiguous and thus did not waive bargaining.

However, a "zipper" clause which states that a new contract "supersedes all prior agreements, understandings, and past practices" is a sufficiently clear and unmistakable waiver of the union's right to bargain over the employer's discon-tinuance of a bonus program. *TCI of New York,* 301 N.L.R.B. 822 (1991). And the D.C. Circuit has indicated that a "zipper" clause stating that the express terms constitute the "entire agreement" between the parties should be strictly enforced to prevent "oral modifications" of written provisions. *Martinsville Nylon Em-ployees Council v. NLRB,* 969 F.2d 1263 (D.C. Cir. 1992).

4. *See* Nelson & Howard, *The Duty to Bargain During the Term of an Existing Agreement,* 27 Lab. L.J. 573 (1976); Wollett, *The Duty to Bargain over the "Unwritten" Terms and Conditions of Employment,* 36 Texas L. Rev. 863 (1958); Note, *Mid-Term Modification of Terms and Conditions of Employment,* 1972 Duke L.J. 813.

————

NLRB v. Lion Oil Co., 352 U.S. 282, 77 S. Ct. 330, 1 L. Ed. 2d 331 (1957). A union and an employer entered into a collective bargaining agreement to remain in effect for one year and thereafter until canceled. The agreement provided that either party could propose amendments by notifying the other party any time af-ter the first ten months of the contract. If agreement could not be reached on amendment of the contract during the 60-day period following this notification, either party could thereafter terminate the agreement by giving a 60-day written notice to the other. At the end of the first ten months, the union duly served no-tice of its desire to modify the contract. The union never gave the further notice to terminate, and thus the contract remained in effect. Nonetheless, some eight months after its initial modification notice, the union went on strike to back up its demands for amendment. Subsequently, the employer defended against unfair labor practices allegedly committed by it during the strike by asserting that the workers had lost their status as employees under the Act by striking in violation of § 8(d)(4). Section 8(d)(4) provides that a party wishing to modify or terminate a contract must not resort to a strike or lockout "for a period of sixty days after ... notice is given or until the expiration date of such contract, whichever occurs later." The Supreme Court held that when a contract is subject to reopening in midterm, the phrase "expiration date" as used in § 8(d)(4) should be construed to mean both the final termination date and the first date on which the agreement is subject to amendment. Otherwise, an obvious restriction would be imposed on employees' concerted activities, and long-term bargaining relationships would be discouraged. The Court therefore concluded that the union had fully satisfied the notice and waiting requirements of § 8(d), and the strikers had not lost their status as employees.

NOTES

1. Just as the union has the right to strike during the reopener period, the employer may unilaterally implement its final proposal following a valid impasse in negotiations under a reopener clause, assuming that it provides the requisite § 8(d) notices. *See Speedrack Inc.,* 293 N.L.R.B. 1054 (1989); *see also Hydrologics, Inc.,* 293 N.L.R.B. 1060 (1989) (unless the contract states otherwise, the assumption is that the parties intend to make the same economic weapons available in the reopener context as are available at termination of the contract).

2. The "cooling off" provisions of § 8(d) apply only to strikes to compel a modification or termination of the collective agreement. They do not apply to a strike to protest an employer's unfair labor practice, *Mastro Plastics Corp. v. NLRB,* 350 U.S. 270 (1956), or to a walkout caused by dangerous working conditions, *NLRB v. Knight Morley Corp.,* 251 F.2d 753 (6th Cir. 1957), *cert. denied,* 357 U.S. 927 (1958). It has also been held that the strike-notice provisions of § 8(d) are inapplicable to a strike over an issue not covered by the contract, since this is not a strike to change or end the agreement. *Mine Workers Local 9735 v. NLRB,* 258 F.2d 146 (D.C. Cir. 1958); *Cheney Cal. Lumber Co. v. NLRB,* 319 F.2d 375 (9th Cir. 1963).

3. A union that strikes without complying with the 60-day notice requirement has been said to "forfeit" its rights as collective bargaining agent, and the strikers lose their status as employees. *Boeing Airplane Co. v. NLRB,* 174 F.2d 988 (D.C. Cir. 1949). An employer's duty to bargain is also suspended during the period of such a strike. *Wholesale Employees, Dist. 65,* 187 N.L.R.B. 716 (1971). When an employer egged on a union to strike, however, it waived the loss of NLRA protections for employees when the union struck during the 60-day "cooling off" period. *ABC Automotive Prods. Corp.,* 307 N.L.R.B. 248 (1992), *supplemented by* 319 N.L.R.B. 874 (1995).

4. *See generally* Note, *Strike Ban Provisions: Section 8(d) of Taft-Hartley,* 50 Nw. U.L. Rev. 260 (1955); Note, *An Examination of the Sixty-Day Notice Requirement of the Taft-Hartley Act on the Right to Strike,* 44 Geo. L.J. 447 (1956).

On § 8(d)(3)'s requirement of a 30-day notice to mediation agencies, *see Retail Clerks, Local 219 v. NLRB,* 265 F.2d 814 (D.C. Cir. 1959); *Furniture Workers v. NLRB,* 336 F.2d 738 (D.C. Cir.), *cert. denied,* 379 U.S. 838 (1964); *Hooker Chems. & Plastic Corp. v. NLRB,* 573 F.2d 965 (7th Cir. 1978) (employer may lock out after 60-day period despite union's late 30-day notice); Note, *Untimely Notice Under Section 8(d)(3) of the Taft-Hartley Act,* 47 Va. L. Rev. 490 (1961).

SECTION II. The Impact of the Antitrust Laws

Although the Sherman Act was passed in 1890 primarily to combat the monopolistic practices of certain business firms, it soon became a major weapon against the organizational activities of labor unions, especially the boycott in all its forms. In recent years, the antitrust laws have been directed much more at the allegedly restrictive provisions that unions have included in collective agreements with employers and groups of employers. To maintain continuity in showing the development of antitrust theory in the labor field, and to take account of the shift in emphasis from organizational to bargaining activities, we have decided to place all the material on unions and the antitrust laws in this section of the Casebook. As will be seen, however, the earlier cases that are presented deal more with union organization than with collective bargaining. The full text of the Sherman Act appears in *Selected Federal Statutes,* and should be read at this point.

Loewe v. Lawlor ["Danbury Hatters"], 208 U.S. 274, 28 S. Ct. 301, 52 L. Ed. 488 (1908). Action for treble damages brought under § 7 of the Sherman Act. Plaintiffs manufactured hats in Danbury, Connecticut. Their complaint alleged: that they did a substantial interstate business; that defendants were members (officers) of the United Hatters of America, which comprised about 9,000 members organized into a large number of subordinate unions, and which was affiliated with the AFL; that defendants were engaged in a combination to force all fur hat manufacturers in the United States, including plaintiffs, to unionize their shops, and had succeeded as to seventy of the eighty-two such manufacturers; that, in pursuance of such object, defendants had called a strike against plaintiffs and had, through the co-operation of the AFL, instituted a nationwide boycott of plaintiffs' products in the hands of wholesalers and dealers; and that as a result plaintiffs had been damaged to the extent of some $80,000. Defendants' demurrer to the complaint was sustained by the trial court. *Held,* demurrer overruled, and case remanded. "If the purposes of the combination were, as alleged, to prevent any interstate transportation at all, the fact that the means operated at one end before physical transportation commenced and at the other end after the physical transportation ended was immaterial."

NOTES

1. This was the first of several notable boycott cases involving labor decided under the Sherman Act. Final settlement of the case did not occur until several years later. On the trial of the case, plaintiffs obtained a verdict and judgment for $240,000 plus costs, which was affirmed in *Lawlor v. Loewe,* 235 U.S. 522 (1915). In the summer of 1917, the case was settled for about $234,000, of which the AFL furnished $216,000. *See* E. Witte, The Government in Labor Disputes 134, 135 (1932).

The Court's opinion on the first appeal constituted simply an application to labor activities of the principle of literal construction of the Sherman Act which characterized the earliest period of the Act's application. The statute, said the Court, made *every* combination in restraint of interstate commerce illegal. The Court was not concerned with the kind but rather with the effect of the restraint. This was before the announcement of the famous "rule of reason" in *Standard Oil Co. v. United States,* 221 U.S. 1 (1911). On the second appeal of the *Hatters* case, the Court thought that the intervening decision in *Eastern States Retail Lumber Dealers Ass'n v. United States,* 234 U.S. 600 (1914) (which had held a commercial boycott illegal under the Act), made the application of the statute to a labor boycott clear.

2. On the threshold question of whether the Sherman Act was intended by Congress to apply to labor combinations, *see* the following: E. Berman, Labor and the Sherman Act 3-54 (1930); A. Mason, Organized Labor and the Law 122 *et seq.* (1925); Boudin, *The Sherman Act and Labor Disputes,* 39 Colum. L. Rev. 1283 (1939), 40 Colum. L. Rev. 14 (1940); Emery, *Labor Organizations and the Sherman Law,* 20 J. Pol. Econ. 599 (1912); Terborgh, *The Application of the Sherman Act to Trade Union Activities,* 37 J. Pol. Econ. 203 (1929). These discussions indicate that there is, at least, very real doubt whether Congress intended any such result. It seems to be conceded that labor counsel were derelict in the early cases in their presentation of this issue to the Court. "It is a sad commentary on the way labor cases are usually argued, that we cannot recall this point to have ever been clearly brought out in any brief submitted on behalf of labor, at least not in the cases argued in the Supreme Court." Boudin, *supra,* 40 Colum. L. Rev. at 20. Berman declares, "An adequate presentation of the *Hatters'* case to the Supreme Court might have greatly changed the history of labor cases since 1908." E. Berman, *supra,* at 86.

———

Sections 6 and 20 of the Clayton Act of 1914 are reproduced in *Selected Federal Statutes.* They should be read at this point.

Duplex Printing Press Co. v. Deering, 254 U.S. 443, 41 S. Ct. 172, 65 L. Ed. 349 (1921). This suit, which was tried subsequent to the enactment of the Clayton Act in 1914, was brought in the Southern District of New York against defendants individually and as representatives of two locals of the International Association of Machinists. Complainant manufactured printing presses in Michigan which were sold throughout the United States and abroad. In order to force complainant to unionize its factory, and adopt the eight-hour day and the union wage scale, the IAM called a strike at complainant's factory, which resulted in the withdrawal from work of a small number (14) of complainant's employees, and instituted a nationwide boycott of complainant's product, which was supported by threats of secondary strike and other action against customers, haulers, etc. Defendants invoked the anti-injunction provisions of the Clayton Act. From a decree dismissing the bill complainant appealed. *Held,* reversed and remanded. The Court cited the *Hatters'* cases and the *Eastern States Lumber* case as settling that the restraints involved were within the Sherman Act, whether produced by peaceable persuasion or by force. As to the cited provisions of the Clayton Act it held: First, that § 6 was not intended to legalize the activities of a labor combination which were otherwise unlawful; second, that the restrictive provisions of § 20 applied only to protect "parties standing in proximate relation to a controversy such as is particularly described," and hence could not be invoked by members of a labor organization who were not immediate parties to the dispute; and third, that, in any case, § 20 was not intended to immunize the "secondary boycott" against injunction.

Apex Hosiery Co. v. Leader, 310 U.S. 469, 60 S. Ct. 982, 84 L. Ed. 1311 (1940). Apex manufactured hosiery and had a plant in Philadelphia at which it employed 2,500 persons and produced merchandise annually of the value of about $5,000,000. Its principal raw materials were brought in from other states, and it shipped interstate more than eighty percent of its finished product. In April 1937, while the company was operating a nonunion shop, defendant American Federation of Full Fashioned Hosiery Workers made a demand for a closed shop. On May 4, 1937, when only eight of the company's employees were members of the union, it called a strike, and at midday on May 6, while the factory was shut down, members of the union who were employed at other factories in Philadelphia assembled at the plant. When the company again rejected the demand for a closed shop, Leader, the union president, declared a "sit down strike," and the unionists forcibly seized the plant and retained possession until forcibly ejected on June 23, pursuant to an injunction. Manufacture was suspended for more than three months as a result. For damages suffered the company sued and obtained a verdict for $237,310 under the Sherman Act, and judgment was accordingly given for treble this amount. The Third Circuit Court of Appeals reversed on the ground that the effect of defendants' activities on total interstate commerce in hosiery (this plant contributing less than three percent) was not substantial. On certiorari the Supreme Court affirmed.

Stone, J., for the Court, held that while labor organizations are not exempted from the Sherman Act, these particular activities were not within the purview of the statute. The Act was not designed to police violence but looked toward "the prevention of restraints to free competition in business and commercial transactions which tended to restrict production, raise prices or otherwise control the market to the detriment of purchasers or consumers of goods and services...." The Justice stated that "restraints on competition or on the course of trade in the merchandising of articles moving in interstate commerce is not enough, unless the restraint is shown to have or is intended to have an effect upon prices in the market or otherwise to deprive purchasers or consumers of the advantages which they derive from free competition." This case, he said, was not one "of a labor organization being used by combinations of those engaged in an industry as the means or instrument for suppressing competition or fixing prices," and "so far as appears the delay of these shipments [of hosiery] was not intended to have and had no effect on prices of hosiery in the market." He concluded as follows:

> [S]uccessful union activity, as for example consummation of a wage agreement with employers, may have some influence on price competition by eliminating that part of such competition which is based on differences in labor standards. Since, in order to render a labor combination effective it must eliminate the competition from non-union made goods ... an elimination of price competition based on differences in labor standards is the objective of any national labor organization. But this effect on competition has not been considered to be the kind of curtailment of price competition prohibited by the Sherman Act....
>
> [A]ctivities of labor organizations not immunized by the Clayton Act are not necessarily violations of the Sherman Act. Underlying and implicit in all of them is recognition that the Sherman Act was not enacted to police interstate transportation, or to afford a remedy for wrongs, which are actionable under state law, and result from combinations and conspiracies which fall short, both in their purpose and effect, of any form of market control of a commodity, such as to "monopolize the supply, control its price, or discriminate between its would-be purchasers." These elements of restraint of trade ... are wholly lacking here. We do not hold that conspiracies to obstruct or prevent transportation in interstate commerce can in no circumstances be violations of the Sherman Act. Apart from the Clayton Act it makes no distinction between labor and nonlabor cases. We only hold now, as we have previously held both in labor and nonlabor cases, that such restraints are not within the Sherman Act unless they are intended to have, or in fact have, the effects on the market on which the Court relied to establish violation in the *Second Coronado* case....
>
> If, without such effects on the market, we were to hold that a local factory strike, stopping production and shipment of its product interstate, violates

the Sherman Law, practically every strike in modern industry would be brought within the jurisdiction of the federal courts, under the Sherman Act, to remedy local law violations. The Act was plainly not intended to reach such a result, its language does not require it, and the course of our decisions precludes it. The maintenance in our federal system of a proper distribution between state and national governments of police authority and of remedies private and public for public wrongs is of far-reaching importance. An intention to disturb the balance is not lightly to be imputed to Congress. The Sherman Act is concerned with the character of the prohibited restraints and with their effect on interstate commerce. It draws no distinction between the restraints effected by violence and those achieved by peaceful but oftentimes quite as effective means. Restraints not within the Act, when achieved by peaceful means, are not brought within its sweep merely because, without other differences, they are attended by violence. [310 U.S. at 503-04, 512-13.]

UNITED STATES v. HUTCHESON

Supreme Court of the United States
312 U.S. 219, 61 S. Ct. 463, 85 L. Ed. 788 (1941)

MR. JUSTICE FRANKFURTER delivered the opinion of the Court....

Summarizing the long indictment, these are the facts. Anheuser-Busch, Inc., operating a large plant in St. Louis, contracted with Borsari Tank Corporation for the erection of an additional facility. The Gaylord Container Corporation, a lessee of adjacent property from Anheuser-Busch, made a similar contract for a new building with the Stocker Company. Anheuser-Busch obtained the materials for its brewing and other operations and sold its finished products largely through interstate shipments. The Gaylord Corporation was equally dependent on interstate commerce for marketing its goods, as were the construction companies for their building materials. Among the employees of Anheuser-Busch were members of the United Brotherhood of Carpenters and Joiners of America and of the International Association of Machinists. The conflicting claims of these two organizations, affiliated with the American Federation of Labor, in regard to the erection and dismantling of machinery had long been a source of controversy between them. Anheuser-Busch had had agreements with both organizations whereby the Machinists were given the disputed jobs and the Carpenters agreed to submit all disputes to arbitration. But in 1939 the president of the Carpenters, their general representative, and two officials of the Carpenter's local organization, the four men under indictment, stood on the claims of the Carpenters for jobs. Rejection by the employer of the Carpenters' demand and the refusal of the latter to submit to arbitration were followed by a strike of the Carpenters, called by the defendants against Anheuser-Busch and the construction companies, a picketing of Anheuser-Busch, its tenant, and a request, through circular letters and the official publication of the Carpenters, that union members, and their friends, refrain from buying Anheuser-Busch beer.

These activities on behalf of the Carpenters formed the charge of the indictment as a criminal combination and conspiracy in violation of the Sherman Law. Demurrers, denying that what was charged constituted a violation of the laws of the United States, were sustained, 32 F. Supp. 600, and the case came here under the Criminal Appeals Act. Act of March 2, 1907....

Section 1 of the Sherman Law on which the indictment rested is as follows: "Every contract, combination in the form of trust or otherwise, or conspiracy, in restraint of trade or commerce among the several states, or with foreign nations, is hereby declared to be illegal." The controversies engendered by its application to trade union activities and the efforts to secure legislative relief from its consequences are familiar history. The Clayton Act of 1914 was the result.... Section 20 of that Act ... withdrew from the general interdict of the Sherman Law specifically enumerated practices of labor unions by prohibiting injunctions against them—since the use of the injunction had been the major source of dissatisfaction—and also relieved such practices of all illegal taint by the catch-all provision, "nor shall any of the acts specified in this paragraph be considered or held to be violations of any law of the United States." The Clayton Act gave rise to new litigation and to renewed controversy in and out of Congress regarding the status of trade unions. By the generality of its terms, the Sherman Law had necessarily compelled the courts to work out its meaning from case to case. It was widely believed that into the Clayton Act courts read the very beliefs which that Act was designed to remove. Specifically, the courts restricted the scope of § 20 to trade union activities directed against an employer by his own employees. *Duplex Co. v. Deering,* [254 U.S. 443 (1921)]. Such a view, it was urged, both by powerful judicial dissents and informed lay opinion, misconceived the area of economic conflict that had best be left to economic forces and the pressure of public opinion and not subjected to the judgment of courts. *Ibid.,* pp. 485, 486. Agitation again led to legislation and, in 1932, Congress wrote the Norris-La Guardia Act....

The Norris-La Guardia Act removed the fetters upon trade union activities, which, according to judicial construction, § 20 of the Clayton Act had left untouched, by still further narrowing the circumstances under which the federal courts could grant injunctions in labor disputes. More especially, the Act explicitly formulated the "public policy of the United States" in regard to the industrial conflict, and, by its light, established that the allowable area of union activity was not to be restricted, as it had been in the *Duplex* case, to an immediate employer-employee relation. Therefore, whether trade union conduct constitutes a violation of the Sherman Law is to be determined only by reading the Sherman Law and § 20 of the Clayton Act and the Norris-La Guardia Act as a harmonizing text of outlawry of labor conduct.

Were, then, the acts charged against the defendants prohibited or permitted by these three interlacing statutes? If the facts laid in the indictment come within the conduct enumerated in § 20 of the Clayton Act, they do not constitute a crime within the general terms of the Sherman Law because of the explicit command of that section that such conduct shall not be "considered or held to be violations of any law of the United States." So long as a union acts in its self-interest and does not combine with non-labor groups, the licit and the illicit under § 20 are not to be distinguished by any judgment regarding the wisdom or unwisdom, the rightness or wrongness, the selfishness or unselfishness of the end of which the particular union activities are the means. There is nothing remotely within the terms of § 20 that differentiates between trade union conduct directed against an employer because of a controversy arising in the relation between employer and employee, as such, and conduct similarly directed but ultimately due to an internecine struggle between two unions seeking the favor of the same employer....

It is at once apparent that the acts with which the defendants are charged are the kind of acts protected by § 20 of the Clayton Act. The refusal of the Carpenters to work for Anheuser-Busch or on construction work being done for it and its adjoining tenant, and the peaceful attempt to get members of other unions similarly to refuse to work, are plainly within the free scope accorded to workers by § 20 for "terminating any relation of employment," or "ceasing to perform any work or labor," or "recommending, advising or persuading others by peaceful means so to do." The picketing of Anheuser-Busch premises with signs to indicate that Anheuser-Busch was unfair to organized labor, a familiar practice in these situations, comes within the language "attending at any place where any such person or persons may lawfully be, for the purpose of peacefully obtaining or communicating information, or from peacefully persuading any person to work or to abstain from working." Finally, the recommendation to union members and their friends not to buy or use the product of Anheuser-Busch is explicitly covered by "ceasing to patronize ... any party to such dispute, or from recommending, advising, or persuading others by peaceful and lawful means so to do."

Clearly, then, the facts here charged constitute lawful conduct under the Clayton Act unless the defendants cannot invoke that Act because outsiders to the immediate dispute also shared in the conduct. But we need not determine whether the conduct is legal within the restrictions which *Duplex Co. v. Deering* gave to the immunities of § 20 of the Clayton Act. Congress in the Norris-La Guardia Act has expressed the public policy of the United States and defined its conception of a "labor dispute" in terms that no longer leave room for doubt.... Such a dispute, § 13(c), provides, "includes any controversy concerning terms or conditions of employment, or concerning the association or representation of persons in negotiating, fixing, maintaining, changing, or seeking to arrange terms or conditions of employment, regardless of whether or not the disputants stand in the proximate relation of employer and employee." And under § 13(b), a person is "participating or interested in a labor dispute" if he "is engaged in the same industry, trade, craft, or occupation in which such dispute occurs, or has a direct or indirect interest therein, or is a member, officer, or agent of any association composed in whole or in part of employers or employees engaged in such industry, trade, craft or occupation."

To be sure, Congress expressed this national policy and determined the bounds of a labor dispute in an Act explicitly dealing with the further withdrawal of injunctions in labor controversies. But to argue, as it was urged before us, that the *Duplex* case still governs for purposes of a criminal prosecution is to say that that which on the equity side of the court is allowable conduct may in a criminal proceeding become the road to prison. It would be strange indeed that although neither the Government nor Anheuser-Busch could have sought an injunction against the acts here challenged, the elaborate efforts to permit such conduct failed to prevent criminal liability punishable with imprisonment and heavy fines. That is not the way to read the will of Congress, particularly when expressed by a statute which, as we have already indicated, is practically and historically one of a series of enactments touching one of the most sensitive national problems. Such legislation must not be read in a spirit of mutilating narrowness....

The relation of the Norris-La Guardia Act to the Clayton Act is not that of a tightly drawn amendment to a technically phrased tax provision. The underlying aim of the Norris-La Guardia Act was to restore the broad purpose which Congress thought it had formulated in the Clayton Act but which was frustrated, so Congress believed, by unduly restrictive judicial construction. This was authoritatively stated by the House Committee on the Judiciary. "The purpose of the bill is to protect the rights of labor in the same manner the Congress intended when it enacted the Clayton Act, October 15, 1914 (38 Stat. L., 738), which Act, by reason of its construction and application by the Federal courts, is ineffectual to accomplish the congressional intent." H. R. Rep. No. 669, 72d Cong., 1st Sess. 3. The Norris-La Guardia Act was a disapproval of *Duplex Printing Press Co. v. Deering, supra,* and *Bedford Cut Stone Co. v. Journeymen Stone Cutters' Ass'n,* 274 U.S. 37 (1927), as the authoritative interpretation of § 20 of the Clayton Act, for Congress now placed its own meaning upon that section. The Norris-La Guardia Act reasserted the original purpose of the Clayton Act by infusing into it the immunized trade union activities as redefined by the later Act. In this light § 20 removes all such allowable conduct from the taint of being a "violation of any law of the United States," including the Sherman Law....

Affirmed.

MR. JUSTICE MURPHY took no part in the disposition of this case.

NOTE

Justice Stone wrote a separate concurring opinion arguing that under the previous decisions of the Court, especially the *Apex* case, the activities of the defendants did not bring them under the Sherman Act. He therefore did not find it necessary to resort to the reasoning used by Justice Frankfurter. Justice Roberts wrote a dissenting opinion, in which Chief Justice Hughes joined. As to the impact of the Norris-La Guardia Act, he said: "It is sufficient to say, what a reading of the Act makes letter clear, that the jurisdiction of actions for damages authorized by the Sherman Act, and of the criminal offenses denounced by that Act, are not touched by the Norris-La Guardia Act." He added:

> By a process of construction never, as I think, heretofore indulged by this court, it is now found that, because Congress forbade the issuing of injunctions to restrain conduct, it intended to repeal the provisions of the Sherman Act authorizing actions at law and criminal prosecutions for the commission of torts and crimes defined by the anti-trust laws. The doctrine now announced seems to be that an indication of a change of policy in an Act as respects one specific item in a general field of the law, covered by an earlier Act, justifies this court in spelling out an implied repeal of the whole of the earlier statute as applied to conduct of the sort here involved. I venture to say that no court has ever undertaken so radically to legislate where Congress has refused so to do. [312 U.S. at 245.]

For discussions of this case, *see* Cavers, *And What of the "Apex" Case Now?* 8 U. Chi. L. Rev. 516 (1941); Gregory, *The New Sherman-Clayton-Norris-La Guardia Act,* 8 U. Chi. L. Rev. 503 (1941); Nathanson & Wirtz, *The Hutcheson Case: Another View,* 36 Ill. L. Rev. 41 (1941); Teller, *Federal Intervention in Labor Disputes and Collective Bargaining—The Hutcheson Case,* 40 Mich. L. Rev. 24 (1941); Tunks, *A New Federal Charter for Trade Unionism,* 41 Colum. L. Rev. 969 (1941).

ALLEN BRADLEY CO. v. INTERNATIONAL BROTHERHOOD OF ELECTRICAL WORKERS, LOCAL 3

Supreme Court of the United States
325 U.S. 797, 65 S. Ct. 1533, 89 L. Ed. 1939 (1945)

MR. JUSTICE BLACK delivered the opinion of the Court....

Petitioners are manufacturers of electrical equipment. Their places of manufacture are outside of New York City, and most of them are outside of New York state as well. They have brought this action because of their desire to sell their products in New York City, a market area that has been closed to them through the activities of respondents and others.

Respondents are a labor union, its officials, and its members. The union, Local No. 3 of the International Brotherhood of Electrical Workers, has jurisdiction only over the metropolitan area of New York City. It is therefore impossible for the union to enter into a collective bargaining agreement with petitioners. Some of petitioners do have collective bargaining agreements with other unions, and in some cases even with other locals of the IBEW.

Some of the members of respondent union work for manufacturers who produce electrical equipment similar to that made by petitioners; other members of respondent union are employed by contractors and work on the installation of electrical equipment rather than in its production.

The union's consistent aim for many years has been to expand its membership, to obtain shorter hours and increased wages, and to enlarge employment opportunities for its members. To achieve this latter goal—that is, to make more work for its own members—the union realized that local manufacturers, employers of the local members, must have the widest possible outlets for their product. The union therefore waged aggressive campaigns to obtain closed-shop agreements with all local electrical equipment manufacturers and contractors. Using conventional labor union methods, such as strikes and boycotts, it gradually obtained more and more closed-shop agreements in the New York area. Under these agreements, contractors were obligated to purchase equipment from none but local manufacturers who also had closed-shop agreements with Local No. 3; manufacturers obligated themselves to confine their New York City sales to contractors employing the Local's members. In the course of time, this type of individual employer-employee agreement expanded into industry-wide understandings, looking not merely to terms and conditions of employment but also to price and market control. Agencies were set up composed of representatives of all three groups to boycott recalcitrant local contractors and manufacturers and to bar from the area equipment manufactured outside its boundaries. The combination among the three groups, union, contractors, and manufacturers, became highly successful from the standpoint of all of them. The business of New York City manufacturers had a phenomenal growth, thereby multiplying the jobs available for the Local's members. Wages went up, hours were shortened, and the New York electrical equipment prices soared, to the decided financial profit of local contractors and manufacturers. The success is illustrated by the fact that some New York manufacturers sold their goods in the protected city market at one price and sold identical goods outside of New York at a far lower price. All of this took place, as the Circuit Court of Appeals declared, "through the stifling of competition," and because the three groups, in combination as "co-partners," achieved "a complete monopoly which they used to boycott the equipment manufactured by the plaintiffs." Interstate sale of various types of electrical equipment has, by this powerful combination, been wholly suppressed....

[The Court then summarized the historical development of the law dealing with labor under the antitrust statutes.]

The result of all this is that we have two declared congressional policies which it is our responsibility to try to reconcile. The one seeks to preserve a competitive business economy; the other to preserve the rights of labor to organize to better its conditions through the agency of collective bargaining. We must determine here how far Congress intended activities under one of these policies to neutralize the results envisioned by the other.

Aside from the fact that the labor union here acted in combination with the contractors and manufacturers, the means it adopted to contribute to the combination's purpose fall squarely within the "specified acts" declared by § 20 not to be violations of federal law. For the union's contribution to the trade boycott was accomplished through threats that, unless their employers bought their goods from local manufacturers, the union laborers would terminate the "relation of employment" with them and cease to perform "work or labor" for them; and through their "recommending, advising, or persuading others by peaceful and lawful means" not to "patronize" sellers of the boycotted electrical equipment. Consequently, under our holdings in the *Hutcheson* case and other cases which followed it, had there been no union-contractor-manufacturer combination the union's actions here, coming as they did within the exemptions of the Clayton and Norris-La Guardia Acts, would not have been violations of the Sherman Act. We pass to the question of whether unions can, with impunity, aid and abet businessmen who are violating the Act....

... Since union members can, without violating the Sherman Act, strike to enforce a union boycott of goods, it is said they may settle the strike by getting their employers to agree to refuse to buy the goods. Employers and the union did here make bargaining agreements in which the employers agreed not to buy goods manufactured by companies which did not employ the members of Local No. 3. We may assume that such an agreement standing alone would not have violated the Sherman Act. But it did not stand alone. It was but one element in a far larger program in which contractors and manufacturers united with one another to monopolize all the business in New York City, to bar all other businessmen from that area, and to charge the public prices above a competitive level. It is true that victory of the union in its disputes, even had the union acted alone, might have added to the costs of goods, or might have resulted in individual refusals of all of their employers to buy electrical equipment not made by Local No. 3. So far as the union might have achieved this result acting alone, it would have been the natural consequence of labor union activities exempted by the Clayton Act from the coverage of the Sherman Act. *Apex Hosiery Co. v. Leader, supra,* 503. But when the unions participated with a combination of businessmen who had complete power to eliminate all competition among themselves and to prevent all competition from others, a situation was created not included within the exemptions of the Clayton and Norris-La Guardia Acts.

Our holding means that the same labor union activities may or may not be in violation of the Sherman Act, dependent upon whether the union acts alone or in combination with business groups. This, it is argued, brings about a wholly undesirable result—one which leaves labor unions free to engage in conduct which restrains trade. But the desirability of such an exemption of labor unions is a question for the determination of Congress. *Apex Hosiery Co. v. Leader, supra.* It is true that many labor union activities do substantially interrupt the course of trade and that these activities, lifted out of the prohibitions of the Sherman Act, include substantially all, if not all, of the normal peaceable activities of labor unions.... Congress evidently concluded, however, that the chief objective of antitrust legislation, preservation of business competition, could be accomplished by applying the legislation primarily only to those business groups which are directly interested in destroying competition. The difficulty of drawing legislation primarily aimed at trusts and monopolies so that it could also be applied to labor organizations without impairing the collective bargaining and related rights of those organizations has been emphasized both by congressional and judicial attempts to draw lines between permissible and prohibited union activities. There is, however, one line which we can draw with assurance that we follow the congressional purpose. We know that Congress feared the concentrated power of business organizations to dominate markets and prices. It intended to outlaw business monopolies. A business monopoly is no less such because a union participates, and such participation is a violation of the Act....

Respondents objected to the form of the injunction and specifically requested that it be amended so as to enjoin only those prohibited activities in which the union engaged in combination "with any person, firm or corporation which is a non-labor group...." Without such a limitation, the injunction as issued runs directly counter to the Clayton and the Norris-La Guardia Acts. The district court's refusal so to limit it was error.

The judgment of the Circuit Court of Appeals ordering the action dismissed is accordingly reversed and the cause is remanded to the district court for modification and clarification of the judgment and injunction, consistent with this opinion.

Reversed and remanded....

MR. JUSTICE MURPHY, dissenting....

The union here has not in any true sense "aided" or "abetted" a primary violation of the Act by the employers. In the words of the union, it has been "the dynamic force which has driven the employer-group to enter into agreements" whereby trade has been affected. The fact that the union has expressed its self-interest with the aid of others rather than solely by its own activities should not be decisive of statutory liability. What is legal if done alone should not become illegal if done with the assistance of others with the same purpose in mind. Otherwise a premium of unlawfulness is placed on collective bargaining....

NOTES

1. In *Meat & Provision Drivers Local 626 v. United States,* 371 U.S. 94 (1962), the Supreme Court held that grease peddlers, who were independent contractors and who joined the union only for the purpose of bringing the union's power to bear in the successful enforcement of an illegal combination of traffic in yellow grease and who had no other economic interrelationship with the other union members, were properly divested of their union membership.

2. A union and a contractors association agreed to establish an industry promotion fund and to require that all employers covered by local union contracts contribute one percent of their gross labor payroll to the fund, whether or not they were members of the association. Was there a Sherman Act violation? Was the union liable? *See NECA, Inc. v. National Constr. Ass'n,* 678 F.2d 492 (4th Cir. 1982), *cert. dismissed,* 463 U.S. 1234 (1983). What about a union-instituted "targeting program" under which employer-contractors who are both signatories to the union's labor agreements and members of a national multiemployer bargaining group receive contract concessions in order to allow them to compete effectively with nonunion firms? Does this violate the Sherman Act? *See Grinnell Corp. v. Road Sprinkler Fitters Local 669,* 156 L.R.R.M. 2337 (D. Md. 1997), *aff'd without op.,* 133 F.3d 914 (4th Cir. 1998).

3. For general analyses during this period, *see* Cox, *Labor and the Antitrust Laws—A Preliminary Analysis,* 104 U. Pa. L. Rev. 252 (1955); Smith, *Antitrust and Labor,* 53 Mich. L. Rev. 1119 (1955); Sovern, *Some Ruminations on Labor, the Antitrust Laws and Allen Bradley,* 13 Lab. L.J. 957 (1962); Winter, *Collective Bargaining and Competition: The Application of Antitrust Standards to Union Activities,* 73 Yale L.J. 14 (1963); *Report of the Attorney General's National Committee to Study the Antitrust Laws* 304-05 (1955).

4. *The place of the Taft-Hartley Act in the antitrust scheme.* Against a background of controversy dealing with the proper place of labor under the antitrust laws, Congress in 1947 considered amendments to the NLRA. The bill passed by the House, the Conference Committee Report notes, "contained a provision amending the Clayton Act so as to withdraw the exemption of labor organizations under the antitrust laws when such organizations engaged in combination or conspiracy in restraint of commerce where one of the purposes or a necessary effect of the combination or conspiracy was to join or combine with any person to fix prices, allocate costs, restrict production, distribution, or competition, or impose restrictions or conditions, upon the purchase, sale, or use of any product, material, machine, or equipment, or to engage in any unlawful concerted activity." 93 Cong. Rec. 6380 (1947). Explaining omission of such provisions from the enacted bill, the conference report continued: "Since the matters dealt with in this section have to a large measure been effectuated through the use of boycotts, and since the conference agreement contains effective provisions directly dealing with boycotts themselves, this provision is omitted from the conference agreement." 93 Cong. Rec. 6380 (1947).

UNITED MINE WORKERS v. PENNINGTON

Supreme Court of the United States
381 U.S. 657, 85 S. Ct. 1585, 14 L. Ed. 2d 625 (1965)

MR. JUSTICE WHITE delivered the opinion of the Court.

This action began as a suit by the trustees of the United Mine Workers of America Welfare and Retirement Fund against the respondents, individually and as owners of Phillips Brothers Coal Company, a partnership, seeking to recover some $55,000 in a royalty payments alleged to be due and payable under the trust provisions of the National Bituminous Coal Wage Agreement of 1950, as amended, September 29, 1952, executed by Phillips and United Mine Workers of America on or about October 1, 1953, and re-executed with amendments on or about September 8, 1955, and October 22, 1956. Phillips filed an answer and a cross-claim against UMW, alleging in both that the trustees, the UMW and certain large coal operators, had conspired to restrain and to monopolize interstate commerce in violation of §§ 1 and 2 of the Sherman Antitrust Act, 15 U.S.C. §§ 1, 2 (1958 ed.). Actual damages in the amount of $100,000 were claimed for the period beginning February 14, 1954, and ending December 31, 1958.

The allegations of the cross-claim were essentially as follows: Prior to the 1950 Wage Agreement between the operators and the union, severe controversy had existed in the industry, particularly over wages, the welfare fund and the union's efforts to control the working time of its members. Since 1950, however, relative peace has existed in the industry, all as the result of the 1950 wage agreement and its amendments and the additional understandings entered into between UMW and the large operators. Allegedly the parties considered over-production to be the critical problem of the coal industry. The agreed solution was to be the elimination of the smaller companies, the larger companies thereby controlling the market. More specifically, the union abandoned its efforts to control the working time of the miners, agreed not to oppose the rapid mechanization of the mines which would substantially reduce mine employment, agreed to help finance such mechanization and agreed to impose the terms of the 1950 agreement on all operators without regard for their ability to pay. The benefit to the union was to be increased wages as productivity increased with mechanization, these increases to be demanded of the smaller companies whether mechanized or not. Royalty payments into the welfare fund were to be increased also, and the union was to have effective control over the Fund's use. The union and large companies agreed upon other steps to exclude the marketing, production, and sale of nonunion coal. Thus the companies agreed not to lease coal lands to nonunion operators, and in 1958 agreed not to sell or buy coal from such companies. The companies and the union jointly and successfully approached the Secretary of Labor to obtain establishment under the Walsh-Healey Act ... of a minimum wage for employees of contractors selling coal to the TVA, such minimum wage being much higher than in other industries and making it difficult for small companies to compete in the TVA term contract market. At a later time, at a meeting attended by both union and company representatives, the TVA was urged to curtail its spot market purchases, a substantial portion of which were exempt from the Walsh-Healey order. Thereafter four of the larger companies waged a destructive and collusive price-cutting campaign in the TVA spot market for coal, two of the companies, West Kentucky Coal Co. and its subsidiary Nashville Coal Co., being those in which the union had large investments and over which it was in position to exercise control.

The complaint survived motions to dismiss and after a five-week trial before a jury, a verdict was returned in favor of Phillips and against the trustees of the union, the damages against the union being fixed in the amount of $90,000, to be trebled under 15 U.S.C. § 15 (1958 ed.). The trial court set aside the verdict against the trustees but overruled the union's motion for judgment notwithstanding the verdict or in the alternative for a new trial. The Court of Appeals affirmed. 325 F.2d 804. It ruled that the union was not exempt from liability under the Sherman Act on the facts of this case, considered the instructions adequate and found the evidence generally sufficient to support the verdict. We granted certiorari.... We reverse and remand the case for proceedings consistent with this opinion.

I

We first consider UMW's contention that the trial court erred in denying its motion for directed verdict and for judgment notwithstanding the verdict, since a determination in UMW's favor on this issue would finally resolve the controversy. The question presented by this phase of the case is whether in the circumstances of this case the union is exempt from liability under the antitrust laws. We think the answer is clearly in the negative and the union's motions were correctly denied.

The antitrust laws do not bar the existence and operation of labor unions as such. Moreover, § 20 of the Clayton Act ... and § 4 of the Norris-La Guardia Act ... permit a union, acting alone, to engage in the conduct therein specified without violating the Sherman Act. *United States v. Hutcheson,* 312 U.S. 219 (1941)....

But neither § 20 nor § 4 expressly deals with arrangements or agreements between unions and employers. Neither section tells us whether any or all such arrangements or agreements are barred or permitted by the antitrust laws. Thus *Hutcheson* itself stated:

> So long as a union acts in its self-interest *and does not combine with non-labor groups,* the licit and the illicit under § 20 are not to be distinguished by any judgment regarding the wisdom or unwisdom, the rightness or

wrongness, the selfishness or unselfishness of the end of which the particular union activities are the means.

312 U.S. at 232. (Emphasis added.)

And in *Allen Bradley v. IBEW Local 3,* 325 U.S. 797 (1945), this Court made explicit what had been merely a qualifying expression in *Hutcheson* and held that "when the unions participated with a combination of businessmen who had complete power to eliminate all competition among themselves and to prevent all competition from others, a situation was created not included within the exemptions of the Clayton and Norris-La Guardia Acts." *Id.* at 809....

If the UMW in this case, in order to protect its wage scale by maintaining employer income, had presented a set of prices at which the mine operators would be required to sell their coal, the union and the employers who happened to agree could not successfully defend this contract provision if it were challenged under the antitrust laws by the United States or by some party injured by the arrangement. *Cf. Allen Bradley v. IBEW Local 3,* 325 U.S. 797 (1945).... In such a case, the restraint on the product market is direct and immediate, is of the type characteristically deemed unreasonable under the Sherman Act and the union gets from the promise nothing more concrete than a hope for better wages to come.

Likewise, if as is alleged in this case, the union became a party to a collusive bidding arrangement designed to drive Phillips and others from the TVA spot market, we think any claim to exemption from antitrust liability would be frivolous at best. For this reason alone the motions of the unions were properly denied.

A major part of Phillips' case, however, was that the union entered into a conspiracy with the large operators to impose the agreed upon wage and royalty scales upon the smaller, nonunion operators, regardless of their ability to pay and regardless of whether or not the union represented the employees of these companies, all for the purpose of eliminating them from the industry, limiting production and preempting the market for the large, unionized operators. The UMW urges that since such an agreement concerned wage standards, it is exempt from the antitrust laws.

It is true that wages lie at the very heart of those subjects about which employers and unions must bargain and the law contemplates agreements on wages not only between individual employers and a union but agreements between the union and employers in a multi-employer bargaining unit. *NLRB v. Truck Drivers Union,* 353 U.S. 87, 94-96 (1957). The union benefit from the wage scale agreed upon is direct and concrete and the effect on the product market, though clearly present, results from the elimination of competition based on wages among the employers in the bargaining unit, which is not the kind of restraint Congress intended the Sherman Act to proscribe. *Apex Hosiery v. Leader,* 310 U.S. 469, 503-504 (1940).... We think it beyond question that a union may conclude a wage agreement for the multi-employer bargaining unit without violating the antitrust laws and that it may as a matter of its own policy, and not by agreement with all or part of the employers of that unit, seek the same wages from other employers.

This is not to say that an agreement resulting from union-employer negotiations is automatically exempt from Sherman Act scrutiny simply because the negotiations involve a compulsory subject of bargaining, regardless of the subject or the form and content of the agreement. Unquestionably the Board's demarcation of the bounds of the duty to bargain has great relevance to any consideration of the sweep of labor's antitrust immunity, for we are concerned here with harmonizing the Sherman Act with the national policy expressed in the National Labor Relations Act of promoting "the peaceful settlement of industrial disputes by subjecting labor-management controversies to the mediatory influence of negotiation," *Fibreboard Paper Prods. Corp. v. NLRB,* 379 U.S. 203, 211 (1964). But there are limits to what a union or an employer may offer or extract in the name of wages, and because they must bargain does not mean that the agreement reached may disregard other laws. *Teamsters Union v. Oliver,* 358 U.S. 283, 296 (1959)....

We have said that a union may make wage agreements with a multi-employer bargaining unit and may in pursuance of its own union interests seek to obtain the same terms from other employers. No case under the antitrust laws could be made out on evidence limited to such union behavior.[2] But we think a union forfeits its exemption from the antitrust laws when it is clearly shown that it has agreed with one set of employers to impose a certain wage scale on other bargaining units. One group of employers may not conspire to eliminate competitors from the industry and the union is liable with the employers if it becomes a party to the conspiracy. This is true even though the union's part in the scheme is an undertaking to secure the same wages, hours or other conditions of employment from the remaining employers in the industry.

We do not find anything in the national labor policy that conflicts with this conclusion. This Court has recognized that a legitimate aim of any national labor organization is to obtain uniformity of labor standards and that a consequence of such union activity may be to eliminate competition based on differences in such standards. *Apex Hosiery v. Leader,* 310 U.S. 469, 503 (1940). But there is nothing in the labor policy indicating that the union and the employers in one bargaining unit are free to bargain about the wages, hours and working conditions of other bargaining units or to attempt to settle these matters for the entire industry.

---

[2] Unilaterally, and without agreement with any employer group to do so, a union may adopt a uniform wage policy and seek vigorously to implement it even though it may suspect that some employers cannot effectively compete if they are required to pay the wage scale demanded by the union. The union need not gear its wage demands to those which the weakest units in the industry can afford to pay. Such union conduct is not alone sufficient evidence to maintain a union-employer conspiracy charge under the Sherman Act. There must be additional direct or indirect evidence of the conspiracy. There was, of course, other evidence in this case, but we indicate no opinion as to its sufficiency.

On the contrary, the duty to bargain unit by unit leads to a quite different conclusion. The union's obligation to its members would seem best served if the union retained the ability to respond to each bargaining situation as the individual circumstances might warrant, without being strait-jacketed by some prior agreement with the favored employers.

So far as the employer is concerned it has long been the Board's view that an employer may not condition the signing of a collective agreement on the union's organization of a majority of the industry. *American Range Lines, Inc.,* 13 N.L.R.B. 139, 147 (1939).... In such cases the obvious interest of the employer is to ensure that acceptance of the union's wage demands will not adversely affect his competitive position.... Such an employer condition, if upheld, would clearly reduce the extent of collective bargaining.... Permitting insistence on an agreement by the union to attempt to impose a similar contract on other employers would likewise seem to impose a restraining influence on the extent of collective bargaining, for the union could avoid impasse only by surrendering its freedom to act in its own interest *vis-à-vis* other employers, something it will be unwilling to do in many instances. Once again, the employer's interest is a competitive interest rather than an interest in regulating its own labor relations, and the effect on the union of such an agreement would be to limit the free exercise of the employees' right to engage in concerted activities according to their own views of their self-interest. In sum, we cannot conclude that the national labor policy provides any support for such agreements.

On the other hand, the policy of the antitrust laws is clearly set against employer-union agreements seeking to prescribe labor standards outside the bargaining unit. One could hardly contend, for example, that one group of employers could lawfully demand that the union impose on other employers wages that were significantly higher than those paid by the requesting employers, or a system of computing wages that, because of differences in methods of production, would be more costly to one set of employers than to another. The anticompetitive potential of such a combination is obvious, but is little more severe than what is alleged to have been the purpose and effect of the conspiracy in this case to establish wages at a level that marginal producers could not pay so that they would be driven from the industry. And if the conspiracy presently under attack were declared exempt it would hardly be possible to deny exemption to such avowedly discriminatory schemes.

From the viewpoint of antitrust policy, moreover, all such agreements between a group of employers and a union that the union will seek specified labor standards outside the bargaining unit suffer from a more basic defect, without regard to predatory intention or effect in the particular case. For the salient characteristic of such agreements is that the union surrenders its freedom of action with respect to its bargaining policy. Prior to the agreement the union might seek uniform standards in its own self-interest but would be required to assess in each case the probable costs and gains of a strike or other collective action to that end and thus might conclude that the objective of uniform standards should temporarily give way. After the agreement the union's interest would be bound in each case to that of the favored employer group. It is just such restraints upon the freedom of economic units to act according to their own choice and discretion that run counter to antitrust policy....

Thus the relevant labor and antitrust policies compel us to conclude that the alleged agreement between UMW and the large operators to secure uniform labor standards throughout the industry, if proved, was not exempt from the antitrust laws.

II

The UMW next contends that the trial court erroneously denied its motion for a new trial based on claimed errors in the admission of evidence.

In *Eastern R. Conf. v. Noerr Motors*, 365 U.S. 127 (1961), the Court rejected an attempt to base a Sherman Act conspiracy on evidence consisting entirely of activities of competitors seeking to influence public officials. The Sherman Act, it was held, was not intended to bar concerted action of this kind even though the resulting official action damaged other competitors at whom the campaign is aimed. Furthermore, the illegality of the conduct "was not at all affected by any anticompetitive purpose it may have had," *id.* at 140....

We agree with the UMW that both the Court of Appeals and the trial court failed to take proper account of the *Noerr* case....

The jury was instructed that the approach to the Secretary of Labor was legal unless part of a conspiracy to drive small operators out of business and that the approach to the TVA was not a violation of the antitrust laws "unless the parties so urged the TVA to modify its policies in buying coal for the purpose of driving the small operators out of business." If, therefore, the jury determined the requisite anticompetitive purpose to be present, it was free to find an illegal conspiracy based solely on the Walsh-Healey and TVA episodes, or in any event to attribute illegality to these acts as part of a general plan to eliminate Phillips and other distributors similarly situated. Neither finding, however, is permitted by *Noerr* for the reasons stated in that case....

There is another reason for remanding this case for further proceedings in the lower courts. It is clear under *Noerr* that Phillips could not collect any damages under the Sherman Act for any injury which it suffered from the action of the Secretary of Labor. The conduct of the union and the operators did not violate the Act, the action taken to set a minimum wage for government purchases of coal was the act of a public official who is not claimed to be a co-conspirator, and the jury should have been instructed, as UMW requested, to exclude any damages which Phillips may have suffered as a result of the Secretary's Walsh-Healey determinations....

The judgment is reversed and the case remanded for further proceedings consistent with this opinion.

It is so ordered.

MR. JUSTICE DOUGLAS, with whom MR. JUSTICE BLACK and MR. JUSTICE CLARK agree, concurring.

As we read the opinion of the Court, it reaffirms the principles of *Allen Bradley Co. v. Union,* 325 U.S. 797 (1945), and tells the trial judge:

First. On the new trial the jury should be instructed that if there were an industry-wide collective bargaining agreement whereby employers and the union agreed on a wage scale that exceeded the financial ability of some operators to pay and that if it was made for the purpose of forcing some employers out of business, the union as well as the employers who participate in the arrangement with the union should be found to have violated the antitrust laws.

Second. An industry-wide agreement containing those features is prima facie evidence of a violation....

Congress can design an oligopoly for our society, if it chooses. But business alone cannot do so as long as the antitrust laws are enforced. Nor should business and labor working hand-in-hand be allowed to make that basic change in the design of our so-called free enterprise system. If the allegations in this case are to be believed, organized labor joined hands with organized business to drive marginal operators out of existence. According to those allegations the union used its control over West Kentucky Coal Co. and Nashville Coal Co. to dump coal at such low prices that respondents, who were small operators, had to abandon their business. According to those allegations there was a boycott by the union and the major companies against small companies who needed major companies' coal land on which to operate. According to those allegations, high wage and welfare terms of employment were imposed on the small, marginal companies by the union and the major companies with the knowledge and intent that the small ones would be driven out of business.

The only architect of our economic system is Congress. We are right in adhering to its philosophy of the free enterprise system as expressed in the antitrust laws and as enforced by *Allen Bradley v. Union, supra,* until the Congress delegates to big business and big labor the power to remold our economy in the manner charged here.

MR. JUSTICE GOLDBERG, with whom MR. JUSTICE HARLAN and MR. JUSTICE STEWART join, dissenting from the opinion but concurring in the reversal. [Mr. Justice Goldberg's single opinion covers both *Pennington* and *Jewel Tea.* We present portions dealing with *Pennington* here; the part dealing with *Jewel Tea* is presented after the other opinions in that case, reprinted *infra.—Eds.*]

[The opinion first reviewed the history of labor and antitrust.]

In my view, this history shows a consistent congressional purpose to limit severely judicial intervention in collective bargaining under cover of the wide umbrella of the antitrust laws, and, rather, to deal with what Congress deemed to be specific abuses on the part of labor unions by specific proscriptions in the labor statutes. I believe that the Court should respect this history of congressional purpose and should reaffirm the Court's holdings in *Apex* and *Hutcheson*.... Following the sound analysis of *Hutcheson,* the Court should hold that, in order to effectuate congressional intent, collective bargaining activity concerning mandatory subjects of bargaining under the Labor Act is not subject to the antitrust laws. This rule flows directly from the *Hutcheson* holding that a union acting as a union, in the interests of its members, and not acting to fix prices or allocate markets in aid of an employer conspiracy to accomplish these objects, with only indirect union benefits, is not subject to challenge under the antitrust laws. To hold that mandatory collective bargaining is completely protected would effectuate the congressional policies of encouraging free collective bargaining, subject only to specific restrictions contained in the labor laws, and of limiting judicial intervention in labor matters via the antitrust route—an intervention which necessarily under the Sherman Act places on judges and juries the determination of "what public policy in regard to the industrial struggle demands." *Duplex Printing Press Co. v. Deering,* 254 U.S. 443, at 485 (1921) (dissenting opinion of Mr. Justice Brandeis)....

Moreover, mandatory subjects of bargaining are issues as to which strikes may not be enjoined by either federal or state courts. To say that the union can strike over such issues but that both it and the employer are subject to possible antitrust penalties for making collective bargaining agreements concerning them is to assert that Congress intended to permit the parties to collective bargaining to wage industrial warfare but to prohibit them from peacefully settling their disputes....

The Court in *Pennington* today ignores this history of the discredited judicial attempt to apply the antitrust laws to legitimate collective bargaining activity, and it flouts the clearly expressed congressional intent that, since "[t]he labor of a human being is not a commodity or article of commerce," the antitrust laws do not proscribe, and the national labor policy affirmatively promotes, the "elimination of price competition based on differences in labor standards," *Apex Hosiery Co. v. Leader, supra* at 503....

Since collective bargaining inevitably involves and requires discussion of the impact of the wage agreement reached with a particular employer or group of employers upon competing employers, the effect of the Court's decision will be to bar a basic element of collective bargaining from the conference room. If a union and employer are prevented from discussing and agreeing upon issues which are, in the great majority of cases, at the central core of bargaining, unilateral force will inevitably be substituted for rational discussion and agreement. Plainly and simply, the Court would subject both unions and employers to antitrust sanctions, criminal as well as civil, if in collective bargaining they concluded a wage agreement and, as part of the agreement, the union has undertaken to use its best efforts to have this wage accepted by other employers in the industry. Indeed, the decision today even goes beyond this. Under settled antitrust principles which are accepted by the Court as appropriate and applicable, which were the basis for jury instructions in *Pennington,* and which will govern it upon remand, there need not be direct evidence of an express agreement. Rather the existence of such an agreement, express or implied, may be inferred from the conduct of the parties....

In *Pennington,* central to the alleged conspiracy is the claim that hourly wage rates and fringe benefits were set at a level designed to eliminate the competition of the smaller nonunion companies by making the labor cost too high for them to pay. Indeed, the trial judge charged that there was no violation of the Sherman Act in the establishing of wages and welfare payments through the national contract, "provided" the mine workers and the major coal producers had not agreed to fix "high" rates "in order to drive the small coal operators out of business." Under such an instruction, if the jury found the wage scale too "high" it could impute the unlawful purpose of putting the nonunion operators out of business. It is clear that the effect of the instruction therefore, was to invite 12 jurymen to become arbiters of the economic desirability of the wage scale in the Nation's coal industry. The Court would sustain the judgment based on this charge and thereby put its stamp of approval on this role for courts and juries....

To allow a jury to infer an illegal "conspiracy" from the agreed-upon wage scale means that the jury must determine at what level the wages could be fixed without impelling the parties into the ambit of the antitrust laws. Is this not another way of saying that, via the antitrust route, a judge or jury may determine, according to its own motions of what is economically sound, the amount of wages that a union can properly ask for or that an employer can pay? It is clear, as experience shows, that judges and juries have neither the aptitude nor possess the criteria for making this kind of judgment....

As I have discussed, the Court's test is not essentially different from the discredited purpose-motive approach. Only rarely will there be direct evidence of an express agreement between a union and an employer to impose a particular wage scale on other employers. In most cases, as was true of *Pennington,* the trial court will instruct the jury that such an illegal agreement may be inferred from the conduct—"indirect evidence"—of the union and employers. To allow a court or a jury to infer an illegal agreement from collective bargaining conduct inevitably requires courts and juries to analyze the terms of collective bargaining agreements and the purposes and motives of unions and employers in agreeing upon them. Moreover, the evidence most often available to sustain antitrust liability under the Court's theory would show, as it did in *Pennington,* simply that the motives of the union and employer coincide—the union seeking high wages and protection from low-wage, nonunion competition and the employer who pays high wages seeking protection from competitors who pay lower wages. When there is this coincidence of motive, does the illegality of the "conspiracy" turn on whether the Union pursued its goal of a uniform wage policy through strikes and not negotiation? As I read the Court's opinion this is precisely what the result turns on and thus unions are forced, in order to show that they have not illegally "agreed" with employers, to pursue their aims through strikes and not negotiations. Yet, it is clear that such a result was precisely what the National Labor Relations Act was designed to prevent. The only alternative to resolution of collective bargaining issues by force available to the parties under the Court's holding is the encouragement of fraud and deceit. An employer will be forced to take a public stand against a union's wage demands, even if he is willing to accept them, lest a too-ready acceptance be used by a jury to infer an agreement between the union and employer that the same wages will be sought from other employers....

Furthermore, I do not understand how an inquiry can be formulated in terms of whether the union action is unilateral or is a consequence of a "conspiracy" with employers independently of the economic terms of the collective bargaining agreement. The agreement must be admitted into evidence and the Court holds that its economic consequences are relevant. In the end, one way or another, the entire panoply of economic fact becomes involved, and judges and juries under the Court's view would then be allowed to speculate about why a union bargained for increased compensation, or any other labor standard within the scope of mandatory bargaining. It is precisely this type of speculation that Congress has rejected....

USS-Posco Indus. v. Contra Costa County Bldg. & Constr. Trades Council, 31 F.3d 800 (9th Cir. 1994), concerned efforts by a group of California unions to eliminate nonunion construction in Northern California. In an effort to thwart work by BE & K, a nonunion contractor, the unions filed numerous lawsuits against BE & K, made various protests against permits being sought by BE & K, lobbied in favor of environmental ordinances that would require additional permits, and encouraged subcontractors to protest alleged safety violations involving BE & K. The court concluded that a broad antitrust exemption exists for labor organizations that act alone and do not combine with non-labor groups and that exercise their *Noerr-Pennington* right to petition the government for redress of grievances. As a result, it found the challenged union practices immune from antitrust liability. *See also* Comment, *The Antitrust Liability of Labor Unions for Anticompetitive Litigation,* 80 Calif. L. Rev. 757 (1992).

NOTES

1. Embry outbid Ross and succeeded it as a supplier of flight-training services to the government. All or most of Ross's employees were to be taken over by

Embry. Before this occurred, however, Ross negotiated a labor agreement with a union setting a high wage scale that Embry could not meet without defaulting on its new government contract. Ross thus hoped to recover the work. Is *Pennington* applicable or distinguishable? Note that the union has contracted with only a single employer, Ross, and that only a single bargaining unit is involved. *See Embry-Riddle Aeronautical Univ. v. Ross Aviation, Inc.,* 504 F. 2d 896 (5th Cir. 1974). *Cf. Mid-America Regional Bargaining Ass'n v. Carpenters Dist. Council of Will County,* 675 F.2d 881 (7th Cir.), *cert. denied,* 459 U.S. 860 (1982) (hourly pay escrow fund to keep projects working during contract talks).

2. *See generally Minda, Interest Groups, Political Freedom, and Antitrust: A Modern Reassessment of the Noerr-Pennington Doctrine,* 41 Hastings L.J. 905 (1990); Whitehead, *The Labor Exemption From Antitrust As An Ideological Antimony,* 32 Willamette L. Rev. 881 (1996).

AMALGAMATED MEAT CUTTERS & BUTCHER WORKMEN, LOCAL 189 v. JEWEL TEA CO.

Supreme Court of the United States
381 U.S. 676, 85 S. Ct. 1596, 14 L. Ed. 2d 640 (1965)

MR. JUSTICE WHITE announced the judgment of the Court and delivered an opinion, in which THE CHIEF JUSTICE and MR. JUSTICE BRENNAN join.

Like *United Mine Workers v. Pennington,* decided today, this case presents questions regarding the application of §§ 1 and 2 of the Sherman Antitrust Act ... to activities of labor unions. In particular, it concerns the lawfulness of the following restriction on the operating hours of food store meat departments contained in a collective agreement executed after joint multi-employer, multi-union negotiations:

"Market operating hours shall be 9:00 a.m. to 6:00 p.m. Monday through Saturday, inclusive. No customer shall be served who comes into the market before or after the hours set forth above."

This litigation arose out of the 1957 contract negotiations between the representatives of 9,000 Chicago retailers of fresh meat and the seven union petitioners, who are local affiliates of the Amalgamated Meat Cutters and Butcher Workmen of North America, AFL-CIO, representing virtually all butchers in the Chicago area. During the 1957 bargaining sessions the employer group presented several requests for union consent to a relaxation of the existing contract restriction on marketing hours for fresh meat, which forbade the sale of meat before 9 a.m. and after 6 p.m. in both service and self-service markets. The unions rejected all such suggestions, and their own proposal retaining the marketing-hours restriction was ultimately accepted at the final session by all but two of the employers, National Tea Co. and Jewel Tea Co. (hereinafter "Jewel"). Associated Food Retailers of Greater Chicago, a trade association having about 1,000 individual and independent merchants as members and representing some 300 meat dealers in the negotiations, was among those who accepted. Jewel, however, asked the union negotiators to present to their membership, on behalf of it and National Tea, a counter-offer that included provision for Friday night operations. At the same time Jewel voiced its belief, as it had midway through the negotiations, that any marketing-hours restriction was illegal. On the recommendation of the union negotiators the Jewel offer was rejected by the union membership, and a strike was authorized. Under the duress of the strike vote, Jewel decided to sign the contract previously approved by the rest of the industry.

In July 1958 Jewel brought suit against the unions, certain of their officers, Associated, and Charles H. Bromann, Secretary-Treasurer of Associated, seeking invalidation under §§ 1 and 2 of the Sherman Act of the contract provision that prohibited night meat market operations. The gist of the complaint was that the defendants and others had conspired together to prevent the retail sale of fresh meat before 9 a.m. and after 6 p.m. As evidence of the conspiracy Jewel relied in part on the events during the 1957 contract negotiations—the acceptance by Associated of the marketing-hours restriction and the unions' imposition of the restriction on Jewel through a strike threat. Jewel also alleged that it was a part of the conspiracy that the unions would neither permit their members to work at times other than the hours specified nor allow any grocery firm to sell meat, with or without employment of their members, outside those hours; that the members of Associated, which had joined only one of the 1957 employer proposals for extended marketing hours, had agreed among themselves to insist on the inclusion of the marketing-hours limitation in all collective agreements between the unions and any food store operator; that Associated, its members and officers had agreed with the other defendants that no firm was to be permitted to operate self-service meat markets between 6 p.m. and 9 p.m.; and that the unions, their officers and members had acted as the enforcing agent of the conspiracy.

The complaint stated that in recent years the prepackaged, self-service system of marketing meat had come into vogue, that 174 of Jewel's 196 stores were equipped to vend meat in this manner, and that a butcher need not be on duty in a self-service market at the time meat purchases were actually made. The prohibition of night meat marketing, it was alleged, unlawfully impeded Jewel in the use of its property and adversely affected the general public in that many persons find it inconvenient to shop during the day. An injunction, treble damages and attorney's fees were demanded.

The trial judge held the allegations of the complaint sufficient to withstand a motion to dismiss made on the grounds, *inter alia,* that (a) the "alleged restraint [was] within the exclusive regulatory scope of the National Labor Relations Act and [was] therefore outside the jurisdiction of the Court" and (b) the controversy was within the labor exemption to the antitrust laws. That ruling was sustained on appeal. *Jewel Tea Co. v. Meat Cutters, Local 189,* 274 F.2d 271 (7th Cir. 1960), *cert. denied,* 362 U.S. 936 (1960). After trial, however, the District Judge ruled the "record was devoid of any evidence to support a finding of a conspiracy" between Associated and the unions to force the restrictive provision on Jewel. Testing the unions' action standing alone, the trial court found that even in self-service markets removal of the limitation on marketing hours either would inaugurate longer hours and night work for the butchers or would result in butchers' work being done by others unskilled in the trade. Thus, the court concluded, the unions had imposed the marketing-hours limitation to serve their own interests respecting conditions of employment, and such action was clearly within the labor exemption of the Sherman Act established by *Hunt v. Crumboch,* 325 U.S. 821 (1945); *United States v. Hutcheson,* 312 U.S. 219 (1941); *United States v. American Fed. of Musicians,* 318 U.S. 741 (1943). Alternatively, the District Court ruled that even if this was not the case, the arrangement did not amount to an unreasonable restraint of trade in violation of the Sherman Act.

The Court of Appeals reversed the dismissal of the complaint as to both the unions and Associated. Without disturbing the District Court's finding that, apart from the contractual provision itself, there was no evidence of conspiracy, the Court of Appeals concluded that a conspiracy in restraint of trade had been shown. The court noted that "the rest of the industry agreed with the defendant local unions to continue the ban on night operations," while plaintiff resisted, and concluded that Associated and the unions "entered into a combination or agreement, which constituted a conspiracy, as charged in the complaint ... [w]hether it be called an agreement, contract or conspiracy, is immaterial." 331 F.2d 547, 551....

We granted certiorari on the unions' petition ... and now reverse the Court of Appeals....

I

We must first consider the unions' attack on the appropriateness of the District Court's exercise of jurisdiction, which is encompassed in their contention that this controversy is within the exclusive primary jurisdiction of the National Labor Relations Board....

Thus, the unions contend, Jewel could have filed an unfair labor practice charge with the Board on the ground that the unions had insisted on a nonmandatory subject—the marketing-hours restriction. Obviously, classification of bargaining subjects as "terms or conditions of employment" is a matter concerning which the Board has special expertise. Nevertheless, for the reasons stated below we cannot conclude that this is a proper case for application of the doctrine of primary jurisdiction.

To begin with, courts are themselves not without experience in classifying bargaining subjects as terms or conditions of employment. Just such a determination must be frequently made when a court's jurisdiction to issue an injunction affecting a labor dispute is challenged under the Norris-LaGuardia Act, which defines "labor dispute" as including "any controversy concerning terms or conditions of employment," Norris-LaGuardia Act § 13(c)....

Finally, we must reject the unions' primary-jurisdiction contention because of the absence of an available procedure for obtaining a Board determination. The Board does not classify bargaining subjects in the abstract but only in connection with unfair labor practice charges of refusal to bargain. The typical antitrust suit, however, is brought by a stranger to the bargaining relationship, and the complaint is not that the parties have refused to bargain but, quite the contrary, that they have agreed. Jewel's conspiracy allegation in the present case was just such a complaint. Agreement is of course not a refusal to bargain, and in such cases the Board affords no mechanism for obtaining a classification of the subject matter of the agreement. Moreover, even in the few instances when the antitrust action could be framed as a refusal to bargain charge, there is no guarantee of Board action. It is the function of the Board's General Counsel rather than the Board or a private litigant to determine whether an unfair labor practice complaint will ultimately issue. National Labor Relations Act § 3(d).... And the six-month limitation period of § 10(b) of the Act ... would preclude many litigants from even filing a charge with the General Counsel. Indeed, Jewel's complaint in this very case was filed more than six months after it signed the 1957 collective bargaining agreement....

II

Here, as in *United Mine Workers v. Pennington,* the claim is made that the agreement under attack is exempt from the antitrust laws. We agree, but not on the broad grounds urged by the union.

It is well at the outset to emphasize that this case comes to us stripped of any claim of a union-employer conspiracy against Jewel. The trial court found no evidence to sustain Jewel's conspiracy claim and this finding was not disturbed by the Court of Appeals. We therefore have a situation where the unions, having obtained a marketing-hours agreement from one group of employers, have successfully sought the same terms from a single employer, Jewel, not as a result of a bargain between the unions and some employers directed against other employers, but pursuant to what the unions deemed to be in their own labor union interests.

Jewel does not allege that it has been injured by the elimination of competition among the other employers within the unit with respect to marketing hours; Jewel complains only of the union's action in forcing it to accept the same restriction, the union acting not at the behest of any employer but in pursuit of its own policies. It might be argued that absent any union-employer conspiracy against Jewel and absent any agreement between Jewel and any other employer, the Union-Jewel contract cannot be a violation of the Sherman Act. But the issue before us is not the broad substantive one of a violation of the antitrust laws—was there a conspiracy or combination which unreasonably restrained trade or an attempt to monopolize and was Jewel damaged in its business—but whether the agreement is immune from attack by reason of the labor exemption from the antitrust laws. The fact that the parties to the agreement are but a single employer and the unions representing its employees does not compel immunity for the agreement. We must consider the subject matter of the agreement in the light of the national labor policy....

We pointed out in *Pennington* that exemption for union-employer agreements is very much a matter of accommodating the coverage of the Sherman Act to the policy of the labor laws. Employers and unions are required to bargain about wages, hours and working conditions, and this fact weighs heavily in favor of antitrust exemption for agreements on these subjects. But neither party need bargain about other matters and either party commits an unfair labor practice if it conditions its bargaining upon discussions of a nonmandatory subject. *NLRB v. Borg-Warner Corp.*, 356 U.S. 342 (1958). Jewel, for example, need not have bargained about or agreed to a schedule of prices at which its meat would be sold and the union could not legally have insisted that it do so. But if the union had made such a demand, Jewel had agreed and the United States or an injured party had challenged the agreement under the antitrust laws, we seriously doubt that either the union or Jewel could claim immunity by reason of the labor exemption, whatever substantive questions of violation there might be.

Thus the issue in this case is whether the marketing-hours restriction, like wages, and unlike prices, is so intimately related to wages, hours and working conditions that the unions' successful attempt to obtain that provision through bona fide, arms-length bargaining in pursuit of its own labor union policies, and not at the behest of or in combination with nonlabor groups, falls within the protection of the national labor policy and is therefore exempt from the Sherman Act.[5] We think that it is.

The Court of Appeals would classify the marketing hours restriction with the product-pricing provision and place both within the reach of the Sherman Act. In its view, labor has a legitimate interest in the number of hours it must work but

---

[5] The crucial determinant is not the form of the agreement—*e.g.,* prices or wages—but its relative impact on the product market and the interests of union members. Thus in *Teamsters v. Oliver,* 358 U.S. 283 (1959), we held that federal labor policy precluded application of state antitrust laws to an employer-union agreement that when leased trucks were driven by their owners, such owner-drivers should receive, in addition to the union wage, not less than a prescribed minimum rental. Though in form a scheme fixing prices for the supply of leased vehicles, the agreement was designed "to protect the negotiated wage scale against the possible undermining through diminution of the owner's wages for driving which might result from a rental which did not cover his operating costs." *Id.* at 293-294. As the agreement did not embody a "'remote and indirect approach to the subject of wages' ... but a direct frontal attack upon a problem thought to threaten the maintenance of the basic wage structure established by the collective bargaining contract," *id.* at 294, the paramount federal policy of encouraging collective bargaining proscribed application of the state law.

no interest in whether the hours fall in the daytime, in the nighttime or on Sundays. "[T]he furnishing of a place and advantageous hours of employment for the butchers to supply meat to customers are the prerogatives of the employer." 331 F.2d 547, 549. That reasoning would invalidate with respect to both service and self-service markets the 1957 provision that "eight hours shall constitute the basic work day, Monday through Saturday; *work to begin at 9:00 a.m. and stop at 6:00 p.m....*" as well as the marketing-hours restriction.

Contrary to the Court of Appeals, we think that the particular hours of the day and the particular days of the week during which employees shall be required to work are subjects well within the realm of "wages, hours, and other terms and conditions of employment" about which employers and unions must bargain. National Labor Relations Act § 8(d); *see Timken Roller Bearing Co.,* 70 N.L.R.B. 500, 504, 515-516, 521 (1946), *rev'd on other grounds,* 161 F.2d 949 (6th Cir. 1947) (employer's unilateral imposition of Sunday work was refusal to bargain); *Massey Gin & Machine Works, Inc.,* 78 N.L.R.B. 189, 195, 199 (same; change in starting and quitting time); *Camp & McInnes, Inc.,* 100 N.L.R.B. 524, 532 (same; reduction of lunch hour and advancement of quitting time). And, although the effect on competition is apparent and real, perhaps more so than in the case of the wage agreement, the concern of union members is immediate and direct. Weighing the respective interests involved, we think the national labor policy expressed in the National Labor Relations Act places beyond the reach of the Sherman Act union-employer agreements on when, as well as how long, employees must work. An agreement on these subjects between the union and the employers in a bargaining unit is not illegal under the Sherman Act, nor is the union's unilateral demand for the same contract of other employers in the industry.

Disposing of the case, as it did, on the broad grounds we have indicated, the Court of Appeals did not deal separately with the marketing-hours provision, as distinguished from hours of work, in connection with either service or self-service markets. The dispute here pertains principally to self-service markets.

The unions argue that since night operations would be impossible without night employment of butchers, or an impairment of the butchers' jurisdiction, or a substantial effect on the butchers' workload, the marketing-hours restriction is either little different in effect from the valid working-hours provision that work shall stop at 6 p.m. or is necessary to protect other concerns of the union members. If the unions' factual premises are true, we think the unions could impose a restriction on night operations without violation of the Sherman Act; for then operating hours, like working hours, would constitute a subject of immediate and legitimate concern to union members.

Jewel alleges on the other hand that the night operation of self-service markets requires no butcher to be in attendance and does not infringe any other legitimate union concern. Customers serve themselves; and if owners want to forego furnishing the services of the butcher to give advice or to make special cuts, this is not the unions' concern since their desire to avoid night work is fully satisfied and no other legitimate interest is being infringed. In short, the connection between working hours and operating hours in the case of the self-service market is said to be so attenuated as to bring the provision within the prohibition of the Sherman Act.

If it were true that self-service markets could actually operate without butchers, at least for a few hours after 6 p.m., that no encroachment on butchers' work would result and that the workload of butchers during normal working hours would not be substantially increased, Jewel's position would have considerable merit. For then the obvious restraint on the product market—the exclusion of self-service stores from the evening market for meat—would stand alone, unmitigated and unjustified by the vital interests of the union butchers which are relied upon in this case. In such event the limitation imposed by the union might well be reduced to nothing but an effort by the union to protect one group of employers from competition by another, which is conduct that is not exempt from the Sherman Act. Whether there would be a violation of §§ 1 and 2 would then depend on whether the elements of a conspiracy in restraint of trade or an attempt to monopolize had been proved.

Thus the dispute between Jewel and the unions essentially concerns a narrow factual question: Are night operations without butchers, and without infringement of butchers' interests, feasible? The District Court resolved this factual dispute in favor of the unions. It found that "in stores where meat is sold at night it is impractical to operate without either butchers or other employees. Someone must arrange, replenish and clean the counters and supply customer services." Operating without butchers would mean that "their work would be done by others unskilled in the trade," and "would involve an increase in workload in preparing for the night work and cleaning the next morning." 215 F. Supp. at 846. Those findings were not disturbed by the Court of Appeals, which, as previously noted, proceeded on a broader ground. Our function is limited to reviewing the record to satisfy ourselves that the trial judge's findings are not clearly erroneous. Fed. Rules Civ. Proc. 52(a).

The trial court had before it evidence concerning the history of the unions' opposition to night work, the development of the provisions respecting night work and night operations, the course of collective negotiations in 1957, 1959, and 1961 with regard to those provisions, and the characteristics of meat marketing insofar as they bore on the feasibility of night operations without butchers....

The unions' evidence with regard to the practicability of night operations without butchers was accurately summarized by the trial judge as follows:

> [I]n most of plaintiff's stores outside Chicago, where night operations exist, meat cutters are on duty whenever a meat department is open after 6 P.M.... Even in self-service departments, ostensibly operated without employees on duty after 6 P.M., there was evidence that requisite customer services in connection with meat sales were performed by grocery clerks. In

the same vein, defendants adduced evidence that in the sale of delicatessen items, which could be made after 6 P.M. from self-service cases under the contract, 'practically' always during the time the market was open the manager, or other employees, would be rearranging and restocking the cases. There was also evidence that even if it were practical to operate a self-service meat market after 6 P.M. without employees, the night operations would add to the workload in getting the meats prepared for night sales and in putting the counters in order the next day. [215 F. Supp. at 844.]

Jewel challenges the unions' evidence on each of these points—arguing, for example, that its preference to have butchers on duty at night, where possible under the union contract, is not probative of the feasibility of not having butchers on duty and that the evidence that grocery clerks performed customer services within the butchers' jurisdiction was based on a single instance resulting from "entrapment" by union agents. But Jewel's argument—when considered against the historical background of union concern with working hours and operating hours and the virtually uniform recognition by employers of the intimate relationship between the two subjects, as manifested by bargaining proposals in 1957, 1959, and 1961—falls far short of a showing that the trial judge's ultimate findings were clearly erroneous....

Reversed.

MR. JUSTICE DOUGLAS, with whom MR. JUSTICE BLACK and MR. JUSTICE CLARK concur, dissenting.

If we followed *Allen Bradley Co. v. Local Union No. 3,* 325 U.S. 797 (1945), we would hold with the Court of Appeals that this multi-employer agreement with the union not to sell meat between 6 p.m. and 9 a.m. was not immunized from the antitrust laws and that respondent's evidence made out a prima facie case that it was in fact a violation of the Sherman Act.

If, in the present case, the employers alone agreed not to sell meat from 6 p.m. to 9 a.m., they would be guilty of an anti-competitive practice, barred by the antitrust laws. Absent an agreement or conspiracy, a proprietor can keep his establishment open for such hours as he chooses.... That Jewel has been coerced by the unions into respecting this agreement means that Jewel cannot use convenience of shopping hours as a means of competition....

At the conclusion of respondent's case, the District Court dismissed Associated and Bromann from the action, which was tried without a jury, on the ground that there was no evidence of a conspiracy between Associated and the unions. But in the circumstances of this case the collective agreement itself, of which the District Court said there was clear proof, was evidence of a conspiracy among the employers with the unions to impose the marketing-hours restriction on Jewel via a strike threat by the unions. This tended to take from the merchants who agreed among themselves their freedom to work their own hours and to subject all who, like Jewel, wanted to sell meat after 6 p.m. to the coercion of threatened strikes, all of which if done in concert only by businessmen would violate the antitrust laws. *See Fashion Guild v. Federal Trade Comm'n,* 312 U.S. 457, 465 (1941).

In saying that there was no conspiracy, the District Court failed to give any weight to the collective agreement itself as evidence of a conspiracy and to the context in which it was written. This Court makes the same mistake.... Here the contract of the unions with a large number of employers shows it was planned and designed not merely to control but entirely to prohibit "the marketing of goods and services" from 6 p.m. until 9 a.m. the next day. Some merchants relied chiefly on price competition to draw trade; others employed courtesy, quick service, and keeping their doors open long hours to meet the convenience of customers. The unions here induced a large group of merchants to use their collective strength to hurt others who wanted the competitive advantage of selling meat after 6 p.m. Unless *Allen Bradley* is either overruled or greatly impaired, the unions can no more aid a group of businessmen to force their competitors to follow uniform store marketing hours than to force them to sell at fixed prices. Both practices take away the freedom of traders to carry on their business in their own competitive fashion.

My Brother WHITE's conclusion that the concern of the union members over *marketing* hours is "immediate and direct" depends upon there being a necessary connection between marketing hours and working hours. That connection is found in the District Court's finding that "in stores where meat is sold at night it is impractical to operate without either butchers or other employees." It is, however, undisputed that on some nights Jewel does so operate in some of its stores in Indiana, and even in Chicago it sometimes operates without butchers at night in the sale of fresh poultry and sausage, which are exempt from the union ban.

It is said that even if night self-service could be carried on without butchers, still the union interest in store hours would be immediate and direct because competitors would have to stay open too or be put at a disadvantage—and some of these competitors would be non-self-service stores that would have to employ union butchers at night. But *Allen Bradley* forecloses such an expansive view of the labor exemption to the antitrust laws.

MR. JUSTICE GOLDBERG, with whom MR. JUSTICE HARLAN and MR. JUSTICE STEWART join, dissenting from the opinion but concurring in the ... judgment of the Court....

The judicial expressions in *Jewel Tea* represent another example of the reluctance of judges to give full effect to congressional purpose in this area and the substitution by judges of their views for those of Congress as to how free collective bargaining should operate. In this case the Court of Appeals would have held the Union liable for the Sherman Act's criminal and civil penalties because in the court's social and economic judgment, the determination of the hours at which meat is to be sold is a "proprietary" matter within the exclusive control of management and thus the Union had no legitimate interest in bargaining over it. My Brother DOUGLAS, joined by MR. JUSTICE BLACK and MR. JUSTICE CLARK, would affirm this judgment apparently because the agreement was reached through a multi-employer bargaining unit. But, as I have demonstrated above, there is nothing even remotely illegal about such bargaining. Even if an independent conspiracy test were applicable to the *Jewel Tea* situation, the simple fact is that multi-employer bargaining conducted at arm's length does not constitute union abetment of a business combination. It is often a self-defensive form of employer bargaining designed to match union strength....

[M]y Brother WHITE indicates that he would sustain a judgment here, even absent evidence of union abetment of an independent conspiracy of employers, if the trial court had found "that self-service markets could actually operate without butchers, at least for a few hours after 6 p.m., that no encroachment on butchers' work would result and that the workload of butchers during normal working hours would not be substantially increased...." ... Such a view seems to me to be unsupportable. It represents a narrow, confining view of what labor unions have a legitimate interest in preserving and thus bargaining about. Even if the self-service markets could operate after 6 p.m., without their butchers and without increasing the work of their butchers at other times, the result of such operation can reasonably be expected to be either that the small, independent, service markets would have to remain open in order to compete, thus requiring their union butchers to work at night, or that the small, independent, service markets would not be able to operate at night and thus would be put at a competitive disadvantage. Since it is clear that the large, automated self-service markets employ less butchers per volume of sales than service markets do, the Union certainly has a legitimate interest in keeping service markets competitive so as to preserve jobs. Job security of this kind has been recognized to be a legitimate subject of union interest. *See Telegraphers v. Chicago & N.W.R. Co.,* 362 U.S. 330 (1960); *Teamsters Local 24 v. Oliver,* 358 U.S. 283 (1959), 362 U.S. 605 (1960).... The direct interest of the union in not working undesirable hours by curtailing all business at those hours is, of course, a far cry from the indirect "interest" in *Allen Bradley* in fixing prices and allocating markets solely to increase the profits of favored employers.

Indeed, if the Union in *Jewel Tea* were attempting to aid the small service butcher shops and thus save total employment against automation, perhaps at a necessarily reduced wage scale, the case would present the exact opposite union philosophy from that of the Mine Workers in *Pennington.* Putting the opinion of the Court in *Pennington* together with the opinions of my Brothers DOUGLAS and WHITE in *Jewel Tea,* it would seem that unions are damned if their collective bargaining philosophy involves acceptance of automation *(Pennington)* and are equally damned if their collective bargaining philosophy involves resistance to automation *(Jewel Tea).* Again, the wisdom of a union adopting either philosophy is not for judicial determination....

NOTES

1. *See* Cox, *Labor and the Antitrust Laws: Pennington and Jewel Tea,* 46 B.U.L. Rev. 317 (1966); Di Cola, *Labor Antitrust: Pennington, Jewel Tea and Subsequent Meandering,* 33 U. Pitt. L. Rev. 705 (1972); Meltzer, *Labor Unions, Collective Bargaining, and the Antitrust Laws,* 32 U. Chi. L. Rev. 659 (1965); St. Antoine, *Collective Bargaining and the Antitrust Laws,* in Industrial Relations Research Ass'n, Proceedings of the 19th Annual Winter Meeting 66 (1966).

2. Under *Pennington,* is there a distinction between a union's loss of antitrust immunity and its commission of a substantive violation? If so, what added elements must be shown to establish an offense arising out of an agreement with extra-unit implications?

For an extended discussion of the meaning of *Pennington* and its progeny, *see Smitty Baker Coal Co. v. UMW,* 620 F.2d 416 (4th Cir. 1980), *cert. denied,* 449 U.S. 870 (1981). Although the plaintiff small coal operator had won a jury verdict of $1,125,000 in his antitrust suit, he ultimately lost; the Fourth Circuit held, *inter alia,* that proof of predatory intent was an essential element in a *Pennington*-type case and there was no such proof here.

Despite claims by the employer that an ILA bargaining agreement concerning the manning of barges ran afoul of *Pennington,* by setting terms for non-party employers, and *Jewel Tea,* in that it regulated nonmandatory topics to restrain competition, the Second Circuit found the language permissible because it "vitally affected" working conditions and wages. Finding legitimate work preservation objectives present, the court applied the nonstatutory labor exemption to the facts. *Berman Enters. v. ILA Local 333,* 644 F.2d 930 (2d Cir.), *cert. denied,* 454 U.S. 965 (1981).

3. What will be the effect of *Pennington* on "most favored nation" clauses, by which the union agrees to give the signatory employer the benefit of the most favorable terms the union subsequently affords any other employer? *See Dolly Madison Indus.,* 182 N.L.R.B. 1037 (1970), *supra.*

4. What other efforts by unions or employers to obtain uniform labor contracts may be placed in question as a result of *Pennington?* For example, what about several unions coordinating bargaining policy with respect to different units of the same business—or several employers coordinating bargaining strategy, in the absence of a multi-employer unit, such as agreeing on a joint lockout in case one employer is struck?

5. A five-to-four majority of the Supreme Court held that the ordinary "preponderance of evidence" standard is applicable to the establishing of substantive violations in civil antitrust actions against labor unions. Only in proving the authority of individual members, officers, or agents of a union to act on its behalf must a "clear proof" test be met. *Ramsey v. UMW,* 401 U.S. 302 (1971).

6. On remand, the courts held that the small coal operators in *Pennington* and *Ramsey* failed to prove a violation of the antitrust laws. *Lewis v. Pennington,* 257

F. Supp. 815 (E.D. Tenn. 1966), *aff'd*, 400 F.2d 806 (6th Cir.), *cert. denied sub nom. Pennington v. UMW*, 393 U.S. 983 (1968); *Ramsey v. UMW*, 344 F. Supp. 1029 (E.D. Tenn. 1972), *aff'd*, 481 F.2d 742 (6th Cir.), *cert. denied*, 414 U.S. 1067 (1973).

However, other similarly situated coal operators prevailed against the UMW in their treble-damage antitrust suits. *Tennessee Consol. Coal Co. v. UMW*, 416 F.2d 1192 (6th Cir. 1969), *cert. denied*, 397 U.S. 964 (1970) (damages of $1,432,500 recovered, plus $150,000 attorneys' fees); *South-East Coal Co. v. UMW and Consolidation Coal Co.*, 434 F.2d 767 (6th Cir. 1970), *cert. denied*, 402 U.S. 983 (1971) (damages of $7,231,356, plus $335,000 attorneys' fees).

American Federation of Musicians v. Carroll, 391 U.S. 99, 88 S. Ct. 1562, 20 L. Ed. 2d 460 (1968). Respondents were orchestra "leaders," who booked so-called "club-dates," or one-time engagements, for their groups, and then secured enough "side-men," or supporting instrumentalists, to play at the various events. Usually the leaders performed with their orchestras, sometimes only conducting but often also playing an instrument. Under the rules of petitioners, musicians unions to which the respondents belonged, orchestra leaders had to charge purchasers of music minimum prices prescribed in a "price list." The prices were a total of (a) the minimum wage scales for sidemen, (b) a "leader's fee" which was double the sideman's scale in orchestras of four or more, and (c) an additional eight percent to cover social security, unemployment insurance, and other expenses. Respondents sought an injunction against this price floor and treble damages under the Sherman Act. Relying heavily on *Teamsters Local 24 v. Oliver, supra*, as well as on *Jewel Tea*, the Supreme Court held that the action should be dismissed. Justice Brennan, speaking for the Court, stated that "the price floors, including the minimums for leaders, are simply a means for coping with the job and wage competition of the leaders to protect the wage scales of musicians who respondents concede are employees on club-dates, namely sidemen and subleaders." He added that "the price of the product—here the price for an orchestra for a club-date—represents almost entirely the scale wages of the sidemen and the leader. Unlike most industries, except for the 8 percent charge, there are no other costs contributing to the price. Therefore, if leaders cut prices, inevitably wages must be cut." Justices White and Black dissented.

NOTES

1. What are the implications of *Carroll* for a society in which the service industries loom ever more important?

2. A collectively bargained job-subsidy program, whereby a union allowed electrical contractors to base their bids for certain specified jobs on wages lower than the contract rates, with the union making up the difference to employees, was protected by the nonstatutory exemption to the antitrust laws. *Phoenix Elec. Co. v. National Elec. Contractors Ass'n,* 81 F.3d 858 (9th Cir. 1996).

3. An agreement by car dealers to restrict showroom hours is not covered by the nonstatutory antitrust exemption when, despite being a response to union demands, the restrictions are not the result of arm's length bargaining and are intended in part to avoid unionization. *In re Detroit Auto Dealers Ass'n,* 955 F.2d 457 (6th Cir.), *cert. denied,* 506 U.S. 973 (1992).

4. The expulsion of a member of a unionized multiemployer association for violating the association's bylaws by negotiating a separate contract with the union did not violate the Sherman Antitrust Act. *Precision Piping & Instruments v. E.I. Du Pont de Nemours & Co.,* 951 F.2d 613 (4th Cir. 1991).

CONNELL CONSTRUCTION CO. v. PLUMBERS LOCAL 100

Supreme Court of the United States
421 U.S. 616, 95 S. Ct. 1830, 44 L. Ed. 2d 418 (1975)

MR. JUSTICE POWELL delivered the opinion of the Court....

I

Local 100 is the bargaining representative for workers in the plumbing and mechanical trades in Dallas. When this litigation began, it was party to a multiemployer bargaining agreement with the Mechanical Contractors Association of Dallas, a group of about 75 mechanical contractors. That contract contained a "most favored nation" clause, by which the union agreed that if it granted a more favorable contract to any other employer it would extend the same terms to all members of the Association.

Connell Construction Company is a general building contractor in Dallas. It obtains jobs by competitive bidding and subcontracts all plumbing and mechanical work. Connell has followed a policy of awarding these subcontracts on the basis of competitive bids, and it has done business with both union and nonunion subcontractors. Connell's employees are represented by various building trade unions. Local 100 has never sought to represent them or to bargain with Connell on their behalf.

In November 1970, Local 100 asked Connell to agree that it would subcontract mechanical work only to firms that had a current contract with the union. It demanded that Connell sign the following agreement:

> WHEREAS, the contractor and the union are engaged in the construction industry, and
> WHEREAS, the contractor and the union desire to make an agreement applying in the event of subcontracting in accordance with Section 8(e) of the Labor-Management Relations Act;

> WHEREAS, it is understood that by this agreement the contractor does not grant, nor does the union seek, recognition as the collective bargaining representative of any employees of the signatory contractor; and
>
> WHEREAS, it is further understood that the subcontracting limitation provided herein applies only to mechanical work which the contractor does not perform with his own employees but uniformly subcontracts to other firms;
>
> THEREFORE, the contractor and the union mutually agree with respect to work falling within the scope of this agreement that is to be done at the site of the construction, alteration, painting or repair of any building, structure, or other works, that if the contractor should contract or subcontract any of the aforesaid work falling within the normal trade jurisdiction of the union, said contractor shall contract or subcontract such work only to firms that are parties to an executed, current, collective bargaining agreement with Local Union 100 of the United Association of Journeymen and Apprentices of the Plumbing and Pipefitting Industry.

When Connell refused to sign this agreement, Local 100 stationed a single picket at one of Connell's major construction sites. About 150 workers walked off the job, and construction halted. Connell filed suit in state court to enjoin the picketing as a violation of Texas antitrust laws. Local 100 removed the case to federal court. Connell then signed the subcontracting agreement under protest. It amended its complaint to claim that the agreement violated §§ 1 and 2 of the Sherman Act, ... and was therefore invalid. Connell sought a declaration to this effect and an injunction against any further efforts to force it to sign such an agreement.

By the time the case went to trial, Local 100 had submitted identical agreements to a number of other general contractors in Dallas. Five others had signed, and the union was waging a selective picketing campaign against those who resisted.

The District Court held that the subcontracting agreement was exempt from federal antitrust laws because it was authorized by the construction industry proviso to § 8(e) of the National Labor Relations Act.... The court also held that federal labor legislation preempted the State's antitrust laws.... The Court of Appeals for the Fifth Circuit affirmed, 483 F. 2d 1154 (5th Cir. 1973), with one judge dissenting. It held that Local 100's goal of organizing nonunion subcontractors was a legitimate union interest and that its efforts toward that goal were therefore exempt from federal antitrust laws. On the second issue, it held that state law was preempted under *San Diego Building Trades Council v. Garmon*, 359 U.S. 236 (1959). We granted certiorari on Connell's petition.... We reverse on the question of federal antitrust immunity and affirm the ruling on state law preemption.

II

The basic sources of organized labor's exemption from federal antitrust laws are §§ 6 and 20 of the Clayton Act, ... and the Norris-LaGuardia Act.... These statutes declare that labor unions are not combinations or conspiracies in restraint of trade, and exempt specific union activities, including secondary picketing and boycotts, from the operation of the antitrust laws. *See United States v. Hutcheson,* 312 U.S. 219 (1941). They do not exempt concerted action or agreements between unions and nonlabor parties. *UMW v. Pennington,* 381 U.S. 657, 662 (1965). The Court has recognized, however, that a proper accommodation between the congressional policy favoring collective bargaining under the NLRA and the congressional policy favoring free competition in business markets requires that some union-employer agreements be accorded a limited nonstatutory exemption from antitrust sanctions. *Meat Cutters Local 189 v. Jewel Tea Co.,* 381 U.S. 676 (1965).

The nonstatutory exemption has its source in the strong labor policy favoring the association of employees to eliminate competition over wages and working conditions. Union success in organizing workers and standardizing wages ultimately will affect price competition among employers, but the goals of federal labor law never could be achieved if this effect on business competition were held a violation of the antitrust laws. The Court therefore has acknowledged that labor policy requires tolerance for the lessening of business competition based on differences in wages and working conditions. *See UMW v. Pennington, supra* at 666; *Jewel Tea, supra* at 692-693 (opinion of MR. JUSTICE WHITE). Labor policy clearly does not require, however, that a union have freedom to impose direct restraints on competition among those who employ its members. Thus, while the statutory exemption allows unions to accomplish some restraints by acting unilaterally, *e.g., American Federation of Musicians v. Carroll,* 391 U.S. 99 (1968), the nonstatutory exemption offers no similar protection when a union and a nonlabor party agree to restrain competition in a business market. *See Allen Bradley Co. v. IBEW Local 3,* 325 U.S. 797, 806-811 (1945); Cox, *Labor and the Antitrust Laws—A Preliminary Analysis,* 104 U. Pa. L. Rev. 252 (1955); Meltzer, *Labor Unions, Collective Bargaining, and the Antitrust Laws,* 32 U. Chi. L. Rev. 659 (1965).

In this case Local 100 used direct restraints on the business market to support its organizing campaign. The agreements with Connell and other general contractors indiscriminately excluded nonunion subcontractors from a portion of the market, even if their competitive advantages were not derived from substandard wages and working conditions but rather from more efficient operating methods. Curtailment of competition based on efficiency is neither a goal of federal labor policy nor a necessary effect of the elimination of competition among workers. Moreover, competition based on efficiency is a positive value that the antitrust laws strive to protect.

The multiemployer bargaining agreement between Local 100 and the Association, though not challenged in this suit, is relevant in determining the effect that the agreement between Local 100 and Connell would have on the business market. The "most favored nation" clause in the multiemployer agreement promised to eliminate competition between members of the Association and any other subcontractors that Local 100 might organize. By giving members of the Association a contractual right to insist on terms as favorable as those given any competitor, it guaranteed that the union would make no agreement that would give an unaffiliated contractor a competitive advantage over members of the Association. Subcontractors in the Association thus stood to benefit from any extension of Local 100's organization, but the method Local 100 chose also had the effect of sheltering them from outside competition in that portion of the market covered by subcontracting agreements between general contractors and Local 100. In that portion of the market, the restriction on subcontracting would eliminate competition on all subjects covered by the multiemployer agreement, even on subjects unrelated to wages, hours and working conditions.

Success in exacting agreements from general contractors would also give Local 100 power to control access to the market for mechanical subcontracting work. The agreements with general contractors did not simply prohibit subcontracting to any nonunion firm; they prohibited subcontracting to any firm that did not have a contract with Local 100. The union thus had complete control over subcontract work offered by general contractors that had signed these agreements. Such control could result in significant adverse effects on the market and on consumers, effects unrelated to the union's legitimate goals of organizing workers and standardizing working conditions. For example, if the union thought the interests of its members would be served by having fewer subcontractors competing for the available work, it could refuse to sign collective bargaining agreements with marginal firms. *Cf. UMW v. Pennington, supra.* Or, since Local 100 has a well-defined geographical jurisdiction, it could exclude "travelling" subcontractors by refusing to deal with them. Local 100 thus might be able to create a geographical enclave for local contractors, similar to the closed market in *Allen Bradley, supra.*

This record contains no evidence that the union's goal was anything other than organizing as many subcontractors as possible. This goal was legal, even though a successful organizing campaign ultimately would reduce the competition that unionized employers face from nonunion firms. But the methods the union chose are not immune from antitrust sanctions simply because the goal is legal. Here Local 100, by agreement with several contractors, made nonunion subcontractors ineligible to compete for a portion of the available work. This kind of direct restraint on the business market has substantial anticompetitive effects, both actual and potential, that would not follow naturally from the elimination of competition over wages and working conditions. It contravenes antitrust policies to a degree not justified by congressional labor policy, and therefore cannot claim a non-statutory exemption from the antitrust laws.

There can be no argument in this case, whatever its force in other contexts, that a restraint of this magnitude might be entitled to an antitrust exemption if it were included in a lawful collective bargaining agreement. *Cf. UMW v. Pennington, supra* at 664-665; *Jewel Tea, supra* at 689-690 (opinion of MR. JUSTICE WHITE); *id.,* at 709-713, 732-733 (opinion of MR. JUSTICE GOLDBERG). In this case, Local 100 had no interest in representing Connell's employees. The federal policy favoring collective bargaining therefore can offer no shelter for the union's coercive action against Connell or its campaign to exclude nonunion firms from the subcontracting market.

III

Local 100 nonetheless contends that the kind of agreement it obtained from Connell is explicitly allowed by the construction industry proviso to § 8(e) and that antitrust policy therefore must defer to the NLRA. The majority in the Court of Appeals declined to decide this issue, holding that it was subject to the "exclusive jurisdiction" of the NLRB.... This Court has held, however, that the federal courts may decide labor law questions that emerge as collateral issues in suits brought under independent federal remedies, including the antitrust laws. We conclude that § 8(e) does not allow this type of agreement....

Section 8(e) was part of a legislative program designed to plug technical loopholes in § 8(b)(4)'s general prohibition of secondary activities. In § 8(e) Congress broadly proscribed using contractual agreements to achieve the economic coercion prohibited by § 8(b)(4). *See National Woodwork Manufacturers Ass'n,* [386 U.S. 612] at 634. The provisos exempting the construction and garment industries were added by the Conference Committee in an apparent compromise between the House Bill, which prohibited all hot-cargo agreements, and the Senate Bill, which prohibited them only in the trucking industry. Although the garment industry proviso was supported by detailed explanations in both Houses, the construction industry proviso was explained only by bare references to "the pattern of collective bargaining" in the industry. It seems, however, to have been adopted as a partial substitute for an attempt to overrule this Court's decision in *NLRB v. Denver Building & Construction Trades Council,* 341 U.S. 675 (1951). Discussion of "special problems" in the construction industry, applicable to both the § 8(e) proviso and the attempt to overrule *Denver Building Trades,* focused on the problems of picketing a single nonunion subcontractor on a multiemployer building project, and the close relationship between contractors and subcontractors at the jobsite. Congress limited the construction industry proviso to that single situation, allowing subcontracting agreements only in relation to work done on a jobsite. In contrast to the latitude it provided in the garment industry proviso, Congress did not afford construction unions an exemption from

§ 8(b)(4)(B) or otherwise indicate that they were free to use subcontracting agreements as a broad organizational weapon. In keeping with these limitations, the Court has interpreted the construction industry proviso as

> a measure to allow agreements pertaining to certain secondary activities on the construction site because of the close community of interests there, but to ban secondary-objective agreements concerning nonjobsite work, in which respect the construction industry is no different from any other.

National Woodwork Manufacturers Assn., supra at 638-639 (footnote omitted)....

Local 100 does not suggest that its subcontracting agreement is related to any of these policies. It does not claim to be protecting Connell's employees from having to work alongside nonunion men. The agreement apparently was not designed to protect Local 100's members in that regard, since it was not limited to jobsites on which they were working. Moreover, the subcontracting restriction applied only to the work Local 100's members would perform themselves and allowed free subcontracting of all other work, thus leaving open a possibility that they would be employed alongside nonunion subcontractors. Nor was Local 100 trying to organize a nonunion subcontractor on the building project it picketed. The union admits that it sought the agreement solely as a way of pressuring mechanical subcontractors in the Dallas area to recognize it as the representative of their employees.

If we agree with Local 100 that the construction industry proviso authorizes subcontracting agreements with "stranger" contractors, not limited to any particular jobsite, our ruling would give construction unions an almost unlimited organizational weapon. The unions would be free to enlist any general contractor to bring economic pressure on nonunion subcontractors, as long as the agreement recited that it only covered work to be performed on some jobsite somewhere. The proviso's jobsite restriction then would serve only to prohibit agreements relating to subcontractors that deliver their work complete to the jobsite.

It is highly improbable that Congress intended such a result. One of the major aims of the 1959 Act was to limit "top-down" organizing campaigns, in which unions used economic weapons to force recognition from an employer regardless of the wishes of his employees. Congress accomplished this goal by enacting § 8(b)(7), which restricts primary recognitional picketing, and by further tightening § 8(b)(4)(B), which prohibits the use of most secondary tactics in organizational campaigns. Construction unions are fully covered by these sections. The only special consideration given them in organizational campaigns is § 8(f), which allows "prehire" agreements in the construction industry, but only under careful safeguards preserving workers' rights to decline union representation. The legislative history accompanying § 8(f) also suggests that Congress may not have intended that strikes or picketing could be used to extract prehire agreements from unwilling employers.

These careful limits on the economic pressure unions may use in aid of their organizational campaigns would be undermined seriously if the proviso to § 8(e) were construed to allow unions to seek subcontracting agreements, at large, from any general contractor vulnerable to picketing. Absent a clear indication that Congress intended to leave such a glaring loophole in its restrictions on "top-down" organizing, we are unwilling to read the construction industry proviso as broadly as Local 100 suggests. Instead, we think its authorization extends only to agreements in the context of collective bargaining relationships and, in light of congressional references to the *Denver Building Trades* problem, possibly to common-situs relationships on particular jobsites as well.

Finally, Local 100 contends that even if the subcontracting agreement is not sanctioned by the construction industry proviso and therefore is illegal under § 8(e), it cannot be the basis for antitrust liability because the remedies in the NLRA are exclusive. This argument is grounded in the legislative history of the 1947 Taft-Hartley amendments. Congress rejected attempts to regulate secondary activities by repealing the antitrust exemptions in the Clayton and Norris-LaGuardia Acts, and created special remedies under the labor law instead. It made secondary activities unfair labor practices under § 8(b)(4), and drafted special provisions for preliminary injunctions at the suit of the NLRB and for recovery of actual damages in the district courts. Sections 10(*l*), 303.... But whatever significance this legislative choice has for antitrust suits based on those secondary activities prohibited by § 8(b)(4), it has no relevance to the question whether Congress meant to preclude antitrust suits based on the "hot-cargo" agreements that it outlawed in 1959. There is no legislative history in the 1959 Congress suggesting that labor-law remedies for § 8(e) violations were intended to be exclusive, or that Congress thought allowing antitrust remedies in cases like the present one would be inconsistent with the remedial scheme of the NLRA.[16]

We therefore hold that this agreement, which is outside the context of a collective bargaining relationship and not restricted to a particular jobsite, but which nonetheless obligates Connell to subcontract work only to firms that have a con-

---

[16]The dissenting opinion of MR. JUSTICE STEWART argues that § 303 provides the exclusive remedy for violations of § 8(e), thereby precluding recourse to antitrust remedies. For that proposition the dissenting opinion relies upon "considerable evidence in the legislative materials." ... In our view, these materials are unpersuasive. In the first place, Congress did not amend § 303 expressly to provide a remedy for violations of § 8(e).... The House in 1959 did reject proposals by Representatives Hiestand, Alger, and Hoffman to repeal labor's antitrust immunity.... Those proposals, however, were much broader than the issue in this case. The Hiestand-Alger proposal would have repealed antitrust immunity for any action in concert by two or more labor organizations. The Hoffman proposal apparently intended to repeal labor's antitrust immunity entirely. That the Congress rejected these extravagant proposals hardly furnishes proof that it intended to extend labor's antitrust immunity to include agreements with nonlabor parties, or that it thought antitrust liability under the existing statutes would be inconsistent with the NLRA. The bill introduced by Senator McClellan two years later provides even less support for that proposition. Like most bills introduced in Congress, it never reached a vote.

tract with Local 100, may be the basis of a federal antitrust suit because it has a potential for restraining competition in the business market in ways that would not follow naturally from elimination of competition over wages and working conditions.

IV

Although we hold that the union's agreement with Connell is subject to the federal antitrust laws, it does not follow that state antitrust law may apply as well. The Court has held repeatedly that federal law preempts state remedies that interfere with federal labor policy or with specific provisions of the NLRA....The use of state antitrust law to regulate union activities in aid of organization must also be preempted because it creates a substantial risk of conflict with policies central to federal labor law.

In this area, the accommodation between federal labor and antitrust policy is delicate. Congress and this Court have carefully tailored the antitrust statutes to avoid conflict with the labor policy favoring lawful employee organization, not only by delineating exemptions from antitrust coverage but also by adjusting the scope of the antitrust remedies themselves. *See Apex Hosiery Co. v. Leader,* 310 U.S. 469 (1940). State antitrust laws generally have not been subjected to this process of accommodation. If they take account of labor goals at all, they may represent a totally different balance between labor and antitrust policies. Permitting state antitrust law to operate in this field could frustrate the basic federal policies favoring employee organization and allowing elimination of competition among wage earners, and interfere with the detailed system Congress has created for regulating organizational techniques.

Because employee organization is central to federal labor policy and regulation of organizational procedures is comprehensive, federal law does not admit the use of state antitrust law to regulate union activity that is closely related to organizational goals. Of course, other agreements between unions and nonlabor parties may yet be subject to state antitrust laws. *See Teamsters Local 24 v. Oliver, supra* at 295-297. The governing factor is the risk of conflict with the NLRA or with federal labor policy.

V

Neither the District Court nor the Court of Appeals decided whether the agreement between Local 100 and Connell, if subject to the antitrust laws, would constitute an agreement that restrains trade within the meaning of the Sherman

Act. The issue was not briefed and argued fully in this Court. Accordingly, we remand for consideration whether the agreement violated the Sherman Act.[19]

Reversed in part and remanded.

MR. JUSTICE DOUGLAS, dissenting.

While I join the opinion of MR. JUSTICE STEWART, I write to emphasize what is, for me, the determinative feature of the case. Throughout this litigation, Connell has maintained only that Local 100 coerced it into signing the subcontracting agreement. With the complaint so drawn, I have no difficulty in concluding that the union's conduct is regulated solely by the labor laws. The question of antitrust immunity would be far different, however, if it were alleged that Local 100 had conspired with mechanical subcontractors to force nonunion subcontractors from the market by entering into exclusionary agreements with general contractors like Connell. An arrangement of that character was condemned in *Allen Bradley Co. v. Local 3,* IBEW, 325 U.S. 797.... Were such a conspiracy alleged, the multiemployer bargaining agreement between Local 100 and the mechanical subcontractors would unquestionably be relevant. *See United Mine Workers v. Pennington,* 381 U.S. 657, 673 (concurring opinion); *Meat Cutters v. Jewel Tea Co.,* 381 U.S. 676, 737 (dissenting opinion)....

MR. JUSTICE STEWART, with whom MR. JUSTICE DOUGLAS, MR. JUSTICE BRENNAN, and MR. JUSTICE MARSHALL join, dissenting.

As part of its effort to organize mechanical contractors in the Dallas area, the respondent Local Union No. 100 engaged in peaceful picketing to induce the petitioner Connell Construction Co., a general contractor in the building and construction industry, to agree to subcontract plumbing and mechanical work at the construction site only to firms that had signed a collective bargaining agreement with Local 100. None of Connell's own employees were members of Local 100, and the subcontracting agreement contained the Union's express disavowal of any intent to organize or represent them. The picketing at Connell's construction site was therefore secondary activity, subject to detailed and comprehensive

---

[19] In addition to seeking a declaratory judgment that the agreement with Local 100 violated the antitrust laws, Connell sought a permanent injunction against further picketing to coerce execution of the contract in litigation. Connell obtained a temporary restraining order against the picketing on January 21, 1971, and thereafter executed the contract—under protest—with Local 100 on March 28, 1971. So far as the record in this case reveals, there has been no further picketing at Connell's construction sites. Accordingly, there is no occasion for us to consider whether the Norris-LaGuardia Act forbids such an injunction where the specific agreement sought by the union is illegal, or to determine whether, within the meaning of the Norris-LaGuardia Act, there was a "labor dispute" between these parties. If the Norris-LaGuardia Act were applicable to this picketing, injunctive relief would not be available under the antitrust laws. *See United States v. Hutcheson,* 312 U.S. 219 (1941). If the agreement in question is held on remand to be invalid under federal antitrust laws, we cannot anticipate that Local 100 will resume picketing to obtain or enforce an illegal agreement.

regulation pursuant to § 8(b)(4) of the National Labor Relations Act ... and § 303 of the Labor Management Relations Act.... Similarly, the subcontracting agreement under which Connell agreed to cease doing business with nonunion mechanical contractors is governed by the provisions of § 8(e) of the National Labor Relations Act.... The relevant legislative history unmistakably demonstrates that in regulating secondary activity and "hot cargo" agreements in 1947 and 1959, Congress selected with great care the sanctions to be imposed if proscribed union activity should occur. In so doing, Congress rejected efforts to give private parties injured by union activity such as that engaged in by Local 100 the right to seek relief under federal antitrust laws. Accordingly, I would affirm the judgment before us....

II

Contrary to the assertion in the Court's opinion, *ante,* ... the deliberate congressional decision to make § 303 the exclusive private remedy for unlawful secondary activity is clearly relevant to the question of Local 100's antitrust liability in the case before us. The Court is correct, of course, in noting that § 8(e)'s prohibition of "hot cargo" agreements was not added to the Act until 1959, and that § 303 was not then amended to cover § 8(e) violations standing alone. But as part of the 1959 amendments designed to close "technical loopholes" perceived in the Taft-Hartley Act, Congress amended § 8(b)(4) to make it an unfair labor practice for a labor organization to threaten or coerce a neutral employer, either directly or through his employees, where an object of the secondary pressure is to force the employer to enter into an agreement prohibited by § 8(e). At the same time, Congress expanded the scope of the § 303 damage remedy to allow recovery of the actual damages sustained as a result of a union engaging in secondary activity to force an employer to sign an agreement in violation of § 8(e). In short, Congress has provided an employer like Connell with a fully effective private damage remedy for the allegedly unlawful union conduct involved in this case.

The essence of Connell's complaint is that it was coerced by Local 100's picketing into "conspiring" with the union by signing an agreement that limited its ability to subcontract mechanical work on a competitive basis. If, as the Court today holds, the subcontracting agreement is not within the construction industry proviso to § 8(e), then Local 100's picketing to induce Connell to sign the agreement constituted a § 8(b)(4) unfair labor practice, and was therefore also unlawful under § 303(a)[8] .... Accordingly, Connell has the right to sue Local

---

[8] If contrary to the Court's conclusion, see *ante,* at 9-16, Congress intended what it said in the proviso to § 8(e), then the subcontracting agreement is valid and, under the view of the Board and those courts of appeals that have considered the question. Local 100's picketing to obtain the agreement would also be lawful.... Connell would therefore have neither a remedy under § 303 nor one with the Board.

100 for damages sustained as a result of Local 100's unlawful secondary activity pursuant to § 303(b).... Although "limited to actual, compensatory damages," *Local 20, Teamsters v. Morton,* 377 U.S. at 260, Connell would be entitled under § 303 to recover all damages to its business that resulted from the union's coercive conduct, including any provable damage caused by Connell's inability to subcontract mechanical work to nonunion firms. Similarly, any nonunion mechanical contractor who believes his business has been harmed by Local 100 having coerced Connell into signing the subcontracting agreement is entitled to sue the union for compensatory damages; for § 303 broadly grants its damage action to "[w]hoever shall be injured in his business or property" by reason of a labor organization engaging in a § 8(b)(4) unfair labor practice.[9]

Moreover, there is considerable evidence in the legislative materials indicating that in expanding the scope of § 303 to include a remedy for secondary pressure designed to force an employer to sign an illegal "hot cargo" clause and in restricting the remedies for violation of § 8(e) itself to those available from the Board, Congress in 1959 made the same deliberate choice to exclude antitrust remedies as was made by the 1947 Congress....

The Landrum-Griffin Bill, H.R. 8400, 86th Cong., 1st Sess., which, as amended, was enacted as the Labor-Management Reporting and Disclosure Act of 1959, by contrast, clearly provided that the new secondary boycott and "hot cargo" provisions were to be enforced solely through the Board and by use of the § 303 damage remedy. *See* 105 Cong. Rec. 14347-14348; II 1959 Leg. Hist. 1522-1523. Recognizing this important difference, Representative Alger proposed to amend the Landrum-Griffin Bill by adding, as an additional title, the antitrust provisions of H.R. 8003. 105 Cong. Rec. 15532-15533; II 1959 Leg. Hist. 1569. Representative Alger once again stated that his proposed amendment

---

It would seem necessarily to follow that conduct specifically authorized by Congress in the National Labor Relations Act could not by itself be the basis for federal antitrust liability, unless the Court intends to return to the era when the judiciary frustrated congressional design by determining for itself "what public policy in regard to the industrial struggle demands." *Duplex Printing Press Co. v. Deering,* 245 U.S. 443, 485 (Brandeis, J., dissenting). *See United States v. Hutcheson,* 312 U.S. 219. In my view, however, even if Local 100's conduct was unlawful, Connell may not seek to invoke the sanctions of the antitrust laws. Accordingly, I find it unnecessary to decide in this case whether the subcontracting agreement entered into by Connell and Local 100 is within the ambit of the construction industry proviso to § 8(e), and if it is, whether it was permissible for Local 100 to utilize peaceful picketing to induce Connell to sign the agreement.

[9] If Connell and Local 100 had entered into a purely voluntary "hot cargo" agreement in violation of § 8(e), an injured nonunion mechanical subcontractor would have no § 303 remedy because the union would not have engaged in any § 8(b)(4) unfair labor practice. The subcontractor, however, would still be able to seek the full range of Board remedies available for a § 8(e) unfair labor practice. Moreover, if Connell had truly agreed to limit its subcontracting without any coercion whatsoever on the part of Local 100, the affected subcontractor might well have a valid antitrust claim on the ground that Local 100 and Connell were engaged in the type of conspiracy aimed at third parties with which this Court dealt in *Allen Bradley Co. v. Local Union No. 3,* 325 U.S. 797....

would make it unlawful for an individual local union to "[e]nter into any arrangement—voluntary or coerced—with any employer, groups of employers, or other unions which cause product boycotts, price fixing, or other types of restrictive trade practices." 105 Cong. Rec. 15533; II 1959 Leg. Hist. 1569.

Representative Griffin responded to Representative Alger's proposed amendment by observing that it

> serves to point out that the substitute [the Landrum-Griffin Bill] is a minimum bill. It might be well at this point to mention some provisions that are not in it.
>
> There is no antitrust law provision in this bill....

105 Cong. Rec. 15535; II 1959 Leg. Hist. 1571-1572.

The Alger amendment was rejected, as were additional efforts to subject proscribed union activities to the antitrust laws and their sanctions. *See, e.g.,* 105 Cong. Rec. 15853 (amendment offered by Rep. Hoffman); II 1959 Leg. Hist. 1685. The House then adopted the Landrum-Griffin Bill over protests that it "does not go far enough, that it needs more teeth, and that more teeth are going to come in the form of legislation to bring union activities under the antitrust laws." 105 Cong. Rec. 15858 (remarks of Rep. Alger); II 1959 Leg. Hist. 1690....

The judicial imposition of "independent federal remedies" not intended by Congress, no less than the application of state law to union conduct that is either protected or prohibited by federal labor law, threatens "to upset the balance of power between labor and management expressed in our national labor policy." *Local 20, Teamsters v. Morton,* 377 U.S. at 260....

NOTES

1. Is *Connell* consistent with *Jewel Tea* and earlier cases in the standard it uses for distinguishing between agreements properly concerned with wages, hours, and other components of the labor market, and agreements improperly concerned with the product market? Has the judiciary once again undertaken to weigh the workers' interests in their jobs against the public's interest in a competitive economy? Is such balancing necessarily bad?

2. Would the result have been different in *Connell* if the union's subcontracting clause had been part of a collective bargaining agreement with the employer? If it had been limited to particular job sites? If it had not been limited to one particular union? If two (or all three) of those conditions had been met? How might that have affected the anticompetitive thrust of the clause? *Compare Woelke & Romero Framing, Inc. v. NLRB,* 456 U.S. 645 (1982), *supra.*

3. When it is alleged that a building trades council and its member unions have conspired with non-labor entities to force nonunion general contractors and subcontractors out of a construction market, neither the statutory nor the nonstatutory exemption will apply. *See Altemose Constr. Co. v. Building & Constr.*

Trades Council, 751 F.2d 653 (3d Cir. 1985), *cert. denied,* 475 U.S. 1107 (1986). However, when the restriction being challenged under the antitrust laws is contained in a valid prehire agreement clause which is protected by the construction industry proviso to § 8(e), the nonstatutory exemption will usually provide immunity. *See A.L. Adams Constr. Co. v. Georgia Power Co.,* 733 F.2d 853 (11th Cir. 1984), *cert. denied,* 471 U.S. 1075 (1985).

When, if ever, should a clause protected by the construction industry proviso to § 8(e) be found to constitute an antitrust violation? Only if there is evidence of an anticompetitive intent? In an en banc opinion in *Sun-Land Nurseries v. Southern Cal. Dist. Council of Laborers,* 793 F.2d 1110 (1986) (four judges dissenting), cert. denied, 479 U.S. 1090 (1987), the Ninth Circuit held that a subcontracting provision sheltered by the § 8(e) proviso is not enough by itself to raise a triable issue of antitrust liability, because some anticompetitive effect is the natural consequence of such a restrictive clause. Other evidence of anticompetitive intent and conduct is necessary. *Accord, Laborers Local 210 v. Associated Gen. Contrs.,* 844 F.2d 69 (2d Cir. 1988).

4. Even if a union's conduct may have violated § 8(b)(4)(B) ("secondary boycott") and § 8(e) ("hot cargo") of the NLRA, the nonstatutory exemption was still applicable if the union was engaged in a legitimate campaign to organize certain small nonunion truckers, and in pursuit of that objective was coercing major unionized trucking firms to enter into discrete (noncollective) agreements not to "interline business" with those particular nonunion companies. Here, the union's conduct was not shown to have created "substantial anticompetitive effects tangential or unrelated to the legitimate central purpose of organizing." *Richards v. Neilson Freight Lines,* 810 F.2d 898 (9th Cir. 1987).

5. How should the Longshoremen's "containerization" case, *NLRB v. ILA,* 447 U.S. 490 (1980), *supra,* have been analyzed if it had been brought as an antitrust case instead of as a secondary boycott case? *See Consolidated Express, Inc. v. New York Shipping Ass'n,* 602 F.2d 494 (3d Cir. 1979), *vacated and remanded,* 448 U.S. 902 (1980), *on remand,* 641 F.2d 90 (3d Cir.), *mandamus denied,* 451 U.S. 905 (1981), *noted in* 61 B.U.L. Rev. 1037 (1981); 80 Colum. L. Rev. 645 (1980); 64 Minn. L. Rev. 1275 (1980).

6. With one Justice dissenting, the Supreme Court disposed of an unusual "reverse *Connell*" case by holding that a union failed to state a claim for damages under the federal antitrust laws when it alleged that a multiemployer association, which was a party to a collective bargaining agreement with the union, had coerced certain third parties and some of the association's members to enter into business relationships with nonunion contractors and subcontractors. *Associated Gen. Contrs. v. California State Council of Carpenters,* 459 U.S. 519 (1983). Although the union contended the association's actions had adversely affected the trade of certain unionized firms, thereby restraining the union's business activities, the Court pointed out that the union was neither a consumer nor a competitor in the relevant market, and that there was only a tenuous, speculative, and casual relationship between the union's alleged injury and the alleged restraint. The Court thus managed to sidestep the knotty substantive problems of commercial restraints and of statutory and nonstatutory exemptions, which had so troubled the Ninth Circuit below. 648 F.2d 527 (1980). *Compare Carpenters Local 1846 v. Pratt-Farnsworth, Inc.,* 690 F.2d 489 (5th Cir. 1982), *cert. denied,* 464 U.S. 932 (1983) (exclusionary "double-breasted" operations in construction industry as antitrust violation).

7. *See generally* Casey & Cozzillio, *Labor-Antitrust: The Problems of Connell and a Remedy that Follows Naturally,* 1980 Duke L.J. 235; Conway, *Broadening Labor's Antitrust Liability While Narrowing Its Construction Industry Proviso Protection,* 27 Cath. U. L. Rev. 305 (1978); Gifford, *Redefining the Antitrust Labor Exemption,* 72 Minn. L. Rev. 1379 (1988); Goldman, *The Labor Exemption to the Antitrust Laws: A Radical Proposal,* 66 Or. L. Rev. 153 (1987); Handler & Zifchak, *Collective Bargaining and the Antitrust Laws: The Emasculation of the Labor Exemption,* 81 Colum. L. Rev. 459 (1981); Lande & Zerbe, *Reducing Unions' Monopoly Power: Costs and Benefits,* 28 J.L. & Econ. 297 (1985); Leslie, *Principles of Labor Antitrust,* 66 Va. L. Rev. 1183 (1980); St. Antoine, *Connell: Antitrust Law at the Expense of Labor Law,* 62 Va. L. Rev. 603 (1976); Symposium, *The Application of Antitrust Laws to Labor-Related Activities,* 21 Duquesne L. Rev. 331 (1983). More specialized labor antitrust problems are discussed in Craver, *The Application of Labor and Antitrust Laws to Physician Unions: The Need for a Re-Evaluation of Traditional Concepts in a Radically Changing Field,* 27 Hastings L.J. 55 (1975); Forst, *Labor Union Representation on Boards of Corporate Competitors: An Antitrust Analysis,* 7 J. Corp. L. 421 (1982); Note, *Labor Unions in the Boardroom: An Antitrust Dilemma,* 92 Yale L.J. 106 (1982).

BROWN v. PRO FOOTBALL, INC.

Supreme Court of the United States
518 U.S. 231, 116 S. Ct. 2116, 135 L. Ed. 2d 521 (1996)

JUSTICE BREYER delivered the opinion of the Court.

The question in this case arises at the intersection of the Nation's labor and antitrust laws. A group of professional football players brought this antitrust suit against football club owners. The club owners had bargained with the players' union over a wage issue until they reached impasse. The owners then had agreed among themselves (but not with the union) to implement the terms of their own last best bargaining offer. The question before us is whether federal labor laws shield such an agreement from antitrust attack. We believe that they do. This Court has previously found in the labor laws an implicit antitrust exemption that applies where needed to make the collective-bargaining process work. Like the Court of Appeals, we conclude that this need makes the exemption applicable in this case.

I

We can state the relevant facts briefly. In 1987, a collective-bargaining agreement between the National Football League (NFL), a group of football clubs, and the NFL Players Association, a labor union, expired. The NFL and the Players Association began to negotiate a new contract. In March 1989, during the negotiations, the NFL adopted Resolution G-2, a plan that would permit each club to establish a "developmental squad" of up to six rookie or "first-year" players who, as free agents, had failed to secure a position on a regular player roster. See App. 42. Squad members would play in practice games and sometimes in regular games as substitutes for injured players. Resolution G-2 provided that the club owners would pay all squad members the same weekly salary.

The next month, April, the NFL presented the developmental squad plan to the Players Association. The NFL proposed a squad player salary of $1,000 per week. The Players Association disagreed. It insisted that the club owners give developmental squad players benefits and protections similar to those provided regular players, and that they leave individual squad members free to negotiate their own salaries.

Two months later, in June, negotiations on the issue of developmental squad salaries reached an impasse. The NFL then unilaterally implemented the developmental squad program by distributing to the clubs a uniform contract that embodied the terms of Resolution G-2 and the $1,000 proposed weekly salary. The League advised club owners that paying developmental squad players more or less than $1,000 per week would result in disciplinary action, including the loss of draft choices.

In May 1990, 235 developmental squad players brought this antitrust suit against the League and its member clubs. The players claimed that their employers' agreement to pay them a $1,000 weekly salary violated the Sherman Act. See 15 U.S.C. § 1 (forbidding agreements in restraint of trade). The Federal District Court denied the employers' claim of exemption from the antitrust laws; it permitted the case to reach the jury; and it subsequently entered judgment on a jury treble-damage award that exceeded $30 million. The NFL and its member clubs appealed.

The Court of Appeals (by a split 2-to-1 vote) reversed. The majority interpreted the labor laws as "waiv[ing] antitrust liability for restraints on competition imposed through the collective-bargaining process, so long as such restraints operate primarily in a labor market characterized by collective bargaining." 50 F.3d 1041, 1056 (C.A.D.C.1995). The Court held, consequently, that the club owners were immune from antitrust liability. We granted certiorari to review that determination. Although we do not interpret the exemption as broadly as did the Appeals Court, we nonetheless find the exemption applicable, and we affirm that Court's immunity conclusion.

II

The immunity before us rests upon what this Court has called the "nonstatutory" labor exemption from the antitrust laws. *Connell Constr. Co. v. Plumbers*, 421 U.S. 616, 622 (1975); see also *Meat Cutters v. Jewel Tea Co.*, 381 U.S. 676 (1965); *Mine Workers v. Pennington*, 381 U.S. 657 (1965). The Court has implied this exemption from federal labor statutes, which set forth a national labor policy favoring free and private collective bargaining, see 29 U.S.C. § 151; *Teamsters v. Oliver*, 358 U.S. 283, 295 (1959); which require good-faith bargaining over wages, hours and working conditions, see 29 U.S.C. §§ 158(a)(5), 158(d); *NLRB v. Borg-Warner Corp.*, 356 U.S. 342, 348-349 (1958); and which delegate related rulemaking and interpretive authority to the National Labor Relations Board, see 29 U.S.C. § 153; *San Diego Building Trades Council v. Garmon*, U.S. 236, 242-245 (1959).

This implicit exemption reflects both history and logic. As a matter of history, Congress intended the labor statutes (from which the Court has implied the exemption) in part to adopt the views of dissenting justices in *Duplex Printing Press Co. v. Deering*, 254 U.S. 443 (1921), which justices had urged the Court to interpret broadly a different explicit "statutory" labor exemption that Congress earlier (in 1914) had written directly into the antitrust laws. *Id.*, at 483-488 (Brandeis, J., joined by Holmes and Clarke, JJ., dissenting) (interpreting § 20 of the Clayton Act); see also *United States v. Hutcheson*, 312 U.S. 219, 230-236 (1941) (discussing congressional reaction to *Duplex*). In the 1930s, when it subsequently enacted the labor statutes, Congress, as in 1914, hoped to prevent judicial use of antitrust law to resolve labor disputes—a kind of dispute normally inappropriate for antitrust law resolution.... The implicit ("nonstatutory") exemption interprets the labor statutes in accordance with this intent, namely, as limiting an antitrust court's authority to determine, in the area of industrial conflict, what is or is not a "reasonable" practice. It thereby substitutes legislative and administrative labor-related determinations for judicial antitrust-related determinations as to the appropriate legal limits of industrial conflict. *See Jewel Tea, supra,* at 709-10.

As a matter of logic, it would be difficult, if not impossible, to require groups of employers and employees to bargain together, but at the same time to forbid them to make among themselves or with each other any of the competition-restricting agreements potentially necessary to make the process work or its results mutually acceptable. Thus, the implicit exemption recognizes that, to give effect to federal labor laws and policies and to allow meaningful collective bargaining to take place, some restraints on competition imposed through the bargaining process must be shielded from antitrust sanctions. See *Connell, supra,* at 622 (federal labor law's "goals" could "never" be achieved if ordinary anticompetitive effects of collective bargaining were held to violate the antitrust laws); *Jewel Tea, supra,* at 711 (national labor law scheme would be "virtually destroyed" by the routine imposition of antitrust penalties upon parties engaged in collective bargaining); *Pennington, supra,* at 665 (implicit exemption necessary to harmonize Sherman Act with "national policy ... of promoting 'the peaceful settlement of industrial disputes by subjecting labor-management controversies to the mediatory influence of negotiation'")....

The petitioners and their supporters concede, as they must, the legal existence of the exemption we have described. They also concede that, where its application is necessary to make the statutorily authorized collective-bargaining process work as Congress intended, the exemption must apply both to employers and to employees.... Nor does the dissent take issue with these basic principles.... Consequently, the question before us is one of determining the exemption's scope: Does it apply to an agreement among several employers bargaining together to implement after impasse the terms of their last best good-faith wage offer? We assume that such conduct, as practiced in this case, is unobjectionable as a matter of labor law and policy. On that assumption, we conclude that the exemption applies.

Labor law itself regulates directly, and considerably, the kind of behavior here at issue—the postimpasse imposition of a proposed employment term concerning a mandatory subject of bargaining. Both the Board and the courts have held that, after impasse, labor law permits employers unilaterally to implement changes in preexisting conditions, but only insofar as the new terms meet carefully circumscribed conditions. For example, the new terms must be "reasonably comprehended" within the employer's preimpasse proposals (typically the last rejected proposals), lest by imposing more or less favorable terms, the employer unfairly undermined the union's status.... The collective-bargaining proceeding itself must be free of any unfair labor practice, such as an employer's failure to have bargained in good faith.... These regulations reflect the fact that impasse and an accompanying implementation of proposals constitute an integral part of the bargaining process. See *Bonanno Linen Serv., Inc.,* 243 N.L.R.B. 1093, 1094 (1979) (describing use of impasse as a bargaining tactic), *enf'd,* 630 F.2d 25 (C.A.1 1980), *aff'd,* 454 U.S. 404 (1982)....

Although the caselaw ... focuses upon bargaining by a single employer, no one here has argued that labor law does, or should, treat multiemployer bargaining differently in this respect. Indeed, Board and court decisions suggest that the joint implementation of proposed terms after impasse is a familiar practice in the context of multiemployer bargaining.... We proceed on that assumption.

Multiemployer bargaining itself is a well-established, important, pervasive method of collective bargaining, offering advantages to both management and labor. See Appendix (multiemployer bargaining accounts for more than 40% of major collective-bargaining agreements, and is used in such industries as construction, transportation, retail trade, clothing manufacture, and real estate, as well as professional sports); *NLRB v. Truck Drivers,* 353 U.S. 87, 95 (1957) (*Buffalo Linen*) (Congress saw multiemployer bargaining as "a vital factor in the effectuation of the national policy of promoting labor peace through strengthened collective bargaining"); *Charles D. Bonanno Linen Service, Inc. v. NLRB*, 454 U.S. 404, 409, n. 3 (1982) (*Bonanno Linen*) (multiemployer bargaining benefits both management and labor, by saving bargaining resources, by encouraging development of industry-wide worker benefits programs that smaller employers could not otherwise afford, and by inhibiting employer competition at the workers' expense).... The upshot is that the practice at issue here plays a significant role in a collective-bargaining process that itself comprises an important part of the Nation's industrial relations system.

In these circumstances, to subject the practice to antitrust law is to require antitrust courts to answer a host of important practical questions about how collective bargaining over wages, hours and working conditions is to proceed—the very result that the implicit labor exemption seeks to avoid. And it is to place in jeopardy some of the potentially beneficial labor-related effects that multiemployer bargaining can achieve. That is because unlike labor law, which sometimes welcomes anticompetitive agreements conducive to industrial harmony, antitrust law forbids all agreements among competitors (such as competing employers) that unreasonably lessen competition among or between them in virtually any respect whatsoever. See, *e.g.*, *Paramount Famous Lasky Corp. v. United States*, 282 U.S. 30 (1930) (agreement to insert arbitration provisions in motion picture licensing contracts). Antitrust law also sometimes permits judges or juries to premise antitrust liability upon little more than uniform behavior among competitors, preceded by conversations implying that later uniformity might prove desirable, ... or accompanied by other conduct that in context suggests that each competitor failed to make an independent decision....

If the antitrust laws apply, what are employers to do once impasse is reached? If all impose terms similar to their last joint offer, they invite an antitrust action premised upon identical behavior (along with prior or accompanying conversations) as tending to show a common understanding or agreement. If any, or all, of them individually impose terms that differ significantly from that offer, they invite an unfair labor practice charge. Indeed, how can employers safely discuss their offers together even before a bargaining impasse occurs? A preimpasse discussion about, say, the practical advantages or disadvantages of a particular proposal, invites a later antitrust claim that they agreed to limit the kinds of action each would later take should an impasse occur. The same is true of postimpasse discussions aimed at renewed negotiations with the union. Nor would adherence to the terms of an expired collective-bargaining agreement eliminate a potentially plausible antitrust claim charging that they had "conspired" or tacitly "agreed" to do so, particularly if maintaining the status quo were not in the immediate economic self-interest of some.... All this is to say that to permit antitrust liability here threatens to introduce instability and uncertainty into the collective-bargaining process, for antitrust law often forbids or discourages the kinds of joint discussions and behavior that the collective-bargaining process invites or requires.

We do not see any obvious answer to this problem. We recognize, as the Government suggests, that, in principle, antitrust courts might themselves try to evaluate particular kinds of employer understandings, finding them "reasonable" (hence lawful) where justified by collective-bargaining necessity. But any such evaluation means a web of detailed rules spun by many different nonexpert antitrust judges and juries, not a set of labor rules enforced by a single expert administrative body, namely the Labor Board. The labor laws give the Board, not antitrust courts, primary responsibility for policing the collective-bargaining process. And one of their objectives was to take from antitrust courts the authority to determine, through application of the antitrust laws, what is socially or economically desirable collective-bargaining policy. See *supra*, at 3-4; see also *Jewel Tea*, 381 U.S., at 716-719 (opinion of Goldberg, J.).

III

Both petitioners and their supporters advance several suggestions for drawing the exemption boundary line short of this case. We shall explain why we find them unsatisfactory.

A

Petitioners claim that the implicit exemption applies only to labor-management *agreements*—a limitation that they deduce from caselaw language, see, *e.g.*, *Connell*, 421 U.S., at 622 (exemption for "some union-employer *agreements*") (emphasis added), and from a proposed principle—that the exemption must rest upon labor-management consent. The language, however, reflects only the fact that the cases previously before the Court involved collective-bargaining agreements, see *Connell, supra*, at 619-620; *Pennington*, 381 U.S., at 660; *Jewel Tea, supra*, at 679-680; the language does not reflect the exemption's rationale. See 50 F.3d, at 1050.

Nor do we see how an exemption limited by petitioners' principle of labor-management consent could work. One cannot mean the principle literally—that the exemption applies only to understandings embodied in a collective-bargaining agreement—for the collective-bargaining process may take place before the making of any agreement or after an agreement has expired. Yet a multiemployer bargaining process itself necessarily involves many procedural and substantive understandings among participating employers as well as with the union. Petitioners cannot rescue their principle by claiming that the exemption applies only insofar as both labor and management consent to those understandings. Often labor will not (and should not) consent to certain common bargaining positions that employers intend to maintain. *Cf.* Areeda & Hovenkamp, Antitrust Law, at ¶ 229'd, p. 277 (Supp.1995) ("[J]oint employer preparation and bargaining in the context of a formal multi-employer bargaining unit is clearly exempt"). Similarly, labor need not consent to certain tactics that this Court has approved as part of the multiemployer bargaining process, such as unit-wide lockouts and the use of temporary replacements. See *NLRB v. Brown*, 380 U.S. 278, 284 (1965); *Buffalo Linen*, 353 U.S., at 97.

Petitioners cannot save their consent principle by weakening it, as by requiring union consent only to the multiemployer bargaining process itself. This general consent is automatically present whenever multiemployer bargaining takes place.... As so weakened, the principle cannot help decide *which* related practices are, or are not, subject to antitrust immunity.

B

The Solicitor General argues that the exemption should terminate at the point of impasse. After impasse, he says, "employers no longer have a duty under the labor laws to maintain the status quo," and "are free as a matter of labor law to negotiate individual arrangements on an interim basis with the union." Brief for United States et al. as *Amici Curiae* 17.

Employers, however, are not completely free at impasse to act independently. The multiemployer bargaining unit ordinarily remains intact; individual employers cannot withdraw. *Bonanno Linen*, 454 U.S., at 410-413. The duty to bargain survives; employers must stand ready to resume collective bargaining.... And individual employers can negotiate individual interim agreements with the union only insofar as those agreements are consistent with "the duty to abide by the results of group bargaining." *Bonanno Linen*, *supra*, at 416. Regardless, the absence of a legal "duty" to act jointly is not determinative. This Court has implied antitrust immunities that extend beyond statutorily *required* joint action to joint action that a statute "expressly or impliedly allows or assumes must also be immune." 1 P. Areeda & D. Turner, Antitrust Law ¶ 224, p. 145 (1978)....

More importantly, the simple "impasse" line would not solve the basic problem we have described above.... Labor law permits employers, after impasse, to engage in considerable joint behavior, including joint lockouts and replacement hiring. See, *e.g.*, *Brown*, *supra*, at 289 (hiring of temporary replacement workers after lockout was "reasonably adapted to the achievement of a legitimate end—preserving the integrity of the multiemployer bargaining unit"). Indeed, as a general matter, labor law often limits employers to four options at impasse: (1) maintain the status quo, (2) implement their last offer, (3) lock out their workers (and either shut down or hire temporary replacements), or (4) negotiate separate interim agreements with the union. See generally 1 Hardin, The Developing Labor Law, at 516-520, 696-699 [3d ed. 1992]. What is to happen if the parties cannot reach an interim agreement? The other alternatives are limited. Uniform employer conduct is likely. Uniformity—at least when accompanied by discussion of the matter—invites antitrust attack. And such attack would ask antitrust courts to decide the lawfulness of activities intimately related to the bargaining process.

The problem is aggravated by the fact that "impasse" is often temporary, see *Bonanno Linen, supra*, at 412 (approving Board's view of impasse as "a recurring feature in the bargaining process ... a temporary deadlock or hiatus in negotiations which in almost all cases is eventually broken, through either a change of mind or the application of economic force"); ... it may differ from bargaining only in degree; ... it may be manipulated by the parties for bargaining purposes, see *Bonanno Linen, supra*, at 413, n. 8 (parties might, for strategic purposes, "precipitate an impasse"); and it may occur several times during the course of a single labor dispute, since the bargaining process is not over when the first impasse is reached.... How are employers to discuss future bargaining positions during a temporary impasse? Consider, too, the adverse consequences that flow from failing to guess how an *antitrust* court would later draw the impasse line. Employers who erroneously concluded that impasse had *not* been reached would risk antitrust liability were they collectively to maintain the status quo, while employers who erroneously concluded that impasse *had* occurred would risk unfair labor practice charges for prematurely suspending multiemployer negotiations....

C

Petitioners and their supporters argue in the alternative for a rule that would exempt postimpasse agreement about bargaining "tactics," but not postimpasse agreement about substantive "terms," from the reach of antitrust. See 50 F.3d, at 1066-1069 (Wald, J., dissenting). They recognize, however, that both the Board and the courts have said that employers can, and often do, employ the imposition of "terms" as a bargaining "tactic." See, *e.g., American Ship Building Co. v. NLRB*, 380 U.S. 300, 316 (1965).... This concession as to joint "tactical" implementation would turn the presence of an antitrust exemption upon a determination of the employers' primary purpose or motive. See, *e.g.*, 50 F.3d, at 1069 (Wald, J., dissenting). But to ask antitrust courts, insulated from the bargaining process, to investigate an employer group's subjective motive is to ask them to conduct an inquiry often more amorphous than those we have previously discussed. And, in our view, a labor/antitrust line drawn on such a basis would too often raise the same related (previously discussed) problems. See *supra*, at 4-5, 9-10; *Jewel Tea*, 381 U.S., at 716 (opinion of Goldberg, J.) (expressing concern about antitrust judges "roaming at large" through the bargaining process).

D

The petitioners make several other arguments. They point, for example, to cases holding applicable, in collective-bargaining contexts, general "backdrop" statutes, such as a state statute requiring a plant-closing employer to make employee severance payments, *Fort Halifax Packing Co. v. Coyne*, 482 U.S. 1

(1987), and a state statute mandating certain minimum health benefits, *Metropolitan Life Ins. Co. v. Massachusetts*, 471 U.S. 724 (1985). Those statutes, however, "'neither encourage[d] nor discourage[d] the collective-bargaining processes that are the subject of the [federal labor laws].'" *Fort Halifax, supra*, at 21 (quoting *Metropolitan Life, supra*, at 755). Neither did those statutes come accompanied with antitrust's labor-related history....

Petitioners also say that irrespective of how the labor exemption applies elsewhere to multiemployer collective bargaining, professional sports is "special." We can understand how professional sports may be special in terms of, say, interest, excitement, or concern. But we do not understand how they are special in respect to labor law's antitrust exemption. We concede that the clubs that make up a professional sports league are not completely independent economic competitors, as they depend upon a degree of cooperation for economic survival. *National Collegiate Athletic Assn. v. Board of Regents of Univ. of Okla.*, 468 U.S. 85, 101-102 (1984); App. 110-115 (declaration of NFL Commissioner). In the present context, however, that circumstance makes the league more like a single bargaining employer, which analogy seems irrelevant to the legal issue before us.

We also concede that football players often have special individual talents, and, unlike many unionized workers, they often negotiate their pay individually with their employers. See *post*, at 5 (STEVENS, J., dissenting). But this characteristic seems simply a feature, like so many others, that might give employees (or employers) more (or less) bargaining power, that might lead some (or all) of them to favor a particular kind of bargaining, or that might lead to certain demands at the bargaining table. We do not see how it could make a critical legal difference in determining the underlying framework in which bargaining is to take place. See generally Jacobs & Winter, Antitrust Principles and Collective Bargaining by Athletes: Of Superstars in Peonage, 81 Yale L.J. 1 (1971). Indeed, it would be odd to fashion an antitrust exemption that gave additional advantages to professional football players (by virtue of their superior bargaining power) that transport workers, coal miners, or meat packers would not enjoy.

The dissent points to other "unique features" of the parties' collective bargaining relationship, which, in the dissent's view, make the case "atypical." *Post*, at 5. It says, for example, that the employers imposed the restraint simply to enforce compliance with league-wide rules, and that the bargaining consisted of nothing more than the sending of a "notice," and therefore amounted only to "so-called" bargaining. *Post*, at 6-7. Insofar as these features underlie an argument for looking to the employers' true purpose, we have already discussed them.... Insofar as they suggest that there was not a genuine impasse, they fight the basic assumption upon which the District Court, the Court of Appeals, the petitioners, and this Court, rest the case. See 782 F. Supp. 125, 134 (D.C.1991); 50 F.3d, at 1056-1057; Pet. for Cert. i. Ultimately, we cannot find a satisfactory basis for distinguishing football players from other organized workers. We therefore conclude that all must abide by the same legal rules.

....

For these reasons, we hold that the implicit ("nonstatutory") antitrust exemption applies to the employer conduct at issue here. That conduct took place during and immediately after a collective-bargaining negotiation. It grew out of, and was directly related to, the lawful operation of the bargaining process. It involved a matter that the parties were required to negotiate collectively. And it concerned only the parties to the collective-bargaining relationship.

Our holding is not intended to insulate from antitrust review every joint imposition of terms by employers, for an agreement among employers could be sufficiently distant in time and in circumstances from the collective-bargaining process that a rule permitting antitrust intervention would not significantly interfere with that process. See, *e.g.*, 50 F.3d, at 1057 (suggesting that exemption lasts until collapse of the collective-bargaining relationship, as evidenced by decertification of the union); *El Cerrito Mill & Lumber Co.*, 316 N.L.R.B. [1005], at 1006-1007 [1995] (suggesting that "extremely long" impasse, accompanied by "instability" or "defunctness" of multiemployer unit, might justify union withdrawal from group bargaining). We need not decide in this case whether, or where, within these extreme outer boundaries to draw that line. Nor would it be appropriate for us to do so without the detailed views of the Board, to whose "specialized judgment" Congress "intended to leave" many of the "inevitable questions concerning multiemployer bargaining bound to arise in the future." *Buffalo Linen*, 353 U.S., at 96; see also *Jewel Tea*, 381 U.S., at 710, n. 18.

The judgment of the Court of Appeals is affirmed.

It is so ordered.

JUSTICE STEVENS, dissenting.

In his classic dissent in *Lochner v. New York*, 198 U.S. 45, 75 (1905), Justice Holmes reminded us that our disagreement with the economic theory embodied in legislation should not affect our judgment about its constitutionality. It is equally important, of course, to be faithful to the economic theory underlying broad statutory mandates when we are construing their impact on areas of the economy not specifically addressed by their texts. The unique features of this case lead me to conclude that the Court has reached a decision that conflicts with the basic purpose of both the antitrust laws and the national labor policy expressed in a series of congressional enactments.

I

The basic premise underlying the Sherman Act is the assumption that free competition among business entities will produce the best price levels. *National Soc. of Professional Engineers v. United States*, 435 U.S. 679, 695 (1978). Collusion among competitors, it is believed, may produce prices that harm consumers. *United States v. Socony-Vacuum Oil Co.*, 310 U.S. 150, 226, n. 59 (1940). Similarly, the Court has held, a market-wide agreement among employers setting wages at levels that would not prevail in a free market may violate the Sherman Act. *Anderson v. Shipowners Assn. of Pacific Coast*, 272 U.S. 359 (1926).

The jury's verdict in this case has determined that the market-wide agreement among these employers fixed the salaries of the replacement players at a dramatically lower level than would obtain in a free market. While the special characteristics of this industry may provide a justification for the agreement under the rule of reason, see *National Collegiate Athletic Assn. v. Board of Regents of Univ. of Okla.*, 468 U.S. 85, 100-104 (1984), at this stage of the proceeding our analysis of the exemption issue must accept the premise that the agreement is unlawful unless it is exempt.

The basic premise underlying our national labor policy is that unregulated competition among employees and applicants for employment produces wage levels that are lower than they should be. Whether or not the premise is true in fact, it is surely the basis for the statutes that encourage and protect the collective-bargaining process, including the express statutory exemptions from the antitrust laws that Congress enacted in order to protect union activities. Those statutes were enacted to enable collective action by union members to achieve wage levels that are higher than would be available in a free market. See *Trainmen v. Chicago R. & I.R. Co.*, 353 U.S. 30, 40 (1957).

The statutory labor exemption protects the right of workers to act collectively to seek better wages, but does not "exempt concerted action or agreements between unions and nonlabor parties." *Connell Constr. Co. v. Plumbers*, 421 U.S. 616, 621-622 (1975). It is the judicially crafted, nonstatutory labor exemption that serves to accommodate the conflicting policies of the antitrust and labor statutes in the context of action between employers and unions. *Ibid.*

The limited judicial exemption complements its statutory counterpart by ensuring that unions which engage in collective bargaining to enhance employees' wages may enjoy the benefits of the resulting agreements. The purpose of the labor laws would be frustrated if it were illegal for employers to enter into industry-wide agreements providing supracompetitive wages for employees....

Consistent with basic labor law policies, I agree with the Court that the judicially crafted labor exemption must also cover some collective action that employers take in response to a collective bargaining agent's demands for higher wages. Immunizing such action from antitrust scrutiny may facilitate collective bargaining over labor demands. So, too, may immunizing concerted employer action designed to maintain the integrity of the multi-employer bargaining unit, such as lockouts that are imposed in response to "a union strike tactic which threatens the destruction of the employers' interest in bargaining on a group basis." *NLRB v. Truck Drivers*, 353 U.S. 87, 93 (1957).

In my view, however, neither the policies underlying the two separate statutory schemes, nor the narrower focus on the purpose of the nonstatutory exemption, provides a justification for exempting from antitrust scrutiny collective action initiated by employers to depress wages below the level that would be produced in a free market. Nor do those policies support a rule that would allow employers to suppress wages by implementing noncompetitive agreements among themselves on matters that have not previously been the subject of either an agreement with labor or even a demand by labor for inclusion in the bargaining process. That, however, is what is at stake in this litigation.

II

In light of the accommodation that has been struck between antitrust and labor law policy, it would be most ironic to extend an exemption crafted to protect collective action by employees to protect employers acting jointly to deny employees the opportunity to negotiate their salaries individually in a competitive market. Perhaps aware of the irony, the Court chooses to analyze this case as though it represented a typical impasse in an unexceptional multiemployer bargaining process. In so doing, it glosses over three unique features of the case that are critical to the inquiry into whether the policies of the labor laws require extension of the nonstatutory labor exemption to this atypical case.

First, in this market, unlike any other area of labor law implicated in the cases cited by the Court, player salaries are individually negotiated. The practice of individually negotiating player salaries prevailed even prior to collective bargaining. The players did not challenge the prevailing practice because, unlike employees in most industries, they want their compensation to be determined by the forces of the free market rather than by the process of collective bargaining. Thus, although the majority professes an inability to understand anything special about professional sports that should affect the framework of labor negotiations, in this business it is the employers, not the employees, who seek to impose a noncompetitive uniform wage on a segment of the market and to put an end to competitive wage negotiations.

Second, respondents concede that the employers imposed the wage restraint to force owners to comply with league-wide rules that limit the number of players that may serve on a team, not to facilitate a stalled bargaining process, or to revisit any issue previously subjected to bargaining. Brief for Respondents 4. The employers could have confronted the culprits directly by stepping up enforcement of roster limits. They instead chose to address the problem by unilaterally forbidding players from individually competing in the labor market.

Third, although the majority asserts that the "club owners had bargained with the players' union over a wage issue until they reached impasse," that hardly constitutes a complete description of what transpired. When the employers' representative advised the union that they proposed to pay the players a uniform wage determined by the owners, the union promptly and unequivocally responded that their proposal was inconsistent with the "principle" of individual salary negotiation that had been accepted in the past and that predated collective bargaining. The so-called "bargaining" that followed amounted to nothing more than the employers' notice to the union that they had decided to implement a decision to replace individual salary negotiations with a uniform wage level for a specific group of players.

Given these features of the case, I do not see why the employers should be entitled to a judicially crafted exemption from antitrust liability. We have explained that the "[t]he nonstatutory exemption has its source in the strong labor policy favoring the association of employees to eliminate competition over wages and working conditions." *Connell Constr. Co.*, 421 U.S., at 622. I know of no similarly strong labor policy that favors the association of employers to eliminate a competitive method of negotiating wages that predates collective bargaining and that labor would prefer to preserve....

The point of identifying the unique features of this case is not, as the Court suggests, to make the case that professional football players, alone among workers; should be entitled to enforce the antitrust laws against anti-competitive collective employer action. Other employees, no less than well-paid athletes, are entitled to the protections of the antitrust laws when their employers unite to undertake anticompetitive action that causes them direct harm and alters the state of employer-employee relations that existed prior to unionization. Here that alteration occurred because the wage terms that the employers unilaterally imposed directly conflict with a pre-existing principle of agreement between the bargaining parties. In other contexts, the alteration may take other similarly anticompetitive and unjustifiable forms.

III

Although exemptions should be construed narrowly, and judicially crafted exemptions more narrowly still, the Court provides a sweeping justification for the exemption that it creates today. The consequence is a newly-minted exemption that, as I shall explain, the Court crafts only by ignoring the reasoning of one of our prior decisions in favor of the views of the dissenting Justice in that case. Of course, the Court actually holds only that this new exemption applies in cases such as the present in which the parties to the bargaining process are affected by the challenged anticompetitive conduct. But that welcome limitation on its opinion fails to make the Court's explanation of its result in this case any more persuasive.

The Court explains that the nonstatutory labor exemption serves to ensure that "antitrust courts" will not end up substituting their views of labor policy for those of either the Labor Board or the bargaining parties. The Court concludes, therefore, that almost any concerted action by employers that touches on a mandatory subject of collective bargaining, no matter how obviously offensive to the policies underlying the Nation's antitrust statutes, should be immune from scrutiny so long as a collective-bargaining process is in place. It notes that a contrary conclusion would require "antitrust courts, insulated from the bargaining process, to investigate an employer group's subjective motive," a task that it believes too "amorphous" to be permissible. *Ante*, at 15.

The argument that "antitrust courts" should be kept out of the collective-bargaining process has a venerable lineage. See *Duplex Printing Press Co. v. Deering*, 254 U.S. 443, 483-488 (1921) (Brandeis, J., joined by Holmes and Clarke, JJ., dissenting). Our prior precedents subscribing to its basic point, however, do not justify the conclusion that employees have no recourse other than the Labor Board when employers collectively undertake anticompetitive action. In fact, they contradict it.

We have previously considered the scope of the nonstatutory labor exemption only in cases involving challenges to anticompetitive *agreements* between unions and employers brought by other employers not parties to those agreements. Even then, we have concluded that the exemption does not always apply. See *Mine Workers v. Pennington*, 381 U.S., at 663.

As *Pennington* explained, the mere fact that an antitrust challenge touches on an issue, such as wages, that is subject to mandatory bargaining does not suffice to trigger the judicially fashioned exemption. *Id.*, at 664. Moreover, we concluded that the exemption should not obtain in *Pennington* itself only after we examined the motives of one of the parties to the bargaining process. *Id.*, at 667.

The Court's only attempt to square its decision with *Pennington* occurs at the close of its opinion. It concludes that the exemption applies because the employers' action "grew out of, and was directly related to, the lawful operation of the bargaining process," "[i]t involved a matter that the parties were required to negotiate collectively," and that "concerned only the parties to the collective-bargaining relationship." *Ante*, at 18.

As to the first two qualifiers, the same could be said of *Pennington*. Indeed, the same was said *and rejected* in *Pennington*. "This is not to say that an agreement resulting from union-employer negotiations is automatically exempt from Sherman Act scrutiny simply because the negotiations involve a compulsory subject of bargaining, regardless of the subject or the form and content of the agreement." 381 U.S., at 664-665.

The final qualifier does distinguish *Pennington*, but only partially so. To determine whether the exemption applied in *Pennington*, we undertook a detailed examination into whether the policies of labor law so strongly supported the agreement struck by the bargaining parties that it should be immune from antitrust scrutiny. We concluded that because the agreement affected employers not parties to the bargaining process, labor law policies could not be understood to require the exemption.

Here, however, the Court does not undertake a review of labor law policy to determine whether it would support an exemption for the unilateral imposition of anticompetitive wage terms by employers on a union. The Court appears to conclude instead that the exemption should apply merely because the employers' action was implemented during a lawful negotiating process concerning a mandatory subject of bargaining. Thus, the Court's analysis would seem to constitute both an unprecedented expansion of a heretofore limited exemption, and an unexplained repudiation of the reasoning in a prior, nonconstitutional decision that Congress itself has not seen fit to override.

The Court nevertheless contends that the "rationale" of our prior cases supports its approach. As support for that contention, it relies heavily on the views espoused in Justice Goldberg's separate opinion in *Meat Cutters v. Jewel Tea Co.*, 381 U.S. 676 (1965). At five critical junctures in its opinion, see *ante*, at 4-5, 10, 15, the Court invokes that separate concurrence to explain why, for purposes of applying the nonstatutory labor exemption, labor law policy admits of no distinction between collective employer action taken in response to labor demands, and collective employer action of the kind we consider here.

It should be remembered that *Jewel Tea* concerned only the question whether an *agreement* between employers and a union may be exempt, and that even then the Court did not accept the broad antitrust exemption that Justice Goldberg advocated. Instead, Justice White, the author of *Pennington*, writing for Chief Justice Warren and Justice Brennan, explained that even in disputes over the lawfulness of agreements about terms that are subject to mandatory bargaining, courts must examine the bargaining process to determine whether antitrust scrutiny should obtain. *Jewel Tea*, 381 U.S., at 688-697. "The crucial determinant is not the form of the agreement—e.g., prices or wages—but its relative impact on the product market *and the interests of union members*." *Id.*, at 690, n. 5 (emphasis added). Moreover, the three dissenters, Justices Douglas, Clark, and Black, concluded that the union was entitled to no immunity at all. *Id.*, at 735-738.

It should also be remembered that Justice Goldberg used his separate opinion in *Jewel Tea* to explain his reasons for dissenting from the Court's opinion in *Pennington*. He explained that the Court's approach in *Pennington* was unjustifiable precisely because it permitted "antitrust courts" to reexamine the bargaining process. The Court fails to explain its apparent substitution in this case of Justice Goldberg's understanding of the exemption, an understanding previously endorsed by only two other Justices, for the one adopted by the Court in *Pennington*.

The Court's silence is all the more remarkable in light of the patent factual distinctions between *Jewel Tea* and the present case. It is not at all clear that Justice Goldberg himself understood his expansive rationale to require application of the exemption in circumstances such as those before us here. Indeed, the main theme of his opinion was that the antitrust laws should not be used to circumscribe bargaining over union demands. *Meat Cutters v. Jewel Tea*, 381 U.S., at 723-725....

Adoption of Justice Goldberg's views would mean, of course, that in some instances "antitrust courts" would have to displace the authority of the Labor Board. The labor laws do not exist, however, to ensure the perpetuation of the

Board's authority. That is why we have not previously adopted the Court's position. That is also why in other contexts we have not thought the mere existence of a collective-bargaining agreement sufficient to immunize employers from background laws that are similar to the Sherman Act. See *Fort Halifax Packing Co. v. Coyne*, 482 U.S. 1 (1987); *Metropolitan Life Ins. Co. v. Massachusetts*, 471 U.S. 724 (1985).

IV

Congress is free to act to exempt the anticompetitive employer conduct that we review today. In the absence of such action, I do not believe it is for us to stretch the limited exemption that we have fashioned to facilitate the express statutory exemption created for labor's benefit so that unions must strike in order to restore a prior practice of individually negotiating salaries....

Accordingly, I respectfully dissent.

NOTES

1. Prior to *Brown*, The Second Circuit held that the nonstatutory exemption shielded a pro basketball league and its member clubs from a player's suit under the antitrust laws for trying to monopolize the market and for conspiring to destroy his career by blacklisting him. *Caldwell v. American Basketball Ass'n*, 66 F.3d 523 (2d Cir. 1995), *cert. denied*, 518 U.S. 1033 (1996). Does *Brown* support this result?

2. Since *Brown*, the courts have shown increased reluctance to inquire into the reasonableness of the parties' bargaining practices. *See Grinnell Corp. v. Road Sprinkler Fitters Local 669*, 156 L.R.R.M. 2337 (D. Md. 1997), *aff'd without opinion*, 133 F.3d 914 (4th Cir. 1998); *Ehredt Underground v. Commonwealth Edison Co.*, 90 F.3d 238 (7th Cir. 1996), *cert. denied*, 117 S. Ct. 685 (1997).

3. For detailed analyses of *Brown, see* Baron, *Labor's Antitrust Touchdown Called Back: United States Supreme Court Reinforces Nonstatutory Labor Exemption From Antitrust Laws*, 33 Tulsa L.J. 401 (1997); Gottesman, *Union Summer: A Reawakened Interest in the Law of Labor*, S. Ct. Rev. 285 (1996). *See generally* Dewey, *Professional Athletes: Affluent Elitists or Victims of the Reserve System? An Emerging Paradox*, 8 Ohio N.U. L. Rev. 453 (1981); Lock, *The Scope of the Labor Exemption in Professional Sports*, 1989 Duke L.J. 339; Note, *Warming the Bench: The Nonstatutory Labor Exemption in the National Football League*, 61 Fordham L. Rev. 1203 (1993); Note, *Releasing Superstars from Peonage: Union Consent and the Nonstatutory Labor Exemption*, 104 Harv. L. Rev. 874 (1991); Note, *Application of the Labor Exemption After the Expiration of Collective Bargaining Agreements in Professional Sports*, 57 N.Y.U. L. Rev. 164 (1982); Highberger, *The Impact of Brown v. Pro Football on the Future of Multiemployer Bargaining Patterns*, 22 Emp. Rel. L.J. 125 (1996).

SECTION III. The Enforcement of the Collective Agreement

ARCHIBALD COX, LAW AND THE NATIONAL LABOR POLICY 85 (1960)

Unless the law is once again to fail to meet the needs of men, the principles determining legal rights and duties under collective bargaining agreements should not be imposed by the courts from above because of precepts learned in other contexts; the governing principles must be drawn out of the institutions of labor relations and shaped to their needs.

This is the way in which our commercial law developed. Two and a half centuries ago Lord Mansfield took the customs and practices of the world of commerce—the law merchant—and incorporated them into the common law administered by courts of general jurisdiction. Perhaps a modern Mansfield may again demonstrate the creative talent of the common law by drawing upon industrial jurisprudence.

A. THE LEGAL STATUS OF THE COLLECTIVE AGREEMENT

The expected outcome of the parties' fulfillment of their bargaining obligations is the execution of a collective labor agreement. Today there are an estimated 150,000 labor contracts in existence in the United States. As of 1980, however, 1,550 agreements covering units of 1,000 or more employees accounted for 6.6 million out of the approximately eighteen million workers under union contract in the industries surveyed. The national picture thus reflects a mixture of concentration and decentralization in bargaining and contract administration. U.S. Bureau of Labor Statistics, Dep't of Labor, Bull. No. 2095, Characteristics of Major Collective Bargaining Agreements iii, 1 (1981). Railroads, airlines, and government were excluded.

Included in *Selected Federal Statutes* is a sample collective agreement. Although labor contracts vary so widely according to the nature, size, and complexity of the particular industry or company involved that no single agreement can be called typical, most of them cover relatively standard subjects. The sample agreement should be read thoroughly at this point in order to gain some acquaintance with its contents.

Until recent years collective agreements were seldom involved in litigation. About 98 percent provide their own grievance and arbitration procedure to resolve disputes over contract interpretation. Court actions have traditionally been regarded as detrimental to healthy labor-management relations in the plant. The paucity of suits for enforcement of collective agreements may be one of the reasons for the delayed and rather sketchy development of theories as to the nature of these instruments.

Early common law decisions advanced at least three separate theories to explain the legal nature of the collective agreement:

1. The labor agreement establishes local customs or usages, which are then incorporated into the individual employee's contract of hire. This seems to have been the orthodox view of the American courts, at least prior to the era of the labor relations acts. *See* Rice, *Collective Labor Agreements in American Law,* 44 Harv. L. Rev. 572, 582 (1931). For historical overview, *see* Symposium, *Origins of the Union Contract,* 33 Lab. L.J. 512 (1982). Under the original form of this theory, the collective agreement itself was not regarded as a contract. It had legal effect only as its terms were absorbed into individual employment contracts. Somewhat similar is the traditional English concept that collective agreements are merely "gentlemen's agreements" or moral obligations not enforceable by the courts. *Young v. Canadian N. Ry.,* [1931] A.C. 83 (P.C.); Wedderburn of Charlton, The Worker and the Law 318-22 (3d ed. 1986). Some American scholars also have voiced an occasional plea that court litigation over collective agreements should be rejected as detrimental to the parties' continuing relationship. *See* Shulman, *Reason, Contract, and Law in Labor Relations,* 68 Harv. L. Rev. 999 (1955). Nevertheless, judicial enforcement at the behest of either employers or unions became generally accepted in this country well before the passage of the LMRA in 1947 and was confirmed by that Act.

2. The collective agreement is a contract that is negotiated by the union as the agent for the employees, who become the principals on the agreement. *Barnes & Co. v. Berry,* 169 F. 225 (6th Cir. 1909); *Maisel v. Sigman,* 123 Misc. 714, 205 N.Y.S. 807 (Sup. Ct. N.Y. County 1924). This so-called agency theory was adopted by a few courts that could not rationalize the enforceability of an instrument executed by an unincorporated association lacking juristic personality. Suits between individual employees and employers were maintainable, however, on the theory the union had merely served as the employees' agent in negotiations.

3. The collective agreement is a third party beneficiary contract, with the employer and union the mutual promisors and promisees, and the employees the beneficiaries. *Marranzano v. Riggs Nat'l Bank,* 184 F.2d 349 (D.C. Cir. 1950); *Yazoo & Miss. Valley R.R. v. Sideboard,* 161 Miss. 4, 133 So. 669 (1931); *H. Blum & Co. v. Landau,* 23 Ohio App. 426, 155 N.E. 154 (1926). Despite arguable shortcomings (is the employer to be left without recourse against the employee beneficiary, who has made no promises?), the third party beneficiary theory became rather widely accepted as the best explanation of the collective agreement in terms of traditional common law concepts. *See* C. Gregory & H. Katz, Labor and the Law 481 (3d ed. 1979).

Today, collective bargaining agreements in industries affecting commerce are enforced as a matter of federal law under § 301 of the LMRA. This means that the Supreme Court's views on the nature of the labor contract are now of primary concern. Two characteristics of the Court's thinking stand out. First, the Court is eclectic in its approach to common law doctrines; it refuses to confine itself to any single theory, but draws upon whatever elements may be helpful in a variety of theories. Second, the Court has emphasized what may be described as the "constitutional" or "governmental" quality of the labor agreement. Thus, the collective agreement has been described as "not an ordinary contract" but rather a "generalized code" for "a system of industrial self-government." *See John Wiley & Sons v. Livingston,* 376 U.S. 543, 550 (1964); *United Steelworkers v. Warrior & Gulf Nav. Co.,* 363 U.S. 574, 578-80 (1960).

The Supreme Court's eclectic approach to the nature of the labor contract is reflected in the following well-known comments by Mr. Justice Jackson in *J.I. Case Co. v. NLRB,* 321 U.S. 332, 334-35 (1944):

> Collective bargaining between employer and the representatives of a unit, usually a union, results in an accord as to terms which will govern hiring and work and pay in that unit. The result is not, however, a contract of employment except in rare cases; no one has a job by reason of it and no obligation to any individual ordinarily comes into existence from it alone. The negotiations between union and management result in what often has been called a trade agreement, rather than in a contract of employment. Without pushing the analogy too far, the agreement may be likened to the tariffs established by a carrier, to standard provisions prescribed by supervising authorities for insurance policies, or to utility schedules of rates and rules for service, which do not of themselves establish any relationships but which do govern the terms of the shipper or insurer or customer relationship whenever and with whomever it may be established....
>
> [H]owever engaged, an employee becomes entitled by virtue of the Labor Relations Act somewhat as a third party beneficiary to all benefits of the collective trade agreement, even if on his own he would yield to less favorable terms. The individual hiring contract is subsidiary to the terms of the trade agreement and may not waive any of its benefits, any more than a shipper can contract away the benefit of filed tariffs, the insurer the benefit of standard provisions, or the utility customer the benefit of legally established rates.

The principal portions of this case are set out in Section I of this Part.

NOTE

Much has been written on the legal nature of the collective agreement, with most commentators noting its unique characteristics and the difficulties and dangers of adopting traditional doctrines developed in other areas of contract law. *See* Chamberlain, *Collective Bargaining and the Concept of Contract,* 48 Colum. L. Rev. 829 (1948); Cox, *The Legal Nature of Collective Bargaining Agreements,* 57 Mich. L. Rev. 1 (1958); Feller, *A General Theory of the Collective Bargaining Agreement,* 61 Calif. L. Rev. 663 (1973); Gregory, *The Law of the*

Collective Agreement, 57 Mich. L. Rev. 635 (1959); Rice, *Collective Labor Agreements in American Law,* 44 Harv. L. Rev. 572 (1931); Shulman, *Reason, Contract, and Law in Labor Relations,* 68 Harv. L. Rev. 999 (1955); Summers, *Collective Agreements and the Law of Contracts,* 78 Yale L.J. 525 (1969).

B. THE ENFORCEMENT OF THE COLLECTIVE AGREEMENT THROUGH THE GRIEVANCE

PROCEDURE AND ARBITRATION LABOR STUDY GROUP, THE PUBLIC INTEREST IN NATIONAL LABOR POLICY 32 (Committee for Economic Development 1961)

A major achievement of collective bargaining, perhaps its most significant contribution to the American workplace, is the creation of a system of industrial jurisprudence, a system under which employer and employee rights are set forth in contractual form and disputes over the meaning of the contract are settled through a rational grievance process usually ending, in the case of unresolved disputes, with arbitration. The gains from this system are especially noteworthy because of their effect on the recognition and dignity of the individual worker. The system helps prevent arbitrary action on questions of discipline, layoff, promotion, and transfer, and sets up orderly procedures for the handling of grievances. Wildcat strikes and other disorderly means of protest have been curtailed and an effective work discipline generally established. In many situations, cooperative relationships marked by mutual respect between management and labor stand as an example of what can be done.

1. THE GRIEVANCE PROCEDURE

The great mass of day-to-day disputes arising during the term of a collective agreement are settled, in actual practice, through the procedure established and administered by the parties themselves. Where satisfactory industrial relations exist under collective bargaining, only a minute percentage of such disputes will even have to go to arbitration. And of those which do, it is extraordinary for the courts to get involved, either in compelling arbitration or in requiring compliance with awards. Since we will be dealing mostly with these exceptional cases, their relatively small role in the total industrial relations picture should be kept in proper perspective.

The grievance procedure is one of the most universal and important provisions in the collective agreement. The grievance procedure has been referred to as the "core of the collective bargaining agreement." L. Hill & C. Hook, Management at the Bargaining Table 199 (1945). *See generally* N. Chamberlain & J. Kuhn, Collective Bargaining 141-61 (2d ed. 1965); S. Slichter, J. Healy & E. Livernash, The Impact of Collective Bargaining on Management 692-738 (1960). Virtually all (99 percent) of the 1,550 major contracts studied in a national survey included such a procedure. U.S. Bureau of Labor Statistics, Dep't of Labor, Bull. No. 2095, Characteristics of Major Collective Bargaining Agreements 112 (1981). It represents the acceptance in labor-management relations of the fundamental notions of due process, and of the virtues of an orderly method of adjusting disputes. The decisions rendered through the established procedure tend to become the industrial case law for the plant. The use of arbitration as the terminal step in the procedure has produced a mass of decisions through which an "industrial jurisprudence" is developing, outside the established judicial system, much as the rules governing negotiable instruments first evolved as part of the "law merchant," and the principles of unfair competition originated with the medieval merchant guilds.

2. VOLUNTARY ARBITRATION

Voluntary arbitration has been defined as a contractual proceeding whereby the parties to any dispute or controversy, in order to obtain a speedy and inexpensive final disposition of the matter involved, select a judge of their own choice and by consent submit their controversy to him for determination. *Gates v. Arizona Brewing Co.,* 54 Ariz. 266, 269, 95 P.2d 49 (1939). *See also* F. Elkouri & E. Elkouri, How Arbitration Works 1-2 (4th ed. 1985); C. Updegraff, Arbitration and Labor Relations 3 (1971). The Supreme Court has observed that while commercial arbitration is a substitute for litigation, labor arbitration is a substitute for industrial strife. *United Steelworkers v. Warrior & Gulf Nav. Co.,* 363 U.S. 574, 578 (1960). For the view that labor arbitration is a substitute for both strikes and litigation ("but in the sense in which a transport airplane is a substitute for a stagecoach"), *see* Shulman, *Reason, Contract, and Law in Labor Relations,* 68 Harv. L. Rev. 999, 1024 (1955). The increasing use in recent years of arbitration in the settlement of labor disputes is a strong indication of a higher degree of maturity in industrial relations. Of 1,550 major collective agreements analyzed in a recent study, for example, about 97 percent provided for the arbitration of grievances between the parties. U.S. Bureau of Labor Statistics, Dep't of Labor, Bull. No. 2095, Characteristics of Major Collective Bargaining Agreements 112 (1981). Today thousands of disputes are settled in voluntary arbitration proceedings without resort to economic pressure or appeals to the sympathy of the public. R. Fleming, The Labor Arbitration Process 27 (1965).

Probably the greatest stimulus toward the use of arbitration to settle industrial grievances was provided by the National War Labor Board during World War II. The Board was given power to settle most types of labor disputes, and it quite regularly ordered the inclusion of arbitration clauses in new contracts whenever the parties were not able to agree upon their grievance procedure. *See generally* Symposium, *An Oral History of the National War Labor Board and Critical Issues in the Development of Modern Grievance Arbitration,* 39 Case W. Res. L. Rev. 501 (1988-89). Although less than ten percent of the labor agreements in effect in the early 1930s provided for arbitration, by 1944 the figures had grown to 73 percent. S. Slichter, J. Healy & E. Livernash, The Impact of Collective Bargaining on Management 739 (1960). *See also* Nolan & Abrams, *American Labor Arbitration: The Early Years, The Maturing Years,* 35 U. Fla. L. Rev. 373, 557 (1983). It is now agreed by an overwhelming majority of both union and management representatives that the good grievance procedure should have arbitration as the terminal point. Jones & Smith, *Management and Labor Appraisals and Criticisms of the Arbitration Process: A Report With Comments,* 62 Mich. L. Rev. 1115, 1116-17 (1964).

The courts in this country have recognized the rights of employees and unions under collective bargaining agreements, but court procedures are ordinarily ill-adapted to the needs of modern labor-management relations, and in addition are costly, prolonged, and technical. *E.g.,* F. Elkouri & E. Elkouri, How Arbitration Works 7-9 (4th ed. 1985); Freidin & Ulman, *Arbitration and the National War Labor Board,* 58 Harv. L. Rev. 309 (1945). One significant deficiency of litigation as a solution to industrial disputes was described by Professor Harry Shulman in this way: "[L]itigation results in a victory, perhaps, results in a decision in any event, which disposes of the particular controversy, but which does not affirmatively act to advance the parties' cooperative effort, which does not affirmatively act to affect their attitudes in their relations with one another. Arbitration can be made to do that." *Quoted in* F. Elkouri & E. Elkouri, How Arbitration Works 7 (rev. ed. 1960). Other advantages of arbitration include the saving of time, expense, and trouble. Arbitration permits self-regulation by business and labor, since it is a private rather than a governmental proceeding.

There are two distinct categories of labor-management arbitration. One is the arbitration of disputes over the substantive terms to be included in a collective agreement. When parties fail to conclude a contract through the usual negotiating sessions, they may agree to break the deadlock by submitting the issues for determination by an arbitrator. This type of arbitration is sometimes called the arbitration of "interests." Today there is a fairly substantial amount of this kind of arbitration, especially by public utilities. M. Copelof, Management-Union Arbitration 10-12 (1948); C. Updegraff & W. McCoy, Arbitration of Labor Disputes 149-50 (2d ed. 1961). Only rarely, however, will unions and employers commit themselves in advance to the arbitration of a new contract by including a provision in their labor agreement that, upon its expiration, arbitration may be invoked to resolve disputes over the terms of a renewal. Less than two percent of the 1,717 major agreements in effect in the early 1960s contained such a provision. U.S. Bureau of Labor Statistics, Dep't of Labor, Bull. No. 1425-1, Major Collective Bargaining Agreements: Grievance Procedures 95.

"Interest" arbitration, agreed to in advance, received a big boost when the Steelworkers and the major steel producers agreed in 1973 to settle unresolved disputes about the terms of their 1974 contracts through final and binding arbitration. Labor Relations Year Book—1973 pp. 32-37 (1974). *See also* Aksen,

The Impetus to Contract Arbitration in the Public Area, in N.Y.U. Twenty-Fourth Annual Conference on Labor 103 (1972); Feller, *The Impetus to Contract Arbitration in the Private Area,* in N.Y.U. Twenty-Fourth Annual Conference on Labor 79 (1972); Fleming, *"Interest" Arbitration Revisited,* 7 U. Mich. J.L. Reform 1 (1973); McAvoy, *Binding Arbitration of Contract Terms: A New Approach to the Resolution of Disputes in the Public Sector,* 72 Colum. L. Rev. 1192 (1972). Twenty-three states and the District of Columbia utilize interest arbitration to resolve public sector labor disputes. *See* Gould, A Primer on American Labor Law 280 n.4 (1994) (listing states).

A number of writers have suggested that interest arbitration might be used in the private sector to expand the utility of collective bargaining, further labor-management cooperation, avoid strikes, and facilitate first contract negotiations. *See* Bavis, *Labor Arbitration as an Industrial Relations Dispute Settlement Procedure in World Labor Markets,* 45 Lab. L.J. 147 (1994); Black & Hosea, *First Contract Legislation in Manitoba: A Model for the United States,* 45 Lab. L.J. 33 (1994); Howlett, *Interest Arbitration in the Public Sector,* 60 Chi.-Kent L. Rev. 815 (1984). Interest arbitration might be profitably employed in second and third contract disputes as well as first contract disputes. *See* Gould, Agenda for Reform: The Future of Employment Relationships and the Law 230 (1993).

The traditional resistance to interest arbitration reflects in part a widespread belief that contract terms directed by a third party will often be unworkable or unrealistic, and that agreement of the parties themselves is ordinarily more effective. F. Elkouri & E. Elkouri, How Arbitration Works 101-04 (4th ed. 1985); Davey, *Hazards in Labor Arbitration,* 1 Ind. & Lab. Rel. Rev. 386, 396 (1948). Furthermore, an absence of definite standards in the arbitration of "interest" disputes is thought to make the arbitral task more difficult. Injudicious use of arbitration in contract negotiation disputes may also impede the development of mature labor-management relationships through collective bargaining. On the other hand, in Great Britain the arbitration of new contract terms is considerably more common than the arbitration of disputes arising under existing contracts. I. Sharp, Industrial Conciliation and Arbitration in Great Britain 444 (1950); Gratch, *Grievance Settlement Machinery in England,* 12 Lab. L.J. 861, 863 (1961). The British apparently feel that outsiders are better equipped to deal with basic wage and hour issues of broad applicability than with individual grievances occurring in a particular local setting.

The task of the arbitrator in an arbitration of interests was well stated by arbitrator Whitley P. McCoy as follows:

> Arbitration of contract terms differs radically from arbitration of grievances. The latter calls for a judicial determination of existing contract rights; the former calls for a determination, upon considerations of policy, fairness, and expediency, of what the contract rights ought to be. In submitting this case to arbitration, the parties have merely extended their negotiations—

they have left it to this board to determine what they should, by negotiation, have agreed upon. We take it that the fundamental inquiry, as to each issue, is: What should the parties themselves, as reasonable men, have voluntarily agreed to?

Twin City Rapid Transit Co., 7 Lab. Arb. Rep. 845, 848 (1947).

Finally, the American rejection of interest arbitration in the private sector is based in part on the view that it would entail an unacceptable intrusion of the government into the workplace. The NLRA is committed to a system of "free collective bargaining" and "private ordering of the workplace" in which government's only role is to ensure that the process of collective bargaining is observed while the terms of the bargain are left to the parties. Is this view of collective bargaining supportable in the current context of heavy governmental regulation of the employment relationship and the workplace? *See* Crain, *Expanded Employee Drug Detection Programs and the Public Good: Big Brother at the Bargaining Table,* 64 N.Y.U. L. Rev. 1286 (1989); Klare, *Workplace Democracy and Market Reconstruction: An Agenda for Legal Reform,* 38 Cath. U. L. Rev. 1 (1988); *see infra* materials in Section IV.C dealing with the tensions between collective bargaining under the NLRA and antidiscrimination mandates.

The other main category of labor-management arbitration is that commonly known as "grievance" arbitration, or, in contradistinction to "interest" arbitration, as the arbitration of "rights." This is the type of arbitration that is customarily provided as the terminal point in contract grievance procedures. It deals with disputes arising during the life of an agreement. The function of the arbitrator in the arbitration of "rights" is quasi-judicial. The arbitrator interprets and applies the provisions of the contract; generally he or she is precluded from adding to or detracting from its terms. Nonetheless, over the years arbitrators have developed somewhat divergent attitudes about the proper approach to the collective agreement. Under a "residual rights" theory the employer retains sole discretion to make managerial decisions affecting employees except as limited, more or less expressly, by the contract. M. Stone, Managerial Freedom and Job Security 5-7 (1964); Killingsworth, *Standards of Arbitral Decision: Jurisdiction,* in Summer Institute on International and Comparative Law, Univ. of Mich. Law School, Lectures on the Law and Labor-Management Relations 228, 230-31 (1951). Under an "implied limitations" theory a union may acquire certain rights as a matter of reasonable inference from different clauses or from the instrument as a whole. *Id.;* Cox, *The Legal Nature of Collective Bargaining Agreements,* 57 Mich. L. Rev. 1, 28-36 (1958); Wallen, *The Silent Contract vs. Express Provisions: The Arbitration of Local Working Conditions,* in National Academy of Arbitrators, Collective Bargaining and the Arbitrator's Role, Proceedings of the Fifteenth Annual Meeting 117-47 (1962). Views also vary under both theories about the weight the arbitrator should give to past practice and bargaining history between the parties, or to notions of essential justice. *E.g.,* R. Fleming, The Labor Arbitration Process 134-98 (1965); Aaron, *The Uses of the Past in Arbitration,* in National Academy of Arbitrators, Arbitration Today, Proceedings of the Eighth Annual Meeting 1 (1955); Mittenthal, *Past Practice and the Administration of Collective Bargaining Agreements,* 59 Mich. L. Rev. 1017 (1961); Wirtz, *Due Process of Arbitration,* in National Academy of Arbitrators, The Arbitrator and the Parties, Proceedings of the Eleventh Annual Meeting 1 (1958).

Arbitration tribunals take several forms: temporary (*ad hoc*) or permanent arbitrators; tripartite boards, boards composed only of neutral or impartial members, or a single arbitrator. F. Elkouri & E. Elkouri, How Arbitration Works 118-35 (4th ed. 1985). Apart from private arrangements made by the parties directly with arbitrators, two important sources of *ad hoc* arbitrators are the American Arbitration Association and the Federal Mediation and Conciliation Service. Both maintain panels of qualified and available arbitrators. The parties then make a selection from lists supplied upon request by the AAA or the FMCS.

As arbitration has matured, it has suffered certain aging pains. Then-Professor Harry T. Edwards declared some years ago that the process had become "too slow and too expensive," with too much "uniformity" and "codification" and an overly "legalistic" approach to day-to-day problems. Thus, a normal case with a one-day hearing cost a union $2200; management would usually pay more. The average time from the filing of a grievance to the issuance of an award runs about two-thirds of a year. These problems may be aggravated by the reluctance of many parties to use new arbitrators. It has been estimated that 90 percent of arbitration cases are heard by 10 percent of the available arbitrators. Labor Relations Year Book—1977 p. 206 (1978). Furthermore, the arbitral ranks are not particularly diverse. For example, only 4.2 to 6.6 percent of labor arbitrators are women. Steen et al., *A Reexamination of Gender Bias in Arbitration Decisions,* 45 Lab. L.J. 298 (1994). The composition of the American Arbitration Association (AAA), often called upon to furnish arbitrators in labor disputes, is predominantly white and male. *See* Jacobs, *Woman Claims Arbiters of Bias are Biased, Too,* Wall St. J., Sept. 19, 1994, at B1 (summarizing basis for a lawsuit filed challenging the ability of private arbitration providers to handle various issues involving discrimination). *See generally* Stallworth & Malin, *Workforce Diversity: A Continuing Challenge For ADR,* Disp. Resol. J., June 1994, at 35.

3. ARBITRATION UNDER THE RAILWAY LABOR ACT

The Railway Labor Act creates special machinery to deal with the various kinds of labor disputes. The National Mediation Board functions as a mediating agency in what we have described as "interests" disputes, and the National Railroad Adjustment Board handles disputes concerning "rights." The Mediation Board has the responsibility, as to disputes within its cognizance which do not concern representation, first, to use its good offices in an attempt to secure an agreement between the parties, and, second, failing in such attempt, to induce the parties to submit their dispute to arbitration under the procedures of § 7 of the RLA.

Arbitration under § 7 is entirely voluntary, in that both parties must agree to submit an "interests" dispute to a board of arbitration. The board's award, however, is enforceable in federal district court.

Adjudication of grievance disputes or disputes concerning "rights" by the Adjustment Board under § 3 is voluntary in the sense that appeal to the Board is apparently optional. But if either party does refer the case, the Board's jurisdiction attaches and it is directed to dispose of the matter. Upon failure of the carrier to abide by an award an appeal may be made to the appropriate district court where the award will be enforced or set aside. In the district court, "the findings and order of the division of the Adjustment Board shall be conclusive on the parties," except for failure to comply with legal requirements or for fraud or corruption.

In setting up the National Railroad Adjustment Board, Congress proceeded on the basis of fifty years of experience with efforts to provide effective methods for settling labor disputes in the railroad industry. The Board is divided into four jurisdictional divisions, of which two have ten members each, one has eight, and the fourth has six. The members are appointed one-half by the carriers and one-half by the brotherhoods, and are compensated by the parties whom they represent. Because of the even division of members, deadlocks are common. In the event of deadlock, the division may select a referee, but if it fails to do so, the National Mediation Board designates the referee. The referee sits with the division as one of its members and hears the case. The award is written by the referee and must receive a majority vote, including the vote of the referee, for adoption by the division.

The airlines are covered by all the provisions of the Railway Labor Act except § 3. Title II of the Act provides for the establishment of special boards of adjustment and a four-member National Air Transport Adjustment Board to handle grievances and disputes between air carriers and their employees over the interpretation or application of the parties' agreements. The powers and duties of the National Air Transport Adjustment Board were to be similar to those of the National Railroad Adjustment Board but it has never been established.

NOTE

The last three decades have produced a torrent of writing on labor arbitration. Works emphasizing the legal problems of arbitration, including its relationship to the courts and the NLRB, will be cited in the sections to follow which deal with the various questions of law. At this point attention will be paid to books and articles concentrating on the practice and procedure of arbitration itself.

Much valuable material on the operation of voluntary labor arbitration is contained in the *Annual Proceedings* of the National Academy of Arbitrators, published by the Bureau of National Affairs. (The National Academy is the professional association of labor arbitrators.) A useful periodical is the American Arbitration Association's *Arbitration Journal.* Texts of selected arbitration awards are published in BNA's *Labor Arbitration Reports* and CCH's *Labor Arbitration Awards,* loose-leaf services with bound cumulations. General studies of arbitration include N. Brand, Labor Arbitration: The Strategy of Persuasion (1987); F. Elkouri & E. Elkouri, How Arbitration Works (4th ed. 1985); O. Fairweather, Practice and Procedure in Labor Arbitration (3d ed. 1990); R. Fleming, The Labor Arbitration Process (1965); P. Hays, Labor Arbitration: A Dissenting View (1966); C. Updegraff, Arbitration and Labor Relations (1971). The developing "substantive law" of arbitral decisions is discussed in W. Baer, Discipline and Discharge under the Labor Agreement (1972); M. Hill & A. Sinicropi, Management Rights: A Legal and Arbitral Analysis (1986); A. Zack & R. Bloch, Labor Agreement in Negotiation and Arbitration (1983). *See also* C. Barreca, A. Miller & M. Zimny, eds., Labor Arbitrator Development—A Handbook (1983); M. Hill & A. Sinicropi, Evidence in Arbitration (1987) and Remedies in Arbitration (1991); A. Zack, Arbitration in Practice (1984); M. Zimny, W. Dolson & C. Barreca, Labor Arbitration: A Practical Guide for Advocates (1990).

Some of the many notable articles on arbitration are Aaron, *Some Procedural Problems in Arbitration,* 10 Vand. L. Rev. 733 (1957); Aaron, *Arbitration Decisions and the Law of the Shop,* 29 Lab. L.J. 536 (1978); Abrams, *The Integrity of the Arbitral Process,* 76 Mich. L. Rev. 231 (1977); Alleyne, *Delawyerizing Arbitration,* 50 Ohio St. L. Rev. 93 (1989); Cooper, *Discovery in Labor Arbitration,* 72 Minn. L. Rev. 1281 (1988); Edwards, *Due Process Considerations in Labor Arbitration,* 25 Arb. J. 141 (1970); Fleming, *Reflections on the Nature of Labor Arbitration,* 61 Mich. L. Rev. 1245 (1963); Fuller, *Collective Bargaining and the Arbitrator,* 1963 Wis. L. Rev. 1; Getman, *Labor Arbitration and Dispute Resolution,* 88 Yale L.J. 916 (1979); Jones, *Evidentiary Concepts in Labor Arbitration: Some Modern Variations on Ancient Legal Themes,* 13 U.C.L.A. L. Rev. 1241 (1966); Jones & Smith, *Management and Labor Appraisals and Criticisms of the Arbitration Process: A Report With Comments,* 62 Mich. L. Rev. 1115 (1964); Nolan & Abrams, *The Future of Labor Arbitration,* 37 Lab. L.J. 437 (1986); Roberts, Waldman, Morris, Simon, *Arbitration in a State of Flux,* in N.Y.U. Twenty-Ninth Annual Conference on Labor 277, 279, 297, 317 (1976) (four separate papers); Symposium, *The Role of Arbitration in Collective Bargaining Dispute Proceedings,* 44 U. Miami L. Rev. 233 (1989).

On the resolution of disputes under the Railway Labor Act, *see* Coleman, *Settling Airline Labor-Management Disputes: Has the Railway Labor Act Become Obsolete?* 58 Geo. Wash. L. Rev. 1073 (1990); Kroner, *Minor Disputes Under the Railway Labor Act: A Critical Appraisal,* 37 N.Y.U.L. Rev. 41 (1962); Mangum, *Grievance Procedures for Railroad Operating Employees,* 15 Ind. & Lab. Rel. Rev. 474 (1962); C. Rehmus, ed., The Railway Labor Act at Fifty: Collective Bargaining in the Railroad and Airline Industries (1976).

C. JUDICIAL ENFORCEMENT OF THE COLLECTIVE AGREEMENT

1. THE ENFORCEMENT OF VOLUNTARY ARBITRATION AGREEMENTS

a. At Common Law

In many states voluntary arbitration may be conducted under either statutory or common law rules. *See generally* F. Elkouri & E. Elkouri, How Arbitration Works 39-46 (4th ed. 1985); C. Updegraff, Arbitration and Labor Relations 23-26 (1971). Although it is usually held that the statute supplements and does not abrogate the common law, at least one state, Washington, has declared that its statute completely supersedes the common-law rules. *Puget Sound Bridge & Dredging Co. v. Lake Wash. Shipyards,* 1 Wash. 2d 401, 96 P.2d 257 (1939). Most arbitrations are in fact conducted outside the statute (if any), with common law principles governing proceedings. In any event, since state arbitration statutes are often very general in nature, their details must be filled in by resort to the common law. The basic principles of common law arbitration have been summarized by the United States Department of Labor as follows:

> Common law arbitration rests upon the voluntary agreement of the parties to submit their dispute to an outsider. The submission agreement may be oral and may be revoked at any time before the rendering of the award. The tribunal, permanent or temporary, may be composed of any number of arbitrators. They must be free from bias and interest in the subject matter, and may not be related by affinity or consanguinity to either party. The arbitrators need not be sworn. Only existing disputes may be submitted to them. The parties must be given notice of hearings and are entitled to be present when all the evidence is received. The arbitrators have no power to subpoena witnesses or records and need not conform to legal rules of hearing procedure other than to give the parties an opportunity to present all competent evidence. All arbitrators must attend the hearings, consider the evidence jointly and arrive at an award by a unanimous vote. The award may be oral, but if written, all the arbitrators must sign it. It must dispose of every substantial issue submitted to arbitration. An award may be set aside only for fraud, misconduct, gross mistake, or substantial breach of a common law rule. The only method of enforcing the common law award is to file suit upon it and the judgment thus obtained may be enforced as any other judgment.

D. Ziskind, Labor Arbitration Under State Statutes 3 (U.S. Dep't of Labor 1943). The common law rule that an agreement to arbitrate future disputes will not be enforced by the courts and is revocable at will by either party was accepted until recently in the majority of American jurisdictions. Gregory & Orlikoff, *The En-*

forcement of Labor Arbitration Agreements, 17 U. Chi. L. Rev. 233, 254 (1950). The National War Labor Board, however, consistently rejected the outmoded common law view that arbitration is to be regarded with hostility as an attempt to supplant the courts. Instead, the Board took the position that agreements for arbitration should be favored and aid given to their enforcement. Freidin & Ulman, *Arbitration and National War Labor Board,* 58 Harv. L. Rev. 309, 315 (1945).

b. State Arbitration Statutes

State arbitration statutes are of three general kinds: (1) general statutes used principally in commercial disputes but often adaptable, with some limitations, to labor disputes; (2) statutes designed specifically for labor disputes, and prescribing the arbitration procedure in some detail; and (3) statutes which merely "promote" arbitration by directing state officials to encourage its use. D. Ziskind, Labor Arbitration Under State Statutes 2-3 (U.S. Dep't of Labor 1943). Massachusetts and Michigan are examples of states having special labor arbitration statutes; New York, on the other hand, simply made its general arbitration statute applicable to labor cases. Mass. Ann. Laws ch. 150C, §§ 1-16 (1989); Mich. Comp. Laws Ann. § 423.9d (1978); N.Y. Civ. Prac. Law § 7501 (McKinney 1980), replacing N.Y. Civ. Prac. Act § 1448. The usual effect of these statutes is to alter the common law rule by making agreements to arbitrate existing and future disputes valid and enforceable.

In 1955 the Conference of Commissioners on Uniform State Laws promulgated a proposed Uniform Arbitration Act, patterned after the New York Act, which would apply to labor-management agreements to arbitrate. By 1992 thirty-five jurisdictions had adopted the act, but several excepted collective agreements from its coverage. 7 Uniform Laws Ann. 1 (Supp. 1988).

The application of federal substantive law under § 301 of the Taft-Hartley Act to union-employer arbitration agreements will make state legislation largely inoperative in industries affecting commerce. State enactments may retain some significance, however, as to procedural matters and as guides in the shaping of the federal law. Smith & Clark, *Reappraisal of the Role of the States in Shaping Labor Relations Law,* 1965 Wis. L. Rev. 411, 456. *See also* Comment, *The Applicability of State Arbitration Statutes to Proceedings Subject to LMRA Section 301,* 27 Ohio St. L.J. 692 (1966).

c. Section 301 of the Labor Management Relations Act

TEXTILE WORKERS UNION v. LINCOLN MILLS

Supreme Court of the United States
353 U.S. 448, 77 S. Ct. 912, 1 L. Ed. 2d 972 (1957)

MR. JUSTICE DOUGLAS delivered the opinion of the Court.

Petitioner-union entered into a collective bargaining agreement in 1953 with respondent-employer, the agreement to run one year and from year to year thereafter, unless terminated on specified notices. The agreement provided that there would be no strikes or work stoppages and that grievances would be handled pursuant to a specified procedure. The last step in the grievance procedure—a step that could be taken by either party—was arbitration.

This controversy involves several grievances that concern work loads and work assignments. The grievances were processed through the various steps in the grievance procedure and were finally denied by the employer. The union requested arbitration, and the employer refused. Thereupon the union brought this suit in the District Court to compel arbitration.

The District Court concluded that it had jurisdiction and ordered the employer to comply with the grievance arbitration provisions of the collective bargaining agreement. The Court of Appeals reversed by a divided vote. 230 F.2d 81....

The starting point of our inquiry is § 301 of the Labor Management Relations Act of 1947....

There has been considerable litigation involving § 301 and courts have construed it differently. There is one view that § 301(a) merely gives federal district courts jurisdiction in controversies that involve labor organizations in industries affecting commerce, without regard to diversity of citizenship or the amount in controversy. Under that view § 301(a) would not be the source of substantive law; it would neither supply federal law to resolve these controversies nor turn the federal judges to state law for answers to the questions. Other courts—the overwhelming number of them—hold that § 301(a) is more than jurisdictional— that it authorizes federal courts to fashion a body of federal law for the enforcement of these collective bargaining agreements and includes within that federal law specific performance of promises to arbitrate grievances under collective bargaining agreements. Perhaps the leading decision representing that point of view is the one rendered by Judge Wyzanski in *Textile Workers Union v. American Thread Co.,* 113 F. Supp. 137 (1953). That is our construction of § 301(a), which means that the agreement to arbitrate grievance disputes, contained in this collective bargaining agreement, should be specifically enforced.

From the face of the Act it is apparent that § 301(a) and § 301(b) supplement one another. Section 301(b) makes it possible for a labor organization, representing employees in an industry affecting commerce, to sue and be sued as an entity in the federal courts. Section 301(b) in other words provides the procedural remedy lacking at common law. Section 301(a) certainly does something more than that. Plainly, it supplies the basis upon which the federal district courts may take jurisdiction and apply the procedural rule of § 301(b). The question is whether § 301(a) is more than jurisdictional.

The legislative history of § 301 is somewhat cloudy and confusing. But there are a few shafts of light that illuminate our problem.

The bills, as they passed the House and the Senate, contained provisions which would have made the failure to abide by an agreement to arbitrate an unfair labor practice. S. Rep. No. 105, 80th Cong., 1st Sess., pp. 20-21, 23; H.R. Rep. No. 245, 80th Cong., 1st Sess., p. 21. This feature of the law was dropped in Conference. As the Conference Report stated, "Once parties have made a collective bargaining contract, the enforcement of that contract should be left to the usual processes of the law and not to the National Labor Relations Board." H.R. Conf. Rep. No. 510, 80th Cong., 1st Sess., p. 42.

Both the Senate and the House took pains to provide for "the usual processes of the law" by provisions which were the substantial equivalent of § 301(a) in its present form. Both the Senate Report and the House Report indicate a primary concern that unions as well as employers should be bound to collective bargaining contracts. But there was also a broader concern—a concern with a procedure for making such agreements enforceable in the courts by either party. At one point the Senate Report, *supra* at 15, states, "We feel that the aggrieved party should also have a right of action in the Federal courts. Such a policy is completely in accord with the purpose of the Wagner Act which the Supreme Court declared was 'to compel employers to bargain collectively with their employees to the end that an employment contract, binding on both parties, should be made....'"

Congress was also interested in promoting collective bargaining that ended with agreements not to strike....

Thus collective bargaining contracts were made "equally binding and enforceable on both parties." *Id.* at 15. As stated in the House Report, *supra* at 6, the new provision "makes labor organizations equally responsible with employers for contract violations and provides for suit by either against the other in the United States district courts." To repeat, the Senate Report, *supra* at 17, summed up the philosophy of § 301 as follows: "Statutory recognition of the collective agreement as a valid, binding, and enforceable contract is a logical and necessary step. It will promote a higher degree of responsibility upon the parties to such agreements, and will thereby promote industrial peace."

Plainly the agreement to arbitrate grievance disputes is the *quid pro quo* for an agreement not to strike. Viewed in this light, the legislation does more than confer jurisdiction in the federal courts over labor organizations. It expresses a federal policy that federal courts should enforce these agreements on behalf of or against labor organizations and that industrial peace can be best obtained only in that way.

To be sure there is a great medley of ideas reflected in the hearings, reports, and debates on this Act. Yet, to repeat, the entire tenor of the history indicates that the agreement to arbitrate grievance disputes was considered as *quid pro quo* of a no strike agreement. And when in the House the debate narrowed to the question whether § 301 was more than jurisdictional, it became abundantly clear that the purpose of the section was to provide the necessary legal remedies. Section 302 of the House bill, the substantial equivalent of the present § 301, was being described by Mr. Hartley, the sponsor of the bill in the House:

"Mr. Barden. Mr. Chairman, I take this time for the purpose of asking the Chairman a question, and in asking the question I want it understood that it is intended to make a part of the record that may hereafter be referred to as history of the legislation.

"It is my understanding that Section 302, the section dealing with equal responsibility under collective bargaining contracts in strike actions and proceedings in district courts contemplates not only the ordinary lawsuits for damages but also such other remedial proceedings, both legal and equitable, as might be appropriate in the circumstances; in other words, proceedings could, for example, be brought by the employers, the labor organizations, or interested individual employees under the Declaratory Judgments Act in order to secure declarations from the Court of legal rights under the contract.

"Mr. Hartley. The interpretation the gentlemen has just given of that section is absolutely correct." 93 Cong. Rec. 3656-3657.

It seems, therefore, clear to us that Congress adopted a policy which placed sanctions behind agreements to arbitrate grievance disputes,[6] by implication rejecting the common law rule discussed in *Red Cross Line v. Atlantic Fruit Co.,* 264 U.S. 109 (1924), against enforcement of executory agreements to arbitrate. We would undercut the Act and defeat its policy if we read § 301 narrowly as only conferring jurisdiction over labor organizations.

The question then is, what is the substantive law to be applied in suits under § 301(a)? We conclude that the substantive law to apply in suits under § 301(a) is federal law which the courts must fashion from the policy of our national labor laws. *See* Mendelsohn, *Enforceability of Arbitration Agreements Under Taft-Hartley Section 301,* 66 Yale L.J. 167. The Labor Management Relations Act expressly furnishes some substantive law. It points out what the parties may or may not do in certain situations. Other problems will lie in the penumbra of express statutory mandates. Some will lack express statutory sanction but will be solved by looking at the policy of the legislation and fashioning a remedy that will effectuate that policy. The range of judicial inventiveness will be determined by the nature of the problem. *See Board of Commissioners v. United States,* 308 U.S. 343, 351 (1939). Federal interpretation of the federal law will govern, not state law. *Cf. Jerome v. United States,* 318 U.S. 101, 104 (1943). But state law, if compatible with the purpose of § 301, may be resorted to in order to find the rule that will best effectuate the federal policy. *See Board of Commissioners v. United*

---

[6]*Association of Westinghouse Salaried Employees v. Westinghouse Corp.,* 348 U.S. 437 (1955), is quite a different case. There the union sued to recover unpaid wages on behalf of some 4,000 employees. The basic question concerned the standing of the union to sue and recover on those individual employment contracts. The question here concerns the right of the union to enforce the agreement to arbitrate which it has made with the employer.

States, supra at 351-352. Any state law applied, however, will be absorbed as federal law and will not be an independent source of private rights.

It is not uncommon for federal courts to fashion federal law where federal rights are concerned. *See Clearfield Trust Co. v. United States,* 318 U.S. 363, 366-367 (1943); *National Metropolitan Bank v. United States,* 323 U.S. 454 (1945). Congress has indicated by § 301(a) the purpose to follow that course here. There is no constitutional difficulty. Article III, § 2 extends the judicial power to cases "arising under ... the Laws of the United States...." The power of Congress to regulate these labor-management controversies under the Commerce Clause is plain. *Houston Texas R. Co. v. United States,* 234 U.S. 342 (1914); *NLRB v. Jones & Laughlin Corp.,* 301 U.S. 1 (1936). A case or controversy arising under § 301(a) is, therefore, one within the purview of judicial power as defined in Article III.

The question remains whether jurisdiction to compel arbitration of grievance disputes is withdrawn by the Norris-La Guardia Act.... Section 7 of that Act prescribes stiff procedural requirements for issuing an injunction in a labor dispute. The kinds of acts which had given rise to abuse of the power to enjoin are listed in § 4. The failure to arbitrate was not a part and parcel of the abuses against which the Act was aimed. Section 8 of the Norris-La Guardia Act does, indeed, indicate a congressional policy toward settlement of labor disputes by arbitration, for it denies injunctive relief to any person who has failed to make "every reasonable effort" to settle the dispute by negotiation, mediation, or "voluntary arbitration." Though a literal reading might bring the dispute within the terms of the Act (*see* Cox, *Grievance Arbitration in the Federal Courts,* 67 Harv. L. Rev. 591, 602-604), we see no justification in policy for restricting § 301(a) to damage suits, leaving specific performance of a contract to arbitrate grievance disputes to the inapposite procedural requirements of that Act. Moreover, we held in *Virginia R. Co. v. System Federation,* 300 U.S. 515 (1937), and in *Graham v. Brotherhood of Firemen,* 338 U.S. 232, 237 (1949), that the Norris-La Guardia Act does not deprive Federal courts of jurisdiction to compel compliance with the mandates of the Railway Labor Act.... The mandates there involved concerned racial discrimination. Yet those decisions were not based on any peculiarities of the Railway Labor Act. We followed the same course in *Syres v. Oil Workers,* 350 U.S. 892 (1955), which was governed by the National Labor Relations Act.... There an injunction was sought against racial discrimination in application of a collective bargaining agreement; and we allowed the injunction to issue. The congressional policy in favor of the enforcement of agreements to arbitrate grievance disputes being clear, there is no reason to submit them to the requirements of § 7 of the Norris-La Guardia Act....

Reversed.

MR. JUSTICE BLACK took no part in the consideration or decision of this case.

MR. JUSTICE BURTON, whom MR. JUSTICE HARLAN joins, concurring in the result.

This suit was brought in a United States District Court under § 301 of the Labor Management Relations Act of 1947, ... seeking specific enforcement of the arbitration provisions of a collective bargaining contract. The District Court had jurisdiction over the action since it involved an obligation running to a union—a union controversy—and not uniquely personal rights of employees sought to be enforced by a union. *Cf. Association of Westinghouse Salaried Employees v. Westinghouse Elec. Corp.,* 348 U.S. 437 (1955). Having jurisdiction over the suit, the court was not powerless to fashion an appropriate federal remedy. The power to decree specific performance of a collectively bargained agreement to arbitrate finds its source in § 301 itself, and in a Federal District Court's inherent equitable powers, nurtured by a congressional policy to encourage and enforce labor arbitration in industries affecting commerce.

I do not subscribe to the conclusion of the Court that the substantive law to be applied in a suit under § 301 is federal law. At the same time, I agree with Judge Magruder in *International Brotherhood v. W. L. Mead, Inc.,* 230 F.2d 576 (1st Cir. 1956), that some federal rights may necessarily be involved in a § 301 case, and hence that the constitutionality of § 301 can be upheld as a congressional grant to Federal District Courts of what has been called "protective jurisdiction."

[MR. JUSTICE FRANKFURTER dissented in a rather unusual 86-page opinion, including the entire relevant legislative history of § 301 of the Taft-Hartley Act and its predecessor bill, the Case bill, in order to prove the point which he had made in *Westinghouse*—that § 301 did not create substantive rights but was only procedural.]

NOTES

1. In *Association of Westinghouse Salaried Employees v. Westinghouse Elec. Corp.,* 348 U.S. 437 (1955), the Supreme Court avoided the constitutional question reached and decided in *Lincoln Mills* by holding that § 301 was not intended to authorize a union to sue on behalf of employees for accrued wage claims, which were described as "uniquely personal rights." Five years after *Lincoln Mills,* in *Smith v. Evening News Ass'n,* 371 U.S. 195, 199 (1962), *infra,* the Court declared that *Westinghouse* was "no longer authoritative as a precedent." The lower federal courts have accordingly allowed unions to maintain actions to enforce the rights of employees in a distribution of the assets of a negotiated pension fund, *UAW v. Textron, Inc.,* 312 F.2d 688 (6th Cir. 1963), to secure for employees wages due under a cost-of-living adjustment clause in a labor contract, *Retail Clerks Local 1222 v. Alfred Lewis, Inc.,* 327 F.2d 442 (9th Cir. 1964), and to enforce the rights of retirees to lump-sum compensation for sick-leave, *SIU de P.R. v. Virgin Islands Port Auth.,* 42 F.3d 801 (3d Cir. 1994).

2. In *Textron Lycoming Reciprocating Engine Div., AVCO Corp. v. UAW*, 118 S. Ct. 1626 (1998), the Supreme Court held that a federal court lacked jurisdiction over a union's suit seeking to have a collective bargaining agreement declared void as a result of alleged fraudulent inducement by the employer. During negotiations leading to a new bargaining agreement, the union repeatedly asked the employer to provide it with any information it possessed regarding plans to contract out unit work. Although the company had already drawn up a subcontracting plan, it said nothing to the union. After the new agreement was concluded, the firm announced plans to contract out half of the bargaining unit jobs. The Court held that § 301 jurisdiction is limited to actions over "suits for violation of contracts" and does not apply to suits seeking to have collective contracts declared void. The Court distinguished the situation where a party brings suit to enforce a bargaining agreement and the defendant raises an affirmative defense questioning the legality of the existing agreement. Since such a suit would initially be to enforce the terms of the contract, § 301 jurisdiction would be available, but not where the initial action merely seeks to have the contract declared invalid.

3. In *UAW v. Hoosier Cardinal Corp.*, 383 U.S. 696, 699-700 (1966), the Supreme Court held that § 301 suits are governed by state statutes of limitations. The Court subsequently held, however, that suits by individual employees against their employer for breach of contract and against their labor organization for breach of the duty of fair representation are subject to the six-months limitations period specified in § 10(b) of the NLRA for unfair labor practice cases. *See Del-Costello v. Teamsters,* 462 U.S. 151 (1983). Should union- and employer-initiated suits to compel arbitration and to obtain the enforcement of arbitral awards be similarly governed by the § 10(b) limitations period, instead of by the different state statutory periods? The Circuits are split on the question. *Compare Teamsters Local 245 v. Kansas City Piggy Back,* 88 F.3d 659 (8th Cir. 1996) ("No"); *Longshoremen (ILA) Local 953 v. Cataneo Inc.,* 990 F.2d 794 (4th Cir. 1993) ("No"); *Service Employees Local 36 v. City Cleaning Co.,* 982 F.2d 89 (3rd Cir. 1992) ("No") *with Communications Workers v. AT&T Co.,* 10 F.3d 887 (D.C. Cir. 1993) ("Yes"); *Cummings v. John Morrell & Co.,* 36 F.3d 499 (6th Cir. 1994) ("Yes"); *Cantrell v. Electrical Workers (IBEW) Local 2021,* 32 F.3d 465 (10th Cir. 1994) ("Yes").

4. The scholarly outpouring generated by *Lincoln Mills* includes Aaron, *On First Looking Into the Lincoln Mills Decision,* in National Academy of Arbitrators, Arbitration and the Law, Proceedings of the Twelfth Annual Meeting 1 (1959); Bickel & Wellington, *Legislative Purpose and the Judicial Process: The Lincoln Mills Case,* 71 Harv. L. Rev. 1 (1957); Cox, *Reflections Upon Labor Arbitration,* 72 Harv. L. Rev. 1482 (1959); Feinsinger, *Enforcement of Labor Agreements—A New Era in Collective Bargaining,* 43 Va. L. Rev. 1261 (1957); Gregory, *The Law of the Collective Agreement,* 57 Mich. L. Rev. 635 (1959). *See* *also* Leonard, *Specific Performance of Collective Bargaining Agreements,* 52 Fordham L. Rev. 193 (1983).

Retail Clerks, Locals 128 & 633 v. Lion Dry Goods, Inc., 369 U.S. 17, 82 S. Ct. 541, 7 L. Ed. 2d 503 (1962). The union and the employers settled a long strike with a "statement of understanding" in which the union conceded it was not then a majority representative entitled to exclusive recognition. The employers agreed to continue wage schedules and other working conditions in effect, and to arbitrate grievances arising under the statement. Subsequently, the employers refused to abide by arbitration awards disposing of two grievances in favor of the union. The union sued for enforcement under § 301. The employers argued the strike settlement agreement was not a "contract" within the meaning of the statute. On certiorari, the Supreme Court held that the union's action could be maintained under § 301 since "[a] federal forum was provided for actions on other labor contracts besides collective bargaining contracts." Section 301 speaks of "contracts," not collective agreements, the Court observed, and the settlement agreement was a contract, even if not a collective agreement. In addition, the Court held that § 301 was not limited to suits by majority representatives but extended to actions on the legitimate agreements of minority unions.

NOTES

1. In *Plumbers v. Plumbers Local 334,* 452 U.S. 615 (1981), the Supreme Court held that a local union was entitled to maintain an action under § 301 for an alleged violation of the union constitution by the international in forcing consolidation of several locals. International union constitutions were held to be contracts between labor organizations, and the federal courts have jurisdiction to resolve disputes arising under them. Arguments advanced before the Court that such matters were "internal union affairs" beyond the scope of the Taft-Hartley Act were rejected by the majority as "wide of the mark." Noting an "obvious and important difference" between substantive regulation by the NLRB of internal union affairs and enforcement by the federal courts of "freely entered into agreements between separate labor organizations," the Court found no impediment to federal judicial action in the latter category. In *Wooddell v. IBEW Local 71,* 502 U.S. 93 (1991), the Court extended its holding in *Plumbers,* ruling that a union member may sue his local under § 301 for a violation of the international constitution. Federal substantive law governed. Thus, although § 301 claims by individual employees for violation of international union constitutions are cognizable, claims for breach of local union constitutions are not. *See Korzen v. Teamsters Local 705,* 75 F.3d 285 (7th Cir. 1996) (distinguishing claims for breach of local union constitutions as actions on contracts between a labor organization and its members from actions on international constitutions, which are agreements among labor organizations).

2. Would § 301 support a suit to enforce an agreement to arbitrate the terms of a new contract? *Compare Boston Printing Pressmen's Union v. Potter Press,* 141 F. Supp. 553 (D. Mass. 1956), *aff'd,* 241 F.2d 787 (1st Cir. 1957), *cert. denied,* 355 U.S. 817 (1957) ("No") *with Builders Ass'n of Kansas City v. Kansas City Laborers,* 326 F.2d 867 (8th Cir. 1964), *cert. denied,* 377 U.S. 917 (1964) *and Pressmen's Local 50 v. Newspaper Printing Corp.,* 399 F. Supp. 593 (M.D. Tenn. 1974), *aff'd,* 518 F.2d 351 (6th Cir. 1975). The Seventh and Ninth Circuits have joined the group supporting the enforceability under § 301 of interest-arbitration agreements and awards. *Sheet Metal Workers Local 20 v. Baylor Heating & Air Conditioning,* 877 F.2d 547 (7th Cir. 1989); *Sheet Metal Workers Local 104 v. Simpson Sheet Metal,* 954 F.2d 1506 (9th Cir. 1992). *See also* Young, *Arbitration of Terms for New Labor Contracts,* 17 W. Res. L. Rev. 1302 (1966); Note, *The Enforceability of the No-Strike and Interest Arbitration Provisions of the Experimental Negotiating Agreement in Federal Courts,* 12 Valparaiso U.L. Rev. 57 (1977).

UNITED STEELWORKERS v. WARRIOR & GULF NAVIGATION CO.

Supreme Court of the United States
363 U.S. 574, 80 S. Ct. 1347, 4 L. Ed. 2d 1409 (1960)

MR. JUSTICE DOUGLAS delivered the opinion of the Court.

Respondent transports steel and steel products by barge and maintains a terminal at Chickasaw, Alabama, where it performs maintenance and repair work on its barges. The employees at that terminal constitute a bargaining unit covered by a collective bargaining agreement negotiated by petitioner union. Respondent between 1956 and 1958 laid off some employees, reducing the bargaining unit from 42 to 23 men. This reduction was due in part to respondent contracting maintenance work, previously done by its employees, to other companies. The latter used respondent's supervisors to lay out the work and hired some of the laid-off employees of respondent (at reduced wages). Some were in fact assigned to work on respondent's barges. A number of employees signed a grievance which petitioner presented to respondent, the grievance reading:

> We are hereby protesting the Company's actions, of arbitrarily and unreasonably contracting out work to other concerns, that could and previously has been performed by Company employees.

> This practice becomes unreasonable, unjust and discriminatory in lieu [*sic*] of the fact that at present there are a number of employees that have been laid off for about 1 and ½ years or more for allegedly lack of work.

Confronted with these facts we charge that the Company is in violation of the contract by inducing a partial lockout, of a number of the employees who would otherwise be working were it not for this unfair practice.

The collective agreement had both a "no strike" and a "no lockout" provision. It also had a grievance procedure which provided in relevant part as follows:

Issues which conflict with any Federal statute in its application as established by Court procedure or matters which are strictly a function of management shall not be subject to arbitration under this section.

Should differences arise between the Company and the Union or its members employed by the Company as to the meaning and application of the provisions of this Agreement, or should any local trouble of any kind arise, there shall be no suspension of work on account of such differences but an earnest effort shall be made to settle such differences immediately in the following manner:

A. For Maintenance Employees:

First, between the aggrieved employees, and the Foreman involved;

Second, between a member or members of the Grievance Committee designated by the Union, and the Foreman and Master Mechanic.

....

Fifth, if agreement has not been reached the matter shall be referred to an impartial umpire for decision. The parties shall meet to decide on an umpire acceptable to both. If no agreement on selection of an umpire is reached, the parties shall jointly petition the United States Conciliation Service for suggestion of a list of umpires from which selection will be made. The decision of the umpire shall be final.

Settlement of this grievance was not had and respondent refused arbitration. This suit was then commenced by the union to compel it.

The District Court granted respondent's motion to dismiss the complaint. 168 F. Supp. 702. It held after hearing evidence, much of which went to the merits of the grievance, that the agreement did not "confide in an arbitrator the right to review the defendant's business judgment in contracting out work." *Id.* at 705. It further held that "the contracting out of repair and maintenance work, as well as construction work, is strictly a function of management not limited in any respect by the labor agreement involved here." *Ibid.* The Court of Appeals affirmed by a divided vote, 269 F.2d 633, the majority holding that the collective agreement had withdrawn from the grievance procedure "matters which are strictly a function of management" and that contracting out fell in that exception....

We held in *Textile Workers v. Lincoln Mills,* 353 U.S. 448, that a grievance arbitration provision in a collective agreement could be enforced by reason of § 301(a) of the Labor Management Relations Act and that the policy to be applied in enforcing this type of arbitration was that reflected in our national labor laws. *Id.* at 456-457. The present federal policy is to promote industrial stabilization through the collective bargaining agreement. *Id.* at 453-454. A major factor in achieving industrial peace is the inclusion of a provision for arbitration of grievances in the collective bargaining agreement.[4]

Thus the run of arbitration cases, illustrated by *Wilko v. Swan,* 346 U.S. 427, becomes irrelevant to our problem. There the choice is between the adjudication of cases or controversies in courts with established procedures or even special statutory safeguards on the one hand and the settlement of them in the more informal arbitration tribunal on the other. In the commercial case, arbitration is the substitute for litigation. Here arbitration is the substitute for industrial strife. Since arbitration of labor disputes has quite different functions from arbitration under an ordinary commercial agreement, the hostility evinced by courts toward arbitration of commercial agreements has no place here. For arbitration of labor disputes under collective bargaining agreements is part and parcel of the collective bargaining process itself.

The collective bargaining agreement states the rights and duties of the parties. It is more than a contract; it is a generalized code to govern a myriad of cases which the draftsmen cannot wholly anticipate. *See* Shulman, *Reason, Contract, and Law in Labor Relations,* 68 Harv. L. Rev. 999, 1004-1005. The collective agreement covers the whole employment relationship. It calls into being a new common law—the common law of a particular industry or of a particular plant. As one observer has put it:[6]

> ... [I]t is not unqualifiedly true that a collective bargaining agreement is simply a document by which the union and employees have imposed upon management limited, express restrictions of its otherwise absolute right to manage the enterprise, so that an employee's claim must fail unless he can point to a specific contract provision upon which the claim is founded. There are too many people, too many problems, too many unforeseeable contingencies to make the words of the contract the exclusive source of rights and duties. One cannot reduce all the rules governing a community like an industrial plant to fifteen or even fifty pages. Within the sphere of collective bargaining, the institutional characteristics and the governmental nature of the collective bargaining process demand a common law of the shop which implements and furnishes the context of the agreement. We must assume that intelligent negotiators acknowledged so plain a need unless they stated a contrary rule in plain words.

---

[4] Complete effectuation of the federal policy is achieved when the agreement contains both an arbitration provision for all unresolved grievances and an absolute prohibition of strikes, the arbitration agreement being the *"quid pro quo"* for the agreement not to strike. *Textile Workers v. Lincoln Mills,* 353 U.S. 448, 455.

[6] Cox, *Reflections Upon Labor Arbitration,* 72 Harv. L. Rev. 1482, 1498-1499 (1959).

A collective bargaining agreement is an effort to erect a system of industrial self-government. When most parties enter into contractual relationship they do so voluntarily, in the sense that there is no real compulsion to deal with one another, as opposed to dealing with other parties. This is not true of the labor agreement. The choice is generally not between entering or refusing to enter into a relationship, for that in all probability preexists the negotiations. Rather it is between having that relationship governed by an agreed-upon rule of law or leaving each and every matter subject to a temporary resolution dependent solely upon the relative strength, at any given moment, of the contending forces. The mature labor agreement may attempt to regulate all aspects of the complicated relationship, from the most crucial to the most minute over an extended period of time. Because of the compulsion to reach agreement and the breadth of the matters covered, as well as the need for a fairly concise and readable instrument, the product of negotiations (the written document) is, in the words of the late Dean Shulman, "a compilation of diverse provisions: some provide objective criteria almost automatically applicable; some provide more or less specific standards which require reason and judgment in their application; and some do little more than leave problems to future consideration with an expression of hope and good faith." Shulman, *supra* at 1005. Gaps may be left to be filled in by reference to the practices of the particular industry and of the various shops covered by the agreement. Many of the specific practices which underlie the agreement may be unknown, except in hazy form, even to the negotiators. Courts and arbitration in the context of most commercial contracts are resorted to because there has been a breakdown in the working relationship of the parties; such resort is the unwanted exception. But the grievance machinery under a collective bargaining agreement is at the very heart of the system of industrial self-government. Arbitration is the means of solving the unforeseeable by molding a system of private law for all the problems which may arise and to provide for their solution in a way which will generally accord with the variant needs and desires of the parties. The processing of disputes through the grievance machinery is actually a vehicle by which meaning and content are given to the collective bargaining agreement.

Apart from matters that the parties specifically exclude, all of the questions on which the parties disagree must therefore come within the scope of the grievance and arbitration provisions of the collective agreement. The grievance procedure is, in other words, a part of the continuous collective bargaining process. It, rather than a strike, is the terminal point of a disagreement....

> A proper conception of the arbitrator's function is basic. He is not a public tribunal imposed upon the parties by superior authority which the parties are obliged to accept. He has no general charter to administer justice for a community which transcends the parties. He is rather part of a system of self-government created by and confined to the parties....

Shulman, *supra* at 1016.

The labor arbitrator's source of law is not confined to the express provisions of the contract, as the industrial common law—the practices of the industry and the shop—is equally a part of the collective bargaining agreement although not expressed in it. The labor arbitrator is usually chosen because of the parties' confidence in his knowledge of the common law of the shop and their trust in his personal judgment to bring to bear considerations which are not expressed in the contract as criteria for judgment. The parties expect that his judgment of a particular grievance will reflect not only what the contract says but, insofar as the collective bargaining agreement permits, such factors as the effect upon productivity of a particular result, its consequence to the morale of the shop, his judgment whether tensions will be heightened or diminished. For the parties' objective in using the arbitration process is primarily to further their common goal of uninterrupted production under the agreement, to make the agreement serve their specialized needs. The ablest judge cannot be expected to bring the same experience and competence to bear upon the determination of a grievance, because he cannot be similarly informed.

The Congress, however, has by § 301 of the Labor Management Relations Act, assigned the courts the duty of determining whether the reluctant party has breached his promise to arbitrate. For arbitration is a matter of contract and a party cannot be required to submit to arbitration any dispute which he has not agreed so to submit. Yet, to be consistent with congressional policy in favor of settlement of disputes by the parties through the machinery of arbitration, the judicial inquiry under § 301 must be strictly confined to the question whether the reluctant party did agree to arbitrate the grievance or did agree to give the arbitrator power to make the award he made. An order to arbitrate the particular grievance should not be denied unless it may be said with positive assurance that the arbitration clause is not susceptible of an interpretation that covers the asserted dispute. Doubts should be resolved in favor of coverage.[7]

We do not agree with the lower courts that contracting-out grievances were necessarily excepted from the grievance procedure of this agreement. To be sure, the agreement provides that "matters which are strictly a function of management shall not be subject to arbitration." But it goes on to say that if "differences" arise or if "any local trouble of any kind" arises, the grievance procedure shall be applicable.

Collective bargaining agreements regulate or restrict the exercise of management functions; they do not oust management from the performance of them.

---

[7] It is clear that under both the agreement in this case and that involved in *American Mfg. Co.,* *supra* at 564, the question of arbitrability is for the courts to decide. *Cf.* Cox, *Reflections Upon Labor Arbitration,* 72 Harv. L. Rev. 1482, 1508-1509 (1959). Where the assertion by the claimant is that the parties excluded from court determination not merely the decision of the merits of the grievance but also the question of its arbitrability, vesting power to make both decisions in the arbitrator, the claimant must bear the burden of a clear demonstration of that purpose.

Management hires and fires, pays and promotes, supervises and plans. All these are part of its function, and absent a collective bargaining agreement, it may be exercised freely except as limited by public law and by the willingness of employees to work under the particular, unilaterally imposed conditions. A collective bargaining agreement may treat only with certain specific practices, leaving the rest to management but subject to the possibility of work stoppages. When, however, an absolute no-strike clause is included in the agreement, then in a very real sense everything that management does is subject to the agreement, for either management is prohibited or limited in the action it takes, or if not, it is protected from interference by strikes. This comprehensive reach of the collective bargaining agreement does not mean, however, that the language, "strictly a function of management," has no meaning.

"Strictly a function of management" might be thought to refer to any practice of management in which, under particular circumstances prescribed by the agreement, it is permitted to indulge. But if courts, in order to determine arbitrability, were allowed to determine what is permitted and what is not, the arbitration clause would be swallowed up by the exception. Every grievance in a sense involves a claim that management has violated some provision of the agreement.

Accordingly, "strictly a function of management" must be interpreted as referring only to that over which the contract gives management complete control and unfettered discretion. Respondent claims that the contracting out of work falls within this category. Contracting out work is the basis of many grievances; and that type of claim is grist in the mills of the arbitrators. A specific collective bargaining agreement may exclude contracting out from the grievance procedure. Or a written collateral agreement may make clear that contracting out was not a matter for arbitration. In such a case a grievance based solely on contracting out would not be arbitrable. Here, however, there is no such provision. Nor is there any showing that the parties designed the phrase "strictly a function of management" to encompass any and all forms of contracting out. In the absence of any express provision excluding a particular grievance from arbitration, we think only the most forceful evidence of a purpose to exclude the claim from arbitration can prevail, particularly where, as here, the exclusion clause is vague and the arbitration clause quite broad. Since any attempt by a court to infer such a purpose necessarily comprehends the merits, the court should view with suspicion an attempt to persuade it to become entangled in the construction of the substantive provisions of a labor agreement, even through the back door of interpreting the arbitration clause, when the alternative is to utilize the services of an arbitrator.

The grievance alleged that the contracting out was a violation of the collective bargaining agreement. There was, therefore, a dispute "as to the meaning and application of the provisions of this Agreement" which the parties had agreed would be determined by arbitration.

The judiciary sits in these cases to bring into operation an arbitral process which substitutes a regime of peaceful settlement for the older regime of industrial conflict. Whether contracting out in the present case violated the agreement is the question. It is a question for the arbiter, not for the courts.

Reversed.

MR. JUSTICE FRANKFURTER concurs in the result.

MR. JUSTICE BLACK took no part in the consideration or decision of this case....

MR. JUSTICE BRENNAN, with whom MR. JUSTICE HARLAN joins, concurring....

The issue in the *Warrior* case is essentially no different from that in *American* [*infra*], that is, it is whether the company agreed to arbitrate a particular grievance. In contrast to *American,* however, the arbitration promise here excludes a particular area from arbitration—"matters which are strictly a function of management." Because the arbitration promise is different, the scope of the court's inquiry may be broader. Here, a court may be required to examine the substantive provisions of the contract to ascertain whether the parties have provided that contracting out shall be a "function of management." If a court may delve into the merits to the extent of inquiring whether the parties have expressly agreed whether or not contracting out was a "function of management," why was it error for the lower court here to evaluate the evidence of bargaining history for the same purpose? Neat logical distinctions do not provide the answer. The Court rightly concludes that appropriate regard for the national labor policy and the special factors relevant to the labor arbitral process, admonish that judicial inquiry into the merits of this grievance should be limited to the search for an explicit provision which brings the grievance under the cover of the exclusion clause since "the exclusion clause is vague and arbitration clause quite broad." The hazard of going further into the merits is amply demonstrated by what the courts below did. On the basis of inconclusive evidence, those courts found that Warrior was in no way limited by any implied covenants of good faith and fair dealing from contracting out as it pleased—which would necessarily mean that Warrior was free completely to destroy the collective bargaining agreement by contracting out all the work.

The very ambiguity of the *Warrior* exclusion clause suggests that the parties were generally more concerned with having an arbitrator render decisions as to the meaning of the contract than they were in restricting the arbitrator's jurisdiction. The case might of course be otherwise were the arbitration clause very narrow, or the exclusion clause quite specific, for the inference might then be permissible that the parties had manifested a greater interest in confining the arbitrator; the presumption of arbitrability would then not have the same force and the Court would be somewhat freer to examine into the merits.

The Court makes reference to an arbitration clause being the *quid pro quo* for a no-strike clause. I do not understand the Court to mean that the application of the principles announced today depends upon the presence of a no-strike clause in the agreement.

MR. JUSTICE FRANKFURTER joins these observations.

[The dissenting opinion of MR. JUSTICE WHITTAKER is omitted.]

United Steelworkers v. American Mfg. Co., 363 U.S. 564, 80 S. Ct. 1343, 4 L. Ed. 2d 1403 (1960). A collective bargaining agreement contained a "standard" arbitration clause covering "any disputes" between the parties "as to the meaning, interpretation and application of the provisions of this agreement." The union agreed not to strike unless the employer refused to abide by a decision of the arbitrator. The contract reserved to management the power to suspend or discipline any employee "for cause." It also provided that the employer would employ and promote employees on "the principle of seniority ... where ability and efficiency are equal." An employee left work due to an injury and later settled a workmen's compensation claim against the company on the basis he was permanently partially disabled. Thereafter the union filed a grievance charging that the employee was entitled to return to his job under the seniority provision. The employer refused to arbitrate and the union sued. The Supreme Court held that arbitration should have been ordered. Declared the Court: "The function of the court is very limited when the parties have agreed to submit all questions of contract interpretation to the arbitrator. It is confined to ascertaining whether the party seeking arbitration is making a claim which on its face is governed by the contract. Whether the moving party is right or wrong is a question of contract interpretation for the arbitrator.... The courts, therefore, have no business weighing the merits of the grievance.... The processing of even frivolous claims may have therapeutic values of which those who are not a part of the plant environment may be quite unaware."

NOTES

1. The two preceding cases, together with *Enterprise Wheel, infra,* are familiarly known as the *Steelworkers Trilogy.* They have evoked a voluminous literature. *See, e.g.,* Aaron, *Arbitration in the Federal Courts: Aftermath of the Trilogy,* 9 U.C.L.A. L. Rev. 360 (1962); Gregory, *Enforcement of Collective Agreements by Arbitration,* 48 Va. L. Rev. 883 (1962); Hays, *The Supreme Court and Labor Law—October Term, 1959,* 60 Colum. L. Rev. 901 (1960); Meltzer, *The Supreme Court, Arbitrability, and Collective Bargaining,* 28 U. Chi. L. Rev. 464 (1961); Smith & Jones, *The Supreme Court and Labor Dispute Arbitration: The Emerging Federal Law,* 63 Mich. L. Rev. 751 (1965); Smith & Jones, *The Impact of the Emerging Federal Law of Grievance Arbitration on Judges, Arbitrators, and Parties,* 52 Va. L. Rev. 831 (1966); Wellington, *Judicial Review of the*

Promise to Arbitrate, 37 N.Y.U. L. Rev. 471 (1962); *Symposium—Arbitration and the Courts,* 58 Nw. U.L. Rev. 466, 494, 521, 556 (1963); *Symposium on Labor Arbitration Thirty Years After the Steelworkers Trilogy,* 66 Chi.-Kent L. Rev. 549 (1990).

2. The lower federal courts appear to be of different minds about the extent to which bargaining history may constitute evidence of an intent to exclude certain claims from arbitration. *Compare IUE v. General Elec. Co.,* 332 F.2d 485 (2d Cir.), *cert. denied,* 379 U.S. 928 (1964) *with Communications Workers v. Pacific Nw. Bell Tel. Co.,* 337 F.2d 455 (9th Cir. 1964). *See also* Lesnick, *Arbitration as a Limit on the Discretion of Management, Union, and NLRB: The Year's Major Developments,* in N.Y.U. Eighteenth Annual Conference on Labor 7, 9-18 (1966).

3. May the parties to a collective bargaining agreement nullify the *Warrior* presumption of arbitrability? *See IUE v. General Elec. Co.,* 407 F.2d 253, 259 (2d Cir. 1968), *cert. denied,* 395 U.S. 904 (1969). *Cf. Teamsters Local 315 v. Union Oil Co.,* 856 F.2d 1307 (9th Cir. 1988), *cert. denied,* 488 U.S. 1043 (1989) (fitness to work as managerial prerogative not subject to arbitration).

4. Are the *Trilogy* rules on arbitrability binding on arbitrators as well as courts? If a court orders arbitration, may the arbitrator subsequently make her own independent determination of arbitrability? *See* Smith & Jones, *supra* note 1, 63 Mich. L. Rev. at 761, and 52 Va. L. Rev. at 871-73.

5. The presumption in favor of arbitrability is broad. *Broadcast Employees v. ABC,* 140 F.3d 459 (2d Cir. 1998), involved a dispute generated by a union's alleged plans to disrupt ABC's broadcasting of sporting events in Hawaii in response to ABC's refusal to recognize the union as the representative of employees in Hawaii. Although the applicable collective contract was limited to the continental U.S., the court found that the clause prohibiting interference with company operations was susceptible to an interpretation covering the asserted dispute. It thus found the controversy subject to arbitral resolution.

AT&T Technologies v. CWA, 475 U.S. 643, 106 S. Ct. 1415, 89 L. Ed. 2d 648 (1986). A contractual provision prescribed the order in which employees were to be laid off "[w]hen lack of work necessitates Layoff." The CWA sought arbitration over layoffs which it claimed were not caused by a "lack of work." AT&T refused to arbitrate, claiming that it had made its reduction-in-force determination pursuant to the authority it possessed under a broad management-rights provision which expressly excluded matters of managerial prerogative from arbitral consideration. The district court, after finding that the union's suggested contractual interpretation was at least "arguable," held that it was for the arbitrator—not the court—to decide whether that interpretation was in fact meritorious. It thus directed the parties to have the arbitrator decide the arbitrability dispute. The Seventh Circuit affirmed this approach. The Supreme Court, however, unanimously rejected this view of the judicial function in such cases. The Supreme Court reaffirmed the principles set forth in the *Steelworkers Trilogy,* and emphasized that district courts, and not arbitrators, are required to resolve substantive arbitrability questions.

> [T]he question of arbitrability—whether a collective-bargaining agreement creates a duty for the parties to arbitrate the particular grievance—is undeniably an issue for judicial determination. Unless the parties clearly and unmistakably provide otherwise, the question of whether the parties agreed to arbitrate is to be decided by the court, not the arbitrator.... It is the court's duty to interpret the agreement and to determine whether the parties intended to arbitrate grievances concerning layoffs predicated on a "lack of work" determination by the Company. If the court determines that the agreement so provides, then it is for the arbitrator to determine the relative merits of the parties' substantive interpretations of the agreement.

NOTES

1. Subsequent cases from the circuit courts reaffirm the principle that arbitrability is for the courts to decide, with "doubts [being] resolved in favor of coverage." *See Carpenters Local 46 v. Zcon Bldrs.*, 96 F.3d 410 (9th Cir. 1996) (district court should not have deferred to an arbitrator's decision that a property development firm, as the alter ego of a construction company, was bound by the arbitration provisions of the latter's collective bargaining agreement; arbitrability issue was for the court, not the arbitrator); *Aircraft Breaking Sys. v. UAW Local 856*, 97 F.3d 155 (6th Cir. 1996), *cert. denied*, 117 S. Ct. 1311 (1997) (arbitrator exceeded his authority in finding no interim collective bargaining agreement existed requiring arbitration after district court had refused to enjoin arbitration on the grounds there was an interim contract that called for arbitration). Even though specific issues are expressly excluded from arbitral coverage, courts will order arbitration when the challenged conduct may have contravened other contractual provisions subject to arbitral resolution so long as it is not unequivocally clear that the parties intended to exclude these disputes entirely from arbitral coverage. *IBEW Local 4 v. KTVI-TV*, 985 F.2d 415 (8th Cir. 1993); *Steelworkers v. ASARCO Inc.*, 970 F.2d 1448, *reh'g denied*, 977 F.2d 576 (5th Cir. 1992). *But cf. Teamsters Local 371 v. Logistics Support Group*, 999 F.2d 227 (7th Cir. 1993) (no arbitration of discharge in absence of "just cause" provision when contract limited arbitration to express provisions); *General Drivers Local 509 v. Ethyl Corp.*, 68 F.3d 80 (4th Cir. 1995) (no arbitration of union's grievance that job-promotion tests discriminated on the basis of race and age where collective bargaining agreement excluded from arbitration "matters affecting wages and rates of pay," because tests in effect determined pay rates).

Must a court rather than an arbitrator decide whether a grievance is arbitrable even when that requires a ruling on the merits of the underlying dispute? *See Independent Lift Truck Bldrs. Union v. Hyster Co.,* 2 F.3d 233 (7th Cir. 1993) ("Yes").

2. Issues on which courts have ordered arbitration include the subcontracting of bargaining unit work, *E.M. Diagnostic Sys. v. Teamsters Local 169,* 812 F.2d 91 (3d Cir. 1987); plant relocation, *Food & Commercial Workers Local 174 v. Hebrew Nat'l Kosher Foods, Inc.,* 818 F.2d 283 (2d Cir. 1987); the dismissal of an impartial arbitrator, *Pitta v. Hotel Ass'n of New York City,* 806 F.2d 419 (2d Cir. 1986); and an employee's violation of a "last chance" agreement (but not the penalty if a violation was found), *Steelworkers v. Lukens Steel Co.,* 969 F.2d 1468 (3d Cir. 1992).

3. The Labor Board held that a union violated the NLRA by demanding the arbitration of grievances seeking to merge three historically separate bargaining units. Such merger is a nonmandatory subject of bargaining, and so the arbitration demands had an illegal objective. The Board did not consider *Bill Johnson's Restaurants, Inc. v. NLRB, supra,* applicable. *Chicago Truck Drivers (Signal Delivery Serv.),* 279 N.L.R.B. 904 (1986).

4. A union may compel arbitration of an employee's discharge even though the employee has already filed a hybrid breach of contract/fair representation action under § 301 against both the union and the employer. *Niro v. Fearn Int'l, Inc.,* 827 F.2d 173 (7th Cir. 1987).

5. *See generally* Reinhardt, Meltzer & Raskin, *Arbitration and the Courts: Is the Honeymoon Over?* in Arbitration 1987—The Academy at Forty 25, 39, 55 (G. Gruenberg ed. 1987) (three separate papers); Note, *Arbitration after Communications Workers: A Diminished Role?* 100 Harv. L. Rev. 1307 (1987).

———

Nolde Bros. v. Bakery & Confectionery Workers Local 358, 430 U.S. 243, 97 S. Ct. 1067, 51 L. Ed. 2d 300 (1977). A union and an employer had a contract providing that "any grievance" between the parties was subject to binding arbitration. After negotiating for three months for a contract renewal, the union exercised its option to cancel the existing agreement by giving a seven-day termination notice. Negotiations continued for four days past the effective date of the termination. Then the company, faced by a threatened strike, informed the union that it was permanently closing its plant. The company paid the employees their accrued wages and vacation pay but rejected the union's demand for severance pay called for in the labor agreement. The employer also declined to arbitrate the severance pay claims on the ground its duty to arbitrate terminated with the contract. The union sued under § 301 to compel arbitration. The Supreme Court, per Chief Justice Burger, held that the issue was arbitrable. "The dispute ..., although arising *after* the expiration of the collective bargaining agreement, clearly arises *under* that contract.... [N]othing in the arbitration clause ... expressly excludes ... a dispute which arises under the contract, but which is based on events that occur after its termination.... By their contract the parties clearly expressed their preference for an arbitral, rather than a judicial interpretation of their obligations...." Justices Stewart and Rehnquist dissented, arguing: "The closing of the [plant] necessarily meant that there was no continuing relationship to protect or preserve.... And the Union's termination of the contract, thereby releasing it from its obligation not to strike, foreclosed any reason for implying a continuing duty on the part of the employer to arbitrate as a *quid pro quo....*"

NOTES

1. In *Litton Fin. Printing Div. v. NLRB,* 501 U.S. 190 (1991), an employer unilaterally modified its operations and laid off some of its most senior employees 10-11 months after the expiration of a contract calling for layoffs on the basis of seniority. The NLRB found an 8(a)(5) violation and directed bargaining but refused to order arbitration. A 5-4 Supreme Court majority agreed that under *Nolde* post-expiration arbitration is required only with respect to "disputes arising under the contract." That would involve facts occurring before the contract expired or "accrued or vested rights." The four dissenting Justices believed that the majority had improperly examined the merits of the contractual dispute in the guise of determining arbitrability.

In *Luden's Inc. v. Local 6*, 28 F.3d 347 (3d Cir. 1994), the court sought to harmonize the seemingly conflicting Supreme Court holdings in *Nolde Bros.* and *Litton Fin. Printing Div.* While *Nolde Bros.* seemed to create a judicial presumption in favor of arbitration with respect to disputes arising under lapsed contracts, *Litton Fin. Printing Div.* suggested that courts have a duty to review the merits of grievance claims to determine if the lapsed agreements actually created the rights being asserted. The Third Circuit decided that it preferred the *Nolde Bros.* approach, as it held that courts determining the arbitrability of grievances arising under lapsed contracts should not reach the merits of the underlying controversies. They should merely decide if the lapsed contracts "arguably" created the obligations the grievants seek to enforce. Since the *Luden's* court found an implied-in-fact collective contract that appeared to continue the grievance-arbitration procedures during the period between formal agreements, it directed arbitration of the grievance in question. *See also McQuestion v. N.J. Transit Rail Opers.*, 30 F.3d 388 (3d Cir. 1994) (while formal collective contract did not exist between parties at time of employee terminations, *de facto* agreement existed that was sufficient to extend National Railroad Adjustment Board jurisdiction over discharge grievances).

2. If an employer's obligation to arbitrate survives the expiration of the contract in certain circumstances, what about the union's obligation not to strike? A court of appeals has held that a no-strike clause did not bar a union's post-contract economic strike, but that the employer remained bound to arbitrate. *Steelworkers v. Fort Pitt Steel Casting Div.,* 635 F.2d 1071 (3d Cir. 1980), *cert. denied,* 451 U.S. 985 (1981). *But cf. Goya Foods, Inc.,* 238 N.L.R.B. 1465 (1978).

3. An economic striker's discharge for picket line misconduct was held arbitrable under a contract that went into effect after the strike ended. The arbitrator would have to decide whether the striker was an employee on the effective date of the contract and thus subject to its just cause provision. *Oil, Chem. & Atomic Workers Local 4-23 v. American Petrofina Co.,* 820 F.2d 747 (5th Cir. 1987).

4. *See generally* Goetz, *Arbitration After Termination of a Collective Bargaining Agreement,* 63 Va. L. Rev. 693 (1977). The principal case and its progeny are noted in 54 U. Colo. L. Rev. 103 (1982); 40 Ohio St. L.J. 187 (1979).

United Steelworkers v. Enterprise Wheel & Car Corp., 363 U.S. 593, 80 S. Ct. 1358, 4 L. Ed. 2d 1424 (1960). A collective bargaining agreement provided for "final and binding" arbitration of any differences about the "meaning and application" of the contract. If a discharge violated the agreement, the company was to "reinstate the employee and pay full compensation." Several workers were dismissed for leaving their jobs to protest the discharge of another employee. An arbitrator found that only a 10-day suspension was warranted. Even though the collective agreement had expired in the meantime, the arbitrator awarded reinstatement and full backpay, with a deduction of 10 days' pay and any sums received from other employment. A court of appeals refused to enforce the reinstatement or the award of backpay beyond the date of the contract's termination. The Supreme Court reversed this ruling, declaring: "The refusal of courts to review the merits of an arbitration award is the proper approach to arbitration under collective bargaining agreements." Speaking through Justice Douglas, the Court went on to say:

> When an arbitrator is commissioned to interpret and apply the collective bargaining agreement, he is to bring his informed judgment to bear in order to reach a fair solution of a problem. This is especially true when it comes to formulating remedies.... Nevertheless, an arbitrator is confined to interpretation and application of the collective bargaining agreement; he does not sit to dispense his own brand of industrial justice. He may of course look for guidance from many sources, yet his award is legitimate only so long as it draws its essence from the collective bargaining agreement. When the arbitrator's words manifest an infidelity to this obligation, courts have no choice but to refuse enforcement of the award.
>
> The opinion of the arbitrator in this case, as it bears upon the award of back pay beyond the date of the agreement's expiration and reinstatement, is ambiguous. It may be read as based solely upon the arbitrator's view of the

requirements of enacted legislation, which would mean that he exceeded the scope of the submission. Or it may be read as embodying a construction of the agreement itself, perhaps with the arbitrator looking to "the law" for help in determining the sense of the agreement. A mere ambiguity in the opinion accompanying an award, which permits the inference that the arbitrator may have exceeded his authority, is not a reason for refusing to enforce the award. Arbitrators have no obligation to the court to give their reasons for an award....

Respondent's major argument seems to be that by applying correct principles of law to the interpretation of the collective bargaining agreement it can be determined that the agreement did not ... provide [for reinstatement and full back pay], and that therefore the arbitrator's decision was not based upon the contract.... This plenary review by a court of the merits would make meaningless the provisions that the arbitrator's decision is final, for in reality it would almost never be final.... It is the arbitrator's construction which was bargained for; and so far as the arbitrator's decision concerns construction of the contract, the courts have no business overruling him because their interpretation of the contract is different from his.

NOTES

1. The first two cases of the *Steelworkers Trilogy* dealt with judicial enforcement of executory agreements to arbitrate; *Enterprise Wheel* dealt with judicial enforcement of an arbitral award. Should a court apply different standards in examining the arbitrator's "jurisdiction" in these two situations? Is there, in any event, a difference between the arbitrator's "jurisdiction" to hear a dispute and his "authority" to render a particular award? The Second Circuit has held that an arbitrator exceeded the scope of the submission when he "added" an implied term to the labor contract on the basis of a past practice which the court found had later been revoked by the employer. *Torrington Co. v. Metal Prod. Workers, Local 1645,* 362 F.2d 677 (2d Cir. 1966). *Torrington* was criticized in Aaron, *Judicial Intervention in Labor Arbitration,* 20 Stan. L. Rev. 41 (1967); Jones, *The Name of the Game is Decision—Some Reflections on "Arbitrability" and "Authority" in Labor Arbitration,* 46 Texas L. Rev. 865 (1968); Meltzer, *Ruminations About Ideology, Law, and Labor Arbitration,* 34 U. Chi. L. Rev. 545 (1967).

In *National Gypsum Co. v. Oil, Chemical & Atomic Workers Int'l Union,* 147 F.3d 399 (5th Cir. 1998), the union grieved the company's unilateral announcement of a change in the workweek which resulted in a loss of overtime pay for employees. The arbitrator ruled in favor of the union, reasoning that the change in workweek was actually a wage change, and since the contract required negotiations over wage changes, the employer had violated the contract by instituting the program unilaterally. The court enforced the award, reasoning that the company's submission to arbitration in spite of the fact that the parties were unable to stipulate to the issue to be resolved by the arbitrator, constituted implied consent to the arbitrator's jurisdiction, allowing the arbitrator to frame the issue under consideration. Since the arbitrator's interpretation of the contract was rational and consistent with the employer's obligations under the NLRA, it was a valid exercise of arbitral authority. *Cf. Pacesetter Construction Co. v. Carpenters 46, Northern California Counties Conference Board,* 116 F.3d 436 (9th Cir.), *cert. denied,* 118 S. Ct. 599 (1997) (refusing to apply to collective bargaining context the rule stated in *First Options of Chicago v. Kaplan,* 514 U.S. 938 (1995) that courts should not assume that parties to a commercial arbitration agreement agreed to arbitrate the issue of arbitrability merely by arguing that issue to the arbitration panel).

On the authority (or lack thereof) of an arbitrator to make a *de novo* determination of an employee's qualifications under a contract giving the employer the right to "determine ability, skill, and qualifications, subject to an employee's right to assert a grievance," *see Houston Lighting & Power Co. v. IBEW Local 66,* 71 F.3d 179 (5th Cir. 1995), *cert. denied,* 117 S. Ct. 52 (1996).

2. A court will not enforce an arbitral award that directly violates enacted law. How should an arbitrator handle a conflict between "the law" and the parties' contract? For contrasting views, *see* Edwards, *Labor Arbitration at the Crossroads: The "Common Law of the Shop" v. External Law,* 32 Arb. J. 65 (1977); Howlett, *The Arbitrator, the NLRB, and the Courts,* in National Academy of Arbitrators, the Arbitrator, the NLRB, and the Courts, Proceedings of the Twentieth Annual Meeting 67 (1967); Meltzer, *supra note 1 [id.* at 1]; Mittenthal, *The Role of Law in Arbitration,* in National Academy of Arbitrators, Developments in American and Foreign Arbitration, Proceedings of the Twenty-First Annual Meeting 42 (1968); Ratner, *Observations on Some Current Issues in Labor Arbitration,* 32 Lab. L.J. 114 (1981).

3. Arbitral awards that draw their essence from the underlying collective contracts continue to be accorded judicial respect. *See American National Can Co. v. United Steelworkers Local No. 3628,* 120 F.3d 886 (8th Cir. 1997) (upholding arbitrator's award in favor of a union that had challenged the employer's decision to contract out work to nonunion employees, despite the fact that the arbitrator refused to follow two prior arbitral awards involving the same parties and the same contract clause); *UTU Local 1589 v. Suburban Transit Corp.,* 51 F.3d 376 (3d Cir. 1995) (sustaining arbitral application of progressive discipline principles under contract clause that simply authorized discharge of employees for "proper cause"); *Champion Boxed Beef Co. v. UFCW Local 7,* 24 F.3d 86 (10th Cir. 1994) (upholding right of arbitrator to reinstate discharged employee due to different treatment of other workers who had previously engaged in similar conduct).

On the other hand, awards that do not appear to draw their essence from contractual provisions or that exceed the remedial powers afforded the arbitrator under the contract are likely to be denied enforcement. *See Interstate Brands Corp. v. Local 441*, 39 F.3d 1159 (11th Cir. 1994), *cert. denied*, 516 U.S. 807 (1995) (arbitrator relied on misinterpretation of external Department of Transportation drug testing regulations when reinstating truck driver who had tested positive for drugs); *Island Creek Coal Co. v. UMW Dist. 28*, 29 F.3d 126 (4th Cir.), *cert. denied*, 513 U.S. 1019 (1994) (voiding unauthorized arbitral award of punitive damages); *Mountaineer Gas Co. v. Oil Workers Local 3-372*, 76 F.3d 606 (4th Cir.), *cert. denied*, 117 S. Ct. 80 (1996) (arbitrator could not reinstate a fifteen-year employee who failed a random drug test when there was a mandatory-termination provision, despite arbitrator's belief in leniency). *But cf. Madison Hotel v. Hotel & Restaurant Employees Local 25*, 128 F.3d 743 (D.C. Cir. 1997) (arbitrator exceeded his authority by issuing a remedy which went beyond the interests of the grievants before him and sought to protect the long-term interests of the entire bargaining unit by requiring the employer to re-create positions it had eliminated in breach of the collective agreement and fill the slots with new hires since none of the aggrieved employees were interested in reinstatement), *reversed on reh'g en banc*, 144 F.3d 855 (D.C. Cir. 1998).

4. The Seventh Circuit held that an arbitrator did not exceed his authority in imposing a severance pay plan on an employer that had breached its labor contract by failing to give the union a six-month notice of the sale of its plant and by failing to negotiate concerning severance pay. *Industrial Workers Local 879 v. Chrysler Marine Corp.*, 819 F.2d 786 (7th Cir. 1987). *See also Synergy Gas v. Sasso*, 853 F.2d 59 (2d Cir.), *cert. denied*, 488 U.S. 994 (1988) (arbitrator could order attorney fees, union dues, and pension fund contributions, in addition to back pay). Would an arbitrator be authorized to "remand" a case to the parties for further negotiations? *Compare AP Parts Co. v. Auto Workers*, 923 F.2d 488 (6th Cir. 1991) *with Phoenix Newspapers v. Teamsters Local 752*, 989 F.2d 1077 (9th Cir. 1993). *See generally* Feller, *The Remedy Power in Grievance Arbitration*, 5 Indus. Rel. L.J. 128 (1982); Fleming, *Arbitrators and the Remedy Power*, 48 Va. L. Rev. 1199 (1962); M. Hill & A. Sinicropi, Remedies in Arbitration (2d ed. 1991).

5. Arbitration by an impartial third party is not essential to judicial enforceability under § 301. An award by a joint labor-management committee may be enforced if it is final and binding under the collective bargaining agreement, even though the procedure employed is not styled "arbitration." *Teamsters Local 89 v. Riss & Co.*, 372 U.S. 517 (1963). But a conspiracy between an employer and an international union to select an arbitrator who was likely to uphold the discharge of an unwanted employee so tainted the proceedings that the award had to be set aside, even though there was no showing that the arbitrator was actually biased or that the local union improperly represented the employee at the arbitration hearing. *Allen v. Allied Plant Maint. Co.*, 881 F.2d 291 (6th Cir. 1989).

6. *See also* Feller, *The Coming End of Arbitration's Golden Age*, in National Academy of Arbitrators, Arbitration—1976, Proceedings of the Twenty-Ninth

Annual Meeting 97 (1976); Kaden, *Judges and Arbitrators: Observations on the Scope of Judicial Review,* 80 Colum. L. Rev. 267 (1980); St. Antoine, *Judicial Review of Labor Arbitration Awards: A Second Look at Enterprise Wheel and Its Progeny,* 75 Mich. L. Rev. 1137 (1977); Wellington, *Judicial Review of the Promise to Arbitrate,* 37 N.Y.U. L. Rev. 471 (1962).

PAPERWORKERS v. MISCO, INC.

Supreme Court of the United States
484 U.S. 29, 108 S. Ct. 364, 98 L. Ed. 2d 286 (1987)

JUSTICE WHITE delivered the opinion of the Court....

I

Misco, Inc., (Misco, or the Company) operates a paper converting plant in Monroe, Louisiana. The Company is a party to a collective-bargaining agreement with the United Paperworkers International Union, AFL-CIO, and its union local (the Union); the agreement covers the production and maintenance employees at the plant. Under the agreement, the Company or the Union may submit to arbitration any grievance that arises from the interpretation or application of its terms, and the arbitrator's decision is final and binding upon the parties. The arbitrator's authority is limited to interpretation and application of the terms contained in the agreement itself. The agreement reserves to management the right to establish, amend, and enforce "rules and regulations regulating the discipline or discharge of employees" and the procedures for imposing discipline. Such rules were to be posted and were to be in effect "until ruled on by grievance and arbitration procedures as to fairness and necessity." For about a decade, the Company's rules had listed as causes for discharge the bringing of intoxicants, narcotics, or controlled substances on to plant property or consuming any of them there, as well as reporting for work under the influence of such substances. At the time of the events involved in this case, the Company was very concerned about the use of drugs at the plant, especially among employees on the night shift.

Isiah Cooper, who worked on the night shift for Misco, was one of the employees covered by the collective-bargaining agreement. He operated a slitter-rewinder machine, which uses sharp blades to cut rolling coils of paper. The arbitrator found that this machine is hazardous and had caused numerous injuries in recent years. Cooper had been reprimanded twice in a few months for deficient performance. On January 21, 1983, one day after the second reprimand, the police searched Cooper's house pursuant to a warrant, and a substantial amount of marijuana was found. Contemporaneously, a police officer was detailed to keep Cooper's car under observation at the Company's parking lot. At about 6:30 p.m., Cooper was seen walking in the parking lot during work hours with two other men. The three men entered Cooper's car momentarily, then walked to another car, a white Cutlass, and entered it. After the other two men later returned to the plant, Cooper was apprehended by police in the backseat of this car with marijuana smoke in the air and a lighted marijuana cigarette in the front-seat ashtray. The police also searched Cooper's car and found a plastic scales case and marijuana gleanings. Cooper was arrested and charged with marijuana possession.

On January 24, Cooper told the Company that he had been arrested for possession of marijuana at his home; the Company did not learn of the marijuana cigarette in the white Cutlass until January 27. It then investigated and on February 7 discharged Cooper, asserting that in the circumstances, his presence in the Cutlass violated the rule against having drugs on the plant premises. Cooper filed a grievance protesting his discharge the same day, and the matter proceeded to arbitration. The Company was not aware until September 21, five days before the hearing before the arbitrator was scheduled, that marijuana had been found in Cooper's car. That fact did not become known to the Union until the hearing began. At the hearing it was stipulated that the issue was whether the Company had "just cause to discharge the Grievant under Rule II.1" and, "[i]f not, what if any should be the remedy." ...

The arbitrator upheld the grievance and ordered the Company to reinstate Cooper with backpay and full seniority. The arbitrator based his finding that there was not just cause for the discharge on his consideration of seven criteria. In particular, the arbitrator found that the Company failed to prove that the employee had possessed or used marijuana on company property: finding Cooper in the backseat of a car and a burning cigarette in the front-seat ashtray was insufficient proof that Cooper was using or possessed marijuana on company property.... The arbitrator refused to accept into evidence the fact that marijuana had been found in Cooper's car on company premises because the Company did not know of this fact when Cooper was discharged and therefore did not rely on it as a basis for the discharge.

The Company filed suit in District Court, seeking to vacate the arbitration award on several grounds, one of which was that ordering reinstatement of Cooper, who had allegedly possessed marijuana on the plant premises, was contrary to public policy. The District Court agreed that the award must be set aside as contrary to public policy because it ran counter to general safety concerns that arise from the operation of dangerous machinery while under the influence of drugs, as well as to state criminal laws against drug possession. The Court of Appeals affirmed, with one judge dissenting....

Because the Courts of Appeals are divided on the question of when courts may set aside arbitration awards as contravening public policy, we granted the Union's petition for a writ of certiorari, ... and now reverse the judgment of the Court of Appeals.

II

The Union asserts that an arbitral award may not be set aside on public policy grounds unless the award orders conduct that violates the positive law, which is not the case here. But in the alternative, it submits that even if it is wrong in this regard, the Court of Appeals otherwise exceeded the limited authority that it had to review an arbitrator's award entered pursuant to a collective-bargaining agreement. Respondent, on the other hand, defends the public policy decision of the Court of Appeals but alternatively argues that the judgment below should be affirmed because of erroneous findings by the arbitrator. We deal first with the opposing alternative arguments.

A. Collective-bargaining agreements commonly provide grievance procedures to settle disputes between union and employer with respect to the interpretation and application of the agreement and require binding arbitration for unsettled grievances. In such cases, and this is such a case, the Court made clear almost 30 years ago that the courts play only a limited role when asked to review the decision of an arbitrator. The courts are not authorized to reconsider the merits of an award even though the parties may allege that the award rests on errors of fact or on misinterpretation of the contract....

The reasons for insulating arbitral decisions from judicial review are grounded in the federal statutes regulating labor-management relations. These statutes reflect a decided preference for private settlement of labor disputes without the intervention of government.... Because the parties have contracted to have disputes settled by an arbitrator chosen by them rather than by a judge, it is the arbitrator's view of the facts and of the meaning of the contract that they have agreed to accept. Courts thus do not sit to hear claims of factual or legal error by an arbitrator as an appellate court does in reviewing decisions of lower courts. To resolve disputes about the application of a collective-bargaining agreement, an arbitrator must find facts and a court may not reject those findings simply because it disagrees with them. The same is true of the arbitrator's interpretation of the contract. The arbitrator may not ignore the plain language of the contract; but the parties having authorized the arbitrator to give meaning to the language of the agreement, a court should not reject an award on the ground that the arbitrator misread the contract.... So, too, where it is contemplated that the arbitrator will determine remedies for contract violations that he finds, courts have no authority to disagree with his honest judgment in that respect. If the courts were free to intervene on these grounds, the speedy resolution of grievances by private mechanisms would be greatly undermined. Furthermore, it must be remembered that grievance and arbitration procedures are part and parcel of the ongoing process of collective bargaining. It is through these processes that the supplementary rules of the plant are established.... Of course, decisions procured by the parties through fraud or through the arbitrator's dishonesty need not be enforced. But there is nothing of that sort involved in this case.

B. The Company's position, simply put, is that the arbitrator committed grievous error in finding that the evidence was insufficient to prove that Cooper had possessed or used marijuana on company property. But the Court of Appeals, although it took a distinctly jaundiced view of the arbitrator's decision in this regard, was not free to refuse enforcement because it considered Cooper's presence in the white Cutlass, in the circumstances, to be ample proof that Rule II.1 was violated. No dishonesty is alleged; only improvident, even silly, factfinding is claimed. This is hardly sufficient basis for disregarding what the agent appointed by the parties determined to be the historical facts.

Nor was it open to the Court of Appeals to refuse to enforce the award because the arbitrator, in deciding whether there was just cause to discharge, refused to consider evidence unknown to the Company at the time Cooper was fired. The parties bargained for arbitration to settle disputes and were free to set the procedural rules for arbitrators to follow if they chose. Section VI of the agreement, entitled "Arbitration Procedure," did set some ground rules for the arbitration process. It forbade the arbitrator to consider hearsay evidence, for example, but evidentiary matters were otherwise left to the arbitrator.... Here the arbitrator ruled that in determining whether Cooper had violated Rule II.1, he should not consider evidence not relied on by the employer in ordering the discharge, particularly in a case like this where there was no notice to the employee or the Union prior to the hearing that the Company would attempt to rely on after-discovered evidence. This, in effect, was a construction of what the contract required when deciding discharge cases: an arbitrator was to look only at the evidence before the employer at the time of discharge. As the arbitrator noted, this approach was consistent with the practice followed by other arbitrators. And it was consistent with our observation in *John Wiley & Sons, Inc. v. Livingston,* 376 U.S. 543, 557 (1964), that when the subject matter of a dispute is arbitrable, "procedural" questions which grow out of the dispute and bear on its final disposition are to be left to the arbitrator.

Under the Arbitration Act, the federal courts are empowered to set aside arbitration awards on such grounds only when "the arbitrators were guilty of misconduct ... in refusing to hear evidence pertinent and material to the controversy." 9 U.S.C. § 10(c). See *Commonwealth Coatings Corp. v. Continental Casualty Co.,* 393 U.S. 145 (1968). If we apply that same standard here and assume that the arbitrator erred in refusing to consider the disputed evidence, his error was not in bad faith or so gross as to amount to affirmative misconduct. Finally, it is worth noting that putting aside the evidence about the marijuana found in Cooper's car during this arbitration did not forever foreclose the Company from using that evidence as the basis for a discharge.

Even if it were open to the Court of Appeals to have found a violation of Rule II.1 because of the marijuana found in Cooper's car, the question remains whether the court could properly set aside the award because in its view discharge was the correct remedy. Normally, an arbitrator is authorized to disagree with the sanction imposed for employee misconduct.... The parties, of course, may limit the discretion of the arbitrator in this respect; and it may be, as the Company argues, that under the contract involved here, it was within the unreviewable discretion of management to discharge an employee once a violation of Rule II.1 was found. But the parties stipulated that the issue before the arbitrator was whether there was "just" cause for the discharge, and the arbitrator, in the course of his opinion, cryptically observed that Rule II.1 merely listed causes for discharge and did not expressly provide for immediate discharge. Before disposing of the case on the ground that Rule II.1 had been violated and discharge was therefore proper, the proper course would have been remand to the arbitrator for a definitive construction of the contract in this respect.

C. The Court of Appeals did not purport to take this course in any event. Rather, it held that the evidence of marijuana in Cooper's car required that the award be set aside because to reinstate a person who had brought drugs onto the property was contrary to the public policy "against the operation of dangerous machinery by persons under the influence of drugs or alcohol." 768 F.2d, at 743. We cannot affirm that judgment.

A court's refusal to enforce an arbitrator's award under a collective-bargaining agreement because it is contrary to public policy is a specific application of the more general doctrine, rooted in the common law, that a court may refuse to enforce contracts that violate law or public policy. *W. R. Grace & Co. v. Rubber Workers,* 461 U.S. 757, 766 (1983); *Hurd v. Hodge,* 334 U.S. 24, 34-35 (1948). That doctrine derives from the basic notion that no court will lend its aid to one who founds a cause of action upon an immoral or illegal act, and is further justified by the observation that the public's interests in confining the scope of private agreements to which it is not a party will go unrepresented unless the judiciary takes account of those interests when it considers whether to enforce such agreements. In the common law of contracts, this doctrine has served as the foundation for occasional exercises of judicial power to abrogate private agreements.

In *W. R. Grace,* we recognized that "a court may not enforce a collective-bargaining agreement that is contrary to public policy," and stated that "the question of public policy is ultimately one for resolution by the courts." 461 U.S., at 766. We cautioned, however, that a court's refusal to enforce an arbitrator's *interpretation* of such contracts is limited to situations where the contract as interpreted would violate "some explicit public policy" that is "well defined and dominant, and is to be ascertained 'by reference to the laws and legal precedents and not from general considerations of supposed public interests.'" *Ibid.* (quoting *Muschany v. United States,* 324 U.S. 49, 66 (1945)).... Two points follow from our decision in *W. R. Grace.* First, a court may refuse to enforce a collective-bargaining agreement when the specific terms contained in that agreement violate public policy. Second, it is apparent that our decision in that case does not otherwise sanction a broad judicial power to set aside arbitration awards as against public policy....

The Court of Appeals made no attempt to review existing laws and legal precedents in order to demonstrate that they establish a "well defined and dominant" policy against the operation of dangerous machinery while under the influence of drugs. Although certainly such a judgment is firmly rooted in common sense, we explicitly held in *W. R. Grace* that a formulation of public policy based only on "general considerations of supposed public interests" is not the sort that permits a court to set aside an arbitration award that was entered in accordance with a valid collective-bargaining agreement.

Even if the Court of Appeals' formulation of public policy is to be accepted, no violation of that policy was clearly shown in this case. In pursuing its public policy inquiry, the Court of Appeals quite properly considered the established fact that traces of marijuana had been found in Cooper's car. Yet the assumed connection between the marijuana gleanings found in Cooper's car and Cooper's actual use of drugs in the workplace is tenuous at best and provides an insufficient basis for holding that his reinstatement would actually violate the public policy identified by the Court of Appeals "against the operation of dangerous machinery by persons under the influence of drugs or alcohol." 768 F.2d, at 743. A refusal to enforce an award must rest on more than speculation or assumption.

In any event, it was inappropriate for the Court of Appeals itself to draw the necessary inference. To conclude from the fact that marijuana had been found in Cooper's car that Cooper had ever been or would be under the influence of marijuana while he was on the job and operating dangerous machinery is an exercise in factfinding about Cooper's use of drugs and his amenability to discipline, a task that exceeds the authority of a court asked to overturn an arbitration award. The parties did not bargain for the facts to be found by a court, but by an arbitrator chosen by them who had more opportunity to observe Cooper and to be familiar with the plant and its problems. Nor does the fact that it is inquiring into a possible violation of public policy excuse a court for doing the arbitrator's task. If additional facts were to be found, the arbitrator should find them in the course of any further effort the Company might have made to discharge Cooper for having had marijuana in his car on company premises. Had the arbitrator found that Cooper had possessed drugs on the property, yet imposed discipline short of discharge because he found as a factual matter that Cooper could be trusted not to use them on the job, the Court of Appeals could not upset the award because of its own view that public policy about plant safety was threatened.[11] In this connection it should also be noted that the award ordered Cooper to be reinstated in his old job or in an equivalent one for which he was qualified. It is by no means

---

[11]The issue of safety in the workplace is a commonplace issue for arbitrators to consider in discharge cases, and it was a matter for the arbitrator in the first instance to decide whether Cooper's alleged use of drugs on the job would actually pose a danger. That is not a problem here, for the arbitrator recognized that being under the influence of marijuana while operating slitter-rewinder machinery was indeed dangerous, and no one disputed this point.

clear from the record that Cooper would pose a serious threat to the asserted public policy in every job for which he was qualified.[12]

The judgment of the Court of Appeals is reversed.

So ordered.

JUSTICE BLACKMUN, with whom JUSTICE BRENNAN joins, concurring.

I join the Court's opinion, but write separately to underscore the narrow grounds on which its decision rests and to emphasize what it is *not* holding today. In particular, the Court does not reach the issue upon which certiorari was granted: whether a court may refuse to enforce an arbitration award rendered under a collective-bargaining agreement on public policy grounds only when the award itself violates positive law or requires unlawful conduct by the employer. The opinion takes no position on this issue. [*See* footnote 12.] Nor do I understand the Court to decide, more generally, in what way, if any, a court's authority to set aside an arbitration award on public policy grounds differs from its authority, outside the collective-bargaining context, to refuse to enforce a contract on public policy grounds. Those issues are left for another day....

NOTES

1. On remand for reconsideration in light of *Misco,* the First Circuit in *S.D. Warren Co. v. Paperworkers Local 1069,* 845 F.2d 3 (1988), reaffirmed its holding that an arbitrator exceeded her authority in setting aside three employees' discharges for violating a rule against drugs on company property. The court pointed out that the contract gave the employer the "sole right" to discharge for "proper cause" and stated that violations of the rule against drugs were "considered causes for discharge." *Misco* was also distinguished in *Iowa Elec. Light & Power Co. v. IBEW Local 204,* 834 F.2d 1424 (8th Cir. 1987) (public policy embodied in federally mandated safety regulations at a nuclear power plant required vacation of an arbitration award reinstating employee discharged for opening a safety door so he could take a shortcut to lunch); *Delta Airlines, Inc. v. Air Line Pilots Ass'n,* 861 F.2d 665 (11th Cir. 1988), *cert. denied,* 493 U.S. 871 (1989) (arbitral award reinstating alcoholic pilot who flew commercial flight while intoxicated contravened state and federal policies prohibiting operation of aircraft while drunk). On the other hand, subsequent to *Misco,* the Third Circuit held public policy did not bar an arbitral reinstatement of a postal employee who had fired two bullets through his supervisor's car windshield. *Postal Serv. v. Letter Carriers,* 839 F.2d 146 (1988). *See also Northwest Airlines v. ALPA,* 808 F.2d 76 (D.C. Cir. 1987), *cert. denied,* 486 U.S. 1014 (1988) (sustaining reinstatement of alcoholic pilot); *Postal Serv. v. Letter Carriers,* 810 F.2d 1239 (D.C. Cir. 1987),

---

[12]We need not address the Union's position that a court may refuse to enforce an award on public policy grounds only when the award itself violates a statute, regulation, or other manifestation of positive law, or compels conduct by the employer that would violate such a law.

cert. dismissed, 485 U.S. 680 (1988) (sustaining reinstatement of letter carrier who had failed to deliver thousands of pieces of mail); *Florida Power Corp. v. IBEW,* 847 F.2d 680 (11th Cir. 1988) (sustaining reinstatement of employee arrested for cocaine possession and drunk driving).

2. In the decade-plus since *Misco,* courts have continued to struggle with the impact of "public policy" and the terms of particular contracts on the enforcement of arbitration awards. On the question of the enforceability of awards which potentially contravene the public policy against illegal drug and alcohol use, or the policies favoring workplace/public safety (which are often linked), *see Stead Motors v. Machinists Lodge 1173,* 886 F.2d 1200 (9th Cir. 1989) (en banc), *cert. denied,* 495 U.S. 946 (1990) (state's general interest in motor vehicle safety not sufficient to nullify award reinstating mechanic who recklessly failed to tighten lug bolts on car's wheels); *Monroe Auto Equip. Co. v. UAW,* 981 F.2d 261 (6th Cir. 1992), *cert. denied,* 508 U.S. 931 (1993) (award reinstating employee who had violated company drug policy not contrary to public policy); *UFCW Local 588 v. Foster Poultry Farms,* 74 F.3d 169 (9th Cir. 1995) (arbitrator's reinstatement of two employees who had been discharged under an employer's random drug-testing program adopted pursuant to Transportation Department regulations did not violate the public policy against drug users driving commercial vehicles, since the arbitrator had not ordered the employer to let the employees drive, and had rescinded the drug testing program pending bargaining with the union over its nonmandatory and discretionary aspects); *IBEW Local 97 v. Niagra Mohawk Power,* 143 F.3d 704 (2d Cir. 1998) (conditional reinstatement of nuclear power plant technician who was terminated for supplying adulterated urine sample for drug test and for testing positive for cocaine did not contravene public policy, since NRC regulations do not prohibit conditional reinstatement of such an individual); *St. Mary Home v. SEIU Dist. 1199,* 116 F.3d 41 (2d Cir. 1997) (arbitrator could reinstate, without back pay, employee of nursing home who had been fired for possessing marijuana with intent to distribute); *Pepsi-Cola Albany Bottling Co. v. International Bhd. of Teamsters Local 669,* 158 L.R.R.M. 2522 (N.D.N.Y. 1998) (reinstatement of truck driver who tested positive for marijuana did not violate public policy or DOT regulations on drug use where the reinstatement is conditioned on driver's successful completion of an employee assistance program and passing all future drug tests). *Cf. Exxon Shipping Co. v. Exxon Seamen's Union,* 993 F.2d 357 (3d Cir. 1993) (award reinstating ship helmsman who tested positive for marijuana contrary to "well defined and dominant" public policy against operation of vessel under influence of drugs, despite absence of proof that worker had used drugs while on duty); *Exxon Corp. v. Esso Workers' Union Inc.,* 118 F.3d 841 (1st Cir. 1997) (overturning arbitrator's award reinstating truck driver in a safety-sensitive position who was discharged after he tested positive for cocaine during a random drug test). *See also Teamsters Local 878 v. Commercial Warehouse Co.,* 84 F.3d 299 (8th Cir. 1996) (arbitrator did not violate public policy against drug use when he awarded three months' back

pay despite sustaining the discharge of an employee who tested positive for cocaine after a workplace accident, where back pay was awarded because of the
employer's "procedural irregularities" during the grievance process); *but cf.
Exxon Corp. v. Baton Rouge OCWU*, 77 F.3d 850 (5th Cir. 1996) (public policy
barred award of back pay to employee discharged for using cocaine, even though
employee was not reinstated and discharge clearly violated labor contract).

For decisions involving awards which potentially conflict with the public policies implicated in the health care setting, *see Highlands Hosp. v. AFSCME Dist.
84*, 151 L.R.R.M. 2629 (W.D. Pa. 1996) (public policy barred arbitration award
reinstating without back pay a health care assistant who pushed elderly Alz-
heimer patient); *DeWitt County v. AFSCME Council 31*, 1998 Ill. App. LEXIS
551 (Ill. App. Ct. 1998) (overturning arbitration award ordering reinstatement of
a nursing aide who struck a resident for taking someone else's glass of milk; the
policy favoring arbitration and freedom of contract must yield to the public policy of protecting the elderly). *Cf. Shelby County Health Care Corp. v. AFSCME
Local 1733*, 967 F.2d 1091 (6th Cir. 1992) (award reinstating workers who engaged in health care facility strike that was not preceded by ten day statutory notice required by § 8(g) not contrary to public policy).

On the problem of arbitral awards which potentially conflict with the policy
against sexual harassment in the workplace, *compare Chrysler Motors Corp. v.
Allied Indus. Workers*, 959 F.2d 685 (7th Cir.), *cert. denied*, 506 U.S. 908 (1992)
(enforcing order reinstating individual who grabbed breasts of female co-worker)
with Newsday, Inc. v. Typographical Union No. 915, 915 F.2d 840 (2d Cir.
1990), *cert. denied*, 499 U.S. 922 (1991) (arbitration award directing reinstatement of male worker who sexually harassed female co-workers violated explicit,
well-defined, and dominant public policy against sexual harassment set forth in
Title VII of Civil Rights Act of 1964). *See* Ray, *Sexual Harassment: Labor Arbitration and the National Labor Policy*, 73 Neb. L. Rev. 812 (1994) (arguing
that reinstatement orders in arbitration cases will not typically violate public
policy against sexual harassment expressed in Title VII because courts have held
that discipline short of discharge can be effective to remedy harassment under
Title VII); *see generally* Elkiss, *And the Winner Is? External Law and its Influence on Arbitration of Sexual Harassment Grievances*, 7 J. Indiv. Emp. Rts. 149
(1998-99); Petersen, *Issues and Standards in Arbitral Approaches to Sexual
Harassment Cases*, 7 J. Indiv. Emp. Rts. 127 (1998-99).

There does exist a public policy against violence in the workplace, but it will
not block enforcement of an arbitral award reinstating an employee who was
physically and emotionally abusive toward fellow employees unless the employer makes a clear showing that the employee was so dangerous and violent
that his reinstatement would necessarily violate that public policy. *See G.B.
Goldman Paper Co. v. United Paperworkers Int'l Union Local 286*, 957 F. Supp.
607 (E.D. Pa. 1997).

3. Some courts are quite deferential to arbitrators' authority to interpret the labor contract. For example, the Ninth Circuit held that an arbitrator could properly infer a "just cause" requirement for discipline from the seniority provision in a collective agreement and from industrial "common law." *SFIC Properties v. Machinists Dist. Lodge 94*, 103 F.3d 923 (9th Cir. 1996), *cert. denied*, 118 S. Ct. 80 (1997). In *Ethyl Corp. v. United Steelworkers*, 768 F.2d 180 (7th Cir. 1985), *cert. denied*, 475 U.S. 1010 (1986), the court explained that arbitrators are not required to interpret bargaining agreements in a literal fashion. They are authorized to read contractual language in light of the perceived intentions of the drafting parties. Arbitration awards based upon well-established past practice may also receive judicial acceptance, despite the absence of some express provision covering the area. *See Chicago Newspaper Pub'rs' Ass'n v. Printing Pressmen Local 7*, 821 F.2d 390 (7th Cir. 1987) (past practice may be applied even if contract states it constitutes parties' "entire agreement").Other courts have been far less deferential. *See, e.g., Bruce Hardwood Floors v. UBC, So. Council of Indus. Workers, Local 2713*, 103 F.3d 449 (5th Cir.), *cert. denied*, 118 S. Ct. 329 (1997) (overturning reinstatement of lying employee, on grounds contract specifically made lying subject to immediate discharge rather than progressive discipline); *Excel Corp. v. UFCW Local 431*, 102 F.3d 1464 (8th Cir. 1996) (arbitrator "erroneously" relied on parol evidence to find seniority provision did not authorize termination of injured employees after they had been on medical leave for 12 months); *Tootsie Roll Indus. v. Bakery Workers Local 1*, 832 F.2d 81 (7th Cir. 1987) (arbitrator may not apply law of the shop to alter a clear "last chance" agreement on the basis of the employer's *general* absenteeism policy).

4. What if the arbitrator's award contravenes positive law? In *Jones Dairy Farm v. UFCW Local P-1236*, 760 F.2d 173 (7th Cir.), *cert. denied*, 474 U.S. 845 (1985), the court sustained an arbitral award that had been based upon external NLRB decisional law reversed by the Labor Board following issuance of the arbitrator's determination, since, absent a showing that the arbitrator "disregarded the law" or committed "gross error," a reviewing court should not overturn the award for mistake of law. *But cf. Trailways Lines v. Joint Council*, 807 F.2d 1416 (8th Cir. 1986) (award "did not draw its essence from the agreement" when arbitrator's analysis was "in large part a verbatim copy" of a prior award involving significantly different facts and contract).

5. Is procedural unfairness by the arbitrator a basis for vacating an award? *See Harvey Alum., Inc. v. United Steelworkers*, 263 F. Supp. 488 (C.D. Cal. 1967); *Valetin v. Postal Serv.*, 787 F.2d 748 (1st Cir. 1986); Note, *Labor Arbitration: Appealing the Procedural Decisions of Arbitrators*, 59 Minn. L. Rev. 109 (1974).

6. *See generally* Craver, *Labor Arbitration as a Continuation of the Collective Bargaining Process*, 66 Chi.-Kent L. Rev. 571, 599-605 (1990); Edwards, *Judicial Review of Labor Arbitration Awards: The Clash Between the Public Policy Exception and the Duty to Bargain*, 64 Chi.-Kent L. Rev. 3 (1988); Estes & Mills, *Judge Reinhardt's Primer on Labor Arbitration: Stead Motors and Public*

Policy Judicial Review, 43 Lab. L. J. 229 (1992); Feller, *Court Review of Arbitration,* 43 Lab. L.J. 539 (1992); Gould, *Judicial Review of Labor Arbitration Awards—Thirty Years of the Steelworkers Trilogy: The Aftermath of AT&T and Misco,* 64 Notre Dame L. Rev. 464 (1989); Meltzer, *After the Labor Arbitration Award: The Public Policy Defense,* 10 Indus. Rel. L.J. 241 (1988); Ray, *Protecting the Parties' Bargain After Misco: Court Review of Labor Arbitration Awards,* 64 Ind. L.J. 1 (1988).

2. THE ENFORCEMENT OF STRIKE BANS AND THE EFFECT OF NORRIS-LA GUARDIA

FELIX FRANKFURTER & NATHAN GREENE, THE LABOR INJUNCTION 36-37, 200-01 (1930)*

The ancient common law action allowed to a master for the forcible taking away of his servant, extended, after the fourteenth century Ordinance and Statute of Labourers to enticement of a servant even without force, was in the middle nineteenth century advanced by an English court to support an action for intentionally inducing breach of a fixed term contract of employment. Eventually, both in America and in England, the traditional limits of "enticement" and of "master and servant" were wholly disregarded in the uses to which the legal categories were put. "Malice" as a requisite of the tort was quickly transformed into a mere word of art; the relationships protected expanded from those based upon a fixed term employment to employments terminable at will. The broad doctrine of "interference with contract relations" has thus been widely invoked in labor controversies....

The restraining order and the preliminary injunction invoked in labor disputes reveal the most crucial points of legal maladjustment. Temporary injunctive relief without notice, or, if upon notice, relying upon dubious affidavits, serves the important function of staying defendant's conduct regardless of the ultimate justification of such restraint.... Moreover, the suspension of strike activities, even temporarily, may defeat the strike for practical purposes and foredoom its resumption, even if the injunction is later lifted.

TEAMSTERS, CHAUFFEURS, WAREHOUSEMEN & HELPERS, LOCAL 174 v. LUCAS FLOUR CO.

Supreme Court of the United States
369 U.S. 95, 82 S. Ct. 571, 7 L. Ed. 2d 593 (1962)

MR. JUSTICE STEWART delivered the opinion of the Court.

The petitioner and the respondent (which we shall call the union and the employer) were parties to a collective bargaining contract within the purview of the National Labor Relations Act. The contract contained the following provisions, among others:

ARTICLE II

The Employer reserves the right to discharge any man in his employ if his work is not satisfactory....

ARTICLE XIV

Should any difference as to the true interpretation of this agreement arise, same shall be submitted to a Board of Arbitration of two members, one representing the firm, and one representing the Union. If said members cannot agree, a third member, who must be a disinterested party shall be selected, and the decision of the said Board of Arbitration shall be binding. It is further agreed by both parties hereto that during such arbitration, there shall be no suspension of work.

Should any difference arise between the employer and the employee, same shall be submitted to arbitration by both parties. Failing to agree, they shall mutually appoint a third person whose decision shall be final and binding.

In May of 1958, an employee named Welsch was discharged by the employer after he had damaged a new fork lift truck by running it off a loading platform and onto some railroad tracks. When a business agent of the union protested, he was told by a representative of the employer that Welsch had been discharged because of unsatisfactory work. The union thereupon called a strike to force the employer to rehire Welsch. The strike lasted eight days. After the strike was over, the issue of Welsch's discharge was submitted to arbitration. Some five months later the Board of Arbitration rendered a decision, ruling that Welsch's work had been unsatisfactory, that his unsatisfactory work had been the reason for his discharge, and that he was not entitled to reinstatement as an employee.

In the meantime, the employer had brought this suit against the union in the Superior Court of King County, Washington, asking damages for business losses caused by the strike. After a trial that court entered a judgment in favor of the employer in the amount of $6,501.60. On appeal the judgment was affirmed by Department One of the Supreme Court of Washington. 57 Wash. 2d 95, 356 P.2d 1 (1960). The reviewing court held that the preemption doctrine of *San Diego Bldg. Trades Council v. Garmon,* 359 U.S. 236 (1959), did not deprive it of jurisdiction over the controversy. The court further held that § 301 of the Labor Management Relations Act of 1947, 29 U.S.C. § 185, could not "reasonably be interpreted as preempting state jurisdiction, or as affecting it by limiting the substantive law to be applied." 57 Wash. 2d, at 102, 356 P.2d, at 5. Expressly applying principles of state law, the court reasoned that the strike was a violation of the collective bargaining contract, because it was an attempt to coerce the employer to forego his contractual right to discharge an employee for unsatisfactory work....

One of [the] issues—whether § 301(a) of the Labor Management Relations Act of 1947 deprives state courts of jurisdiction over litigation such as this—we have decided this Term in *Charles Dowd Box Co. v. Courtney,* 368 U.S. 502 (1962).[9] For the reasons stated in our opinion in that case, we hold that the Washington Supreme Court was correct in ruling that it had jurisdiction over this controversy. There remain for consideration two other issues, one of them implicated but not specifically decided in *Dowd Box.* Was the Washington court free, as it thought, to decide this controversy within the limited horizon of its local law? If not, does applicable federal law require a result in this case different from that reached by the state court? ...

It was apparently the theory of the Washington court that, although *Textile Workers v. Lincoln Mills,* 353 U.S. 448 (1957), requires the federal courts to fashion, from the policy of our national labor laws, a body of federal law for the enforcement of collective bargaining agreements, nonetheless, the courts of the states remain free to apply individualized local rules when called upon to enforce such agreements. This view cannot be accepted. The dimensions of § 301 require the conclusion that substantive principles of federal labor law must be paramount in the area covered by the statute. Comprehensiveness is inherent in the process by which the law is to be formulated under the mandate of *Lincoln Mills,* requiring issues raised in suits of a kind covered by § 301 to be decided according to the precepts of federal labor policy.

More important, the subject matter of § 301(a) "is peculiarly one that calls for uniform law." *Pennsylvania R. Co. v. Public Service Comm.,* 250 U.S. 566, 569 (1919).... The possibility that individual contract terms might have different meanings under state and federal law would inevitably exert a disruptive influence upon both the negotiation and administration of collective agreements. Because neither party could be certain of the rights which it had obtained or conceded, the process of negotiating an agreement would be made immeasurably

---

[9] Since this was a suit for violation of a collective bargaining contract within the purview of § 301(a) of the Labor Management Relations Act of 1947, the preemptive doctrine of cases such as *San Diego Building Trades Council v. Garmon,* 359 U.S. 236 (1959), based upon the exclusive jurisdiction of the National Labor Relations Board, is not relevant.... As pointed out in *Charles Dowd Box Co. v. Courtney,* 368 U.S. at 513, Congress "deliberately chose to leave the enforcement of collective agreements 'to the usual processes of law.'" *See also* H.R. Conf. Rep. No. 510, 80th Cong., 1st Sess. at 52. It is, of course, true that conduct which is a violation of a contractual obligation may also be conduct constituting an unfair labor practice, and what has been said is not to imply that enforcement by a court of a contract obligation affects the jurisdiction of the N.L.R.B. to remedy unfair labor practices, as such. *See generally* Dunau, *Contractual Prohibition of Unfair Labor Practices: Jurisdictional Problems,* 57 Colum. L. Rev. 52 (1957).

more difficult by the necessity of trying to formulate contract provisions in such a way as to contain the same meaning under two or more systems of law which might some day be invoked in enforcing the contract. Once the collective bargain was made, the possibility of conflicting substantive interpretation under competing legal systems would tend to stimulate and prolong disputes as to its interpretation. Indeed, the existence of possibly conflicting legal concepts might substantially impede the parties' willingness to agree to contract terms providing for final arbitral or judicial resolution of disputes.

The importance of the area which would be affected by separate systems of substantive law makes the need for a single body of federal law particularly compelling. The ordering and adjusting of competing interests through a process of free and voluntary collective bargaining is the keystone of the federal scheme to promote industrial peace. State law which frustrates the effort of Congress to stimulate the smooth functioning of that process thus strikes at the very core of federal labor policy. With due regard to the many factors which bear upon competing state and federal interests in this area, ... we cannot but conclude that in enacting § 301 Congress intended doctrines of federal labor law uniformly to prevail over inconsistent local rules.

Whether, as a matter of federal law, the strike which the union called was a violation of the collective bargaining contract is thus the ultimate issue which this case presents. It is argued that there could be no violation in the absence of a no-strike clause in the contract explicitly covering the subject of the dispute over which the strike was called. We disagree.

The collective bargaining contract expressly imposed upon both parties the duty of submitting the dispute in question to final and binding arbitration. In a consistent course of decisions the Courts of Appeals of at least five Federal Circuits have held that a strike to settle a dispute which a collective bargaining agreement provides shall be settled exclusively and finally by compulsory arbitration constitutes a violation of the agreement. The National Labor Relations Board has reached the same conclusion. *W.L. Mead, Inc.*, 113 N.L.R.B. 1040. We approve that doctrine. To hold otherwise would obviously do violence to accepted principles of traditional contract law. Even more in point, a contrary view would be completely at odds with the basic policy of national labor legislation to promote the arbitral process as a substitute for economic warfare. *See United Steelworkers v. Warrior & Gulf Nav. Co.,* 363 U.S. 574 (1960).

What has been said is not to suggest that a no-strike agreement is to be implied beyond the area which it has been agreed will be exclusively covered by compulsory terminal arbitration. Nor is it to suggest that there may not arise problems in specific cases as to whether compulsory and binding arbitration has been agreed upon, and, if so, as to what disputes have been made arbitrable. But no such problems are present in this case. The grievance over which the union struck was, as it concedes, one which it had expressly agreed to settle by submission to final and binding arbitration proceedings. The strike which it called was a violation of that contractual obligation.

Affirmed.

[The dissenting opinion of MR. JUSTICE BLACK is omitted.]

NOTES

1. In *Charles Dowd Box Co. v. Courtney,* 368 U.S. 502 (1962), the Supreme Court held that § 301 of the Taft-Hartley Act did not divest state courts of jurisdiction over a suit for violation of contract between an employer and a labor organization. To the argument that concurrent state court jurisdiction would lead to a disharmony of result incompatible with the *Lincoln Mills* concept of an all-embracing body of federal law, the Court replied: "The legislative history of the enactment nowhere suggests that, contrary to the clear import of the statutory language, Congress intended in enacting § 301(a) to deprive a party to a collective bargaining contract of the right to seek redress for its violation in an appropriate state tribunal.... The legislative history makes clear that the basic purpose of § 301(a) was not to limit, but to expand, the availability of forums for the enforcement of contracts made by labor organizations."

2. Justice Black, dissenting in the principal case, argued that the majority was adding a clause to the contract, on the basis of its own notions of sound policy, that the parties themselves had refused to include. Is there merit in this objection? *See* Wellington, *Freedom of Contract and the Collective Bargaining Agreement,* 112 U. Pa. L. Rev. 467 (1964). *See generally* Koretz, *The Supreme Court and Labor Arbitration, October Term, 1961,* in N.Y.U. Fifteenth Annual Conference on Labor 287 (1962).

BOYS MARKETS, INC. v. RETAIL CLERKS LOCAL 770

Supreme Court of the United States
398 U.S. 235, 90 S. Ct. 1583, 26 L. Ed. 2d 199 (1970)

MR. JUSTICE BRENNAN delivered the opinion of the Court.

In this case we re-examine the holding of *Sinclair Refining Co. v. Atkinson,* 370 U.S. 195 (1962), that the anti-injunction provisions of the Norris-LaGuardia Act preclude a federal district court from enjoining a strike in breach of a no-strike obligation under a collective bargaining agreement, even though that agreement contains provisions, enforceable under § 301(a) of the Labor-Management Relations Act for binding arbitration of the grievance dispute concerning which the strike was called. The Court of Appeals for the Ninth Circuit, considering itself bound by *Sinclair,* reversed the grant by the District Court for the Central District of California of petitioner's prayer for injunctive relief. 416 F.2d 368 (1969). We granted certiorari.... Having concluded that *Sinclair* was erroneously decided and that subsequent events have undermined its continuing validity, we overrule that decision and reverse the judgment of the Court of Appeals.

I

In February 1969, at the time of the incidents that produced this litigation, petitioner and respondent were parties to a collective bargaining agreement which provided, *inter alia,* that all controversies concerning its interpretation or application should be resolved by adjustment and arbitration procedures set forth therein and that, during the life of the contract, there should be "no cessation or stoppage of work, lock-out, picketing or boycotts...." The dispute arose when petitioner's frozen foods supervisor and certain members of his crew who were not members of the bargaining unit began to rearrange merchandise in the frozen food cases of one of petitioner's supermarkets. A union representative insisted that the food cases be stripped of all merchandise and be restocked by union personnel. When petitioner did not accede to the union's demand, a strike was called and the union began to picket petitioner's establishment. Thereupon petitioner demanded that the union cease the work stoppage and picketing and sought to invoke the grievance and arbitration procedures specified in the contract.

The following day, since the strike had not been terminated, petitioner filed a complaint in California Superior Court seeking a temporary restraining order, a preliminary and permanent injunction, and specific performance of the contractual arbitration provision. The state court issued a temporary restraining order forbidding continuation of the strike and also an order to show cause why a preliminary injunction should not be granted. Shortly thereafter, the union removed the case to the federal district court and there made a motion to quash the state court's temporary restraining order. In opposition, petitioner moved for an order compelling arbitration and enjoining continuation of the strike. Concluding that the dispute was subject to arbitration under the collective bargaining agreement and that the strike was in violation of the contract, the District Court ordered the parties to arbitrate the underlying dispute and simultaneously enjoined the strike, all picketing in the vicinity of petitioner's supermarket, and any attempts by the union to induce the employees to strike or to refuse to perform their services.

II

At the outset, we are met with respondent's contention that *Sinclair* ought not to be disturbed because the decision turned on a question of statutory construction which Congress can alter at any time. Since Congress has not modified our conclusions in *Sinclair,* even though it has been urged to do so, respondent argues that principles of *stare decisis* should govern the present case.

[The Court initially discussed the *stare decisis* doctrine, the *Lincoln Mills* holding that the Norris-LaGuardia Act did not preclude specific performance of an employer's promise to arbitrate grievance, and the *Steelworkers Trilogy* preference for arbitration as a dispute resolution technique.]

III

... [I]n *Charles Dowd Box Co. v. Courtney,* 368 U.S. 502 (1962), we held that Congress clearly intended *not* to disturb the pre-existing jurisdiction of the state courts over suits for violations of collective bargaining agreements. We noted that the

> clear implication of the entire record of the congressional debates in both 1946 and 1947 is that the purpose of conferring jurisdiction upon the federal district courts was not to displace, but to supplement, the thoroughly considered jurisdiction of the courts of the various States over contracts made by labor organizations.

Id. at 511....

Subsequent to the decision in *Sinclair,* we held in *Avco Corp. v. Aero Lodge No. 735,* [390 U.S. 557 (1968)], that § 301(a) suits initially brought in state courts may be removed to the designated federal forum under the federal question removal jurisdiction delineated in 28 U.S.C. § 1441. In so holding, however, the Court expressly left open the questions whether state courts are bound by the anti-injunction proscriptions of the Norris-LaGuardia Act and whether federal courts, after removal of a § 301(a) action, are required to dissolve any injunctive relief previously granted by the state courts. *See generally General Electric Co. v. Local Union 191,* 413 F.2d 964 (5th Cir. 1969) (dissolution of state injunction required). Three Justices who concurred expressed the view that *Sinclair* should be reconsidered "upon an appropriate future occasion." 390 U.S. at 562 (STEWART, J., concurring).

The decision in *Avco,* viewed in the context of *Lincoln Mills* and its progeny, has produced an anomalous situation which, in our view, makes urgent the reconsideration of *Sinclair.* The principal practical effect of *Avco* and *Sinclair* taken together is nothing less than to oust state courts of jurisdiction in § 301(a) suits where injunctive relief is sought for breach of a no-strike obligation. Union defendants can, as a matter of course, obtain removal to a federal court, and there is obviously a compelling incentive for them to do so in order to gain the advantage of the strictures upon injunctive relief which *Sinclair* imposes on federal courts. The sanctioning of this practice, however, is wholly inconsistent with our conclusion in *Dowd Box* that the congressional purpose embodied in § 301(a) was to *supplement,* and not to encroach upon, the pre-existing jurisdiction of the state courts. It is ironic indeed that the very provision which Congress clearly intended to provide additional remedies for breach of collective bargaining agreements has been employed to displace previously existing state remedies. We are not at liberty thus to depart from the clearly expressed congressional policy to the contrary.

On the other hand, to the extent that widely disparate remedies theoretically remain available in state, as opposed to federal courts, the federal policy of labor law uniformity elaborated in *Lucas Flour Co.,* is seriously offended. This policy, of course, could hardly require, as a practical matter, that labor law be administered identically in all courts, for undoubtedly a certain diversity exists among the state and federal systems in matters of procedural and remedial detail, a fact which Congress evidently took into account in deciding not to disturb the traditional jurisdiction of the States. The injunction, however, is so important a remedial device, particularly in the arbitration context, that its availability or nonavailability in various courts will not only produce rampant forum-shopping and maneuvering from one court to another but will also greatly frustrate any relative uniformity in the enforcement of arbitration agreements.

Furthermore, the existing scheme, with the injunction remedy technically available in the state courts but rendered inefficacious by the removal device, assigns to removal proceedings a totally unintended function. While the underlying purposes of Congress in providing for federal question removal jurisdiction remain somewhat obscure, there has never been a serious contention that Congress intended that the removal mechanism be utilized to foreclose completely remedies otherwise available in the state courts. Although federal question removal jurisdiction may well have been intended to provide a forum for the protection of federal rights where such protection was deemed necessary or to encourage the development of expertise by the federal courts in the interpretation of federal law, there is no indication that Congress intended by the removal mechanism to effect a wholesale dislocation in the allocation of judicial business between the state and federal courts....

It is undoubtedly true that each of the foregoing objections to *Sinclair-Avco* could be remedied either by overruling *Sinclair* or by extending that decision to the States. While some commentators have suggested that the solution to the present unsatisfactory situation does lie in the extension of the *Sinclair* prohibition to state court proceedings, we agree with Chief Justice Traynor of the California Supreme Court that "whether or not Congress could deprive state courts of the power to give such [injunctive] remedies when enforcing collective bargaining agreements, it has not attempted to do so either in the Norris-LaGuardia Act or section 301." *McCarroll v. Los Angeles County Dist. Council of Carpenters,* 49 Cal. 2d 45, 61, 315 P.2d 322, 332 (1957), *cert. denied,* 355 U.S. 932 (1958)....

An additional reason for not resolving the existing dilemma by extending *Sinclair* to the States is the devastating implications for the enforceability of arbitration agreements and their accompanying no-strike obligations if equitable remedies were not available. As we have previously indicated, a no-strike obligation, express or implied, is the *quid pro quo* for an undertaking by the employer to submit grievance disputes to the process of arbitration. *See Textile Workers Un-*

ion v. Lincoln Mills, supra at 455. Any incentive for employers to enter into such an arrangement is necessarily dissipated if the principal and most expeditious method by which the no-strike obligation can be enforced is eliminated. While it is of course true, as respondent contends, that other avenues of redress, such as an action for damages, would remain open to an aggrieved employer, an award of damages after a dispute has been settled is no substitute for an immediate halt to an illegal strike. Furthermore, an action for damages prosecuted during or after a labor dispute would only tend to aggravate industrial strife and delay an early resolution of the difficulties between employer and union.

Even if management is not encouraged by the unavailability of the injunction remedy to resist arbitration agreements, the fact remains that the effectiveness of such agreements would be greatly reduced if injunctive relief were withheld. Indeed, the very purpose of arbitration procedures is to provide a mechanism for the expeditious settlement of industrial disputes without resort to strikes, lockouts, or other self-help measures. This basic purpose is obviously largely undercut if there is no immediate, effective remedy for those very tactics which arbitration is designed to obviate. Thus, because *Sinclair,* in the aftermath of *Avco,* casts serious doubt upon the effective enforcement of a vital element of stable labor-management relations—arbitration agreements with their attendant no-strike obligations—we conclude that *Sinclair* does not make a viable contribution to federal labor policy.

IV

We have also determined that the dissenting opinion in *Sinclair* states the correct principles concerning the accommodation necessary between the seemingly absolute terms of the Norris-LaGuardia Act and the policy considerations underlying § 301(a). 370 U.S. at 215. Although we need not repeat all that was there said, a few points should be emphasized at this time.

The literal terms of § 4 of the Norris-LaGuardia Act must be accommodated to the subsequently enacted provisions of § 301(a) of the Labor-Management Relations Act and the purposes of arbitration. Statutory interpretation requires more than concentration upon isolated words; rather, consideration must be given to the total corpus of pertinent law and the policies which inspired ostensibly inconsistent provisions. *See Richards v. United States,* 369 U.S. 1, 11 (1962); *Mastro Plastics Corp. v. NLRB,* 350 U.S. 270, 285 (1956); *United States v. Hutcheson,* 312 U.S. 219, 235 (1941).

The Norris-LaGuardia Act was responsive to a situation totally different from that which exists today. In the early part of this century, the federal courts generally were regarded as allies of management in its attempt to prevent the organization and strengthening of labor unions; and in this industrial struggle the injunction became a potent weapon which was wielded against the activities of labor groups. The result was a large number of sweeping decrees, often issued *ex parte,* drawn on an *ad hoc* basis without regard to any systematic elaboration of national labor policy. *See Drivers' Union v. Lake Valley Co.,* 311 U.S. 91, 102 (1940).

In 1932 Congress attempted to bring some order out of the industrial chaos that had developed and to correct the abuses which had resulted from the interjection of the federal judiciary into union-management disputes on the behalf of management. See Declaration of Public Policy, Norris-LaGuardia Act, § 2.... Congress, therefore, determined initially to limit severely the power of the federal courts to issue injunctions "in any case involving or growing out of any labor dispute...." § 4.... Even as initially enacted, however, the prohibition against federal injunctions was by no means absolute. *See* Norris-LaGuardia Act, §§ 7, 8, 9.... Shortly thereafter Congress passed the Wagner Act, designed to curb various management activities which tended to discourage employee participation in collective action.

As labor organizations grew in strength and developed toward maturity, congressional emphasis shifted from protection of the nascent labor movement to the encouragement of collective bargaining and to administrative techniques for the peaceful resolution of industrial disputes. This shift in emphasis was accomplished, however, without extensive revision of many of the older enactments, including the anti-injunction section of the Norris-LaGuardia Act. Thus it became the task of the courts to accommodate, to reconcile the older statutes with the more recent ones.

A leading example of this accommodation process is *Brotherhood of R.R. Trainmen v. Chicago River & Ind. R.R.,* 353 U.S. 30 (1957). There we were confronted with a peaceful strike which violated the statutory duty to arbitrate imposed by the Railway Labor Act. The Court concluded that a strike in violation of a statutory arbitration duty was not the type of situation to which the Norris-LaGuardia Act was responsive, that an important federal policy was involved in the peaceful settlement of disputes through the statutorily-mandated arbitration procedure, that this important policy was imperiled if equitable remedies were not available to implement it, and hence that Norris-LaGuardia's policy of non-intervention by the federal courts should yield to the overriding interest in the successful implementation of the arbitration process.

The principles elaborated in *Chicago River* are equally applicable to the present case. To be sure, *Chicago River* involved arbitration procedures established by statute. However, we have frequently noted, in such cases as *Lincoln Mills,* the *Steelworkers Trilogy,* and *Lucas Flour,* the importance which Congress has attached generally to the voluntary settlement of labor disputes without resort to self-help and more particularly to arbitration as a means to this end. Indeed, it has been stated that *Lincoln Mills,* in its exposition of § 301(a), "went a long way towards making arbitration the central institution in the administration of collective bargaining contracts."

The *Sinclair* decision, however, seriously undermined the effectiveness of the arbitration technique as a method peacefully to resolve industrial disputes without resort to strikes, lockouts, and similar devices. Clearly employers will be wary of assuming obligations to arbitrate specifically enforceable against them when no similarly efficacious remedy is available to enforce the concomitant undertaking of the union to refrain from striking. On the other hand, the central purpose of the Norris-LaGuardia Act to foster the growth and viability of labor organizations is hardly retarded—if anything, this goal is advanced—by a remedial device which merely enforces the obligation that the union freely undertook under a specifically enforceable agreement to submit disputes to arbitration. We conclude, therefore, that the unavailability of equitable relief in the arbitration context presents a serious impediment to the congressional policy favoring the voluntary establishment of a mechanism for the peaceful resolution of labor disputes, that the core purpose of the Norris-LaGuardia Act is not sacrificed by the limited use of equitable remedies to further this important policy, and consequently that the Norris-LaGuardia Act does not bar the granting of injunctive relief in the circumstances of the instant case.

V

Our holding in the present case is a narrow one. We do not undermine the vitality of the Norris-LaGuardia Act. We deal only with the situation in which a collective bargaining contract contains a mandatory grievance adjustment or arbitration procedure. Nor does it follow from what we have said that injunctive relief is appropriate as a matter of course in every case of a strike over an arbitrable grievance. The dissenting opinion in *Sinclair* suggested the following principles for the guidance of the district courts in determining whether to grant injunctive relief—principles which we now adopt:

A District Court entertaining an action under § 301 may not grant injunctive relief against concerted activity unless and until it decides that the case is one in which an injunction would be appropriate despite the Norris-LaGuardia Act. When a strike is sought to be enjoined because it is over a grievance which both parties are contractually bound to arbitrate, the District Court may issue no injunctive order until it first holds that the contract *does* have that effect; and the employer should be ordered to arbitrate, as a condition of his obtaining an injunction against the strike. Beyond this, the District Court must, of course, consider whether issuance of an injunction would be warranted under ordinary principles of equity—whether breaches are occurring and will continue, or have been threatened and will be committed; whether they have caused or will cause irreparable injury to the employer; and whether the employer will suffer more from the denial of an injunction than will the union from its issuance.

370 U.S. at 228. (Emphasis in original.)

In the present case there is no dispute that the grievance in question was subject to adjustment and arbitration under the collective bargaining agreement and that the petitioner was ready to proceed with arbitration at the time an injunction against the strike was sought and obtained. The District Court also concluded that, by reason of respondent's violations of its no-strike obligation, petitioner "has suffered irreparable injury and will continue to suffer irreparable injury." Since we now overrule *Sinclair,* the holding of the Court of Appeals in reliance on *Sinclair* must be reversed. Accordingly, we reverse the judgment of the Court of Appeals and remand the case with directions to enter a judgment affirming the order of the District Court.

It is so ordered.

MR. JUSTICE MARSHALL took no part in the decision of this case.

MR. JUSTICE BLACK, dissenting....

Although Congress has been urged to overrule our holding in *Sinclair,* it has steadfastly refused to do so. Nothing in the language or history of the two Acts has changed. Nothing at all has changed, in fact, except the membership of the Court and the personal views of one Justice. I remain of the opinion that *Sinclair* was correctly decided, and, moreover, that the prohibition of the Norris-LaGuardia Act is close to the heart of the entire federal system of labor regulation. In my view *Sinclair* should control the disposition of this case.

Even if the majority were correct, however, in saying that *Sinclair* misinterpreted the Taft-Hartley and Norris-LaGuardia Acts, I should be compelled to dissent. I believe that both the making and the changing of laws which affect the substantial rights of the people are primarily for Congress, not this Court. Most especially is this so when the law involved is the focus of strongly held views of powerful but antagonistic political and economic interests. The Court's function in the application and interpretation of such laws must be carefully limited to avoid encroaching on the power of Congress to determine policies and make laws to carry them out....

[The concurring opinion of MR. JUSTICE STEWART is omitted. MR. JUSTICE WHITE dissented "for the reasons stated in the majority opinion in *Sinclair Refining Co. v. Atkinson.*"]

NOTES

1. What if the contract contains an express no-strike clause, but no final and binding arbitration clause? What if it contains a final and binding arbitration clause, but no no-strike clause? If both are present, should they be read as coterminous? *Compare Delaware Coca-Cola Bottling Co. v. Teamsters Local 326,* 624 F.2d 1182 (3d Cir. 1980) (Yes), *noted in* 67 Va. L. Rev. 729 (1982) *with Ryder Truck Lines v. Teamsters Local 480,* 727 F.2d 594 (6th Cir.), *cert. denied,* 469 U.S. 825 (1984). What about work stoppage over a dispute that could be submitted to grievance procedures but not to arbitration? *See AT&T v. Communications Workers,* 985 F.2d 855 (6th Cir. 1992). *See generally* Axelrod, *The Application of the Boys Markets Decision in the Federal Courts,* 16 B.C. Ind. & Com. L. Rev. 893 (1975); Gould, *On Labor Injunctions, Unions, and the Judges: the Boys Markets Case,* 1970 Sup. Ct. Rev. 215; Vladeck, *Boys Markets and National Labor Policy,* 24 Vand. L. Rev. 93 (1970); Note, *Express No-Strike Clauses and the Requirement of Clear and Unmistakable Waiver: A Short Analysis,* 70 Cornell L. Rev. 272 (1985).

2. In *Gateway Coal Co. v. Mine Workers,* 414 U.S. 368 (1974), the Supreme Court held that even a strike against allegedly unsafe conditions could be enjoined, when the union could have arbitrated its grievance that a mining company was retaining foremen who had falsified air flow records. Section 502 of the LMRA, which provides that work stoppages because of abnormally dangerous conditions are not "strikes," does not apply in the absence of "ascertainable, objective evidence" of such unsafe conditions. What would constitute "abnormally dangerous" conditions justifying a work stoppage? *See Oil, Chem. & Atomic Workers v. NLRB (TNS Inc.),* 46 F.3d 82 (D.C. Cir.), *cert. denied,* 516 U.S. 821 (1995); Atleson, *Threats to Health and Safety: Employee Self-Help Under the NLRA,* 59 Minn. L. Rev. 647 (1975).

3. *Boys Markets* injunctions are available against employer as well as union breaches of labor contracts which threaten the arbitral process. Thus, unions have obtained injunctions against employers who sought to impose unilateral changes prior to arbitration—if maintenance of the status quo was necessary to preserve the union's arbitral remedy. *See Newspaper & Periodical Drivers' & Helpers Local 921 v. San Francisco Newspaper Agency,* 89 F.3d 629 (9th Cir. 1996); *Rubber Workers Local 884 v. Bridgestone/Firestone, Inc.,* 61 F.3d 1347 (8th Cir. 1995). Generally, however, unions have been unsuccessful in obtaining injunctions to bar unilateral imposition of drug-testing programs. *See Niagra Hooker Employees Union v. Occidental Chem. Corp.,* 935 F.2d 1370 (2d Cir. 1991); *IBEW Local 733 v. Ingalls Shipbuilding Div.,* 906 F.2d 149 (5th Cir. 1990); *but see Oil Workers Local 2-286 v. Amoco Oil Co.,* 885 F.2d 697 (10th Cir. 1989).

4. Justice Black wrote the majority opinion in *Sinclair Refining,* which was overruled in *Boys Markets,* and the full force of his legal argument is better understood from the following passage in the earlier decision:

> The language of § 301 itself seems to us almost if not entirely conclusive of this question. It is especially significant that the section contains no language that could by any stretch of the imagination be interpreted to constitute an explicit repeal of the anti-injunction provisions of the Norris-

LaGuardia Act in view of the fact that the section does expressly repeal another provision of the Norris-LaGuardia Act dealing with union responsibility for the acts of agents....

When the inquiry is carried beyond the language of § 301 into its legislative history, whatever small doubts as to the congressional purpose could have survived consideration of the bare language of the section should be wholly dissipated. For the legislative history of § 301 shows that Congress actually considered the advisability of repealing the Norris-LaGuardia Act insofar as suits based upon breach of collective bargaining agreements are concerned and deliberately chose not to do so.... The House Conference Report expressly recognized that the House provisions for repeal in contract actions of the anti-injunction prohibitions of the Norris-LaGuardia Act had been eliminated in Conference.... And Senator Taft, Chairman of the Conference Committee and one of the authors of this legislation that bore his name, was no less explicit in explaining the results of the Conference to the Senate: "The conferees ... rejected the repeal of the Norris-LaGuardia Act." [370 U.S. at 204.]

5. Assume that sound policy supported the result in *Boys Markets,* but assume further (as seems not unlikely) that Norris-LaGuardia had become such a symbolic issue in the eyes of the labor movement that it was politically hazardous for Congress to tamper with it. Would that have cut for or against the Supreme Court's stepping in to do the job Congress could not face up to? For two thoughtful, contrasting discussions, *see* Wellington & Albert, *Statutory Interpretation and the Political Process: A Comment Upon Sinclair v. Atkinson,* 72 Yale L.J. 1547 (1963), and Bishin, *The Law Finders: An Essay in Statutory Interpretation,* 38 S. Cal. L. Rev. 1 (1965). *See also* Atleson, *The Circle of Boys Market: A Comment on Judicial Inventiveness,* 7 Indus. Rel. L.J. 88 (1985).

6. Should the same standard of presumptive arbitrability applied in the *Steelworkers Trilogy* be used in *Boys Markets* suits? *See* Comment, *Boys Markets Injunctions Against Employers,* 91 Harv. L. Rev. 715 (1978), discussing *Lever Bros. v. Chemical Workers Local 217,* 554 F.2d 115 (4th Cir. 1976). It has been held that neither the expiration of a collective bargaining agreement nor the partial liquidation of an employer's business precludes the issuance of *Boys Markets* injunctions against a union or an employer to preserve the status quo. *Bituminous Coal Operators Ass'n v. Mine Workers,* 585 F.2d 586 (3d Cir. 1978); *Teamsters Local 71 v. Akers Motor Lines,* 582 F.2d 1336 (4th Cir. 1978), *cert. denied,* 440 U.S. 929 (1979). *See also Goya Foods, Inc.,* 238 N.L.R.B. 1465 (1978) (no-strike clause "coterminous" with employer's duty to arbitrate under an expired contract, and strikers may be discharged).

7. *Strike Injunctions Under the Railway Labor Act.* In *Railroad Trainmen v. Chicago River & Ind. R.R.,* 353 U.S. 30 (1957), discussed in *Boys Markets,* the Supreme Court held that the Norris-LaGuardia Act does not prevent an injunction against a strike in a so-called "minor dispute," *i.e.,* one involving a grievance under an existing collective agreement which is subject to statutory arbitration before the National Railroad Adjustment Board. On the other hand, the Court declared in *Railroad Trainmen Lodge 27 v. Toledo, P. & W. R.R.,* 321 U.S. 50 (1944), that Norris-LaGuardia does prevent an injunction in a "major dispute"— one concerning future terms of employment. *See generally* Kroner, *Interim Injunctive Relief Under the Railway Labor Act: Some Problems and Suggestions,* in N.Y.U. Eighteenth Annual Conference on Labor 179 (1966).

A federal district court may include conditions in an injunction against a strike in order to protect employees against a harmful change in working conditions while a dispute is pending before the National Railroad Adjustment Board. *Locomotive Eng'rs v. Missouri-Kan.-Tex. R.R.,* 363 U.S. 528 (1960). A union cannot resort to a strike to enforce its interpretation of a money award by the NRAB in favor of an employee; the RLA provides for enforcement by a court suit. A strike in such circumstances can be enjoined, notwithstanding the Norris-LaGuardia Act. *Locomotive Eng'rs v. Louisville & Nashville R.R.,* 373 U.S. 33 (1963).

8. *United Mine Workers v. Bagwell,* 512 U.S. 821 (1994), involved an acrimonious strike that included unprotected activity. After the strikers engaged in unprotected behavior that had been enjoined by a state court, a contempt proceeding was held that culminated in fines of over $64,000,000. The Virginia Supreme Court found the fines "civil" in nature and rejected UMW claims that a criminal proceeding was required for such substantial penalties. A unanimous Supreme Court reversed. It found the significant fines criminal in nature and held that they could only be imposed after appropriate criminal proceedings.

BUFFALO FORGE CO. v. UNITED STEELWORKERS

Supreme Court of the United States
428 U.S. 397, 96 S. Ct. 3141, 49 L. Ed. 1022 (1976)

[The Buffalo Forge Company operates three separate plant and office facilities in the Buffalo, New York area. The Steelworkers Union has represented the production and maintenance (P&M) employees at these plants for some years. Other locals of the Steelworkers were certified in 1974 to represent the office clerical-technical (O&T) employees of Buffalo Forge at the same three plants. On November 16, 1974, after several months of negotiations looking toward their first collective bargaining agreement, the O&T employees struck and established picket lines at all three locations. The P&M employees honored the picket lines and stopped work.

[The company sued the union under § 301 of the Taft-Hartley Act in Federal District Court for breach of the no-strike clause in the P&M collective agreement, seeking an injunction against the work stoppage. The collective agreement provided for arbitration as follows: "Should differences arise ... as to the meaning and application of the provisions of this Agreement, or should any trouble of any kind arise in the plant, there shall be no suspension of work on account of such differences, but an earnest effort shall be made to settle such differences immediately.... In the event the grievance involves a question as to the meaning and application of this Agreement, and has not been previously satisfactorily adjusted, it may be submitted to arbitration upon written notice of the Union or the Company." The District Court found that the P&M employees had engaged in a sympathy action in support of the O&T employees, but held itself forbidden to enjoin it by the Norris-LaGuardia Act. The Court of Appeals affirmed, and the Supreme Court granted certiorari.]

MR. JUSTICE WHITE delivered the opinion of the Court.

The issue for decision is whether a federal court may enjoin a sympathy strike pending the arbitrator's decision as to whether the strike is forbidden by the express no-strike clause contained in the collective bargaining contract to which the striking union is a party....

.....

II

As a preliminary matter, certain elements in this case are not in dispute. The Union has gone on strike not by reason of any dispute it or any of its members has with the employer but in support of other local unions, of the same international organization, that were negotiating a contract with the employer and were out on strike. The parties involved here are bound by a collective bargaining contract containing a no-strike clause which the Union claims does not forbid sympathy strikes. The employer has the other view, its complaint in the District Court asserting that the work stoppage violated the no-strike clause. The contract between the parties also has an arbitration clause broad enough to reach not only disputes between the Union and the employer about other provisions in the contract but also as to the meaning and application of the no-strike clause itself. Whether the sympathy strike the Union called violated the no-strike clause, and the appropriate remedies if it did, are subject to the agreed-upon dispute-settlement procedures of the contract and are ultimately issues for the arbitrator. [Citing the *Steelworkers Trilogy.*] The employer thus was entitled to invoke the arbitral process to determine the legality of the sympathy strike and to obtain a court order requiring the Union to arbitrate if the Union refused to do so. *Gateway Coal Co. v. United Mine Workers,* 414 U.S. 368 (1974). Furthermore, were the issue arbitrated and the strike found illegal, the relevant federal statutes as construed in our cases would permit an injunction to enforce the arbitral decision. *United Steelworkers of America v. Enterprise Wheel & Car Corp.* [363 U.S. 593 (1960)].

The issue in this case arises because the employer not only asked for an order directing the Union to arbitrate but prayed that the strike itself be enjoined pending arbitration and the arbitrator's decision whether the strike was permissible under the no-strike clause....

The holding in *Boys Markets* was said to be a "narrow one," dealing only with the situation in which the collective bargaining contract contained mandatory grievance and arbitration procedures. 398 U.S. at 253.... The driving force behind *Boys Markets* was to implement the strong congressional preference for the private dispute settlement mechanisms agreed upon by the parties. Only to that extent was it held necessary to accommodate § 4 of the Norris-LaGuardia Act to § 301 of the Labor Management Relations Act and to lift the former's ban against the issuance of injunctions in labor disputes. Striking over an arbitrable dispute would interfere with and frustrate the arbitral processes by which the parties had chosen to settle a dispute. The *quid pro quo* for the employer's promise to arbitrate was the union's obligation not to strike over issues that were subject to the arbitration machinery. Even in the absence of an express no-strike clause, an undertaking not to strike would be implied where the strike was over an otherwise arbitrable dispute. *Gateway Coal Co. v. United Mine Workers, supra; Teamsters Local v. Lucas Flour Co.,* 369 U.S. 95 (1962). Otherwise, the employer would be deprived of his bargain and the policy of the labor statutes to implement private resolution of disputes in a manner agreed upon would seriously suffer.

Boys Markets plainly does not control this case. The District Court found, and it is not now disputed, that the strike was not *over* any dispute between the Union and the employer that was even remotely subject to the arbitration provisions of the contract. The strike at issue was a sympathy strike in support of sister unions negotiating with the employer; neither its causes nor the issue underlying it were subject to the settlement procedures provided by the contract between the employer and respondents. The strike had neither the purpose nor the effect of denying or evading an obligation to arbitrate or of depriving the employer of his bargain. Thus, had the contract not contained a no-strike clause or had the clause expressly excluded sympathy strikes, there would have been no possible basis for implying from the existence of an arbitration clause a promise not to strike that could have been violated by the sympathy strike in this case. *Gateway Coal Co. v. Mine Workers, supra* at 382.[10]

Nor was the injunction authorized solely because it was alleged that the sympathy strike called by the Union violated the express no-strike provision of the contract. Section 301 of the Act assigns a major role to the courts in enforcing collective bargaining agreements, but aside from the enforcement of the arbitration provisions of such contracts, within the limits permitted by *Boys Markets,* the Court has never indicated that the courts may enjoin actual or threatened contract violations despite the Norris-LaGuardia Act. In the course of enacting

---

[10] To the extent that the Court of Appeals, 517 F.2d, at 1211, and other courts ... have assumed that a mandatory arbitration clause implies a commitment not to engage in sympathy strikes, they are wrong.

the Taft-Hartley Act, Congress rejected the proposal that the Norris-LaGuardia Act's prohibition against labor-dispute injunctions be lifted to the extent necessary to make injunctive remedies available in federal courts for the purpose of enforcing collective bargaining agreements.... The allegation of the complaint that the Union was breaching its obligation not to strike did not in itself warrant an injunction....

Here the Union struck, and the parties were in dispute whether the sympathy strike violated the Union's no-strike undertaking. Concededly, that issue was arbitrable. It was for the arbitrator to determine whether there was a breach, as well as the remedy for any breach, and the employer was entitled to an order requiring the Union to arbitrate if it refused to do so. But the Union does not deny its duty to arbitrate; in fact, it denies that the employer ever demanded arbitration. However that may be, it does not follow that the District Court was empowered not only to order arbitration but to enjoin the strike pending the decision of the arbitrator, despite the express prohibition of § 4(a) of the Norris-LaGuardia Act against injunctions prohibiting any person "from ceasing or refusing to perform any work or to remain in any relation of employment." If an injunction could issue against the strike in this case, so in proper circumstances could a court enjoin any other alleged breach of contract pending the exhaustion of the applicable grievance and arbitration provisions even though the injunction would otherwise violate one of the express prohibitions of § 104. The court in such cases would be permitted, if the dispute was arbitrable, to hold hearings, make findings of fact, interpret the applicable provisions of the contract and issue injunctions so as to restore the *status quo ante* or to otherwise regulate the relationship of the parties pending exhaustion of the arbitration process. This would cut deeply into the policy of the Norris-LaGuardia Act and make the courts potential participants in a wide range of arbitrable disputes under the many existing and future collective bargaining contracts, not just for the purpose of enforcing promises to arbitrate, which was the limit of *Boys Markets,* but for the purpose of preliminarily dealing with the merits of the factual and legal issues that are subjects for the arbitrator and of issuing injunctions that would otherwise be forbidden by the Norris-LaGuardia Act.

This is not what the parties have bargained for. Surely it cannot be concluded here, as it was in *Boys Markets,* that such injunctions pending arbitration are essential to carry out promises to arbitrate and to implement the private arrangements for the administration of the contract. As is typical, the agreement in this case outlines the prearbitration settlement procedures and provides that if the grievance "has not been ... satisfactorily adjusted," arbitration may be had. Nowhere does it provide for coercive action of any kind, let alone judicial injunctions, short of the terminal decision of the arbitrator. The parties have agreed to grieve and arbitrate, not to litigate. They have not contracted for a judicial preview of the facts and the law. Had they anticipated additional regulation of their relationships pending arbitration, it seems very doubtful that they would have resorted to litigation rather than to private arrangements. The unmistakable policy of Congress stated in 29 U.S.C. § 173 (d), 61 Stat. 153, is that "Final adjustment by a method agreed upon by the parties is declared to be the desirable method for settlement of grievance disputes arising over the application or interpretation of an existing collective bargaining agreement." *Gateway Coal Co. v. United Mine Workers, supra* at 377. But the parties' agreement to adjust or to arbitrate their differences themselves would be eviscerated if the courts for all practical purposes were to try and decide contractual disputes at the preliminary injunction stage.

The dissent suggests that injunctions should be authorized in cases such as this at least where the violation, in the court's view, is clear and the court is sufficiently sure that the parties seeking the injunction will win before the arbitrator. But this would still involve hearings, findings and judicial interpretations of collective bargaining contracts. It is incredible to believe that the courts would always view the facts and the contract as the arbitrator would; and it is difficult to believe that the arbitrator would not be heavily influenced or wholly preempted by judicial views of the facts and the meaning of contracts if this procedure is to be permitted. Injunctions against strikes, even temporary injunctions, very often permanently settle the issue; and in other contexts time and expense would be discouraging factors to the losing party in court in considering whether to relitigate the issue before the arbitrator.

With these considerations in mind, we are far from concluding that the arbitration process will be frustrated unless the courts have the power to issue interlocutory injunctions pending arbitration in cases such as this or in others in which an arbitrable dispute awaits decision. We agree with the Court of Appeals that there is no necessity here, such as was found to be the case in *Boys Markets,* to accommodate the policies of the Norris-LaGuardia Act to the requirements of § 301 by empowering the District Court to issue the injunction sought by the employer.

The judgment of the Court of Appeals is affirmed.

So ordered.

MR. JUSTICE STEVENS, with whom MR. JUSTICE BRENNAN, MR. JUSTICE MARSHALL, and MR. JUSTICE POWELL join, dissenting....

The Court today holds that only a part of the union's *quid pro quo* is enforceable by injunction.[2] The principal bases for the holding are (1) the Court's literal

---

[2] The enforceable part of the no-strike agreement is the part relating to a strike "over an arbitrable dispute." In *Gateway Coal,* however, my Brethren held that the district court had properly entered an injunction that not only terminated a strike pending an arbitrator's decision of an underlying safety dispute, but also "prospectively required both parties to abide by his resolution of the controversy." *Id.* at 373. A strike in defiance of an arbitrator's award would not be "over an arbitrable dispute"; nevertheless, the Court today recognizes the propriety of an injunction against such a strike.

interpretation of the Norris-LaGuardia Act; and (2) its fear that the federal judiciary would otherwise make a "massive" entry into the business of contract interpretation heretofore reserved for arbitrators. The first argument has been rejected repeatedly in cases in which the central concerns of the Norris-LaGuardia Act were not implicated. The second is wholly unrealistic and was implicitly rejected in *Gateway Coal* when the Court held that "a substantial question of contractual interpretation" was a sufficient basis for federal equity jurisdiction. 414 U.S. at 384. That case held that an employer might enforce a somewhat ambiguous *quid pro quo;* today the Court holds that a portion of the *quid pro quo* is unenforceable no matter how unambiguous it may be. With all respect, I am persuaded that a correct application of the reasoning underlying the landmark decision in *Boys Markets, Inc. v. Clerks Union,* 398 U.S. 235, requires a different result.

....

[There follows a detailed review of the rationale in *Boys Markets.*]

The *Boys Markets* decision protects the arbitration process. A court is authorized to enjoin a strike over a grievance which the parties are contractually bound to arbitrate, but that authority is conditioned upon a finding that the contract does so provide, that the strike is in violation of the agreement, and further that the issuance of an injunction is warranted by ordinary principles of equity. These conditions plainly stated in *Boys Markets* demonstrate that the interest in protecting the arbitration process is not simply an end in itself which exists at large and apart from other fundamental aspects of our national labor policy.

On the one hand, an absolute precondition of any *Boys Markets* injunction is a contractual obligation. A court may not order arbitration unless the parties have agreed to that process; nor can the court require the parties to accept an arbitrator's decision unless they have agreed to be bound by it. If the union reserves the right to resort to self-help at the conclusion of the arbitration process, that agreement must be respected. The court's power is limited by the contours of the agreement between the parties.[17]

On the other hand, the arbitration procedure is not merely an exercise; it performs the important purpose of determining what the underlying agreement actually means as applied to a specific setting. If the parties have agreed to be bound by the arbitrator's decision, the reasons which justify an injunction against a strike that would impair his ability to reach a decision must equally justify an injunction requiring the parties to abide by a decision that a strike is in violation of the no-strike clause.[18] The arbitration mechanism would hardly retain its respect as a method of resolving disputes if the end product of the process had less significance than the process itself....

---

[17] In particular, an implied no-strike clause does not extend to sympathy strikes. See *ante* at n.10.

[18] The Court recognizes that an injunction may issue to enforce an arbitrator's decision that a strike is in violation of the no-strike clause....

In this case, the question whether the sympathy strike violates the no-strike clause is an arbitrable issue. If the court had the benefit of an arbitrator's resolution of the issue in favor of the employer, it could enforce that decision just as it could require the parties to submit the issue to arbitration. And if the agreement were so plainly unambiguous that there could be no bona fide issue to submit to the arbitrator, there must be the same authority to enforce the parties' bargain pending the arbitrator's final decision.

The Union advances three arguments against this conclusion: (1) that interpretation of the collective bargaining agreement is the exclusive province of the arbitrator; (2) that an injunction erroneously entered pending arbitration will effectively deprive the union of the right to strike before the arbitrator can render his decision; and (3) that it is the core purpose of the Norris-LaGuardia Act to eliminate the risk of an injunction against a lawful strike. Although I acknowledge the force of these arguments, I think they are insufficient to take this case outside the rationale of *Boys Markets*.

The *Steelworkers Trilogy* establishes that a collective bargaining agreement submitting all questions of contract interpretation to the arbitrator deprives the courts of almost all power to interpret the agreement to prevent submission of a dispute to arbitration or to refuse enforcement of an arbitrator's award. *Boys Markets* itself repeated the warning that it was not for the courts to usurp the functions of the arbitrator. And *Gateway Coal* held that an injunction may issue to protect the arbitration process even if a "substantial question of contractual interpretation" must be answered to determine whether the strike is over an arbitrable grievance. In each of these cases, however, the choice was between interpretation of the agreement by the court or interpretation by the arbitrator; a decision that the dispute was not arbitrable, or not properly arbitrated, would have precluded an interpretation of the agreement according to the contractual grievance procedure. In the present case, an interim determination of the no-strike question by the court neither usurps nor precludes a decision by the arbitrator. By definition, issuance of an injunction pending the arbitrator's decision does not supplant a decision that he otherwise would have made. Indeed, it is the ineffectiveness of the damage remedy for strikes pending arbitration that lends force to the employer's argument for an injunction. The court does not oust the arbitrator of his proper function but fulfills a role that he never served.

The Union's second point, however, is that the arbitrator will rarely render his decision quickly enough to prevent an erroneously issued injunction from effectively depriving the union of its right to strike. The Union relies particularly upon decisions of this Court that recognize that even a temporary injunction can quickly end a strike. But this argument demonstrates only that arbitration, to be effective, must be prompt, not that the federal courts must be deprived entirely of jurisdiction to grant equitable relief. Denial of an injunction when a strike violates the agreement may have effects just as devastating to an employer as the issuance of an injunction may have to the union when the strike does not violate the agreement. Furthermore, a sympathy strike does not directly further the economic interests of the members of the striking local or contribute to the resolution of any dispute between that local, or its members, and the employer. On the contrary, it is the source of a new dispute which, if the strike goes forward, will impose costs on the strikers, the employer, and the public without prospect of any direct benefit to any of these parties. A rule that authorizes postponement of a sympathy strike pending an arbitrator's clarification of the no-strike clause will not critically impair the vital interests of the striking local even if the right to strike is upheld, and will avoid the costs of interrupted production if the arbitrator concludes that the no-strike clause applies.

Finally, the Norris-LaGuardia Act cannot be interpreted to immunize the union from all risk of an erroneously issued injunction. *Boys Markets* itself subjected the union to the risk of an injunction entered upon a judge's erroneous conclusion that the dispute was arbitrable and that the strike was in violation of the no-strike clause. *Gateway Coal* subjected the union to a still greater risk, for the court there entered an injunction to enforce an implied no-strike clause despite the fact that the arbitrability of the dispute, and hence the legality of the strike over the dispute, presented a "substantial question of contractual interpretation." The strict reading that the Union would give the Norris-LaGuardia Act would not have permitted this result.

These considerations, however, do not support the conclusion that a sympathy strike should be temporarily enjoined whenever a collective bargaining agreement contains a no-strike clause and an arbitration clause. The accommodation between the Norris-LaGuardia Act and § 301(a) of the Labor Management Relations Act allows the judge to apply "the usual processes of the law" but not to take the place of the arbitrator. Because of the risk that a federal judge, less expert in labor matters than an arbitrator, may misconstrue general contract language, I would agree that no injunction or temporary restraining order should issue without first giving the union an adequate opportunity to present evidence and argument, particularly upon the proper interpretation of the collective bargaining agreement; the judge should not issue an injunction without convincing evidence that the strike is clearly within the no-strike clause.[27] Furthermore, to protect the efficacy of arbitration, any such injunction should require the parties to submit the issue immediately to the contractual grievance procedure, and if the union so requests, at the last stage and upon an expedited schedule that assures a decision by the arbitrator as soon as practicable. Such stringent conditions would insure that only strikes in violation of the agreement would be enjoined and that the union's access to the arbitration process would not be foreclosed by the com-

---

[27] Of course, it is possible that an arbitrator would disagree with the court even when the latter finds the strike to be clearly prohibited. But in that case, the arbitrator's determination would govern, provided it withstands the ordinary standard of review for arbitrator's awards. *See United Steelworkers of America v. Enterprise Wheel & Car Corp.*, 363 U.S. 593, 597-599.

bined effect of a temporary injunction and protected grievance procedures. Finally, as in *Boys Markets,* the normal conditions of equitable relief would have to be met.

Like the decision in *Boys Markets,* this opinion reflects, on the one hand, my confidence that experience during the decades since the Norris-LaGuardia Act was passed has dissipated any legitimate concern about the impartiality of federal judges in disputes between labor and management, and on the other, my continued recognition of the fact that judges have less familiarity and expertise than arbitrators and administrators who regularly work in this specialized area. The decision in *Boys Markets* requires an accommodation between the Norris-LaGuardia Act and the Labor Management Relations Act. I would hold only that the terms of that accommodation do not entirely deprive the federal courts of all power to grant any relief to an employer, threatened with irreparable injury from a sympathy strike clearly in violation of a collective bargaining agreement, regardless of the equities of his claim for injunctive relief pending arbitration....

NOTES

1. Doesn't *Buffalo Forge* clearly flout the *Boys Markets* policy of substituting arbitration for strikes? On the other hand, if a Justice was uneasy that *Boys Markets* itself may have come close to flouting the congressional policy expressed in Norris-LaGuardia (*see* Justice Black's majority opinion in *Sinclair Ref.,* quoted *supra,*), might he or she not feel more comfortable in limiting federal injunctions so that the enjoinable no-strike *quid* is coextensive with the arbitration *quo? See, e.g., Westmoreland Coal Co. v. Mine Workers,* 910 F.2d 130 (4th Cir. 1990) (affirming injunction against a work stoppage protesting the employer's discipline of sympathy strikers because issue was arbitrable). In any event, how can the Court justify under a strict *Boys Markets-Buffalo Forge* analysis the federal courts' willingness to "specifically enforce" an arbitrator's order that a union cease striking over an issue not itself subject to arbitration? *See, e.g., New Orleans S.S. Ass'n v. Longshore Workers Local 1418,* 389 F.2d 369 (5th Cir.), *cert. denied,* 393 U.S. 828 (1968); *Pacific Maritime Ass'n v. Longshoremen's Ass'n,* 454 F.2d 262 (9th Cir. 1971).

2. Applying *Buffalo Forge,* the Supreme Court held (6-3) that a *Boys Markets* injunction was unavailable against a longshoremen's union which, despite a no-strike clause, refused to handle cargo destined for the Soviet Union as a political protest against the Russian invasion of Afghanistan. The underlying political dispute was considered "plainly not arbitrable under the collective bargaining agreement." *Jacksonville Bulk Terms., Inc. v. ILA,* 457 U.S. 702 (1982). *See* Rasnic, *Boys Markets and the Labor Injunction Revisited: Jacksonville Bulk Terminals,* 33 Lab. L.J. 704 (1982).

3. In *Cedar Coal Co. v. UMW,* 560 F.2d 1153 (4th Cir. 1977), *cert. denied,* 434 U.S. 1047 (1978), noted in 63 Cornell L. Rev. 507 (1978), the court ruled that some wildcat sympathy strikes in the coal industry may be subject to injunctive relief, despite the Supreme Court's holding in *Buffalo Forge*. Where "the purpose of the strike of Local [A] was to compel [the company] to concede an arbitrable issue to Local [B], with the same employer, the same collective bargaining agreement, the same bargaining unit, and the cause of Local [B] made its own, the *Buffalo Forge* exception to *Boys Markets* should not apply." *Cf. U.S. Steel Corp. v. UMW*, 593 F.2d 201 (3d Cir. 1979), *noted in* 48 Geo. Wash. L. Rev. 124 (1979).

4. When a jury determines in a § 301 damage action that a sympathy strike contravened the contractual no-strike clause, a subsequent arbitral award finding that the general no-strike provision did not apply to sympathy stoppages is not controlling, since the arbitrator is bound by the res judicata effect of the prior jury finding. *See John Morrell & Co. v. UFCW Local 304A*, 913 F.2d 544 (8th Cir. 1990), *cert. denied*, 500 U.S. 905 (1991). *See generally* Note, *Damage Remedies for Sympathy Strikes After Buffalo Forge*, 78 Colum. L. Rev. 1664 (1978).

5. *Buffalo Forge* has provided a feast for the law reviews. *See, e.g.,* Cantor, *Buffalo Forge and Injunctions Against Employer Breaches of Collective Bargaining Agreements*, 1980 Wis. L. Rev. 247; Freed, *Injunctions Against Sympathy Strikes: In Defense of Buffalo Forge*, 54 N.Y.U.L. Rev. 289 (1979); Gould, *On Labor Injunctions Pending Arbitration: Recasting Buffalo Forge*, 30 Stan. L. Rev. 533 (1978); Lowden & Flaherty, *Sympathy Strikes, Arbitration Policy, and the Enforceability of No-Strike Agreements: An Analysis of Buffalo Forge*, 45 Geo. Wash. L. Rev. 633 (1977); Smith, *The Supreme Court, Boys Markets Labor Injunctions, and Sympathy Work Stoppages*, 44 U. Chi. L. Rev. 321 (1977). The case (or its issue) is noted in 76 Colum. L. Rev. 113 (1976); 29 U. Fla. L. Rev. 525 (1977); 53 Texas L. Rev. 1086 (1975).

Complete Auto Transit, Inc. v. Reis, 451 U.S. 401, 101 S. Ct. 1836, 68 L. Ed. 2d 248 (1981). Believing their union was not properly representing them in contract negotiations, a group of employees engaged in a "wildcat" or unauthorized strike in violation of a no-strike clause in the collective bargaining agreement between their employers and the union. Previously, in *Atkinson v. Sinclair Ref. Co.*, 370 U.S. 238 (1962), the Supreme Court had held that § 301 did not authorize a damage action against individual union officers and members when their union was liable for violating a no-strike provision. Now a majority of the Court extended that immunity to situations where the individuals striking in breach of contract were not acting on behalf of the union but in their "personal and nonunion capacity." Justice Brennan, for the Court, recognized that § 301(b) by its terms only "forbids a money judgment entered against a union from being enforced against individual union members." But he declared that "the legislative history of § 301 clearly reveals Congress' intent to shield individual employees from liability for damages arising from their breach of the no-strike clause of a collective bargaining agreement, whether or not the union participated in or authorized the illegality." This was so, he added, "even though it might leave the employer unable to recover for his losses." The Court thought that employer or union discipline of wildcatting workers would constitute a sufficient sanction. It expressly left open the question of whether a *Boys Markets* injunction would be available against wildcatters. Chief Justice Burger and Justice Rehnquist dissented on the grounds that § 301(b) merely "affords individual union members protection against individual liability for collective action," and did not change "the common law rule of contract law of *individual* liability for *individual* conduct." The dissenters regarded such measures as employer discharge or union discipline of wildcat strikers as "no answer; they may be too little and they surely come too late."

NOTES

1. Would a *Boys Markets* injunction have been available against the individual wildcat strikers in *Complete Auto Transit*? *See Hobet Mining, Inc. v. UMW Local 5817,* 143 L.R.R.M. 2302 (S.D. W.Va. 1993). The principal case was noted in 59 Denver L.J. 577 (1982); 49 Tenn. L. Rev. 179 (1981). *See also* Coulson, *Justice Brennan on Wheels: Complete Auto Transit, Best Freight and Clayton v. UAW,* in N.Y.U. Thirty-Fourth Annual Conference on Labor 139 (1981).

2. The Supreme Court held in *Carbon Fuel Co. v. UMW,* 444 U.S. 212 (1979), that an international union which "neither instigates, supports, ratifies, or encourages" wildcat strikes engaged in by local unions in violation of a collective bargaining agreement is not liable in damages to affected employers even if the international "did not use all reasonable means available to it to prevent the strikes or bring about their termination." Why was a judgment against the international union in *Carbon Fuel* so important to the plaintiffs in view of the fact that they had a very substantial judgment against the local unions? Briefs for the coal operators alleged that the "local assets are negligible" and "most Local Unions of the UMWA are, for all practical purposes, judgment proof."

3. At the trial of the *Carbon Fuel* case, the locals were held responsible for the wildcat action of their members on a "mass action" theory—that "large groups of men do not act collectively without leadership and a functioning union must be held responsible for the mass action of its members. However, responsibility for wildcat strikes under this theory will ordinarily be limited to the local union." 582 F.2d 1346 (4th Cir. 1978). Supreme Court review of the judgment against the local was not sought and so *Carbon Fuel* did not afford an opportunity for the Supreme Court to consider the "mass action" theory. Its continuing vitality was accepted in *North River Energy Corp. v. UMW,* 664 F.2d 1184 (11th Cir. 1981); *Consolidation Coal Co. v. UMW Local 1702,* 709 F.2d 882 (4th Cir.), *cert. de-*

nied, 464 U.S. 993 (1983). *Contra, Consolidation Coal Co. v. UMW Local 1261,* 725 F.2d 1258 (10th Cir. 1984); *Philadelphia Marine Trade Ass'n v. Longshoremen (ILA) Local 1291,* 909 F.2d 754 (3d Cir. 1990), *cert. denied,* 498 U.S. 1083 (1991). *See also* Cureton & Kisch, *Union Liability for Illegal Strikes: The Mass Action Theory Redefined,* 87 W. Va. L. Rev. 57 (1984-85).

4. If the employer as well as the union is entitled to refer a matter to arbitration, the union can get a stay of a court suit for damages by the employer, pending arbitration, even though the union has allegedly struck in violation of the contract. *Drake Bakeries, Inc. v. Bakery Workers Local 50,* 370 U.S. 254 (1962). Declared the Court: "We can enforce both the no-strike clause and the agreement to arbitrate by granting a stay until the claim for damages is presented to an arbitrator." In response to the employer's argument that the parties could not have intended to arbitrate "so fundamental a matter as a union strike in breach of contract," the Court said: "Arbitration provisions, which themselves have not been repudiated, are meant to survive breaches of contract, in many contexts, even total breach.... We do not decide in this case that in no circumstances would a strike in violation of the no-strike clause contained in this or other contracts entitle the employer to rescind or abandon the entire contract or to declare its promise to arbitrate forever discharged." The union's right to arbitrate may survive even a prolonged strike. *Packinghouse Workers Local 721 v. Needham Packing Co.,* 376 U.S. 247 (1964).

Has the Supreme Court in *Drake* and *Needham* read the "substantial breach" doctrine out of the federal labor contract law being developed under § 301? *See* Summers, *Collective Agreements and the Law of Contracts,* 78 Yale L.J. 525 (1969). *Cf. Steelworkers Local 14055 v. NLRB (Dow Chem. Co.),* 530 F.2d 266 (3d Cir.), *cert. denied,* 429 U.S. 834 (1976); *Mastro Plastics Corp. v. NLRB, supra,* and accompanying notes.

5. Some years ago a committee of the American Bar Association echoed a common sentiment when it said, "We feel that damage suits are generally not good medicine for labor relations." *See* Fulda, *The No-Strike Clause,* 21 Geo. Wash. L. Rev. 127, 144 (1952) (Report of the Committee on Improvement of Administration of Union-Employer Contracts, ABA Section of Labor Relations Law). Later, however, there appeared to be a trend toward attempting to secure damages for breach of unions' no-strike pledges. *See, e.g.,* Fairweather, *Employer Actions and Options in Response to Strikes in Breach of Contract,* in N.Y.U. Eighteenth Annual Conference on Labor 129 (1966); Bartlett, Newman & Mauro, *Strikes in Violation of the Contract: A Management View; A Union View,* in N.Y.U. Thirty-First Annual Conference on Labor 117 (1978) (two separate papers); Stewart, *No-Strike Clauses in the Federal Courts,* 59 Mich. L. Rev. 673 (1961). One district court awarded punitive as well as compensatory damages under § 301 for a strike in breach of contract. *Sidney Wanzer & Sons v. Milk Drivers, Local 753,* 249 F. Supp. 664 (N.D. Ill. 1966), *noted in* 80 Harv. L. Rev. 903 (1967) and 52 Va. L. Rev. 1377 (1966). But a court of appeals refused to uphold punitive damages under § 301 when an employer violated a contract through a runaway shop. *Shoe Workers Local 127 v. Brooks Shoe Mfg. Co.,* 298 F.2d 277 (3d Cir. 1962). In *Teamsters Local 20 v. Morton,* 377 U.S. 252 (1964), the Supreme Court held that punitive damages could not be recovered for peaceful secondary activities forbidden by § 303 of the LMRA. Are the language and policy of § 301 and § 303 distinguishable on this issue? *See generally* Brandwen, *Punitive-Exemplary Damages in Labor Relations Litigation,* 29 U. Chi. L. Rev. 460 (1962); Ratner, *Damage Actions and the Impact of the Morton Case,* in N.Y.U. Eighteenth Annual Conference on Labor 117 (1966).

D. CONTRACT RIGHTS AND STATUTORY RIGHTS— OVERLAPPING LAW AND FORUMS

1. WITHIN THE FEDERAL SYSTEM

In enacting § 301 of the LMRA, Congress chose not to make breaches of the collective agreement unfair labor practices subject to the jurisdiction of the NLRB; instead, it left the enforcement of the labor contract to "the usual processes of the law." H.R. Conf. Rep. No. 510, 80th Cong., 1st Sess. 42 (1947). Nonetheless, the parties to a labor agreement may include a provision paralleling § 8(a)(3) by forbidding discrimination against employees because of union activity (or because of race or sex, thus paralleling Title VII of the 1964 Civil Rights Act). The parties may also provide for arbitration of disputes about the scope of the bargaining unit. At the same time, the Board regards an employer's unilateral change in working conditions, without bargaining, as a violation of § 8(a)(5)— and where a collective agreement is in existence, that agreement is obviously the standard of many if not all working conditions in a unit. Moreover, § 8(d) makes it part of the duty to bargain to refrain from a strike or lockout to "terminate or modify" a contract prior to its expiration date. The inevitable result of all this is the possibility of overlap, or even conflict, between contractual rights and duties and statutory rights and duties.

The practical implications of this overlap may appear in several contexts: (1) before the NLRB, the respondent may claim (a) the allegation in the charge has already been the subject of an arbitral award in the respondent's favor, which the Board should "honor," or (b) the allegation could be the subject of a grievance under the parties' own contract, and the Board should therefore "defer" to arbitration; or (2) before a court (or arbitrator), the defendant may argue the matter involves an unfair labor practice or representational question subject to the exclusive primary jurisdiction of the Labor Board. The materials to follow deal with these various situations. In the leading case of *Spielberg Mfg. Co.,* 112 N.L.R.B. 1080, 1082 (1955), the Board set forth three general conditions under which it would accord "recognition" to an arbitrator's award: "[T]he proceedings appear to have been fair and regular, all parties had agreed to be bound, and the decision of the arbitration panel is not clearly repugnant to the purposes and policies of the Act." The application (and limitations) of this formula will be considered next.

Analogous but even more sensitive problems arise in the relationship between contract administration and the enforcement of civil rights legislation. *See infra* Section IV.C.

NLRB v. C & C PLYWOOD CORP.

Supreme Court of the United States
385 U.S. 421, 87 S. Ct. 559, 17 L. Ed. 2d 486 (1967)

MR. JUSTICE STEWART delivered the opinion of the Court.

The respondent employer was brought before the National Labor Relations Board to answer a complaint that its inauguration of a premium pay plan during the term of a collective agreement, without prior consultation with the union representing its employees, violated the duties imposed by §§ 8(a)(5) and (1) of the National Labor Relations Act. The Board issued a cease-and-desist order, rejecting the claim that the respondent's action was authorized by the collective agreement....[2]

In August 1962, the Plywood, Lumber, and Saw Mill Workers Local No. 2405 was certified as the bargaining representative of the respondent's production and maintenance employees. The agreement which resulted from collective bargaining contained the following provision:

Article XVII

WAGES

A. A classified wage scale has been agreed upon by the Employer and Union, and has been signed by the parties and thereby made a part of the written agreement. The Employer reserves the right to pay a premium rate over and above the contractual classified wage rate to reward any particular employee for some special fitness, skill, aptitude or the like. The payment of such a premium rate shall not be considered a permanent increase in the rate of that position and may, at the sole option of the Employer, be reduced to the contractual rate....

The agreement also stipulated that wages should be "closed" during the period it was effective and that neither party should be obligated to bargain collectively with respect to any matter not specifically referred to in the contract. Grievance machinery was established, but no ultimate arbitration of grievances or other disputes was provided.

---

[2] The NLRB's order directed respondent to bargain with the union upon the latter's request and similarly to rescind any payment plan which it had unilaterally instituted.

Less than three weeks after this agreement was signed, the respondent posted a notice that all members of the "glue spreader" crews would be paid $2.50 per hour if their crews met specified biweekly (and later weekly) production standards, although under the "classified wage scale" referred to in the above quoted Art. XVII of the agreement, the members of these crews were to be paid hourly wages ranging from $2.15 to $2.29, depending upon their function within the crew. When the union learned of this premium pay plan through one of its members, it immediately asked for a conference with the respondent. During the meetings between the parties which followed this request, the employer indicated a willingness to discuss the terms of the plan, but refused to rescind it pending those discussions.

It was this refusal which prompted the union to charge the respondent with an unfair labor practice in violation of §§ 8(a)(5) and (1). The trial examiner found that the respondent had instituted the premium-pay program in good-faith reliance upon the right reserved to it in the collective agreement. He, therefore, dismissed the complaint. The Board reversed. Giving consideration to the history of negotiations between the parties, as well as the express provisions of the collective agreement, the Board ruled the union had not ceded power to the employer unilaterally to change the wage system as it had. For while the agreement specified different hourly pay for different members of the glue spreader crews and allowed for merit increases for "particular employee[s]," the employer had placed all the members of these crews on the same wage scale and had made it a function of the production output of the crew as a whole.

In refusing to enforce the Board's order, the Court of Appeals did not decide that the premium-pay provision of the labor agreement had been misinterpreted by the Board. Instead, it held the Board did not have jurisdiction to find the respondent had violated § 8(a) of the Labor Act, because the "existence ... of an unfair labor practice [did] not turn entirely upon the provisions of the Act, but arguably upon a good-faith dispute as to the correct meaning of the provisions of the collective bargaining agreement...." 351 F.2d at 228.

The respondent does not question the proposition that an employer may not unilaterally institute merit increases during the term of a collective agreement unless some provision of the contract authorizes him to do so. *See NLRB v. J.H. Allison & Co.,* 165 F.2d 766 (6th Cir. 1948), *cert. denied,* 335 U.S. 814 (1948). *Cf. Beacon Pierce Dyeing Co.,* 121 N.L.R.B. 953 (1958). The argument is, rather, that since the contract contained a provision which *might* have allowed the respondent to institute the wage plan in question, the Board was powerless to determine whether that provision *did* authorize the respondent's action, because the question was one for a state or federal court under § 301 of the Act.

In evaluating this contention, it is important first to point out that the collective bargaining agreement contained no arbitration clause.[9] The contract did provide grievance procedures, but the end result of those procedures, if differences between the parties remained unresolved, was economic warfare, not "the therapy of arbitration." *Carey v. Westinghouse Corp.,* 375 U.S. 261, 272 (1964). Thus, the Board's action in this case was in no way inconsistent with its previous recognition of arbitration as "an instrument of national labor policy for composing contractual differences." *International Harvester Co.,* 138 N.L.R.B. 923, 926 (1962), *aff'd sub nom., Ramsey v. NLRB,* 327 F.2d 784 (7th Cir. 1964), *cert. denied,* 377 U.S. 1003 (1964).

The respondent's argument rests primarily upon the legislative history of the 1947 amendments to the National Labor Relations Act. It is said that the rejection by Congress of a bill which would have given the Board unfair labor practice jurisdiction over all breaches of collective bargaining agreements shows that the Board is without power to decide any case involving the interpretation of a labor contract. We do not draw that inference from this legislative history.

When Congress determined that the Board should not have general jurisdiction over all alleged violations of collective bargaining agreements and that such matters should be placed within the jurisdiction of the courts, it was acting upon a principle which this Court had already recognized:

> The Railway Labor Act, like the National Labor Relations Act, does not undertake governmental regulation of wages, hours, or working conditions. Instead it seeks to provide a means by which agreement may be reached with respect to them.

Terminal Railroad Ass'n v. Brotherhood of Railroad Trainmen, 318 U.S. 1, 6 (1943). To have conferred upon the National Labor Relations Board generalized power to determine the rights of parties under all collective agreements would have been a step toward governmental regulation of the terms of those agreements. We view Congress' decision not to give the Board that broad power as a refusal to take this step.

But in this case the Board has not construed a labor agreement to determine the extent of the contractual rights which were given the union by the employer. It has not imposed its own view of what the terms and conditions of the labor agreement should be. It has done no more than merely enforce a statutory right which Congress considered necessary to allow labor and management to get on with the process of reaching fair terms and conditions of employment—"to provide a means by which agreement may be reached." The Board's interpretation went only so far as was necessary to determine that the union did not agree to

---

[9] The Court of Appeals in this case relied upon its previous decision in *Square D Co. v. NLRB,* 332 F.2d 360 (9th Cir. 1964). But *Square D* involved a collective agreement that provided for arbitration. *See* Note, *Use of Arbitration Clause,* 41 Ind. L.J. 455, 469 (1966).

give up these statutory safeguards. Thus, the Board, in necessarily construing a labor agreement to decide this unfair labor practice case, has not exceeded the jurisdiction laid out for it by Congress.

This conclusion is re-enforced by previous judicial recognition that a contractual defense does not divest the Labor Board of jurisdiction. For example, in *Mastro Plastics Corp. v. NLRB,* 350 U.S. 270 (1956), the legality of an employer's refusal to reinstate strikers was based upon the Board's construction of a "no strike" clause in the labor agreement, which the employer contended allowed him to refuse to take back workers who had walked out in protest over his unfair labor practice....

If the Board in a case like this had no jurisdiction to consider a collective agreement prior to an authoritative construction by the courts, labor organizations would face inordinate delays in obtaining vindication of their statutory rights. Where, as here, the parties have not provided for arbitration, the union would have to institute a court action to determine the applicability of the premium pay provision of the collective bargaining agreement.[15] If it succeeded in court, the union would then have to go back to the Labor Board to begin an unfair labor practice proceeding. It is not unlikely that this would add years to the already lengthy period required to gain relief from the Board. Congress cannot have intended to place such obstacles in the way of the Board's effective enforcement of statutory duties. For in the labor field, as in few others, time is crucially important in obtaining relief....

The legislative history of the Labor Act, the precedent interpreting it, and the interest of its efficient administration thus all lead to the conclusion that the Board had jurisdiction to deal with the unfair labor practice charge in this case. We hold that the Court of Appeals was in error in deciding to the contrary.

The remaining question, not reached by the Court of Appeals, is whether the Board was wrong in concluding that the contested provision in the collective agreement gave the respondent no unilateral right to institute its premium pay plan. In reaching this conclusion, the Board relied upon its experience with labor relations and the Act's clear emphasis upon the protection of free collective bargaining. We cannot disapprove of the Board's approach. For the law of labor agreements cannot be based upon abstract definitions unrelated to the context in which the parties bargained and the basic regulatory scheme underlying that context. *See* Cox, *The Legal Nature of Collective Bargaining Agreements,* 57 Mich. L. Rev. 1 (1958). Nor can we say that the Board was wrong in holding that the union had not foregone its statutory right to bargain about the pay plan inaugurated by the respondent. For the disputed contract provision referred to in-

---

[15]The precise nature of the union's case in court is not readily apparent. If damages for breach of contract were sought, the union would have difficulty in establishing the amount of injury caused by respondent's action. For the real injury in this case is to the union's status as bargaining representative, and it would be difficult to translate such damage into dollars and cents....

creases for "particular employee[s]," not groups of workers. And there was nothing in it to suggest that the carefully worked out wage differentials for various members of the glue spreader crew would be invalidated by the respondent's decision to pay all members of the crew the same wage....

Reversed and remanded.

NOTES

1. Would the result in the principal case have been different if the collective bargaining agreement had contained a provision for final and binding arbitration? If so, on what theory? Does an arbitration clause constitute an agreement to channel collective bargaining in a particular way, or a waiver of a statutory right to bargain? *See, e.g., Timken Roller Bearing Co. v. NLRB,* 161 F.2d 949 (6th Cir. 1947); *Square D Co. v. NLRB,* 332 F.2d 360 (9th Cir. 1964). If so, why wasn't a similar agreement or waiver found in the contract in the principal case, which provided for a grievance procedure and, presumably, permitted a court suit if necessary to resolve disputes? In *NLRB v. Huttig Sash & Door Co.,* 377 F.2d 964 (8th Cir. 1967), a court of appeals, relying on *C & C Plywood,* upheld the Board's jurisdiction to find an employer guilty of an unfair labor practice in unilaterally reducing wages, even though the contract contained an arbitration clause.

2. Why did the "zipper clause" in the principal case play no significant part in the Court's thinking? Is there a difference between a union's waiver of the right to demand bargaining over a change in working conditions proposed by the union, and a union's waiver of the right to object to, or demand bargaining over, a change in working conditions proposed (or imposed) by the employer? Can the "residual rights" theory of the labor contract (*see supra* Section III.B.2) be squared with the principal case? *See, e.g., Ciba-Geigy Pharmaceuticals Div. v. NLRB,* 722 F.2d 1120 (3d Cir. 1983).

3. Would C & C Plywood Corp. have avoided violating § 8(a)(5) if it had bargained with the union before instituting the premium pay rates? Would that depend on whether or not the unilateral granting of premium pay was a breach of contract? What if the union had been offered and had rejected an opportunity to bargain? *See C & S Indus.,* 158 N.L.R.B. 454 (1966), where the Board held an employer's unilateral establishment of an incentive wage system violated § 8(a)(5), even though the union declined to discuss the issue, the labor agreement forbade any change in the method of paying employees without the union's consent, and contract disputes were subject to arbitration.

4. Although a breach of contract as such is not an unfair labor practice, *C & S Indus., supra,* the NLRB will direct a party to "honor" a repudiated contract, *Hyde's Super Mkt.,* 145 N.L.R.B. 1252, *enforced,* 339 F.2d 568 (9th Cir. 1964); *Crescent Bed Co.,* 157 N.L.R.B. 296 (1966). Remedies have included orders to pay any fringe benefits which would have accrued to employees under a contract the employer unlawfully refused to sign, *NLRB v. Strong,* 393 U.S. 357 (1969), and to compensate employees for losses incurred because of a unilaterally imposed rider to an insurance policy, *Scam Instrument Corp.,* 163 N.L.R.B. 284 (1967), *enforced,* 394 F.2d 884 (7th Cir.), *cert. denied,* 393 U.S. 980 (1968). Is it still meaningful to say that the enforcement of collective bargaining agreements is a matter for the courts and not for the NLRB? What policy considerations support the enlargement of the Board's role? Can this be reconciled with the congressional decision not to make breaches of contract unfair labor practices but to subject them to court jurisdiction under § 301 of the LMRA?

Is there a meaningful line between contract breaches that are and are not also § 8(a)(5) violations? *Compare Xidex Corp.,* 297 N.L.R.B. 110 (1989), *enforced,* 924 F.2d 245 (D.C. Cir. 1991) (no § 8(a)(5) violation when an employer refused to arbitrate two individual grievances, since not a "wholesale repudiation" of arbitration) *and Velan Valve Corp.,* 316 N.L.R.B. 1273 (1995) (employer's refusal to arbitrate a grievance protesting the subcontracting of unit work did not violate § 8(a)(5), since it was not a "wholesale repudiation" of the contractual arbitration procedure) *with Rangaire Acquisition Corp.,* 309 N.L.R.B. 1043 (1992), *enforced,* 9 F.3d 104 (5th Cir. 1993) (employer violated § 8(a)(5) by denying extra 15 minutes for lunch break on Thanksgiving, since it constituted a "material, substantial, and significant" change in terms of employment).

In *American Protective Servs.,* 319 N.L.R.B. 902 (1995), a union stated that it intended to submit an employer's final offer to the membership and would be bound by the vote, but would recommend against ratification. After the ballots had been cast but before they were counted, the employer withdrew its proposal. A 2-1 Board majority ruled that the repudiation of the ratification procedure and the withdrawal of the offer violated § 8(a)(5). The dissenter insisted there was no bilateral agreement on the ratification procedure. The union had merely announced its intent, but had not promised, to use that procedure. The Fourth Circuit accepted the dissenter's view and denied enforcement. *American Protective Servs. v. NLRB,* 113 F.3d 504 (4th Cir. 1997).

5. According to the First Circuit, a federal district court's finding that no collective bargaining agreement exists collaterally estops the NLRB from later determining there is an enforceable contract. *NLRB v. Donna-Lee Sportswear Co.,* 836 F.2d 31 (1987).

6. *See generally* Bloch, *The NLRB and Arbitration: Is the Board's Expanding Jurisdiction Justified?* 19 Lab. L.J. 640 (1968); Bond, *The Concurrence Conundrum: The Overlapping Jurisdiction of Arbitration and the NLRB,* 42 S. Cal. L. Rev. 4 (1968); Cushman, *Arbitration and the Duty to Bargain,* 1967 Wis. L. Rev. 612; Lesnick, *Arbitration as a Limit on the Discretion of Management, Union, and NLRB: The Year's Major Developments,* in N.Y.U. Eighteenth Annual Conference on Labor 7, 22-30 (1966); Wollett, *The Agreement and the National Labor Relations Act: Courts, Arbitrators and the NLRB—Who Decides What?* 14 Lab. L.J. 1041 (1963).

MILWAUKEE SPRING DIVISION OF ILLINOIS COIL SPRING CO.

National Labor Relations Board
268 N.L.R.B. 601 (1984), *aff'd sub nom.*
UAW v. NLRB, 765 F.2d 175 (D.C. Cir. 1985)

On 22 October 1982 the ... Board held that Respondent violated the Act [§ 8(a)(1), (3), and (5)] by deciding without the Union's consent to transfer its assembly operations from its unionized Milwaukee Spring facility to its unorganized McHenry Spring facility during the term of a collective-bargaining agreement because of the comparatively higher labor costs under the agreement, and to lay off unit employees as a consequence of that decision....

The Board has reconsidered its Decision and Order in light of the entire record and the oral arguments and has decided to reverse that decision and dismiss the complaint.

I. *Factual Background*

Illinois Coil Spring Company consists of three divisions—Holly Spring, McHenry Spring, and Respondent (Milwaukee Spring). The parties stipulated that, although collectively the four entities are a single employer, each location constitutes a separate bargaining unit.

Respondent, at material times, employed about 99 bargaining unit employees. These employees worked in eight departments, including an assembly operations department and a molding operations department.

The Union has represented Respondent's bargaining unit employees for a number of years. The most recent contract became effective on 1 April 1980, and remained in effect until at least 31 March 1983. The contract contains specific wage and benefits provisions. The contract also provides that the Company "recognizes the Union as the sole and exclusive collective bargaining agent for all production and maintenance employees in the Company's plant at Milwaukee, Wisconsin."

On 26 January 1982 Respondent asked the Union to forgo a scheduled wage increase and to grant other contract concessions. In March, because Respondent lost a major customer, it proposed to the Union relocating its assembly operations in the nonunionized McHenry facility, located in McHenry, Illinois, to obtain relief from the comparatively higher assembly labor costs at Milwaukee Spring. Respondent also advised the Union that it needed wage and benefit concessions to keep its molding operations in Milwaukee viable. On 23 March the Union rejected the proposed reduction in wages and benefits. On 29 March Respondent submitted to the Union a document entitled "Terms Upon Which Milwaukee Assembly Operations Will Be Retained in Milwaukee." On 4 April the Union rejected the Company's proposal for alternatives to relocation and declined to bargain further over the Company's decision to transfer its assembly operations. The

Company then announced its decision to relocate the Milwaukee assembly operations to the McHenry facility.

The parties stipulated that the relocation decision was economically motivated and was not the result of union animus. The parties also stipulated that Respondent has satisfied its obligation to bargain with the Union over the decision to relocate the assembly operations and has been willing to engage in effects bargaining with the Union.[5]

II. *Midterm Modification of Contracts Under Section 8(d)*

A. ... Generally, an employer may not unilaterally institute changes regarding these mandatory subjects before reaching a good-faith impasse in bargaining. Section 8(d) imposes an additional requirement when a collective-bargaining agreement is in effect and an employer seeks to "modif[y] ... the terms and conditions contained in" the contract: the employer must obtain the union's consent before implementing the change. If the employment conditions the employer seeks to change are not "contained in" the contract, however, the employer's obligation remains the general one of bargaining in good faith to impasse over the subject before instituting the proposed change.

Applying these principles to the instant case, before the Board may hold that Respondent violated Section 8(d), the Board first must identify a specific term "contained in" the contract that the Company's decision to relocate modified. In *Milwaukee Spring I,* the Board never specified the contract term that was modified by Respondent's decision to relocate the assembly operations. The Board's failure to do so is not surprising, for we have searched the contract in vain for a provision requiring bargaining unit work to remain in Milwaukee.

Milwaukee Spring I suggests, however, that the Board may have concluded that Respondent's relocation decision, because it was motivated by a desire to obtain relief from the Milwaukee contract's labor costs, modified that contract's wage and benefits provision. We believe this reasoning is flawed. While it is true that the Company proposed modifying the wage and benefits provision of the contract, the Union rejected the proposals. Following its failure to obtain the Union's consent, Respondent, in accord with Section 8(d), abandoned the proposals to modify the contract's wage and benefits provisions. Instead, Respondent decided to transfer the assembly operations to a different plant where different workers (who were not subject to the contract) would perform the work. In

---

[5]The parties' stipulation and the manner in which they briefed this case treat Respondent's relocation decision as a mandatory subject of bargaining. The dissent nevertheless insists on discussing at length what it terms the "threshold issue" of whether Respondent had a duty to bargain over its decision. Based on the facts before us, we find no reason to enter this discussion. We do not find it necessary to decide whether the work relocation here was a mandatory subject of bargaining under the Supreme Court's decision in *First National Maintenance Corp. v. NLRB,* 452 U.S. 666 (1981).

short, Respondent did not disturb the wages and benefits at its Milwaukee facility, and consequently did not violate Section 8(d) by modifying, without the Union's consent, the wage and benefits provisions contained in the contract.[9]

Nor do we find that Respondent's relocation decision modified the contract's recognition clause. In two previous cases, the Board construed recognition clauses to encompass the duties performed by bargaining unit employees and held that employers' reassignment of work modified those clauses. In both instances, reviewing courts found no basis for reading jurisdictional rights into standard clauses that merely recognized the contracts' coverage of specified employees. *Boeing Co.*, 230 NLRB 696 (1977), enf. denied 581 F.2d 793 (9th Cir. 1978); *University of Chicago*, 210 NLRB 190 (1974), enf. denied 514 F.2d 942 (7th Cir. 1975). We agree with the courts' reasoning.

Language recognizing the Union as the bargaining agent "for all production and maintenance employees in the Company's plant at Milwaukee, Wisconsin," does not state that the functions that the unit performs must remain in Milwaukee. No doubt parties could draft such a clause; indeed, work-preservation clauses are commonplace. It is not for the Board, however, to create an implied work-preservation clause in every American labor agreement based on wage and benefits or recognition provisions, and we expressly decline to do so.[10]

In sum, we find in the instant case that neither wage and benefits provisions nor the recognition clause contained in the collective-bargaining agreement preserves bargaining unit work at the Milwaukee facility for the duration of the contract, and that Respondent did not modify these contract terms when it decided to relocate its assembly operations. Further, we find that no other term contained in the contract restricts Respondent's decision-making regarding relocation.

---

[9] *Oak Cliff-Golman* illustrates a midterm modification of wage provisions. In that case, the contract contained wage rates that the respondent unilaterally reduced during the life of the contract. Respondent in the instant case, having unsuccessfully sought the Union's consent to modify the contractual wages and benefits, left those provisions intact....

[10] In *Boeing*, the court stated:

> Since the purpose of the Act is to encourage labor/management peace by resolving differences through collective-bargaining and to stabilize *agreed upon* conditions during the term of a [contract], *Steelworkers v. Warrior and Gulf Co.*, 363 U.S. 574, 578 ... (1960), a rejection of the Board's position here would seem to further the purpose of the Act. Rather than stretching the meaning of a Recognition Clause "impliedly," "implicitly," or "in effect" to cover "functions" (as did the Board), a decision against the Board would encourage the parties affirmatively to negotiate an explicit "Jurisdictional Clause" to be included in the next [contract]. [581 F.2d at 798. Emphasis in original.]

B.[11] Our dissenting colleague and the decision in *Milwaukee Spring I* fail to recognize that decision's substantial departure from NLRB textbook law that an employer need not obtain a union's consent on a matter not contained in the body of a collective-bargaining agreement even though the subject is a mandatory subject of bargaining. *See, e.g., Ozark Trailers,* 161 NLRB 561 (1966). Although the Board found a violation in *Ozark,* it did so grounded on the employer's failure to bargain over its decision to close a part of its operation during the collective-bargaining agreement, transfer equipment to another of its plants, and subcontract out work which had been performed at the Ozark plant. Even though the Board's ultimate conclusion in that case may not here survive the Supreme Court's analysis in *First National Maintenance,* it is instructive to note the Board's recognition that the employer's obligation, absent a specific provision in the contract restricting its rights, was to *bargain* with the union over its decision:

> In the first place, however, as we have pointed out time and time again, an employer's obligation to bargain does not include the obligation to agree, but solely to engage in a full and frank discussion with the collective-bargaining representative in which a bona fide effort will be made to explore possible alternatives, if any, that may achieve a mutually satisfactory accommodation of the interests of both the employer and the employees. If such efforts fail, the employer is wholly free to make and effectuate his decision. [161 NLRB at 568. Footnote omitted.] ...

The rationale of our dissenting colleague adds to the collective-bargaining agreement terms not agreed to by the parties and forecloses the exercise of rational economic discussion and decision-making which ultimately accrue to the benefit of all parties.

C. Accordingly, we conclude that Respondent's decision to relocate did not modify the collective-bargaining agreement in violation of Section 8(d). In view of the parties' stipulation that Respondent satisfied its obligation to bargain over the decision, we also conclude that Respondent did not violate Section 8(a)(5).[13]

---

[11] In agreeing with her colleagues that *Milwaukee Spring I* represented a substantial departure from well-established Board precedent, Member Dennis relies on part III of the decision, and finds it unnecessary to reach the matters discussed in Part II, B.

[13] The dissent's references to "contract avoidance" and "do[ing] indirectly what cannot be done directly" are misleading and deflect the reader's attention from the language of Sec. 8(d). Respondent's action is branded unlawful, even though the dissent fails to identify any term or condition contained in the contract that Respondent modified....

The dissent claims that Respondent's work relocation decision would indirectly modify contractual wage rates. Thus, the dissent would imply a work-preservation clause from the mere fact that an employer and a union have agreed on a wage scale. This revolutionary concept, if adopted, would affect virtually every American collective-bargaining agreement and would undoubtedly come as a surprise to parties that have labored at the bargaining table over work preservation proposals. An agreed-upon wage scale, standing by itself, means only that the employer will pay the stated wages to the extent that the employer assigns work to the covered employees.

III. *The Los Angeles Marine Case*

In reaching a result contrary to that reached here, *Milwaukee Spring* I relied on *Los Angeles Marine Hardware Co.,* 235 NLRB 720 (1978), enfd. 602 F.2d 1302 (9th Cir. 1979).... In holding that, after bargaining to impasse, the respondent was not free to relocate work from one location to another location during the contract term without union consent, *Los Angeles Marine* relied on *Boeing,* which in turn cited *University of Chicago....*

As we stated in part II, A, of this decision, however, we agree with the appellate courts, and not the Board, in the *University of Chicago* and *Boeing* cases. We are also not persuaded that work reassignment decisions and relocation decisions should be treated differently for purposes of determining whether there has been a midcontract modification within the meaning of Section 8(d). Rather, we believe that the same standard applies in both instances, and that the Seventh Circuit correctly stated the governing principles in *University of Chicago,* as follows:

> [U]nless transfers are specifically prohibited by the bargaining agreement, an employer is free to transfer work out of the bargaining unit if: (1) the employer complies with *Fibreboard Paper Products v. NLRB,* 379 U.S. 203 ... (1964), by bargaining in good faith to impasse; and (2) the employer is not motivated by anti-union animus, *Textile Workers v. Darlington Mfg. Co.,* 380 U.S. 263 ... (1965). [514 F.2d at 949.][14]

Consistent with our decision today, we hereby overrule *University of Chicago, Boeing,* and the portion of *Los Angeles Marine* that held that the respondent's transfer of work from one location to another location violated Sections 8(a)(5) and 8(d).

IV. *The Section 8(a)(3) Issue*

In *Milwaukee Spring I,* the Board also found that Respondent's laying off employees as a consequence of its relocation decision violated Section 8(a)(3) notwithstanding that the parties stipulated there was no union animus. Invoking the "inherently destructive" doctrine of *Great Dane Trailers,* the Board apparently held that the 8(a)(3) violation flowed from the finding that the relocation decision violated Section 8(a)(5). Accepting this logic for the purposes of our decision only, we conclude that, having found that Respondent complied with its statutory obligation before deciding to relocate and did not violate Section 8(a)(5), there is no factual or legal basis for finding that the consequent layoff of employees violated Section 8(a)(3).

---

[14] The Seventh Circuit decided *University of Chicago* before the Supreme Court decided *First National Maintenance Corp.* We do not here consider the effect of *First National Maintenance* on *Fibreboard....*

V. *Realistic and Meaningful Collective Bargaining*

Los Angeles Marine and *Milwaukee Spring I* discourage truthful midterm bargaining over decisions to transfer unit work. Under those decisions, an employer contemplating a plant relocation for several reasons, one of which is labor costs, would be likely to admit only the reasons unrelated to labor costs in order to avoid granting the union veto power over the decision. The union, unaware that labor costs were a factor in the employer's decision, would be unlikely to volunteer wage or other appropriate concessions. Even if the union offered to consider wage concessions, the employer might hesitate to discuss such suggestions for fear that bargaining with the union over the union's proposals would be used as evidence that labor costs had motivated the relocation decision.

We believe our holding today avoids this dilemma and will encourage the realistic and meaningful collective bargaining that the Act contemplates. Under our decision, an employer does not risk giving a union veto power over its decision regarding relocation and should therefore be willing to disclose all factors affecting its decision. Consequently, the union will be in a better position to evaluate whether to make concessions. Because both parties will not longer have an incentive to refrain from frank bargaining, the likelihood that they will be able to resolve their differences is greatly enhanced.

VI. *Conclusion*

Accordingly, for all of the foregoing reasons, we reverse our original Decision and Order and dismiss the complaint.

MEMBER ZIMMERMAN, dissenting:

....

There are two issues which must be decided in each plant relocation case. The first issue is whether an employer has a duty to bargain with a union over its relocation decision, or, in other words, whether the relocation decision is a mandatory subject of bargaining. As explained below, I would find such decision to be mandatory where the decision is amenable to resolution through collective bargaining. Here, I would find Respondent's decision to relocate its assembly work from Milwaukee to McHenry amenable to resolution through bargaining and thus a mandatory subject of bargaining. The second issue is whether under Section 8(d) an employer may implement its relocation decision after an impasse in bargaining during the term of the collective-bargaining agreement. As explained below, I would find that Section 8(d) prohibits such a relocation of bargaining unit work in the absence of an agreement with the union, but only where the employer's relocation decision is motivated solely or predominantly by a desire to avoid terms of the collective-bargaining agreement. My colleagues and I apparently agree that if a collective-bargaining agreement contains an applicable work-preservation clause, Section 8(d) requires the employer to obtain the union's consent prior to any transfer of work regardless of the reasons underlying the transfer. The difference, then, between my colleagues and myself is that I find Section 8(d) applicable to other contractual terms. Here, as Respondent's decision was motivated solely by its desire to avoid the wage provisions of the contract, I would find that Respondent is prohibited from implementing its decision without the Union's consent during the term of the collective-bargaining agreement....

... Section 8(d) of the Act prohibits midterm changes in any provision of a collective-bargaining agreement relating to mandatory subjects of bargaining without first obtaining the union's consent. It is well settled, and my colleagues agree, that an employer acts in derogation of its bargaining obligations under Section 8(d), and thereby violates Section 8(a)(5), when it makes any midterm change in the contractual wage rate even though the employer's action is compelled by economic necessity or the employer has offered to bargain with the union over the change and the union has refused. Obviously then, my colleagues and I would agree that had Respondent in this case decided to reduce the wages paid to the assembly employees while continuing to perform the assembly work in Milwaukee, Respondent's decision would violate Section 8(a)(5). Respondent's decision to relocate the assembly work to McHenry would achieve the same result, albeit indirectly: its employees would continue to perform assembly work but at reduced wage rates. The issue then is whether the fact that Respondent decided to relocate the work takes Respondent's decision outside the prescriptions of Section 8(d), or in the words of the administrative law judge in *Los Angeles Marine Hardware Co.,* whether the act allows Respondent "to achieve by indirection that which [it could not] achieve by direct means under Section 8(d) of the Act." ...

In my view the determinative factor in deciding whether an employer's midterm relocation decision is proscribed under Section 8(d) is the employer's motive. Where, as here, the decision is controlled by a desire to avoid a contractual term with regard to a mandatory subject of bargaining, such as wages, then the decision is violative under Sections 8(d) and 8(a)(5), and the employer may not implement the decision during the term of the contract without the union's consent. But where the decision is motivated by reasons unrelated to contract avoidance, then the employer may unilaterally implement its decision after bargaining to impasse with the union....

NOTES

1. The parties in *Milwaukee Spring* acted on the assumption that the relocation decision was a mandatory subject of bargaining. Under the Board's current test in *Dubuque Packing, supra,* would it have been?

2. Where a collective agreement contains a clause that does restrict the transfer of bargaining unit work, an arbitral award enforcing such a provision would generally be entitled to judicial acceptance. *See Teamsters Local 115 v. DeSoto, Inc.,* 725 F.2d 931 (3d Cir. 1984). Furthermore, when a mid-term work transfer contravenes an express work preservation clause and is found to be for the purpose of avoiding negotiated wage obligations, a § 8(a)(5) violation will be found. *See Brown Co.,* 278 N.L.R.B. 783 (1986).

3. In affirming *Milwaukee Spring,* the D.C. Circuit (per Edwards, J.) regarded the employer's work removal as sanctioned either by the managements-rights clause or by implied management-reserved rights. Perhaps most significant was the court's novel treatment of the "zipper" clause, whereby each party waived all further bargaining rights. In effect, the court equated this with a "maintenance of standards" clause, precluding the employer from instituting any unilateral changes during the term of the contract (except under a management-rights theory), regardless of whether it had bargained to impasse. If the employer was not authorized by a union's express or implied waiver to make midterm unilateral changes in a mandatory subject, it would first have to bargain to impasse over the matter. But if by a zipper clause the employer had relinquished the capacity to fulfill the condition precedent to the change, it could never make the change without the union's consent. *See also Mead Corp.,* 318 N.L.R.B. 201 (1995) (zipper clause barred employer's implementation of a retirement incentive plan without the union's consent).

4. *See generally* Green, *Plant Relocation after Milwaukee Spring II and Otis Elevator: The Battleground Shifts to Arbitration,* 2 Lab. Law. 183 (1986). O'Keefe & Touhey, *Economically Motivated Relocations of Work and an Employer's Duties Under Section 8(d) of the National Labor Relations Act: A Three-Step Analysis,* 11 Fordham Urb. L.J. 795 (1983); Wachter & Cohen, *The Law and Economics of Collective Bargaining: An Introduction and Application to the Problems of Subcontracting, Partial Closure, and Relocation,* 136 U. Pa. L. Rev. 1349 (1988); Comment, 44 U. Miami L. Rev. 371 (1989); Note, 33 Cath. L. Rev. 1001 (1984).

––––––

NLRB v. Bildisco & Bildisco, 465 U.S. 513, 104 S. Ct. 1188, 79 L. Ed. 2d 482 (1984). In April 1980 the employer, a partnership in the building supplies business, filed for reorganization under Chapter 11 of the Bankruptcy Act. About half of its employees were covered by a three-year collective bargaining agreement, which was due to expire in April 1982. Beginning in January 1980 the employer defaulted on certain obligations under the contract to pay health and pension benefits and to transmit union dues, and in May 1980 it refused to pay required wage increases. In December 1980 Bildisco, as debtor-in-possession (similar to a trustee in bankruptcy) requested the bankruptcy court for permission to reject the labor agreement, and permission was granted in January 1981. Meanwhile, in mid-summer 1980 the union filed refusal-to-bargain charges against Bildisco for its unilateral actions, and the NLRB found that the employer had violated § 8(a)(5) of the NLRA. With both the bankruptcy and unfair labor practice rulings before it, the Supreme Court held unanimously that a collective bargaining agreement is an "executory contract" subject to rejection under § 365(a) of the Bankruptcy Code. The standard for rejection is that the agreement "burdens the estate" and that "the equities balance in favor of rejecting the labor contract." A divided (5-4) Court further held that a debtor-in-possession does not violate § 8(a)(5) of the NLRA by unilaterally changing the terms of the collective agreement between the date the employer filed the bankruptcy petition and the date the bankruptcy court authorized the rejection.

NOTES

1. Congress responded swiftly to *Bildisco.* Pub. L. 98-353 (1984), 11 U.S.C. § 1113, permits the rejection or modification of a bargaining agreement only when: (1) The employer has made a proposal to the union containing those con-tractual modifications that are necessary to permit the reorganization of the debtor while treating all interested parties equitably; (2) the employer has offered "to confer in good faith in attempting to reach mutually satisfactory modifica-tions"; (3) the bankruptcy court finds that the union has rejected the employer's proposed changes "without good cause"; and (4) the court concludes that "the balance of the equities clearly favors rejection" of the bargaining agreement. The court is obliged to hold a hearing on the employer's petition within 14 days and to issue its determination within 30 days thereafter. Does this stricter standard make it more or less difficult for financially moribund companies to obtain needed concessions at the bargaining table?

2. The 1984 amendment to the Bankruptcy Code has, at least partially, re-stricted the ability of employers to utilize bankruptcy proceedings to abrogate bargaining agreement obligations. In *Wheeling-Pittsburgh Steel Corp. v. United Steelworkers,* 791 F.2d 1074 (3d Cir. 1986), the court ruled that a bankruptcy court erred when it allowed Wheeling-Pittsburgh to void its bargaining agree-ment, since the record did not clearly indicate that the employer-requested con-cessions were "necessary" for successful reorganization under Chapter 11 and were "fair and equitable" to all the parties. The bankruptcy judge "failed to give any persuasive rationale for the disproportionate treatment of the employees who were being asked to take a five-year agreement under a worst-case scenario with-out any possibility for restoration or share in the event of a better-than-anticipated recovery." The court also faulted Wheeling-Pittsburgh's failure to include a "snap back" clause in its proposed agreement which would increase wages if corporate finances improved. *But cf. Teamsters Local 807 v. Carey Transp.,* 816 F.2d 82 (2d Cir. 1987) (rejection of collective bargaining agreement was "necessary" and "fair and equitable" when unionized labor costs were 60 percent above industry average, even though managers and nonunion employees would incur lesser cuts, since compensation of the latter persons was "barely competitive" and their responsibilities had increased).

The Labor Board has recognized that a judicial adjudication of bankruptcy does not ipso facto operate to extinguish the bargaining agreement obligations of the debtor-employer. *See Airport Bus Serv.,* 273 N.L.R.B. 561 (1984). Furthermore, an employer seeking the protection of the Bankruptcy Code is not free to modify its bargaining agreement or to ignore its grievance-arbitration obligations until it obtains bankruptcy court approval. Such an employer is not allowed to take advantage of the automatic stay provision of the Bankruptcy Code (§ 362(a)), since the express requirements of § 1113 must be satisfied before a petitioning company may avoid contractual duties. *See In re Ionosphere Clubs, Inc.,* 922 F.2d 984 (2d Cir. 1990), *cert. denied sub nom. ALPA v. Shugrue,* 502 U.S. 808 (1991). *See also Plabell Rubber Prods.,* 307 N.L.R.B. 1197 (1992).

3. In *NLRB v. Superior Forwarding, Inc.,* 762 F.2d 695 (8th Cir. 1985), the court held that a bankruptcy court possesses the authority to enjoin an NLRB unfair labor practice proceeding pertaining to a debtor-employer's rejection of its bargaining agreement where the Labor Board proceeding would threaten the debtor-employer's estate and interfere with bankruptcy court jurisdiction.

4. *See generally* Craver, *The Impact of Financial Crises Upon Collective Bargaining Relationships,* 56 Geo. Wash. L. Rev. 465 (1988); George, *Collective Bargaining in Chapter 11 and Beyond,* 95 Yale L.J. 300 (1985); Haggard, *The Continuing Conflict Between Bankruptcy and Labor Law: The Issues that Bildisco and the 1984 Bankruptcy Amendments Did Not Resolve,* 1986 B.Y.U. L. Rev. 1; Roukis & Charnov, *Section 1113 of the Bankruptcy Amendments and the Federal Judgeship Act of 1984: A Management-Labor Compromise that Will Not Work,* 37 Lab. L.J. 273 (1986); West, *Life After Bildisco: Section 1113 and the Duty to Bargain in Good Faith,* 47 Ohio St. L.J. 65 (1986). The subject is noted in 56 Fordham L. Rev. 1233 (1988); 80 Geo. L. J. 191 (1991); 134 U. Pa. L. Rev. 1235 (1986); 39 Stan. L. Rev. 1015 (1987); 26 Wm. & Mary L. Rev. 545 (1985).

COLLYER INSULATED WIRE

National Labor Relations Board
192 N.L.R.B. 837 (1971)

The complaint alleges and the General Counsel contends that Respondent violated Section 8(a)(5) and (1) of the National Labor Relations Act, as amended, by making assertedly unilateral changes in certain wages and working conditions. Respondent contends that its authority to make those changes was sanctioned by the collective bargaining contract between the parties and their course of dealing under that contract. Respondent further contends that any of its actions in excess of contractual authorization should properly have been remedied by grievance and arbitration proceeding, as provided in the contract. We agree with Respondent's contention that this dispute is essentially a dispute over the terms and meaning of the contract between the Union and the Respondent. For that reason, we find merit in Respondent's exceptions that the dispute should have been resolved pursuant to the contract and we shall dismiss the complaint.

I. *The Alleged Unilateral Changes*

Respondent manufactures insulated electrical wiring at its plant in Lincoln, Rhode Island. The Union has represented Respondent's production and maintenance employees under successive contracts since 1937. The contract in effect when this dispute arose resulted from lengthy negotiations commencing in December 1968 and concluding with the execution of the contract of September 16, 1969. The contract was made effective from April 1, 1969, until July 2, 1971.

Respondent's production employees have historically been compensated on an incentive basis. The contract provides for a job evaluation plan and for the adjustment of rates, subject to the grievance procedure, during the term of the contract. Throughout the bargaining relationship, Respondent has routinely made adjustments in incentive rates to accommodate new or changed production methods. The contract establishes nonincentive rates for skilled maintenance tradesmen but provides for changes in those rates, also, pursuant to the job evaluation plan, upon changes in or additions to the duties of the classifications. The central issue here is whether these contract provisions permitted certain midcontract wage rate changes which Respondent made in November 1969.

A. *The Rate Increase for Skilled Maintenance Tradesmen:* Since early 1968, Respondent's wage rates for skilled tradesmen have not been sufficiently high to attract and retain the numbers of skilled maintenance mechanics and electricians required for the efficient operation of the plant. The record clearly establishes, and the Trial Examiner found, that other employers in the same region paid "substantially higher rates than those paid by Respondent." In consequence, the number of skilled maintenance workers had declined from about 40 in January 1968 to about 30 in mid-1969, and Respondent had been unable to attract employees to fill the resulting vacancies.

During negotiations, Respondent several times proposed wage raises for maintenance employees over and above those being negotiated for the production and maintenance unit generally. The Union rejected those proposals and the contract did not include any provision for such raises. It is clear, nevertheless, that the matter of the skill factor increase was left open, in *some* measure, for further negotiations after the execution of the agreement. The parties sharply dispute, however, the extent to which the matter remained open and the conditions which were to surround further discussions. The Union asserts, and the Trial Examiner found, that the Union was willing, and made known its willingness, to negotiate further wage adjustments only on a plantwide basis, consistent with the job evaluation system. Respondent insists that it understood the Union's position to be that wage increases for maintenance employees only might still be agreed to by the Union after the signing of the contract, if such increases could be justified under the job evaluation system.

At monthly meetings following conclusion of the contract negotiations, Respondent and the Union continued to discuss the Respondent's desire to raise the rates for maintenance employees. Finally, on November 12, 1969, Respondent informed the Union that five days thence, on November 17, Respondent would institute an upward adjustment of 20 cents per hour. The Union protested and restated its desire for a reevaluation of all jobs in the plant. Respondent's representative agreed to consider such an evaluation on a plantwide basis, upon union agreement to the increase for the skilled tradesmen. The Trial Examiner found that the Union did not agree. The rate increase became effective November 17, 1969.

B. *Reassignment of Job Duties:* One of the production steps, the application of insulating material to conductor, is accomplished through the operation of extruder machines. The insulating material, in bulk, is forced to and through the extruder die by a large worm gear. Each change in the type of insulation used on an extruder requires that the worm gear be removed and cleaned of insulation remaining from the previous production run. The removal, cleaning, and replacement of the worm gear is performed approximately once each week and requires approximately 40 minutes to one hour for each operation. Prior to November 12, 1969, the worm gear removal and cleaning had been performed by a team of two maintenance machinists. On November 12, Respondent directed that future worm gear removals would be performed by a single maintenance machinist with the assistance of the extruder machine operator and helper.

C. *Rate Increases for Extruder Operators:* Respondent's third change, also effective November 17, 1969, produced a rate increase for extruder operators. It had been Respondent's practice to adjust the straight time earnings of extruder operators by a factor representing the amount of time during an eight-hour shift when the extruder was in continuous operation. Under that system, for example, an operator who maintained his machine in continuous operation for eight hours was paid for 10 hours' work. This incentive factor has never been fixed by the contract and Respondent had, in the past, changed the rate for various reasons....

II. *Relevant Contract Provisions*

The contract now in effect between the parties makes provision for adjustment by Respondent in the wages of its employees during the contract term. Those provisions appear to contemplate changes in rates in both incentive and nonincentive jobs. Thus, article IX, section 2, provides:

"The Corporation agrees to establish rates and differentials of pay for all employees according to their skill, experience and hazards of employment, and to review rates and differentials from time to time.... However, no change in the general scale of pay now in existence shall be made during the term of this

Agreement. This Article IX is applicable to the general wage scale, but shall not be deemed to prevent adjustments in individual rates from time to time to remove inequalities or for other proper reasons."

Further evidence of the contractual intent to permit Respondent to modify job rates subject to review through the grievance and arbitration procedures is found in article XIII, section 3, paragraph b, covering new or changed jobs. That paragraph provides that the Union shall have seven days to consider any new rating established by the Company and to submit objections. Thereafter, even absent Union agreement, it vests in the Company authority to institute a new pay rate. The Union, if dissatisfied, may then challenge the propriety of the rate by invoking the grievance procedure which culminates in arbitration.

Finally, the breadth of the arbitration provision makes clear that the parties intended to make the grievance and arbitration machinery the exclusive forum for resolving contract disputes....

IV. *Discussion*

We find merit in Respondent's exceptions that because this dispute in its entirety arises from the contract between the parties, and from the parties' relationship under the contract, it ought to be resolved in the manner which that contract prescribes. We conclude that the Board is vested with authority to withhold its processes in this case, and that the contract here made available a quick and fair means for the resolution of this dispute including, if appropriate, a fully effective remedy for any breach of contract which occurred. We conclude, in sum, that our obligation to advance the purposes of the Act is best discharged by the dismissal of this complaint.

In our view, disputes such as these can better be resolved by arbitrators with special skill and experience in deciding matters arising under established bargaining relationships than by the application by this Board of a particular provision of our statute. The necessity for such special skill and expertise is apparent upon examination of the issues arising from Respondent's actions with respect to the operators' rates, the skill factor increase, and the reassignment of duties relating to the worm gear removal. Those issues include, specifically: (a) the extent to which these actions were intended to be reserved to the management, subject to later adjustment by grievance and arbitration; (b) the extent to which the skill factor increase should properly be construed, under article IX of the agreement, as a "change in the general scale of pay" or, conversely, as "adjustments in individual rates ... to remove inequalities or for other proper reason"; (c) the extent, if any, to which the procedures of article XIII governing new or changed jobs and job rates should have been made applicable to the skill factor increase here; and (d) the extent to which any of these issues may be affected by the long course of dealing between the parties....

The Board's authority, in its discretion, to defer to the arbitration process has never been questioned by the courts of appeals, or by the Supreme Court. Although Section 10(a) of the Act clearly vests the Board with jurisdiction over conduct which constitutes a violation of the provisions of Section 8, notwithstanding the existence of methods of "adjustment or prevention that might be established by agreement," nothing in the Act intimates that the Board must exercise jurisdiction where such methods exist. On the contrary in *Carey v. Westinghouse Electric Corporation,* 375 U.S. 261, 271 (1964), the Court indicated that it favors our deference to such agreed methods....

The policy favoring voluntary settlement of labor disputes through arbitral processes finds specific expression in Section 203(d) of the LMRA....

And of course disputes under Section 301 of the LMRA called forth from the Supreme Court the celebrated affirmation of that national policy in the *Steelworkers Trilogy.*

Admittedly neither Section 203 nor Section 301 applies specifically to the Board. However labor law as administered by the Board does not operate in a vacuum isolated from other parts of the Act, or, indeed, from other acts of Congress. In fact the legislative history suggests that at the time the Taft-Hartley amendments were being considered, Congress anticipated that the Board would "develop by rules and regulations, a policy of entertaining under these provisions only such cases ... as cannot be settled by resort to the machinery established by the contract itself, voluntary arbitration...."[7]

The question whether the Board should withhold its process arises, of course, only when a set of facts may present not only an alleged violation of the Act but also an alleged breach of the collective bargaining agreement subject to arbitration. Thus, this case like each such case compels an accommodation between, on the one hand, the statutory policy favoring the fullest use of collective bargaining and the arbitral process and, on the other, the statutory policy reflected by Congress' grant to the Board of exclusive jurisdiction to prevent unfair labor practices.

We address the accommodations required here with the benefit of the Board's full history of such accommodations in similar cases. From the start the Board has, case by case, both asserted jurisdiction and declined, as the balance was struck on particular facts and at various stages in the long ascent of collective bargaining to its present state of wide acceptance. Those cases reveal that the Board has honored the distinction between two broad but distinct classes of cases, those in which there has been an arbitral award, and those in which there has not.

In the former class of cases the Board has long given hospitable acceptance to the arbitral process.... The Board's policy was refined in *Spielberg Manufactur-*

---

[7] S. Rep. No. 105, 80th Cong., 1st Sess. 23 (1947).

ing Company,[10] where the Board established the now settled rule that it would limit its inquiry, in the presence of an arbitrator's award, to whether the procedures were fair and the result not repugnant to the Act.

In those cases in which no award had issued, the Board's guidelines have been less clear. At times the Board has dealt with the unfair labor practice, and at other times it has left the parties to their contract remedies....

Jos. Schlitz Brewing Co.[12] is the most significant recent case in which the Board has exercised its discretion to defer. The underlying dispute in *Schlitz* was strikingly similar to the one now before us. In *Schlitz* the respondent employer decided to halt its production line during employee breaks. That decision was a departure from an established practice of maintaining extra employees, relief men, to fill in for regular employees during breaktime. The change resulted in, among other things, elimination of the relief man job classification. The change elicited a union protest leading to an unfair labor practice proceeding in which the Board ruled that the case should be "left for resolution within the framework of the agreed upon settlement procedures." The majority there explained its decision in these words:

> Thus, we believe that where, as here, the contract clearly provides for grievance and arbitration machinery, where the unilateral action taken is not designed to undermine the Union and is not patently erroneous but rather is based on a substantial claim of contractual privilege, and it appears that the arbitral interpretation of the contract will resolve both the unfair labor practice issue and the contract interpretation issue in a manner compatible with the purposes of the Act, then the Board should defer to the arbitration clause conceived by the parties....

The circumstances of this case, no less than those in *Schlitz,* weigh heavily in favor of deferral. Here, as in *Schlitz,* this dispute arises within the confines of a long and productive collective bargaining relationship. The parties before us have, for 35 years, mutually and voluntarily resolved the conflicts which inhere in collective bargaining. Here, as there, no claim is made of enmity by Respondent to employees' exercise of protected rights. Respondent here has credibly asserted its willingness to resort to arbitration under a clause providing for arbitration in a very broad range of disputes and unquestionably broad enough to embrace this dispute.

Finally, here, as in *Schlitz,* the dispute is one eminently well suited to resolution by arbitration. The contract and its meaning in present circumstances lie at the center of this dispute. In contrast, the Act and its policies become involved only if it is determined that the agreement between the parties, examined in the light of its negotiating history and the practices of the parties thereunder, did not

---

[10] 112 N.L.R.B. 1080, 1082 (1955).
[12] 175 N.L.R.B. No. 23 (1969).

sanction Respondent's right to make the disputed changes, subject to review if sought by the Union, under the contractually prescribed procedure. That threshold determination is clearly within the expertise of a mutually agreed-upon arbitrator. In this regard we note especially that here, as in *Schlitz,* the dispute between these parties is the very stuff of labor contract arbitration. The competence of a mutually selected arbitrator to decide the issue and fashion an appropriate remedy, if needed, can no longer be gainsaid.

We find no basis for the assertion of our dissenting colleagues that our decision here modifies the standards established in *Spielberg* for judging the acceptability of an arbitrator's award....

It is true, manifestly, that we cannot judge the regularity or statutory acceptability of the result in an arbitration proceeding which has not occurred. However, we are unwilling to adopt the presumption that such a proceeding will be invalid under *Spielberg* and to exercise our decisional authority at this juncture on the basis of a mere possibility that such a proceeding might be unacceptable under *Spielberg* standards. That risk is far better accommodated, we believe, by the result reached here of retaining jurisdiction against an event which years of experience with labor arbitration have now made clear is a remote hazard.

Member Fanning's dissenting opinion incorrectly characterizes this decision as instituting "compulsory arbitration" and as creating an opportunity for employers and unions to "strip parties of statutory rights."

We are not compelling any party to agree to arbitrate disputes arising during a contract term, but are merely giving full effect to their own voluntary agreements to submit all such disputes to arbitration, rather than permitting such agreements to be sidestepped and permitting the substitution of our processes, a forum not contemplated by their own agreement.

Nor are we "stripping" any party of "statutory rights." The courts have long recognized that an industrial relations dispute may involve conduct which, at least arguably, may contravene both the collective agreement and our statute. When the parties have contractually committed themselves to mutually agreeable procedures for resolving their disputes during the period of the contract, we are of the view that those procedures should be afforded full opportunity to function. The long and successful functioning of grievance and arbitration procedures suggests to us that in the overwhelming majority of cases, the utilization of such means will resolve the underlying dispute and make it unnecessary for either party to follow the more formal, and sometimes lengthy, combination of administrative and judicial litigation provided for under our statute. At the same time, by our reservation of jurisdiction, *infra,* we guarantee that there will be no sacrifice of statutory rights if the parties' own processes fail to function in a manner consistent with the dictates of our law....

V. *Remedy*

Without prejudice to any party and without deciding the merits of the controversy, we shall order that the complaint herein be dismissed, but we shall retain jurisdiction for a limited purpose. Our decision represents a developmental step in the Board's treatment of these problems and the controversy here arose at a time when the Board decisions may have led the parties to conclude that the Board approved dual litigation of this controversy before the Board and before an arbitrator. We are also aware that the parties herein have not resolved their dispute by the contractual grievance and arbitration procedure and that, therefore, we cannot now inquire whether resolution of the dispute will comport with the standards set forth in *Spielberg, supra.* In order to eliminate the risk of prejudice to any party we shall retain jurisdiction over this dispute solely for the purpose of entertaining an appropriate and timely motion for further consideration upon a proper showing that either (a) the dispute has not, with reasonable promptness after the issuance of this decision, either been resolved by amicable settlement in the grievance procedure or submitted promptly to arbitration, or (b) the grievance or arbitration procedures have not been fair and regular or have reached a result which is repugnant to the Act.

[The concurring opinion of MEMBER BROWN is omitted.]

MEMBER FANNING (dissenting)....

Clearly ... the effect of the majority's decision is a direction to the parties to arbitrate a grievance which is no longer contractually arbitrable. The complaint is dismissed, but jurisdiction is retained, presumably to give the Union an opportunity to file a grievance under a time-expired contractual provision, with the implicit threat to the Respondent that the Board will assert jurisdiction, upon a proper motion, if Respondent is unwilling now to submit to arbitration. The majority's insistence that the parties' statutory rights cannot be adjudicated in this case except through the authority of an arbitrator verges on the practice of compulsory arbitration. Historically, in this country voluntarism has been the essence of private arbitration of labor disputes. Neither Congress nor the courts have attempted to coerce the parties in collective bargaining to resolve their grievances through arbitration. Compulsory arbitration has been regarded by some as contrary to a free, democratic society. Collective bargaining agreements, such as the one in the instant case, give aggrieved parties the *right* to file grievances and to present their disputes to an arbitrator. The element of compulsion has been deliberately omitted. To establish the principle, as a matter of labor law, that the parties to a collective bargaining agreement must, in part, surrender their protection under this statute as a consequence of agreeing to a provision for binding arbitration of grievances will, in my view, discourage rather than encourage the arbitral process in this country. Many may decide they cannot afford the luxury of such "voluntary" arbitration....

The effect of the majority's decision in the instant case is clearly a reversal of the established *Spielberg* line of cases. In the future applicable standards for review of arbitration awards will not be followed. Neither the existence of an actual award, the fairness of the arbitrator's opinion or its impingement upon the policies of the Act will be considered by the Board in dismissing complaints of this nature. Under the majority's accommodation theory even consideration of the nature and scope of the alleged unfair labor practices, as set forth in ... *Joseph Schlitz, supra,* will not receive the Board's attention. The impact of the majority's decision may be said to go beyond compulsory arbitration. For it means that in the future the Board will not concern itself with the *fact* or the *regularity* of the arbitral process, but will strip the parties of statutory rights merely on the *availability* of such a procedure.

The majority does not frame the primary issue in this case in terms calculated to resolve a particular dispute in a particular case. Rather, a new standard for the nonassertion of jurisdiction is announced, embracing a whole class of employers who have entered into contracts with unions containing a grievance-arbitration clause. In the future, complaints based upon such disputes, without regard to the seriousness of the alleged unfair labor practices, may not be litigated before this Board....

Congress has said that arbitration and the voluntary settlement of disputes are the preferred method of dealing with certain kinds of industrial unrest. Congress has also said that the power of this Board to dispose of unfair labor practices is not to be affected by any other method of adjustment. Whatever these two statements mean, they do not mean that this Board can abdicate its authority wholesale. Clearly there is an accommodation to be made. The majority is so anxious to accommodate arbitration that it forgets that the first duty of this Board is to provide a forum for the adjudication of unfair labor practices. We have not been told that arbitration is the only method; it is one method.

We have recently been told by the Supreme Court that preemption in favor of this Board still exists. It is therefore inappropriate, to say the least, for us to cede our jurisdiction in all cases involving arbitration to a tribunal that may, and often does, provide only a partial remedy.

[The dissenting opinion of MEMBER JENKINS is omitted.]

NOTES

1. The D.C. Circuit recently reaffirmed the *Collyer* deferral doctrine in a § 8(a)(5) case, refusing to enforce a Board order against an employer who stopped providing holiday pay to employees on workers' compensation leave, and chastising the Board for failing to defer to arbitration processes available under the parties' labor contract. In *Burns Int'l Security Servs. v. NLRB,* 146 F.3d 873 (D.C. Cir. 1998), Judge Edwards wrote for the court:

> The relevant inquiry ... is whether Burns acted on a viable claim or right under the parties' CBA in eliminating the holiday pay practice. So long as the employer plausibly claims contractual justification for its actions under the express or implied terms of the CBA, and the matter in dispute is subject to arbitration, then the Board should leave the parties to their contract remedies unless the employer refuses to go to arbitration.

Accordingly, the court overturned the Board's finding that the employees' strike in response to the employer's action was an unfair labor practice strike, eliminating the basis for the Board's ruling that the employer had violated the Act by failing to reinstate the strikers once they made an unconditional offer to return to work.

2. The *Collyer* deferral doctrine was extended to § 8(a)(3) discrimination cases in *National Radio Co.,* 198 N.L.R.B. 527 (1972), another 3-2 decision. In *General Am. Transp. Corp.,* 228 N.L.R.B. 808 (1977), however, then-Chair Betty Murphy voted with Members Fanning and Jenkins to trim back *Collyer* to its original 8(a)(5) dimensions and to refuse to defer to arbitration in cases alleging discrimination against individual employees. She reasoned:

> In cases alleging violations of Section 8(a)(5) and 8(b)(3), based upon conduct assertedly in derogation of the contract, the principal issue is whether the complained-of conduct is permitted by the parties' contract. Such issues are eminently suited to the arbitral process, and resolution of the contract issue by an arbitrator will, as a rule, dispose of the unfair labor practice issue. On the other hand, in cases alleging violations of Section 8(a)(1), 8(a)(3), 8(b)(1)(A), and 8(b)(2), although arguably also involving a contract violation, the determinative issue is not whether the conduct is permitted by the contract, but whether the conduct was unlawfully motivated or whether it otherwise interfered with, restrained, or coerced employees in the exercise of the rights guaranteed them by Section 7 of the Act. In these situations, an arbitrator's resolution of the contract issue will not dispose of the unfair labor practice allegation. Nor is the arbitration process suited for resolving employee complaints of discrimination under Section 7....

Nevertheless, in *United Technologies Corp.,* 268 N.L.R.B. 557 (1984), with Board members reiterating the same arguments, a 3-1 majority overruled *General American Transportation* and revitalized the *National Radio* doctrine favoring deferral in §§ 8(a)(1), 8(a)(3), 8(b)(1)(A), and 8(b)(2) cases. The D.C. Circuit accepted the *United Technologies* approach in *Hammontree v. NLRB,* 925 F.2d 1486 (D.C. Cir. 1991) (en banc). *See generally* Edwards, *Deferral to Arbitration and Waiver of the Duty to Bargain: A Possible Way Out of Everlasting Confusion at the NLRB,* 46 Ohio St. L.J. 23 (1985); Harper, *Union Waiver of Employee Rights Under the NLRA: Part II,* 4 Indus. Rel. L.J. 680 (1981); Lynch, *Deferral,*

Waiver, and Arbitration Under the NLRA: From Status to Contract and Back Again, 44 U. Miami L. Rev. 237 (1989).

3. Does *Collyer* reflect a shift in direction from *C & C Plywood?* What factors must be weighed in assessing the deferral policy? What if the arbitrator's remedial authority is severely limited by the labor contract? *Compare Hoffman Air & Filtration Sys. Div. of Clarkson Indus.,* 312 N.L.R.B. 349 (1993) (declining to defer § 8(a)(1) and related § 8(a)(3) issues to arbitration where the contract prevented the arbitrator from making "any recommendation for future action by the Company or the Union," effectively preventing the imposition of the equivalent of a Board cease-and-desist remedy) *with Roswil, Inc. dba Ramey Supermarkets,* 314 N.L.R.B. 9 (1994) (refusing to defer discharge case to arbitration where the labor contract limited backpay awards to 20 days), *reversed, NLRB v. Roswil, Inc. dba Ramey Supermarkets,* 55 F.3d 382 (8th Cir. 1995) (scope of remedies available to the arbitrator is relevant, but not dispositive of deferral issue). Whether the Board will defer in cases involving alleged statutory violations also depends upon the existence of a question of contract interpretation. In *Public Serv. Co.,* 319 N.L.R.B. 984 (1995), the Board held that it would defer to arbitration the question of whether an employer unlawfully bypassed a union, the recognized bargaining agent under the parties' contract, and dealt directly with the employees, even though the direct dealing was not accompanied by any unilateral change in the terms of employment. The dissent maintained there was no real issue of contract interpretation for the arbitrator to decide; it was essentially a matter of bargaining relationships. Nevertheless, because the arbitrator had the authority to order the employer to honor its contractual obligation to deal with the recognized union rather than with the employees, an adequate remedy existed at arbitration.

What if the arbitrator did not believe the issue was arbitrable, but persuaded by a party's arguments, reached a conclusion on the merits anyhow? In *Doerfer Eng'g v. NLRB,* 79 F.3d 101 (8th Cir. 1996), the court held that the Board had abused its discretion in not honoring an arbitrator's award that an employer could terminate a longstanding practice of allowing employees to use company tools and equipment for personal projects. The NLRB had refused to defer to the arbitrator's decision, relying on the first and last sentences of the arbitrator's opinion which intimated that the grievance was not arbitrable. But the court concluded the arbitrator had actually adjudicated the merits of the dispute. Although the employer had argued to the arbitrator against arbitrability, the union had taken the position before the arbitrator that the matter was arbitrable, and had agreed to be bound by the arbitrator's decision. According to the Eighth Circuit, the union "cannot ... change its position simply because the arbitrator reached an unfavorable conclusion on the merits.... A contrary decision would encourage parties to renege upon their agreement to be bound by an arbitrator's decision and to circumvent the grievance procedure by filing an unfair labor practice charge whenever they felt they had a better chance for favorable resolution before the Board."

Collyer touched off a lively, continuing controversy. *See, e.g.,* Alleyne, *Arbitrators and the NLRB: The Nature of the Deferral Beast,* 4 Indus. Rel. L.J. 587 (1981); Christensen, *Private Judges, Public Rights: The Role of Arbitration in the Enforcement of the National Labor Relations Act,* in J. Correge, V. Hughes & M. Stone, eds., The Future of Labor Arbitration in America 49 (1976); Covington, *Arbitrators and the Board: A Revised Relationship,* 57 N.C. L. Rev. 91 (1978); Getman, *Collyer Insulated Wire: A Case of Misplaced Modesty,* 49 Ind. L.J. 57 (1973); Isaacson & Zifchak, *Agency Deferral to Private Arbitration of Employment Disputes,* 73 Colum. L. Rev. 1383 (1973); Schatzki, *N.L.R.B. Resolution of Contract Disputes Under 8(a)(5),* 50 Texas L. Rev. 225 (1972); Sharpe, *NLRB Deferral to Grievance-Arbitration: A General Theory,* 48 Ohio St. L.J. 595 (1987); Zimmer, *Wired for Collyer: Rationalizing NLRB and Arbitration Jurisdiction,* 48 Ind. L.J. 141 (1973). The Getman piece was a response to Schatzki and Zimmer; their replies are in 49 Ind. L.J. 76, 80 (1973). For judicial approval and qualifications of *Collyer, see Machinists Lodges 700, 743, 1746 v. NLRB,* 525 F.2d 237 (2d Cir. 1975); *IBEW Local 2188 v. NLRB,* 494 F.2d 1087 (D.C. Cir.), *cert. denied,* 419 U.S. 835 (1974).

4. The Board has refused to defer to arbitration, or to honor an award, when the interests of the aggrieved employees were in apparent conflict with the interests of the union as well as of the employer. *Kansas Meat Packers,* 198 N.L.R.B. 543 (1972); *Hendrickson Bros.,* 272 N.L.R.B. 438 (1984), *enforced,* 762 F.2d 990 (2d Cir. 1985); *Gateway Transp. Co.,* 137 N.L.R.B. 1763 (1962) (refusal to honor). *But cf. Roadway Express, Inc. v. NLRB,* 647 F.2d 415 (4th Cir. 1981) (Board improperly failed to defer to union-employer grievance settlement). The Board's refusal to defer to arbitration, however, does not necessarily mean that the employer has no legal obligation to arbitrate. *Teamsters Local 807 v. Regional Import & Export Trucking Co.,* 944 F.2d 1037 (2d Cir. 1991).

5. Should the NLRB honor an arbitrator's award as a whole, or merely any findings of fact or interpretations of contractual provisions which happen also to be essential parts of the unfair labor practice case? What about an issue that the parties had the opportunity but failed to place before the arbitrator? In *Olin Corp.,* 268 N.L.R.B. 573 (1984), the Labor Board announced new standards to be applied when deciding whether to honor a prior arbitral decision under the *Spielberg* doctrine:

> We would find that an arbitrator has adequately considered the unfair labor practice if (1) the contractual issue is factually parallel to the unfair labor practice issue, and (2) the arbitrator was presented generally with the facts relevant to resolving the unfair labor practice. In the [*sic*] respect, differences, if any, between the contractual and statutory standards of review should be weighed by the Board as part of its determination under the *Spielberg* standards of whether an award is "clearly repugnant" to the Act. And, with regard to the inquiry into the "clearly repugnant" standard, we would

not require an arbitrator's award to be totally consistent with Board precedent. Unless the award is "palpably wrong." i.e., unless the arbitrator's decision is not susceptible to an interpretation consistent with the Act, we will defer.

Finally, we would require that the party seeking to have the Board reject deferral and consider the merits of a given case show that the above standards for deferral have not been met. Thus, the party seeking to have the Board ignore the determination of an arbitrator has the burden of affirmatively demonstrating the defects in the arbitral process or award.

The *Olin Corp.* standard was applied by the D. C. Circuit in *Bakery Workers Local 25 v. NLRB,* 730 F.2d 812 (1984). In *Alpha Beta Co.,* 273 N.L.R.B. 1546 (1985), *aff'd sub nom. Mahon v. NLRB,* 808 F.2d 1342 (9th Cir. 1987), the Labor Board indicated that it will defer to prior labor-management grievance settlements in the same manner in which it will defer to prior arbitral awards under the *Spielberg* doctrine. Nonetheless, the Board will not defer when the facts relevant to the factually parallel unfair labor practice issue were not presented to the arbitrator. *See Wheeling-Pittsburgh Steel Corp.,* 277 N.L.R.B. 1388 (1985), *enforced,* 821 F.2d 342 (6th Cir. 1987).

Derr & Gruenewald Constr. Co., 315 N.L.R.B. 266 (1994), concerned a claim that an employer had violated the NLRA by refusing to hire eight employees who had been referred by the union because of their prior participation in a job site protest regarding allegedly unsafe working conditions. The union had taken the case to arbitration and prevailed. Although the arbitrator had not addressed the specific issue raised before the Labor Board, he had found a contractual violation. The arbitrator ordered the firm to discard its "ineligible for hire" list and to provide three of the eight employees with four hours of pay. The NLRB applied the *Olin Corp.* test and found that the arbitral award was not clearly repugnant to the Act's purposes, despite the limited monetary remedy. Since the adversely affected employees had obtained other jobs through the hiring hall, they had effectively been made whole for their losses. *See also Utility Workers Local 246 v. NLRB (Southern Cal. Edison),* 39 F.3d 1210 (D.C. Cir. 1994) (sustaining *Olin Corp.* shift of burden of proof to party *opposing* Board acceptance of prior arbitral award).

In *Mobil Oil Exploration,* 325 N.L.R.B. No. 18, 156 L.R.R.M. 1273 (1997), the Board refused to defer to a prior arbitral award upholding the discharge of an employee who had been engaged in an ongoing dispute with the union president over union policies. The Board found the award "palpably wrong" and "repugnant to the policies of the NLRA" since the discharge had been precipitated by the employee's exercise of his statutorily protected right to generate group opposition to the union leadership.

6. The Board found an arbitration award "repugnant to the Act," and thus not a basis for deferral, when the arbitrator ordered reinstatement without back pay for a union steward who was improperly suspended for vigorously but legitimately pursuing a grievance, and who was then discharged after she was provoked into refusing to leave the plant. *Cone Mills Corp.,* 298 N.L.R.B. 661 (1990). On the other hand, in *Bath Iron Works Corp.,* 302 N.L.R.B. 898 (1991), the Board deferred to an arbitral award that permitted the employer to adopt a drug testing policy without bargaining with the union, since the policy was found to be a mere extension of preexisting work rules forbidding the use of drugs. *See also Southern Cal. Edison Co.,* 310 N.L.R.B. 1229 (1993).

7. In *Taylor v. NLRB,* 786 F.2d 1516 (11th Cir. 1986), the court indicated that the Board's *Olin Corp.* deferral standards inappropriately divest the NLRB of its unfair labor practice responsibilities under § 10. By presuming, until proven otherwise, that all arbitral proceedings confront and decide every possible unfair labor practice issue, the *Olin Corp.* rules overlook instances where contractual and statutory issues may be factually parallel but involve distinct elements of proof and different questions of factual relevance. They also ignore the practical reality of many bipartite grievance-arbitration proceedings in which individual rights may be negotiated away in the interest of group considerations.

8. Overlapping rights and remedies are treated in the context of two specific workplace problems in Barbash, Tobin, Seitz, Kaynard, Estreicher, *Absenteeism and Incompetence: Facets and Forums,* in N.Y.U. Thirty-Fifth Annual Conference on Labor 241 (1982) (five separate papers). *See generally* Gates & Elder, *Olin Must Not and Will Not Survive,* 38 Lab. L.J. 723 (1987); Henkel & Kelly, *Deferral to Arbitration After Olin and United Technologies: Has the NLRB Gone Too Far?* 43 Wash. & Lee L. Rev. 37 (1986); Levy, *Deferral and the Dissident,* 24 U. Mich. J. L. Ref. 479 (1991); Morris, *NLRB Deferral to the Arbitration Process: The Arbitrator's Awesome Responsibility,* 7 Indus. Rel. L.J. 290 (1985); Page & Sherrick, *The NLRB's Deferral Policy and Union Reform: A Union Perspective,* 24 U. Mich. J. L. Ref. 647 (1991).

Carey v. Westinghouse Electric Corp., 375 U.S. 261, 84 S. Ct. 401, 11 L. Ed. 2d 320 (1964). The IUE sought arbitration with Westinghouse regarding its contractual claim to jurisdiction over work being performed by employees represented by another union. Westinghouse refused to arbitrate on the ground that the controversy concerned a representational matter for the NLRB. Although the IUE could not compel the other labor organization to participate in its arbitral proceeding, the Supreme Court concluded that the lower court should have ordered the requested arbitration.

> Grievance arbitration is one method of settling disputes over work assignments; and it is commonly used, we are told. To be sure, only one of the two unions involved in the controversy has moved the state courts to compel arbitration. So unless the other union intervenes, an adjudication of the ar-

biter might not put an end to the dispute. Yet the arbitration may as a practical matter end the controversy or put into movement forces that will resolve it....

The Court recognized that the Labor Board might still be asked to consider the jurisdictional question following the arbitrator's determination. "Should the Board disagree with the arbiter, by ruling, for example, that the employees involved in the controversy are members of one bargaining unit or another, the Board's ruling would, of course, take precedence...."

NOTES

1. Arbitration took place following the decision in the Carey case. The NLRB subsequently concluded, however, that the ultimate issue of representation could not be decided by the arbitrator through an interpretation of the contract but could be resolved only through the use of Board criteria for unit determination. While giving "some consideration to the award," the Board proceeded to make a different unit allocation. *Westinghouse Elec. Corp.,* 162 N.L.R.B. 768 (1967). Arbitration awards have been recognized, however, in representation proceedings as well as in unfair labor practice cases. *Raley's Inc.,* 143 N.L.R.B. 256 (1963). The Board has stated that although it "only infrequently defers to arbitration in representation proceedings," it was prepared to do so in clarifying a bargaining unit of food service workers to include a working chef, since the issue turned solely on contract interpretation, not statutory policy. *St. Mary's Med. Ctr.,* 322 N.L.R.B. 954 (1997).

2. The courts of appeals are divided on whether the NLRB's jurisdiction preempts that of a court when a § 301 suit seeks an ultimate determination regarding representation, for example, whether the wage and benefit provisions of a collective agreement apply to employees not represented by the union at the time the contract was executed. *See Textile Processors Local 1 v. D.O. Summers Cleaners,* 954 F. Supp. 153 (N.D. Ohio 1997) (discussing cases).

3. To what extent should courts resolve NLRA representational issues that arise in the course of suits to compel arbitration, enforce awards, or otherwise remedy contract breaches? A state court could order arbitration on the accretion issue of whether the collective bargaining agreement at an old plant should be extended to cover a newly opened nonunion facility. A Board regional director's earlier dismissal of the employer's election petition had not resolved a "dispositive representational issue." *Bell Cold Storage v. Teamsters Local 544,* 885 F.2d 436 (8th Cir. 1989). *Compare Teamsters Local 776 v. NLRB,* 973 F.2d 230 (3d Cir. 1992), *cert. denied,* 507 U.S. 959 (1993) (union that obtained arbitral award extending collective contract to employees at new warehouse violated NLRA when it sought enforcement of that award after regional director refused to clarify the existing unit to include the new warehouse personnel). *See also Local 342 v. Valley Engineers,* 975 F.2d 611 (9th Cir. 1992).

The Tenth Circuit held that decertification of a union at an employer's old facility did not moot the union's action to compel arbitration of whether employees at the employer's newly constructed plant were covered by the labor contract at the original facility. *UAW v. Telex Computer Prods.*, 816 F.2d 519 (1987). The same court was prepared to decide the relevant bargaining unit in an action under § 301 by employee benefit trust funds to obtain an employer's allegedly delinquent contributions, at least when the NLRB's jurisdiction had not been invoked concerning the issue. *Trustees of Colorado Ironworkers Trust Fund v. A & P Steel, Inc.*, 812 F.2d 1518 (10th Cir. 1987). But another court of appeals held that a union's decertification by the NLRB terminated an employer's contractual obligation to contribute to employee welfare trust funds. *Sheet Metal Workers Local 206 v. West Coast Sheet Metal Co.*, 954 F.2d 1506 (9th Cir. 1992).

4. A union may maintain a suit under § 301 of the Taft-Hartley Act to enforce the monetary obligations assumed by an employer in the construction industry pursuant to a prehire contract authorized by § 8(f) of the NLRA, even if the union never obtained majority support in the relevant unit prior to the employer's repudiation of the contract. This does not impair the right of the employees to select their own bargaining agent. *Jim McNeff v. Todd*, 461 U.S. 260 (1983).

5. Although a court cannot order tripartite arbitration of a jurisdictional dispute involving an employer and two competing unions unless all three parties agree to participate in that proceeding, it can order arbitration between the employer and the labor organization whose members were not assigned the disputed work. *Miron Constr. Co. v. Operating Eng'rs Local 139*, 44 F.3d 558 (7th Cir.), *cert. denied*, 514 U.S. 1096 (1995). For a spirited debate on the capacity of an arbitrator to induce (or strongarm) the second union into an arbitration in a *Carey* situation, *see* Bernstein, *Nudging and Shoving All Parties to a Jurisdictional Dispute Into Arbitration: The Dubious Procedure of National Steel*, 78 Harv. L. Rev. 784 (1965); Jones, *On Nudging and Shoving the National Steel Arbitration Into a Dubious Procedure*, 79 Harv. L. Rev. 327 (1965); Jones, *An Arbitral Answer to a Judicial Dilemma: The Carey Decision and Trilateral Arbitration of Jurisdictional Disputes*, 11 U.C.L.A. L. Rev. 327 (1964). *See also Industrial Workers v. Kroger Co.*, 900 F.2d 944 (6th Cir. 1990). *Cf. Columbia Broadcasting Sys. v. American Recording & Broadcasting Ass'n*, 414 F.2d 1326 (2d Cir. 1969).

Under the Railway Labor Act, the National Railroad Adjustment Board is authorized (and required) to summon the disputing unions before it in order to dispose of all claims to work assignments in a single proceeding. *Transportation Commun. Employees Union v. Union Pac. R.R.*, 385 U.S. 157 (1966), *noted by* Jones in 15 U.C.L.A. L. Rev. 877 (1968).

———

Smith v. Evening News Ass'n, 371 U.S. 195, 83 S. Ct. 267, 9 L. Ed. 2d 246 (1962). Petitioner, a union member, sued his employer in state court for damages, alleging breach of a provision in the collective contract that there would be no discrimination against any employee because of union activity. The state courts dismissed on the ground that the subject matter was within the exclusive jurisdiction of the NLRB. The Supreme Court reversed. The Court first declared that the authority of the Board to deal with unfair labor practices which also violate collective agreements "is not exclusive and does not destroy the jurisdiction of the courts in suits under § 301." The Court then concluded that an action by an individual employee to collect wages in the form of damages is among those "suits for violation of contracts between an employer and a labor organization" arising under § 301.

NOTES

1. In *Arnold Co. v. Carpenters Dist. Council of Jacksonville,* 417 U.S. 12 (1974), the Supreme Court held that a state court had jurisdiction to enjoin a union's breach of a no-strike clause, even though the breach arguably involved a violation of § 8(b)(4)(D)'s jurisdictional dispute provisions.

2. Although ERISA authorizes multiemployer benefit funds to sue employers directly in federal district court for delinquent contributions, nothing explicitly covers suits for sums accruing after the expiration of a collective agreement. The Supreme Court has held that ERISA does not authorize such suits; the matter is for the NLRB under § 8(a)(5). *Laborers Health & Welfare Trust Fund v. Advanced Lightweight Concrete Co.,* 484 U.S. 539 (1988).

3. *See generally* Dunau, *Contractual Prohibition of Unfair Labor Practices: Jurisdictional Problems,* 57 Colum. L. Rev. 52 (1957); Sovern, *Section 301 and the Primary Jurisdiction of the NLRB,* 76 Harv. L. Rev. 529 (1963). The large question of individual employee rights under a labor agreement will be treated in detail in Section IV, *infra.*

Alexander v. Gardner-Denver Co., 415 U.S. 36, 94 S. Ct. 1011, 39 L. Ed. 2d 147 (1974). A black employee who had been discharged for allegedly poor work performance processed a claim through the contractual grievance-arbitration procedures. At the arbitration hearing, he testified that the employer's action was racially motivated in violation of the bargaining agreement's antidiscrimination provision. The arbitrator ruled that the employee had been terminated for "just cause." He did not specifically address the grievant's discrimination claim. Following his exhaustion of EEOC procedures, the discharged worker commenced a Title VII action in federal district court. Although the employer asserted that the previous arbitral decision should preclude judicial consideration of the plaintiff's Title VII suit, based upon collateral estoppel, res judicata, election of remedies, and waiver theories, the Supreme Court rejected these contentions.

The Court first emphasized the fact that a Title VII litigant vindicates the important congressional policy against employment discrimination, while a grievant processing a claim through grievance-arbitration procedures merely vindicates private contract rights. As a result of this crucial distinction, the Court decided that it would be inappropriate to apply preclusion principles to deprive the plaintiff of de novo judicial consideration of his Title VII allegations.

> [T]he legislative history of Title VII manifests a congressional intent to allow an individual to pursue independently his rights under both Title VII and other applicable state and federal statutes. The clear inference is that Title VII was designed to supplement, rather than supplant, existing laws and institutions relating to employment discrimination. In sum, Title VII's purpose and procedures strongly suggest that an individual does not forfeit his private cause of action if he first pursues his grievance to final arbitration under the nondiscrimination clause of a collective-bargaining agreement.

Even though the Court determined that Alexander was entitled to a trial de novo on his Title VII claim, despite the prior adverse arbitral decision, it did note that where factual issues are involved, a federal district court "may properly accord ... great weight" to the previous factual conclusions of the arbitrator, as long as they are supported by an adequate record.

NOTES

1. On remand, the district court's decision that the discharge was nondiscriminatory was affirmed. *Alexander v. Gardner-Denver Co.,* 519 F.2d 503 (10th Cir. 1975), *cert. denied,* 423 U.S. 1058 (1976).

2. Analyses of *Gardner-Denver* and its implications include Cooper, Meltzer, Coulson, *The Arbitration of Title VII Disputes: The Impact of the Gardner-Denver Case,* in N.Y.U. Twenty-Seventh Annual Conference on Labor 183, 189, 201 (1974) (three separate papers); Edwards, *Arbitration of Employment Discrimination Cases: An Empirical Study,* in National Academy of Arbitrators, Arbitration—1975, Proceedings of the Twenty-Eighth Annual Meeting 59 (1976); Edwards, *Arbitration as an Alternative in Equal Employment Disputes,* 33 Arb. J. 22 (Dec. 1978); Meltzer, *Labor Arbitration and Discrimination: The Parties' Process and the Public's Purposes,* 43 U. Chi. L. Rev. 724 (1976); Siegel, *Arbitration of EEO Issues: A Positive View,* in N.Y.U. Thirty-Second Annual Conference on Labor 139 (1979); Wolfson, *Social Policy in Title VII Arbitrations,* 68 Ky. L.J. 101 (1979-80). *See also* Gould, *Labor Arbitration of Grievances Involving Racial Discrimination,* 118 U. Pa. L. Rev. 40 (1969).

3. What impact does *Gardner-Denver* have on the NLRB's *Collyer* deferral policy? *See Arnold Co. v. Carpenters Dist. Council of Jacksonville,* 417 U.S. 12, 16-17 (1974).

4. If an arbitrator determines that an employee has been discharged for just cause under a collective bargaining agreement, without dealing with any question of discrimination under Title VII, should a federal court in a subsequent Title VII action accord finality to the factual findings underlying the arbitration decision, while reserving to itself the statutory issue of discrimination? Would it make any difference if the employee had presented the question of racial, religious, or sex discrimination to the arbitrator? Would it make any difference if the employee had previously challenged the arbitration award in federal court under § 301 and had lost? *Compare Becton v. Consolidated Freightways,* 687 F.2d 140 (6th Cir. 1982), *cert. denied,* 460 U.S. 1040 (1983) *with Aleem v. General Felt Indus.,* 661 F.2d 135 (9th Cir. 1981).

5. What about the reverse situation, where an employee first litigates in federal court, loses, and subsequently seeks to pursue contractual remedies under a collective bargaining agreement—does *Gardner-Denver* apply? *See Weaver v. Florida Power & Light Co.,* 966 F. Supp. 1157 (S.D. Fla. 1997).

6. An employee whose claim of discriminatory discharge has been rejected by the NLRB may still be able to litigate a charge of racial discrimination based on the same incidents under Title VII. *Tipler v. E.I. Du Pont de Nemours,* 443 F.2d 125 (6th Cir. 1971). Although there is an overlap in the application of the NLRA and the Civil Rights Act, the same issue is not necessarily presented in proceedings under the two statutes.

7. Finding portions of the national labor policy "in tension," the Supreme Court in a 7-2 decision held that claims by employees under the Fair Labor Standards Act for time spent in vehicle maintenance procedures mandated by the employer were not barred because they had been previously adjudicated adversely to the plaintiffs under contractual dispute-resolution procedures. Drawing an analogy between the FLSA rights asserted here and the Title VII rights at the heart of its decision in *Gardner-Denver,* the Court stated: "In sum, the FLSA rights petitioners seek to assert in this action are independent of the collective bargaining process. They devolve on petitioners as individual workers, not as members of a collective organization. They are not waivable." *Barrentine v. Arkansas-Best Freight Sys.,* 450 U.S. 728 (1981); *see also Bernard v. IBP Inc. of Nebraska,* 154 F.3d 259 (5th Cir. 1998) (following *Barrentine* and noting the differences in the remedies available under the FLSA and arbitration).

8. The use of arbitration to resolve employment disputes in nonunion workplaces has become an increasingly popular practice, encouraged by the proliferation of statutes and common law causes of action (such as wrongful discharge) protecting individual employee rights. Employers now routinely ask prospective employees to sign agreements waiving their statutory rights and any claims they may have at common law in exchange for private arbitration. In *Gilmer v. Interstate/Johnson Lane Corp.,* 500 U.S. 20 (1991), the Supreme Court ruled that this practice is valid. In *Gilmer,* an individual employee of a brokerage firm, not covered by a collective bargaining agreement, was required by the rules of the New

York Stock Exchange to arbitrate all controversies arising out of his employment. The Supreme Court held (7-2) that the employee was obliged to take his claim under the Age Discrimination in Employment Act to arbitration rather than being able to go directly to federal court. *Gardner-Denver* was distinguished on three grounds. First, it had involved an agreement to arbitrate contractual claims that did not extend to statutory claims; the arbitrator was authorized only to determine private rights under the collective bargaining agreement. By contrast, the Stock Exchange's arbitral rules specifically empowered arbitrators to resolve external statutory issues. Second, the *Gardner-Denver* situation had involved the grievance and arbitration machinery in a labor contract which could be enforced only by the union, not by the individual employee. A potential conflict of interest thus existed between the union's role as enforcer of majority rights under the contract and the individual employee's statutory rights. Third, the claim in *Gilmer* arose under the Federal Arbitration Act, which reflects a liberal policy favoring arbitration agreements, while the *Gardner-Denver* claim had arisen under a collective bargaining agreement.

Gilmer has been extensively analyzed in the law reviews. The case is noted in 72 B.U. L. Rev. 641 (1992); St. Louis U. L.J. 741 (1992); 37 Vill. L. Rev. 113 (1992). *See generally* Estreicher, *Predispute Agreements to Arbitrate Statutory Employment Claims,* 72 N.Y.U. L. Rev. 1344 (1997); Finkin, *Workers' Contracts Under the United States Arbitration Act: An Essay in Historical Clarification,* 17 Berkeley J. Emp. & Lab. L. 282 (1996); Malin, *Arbitrating Statutory Employment Claims in the Aftermath of Gilmer,* 40 St. Louis U. L.J. 77 (1996); Gorman, *The Gilmer Decision and the Private Arbitration of Public Law Disputes,* 1995 U. Ill. L. Rev. 635; Plass, *Arbitrating, Waiving and Deferring Title VII Claims,* 58 Brooklyn L. Rev. 779 (1992); Shearer, *Arbitrability, Preemption, and Preclusion: Developing Issues in Age Discrimination Claims,* 43 Lab. L.J. 313 (1992); Stallworth & Malin, *Conflicts Arising Out of Workforce Diversity,* Proceedings of the 46th Annual Meeting of the National Academy of Arbitrators 104 (1994); St. Antoine, *Divergent Strategies: Union Organizing and Alternative Dispute Resolution* (IRRA Spring Meeting, April 21-23, 1994), 45 Lab. L.J. 465 (1994); Todd, *Using Arbitration to Avoid Litigation,* 44 Lab. L. J. 3 (1993).

9. What are the implications of *Gilmer* for the unionized sector? If a grievance-arbitration provision authorized arbitrators to apply civil rights statutes, could an employer compel an employee who filed a discrimination suit to take the case to arbitration? The following case takes up these questions.

PRYNER v. TRACTOR SUPPLY CO.

United States Court of Appeals, Seventh Circuit
109 F.3d 354 (7th Cir.), *cert. denied,* 118 S. Ct. 294 (1997)

POSNER, CHIEF JUDGE.

We have consolidated the appeals in two employment discrimination cases that raise the same two issues: Are arbitration clauses in collective bargaining agreements other than in the maritime, railroad, and other transportation industries subject to the Federal Arbitration Act, 9 U.S.C. § 1 et seq.? And can a collective bargaining agreement compel an employee to arbitrate a claim that he may have under one of the federal statutes, such as Title VII of the Civil Rights Act of 1964, the Age Discrimination in Employment Act, or the Americans with Disabilities Act, that confer litigable rights on employees? The first issue is critical to our jurisdiction of these appeals; the second is the issue on the merits—which, of course, we can reach only if we satisfy ourselves that we have jurisdiction.

Each of the two plaintiffs is a former employee of one of the defendants, and each was discharged by his employer in alleged violation of federal law. Pryner is black and complains that he was discharged in violation of Title VII and of 42 U.S.C. § 1981 because of his race and also because he had complained about Tractor Supply's previous racial discrimination against him before he was fired; he also has a claim under the Americans with Disabilities Act.... Sobierajski complains of having been discharged because of his age (58 at the time of the discharge), in violation of the Age Discrimination in Employment Act, and because of a disability, in violation of the ADA.

Both plaintiffs were employed under collective bargaining agreements. [Both agreements forbade discrimination by either the company or the union "on the basis of race, creed, religion, national origin, sex or age," with the agreement covering Sobierajski stating that this was "in accordance with applicable Federal and State law."] Both agreements authorize the employer to impose discipline on an employee, up to and including discharge, for "just cause." And both contain a clause that creates a grievance procedure, making the union the employee's griever and culminating in arbitration if the matter is not resolved in the earlier stages of the procedure, for disputes involving "interpretation or application" of the agreement.

Both Sobierajski and Pryner invoked the grievance procedure in their respective collective bargaining agreements. Pryner's union struck out at the earlier stages of the grievance procedure, and has demanded arbitration. Sobierajski's grievance, however, was abandoned, though whether by his own actions or those of the union is unclear. Pryner and Sobierajski then filed these discrimination suits, seeking damages (including punitive damages in the case of Pryner), attorneys' fees, and reinstatement. The defendants moved to stay the suits pending arbitration of the plaintiffs' claims. The motions were denied ..., and the defendants have appealed from these denials....

The issue of our appellate jurisdiction is whether these two appeals are authorized by the Federal Arbitration Act. The denial of a stay of proceedings before the court asked to grant the stay is not a final decision within the meaning of 28 U.S.C. § 1291, but when it is the denial of a stay of those proceedings pending arbitration it nevertheless is appealable immediately, at least ... if the motion is filed under the arbitration act, which expressly authorizes such appeals. 9 U.S.C. § 16(a)(1)(A). The act covers maritime transactions and transactions involving interstate commerce. But "contracts of employment of seamen, railroad employees, or any other class of workers engaged in foreign or interstate commerce" are specifically excluded by section 1. If "engaged in foreign or interstate commerce" is given its usual modern legal meaning, virtually all employment contracts are within the exclusion, including the two collective bargaining agreements upon which the defendants based their motions for a stay. Some courts so read it.... Others confine the exclusion to collective bargaining agreements.... Others deem the arbitration act superseded with regard to such agreements by section 301 of the Taft-Hartley Act—as did we in *Martin v. Youngstown Sheet & Tube Co.*, 911 F.2d 1239, 1244 (7th Cir.1990), and the cases cited there. But in *International Union of Operating Eng'rs v. Murphy Co.*, 82 F.3d 185, 188-89 (7th Cir.1996), we assumed the opposite (that the arbitration act is not superseded by section 301), without citing *Martin*. And in *Chicago Typographical Union v. Chicago Sun-Times*, 935 F.2d 1501, 1504 (7th Cir.1991), decided between *Martin* and *International Union of Operating Engineers*, we had described the issue of supersession as an open one.

A footnote in *United Paperworkers Int'l Union v. Misco, Inc.*, 484 U.S. 29, 40 n. 9 (1987), says that the arbitration act does not apply to labor arbitration. But the footnote gives no reason; is inconsistent with the Supreme Court's subsequent decision in *Gilmer v. Interstate/Johnson Lane Corp.*, 500 U.S. 20, 25 n. 2 (1991), which expressly left the question open; and goes on to cite with apparent approval our decision in *Pietro Scalzitti Co. v. International Union of Operating Eng'rs*, 351 F.2d 576, 579-80 (7th Cir.1965), which, limiting the exclusion of employment contracts in section 1 to workers engaged in the physical movement of goods in interstate or foreign commerce, holds that the arbitration act applies to labor arbitration in all industries except transportation. See also *Briggs & Stratton Corp. v. Local 232*, 36 F.3d 712, 714-15 (7th Cir.1994); *Cole v. Burns Int'l Security Servs.*, 105 F.3d 1465, 1469 (D.C.Cir.1997); *Asplundh Tree Expert Co. v. Bates*, 71 F.3d 592, 596-602 (6th Cir.1995). This is acknowledged to be the "prevailing view" of the scope of the exclusion by an opponent. Matthew W. Finkin, "'Workers' Contracts' Under the United States Arbitration Act: An Essay in Historical Clarification," 17 Berkeley J. Employment & Labor L. 282, 290 (1996).

But aren't we on both sides of the issue? We have cases like *Martin* that hold that section 301 supersedes the Federal Arbitration Act, a case that assumes it does not (*International Union of Operating Engineers*), and cases such as *Briggs & Stratton* that imply not by confining the exclusion in section 1 to transportation workers and saying nothing about supersession by section 301. This internal conflict is, fortunately, illusory. The cases that say that section 301 supersedes the arbitration act for cases within section 301's domain hold (all but *Martin* itself and *Cleveland v. Porca Co.*, 38 F.3d 289, 296 n. 5 (7th Cir.1994)) only that particular provisions of the act, such as its limitations periods (three months for moving to vacate an award, one year for enforcing it), are superseded, and do not mention the provision allowing interlocutory appeals. We shall see that these holdings are consistent with the act's being generally applicable to collective bargaining agreements provided that the workers covered by the agreement are not engaged in transportation and federal common law created under the aegis of section 301 is used to determine any substantive issues that arise in proceedings to vacate or enforce the arbitration award....

Professor Finkin argues that the prevailing view, which limits the exclusion in section 1 to employment contracts in transportation, is wrong. His review of the legislative history (the arbitration act was passed in 1925) has persuaded him that Congress's intention was to exclude all employment contracts. Yet, as he acknowledges, the impetus for the exclusion came entirely from the seafarers' union, concerned that arbitrators would be less favorably inclined toward seamen's claims than judges were. Judges favored such claims, the union thought, in part because of a tradition that seamen were "wards in admiralty," in part because of peculiarities of maritime law that would make it easy to slip an arbitration clause into a maritime employment contract without the seaman's noticing it, and in part because the maritime employment relation was already heavily regulated by federal law. It was soon noticed that the railroad industry's labor relations were also heavily regulated—by a statute (the Railway Labor Act) that included provisions for compulsory arbitration of many disputes. Motor carriers were not yet comprehensively regulated, but it may have seemed (and was) only a matter of time before they would be: hence the expansion of the exclusion from seamen to railroad to other transportation workers. It seems to us, as it did to the Third Circuit in *Tenney Eng'g, Inc. v. United Electrical, Radio & Machine Workers*, 207 F.2d 450, 452-53 (3d Cir.1953), that this history supports rather than undermines limiting "engaged in foreign or interstate commerce" to transportation. To impress the modern meaning on the quoted term, moreover, would both make the reference to seamen and railroad workers superfluous and give the exclusion a breathtaking scope. It would mean that an arbitration clause in an employment contract between a giant multinational corporation and its chief executive officer would, though plausibly "involving" interstate commerce within the meaning of section 2, not be enforceable in federal court. Such a result would not answer to any concern expressed to or by Congress in the debates leading up to the passage of the arbitration act.

Even if as we believe the collective bargaining agreements in this case are not excluded from the act's coverage by section 1's reference to employment agreements, they might be excluded, as some courts believe, by section 301 of the Taft-Hartley Act. Section 301(a), which makes collective bargaining agreements enforceable in the federal courts, was interpreted in *Textile Workers Union v. Lincoln Mills*, 353 U.S. 448 (1957), to require that principles of federal common law be developed and used to interpret such agreements. There is no reference in section 301 to arbitration, which becomes an issue in a section 301 case only when a collective bargaining agreement happens to contain (as most such agreements do) an arbitration clause. The question is then whether, despite its silence about arbitration, section 301 repealed the Federal Arbitration Act with respect to collective bargaining agreements that would otherwise be within the act's scope. This seems hardly likely, quite apart from the venerable but contested principle that repeals by implication are disfavored and so are to be avoided unless there is no way to reconcile the two statutes....

The cases that decline to apply the arbitration act's three-month statute of limitations to suits under section 301 to set arbitration awards aside stand for nothing more than that while the existence of two statutes both conferring federal jurisdiction over the same claim in the same case is not such an anomaly as would justify holding that one or the other was exclusive, if there are inconsistencies the courts are going to have to make a choice. See *Lander Co. v. MMP Investments, Inc.*, 107 F.3d 476, 481 (7th Cir. 1997). Jurisdictional redundancies are commonplace.... It is true, as mentioned in *Lander* and emphasized in *Harry Hoffman Printing, Inc. v. Graphic Communications, Int'l Union*, 912 F.2d [608] at 611-12 [2d Cir.1990], that the arbitration act reaches only disputes that are within the jurisdiction of the federal courts under some other statute, such as the diversity statute or, as here, section 301 of the Taft-Hartley Act. But all that this means, so far as the jurisdictional issue in the present cases is concerned, is that whenever the arbitration act is properly invoked there are two jurisdictional statutes in play. That is not an argument for refusing to apply one of them. And if the arbitration act is better regarded not as a source of jurisdiction at all but merely as a prescription of procedures for a class of cases otherwise within federal jurisdiction, this would actually strengthen the argument against deeming the act superseded by the presence of a "truly" jurisdictional statute such as section 301.

The arbitration act covers almost the whole field of arbitrable disputes, only a subset of which (and a small one in 1925) grow out of collective bargaining agreements. The act's limitations periods were not designed with such agreements in mind, and may not suit them. When the question arose what the statute of limitations should be in suits under section 301 to challenge arbitration awards based on such agreements (the statute contains no limitations period), the courts cast about for analogous claims from which to "borrow" a limitations period. In so doing they did not hold that section 301 had repealed the arbitration act so far as collective bargaining agreements were concerned; and when in 1988, long after section 301 had been enacted, Congress amended the arbitration act to make denials of stays pending arbitration expressly appealable despite the absence of finality, it did not carve an exception for arbitration pursuant to collective bargaining agreements. Judicial Improvements and Access to Justice Act, Pub.L. No. 100-702, 102 Stat. 4671 (1988). That may have been an oversight, but we suspect not; for no reason is suggested why, if immediate appeals of denials of such stays are a good thing with respect to the arbitration of other types of dispute, they are a bad thing when the dispute is a labor dispute. If anything, the public interest in resolving labor disputes by arbitration, and therefore in allowing erroneous refusals to defer to arbitration to be corrected promptly, is greater than in an ordinary commercial arbitration.

The big thing that section 301 did (besides creating federal jurisdiction over suits to enforce collective bargaining agreements), so far as labor arbitration is concerned, was to ordain the creation of a body of federal common law to govern disputes arising out of such arbitration. Included in that body are limitations periods, which by analogy to the substance-procedure distinction worked out in the wake of the Erie decision fall on the substantive side of the divide. *Guaranty Trust Co. v. York*, 326 U.S. 99, 109-10 (1945). The question whether a particular type of interlocutory order is immediately appealable, however, is a quintessentially procedural question to which the Federal Arbitration Act provides an answer that creates no tension with anything in either section 301 or the common law of collective bargaining agreements that has evolved under it; that in fact effectuates the policy of section 301, which is to encourage the resolution of labor disputes by means other than industrial warfare—and arbitration is prominent among those means.

Our resolution of the jurisdictional issue can be criticized as creating an arbitrary difference between the appeal rights of parties to employment contracts, including collective bargaining agreements, in nontransportation industries and the corresponding appeal rights of parties to collective bargaining agreements and other employment contracts in transportation. Parties to employment contracts in other industries can appeal from orders denying stays pending arbitration. Parties to employment contracts in the transportation industries cannot because, excluded from the Federal Arbitration Act by section 1, they cannot rely on section 16; and section 301 of the Taft-Hartley Act has no provision, corresponding to that section, authorizing interlocutory appeals.... The resulting anomaly (different treatment of labor arbitration in transportation versus nontransportation industries) would be the unavoidable consequence of an interpretation of section 1 of the arbitration act that differentiates between employment contracts in the transportation and nontransportation sectors, and that is a distinction to which this court is committed....

So we may turn at last to the issue on the merits, which is whether a collective bargaining agreement can compel the arbitration of a federal antidiscrimination claim.

Two competing interests have to be considered. One is the interest in allowing unions and employers to establish a comprehensive regime for the adjustment of employment disputes; it argues for allowing the collective bargaining agreement to force all such disputes into the grievance and arbitration groove even when the dispute arises out of a claim that a worker's statutory rights have been infringed. The other is the interest in the effective enforcement of rights designed for the protection of workers whom Congress has classified as belonging to vulnerable groups, generally and in these two cases minority groups—blacks, the disabled, and the aged (though whether persons 40 years old and older, the group protected by the age discrimination law, should be considered a vulnerable segment of the population may certainly be questioned as an original matter). That interest will be impaired if the right to bring suit in federal district court to enforce these rights is taken away from the workers.

Or will it? The employers in our two cases, supported by employer groups that have filed amicus curiae briefs, argue that the workers will actually be better off if the employers' position is adopted. Because the Equal Employment Opportunity Commission has an enormous backlog and limited resources for litigating, the vast majority of workers who have claims under any of the statutes that the Commission enforces have perforce to bring and finance their own lawsuits; they cannot rely on the Commission to do so for them. In contrast, a grievance is prosecuted by the worker's collective bargaining representative (the union) at no cost to the worker. It is true that the plaintiffs in these cases do not wish to abandon their right to invoke the grievance machinery created by the collective bargaining agreements; they just want the option of pursuing judicial remedies on top of or in lieu of their arbitral remedies. But unless the arbitral remedy is exclusive, the company's incentive to agree to negotiate an arbitration clause broad enough to encompass statutory violations will be reduced, as the only effect of such a clause will be to multiply the employee's remedies.

The employers emphasize that these collective bargaining agreements do not take away any of the workers' substantive statutory rights, but merely substitute an arbitral for a judicial proceeding as the means of vindicating the rights. Although the arbitrator's award ... can ... be pleaded as res judicata in the worker's federal district court suit, ... subject to limitations unnecessary to dwell on here, ... this is true if the worker wins before the arbitrator as well as if he loses. So there is no curtailment of his substantive rights. The only difference is the forum; the defendants are right. The plaintiffs riposte that it isn't clear that the collective bargaining agreements in our two cases are completely coextensive with the plaintiffs' statutory rights; and it isn't. But a court can properly stay a suit before it if any issue in the suit is arbitrable, even if some issues are not. The arbitration act says in fact that the court shall stay the suit, not just a piece of the suit, if the suit is "brought upon" an arbitrable issue, 9 U.S.C. § 3, though the cases, perhaps concerned lest the tail wag the dog, treat the question whether to stay the entire case as discretionary in cases involving both arbitrable and nonarbitrable issues.... The defendants concede that to the extent that the rights conferred by the collective bargaining agreements, or the sanctions available to the arbitrators, fall short of fully vindicating the plaintiffs' substantive and remedial statutory rights, the plaintiffs will be free to resume their suits after the arbitrators render their awards, having filed the suits within the statute of limitations. But the findings made by the arbitrators might be entitled to collateral estoppel effect in the resumed suits....

The honey-tongued assurances of the employers' able counsel and their amici, unusually and perhaps opportunistically aligned with the unions' interest in controlling their members' access to remedies, do not persuade us that there is no genuine conflict between employer and employee interests in these cases. The plaintiffs' rights under the collective bargaining agreements are not as extensive as their statutory rights, so that to obtain complete relief they may have to undergo two trials, one before the arbitrator and the other in the district court. And by being forced into binding arbitration they would be surrendering their right to trial by jury—a right that civil rights plaintiffs (or their lawyers) fought hard for and finally obtained in the 1991 amendments to Title VII, and that they also have under the age discrimination and disability acts.

Most important, the grievance and arbitration procedure can be invoked only by the union, and not by the worker. The worker has to persuade the union to prosecute his grievance and if it loses in the early stages of the grievance proceedings to submit the grievance to arbitration. *Vaca v. Sipes*, 386 U.S. 171, 190-91 (1967); cf. *Martin v. Youngstown Sheet & Tube Co., supra*, 911 F.2d at 1244. The defendants point out that if the union arbitrarily refuses to prosecute a grievance, let alone refuses on racial or other invidious grounds to do so, the worker can bring a suit against the union for breach of its duty of fair representation of all members of the bargaining unit. *DelCostello v. Teamsters,* 462 U.S. 151, 164 (1983); *Garcia v. Zenith Electronics Corp.*, 58 F.3d 1171, 1176 (7th Cir.1995).... This raises the spectre of three suits to enforce a statutory right—the suit against the union to force it to grieve and if necessary arbitrate the grievance, the arbitration proceeding, and the resumed district court proceeding if the workers' rights under the collective bargaining agreement are more limited than their statutory rights. In any event, the union has broad discretion as to whether or not to prosecute a grievance. It may take into account tactical and strategic factors such as its limited resources and consequent need to establish priorities, just as other "prosecutors" must do, as well as its desire to maintain harmonious relations among the workers and between them and the employer. *Vaca v. Sipes, supra*, 386 U.S. at 191-92.... Corresponding to this expansive and ill-defined discretion, the scope of judicial review of its exercise is deferential. See, e.g., *Air Line Pilots Ass'n v. O'Neill*, 499 U.S. 65, 78 (1991).... The result is that a worker who asks the union to grieve a statutory violation cannot have great confidence either that it will do so or that if it does not the courts will intervene and force it to do so. While the grievance machinery could in principle offer the worker a cheaper alternative to suing, it seems unlikely that the union would be any more willing to prosecute a marginal case than a lawyer asked to handle it on a contingent-fee basis. Indeed, the union might for strategic reasons decline to prosecute a claim that would have enough merit to enable the worker to retain a lawyer on a contingent-fee basis were the worker not bound to the union.

The essential conflict is between majority and minority rights. The collective bargaining agreement is the symbol and reality of a majoritarian conception of workers' rights. An agreement negotiated by the union elected by a majority of the workers in the bargaining unit binds all the members of the unit, whether they are part of the majority or for that matter even members of the union entitled to vote for union leaders—they need not be. The statutory rights at issue in these two cases are rights given to members of minority groups because of concern about the mistreatment (of which there is a long history in the labor movement, see, e.g., *Steele v. Louisville & Nashville R.R.*, 323 U.S. 192 (1944)) of minorities by majorities. We may assume that the union will not engage in actionable discrimination against minority workers. But we may not assume that it will be highly sensitive to their special interests, which are the interests protected by Title VII and the other discrimination statutes, and will seek to vindicate those interests with maximum vigor. The employers' position delivers the enforcement of the rights of these minorities into the hands of the majority, and we do not think that this result is consistent with the policy of these statutes or justified by the abstract desirability of allowing unions and employers to cut their own deals. And we are given no reason to believe that the ability of unionized workers to enforce their statutory rights outside of the grievance machinery established by collective bargaining agreements is undermining labor relations.

The defendants cite provisions added in the early 1990s to Title VII, the Age Discrimination in Employment Act, and the Americans with Disabilities Act that "where appropriate and to the extent authorized by law, ... arbitration ... is encouraged to resolve disputes arising under" these laws. Pub.L. No. 102-166, § 118, 105 Stat. 1071, 1081 (1991); 42 U.S.C. § 12212. These provisions, a polite bow to the popularity of "alternative dispute resolution" and perhaps a mild sop to the judiciary, which has expressed alarm at Congress's relentless expansion of the jurisdiction of the federal courts, encourage arbitration "where appropriate"— and if we are right it is not appropriate when it is not agreed to by the worker but instead is merely imposed by a collective bargaining agreement that he may have opposed. Nothing in the background of the amendments is inconsistent with this interpretation. It would be at least a mild paradox for Congress, having in another amendment that it made to Title VII in 1991 conferred a right to trial by jury for the first time, Pub.L. No. 102-166, § 102, § 1977A(c), 105 Stat. 1071, 1073 (1991), to have empowered unions, in those same amendments, to prevent workers from obtaining jury trials in these cases. We know that statutes, being products of compromise, frequently reflect inconsistent aims. But if that is the case here, we might expect to find a hint of it in the statutory language or design, or in the legislative history, but we find none.

We are not holding that workers' statutory rights are never arbitrable. They are arbitrable if the worker consents to have them arbitrated. If the worker brings suit, the employer suggests that their dispute be arbitrated, the worker agrees, and the collective bargaining agreement does not preclude such side agreements, there is nothing to prevent a binding arbitration. *Austin v. Owens-Brockway Glass Container, Inc.*, 78 F.3d 875, 879 (4th Cir.1996); *American Italian Pasta*

Co. v. Austin Co., 914 F.2d 1103, 1104 (8th Cir.1990).... All we are holding is that the union cannot consent for the employee by signing a collective bargaining agreement that consigns the enforcement of statutory rights to the union-controlled grievance and arbitration machinery created by the agreement.

Thus far we have analyzed the arbitrability of the disputes in these two cases without reference to the precedents that might be thought to govern the issue, even though the hundreds of pages of briefs are devoted to little else. That in itself is a sign that case law is unlikely to be dispositive of the issue. The authority of a previously decided case is at its greatest when it is apparent that the case does not differ in any material particular from the case in which it is cited as authority; and to show the absence of a material difference usually is easy. When instead a lawyer tries to create a mosaic of case authority from a large number of previous cases all distinguishable from the present one, what purports to be an investigation of case law is really a quest for policies or principles that can be found in the previous cases and are thus legitimate factors to guide the decision of a new case. Those factors we have discussed. Both sides of these appeals also are able to cite a case or two that squarely support their position—cases that really do not differ in any material particular from the present one—but in doing so all they have done is identify a circuit split. Compare *Austin v. Owens-Brockway Glass Container, Inc., supra*, 78 F.3d at 885, with *Varner v. National Super Markets, Inc.*, 94 F.3d 1209, 1213 (8th Cir.1996).

Each side has its favorite Supreme Court case that it has flogged mercilessly to yield the desired holding. *Alexander v. Gardner-Denver Co.*, 415 U.S. 36 (1974), ... held that the arbitration of a contractual right not to be discriminated against does not preclude enforcement of a statutory right. This is not quite the same thing as holding that the worker does not have to go through the arbitration process. But as we mentioned earlier, the parties to our cases all assume that if Pryner and Sobierajski must go through arbitration they also must abide by its result, though one possible result is the arbitrators' concluding that they lack authority under the collective bargaining agreements to render complete, or perhaps any, relief, in which event there would be room for further litigation.

By stressing, somewhat formalistically it might seem, the "distinctly separate nature" of contractual and statutory rights, 415 U.S. at 50, the Supreme Court sowed the possibility of distinguishing Sobierajski's case. For his collective bargaining agreement mentions federal and state law and could therefore be deemed consent to the arbitrators' enforcing statutory as well as contractual rights. The defendants note this, but put most of their weight on the Supreme Court's subsequent decision in *Gilmer v. Interstate/Johnson Lane Corp., supra*.... The Court held that [Gilmer] had to submit his claim of age discrimination to arbitration. Although the arbitration clause was not in the employment contract (if it had been the Court would have had to decide the applicability of the Federal Arbitration Act to nontransportation employment contracts), but in the registration agreement to which the employer was not a party, the employer had required Gilmer to sign the registration agreement as a condition of his employment.

Although the Court did not overrule *Alexander*, it did say that the mistrust of the arbitral process that had permeated that opinion had been "undermined" by subsequent decisions evincing a positive attitude toward arbitration. 500 U.S. at 34 n. 5. It also distinguished *Alexander* from Gilmer's case on three grounds. The first was that the arbitration in *Alexander* had "occurred in the context of a collective-bargaining agreement," creating a "tension between collective representation and individual statutory rights." *Id.* at 35. An attenuated version of that tension was present in *Gilmer* itself, because Gilmer's employer had forced him as a condition of his employment to sign a nonnegotiable form contract with the New York Stock Exchange that contained an arbitration clause. But Gilmer's access to arbitration, if a dispute arose, was not controlled by a union, or any other entity or individual. At all events the Court treated his situation as being different from Alexander's.

The second distinction drawn in *Gilmer* was that the issue in the earlier case had been the preclusive effect of an arbitration award concerning a contractual right on the litigation of a statutory right, rather than (as in *Gilmer*) the enforceability of the agreement to arbitrate the statutory claim. The third distinction was that *Alexander* had not been decided under the Federal Arbitration Act. This was not to say that the act had been totally inapplicable, but only that, as we saw earlier, substantive issues in suits that are within the scope of both the arbitration act and section 301 of the Taft-Hartley Act are governed by section 301. So the third ground of distinction ties back to the first, and like the first puts our two cases on the *Alexander* side of the line—while the second distinction seems to be a distinction without a difference, since the Court assumed, consistent with what we said earlier about the preclusive effects of arbitration awards, that *Gilmer* could not bring an age discrimination suit if he lost the arbitration proceeding. 500 U.S. at 28. But for what the distinction is worth, it tugs our cases a little closer to *Gilmer*, since here as there the issue is the enforceability of the arbitration clause in a collective bargaining agreement rather than the effect of the award in an arbitration of a contractual right on the right to sue to enforce a statutory right.

On balance our case is closer to *Alexander*; but is enough left of *Alexander* to compel a decision in favor of the plaintiffs? Only the Supreme Court can answer that question; and we are timid about declaring decisions by the Supreme Court overruled when the Court has not said so.... The conservative reading of *Gilmer* is that it just pruned some dicta from *Alexander*—and it certainly cannot be taken to hold that collective bargaining agreements can compel the arbitration of statutory rights. That issue was not before the Court or discussed by it. The Court may have so distinguished *Alexander* as to deprive it of any authoritative force; but that is the most it did and by doing so opened what till then had been a closed issue. It did not resolve the issue, which for the reasons stated earlier we believe should be resolved in favor of the plaintiffs' right to sue. The district judges were therefore right to deny the defendants' motions for stays of the judicial proceedings pending arbitration.

Affirmed.

NOTES

1. In a contrary decision, a terminated employee's suit alleging discrimination because of gender and disability was barred by her failure to exhaust the arbitration procedures of a union contract. *Austin v. Owens-Brockway Glass Container, Inc.*, 78 F.3d 875 (4th Cir.), *cert. denied*, 117 S. Ct. 432 (1996). The dissenting judge maintained that *Gardner-Denver*, not *Gilmer,* governed collective bargaining agreements. In accord with *Pryner* are *Varner v. National Super Markets*, 94 F.3d 1209 (8th Cir. 1996), *cert. denied*, 117 S. Ct. 946 (1997), and *Harrison v. Eddy Potash, Inc.*, 112 F.3d 1437 (10th Cir. 1997).

In *Wright v. Universal Maritime Service Corp.*, 121 F.3d 702 (4th Cir. 1997) (unpublished opinion), *cert. granted,* 118 S. Ct. 1162 (1998), the plaintiff employee sued four companies that had denied him work because of his previous disability claim, alleging violations of the Americans With Disabilities Act. Applying *Austin v. Owens-Brockway Glass Container, Inc.,* the Fourth Circuit denied his claim because he was covered by a collective bargaining agreement containing a mandatory arbitration clause. The Supreme Court acknowledged the tension between *Gardner-Denver* and *Gilmer,* but found it unnecessary to resolve the general question of the validity of a union-negotiated waiver of employee rights under antidiscrimination statutes because the waiver at issue fell short of the "clear and unmistakable" standard applicable to union-negotiated waivers of employees' statutory rights to a judicial forum for claims of employment discrimination. 119 S. Ct. 391 (1998). Accordingly, the Court vacated the Fourth Circuit's judgment and remanded the case, explicitly reserving the issue of the enforceability of union-negotiated waivers which *are* clear and unmistakable. *Id.* at 397 n.2. *Austin* and *Wright* are analyzed in Hodges, *Protecting Unionized Employees Against Discrimination: The Fourth Circuit's Misinterpretation of Supreme Court Precedent,* 2 Employee Rights & Emp. Pol'y J. 123 (1998); Kelly, *An Argument For Retaining the Well-Established Distinction Between Contractual and Statutory Claims in Labor Arbitration,* 75 U. Det. L. Rev. 1 (1997); Kim, *Arbitrating Statutory Rights in The Union Setting: Breaking the Collective Interest Problem Without Damaging Labor Relations,* 65 U. Chi. L. Rev. 225 (1998).

2. As the *Pryner* court observed, the typical grievance and arbitration procedure under a collective bargaining agreement may be invoked only by the union, not by the individual employee. What if the collective bargaining agreement grants *both* the union and the individual employee the right to demand arbitration? *See Martin v. Dana Corp.,* 124 F.3d 590 (3d Cir. 1997) (distinguishing *Gardner-Denver* and *Pryner* on these facts); *cf. Brisentine v. Stone & Webster*

Eng'g Corp., 117 F.3d 519 (11th Cir. 1997) (applying *Gardner-Denver* in unionized context, and holding that employee is barred from proceeding on his statutory claims in court by an arbitration clause in a labor contract *only* where (1) he agrees individually to the contract containing the arbitration clause; (2) the arbitration clause authorizes the arbitrator to resolve federal statutory claims; and (3) the agreement gives the employee the right to insist on arbitration if the federal claim is not resolved to his satisfaction).

3. In a decision on an *individual* contract of employment in a nonunionized setting, the D.C. Circuit, per Judge Edwards, held that an employee could be required to arbitrate his Title VII race discrimination claim, provided the employer paid all the arbitrator's fees and the procedure was otherwise fair. *Cole v. Burns Int'l Security Servs.,* 105 F.3d 1465 (D.C. Cir. 1997) (2-1 decision on the fee question). *See also Rojas v. TK Communications,* 87 F.3d 745 (5th Cir. 1996). *Cole* (and apparently *Rojas*) sustained contracts that conditioned employment on an agreement to arbitrate statutory claims. The *Cole* court was careful to distinguish the collective bargaining context. Another court of appeals has declared that such individual waivers by employees of the right of access to the EEOC and the courts must be "knowing." *Prudential Ins. Co. of Am. v. Lai,* 42 F.3d 1299 (9th Cir. 1994), *cert. denied,* 516 U.S. 812 (1995). For commentary, *see* Lanni, *Protecting Public Rights in Private Arbitration,* 107 Yale L.J. 1157 (1998); Stone, *Mandatory Arbitration of Individual Employment Rights: The Yellow Dog Contract of the 1990s,* 73 Denver U. L. Rev. 1017 (1996).

2. SECTION 301 PREEMPTION AND STATE CLAIMS

LINGLE v. NORGE DIVISION OF MAGIC CHEF, INC.

Supreme Court of the United States
486 U.S. 399, 108 S. Ct. 1877, 100 L. Ed. 2d 410 (1988)

JUSTICE STEVENS delivered the opinion of the Court.

In Illinois an employee who is discharged for filing a worker's compensation claim may recover compensatory and punitive damages from her employer. The question presented in this case is whether an employee covered by a collective-bargaining agreement that provides her with a contractual remedy for discharge without just cause may enforce her state law remedy for retaliatory discharge. The Court of Appeals held that the application of the state tort remedy was preempted by § 301 of the Labor Management Relations Act of 1947.... 823 F.2d 1031 (CA7 1987) (en banc). We disagree.

I

Petitioner was employed in respondent's manufacturing plant in Herrin, Illinois. On December 5, 1984, she notified respondent that she had been injured in the course of her employment and requested compensation for her medical expenses pursuant to the Illinois Workers' Compensation Act. On December 11, 1984, respondent discharged her for filing a "false worker's compensation claim." *Id.,* at 1033.

The union representing petitioner promptly filed a grievance pursuant to the collective-bargaining agreement that covered all production and maintenance employees in the Herrin plant. The agreement protected those employees, including petitioner, from discharge except for "proper" or "just" cause, and established a procedure for the arbitration of grievances. The term grievance was broadly defined to encompass "any dispute between ... the Employer and any employee, concerning the effect, interpretation, application, claim of breach or violation of this Agreement." Ultimately, an arbitrator ruled in petitioner's favor and ordered respondent to reinstate her with full back pay.

Meanwhile, on July 9, 1985, petitioner commenced this action against respondent by filing a complaint in the Illinois Circuit Court for Williamson County, alleging that she had been discharged for exercising her rights under the Illinois worker's compensation laws. *See Kelsay v. Motorola, Inc.,* 74 Ill. 2d 172, 384 N.E.2d 353 (1978); *Midgett v. Sackett-Chicago, Inc.,* 105 Ill. 2d 143, 473 N.E.2d 1280 (1984); *see also* Ill. Rev. Stat., ch. 48, ¶ 138.4(h) (1987). Respondent removed the case to the Federal District Court on the basis of diversity of citizenship, and then filed a motion praying that the Court either dismiss the case on pre-emption grounds or stay further proceedings pending the completion of the arbitration. Relying on our decision in *Allis-Chalmers Corp. v. Lueck,* 471 U.S. 202 (1985), the District Court dismissed the complaint. It concluded that the "claim for retaliatory discharge is 'inextricably intertwined' with the collective bargaining provision prohibiting wrongful discharge or discharge without just cause" and that allowing the state-law action to proceed would undermine the arbitration procedures set forth in the parties' contract. 618 F. Supp. 1448, 1449 (S.D. Ill. 1985).

The Court of Appeals agreed that the state-law claim was pre-empted by § 301. In an en banc opinion, over the dissent of two judges, it rejected petitioner's argument that the tort action was not "inextricably intertwined" with the collective-bargaining agreement because the disposition of a retaliatory discharge claim in Illinois does not depend upon an interpretation of the agreement; on the contrary, the Court concluded that "the same analysis of the facts" was implicated under both procedures. 823 F.2d, at 1046. It took note of, and declined to follow, contrary decisions in the Tenth, Third, and Second Circuits. We granted certiorari to resolve the conflict in the Circuits....

II

... In *Textile Workers v. Lincoln Mills,* 353 U.S. 448 (1957), we held that § 301 not only provides federal-court jurisdiction over controversies involving collective-bargaining agreements, but also "authorizes federal courts to fashion a body

of federal law for the enforcement of these collective bargaining agreements."
Id., at 451.

In *Teamsters v. Lucas Flour Co.,* 369 U.S. 95 (1962), we were confronted with
a straightforward question of contract interpretation: whether a collective-
bargaining agreement implicitly prohibited a strike that had been called by the
union. The Washington Supreme Court had answered that question by applying
state-law rules of contract interpretation. We rejected that approach, and held that
§ 301 mandated resort to federal rules of law in order to ensure uniform interpretation to collective-bargaining agreements, and thus to promote the peaceable,
consistent resolution of labor-management disputes.

In *Allis-Chalmers Corp. v. Lueck,* 471 U.S. 202 (1985), we considered whether
the Wisconsin tort remedy for bad-faith handling of an insurance claim could be
applied to the handling of a claim for disability benefits that were authorized by a
collective-bargaining agreement. We began by examining the collective-
bargaining agreement, and determined that it provided the basis not only for the
benefits, but also for the right to have payments made in a timely manner. *Id.,* at
213-216. We then analyzed the Wisconsin tort remedy, explaining that it "exists
for breach of a 'duty devolv[ed] upon the insurer by reasonable implication from
the express terms of the contract,' the scope of which, crucially, is 'ascertained
from a consideration of the contract itself.'" *Id.,* at 216 (quoting *Hilker v. Western Automobile Ins. Co.,* 204 Wis. 1, 16, 235 N.W. 413, 415 (1931)). Since the
"parties' agreement as to the manner in which a benefit claim would be handled
[would] necessarily [have been] relevant to any allegation that the claim was
handled in a dilatory manner," 471 U.S., at 218, we concluded that § 301 preempted the application of the Wisconsin tort remedy in this setting.

Thus, *Lueck* faithfully applied the principle of § 301 pre-emption developed in
Lucas Flour: if the resolution of a state-law claim depends upon the meaning of a
collective-bargaining agreement, the application of state law (which might lead
to inconsistent results since there could be as many state-law principles as there
are States) is pre-empted and federal labor-law principles—necessarily uniform
throughout the nation—must be employed to resolve the dispute.

III

Illinois courts have recognized the tort of retaliatory discharge for filing a
worker's compensation claim, *Kelsay v. Motorola, Inc.,* 74 Ill. 2d 172, 384
N.E.2d 353 (1978), and have held that it is applicable to employees covered by
union contracts, *Midgett v. Sackett-Chicago, Inc.,* 105 Ill. 2d 143, 473 N.E.2d
1280 (1984), *cert. denied,* 474 U.S. 909 (1985). "[T]o show retaliatory discharge,
the plaintiff must set forth sufficient facts from which it can be inferred that (1)
he was discharged or threatened with discharge and (2) the employer's motive in
discharging or threatening to discharge him was to deter him from exercising his
rights under the Act or to interfere with his exercise of those rights." *Horton v.*

Miller Chemical Co., 776 F.2d 1351, 1356 (CA7 1985) (summarizing Illinois state court decisions), *cert. denied,* 475 U.S. 1122 (1986); see *Gonzalez v. Prestress Engineering Corp.,* 115 Ill. 2d 1, 503 N.E.2d 308 (1986). Each of these purely factual questions pertains to the conduct of the employee and the conduct and motivation of the employer. Neither of the elements requires a court to interpret any term of a collective-bargaining agreement. To defend against a retaliatory discharge claim, an employer must show that it had a nonretaliatory reason for the discharge, cf. *Loyola University of Chicago v. Illinois Human Rights Comm'n,* 149 Ill. App. 3d 8, 500 N.E.2d 639 (1986); this purely factual inquiry likewise does not turn on the meaning of any provision of a collective-bargaining agreement. Thus, the state-law remedy in this case is "independent" of the collective-bargaining agreement in the sense of "independent" that matters for § 301 pre-emption purposes: resolution of the state-law claim does not require construing the collective-bargaining agreement.

The Court of Appeals seems to have relied upon a different way in which a state-law claim may be considered "independent" of a collective-bargaining agreement. The court wrote that "the just cause provision in the collective-bargaining agreement may well prohibit such retaliatory discharge," and went on to say that if the state-law cause of action could go forward, "a state court would be deciding precisely the *same issue* as would an arbitrator: whether there was 'just cause' to discharge the worker." 823 F.2d, at 1046 (emphasis added). The Court concluded, "the state tort of retaliatory discharge is inextricably intertwined with the collective-bargaining agreements here, because it implicates the *same analysis of the facts* as would an inquiry under the just cause provisions of the agreements." *Ibid.* (emphasis added). We agree with the Court's explanation that the state-law analysis might well involve attention to the same factual considerations as the contractual determination of whether Lingle was fired for just cause. But we disagree with the Court's conclusion that such parallelism renders the state-law analysis dependent upon the contractual analysis. For while there may be instances in which the National Labor Relations Act pre-empts state law on the basis of the subject matter of the law in question, § 301 pre-emption merely ensures that federal law will be the basis for interpreting collective-bargaining agreements, and says nothing about the substantive rights a State may provide to workers when adjudication of those rights does not depend upon the interpretation of such agreements.[9] In other words, even if dispute resolution

---

[9] Whether a union may *waive* its members' individual, nonpre-empted state-law rights, is, likewise, a question distinct from that of whether a claim is pre-empted under § 301, and is another issue we need not resolve today. We note that under Illinois law, the parties to a collective-bargaining agreement may not waive the prohibition against retaliatory discharge nor may they alter a worker's rights under the state worker's compensation scheme. *Byrd v. Aetna Casualty & Surety Co.,* 152 Ill. App. 3d 292, 298, 504 N.E.2d 216, 221, *app. denied,* 115 Ill. 2d 539, 511 N.E.2d 426 (1987). Before deciding whether such a state law bar to waiver could be pre-empted under federal law by the parties to a collective-bargaining agreement, we would require "clear and

pursuant to a collective-bargaining agreement, on the one hand, and state law, on the other, would require addressing precisely the same set of facts, as long as the state-law claim can be resolved without interpreting the agreement itself, the claim is "independent" of the agreement for § 301 pre-emption purposes.

IV

The result we reach today is consistent both with the policy of fostering uniform, certain adjudication of disputes over the meaning of collective-bargaining agreements and with cases that have permitted separate fonts of substantive rights to remain unpre-empted by other federal labor-law statutes.

First, as we explained in *Lueck*, "[t]he need to preserve the effectiveness of arbitration was one of the central reasons that underlay the Court's holding in *Lucas Flour*." 471 U.S., at 219. Today's decision should make clear that interpretation of collective-bargaining agreements remains firmly in the arbitral realm; judges can determine questions of state law involving labor-management relations only if such questions do not require construing collective-bargaining agreements.

Second, there is nothing novel about recognizing that substantive rights in the labor relations context can exist without interpreting collective-bargaining agreements.

> This Court has, on numerous occasions, declined to hold that individual employees are, because of the availability of arbitration, barred from bringing claims under federal statutes. *See, e.g., McDonald v. West Branch,* 466 U.S. 284 (1984); *Barrentine v. Arkansas-Best Freight System, Inc.,* 450 U.S. 728 (1981); *Alexander v. Gardner-Denver Co.,* 415 U.S. 36 (1974). Although the analysis of the question under each statute is quite distinct, the theory running through these cases is that notwithstanding the strong policies encouraging arbitration, "different considerations apply *where the employee's claim is based on rights arising out of a statute designed to provide minimum substantive guarantees to individual workers." Barrentine, supra,* 450 U.S., at 737.

Atchison, T. & S. F. R. Co. v. Buell, 480 U.S. 557, 565 (1987) (emphasis added).

Although our comments in *Buell,* construing the scope of Railway Labor Act pre-emption, referred to independent *federal* statutory rights, we subsequently rejected a claim that federal labor law pre-empted a *state* statute providing a one-time severance benefit to employees in the event of a plant closing. In *Fort Halifax Packing Co. v. Coyne,* 482 U.S. 1, 21 (1987), we emphasized that "preemption should not be lightly inferred in this area, since the establishment of la-

---

unmistakable" evidence, see *Metropolitan Edison Co. v. NLRB,* 460 U.S. 693, 708 (1983), in order to conclude that such a waiver had been intended. No such evidence is available in this case.

bor standards falls within the traditional police power of the State." We specifically held that the Maine law in question was not pre-empted by the NLRA, "since its establishment of a minimum labor standard does not impermissibly intrude upon the collective-bargaining process." *Id.,* at 23.

The Court of Appeals "recognize[d] that § 301 does not pre-empt state anti-discrimination laws, even though a suit under these laws, like a suit alleging retaliatory discharge, requires a state court to determine whether just cause existed to justify the discharge." 823 F.2d, at 1046, n. 17. The court distinguished those laws because Congress has affirmatively endorsed state antidiscrimination remedies in Title VII of the Civil Rights Act of 1964, 78 Stat. 241, see 42 U.S.C. §§ 2000e-5(c) and 2000e-7, whereas there is not such explicit endorsement of state worker's compensation laws. As should be plain from our discussion in Part III, *supra,* this distinction is unnecessary for determining whether § 301 pre-empts the state law in question. The operation of the anti-discrimination laws does, however, illustrate the relevant point for § 301 pre-emption analysis that the mere fact that a broad contractual protection against discriminatory—or retaliatory—discharge may provide a remedy for conduct that coincidentally violates state law does not make the existence or the contours of the state-law violation dependent upon the terms of the private contract. For even if an arbitrator should conclude that the contract does not prohibit a particular discriminatory or retaliatory discharge, that conclusion might or might not be consistent with a proper interpretation of state law. In the typical case a state tribunal could resolve either a discriminatory or retaliatory discharge claim without interpreting the "just cause" language of a collective-bargaining agreement.

V

In sum, we hold that an application of state law is pre-empted by § 301 of the Labor Management Relations Act of 1947 only if such application requires the interpretation of a collective-bargaining agreement.[12]

The judgment of the Court of Appeals is reversed.

It is so ordered.

---

[12] A collective-bargaining agreement may, of course, contain information such as rate of pay and other economic benefits that might be helpful in determining the damages to which a worker prevailing in a state law suit is entitled. *See Baldracchi v. Pratt & Whitney Aircraft Div., United Technologies Corp.,* 814 F.2d 102, 106 (CA2 1987). Although federal law would govern the interpretation of the agreement to determine the proper damages, the underlying state law claim, not otherwise pre-empted, would stand. Thus, as a general proposition, a state law claim may depend for its resolution upon both the interpretation of a collective-bargaining agreement and a separate state law analysis that does not turn on the agreement. In such a case, federal law would govern the interpretation of the agreement, but the separate state law analysis would not be thereby pre-empted. As we said in *Allis-Chalmers Corp. v. Lueck,* 471 U.S., at 211, "not every dispute ... tangentially involving a provision of a collective-bargaining agreement is pre-empted by § 301...."

NOTES

1. *Tort Claims*: It is not easy to distinguish between cases governed by *Lingle,* in which a state tort claim is not preempted by § 301 because it exists independently of any collective bargaining agreement and requires no interpretation of the labor contract for its enforcement, and cases governed by *Lueck,* in which the supposed state claim is preempted because the existence and scope of the claim would have to be determined by resort to the applicable collective agreement. Some courts apply the § 301 preemption doctrine in an expansive manner. For example, *DeCoe v. General Motors Corp.*, 32 F.3d 212 (6th Cir. 1994), involved a union official's state court defamation and tortious interference claims against his employer and several employees who had allegedly made and discussed false sexual harassment charges regarding the plaintiff. The court found these claims preempted, because resolution of both would involve interpretation and application of bargaining agreement provisions. The collective contract imposed a duty on the employer and individual employees to identify and resolve sexual harassment complaints, and the trial court would have to interpret this section of the contract when it sought to decide whether the individuals who filed charges against the plaintiff had engaged in protected conduct. The tortious interference claim was based on the economic relationship created by the bargaining agreement, and thus the trial court would have to examine that contract to determine what economic relationship existed; *accord, McCormick v. AT&T Techs.,* 934 F.2d 531 (4th Cir. 1991), *cert. denied,* 502 U.S. 1048 (1992). *See also Baker v. Farmers Elec. Coop.,* 34 F.3d 274 (5th Cir. 1994) (claim that employer intentionally inflicted emotional distress by reassigning custodian to journeyman lineman position in retaliation against his participation in prior arbitral proceeding preempted, since resolution of question regarding outrageousness of employer's conduct would involve interpretation of management rights clause of contract); *In re Amoco Petr. Additives Co.,* 964 F.2d 706 (7th Cir. 1992) (state claims for invasion of privacy and intentional infliction of emotional distress based on employer's installation of video camera near entrance to women's locker room preempted, since surveillance was arguably authorized by management rights clause in labor contract, so that interpretation of collective agreement would be required), *dismissal of action aff'd,* 6 F.3d 1176 (7th Cir. 1993); *accord, Johnson v. Beatrice Foods Co.,* 921 F.2d 1015 (10th Cir. 1990). In *Stikes v. Chevron USA,* 914 F.2d 1265 (9th Cir. 1990), *cert. denied,* 500 U.S. 917 (1991), the court ruled that § 301 preempted a claim for infringement of a state constitutional right to privacy by an employee who was terminated when he refused to consent to a search of his car in the company parking lot, since the court could not evaluate the worker's expectation of privacy and the employer's right to search employee vehicles without considering the employment conditions contained in the collective contract.

Other courts are more willing to allow such claims. *Compare Jackson v. Kimel,* 992 F.2d 1318 (4th Cir. 1993); *Albertson's, Inc. v. Carrigan,* 982 F.2d 1478 (10th Cir. 1993); *and Galvez v. Kuhn,* 933 F.2d 773 (9th Cir. 1991) (finding no preemption of employment-related emotional distress claims). *See also Foster v. Albertson's, Inc.,* 835 P.2d 720 (Mont. 1992) (while § 301 preempted suit by sexual harassment victim for breach of implied covenant of good faith and fair dealing since that covenant arose from bargaining agreement, it did not preempt public policy or intentional infliction of emotional distress claims that were independent of collective contract).

2. *Breach of Contract Claims:* In *Caterpillar Inc. v. Williams,* 482 U.S. 386 (1987), a unanimous Supreme Court held that § 301 did not completely preempt a state-law complaint for breach of individual employment contracts and thus did not support removal to federal court. In this instance several employees had left the bargaining unit to become managerial or salaried employees and, in this capacity, had received employer assurances of job security in the event their plant closed. Later, after they had returned to unionized positions, they were notified that the plant was closing and they would be laid off. The Court concluded their complaint was not substantially dependent on an interpretation of the collective bargaining agreement. Similarly, the court in *Loewen Group Int'l v. Haberichter,* 65 F.3d 1417 (7th Cir. 1995), found no preemption of a state claim against a former employee for violating a covenant not to compete contained in an individual employment contract, even though the employee was also subject to a collective bargaining agreement; merely examining the labor contract to see whether any conflict existed was held not to be "interpreting" it for § 301 preemption purposes. *Trans Penn Wax Corp. v. McCandless,* 50 F.3d 217 (3d Cir. 1995), concerned an employer that had allegedly made promises to employees of continued job security on the eve of a decertification election. After the incumbent union was decertified, the employer terminated six employees. The court found that their suit for breach of contract and misrepresentation was not preempted by § 301, because resolution of their claims would not require the interpretation of any bargaining agreement provisions.

On the other hand, the Ninth Circuit found § 301 preemption of a breach of contract claim based on an individual employment contract pertaining to a job covered by a collective bargaining agreement. In *Beals v. Kiewit Pacific Co.,* 114 F.3d 892 (9th Cir. 1997), *cert. denied,* 118 S. Ct. 1036 (1998), the employee was offered an opportunity to relocate from Southern California to Hawaii to work on a project that was covered by a union contract. After accepting the offer (which included moving expenses), the employee moved to Hawaii and began work on the job. Five months later he was terminated. Beals sued the employer for breach of contract and negligent misrepresentation. According to the court, the employer's offer was effective only as part of the labor contract and therefore was preempted because it required interpretation of the collective bargaining agreement, which gave the employer the right to terminate Beals at any time. The negligent misrepresentation claim, however, was not preempted because it was based primarily upon the employer's oral representations, which did not require interpretation of the labor contract (though it did entail comparison of the labor contract's terms to the employer's oral representations in order to assess whether Beals' reliance on the representations was justified).

3. *State Claims Based on the Union's Performance of Its Duty as Employee Representative:* In *IBEW v. Hechler,* 481 U.S. 851 (1987), a unanimous Supreme Court held that an employee's state-law tort claim was preempted when she alleged the union was negligent in failing to provide her with a safe place to work. Eight Justices concluded that the existence and scope of any duty of care on the union's part would have to be determined by resort to the applicable collective bargaining agreement. Thus, plaintiff's state claim was not "sufficiently independent ... to withstand the preemptive force of § 301." Justice Stevens concurred on the grounds plaintiff had alleged "nothing more than a breach of the union's federal duty of fair representation." A recent case pressed this issue further, with the same result. In *BIW Deceived v. Local S6, Int'l Union of Marine & Shipbuilding Workers,* 132 F.3d 824 (1st Cir. 1997), the First Circuit ruled that § 301 preemption blocked a state court action that implicitly asserted that the union had breached its duty of fair representation. The employees' complaint alleged negligence, fraudulent misrepresentation, fraud in inducement, infliction of emotional distress, loss of consortium, intentional nondisclosure, and unjust enrichment against the union, which had (pursuant to its labor contract with the employer) participated in job interviews with the employer and assured employees that they would be employed until expiration of the current union contract, and probably much longer; in reliance upon these assurances, the employees accepted offers of employment, left other jobs and relocated to Maine to work for the employer—only to be laid off shortly thereafter. According to the court, removal to federal court was appropriate where the complaint, "though garbed in state-law raiment, sufficiently asserts a claim implicating the duty of fair representation," a matter governed completely by federal law.

In *Steelworkers v. Rawson,* 495 U.S. 362 (1990), a 6-3 majority of the Supreme Court held that a state wrongful death action brought against a miners' union by the survivors of miners killed in an underground fire was preempted by § 301. The complaint included allegations that the union had been negligent in its inspection activities. The Court reasoned that if the union violated any duty owed the miners in the course of the inspections, the duty arose out of the collective bargaining agreement and was not a duty of care owed by the union to society at large. Furthermore, the survivors' action could not be based on the union's duty of fair representation, since mere negligence, even in the performance of a labor contract, would not ground a claim for breach of that duty. Three Justices, dissenting, agreed with the Supreme Court of Idaho that the survivors' case could be characterized as resting on allegations of the union's active negligence in a voluntary undertaking, as defined in the Restatement (Second) of Torts § 323, not on the union's contractual obligations.

4. *See generally* Brower, *Towards a Unified Accommodation of State Law and Collective Bargaining Agreements: Federalism, Public Rights and Liberty of Contract,* 26 Hous. L. Rev. 389 (1989); Gregory, *The Labor Preemption Doctrine: Hamiltonian Renaissance or Last Hurrah?* 27 Wm. & Mary L. Rev. 507 (1986); Harper, *Limiting Section 301 Preemption: Three Cheers for the Trilogy, Only One for Lingle and Lueck,* 66 Chi.-Kent L. Rev. 685 (1990); Modjeska, *Federalism in Labor Relations—The Last Decade,* 50 Ohio St. L.J. 487 (1989); Stein, *Preserving Unionized Employees' Individual Employment Rights: An Argument Against Section 301 Preemption,* 17 Berkeley J. Emp. & Lab. L. 1 (1996); Weinberg, *The Federal-State Conflict of Laws: "Actual" Conflicts,* 70 Tex. L. Rev. 1743 (1992). *Lingle* is noted in 38 Cath. U. L. Rev. 769 (1989); 41 Hastings L.J. 1149 (1991); 40 Syracuse L. Rev. 1279 (1989); 34 Vill. L. Rev. 1035 (1989); 99 Yale L.J. 209 (1989).

LIVADAS v. BRADSHAW

Supreme Court of the United States
512 U.S. 107, 114 S. Ct. 2068, 129 L. Ed. 2d 93 (1994)

JUSTICE SOUTER delivered the opinion of the Court.

California law requires employers to pay all wages due immediately upon an employee's discharge, imposes a penalty for refusal to pay promptly, precludes any private contractual waiver of these minimum labor standards, and places responsibility for enforcing these provisions on the State Commissioner of Labor (Commissioner or Labor Commissioner), ostensibly for the benefit of all employees. Respondent, the Labor Commissioner, has construed a further provision of state law as barring enforcement of these wage and penalty claims on behalf of individuals like petitioner, whose terms and conditions of employment are governed by a collective-bargaining agreement containing an arbitration clause. We hold that federal law pre-empts this policy, as abridging the exercise of such employees' rights under the National Labor Relations Act (NLRA or Act), 29 U.S.C. § 151 et seq., and that redress for this unlawful refusal to enforce may be had under 42 U.S.C. § 1983.

I

Until her discharge on January 2, 1990, petitioner Karen Livadas worked as a grocery clerk in a Vallejo, California, Safeway supermarket. The terms and conditions of her employment were subject to a collective-bargaining agreement between Safeway and Livadas's union, Local 373 of the United Food and Commercial Workers, AFL-CIO. Unexceptionally, the agreement provided that "disputes as to the interpretation or application of the agreement," including grievances arising from allegedly unjust discharge or suspension, would be subject to binding arbitration. See Food Store Contract, United Food & Commercial Workers Union, Local 373, AFL-CIO, Solano and Napa Counties §§ 18.2, 18.3 (Mar. 1, 1989-Feb. 29, 1992) (Food Store Contract). When notified of her discharge, Livadas demanded immediate payment of wages owed her, as guaranteed to all California workers by state law, see Cal. Lab. Code Ann. § 201 (West 1989), but her store manager refused, referring to the company practice of making such payments by check mailed from a central corporate payroll office. On January 5, 1990, Livadas received a check from Safeway, in the full amount owed for her work through January 2.

On January 9, 1990, Livadas filed a claim against Safeway with the California Division of Labor Standards Enforcement (DLSE or Division), asserting that under § 203 of the Labor Code the company was liable to her for a sum equal to three days' wages, as a penalty for the delay between discharge and the date when payment was in fact received. Livadas requested the Commissioner to enforce the claim.

By an apparently standard form letter dated February 7, 1990, the Division notified Livadas that it would take no action on her complaint:

> It is our understanding that the employees working for Safeway are covered by a collective bargaining agreement which contains an arbitration clause. The provisions of Labor Code Section 229 preclude this Division from adjudicating any dispute concerning the interpretation or application of any collective bargaining agreement containing an arbitration clause. Labor Code Section 203 requires that the wages continue at the "same rate" until paid. In order to establish what the "same rate" was, it is necessary to look to the collective bargaining agreement and 'apply' that agreement. The courts have pointed out that such an application is exactly what the provisions of Labor Code § 229 prohibit.[6]

The letter made no reference to any particular aspect of Livadas's claim making it unfit for enforcement, and the Commissioner's position is fairly taken to be that DLSE enforcement of § 203 claims, as well as other claims for which relief is pegged to an employee's wage rate, is generally unavailable to employees covered by collective-bargaining agreements.

Livadas brought this action in the United States District Court under Rev. Stat § 1979, 42 U.S.C. § 1983, alleging that the nonenforcement policy, reflecting the Commissioner's reading of Labor Code § 229, was pre-empted as conflicting

---

[6] Labor Code § 229 provides: "Actions to enforce the provisions of this article [Labor Code §§ 200-243] for the collection of due and unpaid wages claimed by an individual may be maintained without regard to the existence of any private agreement to arbitrate. This section shall not apply to claims involving any dispute concerning the interpretation or application of any collective bargaining agreement containing such an arbitration agreement." Cf. *Perry v. Thomas*, 482 U.S. 483 (1987) (§ 229 bar to waiver defeated by Federal Arbitration Act policy)....

with Livadas's rights under § 7 of the NLRA, 49 Stat. 452, as amended, 29 U.S.C. § 157, because the policy placed a penalty on the exercise of her statutory right to bargain collectively with her employer. She stressed that there was no dispute about the amount owed and that neither she nor Safeway had begun any grievance proceeding over the penalty.[8] ...

The District Court granted summary judgment for Livadas, holding the labor pre-emption claim cognizable under § 1983, see *Golden State Transit Corp. v. City of Los Angeles*, 493 U.S. 103 (1989) (*Golden State II*), and the Commissioner's policy pre-empted as interfering with her § 7 right, see, e.g., *Golden State Transit Corp. v. Los Angeles*, 475 U.S. 608 (1986) (*Golden State I*), by denying her the benefit of a minimum labor standard, namely the right to timely payment of final wages secured by Labor Code §§ 201 and 203. 749 F. Supp. 1526 (ND Cal. 1990). The District Court treated as irrelevant the Commissioner's assertion that the policy was consistent with state law (e.g., Labor Code § 229) and rejected the defense that it was required by federal law, namely § 301 of the Labor-Management Relations Act, 1947 (LMRA), 61 Stat. 156, 29 U.S.C. § 185(a), which has been read to pre-empt state-court resolution of disputes turning on the rights of parties under collective-bargaining agreements. The District Court explained that resolution of the claim under § 203 "requires reference only to a calendar, not to the [collective-bargaining agreement]," 749 F. Supp., at 1536, and granted petitioner all requested relief. *Id.*, at 1540.

A divided panel of the Court of Appeals for the Ninth Circuit reversed. 987 F.2d 552 (1993). The court acknowledged that federal law gives Livadas a right to engage in collective bargaining and that § 1983 would supply a remedy for official deprivation of that right, but the panel majority concluded that no federal right had been infringed. The court reasoned that the policy was based on the Commissioner's reading of Labor Code § 229, whose function of keeping state tribunals from adjudicating claims in a way that would interfere with the operation of federal labor policy is, by definition, consistent with the dictates of federal law. Noting that Livadas did not assert pre-emption of § 229 itself or object to the California courts' interpretation of it, the majority concluded that her case reduced to an assertion that the Commissioner had misinterpreted state law, an error for which relief could be obtained in California courts.

Livadas could not claim to be "penalized," the Appeals panel then observed, for she stood "in the same position as every other employee in the state when it comes to seeking the Commissioner's enforcement. Every employee ... is subject to an eligibility determination, and every employee ... is subject to the risk that

---

[8] Livadas did file a grievance claiming that the discharge had been improper under the collective-bargaining agreement, ultimately obtaining reinstatement with back pay. While the parties dispute what effect, as a matter of state law, that recovery would have on Livadas's right under § 203, neither the pertinent California statutes nor the Commissioner's policy at issue here depend on whether a claimant's termination was for just cause.

the Commissioner will get it wrong." 987 F.2d, at 559. The Ninth Circuit majority concluded by invoking the "general policies of federal labor law" strongly favoring the arbitration of disputes and reasoning that, "Congress would not want state officials erring on the side of adjudicating state law disputes whenever it is a close call as to whether a claim is preempted." *Id.*, at 560. We granted certiorari, 510 U.S. ___ (1994), to address the important questions of federal labor law implicated by the Commissioner's policy, and we now reverse.

II

A

A state rule predicating benefits on refraining from conduct protected by federal labor law poses special dangers of interference with congressional purpose. In *Nash v. Florida Industrial Comm'n*, 389 U.S. 235 (1967), a unanimous Court held that a state policy of withholding unemployment benefits solely because an employee had filed an unfair labor practice charge with the National Labor Relations Board had a "direct tendency to frustrate the purpose of Congress" and, if not pre-empted, would "defeat or handicap a valid national objective by ... withdrawing state benefits ... simply because" an employee engages in conduct protected and encouraged by the NLRA. *Id.*, at 239; see also *Golden State I, supra,* at 618 (city may not condition franchise renewal on settlement of labor dispute).

This case is fundamentally no different from *Nash.*[11] Just as the respondent State Commission in that case offered an employee the choice of pursuing her unfair labor practice claim or receiving unemployment compensation, the Commissioner has presented Livadas and others like her with the choice of having state-law rights under §§ 201 and 203 enforced or exercising the right to enter into a collective-bargaining agreement with an arbitration clause. This unappetizing choice, we conclude, was not intended by Congress, see *infra*, and cannot ultimately be reconciled with a statutory scheme premised on the centrality of the right to bargain collectively and the desirability of resolving contract disputes through arbitration. Cf. *Metropolitan Life Ins. Co. v. Massachusetts*, 471 U.S. 724, 755 (1985) (state law held not pre-empted because it "neither encourages nor discourages the collective bargaining processes").

---

[11]While the NLRA does not expressly recognize a right to be covered by a collective-bargaining agreement, in that no duty is imposed on an employer actually to reach agreement with represented employees, see 29 U.S.C. § 158(d), a State's penalty on those who complete the collective-bargaining process works an interference with the operation of the Act, much as does a penalty on those who participate in the process. Cf. *Hill v. Florida ex rel. Watson*, 325 U.S. 538 (1945) (State may not enforce licensing requirement on collective-bargaining agents)....

B

1

The Commissioner's answers to this pre-emption conclusion flow from two significant misunderstandings of law. First, the Commissioner conflates the policy that Livadas challenges with the state law on which it purports to rest, Labor Code § 229, assuming that if the statutory provision is consistent with federal law, her policy must be also. But on this logic, a policy of issuing general search warrants would be justified if it were adopted to implement a state statute codifying word-for-word the "good faith" exception to the valid warrant requirement recognized in *United States v. Leon*, 468 U.S. 897 (1984). The relationship between policy and state statute and between the statute and federal law is, in any event, irrelevant. The question presented by this case is not whether Labor Code § 229 is valid under the Federal Constitution or whether the Commissioner's policy is, as a matter of state law, a proper interpretation of § 229. Pre-emption analysis, rather, turns on the actual content of respondent's policy and its real effect on federal rights. See *Nash v. Florida Industrial Comm'n*, 389 U.S. 235 (1967) (holding pre-empted an administrative policy interpreting presumably valid state unemployment insurance law exception for "labor disputes" to include proceedings under NLRB complaints); see also 987 F.2d, at 561 (Kozinski, J., dissenting).

Having sought to lead us to the wrong question, the Commissioner proposes the wrong approach for answering it, defending the distinction drawn in the challenged statutory interpretation, between employees represented by unions and those who are not, as supported by a "rational basis." But such reasoning mistakes a standard for validity under the Equal Protection and Due Process Clauses for what the Supremacy Clause requires. The power to tax is no less the power to destroy, *McCulloch v. Maryland*, 17 U.S. 316 (1819), merely because a state legislature has an undoubtedly rational and "legitimate" interest in raising revenue. In labor pre-emption cases, as in others under the Supremacy Clause, our office is not to pass judgment on the reasonableness of state policy, see, e.g., *Golden State I*, 475 U.S. 608 (1986) (city's desire to remain "neutral" in labor dispute does not determine pre-emption). It is instead to decide if a state rule conflicts with or otherwise "stands as an obstacle to the accomplishment and execution of the full purposes and objectives" of the federal law. *Brown v. Hotel Employees*, 468 U.S. 491, 501 (1984).

That is not to say, of course, that the several rationales for the policy urged on the Court by the Commissioner and *amici* are beside the point here. If, most obviously, the Commissioner's policy were actually compelled by federal law, as she argues it is, we could hardly say that it was, simultaneously, pre-empted; at the least, our task would then be one of harmonizing statutory law. But we entertain this and other justifications claimed, not because constitutional analysis under the Supremacy Clause is an open-ended balancing act, simply weighing the federal interest against the intensity of local feeling, see *id.*, at 503, but because claims of justification can sometimes help us to discern congressional purpose, the "ultimate touchstone" of our enquiry. *Malone v. White Motor Corp.*, 435 U.S. 497, 504 (1978); see also *New York Telephone Co. v. New York Dept. of Labor*, 440 U.S. 519, 533 (1979) (plurality opinion).

2

We begin with the most complete of the defenses mounted by the Commissioner, one that seems (or seemed until recently, at least) to be at the heart of her position: that the challenged policy, far from being pre-empted by federal law, is positively compelled by it, and that even if the Commissioner had been so inclined, the LMRA § 301 would have precluded enforcement of Livadas's penalty claim. The nonenforcement policy, she suggests, is a necessary emanation from this Court's § 301 pre-emption jurisprudence, marked as it has been by repeated admonitions that courts should steer clear of collective-bargaining disputes between parties who have provided for arbitration. See, e.g., *Allis-Chalmers Corp. v. Lueck*, 471 U.S. 202 (1985). Because, this argument runs (and Livadas was told in the DLSE no-action letter), disposition of a union-represented employee's penalty claim entails the "interpretation or application" of a collective-bargaining agreement (since determining the amount owed turns on the contractual rate of pay agreed) resort to a state tribunal would lead it into territory that Congress, in enacting § 301, meant to be covered exclusively by arbitrators.

This reasoning, however, mistakes both the functions § 301 serves in our national labor law and our prior decisions according that provision pre-emptive effect. To be sure, we have read the text of § 301 not only to grant federal courts jurisdiction over claims asserting breach of collective-bargaining agreements but also to authorize the development of federal common-law rules of decision, in large part to assure that agreements to arbitrate grievances would be enforced, regardless of the vagaries of state law and lingering hostility toward extrajudicial dispute resolution, see *Textile Workers v. Lincoln Mills*, 353 U.S. 448, 455-456 (1957); see also *Steelworkers v. Warrior and Gulf Navigation Co.*, 363 U.S. 574 (1960); *Avco Corp. v. Machinists*, 390 U.S. 557, 559 (1968) ("§ 301 ... was fashioned by Congress to place sanctions behind agreements to arbitrate grievance disputes"). And in *Teamsters v. Lucas Flour Co.*, 369 U.S. 95 (1962), we recognized an important corollary to the *Lincoln Mills* rule: while § 301 does not preclude state courts from taking jurisdiction over cases arising from disputes over the interpretation of collective-bargaining agreements, state contract law must yield to the developing federal common law, lest common terms in bargaining agreements be given different and potentially inconsistent interpretations in different jurisdictions. See 369 U.S., at 103-104.

And while this sensible "acorn" of § 301 pre-emption recognized in *Lucas Flour*, has sprouted modestly in more recent decisions of this Court, see, e.g.,

Lueck, supra, at 210 ("If the policies that animate § 301 are to be given their proper range ... the pre-emptive effect of § 301 must extend beyond suits alleging contract violations"), it has not yet become, nor may it, a sufficiently "mighty oak," see *Golden State I*, 475 U.S., at 622 (REHNQUIST, J., dissenting), to supply the cover the Commissioner seeks here. To the contrary, the pre-emption rule has been applied only to assure that the purposes animating § 301 will be frustrated neither by state laws purporting to determine "questions relating to what the parties to a labor agreement agreed, and what legal consequences were intended to flow from breaches of that agreement," *Lueck*, 471 U.S., at 211, nor by parties' efforts to renege on their arbitration promises by "relabeling" as tort suits actions simply alleging breaches of duties assumed in collective-bargaining agreements, *id.*, at 219; see *Republic Steel Corp. v. Maddox*, 379 U.S. 650, 652 (1965) ("Federal labor policy requires that individual employees wishing to assert contract grievances must attempt use of the contract grievance procedure agreed upon by employer and union as the mode of redress") (emphasis omitted).

In *Lueck* and in *Lingle v. Norge Division of Magic Chef, Inc.*, 486 U.S. 399 (1988), we underscored the point that § 301 cannot be read broadly to pre-empt nonnegotiable rights conferred on individual employees as a matter of state law, and we stressed that it is the legal character of a claim, as "independent" of rights under the collective-bargaining agreement, *Lueck, supra*, at 213 (and not whether a grievance arising from "precisely the same set of facts" could be pursued, *Lingle, supra*, at 410) that decides whether a state cause of action may go forward. Finally, we were clear that when the meaning of contract terms is not the subject of dispute, the bare fact that a collective-bargaining agreement will be consulted in the course of state-law litigation plainly does not require the claim to be extinguished, see *Lingle*, 486 U.S., at 413, n. 12 ("A collective-bargaining agreement may, of course, contain information such as rate of pay ... that might be helpful in determining the damages to which a worker prevailing in a state-law suit is entitled").

These principles foreclose even a colorable argument that a claim under Labor Code § 203 was pre-empted here. As the District Court aptly observed, the primary text for deciding whether Livadas was entitled to a penalty was not the Food Store Contract, but a calendar. The only issue raised by Livadas's claim, whether Safeway "willfully failed to pay" her wages promptly upon severance, Cal. Lab. Code Ann. § 203 (West 1989), was a question of state law, entirely independent of any understanding embodied in the collective-bargaining agreement between the union and the employer. There is no indication that there was a "dispute" in this case over the amount of the penalty to which Livadas would be entitled, and *Lingle* makes plain in so many words that when liability is governed by independent state law, the mere need to "look to" the collective-bargaining agreement for damage computation is no reason to hold the state law claim defeated by § 301. See 486 U.S., at 413, n. 12.

Beyond the simple need to refer to bargained-for wage rates in computing the penalty, the collective-bargaining agreement is irrelevant to the dispute (if any) between Livadas and Safeway. There is no suggestion here that Livadas's union sought or purported to bargain away her protections under § 201 or § 203, a waiver that we have said would (especially in view of Labor Code § 219) have to be "'clear and unmistakable'" see *Lingle, supra,* at 409-410, n. 9 (quoting *Metropolitan Edison Co. v. NLRB,* 460 U.S. 693, 708 (1983)) for a court even to consider whether it could be given effect, nor is there any indication that the parties to the collective-bargaining agreement understood their arbitration pledge to cover these state-law claims. See generally *Gilmer v. Interstate/Johnson Lane Corp.,* 500 U.S. 20, 35 (1991); cf. Food Store Contract § 18.8. But even if such suggestions or indications were to be found, the Commissioner could not invoke them to defend her policy, which makes no effort to take such factors into account before denying enforcement.[20]

C

1

Before this Court, however, the Commissioner does not confine herself to the assertion that Livadas's claim would have been pre-empted by LMRA § 301. Indeed, largely putting aside that position, she has sought here to cast the policy in different terms, as expressing a "conscious decision," to keep the State's "hands off" the claims of employees protected by collective-bargaining agreements, either because the Division's efforts and resources are more urgently needed by others or because official restraint will actually encourage the collective-bargaining and arbitral processes favored by federal law. The latter, more ambitious defense has been vigorously taken up by the Commissioner's *amici,* who warn that invalidation of the disputed policy would sound the death knell for other, more common governmental measures that take account of collective-bargaining processes or treat workers represented by unions differently from others in any respect.

---

[20] In holding the challenged policy pre-empted, we note that there is no equally obvious conflict between what § 301 requires and the text of Labor Code § 229 (as against what respondent has read it to mean). The California provision, which concerns whether a promise to arbitrate a claim will be enforced to defeat a direct action under the Labor Code, does not purport generally to deny union-represented employees their rights under §§ 201 and 203. Rather, it confines its preclusive focus only to "disputes concerning the interpretation or application of any collective-bargaining agreement," in which event an "agreement to arbitrate" such disputes is to be given effect. Nor does [*Plumbing, Heating & Piping Employers Council v. Howard,* 53 Cal. App. 3d 828 (1975)], the apparent font of the Commissioner's policy, appear untrue to § 301 teachings: there, an employee sought to have an "unpaid wage" claim do the office of a claim that a collective-bargaining agreement entitled him to a higher wage; that sort of claim, however, derives its existence from the collective-bargaining agreement and, accordingly, falls within any customary understanding of arbitral jurisdiction. See 53 Cal. App. 3d, at 836.

Although there surely is no bar to our considering these alternative explanations, cf. *Dandridge v. Williams*, 397 U.S. 471, 475, n. 6 (1970) (party may defend judgment on basis not relied upon below), we note, as is often the case with such late-blooming rationales, that the overlap between what the Commissioner now claims to be State policy and what the State legislature has enacted into law is awkwardly inexact. First, if the Commissioner's policy (or California law) were animated simply by the frugal desire to conserve the State's money for the protection of employees not covered by collective-bargaining agreements, the Commissioner's emphasis, in the letter to Livadas and in this litigation, on the need to "interpret" or "apply" terms of a collective-bargaining agreement would be entirely misplaced.

Nor is the nonenforcement policy convincingly defended as giving parties to a collective-bargaining agreement the "benefit of their bargain," by assuring them that their promise to arbitrate is kept and not circumvented. Under the Commissioner's policy, enforcement does not turn on what disputes the parties agreed would be resolved by arbitration (the bargain struck), see *Gilmer*, 500 U.S., at 26, or on whether the contractual wage rate is even subject to (arbitrable) dispute. Rather, enforcement turns exclusively on the fact that the contracting parties consented to any arbitration at all. Even if the Commissioner could permissibly presume that state law claims are generally intended to be arbitrated, but cf. *id.*, at 35 (employees in prior cases "had not agreed to arbitrate their statutory claims, and the labor arbitrators were not authorized to resolve such claims"), her policy goes still further. Even in cases when it could be said with "positive assurance," *Warrior & Gulf*, 363 U.S., at 582, that the parties did not intend that state-law claims be subject to arbitration, cf. Food Store Contract § 18.8 (direct wage claim not involving interpretation of agreement may be submitted "to any other tribunal or agency which is authorized and empowered" to enforce it), the Commissioner would still deny enforcement, on the stated basis that the collective-bargaining agreement nonetheless contained "an arbitration clause" and because the claim would, on her view, entail "interpretation," of the agreement's terms. Such an irrebuttable presumption is not easily described as the benefit of the parties' "bargain."

The Commissioner and *amici* finally suggest that denying enforcement to union-represented employees' claims under §§ 201 and 203 (and other Labor Code provisions) is meant to encourage parties to bargain collectively for their own rules about the payment of wages to discharged workers. But with this suggestion, the State's position simply slips any tether to California law. If California's goal really were to stimulate such free-wheeling bargaining on these subjects, the enactment of Labor Code § 219, expressly and categorically prohibiting the modification of these Labor Code rules by "private agreement" would be a very odd way to pursue it. Compare Cal. Lab. Code Ann. § 227.3 (West 1989) (allowing parties to collective-bargaining agreement to arrive at different rule for vacation pay). In short, the policy, the rationales, and the state law are not coherent.

2

Even at face value, however, neither the "hands off" labels nor the vague assertions that general labor law policies are thereby advanced much support the Commissioner's defense here. The former merely takes the position discussed and rejected earlier, that a distinction between claimants represented by unions and those who are not is "rational," the former being less "in need" than the latter. While we hardly suggest here that every distinction between union-represented employees and others is invalid under the NLRA, see *infra*, the assertion that represented employees are less "in need" precisely because they have exercised federal rights, poses special dangers that advantages conferred by federal law will be canceled out and its objectives undermined. Cf. *Metropolitan Life*, 471 U.S., at 756 ("It would turn the policy that animated the Wagner Act on its head to understand it to have penalized workers who have chosen to join a union by preventing them from benefitting from state labor regulations imposing minimal standards on nonunion employers"). Accordingly, as we observed in *Metropolitan Life*, the widespread practice in Congress and in state legislatures has assumed the contrary, bestowing basic employment guarantees and protections on individual employees without singling out members of labor unions (or those represented by them) for disability; see *id.*, at 755; accord, *Lingle*, 486 U.S., at 411-412.

Nor do professions of "neutrality" lay the dangers to rest. The pre-empted action in *Golden State I* could easily have been re-described as following a "hands-off" policy, in that the city sought to avoid endorsing either side in the course of a labor dispute, see *Golden State I*, 475 U.S., at 622 (REHNQUIST, J., dissenting) (city did not seek "to place its weight on one side or the other of the scales of economic warfare"), and the respondent Commission in *Nash* may have understood its policy as expressing neutrality between the parties in a yet-to-be-decided unfair labor practice dispute. See also *Rum Creek Coal Sales, Inc. v. Caperton*, 971 F.2d 1148, 1154 (CA4 1992) (NLRA forbids state policy, under state law barring "aid or assistance" to either party to a labor dispute, of not arresting picketers who violated state trespass laws). Nor need we pause long over the assertion that nonenforcement of valid state law claims is consistent with federal labor law by "encouraging" the operation of collective-bargaining and arbitration process. Denying represented employees basic safety protections might "encourage" collective-bargaining over that subject, and denying union employers the protection of generally applicable state trespass law might lead to increased bargaining over the rights of labor pickets, cf. *Rum Creek, supra*, but we have never suggested that labor law's bias toward bargaining is to be served by forcing employees or employers to bargain for what they would otherwise be entitled to as a matter of course. See generally *Metropolitan Life, supra*, at 757 (Congress did not intend to "remove the backdrop of state law ... and thereby artificially create a no-law area") (emphasis and internal quotation marks omitted).

The precedent cited by the Commissioner and *amici* as supporting the broadest "hands off" view, *Fort Halifax Packing Co. v. Coyne*, 482 U.S. 1 (1987), is not in point. In that case we held that there was no federal pre-emption of a Maine statute that allowed employees and employers to contract for plant-closing severance payments different from those otherwise mandated by state law. That decision, however, does not even purport to address the question supposedly presented here: while there was mention of state latitude to "balance the desirability of a particular substantive labor standard against the right of self-determination regarding the terms and conditions of employment," see 482 U.S., at 22, the policy challenged here differs in two crucial respects from the "unexceptional exercise of the State's police power," *ibid.*, defended in those terms in our earlier case. Most fundamentally, the Maine law treated all employees equally, whether or not represented by a labor organization. All were entitled to the statutory severance payment, and all were allowed to negotiate agreements providing for different benefits. See *id.*, at 4, n. 1. Second, the minimum protections of Maine's plant closing law were relinquished not by the mere act of signing an employment contract (or collective-bargaining agreement), but only by the parties' express agreement on different terms, see *id.*, at 21.

While the Commissioner and her *amici* call our attention to a number of state and federal laws that draw distinctions between union and nonunion represented employees, see, e.g., D. C. Code Ann. § 36-103 (1993) ("Unless otherwise specified in a collective agreement ... whenever an employer discharges an employee, the employer shall pay the employee's wages earned not later than the working day following such discharge"); 29 U.S.C. § 203(o) ("Hours worked" for Fair Labor Standards Act measured according to "express terms of ... or practice under bona fide collective-bargaining agreement"), virtually all share the important second feature observed in *Coyne*, that union-represented employees have the full protection of the minimum standard, absent any agreement for something different. These "opt out" statutes are thus manifestly different in their operation (and their effect on federal rights) from the Commissioner's rule that an employee forfeits his state law rights the moment a collective-bargaining agreement with an arbitration clause is entered into. But cf. *Metropolitan Edison*, 460 U.S., at 708. Hence, our holding that the Commissioner's unusual policy is irreconcilable with the structure and purposes of the Act should cast no shadow on the validity of these familiar and narrowly drawn opt-out provisions....

III

Having determined that the Commissioner's policy is in fact pre-empted by federal law, we find strong support in our precedents for the position taken by

both courts below that Livadas is entitled to seek relief under 42 U.S.C. § 1983
for the Commissioner's abridgment of her NLRA rights....

IV

In an effort to give wide berth to federal labor law and policy, the Commissioner declines to enforce union-represented employees' claims rooted in non-waivable rights ostensibly secured by state law to all employees, without regard to whether the claims are valid under state law or pre-empted by LMRA § 301. Federal labor law does not require such a heavy-handed policy, and, indeed, cannot permit it. We do not suggest here that the NLRA automatically defeats all state action taking any account of the collective-bargaining process or every state law distinguishing union-represented employees from others. It is enough that we find the Commissioner's policy to have such direct and detrimental effects on the federal statutory rights of employees that it must be pre-empted. The judgment of the Court of Appeals for the Ninth Circuit is accordingly

Reversed.

NOTES

1. In *Associated Bldrs. & Contrs. v. IBEW Local 302,* 109 F.3d 1353 (9th Cir. 1997), the Ninth Circuit ruled that § 301 does not preempt a state law challenge by nonunion contractors to the legality of a construction union job targeting program embodied in written agreements between the union-signatory contractors and the unions. Under the job targeting programs operated by six IBEW locals, the locals set aside part of the hourly wage from workers employed on public works projects in a fund and then distributed them as subsidies to other union-signatory contractors who bid on "targeted" projects, reducing their labor costs on projects where they faced nonunion competition. The nonunion contractors' lawsuit alleged that the targeting programs were unlawful under the state prevailing wage laws. Where the only controversy in the case was the legality under state law of the job targeting language in the labor agreements, the court found that there was no need to "interpret" the labor contract in order to resolve the nonunion contractors' state law claims. To rule otherwise would allow parties who wished "to immunize themselves from suit under state-laws of general applicability" to do so "by simply including their unlawful behavior in a labor contract," which "clearly exceeds the scope of section 301 preemption intended by Congress."

2. A union employee's claim under the Montana wrongful discharge statute was held preempted on the ground that it would impose a just cause term on the parties, thus "meddling at the heart of the employer-employee relationship"; the employee was fired for harassing a co-worker after a collective bargaining agreement expired but before negotiations reached an impasse. *Barnes v. Stone Container Corp.,* 942 F.2d 689 (9th Cir. 1991).

3. *Claims Based on State Antidiscrimination Law:* In *Reece v. Houston Lighting & Power Co.,* 79 F.3d 485 (5th Cir.), *cert. denied,* 117 S. Ct. 171 (1996), the court ruled that § 301 barred a state claim for racial discrimination in promotion and training, since provisions of a collective bargaining agreement governing promotions, seniority, and assignment to training would have to be interpreted. *See also Oberkramer v. IBEW-NECA Serv. Center,* 151 F.3d 752 (8th Cir. 1998) (state claims based on municipal ordinance prohibiting sexual orientation discrimination were preempted where a collective bargaining agreement contained a nondiscrimination clause; since state ordinance did not provide for a private cause of action, resolution of the claims would be completely dependent on the antidiscrimination clause in the collective bargaining agreement).

4. In *Hawaiian Airlines v. Norris,* 512 U.S. 246 (1994), the Court unanimously held that the preemption rules applicable to collective contracts negotiated under the Railway Labor Act are the same as those developed under LMRA § 301 for agreements negotiated under the NLRA. The Court thus held that under *Lingle* an airline employee's wrongful termination action based on his refusal to sign a maintenance record for a plane he considered unsafe was not preempted by the RLA, since its resolution would not necessitate the interpretation of bargaining agreement provisions. The fact that the plaintiff might also obtain relief through the "minor" dispute procedures established by the RLA to enforce bargaining agreement terms did not deprive state courts of the right to adjudicate his independent wrongful discharge-public policy claim.

E. SUCCESSOR EMPLOYERS' CONTRACTUAL AND BARGAINING OBLIGATIONS

John Wiley & Sons, Inc. v. Livingston, 376 U.S. 543, 84 S. Ct. 909, 11 L. Ed. 2d 898 (1964). Retail, Wholesale and Department Store District 65 had a collective bargaining agreement with Interscience Publishers which was to expire in January 1962. Interscience had about 80 employees, 40 of whom were covered by the contract. In October 1961 Interscience merged with John Wiley & Sons, a much larger publisher with about 300 employees, all nonunion. Wiley took over essentially the whole Interscience work force, and Interscience ceased to exist as a separate entity. Although the Interscience-District 65 agreement had no successorship clause, the union claimed Wiley was bound to recognize certain "vested" rights of the Interscience employees under their contract. These included seniority, severance pay, and pension fund payments. When Wiley refused these demands, the union sued it to compel arbitration a week before the Interscience contract expired. The Supreme Court unanimously held that "the disappearance by merger of a corporate employer which has entered into a collective bargaining agreement with a union does not automatically terminate all rights of the employees covered by the agreement, and ... in appropriate circumstances, present here, the successor employer may be required to arbitrate." The Court emphasized the "central role of arbitration in effectuating national labor policy" and observed that "a collective bargaining agreement is not an ordinary contract.... [I]t is not in any real sense the simple product of a consensual relationship." The Court acknowledged, however, that the "lack of any substantial continuity of identity in the business enterprise before and after a change" in ownership or corporate structure would eliminate the duty to arbitrate. The Court further held that questions of "procedural arbitrability," that is, whether the steps prerequisite to the duty to arbitrate under the contract have been met, must be decided by the arbitrator and not by the courts.

NOTES

1. An unusually comprehensive study of the problems growing out of *Wiley,* as well as of related successorship issues, is presented by Goldberg, *The Labor Law Obligations of a Successor Employer,* 63 Nw. U.L. Rev. 735 (1969). *See also* Barbash, Feller, Jay, Lippman, *The Labor Contract and the Sale, Subcontracting or Termination of Operations,* in N.Y.U. Eighteenth Annual Conference on Labor 255, 259, 277, 293, 315 (1966) (four separate papers); Christensen, *The Developing Law of Arbitrability,* in Southwestern Legal Foundation, Labor Law Developments, Proceedings of the Eleventh Annual Institute on Labor Law 119 (1965); Platt, *The NLRB and the Arbitrator in Sale and Merger Situations,* in N.Y.U. Nineteenth Annual Conference on Labor 375 (1967); Shaw & Carter, *Sales, Mergers and Union Contract Relations,* in N.Y.U. Nineteenth Annual Conference on Labor 357 (1967).

2. *Wiley* is significant not only for its teachings on successorship, but also for its distinction between "substantive" and "procedural" arbitrability. Extending *Wiley,* the Supreme Court has held that whether a union grievance is barred by "laches" is a question for the arbitrator to decide under a broad arbitration agreement applicable to "any difference" not settled by the parties within 48 hours of occurrence, even if the claim of laches is "extrinsic" to the procedures under the agreement. *Operating Eng'rs Local 150 v. Flair Bldrs., Inc.,* 406 U.S. 487 (1972).

NLRB v. BURNS INTERNATIONAL SECURITY SERVICES, INC.

Supreme Court of the United States
406 U.S. 272, 92 S. Ct. 1571, 32 L. Ed. 2d 61 (1972)

MR. JUSTICE WHITE delivered the opinion of the Court.

Burns International Security Services, Inc. (Burns), replaced another employer, the Wackenhut Corporation (Wackenhut), which had previously provided plant protection services for the Lockheed Aircraft Service Company (Lockheed) located at the Ontario International Airport in California. When Burns began providing security service, it employed 42 guards; 27 of them had been employed by Wackenhut. Burns refused, however, to bargain with the United Plant Guard Workers of America (the union) which had been certified after an NLRB election as the exclusive bargaining representative of Wackenhut's employees less than four months earlier. The issues presented in this case are whether Burns refused to bargain with a union representing a majority of employees in an appropriate unit and whether the National Labor Relations Board could order Burns to observe the terms of a collective bargaining contract signed by the union and Wackenhut which Burns had not voluntarily assumed. Resolution turns to a great extent on the precise facts involved here.

I

The Wackenhut Corporation provided protection services at the Lockheed plant for five years before Burns took over this task. On February 28, 1967, a few months before the change-over of guard employers, a majority of the Wackenhut guards selected the union as their exclusive bargaining representative in a Board election after Wackenhut and the union had agreed that the Lockheed plant was the appropriate bargaining unit. On March 8, the Regional Director certified the union as the exclusive bargaining representative for these employees, and on April 29, Wackenhut and the union entered into a three-year collective bargaining contract.

Meanwhile, since Wackenhut's one-year service agreement to provide security protection was due to expire on June 30, Lockheed had called for bids from various companies supplying these services, and both Burns and Wackenhut submitted estimates. At a pre-bid conference attended by Burns on May 15, a representative of Lockheed informed the bidders that Wackenhut's guards were represented by the union, that the union had recently won a Board election and been certified, and that there was in existence a collective bargaining contract between Wackenhut and the union. Lockheed then accepted Burns' bid, and on May 31, Wackenhut was notified that Burns would assume responsibility for protection services on July 1. Burns chose to retain 27 of the Wackenhut guards, and it brought in 15 of its own guards from other Burns locations.

During June, when Burns hired the 27 Wackenhut guards, it supplied them with membership cards of the American Federation of Guards (AFG), another union with whom Burns had collective bargaining contracts at other locations, and informed them that they must become AFG members to work for Burns, that they would not receive uniforms otherwise, and that Burns "could not live with" the existing contract between Wackenhut and the union. On June 29, Burns recognized the AFG on the theory that it had obtained a card majority. On July 12, however, the UPG demanded that Burns recognize it as the bargaining representative of Burns' employees at Lockheed and that Burns honor the collective bargaining agreement between it and Wackenhut. When Burns refused, the UPG filed unfair labor practice charges, and Burns responded by challenging the appropriateness of the unit and by denying its obligation to bargain.

The Board, adopting the trial examiner's findings and conclusions, found the Lockheed plant an appropriate unit and held that Burns had violated §§ 8(a)(2) and 8(a)(1) of the Act ... by unlawfully recognizing and assisting the AFG, a rival of the UPG; that it had violated §§ 8(a)(5) and 8(a)(1) ... by failing to recognize and bargain with the UPG and by refusing to honor the collective bargaining agreement which had been negotiated between Wackenhut and UPG.

Burns did not challenge the § 8(a)(2) unlawful assistance finding in the Court of Appeals but sought review of the unit determination and the order to bargain and observe the pre-existing collective bargaining contract. The Court of Appeals accepted the Board's unit determination and enforced the Board's order insofar as it related to the finding of unlawful assistance of a rival union and the refusal to bargain, but it held that the Board had exceeded its powers in ordering Burns to honor the contract executed by Wackenhut. Both Burns and the Board petitioned for certiorari, Burns challenging the unit determination and the bargaining order and the Board maintaining its position that Burns was bound by the Wackenhut contract, and we granted both petitions, though we declined to review the propriety of the bargaining unit....

II

We address first Burns' alleged duty to bargain with the union.... Because the Act itself imposes a duty to bargain with the representative of a majority of the employees in an appropriate unit, the initial issue before the Board was whether the charging union was such a bargaining representative....

... In an election held but a few months before, the union had been designated bargaining agent for the employees in the unit and a majority of these employees had been hired by Burns for work in an identical unit. It is undisputed that Burns knew all the relevant facts in this regard and was aware of the certification and of the existence of a collective bargaining contract. In these circumstances, it was not unreasonable for the Board to conclude that the union certified to represent all employees in the unit still represented a majority of the employees and that Burns could not reasonably have entertained a good-faith doubt about that fact. Burns' obligation to bargain with the union over terms and conditions of employment stems from its hiring of Wackenhut's employees and from the recent election and Board certification. It has been consistently held that a mere change of employers or of ownership in the employing industry is not such an "unusual circumstance" as to affect the force of the Board's certification within the normal operative period if a majority of employees after the change of ownership or management were employed by the preceding employer....

It goes without saying, of course, that Burns was not entitled to upset what it should have accepted as an established union majority by soliciting representation cards for another union and thereby committing the unfair labor practice of which it was found guilty by the Board. That holding was not challenged here and makes it imperative that the situation be viewed as it was when Burns hired its employees for the guard unit, a majority of whom were represented by a Board-certified union. *See NLRB v. Gissel Packing Co.,* 395 U.S. 575, 609, 610-616 (1969).

It would be a wholly different case if the Board had determined that because Burns' operational structure and practices differed from those of Wackenhut, the Lockheed bargaining unit was no longer an appropriate one. Likewise, it would be different if Burns had not hired employees already represented by a union certified as a bargaining agent, and the Board recognized as much at oral argument. But where the bargaining unit remains unchanged and a majority of the employees hired by the new employer are represented by a recently certified bargaining agent there is little basis for faulting the Board's implementation of the express mandates of § 8(a)(5) and § 9(a) by ordering the employer to bargain with the incumbent union. This is the view of several courts of appeal and we agree with those courts....

III

It does not follow, however, from Burns' duty to bargain that it was bound to observe the substantive terms of the collective bargaining contract the union had negotiated with Wackenhut and to which Burns had in no way agreed. Section 8(d) of the Act expressly provides that the existence of such bargaining obligation "does not compel either party to agree to a proposal or require the making of a concession." Congress has consistently declined to interfere with free collective bargaining and has preferred that device, or voluntary arbitration, to the imposition of compulsory terms as a means of avoiding or terminating labor disputes....

This history was reviewed in detail and given controlling effect in *H.K. Porter Co. v. NLRB,* 397 U.S. 99 (1970)....

These considerations, evident from the explicit language and legislative history of the labor laws, underlay the Board's prior decisions which until now have consistently held that although successor employers may be bound to recognize and bargain with the union, they are not bound by the substantive provisions of a collective bargaining contract negotiated by their predecessors but not agreed to or assumed by them....

The Board, however, has now departed from this view and argues that the same policies which mandate a continuity of bargaining obligation also require that successor employers be bound to the terms of a predecessor's collective bargaining contract. It asserts that the stability of labor relations will be jeopardized and that employees will face uncertainty and a gap in the bargained-for terms and conditions of employment, as well as the possible loss of advantages gained by prior negotiations, unless the new employer is held to have assumed, as a matter of federal labor law, the obligations under the contract entered into by the former employer. Recognizing that under normal contract principles a party would not be bound to a contract in the absence of consent, the Board notes that in *John Wiley & Sons, Inc. v. Livingston,* 376 U.S. 543, 550 (1964), the Court declared that "a collective bargaining agreement is not an ordinary contract" but is rather an outline of the common law of a particular plant or industry.... The Board contends that the same factors which the Court emphasized in *Wiley,* the peaceful settlement of industrial conflicts and "protection [of] the employees [against] a sudden change in the employment relationship," *Id.* at 549, require that Burns be treated under the collective bargaining contract exactly as Wackenhut would have been if it had continued protecting the Lockheed plant.

We do not find *Wiley* controlling in the circumstances here. *Wiley* arose in the context of a § 301 suit to compel arbitration, not in the context of an unfair labor practice proceeding where the Board is expressly limited by the provisions of § 8(d). That decision emphasized "the preference of national labor policy for arbitration as a substitute for tests of strength between contending forces" and held only that the agreement to arbitrate, "construed in the contest of national labor law," survived the merger and left to the arbitrator, subject to judicial review, the ultimate question of the extent to which, if any, the surviving company was bound by other provisions of the contract. *Id.* at 549, 551.

Wiley's limited accommodation between the legislative endorsement of freedom of contract and the judicial preference for peaceful arbitral settlement of labor disputes does not warrant the Board's holding that the employer commits an unfair labor practice unless he honors the substantive terms of the pre-existing contract. The present case does not involve a § 301 suit; nor does it involve the duty to arbitrate. Rather, the claim is that Burns must be held bound by the contract executed by Wackenhut, whether Burns has agreed to it or not and even though Burns made it perfectly clear that it had no intention of assuming that contract. *Wiley* suggests no such open-ended obligation. Its narrower holding dealt with a merger occurring against a background of state law which embodied the general rule that in merger situations the surviving corporation is liable for the obligations of the disappearing corporation. *See* N.Y. Stock Corporation Law § 90 (1951); 15 W. Fletcher, Private Corporations § 7121 (1961 rev. ed.). Here there was no merger, no sale of assets, no dealings whatsoever between Wackenhut and Burns. On the contrary, they were competitors for the same work, each bidding for the service contract at Lockheed. Burns purchased nothing from Wackenhut and became liable for none of its financial obligations. Burns merely hired enough of Wackenhut's employees to require it to bargain with the union as commanded by § 8(a)(5) and § 9(a). But this consideration is a wholly insufficient basis for implying either in fact or in law that Burns had agreed or must be held to have agreed to honor Wackenhut's collective bargaining contract....

We also agree with the Court of Appeals that holding either the union or the new employer bound to the substantive terms of an old collective bargaining contract may result in serious inequities. A potential employer may be willing to take over a moribund business only if he can make changes in corporate structure, composition of the labor force, work location, task assignment, and nature of supervision. Saddling such an employer with the terms and conditions of employment contained in the old collective bargaining contract may make these changes impossible and may discourage and inhibit the transfer of capital. On the other hand, a union may have made concessions to a small or failing employer that it would be unwilling to make to a large or economically successful firm. The congressional policy manifest in the Act is to enable the parties to negotiate for any protection either deems appropriate, but to allow the balance of bargaining advantage to be set by economic power realities. Strife is bound to occur if the concessions which must be honored do not correspond to the relative economic strength of the parties.

The Board's position would also raise new problems, for the successor employer would be circumscribed in exactly the same way as the predecessor under the collective bargaining contract. It would seemingly follow that employees of the predecessor would be deemed employees of the successor, dischargeable only in accordance with provisions of the contract and subject to the grievance and arbitration provisions thereof. Burns would not have been free to replace Wackenhut's guards with its own except as the contract permitted. Given the continuity of employment relationship, the pre-existing contract's provisions with respect to wages, seniority rights, vacation privileges, pension and retirement fund benefits, job security provisions, work assignments and the like would devolve on the successor....

IV

... [T]he Board's opinion stated that "[t]he obligation to bargain imposed on a successor-employer includes the negative injunction to refrain from unilaterally changing wages and other benefits established by a prior collective bargaining agreement even though that agreement had expired. In this respect the successor-employer's obligations are the same as those imposed upon employers generally during the period between collective bargaining agreements." ... This statement by the Board is consistent with its prior and subsequent cases which hold that whether or not a successor employer is bound by its predecessor's contract, it must not institute terms and conditions of employment different from those provided in its predecessor's contract, at least without first bargaining with the employees' representative.... Thus, if Burns, without bargaining to impasse with the union, had paid its employees on and after July 1, at a rate lower than Wackenhut had paid under its contract or otherwise provided terms and conditions of employment different from those provided in the Wackenhut collective bargaining agreement, under the Board's view, Burns would have committed a § 8(a)(5) unfair labor practice and would be subject to an order to restore to employees what they had lost by this so-called unilateral change....

Although Burns had an obligation to bargain with the union concerning wages and other conditions of employment when the union requested it to do so, this case is not like a § 8(a)(5) violation where an employer unilaterally changes a condition of employment without consulting a bargaining representative. It is difficult to understand how Burns could be said to have *changed* unilaterally any pre-existing term or condition of employment without bargaining when it had no previous relationship whatsoever to the bargaining unit and, prior to July 1, no outstanding terms and conditions of employment from which a change could be inferred. The terms on which Burns hired employees for service after July 1 may have differed from the terms extended by Wackenhut and required by the collective bargaining contract, but it does not follow that Burns changed *its* terms and conditions of employment when it specified the initial basis on which employees were hired on July 1.

Although a successor employer is ordinarily free to set initial terms on which it will hire the employees of a predecessor, there will be instances in which it is perfectly clear that the new employer plans to retain all of the employees in the unit and in which it will be appropriate to have him initially consult with the employees' bargaining representative before he fixes terms. In other situations, however, it may not be clear until the successor employer has hired his full complement of employees that he has a duty to bargain with a union, since it will not be evident until then that the bargaining representative represents a majority of the employees in the union as required by § 9(a) of the Act.... Here, for example, Burns' obligation to bargain with the union did not mature until it had selected its force of guards late in June. The Board quite properly found that Burns refused to bargain on July 12 when it rejected the overtures of the union. It is true that the wages it paid when it began protecting the Lockheed plant on July 1 differed from those specified in the Wackenhut collective bargaining agreement, but there is no evidence that Burns ever unilaterally changed the terms and conditions of employment it had offered to potential employees in June after its obligation to bargain with the union became apparent. If the union had made a request to bargain after Burns had completed its hiring and if Burns had negotiated in good faith and had made offers to the union which the union rejected, Burns could have unilaterally initiated such proposals as the opening terms and conditions of employment on July 1 without committing an unfair labor practice. *Cf. NLRB v. Katz,* 369 U.S. 736, 745 n.12 (1962).... The Board's order requiring Burns to make whole its employees for any losses suffered by reason of Burns' refusal to honor and enforce the contract, cannot therefore be sustained on the ground that Burns unilaterally changed existing terms and conditions of employment, thereby committing an unfair labor practice which required monetary restitution in these circumstances.

Affirmed.

MR. JUSTICE REHNQUIST, with whom THE CHIEF JUSTICE, MR. JUSTICE BRENNAN, and MR. JUSTICE POWELL join, concurring in No. 71-124 and dissenting in No. 71-198.

Although the Court studiously avoids using the term "successorship" in concluding that Burns did have a statutory obligation to bargain with the union, it affirms the conclusions of the Board and the Court of Appeals to that effect which were based entirely on the successorship doctrine. Because I believe that the Board and the Court of Appeals stretched that concept beyond the limits of its proper application, I would enforce neither the Board's bargaining order nor its order imposing upon Burns the terms of the contract between the union and Wackenhut. I therefore concur in No. 71-123 and dissent in No. 71-198....

The rigid imposition of a prior-existing labor relations environment on a new employer whose only connection with the old employer is the hiring of some of the latter's employees and the performance of some of the work which was previously performed by the latter, might well tend to produce industrial peace of a sort. But industrial peace in such a case would be produced at a sacrifice of the determination by the Board of the appropriateness of bargaining agents and of the wishes of the majority of the employees which the Act was designed to preserve. These latter principles caution us against extending successorship, under the banner of industrial peace, step by step to a point where the only connection between the two employing entities is a naked transfer of employees....

Burns acquired not a single asset, tangible or intangible, by negotiation or transfer from Wackenhut. It succeeded to the contractual rights and duties of the plant protection service contract with Lockheed not by reason of Wackenhut's assignment or consent, but over Wackenhut's vigorous opposition. I think the only permissible conclusion is that Burns is not a successor to Wackenhut....

To conclude that Burns was a successor to Wackenhut in this situation, with its attendant consequences under the Board's order imposing a duty to bargain with the bargaining representative of Wackenhut's employees, would import unwarranted rigidity into labor-management relations. The fortunes of competing employers inevitably ebb and flow, and an employer who has currently gained production orders at the expense of another may well wish to hire employees away from that other. There is no reason to think that the best interests of the employees, the employers, and ultimately of the free market are not served by such movement. Yet inherent in the expanded doctrine of successorship which the Board urges in this case is the notion that somehow the "labor relations environment" comes with the new employees if the new employer has but obtained orders or business which previously belonged to the old employer. The fact that the employees in the instant case continue to perform their work at the same situs, while not irrelevant to analysis, cannot be deemed controlling.... Where the relation between the first employer and the second is as attenuated as it is here, and the reasonable expectations of the employees equally attenuated, the application of the successorship doctrine is not authorized by the Labor Management Relations Act.

This is not to say that Burns would be unilaterally free to mesh into its previously recognized Los Angeles County bargaining unit a group of employees such as were involved here who already have designated a collective bargaining representative in their previous employment. Burns' actions in this regard would be subject to the commands of the Labor Management Relations Act, and to the regulation of the Board under proper application of governing principles.... Had the Board made the appropriate factual inquiry and determinations required by the Act, such inquiry might have justified the conclusion that Burns was obligated to recognize and bargain with the union as a representative for its employees at the Lockheed facility.

But the Board, instead of applying this type of analysis to the union's complaints here, concluded that because Burns was a "successor" it was absolutely bound to the mold which had been fashioned by Wackenhut and its employees at Lockheed. Burns was thereby precluded from challenging the designation of Lockheed as an appropriate bargaining unit for a year after the original certification....

I am unwilling to follow the Board this far down the successorship road, since I believe to do so would substantially undercut the principle of free choice of bargaining representatives by the employees and designation of the appropriate bargaining unit by the Board which are guaranteed by the Act.

———————

Howard Johnson Co. v. Hotel & Restaurant Employees Detroit Local Joint Board, 417 U.S. 249, 94 S. Ct. 2236, 41 L. Ed. 2d 46 (1974). The Grissom family operated a restaurant and motor lodge under franchise from Howard Johnson. Howard Johnson purchased the personal property used in the restaurant and motor lodge from the Grissoms, and leased the realty. After hiring only nine of its predecessor's 53 employees, Howard Johnson commenced operation of the establishment with a complement of 45. It refused to recognize the union that had bargained collectively with the Grissoms, and it refused to assume any obligations under the existing labor agreements. The union sued both the Grissoms and Howard Johnson under § 301 to require them to arbitrate the extent of their obligations to the Grissom employees. The Grissoms admitted a duty to arbitrate, but Howard Johnson denied any such duty. The Supreme Court applied *Burns,* even though it dealt with a § 8(a)(5) refusal to bargain charge rather than a § 301 suit for arbitration, and sustained Howard Johnson's refusal to arbitrate. The Court distinguished *Wiley* on the ground it "involved a merger, as a result of which the initial employing entity completely disappeared.... Even more important, in *Wiley* the surviving corporation hired *all* of the employees of the disappearing corporation." The Court stressed that "there was plainly no substantial continuity of identity in the work force hired by Howard Johnson with that of the Grissoms, and no express or implied assumption of the agreement to arbitrate." The question of "successorship" was declared "simply not meaningful in the abstract.... The answer to this inquiry requires analysis of the interests of the new employer and the employees and of the policies of the labor laws in light of the facts of each case and the particular legal obligation which is at issue, whether it be the duty to recognize and bargain with the union, the duty to remedy unfair labor practices, the duty to arbitrate, etc."

NOTES

1. Do *Burns* and *Howard Johnson* sound the death knell of *Wiley,* or are the three cases genuinely distinguishable? If so, on what basis? Because of the different relationships of the various employers? The differences in the remedies sought by the unions? The differences in the proportions of the predecessor's and the successor's employees involved? If the latter, would it make sense to say that in refusal to bargain cases, the critical factor is the percentage (a majority?) of the successor's employees coming *from* the predecessor, while in suits to compel arbitration of the predecessor's contract, the critical factor is the percentage of the predecessor's employees going *to* the successor? *See Boeing Co. v. Machinists,* 504 F.2d 307 (5th Cir. 1974), *cert. denied,* 421 U.S. 913 (1975). Consider the implications of *Golden State Bottling Co.,* 414 U.S. 168 (1973) (successor employer may be jointly and severally liable with predecessor for remedying unfair labor practices); *cf. Peters v. NLRB,* 153 F.3d 289 (6th Cir. 1998) (distinguishing *Golden State Bottling* and ruling that successor employer is not responsible for unfair labor practices committed by predecessor where the sale of assets occurred through receivership, preventing the successor from negotiating for indemnity or for a price that would compensate for the risk of unfair labor practices liability).

2. *Burns* indicated that when it is "perfectly clear" a new employer is going to retain its predecessor's employees, it may have to "consult" with the union before setting new terms of employment. A 3-2 Board majority found this caveat applicable in *Canteen Co.,* 317 N.L.R.B. 1052 (1995), *enforced,* 103 F.3d 1355 (7th Cir. 1997), and concluded a successor employer had violated the Act by unilaterally reducing wage rates. Two members believed that the "perfectly clear" condition was satisfied because the employer had told the union *prior* to the wage reduction that he wanted the predecessor's employees to serve a probationary period. Then-Chair Gould concurred on the grounds that the only condition for the *Burns* caveat was the plan to retain the old unit employees, not their willingness to accept the new employer's terms. Two members dissented, limiting the "perfectly clear" caveat to instances where the new employer fails to inform the predecessor's employees of the new terms by the time he makes an unconditional job offer.

3. A successor employer violates § 8(a)(5) (and § 8(a)(3)) by refusing to bargain with the union that had represented its predecessor's employees, even though the union does not represent a majority of the current work force, if the successor prevented the union from securing a majority by unlawfully discriminating against the predecessor's employees in hiring the new work force. *Pace Indus. v. NLRB,* 118 F.3d 585 (8th Cir. 1997), *cert. denied,* 118 S. Ct. 1299 (1998) (Board may properly infer unlawful motivation where successor employer implements elaborate hiring process involving a 19-prong application and a battery of verbal, numerical, and dexterity tests, resulting in the rehiring of 22 out of 103 of the former employees); *cf. U.S. Marine Corp. v. NLRB,* 944 F.2d 1305 (7th Cir. 1990) (6-5 en banc), *cert. denied,* 503 U.S. 936 (1992). *But cf. NLRB v. Bausch & Lomb, Inc.,* 526 F.2d 817 (2d Cir. 1975) (no "successorship" despite unlawful discrimination in hiring if there is insufficient "continuity of identity" in the two businesses).

What about a successor employer who seeks to avoid a bargaining obligation by hiring a majority of its predecessor's employees but asserts a good faith reasonable doubt regarding whether a majority of the employees it has inherited continue to support the union? *See Allentown Mack Sales & Serv. v. NLRB,* 118 S. Ct. 818 (1998), *supra,* Section II.C.

4. Prior to *Burns* and *Howard Johnson,* courts of appeals had applied *Wiley* to compel arbitration in non-merger situations, *e.g.,* where the successor was a purchaser. *See Steelworkers v. Reliance Universal, Inc.,* 335 F.2d 891 (3d Cir. 1964); *cf. Wackenhut Corp. v. Plant Guard Workers,* 332 F.2d 954 (9th Cir. 1964). Are these decisions still supportable? What if the successor has lawfully recognized and contracted with a union different from the one representing the predecessor's employees? *See McGuire v. Humble Oil & Ref. Co.,* 355 F.2d 352 (2d Cir.), *cert. denied,* 384 U.S. 988 (1966), noted in 66 Colum. L. Rev. 967 (1966); *Machinists v. Howmet Corp.,* 466 F.2d 1249 (9th Cir. 1972). Should it make any difference whether the transfer is a stock purchase or a purchase of physical assets? *See* Jenero & Mennel, *Pitfalls and Opportunities: NLRA and Contractual Considerations When Purchasing A Unionized Company,* 22 Emp. Rel. L.J. 141 (1996); Krupman & Kaplan, *The Stock Purchaser After Burns: Must He Buy the Union Contract?* 31 Lab. L.J. 328 (1980). *See also Graduate Plastics Co. v. UAW District 65,* 991 F.2d 997 (2d Cir. 1993) (foreclosure sale). What about the lease of a manufacturing facility—can a lessee be a successor? *See Harter Tomato Prods. Co. v. NLRB,* 133 F.3d 934 (D.C. Cir. 1998) (yes).

5. *Successorship Clauses in Labor Contracts:* In *Lone Star Steel Co. v. NLRB,* 639 F.2d 545 (10th Cir. 1980), *cert. denied,* 450 U.S. 911 (1981), a successorship clause was held mandatory as a bargaining topic, and the union's insistence to impasse was permissible. Since it went to the effect of the employer decision to transfer its assets, rather than the decision itself, the court found the "vitally affects" test met as to the terms and conditions of the employment of unit members, where the effect of the clause was to ensure the continuing application of the agreed terms. But are such clauses enforceable? *See Local Joint Executive Bd. v. Royal Ctr., Inc.,* 796 F.2d 1159 (9th Cir. 1986), *cert. denied,* 479 U.S. 1033 (1987) (employer who closed business and then sold it several months later was obligated under its collective bargaining agreement, which contained a broad grievance-arbitration clause and a provision that required Royal to obtain a commitment from any purchaser obliging it to honor the terms of the collective contract, to arbitrate the union's grievance concerning its alleged breach of the successorship clause). *See also Wheelabrator Envirotech v. Massachusetts Laborers' Dist. Council, Local 1144,* 88 F.3d 40 (1st Cir. 1996) (enforcing arbitrator's award that a contractor was under an obligation to a union, pursuant to a successorship clause, to compel the contractor's successor to assume the parties' collective bargaining agreement, even though the contractor and the successor were not in privity and the successor had outbid the contractor for a job); *Zady Natey, Inc. v. UFCW Local 27,* 995 F.2d 496 (4th Cir.), *cert. denied,* 510 U.S. 977 (1993) (sustaining arbitral award of damages to employees when seller failed to bind buyer in accordance with successorship clause). *But cf. In re Chateaugay Corp.,* 891 F.2d 1034 (2d Cir. 1989) (successorship clause whereby employer agreed not to sell its "operations" unless buyer assumed the union's contract did not apply to the sale of a permanently closed mine). *See generally* Crain-Mountney, *The Unenforceable Successorship Clause: A Departure from National Labor Policy,* 30 U.C.L.A. L. Rev. 1249 (1983); Crystal, *Successor and Assigns Clauses: Do They Actually Require that a Purchaser Adopt the Seller's Contract?* 33 Lab. L.J. 581 (1982); Rock & Wachter, *Labor Law Successorship: A Corporate Law Approach,* 92 Mich. L. Rev. 203 (1993).

6. Seemingly distinct business entities may be bound by the same bargaining or contractual obligations not only on the basis that one is the "successor" of the other but also on the bases that one is the "alter ego" of the other or that they are actually a "single employer." *Compare Telegraph Workers v. NLRB,* 571 F.2d 665 (D.C. Cir.), *cert. denied,* 439 U.S. 827 (1978) *with Alkire v. NLRB,* 716 F.2d 1014 (4th Cir. 1983) *and NLRB v. Campbell-Harris Elec., Inc.,* 719 F.2d 292 (8th Cir. 1983). Actual control of personnel rather than the identity of the owners is the key to alter ego status. *NLRB v. Omnitest Inspection Servs.,* 937 F.2d 112 (3d Cir. 1991). All three theories are discussed in Comment, *Bargaining Obligations After Corporate Transformation,* 54 N.Y.U. L. Rev. 624 (1979); Note, *Labor Law's Alter Ego Doctrine: The Role of Employer Motive in Corporate Transformations,* 86 Mich. L. Rev. 1024 (1988).

7. Even if logically reconcilable, do *Wiley, Burns,* and *Howard Johnson* vary in their attitudes toward the nature of the collective agreement, and toward the values to be promoted in industrial relations? *See generally* Christensen, *Successorships, Unit Changes, and the Bargaining Table,* in Southwestern Legal Foundation, Labor Law Developments 1973, Proceedings of Nineteenth Annual Institute on Labor Law 197 (1973); Goldstein, *Protecting Employee Rights in Successorship,* 44 Lab. L.J. 18 (1993); Harper, *Defining the Economic Relationship Appropriate For Collective Bargaining,* 39 B.C. L. Rev. 329 (1998); Morris & Gaus, *Successorship and the Collective Bargaining Agreement: Accommodating Wiley and Burns,* 59 Va. L. Rev. 1359 (1973); Murphy, *Successorship and the Forgotten Employee,* in N.Y.U. Thirty-First Annual Conference on Labor 75 (1978); Severson & Willcoxon, *Successorship Under Howard Johnson: Short Order Justice for Employees,* 64 Calif. L. Rev. 795 (1976); Silverstein, *The Fate of Workers in Successor Firms: Does Law Tame The Market?,* 8 Indus. Rel. L.J. 153 (1986); Comment, *The Bargaining Obligations of Successor Employers,* 88 Harv. L. Rev. 759 (1975). *Burns* was noted in 40 U. Chi. L. Rev. 617 (1973) and 71 Mich. L. Rev. 571 (1973), and *Howard Johnson* in 74 Mich. L. Rev. 555 (1976). The subject is noted in 77 Cornell L. Rev. 47 (1991); 79 Geo. L.J. 1549 (1991); 44 U. Miami L. Rev. 403 (1989).

8. *Remedies:* A successor employer that violates its duty to bargain with the union which represented the predecessor's employees, or that unlawfully refuses to hire former employees of the predecessor and leaves the union's continuing majority status uncertain, may be required to restore retroactively the terms of the predecessor's contract (pending bargaining) and to make the discriminatees whole at the pay rates in that contract. The rationale for this is that even though the successor could ultimately reduce the wage rates, the company should not be permitted to benefit from its own wrongful acts—it must bear the burden of proving what wage rates good faith bargaining would have produced. *NLRB v. Staten Island Hotel,* 101 F.3d 858 (2d Cir. 1996); *New Breed Leasing Corp. v. NLRB,* 111 F.3d 1460 (9th Cir.), *cert. denied,* 118 S. Ct. 366 (1997); *Galloway School Lines,* 321 N.L.R.B. 1422 (1996); *Advanced Stretchforming Int'l Inc. v. NLRB,* 323 N.L.R.B. No. 84, 155 L.R.R.M. 1036 (1997).

9. *Jurisdiction:* Upon the merger of three newspapers, the union that had represented the employees of one paper sued the consolidated successor to secure arbitration of a "new agreement" pursuant to the terms of the predecessor's contract. A court of appeals held that the NLRB had exclusive jurisdiction to decide whether the employer had met its bargaining obligations under the labor agreement following the merger and consolidation of operations. The union was not merely asking for arbitration of vested rights under the former contract but for "interest arbitration" and the acquisition of future rights, and thus there was no concurrent court jurisdiction. *Newspaper Guild Local 105 v. Ottaway Newspapers,* 79 F.3d 1273 (1st Cir. 1996).

10. May states regulate in the successorship area? *Compare United Steelworkers v. St. Gabriel's Hosp.,* 871 F. Supp. 335 (D. Minn. 1994) (Minnesota law imposing existing collective contracts on successor employers preempted by federal labor law) *and Commonwealth Edison Co. v. IBEW, Local 15,* 961 F. Supp. 1169 (N.D. Ill. 1997) (Illinois law requiring successor to hire predecessor's employees and comply with successorship clause in predecessor's collective bargaining agreement preempted) *with Washington Serv. Contrs. Coalition v. District of Columbia*, 54 F.3d 811, (D.C. Cir. 1995) (D.C. ordinance requiring successor contractors that perform food, janitorial, building maintenance, and health care services to retain predecessor contractor employees for 90-day transition period not preempted by NLRA).

FALL RIVER DYEING & FINISHING CORP. v. NLRB

Supreme Court of the United States
482 U.S. 27, 107 S. Ct. 2225, 96 L. Ed. 2d 22 (1987)

JUSTICE BLACKMUN delivered the opinion of the Court.[*]

In this case we are confronted with the issue whether the National Labor Relations Board's decision is consistent with *NLRB v. Burns International Security Services, Inc.*, 406 U.S. 272 (1972). In *Burns,* this Court ruled that the new employer, succeeding to the business of another, had an obligation to bargain with the union representing the predecessor's employees. We first must decide whether *Burns* is limited to a situation where the union only recently was certified before the transition in employers, or whether that decision also applies where the union is entitled to a presumption of majority support. Our inquiry then proceeds to three questions that concern rules the Labor Board has developed in the successorship context. First, we must determine whether there is substantial record evidence to support the Board's conclusion that petitioner was a "successor" to Sterlingwale Corp., its business predecessor. Second, we must decide whether the Board's "substantial and representative complement" rule, designed to identify the date when a successor's obligation to bargain with the predecessor's employees' union arises, is consistent with *Burns,* is reasonable, and was applied properly in this case. Finally, we must examine the Board's "continuing demand" principle to the effect that, if a union has presented to a successor a premature demand for bargaining, this demand continues in effect until the successor acquires the "substantial and representative complement" of employees that triggers its obligation to bargain.

I

For over 30 years before 1982, Sterlingwale operated a textile dyeing and finishing plant in Fall River, Mass. Its business consisted basically of two types of dyeing, called, respectively, "converting" and "commission." Under the converting process, which in 1981 accounted for 60% to 70% of its business, Sterlingwale bought unfinished fabrics for its own account, dyed and finished them, and then sold them to apparel manufacturers. In commission dyeing, which accounted for the remainder of its business, Sterlingwale dyed and finished fabrics

---

[*]JUSTICE WHITE joins only Parts I and III of this opinion.

owned by customers according to their specifications. The financing and marketing aspects of converting and commission dyeing are different. Converting requires capital to purchase fabrics and a sales force to promote the finished products. The production process, however, is the same for both converting and commission dyeing.

In the late 1970's the textile-dyeing business, including Sterlingwale's, began to suffer from adverse economic conditions and foreign competition.... Finally, in February 1982, Sterlingwale laid off all its production employees, primarily because it no longer had the capital to continue the converting business. It retained a skeleton crew of workers and supervisors to ship out the goods remaining on order and to maintain the corporation's building and machinery. In the months following the layoff, Leonard Ansin, Sterlingwale's president, liquidated the inventory of the corporation and, at the same time, looked for a business partner with whom he could "resurrect the business.";...

For almost as long as Sterlingwale had been in existence, its production and maintenance employees had been represented by the United Textile Workers of America, AFL-CIO, Local 292 (Union). The most recent collective-bargaining agreement before Sterlingwale's demise had been negotiated in 1978 and was due to expire in 1981. By an agreement dated October 1980, however, in response to the financial difficulties suffered by Sterlingwale, the Union agreed to amend the 1978 agreement to extend its expiration date by one year, until April 1, 1982, without any wage increase and with an agreement to improve labor productivity....

In late summer 1982, however, Sterlingwale finally went out of business. It made an assignment for the benefit of its creditors....

During this same period, a former Sterlingwale employee and officer, Herbert Chace, and Arthur Friedman, president of one of Sterlingwale's major customers, Marcamy Sales Corporation (Marcamy), formed petitioner Fall River Dyeing & Finishing Corp. Chace, who had resigned from Sterlingwale in February 1982, had worked there for 27 years, had been vice-president in charge of sales at the time of his departure, and had participated in collective bargaining with the Union during his tenure at Sterlingwale. Chace and Friedman formed petitioner with the intention of engaging strictly in the commission-dyeing business and of taking advantage of the availability of Sterlingwale's assets and workforce. Accordingly, Friedman had Marcamy acquire from [the creditors] Sterlingwale's plant, real property, and equipment, and convey them to petitioner. Petitioner also obtained some of Sterlingwale's remaining inventory at the liquidator's auction. Chace became petitioner's vice-president in charge of operations and Friedman became its president.

In September 1982, petitioner began operating out of Sterlingwale's former facilities and began hiring employees. It advertised for workers and supervisors in a local newspaper, and Chace personally got in touch with several prospective supervisors. Petitioner hired 12 supervisors, of whom 8 had been supervisors with Sterlingwale and 3 had been production employees there. In its hiring decisions for production employees, petitioner took into consideration recommendations from these supervisors and a prospective employee's former employment with Sterlingwale. Petitioner's initial hiring goal was to attain one full shift of workers, which meant from 55 to 60 employees. Petitioner planned to "see how business would be" after this initial goal had been met and, if business permitted, to expand to two shifts. The employees who were hired first spent approximately four to six weeks in start-up operations and an additional month in experimental production.

By letter dated October 19, 1982, the Union requested petitioner to recognize it as the bargaining agent for petitioner's employees and to begin collective bargaining. Petitioner refused the request, stating that, in its view, the request had "no legal basis." At that time, 18 of petitioner's 21 employees were former employees of Sterlingwale. By November of that year, petitioner had employees in a complete range of jobs, had its production process in operation, and was handling customer orders; by mid-January 1983, it had attained its initial goal of one shift of workers. Of the 55 workers in this initial shift, a number that represented over half the workers petitioner would eventually hire, 36 were former Sterlingwale employees. Petitioner continued to expand its workforce, and by mid-April 1983 it had reached two full shifts. For the first time, ex-Sterlingwale employees were in the minority but just barely so (52 or 53 out of 107 employees).

Although petitioner engaged exclusively in commission dyeing, the employees experienced the same conditions they had when they were working for Sterlingwale. The production process was unchanged and the employees worked on the same machines, in the same building, with the same job classifications, under virtually the same supervisors. Over half the volume of petitioner's business came from former Sterlingwale customers, and, in particular, Marcamy.

On November 1, 1982, the Union filed an unfair labor practice charge with the Board, alleging that in its refusal to bargain petitioner had violated §§ 8(a)(1) and (5) of the National Labor Relations Act. After a hearing, the Administrative Law Judge (ALJ) decided that, on the facts of the case, petitioner was a successor to Sterlingwale.... Thus, in the view of the ALJ, petitioner's duty to bargain arose in mid-January because former Sterlingwale employees then were in the majority and because the Union's October demand was still in effect. Petitioner thus committed an unfair labor practice in refusing to bargain. In a brief decision and order, the Board, with one member dissenting, affirmed this decision.

The Court of Appeals for the First Circuit, also by a divided vote, enforced the order. 775 F.2d 425 (1985)....

Because of the importance of the successorship issue in labor law, and because of our interest in the rules developed by the Board for successorship cases, we granted certiorari.

II

Fifteen years ago in *NLRB v. Burns International Security Services, Inc.,* 406 U.S. 272 (1972), this Court first dealt with the issue of a successor employer's obligation to bargain with a union that had represented the employees of its predecessor. [The Court discussed *Burns.*]

These presumptions [of majority support] are based not so much on an absolute certainty that the union's majority status will not erode following certification, as on a particular policy decision. The overriding policy of the NLRA is "industrial peace." *Brooks v. NLRB,* 348 U.S. [96] 103. The presumptions of majority support further this policy by "promot[ing] stability in collective-bargaining relationships, without impairing the free choice of employees." *Terrell Machine Co.,* 173 N.L.R.B. 1480, 1480 (1969), *enf'd,* 427 F.2d 1088 (CA4), *cert. denied,* 398 U.S. 929 (1970). In essence, they enable a union to concentrate on obtaining and fairly administering a collective-bargaining agreement without worrying that, unless it produces immediate results, it will lose majority support and will be decertified.... The presumptions also remove any temptation on the part of the employer to avoid good-faith bargaining in the hope that, by delaying, it will undermine the union's support among the employees....

The rationale behind the presumptions is particularly pertinent in the successorship situation and so it is understandable that the Court in *Burns* referred to them. During a transition between employers, a union is in a peculiarly vulnerable position. It has no formal and established bargaining relationship with the new employer, is uncertain about the new employer's plans, and cannot be sure if or when the new employer must bargain with it. While being concerned with the future of its members with the new employer, the union also must protect whatever rights still exist for its members under the collective-bargaining agreement with the predecessor employer. Accordingly, during this unsettling transition period, the union needs the presumptions of majority status to which it is entitled to safeguard its members' rights and to develop a relationship with the successor.

The position of the employees also supports the application of the presumptions in the successorship situation. If the employees find themselves in a new enterprise that substantially resembles the old, but without their chosen bargaining representative, they may well feel that their choice of a union is subject to the vagaries of an enterprise's transformation. This feeling is not conducive to industrial peace. In addition, after being hired by a new company following a layoff from the old, employees initially will be concerned primarily with maintaining their new jobs. In fact, they might be inclined to shun support for their former union, especially if they believe that such support will jeopardize their jobs with the successor or if they are inclined to blame the union for their layoff and problems associated with it. Without the presumptions of majority support and with the wide variety of corporate transformations possible, an employer could use a successor enterprise as a way of getting rid of a labor contract and of exploiting the employees' hesitant attitude towards the union to eliminate its continuing presence.

In addition to recognizing the traditional presumptions of union majority status, however, the Court in *Burns* was careful to safeguard "'the rightful prerogative of owners independently to rearrange their businesses.'" *Golden State Bottling Co. v. NLRB,* 414 U.S. 168, 182 (1973), quoting *John Wiley & Sons, Inc. v. Livingston,* 376 U.S. 543, 549 (1964).... Thus, to a substantial extent the applicability of *Burns* rests in the hands of the successor. If the new employer makes a conscious decision to maintain generally the same business and to hire a majority of its employees from the predecessor, then the bargaining obligation of § 8(a)(5) is activated. This makes sense when one considers that the employer *intends* to take advantage of the trained workforce of its predecessor.

Accordingly, in *Burns* we acknowledged the interest of the successor in its freedom to structure its business and the interest of the employees in continued representation by the union. We now hold that a successor's obligation to bargain is not limited to a situation where the union in question has been recently certified. Where, as here, the union has a rebuttable presumption of majority status, this status continues despite the change in employers. And the new employer has an obligation to bargain with that union so long as the new employer is in fact a successor of the old employer and the majority of its employees were employed by its predecessor.

III

We turn now to the three rules, as well as to their application to the facts of this case, that the Board has adopted for the successorship situation. The Board, of course, is given considerable authority to interpret the provisions of the NLRA....

A. In *Burns* we approved the approach taken by the Board and accepted by courts with respect to determining whether a new company was indeed the successor to the old. This approach, which is primarily factual in nature and is based upon the totality of the circumstances of a given situation, requires that the Board focus on whether the new company has "acquired substantial assets of its predecessor and continued, without interruption or substantial change, the predecessor's business operations." *Golden State Bottling Co. v. NLRB,* 414 U.S., at 184. Hence, the focus is on whether there is "substantial continuity" between the enterprises. Under this approach, the Board examines a number of factors: whether the business of both employers is essentially the same; whether the employees of the new company are doing the same jobs in the same working conditions under the same supervisors; and whether the new entity has the same production process, produces the same products, and basically has the same body of customers....

In conducting the analysis, the Board keeps in mind the question whether "those employees who have been retained will understandably view their job

948   COLLECTIVE BARGAINING

situations as essentially unaltered." See *Golden State Bottling Co.,* 414 U.S., at 184; *NLRB v. Jeffries Lithograph Co.,* 752 F.2d 459, 464 (CA9 1985). This emphasis on the employees' perspective furthers the Act's policy of industrial peace. If the employees find themselves in essentially the same jobs after the employer transition and if their legitimate expectations in continued representation by their union are thwarted, their dissatisfaction may lead to labor unrest. See *Golden State Bottling Co.,* 414 U.S., at 184.

... [W]e find that the Board's determination that there was "substantial continuity" between Sterlingwale and petitioner and that petitioner was Sterlingwale's successor is supported by substantial evidence in the record. Petitioner acquired most of Sterlingwale's real property, its machinery and equipment, and much of its inventory and materials. It introduced no new product line. Of particular significance is the fact that, from the perspective of the employees, their jobs did not change. Although petitioner abandoned converting dyeing in exclusive favor of commission dyeing, this change did not alter the essential nature of the employees' jobs, because both types of dyeing involved the same production process. The job classifications of petitioner were the same as those of Sterlingwale; petitioners' employees worked on the same machines under the direction of supervisors most of whom were former supervisors of Sterlingwale. The record, in fact, is clear that petitioner acquired Sterlingwale's assets with the express purpose of taking advantage of its predecessor's workforce.

We do not find determinative of the successorship question the fact that there was a 7-month hiatus between Sterlingwale's demise and petitioner's start-up. Petitioner argues that this hiatus, coupled with the fact that its employees were hired through newspaper advertisements—not through Sterlingwale employment records, which were not transferred to it—resolves in its favor the "substantial continuity" question.... Yet such a hiatus is only one factor in the "substantial continuity" calculus and thus is relevant only when there are other indicia of discontinuity.... Conversely, if other factors indicate a continuity between the enterprises, and the hiatus is a normal start-up period, the "totality of the circumstances" will suggest that these circumstances present a successorship situation....

For the reasons given above, this is a case where the other factors suggest "substantial continuity" between the companies despite the 7-month hiatus. Here, moreover, the extent of the hiatus between the demise of Sterlingwale and the start-up of petitioner is somewhat less than certain. After the February layoff, Sterlingwale retained a skeleton crew of supervisors and employees that continued to ship goods to customers and to maintain the plant. In addition, until the assignment for the benefit of the creditors late in the summer, Ansin was seeking to resurrect the business or to find a buyer for Sterlingwale. The Union was aware of these efforts. Viewed from the employees' perspective, therefore, the hiatus may have been much less than seven months. Although petitioner hired the employees through advertisements, it often relied on recommendations from supervisors, themselves formerly employed by Sterlingwale, and intended the advertisements to reach the former Sterlingwale workforce.

Accordingly, we hold that, under settled law, petitioner was a successor to Sterlingwale. We thus must consider if and when petitioner's duty to bargain arose.

B. In *Burns,* the Court determined that the successor had an obligation to bargain with the union because a majority of its employees had been employed by Wackenhut. The "triggering" fact for the bargaining obligation was this composition of the successor's workforce.[12] The Court, however, did not have to consider the question *when* the successor's obligation to bargain arose: Wackenhut's contract expired on June 30 and Burns began its services with a majority of former Wackenhut guards on July 1. In other situations, as in the present case, there is a start-up period by the new employer while it gradually builds its operations and hires employees. In these situations, the Board, with the approval of the Courts of Appeals, has adopted the "substantial and representative complement" rule for fixing the moment when the determination as to the composition of the successor's workforce is to be made. If, at this particular moment, a majority of the successor's employees had been employed by its predecessor, then the successor has an obligation to bargain with the union that represented these employees.

This rule represents an effort to balance "'the objective of insuring maximum employee participation in the selection of a bargaining agent against the goal of permitting employees to be represented as quickly as possible.'" 775 F.2d, at 430-431, quoting *NLRB v. Pre-Engineered Building Products, Inc.,* 603 F.2d 134, 136 (CA10 1979). In deciding when a "substantial and representative complement" exists in a particular employer transition, the Board examines a number of factors. It studies "whether the job classifications designated for the operation were filled or substantially filled and whether the operation was in normal or substantially normal production." See *Premium Foods, Inc. v. NLRB,* 709 F.2d 623, 628 (CA9 1983). In addition, it takes into consideration "the size of the

---

[12] After *Burns,* there was some initial confusion concerning this Court's holding. It was unclear if workforce continuity would turn on whether a majority of the successor's employees were those of the predecessor or on whether the successor had hired a majority of the predecessor's employees. *Compare* 406 U.S., at 281 ("a majority of the employees hired by the new employer are represented by a recently certified bargaining agent"), *with id.,* at 278 ("the union had been designated bargaining agent for the employees in the unit and a majority of these employees had been hired by Burns"). *See also Howard Johnson Co. v. Hotel Employees,* 417 U.S., at 263 ("successor employer hires a majority of the predecessor's employees"); *Golden State Bottling Co. v. NLRB,* 414 U.S., at 184, n. 6 (same). The Board, with the approval of the Courts of Appeals, has adopted the former interpretation. *See Spruce Up Corp.,* 209 N.L.R.B. 194, 196 (1974), enf'd, 529 F. 2d 516 (CA4 1975); *United Maintenance & Mfg. Co.,* 214 N.L.R.B. 529, 532-534 (1974); *Saks & Co. v. NLRB,* 634 F.2d 681, 684-686, and nn. 2 and 3 (CA2 1980) (and cases cited therein); *see also* Note, *Appropriate Standards of Successor Employer Obligations under Wiley, Howard Johnson, and Burns,* 25 Wayne L. Rev. 1279, 1299 (1979). This issue is not presented by the instant case.

complement on that date and the time expected to elapse before a substantially larger complement would be at work ... as well as the relative certainty of the employer's expected expansion." *Ibid.*

Petitioner contends that the Board's representative complement rule is unreasonable, given that it injures the representation rights of many of the successor's employees and that it places significant burdens upon the successor, which is unsure whether and when the bargaining obligation will arise.... According to petitioner, if majority status is determined at the "full complement" stage, all the employees will have a voice in the selection of their bargaining representative, and this will reveal if the union truly has the support of most of the successor's employees. This approach, however, focuses only on the interest in having a bargaining representative selected by the majority of the employees. It fails to take into account the significant interest of employees in being represented as soon as possible. The latter interest is especially heightened in a situation where many of the successor's employees, who were formerly represented by a union, find themselves after the employer transition in essentially the same enterprise, but without their bargaining representative. Having the new employer refuse to bargain with the chosen representative of these employees "disrupts the employees' morale, deters their organizational activities, and discourages their membership in unions." *Franks Bros. Co. v. NLRB,* 321 U.S. 702, 704 (1944). Accordingly, petitioner's "full complement" proposal must fail.

Nor do we believe that this "substantial and representative complement" rule places an unreasonable burden on the employer. It is true that, if an employer refuses to bargain with the employees once the representative complement has been attained, it risks violating § 8(a)(5). Furthermore, if an employer recognizes the union before this complement has been reached, this recognition could constitute a violation of § 8(a)(2), which makes it an unfair labor practice for an employer to support a labor organization.... And, unlike the initial election situation, ... here the employer, not the Board, applies this rule.

We conclude, however, that in this situation the successor is in the best position to follow a rule the criteria of which are straightforward. The employer generally will know with tolerable certainty when all its job classifications have been filled or substantially filled, when it has hired a majority of the employees it intends to hire, and when it has begun normal production. Moreover, the "full complement" standard advocated by petitioner is not *necessarily* easier for a successor to apply than is the "substantial and representative complement." In fact, given the expansionist dreams of many new entrepreneurs, it might well be more difficult for a successor to identify the moment when the "full complement" has been attained, which is when the business will reach the limits of the new employer's initial hopes, than it would be for this same employer to acknowledge the time when its business has begun normal production—the moment identified by the "substantial and representative complement" rule.

We therefore hold that the Board's "substantial and representative complement" rule is reasonable in the successorship context. Moreover, its application to the facts of this case is supported by substantial record evidence. The Court of Appeals observed that by mid-January petitioner "had hired employees in virtually all job classifications, had hired at least fifty percent of those it would ultimately employ in the majority of those classifications, and it employed a majority of the employees it would eventually employ when it reached full complement." 775 F.2d, at 431-432. At that time petitioner had begun normal production. Although petitioner intended to expand to two shifts, and, in fact, reached this goal by mid-April, that expansion was contingent expressly upon the growth of the business. Accordingly, as found by the Board and approved by the Court of Appeals, mid-January was the period when petitioner reached its "substantial and representative complement." Because at that time the majority of petitioner's employees were former Sterlingwale employees, petitioner had an obligation to bargain with the Union then.

C. We also hold that the Board's "continuing demand" rule is reasonable in the successorship situation. The successor's duty to bargain at the "substantial and representative complement" date is triggered only when the union has made a bargaining demand. Under the "continuing demand" rule, when a union has made a premature demand that has been rejected by the employer, this demand remains in force until the moment when the employer attains the "substantial and representative complement." *See, e.g., Aircraft Magnesium,* 265 N.L.R.B., at 1345, n. 9; *Spruce Up Corp.,* 209 N.L.R.B., at 197.

Such a rule, particularly when considered along with the "substantial and representative complement" rule, places a minimal burden on the successor and makes sense in light of the union's position. Once the employer has concluded that it has reached the appropriate complement, then, in order to determine whether its duty to bargain will be triggered, it has only to see whether the union already has made a demand for bargaining. Because the union has no established relationship with the successor and because it is unaware of the successor's plans for its operations and hiring, it is likely that, in many cases, a union's bargaining demand will be premature. It makes no sense to require the union repeatedly to renew its bargaining demand in the hope of having it correspond with the "substantial and representative complement" date, when, with little trouble, the employer can regard a previous demand as a continuing one....

The judgment of the Court of Appeals is affirmed.

It is so ordered.

JUSTICE POWELL, with whom THE CHIEF JUSTICE and JUSTICE O'CONNOR join, dissenting....

I ...

B. ... The critical question in determining successorship is whether there is "substantial continuity" between the two businesses. *Aircraft Magnesium, a Division of Grico Corp.,* 265 N.L.R.B. 1344, 1345 (1982), enf'd 730 F.2d 767 (CA9 1984). *See also NLRB v. Burns International Security Services, Inc.,* 406 U.S. 272, 279-281 (1972). Here the Board concluded that there was sufficient continuity between petitioner and Sterlingwale, primarily because the workers did the same finishing work on the same equipment for petitioner as they had for their former employer.... In reaching this conclusion, however, the Board, and now the Court, give virtually no weight to the evidence of *dis*continuity, that I think is overwhelming.

In this case the undisputed evidence shows that petitioner is a completely separate entity from Sterlingwale. There was a clear break between the time Sterlingwale ceased normal business operations in February 1982 and when petitioner came into existence at the end of August. In addition, it is apparent that there was no direct contractual or other business relationship between petitioner and Sterlingwale. Although petitioner bought some of Sterlingwale's inventory, it did so by outbidding several other buyers on the open market. Also, the purchases at the public sale involved only tangible assets. Petitioner did not buy Sterlingwale's trade name or good will, nor did it assume any of its liabilities. And while over half of petitioner's business (measured in dollars) came from former Sterlingwale customers, apparently this was due to the new company's skill in marketing its services. There was no sale or transfer of customer lists, and given the 9-month interval between the time that Sterlingwale ended production and petitioner commenced its operations in November, the natural conclusion is that the new business attracted customers through its own efforts. No other explanation was offered.... Any one of these facts standing alone may be insufficient to defeat a finding of successorship, but together they persuasively demonstrate that the Board's finding of "substantial continuity" was incorrect.

The Court nevertheless is unpersuaded. It views these distinctions as not directly affecting the employees' expectations about their job status or the status of the union as their representative, even though the CBA with the defunct corporation had long since expired.... Yet even from the employees' perspective, there was little objective evidence that the jobs with petitioner were simply a continuation of those at Sterlingwale. When all of the production employees were laid off indefinitely in February 1982, there could have been little hope—and certainly no reasonable expectation—that Sterlingwale would ever reopen. Nor was it reasonable for the employees to expect that Sterlingwale's failed textile operations would be resumed by a corporation not then in existence. The CBA had expired in April with no serious effort to renegotiate it, and with several of the employees' benefits left unpaid. The possibility of further employment with Sterlingwale then disappeared entirely in August 1982 when the company liquidated its remaining assets. *Cf. Textile Workers Union v. Darlington Mfg. Co.,* 380 U.S. 263, 274 (1965) (the "closing of an entire business ... ends the employer-employee relationship"). After petitioner was organized, it advertised for workers in the newspaper, a move that hardly could have suggested to the old workers that they would be reinstated to their former positions. The sum of these facts inevitably would have had a negative "effect on the employees' expectations of rehire." See *Aircraft Magnesium,* 265 N.L.R.B., at 1346.... The former employees engaged by petitioner found that the new plant was smaller, and that there would be fewer workers, fewer shifts, and more hours per shift than at their prior job. Moreover, as petitioner did not acquire Sterlingwale's personnel records, the benefits of having a favorable work record presumably were lost to these employees.

In deferring to the NLRB's decision, the Court today extends the successorship doctrine in a manner that could not have been anticipated by either the employer or the employees. I would hold that the successorship doctrine has no application when the break in continuity between enterprises is as complete and extensive as it was here.

II

Even if the evidence of genuine continuity were substantial, I could not agree with the Court's decision. As we have noted in the past, if the presumption of majority support for a union is to survive a change in ownership, it must be shown that there is both a continuity of conditions *and* a continuity of work force. *Howard Johnson Co. v. Hotel Employees,* 417 U.S. 249, 263 (1974). This means that unless a majority of the new company's workers had been employed by the former company, there is no justification for assuming that the new employees wish to be represented by the former union, or by any union at all....

In my view, the Board's decision to measure the composition of the petitioner work force in mid-January is unsupportable. The substantial and representative complement test can serve a useful role when the hiring process is sporadic, or the future expansion of the work force is speculative. But as the Court recognized in *NLRB v. Burns Security Services, Inc.,* in some cases "it may not be clear until the successor employer has hired his full complement of employees that he has a duty to bargain with a union, since it will not be evident until then that the bargaining representative represents a majority of the employees in the unit." 406 U.S., at 295. Indeed, where it is feasible to wait and examine the full complement—as it was here—it clearly is fairer to both employer and employees to do so. The substantial complement test provides no more than an *estimate* of the percentage of employees from the old company that eventually will be part of the new business, and thus often will be an imperfect measure of continuing union support. The risks of relying on such an estimate are obvious. If the "substantial complement" examined by the Board at a particular time contains a disproportionate number of workers from the old company, the result either might be that the full work force is deprived of union representation that a majority favors, or is required to accept representation that a majority does not want. Accordingly, unless the delay or uncertainty of future expansion would frustrate the employees' legitimate interest in early representation—a situation not shown to exist here—there is every reason to wait until the full anticipated work force has been employed....

In prior decisions, courts and the Board have looked not only to the *number* of workers hired and positions filled on a particular date, but also to "the time expected to elapse before a substantially larger complement would be at work ... as well as the relative certainty of the employer's expected expansion." *Premium Foods, Inc. v. NLRB,* 709 F.2d 623, 628 (CA9 1983). See also *St. John of God Hospital, Inc.,* 260 N.L.R.B. 905 (1982). Here the anticipated expansion was both imminent and reasonably definite. The record shows that in January petitioner both expected to, and in fact subsequently did, hire a significant number of new employees to staff its second shift. Although the Court finds that the growth of the work force was "contingent" on business conditions, neither the Administrative Law Judge nor the NLRB made such a finding.[7] In fact, they both noted that by January 15, the second shift already had begun limited operations.... In fact, less than three months after the duty to bargain allegedly arose, petitioner had nearly doubled the size of its mid-January work force by hiring the remaining 50-odd workers it needed to reach full production. This expansion was not unexpected; instead, it closely tracked petitioner's original forecast for growth during its first few months in business. Thus there was no reasonable basis for selecting mid-January as the time that petitioner should have known that it should commence bargaining....

In an effort to ensure that some employees will not be deprived of representation for even a short time, the Court requires petitioner to recognize a union that has never been elected or accepted by a majority of its workers. For the reasons stated, I think that the Court's decision is unfair both to petitioner, who hardly could have anticipated the date chosen by the Board, and to most of petitioner's employees, who were denied the opportunity to choose their union. I dissent.

NOTES

1. *"Substantial Continuity" Between the Enterprises:* The Phoenix Steel Corporation began to shut down its Claymont, Delaware, plant in late 1986. By January of 1987, all production had ceased, and by March, the remaining employees had been terminated. In December of 1987, a Hong Kong investor purchased the mill for $13 million. It formed CitiSteel and spent $25 million to refurbish the facility. It began operations in February of 1989 with 124 employ-

---

[7]The evidence shows that in the textile industry, two shifts are necessary for proper finishing work. *See* 775 F.2d 425, 428 (CA1 1985). Thus, it was clear in mid-January that petitioner would need more employees in the immediate future.

ees—substantially fewer workers than the 1,000 who had been previously employed by Phoenix Steel. CitiSteel had restructured job classifications and required formal cross-training for its employees. Although the Labor Board found CitiSteel a "successor" to Phoenix Steel, the D.C. Circuit rejected this conclusion due to a lack of substantial continuity between Phoenix Steel and CitiSteel. *CitiSteel USA v. NLRB*, 53 F.3d 350 (D.C. Cir. 1995); *cf. Systems Mgt. v. NLRB*, 901 F.2d 297 (3d Cir. 1990) (to negate successorship there must be a "fundamental change" in the nature of the business; changing shift hours from full-time to part-time not enough).

The mere passage of time between the termination of predecessor operations and the commencement of successor operations is insufficient to defeat a successorship finding. *See Coastal Derby Ref. Co. v. NLRB*, 915 F.2d 1448 (10th Cir. 1990) (one-year hiatus); *Nephi Rubber Prods. Corp. v. NLRB*, 976 F.2d 1361 (10th Cir. 1992) (16-month hiatus); *Straight Creek Mining, Inc. v. NLRB*, 160 L.R.R.M. 2001 (6th Cir. 1998) (54-month hiatus). *See generally* Comment, *Fall River: The NLRB's Expansive Successorship Doctrine*, 50 Ohio St. L.J. 181 (1989).

2. In *Banknote Corp. of Am. v. NLRB*, 84 F.3d 637 (2d Cir. 1996), *cert. denied*, 117 S. Ct. 944 (1997), the court concluded that while a bargaining demand by the incumbent union was required in *Fall River Dyeing* before a successor was obligated to bargain, no demand is necessary when the new employer hires its full complement at once, including a clear majority from the former employer's workforce. The *Fall River* rule applies to the gradual hiring of employees during a startup period or the hiring of employees after a prolonged delay between the closing and reopening of a business.

3. An employer that sold all its stock to another company but operated as a going concern with the same management and the same employees was a "continuing" employer, not a successor, and remained bound by the preexisting labor contract. *EPE, Inc. v. NLRB*, 845 F.2d 483 (4th Cir. 1988).

SECTION IV. Fair Representation and Individual Contract Rights

CLYDE W. SUMMERS, INDIVIDUAL RIGHTS IN COLLECTIVE AGREEMENTS AND ARBITRATION, 37 N.Y.U. L. Rev. 362, 393 (1962)

The individual's interest may more often be vitiated without vindictiveness or deliberate discrimination. Incomplete investigation of the facts, reliance on untested evidence, or colored evaluation of witnesses may lead the union to reject grievances which more objective inquiry would prove meritorious. Union officials burdened with institutional concerns may be willing to barter unrelated grievances or accept wholesale settlements if the total package is advantageous, even though some good grievances are lost. Concern for collective interests and the needs for the enterprise may dull the sense of personal injustice.

ARCHIBALD COX, THE DUTY OF FAIR REPRESENTATION, 2 Vill. L. Rev. 151, 167 (1957)

Too strict judicial or administrative supervision through the concept of fair representation would impair the flexibility and adaptability of collective bargaining while substituting governmental decisions for self-determination. Past experience with judicial intervention in labor relations gives little reason to suppose that the judges' decision would be wiser than negotiated settlements. On the other hand, so long as numerical majorities occasionally yield to selfishness or caprice, there will be somewhat the same need for judicial or administrative checks on majority rule in collective bargaining as there is for judicial review of legislative enactments. Whether courts and agencies steer a safe central course between the opposing dangers will probably depend upon their success in developing standards of "fairness."

A. JUDICIAL ENFORCEMENT OF FAIR REPRESENTATION

STEELE v. LOUISVILLE & NASHVILLE RAILROAD

Supreme Court of the United States
323 U.S. 192, 65 S. Ct. 226, 89 L. Ed. 173 (1944).

MR. CHIEF JUSTICE STONE delivered the opinion of the Court.

The question is whether the Railway Labor Act ... imposes on a labor organization, acting by authority of the statute as the exclusive bargaining representative of a craft or class of railway employees, the duty to represent all the employees in the craft without discrimination because of their race, and, if so, whether the courts have jurisdiction to protect the minority of the craft or class from the violation of such obligation.

... Petitioner, a Negro, is a locomotive fireman in the employ of respondent railroad, suing on his own behalf and that of his fellow employees who, like petitioner, are Negro firemen employed by the Railroad. Respondent Brotherhood, a labor organization, is as provided under Section 2, Fourth of the Railway Labor Act, the exclusive bargaining representative of the craft of firemen employed by the Railroad and is recognized as such by it and the members of the craft. The majority of the firemen employed by the Railroad are white and are members of the Brotherhood, but a substantial minority are Negroes who, by the constitution and ritual of the Brotherhood, are excluded from its membership. As the membership of the Brotherhood constitutes a majority of all firemen employed on respondent Railroad and as under Section 2, Fourth, the members, because they are the majority, have the right to choose and have chosen the Brotherhood to represent the craft, petitioner and other Negro firemen on the road have been required to accept the Brotherhood as their representative for the purposes of the Act.

On March 28, 1940, the Brotherhood, purporting to act as representative of the entire craft of firemen, without informing the Negro firemen or giving them opportunity to be heard, served a notice on respondent Railroad and on twenty other railroads operating principally in the southeastern part of the United States. The notice announced the Brotherhood's desire to amend the existing collective bargaining agreement in such manner as ultimately to exclude all Negro firemen from the service. By established practice on the several railroads so notified only white firemen can be promoted to serve as engineers, and the notice proposed that only "promotable," *i.e.,* white, men should be employed as firemen or assigned to new runs or jobs or permanent vacancies in established runs or jobs.

On February 18, 1941, the railroads and the Brotherhood, as representative of the craft, entered into a new agreement which provided that not more than 50 percent of the firemen in each class of service in each seniority district of carrier should be Negroes; that until such percentage should be reached all new runs and all vacancies should be filled by white men; and that the agreement did not sanction the employment of Negroes in any seniority district in which they were not working....

If the Railway Labor Act purports to impose on petitioner and the other Negro members of the craft the legal duty to comply with the terms of a contract whereby the representative has discriminatorily restricted their employment for the benefit and advantage of the Brotherhood's own members, we must decide the constitutional questions which petitioner raises in his pleading.

But we think that Congress, in enacting the Railway Labor Act and authorizing a labor union, chosen by a majority of a craft, to represent the craft, did not intend to confer plenary power upon the union to sacrifice, for the benefit of its members, rights of the minority of the craft, without imposing on it any duty to protect the minority. Since petitioner and the other Negro members of the craft are not members of the Brotherhood or eligible for membership, the authority to act for them is derived not from their action or consent but wholly from the command of the Act....

Section 2, Second, requiring carriers to bargain with the representative so chosen, operates to exclude any other from representing a craft. *Virginian Ry. Co. v. System Federation, supra,* 300 U.S. 545 (1930). The minority members of a craft are thus deprived by the statute of the right, which they would otherwise possess, to choose a representative of their own, and its members cannot bargain individually on behalf of themselves as to matters which are properly the subject of collective bargaining....

The fair interpretation of the statutory language is that the organization chosen to represent a craft is to represent all its members, the majority as well as the minority, and it is to act for and not against those whom it represents. It is a principle of general application that the exercise of a granted power to act in behalf of others involves the assumption toward them of a duty to exercise the power in their interest and behalf, and that such a grant of power will not be deemed to dispense with all duty toward those for whom it is exercised unless so expressed.

We think that Railway Labor Act imposes upon the statutory representative of a craft at least as exacting a duty to protect equally the interests of the members of the craft as the Constitution imposes upon a legislature to give equal protection to the interests of those for whom it legislates. Congress has seen fit to clothe the bargaining representative with powers comparable to those possessed by a legislative body both to create and restrict the rights of those whom it represents, cf. *J.I. Case Co. v. NLRB, supra,* 321 U.S. 335 (1944), but it has also imposed on the representative a corresponding duty. We hold that the language of the Act which we have referred, read in the light of the purposes of the Act, expresses the aim of Congress to impose on the bargaining representative of a craft or class of employees the duty to exercise fairly the power conferred upon it in behalf of all those for whom it acts, without hostile discrimination against them.

This does not mean that the statutory representative of a craft is barred from making contracts which may have unfavorable effects on some of the members of the craft represented. Variations in the terms of the contract based on differences relevant to the authorized purposes of the contract in conditions to which they are to be applied, such as differences in seniority, the type of work performed, the competence and skill with which it is performed, are within the scope of the bargaining representation of a craft, all of whose members are not identical in their interest of merit. Without attempting to mark the allowable limits of differences in the terms of contracts based on differences of conditions to which they apply, it is enough for present purposes to say that the statutory power to represent a craft and to make contracts as to wages, hours and working conditions does not include the authority to make among members of the craft discriminations not based on such relevant differences. Here the discriminations based on race alone are obviously irrelevant and invidious. Congress plainly did not undertake to authorize the bargaining representative to make such discriminations....

The representative which thus discriminates may be enjoined from so doing, and its members may be enjoined from taking the benefit of such discriminatory action. No more is the Railroad bound by or entitled to take the benefit of a contract which the bargaining representative is prohibited by the statute from making. In both cases the right asserted, which is derived from the duty imposed by the statute on the bargaining representative, is a federal right implied from the statute and the policy which it has adopted....

So long as a labor union assumes to act as the statutory representative of a craft, it cannot rightly refuse to perform the duty, which is inseparable from the power of representation conferred upon it, to represent the entire membership of the craft. While the statute does not deny to such a bargaining labor organization the right to determine eligibility to its membership, it does require the union, in collective bargaining and in making contracts with the carrier, to represent non-union or minority union members of the craft without hostile discrimination, fairly, impartially, and in good faith. Wherever necessary to that end, the union is required to consider requests of non-union members of the craft and expressions of their views with respect to collective bargaining with the employer and to give to them notice of an opportunity for hearing upon its proposed action....

We conclude that the duty which the statute imposes on a union representative of a craft to represent the interests of all its members stands on no different footing and that the statute contemplates resort to the usual judicial remedies of injunction and award of damages when appropriate for breach of that duty.

The judgment is accordingly reversed and remanded for further proceedings not inconsistent with this opinion.

Reversed.

MR. JUSTICE BLACK concurs in the result.

MR. JUSTICE MURPHY, concurring.

The economic discrimination against Negroes practiced by the Brotherhood and the railroad under color of Congressional authority raises a grave constitutional issue that should be squarely faced....

The constitutional problem inherent in this instance is clear. Congress, through the Railway Labor Act, has conferred upon the union selected by a majority of a craft or class of railway workers the power to represent the entire craft or class in all collective bargaining matters. While such a union is essentially a private organization, its power to represent and bind all members of a class or craft is derived solely from Congress. The Act contains no language which directs the manner in which the bargaining representative shall perform its duties. But it cannot be assumed that Congress meant to authorize the bargaining representative to act so as to ignore rights guaranteed by the Constitution. Otherwise the Act would bear the stigma of unconstitutionality under the Fifth Amendment in this respect. For that reason I am willing to read the statute as not permitting or allowing any action by the bargaining representative in the exercise of its delegated powers which would in effect violate the constitutional rights of individuals.

NOTES

1. The existence of a duty of fair representation under the NLRA, as well as under the RLA, was established in *Syres v. Oil Workers Local 23,* 350 U.S. 892 (1955) (per curiam).

2. On the standard of fairness, the Supreme Court said at a relatively early point in this line of decisions: "Inevitably differences arise in the manner and degree to which the terms of any negotiated agreement affect individual employees and classes of employees. The mere existence of such differences does not make them invalid. The complete satisfaction of all who are represented is hardly to be expected. A wide range of reasonableness must be allowed a statutory bargaining representative in serving the unit it represents, subject always to complete good faith and honesty of purpose in the exercise of its discretion." *Ford Motor Co. v. Huffman,* 345 U.S. 330, 338 (1953).

3. Does the duty of fair representation impose on a union the affirmative obligation to seek the elimination of an employer's discriminatory employment practices? If so, how far must a union go to discharge its obligation? Is it sufficient to process a grievance or to raise the question in contract negotiations? Or must the union be prepared to strike to back up its demand? *See, e.g., Rubber Workers Local 12 v. NLRB,* 368 F.2d 12 (5th Cir. 1966), *cert. denied,* 389 U.S. 837 (1967); *NLRB v. Longshoremen Local 1367,* 368 F.2d 1010 (5th Cir. 1966), *cert. denied,* 389 U.S. 837 (1967), *enforcing* 148 N.L.R.B. 897 (1964); *Woods v. Graphic Commun.,* 925 F.2d 1195 (9th Cir. 1991) (racial harassment by fellow workers and union steward). *Cf.* Comment, *Affirmative Action Programs: A Violation of a Union's Duty of Fair Representation?* 36 Baylor L. Rev. 155 (1984).

4. For further discussion of the development of the concept of fair representation, *see* Clark, *The Duty of Fair Representation: A Theoretical Structure,* 51 Texas L. Rev. 1119 (1973); Cox, *The Duty of Fair Representation,* 2 Vill. L. Rev 151 (1957); Murphy, *The Duty of Fair Representation Under Taft-Hartley,* 30 Mo. L. Rev. 373 (1965); Sovern, *The National Labor Relations Act and Racial Discrimination,* 62 Colum. L. Rev. 563 (1962); Wellington, *Union Democracy and Fair Representation: Federal Responsibility in a Federal System,* 67 Yale L.J. 1327 (1958). *See also* Klare, *The Quest for Industrial Democracy and the Struggle Against Racism: Perspectives from Labor Law and Civil Rights Law,* 61 Or. L. Rev. 157 (1982).

VACA v. SIPES

Supreme Court of the United States
386 U.S. 171, 87 S. Ct. 903, 17 L. Ed. 2d 842 (1967)

[Owens, a long-time high blood pressure patient, returned from a half-year sick leave to resume his heavy work in a meat-packing plant of Swift & Company. Although Owens' family physician and another outside doctor certified his fitness, the company doctor concluded Owens' blood pressure was too high to permit reinstatement and he was permanently discharged. Owens' Union processed a grievance through to the fourth step of the procedure established by the collective bargaining agreement. The union then sent Owens to a new doctor at union expense to "get some better medical evidence so that we could go to arbitration." When this examination did not support Owens' position, the union's executive board voted not to take the grievance to arbitration. Union officers suggested that Owens accept Swift's offer of referral to a rehabilitation center, but Owens declined and demanded arbitration. The union stood by its refusal. Owens thereupon brought a class action in a Missouri state court against petitioners as officers and representatives of the union, alleging that the union had "arbitrarily, [and] capriciously" failed to take his case to arbitration. A jury verdict in his favor was sustained by the Missouri Supreme Court in the amount of $7,000 compensatory and $3,000 punitive damages.]

MR. JUSTICE WHITE delivered the opinion of the Court.

... Although we conclude that state courts have jurisdiction in this type of case, we hold that federal law governs, that the governing federal standards were not applied here, and that the judgment of the Supreme Court of Missouri must accordingly be reversed....

II

Petitioners challenge the jurisdiction of the Missouri courts on the ground that the alleged conduct of the Union was arguably an unfair labor practice and within the exclusive jurisdiction of the NLRB. Petitioners rely on *Miranda Fuel Co.,* 140 N.L.R.B. 181 (1962), enforcement denied, 326 F.2d 172 (2d Cir. 1963), where a sharply divided Board held for the first time that a union's breach of its statutory duty of fair representation violates NLRA § 8(b), as amended. With the NLRB's adoption of *Miranda Fuel,* petitioners argue, the broad pre-emption doctrine defined in *San Diego Building Trades Council v. Garmon,* 359 U.S. 236 (1959), becomes applicable. For the reasons which follow, we reject this argument.

It is now well established that, as the exclusive bargaining representative of the employees in Owens' bargaining unit, the Union had a statutory duty fairly to represent all of those employees, both in its collective bargaining with Swift, *see Ford Motor Co. v. Huffman,* 345 U.S. 330 (1953); *Syres v. Oil Workers,* 350 U.S. 892 (1955), and in its enforcement of the resulting collective bargaining agreement, see *Humphrey v. Moore,* 375 U.S. 335 (1964). The statutory duty of fair representation was developed over 20 years ago in a series of cases involving alleged racial discrimination by unions certified as exclusive bargaining representatives under the Railway Labor Act, *see Steele v. Louisville & N.R.R.,* 323 U.S. 192 (1944); *Tunstall v. Brotherhood of Locomotive Firemen,* 323 U.S. 210 (1944), and was soon extended to unions certified under the NLRA, *see Ford Motor Co. v. Huffman, supra.* Under this doctrine, the exclusive agent's statutory authority to represent all members of a designated unit includes a statutory obligation to serve the interests of all members without hostility or discrimination toward any, to exercise its discretion with complete good faith and honesty, and to avoid arbitrary conduct. *Humphrey v. Moore,* 375 U.S. at 342 (1964). It is obvious that Owens' complaint alleged a breach by the Union of a duty grounded in federal statutes, and that federal law therefore governs his cause of action. *E.g., Ford Motor Co. v. Huffman, supra.*

Although NLRA § 8(b) was enacted in 1947, the NLRB did not until *Miranda Fuel* interpret a breach of a union's duty of fair representation as an unfair labor practice....

A. In *Garmon,* this Court recognized that the broad powers conferred by Congress upon the National Labor Relations Board to interpret and to enforce the complex Labor Management Relations Act necessarily imply that potentially conflicting "rules of law, of remedy, and of administration" cannot be permitted to operate. 359 U.S. at 242.... Consequently, as a general rule, neither state nor federal courts have jurisdiction over suits directly involving "activity [which] is arguably subject to § 7 or 8 of the Act." *San Diego Building Trades Council v. Garmon,* 359 U.S. at 245.

This pre-emption doctrine, however, has never been rigidly applied to cases where it could not fairly be inferred that Congress intended exclusive jurisdiction to lie with the NLRB....

A primary justification for the pre-emption doctrine—the need to avoid conflicting rules of substantive law in the labor relations area and the desirability of leaving the development of such rules to the administrative agency created by Congress for that purpose—is not applicable to cases involving alleged breaches of the union duty of fair representation. The doctrine was judicially developed in *Steele* and its progeny, and suits alleging breach of the duty remained judicially cognizable long after the NLRB was given unfair labor practice jurisdiction over union activities by the LMRA. Moreover, when the Board declared in *Miranda Fuel* that a union's breach of its duty of fair representation would henceforth be treated as an unfair labor practice, the board adopted and applied the doctrine as it had been developed by the federal courts. Finally, as the dissenting Board members in *Miranda Fuel* have pointed out, fair representation duty suits often require review of the substantive positions taken and policies pursued by a union in its negotiation of a collective bargaining agreement and its handling of the grievance machinery; as these matters are not normally within the Board's unfair labor practice jurisdiction, it can be doubted whether the Board brings substantially greater expertise to bear on these problems than do the courts, which have been engaged in this type of review since the *Steele* decision.

In addition to the above considerations, the unique interests served by the duty of fair representation doctrine have a profound effect, in our opinion, on the applicability of the pre-emption rule to this class of cases.... This Court recognized in *Steele* that the congressional grant of power to a union to act as exclusive collective bargaining representative, with its corresponding reduction in the individual rights of the employees so represented, would raise grave constitutional problems if unions were free to exercise this power to further racial discrimination.... Since that landmark decision, the duty of fair representation has stood as a bulwark to prevent arbitrary union conduct against individuals stripped of traditional forms of redress by the provisions of federal labor law. Were we to hold, as petitioners and the government urge, that the courts are pre-empted by the

NLRB's *Miranda Fuel* decision of this traditional supervisory jurisdiction, the individual employee injured by arbitrary or discriminatory union conduct could no longer be assured of impartial review of his complaint, since the Board's General Counsel has unreviewable discretion to refuse to institute an unfair labor practice complaint.... For these reasons, we cannot assume from the NLRB's tardy assumption of jurisdiction in these cases that Congress, when it enacted NLRA § 8(b) in 1947, intended to oust the courts of their traditional jurisdiction to curb arbitrary conduct by the individual employee's statutory representative.

B. There are also some intensely practical considerations which foreclose preemption of judicial cognizance of fair representation duty suits, considerations which emerge from the intricate relationship between the duty of fair representation and the enforcement of collective bargaining contracts. For the fact is that the question of whether a union has breached its duty of fair representation will in many cases be a critical issue in a suit under LMRA § 301 charging an employer with a breach of contract. To illustrate, let us assume a collective bargaining agreement that limits discharges to those for good cause and that contains no grievance, arbitration or other provisions purporting to restrict access to the courts. If an employee is discharged without cause, either the union or the employee may sue the employer under LMRA § 301. Under this section, courts have jurisdiction over suits to enforce collective bargaining agreements even though the conduct of the employer which is challenged as a breach of contract is also arguably an unfair labor practice within the jurisdiction of the NLRB. *Garmon* and like cases have no application § 301 suits. *Smith v. Evening News Ass'n,* 371 U.S. 195 (1962).

The rule is the same with regard to pre-emption where the bargaining agreement contains grievance and arbitration provisions which are intended to provide the exclusive remedy for breach of contract claims. If an employee is discharged without cause in violation of such an agreement, that the employer's conduct may be an unfair labor practice does not preclude a suit by the union against the employer to compel arbitration of the employee's grievance; the adjudication of the claim by the arbitrator; or a suit to enforce the resulting arbitration award. *See, e.g., Steelworkers v. American Mfg. Co.,* 363 U.S. 564 (1960).

However, if the wrongfully discharged employee himself resorts to the courts before the grievance procedures have been fully exhausted, the employer may well defend on the ground that the exclusive remedies provided by such a contract have not been exhausted. Since the employee's claim is based upon breach of the collective bargaining agreement, he is bound by terms of that agreement which govern the manner in which contractual rights may be enforced. For this reason, it is settled that the employee must at least attempt to exhaust exclusive grievance and arbitration procedures established by the bargaining agreement. *Republic Steel Corp. v. Maddox,* 379 U.S. 650 (1965). However, because these contractual remedies have been devised and are often controlled by the union and the employer, they may well prove unsatisfactory or unworkable for the individual grievant. The problem then is to determine under what circumstances the individual employee may obtain judicial review of his breach-of-contract claim despite his failure to secure relief through the contractual remedial procedures....

[W]e think the wrongfully discharged employee may bring an action against his employer in the face of a defense based upon the failure to exhaust contractual remedies, provided the employee can prove that the union as bargaining agent breached its duty of fair representation in its handling of the employee's grievance. We may assume for present purposes that such a breach of duty by the union is an unfair labor practice, as the NLRB and the Fifth Circuit have held. The employee's suit against the employer, however, remains a § 301 suit, and the jurisdiction of the courts is no more destroyed by the fact that the employee, as part and parcel of his § 301 action, finds it necessary to prove an unfair labor practice by the union, than it is by the fact that the suit may involve an unfair labor practice by the employer himself. The court is free to determine whether the employee is barred by the actions of his union representative, and, if not, to proceed with the case. And if, to facilitate his case, the employee joins the union as defendant, the situation is not substantially changed. The action is still a § 301 suit, and the jurisdiction of the courts is not pre-empted under the *Garmon* principle. This, at the very least, is the holding of *Humphrey v. Moore* with respect to pre-emption, as petitioners recognize in their brief. And, insofar as adjudication of the union's breach of duty is concerned, the result should be no different if the employee, as Owens did here, sues the employer and the union in separate actions. There would be very little to commend a rule which would permit the Missouri courts to adjudicate the Union's conduct in an action against Swift but not in an action against the Union itself.

For the above reasons, it is obvious that the courts will be compelled to pass upon whether there has been a breach of the duty of fair representation in the context of many § 301 breach-of-contract actions. If a breach of duty by the union and a breach of contract by the employer are proven, the court must fashion an appropriate remedy. Presumably, in at least some cases, the union's breach of duty will have enhanced or contributed to the employee's injury. What possible sense could there be in a rule which would permit a court that has litigated the fault of employer and union to fashion a remedy only with respect to the employer? Under such a rule, either the employer would be compelled by the court to pay for the union's wrong—slight deterrence indeed, to future union misconduct—or the injured employee would be forced to go to two tribunals to repair a single injury. Moreover, the Board would be compelled in many cases either to remedy injuries arising out of a breach of contract, a task which Congress has not assigned to it, or to leave the individual employee without remedy for the union's wrong. Given the strong reasons for not pre-empting duty of fair representation suits in general, and the fact that the courts in many § 301 suits must adjudicate whether the union has breached its duty, we conclude that the courts may also fashion remedies for such a breach of duty....

III

Petitioners contend, as they did in their motion for judgment notwithstanding the jury's verdict, that Owens failed to prove that the Union breached its duty of fair representation in its handling of Owens' grievance. Petitioners also argue that the Supreme Court of Missouri, in rejecting this contention, applied a standard that is inconsistent with governing principles of federal law with respect to the Union's duty to an individual employee in its processing of grievances under the collective bargaining agreement with Swift. We agree with both contentions.

A. ... Quite obviously, the question which the Missouri Supreme Court thought dispositive of the issue of liability was whether the evidence supported Owens' assertion that he had been wrongfully discharged by Swift, regardless of the Union's good faith in reaching a contrary conclusion. This was also the major concern of the plaintiff at trial: the bulk of Owens' evidence was directed at whether he was medically fit at the time of discharge and whether he had performed heavy work after that discharge.

A breach of the statutory duty of fair representation occurs only when a union's conduct toward a member of the collective bargaining unit is arbitrary, discriminatory, or in bad faith. *See Humphrey v. Moore, supra; Ford Motor Co. v. Huffman, supra.* There has been considerable debate over the extent of this duty in the context of a union's enforcement of the grievance and arbitration procedures in a collective bargaining agreement.... Some have suggested that every individual employee should have the right to have his grievance taken to arbitration. Others have urged that the Union be given substantial discretion (if the collective bargaining agreement so provides) to decide whether a grievance should be taken to arbitration, subject only to the duty to refrain from patently wrongful conduct such as racial discrimination or personal hostility.

Though we accept the proposition that a union may not arbitrarily ignore a meritorious grievance or process it in perfunctory fashion, we do not agree that the individual employee has an absolute right to have his grievance taken to arbitration regardless of the provisions of the applicable collective bargaining agreement.... In providing for a grievance and arbitration procedure which gives the union discretion to supervise the grievance machinery and to invoke arbitration, the employer and the union contemplate that each will endeavor in good faith to settle grievances short of arbitration. Through this settlement process, frivolous grievances are ended prior to the most costly and time-consuming step in the grievance procedures. Moreover, both sides are assured that similar complaints will be treated consistently, and major problem areas in the interpretation of the collective bargaining contract can be isolated and perhaps resolved. And finally, the settlement process furthers the interest of the union as statutory agent and as coauthor of the bargaining agreement in representing the employees in the enforcement of that agreement....

For these same reasons, the standard applied here by the Missouri Supreme Court cannot be sustained. For if a union's decision that a particular grievance lacks sufficient merit to justify arbitration would constitute a breach of the duty of fair representation because a judge or jury later found the grievance meritorious, the union's incentive to settle such grievances short of arbitration would be seriously reduced. The dampening effect on the entire grievance procedure of this reduction of the union's freedom to settle claims in good faith would surely be substantial. Since the union's statutory duty of fair representation protects the individual employee from arbitrary abuses of the settlement device by providing him with recourse against both employer (in a § 301 suit) and union, this severe limitation on the power to settle grievances is neither necessary nor desirable....

B. Applying the proper standard of union liability to the facts of this case, we cannot uphold the jury's award, for we conclude that as a matter of federal law the evidence does not support a verdict that the Union breached its duty of fair representation....

In administering the grievance and arbitration machinery as statutory agent of the employees, a union must in good faith and in a nonarbitrary manner, make decisions as to the merits of particular grievances. *See Humphrey v. Moore,* 375 U.S. 335, 349-350 (1964); *Ford Motor Co. v. Huffman,* 345 U.S. 330, 337-339 (1953). In a case such as this, when Owens supplied the Union with medical evidence supporting his position, the Union might well have breached its duty had it ignored Owens' complaint or had it processed the grievance in a perfunctory manner. *See* Cox, *Rights under a Labor Agreement,* 69 Harv. L. Rev., at 632-634. But here the Union processed the grievance into the fourth step, attempted to gather sufficient evidence to prove Owens' case, attempted to secure for Owens less vigorous work at the plant, and joined in the employer's efforts to have Owens rehabilitated. Only when these efforts all proved unsuccessful did the Union conclude both that arbitration would be fruitless and that the grievance should be dismissed. There was no evidence that any Union officer was personally hostile to Owens or that the Union acted at any time other than in good faith. Having concluded that the individual employee has no absolute right to have his grievance arbitrated under the collective bargaining agreement at issue, and that a breach of the duty of fair representation is not established merely by proof that the underlying grievance was meritorious, we must conclude that that duty was not breached here.

IV

In our opinion, there is another important reason why the judgment of the Missouri Supreme Court cannot stand. Owens' suit against the Union was grounded on his claim that Swift had discharged him in violation of the applicable collective bargaining agreement....

The appropriate remedy for a breach of a union's duty of fair representation must vary with the circumstances of the particular breach. In this case, the employee's complaint was that the Union wrongfully failed to afford him the arbitration remedy against his employer established by the collective bargaining agreement. But the damages sought by Owens were primarily those suffered because of the employer's alleged breach of contract. Assuming for the moment that Owens had been wrongfully discharged, Swift's only defense to a direct action for breach of contract would have been the Union's failure to resort to arbitration, *compare Republic Steel Corp. v. Maddox,* 379 U.S. 650 (1965), *with Smith v. Evening News Ass'n,* 371 U.S. 195 (1962), and if that failure was itself a violation of the Union's statutory duty to the employee, there is no reason to exempt the employer from contractual damages which he would otherwise have had to pay.... The difficulty lies in fashioning an appropriate scheme of remedies.

Petitioners urge that an employee be restricted in such circumstances to a decree compelling the employer and the union to arbitrate the underlying grievance. It is true that the employee's action is based on the employer's alleged breach of contract plus the union's alleged wrongful failure to afford him his contractual remedy of arbitration. For this reason, an order compelling arbitration should be viewed as one of the available remedies when a breach of the union's duty is proved. But we see no reason inflexibly to require arbitration in all cases....

A more difficult question is, what portion of the employee's damages may be charged to the union: in particular, may an award against a union include, as it did here, damages attributable solely to the employer's breach of contract? We think not. Though the union has violated a statutory duty in failing to press the grievance, it is the employer's unrelated breach of contract which triggered the controversy and which caused this portion of the employee's damages. The employee should have no difficulty recovering these damages from the employer, who cannot, as we have explained, hide behind the union's wrongful failure to act; in fact, the employer may be (and probably should be) joined as a defendant in the fair representation suit, as in *Humphrey v. Moore, supra.* It could be a real hardship on the union to pay these damages, even if the union were given a right of indemnification against the employer. With the employee assured of direct recovery from the employer, we see no merit in requiring the union to pay the employer's share of the damages.

The governing principle, then, is to apportion liability between the employer and the union according to the damage caused by the fault of each. Thus, damages attributable solely to the employer's breach of contract should not be charged to the union, but increases if any in those damages caused by the union's refusal to process the grievance should not be charged to the employer. In this case, even if the Union had breached its duty, all or almost all of Owens' damages would still be attributable to his allegedly wrongful discharge by Swift. For these reasons, even if the Union here had properly been found liable for a breach of duty, it is clear that the damage award was improper.

Reversed.

MR. JUSTICE FORTAS, with whom THE CHIEF JUSTICE and MR. JUSTICE HARLAN join, concurring in the result.

1. In my view, a complaint by an employee that the union has breached its duty of fair representation is subject to the exclusive jurisdiction of the NLRB. It is a charge of unfair labor practice. *See Miranda Fuel Co.,* 140 N.L.R.B. 181 (1962); *Rubber Workers Local 12,* 150 N.L.R.B. 312, *enforced,* 368 F.2d 12 (5th Cir. 1966). As is the case with most other unfair labor practices, the Board's jurisdiction is pre-emptive.... There is no basis for failure to apply the pre-emption principles in the present case, and, as I shall discuss, strong reason for its application. The relationship between the union and the individual employee with respect to the processing of claims to employment rights under the collective bargaining agreement is fundamental to the design and operation of federal labor law. It is not "merely peripheral," as the Court's opinion states. It "presents difficult problems of definition of status, problems which we have held are precisely 'of a kind most wisely entrusted initially to the agency charged with the day-to-day administration of the Act as a whole.'" *Iron Workers v. Perko,* 373 U.S. at 706. Accordingly, the judgment of the Supreme Court of Missouri should be reversed and the complaint dismissed for this reason and on this basis. I agree, however, that if it were assumed that jurisdiction of the subject matter exists, the judgment would still have to be reversed because of the use by the Missouri court of an improper standard for measuring the union's duty, and the absence of evidence to establish that the union refused further to process Owens' grievance because of bad faith or arbitrarily.

2. I regret the elaborate discussion in the Court's opinion of problems which are irrelevant. This is not an action by the employee against the employer, and the discussion of the requisites of such an action is, in my judgment, unnecessary. The Court argues that the employee could sue the employer under LMRA § 301; and that to maintain such an action the employee would have to show that he has exhausted his remedies under the collective bargaining agreement, or alternatively that he was prevented from doing so because the union breached its duty to him by failure completely to process his claim. That may be; or maybe all he would have to show to maintain an action against the employer for wrongful discharge is that he demanded that the union process his claim to exhaustion of available remedies, and that it refused to do so. I see no need for the Court to pass upon that question, which is not presented here, and which, with all respect, lends no support to the Court's argument. The Court seems to use its discussion of the employee-employer litigation as somehow analogous to or supportive of its conclusion that the employee may maintain a court action against the union. But I do not believe that this follows. I agree that the NLRB's unfair labor prac-

tice jurisdiction does not preclude an action under § 301 against the employer for wrongful discharge from employment. *Smith v. Evening News Ass'n,* 371 U.S. 195 (1962). Therefore, Owens might maintain an action against his employer in the present case. This would be an action to enforce the collective bargaining agreement, and Congress has authorized the courts to entertain actions of this type. But his claim against the union is quite different in character, as the Court itself recognizes. The Court holds—and I think correctly if the issue is to be reached—that the union could not be required to pay damages measured by the breach of the employment contract, because it was not the union but the employer that breached the contract. I agree; but I suggest that this reveals the point for which I contend: that the employee's claim against the union is not a claim under the collective bargaining agreement, but a claim that the union has breached its statutory duty of fair representation. This claim, I submit, is a claim of unfair labor practice and it is within the exclusive jurisdiction of the NLRB....

3. If we look beyond logic and precedent to the policy of the labor relations design which Congress has provided, court jurisdiction of this type of action seems anomalous and ill-advised. We are not dealing here with the interpretation of a contract or with an alleged breach of an employment agreement. As the Court in effect acknowledges, we are concerned with the subtleties of a union's statutory duty faithfully to represent employees in the unit, including those who may not be members of the union. The Court—regrettably, in my opinion—ventures to state judgments as to the metes and bounds of the reciprocal duties involved in the relationship between the union and the employee. In my opinion, this is precisely and especially the kind of judgment that Congress intended to entrust to the Board and which is well within the pre-emption doctrine that this Court has prudently stated.... The nuances of union-employee and union-employer relationships are infinite and consequential, particularly when the issue is as amorphous as whether the union was proved guilty of "arbitrary or bad-faith conduct" which the Court states as the standard applicable here. In all reason and in all good judgment, this jurisdiction should be left with the Board and not be placed in the courts, especially with the complex and necessarily confusing guidebook that the Court now publishes....

[The dissenting opinion of MR. JUSTICE BLACK is omitted.]

NOTES

1. Prior to the principal case, the lower courts had developed at least two main approaches to an individual employee's right to take a grievance to arbitration. Under one line of cases, illustrated by *Donnelly v. United Fruit Co.,* 40 N.J. 61, 190 A.2d 825 (1963), an employee was regarded as having a "statutorily vested right" under § 9(a) to invoke the grievance procedure, including the final step of arbitration, if the union failed to press the claim. Under a second group of decisions, represented by *Black-Clawson Co. v. Machinists Lodge 355,* 313 F.2d 179

(2d Cir. 1962), an individual employee could not compel the employer to arbitrate a grievance unless the contract specifically so provided; § 9(a) was deemed merely to permit but not require an employer to hear and adjust employee grievances.

2. The Supreme Court ended a long debate over whether a union's negligence alone could constitute unfair representation when it declared in *Steelworkers v. Rawson,* 495 U.S. 362, 372-73 (1990): "The courts have in general assumed that mere negligence, even in the enforcement of a collective-bargaining agreement, would not state a claim for breach of the duty of fair representation, and we endorse that view today."

3. The Supreme Court elaborated on its *Vaca* rule for calculating damages against a union guilty of unfair representation in *Czosek v. O'Mara,* 397 U.S. 25 (1970). Said the Court: "Assuming a wrongful discharge by the employer independent of any discriminatory conduct by the union and a subsequent discriminatory refusal by the union to process grievances based on the discharge, damages against the union for loss of employment are unrecoverable except to the extent that its refusal to handle the grievances added to the difficulty and expense of collecting from the employer." But in *Bowen v. United States Postal Serv.,* 459 U.S 212 (1983), a sharply divided (5-4) Supreme Court limited to Railway Labor Act cases the *Czosek v. O'Mara* formula for calculating damages against unions that breach their duty of fair representation. When an employer subject to the NLRA wrongfully discharges an employee and the union aggravates the harm by improperly declining to arbitrate the case, damages must be apportioned between the parties. The union will be liable to the extent it increased the employee's losses. For example, the union may be responsible for the backpay that accrues after the date of the hypothetical arbitration decision that would have reinstated the employee. *Czosek* was distinguished on the basis that the RLA provides employees with an alternative statutory remedy, if the union refuses to process their grievance. *See* VanderVelde, *Making Good on Vaca's Promise: Apportioning Backpay to Achieve Remedial Goals,* 32 U.C.L.A. L. Rev. 302 (1984).

In *Bridge, Structural, and Ornamental Iron Workers Local 377 and Bryant,* 326 N.L.R.B. No. 54 (1998), the Board ruled that an employee is entitled to make-whole monetary relief from a union for breach of its duty of fair representation only if the Board General Counsel proves that the grievance was meritorious. Further, a union that fails to pursue such a grievance is liable only for the increase in damages caused by its breach, and not the damages caused by the employer's violation of the labor contract. The Board abandoned its previous approach in *Rubber Workers Local 250 (Mach-Wayne Closures),* 290 N.L.R.B. 817 (1988)—allowing a make-whole remedy if the General Counsel showed that the employee's grievance was not "clearly frivolous"—because it risked "imposing essentially punitive liability on the union and granting a windfall to the grievant." Such an allocation of evidentiary burdens, the Board concluded, conflicted with "the essentially remedial character of the Act."

4. Certain employee rights, such as the right to vacation pay or retirement benefits, have been held for some time to "vest," or survive the expiration of the labor agreement. *See, e.g., In re Wil-Low Cafeterias, Inc.,* 111 F.2d 429 (2d Cir. 1940); *Vallejo v. American R.R. of Puerto Rico,* 188 F.2d 513 (1st Cir. 1951); *Hauser v. Farwell, Ozmun, Kirk & Co.,* 299 F. Supp. 387 (D. Minn. 1969). *But cf. Battle v. Clark Equip. Co.,* 579 F.2d 1338 (7th Cir. 1978) (supplemental unemployment benefits subject to reduction). Seniority rights have been placed in a different category. They can be cut off by an employer's moving its plant, or by an agreement between employer and union. *Oddie v. Ross Gear & Tool Co.,* 305 F.2d 143 (6th Cir.), *cert. denied,* 371 U.S. 941 (1962); *Humphrey v. Moore,* 375 U.S. 335 (1964). Is this distinction between individual rights and collective rights sound? What relationship might it have to the Court's conception of the grievance and arbitration process under a labor contract as articulated in *Vaca v. Sipes? See* Aaron, *Reflections on the Legal Nature and Enforceability of Seniority Rights,* 75 Harv. L. Rev. 1532 (1962); Blumrosen, *Seniority Rights and Industrial Change: Zdanok v. Glidden Co.,* 47 Minn. L. Rev. 505 (1962); Feinberg, Katz, Shaw, *Do Contract Rights Vest?* in National Academy of Arbitrators, Labor Arbitration and Industrial Change, Proceedings of the Sixteenth Annual Meeting 192, 223, 231 (1963) (three separate papers).

5. The Supreme Court held in *Breininger v. Sheet Metal Workers Local 6,* 493 U.S. 67 (1989), that the NLRB did not have exclusive jurisdiction over a union member's claim that his union violated its duty of fair representation by discriminating against him in job referrals through a union hiring hall. Barring federal jurisdiction because of specialized Board expertise, said the Court, "would remove an unacceptably large number of fair representation claims from federal courts."

6. *See generally* Blumrosen, *The Worker and Three Phases of Unionism: Administrative and Judicial Control of the Worker-Union Relationship,* 61 Mich. L. Rev. 1435 (1963): Cox, *Rights Under a Labor Agreement,* 69 Harv. L. Rev. 601 (1956); Feller, *A General Theory of the Collective Bargaining Agreement,* 61 Calif. L. Rev. 663 (1973); Gregory, *A Call for Supreme Court Clarification of the Union Duty of Fair Representation,* 29 St. Louis U.L.J. 45 (1984); Hanslowe, *The Collective Agreement and the Duty of Fair Representation,* 14 Lab. L.J. 1052 (1963); Kirby, *Individual Rights in Industrial Self-Government: A "State Action" Analysis,* 63 Nw. U. L. Rev. 4 (1968); Summers, *Collective Power and Individual Rights in the Collective Agreement—A Comparison of Swedish and American Law,* 72 Yale L.J. 421 (1963); Lewis, *Fair Representation in Grievance Administration: Vaca v. Sipes,* 1967 Sup. Ct. Rev. 81.

———————

Air Line Pilots Ass'n v. O'Neill, 499 U.S. 65, 111 S. Ct. 1127, 113 L. Ed. 2d 51 (1991). The Air Line Pilots settled a bitter two-year strike against Continental Airlines by an agreement that gave striking pilots three different options. By hindsight it appeared that the deal arranged by the union was worse than if the strike had simply been terminated and the pilots left to seek reemployment in the order of seniority. A group of former strikers sued ALPA for breach of the duty of fair representation. The Supreme Court first held that the tripartite standard of unfair representation established in *Vaca v. Sipes*—"arbitrary, discriminatory, or in bad faith"—applies to union contract negotiation as well as to contract administration. The Court then reversed a court of appeals' ruling against ALPA, declaring that "the final product of the bargaining process may constitute evidence of a breach of duty only if it can be fairly characterized as so far outside a 'wide range of reasonableness' ... that it is wholly 'irrational' or 'arbitrary.'"

NOTES

1. To what extent should a union, even if acting in accordance with its honest judgment, be allowed to sacrifice individual interests for the sake of the group? Should a union be able to trade off or compromise some claims in order to gain concessions on others? Does it make any difference whether the abandoned grievance involves a discharge, minor discipline, seniority, or wages allegedly accrued and owing? Is it relevant that an arbitration with a single day's hearing may cost a union $2200 and an employer more? Perhaps the most poignant reported instance of conflict between individual and group interests is *Union News Co. v. Hildreth,* 295 F.2d 658 (6th Cir. 1961). A lunch counter employing twelve persons suffered unexplained losses of food or money and suspected dishonesty among the workers. The employer threatened to fire the entire crew. Rather than have this happen, the union acquiesced in the employer's trial layoff of five employees. Losses dropped, the five employees were permanently discharged, and the union refused to process a grievance on behalf of one protesting worker, even though there was no direct proof of her dishonesty. Did the union act so improperly that a court should intervene? *See also Aguinaga v. Food Workers,* 993 F.2d 1463 (10th Cir. 1993) (union wrongfully "bartered away" employees' contract rights for extraneous institutional or political reasons), *cert. denied,* 510 U.S. 1072 (1994). What about a union's adhering strictly to seniority to the exclusion of all other considerations in contesting an employer's promotion decisions? *See Smith v. Hussmann Refrig. Co.,* 619 F.2d 1229 (8th Cir. 1980) (en banc), *cert. denied,* 449 U.S. 839 (1981), *noted in* 76 Nw. U. L. Rev. 519 (1981).

Most courts, however, extend wide latitude to unions seeking to negotiate the best deal for the majority, even at the expense of individual rights. *Cleveland v. Porca Co.,* 38 F.3d 289 (7th Cir. 1994), involved employees who lost their jobs after the sale of a company plant. Although the union had obtained an arbitral award finding that the seller had violated its bargaining agreement by failing to require the purchaser to assume the existing contract, the court found no fair representation breach when union officials negotiated a settlement agreement that permitted the termination of some plant workers. The arbitral award was ambiguous, and the union officials sought in good faith to obtain the best deal they could get. *See also Danylchuk v. Des Moines Register & Tribune Co.,* 128 F.3d 653 (8th Cir. 1997) (sustaining right of union to agree to drop pending discharge grievance as condition for achieving new bargaining agreement); *Considine v. Newspaper Agency Corp.,* 43 F.3d 1349 (10th Cir. 1994) (courts must accord union negotiators wide latitude when they negotiate agreements that compromise the rights of some unit members for the benefit of the rest); *Firemen & Oilers Local 320 (Philip Morris, U.S.A.),* 323 N.L.R.B. No. 10, 154 L.R.R.M. 1185 (1997) (union did not violate its duty of fair representation in negotiating a change from craft to plant seniority, even though this benefitted six employees at the expense of four others and was secured at the sole urging of the employees who would gain).

2. What if the burdens of a union trade-off sacrificing the rights of a numerical minority of employees to benefit the numerical majority fall disproportionately upon a group that has historically been disadvantaged in the union structure, such as people of color or women? *See generally Lewis v. Tuscan Dairy Farms,* 25 F.3d 1138 (2d Cir. 1994) (union agreements that arbitrarily and invidiously sacrifice the employment rights of unit members breach the duty of fair representation); *see, e.g., Woods v. Graphic Communications Union,* 925 F.2d 1195 (9th Cir. 1991) (union failure to file grievances on behalf of black employees complaining about the plant's racially hostile atmosphere); *Jones v. Cassens Transp.,* 617 F. Supp. 869 (E.D. Mich.1985), *rev'd on other grounds,* 838 F.2d 856 (6th Cir. 1988), *reh'g denied,* 873 F.2d 1088 (6th Cir.), *cert. denied,* 493 U.S. 964 (1989) (union worked to save jobs of male employees during a layoff at the expense of female employees' jobs). *See also Union Found Liable for Sex Bias After It Failed to Represent Woman,* Daily Lab. Rep. (BNA) No. 186, at A-6 (Sept. 26, 1995) (describing federal court ruling under Title VII that a local union was liable for its failure to press a female worker's sexual harassment claims—which included rape by a male union member—"in deference to the perceived desires of [the local's] male membership").

3. How far should the union's duty extend? *Bernard v. Air Line Pilots Ass'n,* 873 F.2d 213 (9th Cir. 1989), involved a merger between union and nonunion airlines. The labor organization that represented the pilots of the unionized carrier was found to owe a duty of fair representation to the pilots of the nonunion carrier when it negotiated a seniority integration agreement affecting the employment rights of the pilots from both carriers. On the other hand, a union was held not to have breached its duty of fair representation when it waived the shutdown damage claims of pilots "as a group" against a bankrupt airline and refused to press the demands of individual pilots. The union got a quid pro quo in the employer's agreement to resume limited flight operations. *Burkevich v. Air Line*

Pilots Ass'n, 894 F.2d 346 (9th Cir. 1990). *See also Rakestraw v. United Airlines,* 981 F.2d 1524 (7th Cir. 1992), *cert. denied,* 510 U.S. 906 (1993) (pilots union did not breach fair representation duty when it agreed to dovetail by date of original employment seniority rights of pilots of smaller airline acquired by United even though this favored more senior United pilots).

4. In *Plumbers Local 32 v. NLRB,* 50 F.3d 29 (D.C. Cir.), *cert. denied,* 516 U.S. 974 (1995), the court held that a union that failed to use objective standards to determine the workers to be referred by its exclusive hiring hall, to the detriment of nonmembers, violated its duty of fair representation. When a union assumes the dual role of employer and representative, it may be held to a higher standard than when it simply acts as a bargaining agent.

5. Courts and the Board sometimes seem more willing to intervene and find breaches of the duty of fair representation based on union conduct in grievance-processing even if the union tactics are calculated to benefit the membership as a whole. In *Achilli v. John J. Nissen Baking Co.,* 989 F.2d 561 (1st Cir. 1993), a bakery driver was discharged for engaging in an unauthorized work stoppage when he refused to carry "add-on" pastry orders. The court found that his union breached its duty of fair representation when it failed to disclose at the worker's arbitral hearing that he had merely been following a union order that bakery drivers ignore employer procedures regarding "add-on" pastry orders. Similarly, the Board held in *AFGE Local 888 (Bayley-Seton Hosp.),* 308 N.L.R.B. 646 (1992), that an incumbent union violated the NLRA when, after a rival labor organization was certified as the representative of the same unit, it refused to continue to process unit grievances that arose before the expiration of the incumbent's bargaining agreement.

6. A railroad union did not violate the duty of fair representation by being unfamiliar with laws dealing with subjects beyond the negotiation or administration of collective bargaining agreements, such as an employer's reporting obligations concerning job vacancies. *Barker v. Chesapeake & O.R.R.,* 959 F.2d 1361 (6th Cir.), *cert. denied,* 506 U.S. 1000 (1992).

HINES v. ANCHOR MOTOR FREIGHT, INC.

Supreme Court of the United States
424 U.S. 554, 96 S. Ct. 1048, 47 L. Ed. 2d 231 (1976)

MR. JUSTICE WHITE delivered the opinion of the Court.

The issue here is whether a suit against an employer by employees asserting breach of a collective bargaining contract was properly dismissed where the accompanying complaint against the Union for breach of duty of fair representation has withstood the Union's motion for summary judgment and remains to be tried.

I

Petitioners, who were formerly employed as truck drivers by respondent Anchor Motor Freight, Inc. (Anchor), were discharged on June 5, 1967. The applicable collective bargaining contract forbade discharges without just cause. The company charged dishonesty. The practice at Anchor was to reimburse drivers for money spent for lodging while the drivers were on the road overnight. Anchor's assertion was that petitioners had sought reimbursement for motel expenses in excess of the actual charges sustained by them. At a meeting between the company and the union, Local 377, International Brotherhood of Teamsters (the Union), which was also attended by petitioners, Anchor presented motel receipts previously submitted by petitioners which were in excess of the charges shown on the motel's registration cards; a notarized statement of the motel clerk asserting the accuracy of the registration cards; and an affidavit of the motel owner affirming that the registration cards were accurate and that inflated receipts had been furnished petitioners. The Union claimed petitioners were innocent and opposed the discharges. It was then agreed that the matter would be presented to the joint arbitration committee for the area, to which the collective-bargaining contract permitted either party to submit an unresolved grievance.[2]

Pending this hearing, petitioners were reinstated. Their suggestion that the motel be investigated was answered by the Union representatives' assurances that "there was nothing to worry about" and that they need not hire their own attorney.

A hearing before the joint area committee was held on July 26, 1967. Anchor presented its case. Both the Union and petitioners were afforded an opportunity to present their case and to be heard. Petitioners denied their dishonesty, but neither they nor the Union presented any other evidence contradicting the documents presented by the company. The committee sustained the discharges. Petitioners then retained an attorney and sought rehearing based on a statement by the motel owner that he had no personal knowledge of the events, but that the discrepancy between the receipts and the registration cards could have been attributable to the motel clerk's recording on the cards less than was actually paid

---

[2] The contractual grievance procedure is set out in Art. 7 of the Central Conference Area Supplement to the National Master Agreement. App. 226-233. Grievances were to be taken up by the employee involved and if no settlement was reached, were then to be considered by the business agent of the local union and the employer representative. If the dispute remained unresolved, either party had the right to present the case for decision to the appropriate joint area arbitration committee. These committees are organized on a geographical area basis and hear grievances in panels made up of an equal number of representatives of the parties to the collective-bargaining agreement. Cases that deadlocked before the joint area committee could be taken to a panel of the national joint arbitration committee, composed like the area committee panels of an equal number of representatives of the parties to the agreement. If unresolved there, they would be resolved by a panel including an impartial arbitrator. The joint arbitration committee for the Detroit area is involved in this case.

and retaining for himself the difference between the amount receipted and the amount recorded. The committee, after hearing, unanimously denied rehearing "because there was no new evidence presented which would justify reopening this case."

There were later indications that the motel clerk was in fact the culprit; and the present suit was filed in June 1969, against Anchor, the Union and its International. The complaint alleged that the charges of dishonesty made against petitioners by Anchor were false, that there was no just cause for discharge and that the discharges had been in breach of contract. It was also asserted that the falsity of the charges could have been discovered with a minimum of investigation, that the Union had made no effort to ascertain the truth of the charges and that the Union had violated its duty of fair representation by arbitrarily and in bad faith depriving petitioners of their employment and permitting their discharge without sufficient proof.

The Union denied the charges and relied on the decision of the joint area committee. Anchor asserted that petitioners had been properly discharged for just cause. It also defended on the ground that petitioners, diligently and in good faith represented by the Union, had unsuccessfully resorted to the grievance and arbitration machinery provided by the contract and that the adverse decision of the joint arbitration committee was binding upon the Union and petitioners under the contractual provision declaring that "[a] decision by a majority of a Panel of any of the Committees shall be final and binding on all parties, including the employee and/or employees affected." Discovery followed, including a deposition of the motel clerk revealing that he had falsified the records and that it was he who had pocketed the difference between the sums shown on the receipts and the registration cards. Motions for summary judgment filed by Anchor and the Unions were granted by the District Court on the ground that the decision of the arbitration committee was final and binding on the employees and "for failure to show facts comprising bad faith, arbitrariness or perfunctoriness on the part of the Unions." Although indicating that the acts of the Union "may not meet professional standards of competency, and while it might have been advisable for the Union to further investigate the charges ...," the District Court concluded that the facts demonstrated at most bad judgment on the part of the Union, which was insufficient to prove a breach of duty or make out a prima facie case against it....

After reviewing the allegations and the record before it, the court of appeals concluded that there were sufficient facts from which bad faith or arbitrary conduct on the part of the local Union could be inferred by the trier of fact and that petitioners should have been afforded an opportunity to prove their charges.[4] To

---

[4] As summarized by the Court of Appeals, the allegations relied on were:

"They consist of the motel clerk's admission, made a year after the discharge was upheld in arbitration, that he, not plaintiffs, pocketed the money; the claim of the union's failure to investigate the motel clerk's original story implicating plaintiffs despite their requests; the

this extent the judgment of the district court was reversed. The Court of Appeals affirmed the judgment in favor of Anchor and the International....

It is this judgment of the court of appeals with respect to Anchor that is now before us on our limited grant of the employees" petition for writ of certiorari.... We reverse that judgment....

III

Even though under *Vaca* the employer may not insist on exhaustion of grievance procedures when the union has breached its representation duty, it is urged that when the procedures have been followed and a decision favorable to the employer announced, the employer must be protected from relitigation by the express contractual provision declaring a decision to be final and binding. We disagree. The union's breach of duty relieves the employee of an express or implied requirement that disputes be settled through contractual grievance procedures; if it seriously undermines the integrity of the arbitral process the union's breach also removes the bar of the finality provisions of the contract....

Anchor would have it that petitioners are foreclosed from judicial relief unless some blameworthy conduct on its part disentitles it to rely on the finality rule. But it was Anchor that originated the discharges for dishonesty. If those charges were in error, Anchor has surely played its part in precipitating this dispute. Of course, both courts below held there were no facts suggesting that Anchor either knowingly or negligently relied on false evidence. As far as the record reveals it also prevailed before the joint committee after presenting its case in accordance with what were ostensibly wholly fair procedures. Nevertheless there remains the question whether the contractual protection against relitigating an arbitral decision binds employees who assert that the process has fundamentally malfunctioned by reason of the bad-faith performance of the union, their statutorily imposed collective bargaining agent.

Under the rule announced by the court of appeals, unless the employer is implicated in the Union's malfeasance or has otherwise caused the arbitral process to err, petitioners would have no remedy against Anchor even though they are successful in proving the Union's bad faith, the falsity of the charges against them and the breach of contract by Anchor by discharging without cause. This rule would apparently govern even in circumstances where it is shown that a union has manufactured the evidence and knows from the start that it is false; or even if, unbeknownst to the employer, the union has corrupted the arbitrator to

account of the union officials' assurances to plaintiffs that 'they had nothing to worry about' and 'that there was no need for them to investigate'; the contention that no exculpatory evidence was presented at the hearing; and the assertion that there existed political antagonism between local union officials and plaintiffs because of a wildcat strike led by some of the plaintiffs and a dispute over the appointment of a steward, resulting in denunciation of plaintiffs as 'hillbillies' by Angelo, the union president," 506 F.2d 1153, 1156 (CA6 1974).

the detriment of disfavored Union members. As is the case where there has been a failure to exhaust, however, we cannot believe that Congress intended to foreclose the employee from his § 301 remedy otherwise available against the employer if the contractual processes have been seriously flawed by the union's breach of its duty to represent employees honestly and in good faith and without invidious discrimination or arbitrary conduct.

It is urged that the reversal of the court of appeals will undermine not only the finality rule but the entire collective bargaining process. Employers, it is said, will be far less willing to give up their untrammeled right to discharge without cause and to agree to private settlement procedures. But the burden on employees will remain a substantial one, far too heavy in the opinion of some. To prevail against either the company or the Union, petitioners must show not only that their discharge was contrary to the contract but must also carry the burden of demonstrating breach of duty by the Union. As the District Court indicated, this involves more than demonstrating mere errors in judgment.

Petitioners are not entitled to relitigate their discharge merely because they offer newly discovered evidence that the charges against them were false and that in fact they were fired without cause. The grievance processes cannot be expected to be error-free. The finality provision has sufficient force to surmount occasional instances of mistake. But it is quite another matter to suggest that erroneous arbitration decisions must stand even though the employee's representation by the union has been dishonest, in bad faith or discriminatory; for in that event error and injustice of the grossest sort would multiply. The contractual system would then cease to qualify as an adequate mechanism to secure individual redress for damaging failure of the employer to abide by the contract. Congress has put its blessing on private dispute settlement arrangements provided in collective agreements, but it was anticipated, we are sure, that the contractual machinery would operate within some minimum levels of integrity. In our view, enforcement of the finality provision where the arbitrator has erred is conditioned upon the Union's having satisfied its statutory duty fairly to represent the employee in connection with the arbitration proceedings. Wrongfully discharged employees would be left without jobs and without a fair opportunity to secure an adequate remedy.

Except for this case the courts of appeals have arrived at similar conclusions. As the Court of Appeals for the Ninth Circuit put it in *Margetta v. Pam Pam Corp.*, 501 F.2d 179, 180 (1974): "To us, it makes little difference whether the union subverts the arbitration process by refusing to proceed as in *Vaca* or follows the arbitration trail to the end, but in doing so subverts the arbitration process by failing to fairly represent the employee. In neither case does the employee receive fair representation."

Petitioners, if they prove an erroneous discharge and the Union's breach of duty tainting the decision of the joint committee, are entitled to an appropriate remedy against the employer as well as the Union. It was error to affirm the district court's final dismissal of petitioners' action against Anchor. To this extent the judgment of the court of appeals is reversed.

So ordered.

MR. JUSTICE STEVENS took no part in the consideration or decision of this case.

[The concurring opinion of MR. JUSTICE STEWART and the dissenting opinion of MR. JUSTICE REHNQUIST, with whom THE CHIEF JUSTICE joined, are omitted.]

NOTES

1. *Scope of the Union's Duty in Grievance Processing:* When union officials with access to relevant employer information fail to conduct even cursory investigations of employee grievances, they may be found guilty of fair representation breaches. *See, e.g., Cruz v. IBEW Local 3*, 34 F.3d 1148 (2d Cir. 1994). *See also Beavers v. Paperworkers Local 1741*, 72 F.3d 97 (8th Cir. 1995) (allegation that discharge grievance was rejected in arbitration as untimely states a claim for breach of duty of fair representation). Aside from cases involving perfunctory handling of grievances, however, courts generally remain reluctant to second-guess union handling of the grievance process. *See, e.g., Smith v. United Parcel Serv.*, 96 F.3d 1066 (8th Cir. 1996) (union did not breach its duty of fair representation when it failed to get an expert witness to challenge the reliability of a drug test given an employee); *Baxter v. Paperworkers Local 7370*, 140 F.3d 745 (8th Cir. 1998) (denying grievants the right to be represented by their own private attorneys in discharge arbitration proceedings is not ipso facto arbitrary nor a breach of the union's duty of fair representation); *accord, Garcia v. Zenith Electronics Corps.*, 58 F.3d 1171 (7th Cir. 1995).

In determining the scope of the duty of fair representation, does it remain relevant that the doctrine may have initially been inferred in *Steele* in order to avoid constitutional questions that would otherwise have arisen from the congressional grant of exclusive recognition to majority bargaining agents?

2. Should a union attorney be immune from legal malpractice liability for failing to represent an individual employee adequately? (Hint: what is the individual liability of union agents under *Atkinson v. Sinclair Ref. Co.* (*supra* at *Complete Auto Transit, Inc. v. Reis* discussion). *See Arnold v. Air Midwest Inc.*, 100 F.3d 857 (10th Cir. 1996).

3. *Right To Jury Trial:* An individual who seeks compensatory damages for lost wages and benefits in a fair representation suit prosecuted against a labor organization is entitled to a jury trial under the Seventh Amendment, since such monetary relief is of a legal, rather than a restitutionary, nature. *Teamsters Local 391 v. Terry,* 494 U.S. 558 (1990). The same jury privilege applies to both the contractual and fair representation issues in a *Vaca v. Sipes* suit against an employer and representative union, when a plaintiff seeks both equitable and legal relief. The jury must determine the common legal issues before the trial court considers the equitable questions. *See Brownlee v. Yellow Freight Sys.*, 921 F.2d 745 (8th Cir. 1990); *Black v. Ryder*, 930 F.2d 505 (6th Cir. 1991).

4. *Damages:* The Supreme Court has held, apparently as a blanket rule (5-4), that punitive damages are not available against unions for breach of the duty of fair representation in processing grievances. *IBEW v. Foust*, 442 U.S. 42 (1979), *noted in* 32 Hastings L.J. 1041 (1981). What about damages for emotional distress resulting from unfair representation? *See, e.g., Baskin v. Hawley*, 807 F.2d 1120 (2d Cir. 1986).

5. *Statute of Limitations:* In *DelCostello v. Teamsters*, 462 U.S. 151 (1983), the Supreme Court ruled that the NLRA's § 10(b) six-month statute of limitations governs an employee's *Vaca-Sipes* or *Hines-Anchor Motor Freight* suit against both employer and union, alleging employer breach of contract under § 301 of Taft-Hartley and union breach of the duty of fair representation. The Court concluded that "state limitations periods for vacating arbitration awards fail to provide an aggrieved employee with a satisfactory opportunity to vindicate his rights under § 301 and the fair representation doctrine." *UAW v. Hoosier-Cardinal Corp., supra,* was distinguished as a "straightforward breach of contract suit under § 301" brought by a union, while *DelCostello* was a "hybrid § 301/fair representation claim" having "no close analogy in ordinary state law." The six-month limitations period has also been held applicable to a fair representation suit against a union alone. *Johnson v. Graphic Commun. Workers*, 930 F.2d 1178 (7th Cir.), *cert. denied*, 502 U.S. 862 (1991). *See* Gallagher & Veglahn, *The Statute of Limitations Period in Duty of Fair Representation Cases: A Clarification*, 38 Lab. L.J. 776 (1987).

6. For thoughtful analyses of the issues surrounding the duty of fair representation, *see* Cheit, *Competing Models of Fair Representation: The Perfunctory Processing Cases*, 24 B.C. L. Rev. 1 (1982); Finkin, *The Limits of Majority Rule in Collective Bargaining*, 64 Minn. L. Rev. 183 (1980); Freed, Polsby & Spitzer, *Unions, Fairness and the Conundrums of Collective Choice*, 56 S. Cal. L. Rev. 461 (1983); Goldberg, *The Duty of Fair Representation: What the Courts Do in Fact*, 34 Buffalo L. Rev. 89 (1985); Harper & Lupu, *Fair Representation as Equal Protection*, 98 Harv. L. Rev. 1212 (1985); Hyde, *Democracy in Collective Bargaining*, 93 Yale L.J. 793 (1984); The Changing Law of Fair Representation (J. McKelvey ed. 1985); Malin, *The Supreme Court and the Duty of Fair Representation*, 27 Harv. C.R.-C.L. L. Rev. 127 (1992); Summers, *The Individual Employee's Rights Under the Collective Agreement: What Constitutes Fair Representation?* 126 U. Pa. L. Rev. 251 (1977); VanderVelde, *A Fair Process Model for the Union's Fair Representation Duty*, 67 Minn. L. Rev. 1079 (1983).

Clayton v. United Automobile Workers, 451 U.S. 679, 101 S. Ct. 2088, 68 L. Ed. 2d 538 (1981). The UAW withdrew its request for the arbitration of an employee's discharge. Although the union's constitution required aggrieved members to exhaust internal appeals procedures before seeking redress from a court, the employee immediately sued the union under § 301 of the LMRA, alleging breach of the duty of fair representation. The Supreme Court held that exhaustion of internal remedies will not be required when a union appeals procedure cannot result in reactivation of the employee grievance or an award of complete relief. The latter might include reinstatement as well as backpay. Even though the union could provide full monetary relief, only the employer could grant reinstatement.

NOTES

1. Shortly after *Clayton* was decided, the UAW secured the agreement of a number of the employers with which it bargains that they would permit the reactivation of employees' grievances in situations where the Public Review Board, the International Executive Board, or the Convention Appeals Committee found the union had breached its duty of fair representation. *See, e.g.,* GM-UAW 1982 National Agreement, p. 321; *see also Monroe v. UAW,* 723 F.2d 22 (6th Cir. 1983) (requiring exhaustion of such internal union procedures).

2. Where an employee is required to exhaust internal union procedures before seeking judicial redress, the six-month statute of limitations period will be tolled until the internal union procedures are over. *See Frandsen v. BRAC,* 782 F.2d 674 (7th Cir. 1986). But the First Circuit has held that the pendency of arbitration proceedings did not toll the statute in a hybrid § 301 action when employees were not obliged to exhaust contractual grievance procedures or internal union appeals. *Arriaga-Zajas v. Garment Workers Puerto Rico Council,* 835 F.2d 11 (1st Cir. 1987), *cert. denied,* 486 U.S. 1033 (1988). What is necessary to "exhaust" intraunion procedures? *See, e.g., Stafford v. Ford Motor Co.,* 835 F.2d 1227 (8th Cir. 1987) (sufficient for member to send letter to international president requesting a "new trial").

3. *See generally* Fox & Sonenthal, *Section 301 and Exhaustion of Intra-Union Appeals: A Misbegotten Marriage,* 128 U. Pa. L. Rev. 989 (1980); Gould, *The Supreme Court's Clayton Decision: Its Issues and Implications,* 8 Employee Rel. L.J. 110 (1982); Jacobs, *The Duty of Fair Representation: Minorities, Dissidents and Exclusive Representation,* 59 B.U.L. Rev. 857 (1979). *Clayton* is noted in 46 Albany L. Rev. 1069 (1982) and 31 Cath. U. L. Rev. 311 (1982).

———————

Glover v. St. Louis-San Francisco Railway, 393 U.S. 324, 89 S. Ct. 548, 21 L. Ed. 2d 519 (1969). Black and white railroad employees sued their union and employer, claiming that racial discrimination practiced by the railroad with the sub rosa agreement of certain union officials kept the plaintiffs from securing higher paying jobs. The defendants moved to dismiss on the ground that the plaintiffs had not exhausted their administrative remedies under the contract grievance procedure, in the union constitution, or before the National Railroad Adjustment Board. Plaintiffs responded that they had tried in vain to present their grievances to union and company officials. The Supreme Court held that since the union and the employer were allegedly scheming together to bar the blacks from promotion, the employees should not be required to pursue further any relief administered by the union, the company, or both. Even though the Railroad Adjustment Board ordinarily has exclusive jurisdiction under § 3 First (i) of the Railway Labor Act to interpret collective bargaining agreements, it too was suspect here since its membership is largely chosen by the railroads and the brotherhoods.

NOTES

1. For further rulings on the need to exhaust administrative remedies before suing, or on the elimination of such a requirement because of futility, *see Andrews v. Louisville & N.R.R.*, 406 U.S. 320 (1972); *Steinman v. Spector Freight Sys.*, 441 F.2d 599 (2d Cir. 1971). *See generally* Simpson & Berwick, *Exhaustion of Grievance Procedures and the Individual Employee*, 51 Texas L. Rev. 1179 (1973).

2. The contract in *Groves v. Ring Screw Works*, 498 U.S. 168 (1990), contained a grievance procedure that did not culminate in binding arbitration. If a grievance was not mutually resolved, the union retained the right to strike. Several workers were discharged, and they exhausted the available grievance procedures without success. They then commenced a § 301 breach of contract action against their employer. A unanimous Supreme Court held that they could prosecute their § 301 suit against the employer. The Court refused to find that the contract provision preserving the union's right to resort to economic weapons divested the courts of jurisdiction to hear unresolved contract claims.

3. May a union and employer write into a contract a clause foreclosing individual actions and restricting the right to maintain suit on employee claims to the union? *Cf. Elgin, Joliet & E. Ry. v. Burley*, 325 U.S. 711, 729 (1945) (union cannot, under the RLA, bind employee by grievance settlement of accrued monetary claim without his authorization: "It would be difficult to believe that Congress intended ... to submerge wholly the individual and minority interest, with all power to act concerning them, in the collective interest and agency, not only in forming the contracts which govern their employment relation, but also in giving effect to them and to all other incidents of that relation"). *But see* Feller, *A General Theory of the Collective Bargaining Agreement*, 61 Calif. L. Rev. 663, 774-92, 835-36 (1973).

B. UNFAIR REPRESENTATION AS AN UNFAIR LABOR PRACTICE

Miranda Fuel Co., 140 N.L.R.B. 181 (1962). During a fuel company's slack season, from April 15 to October 15, employees subject to unsteady employment were entitled under a collective bargaining agreement to a leave of absence without loss of seniority. One employee, Lopuch, obtained the employer's permission to leave at the end of work on April 12, a Friday. Lopuch became ill in mid-October and did not return until October 30. He had a doctor's certificate, however, and the company excused the late return. At the urging of other employees, the union demanded that Lopuch be reduced from the middle to the bottom of the seniority list for violating the contract by his lateness. When the union learned about the excused illness, it changed its claim and relied instead on Lopuch's early departure. The employer reluctantly acquiesced in the seniority reduction even though the contract did not call for it. The Board held (3-2) that the demotion was due to "irrelevant, unfair or invidious reasons," and that it violated the union's duty of fair representation under § 9(a) of the NLRA. Moreover, although Lopuch was a union member himself, the Board majority found that the union had violated § 8(b)(1)(A) and (b)(2). It reasoned that the union's duty to represent all employees fairly and impartially under § 9(a) is incorporated into employees' § 7 rights "to bargain collectively through representatives of their own choosing." Unfair representation, whether or not influenced by an employee's union activities, violates § 8(b)(1)(A), and attempts to secure employer participation violates § 8(b)(2). Employer complicity is in turn violative of §§ 8(a)(3) and 8(a)(1).

NOTES

1. Enforcement was denied in *NLRB v. Miranda Fuel Co.,* 326 F.2d 172 (2d Cir. 1963). Judge Medina agreed with the Board's dissenting members that "discrimination for reasons wholly unrelated to 'union membership, loyalty ... or the performance of union obligations' is not sufficient to support findings of violations of [§ 8] of the Act." Judge Lumbard concurred, finding insufficient evidence of any breach of the union's duty of fair representation, and thus he did not have to consider its status as a possible § 8(b)(1) violation. Judge Friendly dissented, but also avoided the unfair representation issue. He read "discrimination" broadly as any distinction made without a proper basis, and argued that any demonstration of union power causing an employer to discriminate was sufficient "encouragement of union membership" to be grounds for finding violations of § 8(b)(2) and (a)(3).

2. In *Metal Workers Local 1 (Hughes Tool Co.),* 147 N.L.R.B. 1573 (1964), the NLRB held that a union's outright rejection of an employee's grievance for racial reasons violated §§ 8(b)(1)(A), (b)(2), and (b)(3), and that the joint certification issued to a white local and a black local should be rescinded because they had entered into racially discriminatory contracts. Chairman McCulloch and Member Fanning, who had dissented in *Miranda,* concurred in the rescission of the certification and in the finding of a § 8(b)(1)(A) violation, the latter on the narrow ground that the black employee had been discriminated against because he was not a member of the white local. In rejecting once again the concept of unfair representation as an unfair labor practice, McCulloch and Fanning elaborated on the rationale for their *Miranda* dissent:

> Section 7 was part of the Wagner Act which in its unfair labor practice section was aimed only at employer conduct. The Wagner Act also contained the present § 9(a). It hardly seems reasonable to infer, in these circumstances, that § 7 contained a protected implied right to fair representation against the bargaining representative, when the entire Wagner Act did not make any conduct by a labor organization unlawful. Section 7 was continued substantially unchanged in the Taft-Hartley Act except for the addition of the "right to refrain" clause, which is not material to our problem. Although the Taft-Hartley Act added union unfair labor practices to the list of prohibited conduct, neither the Act nor the legislative history contains any mention of the duty of fair representation, despite the fact that the *Steele* and *Wallace* decisions were well known, having been issued 3 years previously. Again, although in the interval between the dates of the Taft-Hartley and Landrum-Griffin Acts, there were additional court decisions and articles by learned commentators in the law journals dealing with the legal problems of fair representation, Congress made no change in the wording of § 7, and ignored the problem completely in adding a "Bill of Rights" section to the existing statute. If Congress had really intended that violation of the duty of fair representation should be an unfair labor practice, it would seem that the 1959 revision afforded it an opportunity to clear up the uncertainty. Instead it remained silent. We do not believe that realistically this silence can be interpreted as in any way favorable to the contention that the right to fair representation is a protected § 7 right. There are practical reasons for believing that, if there had been any contemporary understanding that the Act had made it an unfair labor practice for a union to fail in its duty of fair representation, the opposition would have been both strong and loud.
>
> There is another and more important reason why the Board should not undertake to police a union's administration of its duties without a clear mandate from Congress. The purpose of the Act is primarily to protect the organizational rights of employees. But apart from the obligation to bargain in good faith, "Congress intended that the parties would have wide latitude in their negotiations, unrestricted by any governmental power to regulate the substantive solution of their differences." Before *Miranda,* it was assumed that contract or grievance decisions by employers and unions were immune

from examination by the Board unless they were influenced by union considerations. But, under the underlying reasoning of the *Miranda* majority and that of the present decision, the Board is now constituted a tribunal to which every employee who feels aggrieved by a bargaining representative's action, whether in contract negotiations or in grievance handling, may appeal, regardless of whether the decision has been influenced in whole or in part by considerations of union membership, loyalty, or activity. The Board must determine on such appeal, without statutory standards, whether the representative's decision was motivated by "unfair or irrelevant or invidious" considerations and therefore to be set aside, or was within the "wide range of reasonableness ... allowed a statutory representative in serving the unit it represents ..." and to be sustained. Inevitably, the Board will have to sit in judgment on the substantive matters of collective bargaining, the very thing the Supreme Court has said the Board must not do, and in which it has no special experience or competence.

3. Despite the rebuff by the court of appeals in *Miranda,* the NLRB persisted in treating unfair representation as an unfair labor practice, and other courts proved more receptive to this view. In a racial discrimination case, the Fifth Circuit upheld the Board's theory that union unfair representation is a violation of § 8(b)(1)(A) of the NLRA, but did not pass on the Board's contention that it is also a violation of § 8(b)(2) and (b)(3). *Rubber Workers Local 12 v. NLRB,* 368 F.2d 12 (5th Cir. 1966), *cert. denied,* 389 U.S. 837 (1967). *Accord: Teamsters Local 568 v. NLRB,* 379 F.2d 137 (D.C. Cir. 1967), involving a nonracial situation; *NLRB v. Glass Bottle Blowers Local 106,* 520 F.2d 693 (6th Cir. 1975) (sexually segregated locals). *Cf. NLRB v. Longshoremen Local 1581 (Manchester Term. Corp.),* 489 F.2d 635 (5th Cir.), *cert. denied,* 419 U.S. 1040 (1974) (§ 8(b)(2) violation for union to discriminate against Mexican citizens in job transfers). Although the Supreme Court has never squarely ruled on the question, its tacit acceptance of the Labor Board's unfair representation doctrine in *Vaca v. Sipes, supra,* has tended to still further debate. *See generally* Albert, *NLRB-FEPC?* 16 Vand. L. Rev. 547 (1963); Meltzer, *The National Labor Relations Act and Racial Discrimination: The More Remedies, The Better?* 42 U. Chi. L. Rev. 1 (1974); Murphy, *NLRB, the EEOC, and Baby Makes Three: Today's Concerns—Problems or Solutions for Tomorrow,* in N.Y.U. Thirty-Second Annual Conference on Labor 191 (1979); Sherman, *Union's Duty of Fair Representation and the Civil Rights Act of 1964,* 49 Minn. L. Rev. 771 (1964); Sovern, *Race Discrimination and the National Labor Relations Act: The Brave New World of Miranda,* in N.Y.U. Sixteenth Annual Conference on Labor 3 (1963).

4. Sex discrimination by a union is also unfair representation in violation of § 8(b)(1)(A) and (b)(2), and a participating employer violates § 8(a)(3) and (a)(1). *Pacific Maritime Ass'n,* 209 N.L.R.B. 519 (1974). But an employer's unilateral sex discrimination is not an unfair labor practice. *Jubilee Mfg. Co.,* 202 N.L.R.B. 272 (1973), *aff'd,* 504 F.2d 271 (D.C. Cir. 1974).

5. In an unprecedented decision, a court of appeals held that racial discrimination by an employer acting on its own violates § 8(a)(1) where it has the effect of "producing a docility in its victims which inhibits the exercise of their § 7 rights." *Packinghouse Workers v. NLRB (Farmers' Coop. Compress),* 416 F.2d 1126 (D.C. Cir.), *cert. denied,* 396 U.S. 903 (1969). For the case on remand, *see Farmers' Coop. Compress,* 194 N.L.R.B. 85 (1971). *See also* Boyce, *Racial Discrimination and the NLRA,* 65 Nw. U.L. Rev. 232 (1970); Leiken, *The Current and Potential Equal Employment Role of the NLRB,* 1971 Duke L.J. 833.

6. For Board findings of union unfair representation in situations not involving race or sex discrimination, *see Barton Brands, Ltd.,* 228 N.L.R.B. 889 (1977) ("endtailing" rather than "dovetailing" of seniority lists upon merger of two plants for no objectively justifiable reason beyond currying political favor with members of larger unit); *Teamsters Local 860 (The Emporium),* 236 N.L.R.B. 844 (1978), *enforced,* 652 F.2d 1022 (D.C. Cir. 1981) (failure to inform employees that employer had flatly stated the wage increase sought would result in the abolition of the unit); *Teamsters Local 282 (Transit Mix Concrete Corp.),* 267 N.L.R.B. 1130 (1983) (failure to advise employees of the terms of an arbitration award that altered seniority procedures). *Cf. Strick Corp.,* 241 N.L.R.B. 210 (1979) (no violation of duty where union acquiesced in employer's "adamant demand" for contract clause superseding an arbitration award that granted reemployment preferences and seniority rights to discharged strikers).

7. When a union has failed to represent employees fairly in grievance handling, it may be required to pay for outside legal counsel to process their case through arbitration. *See NLRB v. Teamsters Local 396 (United Parcel Serv.),* 509 F.2d 1075 (9th Cir.), *cert. denied,* 421 U.S. 976 (1975).

C. UNION REPRESENTATION AND ANTIDISCRIMINATION LAW

Beginning in the 1960s, Congress enacted a series of statutes prohibiting discrimination in employment. Protection was first extended to employees who suffered discrimination on the basis of race, color, religion, sex, or national origin. *See* Title VII of the Civil Rights Act of 1964, 42 U.S.C. § 2000 *et seq.* (Title VII). Subsequently, Congress enacted separate statutes affording employees protection against age discrimination, *see* Age Discrimination in Employment Act, 29 U.S.C. §§ 621-634 (1967) (ADEA), and disability discrimination, *see* Rehabilitation Act of 1973, 29 U.S.C. §§ 701-796 (Rehabilitation Act), and The Americans With Disabilities Act of 1990, 42 U.S.C. §§ 12101-12213 (ADA). Because these statutes confer rights on employees individually and as a class vis-à-vis both employers and unions, they are relevant to the study of labor law. Accordingly, we treat them here. Issues surrounding the tension between collective and individual rights, raised previously in sections of this text dealing with exclusivity, majority rule, the duty of fair representation, and § 301 preemption of individual claims find their sharpest focus here. Our treatment of antidiscrimination law, however, is necessarily brief: civil rights legislation, including such matters as proof and remedies, has now become so extensive and complex that it calls for coverage in a separate course on employment discrimination. *See, e.g.,* A. Smith, C. Craver & L. Clark, Employment Discrimination Law (4th ed. 1994).

1. AN OVERVIEW OF TITLE VII

a. Substance

Title VII of the Civil Rights Act of 1964 is the centerpiece of federal antidiscrimination law. It prohibits discrimination on the basis of "race, color, religion, sex, or national origin" by employers, labor organizations, and employment agencies. It is an unlawful employment practice for an employer to "fail or refuse to hire or to discharge any individual, or otherwise to discriminate against any individual with respect to ... compensation, terms, conditions, or privileges of employment," or "to limit, segregate, or classify ... employees or applicants for employment in any way which would deprive or tend to deprive any individual of employment opportunities or otherwise adversely affect [his/her] status as an employee, because of the individual's race, color, religion, sex, or national origin." (§ 703(a)) It is an unlawful employment practice for a labor organization to "exclude or to expel from its membership, or otherwise to discriminate against, any individual," "limit, segregate or classify its membership or applicants for membership, or to classify or fail or refuse to refer for employment any individual, in any way which would deprive or tend to deprive any individual of employment opportunities, or ... limit such employment opportunities or otherwise adversely affect [his/her] status as an employee or an applicant," or "to cause or attempt to cause an employer to discriminate against an individual ... because of an individual's race, color, religion, sex, or national origin." (§ 703(c).) Title VII was amended significantly by the Civil Rights Act of 1991, P.L. 102-66, 105 Stat. 1071, primarily on the issues of remedies available and methods/burdens of proof (*see infra*).

The Pregnancy Discrimination Act (PDA) was enacted in 1978 as an amendment to Title VII (codified as § 701(k)). It was intended to clarify that discrimination on the basis of pregnancy, childbirth, or related medical conditions is a form of sex discrimination actionable under Title VII. The amendment was necessary because the Supreme Court had interpreted Title VII as not prohibiting an employer disability leave plan that covered all disabilities except those associated with or arising out of pregnancy. The Court reasoned that discrimination on the basis of pregnancy was not sex-based discrimination because at any given time there were both men and (non-pregnant) women who benefitted from the disability plan—thus, the exclusion of pregnancy was *not* a simple pretext for discrimination against women. *General Electric Co. v. Gilbert,* 429 U.S. 125 (1976). *Gilbert* is specifically overruled by the PDA.

Title VII's "because of sex" language also encompasses sexual harassment, whether by a member of the same sex or the opposite sex as the victim, where members of one sex are exposed to disadvantageous terms of conditions of employment to which members of the other sex are not exposed, resulting in a hostile or abusive work environment. *Meritor Savings Bank v. Vinson,* 477 U.S. 57 (1986); *Oncale v. Sundowner Offshore Services,* 118 S. Ct. 998 (1998). To ground a claim of hostile work environment sexual harassment, the conduct (1) must be "severe or pervasive enough to create an objectively hostile or abusive work environment—an environment that a reasonable person would find hostile or abusive"; and (2) must "actually alter ... the conditions of the victim's employment" in that the victim "subjectively perceive[s] the environment to be abusive." It is not necessary, however, that the conduct "seriously affect employees' psychological well-being." The determination depends on all the circumstances, including the frequency and severity of the conduct, whether it is physically threatening or humiliating or is merely an offensive utterance, and whether it interferes unreasonably with an employee's work performance. *Harris v. Forklift Sys.,* 510 U.S. 17 (1993). Employers are vicariously liable for supervisor harassment if the harassment culminates in a tangible employment action (such as discharge, discipline or demotion). Where the supervisor takes no tangible employment action, the employer is vicariously liable if it acted negligently in failing to prevent continued harm, or assisted the supervisor in carrying out the harassment by virtue of maintaining his or her managerial authority. Employers defending against tangible employment actions by supervisors may negate liability by showing (1) that the employer exercised reasonable care to prevent and correct promptly any sexually harassing behavior (such as by maintaining an antiharassment policy with complaint procedures), and (2) the plaintiff unreasonably failed to take advantage of preventive or corrective opportunities provided by the employer. *Burlington Industries, Inc. v. Ellerth,* 118 S. Ct. 2257 (1998); *Faragher v. City of Boca Raton,* 118 S. Ct. 2275 (1998).

Sexual orientation is not a protected category under Title VII, and federal courts have traditionally held that Title VII's prohibition against sex discrimination does not include sexual orientation discrimination, *see, e.g., Smith v. Liberty Mut. Ins. Co.,* 569 F.2d 325 (5th Cir. 1978); *DeSantis v. Pacific Tel. & Tel. Co.,* 608 F.2d 327 (9th Cir. 1979). State statutory schemes in 10 states offer explicit protection to gays and lesbians in the employment context. States with such laws are California, Connecticut, Hawaii, Massachusetts, Minnesota, New Hampshire, New Jersey, Vermont, Rhode Island, and Wisconsin. The District of Columbia also has such a statute. Many cities have parallel laws. *Romer v. Evans,* 517 U.S. 620 (1996) establishes that states may not legislate (by constitutional amendment or otherwise) to nullify local lawmaking protecting against sexual orientation discrimination; to do so runs afoul of the federal equal protection clause by creating a status-based distinction whose breadth is so remarkable that the Justices concluded that efforts like Colorado's Amendment 2 "seem ... inexplicable by anything but animus toward the class that [they] affect."

b. Coverage

Covered employers include all of those engaged in business affecting commerce with 15 or more employees, and unions with 15 or more members. Individual employees are covered only in their capacity to act as agents of the employer; most courts refuse to assess individual liability against employees under Title VII or other antidiscrimination statutes. *See, e.g, Williams v. Banning,* 72 F.3d 552 (7th Cir. 1995). State and local governments acting as employers are covered. The federal government as employer is excluded from coverage under the main body of Title VII, but is covered by a separate amendment outlining different substantive procedures for enforcement. Employers who do business outside the U.S. are covered when their employees abroad are American citizens (though they are not required to engage in practices that would violate the laws of the host country). Covered employees include all who are paid workers and are not independent contractors, except military personnel.

c. Procedure

The EEOC is charged with administering and enforcing Title VII. This means that claims under Title VII must be filed first with the Equal Employment Opportunity Commission (EEOC); plaintiffs may proceed to court only after they have exhausted the administrative procedures required by the EEOC. At the close of its investigation and conciliation procedures, the EEOC may choose to bring suit itself, or to issue the plaintiff a right-to-sue letter, at which point the plaintiff who wishes to pursue the claim may proceed with a private attorney in court. State courts have concurrent jurisdiction with federal courts to hear Title VII actions. *Yellow Freight Sys. v. Donnelly,* 494 U.S. 820 (1990). If a state has parallel state remedies (under a Human Rights Act, for example), the plaintiff must exhaust those avenues of relief first, before proceeding to the EEOC.

d. Remedies

Equitable remedies, including reinstatement and back pay, injunctive relief, and attorneys' fees and costs form the centerpiece of the remedies available on Title VII claims. The 1991 Civil Rights Act amended the statute to provide for compensatory damages in cases of intentional discrimination. The statute imposes caps on compensatory damages that are tied to the size of the employer: $50,000 for employers with 15-100 employees; $100,000 for employers with 101-200 employees; $200,000 for employers with 201-500 employees; and $300,000 for employers with more than 500 employees. Compensatory damages are enumerated as including future pecuniary losses, emotional pain, suffering, inconvenience, mental anguish, and loss of enjoyment of life. The 1991 amendments also permit the recovery of punitive damages where the discriminatory practice was engaged in "with malice" or "with reckless indifference" to the rights protected under the statute. There is a right to a jury trial in Title VII cases where compensatory or punitive damages are sought.

e. Theories of Liability

Two types of discrimination are prohibited by Title VII, intentional discrimination (disparate treatment) and unintentional discrimination (disparate impact).

(1) *Disparate Treatment*: The plaintiff must prove that the employer failed to treat the plaintiff the same as other applicants or employees *because of* the plaintiff's race, color, religion, sex, or national origin. Disparate treatment is typically proved by direct evidence of discriminatory animus (statements of bigotry accompanying or otherwise causally linked to a negative employment decision, for example) or by circumstantial evidence (where an inference of discriminatory animus arises from the defendant's action). In either event, the focus is on the *intent* of the employer. If the plaintiff proves intentional discrimination by direct evidence, the defendant may present evidence that there were other legitimate factors that affected the decision; if the defendant carries the burden of persuasion on that point, the case is said to be a "mixed motive" case combining legitimate and illegitimate bases for the employment action. Section 703(m) provides that liability attaches when the plaintiff establishes the existence of illegitimate factors, even though other factors also motivated the practice; however, § 706(g) limits the available remedies if the defendant successfully persuades the court that it would have taken the same adverse action in the absence of the impermissible motivating factor—in this situation, remedies are limited to declaratory relief, affirmative relief that does not include hiring or reinstatement, and attorneys' fees. *See Price Waterhouse v. Hopkins,* 490 U.S. 228 (1989); Civil Rights Act of 1991, 42 U.S.C. § 2000e-5(g)(2)(B).

If the plaintiff proves intentional discrimination by circumstantial evidence, there is a three-part process: (1) plaintiff proves differential treatment on the basis of one of the protected categories, so that an inference of discriminatory intent arises; (2) defendant must articulate a legitimate business purpose for the adverse decision, which then dispels the inference of improper motive; and (3) plaintiff produces evidence to show that the defendant's articulated reason was a pretext to hide discriminatory animus (e.g., by showing that similarly situated employees were treated differently). *See McDonnell Douglas Corp. v. Green,* 441 U.S. 792 (1973); *Texas Dep't of Community Affairs v. Burdine,* 450 U.S. 248 (1981); *St. Mary's Honor Center v. Hicks,* 509 U.S. 502 (1993).

(2) *Disparate Impact:* Because Congress sought to remove barriers to equality of opportunity in employment that are structural—the product of a history of dis-

crimination—Title VII reaches beyond intentional discrimination to unintentional discrimination in the form of practices which operate to "freeze the status quo" of prior discrimination. Accordingly, plaintiffs may proceed on a disparate impact theory of discrimination. To do so, plaintiff must prove that the defendant acted in such a way or utilized a hiring device that disproportionately disadvantages a group defined by race, color, religion, sex, or national origin. Proof of discriminatory motive is not required. This method of proving discrimination targets hiring practices that are "fair in form but discriminatory in operation." *See Griggs v. Duke Power Co.,* 401 U.S. 424 (1971). Thus, for example, a union rule requiring the sponsorship of new members by current members may contravene Title VII if it disproportionately limits the membership opportunities of minority candidates. *See EEOC v. Steamship Clerks Union,* 48 F.3d 594 (1st Cir.), *cert. denied,* 516 U.S. 814 (1995).

Plaintiff typically proves his/her case with evidence of the impact on the relevant group disadvantaged by the practice (often statistical evidence), or by using applicant flow evidence. Many courts utilize a four-fifths rule of thumb to assess the sufficiency of the disparity: that is, a selection rate for any protected group that is less than eighty percent of the rate for the group with the highest rate is regarded as evidence of adverse impact of the selection procedure employed. *See Uniform Guidelines on Employee Selection Procedures,* 43 Fed. Reg. 38290 (Aug. 25, 1978). Plaintiff must identify the particular practice or practices that caused the disparate impact, unless they are not capable of separation for analysis. A three-pronged process is followed in disparate impact cases: (1) Plaintiff must show that a specific selection procedure has a disproportionate impact on a protected group; (2) the burden of production and persuasion then shifts to the defendant to show that the challenged practice is job-related and that the disparate impact is justified by business necessity; and (3) if defendant succeeds in carrying its burden, the burden shifts back to plaintiff to show that the employer failed to use a selection device that is equally effective but has a lesser disparate impact.

Section 703(k)(1)(A) of the Civil Rights Act of 1991, 105 Stat. 1071 (1991), codified the requirement established in *Wards Cove Packing Co. v. Antonio,* 490 U.S. 642 (1989) that plaintiffs challenging multi-factor selection procedures identify the specific component(s) causing the disparate impact, unless they can convince courts that the overall procedures are incapable of analytical separation, but overturned another portion of *Wards Cove* which had placed the burden of persuasion on the plaintiff even after disparate impact was established. The Act reimposed the burden of persuasion concerning business justification on respondents in disparate impact cases: once the plaintiff demonstrates disparate impact, the respondent must demonstrate that the "challenged practice is job related for the position in question and consistent with business necessity." The stated purpose was to codify the concepts enunciated in *Griggs.*

f. Employer Defenses

Title VII provides for several affirmative defenses. Three important defenses are: the bona fide occupational qualification defense (BFOQ) (§ 703(e)), the business necessity defense (§ 703(k)(1)(A)), and the bona fide seniority or merit system defense (§ 703(h)).

The BFOQ defense, available to disparate treatment claims under Title VII, allows intentional classification of employees or applicants where reasonably necessary to the normal operation of that particular business or enterprise. This defense is not available to claims of race discrimination; it is limited to sex, national origin, and religion. It applies only to qualifications that affect an employee's ability to do the job. For example, in *Dothard v. Rawlinson,* 433 U.S. 321 (1977), the Supreme Court upheld an Alabama regulation excluding women from "contact" guard positions in all-male prisons. Although noting that the bona fide occupational qualification (BFOQ) provision of § 703(e) of the Civil Rights Act is "an extremely narrow exception" to the general prohibition of discrimination on the basis of sex, the Court found it applicable in view of the very real risk of attacks on women guards under the conditions in Alabama prisons which a federal court had stated were characterized by rampant violence and a jungle atmosphere. Customer preference is not a BFOQ, even where documented (unless customer bodily privacy concerns are implicated). *See Diaz v. Pan Am World Airways,* 442 F.2d 385 (5th Cir.), *cert. denied,* 404 U.S. 950 (1971) (sex is not a BFOQ for flight attendant positions despite customer preference).

The business necessity defense, available to disparate impact claims under Title VII, is a broader concept than the BFOQ defense but analytically parallel to it. More latitude is given to defendants making this defense than to those raising the BFOQ defense, probably because the nature of plaintiff's proof in the disparate impact case is less convincing to courts than plaintiff's proof in a disparate treatment case.

Finally, Title VII insulates from liability employment decisions predicated upon a bona fide seniority system, as long as the seniority or merit system was not intended to discriminate. In *International Brotherhood of Teamsters v. United States,* 431 U.S. 324 (1977), the Government alleged that a large national motor carrier had violated Title VII by a pattern or practice of discrimination against black and Hispanic employees, and that a union had violated the Act by agreeing with the employer to maintain a seniority system that perpetuated the effects of past racial and ethnic discrimination. The Supreme Court affirmed the lower courts' decisions that a pattern or practice of discrimination had been established, but found the practice justified by the employer's bona fide seniority system. Although seniority for purposes of job assignments, layoffs, and recalls was based on time spent in a particular bargaining unit, which tended to lock minorities into their inferior jobs by discouraging transfers, the Court was persuaded that Congress had considered the effect of such a seniority system and had made provision in § 703(h) for differential credit for seniority obtained under discriminatory conditions predating the Act. The seniority system was bona fide because it applied equally to all racial and ethnic groups, and was not negotiated for any illegal purpose. Justices Marshall and Brennan dissented on the seniority issue. Applying *Griggs,* they insisted that the system operated to "freeze" the status quo of prior discrimination by awarding the choicest jobs to "those possessing a credential—seniority—which, due to past discrimination, blacks and Spanish-speaking employees were prevented from acquiring."

Subsequently, the Court held (5-4) that § 703(h) applies to protect seniority systems adopted after the effective date of the 1964 Civil Rights Act as well as those adopted earlier. *See American Tobacco Co. v. Patterson,* 456 U.S. 63 (1982). Absent proof of an actual motive to discriminate on the part of those who negotiated or maintained the system, seniority systems are bona fide. *Pullman-Standard v. Swint,* 456 U.S. 273 (1982). A cause of action arises (and the statute of limitations starts running) not only when a seniority system is adopted but also when individuals become subject to it or are injured by application of the system. *Cf. United Airlines v. Evans,* 431 U.S. 553 (1977) (finding flight attendant's Title VII claim time-barred where she was originally forced to resign under a no-marriage rule, then rehired as a new employee without seniority for her past service after the discriminatory rule was eliminated; the fact that males hired in the interim had more seniority despite their lesser total service did not constitute discrimination, since "this disparity was not a consequence of sex," and concluding that although the seniority system gave present effect to a past act of discrimination, "mere continuity" of the seniority system's impact was not enough to ground a claim where no present *violation* existed).

g. Affirmative Action Programs

Does Title VII operate to bar race conscious actions by unions and employers that are designed to redress the lingering effects of discrimination? "Affirmative action" programs for the benefit of minorities and women in recruitment, training, hiring, promotion, etc., may have various origins. For example, they may be undertaken voluntarily by unions or employers, or imposed pursuant to Executive Order 11246 (prohibiting employment discrimination by government contractors and requiring affirmative action to ensure appropriate representation of women and minorities as a condition for obtaining a government contract), or mandated by a court order as a remedy for a specific statutory violation.

(1) *Voluntary programs:* In *United Steelworkers v. Weber,* 443 U.S. 193 (1979), the Supreme Court upheld an affirmative action plan—collectively bargained by an employer and a union—that reserved for black employees 50 percent of the openings in an in-plant craft training program until the percentage of black craft workers in the plant was commensurate with the percentage of blacks in the local labor force. The Court reasoned:

It would be ironic indeed if a law triggered by a Nation's concern over centuries of racial injustice and intended to improve the lot of those who had "been excluded from the American dream for so long," 110 Cong. Rec., at 6552 (remarks of Sen. Humphrey), constituted the first legislative prohibition of all voluntary, private, race-conscious efforts to abolish traditional patterns of racial segregation and hierarchy.

Although the Court refused to define with precision the line of demarcation between permissible and impermissible affirmative action plans, it observed that the challenged Kaiser-USWA affirmative action plan fell on the permissible side of the line because the purposes of the plan mirrored those of the statute: "to break down old patterns of racial segregation and hierarchy," and to "open employment opportunities for Negroes in occupations which have been traditionally closed to them." Additionally, the plan did not unnecessarily trammel the interests of the white employees, for example by requiring the discharge of white workers and their replacement with new black hires. Nor did the plan create an absolute bar to the advancement of white employees. Finally, the plan was a temporary measure, not intended to maintain racial balance, but simply to eliminate a manifest racial imbalance.

Dissenting, Justice Rehnquist wrote:

In passing Title VII Congress outlawed *all* racial discrimination, recognizing that no discrimination based on race is benign, that no action disadvantaging a person because of his color is affirmative. With today's holding, the Court introduces into Title VII a tolerance for the very evil that the law was intended to eradicate, without offering even a clue as to what the limits on that tolerance may be. We are told simply that Kaiser's racially discriminatory admission quota "falls on the permissible side of the line." By going not merely *beyond,* but directly *against* Title VII's language and legislative history, the Court has sown the wind. Later courts will face the impossible task of reaping the whirlwind.

In *Johnson v. Santa Clara County Transp. Agency,* 480 U.S. 616 (1987), the Court sustained against a Title VII challenge a voluntary affirmative action plan adopted by a public employer. The plan authorized the consideration of ethnicity and sex in evaluating qualified candidates for jobs in which minorities and women were poorly represented. The Court found the *Weber* test applicable and satisfied: there was a "manifest imbalance" that reflected underrepresentation of women in "traditionally segregated job categories." Sex could be taken into account as one factor in a "moderate, flexible, case-by-case approach to effecting a gradual improvement in the representation of minorities and women." *Cf. Taxman v. Piscataway Bd. of Educ.,* 91 F.3d 1547 (3d Cir. 1996), *cert. petition dismissed as moot,* 118 S. Ct. 595 (1997) (use of "racial diversity" as a tie-breaking factor in layoff decisions which resulted in layoff of a white teacher violated Title VII).

Section 116 of the 1991 Civil Rights Act provides that nothing in its amendments should "affect court-ordered remedies, affirmative action, or conciliation agreements, that are in accordance with the law."

(2) *Imposed by Executive Order 11246:* In *Adarand Constr. Inc. v. Pena,* 515 U.S. 200 (1995), the Court applied a strict scrutiny analysis to assess the constitutionality of federally-encouraged racial preferences for subcontractors employed on federally funded construction projects. Racial classifications—even "benign" classifications designed to enhance rather than restrict opportunities available to minorities—imposed by federal, state, or local government actors are thus constitutional only if they are "narrowly tailored measures that further compelling governmental interests." *Adarand* raises serious questions about the continuing validity of programs instituted pursuant to Executive Order 11246. *Cf. Contractors Ass'n of Eastern Pennsylvania v. Shultz,* 442 F. 2d 159 (3d Cir.), *cert. denied,* 404 U.S. 854 (1971) (upholding affirmative action plan implemented by federal contractors under Executive Order 11246 against constitutional attack and finding the plan neither violative of Title VII nor inconsistent with the NLRA).

(3) *Mandated by Court Order as a Remedy for a Violation:* In the situation of a proven violation, most courts of appeals were initially prepared to require "quota" hiring or similar numerically oriented remedial action. But in *Firefighters Local 1784 v. Stotts,* 467 U.S. 561 (1984), which involved the attempted modification of a seniority system to avoid black layoffs, a majority of the Supreme Court indicated that § 706(g) of the CRA limits court-ordered make-whole relief to the actual victims of illegal discrimination. Then, two years later, a 5-4 majority of the Court concluded that § 706(g) did not prevent a court from setting certain nonwhite membership percentage goals in a union as a remedy for "pervasive and egregious" discrimination, even though nonvictims would benefit. *Sheet Metal Workers Local 28 v. EEOC,* 478 U.S. 421 (1986). *See also United States v. Paradise,* 480 U.S. 149 (1987) (upholding by 5-to-4 a one-for-one promotion "quota" for black troopers in the state police against an equal protection challenge under the Constitution; the proven discrimination was described as "blatant and continuous," and "pervasive, systematic, and obstinate").

2. THE AGE DISCRIMINATION IN EMPLOYMENT ACT (ADEA)

The ADEA was enacted in 1967, and prohibits discrimination in employment on the basis of age. The heart of the prohibition against discrimination is contained in § 4(a), and it is parallel to the Title VII prohibition except for the substitution of the word "age" as the prohibited basis of discrimination. The covered class of employees protected under this statute is limited to those who are 40 years of age or older (§ 12 (a)). There is no action for reverse age discrimination against the young (unlike the reverse sex and race discrimination claims available under Title VII). However, if a person in the protected class is replaced with another person in the same class (e.g., 56-year-old replaced by 40-year-old) an action will lie, at least if the replacement is "substantially younger" and the plaintiff can demonstrate that the reason for his loss of employment is because of his age. *O'Connor v. Consolidated Coin Caterers Corp.*, 517 U.S. 308 (1996). In addition, the Older Workers Benefit Protection Act, Pub. L. 101-433, 104 Stat. 978 (1990) prohibits age discrimination with respect to employee benefit plans.

Employers with 20 or more workers, engaged in industries affecting interstate commerce, state and local political divisions, the federal government, employment agencies, and unions are covered under the ADEA. As with Title VII, the EEOC is the enforcing agency. Remedies are similar to those available under Title VII except that the ADEA does not allow pain and suffering damages, but does allow double damages as liquidated damages when a defendant has willfully violated the Act. Jury trial is available.

a. Theories of Liability

Disparate treatment is available in all circuits, and it proceeds along the same analytical path as Title VII cases in terms of elements, proof and the shifting of burdens. In *Hazen Paper Co. v. Biggins,* 507 U.S. 604 (1993), where intentional discrimination was alleged under the Age Discrimination in Employment Act (ADEA), a majority of the Supreme Court suggested in dictum that the disparate impact model of *Griggs* may not apply under ADEA. The Courts of Appeals are split on the question whether the ADEA will support claims of disparate impact. The theory has been accepted in the 2nd, 8th, and 9th Circuits, but rejected in the 3rd, 4th, 7th, 10th, and D.C. Circuits. *Compare Ellis v. United Airlines,* 73 F.3d 999 (10th Cir.), *cert. denied,* 517 U.S. 1245 (1996), and cases cited therein *with Smith v. City of Des Moines,* 99 F.3d 1466 (8th Cir. 1996) *and Mangold v. California Pub. Utilities Comm'n,* 67 F.3d 1470, 1474 (9th Cir. 1995).

b. Defenses

Defenses are parallel to those available under Title VII, including the bona fide seniority system defense (i.e. where the employer has complied with the terms of a bona fide seniority system or employee benefit plan that is not being used to involuntarily retire an employee because of age). The BFOQ defense is treated similarly, allowed only if the employer can show that age is a BFOQ reasonably necessary to the normal operation of the particular business. Stereotyped assumptions will not suffice (e.g. a job cannot be restricted to younger workers because it requires long hours or heavy work, or because older workers are presumed to be rigid or inflexible). Considerations of public safety are often compelling to courts, however, if the employer can show that some members of the age-defined group cannot perform the job safely and efficiently (e.g. airline pilots). *Compare Usery v. Tamiami Trail Tours, Inc.,* 531 F.2d 224 (5th Cir. 1976) (age upheld as BFOQ for intercity bus drivers) *with Houghton v. McDonnell Douglas Corp.,* 553 F.2d 561 (8th Cir.), *cert. denied,* 434 U.S. 966 (1977) (age not upheld as BFOQ for test pilots). *See also Western Air Lines v. Criswell,* 472 U.S. 400 (1985).

Cost-cutting justifications for terminating older employees are acceptable non-discriminatory reasons for termination, but only if the employer can show that its action was not a pretext for age discrimination. In *Hazen Paper Co. v. Biggins,* 507 U.S. 604 (1993), the Supreme Court held that an employer does not violate ADEA simply by firing an older worker to prevent his pension benefits from vesting on the basis of years of service. Age and years of service are analytically distinct in a disparate treatment case.

3. THE AMERICANS WITH DISABILITIES ACT (ADA)

The Americans with Disabilities Act of 1990, 42 U.S.C. § 12101 *et seq.,* prohibits discrimination in employment against qualified individuals because of their physical or mental disabilities. Employers are obliged to make reasonable accommodations for disabilities when that can be accomplished without undue hardship to the operation of the business. The ADA mirrors the Rehabilitation Act of 1973, which applies to federal departments, agencies, and other executive instrumentalities. The ADA expands the antidiscrimination concept expressed in the Rehabilitation Act into the private sector. The antidiscrimination provisions of the ADA applicable to employment (Title I) took effect in July 1992 for private sector employers with 25 or more employees; and in July 1994 became applicable to employers with 15 or more employees (the same as Title VII). The ADA also applies to labor unions, state and local government employers, and the U.S. Congress; federal employees remain covered by the Rehabilitation Act. The ADA is enforced through the EEOC utilizing the procedures set forth in Title VII. Compensatory and punitive damages may be awarded under 42 U.S.C. § 1981A, subject to the same limitations as those applicable to Title VII. In addition, damages may not be awarded to an employer who has endeavored in good faith to achieve a reasonable accommodation for the disabled worker. Remedies are the same as those available under Title VII.

The ADA prohibits discrimination in employment (job application procedures, hiring, advancement, discharge, compensation, job training, and other terms, conditions, and privileges of employment) against a "qualified individual" with a "disability," because of the disability (§ 102(a)). Discrimination is defined to include "not making reasonable accommodations to the known physical or mental limitations of an otherwise qualified individual with a disability," unless "the accommodation would impose an undue hardship on the operation of the business." (§ 102(b)(5)(A)). Both intentional and unintentional discrimination are prohibited. *See Alexander v. Choate,* 469 U.S. 287 (1985). Preemployment medical examinations and questionnaires are prohibited with regard to the existence, nature or severity of a covered impairment, although the employer may ask whether the applicant is able to perform essential job-related functions (climb a telephone pole, drive a truck, etc.). Following a conditional offer of employment, the employer may require a pre-placement medical examination or completion of a questionnaire, as long as it is job-related and consistent with business necessity and given to all entering employees in the same job category (§ 102 (d)).

"Disability" means (1) a physical or mental impairment that substantially limits one or more major life activities of the individual, or (2) a person who has a record of such an impairment, or (3) a person who is regarded as having such an impairment (§ 3(2)). Homosexuality, bisexuality, and certain behavioral disorders are explicitly excluded from this definition. The existence of an impairment is to be determined without regard to mitigating measures such as medicines, or assistive or prosthetic devices (e.g., an epileptic whose condition is completely controlled by medication is still considered to have an impairment). Employees or applicants who are currently engaging in the illegal use of drugs are *not* covered; drug addicts who are not currently using drugs and have been rehabilitated or are currently in rehabilitation *are* covered (§ 104). Impairment does include persons who have asymptomatic HIV infection but who have not yet developed full-blown AIDS. *Bragdon v. Abbott*, 118 S. Ct. 2196 (1998). Impairment does not include characteristics such as left-handedness, height, or weight if they are within "normal" range and are not the result of a physiological disorder—i.e., minor impairments, *see Roth v. Lutheran General Hospital,* 57 F.3d 1446 (7th Cir. 1995) (strabismus); nor does it include temporary impairments, *see Rogers v. International Marine Terminals, Inc.,* 87 F.3d 755 (5th Cir. 1996) (ankle injury); nor does it include common personality traits such as poor judgment or a quick temper where these are not symptoms of a mental or psychological disorder, *see Greenberg v. New York State,* 919 F. Supp. 637 (E.D.N.Y. 1996) (inability to perform under stress); advanced age and pregnancy (except for unusual conditions associated with pregnancy) are not impairments, *see, e.g., Wenzlaff v. NationsBank,* 940 F. Supp. 889 (D. Md. 1996). Alcoholism *is* an impairment. However, the behavioral consequences of an impairment that affect job performance may not be covered (e.g., drunk driving on the job, tardiness due to depression, etc.)

"Major life activities" include caring for oneself, walking, seeing, hearing, speaking, breathing, learning, working, and reproduction. The breadth of this list, and the fact that it is not exhaustive, partially explain the extensive litigation under the ADA so far on what constitutes a covered impairment.

"Substantially limits" refers to the impact of the impairment on one or more major life activities, which impact must be long term or permanent in nature. The impairment must significantly restrict the duration, manner or condition under which an individual can perform a particular major life activity relative to the average person in the general population.

"Qualified individual with a disability" means an individual with a disability who, with or without reasonable accommodation, can perform the essential functions of the employment position that the individual holds or desires (§ 101(8)). "Reasonable accommodation" includes any change in the work environment or in the way things are customarily done that enables an individual with a disability to enjoy equal employment opportunities. These may include permitting the use of leave for treatment, providing reserved parking spaces, providing personal assistants (page turners, readers, travel attendants), providing equipment, aids or services, job restructuring (reallocation of nonessential job functions), reassignment to a vacant position, making the physical workplace accessible, etc. (*see* § 101(9), nonexhaustive list); *see, e.g., Vande Zande v. State of Wisconsin Dep't of Admin.,* 44 F.3d 538 (7th Cir. 1995).

"Undue hardship" means "an action requiring significant difficulty or expense," when considered in light of the nature and cost of the accommodation needed, the overall financial resources of the employer, the impact of the accommodation on the operation of its facility, and the type of operation (§ 101(10)).

4. CURRENT ISSUES REFLECTING THE TENSION BETWEEN LABOR LAW AND ANTIDISCRIMINATION LAW

The tension between majority rights protected under the labor laws and individual rights against discrimination conferred by antidiscrimination laws has often arisen in the context of race and sex discrimination that is either furthered by union practice or perpetrated by union members, albeit with the tolerance of the employer. For example, a number of recent cases involve hostile work environment sexual harassment perpetrated by male union members against their female peers. In such cases, what role should the union play? Should it adhere to its traditional role of defending the job security of accused harassers who are discharged for sexual harassment after the victims complain to the employer? *See, e.g., Ellison v. Brady,* 924 F.2d 872 (9th Cir. 1991) (union represented harasser in grievance against company for involuntary transfer following sexual harassment complaints by female coworker). If it does not do so, what are the risks? While liability under Title VII may not lie, *see Catley v. Graphic Communications Int'l Union Local 277-M,* 982 F. Supp. 1332 (E.D. Wis. 1997) (union's mere acquiescence to discriminatory conduct that is responsibility of employer does not render it liable under Title VII); *York v. AT&T Co.,* 95 F.3d 948 (10th Cir. 1996) (union's statutory duty of fair representation does not oblige it to take action on every grievance; mere inaction will not ground liability unless union had knowledge that prohibited discrimination occurred and made a decision not to assert the discrimination claim)); *but cf. Woods v. Graphic Communications Int'l Union,* 925 F.2d 1195 (9th Cir. 1991) (union may be liable for acquiescing in a racially discriminatory work environment through deliberate choice not to process grievances), are there any risks for the union in failing to take a more proactive role in attempting to mediate between the conflicting interests of its male and female members? *See Robinson v. Jacksonville Shipyards, Inc.,* 760 F. Supp. 1486 (M.D. Fla. 1991) (woman employee challenging hostile work environment was represented by the National Organization for Women's Legal Defense Fund, while the union defended the right of its male members to have pornography in the workplace, telling management that it would grieve any rule barring such pornography from the shipyards on the grounds that such a rule would burden its male members' rights to free expression; court ordered employer to implement a sexual harassment policy drafted by NOWLDF). *See generally* Crain, *Women, Labor Unions, and Hostile Work Environment Sexual Harassment: The Untold Story,* 4 Tx. J. of Women & L. 9 (1995).

Another vexing problem stemming from the tension between majority rights protected under a collective bargaining agreement and individual minority rights protected by employment discrimination statutes has arisen in the context of individual employee requests for employer accommodation under the Americans With Disabilities Act. The question in these cases is whether seniority rights guaranteed under the collective bargaining agreement trump statutorily-created individual rights. A majority of the courts that have confronted this issue have concluded that an accommodation that violates a collective bargaining agreement is *per se* unreasonable. In *Eckles v. Consol. Rail Corp.,* 94 F. 3d 1041 (7th Cir.), *cert. denied,* 117 S. Ct. 1318 (1997), the Seventh Circuit confronted the potential conflict between the ADA and the operation of collectively bargained seniority systems under the RLA. The employee had requested accommodations to his epilepsy under the ADA (a transfer and a preference in scheduling which would have entailed bumping a senior employee from the desired job) which infringed on the seniority rights of the other employees guaranteed in the collective bargaining agreement between the employer and the union. Relying on cases decided under the Rehabilitation Act of 1973 (on which the ADA was modeled), and case law dealing with the requirement of reasonable accommodation to employee religion under Title VII, the court concluded that the ADA does not require disabled employees to be accommodated by sacrificing the collectively bargained seniority rights of other employees; such seniority rights have "pre-existing special status in the law." *Accord, Benson v. Northwest Airlines, Inc.,* 62 F.3d 1108 (8th Cir. 1995); *Willis v. Pacific Maritime Ass'n,* 162 F.3d 561 (9th Cir. 1998). *See also Daugherty v. City of El Paso,* 56 F.3d 695 (5th Cir.), *cert. denied,* 116 S. Ct. 1263 (1996); *Milton v. Scrivner, Inc.,* 53 F.3d 1118 (10th Cir. 1995) (refusing to uphold individual employee requests for accommodations under the ADA where collectively bargained seniority rights would be sacrificed, but stopping short of adopting a *per se* rule). *But cf. Aka v. Washington Hospital Center,* 116 F.3d 876 (D.C. Cir.) (ruling that majority rights do not automatically trump the interests of the disabled; instead, the court must make an individual determination" in light of the specific nature of the requested determinations in each case, including—but not limited to—the degree to which the accommodation might disrupt the workforce by upsetting settled expectations under the collective bargaining agreement, or by undermining the operational structure instituted by the agreement."), *vacated and reh'g en banc granted,* 124 F.3d 1302 (1997), *op. reinstated in part on reh'g,* 156 F.3d 1284 (1998) (declining to rule on whether a *per se* or a balancing approach is more appropriate, and remanding for a determination whether the proposed accommodation actually conflicted with the seniority system).

For scholarly analysis of this dilemma, *see* Dealy, *Compulsory Arbitration in the Unionized Workplace: Reconciling Gilmer, Gardner-Denver and the Americans With Disabilities Act,* 37 B.C.L. Rev. 479 (1996); Dubault, *The ADA and the NLRA: Balancing Individual and Collective Rights,* 70 Ind. L.J. 1271 (1995); O'Melveny, *The Americans With Disabilities Act and Collective Bargaining Agreements: Reasonable Accommodations or Irreconcilable Conflicts?,* 82 Ky. L.J. 219 (1993-94); Schur, *Do Seniority Rights "Trump" the ADA?: Conflicts Between Collective Bargaining Agreements and the Duty to Accommodate Disabled Workers,* 7 J. Indiv. Emp. Rts. 167 (1998-99). *See generally* Bales, *The Discord Between Collective Bargaining and Individual Employment Rights: Theoretical Origins and a Proposed Solution,* 77 B.U. L. Rev. 687 (1997).

PART FIVE

INTERNAL UNION AFFAIRS

A.J. MUSTE, FACTIONAL FIGHTS IN TRADE UNIONS, in AMERICAN LABOR DYNAMICS 332-33 (J. Hardman ed. 1928)*

In the first place the trade union seeks to combine within itself two extremely divergent types of social structure, that of an army and that of a democratic town meeting. The union is a fighting instrument and exhibits always more or less definitely a tendency to take on the characteristics of armed forces and warfare in its structure and activities. There are generals, spies, military secrets, battles, armistices, treaties, breaches of diplomatic relations with the enemy and so on. The union seeks to assert in industry and over its actual and potential membership those prerogatives of a sovereign state, the right to conscript and the right to tax.

But the trade-union army elects its own generals, elects them in many instances annually or on the eve of battle. The army votes on the declaration of war and on the terms of armistice and peace. The reports of confidential agents are made to large committees, on which not infrequently the confidential agents of the enemy occupy prominent positions.

Now this situation is bound to continue indefinitely. Whatever be the manner of the warfare, the union must wage war to gain and to maintain tolerable conditions for its membership. It must develop something of the solidarity, discipline, and capacity for swift striking that an army has. On the other hand, the state and other agencies mainly concerned with the maintenance of the status quo in industry will take good care to insist that the union must remain "a purely voluntary agency" and to deprive it of the right to use instruments of coercion such as they themselves employ.

WILLIAM M. LEISERSON, AMERICAN TRADE UNION DEMOCRACY 54, 77, 79 (1959)**

If labor organizations also exercise autocratic powers over their members, then workers may merely be substituting dictatorial rule of union officials for the arbitrary authority of the employer or his managers. Does "industrial democracy" tend to maintain the traditions and liberties of American democratic government, or is it moving in the direction of what in other countries is called "people's democracy"? Increasingly, as organized labor grows in power and influence, ques-

---

*Copyright © 1928. Reprinted by permission of Harcourt Brace Jovanovich, Inc.
**Reprinted by permission of Columbia University Press, New York, New York.

tions are being asked as to the kind of democracy that is being furthered by the economic and political programs of union organizations....

In a sense we are betting on the democracy of American labor organizations. The assumption is general that democratic political institutions can hardly be maintained without free trade unions. Their primary objective, collective bargaining—now established by law as the national labor policy—is considered essential to democracy in industrial relations. If, however, the unions are not the inherently democratic organizations we assume them to be, if industrial democracy must indeed be a one-party system of democracy, then organized labor may be leading to a society marked by more authoritarianism than liberty, while it is being protected and supported as a movement essential to a fuller democracy....

But this is not the whole picture. Democratic traditions are strong in American labor unions, and their strivings for subjecting management to rules of law embodied in working agreements made jointly with representatives of employees are certainly in line with these traditions. Basic democratic rights, such as equal application of laws, equality of opportunity, and individual freedom make it necessary that those who have economic or other power to oppress shall be restrained to enlarge the liberties of those who are disadvantaged. When employers are free to run their industries as they please, employees are not free in their workplaces. Forcing managements to bargain with unions chosen by employees places limits on their freedom in order that workers shall have freedom to a voice in making the shop rules that govern them. Thus is liberty enlarged and balanced. It may well be that the restrictions which union governments impose on the liberties of their members and on nonunionists will work out to provide greater freedom for all employees.

———

Organizing employees and representing them in collective bargaining have traditionally been the primary functions of labor unions, and unions, as institutions, have been built up around these functions. Like other institutions, however, labor organizations tend to develop both external and internal relationships and problems which, while necessarily colored by their main functions, are nevertheless distinct. These relationships and problems form the subject matter of Part Five. We look here at the union as a "going concern," and our aim is to trace the law applicable to the institutional phases of unionism. For a thoughtful challenge to conventional historiography, *see* Forbath, *The Shaping of the American Labor Movement,* 102 Harv. L. Rev. 1109 (1989).

A more or less consistent general pattern of development emerges. In the earlier days of the labor movement the law took a largely "hands-off" position; legislatures were unconcerned, and the courts interfered in union affairs as little as possible. The often iterated dogma were these: the union is not a legal entity and can therefore neither sue nor be sued in its common name; property may not be held by the union as an entity separate from its members; disputes between unions and their members are ordinarily best left to settlement within the union structure; exhaustion of intraunion remedies must precede resort to the courts.

Before long, however, most of these common-law doctrines were well peppered with exceptions, or, in some instances, discarded entirely. The courts began to see that the growth of unions in numbers and power made anomalous a view which would classify them with social and benevolent societies and fraternal organizations, and which would consider their affairs as of little public concern. Then came the labor relations acts, which established the broad right of a union selected by the majority of employees in a bargaining unit to represent all employees in the unit, whether or not they belong to the union. This enlargement of power more than any other circumstance has tended to focus attention upon the subject of union responsibilities and duties.

Pressure for legislation came to a head as the result of the disclosures of the McClellan Committee from 1957 to 1959, and Congress took a long step toward comprehensive regulation of internal union affairs in the enactment of the Labor-Management Reporting and Disclosure Act in 1959. We shall examine this labor reform legislation against the background of the common law and the labor relations acts.

SECTION I. The Legal Status of Unions

A. THE LEGAL BASIS FOR JUDICIAL INTERVENTION IN THE INTERNAL AFFAIRS OF UNIONS

Even though historically labor unions have been considered voluntary associations, theoretically putting them in the same category as churches and fraternal groups, the labor unions of today both in structure and function bear little resemblance to these other voluntary associations. Nevertheless, a traditional reluctance to interfere still remains an underlying attitude in the minds of judges. They have, however, recognized the necessity of judicial intervention in internal union affairs to protect the rights of union members.

The courts show a continuing preoccupation with the legal nature of the action in discipline cases. About sixty years ago Professor Zechariah Chafee analyzed three possibilities and emphasized one as the proper basis of suit: (1) the action sounds in contract, the constitution and bylaws of a union being in effect a contract between the organization and its members; (2) the action is one for the protection of property rights (in union funds, in one's job, etc.); and (3) the one favored by Professor Chafee—a complaint of wrongful discipline is a tort action, and the rights to be protected are the status of the member in the union and his right to work. Chafee, *The Internal Affairs of Associations Not for Profit*, 43 Harv. L. Rev. 993, 1001-07 (1930). *See also* Summers, *Legal Limitations on Union Discipline*, 64 Harv. L. Rev. 1049, 1050-58 (1951); Summers, *The Law of*

Union Discipline: What the Courts Do in Fact, 70 Yale L.J. 175 (1960); Comment, *The Union Judgment Rule,* 54 U. Chi. L. Rev. 980 (1987).

Despite Professor Chafee's contrary view, most of the recent cases seem to assume that the action is in contract. A wrongful expulsion or discipline is viewed as a breach of the union's implied promise to maintain the member's standing as long as he or she respects valid union rules. Illustrative decisions are *Polin v. Kaplan,* 257 N.Y. 277, 177 N.E. 833 (1931), from New York, *Cason v. Glass Bottle Blowers Ass'n,* 37 Cal. 2d 134, 231 P.2d 6 (1951), from California, and *Int'l Printing Pressmen v. Smith,* 145 Tex. 399, 198 S.W.2d 729 (1946), from Texas. The last-cited decision, besides going extensively into the reasons why the case sounds in contract, shows that the issue is not without practical importance. Since there had been a lapse of more than two years but less than four in the bringing of the action, the suit would have been barred if classified as a tort action, but not if classified as a contract action based on a written instrument. For an indication that Professor Chafee's tort theory still retains some vitality, however, *see Hurwitz v. Directors Guild,* 364 F.2d 67 (2d Cir. 1966), *cert. denied,* 385 U.S. 971 (1966) (broad non-Communist oath an unreasonable requirement for continued membership).

In *Machinists v. Gonzales,* 356 U.S. 617, 618 (1958), the United States Supreme Court had this to say:

> The crux of the claim sustained by the California court was that under California law membership in a labor union constitutes a contract between the member and the union, the terms of which are governed by the constitution and by-laws of the union, and that state law provides, through mandatory reinstatement and damages, a remedy for breach of such contract through wrongful expulsion. This contractual conception of the relation between a member and his union widely prevails in this country and has recently been adopted by the House of Lords in *Bonsor v. Musicians' Union,* [1956] A.C. 104. It has been the law of California for at least half a century.

The possibility that the federal courts will become major adjudicators of members' rights under union constitutions was opened up in *Plumbers v. Plumbers Local 334,* 452 U.S. 615 (1981). *See also Rubber Workers Local 1075 v. Rubber Workers,* 716 F.2d 182 (3d Cir. 1983); *ILA Local 1516 v. ILA,* 815 F.2d 637 (11th Cir. 1987). Previously it had been held that a union constitution was not a "contract" under § 301 so as to ground jurisdiction in a purely internal dispute between a member and his organization. *Hotel & Restaurant Employees Local 400 v. Svacek,* 431 F.2d 705 (9th Cir. 1970). In *Plumbers* the Supreme Court held that a local could sue its international under § 301 for allegedly violating the union constitution by forcing several locals to consolidate. In *Woodell v. IBEW Local 71,* 502 U.S. 93 (1991), the Court ruled further that a union member could sue his local and its officers under § 301 on the basis of the international constitution as a "contract ... between ... labor organizations." *See also Shea v.*

McCarthy, 953 F.2d 29 (2d Cir. 1992) (equitable action against union and its officers under § 301).

Leading decisions propounding the property theory of union members' rights include *Heasley v. Operative Plasterers,* 324 Pa. 257, 188 A. 206 (1936), from Pennsylvania, and *Crossen v. Duffy, 90 Ohio App. 252, 103 N.E.2d 769 (1951), from Ohio. In Bires v. Barney,* 203 Or. 107, 277 P.2d 751 (1954), where the suspension of members and officers of a local union by a parent union did not sever their membership in the union but merely deprived them of the right to visit lodges, the Oregon courts refused to intervene when the suspended members and officers sued for reinstatement, on the ground no property rights were jeopardized.

One of the recommendations of the McClellan Committee in 1958, as the result of its investigations into improper practices involving unions, was that measures should be taken to encourage more "democracy" in internal union affairs. The bill (S. 1555) reported out by the Senate Labor Committee in 1959 contained provisions requiring reporting and disclosure by unions to their members and regulating union elections. However, Senator McClellan introduced an amendment to the committee bill providing explicitly a "Bill of Rights" for members of labor organizations, and this was adopted, with modifications, becoming Title I of the Labor-Management Reporting and Disclosure Act of 1959 (reproduced in *Selected Federal Statutes*). Most noteworthy in this Act is the emphasis, not upon contract and property rights, but upon the analogy between the rights of union members and the rights of citizens in a political democracy, protected by constitutional freedoms. The dominant idea in the Eighty-Sixth Congress was that labor unions are of such great public importance that legislation to protect union members in the exercise of basic liberties in the democratic process is essential—a far cry indeed from the concept of a labor union as a private voluntary association like a social club.

The various rights guaranteed by Title I of the LMRDA will be treated in detail later in this Part.

B. SUITS BY AND AGAINST UNIONS

Judge-made law—the "pure" common law—holds as a general rule that those unions which are voluntary, unincorporated associations have no legal being apart from their members, and may therefore neither sue nor be sued in their common names. The relatively few unions which are incorporated have, of course, the same legal status as other corporations. *See, e.g., Faultless Caster Corp. v. UEW-CIO,* 119 Ind. App. 330, 86 N.E.2d 703 (1949). The statutory situation, however, both state and federal, is different. Although limited by its terms to suits by and against unions for violations of collective agreements, § 301 of the LMRA aptly represents the current statutory trend toward recognizing even unincorporated labor unions as legal entities. A further measure of the development of the law in this respect may be gathered from a statement by the National Labor Relations Board: "The common law concept of an unincorporated labor organization as a group of individuals having no separate entity apart from its members has been discarded—to the extent that it was not already outmoded in modern jurisprudence—by the Labor Management Relations Act, 1947. It is clear that the Act treats labor organizations, for all practical purposes, as juridical entities." *Longshoremen's Union,* 79 N.L.R.B. 1487 (1948). *See also Freight Drivers Local 600 v. Gordon Transps., Inc.,* 576 F.2d 1285 (8th Cir.), *cert. denied,* 439 U.S. 1002 (1978) (local union is "person" entitled to file under § 4(a) of the Bankruptcy Act).

The "strict" common-law view on the suability of unions applies both at law (*e.g., Walker v. Brotherhood of Locomotive Eng'rs,* 186 Ga. 811, 190 S.E. 146 (1938); *Pickett v. Walsh,* 192 Mass. 572, 78 N.E. 753 (1906); the authorities are gathered in Annot., 27 A.L.R. 786 (1923), and Annot., 149 A.L.R. 508 (1944)) and in equity. *Forest City Mfg. Co. v. ILGWU, Local 104,* 233 Mo. App. 935, 111 S.W.2d 934 (1938). Nonetheless, many courts have maneuvered around the rule by using such devices as the class or representative action to permit suits in equity by and against unions. *Smith v. Arkansas Motor Freight Lines,* 214 Ark. 553, 217 S.W.2d 249 (1949); *Donahue v. Kenney,* 327 Mass. 409, 99 N.E.2d 155 (1951). Statutes in about half the states specifically provide for class or representative actions. *See* Sellers, *Suability of Trade Unions as a Legal Entity,* 33 Calif. L. Rev. 444, 447 (1945). On the question whether such statutes permit actions at law for damages, as well as suits in equity, *see Jackson v. International Oper. Eng'rs,* 307 Ky. 485, 211 S.W.2d 138 (1948), and cases cited. An "estoppel" theory has also been invoked to hold a union subject to suit by its members for wrongful expulsion. *Nissen v. International Bhd. of Teamsters,* 229 Iowa 1028, 295 N.W. 858 (1941). These roundabout approaches of the state courts were eschewed by the United States Supreme Court in *United Mine Workers v. Coronado Coal Co.,* 259 U.S. 344 (1922). After pointing out the practical acceptance of labor unions as entities separate from their members, and the existence of a considerable body of federal legislation recognizing unions for various legal purposes, the Court met the issue head-on and declared: "In this state of federal legislation, we think that such organizations are suable in the federal courts...." This bold action by the Supreme Court did not affect the states' common law rules, but it did succeed in establishing a different rule for the federal courts. *See also* Dodd, *Dogma and Practice in the Law of Associations,* 42 Harv. L. Rev. 977 (1929); Sturges, *Unincorporated Associations as Parties to Actions,* 33 Yale L.J. 383 (1924); Note, *Unions as Juridical Persons,* 66 Yale L.J. 712 (1957).

Apart from § 301 of the LMRA, the federal provision bearing most directly on suability is Rule 17(b) of the Federal Rules of Civil Procedure. "[C]apacity to sue or be sued," this rule provides, "shall be determined by the law of the state in which the district court is held; except that a partnership or other unincorporated association, which has no such capacity by the law of such state, may sue or be sued in its common name for the purpose of enforcing for or against it a substantive right existing under the Constitution or laws of the United States."

State laws on "suability" vary considerably. Some, like New York, permit an action by or against designated officers of an association in their representative capacity. N.Y. Gen. Ass'ns Law §§ 12, 13 (McKinney 1942, Supp. 1988). Others—California, for example—provide for suit in the name which an unincorporated association has assumed. Cal. Civ. Pro. Code § 388 (Deering 1972). A few states, such as Florida, have made unions legal entities, at least for purposes of suit, by express statutory provision. Fla. Stat. Ann. § 447.11 (1984).

As has already been seen, § 301 of the LMRA enables unions to sue or be sued as legal entities in the federal courts for breach of union-employer contracts, regardless of diversity of citizenship or the amount in controversy. Section 303 also provides that unions may be sued as entities by persons injured by such conduct as secondary boycotts or jurisdictional strikes. The NLRB is empowered by § 10(c) of the NLRA to require back pay of labor organizations responsible for discrimination against individual employees. Another instance of congressional treatment of unions as legal entities is § 102 of the Labor-Management Reporting and Disclosure Act of 1959, which provides for private suits in federal court to enforce the "Bill of Rights" of union members.

Despite the *Coronado* decision, the Supreme Court unanimously held in *United Steelworkers v. R.H. Bouligny, Inc.*, 382 U.S. 145 (1965), that unions are not entities to the extent of possessing "citizenship" sufficient to support federal diversity jurisdiction, without regard to the citizenship of their members. Lower federal courts have ruled that a union has the citizenship of all its members. *Underwood v. Maloney*, 256 F.2d 334 (3d Cir. 1958), *cert. denied*, 358 U.S. 864 (1958); *Lloyd A. Fry Roofing Co. v. Textile Workers*, 152 F. Supp. 19 (E.D. Pa. 1957). *See also* Cohn, *Problems in Establishing Federal Jurisdiction Over an Unincorporated Labor Union*, 47 Geo. L.J. 491, 509 (1959).

Whether a union can be sued in its common name is only part of the problem of union suability. How is service of process to be effected? From what persons or funds may a money judgment be collected? How is individual or organizational responsibility established? The answers are somewhat analogous to (and as variable as) the answers concerning "suability"—with the common law and the current statutory situation providing the main contrasts, and with the rules of the *Coronado* case falling somewhere in between.

SECTION II. The Civil Liberties of Members

S. LIPSET, M. TROW & J. COLEMAN, UNION DEMOCRACY: THE INTERNAL POLITICS OF THE INTERNATIONAL TYPOGRAPHICAL UNION 347 (1956, 1962)

It is likely that industrial unions must be dictatorial if they are to survive. The dictator is necessary to arbitrate interest conflicts which can not be settled by simply counting which interest group has more members.... [T]he minority crafts in the late-nineteenth-century ITU seceded because they felt that they could not get the ITU to fight their battles. As a general proposition, we may assert that one of the necessary conditions for a sustained democratic political system in an occupational group is that it be so homogeneous that only ideology and not the more potent spur of self-interest divides its members. It is an important property of the ITU's political system that in those "foreign policy" areas where the most important questions are raised, the self-interest of the members is rarely involved, and relatively altruistic ideological commitments dominate political conflict.

ARCHIBALD COX, INTERNAL AFFAIRS OF LABOR UNIONS UNDER THE LABOR REFORM ACT OF 1959, 58 Mich. L. Rev. 819, 830 (1960)

An autocratic union may serve the material demands of its members by bargaining effectively for higher wages and increased benefits. It may establish a measure of job security. None except a democratic union, however, can achieve the idealistic aspirations which justify labor organizations. Collective bargaining may limit the employer's power by substituting a negotiated agreement for arbitrary tyranny of the boss, but it scarcely extends the rule of law to substitute an autocratic union. Only in a democratic union can workers, through chosen representatives, participate jointly with management in the government of their industrial lives even as all of us may participate, through elected representatives, in political government.

CLYDE W. SUMMERS, THE IMPACT OF LANDRUM-GRIFFIN IN STATE COURTS, in N.Y.U. THIRTEENTH ANNUAL CONFERENCE ON LABOR 333, 335 (1960)

All of the elaborate arguments that union democracy was unnecessary, unworkable, or even unfortunate have been deliberately rejected. Financial integrity is not enough; the decisions as to dues and expenditures must be democratically made. Officers must be more than honest and responsible; they must be chosen by the members in an open election after free debate. Union members are guaranteed equal rights, freedom of speech and assembly, and due process within the union. Although the statute leaves undefined the exact amount of individual right to be protected, and cannot guarantee the full realization of the democratic process, the policy thrust of the statute is clear and strong. The public has an interest in union democracy.

THE NEW YORK TIMES, August 29, 1966, at 38, col. 4

The Federal Government's chief mediator has predicted that the public can expect more difficult labor disputes in the future....

William E. Simkin, director of the Mediation and Conciliation Service, [stated his belief] ... in a report on his agency's activities for the fiscal year ended June 30, 1966 ... that there is major significance in the growth of rank-and-file revolt against contracts negotiated by union leaders.

Mr. Simkin gives "some credence to the fears of union leaders" that Congress, in passing the Landrum-Griffin Act "to restore more democracy to unionism and curb bossism went too far in the other direction of encouraging rebel movements."

As often as not, in Mr. Simkin's opinion, "pure and simple habit" prompts rank-and-file rejection of negotiated contracts because they feel that by turning down offers "they will eventually get something better."

A. THE RIGHT OF ADMISSION

Mayer v. Journeymen Stonecutters' Ass'n, 47 N.J. Eq. 519, 20 A. 492 (1890). This was a suit brought by two journeymen stonecutters and a group of master stonecutters who employed journeymen. Defendant stonecutters' association controlled most employment opportunities in the relevant area. It implemented its position, as the court put it, "by denunciations and persecution applied to the offending workmen," who sought jobs without membership, "and boycotting and strikes applied to the offending employers." Complainants asked the court to require the association to admit to membership the complaining journeymen, as well as all other journeymen in the area. *Held,* relief denied. In so ruling, the court pointed out that there was no showing of a proper request by complainant journeymen for admission. But the court went on to say (47 N.J. Eq. at 523-24):

> But if it were otherwise, has this court power to require the admission of a person to membership in a voluntary association, when it has been denied by the society? These organizations are formed for purposes mutually agreed upon; their right to make by-laws and rules for the admission of members and the transaction of business is unquestionable. They may require such qualifications for membership, and such formalities of election, as they choose. They may restrict membership to the original promoters, or limit the number to be thereafter admitted. The very idea of such organizations is association mutually acceptable, or in accordance with regulations agreed upon. A power to require the admission of a person in any way ob-

jectionable to the society is repugnant to the scheme of its organization. While courts have interfered to inquire into and restrain the action of such societies in the attempted exclusion of persons who have been regularly admitted to membership, no case can, I think, be found where the power of any court has been exercised, as sought in this case, to require the admission of any person to original membership in any such voluntary association. Courts exist to protect rights, and where the right has once attached they will interfere to prevent its violation; but no person has any abstract right to be admitted to such membership. That depends solely upon the action of the society, exercised in accordance with its regulations, and, until so admitted, no right exists which the courts can be called upon to protect or enforce.

NOTE

This represents the orthodox view, predicated on the notion that a trade union is like any other voluntary association and can thus fix its own admission standards. In the context of modern developments regarding the closed and union shop, there are significant judicial and legislative trends in the direction of requiring an "open" union. Thus, for example, in *James v. Marinship Corp.*, 25 Cal. 2d 721, 155 P.2d 329 (1944), it was held in effect that a union could not exercise union shop privileges and at the same time arbitrarily deny membership or impose "second class membership." This principle is also embodied (at least as to each individual employee) in §§ 8(a)(3) and 8(b)(2) of the NLRA and in § 2, Eleventh of the RLA. *See generally* Summers, *The Right to Join a Union,* 47 Colum. L. Rev. 33 (1947); Blumrosen, *Legal Protection Against Exclusion From Union Activities,* 22 Ohio St. L.J. 21 (1961); Lang, *Toward a Right to Union Membership,* 12 Harv. C.R.-C.L.L. Rev. 31 (1977).

———————

Directors Guild of America, Inc. v. Superior Court of Los Angeles County, 64 Cal. 2d 42, 409 P.2d 934 (1966). Plaintiff had been assured employment as an assistant director in a television series. He sought admission to defendant union, which allegedly controlled production jobs in the industry through oral agreements with many producers. Although plaintiff tendered the requisite dues and fees and fulfilled the formal membership requirements, he was refused admission pursuant to the union's nepotism policy. The court declined relief on the ground that the "crux" of plaintiff's action was job discrimination, not denial of union membership, and that federal law thus preempted. But a state remedy would have been appropriate if plaintiff had actually been employed and had then been arbitrarily refused membership, thereby making the dispute focus on purely internal union matters. Reasoned the court (64 Cal. 2d at 52-54):

The decisions of this court thus recognize that membership in the union means more than mere personal or social accommodation. Such membership affords to the employee not only the opportunity to participate in the negotiation of the contract governing his employment but also the chance to engage in the institutional life of the union. Although in the case which involves interstate commerce the union must legally give fair representation to all the appropriate employees, whether or not they are members of the union, the union official, in the nature of political realities, will in all likelihood more diligently represent union members, who can vote him out of office, than employees whom he must serve only as a matter of abstract law.

Our decisions further recognize that the union functions as the medium for the exercise of industrial franchise. As Summers puts it, "The right to join a union involves the right to an economic ballot." (*The Right to Join a Union* (1947) 47 Colum. L. Rev. 33.) Participation in the union's affairs by the workman compares to the participation of the citizen in the affairs of his community. The union, as a kind of public service institution, affords to its members the opportunity to record themselves upon all matters affecting their relationships with the employer; it serves likewise as a vehicle for the expression of the membership's position on political and community issues. The shadowy right to "fair representation" by the union, accorded by the Act, is by no means the same as the hard concrete ability to vote and to participate in the affairs of the union.

The above grounds for condemnation of arbitrary rejection from membership apply as forcefully to the situation in which the union does not have a union shop contract as to that in which it does. The need of the worker for union participation is not reduced because the union does not enjoy a union shop; the basis for membership lies in the right and desirability of representation, not in the union's economic control of the job.

Our analysis applies, however, only to union membership for those employed in the appropriate craft or industry. To hold that a union must admit *all* persons who seek membership but are not employed in the craft or industry whose employees are represented by the union would raise serious social and economic questions. Any such sweeping ruling would subject the union to an influx of unemployed persons who could distort its function from representation of those working in the relevant craft or industry to purposes alien to such objectives. It would set up for state courts a test as to the scope of the union's obligation of representation which would conflict with the National Labor Relation Board's counterpart concept of the appropriate bargaining unit. It could gravely affect the basic structure of the union.

NOTE

The California view has not carried the day. In the absence of a statute regulating union membership policies, the following decision still represents the majority position on the issue.

OLIPHANT v. BROTHERHOOD OF LOCOMOTIVE FIREMEN & ENGINEMEN

United States District Court, Northern District of Ohio, Eastern Division
156 F. Supp. 89 (1957),
aff'd, 262 F.2d 359 (6th Cir. 1958), *cert. denied,* 359 U.S. 935 (1959)

JONES, CHIEF JUDGE. This is an action brought by several Negro firemen employed by various southern railroads seeking an order from this court compelling the Brotherhood of Locomotive Firemen and Enginemen to admit them to membership. The Brotherhood has been certified as exclusive bargaining representative for these men, but the constitution of the Brotherhood forbids the admission of Negroes to membership....

The real question is whether Federal action has deprived these Negro citizens of liberty or property without due process of law. It is the considered judgment of this court, without dealing with the question of whether the alleged right to become a member of a labor organization certified as exclusive bargaining representative is concerned with liberty or property, that sufficient Federal action is not shown to enable the courts to declare the Railway Labor Act, or any part thereof, an unconstitutional deprivation of liberty or property. The purpose of the Act was and is to promote industrial peace. Apparently the Act itself would not have been acceptable to the Congress if Negro membership in the agent had been required. In short, the representatives of all the people could not agree that any control over the membership was essential to the major purpose of the Act. However, expedience does not remove the taint of unconstitutionality, if such there be.

As is mentioned above, the Federal action taken by an agency of the Congress, was the certification of the Brotherhood of Locomotive Firemen and Enginemen as exclusive bargaining representative for the bargaining unit involved, which included persons who were not acceptable to membership under the Constitution of the Brotherhood. Actions by the Brotherhood can be attributed to the Congress only if the act of certification clothes the Brotherhood with some or all of the attributes of a Federal agency. The court is satisfied that this act is not sufficient to change the character of the organization from that of a private association to that of a governmental agency.

The court can feel that a situation is unjust and may need some remedial action, but unless upon sound equitable principles relief can be granted, the remedy does not lie with the courts.... To compel by judicial mandate membership in voluntary organizations where the Congress has knowingly and expressly permitted the bargaining agent to prescribe its own qualifications for membership would be usurping the legislative function....

Accordingly, for the reason that there is not sufficient Federal action to render the membership policies of this Brotherhood subject to judicial control, plaintiffs must be denied the relief requested....

NOTES

1. In denying the petition for certiorari in the *Oliphant* case, the Supreme Court said it was making this denial "in view of the abstract context in which the questions sought to be raised are presented by this record." For further discussion of the *Oliphant* case, *see* Wellington, *The Constitution, the Labor Union, and "Governmental Action,"* 70 Yale L.J. 345 (1961).

2. The National Labor Relations Act does not directly regulate admission to union membership. Section 8(b)(1)(A) states "this paragraph shall not impair the right of a labor organization to prescribe its own rules with respect to the acquisition or retention of membership therein." Section 8(b)(5), however, does prohibit excessive or discriminatory initiation fees by unions having union shop contracts. In addition, a proviso to § 8(a)(3) prevents enforcement of "union security" agreements against employees discriminatorily denied membership. *See* Shea, *Unions, Union Membership, and Union Security,* 11 Seton Hall Legis. J. 1 (1987).

3. Admission to union membership was not dealt with by the Labor-Management Reporting and Disclosure Act of 1959. Senator McClellan had included the following provision in his original bill (S. 1137, 86th Cong., 1st Sess. (1959)):

"Section 101(2). Eligibility for Membership.—Every person who meets the reasonable qualifications uniformly prescribed by a labor organization for membership therein shall be eligible for and admitted to membership in such organization...."

This provision was not included in the "Bill of Rights" amendment introduced by Senator McClellan and enacted, in modified form, as Title I of the LMRDA. What would have been the practical consequences of such a provision? What reasons could be given for its omission?

4. In *Betts v. Easley,* 161 Kan. 459, 169 P.2d 831 (1946), black members of a bargaining unit who, under the constitution of the union certified as their bargaining agent, were ineligible for equal membership with whites, sued to enjoin their exclusion and their segregation in separate lodges. In sustaining their cause of action the court stated:

The case here does not, under the allegations, involve denial of seniority rights, as in the *Steele* case, but it does involve a similar issue of racial discrimination. The petition alleges not only that Negro employees are denied the right to take part in such local affairs of the union as the election of officers and the fixing of dues, but are denied the right to participate in determining the position to be taken by the union, as bargaining agent for all employees, as to wages, hours, working conditions, and other such matters vitally affecting their economic welfare. Such denial is repugnant to every American concept of equality under the law. It is abhorrent both to the letter and the spirit of our fundamental charter. Never was it more important than now to reject such racial discrimination and to resist all erosions of individual liberty. The acts complained of are in violation of the Fifth Amendment.

5. Could a union deny membership to an individual who refused to take an oath disavowing support for revolutionary causes? *See Hovan v. Carpenters,* 704 F.2d 641 (1st Cir. 1983).

6. Section 703(c) of the Civil Rights Act of 1964, 42 U.S.C. § 2000e-2, forbids any labor organization having 15 or more members "to exclude or to expel from its membership, or otherwise to discriminate against, any individual because of his race, color, religion, sex, or national origin." *See generally* W. Gould, Black Workers in White Unions (1977); R. Marshall, The Negro and Organized Labor (1965); M. Sovern, Legal Restraints on Racial Discrimination in Employment (1966). *See supra* Part Four, Section IV.C.

B. GENERAL SCOPE AND COVERAGE OF THE LMRDA

Before Congress passed the Labor-Management Reporting and Disclosure Act of 1959 (the "Landrum-Griffin Act"), state courts relied on such concepts as the contract and property rights of union members to afford them a measure of protection against arbitrary action on the part of their organizations. *See generally* Summers, *Legal Limitations on Union Discipline,* 64 Harv. L. Rev. 1049 (1951); Summers, *The Law of Union Discipline: What the Courts Do in Fact,* 70 Yale L.J. 175 (1960); Witmer, *Civil Liberties and the Trade Union;* 50 Yale L.J. 621 (1941). For a skeptical appraisal, *see* Magrath, *Democracy in Overalls: The Futile Quest for Union Democracy,* 12 Ind. & Lab. Rel. Rev. 503 (1959). The principles developed in these common law decisions remain highly significant, since § 603 of the LMRDA makes clear that, unlike the NLRA in the field of labor-management relations, this first major federal intervention in the area of internal union affairs leaves almost entirely intact the body of state law already in existence. *See* Summers, *Pre-emption and the Labor Reform Act—Dual Rights and Remedies,* 22 Ohio St. L.J. 119 (1961). In the pages to follow, state and federal safeguards for union members will be treated together. Because Title I (the "Bill of Rights") of the LMRDA provides a convenient and fairly comprehensive catalogue of the principal rights guaranteed union members, the breakdown made by Title I will be observed in the discussion of the various membership rights.

SHEET METAL WORKERS INTERNATIONAL ASS'N v. LYNN

Supreme Court of the United States
488 U.S. 347, 109 S. Ct. 639, 102 L. Ed. 2d 700 (1989)

JUSTICE MARSHALL delivered the opinion of the Court.

In *Finnegan v. Leu,* 456 U.S. 431 (1982), we held that the discharge of a union's appointed business agents by the union president, following his election over the incumbent for whom the business agents had campaigned, did not violate the Labor-Management Reporting and Disclosure Act of 1959.... The question presented in this case is whether the removal of an elected business agent, in retaliation for statements he made at a union meeting in opposition to a dues increase sought by the union trustee, violated the LMRDA. The Court of Appeals for the Ninth Circuit held that the LMRDA protected the business agent from removal under these circumstances. We granted certiorari to address this important issue concerning the internal governance of labor unions, and now affirm.

I

In June 1981, respondent Edward Lynn was elected to a 3-year term as a business representative of petitioner Local 75 of the Sheet Metal Workers' International Association (Local), an affiliate of petitioner Sheet Metal Workers' International Association (International). Lynn was instrumental in organizing fellow members of the Local who were concerned about a financial crisis plaguing the Local. These members, who called themselves the Sheet Metal Club Local 75 (Club), published leaflets that demonstrated, on the basis of Department of Labor statistics, that the Local's officials were spending far more than the officials of two other sheet metal locals in the area. The Club urged the Local's officials to reduce expenditures rather than increase dues in order to alleviate the Local's financial problems. A majority of the Local's members apparently agreed, for they defeated three successive proposals to increase dues.

Following the third vote, in June 1982, the Local's 17 officials, including Lynn, sent a letter to the International's General President, requesting that he "immediately take whatever action [is] ... necessary including, but not limited to, trusteeship to put this local on a sound financial basis." Invoking his authority under the International's constitution, the General President responded by placing the Local under a trusteeship and by delegating to the trustee, Richard Hawkins, the authority "to supervise and direct" the affairs of the Local, "including, but not limited to, the authority to suspend local union ... officers, business managers, or business representatives." Art. 3, § 2(c), Constitution and Ritual of the Sheet Metal Workers' International Association, Revised and Amended by Authority of the Thirty-Fifth General Convention, St. Louis, Missouri (1978).

Within a month of his appointment, Hawkins decided that a dues increase was needed to rectify the Local's financial situation. Recognizing that he lacked authority to impose a dues increase unilaterally, Hawkins prepared a proposal to that effect which he submitted to and which was approved by the Local's executive board. A special meeting was then convened to put the dues proposal to a membership vote. Prior to the meeting, Hawkins advised Lynn that he expected Lynn's support. Lynn responded that he first wanted a commitment to reduce expenditures. Which Hawkins declined to provide. Lynn thus spoke in opposition to the dues proposal at the special meeting. The proposal was defeated by the members in a secret ballot vote. Five days later, Hawkins notified Lynn that he was being removed "indefinitely" from his position as business representative specifically because of his outspoken opposition to the dues increase.

After exhausting his intraunion remedies, Lynn brought suit in District Court under § 102 of the LMRDA, claiming *inter alia* that his removal from office violated § 101(a)(2), the free speech provision of Title I of the LMRDA. The District Court granted summary judgment for petitioners, reasoning that, under *Finnegan v. Leu, supra,* "[a] union member's statutory right to oppose union policies affords him no protection against dismissal from employment as an agent of the union because of such opposition."

The Court of Appeals for the Ninth Circuit reversed....

II

The LMRDA "was the product of congressional concern with widespread abuses of power by union leadership." *Finnegan,* 456 U.S., at 435. The major reform bills originally introduced in the Senate, as well as the bill ultimately reported out of the Committee on Labor and Public Welfare, S. 1555, 86th Cong., 1st Sess. (1959), dealt primarily with disclosure requirements, elections, and trusteeships. The legislation that evolved into Title I of the LMRDA, the "Bill of Rights of Members of Labor Organizations," was adopted as an amendment on the Senate floor by "legislators [who] feared that the bill did not go far enough because it did not provide general protection to union members who spoke out against the union leadership." *Steelworkers v. Sadlowski,* 457 U.S. 102, 109 (1982). "[D]esigned to guarantee every member equal voting rights, rights of free speech and assembly, and a right to sue," *ibid.,* the amendment was "aimed at enlarged protection for members of unions paralleling certain rights guaranteed by the Federal Constitution." *Finnegan,* 456 U.S., at 435. In providing such protection, Congress sought to further the basic objective of the LMRDA: "ensuring that unions [are] democratically governed and responsive to the will of their memberships." *Id.,* at 436; *see also Reed v. United Transportation Union, ante,* at 325; *Sadlowski, supra,* at 112.

We considered this basic objective in *Finnegan,* where several members of a local union who had held staff positions as business agents were discharged by the local's newly elected president. The business agents had been appointed by the incumbent president and had openly supported him in his unsuccessful re-election campaign. They subsequently sought relief under § 102 of the LMRDA, claiming that discharge from their appointed positions constituted an "infringement" of their free speech and equal voting rights as guaranteed by Title I.

We held that the business agents could not establish a violation of § 102 because their claims were inconsistent with the LMRDA's "overriding objective" of democratic union governance. 456 U.S., at 441. Permitting a victorious candidate to appoint his own staff did not frustrate that objective; rather, it ensured a union's "responsiveness to the mandate of the union election." *Ibid.* We thus concluded that the LMRDA did not "restrict the freedom of an elected union leader to choose a staff whose views are compatible with his own." *Ibid.* In rejecting the business agents' claim, we did not consider whether the retaliatory removal of an elected official violates the LMRDA and, if so, whether it is significant that the removal is carried out under a validly imposed trusteeship. It is to these questions that we now turn.[5]

A. Petitioners argue that Lynn's Title I rights were not "infringed" for purposes of § 102 because Lynn, like other members of the Local, was not prevented from attending the special meeting, expressing his views on Hawkins' dues proposal, or casting his vote, and because he remains a member of the Local. Under this view, Lynn's status as an elected, rather than an appointed, official is essentially immaterial and the loss of union employment cannot amount to a Title I violation.

This argument is unpersuasive. In the first place, we acknowledged in *Finnegan* that the business agents' Title I rights had been interfered with, albeit indirectly, because the agents had been forced to choose between their rights and their jobs. See *id.,* at 440, 442. This was so even though the business agents were not actually prevented from exercising their Title I rights. The same is true here. Lynn was able to attend the special meeting, to express views in opposition to Hawkins' dues proposal, and to cast his vote. In taking these actions, Lynn "was exercising ... membership right[s] protected by section 101(a)." 804 F.2d, at 1479. Given that Lynn was removed from his post as a direct result of his decision to express disagreement with Hawkins' dues proposal at the special meeting, and that his removal presumably discouraged him from speaking out in the future, Lynn paid a price for the exercise of his membership rights.

This is not, of course, the end of the analysis. Whether such interference with Title I rights gives rise to a cause of action under § 102 must be judged by reference to the LMRDA's basic objective: "to ensure that unions [are] democrati-

---

[5] The business agents in Finnegan also claimed that their discharge violated § 609 of the LMRDA, which makes it unlawful for a union or its officials "to fine, suspend, expel, or otherwise discipline any of its members for exercising any right to which he is entitled under the provisions of this Act." We rejected this claim, holding that "removal from appointive union employment is not within the scope of those union sanctions explicitly prohibited by § 609." 456 U.S., at 439.

Lynn's complaint makes reference to § 609, but the Court of Appeals' analysis of his Title I claim is limited to a discussion of § 102. Lynn's § 609 claim is not before the Court, nor are the other claims rejected by the lower courts.

cally governed, and responsive to the will of the union membership as expressed in open, periodic elections." *Finnegan,* 456 U.S., at 441. In *Finnegan,* this goal was furthered when the newly elected union president discharged the appointed staff of the ousted incumbent. Indeed, the basis for the *Finnegan* holding was the recognition that the newly elected president's victory might be rendered meaningless if a disloyal staff were able to thwart the implementation of his programs. While such patronage-related discharges had some chilling effect on the free speech rights of the business agents, we found this concern outweighed by the need to vindicate the democratic choice made by the union electorate.

The consequences of the removal of an elected official are much different. To begin with, when an elected official like Lynn is removed from his post, the union members are denied the representative of their choice. Indeed, Lynn's removal deprived the membership of his leadership, knowledge and advice at a critical time for the Local. His removal, therefore, hardly was "an integral part of ensuring a union administration's responsiveness to the mandate of the union election." *Ibid.; see also Wirtz v. Hotel Employees,* 391 U.S. 492, 497 (1968).

Furthermore, the potential chilling effect on Title I free speech rights is more pronounced when elected officials are discharged. Not only is the fired official likely to be chilled in the exercise of his own free speech rights, but so are the members who voted for him. See *Hall v. Cole,* 412 U.S. 1, 8 (1973). Seeing Lynn removed from his post just five days after he led the fight to defeat yet another dues increase proposal,[6] other members of the Local may well have concluded that one challenged the union's hierarchy, if at all, at one's peril. This is precisely what Congress sought to prevent when it passed the LMRDA. "It recognized that democracy would be assured only if union members are free to discuss union policies and criticize the leadership without fear of reprisal." *Sadlowski,* 457 U.S., at 112. We thus hold that Lynn's retaliatory removal stated a cause of action under § 102.[7]

B. Petitioners next contend that, even if the removal of an elected official for the exercise of his Title I rights ordinarily states a cause of action under § 102, a different result obtains here because Lynn was removed during a trusteeship lawfully imposed under Title III of the LMRDA.

---

[6] There is no suggestion that Lynn's speech in opposition to the dues increase contravened any obligation property imposed upon him as an elected business agent of the Local.

[7] In reaching this conclusion, we reject petitioners' contention that a union official must establish that his firing was part of a systematic effort to stifle dissent within the union in order to state a claim under § 102. Although in Finnegan we noted that a § 102 claim might arise if a union official were dismissed "as 'part of a purposeful and deliberate attempt ... to suppress dissent within the union,'" 456 U.S., at 441, quoting Schonfeld v. Penza, 477 F. 2d 899, 904 (CA2 1973), we did not find that this constituted the only situation giving rise to a § 102 claim. We merely stated that we did not have such a case before us, and that we expressed no view as to its proper resolution. 456 U.S., at 441. Likewise, we explicitly reserved the question "whether a different result might obtain in a case involving nonpolicymaking and nonconfidential employees." *Id.,* at 441, n. 11.

We disagree. In the first place, we find nothing in the language of the LMRDA or its legislative history to suggest that Congress intended Title I rights to fall by the wayside whenever a trusteeship is imposed. Had Congress contemplated such a result, we would expect to find some discussion of it in the text of the LMRDA or its legislative history. Given Congress' silence on this point, a trustee's authority under Title III ordinarily should be construed in a manner consistent with the protections provided in Title I. See *McDonald* v. *Oliver,* 525 F.2d 1217, 1229 (CA5), cert. denied, 429 U.S. 817 (1976); *United Brotherhood of Carpenters & Joiners v. Brown,* 343 F.2d 872, 882-883 (CA10 1965); *Carpenters v. Dale,* 118 LRRM 3160, 3167 (CD Cal. 1985).

Whether there are any circumstances under which a trustee acting pursuant to Title III can override Title I free speech rights is a question we need not confront. Section 101(a)(3) of Title I, 29 U.S.C. § 411(a)(3), guarantees to the members of a local union the right to vote on any dues increase, and, as petitioners conceded at oral argument, this critical Title I right does not vanish with the imposition of a trusteeship. A trustee seeking to restore the financial stability of a local union through a dues increase thus is required to seek the approval of the union's members. In order to ensure that the union members' democratic right to decide on a dues proposal is meaningful, the right to exchange views on the advantages and disadvantages of such a measure must be protected. A trustee should not be able to control the debate over an issue which, by statute, is beyond his control.

In the instant case, Lynn's statements concerning the proposed dues increase were entitled to protection. Petitioners point to nothing in the International's constitution to suggest that the nature of Lynn's office changed once the trusteeship was imposed, so that Lynn was obligated to support Hawkins' positions. Thus, at the special meeting, Lynn was free to express the view apparently shared by a majority of the Local's members that the best solution to the Local's financial problems was not an increase in dues, but a reduction in expenditures. Under these circumstances, Hawkins violated Lynn's Title I rights when he removed Lynn from his post.[11]

III

For the reasons stated herein, we conclude that Lynn's removal from his position as business representative constituted a violation of Title I of the LMRDA. Accordingly, the judgment of the Court of Appeals is

Affirmed.

---

[11]Lynn's post-trusteeship status thus was much the same as it was before the trusteeship. We do not address a situation where an international's constitution provides that, when a trusteeship is imposed, elected officials are required to support the trustee's policies and thus may occupy a status similar to the appointed officials in Finnegan. Cf. § 101(b), Title I, 73 Stat. 523, 29 U.S.C. § 411(b).

JUSTICE KENNEDY took no part in the consideration or decision of this case.

JUSTICE WHITE, concurring in the judgment.

Finnegan v. Leu, 456 U.S. 431, 436-437 (1982), observed that, "It is readily apparent, both from the language of these provisions and from the legislative history of Title I, that it was rank-and-file union members—not union officers or employees, as such—whom Congress sought to protect" (footnote omitted). If that is so and if a case involves speech in the capacity of an officer, it should make no difference that the officer is elected rather than appointed. But in *Finnegan,* it was asserted that the officer was removed because of his campaign activities, as a member, in a union election, which was speech protected by Title I. In response, the Court said that under the union constitution the newly elected president had power to appoint and remove officers and that he was entitled to start out with officers in whom he had confidence. This was sufficient to dispose of the officers' claim under Title I.

In the case before us, the speech for which respondent was removed was also speech in the capacity of a member. The duties of a union business agent are defined in the union constitution. Those duties relate primarily to collective bargaining and administering the collective-bargaining contract. They do not seem to include supporting the union president's proposal to increase union dues; and if they did, I am not so sure that respondent would have spoken out against the dues increase at all.

In this case, unlike *Finnegan,* respondent was not discharged by an incoming elected president with power to appoint his own staff, but by a trustee whose power to dismiss and appoint officers, for all that is shown here, went no farther than the Local's president to discharge for cause, *i.e.,* for incompetence or other behavior disqualifying them for the tasks they were expected to perform as officers. Respondent's speech opposing the dues increase was the speech of a member about a matter the members were to resolve, and there is no countervailing interest rooted in union democracy that suffices to override that protection.

Thus, I doubt that resolution of cases like this turns on whether an officer is elected or appointed. Rather its inquiry is whether an officer speaks as a member or as an officer in discharge of his assigned duties. If the former, he is protected by Title I. If the latter, the issue becomes whether other considerations deprive the officer/member of the protections of that Title.

NOTES

1. In a case that was said not to "fall neatly within either *Finnegan* or *Lynn,*" a union business agent was appointed by a local executive board. After the international imposed a trusteeship, it dismissed the business agent from his position and issued him a membership withdrawal card, preventing him from running for union office. The Sixth Circuit held the individual had standing to sue the international under the LMRDA because he was disciplined in a way that affected his membership rights. *Thompson v. OPEIU,* 74 F.3d 1492 (6th Cir.), *cert. denied,* 117 S. Ct. 482 (1996).

2. Could an *incumbent* president discharge business agents appointed by him for opposing him in an election? Is it of any significance that nearly all unions are "one party" organizations? In *Cotter v. Owens,* 753 F.2d 223 (2d Cir. 1985) the court indicated that a § 102 suit might be available if plaintiff's removal was not an isolated act of retaliation for political disloyalty but was instead part of a "purposeful and deliberate" attempt to suppress membership dissent. But an appointed union officer does not have a right under the LMRDA to retain her position while she seeks an elective office. *Tucker v. Bieber,* 900 F.2d 973 (6th Cir.), *cert. denied,* 498 U.S. 848 (1990). The status of union officials is noted in 32 Cath. U. L. Rev. 287 (1982); 57 Fordham L. Rev. 601 (1989). A key concept in the LMRDA's "Bill of Rights" is that the rights protected are specific, and most courts have been hesitant to enlarge the list beyond those prescribed. Should Title I be held to require a union to hold general membership meetings? *See Grant v. Chicago Truck Drivers,* 806 F.2d 114 (7th Cir. 1986) ("No"). To grant dissident members' access to the union's mailing list? *See Carothers v. Presser,* 818 F.2d 926 (D.C. Cir. 1987) ("No"). To provide a Spanish-English translator at monthly meetings when 48 percent of the members do not speak English? *See Zamora v. Hotel Employees Local 11,* 817 F.2d 566 (9th Cir. 1987) ("Yes"). *See also* Gregory, *Union Leadership and Workers' Voices: Meeting the Needs of Linguistically Heterogeneous Union Members,* 58 U. Cin. L. Rev. 115 (1989).

3. *Membership under Title I.* Most of the provisions of Title I may be invoked only by union members. Section 3(o) of the LMRDA defines "member" as "any person who has fulfilled the requirements for membership in such organization...." In *Hughes v. Iron Workers, Local 11,* 287 F.2d 810 (3d Cir.), *cert. denied,* 368 U.S. 829 (1961), an iron worker, who was a member of both his international and his home local union, moved to another area and requested that his membership be transferred to a sister local. The Third Circuit held that the fulfillment of the intraunion membership requirements was all § 3(o) required, even though the plaintiff had not been formally admitted into membership by the sister local. *But cf. Phelan v. Plumbers Local 305,* 973 F.2d 1050 (2d Cir. 1992), *cert. denied,* 507 U.S. 972 (1993), which held that a union member who had only "travelers'" rights in a sister local could not sue the latter under § 102 for political retaliation because the LMRDA "regulates only the relationship between the union and its members."

4. *Voting rights.* Section 101(a)(1)'s provision on nominating and voting rights has produced much litigation. The courts have been practically unanimous that this section does not encompass a pre-election right to run for union office. *See, e.g., Mamula v. Steelworkers, Local 1211,* 304 F.2d 108 (3d Cir.), *cert. denied,* 371 U.S. 823 (1962); *cf. Calhoon v. Harvey,* 379 U.S. 134 (1964), *infra.* Much more troublesome have been questions concerning the right to vote itself. Does § 101(a)(1) give federal district courts jurisdiction to supervise union elections?

The court in *Robins v. Rarback*, 325 F.2d 929 (2d Cir. 1963), *cert. denied*, 379 U.S. 974 (1965), said nothing in the legislative history of the Act suggested "that the protection of the right to vote in Title I authorizes the federal courts to enter freely upon the field of supervision of union elections, in total disregard of the limitations imposed on that power by Title IV." On the other hand, in *Beckman v. Iron Workers Local 46*, 314 F.2d 848 (7th Cir. 1963), the court held that a federal district court had jurisdiction under § 101(a)(1) to grant a preliminary injunction restraining a union from counting ballots where alleged election irregularities, *i.e.*, ballot stuffing, indicated that union members were being deprived of their right to vote in substance, if not in form. And an international union may have violated the equal voting rights provision of the LMRDA if it manufactured a pretext for ordering the rerun of a local election after the members chose a slate of delegates belonging to a dissident political faction. *UAW Local 594 v. UAW*, 956 F.2d 1330 (6th Cir. 1992). However, a union did not violate the LMRDA's guarantee of equal rights when it conducted a vote by geographical districts on an employer's proposal to distribute certain productivity funds among the employees, with the outcome in each district determinative for that district. The court rejected the argument that this procedure was too favorable to the minority position. *Fulk v. UTU*, 81 F.3d 733 (7th Cir. 1996).

In *Cleveland Orchestra Comm. v. Cleveland Fed'n of Musicians*, 303 F.2d 229 (6th Cir. 1962), § 101(a)(1) was held not to grant symphony musicians an independent right to ratify contracts executed by their union with an orchestra, where the union's constitution and bylaws did not provide for such ratification. A union's failure to disclose the nonmonetary terms of a new contract before submitting it for membership ratification was ruled not violative of the § 101(a)(1) equal voting rights and (a)(2) free speech provisions of the LMRDA in *Ackley v. Teamsters Western Conf.*, 958 F.2d 1463 (9th Cir. 1992). The Labor Board has held that an employer has no standing to challenge a union's ratification of a contract as invalid under the organization's constitution and bylaws. *Newton Corp.*, 280 N.L.R.B. 350 (1986), *enforced*, 819 F.2d 677 (6th Cir. 1987). *See generally* Hyde, *Democracy in Collective Bargaining*, 93 Yale L.J. 793 (1984); Klare, *Workplace Democracy and Market Reconstruction*, 38 Cath. U. L. Rev. 1 (1988); Levy, *Membership Rights in Union Referenda to Ratify Collective Bargaining Agreements*, 4 Hofstra Lab. L.J. 225 (1987); Schwartz, *The Judicial Imperative—Court Intervention and the Protection of the Right to Vote in Unions*, 4 Hofstra Lab. L.J. 269 (1987).

5. *Remedies.* The courts of appeals have generally allowed punitive damages under Title I. *Boilermakers v. Braswell*, 388 F.2d 193 (5th Cir.), *cert. denied*, 391 U.S. 935 (1968); *Morrissey v. NMU*, 544 F.2d 19 (2d Cir. 1976); *Bise v. IBEW Local 1969*, 618 F.2d 1299 (9th Cir. 1979), *cert. denied*, 449 U.S. 904 (1980); *Quinn v. DiGiulian*, 739 F.2d 637 (D.C. Cir. 1984) ("actual malice" or "wanton indifference" to members' rights being the test). *But cf. McGraw v. Plumbers Local 43*, 216 F. Supp. 655 (E.D. Tenn. 1963), *aff'd*, 341 F.2d 705 (6th Cir.

1965). For an important limitation on the relief available under Title I, *see Tomko v. Hilbert*, 288 F.2d 625, 629 (3d Cir. 1961): "Private misconduct which incidentally may frustrate appellant's rights as a union member does not give rise to an action under the bill-of-rights section." *But cf. Roganovich v. United States*, 318 F.2d 167 (7th Cir.), *cert. denied*, 375 U.S. 911 (1963) (§ 610's criminal sanctions for violent interference with rights under the Act are applicable against individual union members as well as against union officers or agents). *See also Morrisey v. NMU, supra*, holding individual officers liable, "at least" when "acting under the color of union authority." A union member who vindicates his right of free speech under Title I of the LMRDA renders a substantial service to his union as an institution and to all its members, and thus counsel fees may properly be awarded to a successful plaintiff in a suit brought under § 102 of the Act. *Hall v. Cole*, 412 U.S. 1 (1973).

The Supreme Court has held that suits alleging violations of LMRDA free speech rights are governed by state general or residual personal injury statutes of limitation, rather than the six-month limitations period contained in § 10(b) of the NLRA. *See Reed v. United Transp. Union*, 488 U.S. 319 (1989). A court of appeals has extended this rule to § 101(a)(1) equal rights claims. *George v. Teamsters Local 639*, 100 F.3d 1008 (D.C. Cir. 1996). The Court has also ruled that a union member suing his union under Title I for lost wages, as well as for injunctive relief, is entitled to a jury trial. *Wooddell v. IBEW Local 71*, 502 U.S. 93 (1991).

The courts are divided on whether local unions have standing to sue on behalf of their members for violations of free speech and other rights under Title I of the LMRDA. See, e.g., *Carpenters Local 42-L v. Carpenters*, 73 F.3d 958 (9th Cir. 1996), and cases cited therein.

6. *Job discrimination.* In *Breininger v. Sheet Metal Workers Local 6*, 493 U.S. 67 (1989), the Supreme Court held that discrimination in job referrals through a union hiring hall is not "discipline" under §§ 101(a)(5) and 609 of the LMRDA. Earlier, several courts of appeals had ruled that a claim of discrimination in employment because of ouster from union membership is subject to exclusive NLRB jurisdiction and may not be the basis of a Landrum-Griffin action. *Spica v. ILGWU*, 420 Pa. 427, 218 A.2d 579 (1966); *Knox v. UAW*, 351 F.2d 72 (6th Cir. 1965); *Barunica v. Hatters, Local 55*, 321 F.2d 764 (8th Cir. 1963). *But cf. Figueroa v. NMU*, 342 F.2d 400 (2d Cir. 1965); *Rekant v. Shochtay-Gasos Union*, 320 F.2d 271 (3d Cir. 1963); *Murphy v. Operating Eng'rs Local 18*, 774 F.2d 114 (6th Cir. 1985), *cert. denied*, 475 U.S. 1017 (1986). *See generally* Arlook, *Federal Preemption and Landrum-Griffin*, in N.Y.U. Thirteenth Annual Conference on Labor 89 (1960).

7. General discussions of the background and effect of the Landrum-Griffin Act are provided by Aaron, *The Labor-Management Reporting and Disclosure Act of 1959*, 73 Harv. L. Rev. 851 (1960); Cox, *Internal Affairs of Labor Unions Under the Labor Reform Act of 1959*, 58 Mich. L. Rev. 819 (1960); Smith, *The*

Labor-Management Reporting and Disclosure Act of 1959, 46 Va. L. Rev. 195 (1960); Summers, *American Legislation for Union Democracy,* 25 Mod. L. Rev. 273 (1962). On Title I in particular, *see* Aaron, *The Union Member's "Bill of Rights": First Two Years,* 1 Ind. Rel. 47 (February 1962); Dunau, *Some Comments on the Bill of Rights of Members of Labor Organizations,* in N.Y.U. Fourteenth Annual Conference on Labor 77 (1961). For contrasting appraisals of the Act after several years in operation, *see* Murphy, *Major Developments of the Year Under the Landrum-Griffin Act,* in N.Y.U. Eighteenth Annual Conference on Labor 31 (1966); St. Antoine, *Landrum-Griffin, 1965-1966: A Calculus of Democratic Values,* in N.Y.U. Nineteenth Annual Conference on Labor 35 (1967); Symposium, *Current Issues in Union Democracy Law,* 4 Hofstra Lab. L.J. 217 (1987). Comparative evaluations of American and foreign legislation are found in Kahn-Freund, *Trade Union Democracy and the Law,* 22 Ohio St. L.J. 4 (1961); Summers, Aaron, Grunfield, Saratier, Magrez, *Internal Relations Between Unions and Their Members,* 18 Rutgers L. Rev. 236, 279, 343, 375, 394 (1964) (five separate papers). Comprehensive studies are J. Bellace & A. Berkowitz, The Landrum-Griffin Act: Twenty Years of Federal Protection of Union Members' Rights (1979); Hartley, *The Framework of Union Democracy in Union Government,* 32 Cath. U.L. Rev. 13 (1982); D. McLaughlin & A. Schoomaker, The Landrum-Griffin Act and Union Democracy (1979). *See also* Symposium, *The Government and Union Democracy,* 24 U. Mich. J. L. Ref. 469 (1991).

C. FREE SPEECH AND POLITICAL ACTION

SALZHANDLER v. CAPUTO

United States Court of Appeals, Second Circuit
316 F.2d 445 (1963), *cert. denied,* 375 U.S. 946 (1963)

LUMBARD, CHIEF JUDGE.... Solomon Salzhandler, a member of Local 442, Brotherhood of Painters, Decorators & Paperhangers of America, brought suit in the district court following the decision of a Trial Board of the union's New York District Council No. 9 that he had untruthfully accused Isadore Webman, the president of the local, of the crime of larceny. The Trial Board found that Salzhandler's "unsupported accusations" violated the union's constitution which prohibited "conduct unbecoming a member ...," "acts detrimental to ... interests of the Brotherhood," "libeling, slandering ... fellow members [or] officers of local unions" and "acts and conduct ... inconsistent with the duties, obligations and fealty of a member."

Salzhandler's complaint alleged that his charges against Webman were an exercise of his rights as a member of the union and that the action of the Trial Board was in violation of the provisions of the LMRDA under which he was entitled to relief.

The undisputed facts developed during the trial in the district court amply support Salzhandler's claims for relief.

Salzhandler was elected financial secretary of Local 442 in 1953. He was reelected thereafter and at the times in question he was serving a three-year term which was to end June 30, 1962. His weekly compensation as an officer was $35, of which $25 was salary and $10 was for expenses. The dispute giving rise to this suit was touched off in November 1960 by Salzhandler's distribution to members of Local 442 of a leaflet which accused Webman of mishandling of union funds.

Prior to the audit each July, Salzhandler obtained the checks for the auditor. In going over the union's checks in July 1960 Salzhandler noticed that two checks, one for $800 and one for $375, had been drawn to cover the expenses of Webman and one Max Schneider at two union conventions to which they were elected delegates. The $800 check, drawn on August 21, 1959 to Webman's order, was endorsed by Webman and his wife. The $375 check, drawn on March 4, 1960 to "Cash," was likewise endorsed by Webman and his wife. Schneider's endorsement did not appear on either check. Schneider had died on May 31, 1960.

On July 15, 1960 two checks, each for $6, were drawn as refunds of dues paid by Max Schneider and another deceased member. Such checks were ordinarily mailed to the widows. Webman, however, brought the two checks to Salzhandler and told him to deposit them in a special fund for the benefit of the son of Max Schneider. Salzhandler refused to do this because the checks were not endorsed. Thereafter Sol Feldman and W. Shirpin, who were trustees of the local, each endorsed one of the checks and Salzhandler made the deposit as Webman had requested.

In November 1960 Salzhandler distributed to members of the local a leaflet which accused Webman of improper conduct with regard to union funds and of referring to members of the union by such names as "thieves, scabs, robbers, scabby bosses, bums, pimps, f-bums, [and] jail birds." Attached to the leaflet were photostats of the four checks. With regard to the convention checks, Salzhandler wrote:

> The last convention lasted five days, Monday August 31, to Friday, September 4, 1959. The delegates of 442 presented their credentials Monday, August 31, and on Thursday, September 3, as soon as they got the mileage fare, they disappeared. They were absent at Thursday afternoon session. The most the chairman should have gotten was a week's pay and allowance—$250.00. The auditor's report shows he got $200 in pay and $300 in expenses—$500, or twice what was coming to him, and also $300 as expenses for the Business Agent. The check was made out to *Cash* for $800 (photostat enclosed). So was the voucher. It does not indicate that Max Schneider got any of it. The same goes for a check made out *only* to I. Webman on March 4, 1960 for another convention, where the chairman was to get $250,

but got $375. It does not indicate Schneider got his share. Were the checks legal?

The leaflet also branded Webman as a "petty robber" of the two $6 checks:

> To prove himself most unworthy of any trust, he performed the cheapest petty act ever. Two widows were refunded each $6.00 for overpayment of dues. Two checks were issued to that effect. The petty robber had two of his friends sign their names and the chairman declared these two checks as contributions to the special tax for Michael Schneider—photostats of checks enclosed.

On December 13, 1960, Webman filed charges against Salzhandler with the New York District Council No. 9 of the union, alleging that Salzhandler had violated the union constitution, § 267, by libelling and slandering him in implying that he, Webman, had not reimbursed Max Schneider for convention expenses, and that he had been a "petty robber" in causing the two $6 checks to be deposited in the Michael Schneider fund, rather than being paid over to the two widows. The charge went on to state that Salzhandler was guilty of "acts and conduct inconsistent with the duties, obligations and fealty of a member or officer of the Brotherhood" and that the net effect of the leaflet was untruthfully to accuse an officer of the union of the crime of larceny. For over six hours on the evening of February 23, 1961, Salzhandler was tried by a five-member Trial Board of the District Council. As the union rules permitted, Salzhandler was represented by a union member who was not a lawyer. At the trial, Webman introduced the leaflet. Salzhandler produced the photostats and was questioned by the Trial Board. Webman's witnesses testified that the convention expenditures were approved by the membership. Salzhandler produced three witnesses who testified that Webman had called members names as alleged in the leaflet.

Not until April 2, 1961 did Salzhandler receive notice of the Trial Board's decision and his removal from office and this was from a printed postal card mailed to all members:

> By a decision of the Trial Committee of District Council 9, Sol Saltzhandler [sic] is no longer Financial Secretary of Local Union 442.

Thereafter, on April 4, the District Council mailed to Salzhandler only the final paragraph of its five page "Decision" which read as follows:

> It is our decision that Brother Solomon Salzhandler be prohibited from participating in the affairs of L.U. 442, or of any other Local Union of the Brotherhood, or of District Council 9, for a period of five (5) years. He shall not be permitted during that period to attend meetings of L.U. 442, to vote on any matter, to have the floor at any meeting of any other Local Union affiliated with the District Council, or to be a candidate for any position in any local Union or in the District Council. In all other respects, Brother Salz-

handler's rights and obligations as a member of the Brotherhood shall be continued.

Salzhandler did not receive a copy of the full opinion of the Trial Board until after this action was commenced on June 14, 1961. Meanwhile, as the union constitution required appeal within 30 days, Salzhandler filed intraunion appeals with the Secretary-Treasurer of the Council and the General Secretary-Treasurer of the Brotherhood on April 12 and 28. At the time this action was brought, plaintiff had received no word regarding said appeals.

On May 15, 1961, Salzhandler attempted to attend a meeting of the local but was prevented from doing so by Webman. The complaint alleges that Webman assaulted Salzhandler and used violence in removing him.

This action was commenced in the federal court under the Labor-Management Reporting and Disclosure Act of 1959, § 102, requesting a nullification of the order of the Trial Board, reinstatement in the position as financial secretary, and damages.

Judge Wham dismissed the complaint holding that the Trial Board's conclusion that the leaflet was libelous was sufficiently supported by the evidence. He went further, however, and made an independent finding that the statements were, in fact, libelous. The court held, as a matter of law, that "The rights accorded members of labor unions under Title I of the Labor-Management Reporting and Disclosure Act of 1959 ... do not include the right of a union member to libel or slander officers of the union." We do not agree.

The LMRDA of 1959 was designed to protect the rights of union members to discuss freely and criticize the management of their unions and the conduct of their officers. The legislative history and the extensive hearings which preceded the enactment of the statute abundantly evidence the intention of the Congress to prevent union officials from using their disciplinary powers to silence criticism and punish those who dare to question and complain. The statute is clear and explicit [quoting §§ 101(a)(1), 101(a)(2), 102, and 609].

Appellees argue that just as constitutionally protected speech does not include libelous utterances, *Beauharnais v. Illinois,* 343 U.S. 250, 266 (1952), the speech protected by the statute likewise does not include libel and slander. The analogy to the First Amendment is not convincing. In *Beauharnais,* the Supreme Court recognized the possibility that state action might stifle criticism under the guise of punishing libel. However, because it felt that abuses could be prevented by the exercise of judicial authority, 343 U.S. at 263-264, the court sustained a state criminal libel statute. But the union is not a political unit to whose disinterested tribunals an alleged defamer can look for an impartial review of his "crime." It is an economic action group, the success of which depends in large measure on a unity of purpose and sense of solidarity among its members.

The Trial Board in the instant case consisted of union officials, not judges. It was a group to which the delicate problems of truth or falsehood, privilege, and "fair comment" were not familiar. Its procedure is peculiarly unsuited for drawing the fine line between criticism and defamation, yet, were we to adopt the view of the appellees, each charge of libel would be given a trial de novo in the federal court—an impractical result not likely contemplated by Congress, see 105 Cong. Rec. 6026 (daily ed. April 25, 1959) (colloquy between Senator Goldwater and Senator Clark)—and such a Trial Board would be the final arbiter of the extent of the union member's protection under § 101(a)(2).

In a proviso to § 101(a)(2), there are two express exceptions to the board rule of free expression. One relates to "the responsibility of every member toward the organization as an institution." The other deals with interference with the union's legal and contractual obligations.

While the inclusion of only two exceptions, without more, does not mean that others were intentionally excluded, we believe that the legislative history supports the conclusion that Congress intended only those exceptions which were expressed.[8]

The expression of views by Salzhandler did not come within either exception in the proviso to § 101(a)(2). The leaflet did not interfere in any way with the union's legal or contractual obligations and the union has never claimed that it did. Nor could Salzhandler's charges against Webman be construed as a violation of the "responsibility of every member toward the organization as an institution." Quite the contrary; it would seem clearly in the interest of proper and honest management of union affairs to permit members to question the manner in which the union's officials handle the union's funds and how they treat the union's members. It is that interest which motivated the enactment of the statute and which would be immeasurably frustrated were we to interpret it so as to compel each dissatisfied and questioning member to draw, at the peril of union discipline, the thin and tenuous line between what is libelous and what is not. This is especially so when we consider that the Act was designed largely to curtail such vices as the mismanagement of union funds, criticism of which by union members is always likely to be viewed by union officials as defamatory.

The union argues that there is a public interest in promoting the monolithic character of unions in their dealings with employers. But the Congress weighed this factor and decided that the desirability of protecting the democratic process

---

[8] As initially introduced before the Senate, the freedom of speech section was absolute in form. *See* 105 Cong. Rec. 5810 (daily ed. April 22, 1959). The section was in fact passed in that form. *Id.* at 5827. Later the question came to be reconsidered and the free speech section was amended to include the two express exceptions. *Id.* at 6030 (daily ed. April 25, 1959). In effect, the section as initially passed took away the power of unions to punish for expressions of views. The subsequent amendment restored that power in only two situations.

We are referred to certain statements made during the debate in the Senate which allegedly indicate that "reasonable restraints" on speech were intended. *See, e.g.,* 105 Cong. Rec. 6022 (daily ed. April 25, 1959) (remarks of Senator Kuchel). We find these statements to be ambiguous and we are not persuaded that exceptions other than those specified were intended.

within the unions outweighs any possible weakening of unions in their dealings with employers which may result from the freer expression of opinions within the unions.

The democratic and free expression of opinion in any group necessarily develops disagreements and divergent opinions. Freedom of expression would be stifled if those in power could claim that any charges against them were libelous and then proceed to discipline those responsible on a finding that the charges were false. That is precisely what Webman and the Trial Board did here when they punished Salzhandler with a five-year ban of silence and stripped him of his office.

So far as union discipline is concerned Salzhandler had a right to speak his mind and spread his opinions regarding the union's officers, regardless of whether his statements were true or false. It was wholly immaterial to Salzhandler's cause of action under the LMRDA whether he spoke truthfully or not, and accordingly Judge Wham's views on whether Salzhandler's statements were true are beside the point. Here Salzhandler's charges against Webman related to the handling of union funds; they concerned the way the union was managed. The Congress has decided that it is in the public interest that unions be democratically governed and toward that end that discussion should be free and untrammeled and that reprisals within the union for the expression of views should be prohibited. It follows that although libelous statements may be made the basis of civil suit between those concerned, the union may not subject a member to any disciplinary action on a finding by its governing board that such statements are libelous. The district court erred in dismissing the complaint.

Accordingly, we reverse the judgment of the district court and direct entry of judgment for the plaintiff which, among other things, should assess damages and enjoin the defendants from carrying out any punishment imposed by the District Council Trial Board.

NOTES

1. The principal case was followed in *Boilermakers v. Rafferty,* 348 F.2d 307 (9th Cir. 1965), which involved the distribution of handbills allegedly containing false statements about another member. *See also Black v. Ryder/P.I.E. Nationwide,* 970 F.2d 1461 (6th Cir. 1992) (picketing of union hall to protest local leadership).

2. Title I's free speech provisions were held to preclude a national union from refusing to publish in its national journal a paid advertisement by local members opposing ratification of a collective bargaining agreement negotiated by the national body. *Knox County Local Rural Letter Carriers v. Rural Letter Carriers,* 115 L.R.R.M. 2980 (6th Cir. 1984). *See also Shimman v. Miller,* 995 F.2d 651 (6th Cir. 1993), *cert. denied,* 510 U.S. 1093 (1994) (local newsletter refused to publish member's letter responding to editor's criticism; newsletter was "public forum" for members' views); *but cf. Laborers' Local 324 v. NLRB*, 123 F.3d 1176 (9th Cir. 1997) (upholding union rule banning distribution of literature at union hiring halls where applied to block distribution of newsletter critical of union, since rule was neutral on its face), discussed further *supra* Note 1 following the *NLRB v. Allis-Chalmers* opinion in Part Three, Section III.B. *See generally* Jacobs & Spring, *Fair Coverage in Internal Union Periodicals*, 4 Indus. Rel. L.J. 204 (1981); Note, *Free Speech and Union Newspapers: Internal Democracy and Title I Rights*, 20 Harv. C.R.-C.L.L. Rev. 485 (1985).

3. "Selective prosecution" of a union member who refused picket-line duty during a strike but who also strongly opposed the strike at union meetings violated the free speech guarantee of § 101(a)(2), since other members refusing picket-line duty were not similarly disciplined. *Massey v. Inland Boatmen's Union*, 886 F.2d 1188 (9th Cir. 1989). Removing an employee from his position as union shop steward and causing him to be fired in retaliation for his participation in demonstrations in front of the union's District Council office protesting the union's layoff of three business agents is an act of union discipline which potentially violates the employee's free speech rights under § 101(a)(2) of the LMRDA. *Maddalone v. Local 17, United Bhd. of Carpenters & Joiners of Am.*, 152 F.3d 178 (2d Cir. 1998).

4. The proviso to § 101(a)(2) is generally assumed to cover such matters as the advocacy of a union schism or a wildcat strike. In *Aircraft Mechanics v. TWU Local 514*, 98 F.3d 597 (10th Cir. 1996), the court sustained the right of a labor organization to discipline a member who supported a rival union and sought displacement of the incumbent union, since the organization acted in reasonable defense of its institutional integrity. Would urging the nonpayment of dues, in the good faith but mistaken belief they were illegally imposed, violate a member's "responsibility ... toward the organization as an institution"? Would the proviso apply to criticism of a union administration so severe as to discredit the organization in the eyes of the public or of its membership? *Compare Farowitz v. Musicians, Local 802*, 241 F. Supp. 895 (S.D.N.Y. 1965) *with Deacon v. Operating Eng'rs Local 12*, 59 L.R.R.M. 2706 (S.D. Cal. 1965). What about active support of the Communist Party? *See Rosen v. Painters Dist. Council 9*, 50 CCH Lab. Cas. ¶ 19,245 (S.D.N.Y. 1964). What about teaching an apprenticeship course sponsored by nonunion firms? *See Halsell v. Bricklayers Local 5*, 530 F. Supp. 803 (N.D. Tex. 1982), *aff'd*, 706 F.2d 313 (5th Cir.), *cert. denied*, 464 U.S. 895 (1983). A union has been enjoined from enforcing a constitutional prohibition of "dishonest or questionable practices to secure the election or defeat of any candidate for office" against members opposing the reelection of incumbent officers, on the ground the provision was so vague that a member would be in peril of violating it whenever she exercised her speech rights under the Act. *Semancik v. UMW District 5*, 466 F.2d 144 (3d Cir. 1972). Discipline for advocating dual unionism was upheld in *Ferguson v. Iron Workers*, 854 F.2d 1169 (9th Cir. 1988). *Cf. Sheet Metal Workers Local 22 (Miller Sheet Metal)*, 296 N.L.R.B.

1146 (1989) (fine for dual unionism does not violate § 8(b)(1)(A) of the NLRA so long as member is not impeded in invoking Labor Board's processes on behalf of second union). *But cf. Machinists Lodge 702 v. Loudermilk,* 444 F.2d 719 (5th Cir. 1971) (fine invalid).

5. For a sharp debate on the *Salzhandler* doctrine, *see* Hall, *Freedom of Speech and Union Discipline: The Implications of Salzhandler,* in N.Y.U. Seventeenth Annual Conference on Labor 349 (1964); Sigal, *Freedom of Speech and Union Discipline: The "Right" of Defamation and Disloyalty, id.* at 367. *See also* Atleson, *A Union Member's Right of Free Speech and Assembly: Institutional Interests and Individual Rights,* 51 Minn. L. Rev. 403 (1967); Beaird & Player, *Free Speech and the Landrum-Griffin Act,* 25 Ala. L. Rev. 577 (1973).

6. Leading common law decisions by state courts on the right of union members to engage in free speech or political activity without being subjected to reprisals are *Mitchell v. Machinists,* 196 Cal. App. 2d 796, 16 Cal. Rptr. 813 (1961); *DeMille v. American Fed'n of Radio Artists,* 31 Cal. 2d 139, 187 P.2d 769 (1947), *cert. denied,* 333 U.S. 876 (1948); *Crossen v. Duffy,* 90 Ohio App. 252, 103 N.E.2d 769 (1951); *Madden v. Atkins,* 4 N.Y.2d 283, 151 N.E.2d 73 (1958). The first two cases involved public issues outside the union; the latter two dealt with political activity within the union.

UNITED STEELWORKERS v. SADLOWSKI

Supreme Court of the United States
457 U.S. 102, 102 S. Ct. 2339, 72 L. Ed. 2d 707 (1982)

JUSTICE MARSHALL delivered the opinion of the Court.

In this case, we confront the question whether § 101(a)(2) of the Labor-Management Reporting and Disclosure Act of 1959 precludes the membership of a union from adopting a rule that prohibits candidates for union office from accepting campaign contributions from nonmembers. The United States Court of Appeals for the District of Columbia held that such a rule violated § 101(a)(2). *Sadlowski v. United Steelworkers of America,* 645 F.2d 1114 (1981). We granted certiorari and now reverse.

I

A. Petitioner United Steelworkers of America (USWA), a labor organization with 1,300,000 members, conducts elections for union president and other top union officers every four years. The elections for these officers are decided by referendum vote of the membership. In the 1977 election, which was hotly contested, two candidates ran for president: respondent Edward Sadlowski, Jr., the Director of USWA's largest District, and Lloyd McBride, another District Director. Both Sadlowski and McBride headed a slate of candidates for the other top union positions.

McBride was endorsed by the incumbent union leadership, and received substantial financial support from union officers and staff. Sadlowski, on the other hand, received much of his financial support from sources outside the union. During the campaign, the question whether candidates should accept contributions from persons who were not members of the union was vigorously debated. The McBride slate contended that outsider participation in USWA elections was dangerous for the union. App. 27, n.2, 298. *See also* App. 129, 398; *see generally* App. 40-48. McBride ultimately defeated Sadlowski by a fairly wide margin— 57% to 43%. The other candidates on the McBride slate won by similar margins.

After the elections, union members continued to debate the question whether outsider participation in union campaigns was desirable. This debate was finally resolved in 1978, when USWA held its biennial Convention. The Convention, which consists of approximately 5,000 delegates elected by members of USWA's local unions, is USWA's highest governing body. At the 1978 Convention, several local unions submitted resolutions recommending amendment of the USWA Constitution to include an "outsider rule" prohibiting campaign contributions by nonmembers. The union's International Executive Board also recommended a ban on nonmember contributions. Acting on the basis of these recommendations, the Convention's Constitution Committee proposed to the Convention that it adopt an outsider rule. After a debate on the floor of the Convention, the delegates, by a margin of roughly 10 to 1, voted to include such a rule in the Constitution. App. 35-36, 81-105.

The outsider rule, Article V, § 27 of the USWA Constitution, provides in pertinent part:

> Sec. 27. No candidate (including a prospective candidate) for any position set forth in Article IV, Section 1, and supporter of a candidate may solicit or accept financial support, or any other direct or indirect support of any kind (except an individual's own volunteered personal time) from any nonmember. USWA Const. Art. V, § 27.

Section 27 confers authority upon the International Executive Board to adopt regulations necessary to implement the provision. It also creates a Campaign Contribution Administrative Committee, consisting of three "distinguished, impartial" nonmembers to administer and enforce the provision. *Id.* The Committee may order a candidate to cease and desist from conduct that breaches § 27, and may declare a candidate disqualified. Its decisions are final and binding.

B. In October 1979, Sadlowski and several other individuals filed suit against USWA in the United States District Court for the District of Columbia. They claimed, *inter alia,* that the outsider rule violated the "right to sue" provision of Title I of the LMRDA, § 101(a)(4), because it would prohibit a candidate from accepting nonmember contributions to finance campaign-related litigation. Both sides moved for summary judgment. The District Court found that the rule violated § 101(a)(4). *Sadlowski v. USWA,* 507 F. Supp. 623, 625 (D.D.C. 1981). The

District Court further decided to invalidate the rule *en toto,* because the portion of the rule that "limits meaningful access to the courts ... cannot be separated or isolated from the rule in its entirety." *Id.*

The United States Court of Appeals for the District of Columbia Circuit affirmed. The Court agreed that Article V, § 27 violated the right to sue provision. However, it chose not to decide whether this violation alone justified an injunction restraining enforcement of the entire rule. It accepted respondents' argument, first raised on appeal, that the outsider rule also violated the § 101(a)(2) "freedom of speech and assembly" provision, and that this violation justified the injunction....

II

... A. At the outset, we address respondents' contention that this case can be resolved simply by reference to First Amendment law. Respondents claim that § 101(a)(2) confers upon union members rights equivalent to the rights established by the First Amendment. They further argue that in the context of a political election, a rule that placed substantial restrictions on a candidate's freedom to receive campaign contributions would violate the First Amendment. Thus, a rule that substantially restricts contributions in union campaigns must violate § 101(a)(2). We are not persuaded by this argument. In light of the legislative history, we do not believe that § 101(a)(2) should be read as incorporating the entire body of First Amendment law, so that the scope of protections afforded by the statute coincides with the protections afforded by the Constitution.

[The Court discussed the legislative history of Title I of the LMRDA.]

This history reveals that Congress modelled Title I after the Bill of Rights, and that the legislators intended § 101(a)(2) to restate a principal First Amendment value—the right to speak one's mind without fear of reprisal. However, there is absolutely no indication that Congress intended the scope of § 101(a)(2) to be identical to the scope of the First Amendment. Rather, Congress' decision to include a proviso covering "reasonable" rules refutes that proposition. First Amendment freedoms may not be infringed absent a compelling governmental interest. Even then, any government regulation must be carefully tailored, so that rights are not needlessly impaired. *Brown v. Hartlage,* 456 U.S. 45, 53-54 (1982). Union rules, by contrast, are valid under § 101(a)(2) so long as they are reasonable; they need not pass the stringent tests applied in the First Amendment context.

B. To determine whether a union rule is valid under the statute, we first consider whether the rule interferes with an interest protected by the first section of § 101(a)(2). If it does, we then determine whether the rule is "reasonable" and thus sheltered by the proviso to § 101(a)(2). In conducting these inquiries, we find guidance in the policies that underly [underlie] the LMRDA in general and

Title I in particular. First Amendment principles may be helpful, although they are not controlling....

Applying this form of analysis here, we conclude that the outsider rule is valid. Although it may limit somewhat the ability of insurgent union members to wage an effective campaign, an interest deserving some protection under the statute, it is rationally related to the union's legitimate interest in reducing outsider interference with union affairs.

(1) An examination of the policies underlying the LMRDA indicates that the outsider rule may have some impact on interests that Congress intended to protect under § 101(a)(2). Congress adopted the freedom of speech and assembly provision in order to promote union democracy. It recognized that democracy would be assured only if union members are free to discuss union policies and criticize the leadership without fear of reprisal. Congress also recognized that this freedom is particularly critical, and deserves vigorous protection, in the context of election campaigns. For it is in elections that members can wield their power, and directly express their approval or disapproval of the union leadership.

The interest in fostering vigorous debate during election campaigns may be affected by the outsider rule. If candidates are not permitted to accept contributions from persons outside the union, their ability to criticize union policies and to mount effective challenges to union leadership may be weakened. Restrictions that limit access to funds may reduce the number of issues discussed, the attention that is devoted to each issue, and the size of the audience reached. *Cf. Buckley v. Valeo,* 424 U.S. 1, 14 (1976) (per curiam) (First Amendment freedom of expression and association may be "diluted if it does not include the right to pool money through contributions, for funds are often essential if 'advocacy' is to be truly or optimally 'effective'").

Although the outsider rule does affect rights protected by the statute, as a practical matter the impact may not be substantial. Respondents, as well as the Court of Appeals, suggest that incumbents have a large advantage because they can rely on their union staff during election campaigns. Challengers cannot counter this power simply by seeking funds from union members; the rank-and-file cannot provide sufficient support. Thus, they must be permitted to seek funds from outsiders. In fact, however, the rank-and-file probably can provide support. The USWA is a very large union whose members earn sufficient income to make campaign contributions. *See* App. 118-120. Requiring candidates to rely solely on contributions from members will not unduly limit their ability to raise campaign funds. Uncontradicted record evidence discloses that challengers have been able to defeat incumbents or administration-backed candidates, despite the absence of financial support from nonmembers. *See* App. 25, 118-119.

In addition, although there are undoubtedly advantages to incumbency, *see Hall v. Cole,* 412 U.S., at 13, respondents and the Court of Appeals may overstate those advantages. Staff employees are forbidden by § 401(g) of the LMRDA and by internal USWA rules from campaigning on union time or from using union funds, facilities, or equipment for campaign purposes. App. 110-117; *see* 29 CFR § 452.76 (1981). Staff officers have a contractual right to choose whether or not to participate in any USWA campaign without being subjected to discipline or reprisal for their decision. *See* App. 107-110, 115-117, 228, 384-385. Indeed, USWA elections have frequently involved challenges to incumbents by members of the staff. Many of these challenges have been successful. App. 108, 201-216.

The impact of the outsider rule on rights protected under § 101(a)(2) is limited in another important respect. The union has stated that the rule would not prohibit union members who are not involved in a campaign from using outside funds to address particular issues. That is, members could solicit funds from outsiders in order to focus the attention of the rank-and-file on a specific problem. The fact that union members remain free to seek funds for this purpose will serve as a counter to the power of entrenched leadership, and ensures that debate on issues that are important to the membership will never be stifled.

(2) Although the outsider rule may implicate rights protected by § 101(a)(2), it serves a legitimate purpose that is clearly protected under the statute. The union adopted the rule because it wanted to ensure that nonmembers do not unduly influence union affairs. USWA feared that officers who received campaign contributions from nonmembers might be beholden to those individuals and might allow their decisions to be influenced by considerations other than the best interests of the union. The union wanted to ensure that the union leadership remained responsive to the membership. *See* App. 210; *see also* App. 61-62, 81-97, 275, 303, 304. An examination of the policies underlying the LMRDA reveals that this is a legitimate purpose that Congress meant to protect.

Evidence that Congress regarded the desire to minimize outsider influence as a legitimate purpose is provided by the history to Title I. On the Senate floor, Senator McClellan argued that a bill of rights for union members was necessary because some unions had been "invaded" or "infiltrated" by outsiders who had no interest in the members but rather had seized control for their own purposes. 2 Leg. Hist. 1097-1100. He stated that the strongest support for the bill of rights provisions "should come from traditional union leaders. It will protect them from the assaults of those who would capture their unions." *Id.*, at 1097.... It is true that Senator McClellan was particularly concerned about infiltration of unions by racketeers: he described situations in which "thugs and hoodlums" had taken over unions so that they could exploit the members for pecuniary gain. *Id.*, at 1097. However, his statements also indicate a more general desire to ensure that union members, and not outsiders, control the affairs of their union.

Additional evidence that Congress regarded the union's desire to maintain control over its own affairs as legitimate is provided by the history of other sections of the LMRDA. In drafting Titles II through VI, Congress was guided by the general principle that unions should be left free to "operate their own affairs, as far as possible." S. Rep. No. 1684, 85th Cong., 2d Sess. 4-5 (1958). It believed that only essential standards should be imposed by legislation, and that in establishing those standards, great care should be taken not to undermine union self-government. Given certain minimum standards, "individual members are fully competent to regulate union affairs." *Id.* Thus, for example, in Title IV, which regulates the conduct of union elections, Congress simply set forth certain minimum standards. So long as unions conform with these standards, they are free "to run their own elections." *Wirtz v. Bottle Blowers Assn.,* 389 U.S., at 471. Congress' desire to permit unions to regulate their own affairs and to minimize governmental intervention suggests that it would have endorsed union efforts to reduce outsider influence.

Indeed, specific provisions contained in Title IV provide support for our conclusion that the outsider rule serves a legitimate and protected purpose. Section 401(g) prohibits the use of employer as well as union funds in election campaigns. This ban reflects a desire to minimize the danger that employers will influence the outcome of union elections. A union rule that seeks to reduce the influence of outsiders other than employers is clearly consistent with that goal. *See also* § 403 of Title IV of the LMRDA, 29 U.S.C. § 843 (authorizing unions to establish their own election rules).

Respondents argue that even if the desire to reduce outside influence is a legitimate purpose, the rule is not rationally related to that purpose. They contend, first, that the union could simply have established contribution ceilings, rather than placing an absolute ban on nonmember contributions. However, USWA feared not only that a few individual nonmembers would make large contributions, but that outsiders would solicit many like-minded persons for small contributions which, when pooled, would have a substantial impact on the election. This fear appears to have been reasonable. In the 1977 election, Sadlowski received a significant percentage of his campaign funds from individuals who made contributions after receiving mail solicitations signed by prominent nonmembers. App. 128-129, 350-353.

Respondents also contend that even if the union was justified in limiting contributions by true outsiders, it need not have limited contributions by relatives and friends. Again, however, the USWA had a reasonable basis for its decision to impose a broad ban. An exception for family members and friends might have created a loophole that would have made the rule unenforceable: true outsiders could simply funnel their contributions through relatives and friends. *See* App. 32. *Cf. Buckley v. Valeo,* 424 U.S., at 53 n.59 (Congress could constitutionally subject family members to the same limitations as nonfamily members).

Finally, respondents contend that USWA could simply have required that candidates for union office reveal the sources of their funds. But a disclosure rule, by itself, would not have solved the problem. Candidates who received such funds might still be beholden to outsiders. A disclosure requirement ensures only that union members know about this possibility when they cast their votes. It does not eradicate the threat of outside influence.

III

As an alternative basis for sustaining the result below, respondents ask this Court to hold that the outsider rule impermissibly encroaches upon its members' right, guaranteed by § 101(a)(4) of the LMRDA, to institute legal proceedings, and that the appropriate remedy for this violation is an injunction striking down the rule *en toto*. However, unlike the District Court and the Court of Appeals, we do not believe that the union's rule violates the right to sue provision.

Section 101(a)(4) provides that a union may not "limit the right of any member thereof to institute an action in any court, or in a proceeding before any administrative agency." The outsider rule would clearly violate this provision if it prohibited union members from accepting financial or other support from nonmembers for the purpose of conducting campaign-related litigation. In our view, however, the outsider rule simply does not apply where a member uses funds from outsiders to finance litigation.

The language of the rule contains no reference to litigation. In addition, the debates leading up to the passage of the rule do not contain any indication that the union intended the rule to apply in this context. But what is most persuasive, the Campaign Contribution Administration Committee (the Committee)—which was given authority to make final and binding interpretations of the outsider rule—has issued an opinion concerning the impact of the outsider rule on the right to sue. In this opinion, it holds that "the limitations imposed by Section 27 do not apply to the financing of lawsuits by non-members for the purpose of asserting the legal rights of candidates or other union members in connection with elections." App. 455; see also App. 456-458.

The Court of Appeals expressed concern about a regulation contained in the USWA's Election Manual which provides that although the outsider rule "does not prohibit the candidate's use of financial support or services from nonmembers to pay fees for legal or accounting services performed in ... securing ... legal rights of candidates," it does prohibit "[a]ctivities which are designed to extract political gain from legal proceedings." App. 495. According to the Court of Appeals, the reference to "activities" might include steps in the legal proceedings themselves, and might prohibit outside assistance to finance a lawsuit even if it was brought in good faith, if it was designed to extract political gain. USWA has explained, however, that this language is intended to cover only nonlitigation activities that in some way refer to litigation, such as mailing a flyer announcing a legal victory, or some information learned during discovery.

IV

We hold that USWA's rule prohibiting candidates for union office from accepting campaign contributions from nonmembers does not violate § 101(a)(2). Although it may interfere with rights Congress intended to protect, it is rationally related to a legitimate and protected purpose, and thus is sheltered by the proviso to § 101(a)(2). We reverse the decision below and remand for further proceedings consistent with this opinion.

It is so ordered.

JUSTICE WHITE, with whom THE CHIEF JUSTICE, JUSTICE BRENNAN, and JUSTICE BLACKMUN join, dissenting.

The question before us is what Congress intended when in 1959 it passed § 101(a)(2), the Bill of Rights provision of the LMRDA. That question is best answered by identifying the problem that Congress intended to solve by adopting the provision. The answer, in turn, is not at all difficult to discover.

After long and careful examination and hearings dealing with the labor union movement, Congress found that too often unions were run by entrenched, corrupt leaders who maintained themselves and discouraged challenge by any means available, including violence and threats. As Senator McClellan explained: "[T]he records of our committee's investigations show over and over again that a rank-and-file member dare not risk any opposition to a corrupt or autocratic leadership. If he does, he may be beaten, his family threatened, his property destroyed or damaged, and he may be forced out of his job—all of these things can happen and have happened." 105 Cong. Rec. 5806 (1959). And again, "Members had better not offer any competition. They had better not seek election. They had better not aspire to the presidency or the secretaryship, or they will be expelled or disciplined." *Id.,* at 6478.

This was the problem that Congress meant to solve. As Senator McClellan stated, its goal was to end "autocratic rule by placing the ultimate power in the hands of the members, where it rightfully belongs so that they may be ruled by their free consent, may bring about a regeneration of union leadership. I believe the unions should be returned to those whom they were designed to serve; they should not be left to the hands of those who act as masters." 2 Legislative History of the LMRDA (NLRB 1959) 1099.

What Congress then did was to guarantee the union member's right to run for election, § 401(e), and to guarantee him freedom of speech and assembly. § 101(a)(2). There is no question, and the Court concedes as much, that the Act created statutory protection for the union member's right effectively to run for union office. Without doubt, § 101(a)(2) was not only aimed at protecting the member who speaks his mind on union affairs, even if critical of the leadership, but was also "specifically designed to protect the union member's right to seek higher office within the union." *Hall v. Cole,* 412 U.S. 1, 14 (1973). The LMRDA was a major effort by Congress "to insure union democracy." S. Rep. No. 187, 86th Cong., 1st Sess. 2 (1959). The chosen instrument for curbing the abuses of entrenched union leadership was "free and democratic elections." *Steelworkers v. Usery,* 429 U.S. 305, 309 (1977). The abuses of "entrenched union leadership" were to be curbed, among other means, by the "check of democratic elections." *Wirtz v. Hotel Employees,* 391 U.S. 492, 499 (1968). These elections were to be modeled on the "political elections in this country." *Wirtz v. Hotel Employees, supra,* at 504; *Steelworkers v. Usery, supra,* at 309.

The member's right to run for office and to speak and assemble was to be subject to reasonable union rules, but the reasonableness of a particular rule must surely be judged with reference to the paradigmatic situation that Congress intended to address by guaranteeing free elections: a large union with entrenched, autocratic leadership bent on maintaining itself by fair means or foul. We do not by any means suggest that the USWA had or has the characteristics that led to the enactment of § 101(a)(2), but it is clear that the section should be construed with reference to those unions with the kind of leadership that caused the congressional response. Such a leadership is not only determined to discourage opposition; it also has at its disposal all the advantages of incumbency for doing so, including the facilities of the union. Those leaders have normally appointed the union staff, the bureaucracy that makes the union run. The staff is dependent upon and totally loyal to the leadership. It amounts to a built-in campaign organization that can be relied upon to make substantial contributions and to solicit others for more. Such a management is in control of the union's communication system and has immediate access to membership lists and to the members themselves. Obviously, even if the incumbents eschew violence, threats or intimidation, mounting an effective challenge would be a large and difficult endeavor. And if those in office are as unscrupulous as Congress often found them to be, the dimensions of the task facing the insurgent are exceedingly large. But Congress intended to help the members help solve these very difficulties by guaranteeing them the right to run for office and to have free and open elections in the American tradition.

It is incredible to me that the union rule at issue in this case can be found to be a reasonable restriction on the right of Edward Sadlowski to speak, assemble, and run for union office in a free and democratic election. The scope and stringency of the rule cannot be doubted. It forbids any candidate for union office and his supporters from soliciting or accepting financial support from any non-member. The candidate cannot accept contributions from members of his family, relatives, friends, or well-wishers unless they are members of the union. Retired members such as Edward Sadlowski, Sr., may not contribute, neither may members not in good standing. Even a fully secured loan from a non-member with a standard rate of interest is forbidden under the rule. The rule goes even further. It forbids the acceptance of "any other direct or indirect support of any kind from any non-member", except an individual's volunteered personal time. The regulations issued under the rule clearly show that the union intends to prohibit, as far as it is within its power to do so, all non-member contributions on behalf of a member running for union office. These regulations specify:

> When prohibited support is contributed, there will be a presumption that it was accepted by the candidate or his supporters, unless they have taken af-

firmative steps in good faith to dissuade the non-member from providing such support and have taken action to correct the effects of the prohibited support.

A candidate unable to rebut this presumption may be disqualified, fined, suspended, or expelled. This is a draconian rule. How could any candidate "correct the effects of the prohibited support"? The rule thus goes far beyond the limitations on contributions approved in *Buckley v. Valeo,* 424 U.S. 1 (1976), and severely limits expenditures as well. The candidate may actually be denied his statutory right to run for office because non-members have exercised their own First Amendment rights.

....

Restrictions such as this are a far cry from the free and open elections that Congress anticipated and are wholly inconsistent with the way elections have been run in this country. The Court has long recognized the close relationship between the ability to solicit funds and the ability to express views. "[W]ithout solicitation, the flow of ... information and advocacy would likely cease." *Village of Schaumberg v. Citizens for a Better Environment,* 444 U.S. 620, 632 (1980).

In *Thomas v. Collins,* 323 U.S. 516 (1945), the Court held that the First Amendment barred enforcement of a state statute requiring a permit before soliciting membership in any labor organization. Solicitation and speech were deemed to be so intertwined that a prior permit could not be required. The Court conceded that the "collection of funds" might be subject to reasonable regulation, but concluded that such regulation "must be done and the restriction applied, in such a manner as not to intrude upon the rights of free speech and assembly." *Id.,* at 540-541.

Specifically with regard to elections and campaign financing, the Court observed in *Buckley v. Valeo, supra,* at 19:

> A restriction on the amount of money a person or group can spend on political communication during a campaign necessarily reduces the quantity of expression by restricting the number of issues discussed, the depth of their exploration, and the size of the audience reached. This is because virtually every means of communicating ideas in today's mass society requires the expenditure of money....

It goes without saying that running for office in a union with 1.3 million members spread throughout the United States and Canada requires a substantial war chest if the campaign is to be effective and to have any reasonable chance of succeeding. Attempting to unseat the incumbents of union office is a substantial undertaking. As we noted in *United Steelworkers v. Usery, supra,* at 311, there is no permanent opposition party within the union. There is only a one-party system consisting of the union's incumbent officers and hired staff all controlled from the top down. "The full-time officers collectively, under the direction of the top officer, constitute the sole political machine for the preservation of their offices and power." Edelstein and Warner, Comparative Union Democracy, p. 39 (1979). The union involved in this case has some 30 elected positions, its president appoints more than 1,500 office and field staff and salaries and expenses for union personnel in 1978 totalled over 37 million dollars. App. 141.

Thus, in the best of circumstances, the role of the challenger is very difficult. And if one keeps in mind that Congress intended to give the challenger a fair chance even in a union controlled by unscrupulous leaders with an iron grip on the staff and a willingness to employ means both within and without the law, it is wholly unrealistic to confine the challenger to financial support garnered within the union. Surely, Congress never intended that a union should be permitted to impose such a limitation....

In addressing itself to union elections, Congress forbade union and employer contributions, but went no further in restricting contributions or expenditures to or on behalf of union candidates for office. The majority emphasizes that Congress was concerned about the control of unions by outsiders and asserts that the challenged rule serves the congressional purpose. It is true, as Senator McClellan explained, that "impositions and abuses ... have been perpetrated upon the working people of many of our states by the thugs who have muscled into positions of power in labor unions and who masquerade [as] labor leaders and as friend of working people...." 2 Leg. Hist. of the LMRDA 1097. But the remedy which he proposed and which was adopted was to end "autocratic rule by placing the ultimate power in the hands of the members," *id.,* at 1099, and by giving them sufficient statutory protection to participate in a fair election to unseat an entrenched leadership.

Yet the majority somehow finds the absolute, unbending, no-contribution rule to be a reasonable regulation of the member's right to seek office and of the free and open elections that Congress anticipated. This, in spite of the availability of other means to satisfy the union's legitimate concerns about outsiders controlling their affairs through those whose campaigns they have financed. A requirement of disclosure of all contributions, together with a ceiling on contributions, would avoid outside corruption without trampling on the rights of members to raise reasonable sums for election campaigns. Such rules would honor both purposes of the legislation: protecting against outside influence and empowering members to express their views and to challenge established leadership. As I see it, the rule at issue contradicts the values the statute was designed to protect and thwarts its purpose.

I respectfully dissent.

NOTE

Both majority and dissenting opinions seem to assume that under the proviso to § 101(a)(2), members' free speech rights are subject to "reasonable union rules." Is that what the statute says? Does *Sadlowski* undermine *Salzhandler, supra*? The principal case is noted in 96 Harv. L. Rev. 288 (1982) and 68 Iowa L. Rev. 831 (1983). *See also* James, *Union Democracy and the LMRDA: Autocracy and Insurgency in National Union Elections,* 13 Harv. C.R.-C.L. L. Rev. 247 (1978).

D. FINANCIAL EXACTIONS

American Federation of Musicians v. Wittstein, 379 U.S. 171, 85 S. Ct. 300, 13 L. Ed. 2d 214 (1964). At a national convention, a union approved a dues increase in accordance with its constitutional procedure whereby the votes of the delegates were weighted to reflect the number of members in a local that each delegate represented. Although a roll call showed that the recommendation had carried in terms of a membership count, less than half of the delegates present voted in favor of the proposal. Certain union members challenged the validity of the enactment under § 101(a)(3)(B) of the LMRDA, which provides that the dues of an international union "shall not be increased ... except ... by majority vote of the delegates voting at a regular convention." The Supreme Court held that that Act did not prohibit the union's weighted system of voting. The Court pointed out that the literal language of the statute did not foreclose this method, and that the legislative history showed sponsors of the Act favored weighted voting as the most democratic procedure. Added the Court: "Section 101(a)(3)(B), as well as Title IV, authorizes a representative system of government and does not require a town meeting for action by an international or national union."

NOTES

1. Many international constitutions set the dues rate, or a minimum dues rate, for local unions. In light of § 101(a)(3), may a duly constituted international convention increase these rates and put them into effect without submitting the issue to a vote of the locals' members? *See Ranes v. Office Employees, Local 28,* 317 F.2d 915 (7th Cir. 1963) *(Held:* Yes). *Cf. King v. Randazzo,* 346 F.2d 307 (2d Cir. 1965). Could the international effect such an increase through secret ballot votes at a series of duly notified local union membership meetings? *See Telephone Workers, Local 2 v. Telephone Workers,* 362 F.2d 891 (1st Cir.), *cert. denied,* 385 U.S. 947 (1966).

Turner v. Dempster, 743 F.2d 1301 (9th Cir. 1984), *cert. denied,* 470 U.S. 1005 (1985), held that a member stated a claim under the "equal rights and privileges" clause of Title I when he challenged a referendum amending the union constitution to increase dues and a rule which only allowed individuals with six years of employment experience on ships at sea to vote in constitutional referenda.

2. Must the procedures for setting so-called per capita taxes, payable directly by local unions (rather than by individual members) to their internationals, conform to the requirements of § 101(a)(3)? *Compare Ranes v. Office Emps. Local 28, supra, with Telephone Workers, Local 2 v. Telephone Workers, supra. See also Patterson v. Carpenters,* 906 F.2d 510 (10th Cir. 1990) (vote on per capita fee paid to district council must provide local members genuine option to vote against any increase).

3. Section 101(a)(3) of the LMRDA is directed at increases in dues and fees, and does not require a union to hold a membership vote before terminating a special assessment and the organizing drive being funded by it. *Corea v. Welo,* 937 F.2d 1132 (6th Cir. 1991). *See also Moore v. IBEW Local 569,* 989 F.2d 1534 (9th Cir. 1993), *cert. denied,* 510 U.S. 1117 (1994) (international union president did not violate § 101(a)(3) when he withheld approval of proposed bylaw that would have decreased local union dues, since that section only applies to dues increases and not dues decreases).

E. THE RIGHT TO SUE; EXHAUSTION OF INTRAUNION REMEDIES

DETROY v. AMERICAN GUILD OF VARIETY ARTISTS

United States Court of Appeals, Second Circuit
286 F.2d 75 (1961), *cert. denied,* 366 U.S. 929 (1961)

LUMBARD, CHIEF JUDGE. The appellant, manager and trainer of a troupe of chimpanzees with which he performs professionally under the name of the "Marquis Family" in theaters, night clubs, circuses, on television, and in motion pictures, instituted this proceeding under § 102 of the Labor-Management Reporting and Disclosure Act of 1959, ... demanding injunctive relief and damages for an alleged violation of the procedural rights granted union members by § 101(a)(5) of the Act.... Upon a motion for summary judgment, the district court dismissed the complaint on the ground that under § 101(a)(4) the plaintiff could bring no court action against a labor union without first exhausting the internal remedies provided by the union, and that in this case the defendant union had established reasonable procedures by its constitution whereby claims against it by members could be heard within the four-month period permitted by the law.

The controversy between the appellant and the American Guild of Variety Artists, a labor union representing variety entertainers in the United States and Canada, arose out of a breach-of-contract claim made against the appellant by a resort hotel in Las Vegas, Nevada. After failing to settle the dispute by negotiation, the AGVA requested the parties to submit it to arbitration, which they did. A panel of three, one selected by each of the parties to the dispute and the third chosen by the two so designated, met in Los Angeles County, California, on January 12, 1960, and decided in favor of the hotel. The union then advised the appellant that if he did not abide by the award, it would place him on the "National Unfair List" appearing in its monthly periodical "AGVA News." The appellant replied that he intended to move to vacate the arbitration award in the California courts, but never began any such proceedings. When the three months provided by California law for vacating arbitration awards had elapsed, the union proceeded to publish the appellant's name in the August 1960 issue of the periodical under a heading which read as follows:

Notice to Members

The rules require that you may not work for any employer, agent, booker or third party who is marked "Unfair" by AGVA. Violation of these rules subjects you to disciplinary action.

Notice to Agents

.... You are not authorized to book AGVA members in unfair establishments or book performers not in good standing in AGVA. Violation of rules subjects you to revocation of your franchise.

The appellant then began this proceeding in the Southern District of New York, claiming that the listing amounted to disciplinary action within the meaning of § 101(a)(5) of the Labor-Management Reporting and Disclosure Act of 1959, ... and that he was, therefore, entitled to specific written charges, a reasonable time to defend, and a full and fair hearing before having his name placed on the list.

The appellant did not, however, seek to utilize the procedure made available by Article XX of the Constitution of the AGVA. This article, entitled "Claims of Members," establishes procedures whereby claims asserted against the union are heard and determined by its Board or Executive Committee. Thus, the first issue before us now is whether the proviso in § 101(a)(4), which protects the right of a union member to sue his union, "Provided, That any such member may be required to exhaust reasonable hearing procedures (but not to exceed a four-month lapse of time) within such organization, before instituting legal or administrative proceedings against such organizations or any officer thereof," required of the appellant in this case that he first have recourse to the internal procedures established by the union's constitution. The exhaustion proviso of § 101(a)(4) does not appear in § 102, which grants members who claim that their rights under § 101 have been infringed a federal forum in which to litigate their disputes with the union. It might also appear from the rejection by the House of Representatives of H.R. 8342, the bill originally reported out of the Committee on Education and Labor, which explicitly provided for exhaustion of internal remedies in § 102, that Congress did not mean to have the exhaustion doctrine apply to the rights granted by § 101, except where, as in the case of the right to sue, it was expressly provided. However, the broad language of the proviso in § 101(a)(4) includes suits instituted against labor unions in any court on any claim. Absent a clear directive by Congress, the policy formulated over a course of time by courts reluctant to interfere in the internal affairs of private organizations should not be superseded. We hold, therefore, that the provision in § 101(a)(4) applies, as well, to suits brought in the federal courts for violations of the rights secured by § 101.

Judge Dimock in this case read § 101(a)(4) as imposing upon the union member an absolute duty to exhaust union remedies before applying to the federal courts. The legislative history of the section indicates, however, that Congress had no intention of establishing such a rule.[2]

The statute provides that any member of a labor organization "may be required" to exhaust the internal union remedies, not that he "must" or "is required to" exhaust them. When read in light of the statements made on the floor of Congress by the authors of the statute, it appears clear that the proviso was incorporated in order to preserve the exhaustion doctrine as it had developed and would continue to develop in the courts, lest it otherwise appear to be Congress' intention to have the right to sue secured by § 101 abrogate the requirement of prior resort to internal procedures. In addition, the proviso dictated an outside limit beyond which the judiciary cannot extend the requirement of exhaustion—no remedy which would require proceedings exceeding four months in duration may be demanded. We therefore construe the statute to mean that a member of a labor union who attempts to institute proceedings before a court or an administrative agency may be required *by that court or agency* to exhaust internal remedies of less than four months' duration before invoking outside assistance.

---

[2] For example, one of the authors of the bill passed by the House, Representative Griffin, expressed a clear opinion on the question. He said:

"The proviso which limits exhaustion of internal remedies is not intended to impose restrictions on a union member which do not otherwise exist, but rather to place a maximum on the length of time which may be required to exhaust such remedies. In other words, existing decisions which require, or do not require, exhaustion of such remedies are not to be affected except as a time limit of 4 months is superimposed. Also, by use of the phrase 'reasonable hearing procedures' in the proviso, it should be clear that no obligation is imposed to exhaust procedures where it would obviously be futile or would place an undue burden on the union member." 105 Daily Cong. Rec. App. A7915 (Sept. 4, 1959).

The statement made by Senator Kennedy, who introduced the original bill to which §§ 101-105 were added as amendments on the Senate floor, is also representative of the attitude taken by those who instituted the legislation. He said:

"Nor is it the intent or purpose of the provision to invalidate the considerable body of State and Federal court decisions of many years standing which require, or do not require, the exhaustion of internal remedies prior to court intervention depending upon the reasonableness of such requirements in terms of the facts and circumstances of a particular case.... The doctrine of exhaustion of reasonable internal union remedies for violation of union laws is just as firmly established as the doctrine of exhausting reasonable administrative agency provisions prior to action by courts." 105 Daily Cong. Rec. 16414 (Sept. 3, 1959).

Section 102, under which the appellant instituted his proceeding, provides for enforcement by federal courts of rights secured by federal law. We are not in this case, therefore, bound by the doctrine of exhaustion as developed in the New York, Nevada, or California courts with respect to suits against unions brought in the courts of those states by union members. In enforcing rights guaranteed by the new statute, whether or not similar rights would be enforced under state law by state courts, the federal courts may develop their own principles regarding the time when a union's action taken in violation of § 101 is ripe for judicial intervention.... The rules formulated by various state courts may suggest helpful avenues of approach, *cf. Textile Workers Union of America v. Lincoln Mills,* 1957, 353 U.S. 448, 457, but the authority granted to the federal courts by Congress to secure the rights enumerated in § 101 of the 1959 Act is accompanied by the duty to formulate federal law regarding a union member's obligation to exhaust the internal union remedies before seeking judicial vindication of those rights.

If we look to the substantial body of state law on the subject, we find that the general rule requiring exhaustion before resort to a court has been almost entirely swallowed up by exceptions phrased in broad terms. *See* Annotation, 168 A.L.R. 1462 (1947); Summers, *Legal Limitations on Union Discipline,* 64 Harv. L. Rev. 1049, 1086-92 (1951). Rather than decide whether exhaustion is proper by determining whether the union's action can be characterized as "void" (*e.g., Tesoriero v. Miller,* 1949, 274 App. Div. 670, 88 N.Y.S.2d 87) or as "affecting property rights" (*e.g., Sheet Metal Workers, Local 65 v. Nalty,* 6 Cir., 1925, 7 F.2d 100), we believe it preferable to consider each case on its own facts.

The congressionally approved policy of first permitting unions to correct their own wrongs is rooted in the desire to stimulate labor organizations to take the initiative and independently to establish honest and democratic procedures. *See* Cox, *The Role of Law in Preserving Union Democracy,* 72 Harv. L. Rev. 609, 615 (1959). Other policies, as well, underlie the exhaustion rule. The possibility that corrective action within the union will render a member's complaint moot suggests that, in the interest of conserving judicial resources, no court step in before the union is given its opportunity. Moreover, courts may find valuable the assistance provided by prior consideration of the issues by appellate union tribunals. *See* Summers, *The Law of Union Discipline: What the Courts Do in Fact,* 70 Yale L.J. 175, 207 (1960). Congress has provided a safeguard against abuse by a union of the freedom thus granted it by not requiring exhaustion of union remedies if the procedures will exceed four months in duration. But in any case, if the state of facts is such that immediate judicial relief is warranted, Congress' acceptance of the exhaustion doctrine as applied to the generality of cases should not bar an appropriate remedy in proper circumstances.

The affidavits and exhibits submitted in the district court on the motion for summary judgment establish that the only hearing given the appellant before his name was placed on the National Unfair List was that of the arbitration proceeding. The union was not a party to the arbitration, and the issue decided by the arbitrators was not whether the appellant should be disciplined by the union but whether he owed an obligation to an employer with whom he had contracted. It is undisputed that no hearing was held in which the appellant could respond to the union's intention of taking disciplinary action. Quite clearly, a hearing in which some liability between a union member and a third party is determined is not the type of hearing demanded by § 101(a)(5). At no time was the appellant given the opportunity of arguing before the union's hearing board that placing him on the Unfair List exceeded the powers granted to the union by its constitution, nor could he raise other mitigating circumstances in response to an expressed intention to place his name on such a list. The facts on their face, therefore, reveal a violation of the rights guaranteed union members by § 101(a)(5). If the question before us were whether the union's constitution authorized the listing of the appellant's name on an unfair list after a hearing with due procedural safeguards, a union tribunal might provide some insight to aid our decision. But no prior consideration by such a tribunal is necessary or helpful on the question whether the treatment of the appellant violated § 101(a)(5).

In addition, the particular form of the disciplinary action makes it difficult for the union to provide an adequate remedy. The appellant, from the date his name appeared on the list, was virtually barred from employment by those dealing regularly with the AGVA. Since he is an independent contractor whose weekly pay varies according to the terms of the contracts he signs with his employers, the precise extent of damages suffered by the appellant as a result of the listing can never be determined. Even were the union to permit him to present his case before a review board, the board could merely order his name removed from the list and, in order to provide a more satisfactory remedy, award as damages for the period during which he was barred from employment a sum which, at best, could only be an approximation. It appears unlikely that Congress intended that its expressed desire to provide minimum safeguards against arbitrary union discipline be avoided by the union's imposition of a sanction which has its most severe effect within a four-month period, if the consequences of such action cannot be precisely measured in order to assess damages. Early judicial intervention providing an adequate remedy by means of the court's power to enjoin further violations is therefore proper....

Moreover, it is by no means clear that the union's own rules afforded the appellant a remedy within the organization.... No provision is made anywhere for any proceeding either before or after the printing of a member's name on the National Unfair List. The union maintains that Article XX of its Constitution, entitled "Claims of Members," provides a means for reviewing the correctness of this sanction. The constitution's separate provision for disciplinary proceedings in Article XVII, however, suggests that Article XX was not intended to provide an alternate procedure for review of a union's sanctions against its members, but merely to grant a forum for other monetary claims against the union. Moreover, after the arbitration award the appellant notified the Western Regional Director of the union by telegram that he intended "appealing to the National Board," and was told in a reply letter that "the decision of the arbitrators is final and ... you cannot appeal this to the National Board of AGVA." Although this response referred not to the disciplinary measure but to the arbitrators' decision, neither that letter nor the later notification that he was being placed on the National Unfair List notified the appellant that any specific review procedure was available. Thus, an attempt to proceed under Article XX might not have proved futile, but it would have been quite uncertain. When asserting what is clearly a violation of a federal statute, a union member should not be required to first seek out remedies which are dubious. Only resort to those expressly provided in the union's constitution or those clearly called to his attention by the union officials should be demanded of him.

Taking due account of the declared policy favoring self-regulation by unions, we nonetheless hold that where the internal union remedy is uncertain and has not been specifically brought to the attention of the disciplined party, the violation of federal law clear and undisputed, and the injury to the union member immediate and difficult to compensate by means of a subsequent money award, exhaustion of union remedies ought not to be required. The absence of any of these elements might, in light of congressional approval of the exhaustion doctrine, call for a different result. The facts of this case, however, warrant immediate judicial intervention.

Nor can we agree with the union's claim that the listing of the appellant's name did not constitute discipline within the meaning of § 101(a)(5). If a union such as the AGVA undertakes to enforce the contracts made by its members with employers, it does so because such enforcement is to the ultimate benefit of all the members, in that it promotes stability within the industry. A breach of contract or a refusal to abide by an arbitration award, therefore, is not damaging merely to the employer but to the union as well, and the union's listing of those of its members who do violate their contracts is an act of self-protection. In thus furthering its own ends the union must abide by the rules set down for it by Congress in § 101(a)(5), and any member against whom steps are taken by the union in the interest of promoting the welfare of the group is entitled to these guarantees.

In passing on the motions for summary judgment and for a temporary injunction, the district court had before it only the complaint and the affidavits of the appellant and various officers of the union. The undisputed facts of the case require that a temporary injunction issue ordering the union to remove the appellant's name from its Unfair List where it is now retained in apparent violation of § 101(a)(5).

We reverse the order of the district court dismissing the complaint and remand the case with instructions to grant the temporary injunction requested by the appellant.

NOTES

1. Legislative history and early judicial authority can be found to the effect that the four-month limitation in § 101(a)(4) "relates to restrictions imposed by unions rather than the rules of judicial administration or the action of Government agencies." *See, e.g.,* 105 Cong. Rec. 17,899 (1959) (remarks of Sen. Kennedy); *Mamula v. Steelworkers,* 414 Pa. 294, 200 A. 2d 306, *cert. denied,* 379 U.S. 17 (1964). Nonetheless, the *Detroy* analysis has prevailed. In *NLRB v. Marine & Shipbuilding Workers,* 391 U.S. 418 (1968), the Supreme Court concluded that the proviso to § 101(a)(4) was "not a grant of authority to unions more firmly to police their members but a statement of policy that the public tribunals whose aid is invoked may in their discretion stay their hands for four months, while the aggrieved person seeks relief within the union." *See also Operating Eng'rs Local 3 v. Burroughs,* 417 F.2d 370 (9th Cir. 1969), *cert. denied,* 397 U.S. 916 (1970).

2. Exhaustion of internal remedies has been dispensed with as a prerequisite to suit where union disciplinary action was "void" because based on an offense not specified in the union constitution, *Simmons v. Textile Workers, Local 713,* 350 F.2d 1012 (4th Cir. 1965), where exhaustion was deemed "futile" because of union hostility toward the member, *Farowitz v. Musicians, Local 802,* 241 F. Supp. 895 (S.D.N.Y. 1965), or where adequate relief—compensatory and punitive damages—was not available through internal union processes, *Maddalone v. Local 17, United Bhd. of Carpenters & Joiners of Am.,* 152 F.3d 178 (2d Cir. 1998). But the mere fact that a final union decision might not be obtainable within four months does not enable a member to bring suit immediately, where there is no showing the member would be harmed by pursuing an intraunion remedy for the statutory period. *Harris v. ILA Local 1291,* 321 F.2d 801 (3d Cir. 1963).

A union cannot defend against a member's suit by contending he failed to exhaust internal remedies when consideration of his intraunion appeal was refused because he had not first paid certain contested "working dues" and the fine imposed on him. *Chadwick v. IBEW Local 175,* 674 F.2d 939 (D.C. Cir. 1982).

3. Section 101(a)(4) provides that "no labor organization shall limit the right of any member thereof to institute an action in any court ..., irrespective of whether or not the labor organization or its officers are named as defendants ...." In *Moore v. IBEW Local 569,* 53 F.3d 1054 (9th Cir. 1995), *cert. denied,* 516 U.S. 1111 (1996), the court voided a bargaining agreement provision that authorized the employer to obtain attorney fees from employees who unsuccessfully challenged grievance-arbitration awards, because the court found that a union could not agree to a contractual provision that restricted the § 101(a)(4) right of employees to prosecute legal actions.

In *Pawlak v. Greenawalt,* 628 F.2d 826 (3d Cir. 1980), *cert. denied,* 449 U.S. 1083 (1981), the court held unlawful a union's constitutional provision which authorized assessment of litigation costs as a fine against members who unsuccessfully sue the union without exhaustion of internal union remedies. Finding such a provision impermissibly limits a member's right to sue, in violation of the Landrum-Griffin Act, the court rejected the union contention that the right to sue is exempted from internal discipline only where the suit "touches a part of the public domain," and not, as in the case at bar, where the suit is strictly internal. The external/internal distinction was found irrelevant to suits brought under Landrum-Griffin, which, unlike the Taft-Hartley Act, was designed specifically to regulate internal union affairs.

4. *See generally* Beaird & Player, *Exhaustion of Intra-Union Remedies and Access to Public Tribunals Under the Landrum-Griffin Act,* 26 Ala. L. Rev. 519 (1974); Boyle, *The Labor Bill of Rights and the Doctrine of Exhaustion of Remedies—A Marriage of Convenience,* 16 Hastings L.J. 590 (1965); O'Donoghue, *Protection of a Union Member's Right to Sue Under the Landrum-Griffin Act,* 14 Cath. U. L. Rev. 215 (1965); Vorenberg, *Exhaustion of Intraunion Remedies as a Condition Precedent to Appeal to the Courts,* 2 Lab. L.J. 487 (1951). Common-law cases are gathered in a comprehensive annotation in 168 A.L.R. 1462 (1947).

5. In *UAW v. National Right to Work Legal Defense & Educ. Found.,* 590 F.2d 1139 (D.C. Cir. 1978), a court of appeals held that the second proviso in § 101(a)(4) of the LMRDA, which prohibits the financing by "interested" employers of members' suits against their union, does not apply to "the legitimate litigation program of a bona fide, independent legal aid organization, even though the organization receives contributions from interested employers." The financing proviso to § 101(a)(4) has also been read to mean that while employers are forbidden to finance the institution of suits by employees against their union, employers are free to finance a defense or counterclaim by employees. *IBEW Local 336 v. Illinois Bell Tel. Co.,* 496 F.2d 1 (7th Cir.) *cert. denied,* 419 U.S. 879 (1974). Would different rulings in these cases have posed substantial constitutional questions?

F. PROCEDURAL DUE PROCESS

1. INTRAUNION SAFEGUARDS

LEO BROMWICH, UNION CONSTITUTIONS, A REPORT TO THE FUND FOR THE REPUBLIC 29-33 (1959)*

In civil society, the phrase "due process" is the summary of an extensive body of law. In briefest form, it states society's determination to give an accused person a fair opportunity to present his defense and is grounded upon the existence of an independent judiciary capable of following its own views in rendering the verdict. How do these conceptions apply to the society of union men and women?

It should already be apparent that the procedural rights of an accused union member are of paramount importance. Given the enormous power of the international president and the many limitations upon rank-and-file control of the union administration, clear and defined rights are essential to any union member who wishes to speak, and criticize, freely. The points that must be examined in determining how the unions handle this problem are fairly obvious. They revolve around the composition of the union tribunals and appellate boards, the time span for appellate procedure, the difference in the regulations regarding the disciplining of an international officer as against a rank-and-file member of a local union. Again, it should be noted that even these important questions are not enough for a full examination of internal union democracy. The presence of good procedure does not guarantee justice, nor is its absence proof of minority control.

A number of unions in our sample have fairly detailed trial procedures indicative of serious concern for due process. These include the International Printing Pressmen, the Mine, Mill and Smelter Workers, and the Upholsterers. In two cases, those of the International Typographical Union and the United Automobile Workers, important constitutional points are spelled out in a way that makes them representative of some of the best of the union trial practices. Although there is considerable variation, even among the better constitutions, an examination of the constitutions of these two unions should give us some idea of the proper type of procedural safeguards.

The constitution of the ITU provides penalties for specific offenses ranging from reprimand or a small fine to expulsion. There is also a category of "violation of laws of the local or international union," "conduct unbecoming a union member," and "malfeasance in office," but the allegations "must be sufficiently specific as to the provisions of union law violated," and the "acts which constitute the basis for the charges" must be cited to permit the defendant to prepare a proper defense. The accusing party must deliver the complaint to the local president within 30 days of the time he became aware of the charge, and the accused has five days in which to answer (though he may waive this right without prejudice to his case).

The charges are discussed at the next meeting of the local. If they are found "cognizable" by the majority of the members present, an investigating committee is appointed by the president of the local. This committee reports at the next regular meeting, and a vote is taken as to whether the case should be prosecuted or dropped. If the vote is to continue the case, the president of the local may appoint a trial committee of three or five members; but if either party to the proceedings objects to the appointment of the committee, its membership is selected by a drawing of lots.

The trial committee is required to notify both parties of the time and place of the hearing. Representation by counsel is permitted, provided that the counsel is a member of the union. After the hearings, the trial committee reports its findings at the next meeting of the local. The members then discuss the verdict, and two-thirds of the members present are required to return a judgment of guilty (voting is by secret ballot). If the accused is found guilty, a vote is then taken on the penalty recommended by the trial committee or, if that is amended, on the heaviest penalty proposed. In order to expel, three-fourths of those present and voting must be in favor. If there is an acquittal, all expenses incurred in connection with the trial are borne by the union (the fees chargeable to counsel should not be in excess of the pay time lost at union scale).

The appeal process in the ITU reflects the same concern for due process. Briefs are filed with the president of the local, time is stipulated for answer and rebuttal, and all documents are forwarded to the international executive council. Unless it is extended by the international president, the maximum time for the filing of documents is 50 days. Appeal from an executive council decision is to the next convention of the international union, but full compliance with the decisions of the lower tribunals is expected pending appeal. A subordinate union, or members not satisfied with the verdict of the convention, may appeal to the courts, but only upon first depositing a bond with the executive council to cover the costs that might be incurred by the international in defending the action. Failure to exhaust these procedural remedies before going into court is punishable by summary expulsion.

In the case of the trial of an international officer, there are somewhat different rules. An international officer of the union may be suspended by the international president or impeached by the executive council. The officer is furnished with a detailed statement of the charges, and the trial board is composed of the presidents of the five largest locals. The decision of this trial board must be rendered within 30 days from the date of suspension, and it can be appealed to the next convention.

There are, of course, some imperfections in this process, but, on the whole, it represents a serious concern for the rights of the members. Thus, the allowance of a "blanket" clause (conduct "unbecoming" a union member, etc.) is, on its face, a violation of the due process requirement of specificity, but then the violation must be fully described. The provision that the accused may select his counsel only among the union members is a limit upon freedom, but in the absence of technical rules of pleading and evidence it will not normally be too serious. The major difficulty is that the trial procedure is placed completely in the hands of officers and union members. Not until the trial and appellate procedures are fully exhausted is there the prospect of judgment by a neutral tribunal.

The United Automobile Workers, whose trial provisions roughly approximate those of the ITU in concern for due process, has addressed itself to this problem of neutral, disinterested judgment. The UAW has a public review board composed of seven "impartial persons of good public repute" who are selected for this service by the international president and approved by the international convention. This board is primarily an appellate body, though it does have original jurisdiction in a few cases. It receives copies of all complaints lodged with the international executive board. If the appellant is dissatisfied with the decision of the executive board, he may then appeal to the public review board. In addition, the board is empowered to act directly on a matter "if it concludes that there is substance to the original complaint and that the action of the International Executive Board does not satisfactorily meet the problem." Thus, a serious attempt is made to keep the judicial decisions of the local and international officers under constant surveillance of a body whose independence cannot be matched by any union tribunal. Yet in the entire labor movement the Upholsterers is the only other union with such independent public review system. [The situation remains essentially unchanged thirty years later. In the intervening period a handful of unions experimented with public review boards, but their efforts were generally abortive. Even the Upholsterers' board has fallen into disuse.—*Eds.*]

Unfortunately, there are a good number of unions whose procedural rules do not match those of the ITU, the UAW, and the Upholsterers. In the Teamsters, for instance, the executive board of the local is given original jurisdiction in the trial of union members; the general executive board has appellate jurisdiction for the five-year interval between conventions, and charges against international officers are heard by the executive board. The Hod Carriers, the Bakery and Confectionery Workers, and the International Union of Operating Engineers have similar provisions concentrating power in the hands of the local and international executive boards....

RICHARD BOYLE v. UAW LOCAL 157

UAW Public Review Board
Case No. 385 (1977)

Richard Boyle, a member of Local 157, appeals his conviction on charges of conduct unbecoming a union member by reason of his allegedly having provided information to his employer which jeopardized the job of a co-worker.

On May 14, 1973, a trial committee found Boyle and Peter E. Folts guilty of conduct unbecoming a union member. The convictions ultimately were sustained by the Local membership and the Local Joint Council....

[Boyle processed an appeal to the International Executive Board, including a hearing before an IEB Appeals Committee.]

The prejudice which accrued to appellant as a result of the failure of the Local Union Executive Board to notify him that it had found the charges[*] against him

---

[*] The charges read:

> We the undersigned hereby charge Union Members Richard Boyle and Peter Folts with conduct unbecoming a Union Member. Specifically, we charge that the two above named individuals did deliberately give detailed information, both verbal and written, to foreman Dan Harvey on alleged improper activities of Union Member George Lewis. These records and statements dealt with alleged absences from his work area by Brother Lewis and alleged improper performance of his job. We feel that the actions of Peter Folts and Richard Boyle were

to satisfy the requirements of Article 31, § 1 of the Constitution was cured at the point that he was permitted to appeal the adequacy of the charges to the International Executive Board. The International Executive Board has now reviewed those charges and has found that they conform to the requirements of Article 31, § 3, that is, they are not deficient under any of the tests set forth therein, whereupon it proceeded to the issues relating to appellant's conviction on the charges, which conviction it has also sustained. Appellant has now requested review of the IEB's decision by the Public Review Board.

We agree with the International Executive Board that the charges satisfy the requirements of Article 31, § 3. The charges allege that appellant Boyle deliberately gave detailed information verbally and in writing to a foreman concerning alleged absences and improper performance of his job by a fellow member. The date of the alleged action was specified to have been March 8, 1973. We conclude that these charges were framed in sufficient detail to enable appellant to prepare a defense and to satisfy the requirements of Article 31, § 1 of the Constitution that the charges state the exact nature of the alleged offense and the period of time in which the offense took place. Finally, the charges were timely filed.

We concur in the conclusion of the Local Executive Board that the act of providing information to management concerning the activities of a fellow worker which would place that fellow worker in jeopardy of losing his job does constitute conduct unbecoming a union member. The charge is not that appellant provided information in response to interrogation by management, but rather that he spontaneously generated it, an activity which is not normally part of an employee's responsibility and, as such, is in contravention of the pledge which the members have made to each other in Article 2, § 1 of the Constitution, "to maintain and protect the interests of workers under the jurisdiction" of the UAW.

Finally, we agree that the charges do not involve a question which should have been decided by the membership rather than the trial procedure. The charges clearly allege a misconduct on the part of appellant. The Constitution requires that such alleged misconduct be processed under the trial provisions of Article 31 of the Constitution.

We turn now to the question as to whether there is sufficient evidence in the record to sustain the trial committee's verdict of guilt on the charges. Boyle's principal challenge to his conviction is based upon his claim that the record is

---

designed to result in and well may result in severe damage to Brother Lewis's job security. We further feel that in taking the actions above mentioned Richard Boyle and Peter Folts have improperly assumed the clear function of management, that being the direction of the work forces and the giving of discipline. The specific action of giving the above mentioned information to management took place on 3/8/73. However, the records were maintained over a longer and undetermined amount of time. We ask that Union Members Peter Folts and Richard Boyle be brought to trial for the indicated offenses as provided in Article 31, of the UAW International Constitution.

insufficient to enable an appellate body to review the evidence. Specifically, he complains of a lack of a transcript of the trial committee proceedings but there was a tape made and although appellant claims that the tape is inaudible, the International Executive Board Appeals Committee which reviewed this case stated it listened to the tapes and, furthermore, heard an oral recitation of the evidence presented against appellant. Appellant, on the other hand, did not appear at that portion of the Appeals Committee's proceedings wherein it dealt with the question of his guilt or innocence of the charges against him.

There is no requirement under the Constitution, however, that a transcript of trial committee proceedings be made. A union trial proceeding ought not be equated with a criminal proceeding. While it is important that fundamental principles of due process be observed, the procedures are much less formal. Neither side is schooled in the subtleties of criminal procedure; rules of evidence are not enforced. Basically the "trial" consists of each side telling its story and the trial committee deciding, on the basis of what it has heard, whether the charges have been proved. In this instance, the trial committee was satisfied that the evidence sustained the charges against appellant. That decision has been reviewed by the general membership, the Local General Council, and the International Executive Board, all of whom have concurred in its findings.

There is nothing in the record to show that appellant was treated unfairly. He was given adequate notice of the charges against him and they were sufficiently detailed to enable him to prepare a defense. We should reverse that conviction only when we find that the Constitutional procedures had not been followed or that there was insufficient evidence in the record upon which a conviction could be sustained. We have found that the Constitutionally mandated procedures have now been followed, that the evidence which is reflected in the record does provide a sufficient basis upon which an impartial trial committee could have concluded that Boyle had taken the actions ascribed to him, and that such actions constituted conduct unbecoming a union member.

The matters raised for the first time in appellant's second letter to the PRB provide no basis for a different result. The assertion that the co-worker did not in fact lose his job is certainly no proof that it was not placed in jeopardy. And the claim of a purpose to discriminate against appellant for political reasons is made without an offer of any supporting evidence. Appellant having failed to present and make a record on either matter before the Local and International reviewing bodies, the PRB cannot investigate and determine the issues initially now.

Affirmed.

NOTE

For further discussion of the UAW Public Review Board, *see* J. Stieber, W. Oberer & M. Harrington, Democracy and Public Review, A Report to the Center for the Study of Democratic Institutions (1960); Brooks, *Impartial Public Review*

of Internal Union Disputes: Experiment in Democratic Self-Discipline, 22 Ohio
St. L.J. 64 (1961); Klein, *UAW Public Review Board Report,* 18 Rutgers L. Rev.
304 (1964); Oberer, *Voluntary Impartial Review of Labor: Some Reflections,* 58
Mich. L. Rev. 55 (1959). *Cf. Clayton v. United Auto Workers,* 451 U.S. 679
(1981), *supra. See also* U.S. Bureau of Labor Statistics, Dep't of Labor, Bull. No.
1350, Disciplinary Powers and Procedures in Union Constitutions (1963); Klein,
Linn, Feller, *Public Review Boards: Their Place in the Process of Dispute Resolutions,* in National Academy of Arbitrators, Arbitration—1974, Proceedings of
the Twenty-seventh Annual Meeting 189, 205, 221 (1975) (three separate papers).

2. LEGAL SAFEGUARDS

INTERNATIONAL BROTHERHOOD OF
BOILERMAKERS v. HARDEMAN

Supreme Court of the United States
401 U.S. 233, 91 S. Ct. 609, 28 L. Ed. 2d 10 (1971)

MR. JUSTICE BRENNAN delivered the opinion of the Court....

Respondent was expelled from membership in petitioner union and brought
this action under § 102 [of the LMRDA] in the District Court for the Southern
District of Alabama. He alleged that in expelling him the petitioner violated
§ 101(a)(5) of the Act....

A jury awarded respondent damages of $152,150. The Court of Appeals for
the Fifth Circuit affirmed. 420 F.2d 485 (1969). We granted certiorari limited to
the questions whether the subject matter of the suit was preempted because exclusively within the competence of the National Labor Relations Board and, if
not preempted, whether the courts below had applied the proper standard of review to the union proceedings.... We reverse.

The case arises out of events in the early part of October 1960. Respondent,
George Hardeman, is a boilermaker. He was then a member of petitioner's Local
Lodge 112. On October 3, he went to the union hiring hall to see Herman Wise,
business manager of the Local Lodge and the official responsible for referring
workmen for jobs. Hardeman had talked to a friend of his, an employer who had
promised to ask for him by name for a job in the vicinity. He sought assurance
from Wise that he would be referred for the job. When Wise refused to make a
definite commitment, Hardeman threatened violence if no work was forthcoming
in the next few days.

On October 4, Hardeman returned to the hiring hall and waited for a referral.
None was forthcoming. The next day, in his words, he "went to the hall ... and
waited from the time the hall opened until we had the trouble. I tried to make up
my mind what to do, whether to sue the local or Wise or beat hell out of Wise,
and then I made up my mind." When Wise came out of his office to go to a local
jobsite, as required by his duties as business manager, Hardeman handed him a

copy of a telegram asking for Hardeman by name. As Wise was reading the telegram, Hardeman began punching him in the face.

Hardeman was tried for this conduct on charges of creating dissension and working against the interest and harmony of the Local Lodge, and of threatening and using force to restrain an officer of the Local Lodge from properly discharging the duties of his office. The trial committee found him "guilty as charged," and the Local Lodge sustained the finding and voted his expulsion for an indefinite period. Internal union review of this action, instituted by Hardeman, modified neither the verdict nor the penalty. Five years later, Hardeman brought this suit alleging that petitioner violated § 101(a)(5) by denying him a full and fair hearing in the union disciplinary proceedings.

I

We consider first the union's claim that the subject matter of this lawsuit is, in the first instance, within the exclusive competence of the National Labor Relations Board. The union argues that the gravamen of Hardeman's complaint—which did not seek reinstatement, but only damages for wrongful expulsion, consisting of loss of income, loss of pension and insurance rights, mental anguish and punitive damages—is discrimination against him in job referrals; that any such conduct on the part of the union is at the very least arguably an unfair labor practice under §§ 8(b)(1)(A) and 8(b)(2) of the National Labor Relations Act....

We think the union's argument is misdirected.... There is no attempt, in this lawsuit, to apply state law to matters preempted by federal authority. Nor is there an attempt to apply federal law of general application, which is limited in the particular circumstances by the National Labor Relations Act. Nor is there an attempt to have the district court enforce the provisions of the National Labor Relations Act itself, without guidance from the NLRB.... The critical question in this action is whether Hardeman was afforded the rights guaranteed him by § 101(a)(5) of the LMRDA. If he was denied them, Congress has said that he is entitled to damages for the consequences of that denial. Since these questions are irrelevant to the legality of conduct under the National Labor Relations Act, there is no danger of conflicting interpretation of its provisions. And since the law applied is federal law explicitly made applicable to such circumstances by Congress, there is no danger that state law may come in through the back door to regulate conduct that has been removed by Congress from state control. Accordingly, this action was within the competence of the district court.

II

Two charges were brought against Hardeman in the union disciplinary proceedings. He was charged with violation of Article 13, § 1, of the Subordinate Lodge Constitution, which forbids attempting to create dissension or working against the interest and harmony of the union, and carries a penalty of expulsion.

He was also charged with violations of Article 12, § 1, of the Subordinate Lodge By-Laws, which forbids the threat or use of force against any officer of the union in order to prevent him from properly discharging the duties of his office; violation may be punished "as warranted by the offense." Hardeman's conviction on both charges was upheld in internal union procedures for review.

The trial judge instructed the jury that "whether or not he [respondent] was rightfully or wrongfully discharged or expelled is a pure question of law for me to determine." He assumed, but did not decide, that the transcript of the union disciplinary hearing contained evidence adequate to support conviction of violating Article 12. He held, however, that there was no evidence at all in the transcript of the union disciplinary proceedings to support the charge of violating Article 13. This holding appears to have been based on the Fifth Circuit's decision in *Boilermakers v. Braswell,* 388 F.2d 193 (5th Cir. 1968). There the Court of Appeals for the Fifth Circuit had reasoned that "penal provisions in union constitutions must be strictly construed," and that as so construed Article 13 was directed only to "threats to the union as an organization and to the effective carrying out of the union's aims," not to merely personal altercations. 388 F.2d at 199. Since the union tribunals had returned only a general verdict, and since one of the charges was thought to be supported by no evidence whatsoever, the trial judge held that Hardeman had been deprived of the full and fair hearing guaranteed by § 101(a)(5). The Court of Appeals affirmed, simply citing *Braswell....*

We find nothing in either the language or the legislative history of § 101(a)(5) that could justify such a substitution of judicial for union authority to interpret the union's regulations in order to determine the scope of offenses warranting discipline of union members. Section 101(a)(5) began life as a floor amendment to S. 1555, the Kennedy-Ervin Bill, in the Eighty-Sixth Congress. As sponsored by Senator McClellan, and as adopted by the Senate on April 22, 1959, the amendment would have forbidden discipline of union members "except for breach of a published written rule of [the union]." 105 Cong. Rec. 6476, 6492-6493. But this language did not long survive. Two days later, a substitute amendment was offered by Senator Kuchel, who explained that further study of the McClellan amendment had raised "some rather vexing questions." *Id.* at 6720. The Kuchel substitute, adopted the following day, deleted the requirement that charges be based upon a previously published, written union rule; it transformed Senator McClellan's amendment, in relevant part, into the present language of § 101(a)(5). *Id.* at 6720, 6727. As so amended, S. 1555 passed the Senate on April 25. *Id.* at 6745. Identical language was adopted by the House, *id.* at 15884, 15891, and appears in the statute as finally enacted.

The Congress understood that Senator Kuchel's amendment was intended to make substantive changes in Senator McClellan's proposal. Senator Kennedy had specifically objected to the McClellan amendment because

> [i]n the case of ... the ... official who bribed a judge, unless there were a specific prohibition against bribery of judicial officers written into the constitution of the union, then no union could take disciplinary action against [an] officer or member guilty of bribery.
>
> ....
>
> It seems to me that we can trust union officers to run their affairs better than that.

Id. at 6491. Senator Kuchel described his substitute as merely providing "the usual reasonable constitutional basis" for union disciplinary proceedings: union members were to have "constitutionally reasonable notice and a reasonable hearing." *Id.* at 6720. After the Kuchel amendment passed the Senate, Senator Goldwater explained it to the House Committee on Labor and Education as follows:

> [T]he bill of rights in the Senate bill require[s] that the union member be served with written charges prior to any disciplinary proceedings but it does not require that these charges, to be valid, must be based on activity that the union had proscribed prior to the union member having engaged in such activity.

Labor-Management Reform Legislation, Hearings before a Joint Subcommittee of the House Committee on Education and Labor, 86th Cong., 1st Sess. pt. 4, p. 1595 (1959). And Senator McClellan's testimony was to the same effect. *Id.* pt. 5, 2235-2236, 2251, 2285.

We think that this is sufficient to indicate that § 101(a)(5) was not intended to authorize courts to determine the scope of offenses for which a union may discipline its members. And if a union may discipline its members for offenses not proscribed by written rules at all, it is surely a futile exercise for a court to construe the written rules in order to determine whether particular conduct falls within or without their scope.

Of course, § 101(a)(5)(A) requires that a member subject to discipline be "served with written specific charges." These charges must be, in Senator McClellan's words, "specific enough to inform the accused member of the offense that he has allegedly committed." Where, as here, the union's charges make reference to specific written provisions, § 101(a)(5)(A) obviously empowers the federal courts to examine those provisions and determine whether the union member had been misled or otherwise prejudiced in the presentation of his defense. But it gives courts no warrant to scrutinize the union regulations in order to determine whether particular conduct may be punished at all.

Respondent does not suggest, and we cannot discern, any possibility of prejudice in the present case. Although the notice of charges with which he was served does not appear as such in the record, the transcript of the union hearing indicates that the notice did not confine itself to a mere statement or citation of the written regulations that Hardeman was said to have violated: the notice appears to have contained a detailed statement of the facts relating to the fight which formed the basis for the disciplinary action. Section 101(a)(5) requires no more.

III

There remains only the question whether the evidence in the union disciplinary proceeding was sufficient to support the finding of guilt. Section 101(a)(5)(C) of the LMRDA guarantees union members a "full and fair" disciplinary hearing, and the parties and the lower federal courts are in full agreement that this guarantee requires the charging party to provide some evidence at the disciplinary hearing to support the charges made. This is the proper standard of judicial review. We have repeatedly held that conviction on charges unsupported by any evidence is a denial of due process ... and we feel that § 101(a)(5)(C) may fairly be said to import a similar requirement into union disciplinary proceedings. Senator Kuchel, who first introduced the provision, characterized it on the Senate floor as requiring the "usual reasonable constitutional basis" for disciplinary action, 105 Cong. Rec. 6720, and any lesser standard would make useless § 101(a)(5)(A)'s requirement of written, specific charges. A stricter standard, on the other hand, would be inconsistent with the apparent congressional intent to allow unions to govern their own affairs, and would require courts to judge the credibility of witnesses on the basis of what would be at best a cold record.

Applying this standard to the present case, we think there is no question that the charges were adequately supported. Respondent was charged with having attacked Wise without warning, and with continuing to beat him for some time. Wise so testified at the disciplinary hearing, and his testimony was fully corroborated by one other witness to the altercation. Even Hardeman, although he claimed he was thereafter held and beaten, admitted having struck the first blow. On such a record there is no question but that the charges were supported by "some evidence."

Reversed.

[The concurring opinion of MR. JUSTICE WHITE and the dissenting opinion of MR. JUSTICE DOUGLAS are omitted.]

———————

Parks v. IBEW, 314 F.2d 886, 911-13 (4th Cir. 1963), *cert. denied,* 372 U.S. 976 (1963). In the course of a lengthy opinion sustaining an international union's revocation of a local's charter for engaging in a strike without international authorization, the court of appeals made the following comments on the elements of a "fair hearing" in union disciplinary proceedings:

The common law clearly requires that, to be valid, expulsion of a member or a subordinate body must be rendered after a "fair hearing...." ... The elements of such a "fair hearing" often resemble constitutional due process requirements and generally encompass full notice and a reasonable opportunity to be heard—including the right to present evidence and the right to confront and cross-examine witnesses. There is also a body of law requiring trial of an accused before an unbiased tribunal. Some commentators seem to think that the courts should play a more active role in reviewing not only specific bias, e.g., prejudgment or use of discipline pretextuously, but also built-in bias, e.g., combined prosecuting and judicial functions and use of "yes men." They have, however, generally recognized either that the courts have not been empowered to do this or that they are unable to reach such bias for it "is an inevitable product of the procedure itself...."

The real basis for the argument that the IP [International President] was biased is that he was, in a sense, both prosecutor and judge. It is quite true that he ordered the charges to be brought and conferred with the International's General Counsel in their formulation as well as in the preparation of the revocation order. But it is also true that the basis for the charges was that the Local had struck in defiance of his repeated admonitions and had rejected his collective bargaining orders. And there can be no doubt that the Constitution vested in the IP these combined prosecuting and judicial functions....

It may well be thought desirable for unions to adopt hearing procedures that keep trial functions separate, but the federal courts are not empowered so to restructure the disciplinary procedures of unions.... Some unions, like the United Automobile Workers, have responded to the pressure for fairness in internal trial proceedings by establishing, essentially external to the union organization, independent public review boards having the final word in disciplinary matters. Such unions would appear to have gone far to separate prosecuting and ultimate judicial functions. But, in the absence of a clear congressional authorization, it is not for the federal courts to compel such measures....

Separation of functions is not an absolute due process prerequisite to fairness in administrative proceedings, see 2 Davis, Administrative Law Treatise § 13.02; in internal union proceedings it traditionally, and under the LMRDA, has also not been deemed a requirement of fairness. Courts, federal courts especially, are justified in ruling a union tribunal biased only upon a demonstration that it has been substantially actuated by improper motives—in other words, only upon a showing of specific prejudice.

NOTES

1. Section 101(a)(5)'s guarantee of a "full and fair hearing" was held to include the right to confront and cross-examine opposing witnesses in *Anderson v. Carpenters,* 53 L.R.R.M. 2793, 47 CCH Lab. Cas. ¶ 18,400 (D. Minn. 1963). But an accused in a union proceeding is not entitled to be represented by legal counsel. *Smith v. General Truck Drivers Local 467,* 181 F. Supp. 14 (S.D. Cal. 1960). Furthermore, informality or minor departures from prescribed procedures are not fatal defects so long as there is adequate notice of the charges and a full opportunity to be heard. *Null v. Carpenters Dist. Council,* 239 F. Supp. 809 (S.D. Tex. 1965); *Anderson v. Carpenters,* 59 L.R.R.M. 2684, 51 CCH Lab. Cas. ¶ 19,747 (D. Minn. 1965). Charges must be drafted with reasonable particularity as to time, place, and circumstances. Failure to comply with this requirement as to each charge on which a finding of guilt is rendered may invalidate the penalty, even though conviction on the other charges only might have justified it. *Gleason v. Hotel & Restaurant Employees Local 11,* 422 F.2d 342 (2d Cir. 1970).

2. In *Cornelio v. Carpenters Dist. Council,* 243 F. Supp. 126 (E.D. Pa. 1965), *aff'd,* 358 F.2d 728 (3d Cir. 1966), *cert. denied,* 386 U.S. 975 (1967), the court found no cause of action in the allegation that a member's accusers were persons of influence in the union (they were business agents). But when members of a union trial board have expressed prehearing opinions indicating a bias or are individuals who were previously affected adversely by the actions of the subject of the trial board hearing, their participation in the proceeding would violate the subject's right under § 101(a)(5) of the LMRDA to a full and fair hearing. *See Goodman v. Laborers,* 742 F.2d 780 (3d Cir. 1984). Similarly, there was a violation of the full and fair hearing requirement when a national union president initiated an investigation against a local president who was a former political rival, determined probable cause, and served as final adjudicator. The court noted, however, that in such a civil proceeding, the union's "combination of investigative, prosecutorial, and adjudicatory functions in the [national] President does not, by itself, violate the LMRDA." *Wildberger v. AFGE,* 86 F.3d 1188 (D.C. Cir. 1996).

3. To what extent should the courts review the findings of fact of union tribunals in disciplinary cases? *See Vars v. Boilermakers,* 320 F.2d 576, 578 (2d Cir. 1963): "Thus, although the courts may be without power to review matters of credibility or of strict weight of the evidence, a close reading of the record is justified to insure that the findings are not without any foundation in the evidence."

4. What constitutes "discipline" under § 101(a)(5)? In *Allen v. Armored Car Chauffeurs Local 820,* 185 F. Supp. 492 (D.N.J. 1960), it was held that a union's failure to process an employee's grievance was not within the purview of § 101(a)(5). The court stated: "The disciplinary action of which this court is given jurisdiction ... is not discharge from employment, but the discipline of a member by the Union as to his membership." *Id.* at 494-95. *See also Breininger* *v. Sheet Metal Workers Local 6,* 493 U.S. 67 (1989) (discrimination in referral through a union hiring hall is not "discipline" under the LMRDA). *But cf. Schermerhorn v. Local 100, Transport Workers Union,* 91 F.3d 316 (2d Cir. 1996) (reprimands issued to plaintiffs after hearings conducted by a union committee constituted "discipline" under the LMRDA); *Scovile v. Watson,* 338 F.2d 678, 680 (7th Cir. 1964), *cert. denied,* 380 U.S. 963 (1965) ("a refusal by the union ... to prosecute an arbitration grievance might be considered as a disciplinary measure relating to the employee's membership in the union"); *Detroy v. American Guild of Variety Artists,* 286 F.2d 75 (2d Cir.), *cert. denied,* 366 U.S. 929 (1961), *supra.* In *English v. Cowell,* 969 F.2d 465 (7th Cir. 1992), the court recognized that a union's termination of an individual's membership because of that person's felony conviction constituted "discipline" that triggered the § 101(a)(5) due process protections. *See generally* Beaird & Player, *Union Discipline of Its Membership Under Section 101(a)(5) of Landrum-Griffin: What Is "Discipline" and How Much Process Is Due?* 9 Ga. L. Rev. 383 (1975); Etelson & Smith, *Union Discipline Under the Landrum-Griffin Act,* 82 Harv. L. Rev. 727 (1969); Note, *Facial Adjudication of Disciplinary Provisions in Union Constitutions,* 91 Yale L.J. 144 (1981).

5. The common-law cases on due process in union proceedings are collected in Annot., 21 A.L.R.2d 1397 (1952).

SECTION III. Union Administration

SENATE COMMITTEE ON LABOR AND PUBLIC WELFARE

S. Rep. No. 187 on S. 1555, 86th Cong., 1st Sess. 5-6 (1959)

A strong independent labor movement is a vital part of American institutions. The shocking abuses revealed by recent investigations have been confined to a few unions. The overwhelming majority are honestly and democratically run. In providing remedies for existing evils the Senate should be careful neither to undermine self-government within the labor movement nor to weaken unions in their role as the bargaining representatives of employees.

It is plain that the trade union movement in the United States is facing difficult internal problems and—because of these internal problems—tensions with the surrounding community. The problems of this now large and relatively strong institution are not unlike the difficulties faced by other groups in American society which aspire to live by the same basic principles and values within their group as they hold ideal for the whole community. But equal rights, freedom of choice, honesty, and the highest ethical standards are built into changing institutions only after struggle. Trade unions have grown well beyond their beginnings as relatively small, closely knit associations of workingmen where personal, fraternal relationships were characteristic. Like other American institutions some unions have become large and impersonal; they have acquired bureaucratic tendencies and characteristics; their members like other Americans have sometimes become apathetic in the exercise of their personal responsibility for the conduct of union affairs. In some few cases men who have risen to positions of power and responsibility within unions have abused their power and neglected their responsibilities. In some cases the structure and procedures necessary for trade unions while they were struggling for survival are ill adapted to their new role and to changed conditions; they are not always conducive to efficient, honest, and democratic practices.

Whatever the causes, the problems are recognized by those within as well as those outside the union movement. The action of the American Federation of Labor-Congress of Industrial Organizations in recognizing the importance of adherence to traditional principles of ethical conduct and trade union democracy and in formulating and implementing codes of ethical practices to carry out these established principles, is a dramatic and convincing demonstration of the trade union movement's desire to conduct its internal affairs democratically and in accordance with high standards of trust. Nevertheless, effective measures to stamp out crime and corruption and guarantee internal union democracy, cannot be applied to all unions without the coercive powers of government, nor is the present machinery of the federation demonstrably effective in policing specific abuses at the local level....

The internal problems currently facing our labor unions are bound up with a substantial public interest. Under the National Labor Relations Act and the Railway Labor Act, a labor organization has vast responsibility for economic welfare of the individual members whom it represents. Union members have a vital interest, therefore, in the policies and conduct of union affairs....

NOTES

1. Prior to the passage of the Labor-Management Reporting and Disclosure Act of 1959, the union constitution was usually the primary standard as to substantive rights in suits involving union administration. *See, e.g., O'Neill v. Plumbers,* 348 Pa. 531, 36 A.2d 325 (1944) (alleged dictatorial control of local by international). In cases of alleged fraud on the part of officers, courts intervened on the basis of such theories as breach of trust or deprivation of property rights. *Collins v. IATSE,* 136 N.J. Eq. 395, 42 A.2d 297 (1945); *id.,* 119 N.J. Eq. 230, 182 A. 37 (1935); *Dusing v. Nuzzo,* 177 Misc. 35, 29 N.Y.S.2d 882 (Sup. Ct.), *modified and aff'd,* 263 App. Div. 59, 31 N.Y.S.2d 849 (1941). The remedy was often threefold: an accounting; the appointment of a receiver; and an election under the supervision of a court officer. *See, e.g., Iron Workers Local 11 v. McKee,* 114 N.J. Eq. 555, 169 A. 351 (1933); *cf. English v. Cunningham,* 269 F.2d 517 (D.C. Cir.), *cert. denied,* 361 U.S. 897 (1959). *See generally* Chamberlain, *The Judicial Process in Labor Unions,* 10 Brooklyn L. Rev. 145 (1940).

2. Comprehensive studies of the internal administration of labor organizations include M. Estey, P. Taft & M. Wagner, Eds., Regulating Union Government (1964); J. Grodin, Union Government and the Law (1961); W. Leiserson, American Trade Union Democracy (1959); National Industrial Conference Board, Handbook of Union Government, Structure and Procedure (1955); P. Taft, The Structure and Government of Labor Unions (1962). Perhaps the most penetrating analysis of the government of a single international is S. Lipset, M. Trow & J. Coleman, Union Democracy: The Internal Politics of the International Typographical Union (1956). A special perspective is provided by Bohlander, *How the Rank and File View Local Union Administration—A Survey,* 8 Employee Rel. L.J. 217 (1982).

A. ELECTION OF OFFICERS

CALHOON v. HARVEY

Supreme Court of the United States
379 U.S. 134, 85 S. Ct. 292, 13 L. Ed. 2d 190 (1964)

MR. JUSTICE BLACK delivered the opinion of the Court....

The respondents, three members of District No. 1, National Marine Engineers' Beneficial Association, filed a complaint in Federal District Court against the union, its president and its secretary-treasurer, alleging that certain provisions of the union's bylaws and national constitution violated the Act in that they infringed "the right of members of defendant District No. 1, NMEBA, to nominate candidates in elections of defendant, which right is guaranteed to each member of defendant, and to each plaintiff, by § 101(a)(1) of the LMRDA...." It was alleged that § 102 of Title I of the Act gave the District Court jurisdiction to adjudicate the controversy. The union bylaws complained of deprived a member of the right to nominate anyone for office but himself. The national constitution in turn provided that no member could be eligible for nomination or election to a full-time elective office unless he had been a member of the national union for five years and had served 180 days or more of seatime in each of two of the preceding three years on vessels covered by collective bargaining agreements with the national or its subsidiary bodies. On the basis of these allegations respondents asked that the union be enjoined from preparing for or conducting any election until it revised its system of elections so as to afford each of its members a fair opportunity to nominate any persons "meeting fair and reasonable eligibility requirements for any or all offices to be filled by such election."

The union moved to dismiss the complaint on the grounds that (1) the court lacked jurisdiction over the subject matter, and (2) the complaint failed to state a claim upon which relief could be granted. The District Court dismissed for want of "jurisdiction," holding that the alleged conduct of the union, even if true, failed to show a denial of the equal rights of all members of the union to vote for or nominate candidates guaranteed by § 101(a)(1) of Title I of the Act, so as to give the District Court jurisdiction of the controversy under § 102. The allegations, said the court, showed at most imposition of qualifications of eligibility for nomination and election so restrictive that they might violate § 401(e) of Title IV by denying members a reasonable opportunity to nominate and vote for candidates. The District Court further held that it could not exercise jurisdiction to protect § 401(e) rights because § 402(a) of Title IV provides a remedy, declared by § 403 to be "exclusive," authorizing members to vindicate such rights by challenging elections after they have been held, and then only by (1) first exhausting all remedies available with the union, (2) filing a complaint with the Secretary of Labor, who (3) may, after investigating the violation alleged in the complaint, bring suit in a United States District Court to attack the validity of the election. The Court of Appeals reversed, holding that "the complaint alleged a violation of § 101(a)(1) and that federal jurisdiction existed under § 102." 324 F.2d 486, 487....

I

Jurisdiction of the District Court under § 102 of Title I depends entirely upon whether this complaint showed a violation of rights guaranteed by § 101(a)(1), for we disagree with the Court of Appeals' holding that jurisdiction under § 102 can be upheld by reliance in whole or in part on allegations which in substance charge a breach of Title IV rights. An analysis and understanding of the meaning of § 101(a)(1) and of the charges of the complaint is therefore essential to a determination of this issue. Respondents charge that the bylaws and constitutional provisions referred to above infringed their right guaranteed by § 101(a)(1) to nominate candidates. The result of their allegations here, however, is an attempt to sweep into the ambit of their right to sue in federal court if they are denied an equal opportunity to nominate candidates under § 101(a)(1), a right to sue if they are not allowed to nominate anyone they choose regardless of his eligibility and qualifications under union restrictions. But Title IV, not Title I, sets standards for eligibility and qualifications of candidates and officials and provides its own separate and different administrative and judicial procedure for challenging those standards. And the equal-rights language of § 101(a)(1) would have to be stretched far beyond its normal meaning to hold that it guarantees members not just a right to "nominate candidates," but a right to nominate anyone, without regard to valid union rules....

Plainly, [§ 101(a)(1)] is no more than a command that members and classes of members shall not be discriminated against in their right to nominate and vote. And Congress carefully prescribed that even this right against discrimination is "subject to reasonable rules and regulations" by the union. The complaining union members here have not been discriminated against in any way and have been denied no privilege or right to vote or nominate which the union has granted to others. They have indeed taken full advantage of the uniform rule limiting nominations by nominating themselves for office. It is true that they were denied their request to be candidates, but that denial was not a discrimination against their right to nominate, since the same qualifications were required equally of all members. Whether the eligibility requirements set by the union's constitution and bylaws were reasonable and valid is a question separate and distinct from whether the right to nominate on an equal basis given by § 101(a)(1) was violated. The District Court therefore was without jurisdiction to grant the relief requested here unless, as the Court of Appeals held, the "*combined* effect of the eligibility requirements and the restriction to self-nomination" are to be considered in determining whether § 101(a)(1) has been violated.

II

We hold that possible violations of Title IV of the Act regarding eligibility are not relevant in determining whether or not a district court has jurisdiction under § 102 of Title I of the Act. Title IV sets up a statutory scheme governing the election of union officers, fixing the terms during which they hold office, requiring that elections be by secret ballot, regulating the handling of campaign literature, requiring a reasonable opportunity for the nomination of candidates, authorizing unions to fix "reasonable qualifications uniformly imposed" for candidates, and attempting to guarantee fair union elections in which all the members are allowed to participate. Section 402 of Title IV, as has been pointed out, sets up an exclusive method for protecting Title IV rights, by permitting an individual member to file a complaint with the Secretary of Labor challenging the validity of any election because of violations of Title IV. Upon complaint the Secretary investigates and if he finds probable cause to believe that Title IV has been violated, he may file suit in the appropriate district court. It is apparent that Congress decided to utilize the special knowledge and discretion of the Secretary of Labor in order best to serve the public interest. *Cf. San Diego Building Trades Council v. Garmon,* 359 U.S. 236, 242 (1959). In so doing Congress, with one exception not here relevant, decided not to permit individuals to block or delay union elections by filing federal-court suits for violations of Title IV. Reliance on the discretion of the Secretary is in harmony with the general congressional policy to allow unions great latitude in resolving their own internal controversies, and, where that fails, to utilize the agencies of government most familiar with union problems to aid in bringing about a settlement through discussion before resort to the courts. Without setting out the lengthy legislative history which preceded the passage of this measure, it is sufficient to say that we are satisfied that the Act itself shows clearly by its structure and language that the disputes here, basically relating as they do to eligibility of candidates for office, fall squarely within Title IV of the Act and are to be resolved by the administrative and judicial procedures set out in that Title.

Accordingly, the judgment of the Court of Appeals is reversed and that of the District Court is affirmed....

MR. JUSTICE DOUGLAS would affirm the judgment of the Court of Appeals for the reasons stated in its opinion as reported in 324 F.2d 486.

MR. JUSTICE STEWART, whom MR. JUSTICE HARLAN joins, concurring.

This case marks the first interpretation by this Court of the significant changes wrought by the Labor-Management Reporting and Disclosure Act of 1959 increasing federal supervision of internal union affairs. At issue are subtle questions concerning the interplay between Title I and Title IV of that Act. In part, both seem to deal with the same subject matter: Title I guarantees "equal rights and privileges ... to nominate candidates"; Title IV provides that "a reasonable opportunity shall be given for the nomination of candidates." Where the two Titles of the legislation differ most substantially is in the remedies they provide. If a Title I right is at issue, the allegedly aggrieved union member has direct, virtually immediate recourse to a federal court to obtain an adjudication of his claim and an injunction if his complaint has merit. 73 Stat. 523, 29 U.S.C. § 412 (1958 ed., Supp. V). Vindication of claims under Title IV may be much more onerous. Federal court suits can be brought only by the Secretary of Labor, and then, only after the election has been held....

The Court precludes the District Court from asserting jurisdiction over this complaint by focusing on the fact that one of the imposed restrictions speaks in terms of eligibility. And since these are "possible violations of Title IV of the Act regarding eligibility" they "are not relevant in determining whether or not a district court has jurisdiction under § 102 of Title I of the Act." By this reasoning, the Court forecloses early adjudication of claims concerning participation in the election process. But there are occasions when eligibility provisions can infringe upon the right to nominate. Had the NMEBA issued a regulation that only Jesse Calhoon was eligible for office, no one could place great store on the right to self-nomination left to the rest of the membership. This Court long ago recognized the subtle ways by which election rights can be removed through discrimination at a less visible stage of the political process. The decisions in the *Texas Primary Cases* were founded on the belief that the equal right to vote was impaired where discrimination existed in the method of nomination. *Smith v. Allwright,* 321 U.S. 649 (1944); *Nixon v. Herndon,* 273 U.S. 536 (1927). *See United States v. Classic,* 313 U.S. 299 (1941). No less is the equal right to nominate infringed where onerous burdens drastically limit the candidates available for nomination. In scrutinizing devices designed to erode the franchise, the Court has shown impatience with arguments founded in the form of the device. *Gomillion v. Lightfoot,* 364 U.S. 339, 345 (1960). If Congress has told the courts to protect a union member from infringement of his equal right to nominate, the courts should do so whether such discrimination is sophisticated or simple-minded. *Lane v. Wilson,* 307 U.S. 268, 275 (1939).

After today, simply by framing its discriminatory rules in terms of eligibility, a union can immunize itself from pre-election attack in a federal court even though it makes deep incursions on the equal right of its members to nominate, to vote, and to participate in the union's internal affairs....

Nonetheless, the Court finds a "general congressional policy" to avoid judicial resolution of internal union disputes. That policy, the Court says, was designed to limit the power of individuals to block and delay elections by seeking injunctive relief. Such an appraisal might have been accurate before the addition of Title I, but it does not explain the emphasis on prompt judicial remedies there provided. In addition to the injunctive relief authorized by § 102 and the savings provisions of § 103, § 101(a)(4) modifies the traditional requirement of exhausting internal remedies before resort to litigation. Even § 403 is not conclusive on the elimination of pre-election remedies. At the least, state-court actions may be brought in advance of an election to "enforce the constitution and bylaws." And as to federal courts, it is certainly arguable that recourse through the Secretary of Labor is the exclusive remedy only after the election has been held. By reading Title I rights so narrowly, and by construing Title IV to foreclose absolutely pre-election litigation in the federal courts, the Court sharply reduces meaningful protection for many of the rights which Congress was so assiduous to create. By so simplifying the tangled provisions of the Act, the Court renders it virtually impossible for the aggrieved union member to gain a hearing when it is most necessary—when there is still an opportunity to make the union's rules comport with the requirements of the Act.

My difference with the Court does not reach to the disposition of this particular case. Whether stated in terms of restrictions on the right to nominate or in terms of limitations on eligibility for union office, I think the rules of a labor organization would operate illegally to curtail the members' equal right to nominate within the meaning of Title I only if those rules effectively distorted the basic democratic process. The line might be a shadowy one in some cases. But I think that in this case the respondents did not allege in their complaint nor demonstrate in their affidavits that this line was crossed. I would therefore remand the case to the District Court with directions to dismiss the complaint for failure to state a claim for relief.

NOTES

1. Is this decision a holding that even *unreasonable* limitations on voting and nominating do not violate § 101(a)(1), so long as the limitations are not discriminatory? *See generally* Levy, *Electing Union Officers Under the LMRDA,* 5 Cardozo L. Rev. 737 (1984); Note, *Union Elections Under the LMRDA,* 74 Yale L.J. 1282 (1965).

2. Following the principal case, federal district courts have held that Title IV rather than Title I governs a local's procedure for nominating delegates to an international convention, *Paravate v. Insurance Workers Local 13,* 59 L.R.R.M. 2169 (W.D. Pa. 1965), and an international's action in voiding a local election, *Carpenters Local 115 v. Carpenters,* 247 F. Supp. 660 (D. Conn. 1965). But Title I jurisdiction has been sustained where "associate members" were allegedly denied the "equal right" to vote and nominate candidates, even though the relief requested included the setting aside of elections already conducted, a remedy within the exclusive domain of Title IV. The court explained that at least some relief would be available under Title I. *O'Brien v. Paddock,* 246 F. Supp. 809 (S.D.N.Y. 1965). *See also Beckman v. Iron Workers Local 46,* 314 F.2d 848 (7th Cir. 1963) (upholding under § 101(a)(1) a preliminary injunction against counting ballots where voting irregularities were alleged); *Schonfeld v. Penza,* 477 F.2d 899 (2d Cir. 1973) (removal of union officer and declaration of his future ineligibility are bases for Title I jurisdiction when such actions can fairly be said to form part of scheme to suppress dissent); *Murphy v. Operating Eng'rs Local 18,* 774 F.2d 114 (6th Cir. 1985), *cert. denied,* 475 U.S. 1017 (1986) (unfair coverage of dissidents in union newsletter). *But cf. Robins v. Rarback,* 325 F.2d 929 (2d Cir. 1963), *cert. denied,* 379 U.S. 974 (1965). *See also* Harris, *Titles I and IV of the LMRDA: A Resolution of the Conflict of Remedies,* 42 U. Chi. L. Rev. 166 (1974); Note, *Pre-Election Remedies Under the Landrum-Griffin Act,* 74 Colum. L. Rev. 1105 (1974).

3. After an election has been conducted, the Secretary of Labor has exclusive authority to challenge it. But prior to an election, § 403 of the LMRDA expressly recognizes "[e]xisting rights and remedies to enforce the constitution and bylaws of a labor organization with respect to elections." Commentators have argued that the union constitution is to be interpreted as a matter of federal substantive law in pre-election suits. *See* Summers, *Preemption and the Labor Reform Act—Dual Rights and Remedies,* 22 Ohio St. L.J. 119, 136-38 (1961); Note, *Election Remedies Under the Labor-Management Reporting and Disclosure Act,* 78 Harv. L. Rev. 1617, 1630 (1965); Note, *Union Elections Under the LMRDA,* 74 Yale L.J. 1282, 1293-94 (1965). The courts, however, have assumed that pre-election actions to enforce a union's electoral rules are governed by state substantive law. *Libutti v. DiBrizzi,* 343 F.2d 460 (2d Cir. 1965); *Wittstein v. Musicians,* 59 L.R.R.M. 2335, 51 CCH Lab. Cas. ¶ 19,684 (S.D.N.Y. 1965); *McArthy v. Machinists Lodge 9,* 252 F. Supp. 350 (E.D. Mo. 1966). *But cf. Wooddell v. IBEW Local 71,* 502 U.S. 93 (1991) (*international* constitution is governed by federal law).

4. Section 401(c) of the LMRDA permits pre-election suits by candidates in union elections to enforce certain specified rights, such as the nondiscriminatory use of membership lists to distribute campaign propaganda. Section 601(a) gives the Secretary of Labor investigatory powers to determine whether any person "has violated or is about to violate any provision of this Act (except Title I ...)." In his bitter (and ultimately fatal) election campaign of 1969 against an entrenched and allegedly corrupt UMW leadership, Joseph Yablonski sought to pursue both these routes. He had limited success in court and was rebuffed by the Secretary of Labor. *See Yablonski v. UMW,* 305 F. Supp. 868, 876 (D.D.C. 1969); *cf. Hodgson v. United Mine Workers of Am.,* 344 F. Supp. 17 (D.D.C. 1972) (invalidating election). For sharply differing views on the Secretary's proper role, *compare* Rauh, *LMRDA—Enforce It or Repeal It,* 5 Ga. L. Rev. 643 (1971) *with* Silberman & Driesen, *The Secretary and the Law: Preballoting Investigations Under the Landrum-Griffin Act,* 7 Ga. L. Rev. 1 (1972).

According to the Supreme Court, a candidate's reasonable request for mailing labels to permit the distribution of election literature prior to a nominating convention must be granted under § 401(c), despite the union's contention that it had a reasonable rule prohibiting preconvention mailings. *Masters, Mates & Pilots v. Brown,* 498 U.S. 466 (1991). However, the Second Circuit has held that nonemployee candidates in a union election could not enter an employer's premises to campaign without showing that access was "the only" reasonable means of communicating with union member employees. *United States v. Teamsters,* 955 F.2d 171 (2d Cir. 1992).

5. The Secretary of Labor's decision not to file suit to set aside a union election is subject to judicial review under the Administrative Procedure Act, 5 U.S.C. §§ 702 and 704, as "final agency action" for which there is no other adequate judicial remedy. The scope of review is sharply limited, however, and does not encompass a trial-type inquiry into the factual basis of the Secretary's decision. The court must simply determine, after examining the statement of reasons for refusing to file an action that the Secretary is required to furnish both court and complainant, whether the refusal was so irrational as to be arbitrary and capricious. *Dunlop v. Bachowski,* 421 U.S. 560 (1975). The Secretary of Labor's refusal to bring suit to overturn the Steelworkers' election of 1977 was held not arbitrary and capricious in *Sadlowski v. Marshall,* 464 F. Supp. 858 (D.D.C.), *aff'd,* 106 L.R.R.M. 2968 (D.C. Cir. 1979), *cert. denied,* 447 U.S. 905 (1980). However, in *Doyle v. Brock,* 821 F.2d 778 (D.C. Cir. 1987), failure to challenge an attendance requirement disqualifying 97 percent of membership was arbitrary and capricious. The Department of Labor has amended 29 C.F.R. § 452.38 to codify the ruling of *Doyle v. Brock,* so that a requirement of meeting attendance which disqualifies a large percentage of members may alone be an unreasonable qualification for union office. 60 Fed. Reg. 57178 (Nov. 14, 1995). *See generally* Hopson, *Judicial Review of the Secretary of Labor's Decision Not to Sue to Set Aside an Election Under Title IV of the LMRDA,* 18 Wayne L. Rev. 1281 (1972).

6. The Supreme Court has ruled that a union member who filed the initial complaint with the Secretary of Labor may intervene in the Secretary's Title IV action to set aside the election. Intervention is confined, however, to the claims of illegality presented by the Secretary's complaint. While agreeing that the Secretary's suit is the exclusive remedy, the Court said: "There is no evidence whatever that Congress was opposed to participation by union members in the litigation, so long as that participation did not interfere with the screening and centralizing functions of the Secretary." *Trbovich v. UMW,* 404 U.S. 528 (1972), *noted in* 41 Geo. Wash. L. Rev. 560 (1973).

7. In *Teamsters Local 82 v. Crowley,* 467 U.S. 526 (1984), the Supreme Court held that while a district court possesses the authority to provide appropriate relief for Title I violations that involve the election process, it does not have the power to enjoin an ongoing union election and to supervise a new election, since such action would interfere with the exclusive authority of the Secretary of Labor over elections specified in Title IV.

8. Even though secret ballot violations "may have affected" the outcome of an election, a federal court has the inherent equitable power to withhold the remedy of a new election where the incumbent faction, knowing it was losing the election, committed intentional and blatant violations of the LMRDA in order to use them as a basis for challenging the election. *Marshall v. Steelworkers Local 1010,* 664 F.2d 144 (7th Cir. 1981).

Hodgson v. Steelworkers Local 6799, 403 U.S. 333, 91 S. Ct. 1841, 29 L. Ed. 2d 510 (1971). An unsuccessful candidate for president of a local union protested the election to both the local and the international. He based his protest on several matters, including the use of union facilities to prepare campaign materials for the incumbent president, who was reelected. After failing to obtain relief through internal union procedures, the candidate filed a complaint with the Secretary of Labor under § 402(a) of the LMRDA. The complaint repeated the charge about the use of union facilities. It also raised, for the first time, an additional objection concerning a requirement in the union constitution that candidates for certain local offices must have attended at least one-half of the regular meetings of the local during the thirty-six months immediately preceding the election. Although the attendance requirement had not been challenged in the candidate's internal union protests, the Secretary included it as a basis for setting aside the election in a suit brought in federal district court. The Supreme Court held (7-2) that under these circumstances the Secretary was barred from challenging the attendance rule in a § 402(b) action. The Court reasoned: "The requirement of § 402(a) that a union member first seek redress of alleged election violations within the union before enlisting the aid of the Secretary, was ... designed to harmonize the need to eliminate election abuses with a desire to avoid unnecessary governmental intervention.... To accept [the Secretary's] contention that a union member, who is aware of the facts underlying an alleged violation, need not first protest this violation to his union before complaining to the Secretary, would be needlessly to weaken union self-government."

NOTES

1. In *Wirtz v. Laborers Local 125,* 389 U.S. 477 (1968), the Supreme Court held that the Secretary of Labor could challenge the validity of a general election of union officers on the basis that ineligible persons had voted, even though the only intraunion protest related to a subsequent runoff election for a single office. Here "respondent union had fair notice from the violation charged by [complainant] in his protest of the runoff election that the same unlawful conduct also occurred at the earlier election." A federal district court has held that the Secretary may litigate alleged Title IV violations discovered during his investigation, despite the complainant's failure to present them directly to the union, under two conditions: (1) the member was ignorant of the facts when he filed his protest, and (2) the alleged violations arose from the same transactions about which the member protested to the union. *Hodgson v. Teamsters Local 734,* 336 F. Supp. 1243 (N.D. Ill. 1972). *See also Dole v. UAW,* 970 F.2d 1562 (6th Cir. 1992) (Secretary may sue after members took reasonable steps to obtain relief within union, in absence of internal procedures "responsive to protests involved" and "legally sufficient" to provide remedy). *But cf. Brock v. Operating Eng'rs Local 369,* 790 F.2d 508 (6th Cir. 1986) (no excuse of exhaustion requirement because of complainants' lack of knowledge).

2. In *Donovan v. Teachers Local 6,* 747 F.2d 711 (D.C. Cir. 1984), the court held that the Secretary of Labor's failure to reopen the nominating process in a court-ordered supervised rerun election for union officers did not violate § 401(c) of the LMRDA by impermissibly infringing the right of members to nominate candidates for "any election."

3. If a union holds its next regular election while a challenge to a previous election is still pending, this does not deprive the Secretary of his right to a court order declaring the challenged election void and directing the conduct of a new election under his supervision. *Wirtz v. Glass Bottle Blowers Local 153,* 389 U.S. 463 (1968). But a federal court in its discretion may decline to order the rerun of an election after a union repeals its unlawful meeting attendance bylaw and holds an untainted intervening election. *McLaughlin v. Boilermakers Lodge 647,* 876 F.2d 648 (8th Cir. 1989).

4. *See generally* Note, *Union Elections and the LMRDA: Thirteen Years of Use and Abuse,* 81 Yale L.J. 407 (1972); Note, *The Enforcement Power of the Secretary of Labor Under Section 402 of the LMRDA,* 1971 U. Ill. L.F. 745.

STEELWORKERS LOCAL 3489 v. USERY

Supreme Court of the United States
429 U.S. 305, 97 S. Ct. 611, 50 L. Ed. 2d 502 (1977)

MR. JUSTICE BRENNAN delivered the opinion of the Court.

The Secretary of Labor brought this action in the District Court for the Southern District of Indiana under § 402(b) of the Labor-Management Reporting and

Disclosure Act of 1959 (LMRDA) ... to invalidate the 1970 election of officers of Local 3489, United Steelworkers of America. The Secretary alleged that a provision of the Steelworkers' International Constitution, binding on the Local, that limits eligibility for local union office to members who have attended at least one-half of the regular meetings of the local for three years previous to the election (unless prevented by union activities or working hours), violated § 401(e) of the LMRDA .... The District Court dismissed the complaint, finding no violation of the Act. The Court of Appeals for the Seventh Circuit reversed. 520 F.2d 516.... We affirm.

I

At the time of the challenged election, there were approximately 660 members in good standing of Local 3489. The Court of Appeals found that 96.5% of these members were ineligible to hold office, because of failure to satisfy the meeting-attendance rule. Of the 23 eligible members, nine were incumbent union officers. The Secretary argues, and the Court of Appeals held, that the failure of 96.5% of the local members to satisfy of the meeting-attendance requirement, and the rule's effect of requiring potential insurgent candidates to plan their candidacies as early as 18 months in advance of the election when the reasons for their opposition might not have yet emerged, established that the requirement has a substantial antidemocratic effect on local union elections. Petitioners argue that the rule is reasonable because it serves valid union purposes, imposes no very burdensome obligation on the members, and has not proved to be a device that entrenches a particular clique of incumbent officers in the local.

II

The opinions in three cases decided in 1968 have identified the considerations pertinent to the determination whether the attendance rule violates § 401(e). *Wirtz v. Hotel Employees,* 391 U.S. 492; *Wirtz v. Bottle Blowers Assn.,* 389 U.S. 463; *Wirtz v. Laborers' Union,* 389 U.S. 477.

The LMRDA does not render unions powerless to restrict candidacies for union office. The injunction in § 401(e) that "every member in good standing shall be eligible to be a candidate and to hold office" is made expressly "subject to ... reasonable qualifications uniformly imposed." But "Congress plainly did not intend that the authorization ... of 'reasonable qualifications ...' should be given a broad reach. The contrary is implicit in the legislative history of the section and in its wording ...." *Wirtz v. Hotel Employees, supra* at 499. The basic objective of Title IV of the LMRDA is to guarantee "free and democratic" union elections modeled on "political elections in this country" where "the assumption is that voters will exercise common sense and judgment in casting their ballots." 391 U.S. at 504. Thus, Title IV is not designed merely to protect the right of a union member to run for a particular office in a particular election. "Congress emphatically asserted a vital public interest in assuring free and democratic union elections that transcends the narrower interest of the complaining union member." *Wirtz v. Bottle Blowers Assn., supra* at 475; *Wirtz v. Laborers' Union, supra* at 483. The goal was to "protect the rights of rank-and-file members to participate fully in the operation of their union through processes of democratic self-government, and, through the election process, to keep the union leadership responsive to the membership." *Wirtz v. Hotel Employees, supra* at 497.

Whether a particular qualification is "reasonable" within the meaning of § 401(e) must therefore "be measured in terms of its consistency with the Act's command to unions to conduct 'free and democratic' union elections." 391 U.S. at 499. Congress was not concerned only with corrupt union leadership. Congress chose the goal of "free and democratic" union elections as a preventive measure "to curb the possibility of abuse by benevolent as well as malevolent entrenched leadership." *Id.* at 503. *Hotel Employees* expressly held that that check was seriously impaired by candidacy qualifications which substantially deplete the ranks of those who might run in opposition to incumbents, and therefore held invalid the candidacy limitation there involved that restricted candidacies for certain positions to members who had previously held union office. "Plainly, given the objective of Title IV, a candidacy limitation which renders 93% of union members ineligible for office can hardly be a 'reasonable qualification.'" *Id.* at 502.

III

Applying these principles to this case, we conclude that here too the antidemocratic effects of the meeting-attendance rule outweigh the interests urged in its support. Like the bylaw in *Hotel Employees,* an attendance requirement that results in the exclusion of 96.5% of the members from candidacy for union office hardly seems to be a "reasonable qualification" consistent with the goal of free and democratic elections. A requirement having that result obviously severely restricts the free choice of the membership in selecting its leaders.

Petitioners argue, however, that the bylaw held violative of § 401 (e) in *Hotel Employees* differs significantly from the attendance rule here. Under the *Hotel Employees* bylaw no member could assure by his own efforts that he would be eligible for union office, since others controlled the criterion for eligibility. Here, on the other hand, a member can assure himself of eligibility for candidacy by attending some 18 brief meetings over a three-year period. In other words, the union would have its rule treated not as excluding a category of member from eligibility, but simply as mandating a procedure to be followed by any member who wishes to be a candidate.

Even examined from this perspective, however, the rule has a restrictive effect on union democracy.[6] In the absence of a permanent "opposition party" within the union, opposition to the incumbent leadership is likely to emerge in response to particular issues at different times, and member interest in changing union leadership is therefore likely to be at its highest only shortly before elections. Thus it is probable that to require that a member decide upon a potential candidacy at least 18 months in advance of an election when no issues exist to prompt that decision may not foster but discourage candidacies and to that extent impair the general membership's freedom to oust incumbents in favor of new leadership.

Nor are we persuaded by petitioners' argument that the Secretary has failed to show an antidemocratic effect because he has not shown that the incumbent leaders of the union became "entrenched" in their offices as a consequence of the operation of the attendance rule. The reasons why leaderships become entrenched are difficult to isolate. The election of the same officers year after year may be a signal that antidemocratic election rules have prevented an effective challenge to the regime, or might well signal only that the members are satisfied with their stewardship; if elections are uncontested, opposition factions may have been denied access to the ballot, or competing interests may have compromised differences before the election to maintain a front of unity. Conversely, turnover in offices may result from an open political process, or from a competition limited to candidates who offer no real opposition to an entrenched establishment. But Congress did not saddle the courts with the duty to search out and remove improperly entrenched union leaderships. Rather, Congress chose to guarantee union democracy by regulating not the results of a union's electoral procedure, but the procedure itself. Congress decided that if the elections are "free and democratic," the members themselves are able to correct abuse of power by entrenched leadership. Procedures that unduly restrict free choice among candidates are forbidden without regard to their success or failure in maintaining corrupt leadership.

Petitioners next argue that the rule is reasonable within § 401 (e) because it encourages attendance at union meetings, and assures more qualified officers by limiting election to those who have demonstrated an interest in union affairs, and are familiar with union problems. But the rule has plainly not served these goals. It has obviously done little to encourage attendance at meetings, which continue to attract only a handful of members.[8] Even as to the more limited goal of en-

---

[6] Petitioners argue that attendance at 18 relatively short meetings over three years is no very onerous burden on a union member. But this argument misconceives the evil at which the statute aims. We must judge the eligibility rule not by the burden it imposes on the individual candidate, but by its effect on free and democratic processes of union government. Wirtz v. Hotel Employees, 391 U.S. at 499.

[8] Attendance at Local 3489's meetings averages 47 out of approximately 660 members. There is no indication in the record that this total represents a significant increase over attendance before the institution of the challenged rule.

couraging the attendance of potential dissident candidates, very few members, as we have said, are likely to see themselves as such sufficiently far in advance of the election to be spurred to attendance by the rule.

As for assuring the election of knowledgeable and dedicated leaders, the election provisions of the LMRDA express a congressional determination that the best means to this end is to leave the choice of leaders to the membership in open democratic elections, unfettered by arbitrary exclusions. Pursuing this goal by excluding the bulk of the membership from eligibility for office, and thus limiting the possibility of dissident candidacies, runs directly counter to the basic premise of the statute. We therefore conclude that Congress, in guaranteeing every union member the opportunity to hold office, subject only to "reasonable qualifications," disabled unions from establishing eligibility qualifications as sharply restrictive of the openness of the union political process as is petitioners' attendance rule.

IV

Finally, petitioners argue that the absence of a precise statement of what the Secretary of Labor and the courts will regard as reasonable prevents the drafting of a meeting-attendance rule with any assurance that it will be valid under § 401 (e). The Secretary, to whom Congress has assigned a special role in the administration of the Act, *see Calhoon v. Harvey,* 379 U.S. 134, 140 (1964); *Dunlop v. Bachowski,* 421 U.S. 560 (1975), has announced the following view:

> Experience has demonstrated that it is not feasible to establish arbitrary guidelines for judging the reasonableness of [a meeting attendance eligibility requirement]. Its reasonableness must be gauged in the light of all the circumstances of the particular case, including not only the frequency of meetings, the number of meetings which must be attended and the period of time over which the requirement extends, but also such factors as the nature, availability and extent of excuse provisions, whether all or most members have the opportunity to attend meetings, and the impact of the rule, i.e., the number or percentage of members who would be rendered ineligible by its application.

29 CFR § 452.38 (a) (1976). Obviously, this standard leads to more uncertainty than would a less flexible rule. But in using the word "reasonable," Congress clearly contemplated exactly such a flexible result. Moreover, on the facts of this case and in light of *Hotel Employees,* petitioners' contention that they had no way of knowing that a rule disqualifying over 90% of a local's members from

office would be regarded as unreasonable in the absence of substantial justification is unpersuasive.[9]

Affirmed.

MR. JUSTICE POWELL, with whom MR. JUSTICE STEWART and MR. JUSTICE REHNQUIST join, dissenting....

As this holding seems to me an unwarranted interference with the right of the union to manage its own internal affairs, I dissent.

Stated broadly, the purpose of Title IV of the Act is to insure "free and democratic" elections. But

> [t]he legislative history [of the Act] shows that Congress weighed how best to legislate against revealed abuses in union elections without departing needlessly from its long-standing policy against unnecessary governmental intrusion into internal union affairs.

Wirtz v. Bottle Blowers Assn., 389 U.S. 463, 470-471 (1968); *Wirtz v. Hotel Employees,* 391 U.S. 492, 496 (1968). Section 401(e) reflects a congressional intent to accommodate both of these purposes. It provides that a labor organization may set "reasonable qualifications uniformly imposed" for members in good standing who wish to be candidates and to hold office. There is no contention that the attendance rule in question was not "uniformly imposed." Nor does the rule render ineligible for office any member who displays enough interest to attend half of his local's meetings.

The Court nevertheless, relying heavily on *Hotel Employees,* holds that this rule imposes an unreasonable qualification, violative of § 401(e). *Hotel Employees* involved a "prior office" rule that limited candidates for local union office to members who previously had held elective union office. The Court's opinion in that case emphasized that the effect of the prior-office rule was to disqualify 93.1% of the union's membership. In this case, the respondent argues that *Hotel Employees* enunciated a *per se* "effects" rule, requiring invalidation of union elections whenever an eligibility rule disqualifies all but a small percentage of the union's membership. Although the Court today does not in terms adopt a *per se* "effects" analysis, it comes close to doing so. The fact that 96.5% of Local 3489's members chose not to comply with its rule was given controlling weight.

In my view, the Court has extended the reach of *Hotel Employees* far beyond the holding and basic rationale of that case. Indeed, the rule there involved was

---

[9] Also unpersuasive is the argument that a union cannot know in advance how many of its members will be disqualified by a meeting-attendance rule. While the precise number may not be predictable, petitioners must have had some awareness of the general attendance rate at union meetings, and if Local 3489's attendance rate is at all typical (and there is no contention that it is not), it should have been fairly obvious that a rule disqualifying all who had not maintained 50% attendance for three years, admittedly one of the most stringent such rules among labor unions, would have a significant antidemocratic impact.

acknowledged to be a sport—"virtually unique in trade union practice." 391 U.S., at 505. It was a rule deliberately designed, as intimated by the Court's opinion, to entrench union leadership. *Id.* at 499. Moreover, the general effect of the rule in *Hotel Employees* was predictable at the time the rule was adopted. By limiting eligibility to members who held or previously had held elective office, the disqualification of a large proportion of the membership was a purposeful and inevitable effect of the structure of the rule itself. The attendance rule before the Court today has no comparable feature. No member is precluded from establishing eligibility. Nor can the effect of the rule be predicted, as any member who demonstrates the requisite interest in union affairs is eligible to seek office. In short, the only common factor between the prior-office rule in *Hotel Employees* and that before the Court today is the similarity in the percentage of ineligible members. But in one case the effect was predetermined for the purpose of perpetuating control of a few insiders, whereas here the effect resulted from the free choice—perhaps the indifference—of the rank and file membership....

Although the opinion of the Court today discounts the weight to be given these purposes, I agree ... that at least facially they serve legitimate and meritorious union purposes: (i) encouraging attendance at meetings; (ii) requiring candidates for office to demonstrate a meaningful interest in the union and its affairs; and (iii) assuring that members who seek office have had an opportunity to become informed as to union affairs. One may argue that requiring attendance at 18 of the 36 meetings prior to the election goes beyond what may be necessary to serve these purposes. But this is a "judgment call" best left to the unions themselves absent a stronger showing of potential for abuse than has been made in this case.

The record in this case is instructive. Twenty-three members were eligible to run for office in the 1970 election. These were members who were nominated and who also had complied with the attendance requirement. The record does not show, and indeed no one knows, how many members were eligible under the rule but who were not nominated. Three candidates competed for the office of president, four for the three trustee offices, and six ran unopposed for the remaining offices. Of the 10 officers elected, six were incumbents. Nonincumbents were elected to the offices of vice president, treasurer, recording secretary, and the minor office of guide. There was no history of entrenched leadership and no evidence of restrictive union practices precluding free and democratic elections. Indeed, the record is to the contrary. Five different presidents had been elected during the preceding 10 years, and an estimated 40 changes in officers had occurred in the course of four separate elections. Bernard Frye, who initiated this case by complaint to the Secretary, won the presidency in an election subsequent to 1970 and thereafter lost it.

In the final analysis, respondent, who bears the burden of proving that the rule is "unreasonable," rests his entire case on a facial attack upon the attendance rule itself, an attack supported by a statistical "effects test" that at best is ambiguous and one that could invalidate almost any attendance requirement that served legitimate union purposes. In my view, the respondent has failed to prove that the rule is unreasonable....

NOTES

1. *Eligibility for office.* Prior to the decision in the principal case, a variety of other conditions on eligibility for union office had been found unreasonable and invalid under § 401(e), at least where they had the effect in actual operation of disqualifying a substantial portion of a union's membership. These included: (a) a requirement that monthly or quarterly dues be paid in advance during the entire one-year or two-year period preceding the election, *Wirtz v. Operating Eng'rs Local 406,* 254 F. Supp. 962 (E.D. La. 1966) (only 3 percent of membership eligible); *Wirtz v. Operating Eng'rs Local 9,* 254 F. Supp. 980 (D. Colo. 1965), *aff'd,* 366 F.2d 911 (10th Cir. 1966), *vacated as moot,* 387 U.S. 96 (1967) (87 percent of membership ineligible); *but cf. Donovan v. Transport Workers Local 500,* 111 L.R.R.M. 2499 (S.D. Fla. 1982) (court rejected Secretary's view that any requirement barring over 70 percent of union members from candidacy is per se unreasonable); (b) parent local membership as distinguished from branch local membership, where transfer from branch to parent local required payment of initiation fees ranging from $75 to $90, *Hodgson v. Operating Eng'rs Local 18,* 440 F.2d 485 (6th Cir. 1971) (60 percent of membership in branches); (c) membership on the union's board of directors for at least six months, *Wirtz v. Office Employees Ass'n,* 60 L.R.R.M. 2215 (N.D. Ind. 1965); (d) a requirement that a member prove his eligibility for an officer's bond of the type prescribed by § 502 of the LMRDA, *Wirtz v. Carpenters Local 559,* 61 L.R.R.M. 2618 (W.D. Ky. 1966); and (e) a requirement that a declaration of candidacy be filed four months prior to the nomination meeting, *Wirtz v. Operating Eng'rs Local 30,* 242 F. Supp. 631 (S.D.N.Y. 1965), *vacated as moot,* 366 F.2d 438 (2d Cir. 1966). *See also Donovan v. Sailor's Union of the Pac.,* 739 F.2d 1426 (9th Cir. 1984), *cert. denied,* 471 U.S. 1004 (1985) (restricting candidacy to persons who had been union members for three years unreasonable).

Courts of appeals have held that a union may lawfully require the payment of strike assessments as a condition for voting and running for office, *Department of Labor v. Aluminum Workers Local 200,* 941 F.2d 1172 (11th Cir. 1991), and that a union may disqualify from running for office any member who applied for a supervisory position within the preceding two years, *Martin v. Letter Carriers Branch 419,* 965 F.2d 61 (6th Cir. 1992). *Cf. Martin v. IATSE Local 412,* 815 F. Supp. 441 (M.D. Fla. 1993) (local violated § 401(e) and international constitution by allowing manager at place of employment to run for union president), *aff'd sub. nom Reich v. IATSE,* 32 F.3d 512 (11th Cir. 1994).

How can one determine whether a given qualification is designed to ensure that candidates will be well-versed and active in a union's affairs, or is designed to deter dissidents and benefit incumbents? Is it best simply to rely on a rule's effects, in terms of the percentage of members disqualified for office? *See generally* Barnard, *Restrictions on the Right to Be a Candidate and Hold Union Office—The "Reasonable Qualifications" Exception in the Labor-Management Reporting and Disclosure Act,* 18 Wayne L. Rev. 1239 (1972); Cohen, *The Secretary of Labor's Court Challenge to the Steelworkers' Meeting Attendance Rule: A Case Study of the Conflict Between Internal Union Self-Government and the Administration of the Landrum-Griffin Act,* N.Y.U. Twenty-sixth Annual Conference on Labor 259 (1974); James, *Union Democracy and the LMRDA: Autocracy and Insurgency in National Union Elections,* 13 Harv. C.R.-C.L.L. Rev. 247 (1978); Plummer, *LMRDA Title IV's § 401(e): The Issue of "Broad Reach" in the Process of Guaranteeing a Reasonable Opportunity to Run for Union Office,* 43 Cath. U. L. Rev. 867 (1994).

Could a predominantly white union, as an affirmative action measure, set aside a certain percentage of seats on the organization's executive board for members of various minority groups? *See Donovan v. Illinois Educ. Ass'n,* 667 F.2d 638 (7th Cir. 1982).

2. *Denial of office.* Does § 402(b) confine the Secretary to an action to "set aside" an election, or may he sue to have installed a duly elected candidate who has been illegally denied his office? *Cf. Wirtz v. Teamsters Local 73,* 257 F. Supp. 784 (N.D. Ohio 1966). *See generally* Fox, *Title IV's "Never Land"—When and How Victorious Insurgents Are to Be Installed in Union Office,* 4 Hofstra Lab. L.J. 299 (1987).

3. *Removal from office.* Pursuant to § 401(h) and (i), the Secretary has issued regulations prescribing minimum standards for the procedures which must be made available to enable the removal of an elected local officer guilty of serious misconduct. *See* 29 C.F.R. §§ 417.1-417.25 (1988).

4. *See generally* Beaird, *Union Officer Election Provisions of the Labor-Management Reporting and Disclosure Act of 1959,* 51 Va. L. Rev. 1306 (1965). The Secretary of Labor's interpretations of the election provisions of the LMRDA are contained in 29 C.F.R. §§ 452.1-452.138 (1988). For an extensive analysis of state court decisions on union elections, still of major significance in private pre-election suits, *see* Summers, *Judicial Regulation of Union Elections,* 70 Yale L.J. 1221 (1961).

B. FIDUCIARY DUTIES OF OFFICERS

HIGHWAY TRUCK DRIVERS, LOCAL 107 v. COHEN

United States District Court, Eastern District of Pennsylvania
182 F. Supp. 608 (1960), *aff'd per curiam,* 284 F.2d 162
(3d Cir. 1960), *cert. denied,* 365 U.S. 833 (1961)

CLARY, DISTRICT JUDGE. This is a private suit brought under the recently enacted Labor Management Reporting and Disclosure Act of 1959.... That Act establishes a fiduciary responsibility on the part of officers of a labor organization

[§ 501(a)], and further provided for a suit in a Federal district court to enforce these responsibilities [§ 501(b)]. The present suit has been brought under § 501(b) to enforce certain of these duties.

The moving parties are nine rank-and-file members of Highway Truck Drivers and Helpers, Local 107, of the International Brotherhood of Teamsters, Chauffeurs, Warehousemen and Helpers of America (hereinafter referred to as "Local 107"), who were given leave by this Court on November 12, 1959 to file a complaint against the defendants, the governing officers of Local 107. The complaint charged the defendants with a continuing mass conspiracy to cheat and defraud the union of large sums of money—the conspiracy alleged to have begun in 1954 and continued to the present time.

The defendants have yet to answer these very serious charges. Having been unsuccessful in first opposing the plaintiffs' petition for leave of this Court to sue, defendants now move to have the complaint dismissed. They are supported in this motion by counsel for Local 107, which has been allowed to intervene as a party defendant. This motion to dismiss is presently before the Court along with the plaintiffs' prayer for a preliminary injunction to prohibit the defendants from using union funds to defray the legal costs and other expenses being incurred by the defendants (and several other members of Local 107) in the defense of civil and criminal actions brought against them in the Courts of Pennsylvania and also the present suit in our own Court.

If the only matter before the Court were the motion to dismiss discussed above, the Court might be disposed to grant the motion. However, there is another facet to the case which prevents the dismissal of the action. That facet relates to the motion for a preliminary injunction to prohibit the defendants from using union funds to defray the expense of legal fees in civil and criminal actions which have been brought against them in the Courts of Pennsylvania as well as to defray legal costs of the present action. The charges in those cases, in essence, grow out of alleged misappropriation of funds by the officers, and the plaintiffs maintain that such expenditures are in violation of the fiduciary duties imposed upon officers of a labor union by § 501(a) of the Act, *supra*, and that unless such expenditures are enjoined the union will suffer irreparable harm thereby.

Shortly after the effective date of the Act and the institution of suits, criminal and civil, in the local Courts against the defendants, the union at a regular monthly meeting, with few dissenting votes, adopted a resolution authorizing the union to bear "Legal costs of such actions [against the officers] which are in reality not directed at our officers but are directed at us, the members of Local 107, our good contracts, our good wages and our good working conditions."

The question, therefore, which faces us is: Does the expenditure of union funds to pay for legal fees in the defense of both criminal and civil actions brought against the various defendant officers for an alleged conspiracy to cheat and defraud their union of large sums of money constitute a breach of that fiduciary duty imposed upon them by § 501(a), *supra*, notwithstanding the purported authorization of such expenditures by a resolution of the union membership passed at a regular union meeting?

At the hearing on the preliminary injunction, it was brought out that within the limit of some four or five weeks after the adoption of the resolution the union, pursuant to the resolution, paid upwards of $25,000 to the attorneys representing the defendants. It is also clear that counsel for the union has advised the officers that such expenditures are proper. We are, therefore, with the payment of those large sums of money already accomplished and threatened further payments about to occur, in a position factually to pass upon the merits of the plaintiffs' contention....

Section 501, with which we are particularly concerned, is entitled "Fiduciary responsibility of officers of labor organizations." This section ... attempts to define in the broadest terms possible the duty which the new federal law imposes upon a union official. Congress made no attempt to "codify" the law in this area. It appears evident to us that they intended the federal courts to fashion a new federal labor law in this area, in much the same way that the federal courts have fashioned a new substantive law of collective bargaining contracts under § 301(a) of the Taft-Hartley Act, 29 U.S.C. § 185(a). *See Textile Workers Union of America v. Lincoln Mills,* 1957, 353 U.S. 448. In undertaking this task the federal courts will necessarily rely heavily upon the common law of the various states. Where that law is lacking or where it in any way conflicts with the policy expressed in our national labor laws, the latter will of course be our guide....

In determining whether or not the expenditures now sought to be enjoined violate the fiduciary responsibility of an officer of a labor organization we must necessarily determine the legal effect of the September 20th Resolution. This goes to the heart of the present problem and appears to be the main ground on which the defendants seek to avoid the injunction.

The plaintiffs assert that the Resolution authorizing such expenditures is encompassed within the express prohibition of § 501(a) against any "general exculpatory resolution." Although not expressly purporting to absolve the defendants of guilt, plaintiffs argue that the Resolution *in effect* does just this. Unfortunately the Act does not define the phrase "general exculpatory resolution." ...

[I]t is not necessary for a resolution to read "The officers are hereby absolved of all responsibility created by the Act" before a court will strike it down as "exculpatory" under § 501(a). Nor must a court accept at face value the stated purposes of a resolution when reason and common sense clearly dictate a different purpose. Nevertheless in my interpretation of § 501(a), the Resolution under discussion is *not* one "purporting to relieve any [officer] of liability for breach of the duties declared by this section...."

We must distinguish between a resolution which purports to *authorize* action which is beyond the power of the union to do and for that reason in violation of § 501(a) when done by an officer (such as the present Resolution) and a resolution which purports to *relieve* an officer of liability for breach of the duties declared in § 501(a). At times this distinction may be a fine one. Very often the result will be the same. Nevertheless we feel that such a distinction should be made here unless the "exculpatory" provision is to be read as a mere "catchall" phrase.[6]

We turn then to the question of whether the September 20th Resolution is valid, i.e., conforms with the law of Pennsylvania and the Federal Labor laws. *See International Union of Operating Engineers, A.F.L.-C.I.O. v. Pierce,* Tex. Civ. App., 1959, 321 S.W.2d 914, at page 917-918. If it is inconsistent with either, we think it follows that the present expenditures by the defendants violate that provision in § 501(a) which imposes upon them a strict duty to "expend [union funds] in accordance with its constitution and bylaws and any resolutions of the governing bodies adopted thereunder ...."—since we read this sentence to authorize only those expenditures made pursuant to a *lawful* bylaw or resolution....

In answering this question of whether an act is ultra vires, we look first to the Constitution of Local 107. Article I, § 2, sets forth the "objectives" of the organization in broad terms. These objectives might be summed up as an effort to organize workmen, to educate them, to improve their condition and to improve the industry in which they work. The defendants pointed to no more specific provision in the constitution (nor can we find any) which would authorize the type of expenditure dealt with here.

It is true that from the general objectives and purposes of a particular trade union, certain ancillary powers reasonably necessary for their attainment may be implied. In determining whether a particular act falls within this admittedly broad latitude of action, the Court must take into consideration all of the factors surrounding it, i.e., the stated purpose of the action, its immediate effect, its possible future benefit to the union, etc. This is necessary in order to determine whether the union, in light of the authority derived from its constitution, has a sufficient interest in the action to empower it to so act. If it has, a court of law will not interfere regardless of the wisdom or propriety of the act. If it has not, a court of law must intervene at the behest of a single union member....

... Although this question again has not been passed upon in Pennsylvania, several other jurisdictions when faced with the problem have concluded that such expenditures are improper....

In light of the foregoing and upon consideration of the situation surrounding the present expenditures, in particular the nature and seriousness of the charges brought against the defendants by the State of Pennsylvania as well as by individual members of their unions, the Court feels that such expenditures to pay for

---

[6] We might point out in this regard that the original Senate version of the Act (i.e., The Kennedy-Ives Bill, S. Rep. No., 187, 86th Cong., First Session, 1959) contained a somewhat similar prohibition against any exculpatory resolution and *also* contained a clause prohibiting unions from paying the legal fees or fines of any person indicted or convicted of a violation of the Bill.

the legal expenses incurred by the defendant officers in the criminal and civil suits brought against them individually are expenses to be borne by the officers themselves and are beyond the power of Local 107 to make. Being beyond the powers of the union as derived from its Constitution, it follows that a mere majority vote at a regular union meeting can not authorize such expenditures....

There are undoubtedly situations in which a suit against a union officer would have a direct and injurious effect upon the union itself or would in reality be directed at the union. In such a situation the union would have the power to lend its financial support to such officer. When the question of whether the union has a sufficient interest to spend large sums of money to defend such a suit arises, it must ultimately be resolved by the court. Although a court will allow wide latitude to those in control of the union, it can not, by allowing unlimited latitude, abandon the right of a minority to see that the union spends its monies in accordance with its lawful aims and purposes as expressed in its Constitution and by-laws. Particularly is this true today, when the voice of the individual employee in fixing his own wages, hours and working conditions has necessarily been surrendered to the voice of the collective bargaining unit.

There is a further reason why the present Resolution is no defense here. Aside from its validity under Pennsylvania law, it is inconsistent with the aims and purposes of the Labor Management Reporting and Disclosure Act and violates the spirit of that Act. A stated purpose of the Act is "to *eliminate* ... improper practices on the part of labor organizations .... and their officers." (Emphasis added.) To allow a union officer to use the power and wealth of the very union which he is accused of pilfering, to defend himself against such charges, is totally inconsistent with Congress' effort to eliminate the undesirable element which has been uncovered in the labor-management field. To allow even a majority of members in that union to authorize such action, when, if the charges made against these defendants are true, it is these very members whom the officers have deceived, would be equally inconsistent with the Act. If some of those members have not been deceived by the defendants, but because of the immediate gains in their income and working conditions which Local 107 has won for them, they are content to accept as officers anyone who produces immediate results, regardless of what other wrongs those officers may commit in so doing, this Court would still not feel constrained to bow to their will in the light of its duty both to those members of Local 107 who place honesty above material gain as well as to the millions of others in the labor movement whose cause would be seriously injured by such an attitude.

Although we have not attempted to treat defendants' arguments individually, since we feel they are satisfactorily answered in this opinion, something should be said concerning their argument that the plaintiffs are here asking us to do that which Congress specifically refused to do when it failed to adopt subsection 107(b) of the original Senate version of the Labor Bill (The Kennedy-Ives Bill), which specifically prohibited "both unions and employers from directly or indirectly paying or advancing the costs of defense, of any of their officers ... who [are] indicted for ... any violation of any provision of the Bill." S. Rep. No. 187, 86th Cong., First Session, 1959, U.S. Code Cong. and Adm. News 1959, at 2318....

[We] are not persuaded by their argument here.

First, the language contained in the Kennedy-Ives Bill is much broader than our holding in the present case. It is essential to an understanding of our position in this case that this point be made clear. That section quoted above would foreclose financial aid by the union to an officer in suits under the Act, under *any* circumstances. In our case we have expressly limited our holding *to the facts before us*. In the light of all of these facts we do not feel that the several actions brought against the defendants involve any question of sufficient interest to Local 107 to warrant their expending large sums of union money to pay the legal costs of the defendants in these suits. That Congress refused to foreclose the right of a union under *any* circumstances to lend financial aid to an officer when sued under any section of the Kennedy-Ives Bill is not, we feel, a strong argument for the conclusion that under *no* circumstances could a union be prohibited from lending financial aid to an accused officer....

Finally, even assuming that Congress intended to leave a union free to use its funds for the purpose of paying its officers legal expenses in actions brought against them under the new Act, if under the law of Pennsylvania, the state in which the union membership contractual relationship arose, such expenditures are illegal, a union officer could not consistent with his duty to the union (which duties ultimately flow from its Constitution) expend union funds for this purpose. This would follow unless we interpret the omission of this prohibition as creating an affirmative federal right in a union to so spend its funds, which right is intended to supersede any state law to the contrary. We flatly reject such an interpretation of the new Act....

A formal order will be entered enjoining the defendants from expending union funds for the defense of the cases presently pending against the defendants in either the Courts of the Commonwealth of Pennsylvania or in this Court. This ruling in no way attempts to pass upon the question of whether or not Local 107 may with propriety, by appropriate resolution, reimburse its officers for their legal expenses in the event they are exonerated from any wrongdoing in connection with the handling of union funds involved in the actions presently pending.

NOTES

1. In July 1961 the International Brotherhood of Teamsters amended its constitution to authorize the international and local unions to pay the cost of defending officers and employees in criminal or civil actions. Was this a "general exculpatory provision ... void as against public policy" under § 501(a)? *See Highway Truck Drivers Local 107 v. Cohen,* 215 F. Supp. 938 (E.D. Pa. 1963), *aff'd*, 334 F.2d 378 (3d Cir.), *cert. denied*, 379 U.S. 921 (1964). *See also Morrissey v. Curran*, 423 F.2d 393 (2d Cir.), *cert. denied*, 399 U.S. 928 (1970).

2. To what extent should a court defer to a union's own interpretation of its constitution, for example, when the authorization for a particular payment is challenged? *See, e.g., Gabauer v. Woodcock*, 594 F.2d 662 (8th Cir.) (en banc), *cert. denied*, 444 U.S. 841 (1979) (contributions to political and activist groups), *noted in* 93 Harv. L. Rev. 608 (1980).

3. In *Gurton v. Arons*, 339 F.2d 371, 375 (2d Cir. 1964), the court declared: "A simple reading of [§ 501] ... shows that it applies to fiduciary responsibility with respect to the money and property of the union and that it is not a catch-all provision under which union officials can be sued on any ground of misconduct with which the plaintiffs choose to charge them." *See also Yanity v. Benware*, 376 F.2d 197 (2d Cir.), *cert. denied*, 389 U.S. 874 (1967). *But cf. Johnson v. Nelson*, 325 F.2d 646, 651 (8th Cir. 1963) (refusal to sign checks approved by the membership; "§ 501 imposes fiduciary responsibility in its broadest application and is not confined in its scope to union officials only in their handling of money and property affairs"); *Moschetta v. Cross*, 48 L.R.R.M. 2669 (D.D.C. 1961) (refusal to hold special convention previously called in accordance with union's constitution); *Sabolsky v. Budzanoski*, 457 F.2d 1245 (3d Cir.), *cert. denied*, 409 U.S. 853 (1972) (failure to disband nonfunctioning locals as required by union's constitution); *Cefalo v. Moffett*, 333 F. Supp. 1283 (D.D.C.), *modified in part*, 449 F.2d 1193 (D.C. Cir. 1971) (merger of unions). What factors militate for or against an expansive reading of § 501? *See generally* Clark, *The Fiduciary Duties of Union Officials Under Section 501 of the LMRDA*, 52 Minn. L. Rev. 437 (1967); Leslie, *Federal Courts and Union Fiduciaries*, 76 Colum. L. Rev. 1205 (1976); Note, *The Fiduciary Duty Under Section 501 of the LMRDA*, 75 Colum. L. Rev. 1189 (1975). For a skeptical view from an economics perspective, *see* Schwab, *Union Raids, Union Democracy, and the Market for Union Control*, 1992 U. Ill. L. Rev. 367. *See also* Pope, *Two Faces, Two Ethics: Labor Union Lawyers and the Emerging Doctrine of Entity Ethics*, 68 Or. L. Rev. 1 (1989).

Section 501 has been held unavailable to union members seeking damages, an accounting, and an injunction against union officers who contributed union funds to partisan political activities and social causes, when the union's constitution and governing resolutions authorized such expenditures. *McNamara v. Johnston*, 522 F.2d 1157 (7th Cir. 1975), *cert. denied*, 425 U.S. 911 (1976).

Should union officials be held personally liable for unauthorized payments to third parties, when the officials themselves do not profit from the transaction? *Compare Richardson v. Tyler*, 309 F. Supp. 1020 (N.D. Ill. 1970) *with Morrissey v. Curran*, 336 F. Supp. 1107 (S.D.N.Y. 1972), *aff'd*, 483 F.2d 480 (2d Cir. 1973), *cert. denied*, 414 U.S. 1128 (1974).

4. Exhaustion of internal union remedies has been held not a prerequisite to a member's suit under § 501(b), as long as the specific procedural requirements of that section are met. *Horner v. Ferron*, 362 F.2d 224 (9th Cir.), *cert. denied*, 385

U.S. 958 (1966); *Holdeman v. Scheldon,* 204 F. Supp. 890 (S.D.N.Y.), *aff'd,* 311 F.2d 2 (2d Cir. 1962). *Contra, Penuelas v. Moreno,* 198 F. Supp. 441 (S.D. Cal. 1961). It has also been held that a union member's failure to request his local to sue alleged union wrongdoers did not bar his court action against the local's officers for breach of their fiduciary duties. *Quinn v. DiGiulian,* 97 CCH Lab. Cas. ¶ 10,163 (D.D.C. 1983), *aff'd,* 739 F.2d 637 (D.C. Cir. 1984).

5. *Litigation costs.* Should union officers sued under § 501 be entitled to retain counsel paid for by the union? *See Tucker v. Shaw,* 378 F.2d 304 (2d Cir. 1967); *Kerr v. Shanks,* 466 F.2d 1267 (9th Cir. 1972), *cert. denied,* 412 U.S. 918 (1973). What about a union's paying a defendant officer's legal fees after he has been exonerated? *See Morrissey v. Segal,* 526 F.2d 121 (2d Cir. 1975). *See also* Bartosic & Minda, *Union Fiduciaries, Attorneys, and Conflicts of Interest,* 15 U.C. Davis L. Rev. 227 (1981); Note, *Counsel Fees for Union Officers Under the Fiduciary Provision of Landrum-Griffin,* 73 Yale L.J. 443 (1964). May successful plaintiffs in § 501 actions be awarded attorneys' fees and other expenses even if there is no monetary recovery? *See Kerr v. Shanks, supra; Bakery Workers v. Ratner,* 335 F.2d 691 (D.C. Cir. 1964).

6. *Bonding.* Section 502 of the LMRDA requires the bonding of union personnel handling the organization's funds or property. An analysis of the section as it was originally enacted is contained in Dugan, *To Bond or Not to Bond—Section 502 of the Landrum-Griffin Act,* 12 Lab. L.J. 536 (1961). In 1965, § 502 was amended to allow coverage by a standard "honesty" bond rather than the more expensive "faithful performance" bond formerly required, and to permit the use of a wider range of surety companies.

C. REPORTING AND DISCLOSURE

About a dozen states require labor unions to register or file organizational and financial reports: Alabama, Alaska, Arkansas, Connecticut, Florida, Kansas, New Hampshire, New Mexico, North Dakota, South Dakota, Washington, and Wisconsin. 4 Lab. Rel. Rep. SLL 1:150 (1993). *See generally* C. Killingsworth, State Labor Relations Acts 99-100 (1948); Aaron & Komaroff, *Statutory Regulation of Internal Union Affairs I,* 44 Ill. L. Rev. 425, 460-61 (1949). In addition, the tremendous growth of welfare and pension funds during and after World War II, coupled with legislative investigations revealing loose practice in their administration, led several states to enact laws setting standards for such funds and requiring reporting and disclosure: Connecticut, Massachusetts, Nevada, New York, and Wisconsin. 4 Lab. Rel. Rep. SLL 1:185 (1993).

Today the most important regulatory and reporting measures in these areas are two federal laws, the Employee Retirement Income Security Act of 1974, 88 Stat. 829 (1974), 29 U.S.C. §§ 1001—1381 (*see generally* Fasser, Levin, Greenberg, *Pension Reform: Its Impact on the Bargaining Scene,* in N.Y.U. Twenty-eighth Annual Conference on Labor 59, 67, 85 (1976) (three separate papers);

Sickles, Donaldson, Gertner, Fillion & Trebilcock, *The Employee Retirement Income Security Act of 1974: Labor Law Considerations,* 17 Wm. & Mary L. Rev. 205, 215, 233, 251 (1975) (four separate papers)) and the Labor-Management Reporting and Disclosure Act of 1959 (*see generally* Aaron, *The Labor-Management Reporting and Disclosure Act of 1959,* 73 Harv. L. Rev. 851, 877-94 (1960); Naumoff, *Reporting Requirements Under the Labor-Management Reporting and Disclosure Act,* in N.Y.U. Fourteenth Annual Conference on Labor 129 (1961)). The former replaced the Welfare and Pension Plan Disclosure Act of 1958, 72 Stat. 997 (1958), as amended (*see generally* BNA, Federal-State Regulation of Welfare Funds (1962)), which was primarily a reporting statute, with elaborate regulation of all employee benefit plans maintained by employers and unions in interstate commerce. Pensions, for example, must meet minimum vesting, benefit accrual, and funding requirements. Stiff fiduciary obligations are imposed on all plan trustees and administrators. Enforcement is through civil suit by a plan participant or beneficiary or by the Secretary of Labor. Criminal sanctions apply to willful violations.

As has been seen, the LMRDA as finally passed was much more than a disclosure measure. But reporting provisions remain a central feature of the Act. Title II prescribes five different types of reports: (1) union organizational reports; (2) union financial reports; (3) "conflict of interest" reports by union officers and employees; (4) employer reports on such matters as payments to union representatives and payments to influence employees in the exercise of their collective rights; and (5) reports by labor relations consultants on agreements to so influence employees, or to inform employers about employee or union activities in a labor dispute. The courts are divided on whether labor consultants engaged in "persuader" activities for employer clients must report *all* compensation from all employer clients for labor relations services, whether persuader or nonpersuader. *Compare Douglas v. Wirtz,* 353 F.2d 30 (4th Cir. 1965), *cert. denied,* 383 U.S. 909 (1966) *and Price v. Wirtz,* 412 F.2d 647 (5th Cir. 1969) *with Donovan v. Rose Law Firm,* 768 F.2d 964 (8th Cir. 1985). *See generally* Beaird, *Reporting Requirements for Employers and Labor Relations Consultants in the Labor-Management Reporting and Disclosure Act of 1959,* 53 Geo. L.J. 267 (1965). On lawyer consultants in particular, *see* Craver, *The Application of the LMRDA "Labor Consultant" Reporting Requirements to Management Attorneys: Benign Neglect Personified,* 73 Nw. U. L. Rev. 605 (1978). The reporting obligations are subject to criminal sanctions and to a civil suit by the Secretary of Labor for an injunction or other appropriate remedy.

The information contained in union organizational and financial reports must be made available to the members of the union. Under § 201(c) of the LMRDA a member may sue to inspect a union's books and records to verify its financial reports, but not in order to make an "intelligent vote" on a proposed increase in dues and fees. *Flaherty v. Warehousemen Local 334,* 574 F.2d 484 (9th Cir. 1978). *Cf. Mallick v. IBEW,* 749 F.2d 771 (D.C. Cir. 1984). *Stomper v. Amalga-*

mated Transit Union, 27 F.3d 316 (7th Cir. 1994), involved union members who sued their union under LMRDA § 201(c) seeking to inspect union records. The union quickly provided most of the information being sought, and the members abandoned their claim for the rest. Although the district court awarded the members attorney fees, the Seventh Circuit reversed. The fact that the members had failed to obtain a favorable judgment precluded any award of attorney fees.

To relieve smaller unions of the mountainous paper work involved in detailed financial reporting, the Secretary of Labor, exercising his discretion under § 208, has authorized simplified reports for unions having annual gross receipts of less than $100,000.

The so-called "goldfish bowl" philosophy underlying the union reporting requirements is reflected in the following statement.

HOUSE COMMITTEE ON EDUCATION AND LABOR

H.R. Rep. No. 741 on H.R. 8342, 86th Cong., 1st Sess. 7-9 (1959)

The members of a labor organization are the real owners of the money and property of such organizations and are entitled to a full accounting of all transactions involving such money and property. Because union funds belong to the members they should be expended only in furtherance of their common interest. A union treasury should not be managed as though it were the private property of the union officers, however well intentioned such officers might be, but as a fund governed by fiduciary standards....

... [T]he rules governing the conduct of the union's business, such as dues and assessments payable by members, membership rights, disciplinary procedures, election of officers, provisions governing the calling of regular and special meetings—all should be known to the members. Without such information freely available it is impossible that labor organizations can be truly responsive to their members.

It is the purpose of this bill to insure that full information concerning the financial and internal administrative practices and procedures of labor organizations shall be, in the first instance available to the members of such organizations. In addition, this information is to be made available to the Government, and through the Secretary of Labor, is to be open to inspection by the general public. By such disclosure, and by relying on voluntary action by members of labor organizations, it is hoped that a deterrent to abuses will be established....

The committee believes that union members armed with adequate information and having the benefit of secret elections, as provided for in title IV of this bill, will be greatly strengthened in their efforts to rid themselves of untrustworthy or corrupt officers. In addition, the exposure to public scrutiny of all vital information concerning their operation of trade unions will help deter repetition of the financial abuses disclosed by the McClellan committee. Where union financial and other practices do not meet reasonable standards, although not willfully dishonest, this bill would have a remedial effect. Under provisions of the committee bill, both labor organizations and their officers are under obligation to make full and accurate reports, subject to criminal penalties.

NOTE

The courts have taken a generous view of the Secretary of Labor's investigatory powers under § 601 of the LMRDA. Thus, it has consistently been recognized that the Secretary need not find "probable cause" to believe a violation has occurred before issuing a subpoena, and the scope of the subpoena issued may be quite broad. *See, e.g., Goldberg v. Truck Drivers Local 299,* 293 F.2d 807 (6th Cir.), *cert. denied,* 368 U.S. 938 (1961); *Teamsters v. Wirtz,* 346 F.2d 827, 831 (D.C. Cir. 1965); *Wirtz v. Teamsters Local 191,* 321 F.2d 445 (2d Cir. 1963). Moreover, regardless of the allowable scope of an action by the Secretary under § 402 to invalidate a union election, his investigation of the election under § 601 is not restricted to the items complained about by a member. *Operating Eng'rs Local 57 v. Wirtz,* 346 F.2d 552 (1st Cir. 1965); *Wirtz v. Teamsters Local 191, supra.*

A subpoena has even been sustained under § 601 for the purpose of investigating an alleged misuse of union funds in violation of § 501(a), although the latter provision is enforceable by private parties or the Attorney General and not by the Secretary. *Teamsters v. Wirtz, supra.* Similarly, in *Operating Eng'rs Local 57 v. Wirtz, supra,* the Secretary's power to investigate was held not to be limited to the matters required to be reported by the Act. The Secretary's right of inspection, however, may be subject to other statutory policies against total disclosure in certain circumstances. *See, e.g., Teamsters v. Goldberg,* 303 F.2d 402 (D.C. Cir.), *cert. denied,* 370 U.S. 938 (1962) (union membership lists).

Are these decisions likely to be affected by the Supreme Court's invalidation of warrantless OSHA inspections in *Marshall v. Barlow's, Inc., supra?* See *Donovan v. Lone Steer, Inc.,* 464 U.S. 408 (1984). Many union officials have asserted that the Secretary of Labor's roving commission to investigate under the LMRDA is the most objectionable single feature of the Act. Why might this be?

D. TRUSTEESHIPS; PARENT-LOCAL RELATIONS

SECRETARY OF LABOR, UNION TRUSTEESHIPS: REPORT TO THE CONGRESS UPON THE OPERATION OF TITLE III OF THE LABOR-MANAGEMENT REPORTING AND DISCLOSURE ACT 5-11 (1962)*

Background

A trusteeship is any method of supervision or control whereby a labor organization suspends the autonomy otherwise available to a subordinate body under its constitution or bylaws. The practice of imposing trusteeships by unions dates back to the 19th century, but was extremely rare until the development of strong national unions.

During hearings of the McClellan Committee it was disclosed that the power to impose trusteeship was used sometimes for the purpose of "milking" local treasuries or undemocratically controlling votes to perpetuate power....

Provisions covering trusteeships were enacted as title III of the Labor-Management Reporting and Disclosure Act of 1959.... This title prescribes conditions under which trusteeships may be established and continued, requires reporting and public disclosure of their stewardship by any labor organization, makes it a crime either to count the votes of delegates of the trusteed union unless democratically elected, or to transfer funds to the supervisory body, and provides redress for the union member or subordinate body either directly in court or through the Secretary of Labor.

The discussions and committee deliberations in Congress recognized that union trusteeships, although sometimes used to control subordinated organizations illegally, most often are used to provide assistance to subordinates in difficulties, to assist in maintenance and stability, and to promote rather than stifle union democracy....

Conclusions

Operation of the trusteeship provisions of the Labor-Management Reporting and Disclosure Act during the first 2½ years supports the following conclusions:

1. Establishment of trusteeships has never been a widespread practice, except in a few unions. When the Act became effective, trusteeships existed in less than 1 percent of the covered unions. Now, less than half that percentage are involved.

2. The Act has been effective in correcting the malpractices disclosed by the McClellan Committee. Further, a large number of trusteeships, while not corrupt, were unnecessarily continued and have now been terminated.

---

*Submitted in September 1962 in accordance with § 305 of the LMRDA; the full report contains much valuable information.—*Eds.*

3. Since enactment of the law, many national union constitutions have been amended to provide greater safeguards against unnecessary suspension of autonomy.

4. Indications are that the Act has not substantially hindered unions from establishing essential trusteeships.

5. The reporting and disclosure of the facts surrounding trusteeships, and the active cooperation of the vast majority of unions and union officers, have resulted in substantial compliance with the law with a minimum need for enforcement.

NOTES

1. At common law, the right of a local union to "secede" from an international, the power of the international to impose a trusteeship to prevent such disaffiliation, and the rights of the respective parties in the assets of the secessionist local, were largely determined as matters of contract law, in accordance with the terms of the particular union constitution insofar as that did not offend public policy. *See, e.g., Harker v. McKissock,* 7 N.J. 323, 81 A.2d 480 (1951), and cases cited; Comment, *Effects of a Union Split Upon Property Rights,* 1952 Wis. L. Rev. 139.

2. During the late 1940s and the 1950s a number of international unions were expelled from the AFL, the CIO, or the AFL-CIO for Communism or corruption. In several decisions the courts relied on the international's loss of affiliation with the parent federation as a breach of a "material implied condition" or as a "frustration" of the international-local contractual relationship, thus enabling the local to disaffiliate from the international and retain its property. *See, e.g., American Bakery Workers Local 240 v. Bakery Workers Local 240,* 58 L.R.R.M. 2744, (Colo. Dist. Ct. 1965); *UE Local 1140 v. UE,* 232 Minn. 217, 45 N.W.2d 408 (1950); *Crocker v. Weil,* 227 Or. 260, 361 P.2d 1014 (1961). *See also* Summers, *Union Schism in Perspective: Flexible Doctrines, Double Standards, and Projected Answers,* 45 Va. L. Rev. 261 (1959).

3. Common-law rights and remedies regarding parent-local relations, including "trusteeships," remain significant despite the enactment of the LMRDA. Under § 306 of the Act, federal jurisdiction becomes exclusive only when the Secretary of Labor files a complaint challenging a trusteeship.

Recently, interest in amending the LMRDA has surfaced because of the amenability of the trusteeship provision to abuse by international and national unions which seek to take control of a local union's finances either to loot the local's treasury or to control its votes in national elections. *See House Panel Asks Drafter of LMRDA to Propose Changes To 1959 Statute,* Daily Lab. Rep. (BNA) No. 86, May 5, 1998, at A-11; *Authorities on Union Democracy Enlisted to Write Fawell's LMRDA Bill,* Daily Lab. Rep. (BNA) No. 229, Nov. 30, 1998, at C-1.

UNITED BROTHERHOOD OF CARPENTERS v. BROWN

United States Court of Appeals, Tenth Circuit
343 F.2d 872 (1965)

[The United Brotherhood imposed a trusteeship on Local 201 for failing to comply with the General President's order to affiliate with a union district council and for failing to raise membership dues from $5.80 to $8.00 per month as required by the bylaws of the district council. Individual members of Local 201 sued to have the trusteeship removed.]

HILL, CIRCUIT JUDGE.... Appellants contend that the judgment must be reversed and the action dismissed because plaintiffs have not exhausted the administrative remedy available to them under the provisions of § 304(a) of the [LMRDA]. The argument is that plaintiffs were required to first file a complaint with the Secretary of Labor in accordance with § 304(a) and exhaust that remedy before proceeding in court with this lawsuit. There is authority to support that argument. *E.g., Cox v. Hutcheson,* 204 F. Supp. 442 (S.D. Ind. 1962); ... *Rizzo v. Ammond,* 182 F. Supp. 456 (D.N.J. 1960). But, there is also authority supporting the view that a local union member need not exhaust the administrative remedy provided in § 304(a) before bringing suit in the district court under that section. *Parks v. International Brotherhood of Electrical Workers,* 314 F.2d 886, 923, 924 (4th Cir. 1963), *cert. denied,* 372 U.S. 976 (1963); ... *Executive Board, IBEW, Local 28 v. IBEW,* 184 F. Supp. 649 (D. Md. 1960). We believe the latter view is the better rule for the reasons set forth in Judge Watkins' excellent analysis of § 304(a) in the *Executive Board* case, *supra,* 184 F. Supp. at 655-659. We can add nothing to that discussion and accordingly hold that appellants were not required to exhaust the administrative remedy provided in § 304(a) before instituting this action....

Appellants also contend that the judgment must be reversed and the action dismissed for the reason that the plaintiffs have failed to exhaust the internal remedies afforded by United Brotherhood's Constitution and Laws as required by § 101(a)(4) of the Act.... We do not agree. Section 101(a)(4) is applicable only where individual violations of the so-called Bill of Rights provisions are alleged and does not apply where, as here, the validity of a trusteeship is being challenged. As the Supreme Court said in *Calhoon v. Harvey, supra,* 379 U.S. at 138: "Jurisdiction of the district court under § 102 of Title I depends entirely upon whether this complaint showed a violation of rights guaranteed by § 101(a)(1)...." In any event, the requirement that internal remedies be exhausted is subject to certain exceptions that are applicable here....

The basic issue in this case is, of course, the validity of the trusteeship imposed upon Local 201 by United Brotherhood. That issue must be determined by reference to § 302 of the Act, ... which provides that a trusteeship may be established and administered by a labor organization over its subordinate body "... only in accordance with the constitution and bylaws of the organization which has assumed trusteeship...." The statute is mandatory in its terms and has nullified or removed whatever inherent power an international union had prior to its enactment to impose such a trusteeship. Unless the constitution and bylaws of the parent organization make provision therefor, such organization has no power to establish a trusteeship over a subordinate body. *Flight Engineers Int'l Ass'n v. Continental Air Lines, Inc.,* 297 F.2d 397 (9th Cir. 1961), *cert. denied,* 369 U.S. 871 (1962). An examination of the constitution and bylaws of United Brotherhood discloses that there is no specific provision authorizing it to impose a trusteeship on any of its subordinate local unions.

It is suggested, however, that United Brotherhood's power to impose the trusteeship in question may be derived from the general authority granted to it in §§ 6B and 6D of its Constitution and Laws, as implemented by the provision in § 10K, which empowers the General Executive Board "... to take such action as it is necessary and proper for the welfare ..." of the national union. Appellant's argument is that while its constitution and laws do not specifically grant it the authority to impose trusteeships, such authority may be implied from §§ 6B, 6D and 10K and that implied authority is sufficient. We do not agree. The legislative history of § 302 of the Act clearly discloses an intent on the part of Congress "... that there should be a 'limitation on the right of internationals to place local unions in trusteeship'" and one of those limitations was that "... the trusteeship must conform to the constitution and bylaws of the labor organization." 2 U.S. Code Cong. & Adm. News, 86th Cong., 1st Sess., 1959, pp. 2333-2334. Obviously, a trusteeship cannot conform to the constitution and bylaws of a labor organization where, as here, the constitution and bylaws make no provision for trusteeships. We think the statute not only contemplates, but requires, more than some vague general reference to the effect that the parent organization shall have power to take such action as is necessary and proper for its welfare. It requires at the very least that the organization's constitution and bylaws set forth the circumstances under which a trusteeship may be established over its local unions and the manner or procedure in which it is to be imposed. It goes without saying, of course, that the constitution and bylaws in that respect must not conflict with applicable provisions of the Act.

A second limitation upon the imposition of trusteeships is that under § 302 it must be for one of the following purposes: (1) To correct corruption or financial malpractice; (2) to assure the performance of collective bargaining agreements or other duties of a bargaining representative; or (3) to restore democratic procedures, or otherwise carry out the legitimate objects of the labor organization. Congress recognized that the use of trusteeships by an international union is a particularly effective device for the maintenance of order within the organization and that "... they have been widely used to prevent corruption, mismanagement of union funds, violation of collective bargaining agreements, infiltration of Communists; in short, to preserve the integrity and stability of the organization itself...." But, Congress also recognized that "... in some instances trusteeships have been used as a means of consolidating the power of corrupt union officers, plundering and dissipating the resources of local unions, and preventing the growth of competing political elements within the organization." 2 U.S. Code Cong. & Adm. News, 86th Cong., 1st Sess., 1959, p. 2333. To preserve the legitimate use of trusteeships, Congress in enacting § 302 enumerated the purposes for which a trusteeship could be imposed in language of a broad and general nature. However, in order to prevent their misuse, Congress obviously intended those purposes to have limitations as well and therefore in determining whether a particular case meets the test, the statute must be construed in the light of the various other provisions of the Act.

The purpose of the Act as a whole is not only to stop and prevent outrageous conduct by thugs and gangsters but also to stop lesser forms of objectionable conduct by those in positions of trust and to protect democratic processes within union organizations.... To accomplish that purpose, a "Bill of Rights of Members of Labor Organizations" was incorporated into the Act. Thus, the rights of individual members of a labor union are protected by federal statute with a view to allowing those members to conduct local matters with a minimum of outside interference. In short, local affairs are to be governed by local members under democratic processes.

With this background in mind we turn to a consideration of the purposes for which the instant trusteeship was imposed. The trial court found, and the evidence confirms, that United Brotherhood established the trusteeship over Local 201 because it would not affiliate with the District Council and would not raise its dues. The court also found, and the evidence shows, that it was not imposed because of "dissension" within the local union. The result is that the trusteeship was established for the purposes of affiliating Local 201 with the District Council and raising the dues of its membership. In determining whether these are proper purposes under § 302, we must remember that a majority of the local membership consistently voted against having anything to do with the District Council and on at least two occasions, by secret ballot, voted against the proposal to raise the monthly dues. We must also remember that the provisions of [§ 101] were designed to afford them protection in that respect. Under these circumstances, we have no hesitancy in holding that the purposes for which this trusteeship was imposed do not fall within any of the categories set forth in § 302. Beyond question, they do not come under the category of correcting corruption or financial malpractice and have nothing whatever to do with collective bargaining. It is also clear to us that the specified purposes are not within the category of restoring democratic processes or otherwise carrying out the legitimate objects of United Brotherhood. To the contrary, the imposition of the trusteeship in question could have no other effect than to stifle democratic processes by, in effect, voiding the results of the properly conducted elections on the issues involved. If we were to hold that the asserted purposes were proper, this court would be placed in the position of allowing a national union to establish a trusteeship over a local union because the members of the local union insisted upon exercising a right granted them by statute. This would in effect nullify and frustrate not only the plain purpose but the express terms of the Act.

It is true that there is a presumption as to the validity of a trusteeship for a period of eighteen months from the date of its establishment. [§ 304(c).] But, it is quite clear from the statute itself and from the legislative history that Congress intended for the presumption of validity to be available only where the trusteeship has been established "... in conformity with the procedural requirements of its [the labor organization's] constitution and bylaws and authorized or ratified after a fair hearing either before the executive board or before such other body as may be provided in accordance with its constitution or bylaws...." [§ 304(c)]; 2 U.S. Code Cong. & Adm. News, 86th Cong., 1st Sess., 1959, p. 2334. Since the trusteeship in this case was not established in conformity with the constitution and bylaws, the presumption is not available to appellants....

NOTES

1. *Compare Carpenters Local 1302 v. Carpenters,* 477 F.2d 612 (2d Cir. 1973), where the Second Circuit, per Judge Hays, sustained an international's imposition of a trusteeship to prevent a local from disaffiliating from a local Metal Trades Council and seeking separate bargaining rights. The international had concluded that the local's action would have a detrimental effect on well-established collective bargaining. Judge Oakes dissented. *See also Local Union 144, SEIU v. Stern,* 158 L.R.R.M. 2495 (S.D.N.Y. 1998) (trusteeship properly imposed for financial mismanagement and insolvency).

2. The elimination of racial segregation has been held a legitimate basis for imposing a trusteeship aimed at effecting a merger of a white local and a neighboring black local. *Musicians Local 10 v. Musicians,* 57 L.R.R.M. 2227 (N.D. Ill. 1964); *cf. Daye v. Tobacco Workers Union,* 234 F. Supp. 815 (D.D.C. 1964).

3. What is the effect of a valid trusteeship? In *Blassie v. Poole,* 58 L.R.R.M. 2359 (E.D. Mo. 1965), it was held that an international, having established a legitimate trusteeship, could suspend the local union's constitution and bylaws, remove local officers and employees, and proceed to manage the organization's affairs without calling general membership meetings. Such actions would not violate §§ 101(a)(1), 101(a)(2), 202(a), or 501(a) of the LMRDA.

4. Would an international's revocation of a local's charter and its reissuance to a new organization constitute a "trusteeship" within the meaning of Title III? *See Parks v. IBEW,* 314 F.2d 886 (4th Cir.), *cert. denied,* 372 U.S. 976 (1963). *Cf. Carpenters Local 267 v. Carpenters,* 992 F.2d 1418 (6th Cir. 1993). What about the forced merger of several separate locals into one? *Compare San Filippo v. Carpenters,* 525 F.2d 508 (2d Cir. 1975) *with Carpenters Local 48 v. Carpenters,* 920 F.2d 1047 (1st Cir. 1990). What if all the local's members have resigned before the international attempts to install the "trusteeship"? *See Tile, Marble &*

Terrazzo Finishers v. TMT Finishers Local 32, 896 F.2d 1404 (3d Cir. 1990). *Stevens v. Carpenters Dist. Council,* 20 F.3d 720 (7th Cir. 1994), concerned a suit by union members claiming that the international union had imposed a trusteeship on their local union without complying with provisions in the international union constitution. The plaintiffs sought restoration of the pre-trusteeship bylaws and election procedures. The court found that their suit was moot, however, since the trusteeship had ceased to exist when permanent delegates to the district council were elected and the temporary trusteeship-imposed bylaws were replaced by measures enacted by the newly elected district council.

5. Could a parent union secure an injunction in federal court to *enforce* a trusteeship over a local, in order to prevent an unlawful strike? What would be the basis of jurisdiction? What would be the effect of the Norris-La Guardia Act? *See Letter Carriers v. Sombrotto,* 449 F.2d 915 (2d Cir. 1971). A federal district court does not have jurisdiction under Title III of the LMRDA to enjoin an international union from conducting a hearing, required by its constitution, to determine whether it should impose a trusteeship on a subordinate body. *Laborers v. Mail Handlers Div.,* 880 F.2d 1388 (D.C. Cir. 1989).

6. *See generally* Anderson, *Landrum-Griffin and the Trusteeship Imbroglio,* 71 Yale L.J. 1460 (1962); Beaird, *Union Trusteeship Provisions of the Labor-Management Reporting and Disclosure Act of 1959,* 2 Ga. L. Rev. 469 (1968); Bellace, *Union Trusteeships: Difficulties in Applying Sections 302 and 304(c) of the Landrum-Griffin Act,* 25 Am. U.L. Rev. 337 (1976); Summers, *Union Trusteeships and Union Democracy,* 24 U. Mich. J. L. Ref. 689 (1991); Note, *A Fair Hearing Requirement for Union Trusteeships Under the LMRDA,* 40 U. Chi. L. Rev. 873 (1973).

SECTION IV. Unions and the Public

A. THE REGULATION OF RACKETEERING AND COMMUNIST ACTIVITY

1. BRIBERY, EXTORTION, AND CORRUPTION

ARROYO v. UNITED STATES

Supreme Court of the United States
359 U.S. 419, 79 S. Ct. 864, 3 L. Ed. 2d 915 (1959)

MR. JUSTICE STEWART delivered the opinion of the Court.

The petitioner, a representative of employees in an industry affecting commerce, was convicted in the United States District Court for Puerto Rico of violating § 302(b) of the [LMRA] by receiving $15,000 from two of their employers....

The facts are substantially undisputed. In 1953 the petitioner was president of a union which represented the employees of two affiliated corporations. In that capacity he negotiated a collective bargaining agreement with the employers. This agreement provided for the establishment of a welfare fund, which, it is unquestioned, met the requisite criteria of § 302(c)(5) of the Act. It was agreed that the petitioner would be the union representative on the joint committee which was to administer the fund. After the agreement was signed, the petitioner told the employers' representative that there was to be a union meeting that evening, and that he wanted to exhibit the welfare fund checks to the union members. Accordingly, the petitioner was given two checks for $7,500. Attached vouchers identified the checks as the employers' contributions to the welfare fund.

Instead of subsequently depositing the checks in the existing welfare fund bank account, however, the petitioner used them to open an account in the name of the fund in another bank. A few days thereafter, he gave the bank a purported resolution from the union's board of directors authorizing withdrawals from this account upon his signature alone. As soon as the employers learned what had happened, they attempted to secure performance of the agreement for joint administration of the fund. Over a period of several months, however, the petitioner used the money for his own personal purposes and, after transferring the funds to another account, for nonwelfare union purposes as well.

The Government does not maintain that embezzlement by an employee representative from an employer-financed welfare fund would violate the federal statute under which the petitioner was convicted. It contends, however, that in this case the jury could properly find that the petitioner when he accepted the two checks intended to use the funds for his personal purposes, and that he was therefore guilty not of embezzlement, but of conduct amounting to larceny by trick. We agree that the evidence could properly support an inference that the petitioner's purpose from the outset was to appropriate the two checks for his own use. We cannot agree, however, that this conduct violated § 302(b) of the Act.

Section 302(b) is a reciprocal of § 302(a), applicable to employers.... The good faith of the employers in delivering the two checks to the petitioner—their intent that the money go to the welfare fund created by the collective bargaining agreement—was not questioned throughout the trial and is not questioned here. The sole purpose of the delivery of the checks, therefore, was to make a lawful payment. What the petitioner received were checks "paid to a trust fund." The transaction, therefore, was within the precise language of § 302(c), and thus was not a violation of § 302(b).

This is not to say that the statute requires mutuality of guilt for the conviction of either the employer or the representative of employees. An employer might be guilty under subsection (a) if he paid money to a representative of employees even though the latter had no intention of accepting.... A representative might be guilty if he coerced payments from an innocent and unwilling employer.... Both would be guilty if the payment were ostensibly made for one of the lawful purposes specified in § 302(c) if both knew that such a purpose was merely a sham.

The present case, however, is not an analogue to any of those situations. The checks were drawn by the employers and delivered to the petitioner as payment to a union welfare fund. Their receipt by him, therefore, was not a violation of the federal statute, whether his intent to misappropriate existed at the time of receipt or was formed later....

Throughout the debates in the Seventy-ninth and Eightieth Congresses there was not the slightest indication that § 302 was intended to duplicate state criminal laws. Those members of Congress who supported the amendment were concerned with corruption of collective bargaining through bribery of employee representatives by employers, with extortion by employee representatives, and with the possible abuse by union officers of the power which they might achieve if welfare funds were left to their sole control. Congressional attention was focused particularly upon the latter problem because of the demands which had then recently been made by a large international union for the establishment of a welfare fund to be financed by employers' contributions and administered exclusively by union officials. *See United States v. Ryan*, 350 U.S. 299.

Congress believed that if welfare funds were established which did not define with specificity the benefits payable thereunder, a substantial danger existed that such funds might be employed to perpetuate control of union officers, for political purposes, or even for personal gain. *See* 92 Cong. Rec. 4892-4894, 4899, 5181, 5345-5346; S. Rep. No. 105, 80th Cong., 1st Sess., at 52; 93 Cong. Rec. 4678, 4746-4747. To remove these dangers, specific standards were established to assure that welfare funds would be established only for purposes which Congress considered proper and expended only for the purposes for which they were established. *See* Cox, *Some Aspects of the Labor Management Relations Act, 1947,* 61 Harv. L. Rev. 274, 290. Continuing compliance with these standards in the administration of welfare funds was made explicitly enforceable in federal district courts by civil proceedings under § 302(e). The legislative history is devoid of any suggestion that defalcating trustees were to be held accountable under federal law, except by way of the injunctive remedy provided in that subsection.

Without doubt the petitioner's conduct was reprehensible and immoral. It can be assumed also that he offended local criminal law. But, for the reasons stated, we hold that he did not criminally violate § 302(b) of the Labor Management Relations Act of 1947.

Reversed.

MR. JUSTICE CLARK, with whom MR. JUSTICE FRANKFURTER, MR. JUSTICE DOUGLAS, and MR. JUSTICE WHITTAKER join, dissenting....

I am sure that the Court agrees that the petitioner's conduct came within the "broad prohibition" of § 302(b). The only question, therefore, is whether he may properly be exculpated by the provisions of subsection (c)(5).... Two conclusions, implicitly drawn by the jury, emerge as indisputable when the evidence is compared with this subsection. In the first place, the statutory exception applies only when the money or other thing of value is "paid to a trust fund," and it is clear that insofar as a lawful fund was in existence the checks were not "paid" to it. They were made out payable to the union. Neither the checks nor the money from them ever came near the bona fide trust fund account at the Banco de Ponce. From the moment they were received by petitioner, he had complete control over them.

Secondly, even a casual reading of the subsection shows, as I am sure the Court itself would agree, that the spurious fund established by the petitioner in the National City Bank failed to comply with the statute in almost every respect. Since the checks were deposited in a union account and subject to the control of petitioner, the payments were not held in trust, as required by the subsection. Moreover, the fund which he created by depositing the checks was not subject to the administration of both the employees and the employers, but was subject to the sole control of the petitioner. As the judge instructed the jury, "a plan does not exist, lawfully exist, until it meets all those requirements" of the subsection. Since the sole purpose of the exception as set out in the Act was to permit the creation of a bona fide trust fund, it is obvious that the purposes of the Act were not complied with here because petitioner established no trust fund whatsoever. On the contrary, the checks were made payable to, and deposited in the name of, the union of which the petitioner was the President. His was the only authorized signature permitting withdrawals from the fund. In fact, the receipt of the checks by the petitioner as trust fund moneys was merely a sham. It does not matter what the intent of the employers was in delivering the checks since, as the Court itself says, the statute does not require mutuality of guilt. The petitioner, by receiving the checks from the employers and through artifice and deceit, has deprived the employees of their benefits and stands guilty under § 302(b) of the Act....

NOTES

1. In *Walsh v. Schlecht,* 429 U.S. 401 (1977), the Supreme Court held that a provision in a construction industry collective agreement between a general contractor and the carpenters' union did not violate § 302(a)(1) of the Taft-Hartley Act but was permitted by § 302(c)(5) and (6). The agreement provided that when the general contractor used signatory carpenter subcontractors, they would be required to pay contributions at an aggregate rate of 96 cents per hour worked by carpenter employees to certain joint-trusteed pension and welfare funds. When he used a non-signatory carpenter subcontractor, he either had to require the sub to be bound by the agreement or else he had to maintain daily records of the subcontractor employees' hours and make the payments into the trust funds himself. The Court's interpretation was that the provision merely required the general contractor to make payments into the trust funds *measured* by the hours of carpentry work performed. If the provision were interpreted to require payments "on behalf of" or "for the benefit of" the employees of non-signatory carpenter employers, it would have run afoul of § 302(a)(1) and it would not have been protected by § 302(a)(5), since the employees of non-signatory employers are ineligible for benefits under such trust funds.

Nor is LMRA § 302 violated when union committee members and grievance chairs take leaves without losing wages or benefits to devote their full time to union business. Section 302(c)(1) permits payments "as compensation for, *or by reason of*, ... service as an employee" (emphasis supplied). *Caterpillar, Inc. v. United Auto Workers*, 107 F.3d 1052 (3d Cir. 1997) (en banc), *cert. pet. dismissed as moot*, 118 S. Ct. 1350 (1998). *See also BASF Wyandotte Corp. v. Chemical Workers Local 227*, 791 F.2d 1046 (2d Cir. 1986) (sustaining the legality of a "no-docking" provision which required an employer to pay the union president and secretary for an aggregate of four hours each day spent conducting union business during normal working hours on company premises); *National Fuel Gas Distribution Corp.*, 308 N.L.R.B. 841 (1992) (continued fringe benefits allowed during union officers' unpaid leaves).

2. Does § 302(c)'s authorization for employer payments to joint union-employer trust funds maintained for certain specified purposes exclude by necessary implication payments to all other types of funds (for example, "industry promotion funds")? *Compare Plasterers Local 2 v. Paramount Plastering, Inc.*, 310 F.2d 179 (9th Cir. 1962), *cert. denied*, 372 U.S. 944 (1963) *with South La. Chapter, Nat'l Elec. Contractors Ass'n v. IBEW Local 130*, 177 F. Supp. 432 (E.D. La. 1959). What about payments to a jointly administered trust fund providing welfare benefits for *retired* employees? Or including union officers and employees along with bargaining unit employees as beneficiaries? *See Blassie v. Kroger Co.*, 345 F.2d 58 (8th Cir. 1965); *Trailways Lines v. Transit Union Joint Council*, 785 F.2d 101 (3d Cir.), *cert. denied*, 479 U.S. 932 (1986). *See also* Goetz, *Employee Benefit Trusts Under Section 302 of the Labor Management Relations Act*, 59 Nw. U.L. Rev. 719 (1965).

Problems of perceived overbreadth in § 302 have been dealt with by amendments adding new individual exceptions to subsection (c), for example, to authorize prepaid legal services plans. Does this seem an appropriate approach or does it suggest a fundamental defect in the structure of § 302? *See generally* Goetz, *Developing Federal Labor Law of Welfare and Pension Funds*, 55 Cornell L. Rev. 911 (1970); Note, *Taft-Hartley Regulation of Employer Payments to Union Representatives: Bribery Extortion and Welfare Funds Under Section 302*, 67 Yale L.J. 732 (1958).

In *NLRB v. Amax Coal Co.*, 453 U.S. 322 (1981), the Supreme Court held that employer-selected trustees of a § 302(c)(5) trust fund are not collective bargaining representatives but owe complete loyalty to the beneficiaries of the trust. Therefore, the UMW did not violate § 8(b)(1)(B) in bargaining to impasse and striking in order to get Amax to contribute to an established multi-employer trust fund for the employees of its new surface mine.

Section 302 of the LMRA provides no private cause of action for damages, but only criminal sanctions and those civil remedies necessary to "restrain violations." The latter may include damages incidental to equitable relief. *Bakerstown Container Corp. v. Teamsters,* 884 F.2d 105 (3d Cir. 1989).

3. The Hobbs Anti-Racketeering Act, 18 U.S.C. § 1951 subjects anyone who "obstructs ... commerce ... by robbery or extortion" to a $10,000 fine and 20 years imprisonment. For definitional issues, *see United States v. Enmons,* 410 U.S. 396 (1973) (violence during lawful strike to secure legitimate bargaining demands); *United States v. Green,* 350 U.S. 415 (1956) (violence to obtain pay for unwanted and superfluous services).

What is the relationship between the Hobbs Act and the ban on "featherbedding" in § 8(b)(6) of the NLRA? *See* Note, *Labor Violence and the Hobbs Act: A Judicial Dilemma,* 67 Yale L.J. 325 (1957); Note, *Featherbedding and the Federal Anti-Racketeering Act,* 26 U. Chi. L. Rev. 150 (1958).

4. Section 602 of the LMRDA outlaws "extortionate picketing." When the provision was under consideration in 1959, Senator Kennedy explained it as follows:

> There has always been some question as to whether the Hobbs Act applied to cases in which violence did not take place....
>
> This provision would not weaken or change the Hobbs Act. It would merely provide that when there is any question as to whether the Hobbs Act applies in cases in which violence does not occur—as in the case of shakedown picketing—adequate sanctions are provided. [105 Cong. Rec. 6530 (1959)].

5. When a court finds mobster domination of a labor organization in violation of the Racketeer Influenced and Corrupt Organizations Act, 18 U.S.C. § 1961, it may impose a judicial trusteeship and direct the removal of the culpable union officials. *See United States v. Teamsters Local 560,* 780 F.2d 267 (3d Cir. 1985), *cert. denied,* 476 U.S. 1140 (1986); *id.,* 974 F.2d 315 (3d Cir. 1992). In June 1988 the Justice Department filed suit under RICO, seeking a trusteeship over the 1.7 million-member International Brotherhood of Teamsters. A settlement reached in March 1989 left the Teamsters' top officers in place but provided for the future election of national officials by a secret vote of the entire membership, rather than by delegates at a convention, under the supervision of court-appointed officers. *United States v. Teamsters,* 931 F.2d 177 (2d Cir. 1991); *id.,* 998 F.2d 120 (2d Cir. 1993). The saga continues. *See U.S. v. Teamsters,* 158 L.R.R.M. 2677 (S.D.N.Y. 1998).

The D.C. Circuit has held RICO inapplicable to a recognition strike that involved acts of vandalism and a business agent's threat to "burn the company buses," when there was no evidence to indicate that the labor organization or its agents "participated" directly or indirectly in the affairs of the "enterprise" being conducted by the struck bus company. *Yellow Bus Lines v. Teamsters Local 639,* 913 F.2d 948 (D.C. Cir. 1990) (en banc), *cert. denied,* 501 U.S. 1222 (1991).

6. *See generally* Blakey & Goldstock, *"On the·Waterfront": RICO and Labor Racketeering,* 17 Am. Crim. L. Rev. 341 (1980); Cohen & Yellig, *Efforts to Apply the Federal Crime of Extortion to Labor-Related Violence,* 72 J. Crim. L. 499 (1981); Goldberg, *Cleaning Labor's House: Institutional Reform Litigation in the Labor Movement,* 1989 Duke L.J. 903; Kannar, *Making the Teamsters Safe for Democracy,* 102 Yale L.J. 1645 (1993); Mastro, Bennett & Donlevy, *Private Plaintiffs' Use of Equitable Remedies Under the RICO Statute: A Means to Reform Corrupted Labor Unions,* 24 U. Mich. J.L. Ref. 571 (1991); Shade, *The Problem of Union Corruption and the Labor-Management Reporting and Disclosure Act of 1959,* 38 Texas L. Rev. 468 (1960). RICO problems are noted in 92 Colum. L. Rev. 103 (1992); 58 Geo. Wash. L. Rev. 125 (1989); 137 U. Pa. L. Rev. 929 (1989). *See also* P. Taft, Corruption and Racketeering in the Labor Movement (1958).

2. RESTRICTIONS ON HOLDING OFFICE

Section 9(h) of the National Labor Relations Act, as added by the Taft-Hartley Act in 1947, required union officers to file non-Communist affidavits before their organizations could have access to the processes of the National Labor Relations Board. The constitutionality of this provision was upheld by the Supreme Court in *American Commun. Ass'n v. Douds,* 339 U.S. 382 (1950). Section 9(h) was repealed in 1959 by the Labor-Management Reporting and Disclosure Act, which replaced the conditional limitation with an outright prohibition. Under § 504(a) of the LMRDA, no person may be a union officer or employee for a maximum period of thirteen years from the time he was convicted of, or held membership in the Communist party, or from the time he was convicted of, or was imprisoned for, any of several specified crimes. Violation of § 504 is declared a criminal offense.

In *United States v. Brown,* 380 U.S. 278 (1965), the Supreme Court held, with four justices dissenting, that § 504 was unconstitutional as a bill of attainder insofar as it applied to Communist Party members. *See generally* D. Saposs, Communism in American Unions (1959). *Douds* was distinguished in part on the ground it imposed an administrative restraint on the union rather than a criminal penalty on the individual officer. Although the Court made no reference to § 504's similar disqualification of persons convicted of various enumerated offenses, the emphasis on the evils of proscribing anyone simply on the basis of membership in a "political group" suggests that *Brown* would not be dispositive of the constitutionality of the section's anti-convict ban. Furthermore, § 504 would apparently not be vulnerable to attack as *ex post facto* legislation in its application to persons committing crimes prior to the passage of the LMRDA. In *DeVeau v. Braisted,* 363 U.S. 144 (1960), the Supreme Court upheld a somewhat similar New York law, reasoning that it was designed primarily to safeguard unions against future abuses and not to punish the disqualified officials for past offenses.

In construing § 504's list of disqualifying offenses, the courts have taken a rather broad view toward including both federal and state crimes analogous to those specified. *E.g., Berman v. Teamsters, Local 107,* 237 F. Supp. 767 (E.D. Pa. 1964) (conspiracy to cheat and defraud as "grand larceny"); *Postma v. Teamsters, Local 294,* 229 F. Supp. 655 (N.D.N.Y.), *aff'd per curiam,* 337 F.2d 609 (2d Cir. 1964) (Hobbs Act violation as "extortion"). It has also been held that the term "imprisonment" as used in § 504(a) includes any period of parole, *Serio v. Liss,* 300 F.2d 386 (3d Cir. 1961), and "conviction" includes a guilty plea followed by a sentence of probation, *Harmon v. Teamsters Local 371,* 832 F.2d 976 (7th Cir. 1987).

Section 803 of the Comprehensive Crime Control Act of 1984, 98 Stat. 1976, 2133 (1984), amended § 504(a) of the LMRDA to add more disqualifying offenses for union personnel and to extend the disbarment period from five to thirteen years, and amended § 504(b) to increase the maximum penalty for willful violations from one year to five years. Section 504(c) was modified to require union officials convicted of labor racketeering activities to leave their union posts immediately without being permitted to await the outcome of post-conviction appeals. The 1984 Act also amended § 302(d) of the LMRA to provide that willful violations involving labor bribery or unlawful payoffs in excess of $1000 shall constitute felonies punishable by fines of up to $15,000 and/or imprisonment for up to five years. *See generally* Panter, *The Changes Accomplished by the Labor Racketeering Amendments of the Comprehensive Crime Control Act of 1984,* 36 Lab. L.J. 744 (1985).

United States v. Hughes, 964 F.2d 536 (6th Cir. 1992), *cert. denied,* 113 S. Ct. 1254 (1993), involved a union official who had been convicted in 1987 of having filed false LM-2 reports in 1982 and 1983. The 1984 amendment to § 504(a) barred union officials convicted thereafter of such violations from holding union office. The court held that the official's conviction after the change in the law caused him to be subject to the amended bar, even though his 1982 and 1983 conduct was not then subject to the § 504(a) preclusion.

B. UNION POLITICAL ACTION

Political action has been characteristic of the labor movement since its earliest days in this country. *See generally* F. Dulles, Labor in America 35-52 (1960); M. Karson, American Labor Unions and Politics, 1900-1918 (1958); J. Rayback, A History of American Labor 23-36 (1959); C. Rehmus & D. McLaughlin, Labor and American Politics (1967). There are traces of organized political activity on the part of unions as far back as the late 1820s and early 1830s, when workers' parties emerged briefly in Philadelphia, New York, and New England. Toward the end of the nineteenth century, the American Federation of Labor was formed, and, influenced by its first leader, Samuel Gompers, it adopted the political strategy of "rewarding" labor's friends and "punishing" its enemies, regardless of party affiliation. This became the traditional union approach to partisan politics, although in recent times organized labor has increasingly tended to support Democratic candidates.

Today virtually every labor organization—local or international—includes political action among its stated objectives. Unions have many reasons for being interested in politics in general and legislation in particular. They have a stake in wage and hour laws and in the laws governing the work of minorities, women, and children, not only for altruistic reasons but also because unregulated competition from any exploited class poses a constant threat to union standards. Social security in all its forms is one of the greatest desires of working people. Government policies on taxation, spending, and price control are also of vital significance, affecting as they do the distribution and purchasing power of income. And unions are naturally concerned about promoting labor relations legislation that will ensure the right to organize and bargain collectively. Since the merger of the AFL and the CIO in 1955, intensified political activity by the AFL-CIO Committee on Political Education (COPE) has been one of the more substantial accomplishments of the reunited federation.

Four states currently have laws restricting union political contributions or expenditures: Indiana, New Hampshire, Pennsylvania and Texas. 4 Lab. Rel. Rep. SLL 1:146 (1993). Enactments or proposals in other states have been invalidated by the courts. *See Alabama State Fed'n of Labor v. McAdory,* 246 Ala. 1, 18 So. 2d 810 (1944), *cert. dismissed,* 325 U.S. 450 (1945); *AFL v. Reilly,* 113 Colo. 90, 155 P.2d 145 (1944); *Bowe v. Secretary of Commonwealth,* 320 Mass. 230, 69 N.E.2d 115 (1946); *AFL v. Bain,* 165 Or. 183, 106 P.2d 544 (1940). In addition, § 304 of the Taft-Hartley Act (formerly 18 U.S.C. § 610; reenacted with amendments as 2 U.S.C. § 441(b)) forbade a labor organization to make a contribution or expenditure "in connection with" any federal election. But the Supreme Court held in *United States v. CIO,* 335 U.S. 106 (1948), that, in order to avoid constitutional questions, § 304 would not be interpreted as prohibiting an endorsement of a political candidate carried in a union newspaper circulated chiefly among the union's own membership. That decision set the pattern for restrictive readings of the statute. Section 304 has since been held inapplicable to political advertising through the commercial press and radio by a small union having no newspaper of its own, *United States v. Painters Local 481,* 172 F.2d 854 (2d Cir. 1949), and to payments to union employees for time spent in political work. *United States v. Laborers Local 264,* 101 F. Supp. 869 (W.D. Mo. 1951). In *United States v. UAW,* 352 U.S. 567 (1957), however, the Supreme Court sustained under § 304 an indictment charging a union with having used union dues to sponsor commercial television broadcasts to influence the electorate in a congressional election. In the UAW case the Court refused to deal with the constitutional questions until after a trial. On remand to the district court for trial, the jury returned a verdict of not guilty. 41 L.R.R.M. 52 (1958).

PIPEFITTERS LOCAL 562 v. UNITED STATES

Supreme Court of the United States
407 U.S. 385, 92 S. Ct. 2247, 33 L. Ed. 2d 11 (1972)

MR. JUSTICE BRENNAN delivered the opinion of the Court.

Petitioners—Pipefitters Local Union No. 562 and three individual officers of the Union—were convicted by a jury in the United States District Court for the Eastern District of Missouri of conspiracy under 18 U.S.C. § 371 to violate 18 U.S.C. § 610....

The indictment charged, in essence, that petitioners had conspired from 1963 to May 9, 1968, to establish and maintain a fund that (1) would receive regular and systematic payments from Local 562 members and members of other locals working under the Union's jurisdiction; (2) would have the appearance, but not the reality of being an entity separate from the Union; and (3) would conceal contributions and expenditures by the Union in connection with federal elections in violation of § 610.

The evidence tended to show, in addition to disbursements of about $150,000 by the fund to candidates in federal elections, an identity between the fund and the Union and a collection of well over $1 million in contributions to the fund by a method similar to that employed in the collection of dues or assessments. In particular, it was established that from 1949 through 1962 the Union maintained a political fund to which Union members and others working under the Union's jurisdiction were in fact required to contribute and that the fund was then succeeded in 1963 by the present fund, which was, in form, set up as a separate "voluntary" organization. Yet, a principal Union officer assumed the role of director of the present fund with full and unlimited control over its disbursements. The Union's business manager, petitioner Lawler, became the first director of the fund and was later succeeded by petitioner Callanan, whom one Local 562 member described as "the Union" in explaining his influence within the local. Moreover, no significant change was made in the regular and systematic method of collection of contributions at a prescribed rate based on hours worked, and Union agents continued to collect donations at jobsites on Union time. In addition, changes in the rate of contributions were tied to changes in the rate of members' assessments. In 1966, for example, when assessments were increased from 2½% to 3¾% of gross wages, the contribution rate was decreased from $1 to 5 per day worked with the result that the change did not cause, in the words of the Union's executive board, "one extra penny cost to members of Local Union 562." At the same time, the contribution rate for nonmembers, who were not required to pay the prescribed travel card fee for working under Local 562's jurisdiction, remained the same at $2 per day worked, approximately matching the total assessment and contribution of members. Finally, in addition to political contributions, the fund used its monies for nonpolitical purposes, such as aid to financially distressed members on strike, and for a period of a few months, upon the vote of its members, even suspended collections in favor of contributions to a separate gift fund for petitioner Callanan. Not surprisingly, various witnesses testified that during the indictment period contributions to the fund were often still referred to as—and actually understood by some to be—assessments, or that they paid their contributions "voluntarily" in the same sense that they paid their dues or other financial obligations.

On the other hand, the evidence also indicated that the political contributions by the fund were made from accounts strictly segregated from Union dues and assessments and that donations to the fund were not, in fact, necessary for employment or Union membership. The fund generally required contributors to sign authorization cards, which contained a statement that their donations were "voluntary ... [and] no part of the dues or financial obligations of Local Union No. 562 ...," and the testimony was overwhelming from both those who contributed and those who did not, as well as from the collectors of contributions, that no specific pressure was exerted, and no reprisals were taken, to obtain donations. Significantly, the Union's attorney who had advised on the organization of the fund testified on cross-examination that his advice had been that payments to the fund could not be made a condition of employment or Local 562 membership, but it was immaterial whether contributions appeared compulsory to those solicited.

Under instructions to determine whether on this evidence the fund was in reality a Union fund or the contributors' fund, the jury found each defendant guilty. The jury also found specially that a willful violation of § 610 was not contemplated, and the trial court imposed sentence accordingly. The Union was fined $5,000, while the individual defendants were each sentenced to one year's imprisonment and fined $1,000....

After we heard oral argument, the President on February 7, 1972, signed into law the Federal Election Campaign Act of 1971, which in § 205 amends 18 U.S.C. § 610, *see infra,* at 409-410, effective April 7, 1972. *See* Federal Election Campaign Act of 1971, § 406, 86 Stat. 20. We, accordingly, requested the parties to file supplemental briefs addressing the impact of that amendment on this prosecution. Having considered those briefs, we now hold that § 205 of the Federal Election Campaign Act merely codifies prior law with one possible exception pertinent to this case; that the change in the law, if in fact made, does not in any event require this prosecution to abate; but that the judgment below must, nevertheless, be reversed because of erroneous jury instructions. This disposition makes decision of the constitutional issues premature, and we therefore do not decide them....

I

We begin with an analysis of § 610.

First. The parties are in agreement that § 610, despite its broad language, does not prohibit a labor organization from making, through the medium of a political fund organized by it, contributions or expenditures in connection with federal elections, so long as the monies expended are in some sense volunteered by those asked to contribute....

The antecedents of § 610 have previously been traced in *United States v. Auto Workers* [352 U.S. 567 (1957)] and *United States v. CIO* [335 U.S. 106 (1948)]. We need recall here only that the prohibition in § 313 of the Federal Corrupt Practices Act of 1925, 43 Stat. 1074, on contributions by corporations in connection with federal elections was extended to labor organizations in the War Labor Disputes Act of 1943, 57 Stat. 163, but only for the duration of the war. As the Court noted in *CIO, supra,* at 115, "It was felt that the influence which labor unions exercised over elections through monetary expenditures should be minimized, and that it was unfair to individual union members to permit the union leadership to make contributions from general union funds to a political party which the individual member might oppose." The prohibition on contributions was then permanently enacted into law in § 304 of the Labor Management Relations Act, 1947, ... with the addition, however, of a proscription on "expenditures" and an extension of both prohibitions to payments in connection with federal primaries and political conventions as well as federal elections themselves. Yet, neither prohibition applied to payments by union political funds in connection with federal elections so long as the funds were financed in some sense by the voluntary donations of the union membership. Union political funds had come to prominence in the 1944 and 1946 election campaigns and had been extensively studied by special committees of both the House and the Senate. Against the backdrop of the committee findings and recommendations, the Senate debates upon the reach of § 304 attached controlling significance to the voluntary source of financing of the funds. The unequivocal view of the proponents of § 304 was that the contributions and expenditures of voluntarily financed funds did not violate that provision....

Senator Taft's view that a union cannot violate the law by spending political funds volunteered by its members was consistent with the legislative history of the War Labor Disputes Act and an express interpretation given to that Act by the Attorney General in 1944. His view also reflected concern that a broader application of § 610 might raise constitutional questions of invasion of First Amendment freedoms, and he wished particularly to reassure colleagues who had reservations on that score and whose votes were necessary to override a predictable presidential veto, see 93 Cong. Rec. 7485, of the Labor Management Relations Act. We conclude, accordingly, that his view of the limited reach of § 610, entitled in any event to great weight, is in this instance controlling.... We therefore hold that § 610 does not apply to union contributions and expenditures from political funds financed in some sense by the voluntary donations of employees. *Cf. United States v. Auto Workers,* 352 U.S. at 592; *United States v. CIO,* 335 U.S. at 123....

Second. Where the litigants part company is in defining precisely when political contributions and expenditures by a union political fund fall outside the ambit of § 610. The Government maintains, first, that a valid fund may not be the alter ego of the sponsoring union in the sense of being dominated by it and serving its purposes, regardless of the fund's source of financing.... The requirement that the fund be separate from the sponsoring union eliminates, in the Government's view, "the corroding effect of money employed in elections by aggregated powers," *United States v. Auto Workers,* 352 U.S. at 582, which this Court has found to be one of the dual purposes underlying § 610. *See id., passim; United States v. CIO,* 335 U.S. at 113, 115. The Government urges, secondly, that in accordance with the legislative intent to protect minority interests from overbearing union leadership, which we have found to be the other purpose of § 610, see *ibid.,* the fund may not be financed by monies actually required for employment or union membership *or* by payments that are effectively assessed, that is, solicited in circumstances inherently coercive. Petitioners, on the other hand, contend that, to be valid, a political fund need not be distinct from the sponsoring union and, further, that § 610 permits the union to exercise institutional pressure, much as recognized charities do, in soliciting donations....

We think that neither side fully and accurately portrays the attributes of legitimate political funds. We hold that such a fund must be separate from the sponsoring union only in the sense that there must be a strict segregation of its monies from union dues and assessments. We hold, too, that, although solicitation by union officials is permissible, such solicitation must be conducted under circumstances plainly indicating that donations are for a political purpose and that those solicited may decline to contribute without loss of job, union membership, or any other reprisal within the union's institutional power. Thus, we agree with the second half of the Government's position, but reject the first.

As Senator Taft's remarks ... indicate, ... the test of voluntariness under § 610 focuses on whether the contributions solicited for political use are knowing free-choice donations. The dominant concern in requiring that contributions be voluntary was, after all, to protect the dissenting stockholder or union member. Whether the solicitation scheme is designed to inform the individual solicited of the political nature of the fund and his freedom to refuse support is, therefore, determinative.

Nowhere, however, has Congress required that the political organization be formally or functionally independent of union control or that union officials be barred from soliciting contributions or even precluded from determining how the monies raised will be spent. The Government's argument to the contrary in the first half of its position is based on a misunderstanding of the purposes of § 610.

When Congress prohibited labor organizations from making contributions or expenditures in connection with federal elections, it was, of course, concerned not only to protect minority interests within the union but to eliminate the effect of aggregated wealth on federal elections. But the aggregated wealth it plainly had in mind was the general union treasury—not the funds donated by union members of their own free and knowing choice. Again, Senator Taft adamantly maintained that labor organizations were not prohibited from expending those monies in connection with federal elections. Indeed, Taft clearly espoused the union political organization merely as an alternative to permissible direct political action by the union itself through publications endorsing candidates in federal elections. The only conditions for that kind of direct electioneering were that the costs of publication be financed through individual subscriptions rather than through union dues and that the newspapers be recognized by the subscribers as political organs that they could refuse to purchase. Neither the absence of even a formally separate organization, the solicitation of subscriptions by the union, nor the method for choosing the candidates to be supported was mentioned as being material. Similarly, the only requirements for permissible political organizations were that they be funded through separate contributions and that they be recognized by the donors as political organizations to which they could refuse support....

Third. Arguably, however, there is one change effected by § 205 material to this case, and that is with regard to the *use* of general union monies for the establishment, administration, and solicitation of contributions for political funds. Section 304 of the Labor Management Relations Act may be interpreted to prohibit such use, while the Hansen amendment plainly permits it....

Thus, § 205 may in one respect have impliedly repealed the substantive law relating to this prosecution. But we need not now decide that question, because even if there has been such an implied repeal, it would not affect this prosecution for reasons to which we now turn....

II

[The Court concluded that there need be no abatement of the prosecution because of the federal saving statute, 1 U.S.C. § 109.]

III

The Government urges:

> The essential charge of the indictment and the theory on which the case was tried was that the [Pipefitters] Fund, although formally set up as an entity independent of Local 562, *was in fact a union fund, controlled by the union,* contributions to which were assessed by the union as part of its dues structure, collected from non-members in lieu of dues, and expended, when

deemed necessary, for union purposes and the personal use of the directors of the Fund. Brief for the United States 23 (emphasis added)....

This was indeed, as we shall shortly see, the theory on which the indictment was drawn, the jury was instructed, and petitioners' convictions were affirmed. It is also the construction of § 610 that we have rejected in favor of the Government's narrower construction that the prerequisite for a permissible political fund is simply that it not be financed by actual or effective dues or assessments.... On the other hand, we find that the indictment may be read to allege not only that the Pipefitters fund was "a union fund, controlled by the union," but that "contributions to [it] were assessed by the union as part of its dues structure, [and were] collected from non-members in lieu of dues ...." ... [H]owever, we do not now construe the indictment as making this essential allegation, but leave that question open for determination on remand. We hold now only that the jury instructions failed to require proof of the essential element for conviction, and hence reverse the judgment below....

Second. The jury instructions embody an interpretation of § 610 that is plainly erroneous. The trial court refused requests by petitioners for instructions that the jury should acquit if it found that contributions to the Pipefitters fund were made voluntarily. Adopting a contrary view, the court instructed the jury, over petitioners' objections, that it should return verdicts of guilty if the fund "was in fact a union fund, ... the money therein was union money, and ... the real contributor to the candidates was the union." "In determining whether the Pipefitters Voluntary Fund was a bona fide fund, separate and distinct from the union or a mere artifice or device," the jury was further instructed to "take into consideration all the facts and circumstances in evidence, and in such consideration ... [to] consider" 19 factors, several of which related to the regularity, rate, method of collection, and segregation from Union monies of payments to the fund. Others concerned the kinds of expenditures the fund made and the Union's control over them. Still others involved whether the payments to the fund were made voluntarily. In the latter regard the court charged (emphasis added):

> A great deal of evidence has been introduced on the question of whether the payments into the Pipefitters Voluntary ... Fund by members of Local 562 and others working under its jurisdiction were voluntary or involuntary. This evidence is relevant for your consideration, along with all other facts and circumstances in evidence, in determining whether the fund is a union fund. *However, the mere fact that the payments into the fund may have been made voluntarily by some or even all of the contributors thereto does not, of itself, mean that the money so paid into the fund was not union money....*

The instructions, as the Court of Appeals confirmed, clearly permitted the jury to convict without finding that donations to the Pipefitters fund had been actual or effective dues or assessments. This was plain error.

The judgment of the Court of Appeals as to petitioners Callanan and Lawler is vacated, and the case is remanded to the District Court with directions to dismiss the indictment against them.... The judgment of the Court of Appeals as to petitioners Local 562 and Seaton is reversed, and the case is remanded to the District Court for proceedings as to them consistent with this opinion.

It is so ordered.

MR. JUSTICE BLACKMUN took no part in the consideration or decision of this case.

MR. JUSTICE POWELL, with whom THE CHIEF JUSTICE joins, dissenting.

The decision of the Court today will have a profound effect upon the role of labor unions and corporations in the political life of this country. The holding, reversing a trend since 1907, opens the way for major participation in politics by the largest aggregations of economic power, the great unions and corporations. This occurs at a time, paradoxically, when public and legislative interest has focused on limiting—rather than enlarging—the influence upon the elective process of concentrations of wealth and power.

I

... In its preoccupation with the legislative history, the Court has overlooked the central point involved in this case: that the conviction of petitioners accords with the plain language of the controlling statute. Nor does the majority demonstrate an ambiguity in that statutory language that makes relevant its long journey into the legislative history.

The operative language of § 610 states that: "It is unlawful ... for any corporation whatever, or any labor organization to make a contribution or expenditure in connection with" any federal election. Despite this unqualified proscription, the majority opinion sustains the right of unions and corporations to make political contributions *directly,* provided only that the funds therefor come voluntarily from members, employees, or stockholders and are maintained separately from the other funds of the union or corporation....

If words are given their normal meaning, the statute and the Court's holding flatly contradict each other. One says that it shall be unlawful for a union to make a political contribution or expenditure. The other says this is perfectly lawful, so long as the funds which the union contributes or expends were donated freely and knowingly. The Court has simply added a qualification, not found in the statutory language, which significantly changes the meaning of this Act of the Congress.

The Court's holding, moreover, directly counters the purposes for which § 610 was enacted. Congress passed this legislation to restrict and minimize the influence corporations and unions might exert on elections....

The two principal motivations for the enactment of § 610, as identified in *CIO,* are (i) the minimizing of influence of labor unions (as well as corporations) on elections "through monetary expenditures"; and (ii) the elimination of the unfairness "to individual union members" of allowing union management to make political contributions from general union funds. It seems self-evident that both of these legislative purposes will be frustrated by the Court's holding that, despite the language of the statute forbidding union contributions, unions may now make political contributions and expenditures, provided only that the source of a fund is voluntary....

II

Accepting, as I think we must, § 610 as written, the issue in this case is whether the political fund of Local 562 was in reality a sham or subterfuge through which the union itself made the contributions forbidden by the statute. The indictment in this case was framed on this basis, and the jury was so instructed. The question properly addressed by the Court of Appeals was "whether the contributions or expenditures were [in fact] made by a labor organization." 434 F.2d 1116, 1121 (1970). After summarizing the evidence submitted to the jury on this issue, the Court of Appeals concluded:

> There is substantial evidence to support a jury finding that the fund was not a bona fide separate and distinct entity but was in fact a device set up to circumvent the provisions of § 610 and that the fund constituted union money.

434 F.2d, at 1121.

The majority opinion of this Court does not contest this view. It concludes, rather, that the jury was erroneously instructed, and that accordingly the verdict and judgment must be set aside. If a new trial is held, the jury must be instructed in accordance with the Court's interpretation of § 610 that a union may lawfully make political contributions from a fund it collects and administers so long as the payments into it are voluntary.

It is from this interpretation of § 610—one which in my view will render the statute largely ineffectual—that I dissent....

NOTES

1. Prior to the decision in the principal case, a federal district court had held that § 304 did not prohibit union contributions or expenditures from that portion of membership dues voluntarily designated for political purposes by individual members. *United States v. Teamsters Local 688,* 47 L.R.R.M. 2005 (E.D. Mo. 1960). Is that ruling still the law? *See Barber v. Gibbons,* 367 F. Supp. 1102 (E.D. Mo. 1973).

2. The implications of *Pipefitters* are probed in Note, *Of Politics, Pipefitters, and Section 610: Union Political Contributions in Modern Context,* 51 Texas L. Rev. 936 (1973). For analyses of earlier developments, *see* Kallenbach, *The Taft-Hartley Act and Union Political Contributions and Expenditures,* 33 Minn. L.

Rev. 1 (1948); Ruark, *Labor's Political Spending and Free Speech,* 53 Nw. U.L. Rev. 61 (1958).

3. In *Buckley v. Valeo,* 424 U.S. 1 (1976), the Supreme Court addressed the constitutionality of the Federal Election Campaign Act of 1971 and 1974. The Court invalidated limitations on individual political campaign expenditures but sustained various limitations on political contributions. Subsequently, in *First Nat'l Bank of Boston v. Bellotti,* 435 U.S. 765 (1978), the Court held that a state statute forbidding expenditures by banks and certain business corporations for the purpose of influencing votes on referendum proposals, other than those affecting the business of the corporation, was an unconstitutional abridgment of free speech. Do *Buckley* and *Bellotti* taken together cast serious doubt on the constitutionality of the anti-expenditure provisions of Taft-Hartley's § 304 (reenacted as 2 U.S.C. § 441(b))? *Buckley* is noted in 76 Colum. L. Rev. 862 (1976); 90 Harv. L. Rev. 171 (1976); 75 Mich. L. Rev. 627 (1977); 1976 Sup. Ct. Rev. 1. *See also* Fleishman, *The 1974 Federal Elections Campaign Act Amendments: The Shortcomings of Good Intentions,* 1975 Duke L.J. 851.

4. For restrictions on a union's use for political purposes of dues money collected under a union security agreement, *see Ellis v. Railway Clerks,* 466 U.S. 435 (1984), *supra.*

Table of Cases

Principal cases and page locations are set out in italics.
See text for subsequent history citations.

A

B

D

F

I

J

K

N

Q

R

S

T

U

X

Y

Z

Index

A

E

ECONOMIC COERCION/INDUCEMENT, pp. 112 to 116.

ECONOMIC STRIKES, pp. 198 to 202, 216.

EEOC, p. 989.

ELECTION OF OFFICERS, pp. 1067 to 1083, 1106, 1107.

EMERGENCY DISPUTES.
Choice-of-procedures approach, pp. 555, 557.
Compulsory arbitration, pp. 556, 558.
Generally, pp. 550 to 558.
Graduated strike, p. 558.
Non-stoppage strike, p. 558.
Railroad/airline disputes, pp. 553, 554.
State laws, p. 554.
Taft-Hartley provisions, pp. 551 to 553.

EMPLOYEE COMMITTEES, pp. 120 to 123.

EMPLOYEE REPRESENTATION PLANS, p. 118.

EMPLOYEES VS. INDEPENDENT CONTRACTORS, pp. 51 to 53.

EMPLOYER ACCOMMODATION, p. 1000.

EMPLOYER DISCRIMINATION.
Concerted activities, pp. 172 to 217. (*See* CONCERTED ACTIVITIES).
Due objector cases, pp. 153 to 168.
Encouraging union membership, pp. 134 to 172.
Hiring halls, pp. 134 to 142.
Judicial review, pp. 131 to 133.
Lockouts, pp. 217 to 240.
Mixed motive cases, p. 133.
Plant closings, pp. 240 to 249, 714.
Proof, pp. 128 to 134.
Remedies, pp. 249 to 260.
Right-to-work legislation, pp. 168 to 172.
Runaway shops, p. 248.
Superseniority to union officials, pp. 141, 142.
Union security, pp. 142 to 168.

EMPLOYER UNILATERAL ACTION, pp. 659 to 667.

EQUAL EMPLOYMENT OPPORTUNITY COMMISSION (EEOC), p. 989.

EQUAL EMPLOYMENT OPPORTUNITY LAWS, pp. 43, 44.

EXCLUSIONS FROM COVERAGE, pp. 51 to 58.

K

KNIGHTS OF LABOR, pp. 8, 9.

L

LABOR MANAGEMENT RELATIONS ACT. (*See* TAFT-HARTLEY ACT).

LABOR-MANAGEMENT REPORTING AND DISCLOSURE ACT. (*See* LANDRUM-GRIFFIN ACT).

LACHES, p. 930.

LANDRUM-GRIFFIN ACT.
Due/fees, p. 1045.
Generally, pp. 41, 42.
Hot cargo agreements, pp. 510 to 512.
Internal union affairs, pp. 1016 to 1026.

LEGAL NATURE OF COLLECTIVE AGREEMENT, pp. 789 to 792.

LESBIANS, p. 988.

LEWIS, JOHN L., p. 35.

LIMITATION PERIODS.
Fair representation, pp. 980, 981.
LMRDA violations, p. 1025.

LITTLE WAGNER ACTS, p. 58.

LOCKOUTS, pp. 217 to 240.

M

MAIL BALLOTS, p. 293.

MAINTENANCE OF MEMBERSHIP, p. 143.

MAJORITY RULE, pp. 601 to 612.

MAKE-WHOLE REMEDY, pp. 653 to 658.

MANAGEMENT FUNCTION CLAUSE, pp. 630 to 636.

MANAGERIAL EMPLOYEES, pp. 55, 56.

MANDATORY SUBJECTS OF BARGAINING, pp. 676 to 690.

MASS ACTION THEORY, p. 859.

MASS PICKETING, p. 391.